BOOKS BY ROBERT C. TUCKER

Philosophy and Myth in Karl Marx
The Soviet Political Mind
The Marxian Revolutionary Idea
Stalin as Revolutionary: A Study in History and Personality
Politics as Leadership
Political Culture and Leadership in Soviet Russia: From Lenin to Gorbachev
The Marx-Engels Reader *(editor)*
The Lenin Anthology *(editor)*
Stalinism: Essays in Historical Interpretation *(editor)*
The Great Purge Trial *(co-editor)*

STALIN

IN POWER

STALIN

IN POWER

THE REVOLUTION FROM ABOVE
1928–1941

Robert C. Tucker

W · W · NORTON & COMPANY

NEW YORK · LONDON

FRONTISPIECE PHOTOGRAPH: Stalin reviewing the Revolution Day parade, 7 November 1934.

FIRST EDITION

THE TEXT OF THIS BOOK *is composed in Times Roman, with the display set in York and Wolf Antiqua. Composition and manufacturing by the Maple Vail Book Manufacturing Group. Book design by Marjorie J. Flock.*

ISBN 0-393-02881-X

W.W. Norton & Company, Inc., 500 Fifth Avenue, New York, N.Y. 10110
W.W. Norton & Company, Ltd., 37 Great Russell Street, London WC1B 3NU

1 2 3 4 5 6 7 8 9 0

924037

*To Liza, Robert, and their
generation of young Russianists*

CONTENTS

Photographs follow pages 222 and 440.

PREFACE

THE SOVIET SYSTEM took shape under the impact not of one revolution but of two.

We have it on Stalin's authority that the second started as a revolution from above. The official *Short Course* of party history, prepared under his personal direction and published in 1938, characterized the rural collectivization of 1929–33 as an expropriation of the kulaks comparable to the Bolshevik expropriation of the capitalists in 1918, and went on: "This was a profound revolution, a leap from an old qualitative state of society to a new qualitative state, equivalent in its consequences to the revolution of October 1917. The distinguishing feature of this revolution is that it was accomplished *from above,* on the initiative of the state, and directly supported *from below,* by the millions of peasants, who were fighting to throw off kulak bondage and to live in freedom in the collective farms."

The claim that collectivization had mass peasant support from below was false, but Stalin's description of it as a revolution from above was accurate. Furthermore, this term is applicable to the second revolution as a whole, including the phase in the later 1930s when massive terror transformed the single-party state inherited from Lenin into an absolute autocracy. The revolution from above was a state-initiated, state-directed, and state-enforced process, which radically reconstituted the Soviet order as it had existed in the 1920s. State power was the driving force of economic, political, social, and cultural change that was revolutionary in rapidity of accomplishment, forcible methods, and transformative effect. The statist character of this revolution is not obviated by the facts that not a few willingly assisted it, most acquiesced in it, and many were, in a career sense, its beneficiaries.

The aim of this book is to show how and why this second revolution took place, how it developed in stages and with what consequences, and what parts Stalin and others played in it and why. As an interpretive history, the book has a central theme: that the second revolution was basically a reversion to a developmental mode that had existed in earlier Russian history. It was a return to a state-sponsored revolution from above, aimed primarily at making Russia a mighty military-industrial power able to fend for itself in an unfriendly international setting and to expand its borders as opportunity allowed.

The tendency for a social revolution to be followed by a return to normalcy is a phenomenon made familiar by the Thermidorian reaction in the aftermath of the French Revolution of 1789. Some participant observers, most notably Lev Trotsky, saw signs of a Russian Thermidor in the rise during the mid-1920s of a conservatively inclined Soviet bureaucratic stratum. Their view, however, was confounded when Stalin led the Soviet party-state into the second revolution at the outset of the 1930s. What occurred in Russia's case was not a relapse into prerevolutionary normalcy, not a return to the Russia of the last tsars, but a revival of a state-building process that had occurred much earlier in the country's history. Inevitably, this resuscitated various old-regime practices, which places a strong counterrevolutionary stamp on Stalin's revolution.

To say this is not to deny that much of what went on in the 1930s moved Russia to modernity. Stalin's Russia of the 1930s rapidly industrialized in the drive for expanded military power, as Tsar Peter's Russia had tried to do in the early eighteenth century. Urbanization proceeded apace. Stalin sent the nation to school, emphasizing technical and vocational education. And there were technological achievements of note, especially in such fields as aviation. None of this, however, contradicts this book's thesis.

Certain preconditions had to exist for the reversion to a long-past developmental mode to take place. One was the pattern of state-sponsored revolutionary change in Russia's earlier history. Yet, patterns out of a nation's past do not reappear simply because once they were there. They may recur, however, if powerful living leaders find them relevant to problems confronting the nation in their own time, and if they succeed in putting into effect resulting policies.

With one exception, the Bolshevik leaders were not disposed to look to the distant Russian past as a source of instruction about present policy. That exception was Stalin. He alone had the potential for leadership that would take cues from old Russia's developmental mode. What kind of man was he that he differed so sharply from the others in this respect? He was, as we shall see, a Bolshevik of the radical right, who blended his version of Leninist revolutionism with Great Russian nationalism. The mixture produced the peculiar idea of a forcible revolution from above as the right formula for socialism in Soviet Russia, and Stalin acted on it.

Although this book is the sequel to my *Stalin as Revolutionary, 1879–1929: A Study in History and Personality*, it is designed to be read on its own as an account of both the background and the events of 1928–41. The interpretation had been worked out, and the great bulk of the book had been written in draft, when Mikhail Gorbachev became Soviet leader in 1985. The reform movement that he initiated has opened up the past, especially the Stalin era, to history writing, and much material of use to scholars has come out recently, but no change in the interpretation presented in this book has been necessitated; rather, the new Soviet materials have been corroborative. Insofar as previously unknown facts of significance about Stalin and the period covered in this work have appeared, I have incorporated them in these pages along with references to the sources.

ACKNOWLEDGMENTS

W HEN A BOOK has been in preparation for over fifteen years, as this one has, the number of debts of gratitude to persons and institutions grows correspondingly long.

First among the institutions to which thanks are due is Princeton University's Center of International Studies, under whose auspices the book was written and whose staff has rendered invaluable service in its preparation. Thanks are also due to the National Endowment for the Humanities, the Rockefeller Foundation, the National Council for Soviet and East European Research, the Institute for Advanced Study, the Harriman Institute for Advanced Study of the Soviet Union, the Kennan Institute for Advanced Russian Studies, and Indiana University's Institute for Advanced Study, all of which provided fellowships or facilities or both. Harvard provided access to its Trotsky Archive, the Hoover Institution to its Boris I. Nicolaevsky Collection, and Columbia University to its Bakhmetieff Collection. Grants from the International Research and Exchanges Board enabled me to pursue research on Stalin in the Soviet Union for a month in 1977 and four months in 1989, very much to this book's benefit.

Among the many persons who have helpfully contributed to my work on this volume, I should list:

My wife, Evgenia Pestretsova Tucker of Princeton University, who was very supportive throughout and commented on draft chapters as they emerged.

Professor George F. Kennan of the Institute for Advanced Study, who shared personal memories of the 1930s in Moscow with me and advised me on various questions concerning the book.

Professor Lars T. Lih of Wellesley College, who read the entire completed manuscript and responded with a detailed and penetrating chapter-by-chapter critical appraisal containing comments, questions, and suggestions for one or another revision, many of which I adopted.

Professor Stephen F. Cohen of Princeton University, who brought to my attention various materials pertaining to subjects taken up in this book.

Professor Richard Wortman of Columbia University, Professor Michael Kraus of Middlebury College, and professors Cohen and Caryl Emerson of Princeton University, who gave me comments on individual draft chapters.

George Moraitis, M.D., of Chicago, a psychoanalyst with special interest in biography, who evaluated Khrushchev's appraisal of Stalin and commented on several draft chapters of this volume; Joseph Wm. Slap, M.D., of Philadelphia, and Otto Kernberg, M.D., of New York, all of whom discussed with me from their perspectives various problems of interpreting Stalin; and the late Karen Horney, whom I never met but whose psychological thought informs in a deep way the portrait of Stalin as a person presented in these pages.

Professor Niels Erik Rosenfeldt of the University of Copenhagen, who has provided me with materials on Stalin's personal chancellery in the 1920s and 1930s and been helpful with his advice.

Professor Mikhail Gefter and Roy A. Medvedev, of Moscow, with whom I have conversed on problems facing the historian of the Stalin period; the late Evgeni Gnedin and the late Elkon Leikin of Moscow, who shared personal memories of that time with me; and Professor D. A. Volkogonov of Moscow, who shared with me some materials gleaned in his research on Stalin.

Professor Ruslan Skrynnikov of Leningrad University, with whom I have conversed and corresponded for many years on the links across time between his biographical subject, Ivan Grozny, and mine, and who has provided me with rare photos of the 1930s.

Ambassador Hans von Herwarth of Küps in West Germany, who gave me his views and written materials bearing on perceptions in the German Embassy in Moscow in the 1930s of events taking place in Soviet policy.

Professor Michal Reiman of the Free University of Berlin, who brought to my attention various materials on Soviet-German relations in the 1930s.

Dr. Bianka Pietrow of the University of Tübingen, who assisted me in my research on Soviet-German relations in the archives of the Foreign Ministry in Bonn.

Professor Darrell P. Hammer of Indiana University, Professor Robert Sharlet of Union College, and Professor Robert M. Slusser of Michigan State University, who corresponded with me on issues facing the researcher of the Soviet 1930s.

Robert Conquest of the Hoover Institution, who corresponded with me on questions concerning Stalin's Terror of the later 1930s.

Theodore Draper of Princeton, who shared with me, from personal memory and his perspective as an historian of American Communism, insights into foreign Communists' perceptions of the Popular Front in 1935–36.

Professor Dodona Kiziria of Indiana University, who advised me on pathways of research into Stalin's influence on the Soviet cinema.

Natalya Kirshon of California, who made available to me Stalin's talk in the Kremlin on the twentieth anniversary of the October Revolution as recorded by her father, General R. P. Khmelnitsky, who was Voroshilov's adjutant.

Other colleagues who have conversed or corresponded with me on themes and problems of the historian of the Stalin period, or shared memories of that time.

The many Princeton graduate students and undergraduates who, over the years, have helped me as research assistants under the university's work-study program or on a private basis.

My editor at W. W. Norton, Mr. James L. Mairs, and Norton's president, Mr. Donald Lamm, for all the ways in which they have been of help, not least by patiently awaiting a long-overdue book.

Irina Rybacek, whose editorial assistance with the manuscript was invaluable and who prepared the Bibliography.

STALIN
IN POWER

CALIGULA: Tell me, my young friend. What exactly *is* a tyrant?
SKIPIO: A blind soul.
CALIGULA: That's a moot point. I should say the real tyrant is a
man who sacrifices a whole nation to his ideal or his ambition.

—ALBERT CAMUS, *Caligula*

Men live in dreams and in realities
—MILOVAN DJILAS, *Conversations With Stalin* 1962

INTRODUCTION:
TOWARD A NEW OCTOBER

THE FIRST revolution was made possible by the rebellious movement that arose in Russia toward the close of World War I. The poet Alexander Blok captured the elemental character of this revolution when he likened it to a Russian blizzard. There were the coups and turmoil of 1917 along with the following three years of civil strife, foreign intervention, and that complex of emergency measures—partly necessitated by the situation and partly inspired by radical Marxist aims—which the Bolsheviks later named "War Communism." The first revolution was this social epoch as a whole. What is called the October Revolution, the coup of 6–7 November (25–26 October old style) 1917, by which Lenin and his party took state power, was a pivotal episode in it.

The blizzard subsided around the end of 1920. Having defeated the White forces in the Civil War, the Bolsheviks now faced a restive people, more than four-fifths of them peasants, in a hungry and war-ravaged land.

In early 1921 they crushed a rebellion of sailors and workers who raised the banner of "Soviets without Bolsheviks!" at the Kronstadt naval base near Petrograd. At their Tenth Party Congress, in March of that year, they adopted the New Economic Policy (NEP), which legalized trade, restored a money economy, and substituted a tax in kind, subsequently in money, for the confiscatory food requisitioning practiced during the Civil War. The NEP permitted nearly 25 million peasant proprietors to work their holdings on nationalized land and market their surplus produce. Private entrepreneurs, the "Nepmen," acquired a free hand in small-scale industry and service trades. A period of relative stability and prosperity ensued.

Lenin's death in 1924 aggravated party battles over power and policy already going on in anticipation of that event. In alliance with the moderate wing led by Alexei Rykov, Nikolai Bukharin, and Mikhail Tomsky, Stalin engaged in a protracted contest with the Left opposition headed by Trotsky. In 1926 Trotsky's defeated faction joined forces with the group led by Grigori Zinoviev and Lev Kamenev and formed the United opposition, but Stalin again prevailed and later that year Trotsky, Zinoviev, and Kamenev were expelled from the Politburo. In October 1927 the United opposition's leaders were expelled from the party and banished to remote areas. By then twilight was descending on NEP society, and during the transitional year of 1928 the rumblings of a huge new upheaval—the second revolution— grew audible.

Stalin now began a bitter fight against the leaders of the moderate group. Outmaneuvered and politically overcome, the latter went down to defeat and in November 1929 they publicly recanted their "Right devia- tionist" views. Organized opposition to Stalin was finally at an end in the party. The general secretary emerged victorious from his long fight for supremacy. By convenient coincidence, his fiftieth birthday came shortly after, on 21 December 1929, and was marked by a public celebration of him as Lenin's successor and the party's "best Leninist." So began what would go down in history as Stalin's personality cult.

There already existed a cult of Lenin, whom the Bolsheviks genuinely venerated as their *vozhd'* (a strong word for leader in Russian). They had political need for a unifying symbol and for continuing guidance by Lenin through his writings, and so they pronounced him eternally alive in his teachings and example. They began to consider themselves a community of Lenin loyalists and to view the Communist party as a revolutionary community of the elect. Stalin was only putting this idea in simple terms when he said at the time of Lenin's death, in what became known as his "oath" speech: "Comrades, we Communists are people of a special sort. We are cut of special cloth. We are the ones who form the army of the great proletarian strategist, the army of Comrade Lenin.[1]"

Now that he had achieved dominance in the party oligarchy and public recognition as Lenin's successor, a combination of *Realpolitik* and psychological need drove Stalin to transform the already existing Lenin cult into a dual one, to remold the party into a community of Lenin-Stalin loyalists. Politically, this promised to make his power position more impregnable than it was at the start of the 1930s. But important as it was, the political motive alone does not provide a sufficient explanation. Abundant evidence indicates that Stalin needed a cult as a prop for his psyche as well as for his power. He craved the hero worship that Lenin found repugnant. On the one hand, his stunning success in the leadership contest could not but confirm him in a sense of himself as a revolutionary statesman of genius, *sans peur et sans reproche,* and raise the expectation that he, the second Lenin, would enjoy something comparable to the devotion and admiration lavished on the first Lenin. On the other hand, behind his customary show of self-assurance he was inwardly insecure. This insecurity was rooted in his self-idealizing and the inevitable disparities between the ideal Stalin of his imagination and the man he actually was.

Many have seen Stalin as primarily a power seeker. That view is not so much wrong as incomplete. He was a formidable master of the techniques of accumulating power. His secretiveness, capacity to plan ahead, to conspire, to dissimulate, and to size up others as potential accessories or obstacles on his path, stood him in good stead here. But power for power's own sake was never his aim. His life in politics was a never-ending endeavor to prove himself a revolutionary hero, as Lenin did before him, and receive, again as Lenin had before him, the plaudits of a grateful party for his exploits as a leader. Power was a prime means to Stalin's supreme goal: fame and glory.

Diminutive in stature (not over five feet four inches tall), stocky in build, with a blotchy face and a crooked left arm resulting from a childhood injury, he was outwardly undemonstrative, at times withdrawn, and in private spoke in so low a voice that listeners, even when close, sometimes had to strain to follow what he said. The sole surviving child of four born to Ekaterina Djugashvili, he grew up in a hovel in the small town of Gori in the Russian Empire's Transcaucasian colony of Georgia. Although notably reticent about his early life and family background, he stated once in private conversation that his father was a priest, which would mean that Ekaterina's often absent husband, Vissarion Djugashvili, a shoemaker by trade, was not his real father.[2] He learned Russian in the local church school, where his mother worked part-time as a cleaning woman. Then he went on, with a scholarship, to the Russian Orthodox theological seminary in the Georgian capital city of Tiflis (Tbilisi in Georgian); Ekaterina wanted him to be a priest.

His wretched childhood, particularly the beatings inflicted on him and on his mother in his presence by the heavy-drinking Vissarion, evidently generated in young Stalin the basic anxiety that can lead a child to develop a neurotic personality. What does this mean? A person whose adverse emotional experiences in childhood cause basic anxiety, meaning a sense of being isolated and helpless in a potentially hostile world, tends to seek and find a rock of inner security by forming an idealized image of himself, for example, as a great warrior. Gradually and unconsciously, if the anxiety-causing conditions do not change, the young person moves from self-idealizing to adopting the idealized self as his true identity, the person he believes himself to be. From then on his energies are invested in the unceasing effort to prove the ideal self in action and gain others' affirmation of it. Karen Horney calls this the search for glory.[3]

What is known of Djugashvili's boyhood shows that he developed an idealized image of himself, first as a warrior-avenger named "Koba." Then, during the subsequent years in the Tiflis seminary, when he entered the local revolutionary underground, his ideal self became a revolutionary one. It was then, too, that the vindictive streak already manifested in him in boyhood grew into a settled character trait. Toward those who failed to treat him as befitted the claims of his ideal self he showed a smoldering animosity that earned him, even in those early years, the reputation among fellow revolutionaries of being a difficult character. Later, among Bolsheviks who knew him well, his vengefulness became proverbial. Along with the search for glory, a need for vindictive triumph over those marked down in his mind as enemies was one of his distinctive characteristics.

Djugashvili's self-idealizing as a revolutionary was greatly reinforced in the early 1900s, when he found in Lenin, the distant chief of the Bolshevik faction of the Russian Empire's Marxist party, a hero with whom he identified and who represented all that he too aspired to be. Because of Lenin's striking Russianness as a radical type, the Lenin-identification resulted in the Russification of Djugashvili's national self-consciousness as an activist in a movement that in later years he called "Russian Bolshevism" and saw as a very Russian phenomenon. Since the identity-figure was Russian, he had to become Russian too. He fashioned a Russian revolutionary persona for himself as "Stalin," a name signifying man of steel and resembling "Lenin." Yet his ideal Stalin self as a Russian was going to be in conflict all his life with his ineradicably Georgian actual self as Djugashvili, a man who spoke Russian with an audible Georgian accent (which may explain why he spoke it so softly).

So Stalin, unlike many of his fellow Old Bolsheviks (party members who joined before 1917), developed a proud sense of membership in Russia as a nation. The Russia of which he first felt a part was the revolutionary nation of the antistate insurrection of 1905. In August 1917 he showed his pride in this nation by espousing in his speech to the Bolshe- viks' Sixth Party congress a "creative Marxism," based on the maxim that Russia might show Europe the way to socialist revolution, as opposed to the "dogmatic Marxism" which assumed that Europe would show Russia the way.[4] Subsequent events, culminating in the October victory, con- firmed to him the validity of his Russocentric view of the nascent world revolution.

The Civil War, during which he became a statesman of a revolution- ary Russian nation at war against foreign and domestic foes, was a forma- tive time in Stalin's political life. The militarized culture of the Civil War later showed in his authoritarian propensity to issue commands, his ex- political-commissar's ruthlessness, his habitual style of dress (party tunic and high Russian leather boots), his ready coarseness of expression, and even in later reminiscences, as when he recalled with relish how a unit of Red Army soldiers scoured Odessa in 1920 in search of the insidious "Entente" that they had heard was responsible for the war they were fight- ing.[5]

In the early 1920s Stalin could see himself as a leader of a revolution- ary Russian nation with a revolutionary Russian state at its head. This attitude was reinforced by the centralizing role he played as commissar for nationality affairs in Lenin's government. He helped supervise the reincor- poration, frequently by forcible means, of minority-inhabited borderlands of the former Russian Empire, including his native Georgia, into the new multinational Soviet Russian state. Although Lenin carried prime respon- sibility for the centralizing policy that reintegrated independence-seeking borderlands, so far as possible, into Soviet Russia, he and most of his other top Bolshevik colleagues did not proudly think of themselves, in Stalin's way, as representatives of a resurrected *Russian* statehood.

Yet, the Bolshevik Revolution, although it produced a regime that defined itself in class terms, was no exception to the tendency of the republican revolutions of modern times to be followed by a groundswell of national consciousness. As early as 1921 a Bolshevik delegate from the Ukraine to the Tenth Party Congress in Moscow, V. P. Zatonsky, deplored the fact that the Revolution had awakened a national movement in Russia. By transforming that country from a backwater of Western Europe into the forefront of a world movement, he said, it had instilled a spirit of "Russian Red patriotism" in the hearts of many Bolsheviks, who tended not simply to take pride in being Russian but to think of themselves first and foremost as Russians and to see the new state more as a new "Russia One and Indivisible" than as a Soviet system and federation.[6] Not for hardheaded political reasons alone, but likewise because his Bolshevik revolutionism was merged with Russian nationalism, Stalin was a leading figure among the party's "Russian Red patriots."

If an individual has found what he regards as his true identity in an ideal self that he feels driven to prove in practice, he must devise modes of enacting that self-identity. In a way, he must become a playwright who creates the roles that he then seeks to play in life. He will inevitably draw upon his culture as well as his personal creativity in the process. So it was with Stalin and to this we must trace his lifelong passion for drama. The culture on which he drew as a playwright in this peculiar sense was his revolutionary political culture as a Bolshevik and, more and more as time went on, past Russian culture as well. The obsessive interest he took in history, Russia's in particular, was part of this process.

His inner world, it appears, was one of dramatic fantasies in which he played a heroic part as a fighter for the just revolutionary cause in a protracted struggle culminating in triumph over powerful, scheming, hate-fully villainous hostile forces. These counterrevolutionary forces also had to be anti-Stalin because in him, as in Lenin before him, the revolutionary cause was personified and the movement had a leader of genius. Thus their enmity toward him was rationalized in his mind in accordance with the exalted view he took of himself. In the course of besting the enemies he would demonstrate, to himself and others, that he was indeed the Stalin of his imagination, a revolutionary politician and Marxist thinker as great as or greater than Lenin, a diplomatist of unsurpassed skill and craft, a superb military strategist, and a national statesman of Russia on a par with the most eminent ones that this great nation had produced in its long history. And by 1929, although he was not yet autocratic master of the regime, his power position and capacity to manipulate policy were sufficiently potent that he could make all sorts of things happen in Russia by enacting his self-designed roles. His hero-scripts, we may call them.

Despite Stalin's formidable accomplishments in the first fifty years of life, up to the late 1920s, he had not been able to enact his hero-scripts. He did not star in his early revolutionary career and in his performance during the testing year of 1917, or prove himself a hero in the Civil War. Nor did he win renown as a Marxist thinker by his publications. On a more personal plane, his actual self as a Georgian-born man with Georgian-accented Russian speech was as far apart from his arrogated Russian self as his actual appearance was apart from the tall and handsome Stalin of portraits soon to come.

To face such disparities threatened to arouse self-accusations, self-hate, and self-condemnation, and he developed a system of inner defense against that. He could remember the past not as it really happened but in a way that was consonant with what a hero-script required. He could rationalize away this or that discrepancy between his ideal and actual selves by, for example, making out some rude behavior on his part to have been a merited response to actions by an enemy of the party. Above all, he could and did deny the disparities, repress them from conscious awareness. As a result the structure of his self-esteem was shaky. It needed reassurance from party comrades that he was the ideal Stalin, and he formed a concept of the party embodying this need.

In this concept—his ideal party, we may call it—true Bolsheviks were those who saw him as he saw himself and rendered fealty accordingly. The party was a kind of political family for which he was a cult object. Here we may note that he had hardly known a father. In adult life he had little to do with his religious Georgian mother and did not even attend her funeral when she died in Tiflis in 1938. His Georgian first wife, by whom he fathered a son named Yakov, was not a politically engaged person and he saw her rarely because of his immersion in party affairs and his first exile. His second wife, Nadezhda Alliluyeva, was a party comrade twenty years younger than he and the hostess of a social circle whose members, including her own family, were party people friendly toward him.

A loner always, Stalin was never really alone. The party was his society, his group of meaningful others. At times Stalin characterized the party in terms that it is hard to imagine occurring to any other Bolshevik. In an unfinished paper of 1921 there appears a fragment saying: "The Communist Party as a kind of order of *swordbearers* within the Soviet state, guiding the latter's organs and giving inspiration to their activity."[7] His reference was to the redoubtable military-religious Livonian Order of Knights against which the Russians fought from the thirteenth century, when Prince Alexander Nevsky battled them on frozen Lake Chud, to the Livonian wars of the fifteenth and sixteenth centuries for control of the Baltic seashore. Although it was a Teutonic ruling caste, something of its military-religious nature as a secret order, bound in fealty to its leader, reappeared in Russia in Ivan the Terrible's special guard force, the *oprichnina*. Who but Stalin among the Bolsheviks would have thought of using such a metaphor for the Communist Party?

To the ideal Stalin there corresponded an ideal party in the form of a brotherhood of Bolsheviks who recognized his greatness, accepted him as their *vozhd'*, and would follow him through thick and thin in revolutionary exploits. And now that he had been publicly proclaimed Lenin's rightful successor, he could not help but expect to be treated as "Lenin today."

In order for that to happen, however, Stalin needed to prove himself in action as a Lenin of today. How could he accomplish this? Since it was axiomatic for Bolsheviks that Lenin's supreme service to history was October itself, and October signified a revolutionary transition to a new order,

Stalin was bound to approach the next great task on the agenda of Bolshevism, the building of socialism in Soviet Russia, in a revolutionary manner. He therefore envisioned an October of his own. It was the historically most consequential of his hero-scripts. He would engineer a breakthrough in the world's history comparable in significance to Lenin's October, and this could only be a revolution of the construction of socialism in one country.

The evidence that Stalin's thinking ran along this line as early as the mid-1920s is plain. On 7 November 1925, October's eight anniversary, he published an article in *Pravda* in which he found a direct parallel between the country's current situation and the situation that prevailed in the prelude to October 1917. Both were turning-point times, he said. Then it was a matter of making the transition from bourgeois to proletarian rule; now, of making the transition from a not-yet-socialist economy to a socialist one. Then, the turning-point moment was resolved by the uprising; now, conditions were propitious for an endeavor to transform NEP Russia into a socialist country. And just as the party won victory eight years ago because it showed "Leninist hardness" in the face of untold difficulties in its ranks, so now it would conquer capitalist elements of the economy by showing the "old Leninist hardness" in the face of difficulties and possible vacillations in certain party quarters. A year later Stalin repeated his comparison of the current with the pre-October period, this time with a reference to Zinoviev and Kamenev as vacillators then and now.[8]

How political leaders diagnose the problems of their parties or countries can be an indicator of their likely prescriptions for the policies needed to resolve those situations.[9] Thus Lenin's diagnosis of Russia's situation in April 1917 as revolutionary underlay his prescription to his fellow Bolsheviks of a party policy of opposing the Provisional Government under the slogan of "All power to the Soviets." Now, in the high NEP years of 1925 and 1926, Stalin was diagnosing Soviet Russia's situation as prerevolutionary, implying that an internal revolutionary policy might be needed soon.

The implication was not, or not fully, understood at that time. So habituated was the collective party mind to the idea that building socialism would be an evolutionary process, and so absent was revolutionary thunder from the country's political atmosphere, that Stalin's party colleagues apparently did not divine what the apostle of socialism in one country was saying in his anniversary article and the subsequent repetition of its theme. But these statements were portents of things to come. After acquiring a commanding position in the party oligarchy by the end of 1927, Stalin manipulated events in 1928 to make it appear that Soviet Russia was in a state of external and internal emergency that required a policy of revolutionary advance in the construction of socialism, for which speedy collectivization of the peasants was a necessity. He thereby steered the state into the revolution from above.

In 1931, amid the resulting turmoil, he gave a speech to Soviet managers in which he explained why it was impossible to relax the dizzy developmental tempo then in force:

To reduce the tempo is to lag behind. And laggards are beaten. But we don't want to be beaten. No, we don't want that! The history of old Russia consisted, among other things, in continual beatings for her backwardness. She was beaten by the Mongolian khans. Beaten by the Swedish feudals. Beaten by the Polish-Lithuanian nobles. Beaten by the Anglo-French capitalists. Beaten by all of them—for backwardness. For military backwardness, cultural backwardness, governmental backwardness, industrial backwardness, agricultural backwardness. Beaten because it was profitable and done with impunity. Remember the words of the prerevolutionary poet, "Thou art poor and thou are abundant, thou are mighty and thou art powerless, Mother *Rus'*." Those gentlemen learned well the words of the old poet. They beat her saying, "Thou art abundant, so one can gain at thy expense." They beat her saying, "Thou art poor, powerless, so we can beat and rob thee with impunity." That's the law of exploiters. The wolves' law of capitalism. Thou hast lagged behind, thou art weak, so thou art not in the right, hence one may beat and enslave thee. Thou art mighty, hence thou art in the right, one must watch out for thee. That's why we can no longer lag behind.

We had no fatherland in the past, Stalin went on, but now we do and we shall defend its independence. Do you want our socialist fatherland to be beaten and lose its independence? He concluded: "We have lagged behind the advanced countries by fifty to a hundred years. We must cover that distance in ten years. Either we'll do it or they will crush us."[10]

This famous passage was not only an astute appeal to Soviet Russian patriotism but also a revelation of the speaker's inner world. Here was the Stalin whose Bolshevism blended with Russian nationalism. Here, too, was the self-dramatizing Stalin seeking to realize his hero-script by leading the party and country in a revolution of socialism's construction and thereby saving Mother Russia from the fate of once again being beaten by foreigners.

The vision of being her savior expressed Stalin's inner world in yet another way. It showed that he had turned to Russia's past for ideas about the course to follow in Soviet policy. In a strange manner presently to be clarified, he had gone to school in Russia's history to learn how to be a revolutionary leader in the present.

Part One

—

THE SETTING

The state's influence on the internal system has hardly been so huge in the history of any other country, and in no other period of our history has this shown up so clearly as the period to which we now turn.

—V. O. KLIUCHEVSKY, 1906

1

THE TSARDOM'S RISE

Muscovy Encircled

SINCE TSARISM was a conservative political force during much of the nineteenth century, it tends to be remembered as such. But in the long period of its rise and development, it acted at times as a force for transformation of Russian society.

State-sponsored social change, and tsarist autocracy itself, arose out of national disaster: the overrunning of the Russian lands by Mongol nomads under Batu, grandson of Genghis Khan, in the mid-thirteenth century. The Russian polity had arisen in the ninth century A.D. as a loose federation of principalities centered in the grand principality of Kiev on the Dnieper River trade route from Scandinavia to Constantinople, capital of the Byzantine Empire. The Mongol domination of *Rus'* (the ancient name for Russia) lasted two centuries and changed the course of the nation's history.

The Mongols, whom the Russians called Tatars, founded a state known as the Golden Horde with its capital at Sarai on the lower Volga. The Tatar overlords of the Russian lands gathered tribute and periodically descended on Russian towns with punitive expeditions so as to enforce their exploitative rule by terror. Russian princes were allowed to retain their positions only as tribute-gathering agents of the Tatar khans, to whom they had to travel for permission to be crowned. It was partly because they distinguished themselves in this capacity that the princes of the small northeastern territory of Muscovy grew in power and influence during the two centuries of the Tatar yoke. By 1480 the grand principality of Moscow had overcome Tatar rule and emerged as the nucleus of a new centralized Russian state. It was in this setting that tsarism arose in the fifteenth and sixteenth centuries.

The Tatar overlordship took away the unity of *Rus'*, but not the memory of it. Muscovy's rise as the hegemonic center of the new Russian state system went forward under the banner of national reunification, the "gathering of Russian lands." In symbolic assertion of this program, the Muscovite grand princes proclaimed themselves sovereigns of "Moscow and all of *Rus'*" (that is, Muscovy and all the Russian lands).[1] The gathering process made rapid strides during the long reign of Grand Prince Ivan III in the second half of the fifteenth century, and continued under his immediate successors.

Muscovy's territory grew from an original nucleus of only about 16,000 square miles to about ten times that size on Ivan's accession in 1462 and to about one million square miles in 1533. It went on expanding in the later sixteenth century under Ivan's great-grandson, Ivan IV, known in Russian as Ivan Grozny and in English as Ivan the Terrible. His conquest of the middle Volga with the taking of the Tatar stronghold of Kazan in 1552 opened the way for the later eastward push to the Pacific that created the modern Russian state of Eurasian continental dimensions. Some Russian principalities, such as Yaroslavl, voluntarily submitted to Muscovite suzerainty. The Rostov princes were bought out. But in numerous instances war or the threat of it was employed. Thus Novgorod, with its extensive surrounding territories, was taken by force in the 1470s, and Tver surrendered under siege in 1485.

Although the Muscovite Russian state achieved a recognized place in the existing system of international relations in the latter part of the fifteenth century, the continuing threat of Tatar incursions and the ambitious program of further in-gathering of Russian lands made its international position a difficult one. Hostile or potentially hostile neighbors ringed the new Russian state in most directions. In the northwest it faced Sweden, a major power whose territories included Finland. On the southern Baltic coast lay Livonia, home of the redoubtable Livonian Order of Swordbearers. Directly west, in dynastic union with Catholic Poland and in possession of the Smolensk territory and other lands comprising parts of present-day Soviet Belorussia and the Ukraine, was the Lithuanian state, a rival for the role of unifier of Russia. In Asia Minor, Byzantium was supplanted in the mid-fifteenth century by a new power, Ottoman Turkey, which was extending control over the Balkans. Finally, various offshoots of the declining Golden Horde had to be reckoned with: the Crimean khanate in the south, the Astrakhan khanate in the southeast, and the Kazan khanate on the Volga east of Moscow.

In this situation of encirclement, the Muscovite state's defense and further expansion required both the creation of a formidable military force and skillful diplomacy aimed at keeping potential enemies divided. As George Vernadsky puts it, "the Muscovite government had a perennial diplomatic task of preventing the formation of any coalition of foreign powers against Moscow, and when such a coalition was nevertheless formed, of breaking the unity of potential or actual enemies by a separate agreement with some of them and by opposing to the enemy bloc a coalition of its own."[2] Ivan III, for example, allied Moscow with the nearby Tatar khanate of Kasimov in his unsuccessful struggle to overthrow the khanate of Kazan; and later with the Crimean khanate as a counterweight to the remnant of the Golden Horde and to Poland-Lithuania.

Such was the historical setting of the Russian state-building process. The fundamental fact was the primacy of external concerns. Under pressing need to continually wage war or prepare for war in the interest of self-defense and the conscious policy of aggrandizement, Muscovy became a military camp and underwent transformation into "a military-national state on an elementary economic foundation."[3] The military-national state grew powerful through the binding of the classes of the population in compulsory state service. By means of a system of military land grants modeled, according to P. N. Miliukov, on that practiced in Ottoman Turkey, the Moscow government created a dependent gentry, a "military serving class" whose tenure of the allotted landed estates was conditional upon continuing military service to the state. One of the devices for creating this class was the introduction of military holdings in newly acquired territories. When Ivan III annexed Novgorod, for example, he dispossessed and deported some eight thousand large and small hereditary proprietors and allotted their lands in service tenure to a smaller number of military serving men, many of whom had previously been courtiers in Moscow or one of its domains.[4] Symptomatically, "courtier" *(dvorianin)* became the name by which a nobleman was designated in the Russian language.

The enserfment of the Russian peasantry was another expression of

the state-building process. Before the second quarter of the fifteenth century, the Russian peasant was not bound to the land and could move freely
from place to place at certain times of the year. His freedom of migration
was increasingly curtailed thereafter, in part because of the government's
desire to pin him down to a definite place for tax-gathering purposes. The
same motive inspired governmental measures to attach burghers to their
towns and trades. A further reason for binding the peasant to the land was
the government's search for support from the middle service class at various junctures.[5] By the mid-seventeenth century, the former peasant ten-
ants had become bondsmen or serfs, attached by governmental legislation
to the estates served by their communal villages. The enserfed peasant was
increasingly subject to the *corvée,* or obligation to contribute a specified
portion of his time to work on the nearby landed estate.

Miliukov contrasts the Russian state-building process with the pattern
of historical development in Western Europe. The Russian state system
took shape before having time to emerge, as in the West, from a process
of internal economic development. So it was that "in Russia the state had
huge influence upon the social organization, whereas in the West the social
organization conditioned the state system." European society was built
"from below upward," with a centralized state superimposed upon a previously formed middle layer of feudal landholders, while Russian society
was fashioned "from above downward." Alluding to the seeming inconsistency of this thesis with the Marxist idea that every political system is a
superstructure over a determining socioeconomic base, Miliukov observed
that he was not questioning the importance of economics: "It was precisely
the elementary state of the economic 'base' here in Russia that called forth
the hypertrophy of the state 'superstructure' and conditioned the strong
reverse action of this superstructure upon the 'base' itself."[6]

The Origins of Autocracy

Political absolutism was not an immemorial fixture of Russian life,
but a product of historical circumstances and of Muscovite Russia's state-
building process. One of the circumstances was the prolonged exposure of
the Russians to Tatar rule. The two centures of subjugation left an imprint
upon Russian political attitudes and behavior, accentuating imperiousness
in the ruler and servility in the ruled. The khans were autocrats who
demanded and mercilessly enforced unconditional submission to their will
by all subjects and subordinates. The Russian princely agents were thus
confronted in their own experience with a new model of rulership quite
different from the oligarchical Kievan pattern. In time there appeared a

tendency to emulate the new model, even though the khans themselves remained enemies. The Moscow grand princes, in particular, began to look upon themselves as autocratic rulers to whom their subjects, high and low, owed unquestioning obedience. As the power of the Golden Horde was broken in the fifteenth century, they undertook to succeed the khans as supreme overlords of all the Russian lands. This notion was reflected in the increasing use of the title of tsar (a Russian derivative of "Caesar"), which had previously been applied to the reigning head of the Horde.

The forging of autocracy required political action to clear away obstacles, including the continued presence of a hereditary aristocracy of boyars and the tradition of princely rule in consultation with leading boyars. In the state-building process, the formation of the new military service class went along with the leveling of the old aristocracy. "All higher social elements were now mercilessly overthrown; the Muscovite society was systematically and intentionally leveled, to form the foundation of an autocratic power. Thus, by nothing less than a series of social revolutions, completed nearly with a century (1484 to 1584), was begun the political tradition of autocracy."[7]

When Ivan IV, the future Ivan Grozny, inherited the throne as an infant of three in 1533, the titled aristocrats enjoyed great power. The orphaned grand prince grew up in a Kremlin ruled by boyars and he began to hate them, increasingly becoming prey to suspicion that they were weaving a web of conspiratorial machinations against him. An enormous grandiosity also appeared in his makeup. His sole solace in the early years was the thought of his royal identity and little by little, "he became a sacred being for himself, and in his mind he created a whole theology of political self-adoration in the form of a learned theory of his own tsarist power."[8] His assumption of the title "Tsar of Moscow and All of *Rus'* " in a formal coronation ceremony in 1547 was emblematic of this process. Later, he sought to transform the vision of himself as an absolute autocrat into reality. An adventurer and publicist, Ivan Peresvetov, helped to prompt him into his course by urging action to elevate the lesser nobility and crush the "traitor-grandees."[9] The tsar's receptivity to this idea was enhanced after his severe illness in 1553, during which the grandees showed a preference for his cousin, Prince Andrei Staritsky, as successor.

When the Russian forces suffered a reverse in the Livonian war in 1564, Ivan blamed it on the boyars, many of whom were strongly opposed to the war's continuation. Prince Andrei Kurbsky, commander of the Russian forces in Livonia, then fled to Lithuania in fear of the tsar's wrath. From there he wrote tracts denouncing Ivan for arrogating despotic power and for departing from the old custom of taking counsel with the great boyars. Ivan replied with angry counterdenunciations. He argued that opposition to him was not only treasonable but also sacrilegious. He claimed a God-given right to unquestioning submission to his will on the part of his subjects—his "slaves," as he called them. And he asserted, falsely but with appropriate genealogical claims, that autocracy (in his understanding of it) had always existed in Russia: "From the beginning the Russian autocrats and not the boyars and grandees *(vel'mozhi)* have held their kingdom."[10]

Kurbsky's flight intensified Ivan's long-growing suspicion that the whole boyar class was a hotbed of treason and that he was the intended victim of a conspiracy. No clear evidence of such a conspiracy has emerged,[11] although high-level opposition to Ivan mounted in response to his long, bloody campaign to exterminate "traitors." First he retired to the village of Aleksandrovskaia Sloboda, not far from Moscow, and sent back word that he was resigning the tsardom because a seditious movement had arisen among the boyars threatening the lives of the royal family. The purpose of this maneuver was to extort popular consent to the projected purge.[12] When a deputation from the stunned populace begged Ivan to reconsider his resignation, he agreed on condition that he be given a free hand to deal with traitorous elements as he saw fit. He angrily insinuated that there had been a plot in favor of the Staritsky family, and accused the traitors of having caused the death of his wife Anastasia and of seeking to destroy him.[13]

Ivan then asserted himself as autocrat in a vendetta against enemies. He set up a special new court called the *oprichnina*. It had its own higher administration, troops, finances, and territories. The new courtiers or *oprichniki*, initially numbering a thousand, were recruited mainly from among lowborn nobles and constituted a privileged guard force, a private army of the tsar for war against the treason that he felt was rampant in the land. Becoming chief of the *oprichnina*, Ivan divided the realm between it and the old administration, the *zemshchina*. The latter, however, was placed under an agent of Ivan's, a captive Tatar khan, who signed government decrees as "Tsar of all the Russias," while Ivan now called himself simply "Prince of Moscow Ivan Vasilievich."[14] Thousands of estates were allotted for the maintenance of the *oprichniki*, the displaced previous holders being deported to distant new lands along the frontier.

The *oprichnina* has been called, with good ground, a state within the state. There is also much to be said for Kliuchevsky's description of it as "a higher police for affairs of treason."[15] Like a police force, it had a special uniform and insignia. The *oprichniki* dressed in black and rode black horses, and so became known to contemporaries as the "dark night" and the "pitch darkness." Their insignia consisted of a dog's head and broom attached to the saddle, symbolizing their function of ferreting out treason and sweeping the Russian land clean of it. New members were reportedly inducted into the organization in a semi-conspiratorial initiation ceremony during which the candidate would kiss the cross after taking an oath to forsake not only friends but even parents, and serve Ivan alone. Aleksandrovskaia Sloboda, Ivan's principal residence from now on, became a kind of *oprichnina* capital after being built up as a fortified stronghold where the ever fearful tsar could feel secure from danger. There, in the company of some three hundred leading *oprichniki,* many of whom wore monastic garb and took monastic titles, he led a life in which the ringing of church bells and reading of prayers alternated with wild revels and visits to the dungeon where suspects were tortured. The new private court of Ivan was thus a strange replica of a military-religious order.

Immediately upon his return to Moscow in 1565, Ivan commenced the assault upon the boyars. His reign of terror led by the *oprichnina* went on for seven years. A large number of boyars and their families were executed on suspicion of treason, and their ancestral estates were confiscated. However, the majority of victims of the wholesale executions were persons of humble station—scribes, servants, dog-keepers, monks, and nuns—who could hardly have been involved in a seditious movement of boyars even if one had existed. In 1570 the tsar and his henchmen descended on Novgorod and carried out a fearful slaughter of many of its inhabitants, high and low, on suspicion of treason. The total number of persons murdered during the terror is estimated at four thousand.[16] The evidence has been preserved in books of victims' names that Ivan sent to monasteries so that prayers would be said for their (and his) souls. In the end, he turned his fury on the "pitch darkness" itself. Many leading *oprichniki* were executed, and the organization was disbanded. But the consequences of the long orgy of violence were yet to be felt in full. For it has been suggested that the *oprichnina* terror against imaginary sedition paved the way for the real sedition that devastated Russia not long after Ivan's death, during the interregnum of 1598–1613 known as the Time of Troubles.[17]

It should be noted that this most despotic monarch cultivated a democratic aura. He was, or seemed to be, siding with the middle and lower orders of society against the pretensions of the grandees. Such was the impression fostered by his maneuver of resignation and then reassumption of the tsardom by compact with the people, in order to make war on boyar treason. It was also Ivan who began calling an "assembly of the land" *(Zemskii sobor)* to discuss affairs of state with emissaries of the people; and before such an assembly he promulgated his edict on the *oprichnina* in 1565.

Ivan was fated to be a controversial figure for posterity. He went down in Russian memory as a cruel tyrant. *Oprichnik* became, especially on the lips of revolutionaries, an abusive byword for a police thug. The name of Grozny's chief henchman, Maliuta Skuratov, lingered on in song and story as a synonym for a vicious killer. Yet some historians saw Ivan's terror as the price of progress in creating a powerful centralized Russian state. According to one of them, the antiboyar terror was a "revolution from above" needed for creation of a unified Russian state, and hence was "revolutionary terror."[18]

The Crowned Revolutionary

The binding of all classes in state service could not fully compensate for Russia's backwardness vis-à-vis Western Europe. Consequently, the tsarist compulsory-service state found itself under pressure to lessen its isolation from the West at the very time when it reached its finished form in the seventeenth century. The government brought in foreign engineers and artisans, granted some concessions to foreign industrialists, and sent Russian missions to study conditions in Europe. While doing all this, it also tried to contain the spread of European cultural influence, for example by segregating Moscow's foreign residents in a special district called the "German quarter." Ironically, it was by frequenting the German quarter in his youth and meeting foreigners there that Tsar Peter I (Peter the Great) acquired his passionate interest in European ways. In 1697–98 he spent fifteen months in Europe, traveling under an assumed name in a Russian mission, studying the military arts and navigation, visiting factories, museums, and public buildings (as well as taverns), and working in shipbuilding yards in Holland.

In this restless, ruthless, and dynamic tsar, Russia acquired at its head a revolutionary statesman. Acting decisively but impetuously and without a preconceived plan, he forced through a revolution from above that transformed the Orthodox Muscovite tsardom of the seventeenth century into the Russian Empire of the eighteenth. In doing so, he made the mode of government more dictatorial than ever and intensified the servitude of society to the state. The break with the Orthodox past was symbolized by his moving of the country's capital from semioriental Moscow to St. Petersburg, an entirely new city built at huge cost of life on northern marshlands bordering the Neva River, in proximity to the sea and to Europe. The central structure of government was refashioned along the lines of European monarchical absolutism, and the local administration was reorganized according to Swedish models. The daily life of upper-class Russians was likewise revolutionized in many ways. On returning from Europe in

1698, Peter personally sheared off the beards of palace dignitaries, depriving them of a possession that had religious meaning in old Russian eyes. Later edicts of the tsar-transformer, as he became known, directed the nobles to dress in the European manner and prohibited the further manufacture of clothing of the old Russian type for them. The first Russian newspaper and theater were founded, the first Russian lay educational institution—characteristically, a training school for naval officers—was opened, and a Russian Academy of Science was established.[19]

Legend ascribes to Peter the remark that "We need Europe for a few dozen years, and afterward we must turn our back to her." Without vouching for its authenticity, Kliuchevsky quotes it as indicative of Peter's relationship to Europe: he saw there a source of technology and advanced ways that would enhance the power of Russia, but not a model civilization to be emulated.

It has been calculated that warfare, including the protracted Northern War with Sweden for control of the Baltic shores, filled all but about two of the thirty-five years of Peter's reign. As under previous tsars, the quest for military power in support of the state's external ambitions was a prime moving force in internal policy. Military needs largely motivated the forced secularization of Russian life as well as the industrialization effort that Peter's government pursued with feverish speed.

Dozens of young Russians were sent abroad to study mathematics, natural science, shipbuilding, navigation and the like, while foreign military officers, shipbuilders, mining engineers, skilled workers, legal specialists, and financial experts were invited to help Russia develop itself. Having previously possessed but a small extractive industry and hardly any manufacturing one, the country had over two hundred factories by the end of Peter's reign in 1725, and its cast iron production was among the largest in Europe.[20] These factories were not, observes Kliuchevsky, fully private enterprises but rather "state operations" supervised by government-appointed agents. By virtue of this arrangement the factory owners from the merchant class were given the nobleman's privilege of employing serf labor. Whole villages were attached to factories in much the same way as other serf villages were to their landed estates.[21] Furthermore, prisoners of war, civilians from occupied territories, and state-owned serfs were brought together in what have been called "Peter's forced labor camps" to construct canals on lakes Ladoga, Onega, and elsewhere.[22]

Thus Peter's innovations not only accepted but accentuated the principle of the compulsory-service state. The service obligations of the nobles were tightened by a series of measures culminating in the legislative act of 1722 on the Table of Ranks. This official hierarchy of fourteen military and corresponding civilian ranks made government service the highroad to noble status. Each military officer and civil servant was to start his career on the bottom rung of the ladder, with the possibility of obtaining personal and eventually hereditary nobility on reaching the requisite higher rungs. The Table created an aristocracy of rank *(chin)* and organized the tsarist bureaucracy as a corps of uniformed possessors of rank: *chinovniki.* Since state service was in principle open to persons from any section of society and offered an equal opportunity to rise, this reform of Peter's had a certain democratic quality. At the same time, it hindered the growth of a corporate spirit of independence among the nobles, reinforced their subservience to the crown, and thereby further strengthened the autocracy.

In a classic passage on the Russian state-building process, Kliuchevsky found its causal core in "the unnatural relation of the external policy of the state to the internal growth of the people." He said that "the expansion of the state territory, straining beyond measure the resources of the people, only strengthened the power of the state without elevating the self-consciousness of the people. . . . The state swelled up, and the people grew lean."[23] Peter's reign well illustrates this dictum. Not only the nobility but other social groups and institutions as well were brought into greater subordination to the needs of the bureaucratic state. The Church Statute of 1721 deprived the Russian Orthodox Church of its remaining administrative autonomy by abolishing the patriarchate and placing church administration in the hands of the Holy Synod, a collegial body headed by a lay chief procurator and serving as a government department for the supervision of church affairs. As for the peasant population, its material conditions worsened while its servile status continued unchanged. To secure resources for the waging of his constant wars, Peter increased the financial burden upon the serfs and extended serfdom to some who had so far retained a residue of personal freedom.

The compulsory-service state evolved under Peter into a full-blown police state. A statute of 1721 assigned to the police very extensive functions of surveillance and control over society, economic life, and education. Because of these forcibly implemented radical changes in Russian life many of the tsar's subjects hated him, and some considered him the Antichrist. A whole series of decrees, partly inspired by Peter's keen curiosity to know what his subjects were thinking and saying about him, aimed at inducing private individuals by threat of punishment or promise of reward to turn informers. The dreaded Petrine security police made regular use of the torture chamber to extract information and confessions.

Abandoning the stiff religious solemnity of Muscovite Russian court life for the mobile existence of a secular chief executive, Peter changed the style of tsarist autocratic rule. He adopted the title of emperor, yet spoke of himself as a "servant of the state." He moved among his subjects in the dress of a Dutch seaman, indulged a lifelong passion for mechanical instruments, and parodied religious ritual in revels with a group of companions known as "The Most Drunken Company of Fools and Jesters." But at all times he remained the autocratic master of Russia. Assisted by a group of favored advisers, he dictated the government's actions in all spheres, led the armed forces, conducted foreign relations, and even composed legislative edicts and diplomatic correspondence in his own hand.

Nor did his personal simplicity of demeanor carry with it an inclination to lessen the majesty of the autocratic office. While casting aside some of the Byzantine trappings of sacrosanct monarchy, Peter encouraged the cult of the tsar and promoted the doctrine of his autocratic power. Theofan Prokopovich, his official panegyrist and pamphleteer, propounded a novel theory of monarchical absolutism in a pamphlet written to defend Peter's decree of 1722, which proclaimed the right of the emperor to appoint his own successor at will. Prokopovich's theory held that the divinely appointed monarch could legitimately change his subjects' civil and religious customs and regulate their activities in every sphere because he was obliged to provide for their welfare and happiness. This theory was a fitting ideological monument to the tsar-transformer and to the pattern of regime-directed revolution that found in him its supreme exponent. Tsar Peter was indeed what an expatriate Russian intellectual called him in the mid-nineteenth century: "a revolutionary, albeit a crowned one."[24]

The pressure of external upon internal policy relaxed with Russia's achievement of its commanding world position by the close of the eighteenth century, enabling the government to give more attention to the needs of internal welfare rather than territorial expansion, although the latter continued. The earlier binding of all classes in compulsory state service gave way to a partial unbinding with the release of the nobility from its service obligations in the late eighteenth century. Further unbinding proceeded in slow uneven steps. Not until 1861 was the peasantry released from serfdom. The 1861 Imperial edict inaugurated a time of transforming change (from above) known as the Epoch of Great Reforms. Although they liberalized Russian life, the autocratic, centralized, bureaucratic state structure was too well entrenched, its repressive powers too formidable, the middle class too weak, and the history-bred submissiveness of the people too enduring, for the processes of change to work their way to fruition peacefully. What had developed as a dynamically active governmental power in the state-building process proved so strong as a static force later on that it could successfully block its own thorough transformation, as shown by its capacity to withstand the nationwide insurrectionary movement in 1905.

Only under the unbearable strains of the third year of World War I did the tsarist structure finally buckle and collapse. Russia's belated republican revolution came suddenly in February 1917: the tsar was deposed and the newly created Provisional Government proclaimed democratic liberties and committed itself to the convoking of a constituent assembly to design the new Russian state order. By then, however, the social and political forces that led to the October Revolution and to the victory of Lenin's party had been unleashed. The blizzard had begun.

History knows all sorts of metamorphoses.
—LENIN, 1922

2

LENIN'S LEGACY

The State Builder

L ENIN would not have wanted to go down in history as the founder of
a new centralized Russian state that swelled to vast proportions
after his death. A believing Marxist, he envisaged the coming
socialism and communism as a stateless as well as classless new
society. The task of Marxist revolutionaries, in his view, was to prepare
the way for a popularly administered "commune-state" in which no government would exist as a bureaucratic apparatus of power in charge of
public affairs.

But history has its ironies and one of them is that Lenin did go down
in it as, among other things, a state builder. And he foreshadowed this role
in the very work of political theory, *The State and Revolution,* written in
August and September 1917, in which he sketched the prospectus for a
nonbureaucratic commune-state in the socialist future. In it he likewise
stressed the Marxist idea that workers would form a transitional "dictator-

ship of the proletariat" in the process of overthrowing the capitalist system. Marx and Engels had been vague about the nature of this dictatorship, although they found intimations of it in the revolutionary Paris Commune of 1870.

To give legitimacy in Marxist terms to his intent to seize power for the Bolshevik party in the semi-interregnum that existed in Russia in 1917, Lenin argued in *The State and Revolution* that revolutionaries should smash the established state order rather than take it over intact. On its ruins they must set up a proletarian dictatorship, which he described as "a centralized organization of violence, both to crush the resistance of the exploiters and to *lead* the enormous mass of the population—the peasants, the petite bourgeoisie, and semi-proletarians—in the work of organizing a socialist economy."[1]

The new Russian state that the Bolsheviks inaugurated in October was constitutionally proclaimed a Republic of Soviets. Its government, the Council of People's Commissars (Sovnarkom), was the executive arm of the All-Russian Congress of Soviets. But power in this state did not reside where the Constitution of 1918 said it did—in the soviets (councils) of workers', soldiers', and peasants' deputies. It resided, rather, in the Russian Communist Party, which ruled through the soviets and other governmental and nongovernmental organizations, such as trade unions, via the placement of party members in controlling posts in their directing bodies. True, in the first years the Sovnarkom, headed by Lenin, functioned as the executive arm of government. But even during Lenin's tenure policymaking on major questions tended to gravitate to the party Central Committee and its Politburo, in which Lenin exercised authority by persuasion as the party's *vozhd'*. Old Russia's political culture, in which absolute power lay outside the executive organs of government, has been cited as one cause of this. "If Divine Providence vested the Autocratic Power in the Hands of the Tsar, History vested the Dictatorship of the Proletariat in the hands of party leadership."[2]

With other parties, socialist as well as nonsocialist, outlawed, with the press under party-government control and a system of preliminary censorship established, the Bolsheviks, numbering some 250,000 in 1919, were securely dominant. In the Cheka (subsequently GPU and then OGPU) they created a centralized political police with far-reaching prerogatives. The land, mineral resources, banks, transportation systems, and major industries, were nationalized. A state monopoly of foreign trade was established, and economic administration vested in a Supreme Council of National Economy under the Sovnarkom. The seat of government was moved from Peter's city back to Moscow. Given the background of tsarism's political culture, still fresh in memory and ingrained in living people's

habits of mind and conduct, and the deep-seated tradition of popular submission to authoritarian government, the postrevolutionary situation was
made to order for a resurgence of Russian-style bureaucracy. To Lenin's
intense chagrin, it began to become evident toward the end of his life.

In one special sense Lenin's Bolshevism stood for revolution from
above. He held it to be both necessary and in accordance with Marxism
that the revolutionaries, once propelled by insurrection into the role of a
ruling party, proceed forthwith to form a regime that would use force and
violence to quell the displaced but still active enemies of the Revolution
from the former ruling classes. The taking of power was not the end of the
revolutionary process but a momentous turning point beyond which it must
continue from above insofar as the revolutionary government wielded the
instruments of repression against its still numerous class enemies. This
Lenin argued in his treatise of 1918, *The Proletarian Revolution and the
Renegade Kautsky*. It is also sharply etched in his 1919 prospectus for a
work, never completed, on the proletarian dictatorship. Two passages are
especially notable. First, "the dictatorship of the proletariat is the *continuation* of the class struggle in new forms." Second, "the state is only a
weapon of the proletariat in its class struggle. A special form of cudgel,
rien de plus."[3]

Reasoning so, Lenin never questioned the propriety of terror as one
means of repressing the Revolution's enemies. The Cheka was created in
December 1917 as a political police force mandated to combat counterrevolution. When an armed uprising took place in Penza in August 1918,
Lenin ordered the local authorities to use "merciless mass terror against
kulaks, priests, and White Guards." Then came the "Red Terror" decree
of 5 September 1918, which specified that "the Soviet republic should be
made secure against class enemies by isolating them in concentration
camps."[4] Terrorist acts by Socialist-Revolutionaries (SRs) in 1918, including the assassinations of high Bolshevik officials and of the German
Ambassador, Count Mirbach, and the attempted assassination of Lenin,
were met with terrorist response on a large scale. Lenin and most other
Bol'shevik leaders saw state terror—summary justice, shooting on the
spot, taking of hostages, arbitrary imprisonment, and the like—not simply
as a necessary response to terrorist provocation, but also as a legitimate
instrument of revolutionary action from above.

Any doubt on this point is dispelled by the fact that Lenin continued
to defend the propriety of terror after the end of the Civil War and the
transition to peaceful conditions under the NEP. Law codes were then
being drafted for Soviet Russia. On 17 May 1922, Lenin wrote a letter to
Commissar of Justice D. I. Kursky about the Soviet criminal code. "The
court must not eliminate terror; to promise that would be self-deception or

deception," he said. "It must be grounded and legalized in principle, without duplicity and embellishment. The formula must be as broad as possible because only revolutionary legal consciousness and revolutionary conscience will set conditions, broader or narrow, of application in practice."[5]

The category of persons subject to terror and other forms of repression as class enemies was ominously elastic in Lenin-inspired thought and practice of the revolutionary period. Not only militant monarchists, White Guards, and other representatives of the former ruling classes were included, but also various elements of the worker-peasant majority were singled out on one ground or another. Better-off peasants called "kulaks" were classified as "village bourgeoisie," and a proclamation of Sovnarkom, signed by Lenin and other prominent Bolsheviks in June 1918, declared "merciless war" against them. In proposed amendments to an antikulak decree, Lenin wrote: "Lay it down more precisely that owners of grain who possess surplus grain and do not send it to the depots and places of grain collection will be declared *enemies of the people* and will be subject to imprisonment for a term of not less than ten years, confiscation of their property, and expulsion forever from the community."[6]

But Lenin did not see revolution from above by repression of enemies as the sole or major task of the new regime. Especially after the Civil War ended and the NEP began, the emphasis in Bolshevik politics shifted to what Lenin had foreseen in *The State and Revolution* as the process of party leadership of the "whole people" in organizing a socialist system of society. This was a constructive task, as reflected in the catchphrase for it: "building of socialism."

A Reformist Road to Socialism

The notion of a long-range effort to build socialism involved a momentous modification of the classical Marxist scheme of history. Marx and Engels had envisaged socialist or communist society (terms they used interchangeably) as arising without much delay on the yonder side of the proletarian revolutions with which they believed the societies of advanced capitalism were pregnant. Such revolutions would produce classless societies that would go through a relatively brief transitional phase marked by the preservation of a state in the form of a proletarian dictatorship whose mission would be to take power and subdue the dispossessed bourgeoisie. The state *qua* state had no task of administration or leadership in a society engaged in constructing communism. In the transitional lower stage of communist society, which in later Marxist writings came to be designated "socialism," people would be remunerated according to the amount of work they did, whereas in the higher phase they would be remunerated according to need. The higher stage would emerge as old habits died out and the productive forces yielded the abundance made possible by modern machine industry.

As Lenin and his fellow Bolsheviks saw it, the October Revolution had propelled Russia onto the socialist shore of history, but so economically and culturally backward a country could not, despite the Marxist dictatorship and nationalization of resources, properly be called "socialist," much less "communist." Classes of workers and peasants, with inevitable antagonisms between them, still existed, and so did the state as an apparatus of coercion, whereas socialism meant the end of class divisions and of the state itself in the old sense. Small-scale commodity production, a breeding ground of capitalism, was prevalent throughout this peasant country's agrarian economy. In grim awareness of all this, Lenin said in 1920: "The dictatorship of the proletariat means a persistent struggle—bloody and bloodless, violent and peaceful, military and economic, educational and administrative—against the forces and traditions of the old society. The force of habit in millions and tens of millions is a most formidable force."[7]

Thus NEP Russia, an impoverished and benighted land with its huge majority of peasants—a petit-bourgeois class in mode of life and mentality—had yet to be remade into a socialist Russia. It was passing through a transition period between capitalism and socialism.[8] The transformative process, especially in the continuing absence of socialist revolutions in advanced European countries, would necessarily be a lengthy one. "The generation of people who are now at the age of fifty cannot expect to see a communist society," said Lenin in 1920 to a congress of the Komsomol (Communist Youth League). "But the generation of those who are now fifteen will see a communist society, and will itself build this society. This generation should know that the entire purpose of their lives is to build a communist society."[9]

The building process was to take place within the framework of the NEP, by evolution, not revolution. Lenin could not have been more firm on this point. Revolution, he explained, "is a change which breaks the old order to its very foundations, and not one that cautiously, slowly, and gradually remodels it, taking care to break as little as possible." War Communism had represented a "revolutionary approach" to the building of socialism; it had sought to break up the old system completely at one stroke and replace it with a new one. The NEP signified a "reformist approach," the method of which was "not to *break up* the old social-economic system—trade, petty production, petty proprietorship, capitalism—but to *revive* trade, petty proprietorship, capitalism, while cautiously and gradually getting the upper hand over them, or making it possible to subject them to state regulation *only to the extent* that they revive."

Here this greatest of twentieth-century revolutionaries lectured his party on the importance of gradualism when conditions call for it. "What grounds are there for assuming that the 'great, victorious, world' revolution can and must employ only revolutionary methods? There are none at all." The supreme, perhaps the only danger for a genuine revolutionary, Lenin declared, is that of "exaggerated revolutionism," meaning the failure to observe the limits within which revolutionary methods are appropriate. "True revolutionaries have mostly come a cropper when they began to write 'revolution' with a capital R, to elevate 'revolution' to something almost divine, to lose their heads, to lose the ability to reflect, weigh and ascertain in the coolest and most dispassionate manner at what moment, under what circumstances and in which sphere of action you must act in a revolutionary manner, and at what moment, under what circumstances and in which sphere you must turn to reformist action. True revolutionaries will perish . . . only if they abandon their sober outlook and take it into their heads that the 'great, victorious, world' revolution can and must solve all problems in a revolutionary manner under all circumstances and in all spheres of action. If they do this, their doom is certain. Whoever gets such ideas into his head is lost because he has foolish ideas about a fundamental problem; and in a fierce war (and revolution is the fiercest sort of war) the penalty for folly is defeat."[10]

The shift to a "reformist approach" as against revolutionism was not, as some Bolsheviks thought, a sign of Lenin's weakening as a revolutionary as his health began to fail in the final years of his life. It was a logical consequence of the realization that the force against which the party was pitting itself was the stubborn "force of habit" in tens of millions of people still wedded to old ways in their workaday lives and ethos. One could quell resistant enemies with the cudgel of state power, but the force of habit could not possibly be so quelled. Only by persuasion could this end be accomplished, hence the need for gradualism and a generation-long time span. The building of socialism was necessarily an educative effort. In taking this view, and in persuading the party to adopt it as well, Lenin was only resurrecting the orientation of his seminal early work, *What Is To Be Done?*, on the instilling of Marxist consciousness on a mass scale as the party's chief task in building a revolutionary movement in Russia.[11]

Consistently with the idea of the construction of socialism as an educative effort, Lenin conceived the Bolshevik-ruled republic as a tutelary state or educational polity in which formally nonparty organizations, like the trade unions and local soviets, would function as (in his terminology) "schools of communism." In these organizations, under the guidance of party members consciously dedicated to the socialist goal, people *en masse* would gradually learn to administer the economy and to manage public affairs on their own, without bureaucrats. And Lenin made adoption of Western techniques a part of the learning process. The Bolsheviks must borrow from the Americans their "Taylor system" of scientific management. They must learn, too, from the Germans. "So long as revolution in Germany is slow in 'being born,' " wrote Lenin in 1918, "our task is to learn state capitalism from the Germans, to take it over *with all our might, and not to spare dictatorial methods in taking it over, in still greater mea-sure than Peter hastened the taking over of westernism by barbaric *Rus'*, not shrinking at barbaric means of fighting barbarism."[12]

The Lenin who sought to design a socialist future for NEP Russia in his valedictory programmatic writings of 1921–23 was as utopian in his vision of the end as he was gradualist in his view of the means. His image of the goal showed an affiliation not only with Marx but also with a much earlier generation of Russian radicals typified by Chernyshevsky. Socialist Russia would be a popularly administered, nonbureaucratic society in which class differences would have been overcome, a society with a large-scale machine industry based on electric power and operating according to a plan. The material abundance of this society would be distributed on socialist principles, and all its economic life would be organized along cooperative lines.

This last was the crux: The whole population, peasantry included, must be drawn little by little into the work of cooperatives, and into work-ing cooperatively. In one of his last articles, Lenin called this the "coop-erating of Russia" and said that it would be the work of a whole historical epoch comprising at a minimum one or two generations. He observed that the old cooperative community builders of the nineteenth century, like Robert Owen, had erred not in their vision of a "socialism of cooperatives" but in their belief that it could be created without a political revolution like the one that the Bolsheviks had carried out in Russia. But how was the cooperating of Russia to be realized? Lenin's answer—by a "cultural revolution"—was a restatement of his idea of socialist construction as a learning process. A cultural revolution was necessary. This meant a long-drawn-out effort of "culturalizing," or work of cultural enlightenment, starting with the overcoming of mass illiteracy and aimed at the eventual remaking of the popular—especially the peasant—mentality and ethos in preparation for a socialism of cooperatives.[13]

Lenin saw Russia's industrialization as a necessary premise of the cultural revolution, "for to be cultured we must achieve a certain develop-ment of the material means of production, a certain material base."[14] How important industrialization would be for the "cooperating" of the countryside he had indicated earlier in a famous statement about the large and important stratum of moderately well-off "middle peasants" who neither employed outside hired labor like the much smaller and better-off class of "kulaks" nor were as easily amenable to change as the poor peasants and the hired farm laborers. Of the middle peasant he said: "We must live in peace with him. In a communist society the middle peasant will be on our side when we alleviate and improve his economic conditions. If tomorrow we could supply one hundred thousand first-class tractors, provide them with fuel, provide them with drivers—you know very well that this at present is a fantasy—the middle peasant would say: 'I am for the *kommunia*' [that is, for communism]."[15]

Most probably the persuasive effect of the still-to-be-created tractor industry was in Lenin's mind when he said, in his final article, that the Bolsheviks' only hope lay in industrializing: "Only when we have done this shall we, speaking figuratively, be able to change horses, to change from the peasant, *muzhik* horse of poverty, from the horse of an economy designed for a ruined peasant country, to the horse which the proletariat is seeking and must seek—the horse of large-scale machine industry, of electrification, of the Volkhov power station, etc."[16]

Muscovy Redux

Bolshevik leaders saw their revolutionary republic as a still backward *Rus'* that had made a great leap forward into modernity on the way to the predestined socialist future of all humanity. The perception of movement into modernity was not unfounded. The Revolution, comprising both the February and October phases, made a clean sweep of much that was archaic in the Russian state down to 1917.

It destroyed the tsarist autocracy. It disestablished Russian Orthodoxy (while at the same time founding a new orthodox faith in Marxism-Leninism, as Marxism according to Lenin later came to be called). It secularized and greatly liberalized the institution of marriage and family ties. It abolished the police-administered system of internal passports by which the old regime controlled the residence and movements of its subjects, and eliminated the Pale of Settlement (area of permitted residence) for Russia's Jews. Within the centralized structure of the party-state it supplanted tsarism's outright colonial rule and Russification policies in the outlying regions, inhabited mainly by non-Russian minorities, with at least the forms of governmental autonomy and a certain measure of linguistic and cultural autonomy. It sought wide popular participation in public affairs through the party-directed mass organizations. It proclaimed equality of the sexes

and opened up opportunities for education and careers to people of heretofore lowly station and limited prospects. It publicized the tsarist government's wartime secret treaties and renounced their arrangements for further
territorial aggrandizement. All this underlay Trotsky's statement in 1924:
"Essentially the Revolution means the people's final break with the Asiatic,
with the seventeenth century, with Holy Russia and cockroaches."[17]

That was not so much a statement of fact, however, as a profession of
faith. Lenin, Trotsky, and other revolutionaries in power knew well that
old Holy Russia was still vigorously alive in their country. However strongly
workers had supported the Revolution in their factory committees, peasants by dividing up the landed estates, and soldiers by voting against the
war with their feet, they had not, in their majority, made a final break with
much that old Russia instilled in them. That Russia lived on in churches,
the village *mir,* the patriarchal peasant family, old values, old pastimes,
old outlooks, muddy roads, and very widespread illiteracy. Lenin's call
for a long-drawn-out cultural revolution in the form of a party-led effort to
overcome old Russian ways reflected his understanding of this.

But not everyone shared the belief that the Revolution marked Russia's leap into modernity. Some had a sixth sense that it represented, rather,
her withdrawal from the Europocentric Petersburg period into her premod-
ern past as an outpost of Asia in confrontation with Europe. It was, after
all, chiefly the Western states that intervened on the side of the Whites in
the Civil War, and to the West that most of the Whites fled when their
cause was lost. A vision of Bolshevik-led *Rus'* standing against the West
inspired Blok's poem of 1918, *Scythians,* which begins:

> You're millions. We're hordes and hordes and hordes.
> Just you try and fight with us!
> Yes, we're Scythians! Yes, we're Asiatics
> With slant and greedy eyes!

The writer Boris Pil'niak also saw the 1917 upheaval as a rebellion of
peasant Russia against the Petrine period and a return to the past. "Just a
few days after the Revolution," says the autobiographical character in his
novel of 1919, *The Naked Year,* "Russia . . . was on her way back to the
seventeenth century."[18] Here it may be noted that at a critical moment for
Lenin's regime in the summer months of 1918, when hostile forces were
closing in from all directions, the territory actually under the regime's
control was reduced roughly to that which had comprised the Muscovite
principality in the fifteenth century.[19] No wonder a vision of the revolutionary republic as a Muscovy redux arose in some Russian minds.

Another reason for the Muscovy redux notion was the messianic
theme in Lenin's thought and practice that led to the creation in Moscow

in 1919 of the Third International, or Comintern, as an agency of world revolutionary leadership. The idea had appeared in Lenin's *What Is To Be Done?*, which in 1902 drew a picture of Russia's proletariat making itself "the vanguard of the international proletariat" by overthrowing tsarism. Messianism was an age-old phenomenon in Russia, expressed in the formula of "Moscow the Third Rome," in which the fifteenth-century Russian monk Philotheus claimed for Muscovy the role of bearer of sacred truth for the whole Christian world—after two earlier Romes had fallen, the original one to the barbarians and the second Rome in Constantinople to the Turks. And now in 1919 the Leninist party-state with its capital in Moscow presented itself as a vanguard proletarian dictatorship that was setting an example to follow for all true worker parties, the Communist ones rather than the Social Democratic parties of the Second International. The sacred truth now was Lenin's Marxism, which was to be carried to the world's workers.

The worker revolutions in advanced Western states, on which Lenin had pinned hope in the widespread European crisis at the end of World War I and in which he had seen potential salvation for the revolution in backward Russia, did not materialize. The Comintern's calls for revolutionary uprisings went largely unheeded abroad, and the Red Army's march into Poland in 1920, which Lenin urged as a detonator of revolution in Germany, ended in defeat. So, although the Soviet Republic survived when the Civil War and foreign intervention ended in late 1920, it found itself in what Lenin christened the "hostile capitalist encirclement." Even Bolsheviks could see a parallel with the hostile foreign encirclement of the Muscovite state in its time of emergence.

Furthermore, the diplomacy developed by Lenin had a resemblance, of which he may not have been aware, to the divisive diplomacy that the rising Muscovite state pursued in *its* hostile encirclement. Lenin saw diplomacy as a defensive weapon to ensure the Soviet Republic's survival by keeping its enemies divided. "So long as we have not won the whole world, so long as we remain economically and militarily weaker than what is left of the capitalist world," he said, "we must stick to the rule: be able to exploit the contradictions and antagonisms between the imperialists. If we had not followed this rule, we would long ago have been hanged on separate aspen trees to the capitalists' general joy. Our basic experience in this respect came from concluding the Brest treaty."[20] The treaty of Brest-Litovsk was the territorially costly separate peace that the fledgling Soviet government, at Lenin's insistence, concluded with Germany in early 1918. It was the first and for Lenin the classic case of an agreement with a capitalist government that served Soviet needs, in this instance the Revolution's need to survive.

Abroad, some White Russian intellectuals were rethinking the Revolution that had made émigrés of them. Russian history had known great peasant revolts, notably those led by Stepan Razin in the sixteenth century, Ivan Bolotnikov in the seventeenth, and Emelian Pugachev in the eighteenth. What were Lenin and his leather-jacketed Bolshevik commissars if not the leaders of another such peasant upheaval in the twentieth? And were they really the Marxist transformers of Russia's culture that they proclaimed themselves to be, or unwitting agents of its national regeneration? Was not their revolution reestablishing a strong centralized Russian state? So, might not Bolshevism itself (as distinguished from Marx's and Europe's "Communism") be something as Russian as its very name rather than the un-Russian Jewish phenomenon that many White émigrés thought it was?

Such was the trend of thought among a group of ex-Whites who published a collection of essays in Prague in 1921 under the title *Smena vekh (Change of Landmarks)*. Abandoning the view of their White Russian brethren that Bolshevism was alien to Russia, they spoke of a "Great Russian Revolution" that marked a rebirth of Russian statehood and alone was capable of restoring Russia's prestige as a great power, a revolution whose very internationalism, embodied in Moscow's Third International, was the successor to old Russia's universalistic idea of Moscow the Third Rome. The regime born of the Revolution, they found, was not an anarchic, centrifugal force for the dispersal of the country, but a "centripetal state force" that was cementing it back together after its new Time of Troubles. Its intelligentsia would become imbued with the "mystique of the state," as a result of which the Russian state would finally fulfill its destiny as "God's way on earth."

Nikolai Ustrialov, the group's intellectual leader, wrote that just as the great French Revolution was the Frenchman's pride, along with Descartes and Rousseau, Voltaire and Hugo, Louis XIV and Napoleon, so the great Russian Revolution would be the Russian's pride along with Pushkin and Tolstoy, Dostoyevsky and Gogol, Peter the Great, Russian music and Russian religious thought. Bolshevik efforts to reunite the minority-inhabited borderlands with the center would be assisted by Russian patriots "in the name of a Russia great and indivisible"; and the minority nations would accept Bolshevism, which was Russian culture's "final product," because they were already bearers of Russian culture. Even if it should be mathematically proved, he said, that 90 percent of the revolutionaries were non-Russian, chiefly Jews, it would not change the purely Russian nature of the movement: It was not they who guided the Russian Revolution but vice versa. And now, under the NEP, which Ustrialov called "Bolshevism's economic Brest," Lenin's new Russia was abandoning orthodox Communist positions. *"To save the Soviets, Moscow is sacrificing communism."* It was an "evolution of the revolution," comparable to the French Revolution's path of Thermidor—the ebbing of Jacobin extremism marked by Robespierre's execution on the ninth of Thermidor. On the basis of this interpretation, the *Smena vekh* authors invited their non-Bolshevik confreres now working in Soviet institutions as administrators and specialists to cooperate loyally with Lenin's regime out of Russian patriotic motives. Ustrialov christened such tactics :"national Bolshevism."[21]

Smena vehk was reprinted in Soviet Russia, read carefully and discussed widely by the Bolshevik leaders, and allowed—along with subsequent writings of the group—to circulate among "bourgeois specialists" working for the Soviet regime, many of whom responded positively to its patriotic philosophy. Lenin, having read the original symposium, told his comrades gathered at the Eleventh Party Congress in 1922: "I think that by being straightforward like this, Ustrialov is rendering us a great service. . . . We must say frankly that such candid enemies are useful. We must say frankly that the things Ustrialov speaks about are possible. History knows all sorts of metamorphoses. . . . *Smena vekh* adherents express the sentiments of thousands and tens of thousands of bourgeois, or of Soviet employees whose function it is to operate our New Economic Policy. This is the real and main danger."

It was a danger, he reasoned, of cultural subversion and setback because former officials and other old-regime holdovers working in Soviet institutions might infect their Communist bosses with old Russian bureaucratic habits and ways of thought. Lenin used a powerful metaphor to drive the point home. He recalled how it was recorded in history books that sometimes one nation conquers another. "But what happens to the culture of these nations? Here things are not so simple. If the conquering nation is more cultured than the vanquished nation, the former imposes its culture upon the latter; but if the opposite is the case, the vanquished imposes its culture upon the conquerer."[22] The danger was that instead of the transformation of the still-persisting culture of old Russia, there might take place in time a Russification of the new Bolshevik culture, a relapse of the Revolution into Russianism.

Because he saw the political revolution as the fulcrum by which the Bolsheviks had placed themselves in a position to build socialism in Russia, Lenin never allowed that the October action might have been premature in view of the failure of socialist revolutions to occur in European countries. He anathematized those Menshevik-minded Marxists—"our European philistines," he called them—who considered that it had been a mistake for socialists to take power in so culturally laggard a country as Russia. Defiantly he replied that if a definite level of culture was needed, as they said, for building socialism, "Why cannot we begin by first achieving the prerequisites for that definite level of culture in a revolutionary way, and *then*, with the aid of the workers' and peasants' government and Soviet system, proceed to overtake the other nations?"[23]

Behind the defiant tone, however, there was a worried realization on Lenin's part, as his time grew short, that the gradual transformation of NEP Russia into a socialist society was not the only possibility in the coming period. As he recognized in his speech to the Eleventh Party Congress, there was the alternative possibility that in the contest of cultures, the new would succumb to the old. The formidable force of old Russian habit might prevail in the end. The "conquering nation" (the Bolshevik Revolution) might be subverted from within by the "vanquished nation" (the culture of Russian tsarism). Lenin's disquiet over this possibility deepened into dismay when it became clear to him that the "real and main danger" might lie somewhere else than in Soviet employees of *Smena vekh* outlook or former officials who were insinuating tsarist ways into the Bolsheviks' administration.

It might lie, rather, at the top, in the receptivity of certain high-placed Bolsheviks to those influences, their readiness to abet the retrograde tendencies. In particular, these Bolsheviks were fostering what Lenin called "bureaucratism" and showing, in dealings with minority nations of the republic, a Great Russian chauvinist attitude, or "true Russianism." The worst offender on both counts, it transpired, was the Russified Georgian Bolshevik Stalin, who by 1922 had accumulated great power as the general secretary of the Central Committee and the head of two government agencies, the Commissariat for Nationality Affairs and the Commissariat of Worker-Peasant Inspection. In notes on the nationalities question, dictated 30–31 December 1922 (not long before suffering the stroke that ended his active involvement in state affairs), Lenin assailed Stalin, along with his choleric fellow Georgian Sergo Ordzhonikidze and the Polish-born chief of the Cheka, Felix Dzerzhinsky, as Russified minority-representatives who were overdoing it on the side of "true Russianism." Stalin he stigmatized as a "Great Russian Derzhimorda." These notes were a part of the case he was building for the purpose of unseating Stalin from the general secretaryship at the impending Twelfth Party Congress. The failure of his health in March 1923, however, made his attendance at the congress impossible and enabled Stalin to weather the most serious adversity encountered on his road to power.[24]

Thus, although in his final public speech, in November 1922, Lenin prophesied that "Out of NEP Russia will come a socialist Russia,"[25] his vision of the Russian future grew clouded in the end. Underneath his *apologia* for October and the optimistic projections of his last speeches and articles, there ran an undercurrent of troubled uncertainty about the outcome of the Revolution. He saw that there was a possibility of cultural reversion, that old Russia might rise again in the Soviet Republic, and that Stalin might play a decisively important part in bringing this about. Both perceptions proved prophetic.

So enamored was Lenin of a revolutionary teaching that came from the West, so admiring of Western organizing ways, and so contemptuous of that non-Western land, the Russia of the tsars, that he probably never seriously thought of himself as a Russian national figure. But some others perceived him as that. Among them was Trotsky. "The National Element in Lenin" was his theme in the speech he gave on Lenin's fiftieth birthday in 1920. Lenin's internationalism needed no certifying, Trotsky said in the tribute, "Yet Lenin himself is national to a high degree." He could not direct such a revolution as the one in progress without being organically linked to the main forces of popular life. The greatest revolutionary action in the history of humanity "found for the first time, in Lenin, its national embodiment."[26]

When Lenin died in 1924, Ustrialov wrote colorfully from abroad about the Russian national element in him. "He was, without doubt, Russian from head to foot," he said in his *Smena vekh* paper. "Here's Russia's spirit, the smell of *Rus'*," he went on in a paraphrase of Pushkin's line. "He of course had Razin in him and Bolotnikov and Great Peter himself." And when present hatreds pass away in the end, "People will understand once and for all that *Lenin is ours,* that *Lenin is a true son of Russia,* its national hero alongside Dmitry Donskoy, Peter the Great, Pushkin, and Tolstoy."[27]

Old Russia claimed Lenin in death, and in a way that would have repelled him. Over objections from his widow Krupskaya and some others, a majority of the top party leadership decided to set up a Lenin mausoleum in Red Square featuring his embalmed body. This had overtones of an old Orthodox Russia, which preserved saints' bones as holy relics and made cult figures of deceased and living tsars. The mausoleum became the centerpiece of a civic cult of Lenin, followed by a Lenin Institute to publish his writings, "Lenin corners" in Soviet institutions, and much else besides. The aim in part was to solidify the ruling party's bond with the nation now that its unifier and unique authority figure had passed away. But the posthumous cult of Lenin also reflected the veneration that this truly charismatic leader inspired in his Bolshevik followers.[28] There was a kind of religiosity in it. The party-state, with its Leninist orthodoxy enshrined in the cult, took on more of the character of a church-state. This too entered Lenin's legacy, and makes it less surprising that the Bolshevik who a few years later succeeded him as *vozhd'* was a former theological seminarian.

Diverging Bolshevisms

Despite all that Lenin's followers shared of his teaching, they were a disparate lot with Bolshevik minds of their own, differing political person-alities and cultural predispositions, clashing power interests, and differing views of Soviet Russia's situation. No matter how strongly they stressed the need to "follow the path of Lenin," they were going to take diverging paths. Leading individuals and factions would, in each instance, stress certain parts of Lenin's Bolshevism, disregard or deemphasize others, and transmute still others into something new—claiming all the while that they were upholding Leninist orthodoxy, as Stalin for example did in his lec-tures of 1924 on *The Foundations of Leninism.*

In the familiar account that has come down to us from Trotsky's writings and others, there were two conflicting policy lines in the Bolshe-vik leadership after Lenin's death. The Left wing was for accelerated industrialization at home and active encouragement of revolutions abroad. On the latter point it kept faith with Lenin's view that Russia's socialist revolution could never have final success without support by socialist revolution in one or several advanced countries. The Right wing, while committed to industrializing within the country's means and with due observance of balance between development of heavy and light industry, was oriented, with the later Lenin, on the gradual building of a socialism based on peasant cooperatives, and stood for caution in international af-fairs. Thus, each found something to stress in the complex legacy of Lenin's Bolshevism, but the elements they chose to stress differed.

Because of its tendency to adapt party policy to a traditional Russian institution, the village commune, and its downplaying of world revolution, the party Right represented a moderate Russian national Bolshevism. Al-exei Rykov, a leader of the Right and Lenin's successor as head of the government, has been credited by a knowledgeable source, who worked in the Soviet government in those years, with priority in arriving at the idea of "socialism in one country."[29] His associate in the mid-1920s, Ni-kolai Bukharin, a leading party intellectual and editor of *Pravda,* became the principal expositor of the idea. Since abandoning or even softpedaling the perspective of world revolution was a deviation from Lenin's Bolshe-vism, it was not admissible in public, especially at a time when the Left was charging the Right with "national narrow-mindedness." Bukharin even warned, in public, against a tendency to "spit" on the international revo-lution and said that "such a tendency could give rise to its own special ideology, a peculiar 'national bolshevism' or something else in this spirit."[30]

In private, however, some members of the Right spoke differently. Rykov told his American journalist friend, Reswick, that "if we, a backward people, stop playing at world revolution and organize our national life on the pattern of our traditional rural *mir,* the capitalist world will have no cause to fear us. On the contrary, it will be to their interest to supply Russia with arms, or even to join us if we are attacked by Japan or Germany." Another prominent moderate, Abel Yenukidze, told Reswick that when world revolution failed to materialize, "it was up to us to uncook the *kasha,"* that is, to make far-reaching concessions to private enterprise in industry as well as agriculture, and also said that if Lenin had lived a few years longer he would have corrected his error of 1917 about imminent revolutions abroad.[31]

The national Bolshevism of the Right thus connoted an adaptation of the aims and policies of the regime to the way of life of a predominantly peasant people, and renunciation in practice of the international revolution on which Lenin banked. Because the revolutionary internationalists on the party Left, headed by Trotsky, would not relinquish Lenin's postulate that backward Russia's socialist revolution was dependent for its ultimate success upon revolutions in more advanced countries, the chasm between the two groups was absolutely unbridgeable. Each feared the other more than anything, and it was to this deep division that Stalin owed his capacity to maneuver his way to power by ousting the two groups seriatim.

But apart from the opportunism, did he have his own political orientation distinct from those of his Bolshevik associates on the Left and the Right? In Trotsky's opinion at the outset of the 1930s, which has influenced much scholarship, he did not. He was a "centrist" who in the quest for the only thing that mattered to him—power—aligned himself with the Right and then, when the Left was defeated in 1927, turned against his erstwhile factional allies in a lurch to the left. He accepted the Right's program when he started espousing socialism in one country in late 1924, and then stole the Left's, or a caricature of it, when he struck out on his own in 1928–29.

In opposition to this picture of Stalin, I will contend that he had his own distinctive orientation and that during the 1920s he worked out a policy program that gave concrete expression to it. His politics of coalition with the Right against Trotsky constrained him from openly voicing this conception before the Left opposition's defeat and expulsion at the end of 1927, and even in the ensuing years he refrained from revealing the full extremism of his program. We can, however, piece it together from various statements that he made during that decade. Differing as it did from the positions of both the Left and the Right, this Bolshevism was very much Stalin's own.

His "true Russianism" made of him a national Bolshevik of quite different complexion from the moderates on the party Right who wanted to adapt policy to the village *mir* in organizing a socialism of cooperatives and subtly to downplay international revolution as a policy goal. Even at the height of his tactical alliance with them, Stalin gave indication of this divergence by the studied way in which his speeches stressed eventual resumption of revolution abroad. And while he joined the Right in arguing that Soviet Russia could proceed all the way to socialism in international isolation, there was a difference between his way of advocating this position and theirs, reflecting the difference between his Russian nationalism and theirs. As an attitude of national self-esteem, nationalism comes in two main varieties: patriotic devotion to one's people and their positive national attributes; and chauvinism, an overweening national pride and sense of superiority over other nations. The national Bolshevism of the Right was nationalist in the first way, Stalin's in the second. His was a radical version of Russian national Bolshevism, a blend of Bolshevik revolutionism with the Great Russian chauvinism that Lenin correctly perceived in him in 1922. The strident way in which he, unlike the Right, preached the "one country" doctrine, could have suggested to a perceptive observer that his national Bolshevism differed from theirs. His was a message of pride in Russia's ability to go it alone and blaze a trail to the socialist future for all mankind, just as she had shown Europe the way to revolution in 1917.

His Russian nationalism had an exclusionary aspect: it was anti-Semitic. In the mid-1920s he made covert use of anti-Semitism in the fight against a Left opposition whose major figures, Trotsky and afterward Zinoviev and Kamenev, were Jews (their original surnames were Bronstein, Radomylsky, and Rosenfeld, respectively). He encouraged the baiting of the opposition leaders as Jews in meetings held in factory party cells.[32] He was identifying his faction as the party's Russian faction, and the Trotskyists as the Jewish one. That Jews, no matter how culturally Russified, could not be authentically Russian seems to have become an article of belief with him, revealed, for example, in the quotation marks with which he set off "Russian" when he referred to " 'Russian' Mensheviks of the type of Abramovich and Dan."[33] To the party, the country, and himself, his message was that real Bolsheviks were real Russians, that Bolshevism was no Jewish phenomenon but a Russian national one, and that Lenin as the party's founder and he as Lenin's coming successor exemplified these truths.

In the act of asserting his proud sense of self-identity as a "Russian" Bolshevik, Stalin was ministering to an identity need present in many of the new state's citizens. Expressing his own outlook he was very effectively offering a Soviet Russian nationhood as a collective identity to be proud of, and presenting the socialism-building enterprise as a Russian mission in world history. In the process he was making himself known in the country as a forceful political leader and promoting his stature within the party and beyond.

Stalin saw both Lenin and himself as leaders of a Soviet Russia that was the rightful successor-state to historic Russia. Such was the implication of a memorandum that he addressed to the other Politburo members in 1926. He found it distressing that some Ukrainian intellectuals wanted de-Russification and a cultural orientation *away* from Moscow at a time when workers of the West were looking with admiration *toward* Moscow as the citadel of world revolution and Leninism; and he termed Leninism "the highest achievement of Russian culture."[34] In *Smena vekh* Ustrialov had called Bolshevism the "final product" of Russian culture. The thought was so extraordinary that its repetition by Stalin in similar language five years later strongly suggests inspiration from the earlier passage. To Lenin, for whom there was no such thing as a single Russian national culture, the idea of Leninism or Bolshevism as its "highest achievement" would have appeared grotesque. To Stalin it appeared natural and true. In his view, both Lenin and himself were representative of a Russian culture stretching back through the centuries, exponents of all that was best in it. Such was the direction of Stalin's thought in the 1920s when he had become one of the country's rulers, living among such reminders of its national past as the halls and churches and crenelated battlements of the old citadel by the Moscow River. And it was at this time that he evolved his policy program.

A letter of 1930 (but only made public twenty years later) shows how determined Stalin was to go to school in Russian history in the process of devising a policy for the near Soviet future. He wrote the letter to the unofficial proletarian poet laureate, Demyan Bedny. Some feuilletons in verse by Bedny, occasioned by real incidents, had appeared in the Soviet press shortly before. One of them, "Get Off the Oven-Shelf," responded to reports of a decline of coal output in the Donbas in consequence of mismanagement and low discipline among miners newly recruited from the farms. Another, "Pererva," dealt with a train wreck resulting from a switchman's carelessness at a stopping point on the Moscow-Kursk railway line called Pererva. Bedny's poems found a cause of these misfortunes in the character traits of indolence and slovenliness inherited from Russia's past. To avoid future repetitions, he wrote at the close of the first-named of the two, "We must remake our nature and not whine and lie on the 'ancestral' oven-shelf."

There was a good Leninist precedent for such satiric social criticism: Lenin had set Soviet Russia the task of overcoming the national heritage of "Oblomovism," the slothful day-dreaming existence immortalized long before the Revolution in the hero of Goncharov's novel *Oblomov*. Nevertheless, Bedny came under criticism from the Central Committee for writing the pieces as he did. Concerned over this, he sent Stalin a personal letter in which, with references to the nineteenth-century Russian satirists Gogol and Shchedrin, he defended the writer's right to satirize the dark sides of Soviet life.

In his harshly negative reply, Stalin set forth his credo of Russian national pride:

The whole world recognizes now that the center of the revolutionary movement has shifted from Western Europe to Russia. . . . The revolutionary workers of all countries unanimously applaud the Soviet working class, and first of all the van-guard of the Soviet workers, the *Russian* working class, as its recognized leader, which is carrying through the most revolutionary and active policy ever dreamed of by the proletarians of other countries. *The leaders of the revolutionary workers of all countries are avidly studying the most instructive history of the working class of Russia, its past, the past of Russia,* knowing that in addition to reactionary Russia there existed also a revolutionary Russia, the Russia of Radishchevs and Chernyshevskys, of Zheliabovs and Ulyanovs, of Khalturins and Alexeevs. All this instills (cannot but instill!) in the hearts of the Russian workers a feeling of revolutionary national pride, capable of moving mountains and working miracles.

Instead of grasping all this, what had Bedny done? He had broadcast to the world that "Russia in the past was an abomination of desolation, that present-day Russia is one great 'Pererva,' that 'indolence' and the wish to 'sit on the oven-shelf' are practically a national trait of Russians in general, including Russian workers, who, of course, have not stopped being Russians because they carried out the October Revolution." This, said Stalin, was not Bolshevik criticism but slander, the discrediting of the USSR, the discrediting of the Russian proletariat.[35]

The reference to the "revolutionary" versus the "reactionary" Russia paraphrased a passage from Lenin, whom Stalin invoked as authority for his position. But Lenin's argument had nothing in common with the one Stalin was making to Bedny now. Lenin saw no general Russian culture to be proud of, only the revolutionary record. The Russian national past that Lenin saw as a despotic and slavish one and as such an "abomination of desolation" (to use Stalin's reproving phrase) was for Stalin "most instructive." If any revolutionary leader was avidly studying Russia's past in those days, it was Stalin.

History indeed, as Lenin said, knows all sorts of metamorphoses, especially in the wake of such great breaks in social continuity as Russia's Revolution. The reversion to the tsarist past that Lenin feared did take place, but in a way that he did not foresee and could hardly have imagined. It occurred as it did because his successor found in Russia's distant past a model for policy in the building of socialism—and managed to act on this singular conception.

. . . state power is needed as the lever of transformation. The new state power creates a new legality, a new order which is a revolutionary order.

—Stalin to H. G. Wells, 1934

3

STALIN'S PROGRAM

S TALIN was not simply the executor of the second revolution, as some have thought, but its political designer as well. He embarked upon the bold undertaking consciously and confidently—overconfidently, it soon turned out. He was ready by 1928 with a political orientation that gave him a sense of what was to be done and how to go about it. He acted on an idea formed in its broad contours in advance of the steps he took to set the process of revolutionary change in motion. Whatever its ultimate sources in other minds and other times, it was Stalin who put all the elements together in an original whole. That the consequences were in many ways catastrophic for his country is another important part of our story. But the grand ideas acted on in history by political leaders have far from always been good ones.

Like Lenin and the other Bolshevik leaders, Stalin was committed to the goal of converting NEP Russia into a socialist Russia. Distinctive of his thinking, however, were three further premises that together constituted the core of his approach. First, the engine of change could and should be the revolutionary use of state power. All the resources of the party-state, comprising its commissariats, police, armed forces, hierarchy of party committees and party cells throughout the land, would be deployed, coercively to the extent necessary, in effecting the country's transformation. Second, the prime purpose of this revolutionary use of state power was the augmentation of state power. To transform NEP Russia into a socialist Russia was to construct an industrially and militarily powerful Soviet Russian state owning the instruments of production and capable of fending for itself in a hostile world. Third, because it was necessary to prepare quickly for a coming war, it was imperative to accomplish all these transformations at a maximally swift tempo.

Such, in briefest summary, was Stalin's approach to a revolution from above. If we have remained widely unaware that he had conceived it before he was politically in a position to act upon it, it is partly because Trotsky and others have spread a misconception of him as a political improviser with hardly any interest in ideas, only in his own power, and partly because the exigencies of his political alignment with the party Right in the mid-1920s prevented him from making his position clear then in a comprehensive policy statement.

My interpretation of the tsardom's rise showed the primacy of external over internal policy as a cardinal factor. The demands of external defense and aggrandizement played a crucial part in the early tsars' internal policy of binding all classes in compulsory service to a centralized state. Now again, in Stalin's policy program, the needs of external policy in the "hostile capitalist encirclement" were primary. All else had to be subordinated to the one great task of amassing military-industrial power in a hurry. The imperative of overcoming Mother Russia's age-old weakness in the short space of ten years was the only possible way of saving her from one more beating by foreigners, he told the managers in his speech of 1931. That summarized the policy design that he had worked out in the course of the previous decade.

To Revolution Through War

Unlike the Right's version of national Bolshevism, Stalin's version placed studied emphasis on future Communist revolutions abroad. Not as a precondition for building a completely socialist society in Russia, as the Left believed, but as a precondition for making this outcome "final," that is, irrevocably secure. The spread of the international Communist revolution was needed in order to provide a security guarantee for socialism-building Soviet Russia against the continuing danger of being over-whelmed by hostile forces surrounding her. Stalin argued this in 1926 with utmost clarity:

> To think that the capitalist world can look with indifference on our successes on the economic front, successes that revolutionize the working class of the whole world, is to succumb to an illusion. Therefore, so long as we remain in the capitalist encirclement, so long as the proletariat has not been victorious at least in a number of countries, *we cannot consider our victory final.* Accordingly, no matter what our successes in construction, we cannot consider the land of the proletarian dictatorship guaranteed against dangers from without. So, in order to win conclusively, *we must bring it about that the present capitalist encirclement is replaced by a socialist encirclement,* that the proletariat is victorious in at least several more countries. Only then can our victory be considered final.[1]

Those foreign observers who did not take Stalin's repeated statements to this effect seriously, and who put him down as a national statesman whose only basic concern was the development of the "one country," were setting themselves and their governments up for future surprises.

He kept faith with world revolution, however, in a decidedly un-Leninist way, which arose out of his special form of national Bolshevism. Lenin, and the Left opposition after him, banked on revolutions in "advanced" countries; Stalin's vision of coming revolutions, being Russocentric, was focused on neighboring lands, most of which did not fall into that class.

Writing in 1921, Stalin exposed his view that Soviet Russia, so far a "socialist island," would be better off if it had *"as neighbors* one large industrially developed or several Soviet states.[2] He revealed it again in 1924 when he wrote that the paths of development of the world revolution were "not so simple" as seemed earlier. Once it had been thought that the revolution would develop through the ripening of elements of socialism in the more advanced countries at the same time, but that idea was in need of substantial modification. The more likely prospect was that the world revolution would develop through the revolutionary "falling away" of more countries from the system of imperialist states, following the path of the "first fallen-away country."[3] Two years later, in the above-cited statement about the need for a "socialist encirclement," he indicated where he thought the new fallen-away lands would be located. A "socialist encirclement" would have to consist of countries girdling Russia.

Stalin reconceived the international revolution as a process radiating outward from Soviet Russia into countries that could, by their geographical proximity, become parts of a "socialist encirclement." This would give the Russia-become-socialist a deep defensive glacis and control over territory and resources detached from the capitalist world; and then no foreign intervention could possibly succeed. Reasoning in this way, Stalin foresaw the emergence of a bipolar world. It was a Bolshevik doctrine that the Revolution had split the world into two hostile "camps"; in Stalin's mind, these became two polar "centers of gravity." One, he said in 1925, was "Anglo-America," the other, Soviet Russia.[4] He further spelled it out in an interview with American sympathizers: "In the further course of development of the international revolution and international reaction, two centers will take shape on a world scale: a socialist center attracting to itself the countries gravitating to socialism and a capitalist center attracting to itself the countries gravitating to capitalism.[5]

Because he came to envisage the further progress of international revolution in territorial terms, Stalin's mind turned to diplomacy as a key method of bringing this about. Here again he was keeping faith with Lenin at the same time as he departed from him. Of all Lenin's teachings, none impressed him more deeply than the idea that intercapitalist discords were an invaluable asset to be exploited by Soviet diplomacy. In 1925 he called them "the greatest support of our regime and our revolution" and went on:

This may seem strange but it is a fact, comrades. If the two main coalitions of capitalist countries during the imperialist war in 1917 had not been engaged in mortal combat against one another, if they had not been at one another's throat, not been preoccupied and lacking in time to enter a contest with the Soviet regime, the Soviet regime would hardly have survived then. Struggle, conflicts, and wars between our enemies are, I repeat, our greatest ally.[6]

But if Stalin kept faith with Lenin in attaching supreme importance to the divisive diplomacy, he departed from him in finding a new use for it. In Lenin's mind and practice, diplomacy was a defensive weapon to keep the capitalist cutthroats divided and thus unable to unite against Bolshevik Russia. For Stalin, diplomacy became at once a defensive *and* offensive weapon, with a mission of opening up a path to the revolution's territorial advance in the very process of keeping enemies divided. Lenin had invited such a thought. After citing Brest as the first example of divisive diplomacy, he said: "One should not draw the conclusion that treaties may only be like Brest or Versailles. That is untrue. There can also be a third kind of treaty, advantageous to us." He did not specify the distinguishing feature of the third kind of treaty. Lenin-textualist that he was, Stalin must have pondered the passage carefully. Brest and Versailles had in common, as disadvantageous treaties to Russia and Germany respectively, the loss of vital territorial interests. One could infer that the revolutionary interests to be served by the "third kind of treaty" were territorial ones. Stalin's orientation, unlike Lenin's, disposed him to do just that.

But how could Moscow make use of divisive diplomacy to promote a territorial advance of revolution? Stalin reasoned that it could do so by facilitating the outbreak of war between two sets of enemy states. Such a war would provide Soviet Russia with opportunities to expand its influence into neighboring countries that were candidates for inclusion in the "socialist encirclement."

Bolsheviks had a settled expectation of future wars derived from Lenin's analysis in his treatise of 1915, *Imperialism, the Highest Stage of Capitalism*. Countries in the advanced stage of financier-controlled "monopoly capitalism," it held, are bound to seek colonies as spheres for export of capital because they increasingly lack investment outlets at home. Since the great Afro-Asian hinterland was all partitioned by the end of the nineteenth century, a latecomer in capitalist development like Germany could acquire colonies only by a forcible repartition—whence the World War and equally inevitable future imperialist wars. The very existence of a revolutionary Soviet republic in such a tension-ridden world was a standing provocation. Future wars generated by imperialism could therefore be expected to turn into anti-Soviet coalition wars for socialism's extinction. Hence the post-1920 uneasy coexistence with capitalist countries was inherently no more than a breathing spell, which might be prolonged by a skillful Soviet diplomacy but must one day end in a military collision. Such was the Leninist view.

But the inevitable was not necessarily imminent, and Lenin's projections for internal policy in his last years were not shaped by a felt need for a frantic effort to gird the isolated Soviet state for war. Nor was the official party line of the early post-Lenin period. The Fourteenth Party Congress of 1925 took a sanguine view of the international prospect. Since the immediate postwar crisis of 1919–20, Stalin said in the main report, a certain "temporary stabilization of capitalism" and a temporary ebb in the revolutionary tide had taken place. What at one time had been seen as a short breathing spell had turned into "a whole period of breathing spell." Between the world imperialist camp, now under Anglo-American leadership, and the world anti-imperialist camp, headed by Soviet Russia, a certain balance of power and period of peaceful coexistence had set in. In this situation, Soviet policy aimed to expand trade relations with capitalist countries, work for peace, pursue rapprochement with countries defeated in the World War, and strengthen Soviet ties with the colonial countries and dependencies.[7]

So spoke Stalin in public in December 1925. Speaking in secret before a Central Committee plenum on 19 January of that year, however, he had defined the external situation in ominous terms as reminiscent of the period before the outbreak of the World War. Taking the floor in support of War Commissar Mikhail Frunze's request for increased budgetary appropriations for the Red Army, he saw signs of "new complications" for which it was necessary to be prepared, and said that "the question of intervention is again becoming topical." Anticolonial movements in India, China, Egypt, and the Sudan, as well as revolutionary sentiment among the British workers, were growing stronger and could not help but turn the ruling strata of the great powers against Soviet Russia as the source of anticolonial and revolutionary inspiration. There were growing complications in the Far East, North Africa, and the Balkans, now again a center of Franco-British rivalry as before the World War. So the conditions for a new war were ripening, "And a new war cannot but impinge upon us."

Stalin went on: Because the new war could become an inevitability, not tomorrow or the day after but within a few years, and because war could not fail to aggravate internal revolutionary crises in East as well as West, "the question cannot but arise before us of being ready for anything." Here he turned his attention to neighboring lands. The revolutionary movement was growing in the West and here or there might overthrow the bourgeoisie. But it would be very hard for revolutionaries to hold onto power, as shown by the examples of border countries like Estonia and Latvia. "The question of our army, of its might and preparedness, will certainly face us as a burning question in the event of complications arising in countries surrounding us." The obvious implication was that the Red Army must be strong enough to come to the aid of revolutions in neighboring lands.

Not that Russia should initiate a war, Stalin continued. That was not so, and no one should harbor such a thought. "Our banner remains, as before, the banner of *peace*. But if war begins, we shall not be able to sit with folded hands—we shall have to take action but we will take action last. And we will act so as to throw the decisive weight on the scales, the weight that could be preponderant." It followed, he said, that the army must be prepared, booted, clothed, and trained, that its equipment must be improved, that the chemical arms and air force must be improved, and that in general the Red Army must be raised to the requisite high level. Such was the demand of the international situation.[8]

The war that could become an inevitability, not tomorrow but in a few years, was the event to which Stalin looked forward as an opening to revolutionary advance. He made this clear enough when he spoke in public nine days later, before the Moscow province party conference. Having stated that conflicts and wars between the enemies of Soviet Russia were her "greatest ally," he went on: "But since the pluses of capital in this sphere are, so far, greater than its minuses, and military collisions between the capitalists are not to be expected any day, clearly matters don't yet stand the way we would like with our third ally."[9] In other words, no existing antagonism was deep enough to generate a new interimperialist war.

These words did not imply that Stalin was impatiently awaiting the emergence of such a war. Since some years would be needed, at a minimum, to prepare the country and the army for a war situation, prolongation of the existing international peace was essential for the present. But eventually, with help from divisive diplomacy, the hoped-for "third ally," an interimperialist war, would come, bringing with it the opportunity for Soviet Russia to expand into contiguous areas and thereby promote the fused interests of her security and further progress of international revolution. Such was the direction of Stalin's thought by 1925, if not somewhat earlier.

As shown by his emphatic championing of the war commissar's request for additional appropriations for the Red Army, his mind focused on the problem of how to prepare the country for a war situation "within a few years." To build up the Red Army's strength to the requisite high level, by producing tanks, artillery, and other machines of modern warfare in large quantities, a strong push on the industrialization front was obviously imperative. Such war-oriented industrialization would call for heavy industry to receive priority over the light industries that produce consumer goods. Hence, industrialization was at the top of Stalin's internal policy agenda. The Fourteenth Party Congress, the first at which he assumed Lenin's old role of presenting the main and policy-setting report, resolved "to conduct economic construction with a view to transforming the USSR from a machine- and equipment-importing country into a machine- and equipment-producing country. . . ." The resolution further decreed that "all measures be taken to strengthen the country's defense potential and to increase the might of the Red Army and Red Navy, both at sea and in the air."[10]

Learning From Russia's Past

In thinking about the "how" of this process, Stalin turned to the Russian past. For several reasons, this was a natural tendency of his mind. First, he had come to view himself as a Bolshevik leader who was likewise a Russian national statesman. Second, he was prone, as shown by his reference in 1925 to a similarity of the current international situation with the one preceding the World War, to see situations in terms of historical parallels. Third, there was a parallel between Soviet Russia's situation of isolation in the capitalist encirclement and that of Muscovite *Rus'* in its isolation amid an encirclement of hostile neighbor states. This could suggest that policies pursued by that earlier Russia in building up its defenses were worthy of emulation. And it did to Stalin.

Russian history was a required subject in the Tiflis seminary where he studied for four years in the late 1890s. In his later capacity as a Bolshevik specialist on the national question, he proceeded with self-education in this subject. Evidence of that appears in his treatise of 1913, *Marxism and the National Question,* where he drew a contrast between the historical formation of West European nation-states owing to the rise of capitalism and the appearance in the East of multinational states, Austro-Hungary and Russia, each dominated by representatives of "commanding nations." In Russia, he wrote, "the role of unifier of nationalities was assumed by the Great Russians, who had at their head a historically developed strong and organized aristocratic military bureaucracy."[11]

Stalin returned to this theme in a revealing excursus into history when he addressed the Tenth Party Congress in 1921 as the party's premier authority on the national question. In this address he made a significant addition to the argument by stressing external needs of self-defense in the eastern cases. He said that the rise of unitary national states in Western Europe coincided with the rise of capitalism, whereas in Eastern Europe, where capitalism did not yet exist or was only emerging, "the interests of self-defense against invasion by the Turks, Mongols, and other Eastern peoples called for the immediate formation of centralized states capable of checking the invaders' onslaught. And since in the East of Europe the process of appearance of centralized states went faster than that of the forming of people into nations, there took shape in this region mixed states consisting of several peoples not yet formed into nations but already united in a common state." These latter were "usually composed of one powerful, dominant nation and several weak, subordinate ones. Examples: Austria, Hungary, Russia."[12]

A mind thinking historically in those terms could have perceived a parallel between the tasks of Russia in the past and at present with respect to the "interests of self-defense." Emphasizing as he did the determining role of external danger in Russia's internal development, Stalin could have drawn the conclusion that the international conditions of the 1920s called for a renewed state-building process. But was he in those years really acquainted with such a (to us) recondite matter as Russia's historical state-building process? Even from the fragmentary evidence now on the record, we can say for certain that he was.

A voracious reader, Stalin once told a visitor who noted a pile of books on his office table that his "daily norm" was 500 pages. In 1925 he directed his assistant, Ivan Tovstukha, to organize his personal library and jotted down on a piece of paper (which has been preserved) the classification to be used. "Russian history," "history of other countries," "military affairs," "Lenin and Leninism," and "diplomacy" were among the more than thirty subjects listed. After Stalin's death the books in the personal library bearing markings, underlinings, and marginalia by him were placed in the Central Party Archive in Moscow. From Soviet scholars familiar with these materials we learn that subjects in which Stalin showed keen interest included Russian history, the history of warfare, and past rulers' techniques of absolute rule. Examples from the latter group would be R. Wipper's pro-Ivan *Ivan Grozny,* Yu. Kaz'min's *The Sovereign's Destiny* (a collection of Russian rulers' lore by a Russian émigré living in Bulgaria in the 1920s), and S. Lozinsky's *History of the Ancient World,* in which Stalin underlined a passage on the Roman proscriptions: public lists of condemned persons whom citizens were authorized and obliged to kill on sight.[13]

Other preserved books with Stalin's markings show that he pursued his self-education on Russian history in the larger sense. One is *The State, Bureaucracy, and Absolutism in Russian History.* The Bolshevik author, M. Ol'minsky, published it before 1917 under the pseudonym of M. S. Aleksandrov; a second edition came out in Moscow and Petrograd in 1919. This book offered a compendium of approaches by non-Marxist historians to Russia's past. Reading it studiously, as he did, Stalin became acquainted—if he had not been before—with Kliuchevsky's interpretation of tsarist absolutism as a system in which the nobility was bound in compulsory service to a supra-class state ruled by a tsar-autocrat through a bureaucracy. As a Marxist Ol'minsky-Aleksandrov could not agree with this but went so far as to define absolutism as an independently operating political force which plays off one class against another and uses an organization of faceless, obedient bureaucratic officials as its instrument. He also gave a respectful hearing to Miliukov's argument (cited above in chapter 1) that whereas states in Western Europe were shaped from below upward by society, the Russian state shaped the social system from above downward.[14]

Conclusive further evidence of Stalin's interest in the early Russian state-building process is that he closely followed a public debate about it in the early 1920s. The debaters were M. N. Pokrovsky and Trotsky.

Pokrovsky was not only Soviet Russia's foremost Marxist historian but a political figure of consequence who served as leader of the Communist Academy, rector of the Institute of Red Professors, chairman of the Society of Marxist Historians, and deputy commissar of education under A. V. Lunacharsky. In 1920 he produced a compressed summary of his position in a brilliantly written short work, *Russian History in Briefest Outline,* which went through several editions and became the Soviet school text in Russian history until Stalin had it condemned and proscribed in the 1930s. In its preface Pokrovsky wrote that he too would present the material by reigns, "only in place of a doll in a crown and a cloak the author has taken the real tsar, tsar-capital, which autocratically governed Russia from Ivan the Terrible to Nicholas the Last." The Russian autocracy was "commercial capital in the cap of Monomachus" (the tsar's crown). Commercial capital was the power not only behind the throne but behind serfdom, Russia's imperial expansion, her intitial industrialization, and much else besides.

Pokrovsky's textbook heaped scorn and hatred on the pre-1917 Russian past (the revolutionary movement excepted), by, for example, devoting whole pages to minute factual accounts of the brutal beatings of serfs by their owners or by official wielders of the knout. Other pages graphically described the revolting conditions of filth and overcrowding endured by Russian industrial workers and their families under the old regime. While commenting on "how little personality matters in history," Pokrovsky did not neglect unflattering details about the rulers in person. Of Peter the Great, whom he described in one passage as "the most energetic, most talented, and most remarkable of the Romanovs" ("but also the most cruel"), he wrote at a later point: "Peter, called by sycophantic historians 'the Great,' locked up his wife in a monastery so he could marry Catherine, who had been the maid of a pastor (Lutheran priest) in Estonia. With his own hands he tortured his son Alexei and then gave orders for his secret execution in the dungeon of the Peter and Paul fortress. . . . He died (1725) of syphilis after passing it on to his second wife, who outlived him by only two years. But it is probably hard to say what caused her premature death: syphilis or alcoholism. After getting to the tsarist throne, this former maid, who couldn't even write her own name, spent all day and most of the night with the bottle."[15]

No wonder that Lenin, given his similar view of Russia's past, was delighted with this book. After receiving a prepublication copy in 1920, he wrote a cordial congratulatory note telling Pokrovsky how very much he liked it and saying: "Original structure and exposition. Reads with enormous interest. In my opinion, it will have to be translated into European languages."[16]

In his early major work, *Russian History From the Earliest Times* (1910–13), Pokrovsky treated Russia's developmental pattern as similar to that of Europe. Commercial capitalism was the driving force of Russian development from the sixteenth century until the appearance of industrial capitalism in the eighteenth and its rise to maturity in the later nineteenth. Peter's forced-industrialization policy was a premature effort to transform the commercial-capitalist order into an industrial-capitalist one by coercive means, by the use of the cudgel *(dubinka)*, of which Peter was a "fanatical worshipper." Peter's firm belief in the cudgel as a "tool of economic development" proved illusory. His effort to "drive the Russian bourgeoisie into the capitalist Eden with a cudgel" came to little: the factories mostly collapsed soon after his death. "Here, as in other fields, Peter's autocracy could not create anything, but it did destroy much."[17]

While Pokrovsky's view became dominant in the 1920s, it enjoyed no monopoly—though not for lack of efforts by Pokrovsky to establish one. An early work of Trotsky's, *1905*, a new edition of which came out in Moscow in 1922, offered quite a different view. The introductory chapter argued that the Russian state, having been formed on a primitive economic foundation and being confronted with more advanced foreign states, would have gone under but for the fact that it swallowed up, under pressure from without, a disproportionately large part of the nation's vital juices. "The state did not collapse," he continued, rather "it began to grow, at the price of monstrous pressure upon the nation's economic forces." Thus, the Russian state was compelled to create its own home industry and technology in order to stand up against the better-armed states of Lithuania, Poland, and Sweden. The history of Russia's state economy was "an unbroken chain of efforts—heroic efforts, in a certain sense—aimed at providing the military organization with the means necessary for its continuing existence." The government apparatus was constantly built and rebuilt in the interests of the treasury, whose function was to seize and utilize for its own ends every bit of accumulated labor of the people. As a result, the tsarist "bureaucratic autocracy" emerged as a self-contained organization enjoying an incomparably greater degree of independence from the Russian privileged estates than European absolutism—an outgrowth of estate monarchy—did from its own. In Russia, the pendulum swung much farther in the direction of state power. "In this respect," Trotsky commented, "tsarism represents an intermediate form between European absolutism and Asian despotism, being, possibly, closer to the latter of these two."[18]

Not surprisingly, the new edition of Trotsky's book elicited a very hostile review from Pokrovsky. Accusing Trotsky of espousing the liberal historian Miliukov's idea of a supra-class Russian state, Pokrovsky declared that it was more important to disprove the existence of such a state than to disprove the historical existence of Jesus Christ. The rise of the centralized Russian state and autocracy was not to be explained, as Trotsky did, by the needs of military defense against an external foe. The new Russian state, a creature of commercial capital, clashed with the already established neighbor-states to the West because of its drive to win an economic place in the sun at their expense.[19]

The doughty controversialists debated in two exchanges in *Pravda* in July 1922. Trotsky defended his position concerning Russia's relative economic backwardness and the rise of an exceptionally strong state organization in response to military needs, whether defensive or offensive, and dismissed Pokrovsky's thesis that the interests of commercial capital dominated the autocracy's policies in the sixteenth century as a caricature.[20] In reply, Pokrovsky brought up the heavy artillery of Karl Marx. In *Capital*, Marx had spoken of "usurer capital" and "merchant capital" as forms of capital handed down from the Middle Ages. The rise of industrial capital and the capitalist mode of production in the sixteenth century required "primitive accumulation" by such means as the taking of gold and silver from America, the looting of the East Indies, the African slave trade, the commercial wars of European nations, the rise of the colonial system, and mercantilism. "These methods," wrote Marx in a passage now quoted in italics by Pokrovsky, *"all employ the power of the state, the concentrated and organized force of society, to hasten, hothouse fashion, the transformation of the feudal mode of production into the capitalist mode, and to shorten the transition.* Force is the midwife of every old society pregnant with a new one. It is itself an economic power." Although Marx' was referring here to Spain, Portugal, Holland, France, and England, Pokrovsky brandished the famous words of the master as also applicable, albeit later in time, to Russia.[21]

In the midst of the anti-Trotsky campaign of 1925, Pokrovsky returned to the fray with another polemical article in which, once again, he went back to Marx's *Capital*. In the history of primitive accumulation, Marx had written,

all revolutions are epoch-making that act as levers for the capitalist class in course of formation, but above all, those moments when great masses of men are suddenly and forcibly torn from their means of subsistence, and hurled as free and "unattached" proletarians on the labor-market. The expropriation of the agricultural producer, of the peasant, from the soil, is the basis of the whole process. The history of this expropriation, in different countries, assumes different aspects. . . .

Whereas in England and Western Europe, Pokrovsky went on, the expropriation had taken place by such means as the enclosures, in Russia and elsewhere in Eastern Europe it had found expression in the peasant's enserfment; and the need to enforce serfdom explained the unusual intensity and longevity of the Russian autocracy.[22]

Stalin closely followed the Pokrovsky-Trotsky debate. The evidence of this appears in his private correspondence of 1927 with two students at the Institute of Red Professors, Tsvetkov and Alypov. They solicited his view on the controversial question of the historical rise of the Russian autocracy. In this connection they referred to his words of 1921, which implied to them, understandably, that he would explain the formation of a centralized Russian state *"not* as a result of economic development, but in the interests of combating the Mongols and other peoples of the East."[23] It was a politically as well as historically sensitive question they were putting. For Pokrovsky, then still rector of the Institute of Red Professors and highly influential, *did* explain the rise of the centralized Russian state and autocracy as a result of economic development, whereas Stalin's political archenemy Trotsky had, in the debate, taken a position akin to the one implicit in Stalin's 1921 statement.

In its full form Stalin's reply to Tsvetkov and Alypov shows that they referred specifically to the Pokrovsky-Trotsky debate in requesting a clarification of his views, and that he was fully familiar with it. He stated:

4) As for the question about the theory of the formation of the Russian "autocratic system," I must say that basically I do not share Comrade Trotsky's theory and I consider Comrade Pokrovsky's theory correct in the main, although not devoid of extremes and excesses on the side of an oversimplified economic explanation of the process of formation of the autocracy.[24]

Since Stalin at the time he wrote this letter was in the final stage of his tense political duel with Trotsky, whose downfall was still some months off, he was bound to dissociate himself from Trotsky's position even though he shared the latter's belief in the requirements of national self-defense as the determining factor in the formation of the centralized Russian state. By the same token, Pokrovsky's continuing preeminence as an historical thinker and importance as a political figure, not to mention his services in the anti-Trotsky campaign, made it impolitic at that time for Stalin to reject the Pokrovsky position. All the more significant, therefore, is the fact that his sole substantive critical comment was directed against Pokrovsky, not Trotsky, and moreover was a criticism with which Trotsky would have agreed wholeheartedly. Indeed, an "oversimplified economic explanation of the process of formation of the autocracy" was just what Trotsky had ascribed to Pokrovsky in their *Pravda* exchanges.

There was something in Pokrovsky's articles, however, that Stalin must have found of great interest: the references to Marx on the expropriation of the peasant as the basis of the revolutionary transformation of feudal into capitalist society, on the crucial role of the state power in the transitional process, and on force as the midwife of every old society pregnant with a new one. Whether Stalin had ever read *Capital* is not known. But being conversant with the Trotsky-Pokrovsky controversy, he could not have been unaware of the passages that Pokrovsky quoted from

Marx. All the more so since Trotsky and the Left economist Evgeni Preo-brazhensky had subsequently picked up Marx's "primitive accumulation" idea and coined the phrase "primitive socialist accumulation" as a formula for Soviet industrialization.

Neither Trotsky nor Preobrazhensky contemplated the use of coercion in a revolutionarily swift expropriation of the Soviet peasantry for purposes of creating a socialist Russia. But for Stalin, who thought in Russian historical terms of the need to force the process for the sake of the country's military self-defense in a hostile world, a literal reading of Marx's famous words was tempting. If the state power had been employed forcibly to hasten the transformation of feudal society into capitalist, why not use it in a similar way to hasten the transformation of NEP Russia into socialist Russia via collectivization? If Peter had employed the *dubinka* of state power to drive the Russian bourgeoisie into the capitalistic Eden, why not use that instrument now to drive the Russian peasantry into the socialist hereafter?

In the main, however, Stalin could only be critical of Pokrovsky for his disregard of the influence of external circumstances on Russia's histor-ical development. Pokrovsky's whole historical outlook was unacceptable to him because of its sweeping repudiation of the Russian national past. In 1925 Stalin gave indication of his disdainful attitude. He spoke in a private letter of the "dying away of a whole series of old prominent men of letters and old 'leaders,' " and went on: "The Lunacharskys, Pokrovskys, Gol-denbergs, Bogdanovs, Krasins, and so on—these names come first to my mind as examples of former Bolshevik leaders who subsequently moved off into secondary roles."[25]

Stalin thus saw (if he had not seen before) that *Rus'*, isolated in a hostile encirclement of foreign states, had sought to build a strong state capable of defending the national territory and gathering Russian lands held by external foes. He saw, too, that the state-building effort, sound in conception, had been at best a partial success and at worst a dismal failure in the execution. Finally, drawn as his mind was to historical parallels, he saw history's relevance to the current situation of Soviet Russia isolated in *its* hostile foreign encirclement, and drew the inference for policy: that it was imperatively necessary to build a mighty industrialized Soviet Russian state in a very short time and thus succeed in the state-building enterprise in which the tsars had tried and failed.

All this he tersely summed up in his no-mere-beatings-of-Russia speech to the managers in February 1931, concluding that Russia, to avoid being crushed by a hostile encirclement, must cover in ten years its lag of fifty to a hundred behind the advanced countries. It would be an error, it was suggested earlier, not to see in that message a revelation of the speaker's

inner world as well as an appeal to patriotism. It would be no less an error
to take it as spur-of-the-moment rhetoric unprepared by prior years of
thought about lessons of the past for Russia's present and future. Identifying with Russia as a nation-state, seeing himself as a successor of those
early tsars as well as of Lenin, Stalin saw a likeness in the country's
situation now and in that former hostile encirclement of Tatars, Swedes,
Polish-Lithuanian nobles, and other foreign enemies. Because of the perceived similarity of situations, the former national response—the state-
building process—appeared most instructive to him.

Toward Collectivization

The thought of Russia's backwardness and isolation in a dangerous
world underlay Stalin's warning in January 1925 that the Soviet state must
build armed strength to make it "ready for anything," and do so in a hurry.
It is therefore no coincidence that later in that same year he began defining
the internal situation in eve-of-October terms. A turning-point moment
was at hand in the revolution's development, similar to 1917, he wrote in
his *Pravda* article of 7 November 1925, and just as "Leninist hardness"
had been needed then, so it would be needed now in order to win victory
over the capitalist elements of the economy.

Why would it be necessary again now? Stalin did not directly say,
and even made a bow to the Right by speaking of the need to form a firm
alliance with the middle stratum of the peasantry. But in the next breath he
observed that "mere development of cooperatives in the countryside is now
no longer enough. Now the task is to enlist the million-strong masses of
peasants in cooperatives and to *implant cooperative ownership in the countryside.*" This meant the formation of production collectives as distinguished from the consumer and credit cooperatives that the Right had in
view. It meant the collectivization of peasant-held land and property. Such
a radical change of the rural way of life in NEP Russia could not be
achieved other than by overcoming inevitable peasant resistance. That
Stalin's thinking ran in just such terms was shown when he told the Comintern Executive Committee in a speech of 1926: "Building socialism in
the USSR means overcoming our own Soviet bourgeoisie by our forces in
the course of a struggle."[26] By "our own Soviet bourgeoisie" he meant
primarily the peasantry, its middle and upper strata in particular. A struggle
to collectivize the peasantry, as the basis for swift war-oriented industrialization, was shaping up in Stalin's mind as a great state task for the near
future.

His thinking on this crucial point was influenced by Iuri Larin's *Soviet*

Countryside, a book published in early 1925. The author, a figure of minor prominence in the party, pictured a rural Russia in which an already economically dominant minority of well-off peasants and kulaks was in danger of taking over political control, while the embittered peasant poor were beginning to contemplate a new agrarian revolution (like the "second revolution" of 1918, he said, when a wave of dekulakization occurred in the aftermath of the dispossession of the landlords of 1917). Far from favoring such a development, Larin argued that it could and should be forestalled by the proletarian government forming an alliance with the peasant poor to implant, for their benefit, production collectives *(kolkhozy)* as distinguished from the cooperatives favored by the middle peasantry.[27]

Bukharin opened fire on Larin's scenario as a deviation from Lenin's plan of building a socialism of cooperatives through reliance on the middle peasant as the "central figure" in the countryside. The *kolkhoz* was not the highroad to rural socialism, he contended, and Larin's "second revolution" would mean a wrong kind of class struggle by "knocking out of teeth."[28] Larin rejected the charge of harboring a "diabolical design" for a second revolution. True, when the time came, fifteen or twenty years hence, the regime would expropriate the large private holdings just as it would expropriate, by decree, Nepman-owned factories. By then, however, it would be so strong that there would be no need to terrify the kulaks with the spectre of a second revolution, and "We shall not need any 'second revolutions' in our country."[29]

On the other hand, Larin had an appreciative reader in Stalin, who, in speaking before the Fourteenth Congress in December 1925, made reference to *The Soviet Countryside* and showed textual familiarity with it. Moreover, although then at the height of his tactical alliance with the Right, he spoke respectfully of Larin and merely dissociated himself "to some extent" from the scheme of a "second revolution" against kulak domination.[30] But if Larin harbored no design for a second revolution, Stalin did, and he did not contemplate a fifteen- to twenty-year wait before acting. He showed this, as we have observed, by defining the Soviet situation of 1925–26 as the prelude to an October in the construction of socialism. The word "October" symbolized revolution to Bolshevik minds as unmistakably as any word could.

Bolsheviks who read his portentous statements about the parallel between the prelude to the first October and the current situation seem not to have grasped their implications. So habituated was the collective party mind of that time to Lenin's reformist position, so much was it taken for granted that cooperative agriculture would come about by means other than the coercive use of state power, that the notion of a "second revolution" was not taken seriously and people did not grasp what was in Stalin's mind when, at the height of the NEP, he defined Russia's situation in eve-of-October terms. They did not see that he really meant it when, in delphic statements here and there, he projected the construction of socialism as a class war against the internal bourgeoisie, a war that was rapidly approaching.

He could not help but know that his scenario for collectivization flew in the face of Lenin's impassioned warning against attempting a swift and stormy passage to socialism by rough revolutionary means. For what he contemplated was a revolution in precisely the sense that Lenin had given the term when he defined it as "a change that breaks the old order to its foundations, and not one that cautiously, slowly, and gradually remodels it, taking care to break as little as possible." But Stalin was no more disposed to respect this part of his mentor's political testament than he was willing to heed the postscript relating directly to himself; he probably put them both down as signs of decline in the physically ailing Lenin.

His Lenin, the one with whom he continued to identify and whom he aspired to emulate and outdo, was not the cautious remodeler of society (and would-be purger of Stalin from power) but the great politician and theoretician of revolution, the hero of 1917, the rock-hard advocate of revolutionary terror, the believer in the coercive use of state power in a continuing class struggle from above against the still numerous and highly dangerous enemies of the Revolution. To prove himself a Lenin of that kind, he must lead the party-state in a revolution of socialism's construction. Not that he found nothing he could accept in the Lenin of NEP, who for all his reformism did, after all, chart a course toward industrialization and cooperative agriculture. And was it not Lenin who, toward the end, spoke of overtaking the other nations "with the aid of the workers' and peasants' government"? Few words in the Leninist canon could have carried so much meaning to Stalin.

The New Peter

Because Stalin cast himself as both a Bolshevik revolutionary leader and a Russian national statesman, he could adopt heroes of Russian history as identity figures without ever ceasing to be, in his own mind, a second and greater Lenin. Now, in the mid-1920s, this small man with the penchant for historical analogies and the yearning to be great found a state-building precursor whom he aimed to emulate and outdo: the revolutionary from above, Peter the Great.

What were the sources of his view of Peter? As noted above, Lenin, whose loathing of tsarism and the tsars was intense, on only one occasion made a positive remark—purely incidental—about Peter. He spoke of Russia's need to take over German techniques by dictatorial methods, "in still greater measure than Peter hastened the taking over of westernism by barbaric *Rus'*, not shrinking at barbaric means of fighting barbarism." Stalin was certainly aware of that dictum and must have read some pertinent parts of Pokrovsky. But whereas Lenin's Peter was no hero and Pokrovsky's was despicable, Peter did have an admirer among Russian Marxists: Georgi Plekhanov. Plekhanov took a positive view of Peter's revolutionary activity from above in a little book called *Basic Questions of Marxism*, which, despite its author's gravitation to the Menshevik wing of the party, was read with respect by all Russian Marxists, Stalin undoubtedly included, around the time of its original publication in 1908. It described Russia's transformation under Peter as an example of how accumulated small changes in history lead eventually (as per the dialectic) to qualitative changes, to a "revolutionary leap":

The "type" of Russian social relations changes slowly. . . . Moscow . . . nevertheless remains Asiatic Moscow. Peter appears and carries out a "forcible revolution" in Russia's state life. The new European period of Russian history begins. The Slavophiles cursed Peter as Antichrist just because of the "suddenness" of his revolution. They maintained that in his reformer's zeal he forgot about evolution. . . . But every thinking person will easily realize that the Petrine revolution was necessary by virtue of the historical "evolution" traversed by Russia, that it was prepared by the latter.[31]

This passage may have started Stalin down the road to his rendezvous with the crowned revolutionary.

A sense of affinity between Peter and the Bolsheviks, between his time and theirs, was abroad in Russia during the revolutionary period. It found some slight expression in Lenin's above-cited statement of 1918 and in Ustrialov's remark of 1924 that Lenin himself had an element of "great Peter" in his makeup. In that same year Maximilian Voloshin, a poet living in Russia, included the line "Great Peter was the first Bolshevik" in a poem entitled *Russia*. The poem pictured the Russians as a believing nation with a faith record that ran from the two-fingered sign of the cross among the seventeenth-century schismatics to belief in the tsar to belief in materialism and the International to visions of electrification and a socialist paradise on earth. The same spirit of history that guided Peter's thought and axe, that drove *muzhik* Russia to spread out in three centuries from the Baltic to Alaska, was now leading the Bolsheviks along "age-old Russian paths."[32]

Peter was a cult figure in some historical literature that Stalin perused in the 1920s. *The Forefather of Russia (Praroditel' Rossii)*, an obscure late-nineteenth-century panegyric that he read, presented Peter's revolu-

tion from above as an heroic accomplishment. So did various writers
whose views were summarized by Aleksandrov-Ol'minsky in a part of his
book dealing with Peter's role in history. Here Stalin read that according
to some contemporaries of Peter, he "delivered Russia from nonbeing to
being." He read that the historian S. Boguslavsky put Peter's personality
in the very center of the transformative effort that took place in his time.
He read that according to another historian, I. Engelman, Peter not only
carried through his reforms with an iron hand but grew all the more persistent in the face of incomprehension of them by some persons close to the
throne, resorting to harsh coercive measures.[33]

Stalin may also have read two small books published in Soviet Russia
in 1926. Both presented the revolutionary monarch in an altogether more
favorable light than Pokrovsky did. One came from the pen of the distinguished historian S. F. Platonov, who retired from St. Petersburg University in 1916 after writing the standard Russian history textbook, among
other works, and then resumed scholarly activity in Leningrad in the 1920s
as chairman of the Standing Historical Commission of the Academy of
Sciences. He published several popular historical-biographical studies,
among them *Peter the Great*. This masterpiece of concise writing for the
nonspecialist managed in only 113 pages to give a history of Russian
opinions about Peter, an account of past historiography of his reign, a brief
biography, the story of the reign itself, and a spirited defense of Peter
against contemporary detractors—not including Pokrovsky, however, whom
it would have been dangerous to attack at that time. In referring to Peter's
personal cruelty, Platonov admitted that he was often "the victim of his
own temperament." But as sketched in the book's final pages, his Peter
was a tireless, observant, incessantly mobile, work-loving "administrator-
overseer" *(administrator-khozyain)*, a man of simplicity, a seeker of
knowledge, the architect of a foreign policy of wide scope, and one who
considered himself a servant of the state.[34] Since this was the picture of
Peter later drawn under Stalin's tutelage, it is possible, even likely, that
one of the 3,100 copies of Platonov's little book found its way into his
hands.

The other book presented Peter as the worker-tsar of a dynamic early
Russia now reborn owing to the October Revolution. Entitled *Russia Then
and Now*, it was issued by the State Publishing House in Moscow in 2,000
copies. Its nationalist spirit was revealed in the epigraph—a couplet by a
poet of the Revolution, Valery Briusov: "Over the snowy breadth of former
Russia / There shines a dawn never seen before." The author, N. A.
Gredeskul, a former law professor, was one of those intellectuals who
stayed in Russia during the Revolution and subsequently formed the internal constituency of Ustrialov and the *Smena vekh* circle. But a Commu-

nist's foreword to a book brandished it as an answer and antidote to the *Smena vekh* yearning for a postrevolutionary philistine normalcy. And in fact, Gredeskul's historico-political tract identified Soviet Russia as the resumption and reincarnation of historic Russia precisely on account of its revolutionary dynamism.

Historic Russia was the embattled Russia of the post-Tatar era, the Russia that had "gathered" its purloined lands and formed itself into a "Great Russia" in a centuries-long struggle with the Tatars, Lithuania, Poland, Germany, Turkey, and Sweden. At a certain point in this process, Russia's Europeanizing proved necessary and a "genius" appeared to force it through "from above":

In Peter one must note not only the fact that he was a statesman of genius who drove Russia to "Europeanization," but also that he was a real "worker" who gave time not only to intellectual but to physical work. Peter was one of the most passionate preachers of labor as the fundamental element in life. . . . Peter's activity was "from above." Down below the necessity of "Europeanization" was not very plain and . . . the popular masses were even aroused against it. . . . Yet despite that Peter had a firm base in the popular mass: a base in its social cohesion, in its habit of "bowing to authority," in the tradition of its "trust" in the autocracy. . . . He could boldly "command" from above, he could act cruelly from above against all who stood athwart him, not having to fear disobedience and contrariness from the lower depths, the popular masses.

By Peter's activity from above, wrote Gredeskul, the Moscow tsardom was transformed into the Russian Empire. The tsar-carpenter of genius had no successors worthy of himself. The throne was occupied by nonentities, even half-witted souls, but the Russian Empire, as though by historical inertia, grew and grew, showing huge military strength. Now again, thanks to the Revolution led by Lenin, perhaps the greatest genius of all humanity, this "Siegfried-nation" was on the march under Bolshevik leadership. "There is no 'break' with Russian history. It is now proceeding at full steam, bringing to final fruition all the 'best' that was in the past. It led us to October, and is leading us further by means of October."[35]

Whether or not this book came into Stalin's possession and influenced his thinking, it was a fair expression of the philosophy of Russian history "then and now" that he was working out for himself at that time. Now, as then, an internal revolutionary advance was dictated. Comparable to Peter's revolutionary transformation of the state into the agency of economic development and reshaping of society, Stalin's advance would also be comparable to Lenin's October as a revolutionary breakthrough to socialism. As a leader bent on swiftly overcoming Russia's backwardness through industrial development, Stalin was consciously emulating Peter, but he also saw a large difference between himself and his tsar-predecessor: where the first Peter failed, the new one would succeed.

This we have directly from him. In one of the most important speeches of his fifty-year political career, delivered before an enlarged Central Committee plenum in November 1928, he referred at one point to Russia's history-bequeathed backwardness, which Peter had tried in vain to overcome. "When Peter the Great, conducting business with the more advanced countries in the West, feverishly built mills and factories to supply the army and strengthen the defenses of the country, it was a special sort of effort to leap clear of the confines of backwardness." Under previous ruling classes, no such effort could succeed. It was only the Bolsheviks who could resolve at long last the problem of liquidating Russia's age-old backwardness.[36] Here was Stalin the aspiring state builder, bent on a Petrine course of rapid transformation of the country from above; the Stalin who, a little over two years later, told the Soviet managers why it was not possible to relax the developmental pace.

Out of ingredients reviewed in these pages—including Stalin's drive to go down in history as a revolutionary hero like Lenin and a revolutionary Russian statesman like Peter, his militarized culture of the Civil War, his sense of parallel between the hostile encirclement of then and now, his view of diplomacy as a lever for Soviet expansion into neighboring states under war conditions, his discovery of the revolutionary role of the early Russian state and its tsar-autocrats, Marx's concept of primitive accumulation by the forcible expropriation of the peasantry with the help of the state, and Lenin's notion of the revolutionary use of state power as a cudgel—came Stalin's orientation on a revolution from above in Soviet Russia. What predisposed him, rather than someone else, to cook this peppery dish[37] was not only his peculiarly strong Russian nationalism and the resulting tendency to view the Russian past in a manner not characteristic of other Bolsheviks. His personality played a major role: he would unflinchingly wield the cudgel of state power against masses of human beings, and see himself in the process as a leader acting rightfully in accordance with his, Bolshevism's and Russia's heroic historical mission.

In his youth he had identified with revolutionary Russia against the Russia of the autocratic state. Now he found that in earlier times revolutionary Russia and the Russian state were not the antipodes they became in the later eighteenth and the nineteenth centuries. Rather, the state itself had acted as a revolutionary force; the political superstructure had reshaped the socioeconomic base in the quest for national power to serve the needs of self-defense in a hostile world. The Muscovite and Petrine Russia of the autocratic state and the revolutionary Russia were one and the same. That idea was the lodestar by which he steered during the rest of his life.

Lenin was a state builder in the role of chief organizer of the Soviet party-state. He advocated and practiced revolution from above in repressing real or suspected enemies of the new state. But the idea of the construction of socialism as a revolution from above employing repressive means against large elements of the Revolution's social constituency, especially in a terror-enforced collectivization of the peasantry, never entered his mind. It entered Stalin's because he came to link, if not to equate, the construction of socialism with state building in an historical Russian sense.

Part Two

THE
FIRST
PHASE

4

STARTING THE SECOND
REVOLUTION

STALIN BEGAN unveiling his revolutionary approach as soon as
victory over the Left opposition enabled him to move away from his
alliance with the Right. Reporting in December 1927 to the Fifteenth Party Congress, which sealed the Left's defeat, he recalled
that in introducing the NEP Lenin had posed the question of *Kto-kogo*
(who will vanquish whom?) in the economy—socialism or private capital?
The "who-whom" question had since been resolved in the trade sphere, he
said, and now must be resolved in production as well.[1] Softly and by
indirection, these words tolled the death knell for the NEP.

Because the party was schooled in the later Lenin's evolutionary
approach to building socialism and the Right was still influential, Stalin
could not bring his revolutionary intentions abruptly into the open. He did
so gradually in a year-long series of high-level discussions, showing himself in the process the "genius at dosage" that Bukharin later called him.[2]

Against stiff opposition from the moderate leaders he advanced a policy platform that by early 1929 he was calling the "General Line."

To win the party leadership's acceptance of it required hard persuasion as well as political infighting. In both Stalin used to good advantage the capacity to manipulate events that his party power gave him. He repeatedly contrived circumstances calculated to persuade party members that his diagnosis of the country's external and internal situation was correct, and that an all-out offensive in "socialist construction" was necessary.

The General Line

In advocating his position, Stalin did not explicitly proclaim the need for a new revolutionary upheaval. He simply urged a strenuous effort to speed up industrialization and collectivization in order to overcome the country's backwardness in a short time. He argued that a modern economic structure founded on heavy industry must be created quickly, not only with the aim of constructing socialism, but also because of the harsh dictates of survival in a hostile world. "Either we do this," he said in his report to the Central Committee of November 1928, "or they'll cross us off."[3] At this point he held up Peter's feverish building of plants as an example for emulation.

In Stalin's General Line, breakneck industrialization was predicated on collectivizing agriculture at a revolutionary tempo. Following Peter's example, he looked to the West for aid in Russia's industrialization. He knew that to build the 1,500 plants projected under the Five-Year Plan, which was being drawn up during 1928, would require huge outlays for foreign technology and machinery. The financing of foreign technological assistance on that scale necessitated a correspondingly great increase in Soviet exports, which consisted very largely of raw materials (mainly oil, lumber, and furs) and foodstuffs (mainly grain). The chief item of a potential increase in exports was grain, of which nearly ten million tons had been exported in 1913 and about two million tons a year in 1925–26 and 1926–27.[4] A major reason for the decline from ten to two millions was that the grain surplus in pre-1917 Russia came chiefly from landlords' estates and wealthy kulak farms, which no longer existed, and furthermore, rural Russia of the 1920s was eating better than before.

Stalin reasoned that to export grain on something like old Russia's scale, the Soviet government must not only do everything possible to increase the amount produced but also—and above all—get grain production and distribution under its control. The replacement of the free market by state-controlled agriculture was thus the prime purpose of Stalinist collectivization. The paramount function of the *kolkhoz* was to serve as a device by which the government would extract the foodstuffs required for financing its military-oriented industrialization.

Addressing a closed Central Committee plenum on 9 July 1928, Stalin offered his rationale for collectivization. First, he argued, the country was not guaranteed against military attack, and could not be defended without at least a six-month grain reserve to feed the army. Second, reserves were also needed in case of complications on the internal grain market. Third, there was no guarantee against a bad harvest. Then he said:

Finally, we absolutely must have a reserve for grain export. We must import equipment for industry. We must import agriculture machines, tractors, and spare parts for them. But it is impossible to do this without exporting grain, without accumulating certain hard-currency reserves through grain exports. In prewar times, 500 to 600 million poods of grain were exported yearly. It's true that much was exported because people ate too little. But it must be understood that before the war, there was *twice* as much marketed grain as now. And just because we now have half the marketed grain, there is no grain for export.[5]

Why there was no grain for exporting then will presently be explained.

Lenin had a link-in-the-chain theory of politics. "Political events are always very confused and complicated," as he stated on one occasion. "They can be compared with a chain. To hold the whole chain you must grasp the main link. Not a link chosen at random."[6] In 1917, according to Lenin, the crucial link was Bolshevik advocacy of Russia's withdrawal from the war and the winning of peasant support by taking over the SRs' land reform program. In 1918–19 the main link had been total mobilization for armed defense of the Revolution. Under the NEP, he called trade the main link. Now Stalin, determined to emulate and outdo Lenin by masterminding an October of socialism's construction, saw in early mass collectivization *his* decisive link in the chain.

To understand how radical this idea was, it must be recalled that in 1927, that climacteric year of the NEP, over 99 percent of Soviet Russia's rural population remained uncollectivized. The socioeconomic face of the countryside had, however, changed greatly since 1917. Although the old rural Russian culture persisted in the village *mir,* the revolutionary period had eliminated not only the old landlords but also the 600,000 or so well-to-do peasant proprietors whose farms of 100 to 150 acres had accounted for about a third of the marketed grain and whose pitilessly profiteering ways had earned for them the derogatory name of kulak ("fist").[7] The accepted fourfold classification of the rural population distinguished an upper stratum of relatively prosperous peasants, the kulaks (who used some seasonal hired labor as well as family hands), along with the middle peasant, the poor peasant, and the propertyless farmhand or rural proletarian, but the Soviet "kulak" of the mid-1920s was, with very few exceptions, not the rapacious, "*mir*-devouring" kulak of yore, but simply a relatively well-off peasant who by dint of hard work and ability, as well as favorable circumstances, had raised himself somewhat about the level of the middle-peasant majority. Not surprisingly, Soviet statements showed confusion both in defining the kulak as a socioeconomic category and in estimating his numbers. [8]

Two important facts emerge. First, although a process of economic differentiation did develop in the countryside during the NEP, it did not lead—as some feared it might—to a sharp polarization between prosperous and poor peasants with a concomitant decline in the numerical strength of the middle peasantry. On the contrary, the latter group, comprising those with sown areas ranging from roughly five to twenty-five acres, grew from year to year. Whereas before the Revolution only 20 percent of the peasants were middle peasants, in 1927 their proportion in the total was 62.7 percent. [9] Secondly, despite some growth during the NEP in the numbers of those defined as kulaks, in 1927 they comprised no more than about a million in all, or 3.9 percent, as against 15 percent of the total peasantry before the Revolution; and hemmed in as they were by the discriminatory tax policy that the Soviet authorities applied to them, the Soviet kulaks of the late 1920s were in no position to become an economically and politically dominant group in rural Russia. [10]

Except in comparison with what came later, the NEP was no golden age in the countryside. Farming methods remained backward, based largely on the traditional wooden plough drawn by a horse if the peasant was fortunate enough to own one. Restrictive tax policies made it inopportune for a middle peasant to become too visibly prosperous. There were severe shortages of such essential manufactured goods as shoes, and rural overpopulation sent millions of villagers to the towns each year in search of seasonal jobs that very often were unavailable. [11] Yet, for very many peasants economic conditions improved during the NEP years, and the political atmosphere in the countryside was not, on the whole, unfriendly to the Soviet regime. An observant foreign Communist (whose sympathies lay with the Left) concluded from travels in the countryside in 1927 that "the majority of the peasants were well disposed towards the Soviet power, at any rate they felt no hostility towards it." [12]

A Russian-born American sympathizer with the Revolution, Maurice Hindus, who traveled widely in rural Russia in the 1920s, visiting among other places his native village, was struck by changes in peasant attitudes. The servile *muzhik* of prerevolutionary days, who would bow and remove his hat in the presence of a landlord or official, or even kneel down and kiss their hand if coming to ask a favor, and who felt fear at the very word *pravitel' stvo* (government), was no more. "The Revolution has made him one of the most articulate persons in Russia. . . . He talks of his grievances with no more compunction than he does of the weather or his crops. Indeed, he is the only person in Russia who brushes aside, and with impunity, strictures on freedom of speech." He was not rebellious, Hindus went on. But if hostility to the new regime was not widespread, hostility to collectivized agriculture was. The peasant was not opposed to cooperative societies insofar as they helped him to pursue his individual interests. But communism in the sense of joint production, distribution, and use was anathema, and Hindus could not imagine the peasant accepting anything like that. "A tight-fisted, self-centered individualist, with a deeply ingrained desire for private property, as jealous of his personal possessions as the American or the French farmer is of his, he vigorously shakes his head at the mere suggestion of the communization of the village."[13] The tiny proportion (1.7 percent) of peasant households that had voluntarily joined producer cooperative associations by 1928, in spite of governmental organizing aid and financial inducements, confirms this picture of peasant attitudes.

From a Leninist point of view, the Russia of 1928–29 was not ready for mass collectivization. True, the cooperative movement in the form charted by Lenin had, by the end of 1927, advanced to the point that nearly ten million peasant households, or around 40 percent, were members of consumer cooperatives, and a year later the proportion rose to over 50 percent.[14] But the industrialization that Lenin considered a precondition for collectivizing was still in its infancy. In 1927 the Soviet Union possessed a grand total of 28,000 tractors as compared with the 100,000 that Lenin had envisaged in 1919 as a persuasive inducement for the peasant to join the "kommunia," and its tractor production in 1927–28 came to a mere 1,272.[15] Nor was the cultural revolution, which Lenin likewise considered essential, much more than begun. Thus, from 70 to 85 percent of the rural poor were still illiterate in early 1927.[16]

Stalin was aware of all this. But from his point of view, none of it argued against a crash collectivization drive. This would, he knew, arouse peasant resistance and hence require forcible measures or the threat of them—as any revolution does—and there would be opposition to that in the party. But did not Lenin repeatedly go against party opinion, for example in the pre-October period? Stalin never forgot that he did, and several years later, at the Sixteenth Party Congress, he reminded his party colleagues that they must "master the Leninist line—to go against the current when the situation demands it, when the party's interests demand it. . . . That's just what Leninism in practice, Leninism in leadership, means."

That was said, however, in 1930, after Stalin had already gone against the party current. In 1927–28 he was not yet able openly to flout high-level party opinion. For all his power over the party bureaucracy, he lacked the huge personal authority that enabled Lenin to prevail at certain critical times when he was at odds with the trend of sentiment in higher party circles. Stalin had to proceed with circumspection and employ his wiles. He had to persuade those who politically counted that the country's defenses had to be prepared in a hurry because of external danger, and that his prescription of high-speed industrialization, and of collectivization to support it, was the right policy.

The greatest obstacle that he had to clear away were the members of the Right, who would certainly render all possible resistance to the adoption of his line. This meant their ouster from positions of power and influence as representatives of what would later be called a "Right danger" and a "Right deviation." The defeat of the Right and the gaining of the Central Committee's support for his General Line were therefore interlocked objectives. Progress toward either would facilitate progress toward the other. In the course of his double-edged politics Stalin would be doing something more than preparing the party to embark upon the second revolution; he would be getting it started.

Beating the War Drums

Unless the war danger was really serious, high-speed industrialization and collectivization would not really be necessary. So Stalin had to bring home the reality of the war danger.

In his November 1928 Central Committee speech he admitted that some party members questioned the need for the rapid developmental tempo and the concomitant tension it would create. He replied: "Speaking abstractly, without regard to external and internal circumstances, we could of course proceed at a slower pace. But the fact is, first, that one cannot disregard external and internal circumstances; and second, that if we proceed from the surrounding situation, we cannot help but recognize that it dictates to us a swift tempo of development of our industry." The surrounding situation, he went on, was the capitalist encirclement, as a result of which it was "impossible to uphold the independence of our country without having an adequate industrial base for defense."[17]

Several current events in Soviet foreign relations assisted Stalin in his argument. Soviet monetary aid to British workers in their General Strike of 1926 was followed by raids on Soviet offices in Peking, Shanghai, and London, and the British government used documents taken in the raids as a basis for breaking diplomatic relations with the Soviet Union in May

1927. The assassination of the Soviet envoy to Poland, P. L. Voikov, two weeks later was portrayed in Moscow as evidence of a conspiratorial anti-Soviet cabal rather than the isolated act of a young White Russian émigré, which it appears to have been. Shortly afterward, the international horizon further darkened with the debacle of the Chinese Communist party at the hands of the nationalist Chiang Kai-shek, who had enjoyed Soviet support. On top of all this, France broke off economic negotiations with the USSR and forced the recall of the Soviet envoy, Christian Rakovsky. Intensified press discussion of those events caused genuine fears among the public, and the episode has been labeled the "Soviet war scare of 1926–27."

In June 1927 Foreign Commissar Georgi Chicherin returned home from a visit to Western Europe. He later told the American journalist Louis Fischer: "Everybody in Moscow was talking war. I tried to dissuade them. 'Nobody is planning to attack us,' I insisted. Then a colleague enlightened me. He said, "Shh. We know that. But we need this against Trotsky.""[18] The war danger was thus being played up as part of the anti-Trotskyist campaign then in its culminating phase—to support charges that the opposition was irresponsibly fomenting intraparty dissension at a time of acute international tension. Stalin was in the forefront of this campaign. In July 1927 he opened a *Pravda* article by saying: "It is hardly open to doubt that the basic question of the present is the threat of a new imperialist war. It is not a matter of some undefined and intangible 'danger' of a new war. It is a matter of a real and genuine threat of a new war in general and a war against the USSR in particular."[19]

Because he had a further political motive—to substantiate his policy design—he did not desist from emphasizing the grave danger after the war scare eased. In his Fifteenth Congress report in December 1927 he found the international scene disturbingly reminiscent of the prelude to the World War, "when a murder at Sarajevo led to war." The postwar period of a temporary stabilization of capitalism was ending and preparations for a new war were "going forward full steam." And: "If two years ago it was possible and necessary to speak of a period of a certain equilibrium and of 'peaceful coexistence' between the USSR and the capitalist countries, now we have every ground to assert that *the period of 'peaceful coexistence' is receding into the past,* giving way to a period of imperialist attacks and preparation of intervention against the USSR."[20]

The steady drumbeat of Stalin's invocations of war danger served his interest in the contests against the Left and then against the Right, but it also expressed his purposes in politics. His foreign policy approach, on the other hand, was anything but warlike during this period and after. Although he operated on the assumption that a new war was inevitable and for certain reasons desirable, he was nevertheless concerned to postpone it and make use of the time thus gained for building a powerful heavy industry and war industry with all possible speed.

The Shakhty Case

The effectiveness of political leaders in carrying out their policy intentions depends upon their capacity to persuade other active participants in their political process that their political diagnoses are correct. Whenever objective circumstances do not support these diagnoses, unscrupulous leaders tend to resort to deliberate contrivance, to the fabrication of circumstances that would make it *appear* that the collective situation is what they maintain it is.[21]

Stalin fabricated circumstances in 1928 in order to dramatize the war danger. The passing of the war scare made it important for him to support his thesis with graphic new evidence of imperialist enmity toward the USSR and readiness to intervene in its affairs. Such seeming evidence was devised with police help and put on the public record in the Shakhty case, the curtain raiser of the Stalin era's show trials. It was staged in the Hall of Columns of Moscow's House of Unions (the former Club of the Nobility) in May–July 1928 before an audience of police-picked citizens, with foreign correspondents present. The accused were a group of fifty-three engineers, including three German citizens, who had worked in the coal-mining district of Shakhty in the North Caucasus and in the nearby Donbas in the Ukraine. Most were representatives of the old technical intelligentsia, men of *Smena-vekh* outlook employed as "technical directors" under Soviet managers who were generally party men with little technical knowledge. They were charged with participating in a foreign-based criminal conspiracy to wreck the Soviet coal mining industry and put the Donbas out of action by deliberate mismanagement of operations, causing explosions and arson in mines, factories, and power stations, ruining mine ventilation, importing unneeded equipment, violating labor legislation, and worsening the workers' living conditions. The conspirators were said to have acted on behalf of the Polish, German, and French intelligence services as well as the former mine and factory owners now living in emigration.

In that dawn of Soviet industrialization there was plenty of mismanagement in overstrained Soviet industry, some of it flagrant. Workers, often fresh from the village and ignorant, occasionally damaged or destroyed machinery. Low qualification and incompetence of technically untrained managers caused accidents, including explosions. There may also have been scattered instances of wrecking by individual ill-wishers of the Soviet state—though it is hard to prove. But there was never a deliberate wrecking policy by "bourgeois specialists" as a group.[22] The allegation of a foreign-based counterrevolutionary conspiracy was baseless.

Stalin's key personal role in developing the Shakhty case, in collaboration with a police official from the North Caucasus, one Yefim G. Yevdokimov, is attested by an ex-Soviet source. Yevdokimov, a Chekist of long standing with a prerevolutionary record as a common criminal, was an acquaintance of Stalin's. He came to Moscow in late 1927 with a story about a wrecking conspiracy in Shakhty and was rebuffed by the OGPU chief, V. R. Menzhinsky, for lack of convincing evidence. Then, however, he received encouragement from Stalin, who subsequently took a role of direct supervision in building up the case, over opposition from Premier Rykov and the new head of the Supreme Council of National Economy, Valerian Kuibyshev, both of whom feared the damaging economic and political consequences of this political affair.[23] Those arrested were physically and mentally coerced to confess complicity in the fictional conspiracy. Two of the imprisoned defendants, Boyaryshnikov and Miller, told the writer V. T. Shalamov, whom they met in camp much later, that the methods included the "conveyor" (constant interrogation without allowing the victim to sleep), solitary confinement, and the placing of people in cells with hot or cold floors.[24]

When all was ready, the scene was set in true theatrical fashion. The defendants, judges, prosecutor Nikolai Krylenko and his assistants, stenographers, and police guards with fixed bayonets were stationed on a raised, artificially lighted dais that presented to spectators the appearance of a stage.[25] The presiding judge was a clever, articulate, and opportunist lawyer, Andrei Y. Vyshinsky, who was distrusted by Old Bolsheviks because of his Menshevik past and a record of arresting Bolsheviks in the summer of 1917 while serving as police chief of a borough of Moscow.[26] Stalin had met Vyshinsky, who was three years his junior, when both were imprisoned in Baku in 1907,[27] and later became his political patron. Having become rector of Moscow University during the 1920s, Vyshinsky made his debut in Stalin's high politics during the Shakhty trial, in which he distinguished himself by doing everything possible to back up the prosecution. The trial received a blaze of publicity in the Soviet press. At the end, eleven of the defendants were sentenced to death. Most of the others received prison terms, and a very few, including the Germans (whose presence was supposed to demonstrate the foreign sources of the purported conspiracy), were let off. Six of the eleven sentenced to death received reprieves; the other five innocent people were executed.

In this first show trial of the Stalin era, only ten of the fifty-three defendants made full confessions and implicated the others; another half-dozen made partial confessions; the rest maintained their innocence and fought the charges. One defendant who failed to appear was said by his counsel to be unable to stand trial because he had gone out of his mind. The techniques of compelling confessions and of stage managing the trial were still so imperfect that even a foreign observer sympathetic to the Soviet regime (as Lyons was then) could readily see signs of the inhuman pressures to which the accused had been subjected. One defendant attempted in court to retract his confession, saying "I scarcely knew what I signed." Another, who had at first denied the charges against him, subsequently announced in court that he had signed a confession, whereupon he collapsed when his wife cried out from the relatives' box: "Kolya darling, don't lie! Don't! You know you're innocent."[28]

By its encouragement of what came to be called "specialist baiting," the trial served Stalin's political purposes in the developing battle against the Right and its supporters in government agencies who favored the alliance with the old technical intelligentsia. But a key objective was to dramatize the war danger by persuading people that the hostile capitalist world was *already intervening*—through enemies in their midst who wore masks of loyal citizens. Stalin himself set that line in a speech of April 1928, shortly before the trial opened. He described the alleged conspiracy as "economic counterrevolution" and asserted that international capital, having failed in its military-political intervention in the Civil War, was now attempting "economic intervention" with the aid of various groups of counterrevolutionary bourgeois specialists. "It would be stupid to think that international capital will leave us in peace," he said. "The Shakhty case marks a serious new action of international capital and its agents in our country against the Soviet regime." And further: "We have internal enemies. We have external enemies. This must not be forgotten for a single moment." The lesson? To press ahead with a "revolutionary policy" while maintaining maximum vigilance.[29]

In the political show trial Stalin found a spectacular way of drumming home the war danger to Soviet people without unduly disrupting the Soviet government's relations with foreign states whose assistance in industrialization it was seeking and would be obtaining. Thus the acquittal of the three Germans. He later provided an ideological rationale for these theatrical politics by declaring that "the capitalist encirclement must not be regarded as a simple geographical concept." The hostile encirclement was not only, as its name seemed to imply, out there beyond the borders; it was inside the country as well: "The capitalist encirclement means that around the USSR there are hostile class forces ready to support our class enemies inside the USSR morally and materially, by economic blockade, and, if given the opportunity, by military intervention." The wrecking activities of bourgeois specialists, uncovered "in all branches of our industry," stood as proof.[30]

A further forum for Stalin's harping on the war danger was the long-delayed Sixth Congress of the Communist Third International (Comintern), which opened in Moscow on 11 July 1928, just five days after the Shakhty trial closed, and in the same Hall of Columns. The proceedings, in which some five hundred delegates from fifty-eight parties took part, were dominated by the Russians. Bukharin, who had succeeded Zinoviev as leader of the Comintern, chaired the meeting and delivered the principal speeches. He was also the author of the new Comintern program adopted by this congress, and at its conclusion was elected chairman of the executive committee.

It is a measure of Stalin's tactical skill (and Bukharin's lack of it) that he managed to impress the talented and personable Bukharin into service at this parley as the spokesman of a position that in essentials was Stalin's and contrary to Bukharin's views, thereby making of the latter a hapless accessory in his own and his fellow moderates' coming downfall. In the precongress Politburo discussions there were sharp differences. The theses and program that Bukharin had drafted announced the advent of a postwar "third period," following the 1918–23 revolutionary period and the ensuing era of relative capitalist stabilization. In this Stalin concurred. They differed, however, in that Bukharin did not see the incipient third period as a time of increasing breakdown of the stabilization, whereas Stalin did. For him the third period was characterized by deepening interimperialist antagonisms leading to new wars.[31] The new program duly reflected this position, stating that the third period "inevitably leads to a fresh epoch of wars among the imperialist states. . . ." Policy conclusions were drawn accordingly. The Comintern executed a left turn. Communists were to intensify their fight against Social Democrats as the "main danger."

Some foreign delegates were puzzled by the insistence on the threat of war at a time when no war seemed on the horizon. One was Bertram D. Wolfe, a delegate of the U.S. Communist Party. He could not see the imminent war danger that Bukharin stressed in his report, although, when he returned home from the congress, he reported: ". . . the whole work of the Sixth Congress on every question leads to the same conclusion—that the war danger is the decisive factor in the present situation." Before departing Moscow, the somewhat baffled Wolfe had tried to seek out Bukharin for a chat about the question. He was unable to get even ten minutes alone with him.[32]

What Wolfe did not then know was that Bukharin, desperate over what was going on behind the scenes, had shortly before taken the politically risky step of making contact with the recently expelled Kamenev, who was living at that time in a provincial town not far away. After summoning him to Moscow, Bukharin held a series of clandestine conversations with Kamenev on 8, 11, and 12 July 1928. He apparently wanted to head off a feared reconciliation between Stalin and the party Left, and he informed Kamenev that Politburo members Rykov, Tomsky, and himself were radically at odds with Stalin. Their differences with him were, he said, many times more serious than those between them and Kamenev's group. Concerning the Comintern congress, Bukharin had this to say: "Stalin spoiled the program for me in many places. . . . He's eaten up by the yearning to become a recognized theorist. He thinks that's the only thing he lacks."[33]

Soon after the Comintern congress closed, Stalin opened fire in the Central Committee on what he now began to call the "Right danger" in Russia's Communist Party, with Bukharin's theoretical errors as his chief target of attack.

The Grain Collections Crisis

The 1927 harvest was a normal, average one. Yet, grain collections by the governmental and cooperative purchasing agencies fell off sharply toward the end of the year and as a result the grain exports in 1927–28 virtually ceased. The grain collections crisis enabled Stalin to persuade many in the party's higher ranks that a tough policy was needed to solve the regime's short-term problem. In fact this policy aimed at starting the second revolution.

What caused the grain collections crisis of 1928 has long remained unclear. Now we have some indication that it came about by Stalin's contrivance. But whether he contrived it or not, he made effective use of the crisis of grain procurements so as to justify the need for confiscatory measures, which would be the first battle in a war with the peasants ending in their collectivization.

Under the NEP peasants paid a tax to the state for their use of land, and the state used the tax money to buy the wheat from the peasants. Why then were there suddenly difficulties with grain purchases? It has been alleged—although this has not been definitely confirmed—that Stalin personally, acting with the help of close associates, intervened in two ways: the prices offered for the peasants' grain were lowered and the prices of the manufactured goods delivered to the countryside for sale to the peasants were considerably increased.[34] In any event, the peasants at this time withheld their grain from the market. To obtain what cash they needed for paying off taxes, they sold their technical crops and livestock products, on which prices were not lowered. They expected, reasonably, that by spring their grain would be bought at the previously prevailing higher prices.

Under Stalin's prodding, the party leadership responded to the emergency with coercive and confiscatory measures. Circular letters sent out from Stalin's Central Committee offices in December 1927 and early January 1928 directed local officials to take "extraordinary measures" for extracting the withheld grain, and threatened them if they failed to promptly increase grain procurements.[35] Between 15 January and 8 February, Stalin, like other party leaders, went on a personal trouble-shooting trip in connection with the procurements emergency. Choosing Siberia, he made several stops for discussions with local officials whom he admonished to get tough with kulak grain hoarders by applying Article 107 of the Criminal Code, under which they (as "speculators") could be punished and their grain stocks confiscated. One quarter of the grain so confiscated would go to poor peasants and low-income middle peasants at low state prices or on long-term credit (this, though Stalin did not say so, was a throwback to a technique used under War Communism, when *kombedy,* or "committees of the village poor," received 25 percent of the grain they helped extract from better-off peasants).

Going beyond immediate measures, Stalin lectured the Siberian officials on the urgent need to liberate Soviet industry from "kulak caprices" by going forward in collectivization, with a view to obtaining at least a third of the needed grain from *kolkhozy* and state farms *(sovkhozy)* within the next three or four years. But such "partial collectivization," albeit sufficient to supply the working class and Red Army more or less adequately with grain, would be quite insufficient, he went on, to ensure food supplies for the whole country and the necessary food reserves in the hands of the state, nor would it mean the victory of socialism in the countryside. To eliminate the danger of a restoration of capitalism, it was necessary to proceed from the already accomplished socialization of industry to the "socialization of all agriculture," meaning that all regions of the country without exception must be covered with *kolkhozy* and *sovkhozy* capable of replacing the individual peasants, and not the kulaks alone, as suppliers of grain to the state.[36] In these statements of January 1928, which went unpublished for more than twenty years, Stalin's proposed timetable for the process was not so compressed as the one he would prescribe at the end of 1929, but he made it quite clear that what he contemplated was the radical idea of wholesale collectivization.

Stalin and others later admitted that the "extraordinary measures" used in the procurements campaign of early 1928 harked back to War Communism's system of forcible grain appropriation by allocation of fixed delivery quotas to individual farmsteads. Arrests, posting of interception squads on district boundaries, searches of premises for hidden stores of grain, direct extralegal confiscation of grain so discovered, the closing down of grain markets, and the levying of a compulsory agricultural "loan" in return for grain taken by the local authorities were among the methods now employed. Since the bulk of the withheld grain belonged to the middle peasants and not to the very small minority of farmsteads officially classified as "kulak" (under one-twentieth of the total peasant households), the "extraordinary measures" were mostly applied against that very middle-peasant majority with which, under the ruling canons of NEP, the working-class regime was supposed to remain in alliance.[37] Peasants, especially the better-off ones, began to reason that it made no sense to sow as much grain for the coming year if their stocks were to be subject to confiscation again. What started as a grain collections crisis was now turning into a crisis of the regime's relations with the peasantry.

Inside the party, Stalin found his hard-line course under attack by the moderates. Even his follower Anastas Mikoyan voiced criticism and took the lead in calling for restraint and offering reassurance to the troubled peasantry.[38] Since it was known in party circles throughout the land that Stalin in his December and January circular directives had been the chief advocate of the revived War Communist methods, he could not stand aside as the methods were being modified to placate an aroused peasantry. Accordingly, in a new circular letter dated 13 February 1928, he linked himself with the modification by pooh-poohing rumors that the NEP was being abolished and condemning as "distortions" and "excesses" such practices as grain confiscations, the posting of interception squads, and compulsory levying of the agricultural loan. He took care at the same time, however, to claim that the policy of "extraordinary measures" had been necessary and successful. In sounding the retreat, he was concerned both to establish the rightness of the confiscatory policy that had been followed under his leadership and to keep the way open for further pursuit of it. Meanwhile, so serious did the situation become that in July 1928 grain procurement prices were finally raised (something hitherto resisted by the regime), and between June and August this grain-exporting country imported 250,000 tons of grain from abroad.[39]

Shortages, however, led to the general introduction of food rationing in February 1929. In these conditions, the official declarations of early 1928 on the terminating of extraordinary means of food collection went by the board. Inevitably, as in the previous year, the extortionary procedures affected not alone the kulaks but primarily the far larger number of better-off middle peasants who possessed the bulk of what grain stocks there were. Already tense, the atmosphere in the countryside began to grow violent. In various places, hard-pressed peasants retaliated by murdering procurement agents.[40] Extremist measures on the regime's part were calling forth a retaliatory extremism on the part of some peasants. The more Stalin succeeded in pushing through a policy of strong-arm methods of grain procurement, the more the circumstances themselves changed for the worse, thereby inviting still more strong-arm methods, and so on in a vicious circle. In the end, an all-out drive for collectivization—which Stalin wanted—seemed to many the only course left.

The moderates foresaw trouble and warned against it in very strong terms. In a lengthy brief presented to a closed Central Committee plenum in July 1928, Bukharin argued that the current year's grain collection difficulties stemmed mainly from avoidable faults in planning and in pricing policy. He acknowledged that the extraordinary measures had been necessary, but he pointed out that they had produced a very tense situation in the countryside, and that to continue them would lead to War Communism "without a war." Such a policy would contravene Lenin's basic precept on peasant policy by threatening a "rupture of the bond" with the middle peasant. Should the regime seek to drive the *muzhik* into the commune by force, the outcome might be a kulak-led mass peasant uprising that would destroy the proletarian dictatorship. At this point Stalin drew laughter from the assembly by breaking in derisively with an old Russian folk saying: "Terrible is the dream, but merciful is God."[41]

The moderates (anticipating later historians) offered a basically economic diagnosis of the grain collection difficulties, and proposed to deal with them by such economic methods as increased prices for peasant grain. Stalin rejected that position on two main grounds. First, the needs of industrialization ruled out a price increase since the existing sharp spread between the low prices paid to the peasants for their produce and high ones paid by them for manufactured goods was a basic source of accumulation for industrializing, "something on the order of 'tribute,' something on the order of a supertax." Second, the difficulties had their source not in economics but in a political phenomenon: kulak antagonism to the Soviet regime. The withholding of grain was a move by the kulaks and speculators against the Soviet regime, and as such it called for retaliatory countermeasures and offensive measures.[42]

In order to justify this militant course in the countryside, Stalin now advanced the proposition, henceforth central to his ideology, that class war must intensify with progress toward socialism. Just as there could be no such progress in the sphere of trade without dislodging thousands and thousands of traders who would inevitably resist, or in industry without dislodging thousands and thousands of entrepreneurs who likewise would resist the measures taken against them, so a policy of restricting the capitalist elements in the countryside must result in their efforts to stir up resistance by poor and middle peasants. It followed that "progress toward socialism cannot but lead to resistance by exploiter elements to that progress, and the exploiters' resistance cannot but lead to an inexorable aggravation of the class struggle."[43] This formula provided an ideological rationale for the vicious circle of confiscatory measures—resistance—intensified confiscatory measures that Stalin's own agrarian policy was producing.

The party moderates saw that he was moving toward a rural revolution and were aghast. They knew that nothing but force would drive the mass of peasants into *kolkhozy,* and feared that such an operation would lead to catastrophe. It was in these circumstances that Bukharin called Kamenev to Moscow in July 1928 for clandestine talks. Visibly agitated, he told Kamenev that Stalin was a Genghis Khan whose line spelled ruin for the Revolution. His thesis about the growing intensity of the class struggle on the way to socialism was "idiotic illiteracy." His policy was leading to an uprising that would have to be drowned in blood.[44]

The extreme nervous alarm that Bukharin displayed was in part a reaction to something Stalin had said in the above-mentioned speech. He had used the word "tribute" *(dan')* in referring to the gap between the prices the peasant paid for manufactured goods and those he received for his grain. The word *dan'* historically referred to the tribute that the Russian princes were compelled to exact from their subjects for the benefit of the Tatar khans. The grim associations with which it was freighted may explain why Bukharin now described Stalin as a "Genghis Khan." Stalin's use of *dan'* opened the eyes of his adversaries in the moderate group to the full meaning of his policy design. They must have realized that he was trying to emulate the Muscovite Russian state, which had bolstered its military power by direct exploitation of the population, especially by imposing serfdom on the peasantry. They saw that he was setting course toward a revolution from above in the coercive Russian state-building tradition. And familiar as these well-read Bolshevik leaders were with the texts in which Plekhanov, Miliukov, and others had explained the nature and driving forces of the state-building process, they had no difficulty in understanding the essence of Stalin's collectivization project. When they made their last stand, in February 1929, they ascribed to him a policy of "military-feudal exploitation of the peasantry." In his address to the closed joint plenum of the Central Committee and Central Control Commission in April 1929, which formalized the moderates' defeat, Stalin dismissed the charge as gross slander. His wording was echoed in the resolution of the joint plenum, which said that the "slanderous thrust" about military-feudal exploitation of the peasantry was "taken from the arsenal of the party of Miliukov."[45]

Subsequent events proved that the moderates diagnosed Stalin's peasant policy correctly, and that their forebodings about it were well founded. Why then did they lose and why did Stalin win the battle for the party oligarchy's support at that crucial juncture? The usual answer—his organizational power as general secretary—is no more than an important part of the answer. Another part is that his policy maneuvers brought about a situation in which there seemed to many no way out but the way in which he was pointing. Still another is the skill with which he appealed to the latent antikulak sentiment in the party.

For example, at the November 1928 Central Committee plenum, where Rykov argued for higher prices for grain on the ground that the peasant had cut down his sowings after losing all incentive to produce, Stalin declared: "It's not a matter of caressing the peasant and seeing in this the way to establish correct relations with him, for you won't go far on caresses."[46] During the April 1929 plenum, he clinched his antikulak case by telling a story. At a recent village assembly in Kazakhstan, after an agitator had tried for two hours to persuade the local holders of grain stocks to turn them over, a kulak stepped forth with a pipe in his mouth and said: "Dance a little jig for us, young fellow, and I'll give you two poods." At this point in Stalin's speech, a voice from the plenum audience exclaimed, "the son-of-a-bitch!" and Stalin went on: "Try and persuade people like that. Yes, comrades, a class is a class. There's no getting away from it."[47]

In those decisive Central Committee sessions of 1928, Stalin had the support not only of such prominent figures as Molotov, Ordzhonikidze, Kuibyshev, Voroshilov, Mikoyan, and others, but also of the party secretaries of key areas: the Ukraine (S. V. Kosior), Leningrad (S. M. Kirov), Siberia (R. I. Eikhe), the North Caucasus (A. A. Andreev), the Urals (N. M. Shvernik), the Central Black Earth region (I. M. Vareikis), the Lower Volga (B. P. Sheboldaev), the Middle Volga (M. M. Khataevich), Kazakhstan (F. I. Goloshchekin), and Kharkov (P. P. Postyshev).[48] If somewhat younger than he in years, these men were for the most part Bolsheviks of similar mold, individuals for whom the Civil War and War Communism had been a formative experience of their political lives.

One other fact must be taken into account in explaining Stalin's victory and the moderates' defeat. Despite his tough talk and introduction of the ominous formula about the aggravation of the class struggle on the way to socialism, Stalin made no explicit mention of an impending revolution from above and forebore to reveal that he was prepared to resort to terror in collectivizing. He dismissed the grave fears being voiced by the moderates as groundless, mere alarmism of the weak-nerved in the face of difficulties and the need for a firm policy hand. He presented himself to his fellow party oligarchs as anything but the extremist and gambler that he soon turned out to be. Accordingly, the support that the Central Committee gave to the General Line was support for a far more restrained position than the one Stalin embarked on soon afterward. Proof of this lies in the Five-Year Plan. On the day the April 1929 Central Committee plenum ended in Stalin's conclusive victory, the Sixteenth Party Conference opened. The collectivization envisioned in the Five-Year Plan adopted by it was not at all a blueprint for the rural revolution that Stalin launched before the year was out. It provided that 17.5 percent of the country's total sown area would belong to the "socialized sector" by the end of the plan period, that is, 1933. Far from envisaging that the "individual sector" would be vastly curtailed by then, the conference resolution only specified that it would have ceased its numerical growth.[49]

After two seasons of great difficulty in grain collections, the party leadership as a whole still did not perceive the necessity or possibility of wholesale collectivization in the immediate future whereas Stalin, inspired by his urge to go down in history as a combination of Lenin and Peter the Great, did. For the moment, however, he was content with what he had achieved: the defeat of the Right and formal party approval of at least a limited collectivization plan. The plan as approved was a mandate for change in the direction he desired—change that he intended to accelerate.

Stalin's Leninism

As a Bolshevik, even a Russian national one, Stalin was bound to accept Lenin as the supreme authority. How could he do so while going against Lenin's clearly expressed view that coercive methods must be avoided in the transition to socialism? The Right kept pressing this question in various ways as he started to unveil his revolutionary project during the party debates in 1928. His answer was that "to take Lenin in one part without wanting to take him as a whole is to distort Lenin."[50] This was a way of recalling the party to that other, earlier, class-war Lenin who sponsored forcible food requisitioning, the martial Lenin best exemplified by Lenin's actions in 1917–18, the Lenin who himself wrote "revolution" with a capital R, and who was Stalin's identity-figure.

As a Leninist of that stripe, Stalin invoked Lenin's *Kto-kogo* formula at key points. In his April 1929 polemic against the "Right deviation" he declared that "we live according to Lenin's formula of '*Kto-kogo*': either we shall pin them, the capitalists, to the ground and give them, as Lenin expressed it, final decisive battle, or they will pin our shoulders to the ground."[51] Indeed, Lenin in May 1921 said that the past four years of revolution and Civil War had not been the last decisive battle (referring to the line of "The Internationale" which runs "This is our last, decisive battle"); that would only come with "victory on the economic front."[52] At the Sixteenth Congress in 1930, with a sideswipe at "Bukharin's childish formula about the peaceful growing of capitalist elements into socialism," Stalin said: "Our development has proceeded and continues to proceed according to Lenin's formula—'Kto-kogo.' Either we will overcome and crush them, the exploiters, or else they will overcome and crush us, the workers and peasants of the USSR—that's how the question stands, comrades."[53] Thus did this who-will-beat-whom personality, who lived his whole life according to Lenin's formula in his own stark understanding of it, intone the fighting words again and again in defense of his policy. What needs stressing is that he never lacked for a Lenin text in arguing his case.

If there is any historical "would-have-happened" about which we can be certain, it is that Lenin, had he been living still, would have opposed Stalin's coercive peasant policy of 1928–29 and the forcible mass collectivization that followed. Stalin's opponents were entirely justified in claiming Lenin's authority for their position in the debate over agrarian policy at that time.

In 1919, at the height of War Communism, Lenin pointed out to the Eighth Party Congress that in the countryside, unlike in the towns, one could not simply lop off a top layer of capitalists and be left with a foundation for socialized production. What was left in the countryside after the landlords' elimination were many million small, middle, and large peasants with their addiction to individual farming. Since the small peasants were the regime's rural friends, the key to its agrarian policy must be alliance with the nonexploitative middle peasant, who—being both a proprietor and a working person—was essentially "a class that vacillates." The middle peasant was a large stratum, numbering in the millions, and nothing could be achieved here by coercive means: "*Coercion toward the middle peasantry is a supremely harmful thing*," Lenin declared with heavy emphasis, and added with reference to agrarian policy in general: "*To act here by means of coercion is to ruin the whole cause. Long-term educational work is needed here. To the peasant, who not only in our country but all over the world is a practical person and a realist, we must provide concrete examples to prove that the 'kommunia' is best of all.*"[54] The ensuing growth of the middle peasantry in numbers and its persisting strong disinclination to exchange individual for collective farming added weight to Lenin's warning.

On 20 January 1929, the eve of the fifth anniversary of Lenin's death, when the moderates still enjoyed considerable influence on the editorial board of *Pravda,* Krupskaya published a courageous article in the party paper, "Ilyich on *Kolkhoz* Construction," testifying on her unimpeachable authority that a noncoercive approach to the small farmer was central to Lenin's legacy in agrarian policy. She traced his views back to an article of 1894 by Engels on "The Peasant Question in France and Germany." Engels had foreseen that on coming to power the Communists would not confiscate the small peasant farms but would use state aid to foster their gradual merger into large cooperative farms. Lenin had reread Engels' essay many times, his widow recalled, and was deeply influenced by it. Then she traced Lenin's views on the peasant problem through his culminating article of January 1923, "On Cooperation." She cited the latter at length because, she explained, it was being interpreted nowadays "quite variously." This was her polite way of rebutting Stalin's contention that his collectivization project and Lenin's plan for the "cooperating of Russia" were one and the same.

If we take Lenin's last articles as his political testament, as Bukharin did in accordance with Lenin's own view of the matter, it follows that Stalin's orientation on a second revolution was in conflict with that testament. But before we conclude that there was a complete gulf between "Leninism" and emergent "Stalinism," we must look at the other side of the question. If the party moderates found Lenin's political testament in the reformist later articles, Stalin found it mainly in other Lenin utterances: those of the Lenin whose watch-words were class war and *Kto-kogo.*

Thus, in upholding the need for extortionary measures of grain collection, Stalin recalled that in 1922, when Preobrazhensky proposed to include a statement in the Eleventh Party Congress' resolution on agrarian policy that would renounce *kombedy* (that is, confiscatory) methods against the kulak "once and for all," Lenin objected that ". . . war, for example, can compel a resort to *kombedy* procedures."[55] Even in defending himself against the charge of "military-feudal exploitation of the peasantry" as reflected in his use of the term "tribute," with its Tatar associations, Stalin was able to find a number of passages in which Lenin had used this term (although in quite different contexts), thereby giving it "the right of citizenship in our Marxist literature." In *The Immediate Tasks of the Soviet Government,* for example, Lenin had spoken of "the tribute *(dan')* paid by us for our backwardness in the organizing of nationwide accounting and control from below."[56]

The thesis that the internal class war grows more intense with the approach to socialism is widely regarded as one idea that was truly original with Stalin. Formulated as a *law* of the advance toward socialism, it did carry Stalin's own trademark. Yet, even on this crucial issue Stalin found support in a 1919 Lenin statement that "the destruction of classes is a matter of a long, hard, stubborn *class struggle,* which *after* the overthrow of the power of capital, *after* the destruction of the bourgeois state, *after* the establishing of the proletarian dictatorship *does not disappear* (as the vulgar minds of the old socialism and the old Social Democracy imagine)."[57] Another supportive Lenin text from the first revolutionary period ran: "The strength of the proletariat and the peasantry allied to it grows with the resistance of the bourgeoisie and its retainers. As their enemies, the exploiters, step up their resistance, the exploited mature and gain in strength; they grow and learn and they cast out the 'old Adam' of wage-slavery." This statement appears in an article that Lenin wrote in January 1918 but withheld from publication.[58] Stalin "quoted" it by having it made public for the first time in *Pravda*'s issue of 22 January 1929, when the fifth anniversary of Lenin's death was being marked and Stalin's battle with the Right opposition was at its climax.

In his conversations of July 1928 with Kamenev, Bukharin contemptuously dismissed Stalin's thesis about the growing intensity of the class struggle as "idiotic illiteracy." This was more a revelation of Bukharin's strong feelings in the grim fight he was then waging against Stalin than an objective assessment of the latter's grasp of Leninism. Granted that the thesis was opposed to Lenin's political testament as set forth in the final phase, it was not inconsistent with the revolutionism of that younger Lenin whom Stalin was invoking, a Lenin who still earlier, in 1905, invidiously contrasted "the way of reform" as one of "delay, procrastination, the painfully slow decomposition of the putrid parts of the national organism" with the revolutionary way of "rapid amputation, which is least painful to the proletariat, the path of immediate removal of what is putrescent."[59]

Another document that proved useful was "How to Organize Competition," an essay written by Lenin in January 1918 and withheld from publication. It appeared in *Pravda* on 20 January 1929 under the title "Lenin—Banner of the Millions," sharing space that day with Krupskaya's "Ilyich and *Kolkhoz* Construction."

In one part of this previously unpublished article, Lenin launched into a tirade against "the rich and their hangers-on, and the crooks, the idlers, and the hooligans" and those described as "these dregs of humanity, these hopelessly decayed and atrophied limbs, this contagion, this plague, this ulcer that socialism has inherited from capitalism." He went on: "No mercy to these enemies of the people, the enemies of socialism, the enemies of the toilers! War to the bitter end on the rich and their hangers-on, the bourgeois intellectuals; war on the rogues, the idlers, and the hooligans!" As for the way to wage the war, and "to cleanse the land of Russia of all sorts of harmful insects, of the flea-crooks and bedbug-rich, and so on and so forth," Lenin had these thoughts to offer: "In one place half a score of rich, a dozen crooks, half a dozen workers who shirk their work (in the hooligan manner in which compositors in Petrograd, particularly in the party printing shops, shirk their work) will be put in prison. In another place they will be put to cleaning latrines. In a third place they will be provided with 'yellow tickets' after they have served their time, so that all the people shall have them under surveillance, as *harmful* persons, until they reform. In a fourth place, one out of every ten idlers will be shot on the spot." After appearing in *Pravda* and other soviet papers, this short essay was put out as a pamphlet with a circulation of 3.5 million copies.

Why Lenin chose to withhold it from publication is unknown. Krupskaya's much later statement in her memoirs that he did so because he considered it "unfinished" is not convincing; it is as finished as other quickly written pieces that he did publish.[60] Conceivably, he himself was taken aback by its extremism when he reread it on returning from the brief vacation in Finland during which he wrote the essay. But this question is of no great importance considering that Lenin expressed himself along the same general lines in other statements of that time. The use to which Stalin put the essays shows how valuable they were to him. Ironically, he was able to answer Krupskaya's plea in her dead husband's name for a nonviolent peasant policy by publishing in the very same issue of *Pravda* a statement on the propriety of revolutionary violence from above—signed by Lenin.

Stalin was going to use terror in dealing with all those who in the course of the second revolution would be called "class enemies"—an infinitely more elastic category in his usage than it was in Lenin's. The Leninist legitimacy of such action was important for him to establish, and a means of doing so was to publicize Lenin documents defending the need for terror by a revolutionary government against its enemies. One was the letter that Lenin wrote in 1922 to Commissar of Justice Kursky insisting that the criminal code openly justify the necessity of terror and not simply the limits of it. This letter first received full publicity when it appeared in 1930 in the Central Committee journal *Bol'shevik* under the bold-face title: *Letter to Comrade D. I. Kursky on the Question of Terror,* in a special section called "Lenin and Leninism." An accompanying article, by one I. Cherviak, said it was "of enormous interest" and "of especially topical significance now."[61]

5

THE FIVE-YEAR PLAN
IN FOUR!

STALIN CHOSE the October anniversary, 7 November 1929, to issue a manifesto of the second revolution in a *Pravda* article, "The Year of the Great Turn." It presented events of that year as the opening of a momentous new chapter in history, a revolution of socialism's construction in Soviet Russia.

The USSR was swiftly becoming a metal country, it said. A Soviet heavy industry was being built at a tempo far in excess of what the Right opportunists had thought possible. Collectivization of agriculture was also proceeding very rapidly, refuting Bukharinist arguments that the peasants would not join the collectives, that an accelerated collectivization drive would arouse mass discontent among them, and that the highroad of rural socialism was the formation of cooperative associations rather than true collective farms. The young, large-scale, socialized agriculture, growing now even faster than big industry, had a great future and could show miracles of growth. If accelerated collectivization continued, the USSR would in three years be one of the world's largest grain producers, if not the largest. The Five-Year Plan in industry and agriculture was thus to be seen as a plan for building a socialist society. Stalin concluded: "We are advancing full steam ahead—to socialism, leaving behind the age-old 'Russian' backwardness. . . . And when we have put the USSR on an automobile and the *muzhik* on a tractor, let the worthy capitalists, who boast so much of their 'civilization,' try to overtake us! We shall yet see which countries may then be 'classified' as backward and which as advanced."

The key Russian word in Stalin's manifesto is *perelom,* here translated as "turn." It is difficult to render in English. In medicine it refers to the breaking of a limb or a crisis that occurs in an illness. Figuratively, it means a fundamental shift of direction, a turning point. Lenin's writings of 1917 often used it in that sense. One said: "Every revolution signifies a sharp turn *(perelom)* in the life of huge masses of the people. If such a turn has not occurred, a real revolution cannot take place.[1]

Russia was indeed the scene of a *perelom* in the second half of 1929, but not of the kind meant by Lenin. It was not a peasant movement from below to change the face of the countryside or a worker movement from below to industrialize at a breakneck pace. Rather, the radical transformation of Russia's way of life was being initiated by action of representatives of the regime in the towns and villages, and they in turn were acting under administrative pressure from higher authority in Moscow. The second revolution had started from above: in Stalin's Central Committee headquarters.

NEP Russia went down under an onslaught like one of those undeclared wars that became common in the twentieth century. Even as the change was taking place, no one officially proclaimed the NEP to have ended. Stalin told the Sixteenth Party Congress in June 1930 that the ongoing "offensive of socialism along the whole front" did not signify the repeal of the NEP, but only its "final phase."

Already, however, NEP society was receding into the past and quickly becoming just the memory of a time of relative normalcy and plenty. The Nepmen in the towns were being driven out of business by confiscatory taxes. Many were arrested, and some tortured, in order to reveal where they had hidden real or suspected gold and other valuables that the state could use for foreign exchange. Food rationing, introduced in February 1929, was in force again as under War Communism. Industrialization was proceeding feverishly, and collectivization was advancing in the countryside under the battle cry "Liquidation of the kulaks as a class." The demographic map of the country was changing through the deportation of people to remote areas and the mobilization of tens of thousands of Soviet citizens, especially from the nation's youth, for work on new construction projects in the Urals, Siberia, and elsewhere. Some went willingly and even with enthusiasm; others simply went.

To a foreign journalist who observed these events from Moscow, it was "Russia's iron age."[2] To the ordinary person who lived through it, or died in it, it was simply the *piatiletka* (Five-Year Plan). Histories commonly describe it as the time of forced industrialization and wholesale collectivization. These were the focal processes. But the whole cultural system, comprising the organization of the state, the ways of running the economy, the social structure, justice, the penal system, education, the visual and dramatic arts, literature, and the daily life of the people, was in the throes of rapid change. Not even the traditional way of measuring the passage of time was left untouched. By governmental decree, the seven-day week disappeared for a while (from 25 May to 27 November 1930) in favor of the unbroken workweek, under which the days were no longer named but simply numbered from one through five, and different contingents of workers rested on different sixth days so that plants and other institutions could operate without letup. The resulting disruption of normal family life was emblematic of the period, and the blow to church going was a part of the revived antireligious campaign that also had a place in the offensive along the whole front.

Not by force alone was the second revolution accomplished, especially in the initial phase. At the end of the 1920s, whatever was left of Marxist radicalism in the party and intelligentsia, of revolutionary *élan* in the youth and working class, was mobilized under the banner of building the new socialist Russia. The martial spirit of War Communism was resurrected in the official language of the time. Stalin expressed it in April 1930 when he hailed the first graduating class of the recently founded Industrial Academy in Moscow as "its first arrow shot into the camp of our enemies, into the camp of production routine and technical backwardness." At the opening of the Stalingrad tractor plant in June of that year, his congratulatory message said that "the 50,000 tractors you are going to give the country each year are 50,000 shells blowing up the old bourgeois world and cutting through the road to the new socialist system in the countryside."[3]

The press was filled with phrases like "industrial front," "agricultural front," "battle for coal," "Red offensive," "light cavalry attacks," "militant discipline," and "shock brigades." Literature was the "literary front" where writers enlisted in the class war against bourgeois literary culture and for industrialization; and other intellectual professions were similarly mobilized. Writers' brigades recited in workshops of Moscow plants on All-

Union Shock Worker's Day. The *Literary Gazette* opened a new section of inspirational feature stories under the heading, "Writers on the Front of Socialist Competition."

Not long before his suicide in 1930 the poet Vladimir Mayakovsky, wrote a poem, "The March of the Shock Brigades," which contained the characteristic lines: "Fight today, revolutionary, on the barricades of production." Another of his poems, "The March of Time," inspired Valentin Kataev to pay a visit to the new industrial city in the Urals, Magnitogorsk. The resulting novel, *Time, Forward!,* was a celebration of the *piatiletka* in an account of one day in the building of a new industrial center in the Urals. The main hero, a technologically revolutionary Bolshevik engineer named Margulies, does battle with a conservative-minded old-regime holdover, Nalbandov, who opposes "risky experiments" and "barbaric rapidity of work." Soviet workers build the new complex while the American consulting engineer thinks only of the money he is making, and a touring capitalist tycoon named Roy Roop cries out "Babylon, Babylon!" in fright at the grandiosity of the new world rising there in the wilderness. Meanwhile, the builders of socialism breathe the pure air, "twice cleared by the thunderstorm of two revolutions."

The Plan Is Only the Beginning

The Five-Year Plan went into operation in October 1928, although its formal adoption did not take place until the spring of 1929. The drafting of the plan had started already in 1925. Several earlier variants were rejected because, as a Soviet source much later put it, "The authors of these variants simply could not get it through their heads that it was not simply a matter of developing industry, but of a great industrial revolution."[4]

In putting this idea across, Stalin had the support of such stalwart fellow believers in high-speed industrialization as Ordzhonikidze and Kuibyshev. Even they, however, worked under heavy pressure from the industrialization-obsessed general secretary. From them and others in high places the pressure was transmitted on down to the planning officials, of whom S. G. Stumilin—then in charge of the work of Gosplan (State Planning Commission) in preparing the plan—said that they preferred to "stand" for higher tempos rather than "sit" for lower ones.[5] In Russian, "to sit" is a colloquial expression for doing time in confinement. The comment was not made wholly in jest. The plan was adopted by the Sixteenth Party Conference in April 1929 in an "optimal" variant as opposed to the "starting-point" variant embodying the relatively moderate projections of the professional planners. The "starting-point" variant was subsequently labeled a "wrecking plan" and some planners were imprisoned.

Valerian Kuibyshev, who joined the Politburo in 1927 after succeeding Felix Dzerzhinsky in the previous year as head of the Supreme Council of National Economy, played a prominent part in pushing through the optimal version of the plan. In loyalty to Stalin, he dismissed the charge of "overindustrialization" and overconcentration on the producer-goods industries and overruled the professional economists whose projections were based on economic realism. After rejecting, with Stalin, the plea for balanced economic growth made by Bukharin in his famous *Pravda* article of 20 September 1928, "Notes of an Economist," Kuibyshev would stay in his office late into the night struggling vainly to square the statistical circle of the *piatiletka*. "This is what's been troubling me yesterday and today," he wrote to his wife on 8 October 1928. "I can't balance it out and since I absolutely cannot take the path of cutting down on capital construction (slowing down the tempo), I have to shoulder a virtually unbearable burden in reducing the unit cost of production."[6] Politics was in command; economics was faltering in obedience to impossible orders.

As adopted in the "optimal" variant, the plan was a design for the leap out of backwardness that Stalin credited Peter with attempting. Industrial output was to rise by over 20 percent annually. In reporting this to the Sixteenth Party Conference, Kuibyshev pointed out that industrial growth had reached no more than an annual 8.7 percent in the greatest boom period of the USA, 1850–60, and no more than 8 percent in the years of most rapid economic growth of tsarist Russia. He forebore to mention, however, that the plan in its optimal variant was predicated on four assumptions so uncertain individually that their aggregate was nothing short of an economic miracle: (1) five consecutive good harvests; (2) more external trade than in 1928; (3) a sharp improvement in qualitative performance; and (4) a smaller ratio than previously of military expenditures in the total of state expenditures.[7] The last-named of these assumptions was in no way inconsistent with the general military orientation of the *piatiletka*. It had to do with the maintenance of the army during what the plan presupposed would be a period of continued breathing spell.

In order to understand how subsequent events developed as they did, we must realize that Stalin did not feel constrained by the guidelines of the plan even in the unrealistic version finally adopted in April 1929. For him the plan document was simply a party-approved mandate for the feverish leap out of Russian backwardness, an official charter for the mobilization of the great nation's energies in a single-decade industrial revolution. What had made it worthwhile to pressure the planning officials into adoption of the optimal variant was to get the spirit of maximalism embodied in a Soviet state paper.

Accordingly, not long after the plan was legislated into law, pressure began to be exerted from above for its overfulfillment. In 1929 Soviet economic growth did not keep pace with the plan targets, and the favorable presuppositions of the optimal variant were not being borne out, partly due to the decline of raw material prices on the world market after the onset of the Great Depression. Although a downward revision of the control figures was therefore in order, Stalin and Molotov unexpectedly demanded and obtained an almost twofold increase in them.[8] Then Stalin went before the Sixteenth Congress and espoused the slogan, "The Five-Year Plan in Four Years," adding for good measure that ". . . we can fulfill it for a whole series of branches of industry in three years or even in two and a half years." In practice, as he went on to point out, this meant that pig iron production would reach 17 million tons as against the planned 10 million tons in the final year of the plan period (1932–33); that tractor production would reach 170,000 as against the planned 55,000; that car and truck production would reach 200,000 as against the planned 100,000, and so on. "It may be said that by so basically altering the plan targets, the Central committee is violating the planning principle and undermining the authority of the planning organs," Stalin declared. "But only hopeless bureaucrats can talk that way. For us Bolsheviks, the Five-Year Plan is not something finished and once and for all given. . . . The drawing up of the plan is only *the beginning of planning*."[9]

So, the slogan "The Five-Year Plan in Four!" blanketed the country. Kindergartners marched around their schools waving little banners and chanting:

> Five in four,
> Five in four,
> Five in four,
> *And not in five!*

What it meant, one of them now living in America has said, they did not know.

One of the "hopeless bureaucrats" turned out to be none other than the ardent Stalinist industrializer Kuibyshev, under whose driving pressure the plan had been adopted in its overambitious optimal variant. After going along with Stalin's steep upward revision of the plan targets, he realized in the light of sober computations that this made no sense. At a meeting of the combined presidiums of Gosplan and the Supreme Council of National Economy in August 1930, he produced statistics that "showed the full unreality of the revisions made." Thus, to raise pig iron output to 17 million tons by the last year of the plan period (it was running at 5 million tons during 1930, and would drop to 4.9 million in 1931 as compared with the 10 million called for by the plan prior to its upward revision) would require a budgetarily impossible investment of 2.5 billion rubles in ferrous metal-lurgy alone in 1931. So the target was reduced to the originally set level of 10 million tons, and even this was not reached until the second plan period in 1934.[10]

But Stalin was of no mind to lessen the pressure on the country. In the no-more-beatings-of-Russia speech of February 1931, he went a step further in his economic extremism. The fulfillment of the Five-Year Plan in four years was already assured, he said, and the economic managers' promise to meet the control figures for industrial production in 1931 was by implication an undertaking to fulfill the plan in three years for the basic and decisive branches of industry. Later in the speech he enuncia-ted the fighting motto, "There are no fortresses that Bolsheviks cannot con-quer."[11]

So it was that the plan as such ceased to have meaning in the time of the *piatiletka*. "Bacchanalian planning,"[12] under the direct personal prod-ding of Stalin, supplanted all rational planning principles. Taking advan-tage of the lack of restraints upon his policy-making power, he was acting now in obedience to his urge to succeed where Peter failed and to bring about a second October. The man who had recommended himself to the party during the mid-1920s as a prudent, cautious manager was now at the wheel of the careening car of Soviet industrialization, driven by his inner fantasy about his hero-role in revolutionary history.

Stalin followed Peter's example in looking to the West for aid in Russia's industrialization. A billion and a half rubles in foreign currency were spent in 1928–33 to buy equipment for heavy industry.[13] Numbers of engineers were sent abroad to learn foreign industrial technology, and hundreds of foreign engineers and thousands of foreign skilled workers were brought to Russia on contract. Soviet-made automobiles like the ZIS, and Soviet tractors like the Stalinets 8, were direct copies of American models, in the latter instance the Caterpillar D–7. An exhaustive study lists 217 technical assistance agreements between the USSR and foreign firms for the period 1929–45, and concludes that "no major technology or major plant under construction between 1930 and 1945 has been identified as a purely Soviet effort."[14] The foreign companies involved in this massive technological transfer were American, German, British, Italian, French, Swedish, Norwegian, Danish, Canadian, Swiss, Spanish, Czech, and Manchurian; the listing reads like a Who's Who of world capitalism.

The war-oriented character of Stalin's industrialization was manifest in its geography. The bulk of pre-1917 Russia's industrial development was concentrated in European Russia and the Ukraine plus the oil center of Baku and other mineral-bearing areas of the Transcaucasus. The vast reaches of Siberia, stretching eastward from the Ural mountains, and of arid Kazakhstan to the south, were inclement and sparsely settled, yet mineral-rich and militarily far less vulnerable. With the latter facts in mind, and following a lead provided by the non-Communist Russian engineer, Vasily Grinevetsky, in his book of 1918 on *The Postwar Outlook for Russian Industry*, the Stalinist industrializers made Asian Russia a focal area of the industrialization drive.[15] Thus, one of the biggest projects of the *piatiletka* was the Ural-Kuznetsk combine. Coking coal from the Kuznetsk basin in Siberia was supplied to the great new Magnitogorsk iron-and-steel works built in the iron-rich Urals area. Among many projects involved in the eastward expansion were the tractor plant in the Urals city of Cheliabinsk, combine-producing and other plants in the "Chicago of Siberia," Novosibirsk, and the development of the nonferrous metals industry as well as coal mining in Kazakhstan. Stalin placed special emphasis on all this, and a later Soviet source said that the idea for the Ural-Kuznetsk combine came directly from him.[16] Linked with this geography of war-oriented industrialization was the vast expansion of the forced labor system, which represented an integral part of the revolution from above.

Although the vast majority of those victimized were peasants, not a few of Stalin's victims were engineers from the old intelligentsia. Professional planners responsible for the "starting-point" variant of the plan were among them. The charge that they and others were engaged in a "wrecking" conspiracy on behalf of the capitalist encirclement was dramatized in the next big show trial following the Shakhty case. This was the Industrial Party *(Prompartiia)* trial of November–December 1930.

Its theatrical character is evident from the scenario of the alleged conspiracy, reprinted on the adjoining page from a Soviet English-language translation of the indictment.[17] The plot of this play was "The Plot." The Industrial Party was a fictional organization. According to the indictment, however, it was organized in the later 1920s by members of the old technical intelligentsia, such as Professor Leonid Ramzin, director of Moscow's Thermal Technical Institute, and it had a membership of some two thousand engineers. Originally a coordinating center for wrecking activities in munitions, textiles, shipbuilding, engineering, chemicals, gold mining, oil, and other industries, it developed into an underground political party aiming to prepare the ground by economic sabotage for a *coup d' état* in 1930 or 1931, which was to be supported by French- and British-led military intervention from abroad. In the field of planning, one of its machinations was the advocacy of plans calculated to slacken the pace of economic development, create disproportions leading to an economic crisis, and thereby cause wide popular discontent. The indictment also said that one of the accused "died during the investigation," and that two others were "previously sentenced," that is, available to the OGPU play producers as convicted criminals whose testimony against newly indicted persons could be spun out at will. The rehearsed confessions then "revealed" that on coming to power, the party intended to form a counterrevolutionary government in which the accused Palchinsky (already shot by the time of the trial) would be prime minister, the former Russian industrialist P. P. Ryabushinsky minister of interior, and the well-known historian, Academician E. V. Tarlé, foreign minister. Unfortunately for the play's credibility, it transpired (in the West) that Mr. Ryabushinsky had died in emigration before the time of the Industrial Party's alleged formation.

The Plot

Industrial Wrecking by the Joint Council of Engineers' Organisations, later the Industrial Party.
Wrecking of the Five-Year Plan in order to produce an economic crisis in 1930.
Espionage under the French General Staff.
Disintegration of the Red Army.
Foreign intervention and domestic revolt in 1930—31.
Military dictatorship followed by democratic-capitalist government.

Russians	Special Field
Prof. Leonid Ramsin, Leading Conspirator, and Chief Witness: Indicted.	Power and Fuel.
P. A. Palchinsky, early leader of Plotters' Organisation: already shot for wrecking activities.	Foreign Contacts.
Prof. Charnovsky of the Supreme Economic Council: Indicted.	Metal Industry.
Engineer Hrennikof: died during the investigation.	Metal Industry.
Prof. Fedotof, Textile Institute: Indicted.	Textiles.
Engineer Kupriyanof, Textile Organisation, Section of the S. E. C.: Indicted.	Textiles.
L. G. Rabinovich: Previously sentenced.	Coal.
P. I. Krassovsky: Previously sentenced.	Transport Services
Prof. I. A. Kalinnikof, State Planning Commission and School of Military Aviation: Indicted.	Aviation.
Engineer V. A. Larichef, State Planning Commission: Indicted.	Fuel and oil.

Foreigners.	Special Interests.
Deterding (Dutch Shell)	Oil.
Vickers (England)	Munitions.
Nobel	Oil and Explosives.
Urquhart (former owner of Russian Mines)	Mines.
Col. Lawrence (of Arabia)	
The French General Staff	Espionage and Intervention.
White Russian émigrés.	Restoration of Property.

Since the evidence was the testimony, the staging required that the accused be induced to play their assigned parts in the courtroom political drama. It appears that the means of inducement were mainly twofold: promises of lenient treatment on condition of full cooperation, and threats of dire consequences to the accused or persons close to them, or both, if they refused; the threats were in turn reinforced by physical pressure. The court passed death sentences—in response to feigned popular demand voiced in nationwide party-organized mass meetings—which were then commuted by governmental decree. The star defendant in this case, who incriminated both himself and others, was Professor Ramzin himself. After the trial he was set to work in prison on boiler construction and later released. When another released defendant, the engineer Lurie, refused to speak with him because of what Ramzin had done, the latter broke down in tears, said that he had incriminated himself more than all the others, and that the OGPU had compelled him to testify as he did.[18]

Like the Shakhty case before it, the Industrial Party trial served several political purposes of Stalin's. It helped create an atmosphere of terror in which the technical intelligentsia grew more responsive to pressures for herculean industrial accomplishment. It dislodged the Right's technician friends from posts in the economic organs that could be filled with Stalin-oriented new people. And it fabricated a deadly conspiratorial struggle on the part of a capitalist encirclement that was, in Stalin's terminology, no mere "geographical" fact, thereby underscoring the war menace that served as the backdrop of the whole massive campaign to mobilize people by the millions for self-sacrificing labor to build state power.

Ramzin's reemployment in penal servitude was not an isolated case. Trials of alleged wreckers were accompanied by a wave of behind-the-scenes arrests of technical specialists. They were spurred on by Stalin's own statement in his Sixteenth-Congress report that wrecking activities had been brought to light in "all branches of our industry."[19] The underlying reality is that engineers were being arrested in wholesale numbers in order to whip up production by terror. A clandestine Soviet correspondent of the Berlin-based Menshevik *Socialist Herald* reported in April 1931 that over 7,000 of the country's 35,000 engineers were under arrest. "Technical bureaus" for jailed engineers were set up by the OGPU, initially in Moscow and Kharkov, subsequently in other cities.[20] Aleksandr Solzhenitsyn would one day depict such a Stalinist prison institute, from personal experience, in his novel *The First Circle*.

But engineers were not the only ones accused of being wreckers. The whole of Soviet science, according to an article typical of the time, was honeycombed with "scientific-theoretical wrecking." In economics there were the wrecker theories of planners like B. Bazarov and N. Kondratiev (whose views did not envisage anything like the heroic Stalinist tempos of industrialization as feasible). Wrecking was rife in forestry science, melioration theory, mining science, high tension technology, microbiology, and even in ichthyology, some of whose representatives had reasoned that the five-year plan for fish was unfeasible due to the natural laws of fish reproduction—implying, the article said, that there was no difference between the USSR and a capitalist country (in other words, between Soviet and capitalist fish). As if to make the anticonservationist thrust of the argument explicit, the article went on to attack the Soviet journal *Okhrana prirody (Conservation of Nature)* for concealing its "wrecking innards" with a plea against ploughing up great expanses of partly wooded lands on the new giant state farms, arguing that it would cause agricultural pests to become a danger. Another wrecker article in the same journal expressed nostalgia for the fast disappearing pristine conditions of the Yamskoi steppe, thereby showing that it equated conservation of nature with conservation *from* socialism.[21]

"Cultural Revolution"

All this was emblematic of a process that was touched off by the Shakhty case and went down as the "cultural revolution" of 1928–31, although it had little more than the name in common with the long-range culturalizing program that Lenin envisioned. Indeed, Lenin's conception of cultural revolution was openly attacked—without his name being mentioned.

Thus, a party official in charge of propaganda and agitation, A. I. Krinitsky, attributed to officials of the Commissariat of Education, under Anatoly Lunacharsky, a deeply mistaken "antirevolutionary, opportunist conception of cultural revolution as a peaceful, classless raising of cultural standards—a conception which does not distinguish between bourgeois and proletarian elements of culture . . ., and does not see the fierce struggle of the proletariat against the class antagonist in everyday life, the school, art, science and so on. . . ."[22] What cultural revolution meant now was a series of offensives on the "cultural front." Proletarian class belligerency was its keynote. Illiteracy became the object of attacks by the "cultural army." In government offices there were "social purges" of nonproletarian persons. In higher education there were purges of "socially alien" elements of the student body. Professors as well as engineers in the "bourgeois specialist" category underwent harassment or worse.

Meanwhile, a movement for "proletarian advancement" brought very many Communist party members as well as nonmembers of working-class origin into a higher educational system that was rapidly being expanded along specialized vocational lines to serve the needs of industrialization. Although supported from below by the beneficiaries, who were being mobilized for higher education in party- and trade-union-selected groups of "thousands," the movement of "proletarianization" was an expression of a transformative activity from above. Stalin gave it his personal imprimatur when he told assembled industrialists in June 1931 that the working class "must create for itself its own productive-technical intelligentsia," adding that "not a single ruling class has managed without its own intelligentsia."[23] His evident aim was to form a new elite or subelite ("intelligentsia") of persons trained by and devoted to his regime and capable of taking their places in the increasingly industrialized economy.

The results were impressive. As the industrial work force grew by three millions during the *piatiletka,* the doors to higher education were opened wide. Preference in admissions went to those of working-class background. Total enrollment in higher education rose from 160,000 in 1927–28 to 470,000 in 1932–33, a threefold growth, and the proportion of students of worker origin changed from a fourth to a half. Very many entered as young adults with incomplete secondary schooling and not less than five years of work experience. To cite a particular case of that generation, the future Soviet leader, Leonid Brezhnev, then twenty-four years old, entered in 1930 the Metallurgical Institute in his hometown of Dneprodzerzhinsk in the Ukraine as a worker student.[24]

The "cultural revolution" of 1928–31 was a martial counterpart in all fields of culture—education, science, technology, scholarship, and the arts—to the feverish drive for industrialization and collectivization in the economy; it was the cultural *piatiletka.* Overthrow of the old intelligentsia, of its authority and much of what it stood for, was the watchword. A representative case was what happened in historical scholarship.

Pokrovsky and his disciples unfurled the banner of cultural revolution in this field, opening fire on still active old-regime historians and their followers as the "class enemy on the historical front." Their main targets were professors Platonov and Eugene Tarlé. Since both worked in Leningrad, it was there that they were assailed in a scholarly purge held under the auspices of the Society of Marxist historians in 1931. Platonov was pilloried for seeking, in his *Peter the Great,* to "glorify the idea of monarchy in the picture of the 'great tsar' as a *vozhd'* of the people,"[25] and for another in his series of short biographies in the 1920s, *Ivan Grozny.* Here he called Ivan a tyrant and even described the sadistic pleasure Ivan took in witnessing the agonies of those tortured to death on his orders. The only time the tsar ever grieved and repented, wrote the historian, was when in a fit of rage he killed his own son with a club. But at the same time Platonov's

Ivan was a tsar-transformer who created in the *oprichnina* a weapon against the landowning aristocracy as a class. "Whatever judgment one makes of Grozny's personal conduct," he concluded, "as a statesman and politician he remains a major figure."[26]

"Nationalist" and "monarchist" were among the labels now pinned on Platonov. He was accused of belonging to a historiographical "counterrevolutionary wrecking center" and exiled to the Volga city of Samara (later Kuibyshev). Tarlé, who had also figured in the Industrial Party case, was imprisoned. Had Platonov not died in Samara in 1933, the elderly historian would have—no doubt with amazement—seen himself restored to honor in Stalin's Russia, as was the still living Tarlé. Platonov's prerevolutionary *Outlines of the History of the Troubles in the Moscow State of the XVI–XVII Centuries* (a book favorable to the *oprichnina*) was republished in the year of terror, 1937, in a Soviet edition of 10,000 copies, with a respectful foreword from the Socioeconomic Publishing House about the deceased author. By then, under Stalin's influence, Ivan and Peter were getting recognition as people's tsars.

Militant leftism of 1928–31 in various fields of culture was given a green light by Stalin when, for example, he declared in his concluding speech to the Sixteenth Party Congress in 1930 that they country was still in the period of transition from capitalism to socialism, but it was a vastly different situation from that of a decade ago when Lenin introduced the notion. "Clearly, we have already made entry into the period of socialism. . . ."[27] At a time when the country's leader was speaking in such near millenarian tones, it is no wonder that radical-minded Communists, of whom not a few were still active in those years, anticipated the early advent of things foretold in Marxian doctrine.

The doctrine's founders had envisaged the communist future as a society without a state, for the historical state, in their view, was an instrument of class rule and under communism there would be no division of society into classes. None of the established institutions, such as the family and school, would exist any longer in forms similar to those of the past. In *The State and Revolution*, Lenin had provided a Bolshevik gloss on the Marx-Engels prophecy about the "withering away" of the state in communist society. This would start in the lower (socialist) phase of communist society and be completed in the higher phase when not even the "commune" state proper to socialism would be needed since people would be used to observing the elementary rules of social intercourse "without force, without coercion, without subordination, without the *special apparatus* called the state."[28]

Now, in the time of the "cultural revolution," such leading Old Bolshevik legal theorists as E. B. Pashukanis, P. I. Stuchka, and Nikolai

Krylenko were eager to assist the withering away of NEP legal institutions—as institutions of the transition period *to* socialism—in order to make way for what they called "economic law." The judicial system would close up shop as "comrades' courts" took over more and more of the decreasing volume of their work; and some scholars were saying, according to a Soviet journal published in 1930, that "there is no reason to get absorbed in the study of the state, since it . . . is withering away in the period of the dictatorship of the proletariat."[29] The educational radical V. N. Shulgin advocated the "withering away of the school" in favor of forms of education merged with citizenship and production.[30] Visionary anti-urban planners like Leonard M. Sabsovich foresaw the imminent supplanting of the big cities by a network of new factory communities, linked by electric-powered mass public transport, which would transform Soviet Russia into a federation of small towns and mark the "withering of the centralized state under communism". Some of their ideas were influential in planning the sixty or more new industrial towns that were begun during the *piatiletka*.[31]

Stalin invited and for a time tolerated all this because it served his mobilizational purposes in the big transformative push. But the basic *ideas* of the cultural leftists went against the grain of his national Bolshevism. At the very time when Platonov was being condemned by the Society of Marxist Historians for his favorable view of Tsar Peter, Stalin was cultivating a positive image of Peter in the artistic work of Alexei Tolstoy. At the very time when the legal theorists were discussing the withering away of the state, his thought ran in the opposite direction.

Their perspective was antithetical to his as a Russian national Bolshevik for whom the construction of socialism and state building were one and the same. He indicated as much when he told the Sixteenth Congress in 1930:

We stand for the withering away of the state. And at the same time we stand for the strengthening of the proletarian dictatorship, the most mighty and powerful of all hitherto existing state regimes. The highest development of state power for the purpose of preparing conditions for the withering away of state power—that's the Marxist formula. Contradictory? Yes, "contradictory." But a contradiction of real life, entirely reflecting Marx's dialectic.[32]

This was not Marx's thought, or Lenin's. It was the dialectic of a Soviet Russian state builder and it foreshadowed the quickly approaching time when past preaching of "withering" would be treated as a capital crime.

There were other deep differences between Stalin and the cultural leftists to whom he temporarily gave free rein in pursuance of his ends. He genuinely favored the recruitment of many thousands of workers into a new elite through technical education. But he had no wish to continue a vendetta against "bourgeois" experts once his policy of specialist-baiting in the Shakhty and other cases had done its work. So, in the very speech of June 1931 in which he declared that the working class must create its own new technical intelligentsia, he decried "the harmful and disgraceful phenomenon of specialist-baiting" and proclaimed a new policy of solicitude for the old technical intelligentsia, among whom, he said, "there remain only a small number of active wreckers."[33]

The ideology of the cultural leftists was class oriented; they stood for "proletarian hegemony" and the creation of a literature, art, and more broadly a culture that would be proletarian in spirit and content. Such, in particular, was the viewpoint of the Russian Association of Proletarian Writers (RAPP), which dominated literary life during the *piatiletka* under the energetic, doctrinaire headship of the literary critic Leopold Averbakh. Having coexisted uneasily with other literary groups under the more tolerant cultural dispensation of the NEP era, the RAPP now asserted its militant leftist line as the only valid one. Under the slogan "Either ally or enemy," it attacked the work of the nonparty writers known as "fellow travelers," among them Boris Pil'niak and Alexei Tolstoy. The RAPP leaders were eager to mobilize literature behind the state's goals in the Five-Year Plan, but wanted to fulfill this mission according to their own "Dialectical Materialist Method," which enjoined the writer to show the "living man" in all his inner conflict between good and bad. They thus stood for a certain autonomy of proletarian literature and were uncomfortable with directives from political commissars. One such directive was the call issued in 1931 by Stalin's lieutenant, Lazar Kaganovich, for "a *magnitostroi* of literature," meaning works glorifying construction projects like the one at Magnitogorsk and peopled for didactic purposes with one-dimensional positive heroes and negative villains—the kind of literature subsequently produced under the new literary canon of "socialist realism."[34]

The RAPP was temporarily of use to Stalin because it joined the general attack on the "Right deviation" in 1928–29 and promoted a mobilizational literature in service of the plan. But he was never in sympathy with its leftist line. In a private letter of 2 February 1929 to the playwright Vladimir Bill-Belotserkovsky, who was under attack by the RAPP and had solicited his support, Stalin dismissed as unsound the very idea of applying the concepts "left" and "right" to literature, art, and the theater. It would be better, he said, to employ such straightforward antitheses as "Soviet" versus "anti-Soviet" or "revolutionary versus antirevolutionary." Then he praised the very nonproletarian Mikhail Bulgakov for his *Days of the Turbins* in which the way of Bolshevik revolutionism was shown as the way of Russian patriotism.[35]

RAPP's leftism and "proletarian hegemony" were out of line with

Stalin's national Bolshevism. In 1931, Stalin's assistant Lev Mekhlis, secretary of the editorial board of *Pravda,* published an attack on the RAPP in which he objected to its excessive praise of the proletarian poet Demyan Bedny, whose "Get Off the Oven-Shelf" was, said Mekhlis (echoing Stalins's recently published criticism of it), a rude attack on the Russian people.[36] A further fault with the RAPP's outlook, according to an editorial article by Stalin's young philosophical protégé Pavel Yudin, was the idea that the purpose of the ongoing cultural revolution was to bring into being a "proletarian culture" *on the way* to the socialist culture that would come about when full socialism was attained, whereas "Comrade Stalin defines the proletarian culture in the transition period as socialist in its content."[37] From Stalin's point of view, a "socialist culture" was emerging already and, as Yudin also indicated, selected elements of past national culture were properly a part of it.

The writer Maxim Gorky returned from abroad in 1931 to settle down in Russia. Stalin lionized him and made him the doyen of Soviet literature. Now a reorganization of the literary and artistic world seemed desirable. On 23 April 1932, by what was later revealed to have been Stalin's personal decision, the party Central Committee issued a decree dissolving the RAPP and similar proletarian organizations in the other arts, after which even a phrase like "proletarian literature" went out of use.[38] The decree provided that a single Union of Soviet Writers should be set up to unite all writers upholding the platform of the Soviet regime and striving to participate in the construction of socialism. Nonproletarian and nonparty writers (Gorky himself was one) found welcome in the new organization. But the intention to further politicize literature was evident in the appointment of a political underling of Stalin's, A. S. Shcherbakov, as the new union's secretary and the enshrining of "socialist realism" in its bylaws as mandatory for all Soviet writers.

The State Swells Up

Stalin's dialetical formula "The highest development of state power for the purpose of preparing conditions for the withering away of state power," was a rationalization for the explosive growth of the centralized state during the *piatiletka.* Economic expansion by Stalinist industrialization was expansion of the Soviet state. All the far-flung projects were additions to the fund of state-owned property. Their employees were servants of the state. Most came under administrative subordination to great bureaucratic conglomerates, the people's commissariats. As the state-owned, state-administered industrial economy mushroomed, the Moscow bureaucracy swelled proportionately. The old technical intelligentsia, which disappeared by the thousands into prison technical institutes, was replaced by newly trained graduates of the expanding system of technical education. Other administrators and lower employees joined the ruling centers in great numbers. A new service class was rising by governmental fiat in the revolution from above. No wonder that Stalin had to relegate the contradiction between Marx's theory and Russia's reality to the mysteries of the dialectic.

The people's commissariats were of three types: all-union commissariats, which directed subordinate institutions, including plants, throughout the land; unified commissariats, consisting of a coordinating central commissariat in Moscow that directed subordinate commissariats of the same name in the capitals of each of the union republics; and republic commissariats, autonomously in charge of activities on the territories oı their republics. Under the Soviet Constitution of 1924, there were five all-union ones (Foreign Affairs, Military and Naval Affairs, Foreign Trade, Transport, and Posts and Telegraph) and five unified ones (Food Supply, Labor, Finance, Worker-Peasant Inspection, and the Supreme Economic Council). The *piatiletka* produced a proliferation of state agencies of the centralized kinds, all subject to policies set by the appropriate party Central committee departments.

Especially striking was the growth of the industrial bureaucracy. At the close of 1929, thirty-five "associations" were set up under the Supreme Economic council for planning and directing different branches of the economy. They were huge organizations. Thus the timber industry association, *Soyuzlesprom,* had a thousand production units under its direct control.[39] When Ordzhonikidze took over headship of the council in 1930 from Kuibyshev, who became chief of Gosplan, he formed within it individual sectors, each in charge of several associations. This system having become too unwieldy, the Supreme Council was subdivided in early 1932 into an all-union Commissariat for Heavy Industry (of which Ordzhonikidze became head), an all-union Commissariat for the Timber Industry, and a unified Commissariat for Light Industry that not long afterward also became an all-union one, leaving only small factories in this and other fields under the newly created republic commissariats of local industry.[40] Within the centralized commissariats, the associations became "chief administrations' *(glavki),* each supervising multitudes of enterprises throughout the country. Eventually, various *glavki* grew into independent centralized commissariats for coal, chemicals, munitions, nonferrous metals, textiles, and so on, each with its own *glavki* such as those for linen, silks, and woolens in the Commissariat for Textiles. Mikhail Pervukhin, an industrialist who under Stalin rose to the highest levels of party-state rule, once compared these giant state organizations to capitalist conglomerates in America: "You call it General Electric, we call it the Ministry of the Communications Equipment industry."[41]

What happened in all other areas was the same: growth of the centralized state. The Commissariat for Transport proliferated in 1931 into a Commissariat for Railways, a Commissariat for Water Transport (itself later subdivided into commissariats for maritime and river transport), and a Central Administration of Road and Auto Transport. A Commissariat for the Food Industry emerged from the Commissariat of Supply to which the food industry was transferred with the demise of the Supreme Council. A governmental Committee for Produce Collection, subsequently made into a commissariat of that name, was set up to supervise obligatory deliveries of farm products. Supervision of the tens of thousands of collective and state farms organized in the crash collectivization campaign necessitated the formation of governmental trusts for grain, cattle, sheep, agricultural equipment, and others, which at the end of 1929 were brought under a newly created USSR Commissariat for Agriculture, out of which a separate Commissariat for Grain and Livestock State Farms was detached in 1932. Research in this key area was centralized as well. Acting on orders from Stalin, who wanted agricultural science to be administered from above, the eminent plant biologist Nikolai Vavilov organized in Moscow in 1929 an All-Union Academy of Agricultural Sciences. Its institutes, such as the Potato Institute or the Wheat Institute, prescribed cultivation techniques to be used throughout the huge, climatically diverse country. Within a few years the academy controlled 407 experimental institutions with a total staff of 11,000 researchers.[42] Even the state liquor monopoly was further centralized with the formation by a decree of 1930 of *Soyuzspirt,* an all-union alcoholic and wine beverage association, which took over winery trusts previously under local organs.

Because the state's expansion was heavily involved with the pursuit of war-making power, much growth occurred in the military sphere. The armed forces, whose strength stood at 586,000 in 1927, numbered 1,433,000 men a decade later. The Sovnarkom's old Council of Labor and Defense became a Council of Defense for coordinating all related matters. The Revolutionary Military Council (which had been headed by Trotsky) was abolished and replaced by an advisory Military Council under the Commissariat for Military and Naval Affairs, renamed Defense Commissariat in 1934. A Commissariat for the Defense Industry was created in 1936 to manage the military-industrial complex. In 1937 a Commissariat of the Navy was separated out of the Defense Commissariat to administer the now substantial navy: about five hundred naval vessels had been built in the previous decade, four times the number built by tsarist Russia in the ten years preceding World War I. A. I. Egorov, the commander with whom Stalin served as political commissar on the southwestern front against Poland in 1920, became, as Marshal Egorov, the first chief of the resurrected General Staff.[43]

As the state swelled up at the center, the areas of autonomy of the constituent republics contracted. Constitutionally a federation of sovereign republics, the USSR became, increasingly, a Soviet Muscovy in which the republic governments, whether expanded or diminished in size, served as agents of the center in what came to be known colloquially as "the periphery." In 1930, republic commissariats for internal affairs were abolished. A USSR Procuracy was set up in 1933 with powers of directing the activities of the republic procuracies, and the USSR Supreme Court was endowed with the key functions of issuing directives to the republics' judicial organs and conducting inspections of them. Earlier, the republic commissariats for agriculture became subordinate bodies of the central Commissariat for Agriculture in Moscow, resulting, for example, in a situation where the Ukraine, which produced 80 percent of the country's sugar, had no say in administering sugar production. This agriculturally rich, industrially developed republic, second only to the RSFSR (Russian Soviet Federated Socialist Republic) in population, was especially hard hit by the centralizing tendency, and its leaders vainly tried to check the authoritarian ways of the central commissariats. They also opposed two new legislative proposals issued in 1928, a "Statute on Budget Rights" that failed to guarantee the republics' budgetary authority, and "General Principles of Land Use Construction." The Ukrainian leader Mykola Skrypnik, an Old Bolshevik associate of Lenin's and a founder of the Ukrainian Soviet Republic, pointed out that the latter law made the nationalized land the property of the Union rather than of the republics, and "will mean that the sovereignty of the separate republics will amount only to this, that they will have their governments, but without any territory.[44] His protest was overruled.

In his address to the Sixteenth Congress, Stalin proclaimed the Soviet present an era of the flowering of different cultures that were *"socialist* in content and national in form."[45] The italics were his and important. Centralized statehood was becoming in practice the "socialist content" of the national cultures. In other words, the same state-centralizing tendencies that manifested themselves in the economic administration were at work in the realm of culture. A central governmental Committee for Higher Technological Education was created in 1932 and later transformed into the All-Union Committee for Higher Education, which administered all institutions of higher learning save those under the Sovnarkom committees for the arts and physical culture and the Defense Commissariat's military schools. Following the dissolution of the proletarian organizations for the arts by Stalin's decree of April 1932, single all-union professional organizations were created—the Union of Soviet Writers, the Union of Soviet Artists, the Union of Soviet Musicians, the Union of Soviet Architects—which were organs of the party-state in fact if not in theory. The Sovnarkom Committee on Art Affairs set up in January 1936 was in effect a state ministry for the arts.[46] The Academy of Sciences that Peter founded, having survived the 1917 events and led a semi-autonomous existence at its Leningrad headquarters during the ensuing decade, was transformed in 1929–30 and subsequently became a huge, Moscow-centered all-union state institution for research, serving primarily the industrialization effort.[47]

Meanwhile, the state-regimented Soviet culture grew more and more Russia-oriented. Thus, a younger Ukrainian Communist historian, Matviy Yavorsky, whose school of Ukrainian historiography rejected centralist Russian historical concepts, was expelled from the party and exiled to a remote area in 1930. And Skrypnik, who as the Ukraine's commissar for education in the later 1920s had sponsored a new uniform Ukrainian orthography (for both Eastern and Western Ukraine), under which transliteration of foreign words was made less similar to the Russian way and more similar to that of West European languages, was assailed in 1933 for, among other transgressions, his orthographical nationalism expressed in the detaching of the Ukrainian from the fraternal Russian language.[48] His suicide not long after symbolically marked the dying of meaningful Ukrainian statehood under the rule of Stalin's Russian national Bolshevism.

The Policy of Privilege

As the state swelled up, the mass of the people "grew lean." They did so in the sense of being hungry much of the time, living on rations (when honored), going without desperately needed housing, being overworked, struggling for items of simple necessity, and enduring all manner of hardship on the far-flung sites of industrialization. Living standards, which were supposed to rise during the five-year period, in fact declined. Official statistics glossed this over by recording a growth of 85 percent in the incomes of workers and peasants between 1928 and 1932.[49] But since, as revealed much later, retail sales by state and cooperative stores rose from roughly twelve to forty billion rubles during the same period, without any increase (to put it overconservatively) in the total amount of goods sold, real wages went down drastically owing to inflation.[50]

But not all the people grew lean. Stalin saw to that by introducing a policy of stratification and privilege that enabled higher-level functionaries and their families to lead relatively comfortable lives during that time of bleak austerity. He enunciated this policy at the June 1931 conference of industrialists in his characteristically veiled way. After ordering a halt to further specialist baiting he proclaimed that not only the old technical intelligentsia but a number of other people more important than they were to be accorded solicitous treatment befitting their services to the state. He devoted another part of his speech to a polemic against " 'leftist' egalitarianism *(uravnilovka)* in the sphere of pay." His ostensible point was that existing Soviet wage scales that held down differential remuneration for different forms of labor—skilled and unskilled, heavy and light—must be scrapped in favor of wage differentials that would give workers incentive to stay where they were and thus reduce the disruptive phenomenon of labor turnover in the plants.[51]

In his speech Stalin attributed to Marx and Lenin the view that skilled and unskilled work would be unequally remunerated *under socialism,* the first phase of communist society, although no longer under full communism where the principle of remuneration according to need would prevail. This mangled Marx's position, which had been upheld also by Lenin. The Marxist and Leninist view was that in socialist society people would be differentially remunerated according to the quantity of work performed, but not according to quality or the degree of qualification. Under the NEP, wage differentials according to skill and high rates of pay for the special engineering skills of "bourgeois" specialists were accepted practices. But they were regarded as necessities of NEP society's transition *to* socialism, not as features *of* it.[52] Now, by Stalin's fiat, differentials according to quality of work and qualification were sanctified as socialist. Such a break with Marxism and Leninism was, in addition, a way of making it possible to call the increasingly stratified society emerging in the time of the *piatiletka* "socialist." Stalin's attack on egalitarianism was preparation for the universal introduction of piece work pay that took place in 1932, and for the introduction of a new wage scale that made the pay ratio between the least and most skilled labor, which had been two to one, as high as 3.7 to one.[53]

Stalin's speech opened the way for creation of the Soviet labor aristocracy which soon came into being via the so-called Stakhanov movement. But the legitimizing of wage differentials also provided cover for a policy of making those described by Stalin as "the command staff of our industry," and others in posts of authority, a privileged class. Lenin's legacy in this field was the "party maximum," under which the salary of a party member, no matter what position he held, could not exceed that of a better-paid worker. Having been nullified in practice by various bonuses, the party maximum was quietly shelved in 1929 and formally abolished in 1932 after Stalin emerged as the champion of differentials and nemesis of egalitarianism.[54] No wonder that the watchword "proletarian hegemony" was on the way out.

"Responsible workers," comprising party leaders, higher-ups in the commissariats and other Soviet organizations, their republic and province counterparts, and managerial personnel in the economy, became far more an upper class in the post-NEP austerity than before. Albeit inconspicuously, they lived quite unlike ordinary citizens. Their perquisites included comfortable apartments, chauffeur-driven cars for the top brass, special dining rooms at work, easy access to rest homes and sanatoria at vacation time. Like the foreign specialists working on contract, they were served by a network of special shops where good food and other scarce consumer items, some imported from abroad, were available on coupons at low prices. The ordinary person could obtain such things only in return for pieces of jewelry, gold, or silver in the Torgsin shops set up by the government in the quest for valuables that could be turned into foreign currency. In a society where the hardship experienced by the many was not shared by the favored few, "leftist egalitarianism" was out of place, and the most effective means of disposal was to condemn it, as Stalin did, on the ground that it was un-Marxist.

Higher party and government officials in Moscow and their families formed the peak of the privileged class, topped only by the country's political leaders who lived in buildings on the grounds of the Kremlin. In 1931 construction was completed of a large apartment complex on the Moscow River embankment. It became known as Government House. Into it moved "responsible workers" who during the 1920s had occupied smaller space in the Kremlin or in Moscow hotels. The eleven-story building, in several sections, contained over five hundred multiple-room government-furnished apartments, with central heating, gas, and (a rare luxury for that time) round-the-clock hot water. Each apartment had a telephone— something very hard for Muscovites to obtain in those days. Government House had its own food and general stores, a branch of the Kremlin Polyclinic, a branch of the Kremlin restaurant that served well-cooked food in abundance at very low prices, a theater, and a cinema.[55]

In the month following Stalin's speech to the industrialists, the State Legal Publishing House issued a 350-page handbook of laws and regulations on privileges for specialists; and governmental decrees of 1931 and 1932 mandated separate housing for these people at new construction sites and special dining rooms for engineers and technicians.[56] The privileged conditions provided by Moscow's Government House were replicated, if on a lesser scale, in republic and province capitals and industrial centers throughout the land. A microcosm of the hierarchical new society taking form as a result was the huge iron and steel center at Magnitogorsk in the Urals. John Scott, an unemployed American who went to Russia in 1933 to find a job and stayed on for several years as an ordinary worker, offers an eyewitness picture rather different from the fictional Magnitogorsk of Katayev's *Time, Forward!*

He found himself in what might roughly be described as a four-class society. There was an upper class consisting of the director of this huge new industrial complex, his top-level administrative, technical, and political personnel, plus a few of the most valued prisoner specialists, the secretary of the City Party Committee, and the local head of the OGPU; a middle class consisting of engineers, brigade-leaders, highly skilled workers and foremen, city employees, doctors and teachers; a lower class of ordinary workers as well as low-level office employees (whose numbers proliferated due in part to a very large bookkeeping staff to keep track of workers' performances on piece work pay); and, at the bottom, an underclass of convict laborers numbering about fifty thousand.

The social distance between the classes was reflected in spatial separation as well as differentiated living and working conditions. The convict laborers were isolated from the rest of the city, ate in their own dining halls, went to work under police guard, and did the heaviest work, such as digging foundations, for next to no pay although they had the incentive of higher rations and earlier release to make them work hard. The workers ate a rationed meal once a day in one of a large number of dining halls where the bread ration was two hundred grams. Engineering personnel took their meals in separate, uncrowded dining rooms where the bread serving was three hundred grams. Food for home consumption, chiefly black bread issued on ration cards, was sold to workers in workers' stores and to foremen in foremen's stores.

The ordinary workers lived in wooden barracks, crowded into minuscule, barely furnished rooms; foremen had larger, better furnished ones. Later in the 1930s the barracks were replaced by apartment buildings. The middle class lived in a separate residential section called "socialist city," which consisted of fifty or so large brick and stone apartment buildings with metal roofs and balconies, centering on two open squares with benches, fountains, and playground. Five miles away, in a small suburban world of which the workers had hardly any knowledge, lived the elite, and the foreign engineers working on contract, in some hundred and fifty individual houses equipped with running water and central heating, served by a well-stocked special store where goods were sold at prices far below what workers would pay in their stores for similar items when available. This suburb was informally called "American city."

More members of the local upper class moved into it as the foreign engineers began to depart beginning in 1933. In addition, the director of the works, A. P. Zavenyagin, who was a virtual dictator of this one-industry town, built a dozen large houses for himself and top aides— department heads, chief engineers, and the like. Their rents were paid by the factory as administrative expenses. Chauffeured cars were placed at these people's service, also at factory expense, for hunting trips and theater going as well as business purposes. Zavenyagin's own place, which had a small deer park behind it and a walled garden in front, was something special: a stuccoed brick mansion whose fourteen rooms included a billiard room, a play room for his two sons, a music room, and a large study.[57]

Bolshevik theory envisioned the withering of the state, but Stalin the Russian national Bolshevik saw things differently. Statelessness was no part of his intention, and socialist society in the Stalinist canon was not going to be a classless one. The revolution from above was creating a new, privileged service class whose motto would one day be expressed by its archetypal representative, Georgi Malenkov: "We are all servants of the state."[58]

The Count and the Commissar

"Do you admit a parallel between yourself and Peter the Great?" asked the biographer Emil Ludwig in an interview with Stalin in 1931. Stalin answered: "In no way. Historical parallels are always risky. This parallel is pointless." When Ludwig persisted, saying that Peter had done much to develop his country, Stalin agreed that he had done much to create and consolidate the national state of the landowners and merchants, albeit at the expense of the enserfed peasantry, "which was skinned thrice over." Stalin's aim in life, however, was to elevate the working class, to consolidate an international socialist state rather than a national one, and to be a worthy disciple of Lenin. "As for Lenin and Peter the Great," he added, the latter was a drop of water in the sea while Lenin was a whole ocean."[59]

Ludwig was singularly naive if he expected a man who instinctively parried any attempt at probing his inner thoughts to give a candidly revealing answer to the question about Peter. That was not Stalin's way. He did see a parallel between Peter's role in history and his own, but he said it by indirection, for instance in his Central Committee speech of November 1928. He also contrived to have Peter depicted to the reading public no longer as the premature industrial capitalist and syphilitic sadist of Pokrovsky's textbook, but as an heroically striving fighter against backwardness and tragically frustrated Russian state builder. The instrument of this transformation was Alexei Tolstoy.

An offspring of the nobility (the illegitimate son of a count), Tolstoy emigrated in 1919. In Berlin in 1921, he joined the *Smena vekh* circle and saw in Bolshevism a force for the defense of Russian statehood. Returning to Russia in 1923, he placed his talented pen at the service of the Soviet regime, and became known informally as the "worker-peasant count." He produced a series of Peter-portraits in the form of a story, a stage play in three different versions, a novel, and film scenario. Stalin's direct intervention in 1929 and after led to his progressive idealization of Tsar Peter.

Tolstoy's earlier efforts bespoke a Slavophile-like belief in the essential futility of the Petrine project of transforming Russia. In "Peter's Day," a story written in 1918 and constructed around one day in the life of the tsar-transformer, Peter appears as a brutal, besotted, snot-nosed despot terrorizing old Orthodox *Rus'* in an obsessive lone effort to accomplish the impossible. Of the building of Petersburg, we read: "Who needed it, for what purpose this new misery of blood and sweat and the lost lives of thousands was necessary—the people didn't know." Those overheard to say a questioning word of complaint were betrayed by informers who brought their information to the police hut with the password "word and deed"; and the culprit was then dragged off in chains to the Secret Office of *Preobrazhensky Prikaz,* to be subjected to hideous tortures, sometimes at the hand of the tsar himself. "But to think, even to feel any feeling other than submissiveness, was forbidden. So Tsar Peter, sitting on wastelands and swamps, strengthened the state and remade the country by his awful will alone. . . . Emissaries, sneaks, informers scurried all over the place; wagons loaded with prisoners rattled swiftly along the roads; the whole state was in the grip of fear and terror."[60]

In late 1928, a Soviet writer now, Tolstoy began work on a new Peter portrait. The title of his play, *On the Rack,* evoked the theme of the tsar-transformer torturing Holy Russia. The ultimate futility of the reforming enterprise is vividly shown in the final scene: Peter's beloved frigate, the *Ingermandlandia,* goes down with the rest of his fleet in a great Petersburg flood. As the waters rise higher and higher, Peter, watching through a window, speaks the closing line: "The water approaches. Awful is the end."

Now, however, the tsar is no longer a repellent figure but a tragic hero. We are shown scenes of the new Russia at work on constructive tasks, and Peter's solitude is that of a patriot beset by too many obstacles. He negotiates for the sale of Russian flax to Dutch merchants who have reached Petersburg but discovered en route how dangerous the Swedish warships make it for merchant vessels sailing to the Russian port. He laments: "Sick for a whole month now, and the state is already falling apart. Treason I sense everywhere, it all smells of decomposition. The Swedes, the Swedes, damned darkness. If it weren't for the Swedes, we'd be trading now with Holland and the Germans, with England and the king of France. Ruination—no end to war is visible. In Poland they've made Stanislaw Leszczynski king—and Poland's against us. King Charles seeks our total impoverishment. . . . I want to see people think about the good of the state—not just thieving. They don't give service, they don't work— they just eat. I fear the Russian more than the Swede."[61]

In 1929 the Second Moscow Art Theater undertook a stage production of *On the Rack*. What then happened has been told by a well-known older-generation Russian writer and scholar who left his country during World War II.[62] Although inclined to give Tolstoy's play the green light for public showing, the governmental censoring organization, called the Chief Repertoire Committee, was apprehensive lest it be construed as esoteric monarchist propaganda, and made its approval contingent upon the outcome of a special preview to be witnessed by political leaders as well as literary scholars and followed by a general discussion. Among the political leaders in attendance at the preview was Stalin, who left his box shortly before the end and was escorted by the anxious theater director, Ivan Bersenev, to his car. Noting the leader's early exit, those who spoke first in the ensuing discussion denounced the theater for depicting Peter heroically, and accused it of "monarchism." Then Bersenev took the floor to announce that on the way to his car "Comrade Stalin, in speaking with me, passed the following judgment on the production: 'A splendid play. Only it's a pity that Peter wasn't depicted heroically enough.' " The play was approved for public presentation.

Tolstoy himself confirmed this story in substance when he subsequently recalled that "the production of the first version of 'Peter' in the Second Moscow Art Theater met with a hostile reception in the part of the RAPP and was saved by Comrade Stalin, who gave me the right historical approach to the Petrine epoch."[63] The "right historical approach" was to depict Peter as the hero of a previous great turning point in Russia's history; and the pliable ex-count, a lover of good living and a cynic, was willing to oblige. He and the general secretary became friends. "Iosif Vissarionovich very attentively went over our plans, approved them, and gave directions on which we based our work," he later revealed, and went on to indicate the general sense of Stalin's directions: "The epoch of Peter I was one of the greatest pages in the history of the Russian people. In essence the whole Petrine epoch was permeated with the heroic struggle of the Russian people for its national existence and independence. Dark, uncultured, boyar *Rus'* with its backward technology and patriarchal beards, would have been swallowed up by foreign invaders in no time at all. It was necessary to carry through a decisive revolution in the entire life of the country, to lift Russia to the level of the cultured countries of Europe. And

Peter did this. The Russian people maintained its independence."[64] In sum, Tolstoy's original pessimistic view of Peter's era has undergone a full reversal.

Peter I, the large historical novel on which he began work in 1929, embodied the new optimistic approach. The first part, on the background and Peter's early years, came out in 1930. Now the groaningly oppressed, crisis-ridden Russia is the pre-Petrine one. The inchoate popular yearning is for the great change that the talented, strong-willed, patriotically inspired, boundlessly energetic and eagerly inquisitive young transformer-to-be is destined to initiate against all the aristocratic forces of resistance to modernization. On the mission to Western Europe, Peter is drawn to the working people, not the upper classes. The first part closes with his return and bloody suppression of the Moscow mutiny of the *strel' tsy* (musketeers) in 1698: "All winter the tortures and executions went on. In response, uprisings erupted in Archangel, in Astrakhan, on the Don, and in Azov. The torture chambers filled up, and the snowstorms tossed about thousands of corpses on the walls of Moscow. The whole country was gripped by terror. Everything old crept into dark corners. It was the end of Byzantine Russia. The winds of March brought visions of merchant vessels off the shores of the Baltic Sea."[65]

In the novel's second part, we see the beginning of Russia's transformation, Peter's defeat at Narva, then the first Russian victories over the Swedes in the Northern War, and finally the founding in 1703 of a small fortress to which the name "Piterburkh" is given: "Only an arm's length away was the open sea, rippling gaily in the wind. Off to the West, beyond the sails of the Swedish ships, sea clouds drifted high in the sky, like puffs of smoke from another world."[66] The third part, which remained unfinished, was to have ended with scenes from the battle of Poltava as the victorious outcome and finale of Peter's transformation of Russia.

So Peter became the would-be Stalin of yesteryear, and his revolution from above the partial *piatiletka* of early eighteenth-century Russia. On a short visit to Paris in 1937, Tolstoy, while in his cups, confided his story to an old expatriate friend, the painter Annenkov. While I was working on Peter, he said, "the 'father of the peoples' revised the history of Russia. Peter the Great became, without my knowing it, the 'proletarian tsar' and the prototype of our Iosif! I rewrote it all over again in accordance with the party's discoveries, and now I'm preparing the third and I hope the last variant of this thing, because the second variant also didn't satisfy our Iosif. I already see before my eyes all the Ivan Groznys and sundry Rasputins rehabilitated, become Marxists, and glorified. I don't give a damn! These gymnastics even amuse me! You really do have to be an acrobat. Mishka Sholokhov, Sashka Fadeev, Ilya Ehrenbriuki—they're all acrobats. But they aren't counts! And I'm a count, devil take it. And our aristocracy (may it come apart at the seams!) has produced too few acrobats. Get it? My fate's a very hard one."[67]

In more general as well as more tactful terms, Tolstoy had said the same thing earlier in public: "The start of my work on the novel coincided with the beginning of the fulfillment of the *piatiletka*. For me that work on *Peter* was above all an entry into history through contemporaneity, grasped in a Marxist way." And in notes for a further speech at that time: "The first decade of the eighteenth century presents an astonishing picture of an explosion of creative forces, energy, enterprise. The old world cracks and crumbles. Europe, not having expected anything like that, gazes in fear and amazement on the rising new Russia. Despite the difference in aims, Peter's epoch and ours speak to one another through a kind of burst of forces, through explosions of human energy and willpower directed to liberation from foreign dependence."[68]

Another statement by Tolstoy sounds like an Aesopian message on the kinship of the proletarian tsar with his royal predecessor. In an interview with the editors of the Soviet youth journal *Smena (The Shift)*, he was asked how such a "gigantic figure" as Peter could have sprung from his easy-going, falconry-loving father, Tsar Alexei Mikhailovich. In reply he gave it as his personal opinion, based on a mask of Peter's face taken in 1718 and now in his possession, that Peter was not actually the son of his supposed father. Judging by the facial resemblance, his real father was Patriarch Nikon, an ambitious, intelligent, strong-willed, powerful man who had come from simple peasant stock in the outlying area inhabited by the Mordovian people and had risen rapidly up the ladder from priest to patriarch.[69]

The clever count—apart from knowing that there was no real evidence to support his surmise—was well aware that his ambitious, intelligent, strong-willed, powerful friend Iosif had been born of simple peasant stock in the outlying area of Georgia and had risen from pupil in a school for priests to the post of general secretary.

6

THE MAKING OF A RURAL UPHEAVAL

Stalin's Power

WHEN Rykov, Bukharin, and Tomsky made their defiant last stand during a stormy enlarged session of the Politburo in January–February 1929, they contended that Stalin was arrogating to himself decision-making powers that by Bolshevik tradition were collective and belonged to the Central Committee. "We are against questions of party leadership being decided by one person," they were later quoted as saying. "We are against the replacement of control by a collective with control by a person, even though an authoritative one."[1] By then, however, Stalin's dominance of policy making was indisputable.

In 1930 he further consolidated his commanding position by a series of appointments and demotions. Rykov and Tomsky were dropped from seats on the Politburo, from which Bukharin had been removed in the previous year, although all three retained membership in the Central Committee. Sergei Kirov, Stanislav Kosior, and Lazar Kaganovich—all men of the Stalin faction—were advanced from candidate to full membership of the Politburo, joining Stalin, Molotov, Voroshilov, Kalinin, Kuibyshev, Ordzhonikidze, and Rudzutak as voting members of the high body. Numbers of Rightists on the Central Committee either lost seats or were demoted to candidate status when the committee was reelected at the Sixteenth Congress.

There is no question about Stalin's political ascendancy at that time. But was he a dictator? When Eugene Lyons posed this question in an interview with him in 1931, he answered: "No, I am no dictator. Those who use the word do not understand the Soviet system of government and the methods of the Communist Party. No one man or group of men can dictate. Decisions are made by the party and acted upon by its chosen organs, the Central Committee and the Politburo."[2] When interviewed by Emil Ludwig later that year, Stalin responded to a similar question by saying that Soviet policy was made in the seventy-member Central Committee. This was an "Areopagus" representing the best minds in industry, commerce, military affairs, agriculture, and so on, each having the possibility of correcting someone's individual opinion or proposal.[3]

Stalin's replies to the foreigners' questions misrepresented the extent of his power, yet his disclaimer of dictatorship was not completely unfounded. If a dictator or autocrat may be characterized as a political leader who can decide policy questions arbitrarily and without the likelihood of significant opposition from within the regime that he heads, much less from the society at large, Stalin at the outset of the 1930s was not yet a dictator. He was not beyond having to contend with criticism, dissent, and outright opposition in the Communist Party.

The willingness to voice critical views or to oppose Stalin had its source in the political culture of the regime in which he had risen to supremacy. The Soviet state did not take shape as an autocracy but rather as a party dictatorship which relied on oligarchical decision-making practices in dealing with contentious political issues. It was Lenin who established the role of a political leader standing in a highly authoritative yet nondictatorial relation to the rest of the ruling group. Lenin did not determine policy by autocratic fiat, but rather by gaining majority assent to his policy positions in the Central Committee and its smaller subcommittee, the Politburo. If his views usually prevailed it was because his advocacy of them generally proved persuasive, and also because of the immense personal authority that he enjoyed. Important policy issues were normally resolved through a process of debate in which the members of the high party councils, meeting in closed session, were free to express their own views and oppose those of others, including Lenin, until the questions

were settled by majority vote. To this extent Lenin's legacy in party decision making is correctly expressed in the Soviet phrase "collective leadership."

The leadership that Stalin won in the post-Lenin political contest must
be understood against this background. When the higher party strata gave
him their predominant support against the various oppositions in the post-
Lenin years and accepted him as the party's leader, it was not with a sense
of impending submission to a personal dictatorship. Although prepared to
follow Stalin, this ruling group was, with exceptions, no collection of
sycophantic yes-men. Some servile supporters and pliable careerists had
been promoted to seats on the Central Committee by the efforts of Stalin's
political machine, but there were many who supported Stalin through these
years because, on basic matters, they agreed with him. His heavy-hand-
edness, the "rudeness" that led Lenin finally to urge his removal from the
post of general secretary, was a known fact. But because of the oligarchical
tradition, the prevailing assumption was that Stalin would respect the right
of others in high position to voice their opinions in the appropriate times
and places, and that he would not override the currents of political opinion
at the level of the Politburo and Central Committee.

On the other hand, Stalin was a man of despotic disposition, and
while the Bolshevik oligarchical tradition militated against a leader's dictatorial rule over the party elite, Lenin and his fellow founders of the party-
state had created no institutional safeguards against a dictatorship. Lenin,
although a lawyer by training, did not—especially in the formative first
period after the Revolution—uphold the rule of law either in practice or as
an ideal; he conceived the new polity, rather, as party-proletarian rule
under the guidance of Marxism. Nor was the turn to the NEP marked by a
new spirit of political pluralism in the party to match the new tolerance of
pluralism in the economy. On the contrary, Lenin reasoned that an army is
never so much in danger of panic and hence in need of discipline as in time
of retreat; and with this in mind he forged a tighter intraparty regime rather
than a looser one. His Resolution on Party Unity, which was adopted by
the Tenth Congress in 1921, formally banned factions in the party. Although honored in the breach during the remainder of the 1920s, it proved
a valuable weapon for Stalin against intraparty opposition.

Lenin's place of work was his office in the Kremlin. Employing but a
relatively few administrative aides and a small staff of clerk-stenographers,
he dealt directly by phone and correspondence with party leaders, people's
commissars, their deputies, and others, and devoted the bulk of his time
and energy to the duties of governmental chief executive. He sought to
make of the Sovnarkom, over whose weekly sessions he regularly presided, an engine of day-to-day policy decisions and their implementation.

Its meeting place (as well as that of the Central Committee and Politburo) was the Cabinet Room next to Lenin's office, and it had, as of early 1921, a chancellery, with sixty-five administrative officials who prepared the Sovnarkom meetings and monitored its decisions. The head of the chancellery, which included a Sovnarkom Secretariat employing eight secretaries and typists, was Lenin's chief aide, V. D. Bonch-Bruyevich.[4]

Basic policy questions as well as contentious issues arising on the governmental side were usually decided in meetings of the party Central Committee or Politburo, in which Lenin was only one of several voting members albeit the most influential. One reason why contentious issues often arose was that most commissariats were headed by Bolsheviks of stature and prominence who had strong views that they were willing to defend even if Lenin did not share them. Examples were Trotsky as war commissar, Dzerzhinsky as head of the Cheka, Lunacharsky as commissar of education, and Stalin as commissar for nationality affairs and worker-peasant inspection.

The Sovnarkom did not function as a government for long. The system's built-in bias toward party rule asserted itself. By 1921 the Politburo and Central Committee were operating as the focal center of political authority for the governmental bureaucracy as well as for the party, and the higher party organs in Moscow and around the country were becoming the real government.[5] The failing of Lenin's health during 1922 accelerated the Sovnarkom's eclipse. Stalin, whose main base of operation was the party machine, helped the process along. And as he emerged victorious from the post-Lenin contest for power, he brought the Sovnarkom under his personal control. A resolution of the Sixteenth Party Conference in April 1929 prescribed a purge of the governmental bureaucracy, in which the Right's influence had been strong. In 1930 Rykov was replaced in the premiership by Stalin's confederate, Molotov, so Stalin could now count on the Sovnarkom's full cooperation in his plans and policies. With few exceptions moreover, such as that of Maxim Litvinov at the Foreign Affairs Commissariat, he did not follow Lenin's example of wanting strong-minded men of independent stature to head the government departments.

In addition to holding seats on the policy-making Central Committee and Politburo, as Lenin had, Stalin was the leading figure in the Central Committee's Orgburo, which had charge of party organizational affairs and higher appointments. But his principal role was that of general secretary, the foremost member of the Central Committee Secretariat—the group of party secretaries collectively responsible for directing the party bureaucracy. In 1930, via his lieutenant for party organizational affairs, Kaganovich, Stalin reorganized the Central Committee apparatus. He incorporated into the Central Committee all the directing and overseeing of the far-flung work of industrialization then going at full blast. As reorganized, the Central Committee consisted of a Secret Department serving the Politburo, the Orgburo, and the Secretariat; an Organizational-Instructor Department responsible for appointments of party officials and supervision of the countrywide network of party organizations; an Assignments Department responsible for selecting and allocating administrative, economic, and trade union officials; a Department of Culture and Propaganda, for supervising the press, education, party propaganda, and general culture; a Department of Agitation and Mass Campaigns; and the Lenin Institute. Under Stalin the central party machine was moving beyond its traditional role of providing overall policy guidance for governmental and public institutions to become the supreme executive center for economic development and other spheres of state activity. This shift was reflected in a vast expansion of the responsibilities of the Orgburo, whose published plan of work for 1931, as compared with that for 1928, showed it to have graduated from being a center of supervision of party organizations into the role of a general staff for checking on the fulfillment of all important directives connected with the second revolution.[6]

The Central Committee offices were housed in a sprawling six-story building on Staraya Square not far from the Red Square. By the end of the 1920s Stalin had created there a formidable personal power structure out of all comparison with the modest facilities in the Kremlin that had served Lenin's needs. Its setting was the Central Committee's Secret Department. The latter was set up in 1920 as a service organ for the party's higher bodies. It provided administrative services, including minute taking, for the Politburo (whose meetings were still held at the Kremlin), the Orgburo, and the Secretariat. It handled party documents and correspondence, ran a coding and decoding office, and kept the party's secret archives. When Stalin became general secretary in 1922, he moved his personal staff into this "holy of holies," as a fugitive Soviet official called it.[7]

Stalin made his chief assistant, Ivan Tovstukha, deputy head and then head of the Secret Department. Other members of his personal staff, now called "assistant Central Committee secretaries," received important assignments as well. His assistant Lev Mekhlis replaced Tovstukha as head of the Secret Department for a time in the mid-1920s. Others, including Georgi Malenkov, acted as Politburo secretaries, while still others manned a key unit of the Secret Department, the Central Committee's "Secretariat bureau," which had over one hundred employees by the end of 1925. One of the assistant Central Committee secretaries, Alexander Poskrebyshev, was appointed in 1928 to head Stalin's personal domain within the Secret Department, the "Special Sector" (Osobyi sektor), and in this capacity he served as Stalin's chief assistant for the next twenty-five years.[8]

This personal structure of government provided Stalin not only with his own system of secret information necessary for policy making, but also with mechanisms for implementing policy decisions that he made with the help of his group of executive assistants. Via the Central Committee's system of *nomenklatura,* or lists of posts for which nominees had to be cleared by party authorities at the appropriate level, the Secret Department/ Special Sector was in a position to control higher appointments at sensitive points in the party-state. It exercised oversight of the security police, of foreign affairs, and of economic, cultural, and other branches of internal life. Through a system of subordinate secret departments/special sectors in the republic and province party committees and in the Komsomol, its reach ramified throughout the entire Soviet Union.

Officially mentioned as "Comrade Stalin's secretariat," the corps of executive assistants became known informally to party insiders as "Stalin's cabinet," and this term accurately indicates its innermost nature as an unofficial government subordinate directly and exclusively to Stalin. Each assistant was responsible for following a particular field of activity, such as press and propaganda, party cadres or personnel, foreign policy, military matters, police affairs, and nationalities. As Stalin's desk officer for that area, he would have his own assistants and access to the full range of information available in party channels as well as in the government commissariats. He would prepare position papers and keep Stalin well briefed in preparation for sessions of the higher assemblies.[9] These little-known men with the title "assistant Central Committee secretary" were, in some cases, too young to have had a pre-1917 party past. They were capable, hard-working, reliable, close-mouthed, and totally dedicated to Stalin's service. Among them were such persons of future importance as Malenkov, Mekhlis, and Nikolai Yezhov. Little by little, Stalin began moving his protégés into official positions of power where it was desirable for him to have unquestioning executors of his will. After Bukharin lost the editorship of *Pravda* in 1929, Mekhlis received a commanding position on the editorial board of this most authoritative of Soviet newspapers. Malenkov would take over the key Central Committee Department of Leading Party Organs in the mid-1930s. Yezhov would head the security police in the later 1930s.

The first five stories of the big building on Staraya Square were occupied by various specialized departments; the top floor by the Secretariat and its service staff. The offices of the Central Committee secretaries other than Stalin occupied no more than half of this floor. The other half was Stalin's realm. It was physically sealed off from the rest. The only entrance led into an anteroom that opened onto other offices, including the inner sanctum where Stalin worked. He liked to work alone there. His habit was to study a file of materials on a problem, prepared by one or another of his assistants, and then pace back and forth smoking his pipe as he thought the matter over. After reaching a decision, he would summon a stenographer, to whom he would dictate his decision.[10]

It is attested by diverse sources that one of Stalin's devices for aggrandizing his power was the collection of derogatory information on party figures. An agency that proved useful for this purpose was the Central Party Control Commission. Originally created in 1920 as a kind of high tribunal to adjudicate complaints by party members, it evolved into a disciplinary body. Inside the commission, according to Trotsky, Stalin set up a special group under his supporters Emelian Yaroslavsky and Matvei Shkiriatov. Its task was to comb the surviving tsarist police archives for materials that then went into a special archive "full of all sorts of documents, accusations, libelous rumours against all the prominent leaders without exception."[11] This archive, which appears to have been housed in the extensive quarters of Stalin's Special Sector on the sixth floor, lent itself to obvious political uses on his part. There are also reports from ex-Soviet sources that Stalin's staff tapped the telephones of high-placed persons in order to keep him well informed on their attitudes and actions.

He also sought and acquired a close working relation with the police organization. Liaison with the police, and oversight of its affairs, was an important facet of the work of Stalin's chancellery.[12] But Stalin also acquired direct influence with the police leaders. V. Menzhinsky, Dzerzhinsky's successor at the head of the OGPU, was a sickly man. Hence, a powerful role in OGPU activities devolved upon Genrikh Yagoda, his forceful and resourceful deputy. Yagoda was not initially a Stalin man. He is believed to have leaned toward the Right and, with some others in the police leadership who feared peasant disorders, to have sympathized in 1928 with the opposition to a crash program of collectivization. Later, he became—however unenthusiastically—a helper of Stalin's in the police organization. The need to expiate his erstwhile rightist leanings would have worked to that end.

In order to convert the police connection into greater personal political power, Stalin had to overcome the party's tradition of settling its inner conflicts without resort to police reprisals. In Lenin's time the Bolsheviks had freely wielded the police weapon against members of other parties, but remembering the self-destructive path taken by French Jacobins, they had deliberately avoided the use of lethal methods within their own party. In party lore this unwritten rule against bloodletting among the Bolsheviks was associated with Lenin personally. Its abrogation under Stalin began with the imprisonment and exile of large numbers of Left oppositionists at the close of the 1920s. After expulsion from party membership, they were sentenced under the section of the Criminal Code (Article 58) covering various forms of counterrevolutionary crimes. Reports from oppositionist sources that made their way abroad and were published in Trotsky's Paris-based *Bulletin of the Opposition* spoke of hundreds of arrests in Moscow and other major industrial centers in January 1929; of a thousand or so oppositionists being "taken out of circulation" before the anniversary of the Revolution in November of that year; of further such arrests on a large scale in early 1930 as preparations for the Sixteenth Congress began; and even of a few instances of oppositionists receiving the death penalty. Some of the arrested persons were kept in special-regime prisons known as "isolators." The bulk of them, however, were deported to distant places where they lived in exile colonies under conditions worse than those many of them had experienced as exiled revolutionaries in old Russia. A report that came out in November 1930 said that over 7,000 "Bolshevik-Lenin-ists" (as the oppositionists called themselves) were then in exile, prison, or under surveillance, and that these numbers were growing as arrests and deportations continued.[13]

Stalin's justification of this repressive policy was set forth in a memorandum that he wrote at the beginning of 1929—apparently for the Politburo—and that, with insignificant stylistic changes, appeared in *Pravda* on 24 January 1929 as an unsigned editorial under the title "They've Sunk to This." His argument was that during 1928 the opposition had undergone full transformation *"From an underground antiparty group into an underground anti-Soviet organization,"* and further that *". . . an impassible gulf* has opened up between the former Trotskyist opposition inside the ACP (b) and the present anti-Soviet Trotskyist underground organization outside the ACP (b)."[14] To thus reclassify the Trotskyists from a defeated intraparty opposition into a subversive antistate movement was both to justify the police reprisals and to create a precedent for dealing in the same way with any future intraparty opposition. Stalin did not, to be sure, proclaim this change as a break with Leninist tradition. Rather, he made himself out to be a latter-day Lenin by recalling how Lenin, in his draft of the Resolution on Party Unity at the Tenth Congress, had (with a reference to Menshevik leaflets circulated in Petrograd on the eve of the Kronstadt rising) accused the Mensheviks of taking advantage of discords within the Bolshevik party to stir up trouble for the Soviet regime; and Stalin added: "The Trotskyist organization is now in fact fulfilling the same role that the Menshevik party fulfilled in the USSR at one time in its fight against the Soviet regime." The police measures against an intraparty opposition were thus justified by comparing them with similar measures taken under Lenin against the Menshevik opposition.

At about this time, the decision was taken to deport Trotsky himself, who during 1928 had been in exile in the remote town of Alma-Ata, to a foreign country. In February 1929 he was shipped to Turkey, where he was domiciled on the island of Prinkipo. Some months later, the first issue of Trotsky's *Bulletin of the Opposition* carried what purported to be an inside account from Moscow of the Politburo discussion of this question. The proposal for deportation was said to have been supported by Stalin on several grounds, including the argument that "if Trotsky comes out with attacks on the leadership, we will depict him as a traitor."[15] In Stalin's view, a Trotsky visibly carrying on the political struggle from abroad would dramatize the image of internal Trotskyists as subversives involved in an antistate conspiracy. By the same token, the justification for the use of police repression against party opponents would be strengthened.

In the summer of 1929 events took a further turn in this direction. Yakov Bliumkin, an ardent Trotsky supporter working in the OGPU's counterintelligence division, paid a visit to Trotsky on Prinkipo during a mission abroad, and carried home a message from Trotsky to his fellow oppositionists in Russia. Soon after arriving in Moscow, Bliumkin was arrested, convicted in secret of treason, and executed.[16] It is open to surmise, although supporting evidence is lacking, that Bliumkin was the victim of an intrigue devised in Moscow by Stalin, namely, that his superiors had encouraged him to make contact with Trotsky on Prinkipo. In any event, the attempted transmission of a message from abroad could be interpreted as corroboration of Stalin's picture of a conspiratorial Trotskyist organization; and Bliumkin's execution carried police measures against intraparty opposition for the first time to the point of applying the death penalty.

The upshot is that an anomalous situation existed in the party-state at the turn of the decade. Stalin had succeeded to the role of supreme leader in a system whose practice of deciding policy issues by majority vote in the Politburo and Central Committee he was supposed to respect. Yet, he had amassed so much personal political power that he could manipulate the regime's policy. Consequently, his actual position belied his formal subordination to the party's higher deliberative bodies. This presented no serious problem so long as he and they were broadly in harmony. But when he began to manipulate policy in ways that many of his colleagues had not expected and could not approve, a collision between the formalities and the realities was inevitable.

On the Eve

The Five-Year Plan did not envisage general collectivization during the five years. The goal was far more limited, and for good reason. Those who prepared its agricultural section were doubtless well aware that rapid total collectivization could not be achieved without coercing the middle-peasant majority. There were no party guidelines for that. Lenin had warned in 1919 that anyone who took it into his head to deal with the middle peasant by coercion would "ruin the whole cause." Still earlier, he had said that such a tremendous transformation in the life of the people as joint cultivation on large farms would have to be approached gradually and prudently. Given the peasant's attachment to separate plots of land, he said, it would be "madness" to imagine that cultivation in common could be "decreed and imposed from above" or brought about "at one blow."[17]

As approved in the optimal version in April 1929, the plan provided that collective and state farms would produce 15.5 percent of the gross grain harvest in the final plan year, 1932. Such partial collectivization would be no small accomplishment. But it would not restore Russia to her pre-1914 position as a major world grain exporter, and hence would not provide the Soviet government with the wherewithal to finance the costly imports of machines and technology that were required if the escalating targets on the industrialization side were to be attained. So it could not satisfy Stalin. From his point of view, the state must take complete control of agriculture without delay so as to make feasible a speedy industrial revolution.

Such, on the basis of his statements cited earlier, was the gist of Stalin's reasoning. Still, there were matters of degree. He could have pursued collectivization with a modicum of restraint and a sense of limits. He could have been mindful of Lenin's warnings on this crucial point, which were certainly known to him. If he did not so behave, we can safely rule out stupidity or simple pigheadedness as the reason and turn to his personal motivations for understanding his approach.

Stalin turned fifty in December 1929 just as the decision for all-out collectivization was taking final form. This offered an occasion for publicizing his victory in the contest for the leadership succession. Taking advantage of a convenient precedent in party history—the marking of Lenin's fiftieth birthday at a party meeting in 1920—Stalin's entourage arranged an official celebration of his anniversary, on 21 December, as a major public event. The modest ceremony inflicted on a reluctant Lenin was eclipsed. Stalin was lauded in press articles as Lenin's supremely gifted disciple and rightful successor. The event was made into a symbolic coronation of him as the party's new *vozhd'*.

Where Lenin had shown disapproval of such proceedings, Stalin showed appreciation. He responded with a short public message of thanks in which he placed the eulogistic birthday greetings to the credit of "the great party of the working class that bore me and reared me in its own image and likeness." His message concluded: "You need have no doubt, comrades, that I am prepared in the future, too, to devote to the cause of the working class, the proletarian revolution and world communism, all my strength, all my ability and, if need be, all my blood, drop by drop."[18]

The imagery of Stalin's reference to the Communist Party as his mother is striking. It conveys something more than consciousness of his newly won primacy in the regime: a subconscious feeling that he was taking Lenin's unique place as the mothering party's beloved chief. And the picture of a martyr shedding his blood for the party cause drop by drop was a revelation of this self-dramatizing man's inner life of fantasies in which he played a heroic part. The hero-script that he was now, finally, able to enact was the vision of going down in history as another Lenin by bringing off an October of the construction of socialism, with him as the lone leader who would devise and force through the project against high-level party opposition, as Lenin repeatedly did, and later receive the plaudits due him for the exploit. The October of socialism's construction would be mass collectivization.

That Stalin conceived the collectivization project in such terms is indicated by the fact that at this very moment the party journal *Communist Revolution* described it as a "rural October."[19] And that he was conscious of himself, at this critical moment, as a *vozhd'* acting the part of a Lenin is indicated by an article that must have been prepared around this time although it appeared somewhat later. As an editorial in the party's journal of organizational affairs, it carried a special imprimatur of the general secretary's office. Taking issue with the (unattributed) view that the party in the post-Lenin era could be "an orchestra without a conductor," it argued that Lenin's legacy to Bolshevism was the role of a supreme leader of a party of willing followers. Lenin himself had once said that the will of tens and hundreds of thousands could be expressed in one person, and at all times had genuinely led the movement by innovating sound policies and organizing their implementation. Stalin had shown himself first among equals in carrying on this tradition.[20]

The latter-day Lenin was now innovating the collectivization of agriculture.

Collectivizing from Above

He brought about the radical mode of collectivizing by secretly ordering the local authorities to take actions that by the fall of 1929 gave rural Russia the false appearance of being in the throes of spontaneous revolutionary change. Having contrived these circumstances, he pointed to them in his article on "The Great Turn" to support his public definition of the situation in the countryside as a revolutionary one and his policy of full speed ahead.

The approximately one million peasant households in the 57,000 collectives that had been formed by 1 June, 1929 represented only between three and four percent of the country's peasant population. "Wholesale" collectivization, which in Soviet parlance meant the transformation of all the lands in the area of a whole village or district into collective-farm land, got going in the summer of that year in selected grain-producing areas. Some 911,000 peasant households entered collectives in the July–September quarter of 1929, nearly doubling the number of collectivized peasant families; and in the final quarter of the year, about 2.4 million more households were collectivized, bringing the grand total of peasants brought into collectives to over 25 million—about 20 percent of the peasant population.[21] Nothing like this rate of collectivization had been projected in the plan.

The great leap forward in collectivization after 1 June resulted from increased pressures at the top that brought intensified administrative actions by local officials. The fact that in September–October 1929 many regional party committees formed special collectivization commissions[22] is one indication of the sort of instructions then reaching the rural regions from Stalin's Central Committee Secretariat. Driven by exhortations from above, the local authorities vied with one another in their pushes to collectivize. What Soviet historians would later describe as "unhealthy tendencies" and "gross excesses" were the inevitable and widespread consequence of these exhortations.

Thus, an investigation of the Khoper district in the Lower Volga region, carried out at the beginning of November 1929 by one Baranov, a representative of the USSR *Kolkhoz* Center in Moscow, disclosed that peasants were being intimidated by threats that they would be dispossessed of their land, and that peasant families were being registered in collectives without their knowledge.[23] As Baranov wrote in his report,

A system of shockwork and campaigning methods is being practiced by the local organs. All the organizing has gone on under the slogan, "Who will achieve more." The directives of the district administration are sometimes translated locally into the slogan: "Anybody who doesn't join a collective farm is an enemy of the Soviet regime." No broad mass work has been done. In one case a *kolkhoz* was organized by decision of a village assembly, and those who didn't want to join were asked to submit s special statement on their reasons. There've been cases of big promises of tractors and credits: "You'll get everything—just join the *kolkhoz*." All these factors together yield so far 60 percent and perhaps as I write this letter even 70 percent collectivization. We haven't studied the qualitative aspect of the collective farms. Thus a very great gap exists between the quantitative growth and qualitative organization of big farms. If steps aren't taken right now to consolidate these collectives, the cause may compromise itself. The collectives will begin to disintegrate. It must be taken into account that a very great deal of selling off of livestock is going on in the district. It all places us in an extremely difficult situation.[24]

Along with such administrative pressures upon, mainly, the middle peasants in villages or districts of wholesale collectivization, the greatly accelerated collectivization drive of the summer and fall of 1929 saw rather extensive use of the repressive practice called "dekulakization," which meant the complete expropriation and in most cases exile of kulak households. Instances of it had occurred earlier. For example, in 1928 a "committee of the poor" was formed by the eighteen poorest households of a Ukrainian village whose story was later recounted in emigration by a former inhabitant. The committee would meet in the village soviet, select a victim, and then make an armed raid and strip the kulak family of everything, down to extra clothing its members were wearing. Twenty-one kulak households were so expropriated, their members exiled to Siberia and Kazakhstan, and a commune created with two of the former kulak farms as its base.[25]

In the latter half of 1929, dekulakization was accelerated along with the collectivization drive. First, the authorities sharply increased the already very heavy tax burden on kulaks, whose "resistance"—which term undoubtedly refers to what in many cases was the simple act of raising objections—was followed by their total expropriation. According to Soviet sources, 33,000 kulak households were expropriated in the Ukraine alone before the end of 1929.[26] From a Central Committee decree of 18 July 1929, which must have emanated from Stalin's offices since there was no plenum at that time, we may infer that these and other "dekulakized" households were deported as well as expropriated. For this decree approved a policy of prohibiting the entry of kulaks into collective farms, and many local party organizations thereupon passed decisions to the same effect.[27]

Stalin's moves to accelerate the collectivization drive culminated in a decree that issued from the Central Committee Secretariat on 29 July 1929 and was entitled "On Party Organizational Work in the New Grain Procurement Campaign." It was a directive to party organizations around the country on the procedures to be followed in the 1929–30 grain procurement period, and a document of historic importance because it prescribed what a Soviet historian has called "a decisive change in grain collections policy."[28] The decree systematized the emergency methods brought into play in the winter and spring of 1928 in response to the peasant "grain strike," that is, the allocation of compulsory grain delivery quotas to districts and villages. The change consisted in the adoption of this approach *as a regular policy*. The new line was reflected in official decrees promulgated by the governments of the Russian Federation and the Ukraine on 28 June and 3 July 1929, respectively. What had hitherto been practiced as an emergency measure to meet a crisis situation—compulsory grain delivery quotas for villages and individual farmsteads, along with fixed obligations for the better-off sections of the peasantry in the matter of grain deliveries—was thereby made into law.[29]

Although it was never stated in so many words, this in fact ended the NEP. The essence of the NEP was that after payment of a fixed agricultural tax, initially taken in kind and from 1924–25 in money, the peasant was free to consume the remainder and to sell any surplus to governmental or cooperative procurement agencies or private traders for whatever price he could obtain. Now the Soviet regime was reverting to what was in essence a grain requisitioning system comparable to that of Civil War days, along with virtual expropriation of peasants classified as kulaks. The government decrees just mentioned in effect restricted the free sale of grain by the procedures they prescribed for first-priority sale of grain in fulfillment of state obligations as formalized by village assemblies. These assemblies, we may add, would be acting on instructions coming down to local cadres through party channels from the higher authorities, regional and ultimately central.

This in turn made mass collectivization unavoidable. As Moshkov puts it: "The content and character of these changes were such that *they had to be followed by the beginning of widespread social transformations in the countryside:* otherwise, as Civil War experience showed, the delivery of grain to the state on a planned basis, at prices disadvantageous to the peasants, inevitably led to the reducing of grain production to the consumption minimum."[30] The new system of grain procurements, in other words, deprived the peasant of what the NEP had given him: a real incentive to produce and market grain surpluses. Consequently, Stalin's decision to convert compulsory grain deliveries at low state prices into a system was implicitly a decision for general collectivization.

The November Plenum

Lenin's political leadership was marked by periodic abrupt turns when he thought situations dictated them. As a latter-day Lenin in his own eyes, Stalin probably thought he was taking a leaf from Lenin's book when he initiated the abrupt turn toward mass collectivization in mid-1929. But there was one large difference. Whereas Lenin would proclaim the sharp shift openly and argue the urgent need for it before the appropriate larger party forum, Stalin would move quietly behind the scenes in an attempt to make the change *appear* to be coming spontaneously from below.

So in this case. He took action behind the scenes to set the party on a course toward mass collectivization in the immediate future. Then he came forward in *Pravda* on 7 November 1929 with the article that proclaimed 1929 to be the great turning-point year because of what he said was taking place spontaneously throughout the country: peasants were entering the collective farms no longer in individual groups as before, but by whole villages and districts. Stalin did not mention the administrative pressures that achieved the astonishingly rapid collectivization "movement" he reported. And when he added with heavy emphasis that *"the middle peasant has joined the collectives,"* this was much more a prophecy than a statement of fact.

In reality, the peasants were profoundly troubled by the events brought about by the circular orders emanating from Stalin's Central Committee offices. Maurice Hindus attended a meeting on collectivization in Moscow's Peasant Home in the summer of 1928 and later reported: "Writer after writer with whom I discussed the prospects of the venture was in a skeptical mood. Peasants who were staying in the Moscow Home and dropped in on the meeting laughed at it as at some silly caper of a spoiled child." The peasant, he explained, was essentially an individualist "accustomed to land of his own, a horse of his own, a cow of his own, a way of his own. . . . I have met peasants again and again living in the vicinity of a successful *kolkhoz,* who if left to themselves would not readily part from individual landholding. Never in all my wanderings in Russian villages have I heard so much expression of doubt, of alarm, of disappointment, so much prophecy of doom as in the summer of 1929, when the new movement had attained sweeping proportions."[31]

The middle peasants were not joining the collectives *en masse;* rather, they were holding back as much as they could. At the time of "The Year of the Great Turn," as a later historian recorded, "no deep and general *perelom* in the attitude of the middle peasantry toward collectivization had yet occurred."[32] Eyewitness testimony corroborates this judgment. In late July 1929, E. I. Veger, a Central Committee field officer with experience in northern Russia, reported to the Politburo that the village poor were spearheading collectivization, while the middle peasants were showing notable reluctance to join it. Veger attributed to the peasants such statements as: "The middle peasant—he can exist independently, while need drives us (the poor peasants) into the collective." "The middle peasants—they can wait with collectivization, but we can't." "Only the poor peasant really desires collectivization; the middle peasant—he still thinks he can manage on his own."[33]

When Lenin wrote in 1917 that "a real revolution cannot take place" without a sharp turn in the life of huge masses, he was referring to a spontaneous shift of mass attitude in response to events in a society. In those terms, the great turn that Stalin proclaimed in his article of 7 November 1929 was a false or contrived one. The changes in the countryside were being initiated from above and pushed through locally by administrative measures and intimidation. Stalin's motive is not far to seek. He wanted to scrap the comparatively modest collectivization goals of the *piatiletka* in favor of a second revolution in the countryside, but for such a far-reaching policy shift, he needed the Central Committee's imprimatur. Since "The Year of the Great Turn" appeared on the eve of a plenary session of the Central Committee (due to open on 10 November 1929), a prime purpose of the article clearly was to influence this plenum's deliberations by brandishing the remarkable successes of an ongoing drive for mass collectivization.[34]

Although the proceedings of the week-long November session have not yet been published, we know enough about it from the published resolutions, from writings of Soviet historians after Stalin's death, and from one major speech that was published at the time—Molotov's. Stalin himself is reported to have spoken (although his article of 7 November was his main plenum "speech"), and he intervened from time to time with brief comments, such as: "Now even the blind can see that the *kolkhozy* and *sovkhozy* are growing at an accelerated rate."[35] The chief spokesman of his position, however, was Molotov, then the Central Committee secretary in charge of agriculture. He gave three speeches, one of them on the collectivization movement. Its prominent and exclusive featuring in the post-plenum issue of the Central Committee journal *Bol'shevik* shows beyond a doubt that he was voicing Stalin's views.

This speech is particularly noteworthy for two lines of argument. First, Molotov asserted that the very idea of a *five*-year plan of collectivization was faulty and must be discarded. He declared that to stretch the collectivization over the period of five years would be "a waste of time. For the main agricultural regions and provinces, whatever the different tempos of collectivization in them, we have to think right now in terms not of a five-year period but of the coming year." In arguing the case for scrapping the already adopted five-year program of partial collectivization in favor of a big push to collectivize "in the main" during the coming months, Molotov said that grain procurements had gone so successfully thus far in 1929 that they were already complete in the Ukraine and certain other areas. As a result the government had managed to create an "inviolable" grain reserve fund of over one and one-half million tons. This meant that, organizationally speaking, the period of the upcoming spring sowing campaign would be unprecedentedly favorable for agriculture and specifically for collectivization. The critical time of opportunity was the next five months—November, December, January, February, and March. "Since, for the time being, Messrs. the imperialists are not of a mind directly to attack us, we must use the moment for a decisive shift in economic advance and the collectivization of millions of peasant households."[36]

Molotov further argued that "the mobilization of peasant resources" did not mean, as some mistakenly believed, a mobilization of peasant savings through the agricultural credit system; the poor and middle peasant, after all, had little money. Rather, it meant the direct mobilization of the peasants' "kopecks" in the form of their possessions (dobro). "It is above all a mobilization of means of production, be it pitifully small in the majority of cases and sometimes simply niggardly, but adding up in the aggregate to an enormous amount." So, the very "soul" of the kolkhoz movement lay in the "socialized funds" (that is, collectivized peasant property) without which the collective farm could not exist and which became its "indivisible funds." Here Molotov reinforced his argument by saying that the Soviet state, being poor and having to invest its principal resources in industrialization, was unable to furnish much material assistance for collectivization. Although it would provide what it could, this contribution would only by "chickenfeed" (groshi). So, "The kolkhoz movement can develop as a mass affair only on condition that with the support of the proletarian state it draws into its socialized funds the hundreds of millions and billions of peasant resources (material values). In the growth of these socialized funds lies the essence of the collectivization of the countryside."[37]

The sense of the argument was supremely clear: an industrialization-bent regime too poor to offer serious material inducement to the peasantry to collectivize would nevertheless proceed with immediate collectivization by compelling the peasants themselves to pool their possessions, their means of production. The peasantry, to put Molotov's phrase "mobilization of peasant resources" in less euphemistic terms, would be expropriated. The "material values" owned by the great mass of poor and middle peasants, not to mention kulaks—their draft animals, livestock, ploughs, and other farming implements—would become the property or "indivisible funds" of collective farms that in turn would provide the state, reliably and at nominal prices, with the wherewithal to finance the huge projected "economic advance"—industrialization.

The November plenum was Stalinist in that oppositionist voices were now stilled, Stalin supporters were in full command, and his line, as expressed by Molotov, received the sought-for approval. Bukharin, Rykov, and Tomsky took part in the discussion, but as a beaten ex-opposition rather than as an anti-Stalin group fighting for their own policy line. Very many of the participants took their cue from Stalin's 7 November *Pravda* article. Above all, the plenum's resolutions followed Stalin's new line. One of them even said that "in the wake of the poor peasant *the mass of middle-peasants* has moved into the collective farms." Another, on the economy's control figures for 1929–30, accepted Stalin's proposal in the "Great Turn" article that sown areas of the collective farms be increased to 15 million hectares in 1930.[38]

Still, those who supported Stalin, or not a few of them, were not yet Stalinists in the sense of being automatic yes-men. Heirs to the argumentative inner political culture of the Bolshevik movement, some of the participants at the plenum voiced, albeit circumspectly, certain questions and apprehensions. They were doing so on the assumption that their opinions counted, that they could help shape the Soviet regime's policy, and that they had a duty as members of the ruling group to head off foreseeable and potentially costly errors.

One historian notes that Molotov's call for immediate mass collectivization "alarmed certain members" of the Central Committee, and that "they warned against haste in the collective farm movement, against wholesale conduct of full collectivization." The above-mentioned Baranov letter on the crude administrative pressures by which collectivization was taking place in the Khoper district was read out at the plenum.[39] Concern seems to have been greatest in the minds of officials directly involved in agricultural policy and among party secretaries of some of the chief grain-growing regions, for they were close to the rural scene and knew what was happening. They were aware that rural cadres, obedient to orders from above and seeking to outdo one another in showing what they could accomplish, were reporting the creation of what were actually—in words used by one of the speakers—"paper *kolkhozy*." One high-ranking figure who expressed apprehension was the first party secretary of the Ukrainian Republic, Stanislav Kosior. "We had full-scale collectivization on the territory of dozens of villages," he said, "and then it turned out that all this was sham and artificially created, and that the population wasn't taking part and didn't know anything about it."[40] B. P. Sheboldaev, the party secretary of the Lower Volga region, directly raised and then negatively answered the question: "Are we ready for the collectivization movement that is now developing regionally and apparently will develop on a countrywide basis in the immediate future? I think that we are not now yet ready for this movement."[41]

Stalin was in attendance at the plenum and heard all this, but was unmoved by it. Of him, Molotov, and Kaganovich (the latter was then the Central Committee secretary in charge of organizational matters), Ivnitsky writes: "They were aware that even in the fall of 1929 serious mistakes were made locally (there was forcing of the tempo of collectivization, the voluntary entry principle was violated in organizing collectives, and so on). They did not, however, take firm measures to put a stop to the excesses; rather, they aggravated the errors by their action. Thus . . . when G. N. Kaminsky and S. V. Kosior cited facts in their reports on excesses in collectivization (in the Lower and Middle Volga and in the Ukraine), Stalin paid no attention to this. Nor did he take seriously the letter of the instructor of the USSR *kolkhoz* Center, Baranov, on the excesses in the Khoper district." Stalin's comment on the Baranov letter was: "What do you expect, to organize everything in advance?"[42]

Stalin paid no attention because the phenomena that alarmed numbers of his party colleagues were the direct and deliberate consequence of the instructions that had gone out of his office through party channels to the rural localities, and impelled the authorities at that level to commit the "excesses." Those instructions reflected his strategy for speedy mass collectivization, his approach as distinguished from that of the "alarmed" ones. The real and basic question underlying their alarm was: Would it really be feasible to dispossess the peasant, especially the all-important middle peasant, fiercely attached as he was to his horse, his plough, his livestock, and his assigned plot of land—nationalized though the latter was in law and principle? Would he willingly part with his "resources"? And if not, then what?

Stalin offered an answer, although surely a disingenuous one, in a speech that he gave the following month. Addressing the conference of agrarian Marxists on 27 December 1929, he went back at one point to Engels' old article on the peasant question, the article that Krupskaya had discussed in "Ilyich on *Kolkhoz* Construction" as a profound influence on Lenin's thinking. Stalin quoted Engels as saying in it: "We are firmly on the side of the peasant smallholder; we will do everything possible to enable him to live more tolerably and to ease his transition to association in case he so decides; and in case he is unable to make the decision, we will try to give him *as much time as possible* to think it over *on his own little plot*" (Stalin's italics). How, asked Stalin, was Engels' at first glance excessive caution in this passage to be explained? Answering, he said that Engels had proceeded from the fact that private property in the land was an established institution and the peasant would therefore find it hard to part with "his little plot." Such was the peasantry in the West, in capitalist countries where private ownership of the land exists, Stalin went on. "Understandably, great caution is needed there." In Russia, however, the situation was different: nationalization of the land facilitated the transition of the individual peasant to collectivization. "It's a pity that our agrarian theorists haven't yet tried to bring out with requisite clarity this difference between the peasant's situation in our country and the West."[43]

Kremlin-dweller though Stalin had become, this son of a serf-born mother, a man who had lived at times among peasants during his pre-1917 years as a revolutionary and political exile, knew the mentality of the Russian peasant too well to be taken in by his own argument. His contrasting of Russia with the West, combined with the statement that "great caution" was needed in disturbing peasant land proprietorship in the West, invited the inference that no great caution was called for in Russia. In case the "agrarian Marxists" didn't get the point, Stalin made sure that they would by unveiling in that same speech the slogan that served him as a shorthand formula for his strategy: "liquidation of the kulaks as a class."

The Strategy of Terror

Of the peasant households that had been collectivized by November 1929, the great bulk came from the 30 percent in the poor-peasant and farm-laborer categories. The middle peasantry, constituting a full two-thirds of the peasant population, was still holding back as far as possible. Consequently, the crux of the problem of effecting swift mass collectivization was to get the middle peasants—and their "material values," which in the aggregate were vast compared to the possessions of the peasants in the bottom categories—into the collectives.

Stalin's strategy for accomplishing this was based squarely on Lenin's thesis that the peasantry was essentially a "vacillating class"—drawn to individual farming in that the middle peasant was a proprietor and yet also a potential constituency for rural socialism in that he himself farmed the land in the sweat of his brow and was thus a working person. Lenin drew from this thesis the conclusion that if the middle peasants could be educated to the advantages of cooperation, they would opt for associative forms of farming.

Starting from Lenin's premise, Stalin proceeded with impeccable logic to an opposite conclusion. Given that the middle peasantry was in essence a vacillating class, and given further that the government was unable to offer by way of material assistance anything but the "chicken-feed" of which Molotov had spoken, there remained the option of force: the middle peasant's vacillating would be very quickly ended if he could be shown, vividly and harrowingly, that the only alternative to joining a *kolkhoz* was so fearsome that anything—even the *kolkhoz*—would be preferable. But in order so to terrorize him into collectivization, there had to be a social group, rather indeterminate in size and elastic in definition (elastic enough to admit any recalcitrant middle or even poor peasants), that would be treated with such spectacular ferocity that the mass of middle and the still uncollectivized poor peasants would rush into collectives in order to avoid such a fate. Kulaks were obvious candidates for such victimization. For this purpose, however, the expropriating would have to be carried out on a mass scale under the slogan of "liquidation of the kulaks as a class."

The evidence for his hypothesis about Stalin's thinking begins with his repeated and studied citation of Lenin's view of the peasantry as a vacillating class. Further, through Molotov he telegraphed his inclination to end the middle peasant's vacillation by the stick rather than the carrot. Speaking at a meeting of the Urals province party committee in early 1928, Molotov said: "We must deal the kulak such a blow that the middle peasant will snap to attention before us."[44] Although he made this statement in the context of the grain procurements crisis and offered it as a formula for action to make the middle peasant surrender his grain stocks rather than for collectivizing him, it enunciated with total clarity the strategy of terror that Stalin—whose spokesman Molotov was, then as well as later—would follow in collectivization.

Stalin himself spoke of "such a blow" in his speech of December 1929 to the agrarian Marxists. The Soviet regime, he said, was now making a decisive turn to the policy of dekulakization. If it was not to consist of mere declamation, pinpricks, and idle talk, the new policy meant "breaking" the kulaks as a class. "To take the offensive against the kulaks means to get ready for action and to deal the kulak class *such a blow* that it will no longer rise to its feet. That's what we Bolsheviks call an offensive." To make his point unmistakably plain, Stalin added that it was absurd to think of allowing the kulak to join collective farms. "Of course he can't be admitted to a collective farm. He can't be because he's an accursed enemy of the collective farm movement."[45] Stalin did not explain here—he was speaking for public consumption—that the key purpose of treating the kulak class *per se* as an "accursed enemy" was to cause the middle peasant to "snap to attention." But this was the evident rationale of excluding in principle the possibility of allowing individual kulaks to join collective farms by way of exception. The whole point of *total* exclusion was the exemplary victimizing that lay at the core of the terror strategy.

The crowning evidence on this matter has come from particulars about the special advisory commission that the Politburo set up on 5 December 1929. Its function was not to act as an executive group giving day-to-day direction of collectivization, but to draft a Central Committee decree giving practical effect to the November plenum's decision to proceed with general collectivization in the immediate future. The commission consisted of twenty-one persons, including senior officials of the central agricultural agencies and secretaries of key party committees around the country. Ya. A. Yakovlev, just appointed to head the new all-union Commissariat for Agriculture created by decision of the November plenum, was its chairman. Eight subcommissions were formed to deal with such component problems as the tempo of collectivization, the type of collectives to be set up, the treatment of the kulak, and the mobilization of peasant resources. Working at high speed, the subcommissions produced their recommendations in about ten days' time, and a draft Central Committee decree, discussed and approved by the full commission on 18 December, was submitted to the Politburo on 22 December.[46]

Judging by the contents of its draft, the commission accepted unquestioningly the November plenum's decision to proceed with mass collectivization. But it also displayed a certain amount of the caution that Stalin would indirectly criticize in his 27 December speech as unnecessary in Russian conditions. Its members, or the great majority of them, either did not comprehend the pith of his strategy of terror or, *if* they did, failed to share his position and sought to keep the procedures of collectivization within certain bounds for fear of provoking a bureaucratic "gambling sport" (in the words of the draft) and a resultant chaotic stampede of panic-stricken peasants into paper *kolkhozy*. In a meeting of the subcommission chairmen that was discussing the tempo question, Yakovlev warned in the strongest terms against "any administrative euphoria, obsessions or excessive haste whatever, for in the event of a more or less serious spread of such phenomena, the movement would face the threat of bureaucratization, the frightening off of certain strata of poor and middle peasants from collectivization, and the substitution for real collectivization of a formal, show-case collectivization which we don't need."[47] Reflecting this circumspect approach, the commission's draft specifically prohibited any premature proclaiming of "districts of wholesale collectivization." It called for collectivizing the overwhelming majority of peasant households within a five-year period, collectivizing of major grain-growing regions in two to three years (or even sooner in individual districts and provinces) and collectivizing of major grain-consuming zones (where livestock or technical crops like cotton were mainly grown) in three to four years. Further, it specified that no administrative obstacles should be placed in the way of an individual peasant's withdrawal from a collective farm if he so desired.[48]

On the question of the most desirable type of collective farm, there was some sentiment, especially from the Urals organization, for the commune. But the commission's draft opted for the middle form—the artel or *kolkhoz*. In the artel, it said, the main means of production were socialized "with simultaneous retention under present conditions of the peasant's private property in small equipment, small livestock, milk cows, and so on, where they serve the consumption needs of the peasant family." The commission's reasoning was that this arrangement was best suited to the middle-peasant strata who would form the majority of collective farms and keep for some years their "traits of the individual peasant with his characteristic vacillations."[49]

The thorniest single problem facing the commission was how to deal with the kulak. The new policy of liquidating him as a class was implicit in the November plenum's decisions. But as often happens in political life, the crux of the problem lay in the "how." That the kulaks would all be expropriated was taken for granted. But should anyone officially classified as a kulak be excluded under all circumstances from joining a collective, even if he showed a disposition to accept the new situation and work hard if allowed to join? Considering that the kulaks were among the ablest and most industrious elements in the countryside, there was reason for those Bolsheviks who favored a strategy of heavy pressure—but not of wholesale terror, if it could be avoided—to answer in the affirmative.

The reluctance of a majority of the commission's members to adopt a flatly exclusionary policy was reflected in its draft decree. The kulaks were divided into three different groups: those who would actively resist collectivization; those who would resist but less actively and who would not accommodate themselves to general collectivization; and those willing to submit and cooperate loyally with the new system. The first group would be subject to arrest and deportation to remote parts of the country, by decision of a village assembly or soviet; the second, to resettlement, again by such decision, outside the bounds of the given region; and the third group would be treated as potential collective farm workers with a three to five year probationary period of loss of electoral rights before they could be admitted as regular members. In adopting this differentiated approach, the commission was mindful of the value of keeping the members of kulak families usefully employed in farming when possible. It also reasoned that under this plan the isolating of the "most anti-Soviet elements" would soften the resistance of the rest.[50]

The spirit of the commission's draft decree was thus to proceed with immediate mass collectivization in a manner that would combine firm administrative pressure from above, plus drastic action against the "most anti-Soviet elements," with certain restraints and flexibility designed to reconcile the mass of peasants to their new conditions of life. This was not in accord with Stalin's contemplated strategy of terror. If the great mass of still uncollectivized peasants were to be made to snap to attention, they must be given strong motivation: the desire to avoid for themselves the misery being inflicted upon a minority defined as the class enemy—a minority in which any resisting peasant could find himself and his family included. How could such a strategy be carried through successfully if a whole subclass of kulaks were to be admitted, even on a basis of second-class citizenship, into collective farms, and still others resettled but not in "remote parts"?

That Stalin was in fact thinking in these terms is shown by his negative reception of the draft decree when the commission submitted it on 22 December for the Politburo's consideration. A fortuity of the timing is of possible significance here With the previous day's official hosannas to the "best Leninist" and "rockhard Bolshevik" on his fiftieth birthday still ringing in his mind, Stalin's customary self-assurance may have taken on a tinge of dizziness with success. In any event, he was not content with the draft. He wanted the document to be briefer. He was not satisfied with the proposed timetable for collectivization, particularly in the main grain-growing regions, and did not like the limits of socialization of the peasant's property and the possibility of his withdrawing from the collective. After checking with Molotov, who of course fully agreed with him, Stalin returned the draft decree to the commission with his comments and with instructions to rework it. When the Politburo met on 25 December, presumably for a regular weekly meeting, it deferred discussion of the draft after hearing Stalin's criticisms of it.[51]

The commission submitted a revised version of the draft decree on 2 January 1930. Reflecting Stalin's pressure to shorten the timetable in the main grain-growing regions, it allowed one or two years, not the originally envisaged two or three, for collectivizing the North Caucasus and the Lower and Middle Volga. It also omitted—presumably under pressure from Stalin, who had declared in his speech of 27 December that the kulak must on no account be allowed to join the collective farms—the original draft's provision for potential admission of cooperatively inclined kulaks to the probationary status of workers on collectives. The revised version now stated simply: "The kulak is not to be allowed into collective farms; by decisions of poor and middle peasants uniting in collective farms and of local soviets, the kulaks' means of production are to be confiscated and transferred to the indivisible funds of collective farms, kulaks are to be moved to distant and worst pieces of land, and malicious kulak elements are to be deported from the regions."[52]

Not even in the revised and purportedly final version, however, did the decree prove acceptable to Stalin. Encouraged by his hardline position, and probably directly instigated by him, a commission member named T. R. Ryskulov, who was a vice chairman of the Sovnarkom, then proposed to the Politburo a series of further radicalizing changes in keeping with Stalin's approach: to intensify the tempo of collectivization in stock-growing and technical-crop regions as well as grain-growing ones; to replace the provision on the peasant's preservation of small implements, poultry, and so on, with a "categorical instruction" on socializing possessions "without any restrictions"; and to exclude altogether any provision on voluntary withdrawal. On the latter point, Ryskulov's note said the commission wanted "to supplant the revolutionary character of the collective farms with hyper-voluntariness."[53]

Stalin saw to it that the Ryskulov proposals were adopted. He secured removal of the provisions for private retention of animals and other items, and for the right of voluntary withdrawal from the collective, on the ground that such matters were best dealt with in a model charter of the artel that was to be drafted by the Commissariat for Agriculture. He was in a position to do this because, on 4 January, he personally edited the final text of the decree together with commission chairman Yakovlev.[54] In the process, he also removed the commission's explicit instruction to local party organs not to be carried away by administrative enthusiasm into premature proclaiming of districts of wholesale collectivization. This was replaced by a vague warning against any "decreeing" of the collectivization movement that could threaten to make "real socialist competition in organizing collective farms" into a game of collectivization. Such a formulation left the way open for, if it did not invite, the very phenomenon of bureaucratic competition that the commission wanted to avoid. More important, the revised version's already abbreviated, tough provision on kulak policy was further reduced to the curt statement that in drafting the model charter for the artel as a transitional form of collective on the way to the commune, the Commissariat of Agriculture should take into account "the inadmissibility of allowing kulaks to join the collective farms."[55]

So emerged the decree of 5 January 1930, issued in the name of the Central Committee and entitled "On the Tempo of Collectivization and Measures of State Assistance in Collective Farm Construction." In its brevity, in the timetables specified, in the absence of the calming reassurances to the peasant that the Politburo commission had vainly tried to include in the document, and above all in its ominously brief reference to nonadmission of kulaks, this document bore the brand of Stalin's strategy of terror.

In acting as he did, Stalin was also motivated by an economic consideration. Many of the industrialization projects of the *piatiletka* were in remote and highly inclement parts of the country, which held no attraction for most citizens who were free to choose where they would work. If great numbers of peasants could be unceremoniously shipped to such areas and set to work on the hardest jobs at subsistence rations, their cheap impressed labor would make a big contribution to the industrial side of the second revolution. Here it is noteworthy that the resolution of the November 1929 plenum particularly stressed the importance of timber exports in connection with the need to "force the development of the export branches of the economy." Russia's great forests, and hence its lumbering, are concentrated in the Far North. On the eve of the plan period the USSR had a serious unemployment problem, and the industrialization drive was one way of absorbing surplus manpower, but apart from a relatively small number of enthusiasts among party members and dedicated youth, not many wanted to migrate to the bleak northern forests or the new construction sites in the east.[56]

Remembering Peter's lavish (for his time) use of forced labor in his drive to make Russia great and strong, Stalin was doubtlessly aware of what it would mean to have a large pool of people who could be made to work where they were needed without material incentives that the government could ill afford. This must have made him all the more insistent on a policy not of limited but wholesale deportation of kulaks into the interior, for which purpose the kulak *qua* kulak had to be stigmatized as an "accursed enemy." Besides, as Stalin observed in his speech to the agrarian Marxists, apropos the undesirability of wrapping the new policy of dekulakization in excessive fine print, "When the head's removed, there's no use crying over the hair."[57]

But why did Stalin take the highly incautious step of excluding from the collectivization decree the commission's point about the peasant being permitted to retain minor implements, poultry, a milk cow, and other small property after joining a collective farm? After all, this was a large part of the difference between the regime's preferred form of collective farm, the artel, and the commune. Since the decreed terroristic mass dekulakization would end the vacillating middle peasant's hesitation about joining the collective farm, why not make it easier for him to take this step by giving an explicit assurance—written into the decree by which local officials would be guided in collectivizing—that the peasant would *not* be dispossessed of virtually everything he owned save his cottage and clothes? The answer turns on an ominous phenomenon that had already begun in the last quarter of 1929: the mass slaughter of livestock by peasants who were being pressured into joining collective farms.

To various officials, both local and at the center, the logical countermeasure appeared to be to go at once to the "higher forms" of collective farm in which even small animals, poultry, and the family milk cow would be appropriated for the collective before they could be slaughtered by the peasants. In late December 1929, the governing board of the *Kolkhoz* Center enjoined local officials to pursue "maximum socialization of livestock and poultry in the collective farms," that is, in effect set course not toward the artel but toward the commune.[58] Still earlier, on 10 December, it sent out a telegram to local organizations ordering them to secure 100 percent socialization of draft animals and cows, 80 percent of pigs and 60 percent of sheep before the end of the spring sowing in the regions of wholesale collectivization and in the large collective farms. In other decisions of that time, it prescribed the socialization of domestic poultry, and the raising of the number of communes to the level of 25 percent of the total number of collective farms. Ivnitsky, who reports this information, adds: "Stalin, Molotov, and Kaganovich could not but know about this because all decisions of the USSR *Kolkhoz* Center were sent to them for their information, and G. N. Kaminsky and T. A. Yurkin [the chairmen of the board of the *Kolkhoz* Center in 1929–30] cleared important policy questions of collective farm construction with them."[59]

Stalin, it is plain, was one of the persons in official positions to whom preemptive seizure of the peasants' animals, down to the chickens in the cottage yard, appeared the only way to deal with the situation that the collectivization drive in the second half of 1929 was creating. The Central Committee decree, which would give guidance to local authorities and be known to the public, must not be in contradiction with actual instructions being issued through confidential governmental channels in response to the peasants' already apparent tendency to slaughter their stock rather than turn it over to the collectives. To strike out the Politburo commission's stipulation on retention of some animals was therefore the only course that Stalin could think of taking. The alternative was to beat a retreat in the collectivizing offensive itself—something against which his fighting nature and his whole political orientation rebelled.

What emerges is that Stalin placed his own regime before a *fait accompli*. Acting behind the scenes to give policy direction to the party-state's centralized bureaucracy, he managed to set in motion processes that were acquiring a momentum of their own and threatening to get out of hand. The Politburo commission was attempting to legislate the conduct of a second revolution that was already taking place.

Some Western historians have mistakenly believed that Stalin entered upon this revolution pragmatically, without premeditation, and with no vision of where the country was going under his leadership.[60] Whatever his miscalculations, and they were monumental, he acted with forethought. Here we would do well to hearken to his own words of 1927. Recalling his days as a political exile in northeastern Siberia during the World War, he said: "Have you seen the sort of rowers who row hard in the sweat of their brow but do not see whither the current is carrying them? I've seen such rowers on the Yenisei. They're honest and tireless rowers. The trouble is, they don't see and don't want to see that they can be driven by a wave onto the cliff where destruction threatens them."[61]

The recollection was unwittingly prophetic. Unlike those rowers on the Yenisei, this Bolshevik rower on political waters thought he knew where his boat was heading. He failed, however, to foresee the cataract that lay around the next bend of Russia's troubled history.

The cult of personality acquired such monstrous size because Stalin himself, using all conceivable methods, supported the glorification of his own person.

—N. KHRUSHCHEV, SPEECH TO THE TWENTIETH PARTY CONGRESS

7

THE CULT AND ITS CREATOR

VERY FEW PEOPLE knew that "Stalin" symbolized an ideal self to its bearer and was linked with an image of the party as an order of his faithful swordbearers. This unawareness stemmed in part from Stalin's studied effort to emulate in public Lenin's example of unassuming deportment. In private, moreover, he repeatedly affected disdain for adulation. In 1930, for example, he ended a letter to Ya. Shatunovsky, an Old Bolshevik, by saying, "You speak of your 'devotion' to me. Perhaps that phrase slipped out accidentally. Perhaps. But if it isn't an accidental phrase, I'd advise you to thrust aside the 'principle' of devotion to persons. It isn't the Bolshevik way. Have devotion to the working class, its party, its state. That's needed and good. But don't mix

---

A substantial portion of this chapter appeared in the *American Historical Review* (April 1979) under the title "The Rise of Stalin's Personality Cult."

it with devotion to persons, that empty and needless intellectuals' bauble."[1]

The man behind the mask of modesty was, however, hungry for the devotion he professed to scorn. Party comrades who had known him for long years, as well as observant lower officials whose work brought them into direct contact with him, were aware of this. Around 1930, for example, Eugene Lyons heard the following in a private conversation with a Soviet official who had known Stalin both before and after the Revolution. "Stalin," he said meditatively, "has one weakness. His Achilles' heel. That's his vanity. He may pretend to be annoyed with the hallelujahs of praise. But he does nothing to stop them. He always allows himself to be convinced too readily that the genuflecting is politically useful. He reacts to the mildest slight on his dignity as though it were an electric shock."[2]

An incident from Stalin's home life illustrates the official's comment. There was a caged parrot in one of the rooms of the Kremlin apartment. Stalin, whose custom it was to pace back and forth puffing on his pipe as he thought things out, regularly did so in that room. By uncouth habit, he would spit on the floor now and then as he paced. Once, the parrot imitated him spitting. Incensed rather than amused, Stalin reached into the cage with his pipe and killed the bird with a blow to its head.[3] Small as it is, the episode of the purged parrot reveals something important: how vulnerable Stalin was because of his painfully sensitive self-esteem.

The Sixteenth Party Congress, which met in Moscow in June–July 1930 in the midst of the collectivization drive, reflected Stalin's view of the significance of this drive in its resolution: "If the confiscation of the land from the landowners was the first step of the October Revolution in the countryside, the changeover to collective farms is the second and, moreover, decisive step, which marks a most important stage in building the foundation of a socialist society in the USSR."[4] The rural October called for recognition as such, and for homage to the leader. This thought found willing executors in the Mekhlises and other Stalin men now in charge of the publicity apparatus. The congress saw a new wave of acclaim for Stalin. On the first day, when he gave the main political report, *Pravda* featured on its front page a large drawing showing him in profile, speaking into the microphone, against the background of a picture on the wall of Lenin in profile. No subtlety was needed to grasp the message that Stalin was Lenin today.

Louis Fischer, who covered that event for *The Nation,* concluded his postcongress dispatch by saying: "A good friend might also advise Stalin to put a stop to the orgy of personal glorification of Stalin which has been permitted to sweep the country. . . . I have gone back over the newspapers from 1919 to 1922: Lenin never permitted such antics and he was more popular than Stalin can ever hope to be. . . . If Stalin is not responsible for this performance he at least tolerates it. He could stop it by pressing a button." A Foreign Commissariat press officer, whose duties included the briefing of Stalin on foreign coverage of Soviet affairs, later told Fischer that when he translated the passage just quoted, Stalin responded with an expletive: *svoloch!* (the bastard).[5]

In his vision of the party as his mother or an order of swordbearers, he was its idolized leader. But the actual Bolshevik party of that time was no more a solid phalanx of Stalin enthusiasts than the actual Stalin was the genius leader of his imagination. Although he had won considerable prestige and popularity in the party in the post-Lenin years, Stalin in 1930 was very far from being the cult object that Lenin had been for the Bolsheviks. Party people knew him as the *khozyain* (boss). To many he was a canny and capable leader whose policy positions were, in the prevailing circumstances (or those he had made to appear to prevail), persuasive. He had some reliable old intimates like Voroshilov, some sycophantic followers like Kaganovich, some adoring or at least studiously self-ingratiating protégés in his Central Committee Secretariat, and no doubt very many rank-and-file Communists were ready to render him full fealty. But in higher party circles the attitudes toward him were diverse. There were intimates and underlings who saw or pretended to see him as the idealized Stalin. Others were friendly and supportive without adulating him, still others had reservations about him, still others nourished deep doubts, and some quietly opposed him. Many older Bolsheviks also remembered episodes in his political past that he preferred to forget because of their inconsistency with his idealized image of himself.

Whereas he felt constrained to blot out such discrepancies, the actual party as it existed at the start of the 1930s did not. The danger was that his effort to prove the ideal Stalin in action by masterminding a rural October would have disastrous results, causing the actual party to withdraw much of its support and Stalin to react against it with murderous wrath. The rift between his ideal party and the actual one thus contained seeds of the mass tragedy that would befall the latter before the decade's end.

The Premier Philosopher

After the Sixteenth Congress, the wave of acclaim of Stalin subsided. Although his name appeared often in the press, there was no regular flow of laudatory publicity about him during the rest of 1930 and much of 1931. Shortly afterward the situation changed, as a result of certain steps that he took. The first was in philosophy, where a school of devotées of Hegelian dialectics, led by A. M. Deborin, had been dominant in the later 1920s.

Although Lenin had some philosophical writings to his credit, it was not uncommon then to place him below Plekhanov in philosophy. Deborin's disciples, moreover, tended to rate Deborin as the Engels or Lenin of today in philosophy.[6] As for Stalin, his standing in Marxist philosophy was virtually nil. Evidence on this point exists in the form of a list, published in 1929, of writings with which students entering graduate work in the Communist Academy's Institute of Philosophy were supposed to be familiar. Thirty-three works were listed under dialectical and historical materialism (that is, philosophy): six by Marx and Engels came first, followed by six of Lenin's, then four by Plekhanov, then seven by Deborin. Then came entry number 23, Stalin, *Problems of Leninism,* which even at that low ranking was very probably included for diplomatic reasons, and the list (Western philosophers might be interested to note) ended with Descartes, Hobbes, Hume, and Berkeley.[7]

Stalin could not rest content with this situation. For many years he had nourished pretensions in Marxist philosophy, and during the 1920s he quietly continued to enhance his command of it. He called in Jan Sten, a leading philosopher of the Deborin School, to guide him in the study of dialectics. Thrice-weekly sessions went on from 1925 until some time in 1928, after which Stalin called a halt.[8] Then, in late 1929, he sounded the future Stalin school's characteristic note by telling the conference of agrarian Marxists that Marxist theory must keep in step with the needs of practice.

Not long after that, three young members of the Institute of Red Professors (a key party school), Pavel Yudin, Mark B. Mitin, and V. Ral'tsevich, took up Stalin's theme in a *Pravda* article, arguing that philosophy should apply itself in a new way to theoretical problems of practice in the building of socialism. They lauded Stalin for showing an example of "deepened understanding of Marxist-Leninist dialectics" in his theoretical formulation of the idea of a struggle against both Left and Right deviations; and called for a corresponding two-front struggle in philosophy.[9] Although Deborin was not openly attacked, the article pointed to his school as the enemy on the philosophical second front. The authors were in effect coming forward as the nucleus of a new, Stalin school in Soviet philosophy. Stalin's approbation—if not also inspiration—was reflected in the unusual note published along with the article, saying "The editors associate themselves with the main propositions of the present article."

Soon Stalin intervened personally. On 9 December 1930 he spoke out on philosophical matters in an interview with a group of philosophers from the Institute of Red Professors. Mitin later quoted him as saying that it was necessary to "rake up and dig up all the manure that has accumulated in questions of philosophy and natural science." In particular, it was necessary to "rake up everything written by the Deborinite group—all that is erroneous in the philosophical sector." Deborin's school was a philosophical form of revisionism which, according to Stalin, could be called "Menshevizing idealism." It was necessary, he said further, to expose a number of erroneous philosophical positions of Plekhanov, who had always looked down upon Lenin. Stalin kept emphasizing in the interview that Lenin had raised dialectical materialism to a new plane. Before Lenin, materialism has been atomistic, he said. On the basis of new scientific advances, Lenin produced a Marxist analysis of the theory of matter. But while he created much that was new in all spheres of Marxism, Lenin was very modest and didn't like to talk about his contributions. It was incumbent upon his disciples, however, to clarify all aspects of his innovative role.[10]

Stalin was assuming the role of the premier living Marxist philosopher. Albeit coarsely, he spoke as one philosopher, and *the* authoritative one, to others. He was clearing the way for his self-elevation by mobilizing the subservient young would-be disciples to dethrone Deborin and Plekhanov from their positions of eminence. "Deborinism" along with "Menshevizing idealism" would now become polemical bywords for philosophical heresy, and future lists of mandatory advance reading for graduate students in philosophy would no longer put Stalin in twenty-third place. Deborin's treatises would not figure in them at all.

Stalin did not directly refer in the interview to his own philosophical credentials, although he implied them by his pronouncements. But he employed an indirect strategy of cult building by the way he dealt with Lenin. He combined praise of Lenin as a philosopher with the warning not to be put off by Lenin's modest forbearance to speak about his contributions in this field. This carried the Aesopian message, which did not escape the alert Yudin and Mitin, that *they* should not be put off by Stalin's modesty on the same count. Stalin was promoting Lenin's primacy in philosophy as a vehicle of his own claim to similar primacy.

Before Deborin himself came under attack, he was pressured to cooperate in his own downgrading and his school's obliteration. According to his own subsequent account in a letter to Khrushchev after Stalin died, the head of the Central Committee's Propaganda and Agitation Department (that is, a man of Stalin's apparatus—R. T.) informed him at the close of 1930 that a single authority was now to be established in all fields, philosophy included, and that authority was to be Stalin. Afterward, Mitin, Yudin, and Ral'tsevich visited him and delivered an ultimatum: at a public meeting he must denounce his disciples (Sten, N. A. Karev, I. K. Luppol, and others) as enemies of the people and proclaim Stalin a great philosopher. Deborin refused. His name then figured along with the others in denunciations of his philosophical school.[11]

Other actions followed. Mitin replaced Deborin as editor of the philosophical journal *Under the Banner of Marxism*. In 1931 *Bol'shevik* carried a bitter criticism of "Menshevizing idealism" as found in the *Great Soviet Encyclopedia*. In castigating Deborin and others of his school as carriers of this disease, the *Bol'shevik* author stated: "Materialist dialectics really must be elaborated. But this elaboration must be carried out on the basis of the works of Marx, Engels, Lenin, and Stalin. . . ."[12] Here appeared the holy quartet—Marx, Engels, Lenin, Stalin—which would become the symbolic centerpiece of Stalinist thought and culture, replete with the four huge, equal-sized portraits on the facade of Moscow's Bolshoi Theater for May Day, 7 November, and other special occasions.

The enthronement of Stalin as Communism's first philosopher in succession to Marx, Engels, and Lenin had taken place. Embryonic in this development was the mono-authority regime that became a hallmark of intellectual culture in the Stalin period and distinguished it from pre-Stalinist Bolshevism. To treat Lenin's philosophical writings as sacrosanct dogma, for example, had not been the practice. Starting now, Stalin became not only the first philosopher but also the authority figure in some other fields. In still others a Stalin-surrogate—Andrei Vyshinsky, for example, in law— was, so to speak, subenthroned as the authority figure. Part of the role of such Stalin-surrogates was to glorify Stalin's thought in the process of hunting for heresy and establishing Stalinist truth for their own disciplines. Consequently, those chosen for this role were men who combined intellectual acumen, in most cases, with absolutely reliable servility. Anyone with any independence of mind, no matter how zealous a Communist, was unacceptable.

The second area Stalin selected for building the stately edifice of the Stalin cult was party history. Here he was moving into a field of great political sensitivity, for the annals of the Bolshevik past were the movement's inner sanctum. He was also treading on ground of sacred personal concern, namely, his revolutionary biography.

He made his move in the homely manner that so many people choose in order to set the record straight: he wrote a letter to the editors.

Of Real and Other Bolsheviks

At the outset of the 1930s, research on the history of the Marxist movement was still pursued with a certain freedom, contentious issues were seriously debated, and work of scholarly character was still produced in Soviet Russia. One set of questions, having to do with the German Social Democratic party (SPD) and the pre-1914 Second International, was deemed so important that in 1929 the Communist Academy's Institute of History set up a special study group for it. The group's academic secretary was A. G. Slutsky.

In October 1930 *Proletarian Revolution* printed an article by Slutsky. His main topic was Lenin's position in connection with the internal divisions in the pre-1914 SPD, where a revisionist wing led by Eduard Bernstein was opposed by a dominant centrist group, whose leaders were Karl Kautsky and August Bebel and whose viewpoint was taken by many, Lenin included, as representative of revolutionary Marxism. The German party also had a group of left radicals led by Rosa Luxemburg. Slutsky wrote that she, as early as 1911, grasped and openly discussed the basically "opportunist" nature of Kautskyan centrism, whereas Lenin, although he had shown a certain critical caution toward the Kautsky-Bebel SPD leadership ever since 1907, continued to pin hopes on it. The facts therefore showed "a certain underestimation by Lenin of the centrist danger in the German party before the war."[13]

The publication of this article shows that although a Lenin cult existed in those days, it was still possible in 1930 to publish an article that did not treat Lenin as an infallible, preternaturally foresightful genius beyond human limitations. True, *Proletarian Revolution's* editors—the Old Bolsheviks Saveliev, Adoratsky, Ol'minsky, Baevsky, and Gorin—seemed to sense potential danger, for they inserted an introductory footnote saying they were not in agreement with Slutsky's presentation of Lenin and hence were printing his essay "for purposes of discussion." But clearly they were unprepared for the thunderbolt that its appearance provoked. Stalin was infuriated and wrote a letter of article length entitled "On Some Questions of the History of Bolshevism." It was printed simultaneously in *Proletarian Revolution* and *Bol'shevik* at the end of October 1931.

First, Stalin mauled Slutsky's position into unrecognizability, contending that to accuse Lenin of having underestimated the danger of centrism in the prewar SPD was to accuse him of underestimating the danger of "veiled opportunism," which in turn was to accuse him of not having been a "real Bolshevik" before 1914—since a real Bolshevik could never underestimate the danger of veiled opportunism. It was simply an "axiom" that Bolshevism arose and grew strong in ruthless struggle against all shades of centrism. So the editors should never have accepted Slutsky's "balderdash" and "crooked pettifogging" as a discussion piece; the genuineness of Lenin's Bolshevism was not discussible. Secondly, Stalin protested against Slutsky's favorable treatment of Rosa Luxemburg and the left radicals in the pre-1914 SPD. He was deeply irked by the very idea that Lenin might have had something to learn from these people.

The strong Russian-nationalist tinge of Stalin's Bolshevism made itself felt in his letter. It presented a Russocentric view of the history of the European Marxist movement. It said that the "Russian Bolsheviks" were justified in setting up their own positions as the test of the Marxist revolutionary validity of this or that position of left Social Democrats abroad. Lenin's forecast of 1902, in *What Is To Be Done?*, that the Russian proletariat might yet become "the vanguard of the international revolutionary proletariat" had been brilliantly confirmed by subsequent events. Then and now it was not for Western Marxists to give lessons to their Russian brethren, but vice versa.

To say or imply otherwise, as Slutsky did, was "Trotskyist contraband." To give weight to this ugly charge, Stalin declared Slutsky's thesis about Lenin's pre-1914 underestimation of centrism to be a cunning way of suggesting to the "unsophisticated reader" that Lenin only became a real revolutionary after the war started and he "rearmed" with the help of Trotsky's theory of the growing of the bourgeois-democratic into a socialist revolution (the permanent revolution theory). Lenin himself, Stalin recalled, had written in 1905 that "we stand for uninterrupted revolution" and "we'll not stop halfway." However, contrabandists like Slutsky were not interested in such facts, which were verifiable from Lenin's writings. Slutsky, Stalin noted elsewhere in the letter, had spoken in his article of the unavailability of some Lenin documents pertaining to the period in question. "But who except hopeless bureaucrats can rely on paper documents alone? Who but archive rats fails to realize that parties and leaders must be tested primarily by their *deeds* and not simply by their declarations."

Toward the end of the letter, Stalin's language shifted from the rude to the sinister. In giving Slutsky a forum for his contraband, the editors showed a "rotten liberalism" toward Trotskyist-minded people. This was current among a segment of Bolsheviks who failed to understand that Trotskyism had long since ceased to be a faction of Communism and turned into a forward detachment of the counterrevolutionary bourgeoisie. Here Stalin was repeating in public the argument of the Politburo memorandum he had written in 1929,[14] transferring Trotskyist affiliation or sympathies from the category of a political error to that of a crime against the Soviet state. In concluding his argument Stalin now said, "This is why liberalism toward Trotskyism, even though defeated and masked, is a form of bungling that borders on crime, on treason to the working class." Hence the editors' task was "to put the study of party history onto scientific Bolshevik rails and to sharpen vigilance against Trotskyist and all other falsifiers of the history of our party, systematically ripping off their masks." This was all the more necessary in that certain genuinely Bolshevik party historians were themselves guilty of errors that poured water on the mills of the

Slutskys. Unfortunately, said Stalin at the end, one such person was Comrade Yaroslavsky, whose books on party history, in spite of their merits, contained a number of errors in principle and of historical character.[15] E. Yaroslavsky was the dean of party historians and secretary of the Central Party Control Commission.

Considering what Stalin had said earlier about centrism, it is easy to see why he would have been outraged by Slutsky's argument that Lenin had underestimated the centrist danger in the SPD. To fight against Left and Right deviations was not to be a centrist, Stalin had contended in 1928, any more than it had been centrist of Lenin to combat both Menshevism on the right and the left sectarianism condemned in *Left-Wing Communism*. Centrism meant "adaptation," and on that account was "alien and repulsive to Leninism."[16] How then—no matter what documents the archive rats might turn up—could a real revolutionary, that is, a Bolshevik, ever, even briefly, underestimate the centrist danger? To a mind that so reasoned, Slutsky and his like fully deserved the merciless bawling out that the letter gave them and severe punishment as well. Slutsky was arrested not long after Stalin's letter appeared and spent about twenty years in exile.[17]

But Stalin's letter, in addition to expressing rage, pursued a purpose. It solicited a Stalin cult in party history by the very fact that Stalin produced it and by its tone and content. In writing it (or, conceivably, having it written to his specifications), he arrogated to himself the position of premier party historian and arbiter of contentious issues in that sensitive area. Its publication was Stalin's self-assertion as the supreme authority on the very subject that would form the core of his personality cult as it developed further in the 1930s: Bolshevism's past and the parts that he and others had played in it.

Secondly, in the letter, as in the earlier interview with philosophers, Stalin followed the strategy of cult building via the assertion of Lenin's infallibility. By making the party's previous *vozhd'* an iconographic figure beyond criticism, Stalin's letter implicitly nominated the successor-*vozhd'* for similar treatment. Since he, Stalin, was the man whom the party had saluted in 1929 as its acknowledged chief in succession to Lenin, would it not behoove party historians to be as careful not to find lapses or blemishes in his political past as the letter in effect ordered them to be where *Lenin's* past was concerned? People as experienced as Bolshevik party intellectuals in reading delphic utterances were bound to ask such questions as they pondered or discussed with one another the implications of the letter. Stalin even gave them a broad hint with a phrase used twice in the letter: "Lenin (the Bolsheviks)." Lenin, by Stalin's fiat, stood for real Bolshevik revolutionism as distinct from any and all bogus varieties, left, right, or center.

The words in parenthesis pluralized his revolutionary rectitude. They made it more inclusive without giving names. But anyone with the intelligence to be a party historian could guess whose name ought to follow Lenin's on the list of "Bolsheviks" in Stalin's normative sense of the term.

Thirdly, the letter stated quite explicitly that one should evaluate the party pasts of real revolutionaries not on the basis of documents that archive rats might turn up or fail to, but on the basis of their "deeds." The latter naturally would have to be documented so far as possible. Stalin, as later transpired, was the arch-archive rat of the Soviet Union, or more precisely the leader of a whole pack of them, although his was as much a hunger for destruction or concealment of documents as for their discovery. So, if one thought at all deeply about the implications of his letter, the conclusion was that a party historian should not be guided *a la* Slutsky by what he could document, but by what he knew *a priori* must be true, for example, that Lenin, being a "real Bolshevik," could never have underestimated centrism, or that Stalin, also a "real Bolshevik," could never have taken an un-Bolshevik position at any juncture. The function of documentary materials, or of their concealment, was to help establish such higher truth. To use them otherwise was to be a slanderer and falsifier. Consequently, the message of Stalin's tirade against falsifiers was that one *must* be ready to falsify (in the normal meaning of the word) whenever the party's view of history—as revealed by word from Stalin or his spokesmen—should so dictate.

The cult-building purport of Stalin's letter may be shown further by examining the Yaroslavsky work that it criticized. Stalin did not make clear the nature of the errors to which he was alluding, and Yaroslavsky himself seems to have been somewhat baffled. He wrote Stalin several letters asking clarification but received no answer.[18] It has been remarked, however, that in various party discussions prior to the Stalin letter, Yaroslavsky had defended every Leninist's right to voice his view on "any controversial question" without fear of being branded a "revisionist."[19] From Stalin's standpoint, such a position would certainly be "rotten liberalism," hence an error in principle. As for historical errors, a quick glance through volume 4 of the party history published in 1929 under Yaroslavsky's editorship and devoted to 1917–21 could have indicated to him at least one area of difficulty: while poisonously anti-Trotsky in its account, for instance, of Trotsky's position in the Soviet trade union controversy of 1920, the book treated Trotskyism as the (wrongheaded) faction of Communism that Stalin now said it had "long since" ceased to be; it did not show Trotskyism to be, even incipiently, the forward detachment of the counterrevolutionary bourgeoisie that Stalin declared it to have become. Even its reprinted photos seemed ill chosen in some cases. Here, for example, was Lenin's original fifteen-man Council of People's Commissars with Trotsky on the upper right flanking Lenin (and Rykov, appropriately, flanking Lenin on the left, that is, Lenin's right), while Stalin appeared on the lower left next to the Kremlin wall; and here, on another page, was an old photo of the Soviet delegation to the Brest talks, with Trotsky, its leader, looking handsome and impressive in the top row.[20] What Yaroslavsky may have been a little slow in grasping was that affirmation of Stalin necessitated the retrospective denigration of many others who had played more prominent parts in the Revolution than he.

Further, this volume of the Yaroslavsky-edited party history made brief reference to the well-known fact, acknowledged by Stalin himself in a 1924 speech, that in March 1917, prior to Lenin's return to Russia and the issuance of his "April Theses," Stalin had shared with Muranov and Kamcncv "an erroneous position" on policy toward the Provisional Government (advocacy of mere pressure on it to leave the war). This easily documentable truth of party history as written before 1929 was one of the Yaroslavsky "mistakes" to which Stalin's letter alluded. It became an unfact in party history as rewritten in the 1930s by Yaroslavsky and others. The system of falsification extended to retrospective censorship by or for Stalin of his own earlier writings, for example the deletion from later printings of *Problems of Leninism* of his 1924 reference to the position he took in March 1917. Subservient writers falsified actual party history in conformity with an idealized image of the "real Bolshevik" who *could* not have strayed from the path of revolutionary rectitude—an image representing Stalin's self-concept. The logical groundwork of this system of falsification was laid in Stalin's letter to *Proletarian Revolution*.

The Glorifiers at Work

Hell broke loose on the party history and theory "fronts" as soon as Stalin's letter appeared. The Communist Academy's institutes hastily called meetings to discuss the document's implications for their work. *Proletarian Revolution,* after putting out the issue containing the letter, suspended publication in 1932, and when it reappeared early in 1933 it had a wholly new editorial board.

Soviet archival sources reveal the following facts.[21] All Soviet historical journals received instructions to print the text of Stalin's letter and appropriate editorials on its meaning for their respective areas. In a confidential letter of 26 November 1931 to the editorial board of one such journal, *The Class Struggle,* Mekhlis said that materials in preparation should be written through the prism of Stalin's propositions. The presidium of the Communist Academy met on 31 November to review its affiliates' responses to the Stalin letter. K. G. Lurie, academic secretary of the Society of Marxist Historians, said that Trotskyist contraband had already been brought to light in numerous works. She combined the unmasking of contrabandists with criticism of three well-known party figures—Yaroslavsky, Karl Radek, and I. I. Mints.

Other reports showed that not only party history but all sectors of the "theoretical front" were being brought into line with higher-level authoritative interpretation of Stalin's letter. A representative of literary criticism denounced the "Menshevik-Trotskyist view" of Gorky's writings, without indicating what it was, and said Stalin's letter necessitated criticism of the literary policy—also not identified—of the Second International. One Butaev, representing the Institute of Economics, said it had set up a special brigade to reexamine the economic theory front from the angle of Stalin's letter and "bring to light Trotskyist contraband in the economics literature." Examples were the still prevalent petty-bourgeois and Trotskyist ideas equating socialism with equal remuneration, and the view, voiced in a book issued in 1931, that Ford's factories were a model for Soviet rationalization of labor processes. The legal theorist Pashukanis, speaking for the Institute of Soviet Construction and Law, criticized a textbook by two authors (one of them Butaev) in which no account was taken of what Stalin had said in 1927 about the proletarian state.

The pell-mell rush to ferret out "Trotskyist contraband" and "rotten liberalism" was deeply troubling to various persons in responsible posts. Stalin was not yet an absolute dictator; many in high places failed to realize that he was on the way to becoming one. So, some prominent Old Bolsheviks, including Ol'minsky, Yaroslavsky, V. Knorin, and N. Lukin, sought to restrain those (Yaroslavsky called them "glorifiers" in a handwritten note found decades later in the party archives) who were taking Stalin's letter as a new gospel. Thus, Yaroslavsky warned that there were certain unprincipled people who "want to make capital on this question" (that is, the Stalin letter). But this statement, along with his handwritten note saying "How the glorifiers 'worked me over' in 1931," did not see publication until 1966.[22]

One month after Stalin's letter appeared, his headquarters swung into action against the pleaders for restraint. On 1 December 1931, Kaganovich gave a long speech to the Institute of Red Professors on the occasion of its tenth anniversary. When its text appeared in *Pravda* some days later, it became clear that the speech was meant as an address to the whole Soviet intelligentsia. But "address" isn't the right word; the document may better be described as a many-thousand-worded peremptory command issued by drill sergeant Kaganovich to the army of the intelligentsia, ordering it to snap to attention in the light of General Stalin's letter.

The importance of Stalin's letter, Kaganovich said, did not lie in the insignificant figure of the ex-Menshevik Slutsky, whom Stalin had pulverized in passing; it lay in exposing the rotten liberalism of *Proletarian Revolution*'s editors toward deviations from Bolshevism and distortions of party history. But this journal was not the only weak spot. A still weaker one was Comrade Yaroslavsky's four-volume history. Among his illustrations of the history's grave errors, Kaganovich mentioned its "erroneous and harmful assessment of the role of the Bolsheviks in the first period of 1917, [its] foul slander of the Bolsheviks." This was a veiled rebuke to Yaroslavsky for his reference to Stalin's "erroneous position" in March 1917. Then came a methodological pointer. One had to grasp the "flexibility of Lenin's tactics" in order to comprehend party history, and not look for a passage where Lenin said in so many words, "Kautsky is a bastard." What, in other words, a "real Bolshevik" said or failed to say at a particular time was not the touchstone of historical truth; the documents must be interpreted according to the canons of the "real-Bolshevik-revolutionary-can-do-no-wrong" school.

Kaganovich wound up with an implicit call for an intensification of the ongoing heresy hunt. Difficulties were rife, the fight was not over, the class struggle was continuing. 'Opportunism is now trying to creep into our ranks, covering itself up, embellishing itself, crawling on its belly, trying to penetrate into crannies, and trying in particular to crawl through the gates of the history of our party." Radek was wrong when in his recent speech he described the Comintern as a channel through which many different currents and brooklets flowed into the Bolshevik party. No, the party was no meeting place of turbid brooklets, but a "monolithic stream" with every resource to smash all obstacles on its path. The meaning was as clear as the metaphor was mixed: fall in line or be destroyed.[23]

The pleaders for restraint, and others (who did not plead openly), fell in line. Within twelve days following Kaganovich's speech of 1 December, *Pravda* carried letters of recantation from Radek, Yaroslavsky, and the party historian Konstantin Popov. Radek pleaded guilty to all Kaganovich's charges and joined the attack on "Luxemburgianism." Yaroslavsky acknowledged a whole series of "most gross mistakes" in the four-volume history, including "an unobjective, in essence Trotskyist treatment of the Bolsheviks' position in the February–March period of the Revolution of 1917" (Trotskyist, presumably, because Trotsky was one of those who had called attention to the generally known facts about Stalin's position then). He also disavowed the view, reportedly expressed by Mints in a recent speech, that the authors of the four-volume history had erred because of their objectivity and that what was now being asked of party historians was "not so much objectivity as political expediency." No, lied Yaroslavsky, the party had not and could not demand unobjectivity from historians; the problem with the four-volume work was that it had sinned against objectivity.[24] Resigning himself to the situation, he started work on the glorifying biography of Stalin that would be published later in the 1930s.

The heresy hunt had the character of a witch hunt. Falling in line meant more than pleading guilty to errors. To prove the seriousness of one's recantation, one had to join the chorus of accusers. Only by denouncing others' Trotskyist contraband could one demonstrate one's own real Bolshevism. Such was a law of what was now becoming a ritual part of the political culture. One had to join the hunt to protect oneself from being unmasked as a witch, or to show that one's already exposed witchhood was not an incurable case and was being expiated. Yaroslavsky's public disavowal of his friend Mints was one of many examples.

The letter to *Proletarian Revolution* was a turning point. From the time of its appearance, the glorifying of Stalin became one of Russia's great growth industries. No field of culture was exempted from the task of finding inspiration for its activity in the letter. The February 1932 issue of *For A Socialist Accounting,* for example, discussed its implications in an article that bore the title: "For Bolshevik Vigilance on the Bookkeeping Theory Front." But revolutionary history and Stalin's place in it remained the central concern. A small example, typical of many, was an article published shortly after Stalin's letter appeared. It denounced a book on Comintern history on the ground that Stalin's name was mentioned only twice.[25]

Stalin took a further hand in his self-promotion. Having asserted himself as premier party historian, he delivered another lecture in reply to two party members, Olekhnovich and Aristov, who had written separately to him in response to the letter; and his answers, dated 15 and 25 January 1932, were published in *Bol'shevik* the following August. Olekhnovich, apparently, had tried to show himself more Stalinist than Stalin. He suggested that "Trotskyism *never was* a faction of Communism" but "*all the time* was a faction of Menshevism" although for a certain period of time the Communist party had (wrongly) *regarded* Trotsky and the Trotskyists as real Bolsheviks. In knocking this construction down, Stalin showed the hair-splitting quality of his mind. Undeniably, he said, Trotskyism at one time was a faction of Communism, but forever oscillating between Bolshevism and Menshevism; hence, even when they did belong to the Bolshevik party the Trotskyists had never been "real Bolsheviks." Thus, on the one hand the Trotskyists had never been "real Bolsheviks" (hereby Stalin upheld the normative content of that notion), yet they had, for a while, really formed a faction of the party. The upshot: "In actual fact, Trotskyism was a faction of Menshevism before the Trotskyists joined our party, temporarily became a faction of Communism after the Trotskyists' entry into our party, and again became a faction of Menshevism after the Trotskyists' banishment from our party. 'The dog went back to its puke.' "[26]

These further pronouncements could not but confirm to professionals that they should look to Stalin's writings and sayings as scripture. As if to meet their need, party publications in 1932 started printing early Staliniana, such as Stalin's virtually unknown letter of 1910 to Lenin from Sol'vychegodsk exile and his little known "Letters from the Caucasus" of that same year. Meanwhile, the glorifiers set about rewriting history in accordance with Stalin's canons and in a manner calculated to accentuate his role and merits in the party's revolutionary past while discrediting those of his enemies. The skewed Stalinist version of Bolshevism's biography began to emerge. Grosser falsification still lay ahead.

The rise of the Stalin cult brought not the eclipse of the Lenin cult but its far-reaching modification. Instead of two cults in juxtaposition, there emerged a hyphenate cult of an infallible Lenin-Stalin. In one respect Lenin now "grew" in stature: he became the original Stalinist "real Bolshevik" who *could* not have erred. But by being tied like a Siamese twin to his successor, he was inescapably diminished in certain ways. Only those facets of his life and work that could be connected with Stalin's were available for full-scale idealization, and whatever was not Stalin-referential had to be kept in the background. In effect, parts of Lenin's life had to be deemphasized and other parts rearranged, modified, or touched up to put Stalin in the idealized picture.

Thus Stalin was now portrayed as sharing in Lenin's exploits. He was shown as having been from an early time Lenin's righthand man, on whom the leader leaned for counsel and support at key points in the development of the Revolution and after. The marking, on 5 May 1932, of the twentieth anniversary of *Pravda*'s founding may be taken as an illustration. At the beginning, said *Pravda*'s anniversary editorial, Lenin "wrote articles for the paper nearly every day—with the closest participation and guidance of Comrade *Stalin,* particularly at the time when Lenin was hiding underground." So, in the dual cult, the younger figure emerges as a co-Lenin who naturally takes over when Lenin number one is away from the immediate scene of action.

Yaroslavsky had by now not simply fallen in line but taken a place in the vanguard of the glorifiers. Given an opportunity to contribute an article in commemoration of the twentieth anniversary of the Prague Conference of January 1912, he found a shrewd way of retrospectively portraying Stalin as practically a founder of the Bolshevik party. It was a generally accepted truth, attested by Lenin, that Bolshevism as a political current had existed from 1903, when the Bolshevik-Menshevik schism occurred at the Russian Marxist party's Second Congress. But the Bolshevik party's formal existence as such dated only from the all-Bolshevik Prague Conference, at which Lenin set up what had been a faction as a separate party no longer organizationally tied to the Mensheviks. It was in the aftermath of the Prague Conference that Stalin was elevated (by cooptation, not election) to membership in the party Central Committee. Yaroslavsky obscured the embarrassing fact of Stalin's cooptation by saying: "At the conference a Bolshevik Central Committee was elected in the persons of Lenin, Stalin, Zinoviev, Ordzhonikidze, Belostotsky, Shvartsman, Goloshchekin, Spandarian, and Ia. M. Sverdlov (some of these comrades were coopted into the Central Committee subsequently)." And by writing with heavy emphasis, "The Prague Conference was a *turning-point moment in the history of the Bolshevik party*," he contrived to portray Stalin by indirection as having been present at the party's creation.[27]

It took a while for even clever party ministers of the transformed cult to comprehend and apply its special canons. One zealous glorifier, S. E. Sef, managing secretary of the journal *Marxist Historian,* provisionally gave the title "Marx, Engels, Stalin" to the leading article of a planned special issue for the oncoming fiftieth anniversary, in March 1933, of the death of Marx, but his omission of Lenin was corrected before the issue appeared.[28] Sef had failed to grasp that Lenin *qua* coleader remained a cult-object. In the dual cult, however, the figure of the successor began now to tower over that of the predecessor. For example, a foreign correspondent's count of "political icons" (portraits and busts of leaders) in shop windows along several blocks of Moscow's Gorky Street on 7 November 1933 showed Stalin leading Lenin by 103 to 58.[29]

Stalin's early revolutionary years in Transcaucasia began to attract reverent attention. A pamphlet published in Georgia portrayed the young Stalin as a heroic leader in underground direction of revolutionary activities in Batum in 1901–2.[30] On 14 March 1933, *Pravda* marked the fiftieth anniversary of Marx's death by lauding Stalin's theoretical contributions to materialist dialectics. The phrase "classical works of Marx, Engels, Lenin, and Stalin" was now commonplace. Partizdat, the party publishing house, was savagely criticized for failure to eliminate a series of minor misprints ("as if in a book by Comrade Stalin 'minor' misprints are allowable!"—the critic parenthetically exclaimed) in the latest printing of the fastest selling of the classics, Stalin's collection of articles and speeches, *Problems of Leninism.*[31] Overall figures released in early 1934 show that the classics had been published in 1932–33 in the following numbers: 7 million copies of Marx's and Engels' works, 14 million of Lenin's, and

16.5 million of Stalin's, including two million copies of *Problems of Leninism*. The latter was now well on the way to becoming one of the world's best sellers of the second quarter of the twentieth century. By 1949, 17 million copies of this work were in print in fifty-two languages.

Who were the glorifiers? Very many assisted in the process, ranging from sycophants in Stalin's entourage to obscure ideological workers like Lurie. Some, without doubt, were persons devoted to Stalin or to the man they idealistically perceived him to be; others were simply careerists who often lacked strong qualification in intellectual work but were shrewd and cynical enough to grasp opportunities for self-advancement inherent in the Stalin-glorifying enterprise. One who made his way into the inner circle and rose to dizzy heights of power by exploiting Stalin's susceptibility to adulation and urge to embellish his revolutionary biography was the Georgian secret policeman Lavrenti Beria, who became party chief of the Transcaucasus in 1932 with Stalin's backing. The one quality shared by all the glorifiers, high and low, was servility.

The Need for Enemies

The other side of Stalin's grandiosity was aggression. He was a venomous hater and a nemesis of those whom he hated. This characteristic was, so to speak, the underside of the personality cult.

Extreme self-idealizing such as that seen in Stalin inescapably leads to conflict—within the person and with others. Being at best humanly limited and fallible, such an individual is bound in practice, in his actual self and his performance, to fall short of the ideal self's standards of perfection and supremely ambitious goals of achievement and glory. He will make mistakes, very likely all the greater because of his need to score only spectacular triumphs. For all this he will unconsciously accuse, berate, condemn, and despise himself—unconsciously because he can admit into awareness only those aspects of himself and his life that are, or appear to be, in keeping with his ideal self or that can be rationalized conformably with its dictates. Everything that has to be denied and repressed—the failures, faults, errors, miscalculations, shortcomings, ugly traits, wrongdoing and, it may be, villainies—forms in the aggregate a hated self that remains in the personality system despite its repression.

But self-condemnation and self-hate are no less real for being unconscious. They are so painfully disturbing that the individual feels driven to relieve himself by turning his self-hate outward against others whom he can freely denounce, accuse, despise, condemn, and possibly punish. Such projection of self-hate, along with the faults and misdeeds that have aroused it, means that the individual actually experiences his own failings as those of others and his own self-condemnation as condemnation of others. It is a radical inner defense, which performs a cathartic function. The submerged feelings are admitted into consciousness and expressed openly against people in whom the inner enemy, the hated self, appears embodied. The self-hate comes into awareness as hatred of other people, and is acted upon in aggression against them. Stalin's is a classic case. From youth onward projection became second nature with him, and was no doubt involved in his history of ugly scrapes and resulting reputation among old revolutionaries as a difficult character. In later years, the more there was in his conduct that he had to deny and censor out of consciousness, the more he found to hate, blame, and punish in others.

The self-idealizing individual's suppressed self-hate makes his pride system a shaky structure that requires buttressing by regular reassurance from significant others—persons in the circle of those whose opinions matter to him—that he is in fact the superlative being he considers himself to be. Stalin's circle of significant others comprised all Soviet citizens and in particular those who belonged to the Communist Party; foreign Communists figured in it as well. What he expected of these people, as the cult's transformation in the early 1930s has clearly shown, was affirmation of his idealized political biography and arrogated merits as the authentic reality. A party of "real Bolsheviks" must be a collection of Lenin-*Stalin* glorifiers.

When some significant others failed this test, by speaking or acting in ways that impugned the authenticity of the idealized Stalin, he could only react with violent anger and the resolve to get back at the offenders in some way that would be very painful to them.[32] Unable to accept the possibility that the idealized version of himself was faulty, he had to construe their behavior as a deliberate attempt to malign and besmirch him, and to punish them for it. Whence his proverbial vengefulness, his well-founded reputation among Old Bolshevik associates as a terrible hater. In the clandestine conversation with Kamenev in 1928, Bukharin called it Stalin's "theory of sweet revenge."[33]

There is scarcely any doubt that the slow-burning anger he felt toward those who disaffirmed the ideal Stalin was vastly intensified by his projection upon them of some of the hatred that he unconsciously harbored for himself. The particular others upon whom he projected, and toward whom he experienced, his self-hate were, in other words, likely to be those who had already incurred his vindictive animosity and been marked down in his mind as enemies. Such people were numerous in the party. Only now was the personality cult bringing the idealized Stalin into clear public view as a norm by which any prudent Communist or other Soviet person should be guided in statements made in meetings or in conversations that might be overheard by an undercover police informer. In the more free-spoken party past, before Stalin's ascent to his present pinnacle of power, not a few Communists had aroused his hostility by acting in ways that negated the ideal Stalin. They had called attention to this or that shortcoming in him, or belittled his merits as a revolutionary, or cast doubts on his leadership prowess, or simply taken issue with his views. An extreme case was Trotsky's exclamation at a stormy Politburo session in 1926 that Stalin was posing his candidature to the post of gravedigger of the Revolution—which provoked Trotsky's Left Communist associate, Yuri Piatakov, to ask afterward: "Why did Lev Davidovich say this? Stalin will never forgive him until the third and fourth generation!"[34] Less dramatic but not less serious in ultimate result was an incident involving the eminent Marx scholar, David Riazanov, who approached Stalin after hearing him expound the theory of socialism in one country at a party meeting in the 1920s and said: "Stop it, Koba, don't make a fool of yourself. Everybody knows that theory is not exactly your field."[35] In 1930 Riazanov still held the post of director of the Marx-Engels Institute in Moscow, but his days as director were numbered.

Stalin's mental world was thus sharply split into trustworthy friends and villainous enemies—the former being those who affirmed his idealized self-concept, the latter, those who negated it. People around him were in greater peril than many realized of slipping from the one category to the other if they spoke or acted, even unwittingly, in a manner that triggered his hostility. His daughter has described him in this process. If he was told that someone "has been saying bad things about you" or "opposes you," and that there were facts to prove this, a "psychological metamorphosis" would come over Stalin. Then there was no going back: "Once he had cast out of his heart someone he had known a long time, once he had mentally relegated that someone to the ranks of his enemies, it was impossible to talk to him about that person any more. He was constitutionally incapable of the reversal that would turn a fancied enemy back into a friend."[36]

To understand the irrevocability of Stalin's judgment, we must take account of what it meant to him to classify someone as an enemy. First, it meant that he mentally placed that individual in a category that derived from his political culture as a Bolshevik: counterrevolutionary enemy of the Soviet regime, class enemy, anti-Communist, or "enemy of the people." It was absolutely necessary for Stalin to categorize the offending individual in this way rather than simply as a personal enemy (though he would be that too). For if the individual were an enemy of Communism, then his critical attitude toward Stalin could be construed as opposition to a leader who, by virtue of his genius, was Communism's best defender.

The individual's anti-Stalin feeling would thus appear as recognition by an anti-Communist of the party's great good fortune in having Stalin as its leader, and would thereby be transmuted into a negative form of confirmation of the ideal Stalin. This would in no wise lessen Stalin's vindictive response to that individual but would permit him to experience and act upon it without the slightest questioning of his idealized picture of himself.

Inasmuch, however, as the person in question may have been a Communist of long standing and one who gave every outward appearance of sincere devotion to the party and its cause, it followed that he was—to use a term that came quite readily to Stalin's lips—a two-faced person or "double-dealer" *(dvurushnik),* and hence the most dangerous kind of enemy, a disguised one operating behind a mask of professed party and Soviet loyalty. This was a standard ingredient of Stalin's generalized image of "the enemy." We may speculate that he also poured into it all that he hated within himself, including the very fact that he felt this hate. So the enemy appeared in the Stalinist image as, among other things, a savage Stalin-hater. Naturally, anyone whom Stalin came to view through the lenses of his image of the enemy was powerless to reverse the condemnatory judgment, for any protestations of loyalty were now, for Stalin, simply further evidence of double-dealing.

Stalin was litigious. He became addicted to using the courtroom as a theater of revenge. His favorite form of vindictive triumph over enemies was their condemnation in a public trial as criminals who openly confessed their culpability for wrongdoing in a conspiracy to harm the party and the Communist cause. The awful suffering they endured in the process of being coerced into agreement to play the part of confessed criminals was doubtless, in Stalin's mind, a merited portion of their punishment as foul enemies. Their ultimate destruction was another portion.

Political trials began early in Soviet history. The so-called "demonstration trial," meaning the public use of the courtroom for politically didactic purposes, made its appearance under Lenin with the SR trial in 1922.[37] Under Stalin's guidance, the demonstration trial was transformed into the show trial as it emerged in the Shakhty case and others in the early 1930s. Here the court proceedings become literally a dramatic performance in which not only the judge and the prosecutor but also the defendants play prearranged parts just as actors do on the stage. The crux of the show trial is the confession. The defendants play leading roles by confessing in vivid detail to heinous political crimes committed by themselves and others as part of a great conspiracy.

The diverse purely political motives of the early show trials have been noted: to dramatize the alleged war danger, to stir up the martial spirit of "cultural revolution," to impress on planners and others the need for breakneck industrializing, to dislodge the Rightists' friends from the economic administration, and to combat the "Right deviation." In general, Stalin's commitment to a second revolution made the official image of dangerously active external and internal enemies necessary for justifying the sacrifices that this revolution was exacting from the population. To this extent, his need for enemies was political, not psychological. He might bear no personal grudge against a given victim, as shown by the later release of some victims of the show trials of the early 1930s. But psychological forces came into play as well. Stalin had an idealized image of himself to protect, and scores to settle. Consequently, when he had the power to mobilize the mechanisms of Soviet justice for his own ends, he did so in ways that served the requirements not only of the politics of the revolution from above but also of his personality cult and need for vengeance.

A standard charge against the accused in the early show trials was "wrecking," that is, economic sabotage. Some wrecking did actually occur, such as the case that John Scott personally observed at Magnitogorsk where, one morning, mechanics found bearings and grease cups of a big turbine filled with ground glass put there, as soon transpired, by embittered forced laborers who had been deported as kulaks.[38] But there is no evidence that such acts were widespread. On the other hand, there was a wrecker at work on a huge scale during the *piatiletka*. The record shows that Stalin himself was, albeit unintentionally, a superwrecker in his mismanagement of the developmental effort. For both political and psychological reasons, he needed to find others culpable, to project upon them his heavy responsibility for all the breakdowns and shortages that were rife. So, he spied conscious wreckers lurking in every corner and doing dirty work in the Soviet economy, and became their scourge—to the detriment of the industrialization drive, since the victims were generally not only innocent of the wrecking charge but able, hard-working citizens who had been doing their best to help the drive succeed.

Who Is to Blame?, the title question of Herzen's antiserfdom novel of 1845, became in this way the accursed question of Stalin's Russia. His answer began with a compulsive "Not I!" and proceeded to an accusatory "They, our enemies, are!" To prove this contention in a dramatically persuasive way was, along with the aforementioned political motives, the mission of the political show trials. In numerous other cases, the same general aim was served by the announced meting out of summary justice, without public trial, to officials, technicians, and others charged with wrecking activities. To establish Stalin's blamelessness, others had to be blamed for the consequences of his faults as a leader.

In the trials of the early 1930s, from the Industrial Party case of 1930 through the Menshevik case of March 1931 to the Metro-Vickers case of

April 1933, in which Soviet and British engineers were tried for alleged wrecking in the electrical industry, the politics of Stalin-exculpation were enacted as theater. The defendants, save for the British engineers in the latter case, confessed in lurid detail to the charges. Their confessions were presented to the Soviet and foreign publics as explanation for problems that were generally traceable to the dizzy developmental tempos foisted on the country by Stalin. The USSR's heroic efforts in the construction of socialism were pictured as beset by conspiracies of sabotage supported from abroad and partially carried out, prior to their exposure, by enemies operating behind the masks of loyal Soviet citizens, many occupying responsible positions in industry, planning, trade, and science.

The Menshevik trial of 1931 was a striking case of the politics of Stalin-exculpation and, at the same time, of Stalin's use of the show trial as an instrument of vengeance against individuals marked down in his mind as enemies. Ten prominent Soviet specialists, most with a Menshevik past, were accused of having formed in 1928 a counterrevolutionary conspiratorial "Union Bureau" to direct far-flung wrecking activities in collusion with the (actually existing) Menshevik Delegation Abroad, led by Raphael Abramovitch and others. The defendants were also accused of collaborating with the Industrial Party and with another internal counterrevolutionary group, a *neo-narodnik* "Peasant Labor Party," whose supposed leaders, including the well-known agricultural economists A. V. Chayanov and N. D. Kondratiev, were denounced and tried in 1930 as intellectual inspirers of the "Right deviation."

The "Peasant Labor Party" was fictional in a very special way: it existed in a utopian tale written and published early in the 1920s by the talented Chayanov, who was a man of letters as well as an economist. The Russia of a half-century hence depicted in it was a flourishing land of middle-peasant farms centering in modernized village communes, all under the beneficent rule of a party of peasant labor. Chayanov and numbers of his colleagues, all loyal and valuable thinkers, were arrested after the OGPU deputy chief, Ya. D. Agranov, had the idea—doubtless approved by Stalin—of putting on a show trial in which they would confess to involvement in a real conspiratoral kulak-oriented peasant labor party. Though the victimized men were broken and made to sign confessions by a combination of pressure, torture, and trickery, the case was too flimsy to be made into a police-staged public trial and so was "tried" behind closed doors, and Chayanov perished in confinement.[39]

The defendants in the Menshevik trial included the well-known economist and influential Gosplan figure V. G. Groman, the State Bank economist V. V. Sher, the Supreme Economic Council member A. M. Ginzburg, Commissariat of Trade officials M. P. Yakubovich, A. L. Sokolovsky,

and L. B. Zalkind, the finance official Fen-Yenotaevsky, and N. N. Sukhanov, author of the memoir of 1917 in Petrograd, *Notes on the Revolution*
(1922). Four other defendants, among them V. K. Ikov and I. I. Rubin,
the latter an economist who had worked for several years in the Marx-
Engels Institute, were accused of being associated with the "Union Bureau" although not formally members of it. Abramovitch was said to have
made an illegal visit to Russia in 1928 to assess conditions and to have
directed the "Union Bureau" members to organize action aimed at creating
an economic crisis preparatory to an internal revolt and external military
intervention. The fourteen accused were charged with engaging in such
wrecking activities as: deliberate disorganization of the consumer cooperative supply network; misallocation of products in such a way as to cause
the "appearance" of extreme shortages of goods in certain parts of the
country; the setting of plan targets either too low or too high for purposes
of disorganizing the economy; sabotage of the credit system in the State
Bank; and conscious promotion of disruptive planning estimates in Gosplan.[40] The accused took upon themselves, in short, criminal responsibility
for much of the Stalin-caused chaos, confusion, mismanagement, and
misery of the *piatiletka*.

In fact, there was no Menshevik wrecking conspiracy, and no "Union
Bureau" existed. Abramovitch was able to prove incontrovertibly that he
had been in Western Europe at the time of his alleged illegal trip to Russia
in 1928. It is true that former Mensheviks working in Soviet economic
organizations had been highly critical of the bacchanalian planning that
took over in 1929. Groman in particular had foreseen that Stalin's attempt
to take the citadel of socialism by storm would lead to economic disaster,
and had said so in a discussion group of mostly former Mensheviks that
had met informally during the 1920s and called itself the "League of
Observers."[41]

The only truth in the charge of collusive ties with the Menshevik
Delegation Abroad was that Ikov had corresponded with foreign Mensheviks, and that copies of the Mensheviks' Berlin-based *Socialist Herald*
occasionally came into the hands of the accused persons. As to wrecking,
the only instance involved skulduggery on Stalin's and Mikoyan's part.
Yakubovich, who survived many years of confinement in Stalinist concentration camps and was released and rehabilitated after Stalin died, stated in
a deposition to the Procurator General of the USSR that as chief of the
Manufactured Goods Division of Mikoyan's Commissariat of Trade he
had committed one violation of the governmental decree on the setting
aside of certain contingents of goods for the Magnitogorsk and Kuznetsk
industrialization projects—by allocating these goods to Moscow. But he
did so with extreme reluctance on direct orders from Mikoyan, who in-

formed him orally that these were Stalin's orders and, when Yakubovich hesitated because he was being asked to violate official policy, said: "What, you don't know who Stalin is?" Yakubovich then did as Stalin through Mikoyan had bid him to do, only to read in *Pravda* some days later that he was violating governmental directives by arbitrarily sending elsewhere goods marked for *Magnitostroi*—and to be charged with this wrecking crime in the trial itself.[42] He had been forced by Stalin, via Mikoyan, to take the one action which gave substance to the charge that he was guilty of wrongdoing.

From Yakubovich's deposition and other sources, we learn how the accused—some of whom were men of singular moral and physical strength—were broken down and induced to play their parts in the show trial. Sukhanov, the most cooperative in self-incrimination and the incriminating of others, was deceived by the promise of pardon in return for his services; in subsequent confinement in the Verkhne-Uralsk political isolator he protested the betrayal.[43] Groman, an alcoholic, was induced to cooperate by the withholding and providing of liquor at the requisite times. Ikov, the only defendant actually involved in liaison with Mensheviks abroad, was evidently bribed by promises of leniency; and he—alone of the accused—was set free after only eight years of confinement and allowed in 1939 to reside again in Moscow. Ginzburg and Yakubovich resisted stubbornly. Having endured torture by beating as long as they could and then attempted suicide by opening their veins, they were afterward tortured by deprivation of sleep until they gave in. Even then Yakubovich only ceased resisting after his old comrade, Sher, was brought before him, said that he had confessed to having been a member of the "Union Bureau" and named Yakubovich as a fellow member. At one point, when refusing to agree to a particular charge, Yakubovich said to his interrogator, Nasedkin, "But you must understand, that never did happen and couldn't have," and Nasedkin replied: "I know it didn't happen, but this is Moscow's demand."

Now we come to the final bizarre twist: the "Union Bureau" in a strange way did come into existence—as a counterrevolutionary organization created in and by the Soviet secret police. After Yakubovich had been finally broken, an audience was arranged between him and another accused, M. I. Teitelbaum, who had worked in the Commissariat of Foreign Trade. The interrogator, Apresian, rose and left the room when Yakubovich entered. Teitelbaum told Yakubovich that he had been beaten into confessing to having taken bribes from capitalist firms while traveling abroad, that he couldn't stand the thought of being put on display as a crook, that Apresian had suggested to him that he might change his testimony and confess to having participated in the counterrevolutionary "Union Bureau"—thereby becoming guilty of a political crime rather than bribery.

"Comrade Yakubovich," he went on, "I beseech you, take me into the Union Bureau, so I can die as a counterrevolutionary rather than as a crook and scoundrel!" At this, Apresian returned, snickered, and said: "Well, have you come to terms?" Looking into Teitelbaum's pleading eyes, Yakubovich said: "I agree. I confirm Teitelbaum's participation in the Union Bureau." Apresian then invited Teitelbaum to rewrite his confession accordingly. Yakubovich's deposition adds: "That's how the 'Union Bureau' was created."

Against the majority of the defendant-victims in this and the other early show trials Stalin hardly felt personal enmity, save insofar as he projected upon them, along with his own culpability, repressed loathing of himself for mismanagement of industrialization. But there were some on whom he took revenge as enemies who had maligned him. As mentioned above, Groman had been in private—but in Russia hardly anything was securely private—a vocal critic of Stalin's approach to industrialization. Sukhanov had aroused Stalin's vengefulness by a written slur. In his *Notes on the Revolution,* widely read in Russia in the early 1920s despite its author's Menshevik background, Sukhanov cuttingly described Stalin as a "grey blur" in the revolutionary year of 1917. His condemnation in the trial and ensuing imprisonment could only have seemed merited punishment in Stalin's eyes as well as a way of warning alert party historians not to take a Sukhanov-like view of Stalin in 1917. The Menshevik trial was also a vehicle of Stalin's vengeance against David Riazanov, who was not one of the defendants but whose forced mention by one of them, Rubin, was instrumental in his ruination.

To what lengths Stalin would go in his vindictiveness toward an enemy like Riazanov is shown by the treatment of Rubin, who had worked under Riazanov for several years in the Marx-Engels Institute and venerated his mentor. On being arrested, he was treated with great cruelty (such as lengthy confinement in a punishment cell too small to move in), but refused to confess guilt for crimes he had not committed. The police finally broke him by the savage expedient of bringing him face to face with a person who was a stranger to him and threatening to shoot this person on the spot if Rubin remained stubborn; after two such episodes, each ending in murder, Rubin capitulated. In the trial he testified that, having heard rumors of his impending arrest, he gave to Riazanov for safekeeping a sealed envelope containing materials on the Menshevik conspiracy.[44] Reportedly, Riazanov was then summoned before the Politburo and confronted with a demand by Stalin that he reveal the whereabouts of the incriminating documents, to which he defiantly replied: "You won't find them anywhere unless you've put them there yourself."[45] Expelled from the party and his institute post, Riazanov went to live in the city of Saratov as an exile, and perished in the subsequent purges. Later in 1931, the Marx-Engels Institute was merged with the Lenin Institute and placed under the direction of V. V. Adoratsky, a man whose medium stature in Marxist thought went along with pliability and a realization that safety and success lay in magnifying Stalin's merits as a theorist.

So it was that inner needs of a self-glorifying and vengeful leader were being institutionalized in public life and the workings of the governmental system. The personality cult, now pervasive, was presenting his ideal self to the whole people, giving him reassurance that the grandiose Stalin was real and recognized. His inner defenses were being transformed into outer ones, politicized. His urge to repress certain facts from consciousness was being served by the police repression of individuals whose presence constituted a reminder of those facts. His stringent need not to be reminded or made aware of past or present discrepancies between the ideal Stalin and the actuality was being served by a censored press, a subservient officialdom, a cowed intelligentsia, and a political police force with eyes and ears everywhere in the society. And his projection of his faults and self-hate onto others was being dramatized in courtrooms where people played the parts of confessed enemies of the Soviet regime and were sentenced to be punished with all severity for their crimes. The police producers of these melodramas were following directions received from the chief playwright, Stalin himself.

But how, we may ask, could be reconcile his extreme vindictiveness and the inhumanly cruel treatment of those coerced into playing these fictional roles with the vision of himself as a noble leader of the Communist Party and Russia on the road to socialism? He could do this, it appears, by devising a script that cast him as a hero in his very search for vindictive triumph over his enemies and sanctified all his actions, however unsavory, as necessary means to a just end. It made him out to be a stern, resolute, ever vigilant avenger of the party and people against enemies engaged in a deadly struggle against the Soviet Russian state and Communism.

8

TERROR AND CALAMITY: STALIN'S OCTOBER

TOWARD THE CLOSE of the 1920s, the Soviet Union was still overwhelmingly a peasant country. More than four-fifths of its population of about 150 million lived in some 600,000 hamlets and villages scattered across the vast land. Consequently, when we speak of the "second revolution in the countryside" during the years 1929–33, it must be understood that a whole society was in turmoil.

The upheaval affected the lives of the townspeople by drastically reducing food supplies, but revolutionary changes were afoot in the cities as well. The Nepmen, who had controlled about 80 percent of the country's small-scale industry and over a third of its retail trade as late as 1926–27, went the way of the rural private entrepreneurs. Not only were new plants being built or expanded in many cities, but the industrial revolution was partly an invasion of Russia's open spaces by city people. Here and there an entire new town arose as an outpost of industrializing urbanism in what had been wilderness. A celebrated instance was Komsomolsk-on-the-Amur, a factory town of 70,000 settled in the Soviet Far East. Magnitogorsk was another.

If forced resettlement under police control was the lot of very many displaced peasants and others, confinement and toil in one or another of Russia's now booming network of forced-labor camps was the grimmer fate of many more, lending weight to the hypothesis that the economic uses of huge quantities of unfree labor were an unspoken consideration behind Stalin's terror strategy. The idea and to a small extent the practice of forced labor, together with the notion of its reformative value, had come down from Lenin's time; and concentration camps for the isolation of persons deemed political enemies emerged soon after November 1917. In 1924 Dzerzhinsky proposed to a congress of Soviet justice officials that concentration camps be adapted to a "policy of colonization" by being placed in hitherto undeveloped territories "where it will be possible to compel the inmates, whether they like it or not, to occupy themselves in productive work."[1] But it remained for Stalin to put the proposal into effect, and in such a way that "productive work" meant for countless people simply being worked to death, driven by the desperate desire to earn by their efforts the semistarvation ration on which they were kept. Although the camp network was now placed under a newly formed OGPU agency called the "Chief Administration of Corrective Labor Camps" (GU-LAG), the term "corrective" was quite meaningless because the mass of inmates were treated as enemies whose purpose in life was to work so long as they could survive. Since sentences were normally prolonged on completion, or at best commuted to forced settlement in the camp area, the inmates' status was tantamount to that of slaves.

The number of labor camps rapidly grew from the six in existence in 1930, and the number of inmates soared from an estimated 30,000 in 1928 to nearly 2 million in 1931.[2] Great numbers of camp laborers became "employees" of huge police-run projects like the White Sea-Baltic Sea canal, which was built on the basis of a Stalin-sponsored decision of 1930. Forced labor was used in road building, lumbering, construction, and mining. Often the police contracted this kind of labor out to such institutions as the State Fishing Agency. From 1929 on, it became a part of yearly economic planning under the *piatiletka*.[3]

A branch of the economy in which Stalin showed particular interest was gold mining, a source of hard currency for financing industrialization. An Old Bolshevik, Aleksandr Serebrovsky, became head of the Soviet Gold Trust after being summoned in 1927 for a talk with Stalin. The general secretary had been reading Bret Harte's *Sutter's Gold* and other writings on the California gold rush, and told Serebrovsky that the process that made up the history of California must be applied to Russia's outlying regions. At the beginning, they would mine gold and then gradually change over to the mining of other minerals, coal, oil, iron, and so on.[4] The Urals and areas further to the east are rich in gold. A special new OGPU agency called Dalstroy was set up in 1931–32, with its headquarters in Magadan, to organize and develop gold mining by forced labor in the Kolyma region in northeast Siberia. Under its director, Eduard Berzin, Dalstroy supervised a Siberian "gold rush" of quite different character from the one that fired Stalin's imagination when he read Bret Harte.

Western writers sometimes use the word "modernization" to describe the industrialization and urbanization under the first two five-year plans. Yet the methods used in these developments were a direct throwback, although on an incomparably bigger scale, to those employed over two centuries earlier by Peter when he used serf and convict labor for his government-owned plants and construction projects. The "urbanization" of the Soviet East was chiefly a matter of the GULAG empire's expansion.[5]

The rural revolution was spearheaded by townsmen. In 1930 the Soviet trade unions dispatched 180,000 worker brigades into the countryside to organize collective farms and to repair machines. Another spur to the urban invasion was the selection, by decree of the November 1929 plenum, of 25,000 factory workers who, after hastily organized courses, were sent out as organizers of collective farms. Four-fifths of these "twenty-five-thousanders" were Communist party or Komsomol members.[6] Described in official publicity of the time as volunteers in a grass-roots proletarian movement to give leadership to the rural revolution, many of the twenty-five-thousanders were fired by enthusiasm for the collectivizing cause. Others joined the movement because they were lured by the material rewards. Some of the enthusiasts returned in disgust, saying things like: "There are too many injustices; it is not collectivism, it is pillage."[7]

The Terror Strategy in Action

State terror is triadic. One element of the triad is a political leadership determined to use terror for its purposes. The second is a minority chosen for victimization in so frightful a form that the third element, a far larger body of people, seeing what can happen to the victims, will be motivated to fulfill the leadership's purpose, which may be to render it quiescent or, alternatively, to induce it to take actions that it otherwise would not be disposed to take. A leader's murderous hatred of the victimized people may enter into the motives for terror. In Stalin's October, practical political considerations were initially uppermost although, as we shall see, he became infuriated by the turn that peasant response to his terror policy took.

Molotov anticipated the terror strategy when he spoke in 1928 of dealing the kulak "such a blow" that the middle peasant would "snap to attention before us." The victimized element was the "kulak." The larger body of people which was to be induced to act by joining the collectives was the rest of the peasantry, especially the middle-peasant majority. The victimizing consisted of dispossessing the "kulaks" and, in very many cases, packing them and their families into boxcars for dispatch to unknown distant destinations where they would, if they survived the trip (and very many did not), be forced to labor under wretched conditions on construction sites or in prison camps. The victimizing was officially called "dekulakization."

This term must be used in quotation marks because it was largely a misnomer. Not only was "kulak" vague in Soviet usage; even in official statistics no more than a quite small proportion of the peasantry were kulaks. In poorer villages, of which there were great numbers, there were none at all—if "kulaks" meant peasants who employed hired labor. Yet, if all the peasants were to be terrorized into joining the collectives, there had to be some candidates for victimizing everywhere. Hence in very many cases those chosen for victimizing were simply families who by dint of ability and hard work were a little better-off than their neighbors.

The war novelist Vasil Bykov gives an example from his childhood memory. He was born in 1924 in a poor Belorussian village in which there were no kulaks. Since, however, it was mandatory that some peasants be singled out for victimizing, the village activists chose three of their fellow villagers for "dekulakization": one because he owned not only a cow but also her calf; another because his mare had a foal; and a third because a distant woman relative would come to help him gather the harvest.[8] This case was representative of untold numbers of others. There were exceptions, in one of which a Communist collectivizer from a nearby city would set up a table in the middle of a village, put a list and a pistol on it, call a meeting of all the peasants, and inform them that those who refused to sign up for the *kolkhoz* would go straight to Siberia.[9]

A Soviet governmental decree of 1 February 1930 solicited the active participation of poor peasants and hired hands in "dekulakization" by providing that property confiscated and turned over to the indivisible funds of collective farms would constitute the initial membership contributions of these two groups. This was a measure, reminiscent of Civil War times, to fan class war in the villages by giving the village poor a material incentive to act against their better-off neighbors. How it worked in practice was explained to John Scott and a Russian worker named Popov at Magnitogorsk by one Shabkov, a husky ex-kulak's son who was working with them while living in the "special" section of town:

Just between the three of us, the poor peasants of the village get together in a meeting and decide: "So-and-so has six horses; we couldn't very well get along without those in the collective farm; besides he hired a man last year to help on the harvest." They notify the GPU, and there you are. So-and-so gets five years. They confiscate his property and give it to the new collective farm. Sometimes they ship the whole family out. When they came to ship us out, my brother got a rifle and fired several shots at the GPU officers. They fired back. My brother was killed. All of which, naturally, didn't make it any better for us. We all got five years, and in different places. I heard my father died in December, but I'm not sure.[10]

That elements of the village poor were active in "dekulakizing" is a fact, but it remains a moot question how widespread and willing the partic-ipation was. A Western scholar who himself spent three years (1939–41) in Soviet camps and exile and talked there with people who were in the villages at the beginning of the 1930s, formed the opinion that while in any locality "one can find some people willing to take part in outrages and plunder, particularly if this is sponsored by the authorities," the mass of the peasantry was "deeply shocked by the methods of the 'second agrarian revolution' " and there was no spontaneity like that shown when the big estates were seized by peasants in 1917.[11] Furthermore, the documentary record that we have for one Soviet province shows that by no means all the poor peasants, not to mention the middle ones, were willing accomplices in "dekulakization." Some poor peasants took bribes from wealthier ones for removing their names from the deportation lists. Some collected sig-natures to petitions testifying to the good character of individuals selected for victimizing. Some "considered dekulakization unjust and harmful, refused to vote approval of deportation and expropriation measures, hid kulak property, and warned their kulak friends of pending searches and requisitions."[12]

Collectivization was in essence a gigantic party-and-police operation. The proof lies in the Smolensk party archives, which contain not only documentary material relating to that province but also copies of circular instructions sent out from Moscow to all provinces through confidential party channels. To supervise the operation locally, special troikas were set up in each district consisting of the first secretary of the district party committee, the chairman of the Soviet executive committee, and the head of the local OGPU. They were given two weeks to make inventories of property to be confiscated. At that time, there were many suicides among supposed kulaks, some of whom killed their wives and children before taking their own lives. There were fictitious divorces for the purpose of saving some property and the lives of family members, and numerous peasants engaged in "self-dekulakization" by selling out what possessions they could or leaving them with others, abandoning their homes, and fleeing east. Under a top-secret letter sent out on 12 February 1930 to all district troikas in the Western province's Velikie Luki region, "orientation numbers" of kulaks to be deported were given. "There shall be no oscillation, no concessions to rightist-deviationist attitudes and no pacifism," the directive concluded. [13]

What "dekulakization" meant in human terms we know from numerous eyewitness accounts published abroad, all abundantly supported by the Smolensk documents. One such scene is vividly described in a memoir. The family of a successful young party man and industrial executive, Victor Kravchenko, then living in Dniepropetrovsk in the Ukraine, took in a starving waif named Katya who had been deported with her family on charges that the father was a "kulak accomplice"; all they had owned was a horse, a cow, a heifer, five sheep, some pigs, and a barn. After being pressured and beaten by the local authorities in an effort to squeeze the last bit of grain from him, the father had slaughtered a pig and a calf so that his family could eat, and then was told that slaughtering livestock without permission was a crime. Katya went on:

Then one morning about a year ago . . . strangers came to the house. One of them was from the G.P.U. and the chairman of our Soviet was with him too. Another man wrote in a book everything that was in the house, even the furniture and our clothes and pots and pans. Then wagons arrived and all our things were taken away and the remaining animals were driven to the *kolkhoz*. . . . They put us all in the old church. There were many other parents and children from our village, all with bundles and all weeping. There we spent the whole night, in the dark, praying and crying, praying and crying. In the morning about thirty families were marched down the road surrounded by militiamen. People on the road made the sign of the cross whey they saw us and also started crying. At the station there were many other people like us, from other villages. It seemed like thousands. We were all crushed into a stone barn but they wouldn't let my dog, Volchok, come in though he'd followed us all the way down the road. I heard him howling when I was inside in the dark. After a while we were let out and driven into cattle cars, long rows of them, but I didn't see Volchok anywhere and the guard kicked me when I asked. As soon as our car filled up so that there was no room for more, even standing up, it was locked from the outside. We all shrieked and prayed to the Holy Virgin. Then the train started. No one knew where we were going. [14]

"Kulak accomplice" *(podkulachnik)* was a term then in currency for a peasant who was not by any criterion a kulak but was treated as one on the ground that he was uncooperative in collectivization. The use of such a term was rendered all the more necessary by the solidarity shown by many villagers in the face of the regime's savage assault on the better-off peasants. Considering, further, that the local authorities were under unremitting pressure from higher-ups to fulfill collectivization quotas set for their districts, it is not surprising that on 20 February 1930 "the OGPU reported mounting arrests and dekulakization of middle peasants. . . . The same report noted that poor peasants who had been hired hands before the revolution and who now owned an extra horse or cow, were, in many cases, also being dekulakized."[15]

Following events from Moscow, far from the scenes of terror and confusion that were the outcome of his manipulation of policy over the past two years, Stalin was trying to direct the upheaval. In reporting to the Sixteenth Party Congress some months later, he would liken this "offensive along the whole front" to a military offensive with its unavoidable "breaches and mad dashes on certain sectors of the front."[16] The military metaphor was an apt one. Stalin's party offices became the staff headquarters of the revolution from above. From the end of 1929, the Information Department of the Central Committee every five or six days sent bulletins on the progress of collectivization to him as well as to Molotov and Kaganovich.[17]

The party archives show that the bulletins were factually informative and did not hide negative phenomena. For example, the first secretary of the Central Black Earth province party committee, I. Vareikis, reported to the Central Committee on 18 February 1930 that wholesale collectivization was being accompanied by "mass excesses and methods of coercion toward the middle peasant." In that same month the party secretary of the Moscow province, K. Bauman, reported to the Politburo that "coercive collectivization" had led to a series of peasant outbreaks there.[18]

If Stalin, as the general in command of the great offensive, did not at first respond to such information with corrective measures, it was because the so-called "excesses" were not from his viewpoint excesses; they were his terror strategy in action. With what must have by now been grim determination, he kept his forces engaged in a battle to break the back of peasant resistance to collectivization at a single blow.[19] Having pressed for an optimal version of the Five-Year Plan that he then took as a mandate to raise the objectives of industrialization sky-high, having scrapped the plan's relatively moderate collectivization targets in favor of the rural revolution for which the decree of 5 January 1930 was a prospectus, he now scrapped the latter's one-to-three-year timetable in favor of a three-to-four-month one, an effort to collectivize the bulk of the peasants by the start of spring sowing in mid-April. In this his revolutionary motivation was doubtless stiffened by a sense of desperation over incoming information on the spreading peasant slaughter of livestock. By the beginning of 1930, for example, the number of horses in the country—and in the continuing absence of large numbers of tractors, horses were as essential to collective farming as they had been to private farming—had sharply declined due to slaughter, disease, and lack of feeding.

If Stalin was not to call a hasty retreat in the face of this dangerous development, he had to press forward relentlessly in a make-or-break offensive, and that is what he chose to do. On 16 January 1930 the Soviet government issued a decree giving district authorities the power to confiscate the property of kulaks who destroyed livestock. "Kulaks" in this context already meant any peasant at all. Since very many ordinary peasant families were destroying their livestock, the decree (as in the case of Katya's family) drew large numbers of middle-peasant farmsteads into the vortex of "dekulakization."[20] Further evidence of Stalin's sense of urgency and resulting pressure for preemptive seizure of livestock is the fact that when the model charter of the agricultural artel was adopted by the Commissariat of Agriculture and published in *Pravda* on 6 February 1930, there was no provision in it for peasant retention of some livestock as private property. This in spite of the fact that when a draft of the document was discussed on 14 January at an all-union conference of representatives of regions of wholesale collectivization, the proposal was made to write into the charter a clause on collective-farm families' possession of garden plots and on their right to own productive livestock.[21] Stalin, as discussed earlier, had deleted such a provision from the Politburo commission's draft decree in December on the ground that its proper place was in the model artel charter still to be promulgated. In effect he prescribed the formation of artels that would hardly differ in practice from that (in Soviet terms) "higher form" called the "commune," which to the great majority of peasants was the least tolerable of all three forms; the official terminology of the time recognized this by speaking of "artels of the heightened type," in which all that remained in the peasant's possession was his cottage and articles of domestic use.

Local officials were themselves terrorized by the danger of being accused of "Right deviationism" if they failed to achieve the decisive results demanded of them by Moscow. As a later report of an inquiry into collectivization in the Middle Volga province put it, "the excesses are explained in considerable measure by the fact that district officials, to save themselves from the Right deviation, preferred to go too far rather than not far enough."[22] Given the intense pressure to speed up collectivization and to apply the antislaughter law to any guilty peasant household, whatever its classification, a great wave of indiscriminate repression occurred. Stalin encouraged this both by actions that he took behind the scenes and by two public statements that he made at the time.

One behind-the-scenes action was a statement by G. N. Kaminsky that would not have been made without direct or indirect guidance from Stalin. Shifted on 14 January 1930 from his chairmanship of the *Kolkhoz* Center to the headship of the Central Committee's Agitation and Mass Campaigns Department, in which capacity he was now a direct subordinate of Stalin's, Kaminsky later in that month told a group of representatives of areas of wholesale collectivization: "If you go too far in a certain case and they arrest you, remember that you will have been arrested for the revolutionary cause."[23] While very many people were being arrested then, no available information indicates that overzealous collectivizers were among them. Stalin also personally inspired *Pravda's* fire-breathing editorial of 3 February 1930, which declared that dekulakization must proceed "with maximal *organization and rapidity* in the wholesale collectivization regions" and made the remarkable statement that "the latest collectivization target figure—75 percent of the poor-and-middle peasant households in 1930–31—is not maximal."[24]

The orientation on supermaximalism was reinforced by statements that Stalin published in his own name. One was an article published in *Pravda* on 10 February in reply to questions put to him by students of the higher party school known as the Sverdlov University. One question was whether a two-track policy of "liquidating" in the wholesale-collectivization regions and merely putting restrictive pressures on kulaks elsewhere might not lead to the latter "liquidating themselves" by the squandering (that is, selling off or abandoning) of their property—to which Stalin answered: "Against the 'squandering' of kulak property there is only one antidote: to intensify the collectivizing work in the regions where wholesale collectivization is not in progress." This referred to the less developed, chiefly "national" (that is, of non-Russian nationality) and grain-consuming rural areas, such as large parts of Soviet Central Asia and the Transcaucasus, where the declared official policy had been to allow two or three years for collectivizing. Stalin's statement spurred an already emerging tendency in those areas to emulate the grain-growing regions. "Dekulakization" proceeded not only in the Central Asian and Transcaucasian republics, but even in the Far North. "The hasty conduct of dekulakization," record the historians, "went on all over the place." In some areas, up to 15 percent of the peasant households were affected.[25]

Exactly how many people were uprooted and repressed by "dekulakization" is not known and may never be. According to some estimates, about 1,100,000 peasant households, comprising some seven million people, were expropriated, and about half of these people were deported to labor camps or exile colonies in the far north and Siberia.[26] The agricultural economist V. A. Tikhonov estimates that about three million peasant households were liquidated between 1929 and the end of 1933, leaving no less than 15 million people without shelter. Around two million managed to find work on construction sites. The rest were sent to fell timber in the far north, and about a million able-bodied adults wound up in concentration camps.[27] In any event, the numbers were horrendous.

It must not be imagined that the mass uprooting of people was carried out with cool efficiency and dispatch. Russia is not like that. The overloading of the rail system caused trains to take weeks to deliver their miserable human cargo to eastern and northern places. There was confusion galore, breakdowns occurred, and here and there a kindly person upheld Russian or other honor by risking his or her own well-being to help some victim. Many peasants who could see what was in store for them simply left home to wander through the country in search of food and new lives at something other than forced labor. In the agriculturally rich Ukrainian republic, a region historically more open to Western influence and with stronger traditions of resistance to serfdom than the Great Russian heartland, peasant opposition to collectivization was particularly stiff. So many Ukrainian peasants began to move around in search of better conditions that a Central European Communist who escaped Russia in 1933 remarked, "The Ukrainian village is leading a nomad life."[28] Truly, this was a society in convulsion.

The Emergency and After

Toward the close of February 1930 something serious happened at the summit of power in Moscow. Stalin momentarily lost full control as events in the countryside threatened to get out of hand. His "offensive along the whole front" had plunged the state into an emergency. Alarmed, some high-placed men finally asserted themselves. They called for a retreat and Stalin acquiesced because, it seems, he too could see that there was no alternative.

By then the results of the crash collectivization drive were enormously impressive—on paper. As of 20 February, about 14 million peasant households were officially listed as collectivized.[29] This means that almost ten million peasant families had been forced into collectives in the brief period of approximately seven weeks since 1 January. But the reality behind this seeming miracle was a countryside in chaos. The terror had caused the middle peasant to "snap to attention" in the sense of signing up for collective-farm membership under duress, but it had not persuaded him to cooperate in earnest with the regime. An unknown but quite large number of the hastily created collectives were paper *kolkhozy*. Reports reaching Moscow during January told of very many peasants departing from collectives.

Having been administratively pressured into joining, now they were opting out. More serious still, the livestock slaughter begun by the peasants in the last quarter of 1929 continued on a steeply rising scale in early 1930, and the regime's frantic effort to forestall it by preemptive seizure proved unavailing: it only turned the collective farm into the thrice-dreaded commune and hardened the peasant's sullen resolve to enter it, if he must, without his livestock.

The rural Communist brother of a Russian maid working for the family of a pro-Soviet American journalist in Moscow related his personal experience of having—contrary to his own best judgment—to drive peasants in the Klin district of Moscow province into collectives: "I called a village meeting," he said, "and I told the people that they had to join the collective, that these were Moscow's orders, and if they didn't, they would be exiled and their property taken away from them. They all signed the paper that same night, every one of them. Don't ask me how I felt and how they felt. And the same night they started to do what the other villages of the USSR were doing when forced into collectives—to kill their livestock."[30] According to the official account, it was during the two months of February and March 1930 that the great bulk of the slaughter of the following totals of livestock lost in the 1929–30 economic year took place: one quarter of all cattle, a third of the country's pigs, and more than a quarter of its sheep and goats.[31] Over the whole period of peasant collectivization (1928–33), the statistics of peasant livestock slaughter, revealed after Stalin died, are: 26.6 million head of cattle, or 46.6 percent of the total; 15.3 million head of horses, or 47 percent of the total; and 63.4 million head of sheep, or 65.1 percent of the total.[32]

Nor was peasant resistance passive only. There took place during February and March 1930 what Soviet historians after Stalin have called "anti-*kolkhoz*" and even "anti-Soviet" peasant outbreaks, and the atmosphere in the countryside grew tense in the extreme. Not only were peasants engaging in arson; here and there they were rising up in armed rebellion. There were thirty-eight armed outbreaks in the Central Black Earth province between 17 December 1929 and 14 February 1930. In various places the peasant rebels put forward slogans like: "We're for the Soviet regime, but without Communists!" "Soviet power, but without *kolkhozy!*"[33] In Central Asia, February witnessed thirty-eight outbreaks of violence with 15,000 participants.[34]

So serious were the peasant uprisings in various places that local forces were unable to handle the situation, and men had to be sent out from Moscow to put them down. Khrushchev was told by the chief of the political directorate of the Moscow Military District that strikes and sabotage were taking place throughout the Ukraine and that Red Armymen had to be mobilized to weed the sugar beet crop there. Since the soldiers did not know anything about sugar beet cultivation, the crop was lost.[35] It should be added that what enraged so many peasants to the desperate point of taking up arms against the Soviet authorities was not alone their expropriation, but also the revived official antireligious campaign that accompanied the collectivizing. They were as deeply attached to their village churches as they were to their land, animals, and implements.

Against the backdrop of these ominous developments, some men in high places moved into action. In mid-February 1930 various Politburo members, including Ordzhonikidze and Kalinin, and representatives of the Agricultural Commissariat traveled to key rural regions to investigate matters and help the local authorities get ready for the spring sowing. They were appalled to discover how bad the situation was. The spring sowing was itself an uncertainty; the country faced the possibility of a fearful famine and utter breakdown. On their return to Moscow, a special Central Committee meeting on collectivization was convened on 24 February. The gist of what Ordzhonikidze, Kalinin, and others had to say was that the low-level rural officials were unable to put through collectivization effectively on the basis of the directivess coming from Moscow. They were taking their cues from *Pravda,* said Ordzhonikidze, who had traveled to the Ukraine, and "*Pravda* very often gives wrong instructions."[36] *Pravda* in this context meant Stalin. A particular burden of the meeting's complaint against *Pravda* was its failure to provide clear guidelines on the degree of "socialization" of peasant property and its orientation on accelerating the tempo of collectivization.[37]

What Stalin said at this meeting, or whether he even attended it, the available sources do not reveal. Meanwhile, how confused the situation was at the center at this time is indicated by a message to Moscow from Vareikis, who had reported on 18 February that wholesale collectivization in the Central Black Earth province was being accompanied by mass excesses and coercion of the middle peasant. In a follow-up communication twelve days later, he coupled his announcement of the completing of collectivization in the province with the statement that "many collective farms exist only on paper" and that "mass anti-*kolkhoz* movements" of the peasants were taking place. "In the previous letter," he concluded, "I asked that the report . . . be given to the Central Committee (if possible, to the Politburo). So far, I've had no answer. Does the Central Committee intend to hear the report? If so, when?"[38]

The 24 February meeting, along with Politburo sessions held at that time, brought the decision to modify policy in the face of the dire emergency that Stalin's strategy had created. Still earlier, on 20 February, following a specially convened meeting of representatives of the republics of the Soviet East, the Central Committee issued a decree condemning the mechanical transfer of the high tempos of collectivization in the grain-producing areas to the "national, economically backward regions"; and this call to put the brake on collectivization in most of the minority-nation republics was made public by *Pravda* in its editorial for 27 February. Acting on Ordzhonikidze's recommendation, on 21 February the Ukrainian party's Central Committee ordered the lower-level organizations to stop socializing small productive livestock on the collective farms, and *Pravda* in editorials of 21 and 22 February ordered a halt to indiscriminate collectivizing of livestock down to pigs and poultry. At the insistence of regional party leaders and a number of Politburo members, the Central Committee at the end of February made changes in the model charter of the agricultural artel.[39] As published in a new and longer version in *Pravda* on 2 March 1930, the charter specified—as it had not in the form published on 6 February—that small-scale equipment required for work on peasants' private garden plots, a milk cow and some quantity of sheep, pigs, and poultry were to remain in the possession of collectivized peasant households. Thus, the provision that Stalin had stubbornly resisted was included in an official document.

But none of this met the full needs of the tense situation; a major policy statement was called for. The Politburo commissioned Stalin to prepare it. This was done on the understanding that, in accordance with Bolshevik tradition, he would clear the statement with Politburo colleagues before submitting it for publication. Very likely they, for their own part, reasoned that since he was the field marshal of the collectivizing army, it would only be appropriate for him to be the one to blow the bugle call for retreat. But they failed to reckon with his capacity to outmaneuver them. Having prepared the article, he arranged for its publication without clearing it in advance with other Politburo members.[40] And when Stalin's bugle blew in *Pravda* on the morning of 2 March, the call for retreat was sounded in a way that aroused dismay and indignation in party ranks, high and low.

"Dizzy with Success" was the article's title; the guilt of overzealous local officials for the mistakes being made in the collectivization drive was its pervasive theme. Starting with the boast that the drive itself was a stupendous success in that half the country's peasant households were collectivized on 20 February, which meant that the Five-Year Plan of collectivization had been overfulfilled by more than two times and that "*a radical turn of the countryside to socialism may already be considered assured,*" Stalin said that these successes had their shady side. They intoxicated some people into making "adventuristic attempts to solve all the problems of building socialism 'in a trice.' " Should such "there's-nothing-we-can't-do!" attitudes receive the right of citizenship, the danger of a breakdown of the collective-farm movement could become a reality.

Then Stalin spelled out the mistakes being made. First, it was wrong and stupid to violate the principle of the voluntary character of the *kolkhoz* and mechanically transplant the tempo and methods of collectivization used in the developed regions to underdeveloped ones like "Turkestan" (Stalin used this old tsarist title for Soviet Central Asia), where unwilling peasants were being forced to join collective farms by threats of military force or of being deprived of irrigation water and manufactured goods. There was nothing in common between such an Unter Prishibeev[41] approach and the party's policy. "Who needs these distortions, this decreeing of the collective-farm movement, these unworthy threats against the peasants? Nobody but our enemies!" Next, there were inadmissible attempts to leap beyond the limits of the artel (text in today's *Pravda*) straight to the commune, socializing even homes, small livestock, and poultry in the process. Who but "our accursed enemies" needed such bungling, such stupid and injurious racing ahead? Finally: "I do not even speak of those— pardon the expression—revolutionaries who start the organizing of artels by removing bells from the churches. To take down the church bells— what r-r-revolutionariness!" Having thus aped the later Lenin's sarcasm about ultrarevolutionariness, Stalin concluded with a short lecture on how "The art of leadership is a serious matter. You can't lag behind the movement because to lag behind is to become separated from the masses. But neither can you race ahead, because to race ahead is to lose the masses and isolate yourself."

"I'm not guilty, all the others are," says Chekhov's Unter Prishibeev to the judge in response to his neighbors' complaints against his behavior. So now Stalin. He wasn't guilty, all the others were. They were bungling collectivization. But as they themselves well knew, many having followed his collectivizing strategy with heavy heart and inner protest, Stalin was the archbungler, and he was ascribing to them his very own ways of bungling the job. Many politicians blame their faults on others. Stalin was all the more disposed to do so because of his personal inability to permit any shadow of blame to fall across the image of himself as a leader without blemish. Still, in this instance the accusations were so blatant a falsifying of what had happened that "Dizzy with Success" aroused widespread panic and consternation among rural officialdom. Some actually forbade people to read the article, or had it removed from locally circulated copies of *Pravda;* and in a comment found by historians in the party archives after Stalin's death, a district Komsomol secretary in Siberia said: "Stalin's article is incorrect. It will upset all the work."[42]

If, as suggested above, Stalin lost full control in the latter part of February, now he reasserted it. Not only was he too strongly entrenched for his supremacy to be easily shaken, but in this critical time those in high positions must have been loath to take any action that would show a regime in disarray. Nevertheless, in the very act of alleviating the crisis in the regime's relations with the peasantry, "Dizzy with Success" created elements of a crisis in Stalin's relations with officialdom. Furthermore, it did not satisfactorily alleviate the collectivization crisis itself. For it gave local officials no adequate guidelines for solving the host of new problems that would result from the very relaxation of pressure the article commanded. Accordingly, the main points were set forth in more specific terms in a decree issued by and in the name of the party Central Committee on 14 March and published in the papers on the following day.

In mid-March, Ordzhonikidze, Mikoyan, and other Soviet leaders went to the main agricultural regions to assist efforts to deal with the situation. Special meetings were called, and explanatory articles printed in local newspapers. But the goal of consolidating gains, proclaimed in "Dizzy with Success," was not achieved. The peasants, especially middle peasants, took advantage *en masse* of the party's sudden conversion to the voluntary principle. Between the middle of March and the end of May, eight million households withdrew from the *kolkhozy*. However, the regime managed to hold much of its line of advance in the leading grain-growing regions.

But Stalin's resolve was in no way softened. He dispatched Kaganovich to transmit hard-line instructions by word of mouth to local officials. On 20 March, Kaganovich visited the district party committee's bureau in the town of Kozlov in the Central Black Earth province and instructed it to fight to the end of the sowing period for collectively organized field work, to expel "anti-*kolkhozniki*" from the collectives, allot them pieces of land in far-off places, and give them no credit.[43] In Stalin's eyes, the setback was merely a necessitated tactical maneuver in a protracted campaign. He showed the military character of his political thinking in an article published in *Pravda* on 3 April 1930, in the form of replies to questions from unidentified "comrade collective farmers." It stoutly rejected the idea that the present crackdown on excesses was to be seen as a "retreat." People must understand, it said, that just as in war, an offensive can only be successful when positions taken are consolidated, forces are regrouped as dictated by the changing situation, the rear is strengthened and reserves are brought up so as to guard against unexpected developments, to eliminate the breaches against which no offensive is guaranteed, and thus to prepare the enemy's full liquidation.[44]

Having averted the threat of a breakdown of the spring sowing by its hasty concessions, the regime stabilized the situation. In the fall, Stalin ordered his party-police forces back into the long march of forced collectivization. The statistics resumed their inexorable upward climb: by 1 April 1931, 13 million households; by mid-1932, 14.9 million; by mid-1933, 15.2 million; by mid-1934, 15.7 million; by mid-1935, 17.3 million; by mid-1936, 18.4 million; and by mid-1937, 18.5 million, or 93 percent of the total. The total, however, was now 19.9 million as compared with 25.6 million in mid-1929 on the eve of the big offensive,[45] and this drop of 5.7 million households gives some idea of the toll taken by the terror strategy.

By mid-1933, when 65 percent of the peasant households had been collectivized, with 90 percent or more in the grain-growing regions, Stalin's victory over the peasant was assured. Reporting to the Central Committee in January of that year, he declared that over 200,000 collective farms and about 5,000 grain-growing and livestock-growing state farms had been organized in the past three years or so; that now more than 70 percent of the peasants' cropland was collectivized; and that the Five-Year Plan of collectivization had been fulfilled thrice over.[46]

But Stalin declared that the struggle was not over. The enemy—all sorts of "former people" such as one-time private traders, nobles, priests, kulaks, kulak accomplices, White officers, bourgeois intellectuals, and other anti-Soviet elements masked as "workers" and "peasants"—was still active, only doing his dirty work from within the system, including the collective-farm system, by means of wrecking. Storage depots were being burned down, machines broken; and in their passion for wrecking there were some, including certain professors, who were even inoculating collective- or state-farm cattle with the plague or malignant anthrax and spreading meningitis among horses. Thievery was taking place on a mass scale in factories, on the railways, and in trading enterprises, but especially on the state and collective farms.

Stalin warned his fellow Communists not to turn the collective farm into an "icon" on the ground of its being a socialist form of economic activity. Precisely because it constituted a "ready-made form of mass organization," the collective farm was potentially an even greater danger than the scattered individual peasant farmsteads it had supplanted. It could be penetrated by counterrevolutionary anti-Soviet elements and then used for their purposes, as happened in the North Caucasus where such elements had created "something like *kolkhozy*" as a cover for their underground organizations. No longer openly an enemy, the kulak nowadays pretended to be *for* the collective but only to carry on wrecking work inside it. To detect and render him harmless, "one must possess the capacity to rip the enemy's mask off and show the collective farmers his true counterrevolutionary face."[47] Stalin's statement about collectives becoming fronts for anti-Soviet elements was a veiled reference to peasant disturbances that had taken place not only in the North Caucasus but also in the Ukraine in

1932. One source referring to these events is Khrushchev, who was working at that time in the Moscow city party committee. Kaganovich, then in charge of that committee, suddenly announced that he had to go on business to Krasnodar, a city in the Kuban region of the North Caucasus. It turned out that he had gone to quell a strike of Kuban Cossacks who were refusing to cultivate their land, and that as a result "whole Cossack settlements were picked up and moved forcibly to Siberia."[48] According to an account based on archival materials, Kaganovich on that trip ordered mass repressions against local party, Soviet, and *kolkhoz* officials whom he—following Stalin's orders—held responsible for the breakdown of grain deliveries from that area. In addition to the Cossack villages whose population was deported to northern regions, fifteen other Cossack villages were punished by stoppage of delivery of manufactured goods to them, the closing of their bazaars, and the premature exaction of loans and taxes. The party organizations of the Kuban area were so thoroughly purged that they lost 45 percent of their personnel. Similar operations were carried out, by Kaganovich and Molotov, among others, in the Ukraine and the Don River regions.[49]

One of Stalin's responses to the continuing difficulties with peasants-become-*kolkhozniki* was to set up special new party-police units to oversee the collective-farm bureaucracy itself. Called "political sections," these units were formed in both state farms and in the machine-tractor stations (MTS) that had been developed on a wide scale starting in 1929 as state enterprises to perform mechanized services for the collective farms in return for payments in kind. Some five thousand political sections, employing party members sent out by the Central Committee, were created as extraordinary organs for control of agriculture. The new sections were mixed party-government agencies in that their chiefs—in machine-tractor stations, where the great majority of them were formed—were *ex officio* the deputy directors of the station and, as such, government officials. Furthermore, the section chief's own first deputy was in every case a representative of the OGPU, whose presence made the political section a punitive organ. In many cases, the work of the OGPU deputies (who were outside party control) amounted to purging the personnel of both collective farms and MTS's. One, for example, told his nominal chief, the head of the political section: "I am not subordinate to you. I work according to special GPU orders. They're not your business. I do my own operational work."[50] Already in the early 1930s, the party-state was beginning to be transformed under Stalin into a state whose secret police, securely controlled by him, reigned supreme.

By the spring of 1933 massive further use of the terror strategy no longer appeared necessary to Stalin, and he ordered a policy change in a secret circular instruction that has been preserved in the Smolensk archive. The instruction said that starting in 1929 resistance to the collective-farm movement had made necessary mass arrests and mass deportations, and that the wrecking and mass pilfering of collective- and state-farm property in 1932 had required further intensifying of repressive measures. But now the victory of the collective-farm system was assured, "which makes it possible to stop, as a rule, the use of mass deportations and sharp forms of repression in the countryside." This did not signify, however, a relaxation of the class struggle. That would inevitably grow more sharp. The task was, rather, "to improve the old techniques of the struggle, to rationalize them, and to make our blows more accurate and organized." In fulfillment of this objective, the Stalin-Molotov instruction ordered the immediate cessation of mass deportations.[51]

Not only does this document provide further proof that Stalin's collectivization campaign was waged throughout on the basis of the strategy of terror. It adds importantly to the evidence that the critical situation in the countryside did not really end with the passing of the emergency of early 1930. The state of emergency passed; the crisis of state-regimented agriculture grew chronic.

Hungry Thirty-Three

One reason why Stalin could safely curtail large-scale punitive operations in the spring of 1933 is that by then many rural parts of the country were in the grip of a great famine, which was breaking whatever was left of the peasants' will to resist collectivization. That year went down in popular memory as "hungry thirty-three." Although 1933 was the worst year, the famine started in 1932 and lasted into 1934. The areas most heavily stricken were the grain-producing ones where collectivization was advanced farthest: the Ukraine, the North Caucasus, the Lower and Middle Volga, and Kazakhstan. In Russia proper the areas most affected were the southern Urals, and the Kursk, Tambov, Vologda, and Archangel regions. The Ukraine, with its very large and strongly resistant peasantry, was hardest hit of all.

While peasants and their children were dying of starvation by the millions, the Soviet government was exporting millions of tons of grain to earn foreign currency for industrialization. Grain exports rose from the 2 million metric tons a year in the mid-1920s to 4.8 million in 1930 and to 5.2 million in 1931, but then went down to 1.8 and 1.7 million respectively in 1932 and 1933, and approximately 800,000 tons in 1934.[52] The trade of human lives for technology was rendered all the more tragic by the very

low prices that the exported grain fetched on international markets during
the Great Depression.

This famine was not weather-caused. Although drought occurred in a
number of northeastern regions in 1931 and poor weather conditions caused
(as Stalin told the January 1933 plenum) "certain harvest losses" in areas
of the Ukraine and North Caucasus in 1932, the total amounts of grain
gathered (close to 70 million tons in 1931 and 1932, and 70 million in
1933) were not greatly below the 72- or 73-million ton grain harvests on
which this bread-eating country had lived rather well during most of the
1920s.[53] The famine has variously been described as "organized," "administrative," and "man-made." The man at the center of the causation was
Stalin.

On the heels of the sapping of peasant morale and incentive by collectivization, plus the mass slaughtering of livestock, the Stalin regime made
use of its newly created control devices, the *kolkhoz* and MTS, plus ruthless force, to pump out of the countryside a far greater proportion of the
grain produced, and other agricultural products, than formerly. Whereas
obligatory deliveries to the state at nominal prices amounted to no more
than 14 percent of the grain harvest in the years 1926–28, they came to
22.5 percent in 1929, 26.5 percent in 1930, 33 percent in 1931, and 39.5
percent in the years 1933–36. Meanwhile, deliveries of meat, milk, and
eggs increased while the amounts produced went into decline.[54] Insofar as
the regime could control its own lower officialdom by the threat of arrest
for failure to carry out its orders, no matter at what cost in suffering and
even in damage to agriculture itself—for example, by the taking of seed
grain needed for the coming crop year—there was hardly any limit to its
ability to extract what rural Russia produced. Stalin's boast in January
1933 that the state could now procure over twice as much grain per year as
it could before collectivization attests to this. The point is, it did, and used
the grain to build up its reserves in the event of war, for export, and to feed
the army and town population.

Although the gross grain harvest in 1932 was 69.9 million tons, part
of it went ungathered. The main reason is that peasants, remembering how
virtually all the grain was taken away from them in the previous year,
evaded field work on the *kolkhoz* by all possible means. And before the
grain was gathered, "barbers" roamed the fields, stealthily and normally
by night, and clipped off stalks of grain with scissors. These so-called
"barbers" were chiefly peasant women driven to desperation by the sight
of their starving children. Then, when the grain was gathered and piled in
threshing centers for subsequent compulsory delivery to the state, so-called
"carriers" appeared who would pick up small amounts of grain and stuff
them into pockets or under bosoms. In response came a savage law dated

7 August 1932, set down on paper in Stalin's own handwriting. It prescribed death by shooting, or not less than ten years' deprivation of liberty if there were mitigating circumstances, for stealing state- or collective-farm property, and prohibited amnesty in all such cases. No amounts of stolen goods were specified as those justifying the application of these draconian penalties. Since any amount whatsoever could and often did become the basis of conviction, the law became known informally in the countryside as the "five stalks law." During the first five months after its enactment, 54,545 people were convicted under it, and 2,110 of them were sentenced to be shot.[55]

In various parts of the country—the Ukraine, North Caucasus, and the lower and middle Volga—the collective farms did not fulfill the plan for obligatory deliveries of grain in 1932. When Stalin learned that the local authorities in one district of the Dniepropetrovsk region of the Ukraine were allowing the collective farms to set aside seed and insurance funds of grain, he went into a terrible rage and sent out a circular to all party organs on 7 December 1932 branding the heads of the offending district "deceivers" of the party and crooks following a kulak policy under the banner of their "agreement" with the General Line of the party. His circular demanded their immediate arrest and imprisonment for five or ten year terms in every case, and insisted that "saboteurs" of compulsory grain deliveries in other districts be treated in the same way. By the winter of 1932–33 mass famine stalked the grain-growing regions of the Ukraine, the North Caucasus, the lower and middle Volga, the southern Urals, and Kazakhstan.[56]

Russia's most recent great famine had occurred in 1920–21. Centered in the Volga area, it cost over five million lives. Aid from abroad, in particular through the American Relief Administration under Herbert Hoover, helped cut the death toll and ease the suffering. The aid from abroad was made possible because the Bolsheviks admitted the famine and mobilized domestic and foreign resources to combat it. This time, no relief came, despite efforts of some European groups to organize aid, because Stalin's regime refused to acknowledge—in fact denied—that a famine was taking place. When word of the famine reached foreign journalists in Moscow, a new ruling was introduced banning travel by foreign correspondents in the countryside without special permission from the Foreign Commissariat. The Press Department of this commissariat, then under Konstantin Oumansky, served also as their censoring agency. Unfortunately, some Western journalists in Moscow—including Walter Duranty of *The New York Times,* who was then dean of the press corps, and Louis Fischer of *The Nation*—cooperated with the Soviet cover-up by writing dispatches (and, in Fischer's case, lecturing at home) in ways calculated to blunt the impression created by other reports that a terrible famine was taking place in the Soviet Union.[57]

Later, much information about the famine came out in articles and books by correspondents and other travelers after they left the country and in writings of former Soviet citizens who were able to tell their life-stories abroad. The famine was history, however, by the time most of these accounts came out.[58]

Fedor Belov, then living in his recently collectivized Ukrainian village, writes that the famine was the most terrible thing the Ukrainian people ever experienced, and says: "The peasants ate dogs, horses, rotten potatoes, the bark of trees, grass—anything they could find. Incidents of cannibalism were not uncommon."[59] Fred Beal, a radical American labor organizer who had found refuge in Russia from a threatened jail sentence at home, was at that time a sort of public relations officer with the foreign workers colony at the big tractor plant going up at Kharkov, then the capital city of the Ukraine (later the capital was moved to Kiev). In the spring of 1933 he made a random visit to the village of Chekhuyev, a two-hour train ride from Kharkov. The only person still alive there was a woman who had gone mad. The houses contained only corpses, on some of which rats were feeding. A sign in Russian on one house, in which two men and a child lay dead with an icon beside them, read: "God bless those who enter here, may they never suffer as we have." Another read: "My son. We couldn't wait. God be with you." Other signs had been placed on graves of some who had been buried. One read: "I LOVE STALIN, BURY HIM HERE AS SOON AS POSSIBLE!" When he had occasion to call on G. I. Petrovsky, then the titular president (chairman of the Soviet executive committee) of the Ukranian Republic, Beal reported that men in his factory were saying that peasants were dying all over the country and that five million had died in the present year (1933). What was he to reply? " 'Tell them nothing!' answered President Petrovsky. 'What they say is true. We know that millions are dying. That is unfortunate, but the glorious future of the Soviet Union will justify that. Tell them nothing!' "[60]

Petrovsky's ackowledgment of the famine in a personal conversation with a foreigner was exceptional. Bland denials by high officials of the facts known to all Russians with rural connections—and hardly any lacked them—were the rule. In December 1933, addressing the All-Union Soviet Executive Committee of which he was chairman (and hence the titular president of the Soviet Union), Kalinin said: "Political impostors ask contributions for the 'starving' of Ukraina. Only degraded disintegrating classes can produce such cynical elements." When the leader of the French Radical Party, Eduard Herriot, arrived in Odessa during the famine, he was so guided by functionaries while in the Ukraine and en route to Moscow by train that he could honestly report back in Paris that he had not seen any famine.[61] Earlier, in 1931, a time of widespread hunger but not yet of famine, George Bernard Shaw, accompanied by Lady Astor, made a well-publicized visit to Russia, where he was courted assiduously and dined sumptuously. Then he publicly ridiculed reports that Soviet people were going hungry.

Although the famine afflicted rural Russia primarily, its consequences were also felt in urban Russia—save for Moscow and possibly a few other favored cities. Facing sure starvation in their villages, many peasants came to towns to beg for food. They were driven away by the police, but very many collapsed and died on city streets. Thus the Kharkov tractor plant, located ten miles outside the city, was besieged by begging people. "Not a day passed," writes Beal, "without groups of these disinherited peasants and workers, young and old, men and women, knocking at our doors. They would dig into the garbage boxes and fight like packs of wild dogs for food remains." The workers themselves subsisted on starvation rations (for lunch a bowl of cabbage soup, a slice of bread, and a few ounces of barley gruel), and these were doled out to them in factory restaurants on presentation of a food ticket. The foreign workers in the plant, themselves living on the most meager diet, "were in despair at having to work alongside starving, stupefied, and dazed Russian workers."[62] Food prices on the free market were so high that these goods were mostly an unattainable luxury for all but highly paid specialists.

Khrushchev, who left the Ukraine for Moscow in 1929, reports how Anastas Mikoyan long afterward told him about being visited during the famine by one Comrade Demchenko, first secretary of the Kiev province party committee, who said: "Anastas Ivanovich, does Comrade Stalin— for that matter, does anyone in the Politburo—know what's happening in the Ukraine? Well, if not, I'll give you some idea. A train recently pulled into Kiev loaded with corpses of people who had starved to death. It had picked up corpses all the way from Poltava to Kiev. I think somebody had better inform Stalin about this situation."[63] But Stalin would not listen. When a braver man than Demchenko, R. Terekhov, reported to the Politburo on starvation in villages of Kharkov province, Stalin cut him off with the words: "They tell us, Comrade Terekhov, that you're a good orator, but it transpires that you're a good story-teller. Fabricating such a fairy tale about famine. Thought you'd scare us, but it won't work! Wouldn't it be better for you to leave the posts of province committee and Ukrainian Central Committee secretary and join the Writers' Union: you'll concoct fables and fools will read them."[64]

Stalin knew well that the famine was no fairy tale. Another who had the nerve to tell him about it was the writer Mikhail Sholokhov, a resident of the Veshenskaia district in the Don River region and the author of a pro-collectivization novel, *Virgin Soil Upturned*. The book contained such realistic scenes of "dekulakization" in a Don Cossack village that Stalin's personal permission had been necessary for its publication. Sholokhov wrote to Stalin on 16 April 1933, asking him to send to Veshenskaia some strong-minded Communists to investigate and expose those who had mortally undermined the district's collective-farm economy by taking grain through "disgusting 'methods' of torture, beatings, and humiliation," and those who had inspired them to these actions. Sholokhov wrote further: *"These are not individual instances of excesses, they are the 'method' of carrying out grain deliveries, legalized on a district scale. . . ."*

Stalin began his letter of reply with thanks for revealing that "sometimes our officials, in their desire to bridle the enemy, accidentally strike at friends and descend to sadism." But Sholokhov, he went on, saw only one side of the matter—the other side being that "the esteemed reapers of your district (and not only yours) carried out an 'Italian strike' (sabotage!) and were not averse to leaving the workers and Red Army without bread. That the sabotage was quiet and outwardly inoffensive (no bloodshed) doesn't alter the fact that the esteemed reapers were waging what was in essence a 'quiet' war against the Soviet power. A war of starvation, Comrade Sholokhov. Of course, this in no way justifies the outrages that were, you assure, committed by our officials and those guilty of these outrages must receive due punishment. Still, it's as clear as God's day that the esteemed reapers are not such harmless folk as might appear from a distance."[65]

Stalin's responses to Terekhov and Sholokhov show that he was rationalizing both his sponsorship and condoning of the cruel methods of confiscation and his refusal to acknowledge the fact of famine (which would imply the need to provide relief) by treating the peasants' desperate resistance to starvation as evidence of their acting as enemies in a "quiet war" against the regime. By so doing, he could accomplish the mental feat of reconciling his actions—and inaction—with the inner picture of himself as the hero of a "rural October."

Many of the peasants believed that the regime was deliberately using the famine as a weapon against them.[66] The historical record contains confirmation of this belief by a high party official. M. M. Khataevich, secretary of the Ukrainian Central Committee and the Dniepropetrovsk province committee, met Victor Kravchenko in the countryside while the local party chief was on an inspection trip by car during harvest time in 1933. Kravchenko was one of three hundred party activists in the Dniepropetrovsk province whom the Ukrainian Central Committee had chosen to work in the new political sections and safeguard the gathering of the grain.

While fulfilling his party assignment, he had been horrified to discover near the railway station of a famine-stricken village a cache of thousands of bushels of grain that had been set aside in secret as state reserves, and he had given permission to distribute some grain and milk to the local peasants. Khataevich, having learned of this, berated the young functionary publicly for not having been a disciplined party member. Afterward, he took Kravchenko aside, out of earshot of other officials, and made clear that he had been scolding him "for the record." Then he quietly explained: "A ruthless struggle is going on between the peasantry and our regime. It's a struggle to the death. This year was a test of our strength and their endurance. It took a famine to show them who is master here. It has cost millions of lives, but the collective farm system is here to stay. We've won the war."[67]

Just how many millions of lives were lost remains a subject of research, speculation, and dispute to this day. Informed estimates range from 3 to 4 million famine deaths at the lower end to as many as 7 to 10 million at the higher, and include as many as 3 million children born between 1932 and 1934.[68] Ultimately, however, the toll in death, suffering, and blighted lives resulting from terroristic collectivization and the famine, which constituted both a part and a consequence of it, defies statistical expression. Let it be said simply that Stalin's "October" was one of our violent century's most monstrous crimes against humanity.

Back to *Barshchina*

The antipathy toward the *kolkhoz* was so widespread and not confined to the better-off peasants because many saw in it a revival of serfdom. Serfdom was still a live historical memory, having been abolished only in 1861 and even later in certain outlying parts of the Russian Empire such as Georgia. In the Russia of 1930, a peasant of forty to fifty years of age was likely to have been the child of serf-born parents. Some of the latter were still living. Even if too young to remember serfdom as a personal experience, the generation of serf-born fathers and mothers preserved the memory as passed down to them by their own elders.

There is a profusion of eyewitness testimony by contemporaries that the perception of the *kolkhoz* as a revival of serfdom under Communist auspices was widespread during collectivization. A commonly encountered peasant artifice was the use of the initials "V.K.P." (officially designating the *Vsesoiuznaia Kommunisticheskaia Partiia,* or all-union Communist party) to mean *Vtoroe krepostnoe pravo,* or The Second Serfdom. Another saying was that Russia after the Five-Year Plan would need three tsars: Peter the Great to finish building; Alexander II to emancipate the serfs; and Nikolai II to eliminate the food shortage.[69] Perhaps the most explicit expression of peasant sentiment occurs in a letter found in the Smolensk archives. Sent to the Western province's peasant newspaper, *Our Village,* in late 1929 or early 1930 by one Ivan Chuyunkov, who identified himself as a poor peasant ("I have but one hut, one barn, one horse, 3 dessyatins of land, and a wife and three children"), it told of events in the writer's village of Yushkovo: 'A brigade of soldiers came to us. This brigade went into all the occupied homes, and do you think that they organized a *kolkhoz?* No, they did not organize it. The hired laborers and the poor peasants came out against it and said they did not want *corvée,* they did not want serfdom."[70] Needless to say, *Our Village* let the letter go unpublished.

The peasants' perception of the *kolkhoz* as a second serfdom proved more accurate than many may have realized at first. The old Russian serf's obligatory service could be performed in one or a combination of two forms: *obrok,* the provision to the landowner of a fixed amount of produce during the agricultural year, or *barshchina,* working so many days per year on the landowner's fields. *Barshchina* is the equivalent of the French *corvée.*[71] In the early nineteenth century, landowners who considered themselves progressive might put their serfs on *obrok* as the less onerous form of obligatory service. But both forms remained in use.

As the Soviet *kolkhoz* or "agricultural artel" evolved in the early 1930s, it became necessary to work out a generally accepted method of remuneration of the collective farmer for his yearly work on the collective's fields (as distinct from the time he spent cultivating his private garden plot, normally located beside his cottage). Although in theory a producers' cooperative, the *kolkhoz* was in practice a state-run organization, administered by a chairman and governing board whose elective members were party-chosen officials. Its law of operation was to fulfill fixed obligatory grain or other produce deliveries at government-set nominal prices, to make the required payment in kind for the services performed by the nearby machine-tractor station, to set aside certain quotas of produce for seed, forage, and insurance funds, and, finally, to allocate a portion of its annual produce for sale to the government or on the free market. What remained was subject to distribution among the collective farmers, who were thus in the position of residual recipients of produce and income.

The method of distributing the residue was not initially uniform, as shown by the complaint in an official decree of the Sixth Congress of Soviets in March 1931 that in some places the distribution was being made "by souls" rather than by the quantity and quality of work an individual performed.[72] The regime favored the piece-work method, which was based on the "labor-day" *(trudoden'),* and which aimed at raising the individual's incentive. By the end of 1931, the distribution of the residual income and produce by "labor-days" was an established practice in three-fourths of the *kolkhozy,* and under the model collective-farm charter promulgated in February 1935 the "labor-day" system was prescribed for universal adoption. Each form of agricultural work, such as ploughing, sowing, milking, and so on, was given a certain "labor-day" value based on its relative complexity, difficulty, importance, and the amount of training needed. Thus, one kind of job (say, ordinary field-work) might be given a value of one-half a "labor-day" per day's work; another, more skilled variety, one and one-half.

The average worth of a "labor-day" was determined by the overall amount of the residue in money and kind divided by the total number of "labor-days" accumulated by all the individuals working on the given collective farm. Differences in land fertility, crop weather, amounts of compulsory deliveries, and the willingness of the peasants to work well for the collective, were factors causing the worth of a "labor-day" in one collective to differ from that in another. Belov recalls that in the later 1930s the worth of a "labor-day" on his collective in the Ukraine was usually about three to six kilograms of grain and three to five rubles in cash, but that there were other collectives in the same district whose "labor-day" came to only one to two kilograms of grain and 70 to 90 kopecks in cash. In a year when the rate on his collective turned out to be only one kilogram of grain and 55 kopecks per "labor-day," a member remarked: "You will live, but you will be very, very thin."[73]

Just how "thin" a collective farmer could become is indicated by a revealing episode in which even Stalin, for once, was stumped for a solution. Administrators would dock "labor-days" from a collective farmer's account as punishment for violating regulations. On 4 April 1934, I. A. Akulov, then head of the USSR Procuracy (the government agency charged with, among other things, ensuring observance of the law) sent Stalin a note reporting that heavy fines in "labor-days" were being levied widely, and illegally, on collective farmers for even very slight violations of the farm rules. At times, he said, the fines would total two to three hundred "labor-days" and thus exceed the offender's annual aggregate. How should this be handled? Stalin sent Akulov's message to Premier Molotov with a penned notation: "Comrade Molotov, how should this be handled?"[74]

Since the residual earnings from collective-farm labor were often small and in any event variable, the individual peasant was strongly inclined to spend as much time as possible on his small garden plot, knowing that he could use its produce for his own family's needs and market any surplus. To combat this tendency the regime made it a requirement that all *kolkhozniki* work a certain number of days each month on the collective. Eventually, this practice was codified in a party-government decree of 27

May 1939, which sharply reproved party and government officials for permitting the surreptitious aggrandizement of the private garden plots to the point where they were becoming in many instances the main source of the collective farmer's income rather than the subsidiary source they were supposed to be. To roll back this advance of rural private enterprise, the decree specified the establishment for every able-bodied collective farmer of an "obligatory minimum of labor-days per year." It would be 100 in the cotton-growing regions; 60 in the Moscow, Leningrad, and a series of other specified provinces, 80 in the remainder of the country. Those who failed to fulfill the norms would forfeit their collective-farm membership and the rights it carried.[75]

The resemblance of the "labor-day" system to the *corvée* is immediately apparent to anyone familiar with the history of serfdom and the rural order established under Stalin. But was it so perceived by Russians of Stalin's time? In 1947, this author, struck by the comparison through the reading of old Russian history books while living in Moscow, asked a fifty-year-old Soviet citizen, a native Muscovite of keen intelligence and wide experience but little formal education, the following question: Is there anything in common between what was called *barshchina* in the time of serfdom and the "labor-day" system on Soviet collective farms? Back came the answer, unhesitating, matter-of-fact, categorical: "out-and-out *barshchina.*"[76] One's sense of the collective farm as the serf system in Soviet guise was reinforced in those days by travel in that part of the Moscow province to which members of the foreign colony had access: here and there, a still surviving old manor house had become the central administrative office of a *kolkhoz*.

It is little wonder that, in his shrewdness, the peasant took "V.K.P." in a dual meaning. He had additional reason to do so when the Sovnarkom approved a Statute on Passports, which revived under Soviet auspices (by Stalin's personal decision), the internal passport system that had existed under the tsarist regime and been abolished in 1917. Initially applied to citizens of Moscow, Leningrad, Kharkov, and areas around them, under a decree dated 27 December 1932, the system was extended in early 1933 to citizens throughout the USSR. They received internal passports, renewable at five-year periods, from the age of sixteen. Registration of one's passport with the local police (militia) was made a precondition of legal residence in a town, populated point, or a hundred-kilometer zone along the Western border. According to article 2 of the government decree of 23 April 1933, citizens whose regular place of residence was a rural area (except for state farms and the areas around machine-tractor stations) were not to receive passports.[77]

The aim of the passport system was governmental control over the movement of Soviet citizens. The revolution from above caused enormous commotion below. There was mass migration, forced for the most part but in many instances voluntary. There was widespread confusion, rapid change in ways of living, privation on a massive scale, and the natural striving of many to seek better conditions elsewhere—in another plant or another town. Since certain cities, especially Moscow, were better supplied than most, they were natural centers of attraction. Under the relatively loose administrative regulations of the NEP period, moving around presented no great difficulty. Now that began to change. On 3 September 1930 *Pravda* carried a Central Committee proclamation calling on all party, economic, trade-union, and Komsomol organizations to combat the turnover, the "flitting" from job to job, which was undermining labor discipline and disorganizing production. Enterprises were to secure the attachment (*zakreplenie*) of workers to their jobs by measures ranging from social pressures and material incentives to the boycott of "malicious production deserters." An anonymous article sent from Russia to Trotsky's *Bulletin of the Opposition* acidly described the document as "a real Yuri's day manifesto for the Soviet proletariat."[78] The reference was to the abolition under Tsar Boris Godunov, who ruled from 1598 to 1605, of the Russian peasant's traditional right to move from one landowner's estate to another once a year, around 26 November, St. George-Yuri's day on the old church calendar.

If the Central Committee proclamation of September 1930 made it more difficult for the worker to move from job to job at will, the passport statutes of 1932–33 represented a big further restriction. Having to obtain the registration of the local police in his passport in order to be a legal resident of a given town or area, the Soviet worker could no longer move from place to place without securing managerial consent. Even travelers making stopovers en route were obliged to register their passports with the police for the short time of their stays away from home.

As for the peasant majority of the population, the denial of passports made their enserfment complete. A Soviet citizen in possession of a passport could, at least in theory, move around insofar as he could secure job transfers from management. By bribery he might even obtain the coveted registration for privileged cities like Moscow. But the peasant, having no passport, fairly soon became as securely attached to his village as the bonded peasant serfs of yore had been to theirs. Once again the Russian peasant was bound to the soil of a landowner (the state) and on *barshchina*. The designation of the landed estate as an artel was verbal cover for a revived system of serfdom. Not until 1975 did the Soviet regime modify the passport system in such a way as to confer a passport upon the peasant, thereby graduating him to the same level of governmental restriction as that experienced by other Soviet citizens.

Under Stalin, as under the princes of Muscovy, Russia's development was taking the form of a state-building process in which various strata were being bound in compulsory service to the state power. Kliuchevsky's concise summation of the historical process may be applied without exaggeration to Soviet development in Stalin's time: "The state swelled up; the people grew lean."

The Balance Sheet

In January of "hungry thirty-three," Stalin reported to the Central Committee plenum that the *piatiletka* had been a success. Its basic mission had been to transform the Soviet Union from a weak agrarian country into a mighty industrial power capable of standing on its own, independent of the caprices of world capitalism; to build the economic foundation of a socialist society; to change small-scale dispersed agriculture into large-scale collective farming; and to raise the country's defense potential to the required level for repelling any attempts at military invasion. Not only had all this been accomplished; it had been done in four years and three months instead of the planned five.

The USSR had possessed no tractor industry; now it did. No automobile industry; now it did. No machine building; now it did. No serious agricultural machinery industry; now it did. No aircraft industry; now it did. From last or near last place in electric power, coal, and oil production, it had moved into one of the first places. It had a new coal and iron-and-steel base in the East, new textile industry centers in Central Asia and Western Siberia, and all this on a scale dwarfing West European industry. It had been transformed from an agrarian country whose industrial output was 48 percent of the total in 1928 into an industrial one for which the comparable figure was 70 percent in 1932. The five-year industrial production plan had been fulfilled by 93.7 percent in four years; the heavy-industry part of it, by 108 percent. If the total program had been underfulfilled by 6 percent, this was only because the refusal of nonaggression pacts by neighboring countries and complications in the Far East (the Japanese occupation of Manchuria in 1931) had made it necessary to convert some plants to munitions production for some months to plug gaps in the defense potential. True, these achievements had cost "certain difficulties in the sphere of consumer goods." But if, instead of spending a billion and a half rubles in foreign currency to import equipment for heavy industry, the government had spent half of this to import cotton, leather, wool, rubber, and so on, the USSR would not now have such a powerful heavy industry and would be disarmed in the face of the capitalist encirclement.[79]

Such was Stalin's version of the balance sheet for the previous four years. There is no denying that much had been accomplished. The huge Dnieper River dam and power station was completed. So was—by the use of forced labor—the Turk-Sib railway linking Siberia with Central Asia. The White Sea–Baltic Canal was nearly finished, again by forced labor, and fitted out with a 48-meter portrait of Stalin at the concrete dam of the sixth section. Afterward, some of its more than 100,000 involuntary builders were amnestied with much fanfare, but most were simply shifted to another project, the digging of a canal linking Moscow with the Volga River. Stalin, accompanied by Voroshilov, Kirov, and Yagoda (the latter having supervised the project for him), marked the first canal's completion by cruising through it in July 1933 and bestowing a gracious handshake on the technical managers when they were introduced to him by Yagoda. It is an irony of history that the sixteen-foot-deep waterway proved too shallow for military vessels and little needed for economic purposes, so that when Solzhenitsyn visited it in 1966 he found it in a state of disuse.[80]

Big new industrial complexes like Magnitogorsk and Kuznetsk, the Urals and Kramatorsk heavy machinery plants, the automobile plants in Moscow and Gorky, the tractor plants in Stalingrad, Kharkov, and Cheliabinsk, and hundreds of others were built or at least begun. The five-year education plan represented an organized effort to combat illiteracy. The technical schools and worker study programs set up under the Supreme Economic Council produced a whole new generation of skilled workers and technically trained specialists and administrators. New towns were founded, old ones rebuilt. Semioriental Moscow, known from old as the "forty forties" (forty times forty Orthodox churches), a town of narrow, winding, cobbled streets, was changed into a city of broad thoroughfares fronted by nondescript functional buildings, and its future pride, the metro, was laid under the hard-driving supervision of Kaganovich, for whom it was eventually named, and Khrushchev. One of the city's most revered religious landmarks, the chapel of the Iberian Virgin at the entrance to Red Square, disappeared one night to the shock and horror of many Russians. Another, the great gold-domed Church of Christ the Savior, built in the nineteenth century on a prominent spot by the Moscow River to honor the 1812 victory over Napoleon, was blown up in 1932, unquestionably at Stalin's behest, to make way for a planned Palace of Soviets, which was to be topped by a towering Lenin statue that would make the building a few feet taller than the highest then existing New York skyscraper. But old Russia took passive revenge for the act of destruction: the ground proved too soggy for such a mighty structure, and the palace was never built; the empty space became the site of an outdoor swimming pool.

The achievements were accompanied by large-scale waste not mentioned in Stalin's progress report. Projects begun were not always com-

pleted. Expensive imported machinery was often mishandled or left to rust
in unsheltered places. Famished workers could not be efficient, even with
the special incentives offered under the newly established piece-work system. Nor did the majority of workers respond to the inspirational propaganda in the same spirit as the shock workers whose exploits of "labor
heroism" were celebrated in the Soviet press. The trade unions, which in
Leninist tradition and under Tomsky's leadership had preserved (until about
1927–28) some sense of being potential defenders of worker interests vis-
à-vis management, were now pure Soviet company unions whose mission
was to instill production-mindedness into the working class and to spur it
to greater efforts. In these conditions, many workers resorted to the only
weapon left to them, the surreptitious slow-down. "So extreme was the
despair that all over Russia the workers were engaged in a great spontaneous campaign of silent sabotage," wrote Fred Beal. As for the shock
workers themselves, some were idealists but most were simply "stool-
pigeons" who spied on their fellow-workers.[81]

Stalin was wrong in claiming that the plan in industry had been fulfilled. His claim was made in overall terms, which were misleading because of the rise since 1927 in the prices in terms of which the overall
fulfillment percentages were computed. Plan targets for a whole series of
major products were not fulfilled. Coal production for 1932 was 13.4
million tons as compared with the 22 million projected for the final plan
year; iron ore, 12.1 million as compared with the projected 19; pig iron,
6.2 million tons as compared with the projected 10 (the latter itself having
been reduced from Stalin's wild 17); steel, 5.9 million tons as compared
with the projected 10.4; wool cloth production, 93.3 million meters as
compared with the projected 270 million, and so on. Yet the total employed
labor force in 1932 was 22.8 million as compared with the projected 15.8
million.[82]

The question is, did the accomplishments require Stalin's revolutionary approach and, in particular, collectivization in the form that it took?
On the basis of Soviet materials, including the revealing researches published in 1968–69 by the Soviet scholar A. A. Barsov, some Western
economists have reached a negative answer. Barsov's own conclusion is
that the surplus product redistributed from agriculture to other spheres of
the economy by the end of the *piatiletka,* amounting to about 30 percent of
the centralized net state income used for industrializing, was not greater in
scale than before; the increase was only about 4 percent, and its relative
weight decreased during the five-year period. The bulk of the surplus
product that made rapid industrialization a reality was created by the working class in industry, construction, and transport.[83]

The question, let it be emphasized, is not whether the peasantry made a mighty contribution in blood, sweat, tears, and starvation to the industrial revolution of 1928–33, providing the great bulk of the manpower for the forced-labor empire, having its farm labor exploited in the extreme, and dying by the millions while the food that could have kept people alive was being shipped abroad to pay for foreign machinery and personnel. The question is whether an industrialization drive conducted, as had been contemplated in the 1920s, within the framework of the NEP, with due consideration of the need for balanced economic growth and without the calamity of Stalinist collectivization, could have yielded something like the 50 percent expansion of industrial output achieved during the crucial five years. At this point, an interpretive historian should allow economists to answer in their own words.

Hunter: "A number of alternative paths were available, evolving out of the situation existing at the end of the 1920s, and leading to levels of capacity and output that could have been as good as those achieved by, say, 1936, yet with far less turbulence, waste, destruction, and sacrifice."[84] Millar: "Whatever its merits may have been on other grounds, mass collectivization of agriculture must be reckoned as an unmitigated economic policy disaster. . . . The evidence suggests that the oppressive state agriculture procurement system, rather than serving to extract a net contribution from agriculture as a whole, should be credited with preventing the collectivization disaster from disrupting the industrialization drive."[85]

Stalin calculated that revolutionary collectivization would undergird a herculean industrialization. His calculation was borne out only in the grotesque sense that while collectivization was in fact made to support industrialization, it did so at a cost that was incalculably great in lives, health, morale, and the well-being of a generation, and unnecessary for the bulk of the results achieved.

9

STALIN'S TIME OF TROUBLE

STALIN mentally divided the Communist Party and the Soviet political world into two camps. One, a community of the faithful, consisted of Lenin-Stalin loyalists, the "real Bolsheviks" and real Soviet citizens who showed their fidelity to the regime and Communism by believing in Stalin as the great leader and by upholding his policies through thick and thin.

Arrayed against this community of the faithful was the countercommunity of unbelievers, comprising all those who were anti-Soviet, anti-Bolshevik, and anti-Stalin. Some of them, like the "esteemed reapers" of Stalin's letter to Sholokhov, were overt enemies. Very many others were covert enemies operating behind masks of party and Soviet loyalty. Their prime method of undermining the Communist cause was to oppose Stalin by criticism and sabotage of his policies, and also by belittling his merits as the political man of genius that they knew him to be.

The Anti-Stalin Backlash

The events traced in the preceding chapters caused the community of the faithful to shrink in the early 1930s and the countercommunity to grow. Stalin's popularity plummeted by comparison with his standing in the later 1920s. Then his critics were chiefly members of oppositional groups numbering at most a few thousand. Now, in reaction to the grim times the country was experiencing under his rule, they became far more numerous.

In his own eyes the mastermind of a second October, who deserved grateful recognition as such, Stalin appeared to many others the bungler of collectivization. They were under no inner compulsion to see him as a hero of revolutionary history. From Central Committee meetings and various circular directives that had emanated from his Central Committee offices in 1929 and early in 1930, many in high places and in the regional party leadership were aware of his personal responsibility for the policy that was publicly repudiated in the emergency of February–March 1930. Consequently, an anti-Stalin backlash developed in the early 1930s. Since little about it appeared in the Soviet press, it had a certain muted, even clandestine quality; and not all party members shared it. Still, the critical current had a potent influence on later events.

It found expression in the literary world. In 1931 the journal *Red Virgin Soil* published a story called "Being of Use" by Andrei Platonov, who was not then well known. It told of how in March of 1930 a certain good-hearted poor man, an electrician by trade, boarded a train in Moscow and got off somewhere in central Russia. This nameless wanderer, described as capable of erring but never of lying, moves from *kolkhoz* to *kolkhoz* being of use as an electrician and talking with peasants. Little by little the reader begins to perceive a central Russia countryside devastated by the hurricane of Stalin's collectivization, peopled by peasants in a kind of trance. Reference is made to "hypocritical observance of the voluntary principle." In one place the wanderer remarks that "the excesses in collectivization were not a wholesale phenomenon, some places were free of dizzying mistakes, there the party line didn't get cut off and go into a curving deviation. But unfortunately there weren't too many such places." Proof that an intelligent reader could perceive the anti-Stalin message is that one—Stalin himself—wrote in red pencil on the margin: "Scum!"[1]

In 1933 the poet Osip Mandelstam composed a sixteen-line poetic epigram about Stalin. It ran as follows:

> We live, deaf to the land beneath us,
> Ten steps away no one hears our speeches,

But where there's so much as half a conversation
The Kremlin's mountaineer will get his mention.

His fingers are fat as grubs
And the words, final as lead weights, fall from his lips,

His cockroach whiskers leer
And his boot tops gleam.

Around him a rabble of thin-necked leaders—fawning
half-men for him to play with.

They whinny, purr or whine
As he prates and points a finger,

One by one forging his laws, to be flung
Like horseshoes at the head, the eye or the groin.

And every killing is a treat
For the broad-chested Ossete.

The oral composition traveled from Muscovite mouth to mouth until it reached the police in a version whose second stanza ran:

All we hear is the Kremlin mountaineer,
The murderer and peasant-slayer.

Mandelstam was arrested. When Bukharin, then editor of *Izvestiia,* went to Yagoda to intercede on the poet's behalf, Yagoda recited the epigram to him by heart.[2]

The anti-Stalin backlash showed up in the working class as well. This we know from OGPU reports found in the Smolensk archives. It was one of the tasks of the OGPU, as it had been of the tsarist police, to keep track of public opinion and report on it to the central authorities. A top secret OGPU document dated 27 March 1931, on popular attitudes in the Western province town of Roslavl in connection with the deportations, claimed that the workers "basically" approved these measures, but said that some "betray negative attitudes," that they were talking about the "good old times" and saying, "All this would not have happened if Lenin had been alive." Looking at Lenin's portrait, one worker had said that "were Lenin alive, he would have allowed free trade and eased our lot. Afterwards, he would have instituted a shift toward collectivization—not by force, but by consent and persuasion."[3]

One Old Bolshevik who shared the view of the worker-critics was Krupskaya. Collectivization was not proceeding "in Lenin fashion," she said in a speech of May 1930 before a party conference of Moscow's Bauman district. Its methods had nothing in common with Lenin's cooperative plan. In carrying it out, the leaders of the Central Committee had not consulted with the lower ranks of the party or with the people, and they had no right to blame the local organs for the Central Committee's own mistakes. Kaganovich went down to the Bauman district to handle the situation for Stalin. He said that as a Central Committee member herself, Krupskaya had no right to criticize the Central Committee's line. "Let not N. K. Krupskaya think," declared Kaganovich, "that if she is the wife of Lenin she has a monopoly on Leninism."[4] He also passed word that Krupskaya was to be attacked, and she was from all sides. Khrushchev, then a student at the Industrial Academy in the Bauman district and a staunchly pro-Stalin rising young party functionary, recalled much later how sorry he had felt for Krupskaya, whom he too venerated, when she was being critically assailed at the conference, and how "people avoided her like the plague."[5]

Some of 50,000 letters sent to Stalin between the autumn of 1929 and the spring of 1930 expressed the resentment that "Dizzy With Success" aroused among local party members. One that has been quoted by post-Stalin Soviet historians as typical was written by a worker in Dnieprope-trovsk named Belik, who had taken part in collectivization, and appeared in *Pravda* on 9 June 1930. "Comrade Stalin," he said, "I, an ordinary worker and *Pravda* reader, have regularly been following the newspaper articles! Is the guilty one the person who couldn't help but hear the hue and cry over collectivization and over the question of who should direct the collective farms? All of us, the grass-roots people and the press, over-looked that basic question about the leadership of the collective farms, while Comrade Stalin, in all likelihood, was in deep sleep at that time and didn't hear and see our mistakes. So you too have to be rebuked. But now comrade Stalin shifts all the blame on the local offices, and defends himself and the top group."[6]

What Comrade Belik made bold to say in a letter addressed to Stalin, others were saying informally. The party man from the Klin district of Moscow province told the Fischers apropos "Dizzy With Success": "That was exactly what I had said from the beginning. But our local authorities wouldn't listen because they had orders from Moscow and were afraid to disobey them. Everybody in the village now laughed at me. I wanted to go away and never return."[7]

Some officials even had the temerity to warn Stalin of the "excesses" while they were being committed or, afterward, to call grass roots resent-ment over his article to his attention. A. M. Nazaretian, a secretary of the party committee of the Transcaucasian Federation, repeatedly warned Sta-lin about the likely consequences of the coercive means being used, only to find himself, by Stalin's devices, saddled with blame for those conse-quences and recalled to Moscow. There, without work, he and his wife and children went hungry for several months until Ordzhonikidze interceded for him. Knowing that Ordzhonikidze, along with Kirov and Kuibyshev, would defend this highly regarded Transcaucasian Old Bolshevik if the case came before the Politburo, Stalin agreed to his appointment to a minor official post in the Urals.[8]

A document preserved in the Central State Archive of the October Revolution shows the outrage felt by some workers of Moscow and the nearby factory town of Podolsk against Stalin for his catastrophic mismanagement of the development drive. This anti-Stalin manifesto, bearing four signatures, was approved at a meeting of 273 workers held in Podolsk on 19 September 1930. It said that Stalin, dizzy with power, had lost all capacity of sound judgment. His "criminal activity" of the past two years had nullified all Lenin's achievements and now confronted the proletarian regime with the threat of total ruin. To preserve proletarian power, Stalin must immediately be ousted and put on trial "for countless crimes that he has committed against the proletarian masses."[9] What fate overtook the authors of this then unpublished manifesto is not known.

Dissent also reared its head in public, although in a controlled way. In accordance with party tradition, policy theses were published in advance of the Sixteenth Congress, and on 9 June 1930 *Pravda* published a special "discussion sheet" filled with comments by party members. One became a *cause célèbre*. A party member from Saratov, named Mamaev, argued that wholesale collectivization was premature for lack of agricultural machinery, and aimed some darts directly at Stalin. The latter, Mamaev said, had quite rightly fixed attention on coercive collectivization. But most unfortunately, this came *after* the blundering. "So, somebody did not foresee it. Involuntarily the question arises: whose head grew dizzy?" Speaking up in defense of the maligned lower officials, Mamaev declared: "One should speak of one's own missed shots and not give lessons to the lower party mass." Citing an old saying in Russia, Mamaev went on: "It turns out that 'The tsar is good, but the local *chinovniki* [state officials] are no good.' "

It seems that Mamaev's short article was allowed to appear in the censored party organ to provide occasion for denunciation of the views it expressed. For there appeared in *Pravda* the next day a five-column editorial counterblast obviously prepared in advance, "The Kulak Agents' Network Inside the Party." Mamaev was branded a "kulak agent." His defense of the lower party ranks against the leadership was "demagogy of the worst sort." The article's infuriated tone, its demand that Mamaev's statement and others like it be "burned out without a trace by the hot iron of proletarian Bolshevik self-criticism," probably achieved the intended aim of making plain to the party ranks that criticism of Stalin's leadership was taboo.

Political Opposition

It was less easy to stifle anti-Stalin talk in higher party circles. The stage managing of the Sixteenth Congress fostered an impression of a party hierarchy united in enthusiastic support of Stalin, but it was false. The most one could say is that the congress represented a demonstrative closing of the ranks by a leadership divided about the wisdom of some current policies but reluctant to display division at a time of crisis.

Events soon showed that oppositional currents were running in the party. In late 1930 it came out that two groups had been engaging in "underground factional work" against the General Line. The leaders of this oppositional "right—'left' bloc" ("left" had to be used in quotes to show that no one could really be to the left of the General Line) were, on the one hand, S. I. Syrtsov, then a candidate member of the Politburo as well as a Central Committee member and the premier of the Russian Federation, and, on the other, Central Committee member V. V. Lominadze, who was first party secretary of the Transcaucasian Federation, and L. A. Shatskin, a member of the Central Party Control Commission. Although the former was pictured as a rightist and the latter two as pseudo-leftist, the fact is that all three were Stalin supporters who had soured on his policies and on him.

What this group concretely stood for has to be inferred from pertinent parts of the denunciatory articles that appeared along with the announcement of the expulsion of these leaders from their high posts. One thing is clear: these Bolsheviks began to doubt that Stalin's policies were leading to socialism, and became convinced that the policies were producing a rampant growth of bureaucratism. The Transcaucasian bureaucracy was showing what Lominadze called a "feudal-lord attitude toward the needs and interests of workers and peasants." In their view, the pace of industrialization should be reduced to what was soberly manageable without great wasteful spurts. Syrtsov called the vaunted successes of the *piatiletka* "eyewash" and described the Stalingrad tractor plant as a "Potemkin village."[10] The "bloc" was accused of conspiring to change the party line *and* leadership; according to firsthand testimony, Lominadze even envisaged Stalin's ouster as something to be accomplished at the next party congress.[11] This must have been a sharp blow to Stalin, since the younger fellow Georgian had been his personal protégé and emissary in Comintern affairs in the later 1920s.

By 1932 there was further drastic worsening of conditions in the country. A weary working class was now turning a deaf ear to agitation for more labor heroism. Prices had shot up. Basic goods as well as food were rationed, and not always available on ration cards. Mass manifestations of discontent were reportedly seen even in factories of privileged Moscow. With famine stalking the countryside, people going hungry in the towns, factories everywhere trying to meet the food emergency by the new panacea of rabbit-breeding on factory grounds, collectivized peasants working listlessly for lack of incentive and many (as the saying went) "leaking" out of the collectives when possible, the catastrophe of Stalinist collectivization was beyond intelligent doubt. Now even the lower and middle ranks of Soviet officialdom had largely lost the optimism still felt during the first three plan years and were stricken with what an anonymous Moscow correspondent of the *Bulletin of the Opposition* called "a hangover from the 'economic October.' " Stalin was now a "fallen idol" in the eyes of all but a very small upper stratum of the bureaucracy, wrote another anonymous correspondent from Moscow to the *Bulletin.* He continued that the average Soviet official moved away from Stalin in a passive and expectant way, aligning himself with the party mass by refusing to show enthusiasm for Stalin. To illustrate this point, the correspondent mentioned that Stalin's appearance at Moscow's Bolshoi Theater—always well patronized by officials—on 23 February 1932 "was greeted before my eyes with cold silence."[12]

The grave situation was bringing discredit on the party itself in the eyes of many ordinary people, uninformed as they were about the crucial part that Stalin had played in recent party decisions. "Bolshevism is losing popularity," a young Hungarian Communist resident in the Soviet Union, Mate Zalka, confided to his diary. "The newspapers are pervaded with falsehood. They blame everything on forces abroad. *Pravda*'s lies are terrible. Our ruble is worth a kopeck. This is no crisis, it's worse. We're afraid to speak the truth."[13] Awareness that the public was uninformed about Stalin's personal role in bringing about the catastrophe only intensified the anguish of some highly placed officials and bitterness among middle-ranking party members against Stalin for his silence.

The year 1932 was comparable to 1921 as a time of crisis. Politically conscious people waited for Stalin to come out now, as Lenin had then, with a frank diagnosis of the situation and a prescription for a sharp policy turn designed to alleviate it. They waited in vain. In these circumstances it is hardly surprising that some Soviet politicians saw Stalin's departure from leadership as imperative for the country's well-being.

One informal anti-Stalin group that emerged then was led by A. P. Smirnov, V. N. Tolmachev, and N. B. Eismont, men whose party membership dated from 1896, 1904, and 1907, respectively. Smirnov, the principal figure, had been a Central Committee secretary and agriculture commissar between 1928 and 1930. The Central Committee plenum of

January 1933 approved an earlier Central Control Commission decision to expel Smirnov from the Central Committee and the other two from the party as punishment for having formed an "underground factional group" to change the industrialization and collectivization policies. Long after Stalin's death, it came out that the three men were brought to account for advocating the replacement of Stalin. During the Central Committee's consideration of the case, Stalin declared: "It's only enemies who can say, get rid of Stalin and no harm will come of it."[14]

An anti-Stalin appeal came from the pen of M. I. Riutin, a well-known district party secretary in Moscow who had supported the Right against Stalin at the end of the 1920s. On 21 August 1932 he met with a dozen or so fellow party members in a Moscow apartment to discuss and edit an "Appeal to All Party Members." Two years earlier, then a candidate member of the party Central Committee, Riutin had written a 200-page treatise that reflected the Right's anti-Stalin position and became known in party circles as the "Riutin platform." For that he was expelled from the party and arrested. In January 1931, however, he was released and received back his party card along with a warning not to resume oppositional activity. But he did just that by writing the Appeal in 1932. Some copies went into hand-to-hand circulation.

Riutin compressed into the Appeal's seven or so pages a withering indictment of Stalin for breaking with Leninism, establishing a personal dictatorship, and pursuing policies that had brought the country to the brink of disaster. His reckless tempo of industrialization had disorganized the whole economy, impoverished the people, and undermined their faith in socialism. His terroristic collectivization, mainly aimed against the masses of middle and poor peasants, had reduced the countryside to desperate straits. Hardly more than 30 percent of the 1927 head of livestock survived. Millions of peasants were nomads seeking refuge in overpopulated towns. Famine was looming in 1933. Real Leninism was becoming a forbidden doctrine. The people were muzzled, live Bolshevik thought smothered, the press a monstrous factory of lies. Stalin and his retinue had usurped the party's rights and were promoting sly, sycophantic careerists ready to change their views as commanded. The boldest and more brilliant provocateur could not have done so much to discredit Leninism and socialist construction. Lenin's fears about Stalin had been fully borne out. He was wrecking the Communist cause and his leadership should be terminated as soon as possible.

Someone present at the August meeting turned informer. On 30 September the police raided the apartment and seized the document's original. Riutin was expelled from the party and arrested. Two weeks later the central Party Control Commission's presidium expelled twenty other party members as a Riutin-led "counterrevolutionary group." They included Zinoviev and Kamenev, who had possessed copies of the Riutin Appeal without informing the authorities, the philosopher and historian V. Ter-Vaganian, P. Petrovsky (son of the Ukraine's president), an old Georgian party comrade of Stalin's, Sergei Kavtaradze, the writer Polina Vinograd-skaya, A. Slepkov, D. Maretsky, and the philosopher Jan Sten.[15] All of them became terror victims in a few years' time.

One of the readers of the Appeal was Stalin. It aroused him to such fury that the expulsions and Riutin's arrest could not appease him. He confronted the Politburo with the demand that it sanction Riutin's execution as a terrorist. Amid silence around the Politburo table, Kirov spoke up saying: "Can't do that. Riutin is not a lost man but an errant one. Devil only knows who had a hand in this letter. People won't understand us."[16] Stalin, perhaps sensing the majority's opposition to his demand, let the matter rest, and Riutin got off with a ten-year term—for the present.

Stalin, however, would not let go. When he found that Riutin's confinement in the Suzdal political prison was not sufficiently severe to suit him, he had him moved to a worse regime in the Verhne-Uralsk prison. At some point thereafter Riutin was brought to Moscow in an effort to torture and pressure him into consent to play a part in a public treason trial, but he refused. In 1937, on Stalin's personal orders, he was executed. His two sons, both aeronautical engineers, were likewise done to death. His wife was sent away and killed in a camp near Karaganda in 1947. His 20-year-old daughter and her small child were thrown out of their Moscow lodging onto the street, minus their worldly possessions.[17]

Although Stalin's power was not seriously threatened by the Riutin platform, his pride was. To denounce him as the Revolution's evil genius when he saw himself as the hero-leader of its second stage was to wound him in an almost unendurably painful way. His description of the Riutin document as a call for his assassination was true in a symbolic sense. He could not help viewing the denunciation as character assassination, a deadly blow to his most sensitive and vulnerable spot—the belief in his mission of greatness in history. His response was the only one of which he was capable under those circumstances: to demand the death of his assailant as an enemy not simply of him but of the Revolution. To Stalin the punishment he demanded exactly fit the crime, and he later showed how deeply rankled he was by the ruling group's refusal to sanction it.

Bolshevik Disbelievers

The active opposition of the Lominadzes and Riutins was not all Stalin had to contend with. There was also, especially among Old Bolsheviks, a negative attitude toward the post-NEP society taking shape in the early 1930s. Schooled as they were in what Marx and Lenin had taught about socialism, some found it hard, others impossible, to view the new society as incipiently socialist. Stalin was also versed in the teachings of Marx and Lenin, but in his mind this schooling was overlaid with the orientation on state building.

That he regarded the ongoing revolution from above as an October of socialism's construction is clear. When the Central Committee met in January 1933 to review the results of the Five-year Plan, he not only declared that the Soviet Union had become a mighty and independent industrial power. He claimed that the "economic foundation of a socialist society" had now been built, and asserted that "we have established the principle of socialism in all spheres of the economy by expelling the capitalist elements from it."[18]

At the time Stalin made this claim, much of the countryside was famine-stricken. Millions were being worked to death in the forced-labor camps. Many in the new industrial sites shivered in cold, dark, barrack-like structures for lack of real housing. "Hard was the life of Soviet people then," recalls the writer of a Soviet book of the 1960s. "I remember how ill-clothed our workers were. It wasn't easy to get a new suit or dress on one's ration card. Many who took part in family gatherings brought their own food. Chip-in parties, fraternally egalitarian—this had its charm. The parties ended early: 1 January was a working day, the new *piatiletka* was to start out in shockwork fashion."[19]

All this was not what most Bolsheviks of the older generation meant by "socialism." Even if Stalin had explained more clearly how socialist construction had blended in his mind with state building in the Russian pattern, few of his Old Bolshevik contemporaries could have gone along with him: their minds were not attuned to his acquired sense of Peter's Russia as the rightful ancestor of Lenin's and Stalin's Russia. As they saw it, socialism was not simply a matter of industrialization along with state ownership and planning; or of dislodging capitalist elements from the economy. Many of them assumed that it would mean better living conditions for the workers, not dire poverty; that its building would not necessitate mass terror against the peasants; that it would bring more equality rather than less, less bureaucracy rather than more, and more popular self-management along the lines sketched by Lenin in his picture of the "commune-state"; and that a resurrection of such relics of the tsarist past as penal servitude, *barshchina,* and the passport system was no part of socialist construction. Many Bolsheviks who had been Stalin's supporters tended to believe these things just as much as those whose political sympathies had lain with Trotsky, Zinoviev, Shliapnikov, Bukharin, or others.

Knowing that most of his revolutionary contemporaries couldn't easily reconcile the privation and inequality all around them with their values as socialists of Marxist and Leninist persuasion, Stalin sought to help them doctrinally. His spokesman Molotov (whom some in the party now began to call his "bludgeon") explained to the elite audience gathered at the Seventeenth All-Union Party Conference in February 1932 that socialism need not entail material plenty. It was necessary, said the Soviet premier, to "give rebuff to reasoning like: 'socialism is production for consumption's sake'." Such a viewpoint was "one-sided and incorrect."[20]

The "incorrect" idea had been axiomatic for a generation of Russian socialists. Many Bolsheviks who had never supported Trotsky would have agreed with what he wrote in March 1932: "Is it not monstrous? The country cannot get out of a famine of goods. There is a stoppage of supplies at every step. Children lack milk. But the official oracles announce: 'The country has entered into the period of socialism!' Would it be possible more viciously to compromise the name of socialism?"[21] Those who spoke out in ways that presupposed such thinking came to grief. For example, a one-time revolutionary, now director of a Moscow bread factory, was called to testify at the trial of a worker who had stolen a small amount of bread and was being tried under Stalin's law of August 1932 against theft of state property. Unable to contain himself, the director exclaimed at one point: "If we gave the workers bread, they wouldn't steal." Sent into exile shortly thereafter, he perished in the Terror of the later 1930s. What distinguished him from others of his generation was not his view but the fact that he voiced it.[22]

Growing class inequality was also hard for some people of the old Marxist-Leninist persuasion to stomach. Some Bolshevik managers protested their own privileged position by boycotting the special shops, wearing workers' clothing, and joining the food queues. When this happened in Ivanovo province after wildcat strikes broke out among textile workers in 1932, Kaganovich, who soon arrived on the scene, not only saw to the suppressing of the strikes but punished the protesting managers as well. According to one of them, who later turned up in a camp and told his story to fellow inmate Joseph Berger, Kaganovich explained that "the use of special shops by the privileged was party policy—to boycott them was therefore aggression against the government."[23]

Mostly, however, the disbelievers kept quiet while their disbelief continued. Vasily Yurkin, a Russian intellectual and a Bolshevik since 1914, explained to Berger in the Siberian camp at Mariinsk in 1935 that one should not confuse the events of the first revolutionary era with those taking place now. What had happened in the Civil War was unavoidable, "but what is happening now would have filled Lenin with horror." A worker Communist named Belousov, who had been chairman of the Metal Workers' Union in 1905 and now too was an inmate of the Mariinsk camp, told Yurkin and Berger that he had never taken part in any opposition although much of what he read in the papers "clashed with his secret, ideal image of the party." He had passed time quietly with friends at the Society of Old Bolsheviks in Moscow. And yet: "Can you believe it—when, finally, in 1935, I was arrested, I felt a measure of relief! The fact is that for years past we Old Bolsheviks who lived in this new society, in this new state we had created with our own hands, had been living with fear and horror in our hearts—a horror more intense than anything we had felt in tsarist times." Berger writes of Belousov's confession: "It was the first one of its kind I had heard but I was to listen to many more from the Communists I met in other camps and prisons."[24]

Younger party members might put credence in Stalin's claim of success in socialist construction; these elder ones could not. Their disbelief was something of which he was certainly aware from, among other sources, the OGPU's reports; and it could not fail to arouse his vindictive fury. For indirectly it was a disbelief in him as the leader under whose direction the country was fulfilling Lenin's prophesy that "Out of NEP Russia will come a socialist Russia." Were that not happening, he would not be one of the things that "Stalin" signified to him: architect of socialism. The disbelievers did not understand that their inability to see his creation as the basically socialist society he held it to be was from his standpoint an intolerable affront, no less a blow than it would have been to defame him outright. Unknowingly, many survivors of the revolutionary generation were in grave danger of becoming outcasts from a society still being ruled in the name of their Revolution.

A Death in the Family

Another episode contributed to making 1932 a year of intense personal bitterness for Stalin rather than the time of triumph that he had certainly expected it to be. Not only did dissenting opinion spread widely in party circles; it appeared inside his family. The offender was his wife.

Nadezhda Alliluyeva-Stalina, called Nadya by intimates, was still in her late twenties when Stalin turned fifty in 1929. When they married ten years earlier, she was already an ardent party activist for whom Stalin, as an Old Bolshevik of high standing, was an embodiment of the Revolution that she idealized. Although he was a difficult man to live with, the marriage had so far survived the inevitable strains. Nadya gave him the companionship of a devoted wife and made Zubalovo, their country house outside Moscow, a sociable meeting place for many visiting friends and relatives.[25]

After giving birth to their two children, Vasily and Svetlana, Nadya resumed a professional life while carrying on as mistress of Zubalovo. In 1930 she entered the new Industrial Academy as a chemistry student specializing in synthetic fibers. A serious, diligent, unassuming person, she came to school by streetcar so as not to display her social position. Among those she befriended at that time was the academy's party secretary, Nikita Khrushchev, who in retrospect attributed his successful political career and survival of later purges to the fact that Nadya had spoken well of him to Stalin.[26]

It may have been a combination of Communist idealism and contact with the other students and everyday life at the beginning of the 1930s that turned Nadya against the policies then in force and against her husband as their chief inspirer. She came to the realization, as their daughter later put it, that "my father was not the New Man she had thought when she was young, and she suffered the most terrible, devastating disillusionment."[27] Based on what she was told much later by her old nurse, various relatives, and Nadya's close friend Polina Molotova (Molotov's wife), Svetlana conveys a picture of her mother as having become deeply depressed a few days before she died on 9 November 1932. "My nurse heard my mother say again and again that 'everything bored her,' that she was 'sick of everything' and 'nothing made her happy'."[28] This testimony is in agreement with that of a one-time Soviet official, Alexander Barmine, who recalls having seen Nadya with her brother, Pavel Alliluyev, during the anniversary parade in Red Square on 7 November 1932: "She looked pale and worn, little interested in the proceedings around her. I could see that her brother was deeply concerned."[29]

Most likely Nadya's dejection was evident at the dinner party held on the night of 8 November at the Voroshilovs' to mark the fifteenth anniversary of the Revolution, and Stalin was annoyed. According to the daughter's reconstruction of events, at one point he said to Nadya, "Hey, you, have a drink!" This is consistent with the further reported detail that he doused a cigarette in his wine glass and flipped it across the table at her.[30] Nadya screamed, "Don't you dare 'hey' me!" rose, left the banquet, and headed for home. Polina Molotova went along and walked around the Kremlin grounds with her until Nadya had calmed down enough for Polina to feel that she could safely leave her alone. Nadya retired to her private bedroom in the Stalins' Kremlin apartment where, according to her daughter's later account, she was found the next morning, dead from a self-inflicted bullet shot. It came from a small revolver sent her as a present from Berlin by her brother, Pavel Alliluyev, who had served as military representative with the Soviet trade mission in Germany. She left behind a letter filled with both personal and political accusations against Stalin. He was shocked into numbness by her suicide and infuriated by her accusations, which he took as an act of betrayal. When he approached her open coffin to pay his last respects during the civil leave-taking ceremony in a building on Red Square, he stood there for a moment, then pushed the coffin away from him, and abruptly walked out. He never visited her grave in Moscow's Novo-Devichy cemetery.[31]

A different version of Nadya's death circulated in some Old Bolshevik circles in the 1930s. According to it, Stalin shot or strangled her to death in a fit of rage during a quarrel after he came home from the dinner party later that night.[32] As told to the present writer by a person well-situated to know what some very high-placed persons believed, Stalin in a meeting with Politburo members on the day after Nadya's death said that he took action against her as she menacingly advanced upon him. It could be (we may speculate) that he arrived as she was preparing to commit suicide and that a violent scene ensued in which she came at him with pistol in hand and was slain by him in an ensuing scuffle.

However that may be, Stalin's responsibility for his wife's untimely end is not in question. In whatever manner it physically occurred, hers was a Communist's death of protest against him. His daughter reports that he never got over the shock and to the end of his life went on brooding about the tragedy, imputing the blame to others.

The Birth of the Great-Conspiracy Theory

Nadya's accusatory farewell and death, coming on top of the other hammer blows to Stalin's psychic structure, made the close of 1932 a time of inner crisis. From youth he had tended to be a loner; now he withdrew into himself more than ever and became a recluse. He stopped coming to Zubalovo and started building the country house in Kuntsevo that he occupied for the rest of his life. He moved out of the Kremlin apartment he had shared with Nadya into a smaller one not associated with her. While keeping up some ties with children and relatives, he was no longer regularly surrounded by the society of which Nadya had been a vital hub and hence no longer benefited from its free and easy flow of conversation on Soviet affairs. His more solitary life reflected a change that had come over him. As his daughter puts it, "inwardly things had changed catastrophically. Something had snapped inside my father."[33]

After the shocked numbness and fits of uncontrollable rage at the time of Nadya's death, Stalin recovered his equilibrium and pursued his politi-

cal life, along with a social life of sorts, as before. The price paid for the
equilibrium was, however, a settled inner vision of the Soviet Communist
party and the society as riddled with treason and the potentiality of treason.
Even in the 1920s he had been prone to see the world around him peopled
with enemies engaged in conspiratorial machinations. Now this tendency
took a radical turn for the worse. He began to picture himself as the
intended victim of a great counterrevolutionary conspiracy centered in
certain circles of Bolshevik ill-wishers and ramified through the society. It
was the only way he could mentally come to terms with the situation in
which he found himself.[34]

In the exercise of power Stalin had stumbled. There were notable
successes in industrialization, but the total picture was grim. Taking socialism by storm in the coercive Russian state-building tradition proved in
practice too costly and disruptive a mode of national development. Collectivizing by terror had backfired with consequences that included the worst
famine in Russia's history along with the loss of about half her livestock.
The human cost was beyond calculation. The backlash was testimony to
widespread belief in the party that Stalin was to blame for these misfortunes. To this his reaction was vindictive rage.

It was impossible for him to recognize that he had bungled things and
that there was justice in the criticism of his leadership. That would be the
path of breakdown, of parting company with himself—the idealized Stalin-
self. Since he could not relinquish or seriously scale down his self-concept,
he had to keep his mind's eye firmly fixed on achievements and treat the
costs as unavoidable or caused by others. More, he had to see the changes
wrought during the *piatiletka* as equivalent in their consequences to the
October Revolution, and himself as the architect of a socialist society.
Lenin, the leader of the first October, was adored afterward by the party
he had steered to that triumph. Now he too deserved to be adored. There
were many, especially among ordinary people, who did pay homage to
him—he could see signs of that in the Soviet press, in the growing attention
to his revolutionary biography, his past and present exploits. But many
others saw everything in a negative light. Instead of recognizing an historic
victory, they were belittling the constructive achievements. Instead of
saluting his leadership of genius, they were criticizing him and conspiring
to overthrow him.

Such, it appears, was the direction of Stalin's thinking at this point.
Not being able to see anything in his actions that merited criticism, he had
to perceive the critics and disbelievers as deliberate maligners engaged in
an attempt to sabotage the revolution of socialist construction by besmirch-
ing his leadership and doing everything possible to make the enterprise
fail. He had to see in every Riutin an assassination-scheming counterre-

volutionary, a wrecker, an enemy of the people, all the more dangerous in that he wore a mask of loyalty. Because—as Stalin certainly knew from secret-police reports—criticism of him was rife, he could only conclude that large numbers of persons were plotting his own and the regime's destruction. He naturally thought of individuals he firmly knew to be his enemies as plausible ringleaders of the conspiracy.

Indirect, *ex post facto* evidence that he so reasoned exists in a letter of the party Central Committee, marked top secret and dated 29 July 1936. It was sent as a circular letter to all republic, regional, town, and district party committees, and it concerned "the terrorist activity of the Trotskyist-Zinovievist counterrevolutionary bloc." The bloc was said to have concentrated on "perpetrating terror against very prominent party leaders, in the first instance Comrade Stalin." Of special significance is the date given for the formation of the purported great anti-Soviet conspiracy: *the end of 1932.*[35] Since the letter came from Stalin's headquarters and was indubitably a product of his inspiration, the timing of the alleged conspiracy's inception suggests that the belief in its existence arose in his mind at the time when he was under stress of the events just described.

We have, moreover, some revealing public remarks of Stalin's that go to corroborate the above reconstruction of his thought process. The occasion was a graduating ceremony of the Red Army Academy, held in the Kremlin palace on 4 May 1935. Stalin was the speaker. He began by harking back to the theme of the no-more-beatings speech of 1931. The task had been to move a country ruined by four years of the World War and three of the Civil War, with a semiliterate population and no more than oases of industry in a sea of tiny peasant farmsteads, onto the rails of modern industry and mechanized agriculture. It was a question of EITHER doing this in the shortest possible time and thus strengthening socialism, OR of failing to do it and letting the country lose its independence and become a play object for imperialist powers. The country had experienced then a most cruel famine in the sphere of technology. Only by making sacrifices and introducing the most stringent economy in everything, including nourishment and manufactured goods, could the technology famine be eliminated. Of course, quick and wholesale successes were not to be expected in such a big undertaking; it had been necessary to overcome early setbacks and go forward without wavering toward the great aim.

But not all comrades possessed the requisite nerves, patience, and composure. "Let bygones be bygones," the saying went. "But a man has a memory, and involuntarily you think back on the past when you take stock of the results of our work." Well, Stalin went on, some comrades took fright at the difficulties and called on the party to retreat. "What good do your industrialization and collectivization, your machines, iron and steel, tractors, combines, and automobiles do us," they said. "Better to produce more manufactured goods, better to buy more raw material for consumer goods and give the population more of all those trifles *(melochi)* that enhance people's lives." Of course, said Stalin, the three billion rubles of foreign exchange obtained through cruelest economizing and spent on industry could have been used to raise consumer goods production—at the expense of undermining the foundations of socialism, being disarmed in the face of external enemies, becoming captive of the internal and external bourgeoisie. That too would have been a kind of plan, but a plan of socialism's retreat rather than the plan of offensive that was chosen and that led to the victory of socialism.

But the comrades who were shoved aside in the process did not confine themselves to criticism and passive resistance, Stalin continued. They threatened to raise a revolt in the party against the Central Committee. More than that, they threatened "certain ones among us" with bullets. "Apparently, they reckoned on intimidating us and forcing us to swerve from the Leninist path. These people obviously forgot that we Bolsheviks are people of a special cut. . . . They forgot that we were forged by great Lenin, our *vozhd'*, our teacher, our father, who did not know or recognize fear in struggle. . . . Naturally, we gave no thought to swerving from the Leninist path. We stuck to this path and redoubled the speed of our advance, sweeping aside any and all obstacles. True, along the way we had to do damage to some of these comrades. But that couldn't be helped. I must confess that I too took part in this business."[36]

These impromptu-appearing remarks of 1935 betray a great deal: that Stalin was obsessively troubled by memories of earlier criticism and viewed the critics, or some of them, as plotters of his assassination; that he managed to reconcile the record of the recent past with the indispensable image of himself as the glorious leader of Soviet Russia's march to modernity and socialism; that he cast himself as a hero not only in refusing to relax the pressure but also in suppressing party opponents; that he made himself out to have been a famine-fighter by transferring the famine to the realm of technology while transforming actual mass starvation into cruel "economizing" on nourishment; and that he minimized past privation by treating the missing essentials, like clothing, as life-enhancing "trifles." Finally, his description of the Bolsheviks as "people of a special cut"—the phrase used in his "oath" speech of 1924—shows that he still held to his idealized community concept, the image of the party as a league of warriors united in fidelity to a heroic leader.

That was what Stalin believed that the Bolsheviks ought to be, but not what he thought they all were. As he saw it in the aftermath of the bitter autumn of 1932, the party as then constituted, with a total of 3,200,000 members and candidates, was at best a conglomeration of real Bolsheviks and enemies masquerading under the name. Such was his contention when he addressed the Central Committee plenum called in early January 1933 to assess the results of the *piatiletka*. He coupled the proud claim that the economic foundation of socialism had been built with the dark vision of a party and society swarming with masked enemies, and the demand for a purge.

Here was Stalin's vision: various former people—merchants, industrialists, kulaks and their accomplices, bourgeois intellectuals, and others —were ensconced in Soviet plants, farms, and government offices; some had even wormed their way into the party. Unable to fight openly, they were carrying on stealthy wrecking activities, such as arson, sabotage, thievery, even the inoculating of cattle with the plague and of horses with meningitis. They would go to any length to mobilize backward elements for anti-Soviet purposes. Remnants of the SRs, Mensheviks, bourgeois nationalists, Trotskyists, and Rightists could reactivate themselves in these circumstances. Hence the internal struggle must grow more intense with progress in completing the construction of socialism. The quality that Bolsheviks most needed now was revolutionary vigilance.[37]

Two important conclusions followed from Stalin's diagnosis of the situation. First, the Soviet state, including its punitive organs, must be strengthened. It must not be allowed to begin withering away as Marxist theory foretold. "A strong and mighty dictatorship of the proletariat— that's what we need now to smash to pieces the last remnants of the dying classes and break up their thieving machinations." Some comrades had understood the Marxist thesis about the elimination of classes and resulting disappearance of the state as grounds for torpor and complacency, for the counterrevolutionary theory of the diminishing of class war and weakening of state power. Such people were degenerates or double-dealers who must be kicked out of the party.[38]

The second conclusion was the necessity of a large-scale party purge. This had already been decided by the Politburo, very likely at the time of the Riutin affair under pressure from the enraged Stalin. A special resolution of the January plenum approved the Politburo's decision to conduct a party purge during 1933 and to "organize the work of purging the party in such a way as to ensure iron proletarian discipline in the party and cleanse the party ranks of all unreliable, unstable, and hanger-on elements."[39]

A Central Committee directive of 28 April 1933 made clear the intended scope of the operation. A Central Purge Commission, headed by Jan Rudzutak and numbering among its members Kaganovich, Kirov, Yaroslavsky, and Stalin's rising protégé from the Central Committee apparatus, Yezhov, was to direct a network of republic, regional, and district purge commissions in weeding out all who might be adjudged to fall into one of six broad categories, the first three of which were defined as follows: "(1) class alien and hostile elements who made their way into the party by deceit and remain there in order to demoralize the party ranks; (2) double-dealers who live by deceiving the party, who conceal from it their true aspirations and, covered by a false oath of 'fidelity' to the party, in fact strive to undermine the party's policy; (3) open and hidden violators of the iron discipline of the party and state, who fail to carry out the decisions of the party and state, who cast doubt on or discredit the party's decisions and plans by chatter about their 'lack of realism' and 'impracticability'."[40] Party critics of Stalin and his policies were to be prime targets.

The projected purge was placed in the hands of a specially created purge commission rather than the regular party body for this purpose, the Central Control Commission. Under Kuibyshev from its formation in 1923 until 1926 and under Ordzhonikidze thereafter to 1930, the Central Control Commission had served the Stalin faction well as a disciplinarian arm of the fight against the oppositions. But under Rudzutak after 1930, the agency came under criticisms indicating that Stalin now saw it as an impediment to his full freedom to act against opponents in the party. One criticism was excessive leniency in reinstating party members who appealed to the commission against lower-level expulsion actions.[41]

Although the special new commission was placed under Rudzutak, its creation indicated that Stalin did not trust the established party body to carry out satisfactorily the major purge operation that he envisaged. He wanted an organ that would mercilessly root out the "masked enemies" from Soviet society. He was starting down the road that led to the Terror of the later 1930s.

Stalin in 1929.

Khrushchev in the early 1930s.

Voroshilov, Stalin, Molotov, Kalinin in mid-1930s.

Stalin, Kaganovich, Andreev, Voroshilov, and Comintern chief Dimitrov.

Famine scenes in the Ukraine, early 1930s.

Stalin and aviator Chkalov.

Nikolai Yezhov.

Ordzhonikidze, Voroshilov, Kuibyshev, Stalin, Kalinin, Kaganovich, and Kirov.

Lev Trotsky, later 1930s. *U.S. Information Agency*

Mikhail Tukhachevsky.

Molotov, Stalin, and Litvinov on Kremlin grounds, mid-1930s.

Nadezhda Alliluyeva, circa 1930.

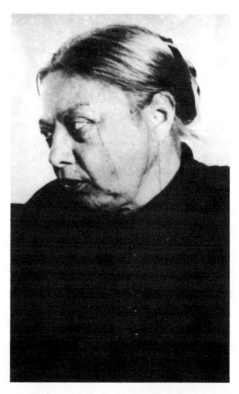

Krupskaya in 1929. *U.S. Information Agency*

Karl Radek, 1935. *Staatsbibliothek Berlin*

Kirov in 1934. *Staatsbibliothek Berlin*

Stalin's last visit to his mother in Georgia.

The Stalin museum in Gori.

Painting of Stalin at Gorky's dacha, early 1930s.

Foreign Commissar Litvinov at work, 1932. *U.S. Information Agency*

German ambassador in Moscow, Count von der Schulenburg.

Alexi Tolstoy, the "worker-peasant count."

Soviet writer Mikhail Sholokhov.

Lavrenti Beria. *David King Collection*

Left, theater director Vsevelod Meyerhold, the "Master."

Stalin's second wife lying in state. *David King Collection*

Henritch Yagoda. *David King Collection*

Grigori Zinoviev. *David King Collection*

Voroshilov, Stalin, and Kalinin at the Sixteenth Party Congress, 1930.

Stalin and Maxim Gorky, 1931.

10

THE DIPLOMACY OF RAPPROCHEMENT WITH GERMANY

O N NO SUBJECT was foreign opinion more inclined to err in the 1930s than on Stalin's foreign policy. The apostle of socialism in one country was widely viewed as a nationalist leader who, in fact if not in theory, had jettisoned international Communist revolution as an aim of Soviet policy. This simplistic thinking, based on the antithesis of "Russian nationalism" versus "international revolution," blocked an understanding of Stalin's foreign policy as a subtle amalgam of both.

In charity to those who erred, it must be said that for reasons of *Realpolitik* Stalin encouraged the misconception. For instance, to a visiting American agricultural engineer whom he invited to his Kremlin office for

A preliminary version of this chapter appeared in *The Slavic Review* (December 1977) under the title "The Emergence of Stalin's Foreign Policy."

an interview in 1929, he admitted, with what the visitor took to be "disarming frankness," that under Trotsky there *had* been an attempt to spread Communism throughout the world, and said that this was the main cause of his break with Trotsky.[1] In 1936, he spoke still more bluntly to the American newspaper executive, Roy Howard. He said, "The export of revolution is nonsense," and dismissed the idea that Soviet Russia had ever harbored world revolutionary intentions as a "tragicomic" misunderstanding.[2]

The exiled Trotsky eagerly seized upon such statements as evidence for his own view that Stalin's foreign policy, being that of a Thermidorian bureaucracy, had in fact renounced world revolution. When Campbell's book came out in 1932 with its account of the 1929 conversation, Trotsky wrote in the *Bulletin of the Opposition:* "The declaration of Stalin is no maneuver and no trick; basically it flows from the theory of socialism in one country."[3] Later, Trotsky sought to sum up Stalinist foreign policy in the phrase "From 'World Revolution' to 'Status Quo'," brandished Stalin's remarks to Roy Howard as proof, and commented: " 'Your tragicomic misunderstanding,' Stalin might have concluded, 'lies in your taking us for the continuers of Bolshevism, when we are in fact its gravediggers.' "[4]

Those who saw the international revolution as a dead letter in Stalin's foreign policy could point not only to such words but also to Soviet actions—and inactions—of the late 1920s and early 1930s. Bukharin said to Kamenev during their clandestine conversation of July 1928, "Externally Stalin is following a rightist policy." Hypercaution was in fact the keynote of the policies pursued abroad at this time and after. Stalin's regime showed an anxious concern for the maintenance of international peace.

When William Bullitt arrived in Moscow in December 1933 as American ambassador, following U.S. recognition of Soviet Russia, Foreign Commissar Litvinov informed him in their first official conversation that the Soviet government wanted to join the League of Nations, an organization long reviled in Soviet publicity as a tool of Anglo-French imperialism. He explained the shift of policy by the desire to secure Russia on its western borders at a time when a Japanese attack was believed imminent in the Far East. The nervousness felt on this score was reflected in Litvinov's suggestion that an American squadron or warship be sent the following spring on a visit to Vladivostok or Leningrad as a gesture of support. At a Kremlin banquet in Bullitt's honor, Stalin solicited 250,000 tons of American steel rails to complete the double-tracking of the Trans-Siberian railway in preparation for trouble with the Japanese, declared that "President Roosevelt is today, in spite of being the leader of a capitalist nation, one of the most popular men in the Soviet Union," and ended by kissing the amazed envoy on the face.[5]

But a foreign policy must be understood in terms of its longer-range perspective as well as the actions of the moment. Stalin was then preoccupied with the second revolution, knew that Soviet society was in no condition to fight, and feared any external complications that could lead to war. Yet preparation of the country for a future war was a primary purpose of his policies, and the war prospect was a revolutionary one as well.

An acute observer would have done well to look through a volume of previously unpublished Lenin writings that came out in Moscow in 1929. One of the documents, a set of notes written by Lenin in early 1918, contained the injunction: "First conquer the bourgeoisie in Russia, then fight with the external, foreign, outside bourgeoisie."[6] The editing of unpublished Lenin documents was considered a matter of such high state importance that the Lenin Institute was a constituent part of the Central Committee apparatus under Stalin. He was undoubtedly aware of the lines just quoted, and the whole record of his conduct of Soviet policy shows that he took them as authoritative guidance.

But before becoming powerful enough to fight the "outside bourgeoisie," Stalin reasoned, Soviet Russia must align herself diplomatically with a section of it. By helping to keep the capitalist world divided against itself, such a policy would provide her with insurance against the dread possibility of having to fight a war for survival against an overwhelming coalition of enemy states. Moreover—according to Leninist theory—tendencies leading toward the outbreak of a new interimperialist war would be strengthened, and such a war, if properly exploited, could offer an opening for revolutionary advance. To prepare the way for moving into neighboring countries destined to constitute parts of the needed "socialist encirclement," Moscow's best bet from Stalin's point of view, was a diplomacy of accord with Germany.

The German Orientation

Interviewing Stalin in December 1931, the German biographer Emil Ludwig said that he had observed in Russia a general enthusiasm for everything American. "You exaggerate," Stalin replied. Although American efficiency and straightforwardness were appreciated, he said, there was no special respect for everything American. If there was any nation toward which Soviet sympathies were strong, it was the Germans. "Our feelings toward the Americans bear no comparison with these sympathies!"[7]

After inquiring why the Russians felt such ardent pro-German sympathies (to which Stalin archly replied, if only because Germany gave the world Marx and Engels), Ludwig said that recent Soviet-Polish talks about a nonaggression treaty had aroused alarm among German politicians. Should Poland's present borders receive official Soviet recognition, it would be deeply disappointing to the German people, which had taken the USSR's opposition to the Versailles system seriously. In his carefully worded response, Stalin stressed that a Soviet-Polish nonaggression agreement would mean nothing more than an undertaking by the two states not to attack one another. It would be neither a recognition of the Versailles system nor a guarantee of Poland's borders. "We have never been Poland's guarantors and never will be, just as Poland has not and will not be a guarantor of ours. Our friendly relations with Germany remain just what they have been so far. Such is my firm conviction. So, the alarm of which you speak is utterly unfounded."[8]

Stalin's German orientation was not rooted in anything personal. His German experience was confined to the two or three months that—as he mentioned to Ludwig—he had spent in Berlin in 1907 while returning from a Bolshevik party congress in London, and he knew only a few words of German. The orientation derived from the legacy of Lenin. The Brest treaty, that primal act of Leninist diplomacy to which the Bolshevik Revolution owed its survival, was an accord between Moscow and Berlin.

Subsequently, Lenin visualized an alliance with Germany as an attractive option for Moscow's divisive diplomacy. "Germany is one of the strongest advanced capitalist countries, and so it cannot put up with the Versailles treaty. Herself imperialist but pinned down, Germany must seek an ally against world imperialism," he said in his speech of 6 December 1920. "Here is a situation we must utilize."[9] Lenin's prevision of a Soviet-German alliance bore fruit in the Rapallo treaty of 1922 providing for full resumption of diplomatic relations, mutual cancellation of economic claims, and most favored nation treatment. This coup of Lenin's divisive diplomacy opened the way for an anti-Versailles partnership between the Soviet and German governments during the 1920s. The relationship, though close, was also uneasy because of conflicting pressures on both partners. On the German side there was a division among influential circles and in the Foreign Ministry between men of Eastern orientation (the *Ostlers*), who saw the Russian connection as vital for Germany's revisionist goals, and those of Western orientation (the *Westlers*), who felt that Germany's interests, the territorial one included, could best be served by cooperation with the West. The German ambassador in Moscow, Count Ulrich von Brockdorff-Rantzau, and the man who succeeded him in that post in 1929, Herbert von Dirksen, were prominent *Ostlers,* as were the military leaders who valued the clandestine use of Soviet soil for military training and testing in collaboration with the Red Army. The German Social Democratic party, on the other hand, was strongly wedded to the Western orientation.[10]

The latter circumstance helps to explain Stalin's extreme antipathy for the SPD. In February 1925 he told a German Communist journalist, Wilhelm Herzog, that a proletarian revolution was out of the question in Germany so long as the SPD had not been exposed, crushed, and reduced to an insignificant minority among the workers. Recalling that Lenin in the pre-October period had insisted on the Mensheviks' elimination as a prime condition of victory, Stalin said that now no firm German revolutionary victory was possible even in the best of external conditions as long as there were, within the working class, two competing parties of equal strength.[11] Stalin's antipathy extended to German Communists of moderate persuasion who favored a common front with amenable left-wing Social Democrats against the fascist danger. One such person was the prominent German party leader Heinrich Brandler, who sought a united front with the SPD left wing looking to possible Communist participation in a coalition government.[12] Later in the month of his interview with Herzog, Stalin numbered Brandler, along with his associate Thalheimer, among the "old" leaders who, like the Lunacharskys and Pokrovskys in Russia, were passing out of the picture now; and stressed the need to eradicate "Brandlerism" from the German Communist party.[13] Brandler's expulsion from party membership came in 1929, by which time it was an official Comintern policy to damn Social Democracy as "social-fascism."

The German alignment was a star by which Stalin steered Soviet diplomacy in the later 1920s and early 1930s. The anti-Entente memories of the Russian Civil War were an enduring influence on his political thinking: the two great adversary poles of attraction in the contemporary world were the Soviet East and the capitalist West led by "Anglo-America." The American-sponsored Dawes plan (regarding German reparations) he assessed in a speech of May 1925 as an American-British-French scheme for looting Germany; and he saw a sign of the unwillingness of "such a cultured nation as Germany" to bear that yoke in the "in essence reactionary fact" of Field Marshal von Hindenburg's election to the German presidency in the previous month.[14]

The now abundantly documented inner history of Moscow-Berlin relations in the later 1920s reveals the picture of a German government adhering generally to the Russian connection in the midst of a tug-of-war of pressures from West and East; and of a Stalin regime nervously fearful lest its German connection be lost due to a combination of the *Westlers'* influence internally and a determined effort by the Versailles powers to lure Berlin into their anti-Soviet camp with economic, political, and territorial concessions. From the talks on renewal of Rapallo that led to the 1926 Treaty of Berlin, through to the talks of early 1931 on the latter's extension, the now available German Foreign Ministry correspondence shows the Soviet side regularly pressing the Germans to reaffirm their adherence to the Rapallo line and periodically taking initiatives to cement political, military, and economic ties with Berlin. Thus the 1931 talks found Litvinov offering the Germans a choice between straight renewal or a stronger treaty whereas the Germans favored simple renewal; and Moscow wanted a five-year extension as against the original Wilhelmstrasse proposal of only six months.[15]

It is true that German dealings with the Russians were bedeviled by many frustrations and that for about a year in 1929–30—during the chancellorship of Herman Müller, the first Social Democrat to hold that post since 1923—severe tensions brought by developments on the Soviet side plunged the partnership into a crisis. The earlier Soviet arrest of five German engineers and placing of three on trial in the Shakhty case was one of the developments.[16] Another was the descent on Moscow, during collectivization, of thousands of Mennonites of German extraction who were fleeing their villages in quest of a new home in Canada and whose plight greatly aroused German public opinion. Significantly, it was Soviet initiatives for better relations which caused the diplomatic crisis to subside in early 1930.

As Weimar Germany entered the time of its death agony, Moscow signed a nonaggression agreement with France in August 1931 with a view to defusing French anti-Sovietism; and in January 1932 it concluded a similar agreement with Poland. In doing so the Narkomindel (as the Foreign Commissariat was called) rejected the Poles' long-standing demand for a clause specifically recognizing the German-Polish border. But it agreed to a general formula defining aggression as any action violating the territorial integrity or political independence of either side.[17] To the worried Germans this looked like an "indirect guarantee" of the eastern borders they aspired one day to revise.

Stalin's forthright statement to Ludwig in December 1931 that the Soviet Union would never be Poland's guarantor was obviously intended to reassure the Germans that whatever phraseology was used in the impending treaty with Poland, they had no cause for alarm. He wanted to emphasize that Moscow's German orientation was still in force.

Stalin and the Nazi Revolution

The Weimar republic went down under the assault of the Great Depression and the Nazi movement, helped along by various political factors: the feebleness of the center forces, the absence of alert and vigorous political leadership on the part of those in authority, and, not least, the tactics pursued by the German Communists on orders from Moscow—from Stalin.

Unemployment in Germany rose steadily from over one million in late 1929 to over six million in 1931–32, the latter number amounting to something like a third of the wage-earning population. Masses of Germans grew responsive to the would-be savior leadership of Adolf Hitler and his National Socialist party, and by the summer of 1932, the Nazis held about a third of the seats in the Reichstag. The stage was now set for the combined propaganda blitz and high-level political maneuvering that brought Hitler to the chancellorship on 30 January 1933. The ensuing "legal revolution" witnessed a wave of Nazi terror, the Reichstag fire of 28 February followed by the Enabling Act ("Law for Removal of the Distress of People and Reich"), and the overthrow of the constitutional order. By the summer of 1933, the Nazi dictatorship was firmly established.[18]

With their mass worker and trade union constituencies, their combined total of close to 40 percent of the Reichstag seats in November 1932 (representing about seven million Social Democratic votes and nearly six million Communist ones), the two parties of the German Left were together a potentially powerful force for preservation of the constitutional order. Whether they could have prevented the Nazi victory by resolutely working in tandem and with other antifascist elements to this end is an unanswerable question. What is certain is that the absence of such cooperation, indeed the strife between the two parties during that critical time, facilitated the downfall of the constitutional order. Not all Communists were blind to the catastrophic character of this strife. As early as September 1930 Trotsky raised his voice from Prinkipo exile to urge the German Communist party (the KPD) to work with the SPD in a united front against fascism. He accurately forewarned that a Nazi victory would mean the crushing of the German working class and an inevitable war against the USSR. Many German Communists took a similar view.[19]

But Stalin had different ideas. By forcing upon the KPD a policy of uncompromising belligerence against Social Democracy ("social-fascism"), he abetted the Nazi victory. A Comintern Executive Committee directive to the German Communists in February 1930 demanded "merciless exposure" of Social Democracy. Under Comintern direction, the German Communist leader Heinz Neumann in the summer of 1930 drafted a new KPD "Program of National and Social Liberation," which promised to annul the Versailles treaty and the Young Plan and denounced the SPD as the treasonable party of Versailles. Competition with the Nazis for the mantle of German nationalism went along with a certain amount of collaboration. In the summer of 1931, for instance the Communists, on orders from Moscow, joined in a Nazi- and rightist-organized plebiscite against the SPD state government in Prussia.[20]

The leaning toward a united antifascist front with the SPD was not entirely confined to the Communist rank-and-file; there were signs of it among the party leaders too. Ernst Thaelmann rebelled at first against the instruction to participate in the anti-SPD Prussian plebiscite. Then he, Hermann Remmele, and Heinz Neumann "were called to Moscow to learn at first hand that this instruction had been issued to the Communist International by Stalin personally."[21] Another former German Communist, who worked in the Comintern offices in Moscow in 1932 and survived a lengthy later incarceration in Soviet concentration camps, recalls that ". . . as early as 1932 there existed in the leadership of the KPD as well as in the Comintern machine a marked readiness to set up a 'united front' with the Social Democrats which would have prevented the victory of National Socialism. But their timid proposals were not adopted. The influence of Stalin—who held fast to his line, while any criticism of it was instantly branded as 'anti-party heresy,' if not as 'provocation by agents of international capitalism'—was decisive."[22]

The SPD leadership, concerned over its ties with the Catholic and center parties, also held back from collaboration with the Communists. By the autumn of 1932, however, the depth of the crisis made the urgency of collaboration clear. An SPD leader, Friedrich Stampfer, obtained an interview with the Soviet envoy in Berlin, Lev Khinchuk, himself a former Russian Menshevik. "Would it be possible to expect the cooperation of Communism in the struggle against National Socialism?" Stampfer asked Khinchuk. Several interviews followed between Stampfer and Soviet Embassy attaché Vinogradov, who finally broke off the exchanges by saying: "Moscow is convinced that the road to Soviet Germany leads through Hitler."[23]

Stalin's decisive personal role in the KPD policies that abetted the Nazi revolution is beyond doubt. Insofar as the possibility existed of heading off this event by encouraging a united front of the German Left and other anti-Nazi forces, he was chiefly responsible for its failure to materialize. To some his decision has seemed an act of monumental political ineptitude stemming from failure to grasp the revolutionary nature of National Socialism or a belief that its victory—as was said in Communist circles at that time—would be short-lived and pave the way to power for German Communism. Such interpretations are unconvincing. The then current version about a short-lived Nazi victory bears earmarks of a convenient rationalization put out by Stalin's headquarters. However inadequate his understanding of Hitler and the Nazi movement may have been in 1930–33, Stalin knew enough about the staying powers of Italian fascism, not to mention Russian Bolshevism, to beware of assuming that the Nazis could not create a stable single-party system and extirpate resistance with ruthless terror. We must take into account that Stalin, for all his doctrinaire cast of mind, was reasonably well informed and given to acting with a carefully thought-out rationale. Although complex, the rationale in this instance is not hard to reconstruct.

First, elemental caution dictated that the German Communists be restrained from any attempt at a seizure of power, no matter how revolutionary the German situation. In the comparable circumstances of 1923, Stalin had argued in a letter to Zinoviev that the German Communists should be restrained on the grounds that their position was not so favorable as the Bolsheviks' in 1917 in Russia and that "if power in Germany were, so to speak, to fall to the street and the Communists picked it up, it would end in failure and collapse."[24] He had ample reason to take the same view in 1932. Even if a coup should initially succeed, the German Communists could not possibly hold out on their own against combined internal and external counterrevolutionary forces. The Soviet Union for its part was in no position to come to their aid or to risk any international complications that might result in early war. Separated from Germany by hostile Poland, preoccupied with its *piatiletka,* stricken by famine, it would be condemned to stand by helplessly and ignominiously while German Communism was being overthrown and destroyed.

For different reasons, Stalin could not look with favor on a KPD bloc with the SPD and other amenable elements to prevent the fall of the Weimar system. Even this policy entailed some small risk of international anti-Soviet complications that had to be avoided at all cost. And supposing the policy succeeded and the Nazis were stopped from taking power, what then? The SPD politicians were inveterate *Westlers,* indeed the chief German force for a Western orientation in foreign policy. As probably the dominant partner in the anti-Nazi coalition, their foreign-policy orientation would be influential. No prospect could have been less pleasing to Stalin.

The only serious remaining possibility was the path that Stalin took. Accepting and even indirectly abetting the Nazi takeover was a course that offered promise along with dangers to the USSR (but in what direction were there no dangers?) and the certainty that German Communism would be repressed. Despite their shrill ideological anti-Bolshevism and anti-Slav racism (along with anti-Semitism, which would not grieve Stalin), the Nazis were no *Westlers.* Their movement was stridently nationalistic, revanchist, illiberal, antidemocratic, antipacifist, and anti-Versailles. They were plainly a bellicose force. Their accession to power might, then, be a harbinger of great tension, if not a new war, between Germany and the West. We have direct testimony that this was what Stalin thought. In a conversation with Heinz Neumann at the end of 1931 he said: "Don't you believe, Neumann, that if the Nationalists seize power in Germany they will be so completely preoccupied with the West that we'll be able to build up socialism in peace?"[25]

Stalin's line of thought and action—or inaction—at this critical juncture was consistent with his war-and-revolution scenario. By accepting if
not actively facilitating the Nazi takeover, he was guiding events in the
direction he had long wanted them to take—toward a war between opposed
imperialist countries in Europe. This was not, as he knew, an early prospect, for it would be a matter of years before the Nazis could rearm
Germany for war. But an early outbreak of war was not something for
which Russia was prepared either. What the Nazi victory portended was
the end of passivity in German foreign policy. A liberal democratic Weimar Germany perpetually poised between *Ostpolitik* and *Westpolitik,* wavering between the Russian connection and the Western alignment into
which she was regularly being drawn by anti-Soviet politicians in America,
Britain, France, and Germany herself, would never go to war against the
West for German interests. A Nazi Germany might. There was of course
the alternate possibility that it would march against Russia. But Stalin
apparently reckoned that he could contain this threat by the devices of
diplomacy.

As the Nazi takeover drew near, Moscow signaled its readiness for it,
indeed its cautious hopefulness. In July 1932 the counselor of the German
Embassy in Moscow, Gustav Hilger, had a talk with Doletsky, the head of
the Soviet news agency TASS. Along with Soviet worries, Doletsky communicated to Hilger "his conviction that healthy political common sense
would win out in a National Socialist government; even the Nazis would
be sensible and continue a policy toward Russia that, in his opinion, was
consonant with the long-range interests of Germany." "His" conviction
was unquestionably the view that Doletsky had been commissioned to
convey informally. He assured Hilger that the Soviet press had been ordered to give no appearance of interfering in Germany's crisis and even to
avoid criticizing German policy. His only fear was that Hitler's accession
might be followed by a disturbed transition period before normal relations
could be reestablished. "The general impression in the German Embassy,"
adds Hilger in his recollections, "was that the Soviet government would
have liked to establish contact with the National Socialists for the purpose
of preventing such temporary difficulties."[26]

A former German Communist writes that a saying was current in
antifascist German circles at that time, "Without Stalin, no Hitler," and
that Zinoviev said to him in early 1933: "Apart from the German Social
Democrats, Stalin bears the main responsibility to history for Hitler's
victory."[27] Be that as it may, Stalin played a part in helping the Nazis to
take power.

First Overtures

Using terror to solidify their power, the Nazis seized on the pretext of the Reichstag fire to hound members of the KPD into exile, concentration camps, or underground. Initially, their relations with Moscow were clouded by a series of ugly incidents in which Nazi toughs invaded the premises of Soviet offices in Berlin. The new authorities hastened, however, to assure the Soviet government that their anti-Communist internal policies had nothing to do with their foreign policy.

Some men in Moscow were apprehensive about the Nazi takeover and inclined to respond in a stiffer way than Stalin wanted. Two top commanders, M. N. Tukhachevsky and Yan Gamarnik, are reported to have proposed right after Hitler's accession that Red Army–*Reichswehr* relations be broken off, and to have been overruled by Stalin.[28] They and others who shared their outlook were not in most cases anti-German or opposed to the German orientation. Ordzhonikidze, for example, was appreciatively aware of the contribution that the 5,000 or more German engineers working in the Soviet Union had made to the *piatiletka*. Tukhachevky and his fellow officers prized the Red Army's connection with the *Reichswehr*. But the rise of the ferociously anti-Communist German radical right to power seemed to jeopardize the long-standing friendly links between the two outcasts of Versailles and show the need for new directions in foreign policy.

A leading figure who reasoned in this fashion was Foreign Commissar Maxim Litvinov. An old Bolshevik of wide foreign experience, who had spent ten pre-revolutionary years in England and returned to Russia in 1918 with an English wife, he was less attached to the German orientation than many other Soviet politicians.[29] Since he was also a Jew, Litvinov could not but harbor extreme antipathy for a force like German National Socialism. Earlier, as the ties with Germany loosened in the prelude to Hitler's taking of power, he had responded to a French initiative for better relations by negotiating the Franco-Soviet nonaggression pact of 1931. Similar accords followed with the border states of Poland, Finland, Latvia, and Estonia. These moves unquestionably had Stalin's approval, and no significant realignment of policy was involved. Still, in the new atmosphere following January 1933, Litvinov and others were bound to be attracted to the idea of a new diplomacy of cooperation with those European states that had cause to fear Hitler's Germany. Stalin, however, had other ideas, and Hitler gave him some encouragement.

On 23 March 1933, the *Fuehrer* declared the Reich ready to cultivate friendly and mutually profitable relations with the Soviet Union. "It is above all the government of the National Revolution who feel themselves in a position to adopt such a positive policy with regard to Soviet Russia," he said further. "The fight against Communism in Germany is our internal affair in which we will never permit interference from outside. Our political relations with other Powers to whom we are bound by common interests will not be affected thereby."[30] In early May, Hitler's government took the symbolic step of ratifying the protocol—signed in 1931 but left unratified by the Brüning and von Papen governments—on an extension of the 1926 Treaty of Berlin. More important, he received Khinchuk a few days before this and made reference to common interests of Germany and Soviet Russia. He said that they were both economic and political because the two countries had the same difficulties and the same enemies. The two countries could complement one another and render mutual services.[31] Stalin must have read this with keen interest.

Moscow's public posture was wary. Its chief commentator on German affairs was Radek, who also served as a behind-the-scenes foreign-policy adviser to Stalin. In articles printed in *Bol'shevik* and *Pravda* in May–June 1933, Radek construed Hitler's conciliatory gestures as a means of gaining time and as a concession to German industrialists concerned to keep Soviet orders during the economic crisis. He also said that Alfred Rosenberg, whom he called "the inspirer of German fascism's foreign policy," had paid an unofficial visit to London to sound out British diehards on a possible deal against the Soviet Union. German fascism was combining its reassurances to Moscow with efforts to build an anti-Soviet coalition.

Stalin did not intend to stand idly by in face of the machinations Radek was describing. He knew that no attack could possibly be imminent at that early stage and was aware of holding strong cards of his own. Hitler had already indicated in his talk with Khinchuk that one common interest, hence potential basis of cooperation, between his Germany and Stalin's Russia were their respective revisionist claims upon different portions of Poland. If Hitler, moreover, were disposed to pursue his revisionist aims in the West by means of war, Stalin was in a position to guarantee him against the specter inherited from 1914–1918— a two-front war. There was also reason to believe that Hitler's policies might be influenced by those very Reichswehr, nationalist, and capitalist circles that had been proponents of the Eastern orientation all along. One of them, General Hans von Seeckt, had argued in a recently published pamphlet that it was useless for Germany to try and drive a wedge between Britain and France and that she needed Russia's friendship for attainment of her revisionist aims.

Radek approvingly quoted the pamphlet at length in one of his articles, clearly implying that the general was talking sense.[32]

Finally, there was in National Socialism, itself a revolutionary movement, a current of admiration for revolutionary Russia. Among the Nazis there were some *Rechtsbolschewisten* (Bolsheviks of the right) who saw Stalin as a true man of power and exponent of Russian nationalism in opposition to the international Communism of those like Trotsky, whom they despised as rootless cosmopolitan Jews. Even Alfred Rosenberg's organ *Weltkampf* spoke in 1929 of Stalin's anti-Semitism and said Russia could not be called a Jewish state since Trotsky had been deposed and non-Jews like Stalin, Kalinin, and Rykov were on the rise.[33]

Sedately, with no show of anxiety or alarm, Stalin signaled his interest in doing business with Berlin. Having reciprocated Hitler's action in ratifying the protocol on extension of the 1926 treaty, the Soviet government published an *Izvestia* editorial on 5 May 1933, which reaffirmed the Rapallo tradition, pointed out that past unfriendly German politics toward the USSR had only weakened Germany, proclaimed Soviet desire for peace and good economic relations with that country, and concluded that the now extended treaty "will have the significance given it by concrete actions of the parties that concluded it."

Not long afterward Stalin began to communicate with Berlin via special channels, bypassing the Foreign Commissariat. In the summer of 1933 his old friend Abel Yenukidze, whose official post was secretary of the Central Executive Committee of Soviets, took a vacation in Germany. In August, after returning, he arranged an outing at his country house for Ambassador Dirksen and the minister-counselor of the German Embassy, Twardowski. They were joined by deputy foreign commissars N. N. Krestinsky and Lev Karakhan. The former had served in the 1920s as Soviet envoy to Berlin.

Yenukidze (described in Dirksen's memoirs as "a fair-haired, blue-eyed, kindly Georgian with definite pro-German leanings") suggested to Dirksen that the National-Socialist reconstruction of the German state could have positive consequences for German-Soviet relations by giving the German government the degree of freedom of action in foreign affairs long enjoyed by the Soviet government. He thought that a German "state political line" was little by little emerging as the "state" elements in the Nazi movement separated from the "agitational" ones. In both Germany and the USSR, however, there were many who put political goals of the party in first place, and these people must be checked by "state-political thinking."[34] Dirksen and Twardowski voiced the view that a *modus vivendi* could be worked out between the Soviet Union and the new German regime, and they suggested that an influential Soviet representative meet with Hitler in furtherance of that aim. It was arranged that Krestinsky, after taking a cure at Kissingen in Germany, should stop in Berlin en route home and seek an interview with the chancellor. Hitler subsequently agreed, after much persuading on the German side, to see Krestinsky. But the latter was directed to return home from Kissingen via Vienna rather than Berlin, and the meeting did not take place—very likely because Litvinov, who had to be brought into the plan, persuaded Stalin that the timing of the meeting would be inopportune.[35]

By then—October 1933—Stalin was taking a further step in his secret diplomacy vis-à-vis Berlin. He opened a communication channel through an individual whom Twardowski, in telegrams to Berlin, called "our Soviet friend." This go-between is believed by a knowledgeable source to have been Radek. Evgeni Gnedin, who served in the Narkomindel during the 1930s, also reports, from personal knowledge, that Radek around this time was placed in charge of a small foreign-policy section attached to Stalin's secretariat. He would order various studies by foreign-affairs specialists and carry out special assignments for Stalin, with whom he was in direct contact.[36]

In place of the Hitler-Krestinsky meeting that did not come off, "our Soviet friend" arranged for a meeting to take place in Moscow, but behind Litvinov's back, between Dirksen and a man Stalin knew he could trust—Molotov. Dirksen, then on leave in Germany, was expecting to return to Moscow for a brief farewell visit whose precise timing was not yet decided. His successor in the Moscow ambassadorship was to be Rudolf Nadolny, a strong *Ostler*. Litvinov was to leave Moscow shortly for Washington and talks with President Roosevelt on U.S. recognition of the USSR. Molotov was scheduled to pay a visit to Ankara.

On 24 October Twardowski sent an urgent wire to Berlin for Dirksen. "Our friend" had brought about a conversation the day before. He considered the atmosphere toward Germany "so improved" that it was desirable for the opportunity of Dirksen's farewell visit to be used "to pick up the threads again," after which "perhaps Nadolny can bury the hatchet once and for all by signing a little protocol." "Our friend" reported to Twardowski that Molotov had given up the trip to Ankara, alluded to Litvinov's forthcoming trip to Washington, and "specifically offered his mediation."[37] Litvinov departed Moscow on 28 October, and Dirksen arrived the following day. Gnedin, the first to reconstruct this episode, which he accurately calls an "intrigue," comments that the ground was thereby prepared, deliberately and behind the back of Litvinov, for rapprochment with Hitler's Germany.[38]

What transpired between Molotov and Dirksen in October 1933 is not known. But judging by the royal farewell that Stalin's court gave to Hitler's envoy, the results could not have been displeasing to the general secretary. Dirksen was given a grand farewell dinner that was attended by many dignitaries who normally avoided contact with foreigners. He received a beautiful onyx bowl as a parting gift, and "Voroshilov ordered one of his generals to hand me his gift of a writing-set in lacquer with a modern design but executed in the famous old technique."[39]

11

THE CONGRESS OF VICTIMS

The Reconciliation Line

THE FOOD CRISIS started to show signs of abating in late 1933, before the famine ended. The improvement was partly deceptive: crop statistics were no longer based on barn yield but on "biological" yield, or what was in the fields before the harvesting with its heavy losses. This created an appearance of fulfillment of the Five-Year Plan's control figures for grain production.[1] Nevertheless, cutting of grain exports and more efficient grain collection—at cruel cost to starving peasants—raised the amount of food available to the town population in 1933. And when it became clear that a fairly good harvest could be expected in the fall, there was huge relief in high circles that, at whatever price, the war of forced collectivization had been won.

As the emergency subsided, talk of Stalin's removal did as well. According to Bukharin's later account to Nicolaevsky, people who only yesterday had been trying to obtain a copy of the Riutin platform were now saying that Stalin had won. From the autumn of 1933, "The groupings were now not for or against Stalin. Everybody emphasized tirelessly his devotion to Stalin. It was rather *a fight for influence over Stalin,* a fight for his soul, so to speak,"[2] said "Old Bolshevik."

The fight was being waged by a group that favored a policy of "reconciliation with the people." Knowing what people had endured during the *piatiletka* and apprehensively aware by now that Hitler's hostile regime was not going to be a quick-passing phenomenon, the promoters of this policy argued that the chief present task was the rebuilding of morale. The home front had to be solidified in face of the threat of Nazi aggression. The austerity of Soviet life must be relieved by more attention to housing and consumer goods. The rampant governmental terror of recent years must be curbed. The Soviet political system must be made at least to appear more democratic so as to dramatize the gulf between Communism as a basically humanistic movement and fascism as a racist, terrorist, and openly antidemocratic one.[3]

The Politburo advocates of the reconciliation line had the support of Maxim Gorky. Although not a holder of party office, or even a party member, he was a man of consequence as Russia's world-renowned man of letters. Having been courted by Stalin in correspondence while still living abroad, Gorky returned to Russia in 1931 to settle down, and was lionized by the regime. An apartment in Moscow and a two-story dacha outside the city were placed at his disposal. Stalin would occasionally pay visits to the apartment, with various Soviet writers in attendance. On one such occasion, in October 1932, he offered his famous characterization of Soviet writers as "engineers of human souls."[4] Gorky rendered valuable service to Stalin by, among other things, sponsoring the visit of 120 Soviet writers to the newly completed Baltic–White Sea Canal and the subsequent collective volume glorifying that forced-labor project as a grandiose experiment in rehabilitating enemies. Stalin, in turn, showed his solicitude for the writer by such niceties as arranging for an elevator to be installed in the country house after learning that Gorky found it hard to negotiate the stairway on foot.[5] Now, in late 1933, Gorky joined the efforts to convert Stalin to the reconciliation line. He even put forward in private the idea of forming a fully loyal second Soviet party consisting of representatives of the intelligentsia who would suggest "changes and remedies."[6]

Foremost among the Politburo proponents of the reconciliation line was, by all accounts, Sergei Kirov. The forty-seven-year-old Leningrad party chief had reached by now a prominent place in political life. His credentials for leadership were strong. A Bolshevik since 1904, a revolutionary with a record of arrests and exile, he came to the fore as a leader in the North Caucasus during the Civil War and joined the Central Committee before Lenin died. He was staunchly pro-Stalin in the later drive against the Trotskyist-Zinovievist opposition. In 1926, following Zinoviev's ouster, he took over the important Leningrad organization for Stalin and joined the Politburo as a candidate member, becoming a full member in 1930. His friendship with Stalin, dating from Civil War days, was close, as witnessed by Stalin's inscription in the copy of *On Lenin and Leninism* that he gave Kirov in 1924: "To my friend and beloved brother, from the author. I. Stalin."[7]

Kirov's prestige arose in part from his personal qualities. Born Sergei Mironovich Kostrikov in the northeast Russian heartland province of Viatka, he was a Russian by nationality and showed the national character traits at their best in his simplicity, straightforwardness, sagacity, and diligence. He had the gift for forceful, pungent, impromptu public speech that Russians prize and Stalin lacked. Although without intellectual pretensions, he was a cultivated man, a reader of books, who was able to make friends with a writer like Gorky. He was also popular with party colleagues of more practical bent, and was widely and affectionately known, as Lenin had been, by his patronymic. "Our Mironych," they called him, and some dubbed Leningrad the "city of Ilyich and Mironych." He was an approachable leader in whose Smolny office all sorts of people received a hearing and often some help.[8]

Kirov was an enthusiast of industrialization and a hard-driving leader not only of Leningrad but of the whole Soviet north during the *piatiletka*. Since Leningrad was a great center of machine building, party leaders and factory heads from all over the union turned to him, and sometimes traveled to him, for help and advice. So there emerged, without any apparent attempt by him to cultivate it, a Kirov constituency across the country. One of his Soviet biographers relates how the vice-commissar of heavy industry, Iosif V. Kosior, was surprised during his visit to the Soviet Far East in 1933 to hear people saying on all sides: "Kirov, Kirov."[9]

That Kirov was tough and unsqueamish is beyond doubt. Since the area under his general supervision included the prisoner-built Baltic–White Sea Canal, he could hardly have been a resister of Stalin's Petrine methods. But neither was he a devotee of them, and where it was in his power he preferred to act with restraint. Collectivization was carried out in Leningrad region with less convulsive haste and far less resulting damage than in the country generally.[10] This was an implicit indictment of Stalin's blitzkrieg collectivization and its consequences. The steady-nerved Kirov is reported to have said of Stalin, "He's an hysteric," in informal remarks of 1930 to a group of Leningrad companions.[11]

Very likely this remark was relayed to Stalin by someone in his network of informers, and it may help to explain the coolness that he began to show toward Kirov. Khrushchev, who became second secretary of the Moscow party organization in 1932, recalls a Politburo meeting at which one of Kirov's subordinates reported on Leningrad's success in building up its economy enough to cut back on rationing. Khrushchev stayed behind briefly when the meeting recessed. "Unintentionally, I was witness to an exchange of sharp words between Stalin and Sergei Mironovich Kirov. Sergei Mironovich said something favorable about his delegation's report on rationing, and Stalin shot back with some insulting remark about the secretary who had delivered the report. I was shocked. In those days I was very idealistic about party morality. I couldn't believe that Stalin, the leader of our party, would behave disrespectfully toward another party member.[12]

If Kirov was the natural leader of the Politburo advocates of the reconciliation line, Ordzhonikidze was the natural coleader. Intimate friends since the Civil War years when they collaborated in the Caucasus, the two men would confer by phone nearly every day. On visits to Moscow, Kirov would stay at the Ordzhonikidzes' apartment where he and Sergo would talk through the night about their problems.[13] In the early 1930s Ordzhonikidze tried to curb the wild extremes of bacchanalian planning and shield the technical intelligentsia from specialist baiting.[14] As a frequent visitor to industrial building sites he knew better than most Politburo members how hard the dire housing shortage was on worker morale, and tried to do what he could about the problem.[15]

Other Politburo members who may be presumed to have supported the reconciliation line include Kuibyshev, the Ukrainian first party secretary Stanislav Kosior, and Yan Rudzutak. It has been speculated that Voroshilov, concerned as defense commissar with army morale, had leanings in this direction. In addition, Kalinin, titular president of the USSR, betrayed his preference for moderation by a widely rumored *cri de coeur* during a Leningrad literary function in 1932 when someone read a poem in praise of Cheka terror. "We are often obliged to resort to terror," he reportedly exclaimed, "but it must never be glorified. It is our tragedy that we are obliged to have recourse to such terrible measures, but there is nothing for which we all yearn more than the abolition of terror."[16]

One other important figure associated with Kirov—although not a participant in the shaping of high policy—was Mikhail Tukhachevsky. This ex-tsarist army officer, who joined the Bolsheviks in 1918 and rose to leadership and renown as a Red commander in the Civil War, was now, at forty-one, in his prime as an innovative military mind of the first order. He ran afoul of Stalin during the Soviet-Polish war of 1920, and remained an object of the general secretary's animosity. In 1928 Stalin dismissed as "nonsense" a far-seeing memorandum in which Tukhachevsky, then Red

Army chief of staff, proposed rapid development of the air and armored forces and reequipping of the army. Tukhachevsky was subsequently assigned to command the Leningrad military district where he formed a fast friendship with Kirov. He also had close ties with Ordzhonikidze and Kuibyshev dating from the Civil War. Only very recently, as external dangers mounted, had Stalin brought him back to Moscow as Voroshilov's deputy and chief of munitions at the Defense Commissariat, with the mission of speeding the Red Army's modernization.[17] Tukhachevsky was undoubtedly at one with Kirov and the others in their views on party policy.

Up to a point, the promoters of the reconciliation line encountered a receptive Stalin. He was not averse to easing pressure on the people and raising morale now that the Rubicon of collectivization and basic industrialization had been crossed. Nor was it hard to convince him that high productivity required some changes in economic policy.

Just before the January 1933 Central Committee session, Ordzhonikidze took a leading metallurgical engineer, Avraam Zaveniagin, to see Stalin. When Stalin asked him what was now paramount in industry, Zaveniagin replied, "making it work" *(osvoenie),* and argued his case with telling examples of newly built plants not yet functioning at close to capacity. Stalin agreed, and incorporated the theme into his speech. The plenum's resolution announced the change of policy: "The First Five-Year Plan was a plan of *construction.* . . . The Second Five-Year Plan, if it wants to count on serious success, must supplement the present slogan of new construction with the new slogan of putting new plants and machinery *into operation.*"[18] The policy shift was also reflected in Stalin's projection of the average annual industrial growth rate under the Second Five-Year Plan at 13–14 percent, which was lower than earlier official projections.

"Making it work" meant more than mastering new technology. Abolition of NEP brought virtually the entire economy under governmental management. To make it function with reasonable efficiency, it was necessary to emphasize budgetary discipline and profitability and to provide more work incentives. One step taken to tap incentives was the organizing of private trade in food produce at state-supervised collective-farm markets where peasants could sell surpluses from their small family garden plots at free prices. This and other adjustments sought to make the statist economic model more flexible and productive.[19] There is no sign that Stalin was opposed.

But the advocates of the new line had their sights set on something more than reconciliation with the people. They also wanted a clearing of the bitter intraparty atmosphere left over from the unrest and recriminations of the recent past, a reconciliation within the party. Here, according to the "Letter of an Old Bolshevik," they met opposition from people in Stalin's immediate entourage, especially Kaganovich and Yezhov, who were fearful that their careers would be wrecked if repressive policies were abandoned.[20]

That there was resistance to a relaxation of the intraparty regime is certain. But the "Letter" goes astray in the location of its source—possibly because Bukharin withheld from Nicolaevsky some of what he understood about Stalin. Certain men in Stalin's entourage were probably unenthusiastic about a reconciliation, but they would not have opposed it if they had seen Stalin definitely inclining in that direction. For they were his instruments.

The real obstacle faced by the reconcilers in their struggle for Stalin's soul lay just there: in him. He could see that an easing of pressure on the people was desirable for morale's sake. But reconciliation inside the party could not have appealed to him. It clashed with his resolve to settle scores with covert enemies. He had made this resolve plain in the very January 1933 plenum speech in which he heralded both a more moderate economic policy and a new party purge.

In the ensuing months Stalin showed no willingness to withdraw that declaration of war against "double-dealers masked as Bolsheviks." Rather, the reverse. Simultaneously with the purge directive of 28 April 1933,[21] there appeared an article by Yaroslavsky describing the planned operation for the first time as a "general purge." Only twice before in party history, in 1921 and 1929, had general purges taken place. In mid-May, *Bol'shevik* editorially explained how the new one would differ from the previous two. Whereas then the enemy was proceeding mainly by frontal attack and battle lines in the class war were stark, now it was a matter of rooting out class-alien and hostile elements who had penetrated the party by deceit and were trying to subvert socialism's construction from within. Powerless to mount an open attack because of the triumph of the General Line, enemies of the party like the Syrtsov-Lominadze, Riutin and Smirnov-Eismont-Tolmachev groups were applying "the tactics of masked, deeply conspiratorial struggle, double-dealing."[22] The purge operation began on 1 June 1933 in the Moscow, Leningrad, and eight other key regions. Specially formed purging commissions set about the rechecking of the more than a million party members living in these localities. Expulsions resulted in about one out of six cases.

Undeterred by the ongoing purge, though doubtless fully aware that they faced an uphill battle, the reconcilers in high councils pressed on with their effort to win Stalin over. Their main method was biographical therapy. By now, perhaps as a result of the burgeoning personality cult, they saw that the idealized Stalin projected in the cult was Stalin as he really wanted and needed to see himself, and that he was enraged by any attitude inconsistent with that picture. Gorky, who could train a sensitive literary imagination on Stalin's character, led the way in drawing the practical conclusion that the best means of disarming the vindictive response was to lavish on Stalin the homage that he took as his due.

So, as "Old Bolshevik" told the story, Gorky sought to persuade Stalin that everybody recognized the genius of his policies, that his position as leader was undisputed, and that generosity to erstwhile opponents would strengthen his position rather than weaken it. "Old Bolshevik" hesitated to say how convincing all this was to Stalin, but felt certain of his receptivity to one line of argument that Gorky used. It involved the verdict of future biographers:

For some time now, Stalin has been concerned not only with making his biography, but also with the desire that it be written in the future in favorable colors. He would like to be depicted not only as strong and ruthless in battle against irreconcilable foes, but also as simple and generous on occasions when the present hard-boiled era makes it possible for him to show himself as he believes himself really to be in the depths of his soul. Hence his efforts to play Haroun-al-Rashid, for was not the latter also from the East, and quite as primitive? At any rate, Gorky knew well how to play upon this string and tried to make use of it for good ends—to diminish Stalin's mistrust, to soften his vindictiveness, etc.

These endeavors did not go unrewarded. Kamenev, whom Gorky held in high esteem, was received by Stalin for a private talk in which he acknowledged and renounced his former oppositionism. Subsequently he was appointed to a leading post in the Academia publishing house. In the summer of 1933, he, Zinoviev, and a number of other former oppositionists were reinstated as party members, making it possible for them to participate in the coming party congress, which was due to open at the end of January 1934.[23]

As that time approached, the reconcilers' efforts were climaxed by a *tour de force* of biographical therapy. When *Pravda* readers opened their paper on New Year's day 1934, they found it largely filled with a work of Stalin-idealization in fictional form, signed by Karl Radek. If the title of master glorifier had been awarded as a prize, the winner would certainly have been this pliant, astute, and journalistically gifted ex-Trotskyist. Entitled "The Architect of Socialist Society," his article purported to be the ninth in a future course of lectures on "The History of the Victory of Socialism," delivered in 1967, the year of the October Revolution's fiftieth anniversary, at a School of Inter-planetary Communications in Moscow.

The world bourgeoisie, the future lecturer began, had not expected the decade after Lenin's death to see the building of socialism in the Soviet

Union. Misled by the experience of former revolutions, whose outstanding original leaders were succeeded by miserable epigones, the bourgeoisie had failed to foresee that Lenin would be succeeded by a leader who combined the audacity of the great insurrectionist with the cool calculation of a mathematician. True, the Stalin period stood firmly on the base of the Lenin: Stalin never aspired to be anything other than the executor of Lenin's testament. To be that, however, he had to take decisions comparable to Lenin's in their boldness and develop Lenin's teachings independently, as Lenin had developed Marx's. He showed his greatness as successor to Marx and Lenin and as a theoretician of Marxism by the way in which he upheld the possibility of building socialism in one country—against disbelievers like Trotsky, Zinoviev, Kamenev, and a certain Rosa Luxemburgian, Karl Radek, who jestingly likened Stalin's idea to the proposal of a benevolent old-Russian provincial governor, in a novel of Saltykov-Shchedrin's, to introduce liberalism in one county. Stalin likewise implemented the socialist idea in great historical battles, thereby founding a fortress of socialism that would facilitate the victory of socialism on the *international* scale. Thus he became the great architect of socialism.

With Stalin at its head, the party summoned the proletariat to storm the heights of industrialization under the Five-Year Plan, and it responded with a great new surge of the sacred feelings with which it had flung itself into the October battles. The situation in the countryside was more difficult because of kulak resistance to collectivization, and because this resistance found an echo in certain strata of the party.

Nevertheless, in mockery of the capitalists' expectation that the collectivization drive would fail, socialism achieved its first world victory in the countryside. Stalin's wager on the *kolkhoz,* based on the common sense of the working peasants and the power of organization, proved as accurate as a geometric design. When many organizers of collectives exceeded the limits of what was possible and useful, Stalin restrained the disorderly forward rush and called a halt to the mistakes that arose from being, as he put it, "dizzy with success." In leading the offensive against the capitalist elements in the countryside, he followed the basic Leninist strategic principle visible in all his political moves: after choosing the correct path, never retreat in the face of difficulties. Thus in 1932 he adamantly repulsed attempts to surrender the properly occupied front in the countryside. The sowing and harvest of the following year showed that the great bulk of the collective farmers had accepted the *kolkhoz.* Some difficulties remained, but the Rubicon was crossed in 1933.

The victory of socialism was won in the face of serious resistance from abroad as well as at home. Prophesying failure for the industrialization drive, the capitalist world took steps to turn the great construction project into a Tower of Babel. At the command of the general staffs of the world bourgeoisie, certain venerable scientists and engineers began to disrupt things, submit fictitious plans, and create bottlenecks to future development, while preparing plans to blow up the whole construction in the event of intervention. But these machinations were foiled by the class vigilance of the proletariat. Young proletarian engineers took the place of the wreckers. Meanwhile, the world capitalist crisis enabled the proletariat to buy the services of thousands of unemployed foreign engineers.

Soviet differed from capitalist industrialization in its furious pace. Fifty years' work was accomplished in five. Yet the growth rates under the Five-Year Plan were not chosen arbitrarily by Stalin. The stern commands issued from the captain's bridge by the navigator of the Revolution reflected his far-sightedness. Stalin and the Central Committee knew that the world bourgeoisie would not want to permit the Soviet Union quietly to construct socialism, for this would accelerate the socialist revolution in the capitalist countries and inspire the colonial masses to fight for liberation. The situation resembled that of a company of troops within sight of an enemy machine gun: it must either retreat or plunge forward through danger and take the position by storm. So, the success achieved in building the foundation of socialism dealt a mortal blow to the crisis-ridden capitalist world.

The ninth lecture closed on a triumphal note, describing as follows the scene on May Day 1933 in Red Square:

On Lenin's Mausoleum, surrounded by his closest comrades-in-arms—Molotov, Kaganovich, Voroshilov, Kalinin, and Ordzhonikidze—stood Stalin in a grey soldier's greatcoat. His calm eyes gazed reflectively at the hundreds of thousands of proletarians marching past Lenin's tomb with the firm step of a shock troop of future conquerors of the capitalist world. He knew that he had *fulfilled the oath taken ten years earlier over Lenin's coffin.* And all the working people of the USSR and the world revolutionary proletariat knew it too. And toward the compact figure of our *vozhd'*, calm as a promontory, flowed waves of love and faith, waves of confidence that there, on Lenin's tomb, was gathered the staff of the future victorious world revolution.

The fictional future lecture was a masterpiece of rationalization and falsification aimed at portraying Stalin's career as the fulfillment of his dream of glory. It was Stalin's life according to what the shrewd Radek perceived was Stalin's own hero-script. Above all it was the *piatiletka* and collectivization as Stalin's October, with an admiringly grateful party and people according him their recognition of his Lenin-like genius. Instead of simply describing the events of recent years as historic, Radek depicted history itself in the act of recording them and paying homage to the hero. This afforded Stalin the special satisfaction of viewing himself in the mirror of time from the vantage-point of more than thirty years hence, and being graphically reassured that posterity would remember and revere him as a giant early leader of the Russian and world revolution. That he was very pleased is evident from the article's prominent featuring in *Pravda* and subsequent issuance as a pamphlet with an initial circulation of 225,000 copies.

There was only one problem: many people did not see Stalin and his achievements as Radek portrayed them, and Stalin knew it.

The Cabal of the Regional Secretaries

The impending assembly of the party elite was anticipated as a big event. The previous, Sixteenth Congress, was held amid the turmoil of collectivization and offered little opportunity for calm deliberation of future policy. Now, with the internal situation stabilized and the crisis atmosphere dispelled, things were different. The very time chosen for the congress's opening—the end of January 1934, a few days following the tenth anniversary of Lenin's death—suggested the special importance attached to it as an occasion for retrospect as well as for charting the future.

As the date drew near, regional and republic party conferences selected delegates to the congress on the ratio of one voting delegate for every 1,500 party members and one nonvoting delegate for every 3,000 candidates for party membership. Voting mandates went to 1,225 elected delegates, and nonvoting mandates to 736. People in positions of authority, both centrally and locally, were foremost among those elected. The natural outcome was a congress whose composition was in some ways strikingly unrepresentative of the 2,800,000-member party as a whole. Stalin's protégé Yezhov, who served as chairman of the congress' credentials commission, observed in his report that 80 percent of the congress delegates were persons who joined the party before the Revolution or during the Civil War, whereas only 10 percent of the total party membership were such party veterans.[24] Putting it otherwise, the overwhelming majority of those elected (1,646 out of 1,966 delegates in both categories) had become Communists in Lenin's time, and Old Bolshevik members of pre-1917 vintage, now a minuscule minority in the total party membership, made up almost 25 percent of the delegates. Like its predecessors of the 1920s, this was a congress dominated by the party's Old Guard. It would be the last.

"Our country has become a country of mighty industry, a country of collectivization, a country of victorious socialism," Molotov declared when he opened the congress with a short speech late in the day on 26 January

1934. The setting was the conference hall of the Great Kremlin Palace. The theme of socialism triumphant was underscored in the title of *Pravda*'s editorial that day, "The Congress of Victors," and the gathering went down in history under that name. Yet, a majority of the victors became victims of the second revolution in the bloody new phase that opened before 1934 was over. Khrushchev revealed in 1956 that 1,108 of the 1,966 delegates were later arrested on charges of "antirevolutionary crimes." What happened to turn the victors' congress into a congress of victims?

There is no evidence that such men as Ordzhonikidze, Kirov, Kuibyshev, and others involved in planning the congress intended it to become an event that would shake the Soviet world. Every indication is that they meant it to confirm the new atmosphere of normalcy and a set of policies that would foster, in that atmosphere, the further rebuilding of popular morale and preparation for new trials that external events seemed to betide. The affair, as they envisaged it, was to constitute a crowning success of the reconciliation line and a pledge of its continuation. This it could best do by being a congress of reconciliation. There would be tributes to the leader by stout supporters and fallen ex-adversaries alike. The picture would emerge of a ruling party reunited around its acknowledged *vozhd'*—and of a *vozhd'* magnanimously accepting the errant but repentant ones back into the party fold.

That such was the intention is shown by the precongress publicity. The Stalin cult came to one of its climaxes in January 1934. The new year opened with Radek's celebration of the Architect. Then and after, the theme of socialism victorious was coupled with that of Stalin the victor. Perhaps the most subtly significant sign that the congress was really planned as a triumph for Stalin was the choice of 26 January as its opening day. This was the tenth anniversary of Stalin's "oath" speech during the days of mourning for Lenin. That the coincidence of dates was no accident became evident before the congress opened. On 21 January, the anniversary of Lenin's death, *Pravda*'s special article for the occasion said: "Looking back on the ten-year path traversed, the party is entitled to declare that the Stalin oath has been fulfilled with honor. *The decade following Lenin's death has been the decade of a great, world-historic victory of Leninism.* Under Stalin's leadership the Bolsheviks have brought it about that SOCIALISM IN OUR COUNTRY HAS WON."

This, too, was the opening theme of *Pravda*'s account the next day of the memorial meeting held in Moscow's Bolshoi Theater with the Politburo present. Further on it described the scene of Stalin's entry onto the stage: "*Stalin!* The appearance of the ardently loved *vozhd'*, whose name is linked inseparably with all the victories scored by the proletariat, by the Soviet Union, was greeted with tumultuous ovations. All rose and it seemed there would be no end of the applause and the cries of 'Hurrah!' and 'Long live our Stalin!' " Then, on the morning of the congress' opening day, Radek made the choice of date more explicit with an *Izvestia* article called "An Oath Fulfilled." It presented the post-Lenin decade as a triumphal Stalin-led march in carrying out every vow made by Stalin ten years ago. Thus he had sworn to uphold the party's unity as the apple of its eye, and now the party enjoyed "steel unity." Lenin's dream of 100,000 tractors had been realized more than twice over. Above all, ten years after Lenin's death, socialism was no longer a commandment but a reality, and the congress opening today would be "a fighting road for the future victors on a world scale."

Radek proved wrong about the party's unity and right, though in an unintended way, about the congress' road being a fighting one. At the very outset, the plans to make it a congress of reconciliation began to go awry.

Shortly before the opening, the regional and minority-republic party secretaries arrived at the heads of their congress delegations. Some of these local leaders were rising younger figures directly linked with Stalin. Representative of this group were Andrei Zhdanov, then thirty-eight and party secretary of Gorky province; Nikita Khrushchev, thirty-nine, who had risen as a Kaganovich protégé to ranking position in the Moscow party organization; and Lavrenti Beria, thirty-five, who had come to Stalin's attention through his work in the Transcaucasian security organs in the 1920s and later, with Stalin's support, had become party secretary of the Transcaucasus. But many other regional secretaries were Old Bolshevik veterans of the prerevolutionary struggle. Some harbored critical feelings toward Stalin. They had seen his defects as a political leader during collectivization and resented his unjust blaming of local people for his own errors. Some had bided their time in hope of effecting a change of leadership at the next party congress. Now, reaching Moscow on the eve of the event, they found the cult reaching grotesque extremes, and did not like it.

As a congress delegate who survived told the story thirty years after, "The abnormal atmosphere that had formed in the party in connection with the personality cult aroused alarm among many Communists. As later transpired, the thought ripened in the minds of certain congress delegates, primarily those who remembered Lenin's testament well, that it was time to shift Stalin from the general secretary post to other work."[25] Those in whose minds the thought ripened reportedly included, among others, Central Committee members I. M. Vareikis, B. P. Sheboldaev, M. D. Orakhelashvili, S. V. Kosior, G. I. Petrovsky, and R. I. Eikhe. They quietly discussed the matter in Ordzhonikidze's and possibly other Moscow apartments as the congress opened.[26] If Stalin was to be deposed from party leadership, now was the time to prepare the move. The congress, as the party's sovereign authority, would end by electing a new Central Committee, which in turn would elect its new standing bodies: Politburo, Orgburo, and Secretariat. One member of the Secretariat, or committee of all-union party secretaries, would become the Central Committee's general secretary. In Kirov the opponents of Stalin had a natural candidate for that post. But in order to succeed, they had to have his cooperation.

As Khrushchev tells the story in his memoirs, Sheboldaev made the approach to Kirov on the group's behalf. The "oldsters," he told Kirov, were saying that the time had come to carry out Lenin's behest to displace Stalin from the post of general secretary because of his personal qualities, and they wanted Kirov to take over the job. There are two versions of what happened next. According to Khrushchev's, Kirov told Stalin about the conversation with Sheboldaev, and Stalin replied: "Thanks, I won't forget you for this."[27] According to Shatunovskaya's version, Stalin learned what had happened and summoned Kirov to see him. Kirov did not deny that he had been approached and said to Stalin that he had brought things to this pass by his own actions. Later he told relatives and friends that now his head was on the block.[28]

Mikoyan, whose memoir account states that Kirov proved his loyalty to Stalin by telling him about the approach, says further that Kirov encountered on Stalin's part "only hostility and vengefulness toward the whole congress and, of course, toward Kirov himself."[29] It is undoubtedly true that the episode aroused Stalin's vengeful hostility toward the congress and that Kirov could no longer appear in his eyes other than as a most dangerous potential rival. But more than that, Stalin's inner vision of the party ranks and especially the higher ones as a hotbed of conspiratorial machinations against him could only be greatly reinforced. After all, this machination was real.

But eventually, despite the ill-starred beginning, the principals played their parts as planned. In fact, the effort to make this a congress of Stalin's reconciliation with the party seems to have been intensified. Not only did Stalin receive tumultuous standing ovations before and after he gave the main congress address—the Central Committee's review-report—on the opening day. The symbolism of oath fulfillment was underlined by arranging for him to give his report not only on the day but at the same hour as his speech ten years before.

In the panegyrics resounding from the rostrum during the following days one could occasionally hear an almost frantic adulatory note, especially in the speeches of the ex-oppositionists who appeared at intervals to castigate themselves for past political sins and to praise their conqueror. Zinoviev saluted Stalin for presiding in practice over the revolution of socialist construction that Lenin had only charted in thought. Kamenev compared the Lenin epoch of 1917–24 with the "Stalin epoch" of 1925–34 as "two equal epochs that must so go down in history." Bukharin said that adoption of his Rightist line at the end of the 1920s would have been a disaster, and acclaimed "the glorious field marshal of the proletarian forces, the best of the best—Comrade Stalin!" Preobrazhensky admitted (with truth) that collectivization in three or four years was something that he and his fellow Left oppositionists had never foreseen, and drew the moral that one should apply to Stalin the motto a comrade had once used of Lenin: "Vote with Ilyich and you won't be wrong." Lominadze, now working in Magnitogorsk, apologized for his bloc with Syrtsov and failure to "grasp the deep, clear, theoretically rich thesis of Comrade Stalin, simple to the point of genius, that the destruction of classes takes place in the process of fiercest class struggle." Tomsky, Rykov, and Radek also joined the parade of the Stalin glorifiers. Few if any leaders in history have heard such extravagant eulogies from vanquished political enemies. Even Vareikis and Petrovsky, participants in the cabal, spoke in respectfully loyal tones albeit with dignity.

The final speaker in the discussion of the report was Kirov. When P. P. Postyshev, who chaired that session, gave him the floor, the delegates greeted him with wild applause and a standing ovation. His address was all that could have been expected of a loyal lieutenant. After saying that Stalin's report must be studied "down to the last comma," he proposed that instead of preparing a resolution on it, the congress should "adopt for execution, as party law, all the theses and conclusions of Comrade Stalin's review-report." The custom, both during and after Lenin's time, had been to set up a commission that would, taking account of the debate, prepare and place before the congress a resolution approving the report and formulating the salient points for policy in the coming period. This time, in response to Kirov's proposal, the congress adopted Stalin's huge report *en toto* as guidance. It was a gesture of collective prostration before him, as if to say that his every word was indispensable.

Toward the end of his speech, Kirov's hearty personality burst through in these words: "Our successes are really tremendous. Damn it all, to put it humanly, you just want to live and live—really, just look what's going on. It's a fact!" Parenthetical interpellations in the transcript give reactions of the assembly: "excitement in the hall," "Laughter, applause," "stormy applause," "noisy applause," "a thunder of applause." The peroration was a reference to the oath speech: "We are fulfilling that vow and will go on fulfilling it, because that vow was given by the great strategist of liberation of the working people of our country and the whole world—Comrade Stalin!" The words referred to Stalin, but the huge standing ovation at the end was meant for Kirov himself and everyone there knew it. Afterward, in the couloirs, delegates asked one another who had been accorded the more demonstrative reception, Kirov or Stalin.[30] Stalin may have asked himself the same question, and his vindictive feeling toward both Kirov and the congress was bound to be aggravated. Once again an unforeseen event—the spontaneous enthusiasm for Kirov—had confounded the calculations of those who wanted to manage Stalin's mind.

Reorganizing the Control System

After the demonstration for Kirov ended, Stalin took the floor to announce that he would abstain from a concluding speech since "The debates at the congress have shown our party leaders' complete unity of views on all questions of party policy." So they had in the sense that no one registered dissent from Stalin's positions. But partly because of the move to please Stalin by demonstratively foregoing the usual effort to distill a major policy statement from the review-report and discussion of it, the congress produced no comprehensive formulation of the party line for the coming period.

It did pass some substantive decisions: a resolution on organizational questions based on Kaganovich's report, a new text of the party rules, and a resolution on the Second Five-Year Plan, which endorsed the shifts in economic policy discussed above. The resolution projected an average annual growth rate of 18.5 percent for consumer goods in 1933–37, as compared with 14.5 percent for producer goods. The congress thus pledged a more measured tempo of economic growth and more attention to people's needs.

Stalin gave the modified economic policy emphatic support. He emerged in the review-report as an exponent of a socialism of plenty. Or rather, gradations of plenty, since he also argued that "Marxism is the enemy of levelling." He espoused the theme of a socialism of prosperity in his characteristic way: by heaping harsh ridicule on those who thought differently, in this case unnamed party members who thought that "socialism can be built on a base of poverty and privation." He also came forward now as a champion of enlarged trade services, and a scourge of Communists who haughtily viewed trade and money as things soon to be supplanted by direct product exchange. Such disdain of trade was a "rundown nobleman's prejudice," not a proper Bolshevik attitude, and all talk of the early advent of product exchange was "leftist nonsense." Money, this instrument of bourgeois economy, had been taken over by the Soviet regime and adapted to the interests of socialism, and would continue to be used for a long time. Direct product exchange could only come about through "ideally developed Soviet trade."

In economic policy Stalin made it clear that he had chosen to follow the reconciliation line. In intraparty affairs, he did not. True, he said the party was unified now as never before. But then he warned against the inference that the struggle was over and that there was no longer any need for an "offensive of socialism." Remnants of antiparty ideologies still had a tenacious hold and were quite capable of resuscitation. The capitalist encirclement was still an active force for ideological subversion. It was wrong to think, as some did, that the classless socialist society would arrive without a fight and by allowing the state to weaken or wither. No, it could come only "through strengthening the organs of the proletarian dictatorship, through intensifying the class struggle, through liquidating the remnants of the capitalist classes, in battles against enemies both internal and external." The argument augured not a policy of reconciliation in the party, but a continuation of the purge. That the purge was in fact scheduled to continue emerged from Rudzutak's report to the congress on behalf of the Central Control Commission and Commissariat of Worker-Peasant Inspection.

Stalin himself gave an oblique but ominous further sign of purge intentions with a proposal in the review-report for a sweeping reorganization of the political control system. The existing arrangement, designed by Lenin, coupled the party's Central Control Commission (CCC) with the government's Commissariat of Worker-Peasant Inspection (WPI) in a combined party-and-government agency whose several missions were to uphold party and state discipline, to serve as a check on the creeping bureaucratism that so alarmed Lenin toward the end, to assuage high-level conflict by having representatives of the CCC-WPI present at Politburo meetings, and to enlist ordinary citizens in the ferreting out of abuses in the work of the party-state machinery. It has been already noted that Stalin placed the 1933 purge in the hands of a specially created purge commission rather than the CCC. He did not like the fact that the CCC responded favorably to many appeals. Other features of the established control system that he found irksome were the obligatory participation of members of the CCC's presidium in the preparation and conduct of Politburo sessions, and the fact that at plenary meetings of the CCC, elder party figures would boldly criticize shortcomings in the administration of industry and agriculture.[31]

The proposed reorganization was virtually a plan for the dismantling of the decade-old control system. The combined agency would be divided into a purely governmental Soviet Control Commission and a Party Control Commission which, though elected by the congress, would be subordinate to the Central Committee. In presenting the plan Stalin stressed that by "control," whether on the governmental or party side, he meant centralized check-up on execution of policy decisions. It was control downward unmodified by control upward: "What we need now is not inspection but check-up on fulfillment of the center's decisions." As for the proposed new Party Control Commission, it would carry out Central Committee assignments and have local agents independent of local organizations. It would chiefly check fulfillment of Central Committee decisions. Its disciplinary powers would extend to the bringing of even Central Committee members to account. Concerning its appellate role, Stalin said nothing.

After Stalin's death it was revealed that shortly before the congress opened, the reorganization plan was approved by the Politburo at a session from which Rudzutak, who always attended its meetings, was absent.[32] Perhaps he preferred not to take part in a session at which his party conscience would compel him to object to a plan that he knew Stalin meant to push through. Afterward, Rudzutak came before a meeting of the CCC presidium looking very upset, reported the impending reorganization, and sat down. There was no discussion of the matter because those present had been made aware that Stalin had categorically rejected a proposal by some CCC members—Rudzutak himself may have been one of them—that his plan be placed before a plenary session of the CCC for discussion.[33]

Hence when he addressed the congress, Rudzutak knew that it was his swan-song as the USSR's chief controller. He wound up his lengthy report by briefly restating Stalin's proposals, largely in Stalin's own words, and took his seat. The ensuing discussion was cut off, without explanation, after only four persons had spoken. Rudzutak's declining of a concluding word was not even stated by him (according to custom), but by the man who chaired that session. Significantly, this was Matvei Shkiriatov, an Old Bolshevik who had long served Stalin as a special assistant for purge matters. Later in the congress, discussion of the planned organization of the control system was resumed by Kaganovich. He expanded on Stalin's philosophy of control as check-up on implementation of policy decisions at the center.

In the discussion of Kaganovich's report, Shkiriatov rose to support Stalin's reorganization plan and speak about the purge. As if to convey that Kirov's own domain had needed an outside overseer of the weeding-out of enemies in 1933, he declared: "I, comrades, purged the Leningrad organization, one of our best organizations, and am acquainted with matters in other organizations where the purge was carried out." The tone, like the man himself, was sinister.

Whither Foreign Policy?

On the eve of the congress, storm clouds were gathered in the Far East where Japan, having occupied Manchuria, was threatening Soviet possession of the Chinese Eastern Railway and raising fears of a possible invasion of Soviet territory. In a press interview of 25 December 1933, Stalin suggested that the League of Nations, long a Soviet bugbear, might have peace-preserving uses.[34] About that time the German Embassy in Moscow got wind of a French initiative toward a possible mutual assistance pact with the USSR, and reported that there was a growing inclination in the Soviet Union, under impact of Far Eastern tensions, to respond positively to the French proposal.[35]

Then, on 29 December, Litvinov gave the Central Executive Committee a wide-ranging address on foreign affairs. The postwar "era of bourgeois pacifism" was now giving way, he said, to a new era of diplomacy in which war and peace were again the dominant issue. He propounded a division of foreign capitalist states into aggressive, unaligned, and those disposed to peace-keeping arrangements. Under the first category he alluded to Germany and Japan. While stating that "With Germany, as with other states, we want to have the best of relations," he pointed to ominous signs of German unfriendliness toward the USSR, including the republication of Hitler's *Mein Kampf* in Germany in a new edition "without any deletions."[36] This referred to the inclusion of chapter 14, with its chilling preview of a future German policy of conquering *Lebensraum* in a Russia whose Bolshevik regime was an agency of international Jewry.

The new German ambassador, a strong *Ostler* Rudolf Nadolny, understandably reacted poorly to the foreign commissar's speech. He said in his first major report to Berlin, sent 9 January 1934, that Litvinov was committed to a decision to switch over to the French group. One of several reasons was that "Litvinov is known to be M. Wallach from Bialystok," that is, Jewish. Policy, however, would be decided by "other important people," among whom, it seemed, "there mostly prevails regret over the falling out with Germany and the desire for reconciliation." Nadolny had been assured—by whom he did not say—that "nothing decisive has yet taken place, that only in case of emergency would the Soviet Union bind itself by treaty to the other side, and that we did not yet have to consider our cause here as lost." Consequently, steps should be taken immediately and energetically, by way of peaceful gestures, to frustrate the intentions of "the sly M. Wallach" aimed at Russia's inclusion in the French ring.[37]

In a postscript sent the next day, Nadolny reported that Radek had taken the opportunity to express himself to "one of our journalists." Radek had cautioned against undue German alarm at the Litvinov speech. Moscow was following a state policy *(Staatspolitik)*, and "Nothing will happen that will permanently block our way to a common policy with Germany." Once the Far Eastern tension subsided, he thought new possibilities would develop with Germany in Europe. Meanwhile, the two must seek common ground. As for the foreign commissar, "You know what Litvinov represents. Over him there is a hard, cautious, and distrustful man endowed with a firm will. Stalin does not know where he stands with Germany. He is uncertain. . . . You must not imagine us to be so foolish that we will fall into the spokes of the wheel of world history. . . . If we carry on a state policy, we must oppose the revision of Versailles at our expense." To underline the latter theme, Radek added misgivings about Nazi machinations in the Baltic and commented that the Baltic states, created by the Entente as a *place d'armes* against the Soviet Union, "are today the most important protective wall for us against the West" (that is, no *place d'armes*). From all this Nadolny drew the conclusion that "Litvinov went too far in his negative attitude," and he urged that "we should utilize this circumstance at once."[38]

Stalin had allowed Litvinov to adumbrate, but without openly espousing, a reorientation of Soviet policy toward collective security in concert with the status-quo powers. At the same time, he was telling the Germans, via Radek, that his real preference was for the German-Soviet collaboration suggested in Hitler's talk with Khinchuk the previous May.

In a suitably circumspect way Stalin repeated this message publicly when he addressed the party congress on 26 January. He echoed Litvinov's theme that the era of "bourgeois pacifism" was ending, but omitted the foreign commissar's tripartite division of foreign states. He stated it as a fact that "things are moving toward a new imperialist war." His discussion of the war prospect showed a mind dominated by the idea that history was repeating itself and generating, as in 1914, an imperialist war that would lead to a new round of revolutions. Of the coming war he said, "It will certainly unleash revolution and place the very existence of capitalism in question in a number of countries as happened during the first imperialist war." Further: "Let not Messrs. bourgeois blame us if, on the morrow of such a war, certain governments near and dear to them, now ruling safely 'by the grace of God,' turn up missing." He even hinted at the whereabouts of some of these revolutions by foreseeing the war-caused downfall of "bourgeois-landowner" governments in a number of countries of Europe and Asia. Among the governments seen in Moscow as reflecting a strong landowner interest were those of Poland and the Baltic states.

Turning to diplomacy, Stalin took special note of a recent change for the better in Soviet relations with France and Poland. But it was not true, he went on, what certain German politicians were saying, that because of German fascism's rise to power the USSR was now orienting itself on France and Poland and had become a supporter of Versailles. Despite all the Soviet lack of rapture for the German fascist regime, fascism had nothing to do with it, as shown by the fact that fascism in Italy did not prevent the USSR from having the best of relations with that country. The difficulty in Soviet-German relations arose from the change in German policy, from the fact that in the contest between different foreign-policy tendencies going on in Germany a new line reminiscent of the kaiser's anti-Russian one and represented by people like Alfred Rosenberg was prevailing over the old line embodied in the Soviet-German treaties. As for the USSR's "supposed reorientation," its sole orientation had been and remained on the USSR alone. "And if the USSR's interests demand rapprochement with these or those countries not concerned to violate peace, we embark upon this course without hesitation."

Stalin was thus unambiguously telling Hitler that whenever his government should be disposed to leave Russia in peace and revive the "old line" of German-Russian collaboration, Russia would be ready to reciprocate. Hitler had referred to common interests between the two states, and Stalin was showing his awareness of them. The signal did not go unheeded. In his cable to Berlin, Nadolny noted Stalin-Litvinov differences: Stalin did not mention relations with the League, did not (like Litvinov) treat Germany in conjunction with Japan, did not indicate a commitment to Poland and France, and preserved an un-Litvinov-like "calm tone and strict matter-of-factness." Nadolny thought that a responsive statement should be made on the German side, lest Francophile tendencies in Moscow receive decisive impetus.[39] Up to a point, Hitler obliged. Addressing the Reichstag on 30 January, he gently reproved "M. Stalin" for expressing in his "last great speech" the fear that forces hostile to the Soviet might be active in Germany.[40]

Stalin evidently wanted his own voice to be the sole congress viewpoint on foreign policy. Litvinov attended as a voting delegate but did not speak. The Comintern's report was given by Dimitry Manuilsky, who had taken charge of Comintern affairs for Stalin after Bukharin's ouster from them in 1929. Apart from justifying the passive policy foisted on the German Communists prior to the Nazi takeover—on the ground that no true revolutionary situation had existed in Germany—he said little in many words. Other speakers touched on foreign affairs glancingly if at all. Yet the congress did convey a viewpoint on foreign policy, and it was at variance with Stalin's.

Litvinov was far from alone in his outlook. A year after January 1933, Hitler's power showed no sign of weakening and his attitude toward Russia and Communism no sign of softening. Various Soviet men of influence were worried and of a mind to raise the banner of antifascism in an effort to make common cause with democratic antifascist forces in European countries. Judging by Kirov's precongress speech in Leningrad, he was among these people and probably foremost among them.

"What is fascism?" he asked at one point, and answered: "The open, utterly unconcealed, terroristic dictatorship of the most reactionary, most chauvinist, and most imperialist elements of finance capital." But finance capital was not the crux. Kirov saw Hitler's movement as a recrudescence in Germany of what pre-1917 Russia had witnessed in the bands of Black Hundred thugs of the nationalist and monarchist radical right: "German fascism, with its pogrom ideology, its anti-Semitism, its views on higher and lower races, very much resembles, in its circle of ideas, the organizations of *the Russian Black Hundreds, the party of Mikhail Arkhangel,* very familiar to us." It is notable that Kirov (whose wife was Jewish) made particular reference to the Nazis' anti-Semitism. He went on to call the fascist ideology a throwback to medieval times, spoke of the public burning of books, and commented that one could not stop the international Communist movement by "burning Communists at the stake, as in the time of the Inquisition." He said some people were seeking a solution for the crisis of capitalism in dismemberment of the USSR, and then named them: "The most clear and straightforward exponents of this policy are two representatives of bellicose imperialism, Araki [Japanese war minister] on the one hand and Hitler on the other. The one dreams of marching to China, the other of 'modestly' seizing the Ukraine along with the Black Sea coast and the Baltic. I repeat, these are the most straightforward and open of our enemies."[41]

Between Kirov's aroused antifascist statement and Stalin's diplomatic probe of Berlin there was a political gulf.[42] The one was getting ready to do business with Hitler, the other to do battle with him. Each, moreover, had allies in his foreign-policy orientation. Molotov and Kaganovich touched on Soviet-German relations in Stalin's way in their precongress speeches. Gorky, on the other hand, who spoke before the Moscow party conference preceding the congress although he was not to be a congress participant, forcefully condemned fascist obscurantism in words similar to Kirov's. Then, at the congress itself, Rudzutak joined the anti-Hitler party. Toward the end of his report on party-state control, he broke into a denunciation of the Nazis. They boasted of destroying Marxism, he said, but so far their only victories in that line consisted in beheading revolutionaries with an ax. That was nothing new. Equally experienced torturers had done their work in tsarist Russia, whose *oprichniki* were a no less brutalized force than the fascists, but could not prevent revolution from sweeping a sixth of the earth.[43]

More outspoken was Bukharin. He combined his praise of Stalin's leadership with an impassioned warning against National Socialism. Devoting the last part of his congress speech to foreign policy, he declared that there were at present two *places d'armes* for aggression against Soviet Russia: Fascist Germany and Imperial Japan. To prove his point, he quoted lengthy passages from *Mein Kampf* on Germany's mission of crushing Russia; Alfred Rosenberg's argument that the essence of the Russian Revolution was the triumph of the "Mongoloid forces" in the Russian national organism; and the Nazi "poet" who had said, "Every time I hear the word 'culture,' I reach for my Browning." He eloquently portrayed the Nazi cult of blood and violence, and wound up by foreseeing for Soviet Russia an inescapable future collision with this irrational force: "This is what stands before us, and these are the ones whom we shall have to face, comrades, in all those stupendous historical battles that history has laid on our shoulders. . . . We shall go into battle for the fate of *humanity*. For that battle we need solidarity, solidarity, and still more solidarity."

Stalin was displeased by Bukharin's eloquent summons to battle. Kirov indicated this by including in his own subsequent congress speech a reproving remark that Bukharin "sang ostensibly according to the notes, but was off key." Yet, he too had sung off Stalin's key in the Leningrad speech, and the assembly as a whole did so when it showed its receptivity to the anti-Nazi message by according Bukharin prolonged applause.[44] The mood of the congress was clearly antifascist.

Meanwhile, developments in other countries were making the tactic of waiting for favorable signs from Hitler untenable for Stalin. On the very day of his congress report, 26 January, Germany moved further away from Russia by concluding a nonaggression pact with Poland. Some days later, events in France dictated a new departure in Soviet policy. Antigovernment agitation led by French fascist and right-wing extremist groups culminated in a huge demonstration and fierce street fighting in Paris on 6 February. The Third Republic was in crisis. In this situation the Communists and their Moscow mentors drew back from the course followed in Germany, where the Communists' left-wing extremism had helped the fascists overthrow the democratic order. On 12 February the French Communists joined the Socialists in a one-day strike against fascism. It was the beginning of the subsequently adopted Communist tactics of the democratic antifascist Popular Front.[45]

For Stalin, however, the tactical turnabout did not signify a conversion to an antifascist outlook similar to Kirov's. Rather, it flowed from his orientation on a European war as the pathway to Russia's emergence into a commanding position on the continent. The existence in Europe of two more or less evenly balanced groups of powers was the prerequisite of that scenario. The rise of fascism in France posed a deadly threat to it. France was the keystone of the anti-German group. The triumph of fascism there would mean the collapse of Stalin's long-term strategy. In these circumstances, his espousal of a united antifascist front in France was of a piece with his earlier resort to fascism-abetting left extremism in Germany. The basic aim was to keep these traditional enemies apart so that they could move onto a collision course.

Even as Stalin gravitated toward the new politics of collective security and the Popular Front, he continued sending signals to Hitler. In early 1934 Voroshilov recalled the German and Soviet armies' past collaboration with nostalgia and urged Ambassador Nadolny to influence his government to follow a less anti-Soviet policy. "Just a few reassuring words from Hitler, he said, would be enough to show the Kremlin that *Mein Kampf* was no longer his basic policy statement."[46]

After the Congress

The congress finished its main business on 8 February and took the evening off to give the delegations a chance to confer. The next day the participants attended a parade on Red Square. In the evening they convened again to elect the new Central Committee and other bodies, including the new Party Control Commission.

It was Bolshevik practice for the delegates to a party congress to be handed a ballot containing a list of nominees for a new Central Committee. A delegate would leave unmarked the names of those nominees for whom he wished to vote, strike out the names of those he was voting against, and turn in the ballot unidentified by name. An absolute majority of votes was required for election.

After the voting on the evening of 9 February, the congress' vote-counting commission worked into the night tallying up the results. Kirov, it turned out, received only three or four negative votes, and Stalin a shockingly high number. Most members of the vote-counting commission were shot in the later Terror, but a few survived in prison and camp. One of the survivors, V. M. Verkhovykh, was vice-chairman of the vote-counting commission. In a written report of 23 November 1960 to the Party Control Committee, he stated that Stalin, Molotov, and Kaganovich received the largest numbers of negative votes, in each case over 100. Although he could not recall the precise number of votes cast against Stalin, he thought it may have been 123 or 125.[47] Other sources with access to inside information have given still higher numbers.[48]

V. P. Zatonsky, who was chairman of the vote-counting commission, informed Kaganovich, who handled organizational matters at the Seventeenth Congress, of what had happened. Kaganovich confidentially passed on this bad news to Stalin, who decreed that in the announcement of the voting results at the final meeting of the congress the next day, the number of votes cast against him be given as three, and that all but three of the ballots with his name crossed out be destroyed.[49] The fact that only 1,059 ballots have turned up in the party archives (166 less than the number of delegates to the Seventeenth Congress with the right to vote)[50] strongly suggests that something like that number were destroyed, as Stalin demanded. But he knew the real facts and could only have been further embittered by them. In his mind the large number of anti-Stalin ballots had to be one more count against the cabal, the congress, and the party as then constituted.

The new Central Committee had seventy-one full and sixty-eight candidate members. Its complexion bears out Khrushchev's information that Stalin approved the slate of nominees.[51] True, quite a few well-known party figures were held over from the past. More than any predecessor, however, this Central Committee was handpicked by Stalin. One significant sign of that was the inclusion, for the first time, of Beria. Old Bolsheviks who were active in the Transcaucasus during the revolutionary period, including Ordzhonikidze and Kirov, despised him. At one point during the Civil War he was imprisoned by the Reds on suspicion of working for the other side. A telegram came from Kirov demanding that he be shot as a traitor to the revolutionary cause. He was saved by the resumption of fighting at that time, but learned of the telegram's existence.[52] The elevation to the Central Committee of this intensely disliked man with a shady political past and a grudge against Kirov was testimony to Stalin's power of having his way.

Along with Beria, two other Stalin protégés—Yezhov and Khrushchev—vaulted the candidate stage straight into full membership of the high body. The secret-police element was bolstered by the advancement of Yagoda from candidate to full membership and the designation as full members of two police officials, Balitsky and Evdokimov, who had not been candidates. Several men of Stalin's entourage were brought in as candidate members: Mekhlis, Tovstukha, Poskrebyshev, and the cavalryman Budenny. Zaveniagin, who had spoken with Stalin about "making it work," became a candidate member, as did M. A. Bagirov, a Transcaucasian client of Beria's and Stalin's. Tukhachevsky, in recognition of his importance as first deputy defense commissar, did as well.

The congress accepted Stalin's plan for the reorganization of the control system, and adopted revised party rules that defined the functions of the new Party Control Commission; its duties were to see to the execution of Central Committee decisions and bring to account violators of party discipline. Concerning appellate functions nothing was said. The congress' resolution on organizational questions specified that the commission's chairman must be a Central Committee secretary—an innovation which meant that the head of the commission would be directly subject to

Stalin's authority as the senior secretary. The sixty-one-member Control Commission elected at the congress as one of the standing bodies had its first plenum on 10 February and elected Kaganovich as its chairman, Yezhov as its vice-chairman, and Shkiriatov as secretary of a special party collegium to examine cases of violation of party ethics and discipline. The placing of the commission under the domination of these three was eloquent testimony to the reality of their chief's postcongress power—and to the fact that he was gearing the machinery for a purge.

On 10 February, after the congress closed, the new Central Committee met for its first plenum and elected its standing bodies. The next day *Pravda* reported the results. Stalin, Molotov, Kaganovich, Voroshilov, Kalinin, Ordzhonikidze, Kuibyshev, Kirov, Andreev, and Kosior were listed (in that order) as full members of the Politburo; Mikoyan, Chubar, Petrovsky, Postyshev, and Rudzutak as candidate members. The Secretariat was reduced to four members; Stalin, Kaganovich, Kirov (who remained secretary of the Leningrad committee), and Zhdanov (relieved of his duties as secretary of the Gorky committee). The Orgburo consisted of Stalin, Kaganovich, Kirov, Zhdanov, Yezhov, Shvernik, Kosarev, Stetsky, Gamarnik, and Kuibyshev, with M. M. Kaganovich (Lazar's plant-director brother) and A. I. Krinitsky as candidates. Stalin's unique status as supreme leader was underscored by the fact that his name came first on all three lists (whereas in 1930, after the Sixteenth Congress, the comparable listing was alphabetized and his name came last or next to last in each case). The point was driven home photographically: a large photo of Stalin dominated the small ones of the other nine full members of the Politburo. In the coverage of the postcongress plenum in 1930, his photo was the same size as the others.

The composition of the standing bodies showed Stalin's influence in their selection. A. A. Andreev, a reliable Stalinist, took Rudzutak's place as a full member of the Politburo; Rudzutak sank to candidate status. Stalin's protégés Yezhov and Zhdanov joined the Orgburo. And with Kaganovich and Zhdanov flanking him as Central Committee secretaries, Stalin was more securely than ever in control of the Secretariat, now cut down from seven members to four.

During this postcongress plenum, it was Stalin himself who nominated Kirov to be one of the members of the new smaller Central Committee Secretariat, and he proposed that Kirov move to Moscow to take up his new secretarial duties (and indeed, Kirov could hardly have discharged them in any but a formal sense without moving to Moscow). To the latter proposal Kirov objected strongly, asking to be permitted to stay in Leningrad for another year or two to help ensure fulfillment of the second Five-Year Plan. Both Ordzhonikidze and Kuibyshev spoke up in favor of this arrangement, and Stalin, infuriated that he was not receiving the usual full support, stalked out of the meeting room in a huff.[53]

One particular point concerning the reconstituted party regime has remained an enigma. Announcements of postcongress plenums in 1922 and after said not only that Stalin was elected a Central Committee secretary, but also that the new Central Committee confirmed him as general secretary. This time there was no reference to such confirmation. From the omission a veteran observer of Soviet politics has inferred that the new Central Committee deprived Stalin of the position of general secretary and all the associated "additional rights" that set him apart from the other Central Committee secretaries.[54] A large interpretation of the history of the Soviet regime in the ensuing years flowed from the hypothesized grave setback of Stalin's fortunes.

The inference, however, was unfounded. First, general secretary was a special title accorded Stalin as the senior Central Committee secretary, not, technically speaking, an office. The office was that of secretary, as indicated by the fact that both before and after 1934 Stalin signed party decrees "Secretary of the Central Committee." Secondly, Soviet official sources testify that Stalin did not cease to be general secretary in February 1934 even though the announcement concerning the postcongress plenum made no mention of his having been confirmed as such. Thirdly, the symbolic evidence cited above and the signs of Stalin's heavy influence in the reshaping of the party regime contradict the notion that his power was reduced by the new Central Committee whose very composition testified to this power.

Why, then, was no mention made after the plenum of Stalin's reconfirmation as general secretary? One possibility is that, still smarting from the failed attempt of some old party comrades to replace him with Kirov as senior party secretary, he demonstratively waved aside formal reconfirmation and that the plenum, in a gesture similar to the congress' enshrining of his entire congress report as its political resolution, then pronounced his status as general secretary to be settled for good and not in need of further formal confirmation. But even if such a gesture was offered, or if formal reconfirmation was omitted on Stalin's initiative, he may well have had a reason for preferring that no public announcement of his "general" status be made at this time.

A possible clue is contained in a statement made by Stalin in 1926. Responding to Trotsky's belated revelations concerning the conflict that had taken place behind the scenes more than four years earlier over Stalin's harsh treatment of a group of leading Georgian Communists headed by Budu Mdivani, Stalin denied that he and Lenin had had a significant disagreement over that matter, and said that people like Mdivani "deserved still more severe treatment that I *as one of the secretaries of the Central Committee* of our party gave them.[55] At the time to which he was referring, he had been general secretary and Molotov and Kuibyshev had been secretaries. By describing himself as "one of the secretaries," Stalin was collectivizing responsibility for actions undertaken by the Central Committee Secretariat at that time and thereby reducing his personal role.

Now again he appeared in *Pravda*'s announcement as, so to speak, just "one of the secretaries," albeit the one whose name came first on the list. We may speculate that he wanted to make his administrative primacy somewhat less conspicuous, to downplay his paramount responsibility for actions that he expected would be taken soon in the Central Committee's name. To parade the fact that he was *general* secretary would make it more difficult to hold aloof and pretend that the coming mass purge was someone else's doing, not his.

To Remake the Party

None of the unexpected occurrences at the congress—the cabal at the start, the pro-Kirov demonstration, the showing of support for an antifascist orientation in foreign policy, and the anti-Stalin votes at the end—threatened to unseat Stalin from power. But they were enough to anger him beyond measure. Knowing as he did that some, perhaps many, of the encomia he had heard came from persons who then voted against him, he must have wondered now just how many were sincere and how much credence he could place in homage from the Radeks and other men of the Bolshevik Old Guard and people under their influence. Because he could not tolerate being outshone, the fervent acclaim for Kirov, the fact that some Old Bolsheviks wanted him to be the party's leader, and his top score in the voting for Central Committee were all, from Stalin's standpoint, black marks against the many Kirov admirers and conclusive cause for turning against Kirov himself. His shock and rage at the humiliating number of anti-Stalin votes had to be all the greater because of the impossibility of knowing just who among the 1,225 voting delegates cast them. Many in all probability were members of the delegations of regional secretaries involved in the cabal, but the voting procedure made it impossible to know. Hence the whole 1,225 fell under a dark cloud of suspicion in Stalin's mind. In this perspective the wonder is not that 1,108 of the "victors" (voting and nonvoting) were arrested subsequently, but that many were not.[56]

What was to have been a congress of reconciliation became one of

Stalin's final estrangement from the Bolshevik party. Instead of being reassured of his unique place in party esteem and fully converted to the reconciliation line, he became more embittered, solitary, vengeful, and dangerous. If his will to vengeance had softened with the passage of time and under the influence of biographical therapy, it must have hardened now. If he had wavered before in his belief that the party was honeycombed with enemies scheming against him, he could do so no longer. Now he knew that treason was rife even in the party's highest organ of authority, the congress.

Not only must Stalin's determination to proceed with the party purge have been steeled. In the aftermath of the congress experiences, what seemed necessary was not simply a continuation of the operation that had been going on in recent months but a purge of a new kind—new in scope and in method. Not a bloodless weeding out as in the past but a purge in which expulsion would mean repression as a traitorous enemy of the Revolution; and not a mere diminution of numbers but a *radical renovation of the party undertaken as the next big task of the revolution from above.* A whole generation of party members who had failed the test of fealty must go, their places to be taken by a new generation of "real Bolsheviks" who would not fail the test, who would recognize Stalin's revolutionary genius, and who would faithfully follow him in politics no matter where he might lead. Let the Zhdanovs and Berias and Khrushchevs who *could* be his devoted supporters and admiring disciples become the new cohort of leaders in a party remade to conform with his community ideal. Let a party of Lenin-*Stalin* worshippers be created.

Testimony from a variety of informed sources supports such a reconstruction of Stalin's thought process. Shortly after the congress, according to the Soviet film director M. I. Romm, Kaganovich remarked among friends that a "mass replacement of leading party cadres" was imminent.[57] Later, in Kiev where he worked, Petrovsky observed to the Ukrainian party leader Kosior that Stalin "for some reason has taken a dislike to the Old Bolsheviks and is up in arms against them."[58] A well-connected secret police officer heard a starker version from the chief of the police organization's foreign division, Slutsky: "Stalin has said that the entire prerevolutionary and war generation must be destroyed as a millstone around the neck of the revolution."[59]

The fullest corroborating testimony came out via "Old Bolshevik." Stalin had grown convinced, he said, that the Old Bolsheviks as a group rejected him in the depths of their hearts and that the majority of those who protested their devotion to him would betray him at the first opportunity. Their hostility stemmed from their psychology as lifelong oppositionists who could not help but be critical of what existed:

In short, we are all critics, destructionists—not builders. This was all to the good—in the past; but now, when we must occupy ourselves with constructive building, it is all hopelessly bad. It is impossible to build anything enduring with such human materials, composed of skeptics and critics. What must be considered now, first and foremost, is the necessity of enduring construction, particularly because Soviet Russia is facing tremendous perturbations, such as will arise inevitably with the coming of war. It was thus that Stalin reasoned.[60]

The conclusion that Stalin drew, "Old Bolshevik" said, was the need to rid the regime of all those infected with the spirit of criticism and to create a new ruling stratum imbued with the psychology of true builders.

This testimony, in addition to confirming the radical character of the final decision, shows how Stalin rationalized it. In fact, however, the Bolshevik ex-revolutionaries were not psychologically unfit to be builders. They had been "destructionists" toward tsarist Russia, but after 1917, they were, as Lenin had been, wholeheartedly committed to rebuilding Russia on socialist lines. They were "skeptics and critics" only of Stalin's crudely coercive approach to the task, its destructive consequences, and the growth of inequality and privilege. In Stalin's rationalization, however, belief in him and his works was the nub of the new ruling stratum's "psychology of true builders."

Because of his Lenin-identification, Stalin always needed to think of himself as acting like Lenin when he embarked upon a major project. So now, ironically, he needed Leninist warrant for destroying the very political generation of which Lenin had been an elder representative figure and idolized leader. More ironically still, such warrant was relatively easy to find. In the Leninist heritage Stalin found much that served him well in justifying a course of action that for Lenin would have been unthinkable.

The purge was integral to Lenin's conception of the party as a revolutionary community of the elect. As the epigraph to his *What Is To Be Done?* he chose a statement in which Lassalle observed to Marx that "a party grows stronger by purging itself." He argued in this work that to be capable of effective action in the tsarist police state, the party must eschew democratic procedures like open election to office and base itself on "complete, comradely, mutual confidence among revolutionaries." Should the confidence prove misplaced, "an organization of real revolutionaries will stop at nothing to rid itself of an unworthy member."[61] After 1917, when membership in what was now a ruling party grew attractive to careerists and the like, Lenin looked to the purge as a means of weeding out such people. He championed the general purge of 1921, which brought the expulsion of almost a third of the 600,000 members of that time; and on one occasion he even called for a "purge of terrorist character"—specifically, summary trial and shooting—for "former officials, landlords, bourgeois and other scum who have attached themselves to the Communists and sometimes commit outrageous and infamous acts of mistreatment of peasants."[62]

In his article for Lenin's fiftieth birthday in 1920, Stalin commented that Lassalle was right in saying that a party becomes stronger by purging himself; and in *The Foundations of Leninism* he treated the party purge as one of those foundations. The purge theme in *What Is To Be Done?* had struck a responsive chord in the young man, who acquired from it a proud consciousness of himself as a member of Lenin's community of the elect. But the notion of an "unworthy member" took on for Stalin a special meaning. The party being the army of Lenin-Stalin, a body of people united in fealty to their leader, a critic of Stalin's was an enemy of the party and as such a candidate for punishment by purge.

He knew very well that to take this course was to go against the current of sentiment in the party as presently constituted. It was to go against the wishes of the great majority of the new Central Committee and of a majority of the Politburo's members. But there was Leninist warrant for that too. Reminiscing about Lenin during the days of mourning in 1924, Stalin praised his flouting of majority party opinion when he was certain of being in the right. Lenin had never been the "prisoner of majorities" at times when majority party opinion conflicted with the proletariat's basic interests, not even when it meant taking a stand against all the others.[63] To be Leninists rather than "tailists," Stalin told the Sixteenth Congress, party people must "grasp the Leninist line—go against the current when the situation, the party's interests, demand it.[64]

To his mind, they certainly demanded it now. No matter that he would be in a minority, even a minority of one. One against *all* the others—there was precedent for that too. At the Fifteenth Congress, when the Left opposition leaders were being expelled, Stalin recalled that in 1903, when it was time for the Russian Marxist party to turn from agreement with the liberals to do mortal battle against them, it had a sextet of leaders in Plekhanov, Zasulich, Martov, Lenin, Akselrod, and Potresov. The sharp turn proved "fatal" to five of the six, leaving only Lenin, one of the youngest, in the leadership. Not only did the old leaders' departure not cause the party to perish, as many warned; it was only by that means that the party had got onto the right road of Bolshevik cohesion for leading the proletariat into revolution. The same thing had happened in 1907–8, when another sharp turn—from open to circuitous methods of revolutionary action—proved "fatal" to leading Bolshevik figures like Aleksinsky, Bogdanov, and Rozhkov. "What did Lenin seek then? One thing only: to rid the party as quickly as possible of the unstable and sniveling elements, so they wouldn't get in the way. That, comrades, is how our party grew."[65]

Thus there was Leninist warrant for a purge that would prove "fatal" to most or even all the still surviving party leaders of Stalin's seniority. Even if he alone of the septet that stood at the helm just after Lenin died— Bukharin, Kamenev, Rykov, Stalin, Tomsky, Trotsky, and Zinoviev— should survive in power, it would only be a repetition of what had happened under Lenin and by his devices in 1903.

The party had grown strong by ridding itself of unstable and sniveling elements at times when a sharp policy turn was needed. After saying this, Stalin went on: "Our party is a living organism. Like every organism, it undergoes a process of metabolism: the old and outworn moves out; the new and growing lives and develops.[66] In brief, party people opposed to him were shit. So he reasoned at the end of 1927. Now, six years later, he believed that the party was swarming with such people; and he knew what to do about it. He was going to organize a terroristic purge.

Part Three

THE
SECOND
PHASE

You, Mr. Wells, appear to proceed from the assumption that all people are good. But I do not forget that many people are evil.

—STALIN, 23 JULY 1934

12

THE COMING OF
THE GREAT PURGE

FROM LATE 1932 Soviet Russia was the scene of a conspiracy to
seize total power by terrorist action. This was the gist of the secret
letter circulated by Stalin's office to party committees in July 1936.[1]
In a way the charge was true. There *was* a conspiracy. It had its
inception in 1932, and took final shape in 1934. It was carefully organized,
and sought total power through terrorist action against much of the party-
state's leadership.

Beyond that point, fact leaves off and fiction begins. Those accused
of being ringleaders of the conspiracy—Zinoviev, Kamenev, Trotsky, and
others—were among its intended victims; and the one named in the letter
as the chief intended victim—Stalin—was the archconspirator. The secret
letter was projective. Through a glass darkly it revealed what happened:
from the time when Stalin came to see himself as the target of a plot by a
multitude of masked enemies, he began conspiring against them. Their
conspiracy was fictional; his was real.

Conspiracy from Above

After the Seventeenth Congress Stalin became more inaccessible than ever in his establishment on Staraya Square. He reduced the daily contacts with officials to the minimum and spent hours alone in his study, pacing back and forth and smoking his pipe. "On such days it was said in his immediate secretariat that Stalin was thinking, that he was working out a new line. And when Stalin was thinking, absolute silence was incumbent upon everybody."[2] "Old Bolshevik" inferred that Stalin was now trying to decide whether to follow Kirov's policy line or that favored by Kaganovich and Yezhov. Actually, Stalin had already chosen his course of action and only needed to work out the intricacies of implementation.

A conspiracy from above has the special resources of the citadel of power—always a great advantage and still greater in the centralized political order of a modern party-state. The Seventeenth Congress enhanced the Soviet citadel's value to Stalin. It yielded a new set of party rules more in keeping with his needs, a party hierarchy more in accordance with his desires, and a new Party Control Commission that he securely controlled. It approved a reorganization of the Central Committee apparatus on the basis of a plan presented by Kaganovich. The various departments were now specialized according to branches of the economy, and each was made responsible for all party activities in its sphere. The nub of power remained the Secret Department, now called Special Sector.[3] Poskrebyshev remained head of it. Each republic and regional party committee had its own special sector, directly subordinate to and in communication with the main one. Via Poskrebyshev and his staff, Stalin thus presided over a personal power structure ramified throughout the country. It possessed extensive personnel files, served as the main conduit of confidential information and directives, and handled liaison with the security police. No better instrument for a conspiracy from above could have been devised.

Whether Stalin took anyone wholly into his confidence is not known and may be doubted; this was a loner's conspiracy. Yet, the executors of his plans had to be apprised of them by stages, and there was need for organizational assistance outside the party apparatus. Even under the direction of the specially appointed purge commission, the 1933 purge had been a limited affair. The party could not be the organ of its own near-total transformation, nor could it handle the arrests, interrogations, trials, executions, and repressions that would accompany a terroristic purge. Inevitably, Stalin turned at this juncture to the security police.

The police leaders were themselves mostly Old Bolsheviks and destined for destruction. But by virtue of their profession, their trained readiness to follow orders, and Stalin's hold on Yagoda, the police establishment was manipulable for his conspiratorial purposes. In early 1934 he invited a group of leading OGPU officials to a meeting in his office. Among those present were Yagoda and the Central Committee person then in charge of liaison with the OGPU, Feldman. Stalin wanted information on the police chiefs' life-style. How well were they housed? What kinds of cars were at their disposal? Did they enjoy the use of good dachas? *"Bezobrazie!* [An outrage]," he exclaimed on hearing their answers. The "best sons" of the Soviet Union must live in a manner befitting the importance of their work. One of the steps then taken was the building of a complex of comfortable dachas and a spacious clubhouse for the police officials' exclusive use at the village of Novogorsk near Moscow.[4] Stalin was seeking to cement his ties with men on whom he knew he would soon have to rely for extraordinary services.

The long-ailing Menzhinsky died in May 1934. On 11 July the press published a governmental decree setting up an all-union People's Commissariat of Internal Affairs (NKVD). Yagoda was appointed head of it, and Ia. S. Agranov and G. E. Prokofiev became his deputies. The OGPU was incorporated into the new commissariat as the Chief Administration of Internal Security. Other divisions were GULAG, the militia or regular police force, the border guard, internal security forces, fire department, and civil registry. The OGPU judicial collegium, which had power of passing summary death sentences, was abolished. The decree specified that state security cases would henceforth be referred to the courts after police investigation. Cases of espionage and the like were to be tried by a military collegium of the Supreme Court. Finally, the NKVD would have a Special Board *(Osoboe soveshchanie)* with right of administrative, that is, nonjudicial, sentencing to terms of up to five years of exile, deportation, or confinement in labor camps.

The police reorganization was presented to the public as a reform measure made possible by enhanced stability of the regime and the full competence of the court system to decide state security cases. In fact, it was a move in Stalin's conspiracy. The provision for treason cases to be judged by a Supreme Court military collegium presaged the staging of a series of treason trials before that collegium under the chairmanship of V. V. Ulrikh, described as an "army military jurist." Further, a statute promulgated in June 1934 introduced the concept of high treason into Soviet legislation as a new rubric covering such previously recognized crimes as espionage, the divulging of military or state secrets, and fleeing abroad. The statute made these crimes punishable by death and contained the savagely punitive provision that family members of service personnel guilty of fleeing abroad were subject to five- to ten-year sentences if they should abet the crime or know of the intention to commit it without reporting this to the authorities, and to sentences of up to five years if innocent of such knowledge.[5] Stalin was putting high treason on the country's agenda, and anticipating circumstances under which Soviet persons would feel pressed to flee abroad, or not to return home when ordered to do so.

Another portent was the Special Board. The decree of 11 July directed the new commissariat to prepare a statute on this organ. Under the statute, issued 5 November 1934, the Special Board was to consist of the people's commissar as chairman, his two deputies, the head of the militia administration, the USSR procurator or his deputy, and one or two others. It was empowered to pass administrative sentence on "persons deemed socially dangerous." No definition of "socially dangerous" was given. The statute was not printed in the late November issue of the periodically published register of new laws, along with other legal acts of its date, but in March 1935 along with laws passed in early 1935.[6] The delay in publication, undoubtedly deliberate, was probably motivated by the desire not to publicize the mission of the newly instituted policy organ—which became an instrument of the wholesale reprisals that began after Kirov's death in December 1934.

The Special Board had a tsarist ancestor. An institution of the same name and character existed in the Russian Ministry of Internal Affairs under the last two tsars. The statute on "Measures to Maintain State Security and Public Tranquility," passed in 1881 after the assassination of Tsar Alexander II, created an *Osoboe soveshchanie* with power of administrative sentencing of persons to exile for terms of one to five years. It consisted of the vice-minister of internal affairs as chairman, two representatives of his ministry, and two representatives of the Ministry of Justice. Its decisions required confirmation by the minister of internal affairs.[7] The main mission of the tsarist Special Board had been to send revolutionaries into exile. Stalin's Special Board soon acquired a similar function, in some cases affecting the same people.

But before the new machinery of repression could be put to work, a justification was needed for the unleashing of terror. Although Lenin was incautious enough to use the phrase "terroristic purge," nothing of that kind had yet occurred in the party. Stalinist repression of the Left, justified by the claim that "Trotskyism" was alien to Bolshevism, fell short of outright terror. Furthermore, the Riutin affair had dramatized the strength of the opposition at Politburo level to bloodshed as a means of settling scores between Bolsheviks. Stalin needed a powerful, politically persuasive excuse for overcoming this opposition.

German events proved instructive to him at this time. The Reichstag fire of the previous year had been played up in the Soviet press for what it may have been: a Nazi-staged crime followed by legislation to authorize summary justice and ensuing terror against Communist and other left-wing elements. On 30 June 1934 Hitler acted again, this time to consolidate his dictatorial power by supressing a large, potentially unruly element in the Nazi movement itself, namely the Storm Troops led by Captain Ernest Röhm. In a swift conspiracy from above that had the support and help of the German military leaders, he brought about the weekend massacre of Röhm and others on the pretext that they were planning a coup. Then he legalized governmental terror with a one-paragraph law that read: "The measures taken on June 30 and July 1 and 2 to strike down the treasonous attacks are justifiable acts of self-defense by the state."[8] It is attested that the Röhm purge greatly interested Stalin and that he attentively read all reports on it from Soviet secret agents in Germany.[9] Also, that at the first Politburo meeting after 30 June, he said: "Have you heard what happened in Germany? Some fellow (molodets!) that Hitler. Knows how to treat his political opponents."[10]

Although Stalin's interest is understandable, the Röhm purge was as much a model of what he could *not* do as it was a source of instruction. To swoop down on his party enemies in an openly terroristic "night of the long knives," as Hitler described his weekend operation in Germany, was out of the question for Stalin. Not only did Bolshevik political culture militate against any such action; it was not Stalin's way to act so. Besides, his enemies were far too numerous to be put out of the way in a single limited operation. What he needed was, rather, a Soviet equivalent of the Reichstag fire: a heinous crime and politically shocking event in which numbers of prominent Old Bolsheviks could be implicated. Once that precipitating event were brought off, an emergency legislative act similar to Hitler's one-sentence law could clear the way for a widening arc of repressions against party members. The bar to terror against the party as then constituted would be broken.

It was natural for Stalin to think of an assassination as the precipitating event. Not only had threatened assassination—his own, by the likes of Riutin—been on his mind for some time. Soviet history contained a suggestive episode that was burned into the memory of Stalin's political generation: the events of 30 August 1918, when SRs murdered the head of the Petrograd Cheka, M. S. Uritsky, and tried to kill Lenin in Moscow. A sharp intensification of the Red Terror ensued then. There was thus a precedent for initiating a cycle of official terror in response to the assassination of a leading Bolshevik (in Leningrad) and the attempted assassination of the supreme leader in Moscow. This pattern reappears in the secret circular letter of July 1936, which accused the imaginary counterrevolutionary organization of murdering Kirov in Leningrad and planning the murder of Lenin's successor in Moscow.

The choice of Kirov as the victim was as inevitable as the decision to use an assassination as the precipitating event. Stalin became enviously hostile toward his one-time friend, had serious differences with him over policy, and feared him as a rival for party leadership. Further, no other leading Communist's death by violence would have so great a shock effect and serve so well to justify the unleashing of terror. Nor would it have escaped Stalin's mind that the Zinoviev-Kamenev group, whose past record of opposition and disgrace made it the best possible Old Bolshevik circle to implicate in the crime, had former adherents in Zinoviev's old stronghold, Leningrad.

"Ivan Vasilievich" and the Bolshevik Grandees

Even in procuring the murder of a comrade as the pretext for a terroristic purge, it would have been out of character for Stalin to recognize his criminality. He had to see himself as a wise and just leader. In being an archvillain, he had to play a heroic part. Once again, Russian history was of help. If Peter served him as a role model in the *piatiletka,* the "terrible tsar," Ivan Grozny, did so in the Great Purge.

What were the sources of his positive image of Ivan? One of them was a book by R. Iu. Wipper, a professor at Moscow University. Wipper, a monarchist then, published a biography of Ivan in 1922 in Moscow. It characterized Ivan as "one of the greatest diplomats of all times" and said it was for the good of Russia that he threw off the oligarchy and promoted service nobles of obscure origin to high places while forcibly transplanting titled magnates to new regions. There really was a "great plot" hatched by the Moscow boyars and Novgorod clergy against the life of Ivan, who therefore "cannot be accused of being oversuspicious." As for the bloody Novgorod events, objective documentary testimony was lacking, and besides ". . . the tsar was then passing through a very difficult period of life, suffering from the consciousness of his isolation, desertion, his encirclement by enemies and traitors, and lack of faithful and reliable supporters." The *oprichnina* was a "weapon against treason," a "progressive institution," and a "great military-administrative reform" called forth by the difficulties of Russia's just war in Livonia for access to the Baltic sea. By convening the *Zemskii sobor* in order to appeal to the patriotism of wide sections of society, especially the army, Ivan "stood forth as a popular monarch in a halo of glory."[11] In sum, a people's tsar.

It is known, as noted earlier,[12] that Stalin read Wipper's book. This is consonant with Wipper's later career and Stalin's views on Ivan. No friend of the Revolution, Wipper emigrated to Latvia in 1923 but returned to Moscow in 1941 (after Latvia's annexation to the USSR) and was made an academician. At that time many Russian émigrés in Latvia were being shipped off to Siberian prison camps, yet Wipper's book on Ivan was reissued in a new edition in 1942, in a third edition in 1944, and received acclaim. Its image of Ivan was now the approved Soviet one. Ivan had become a hero of history in Stalin's Russia. A play about him, written by Alexei Tolstoy in the spirit of Wipper's book, was running in Moscow's Maly Theater in the early 1940s. The noted film producer Sergei Eisenstein was at work on a series of films about Ivan. In this connection he and the actor playing the role of Ivan, N. K. Cherkasov, had a talk with Stalin. Cherkasov later recounted it in his memoirs.

Stalin told them that Ivan was a great and wise ruler who protected the land from penetration of foreign influence and strove to unify Russia. He observed (incorrectly) that Ivan was the first to introduce a monopoly of foreign trade in Russia, adding that after him only Lenin managed that. He stressed the "progressive role" of the *oprichnina,* and said that its leader, Maliuta Skuratov, was a major Russian military commander who died heroically in the struggle with Livonia. But Grozny also made mistakes, Stalin went on, one of them being that he allowed five big feudal families to escape liquidation. Had he not thus failed to carry through the fight against the feudal lords to a finish, there would have been no subsequent Time of Troubles in Russia. The problem was that God got in the way: every time Grozny liquidated a family of feudal lords, a boyar clan, he would repent for a whole year and seek absolution for his sins when what he should have done was to act more decisively!

At the end of the talk Stalin inquired about the projected ending of part two of the Ivan film series. Cherkasov said that it was to end with the Livonian campaign and Ivan's victorious emergence onto the Baltic shore. He would be shown standing at the sea's edge surrounded by his military chiefs, flag-bearers, and fighting men. His innermost youthful dream of seeing "the blue sea, the far sea, the Russian sea" had come true, and gazing into the distance he would conclude the film by saying: "On the seas we stand and will stand!" Stalin smiled at this and gaily exclaimed: "Well, why not! That's the way it actually happened—and a lot better, too!"[13]

Such was Stalin's opinion of Ivan. Though stated in 1947, it was formed many years earlier and certainly by the time with which we are here concerned. Ivan was on Stalin's mind in 1934. At some point in the summer or early fall, around the time of the First Soviet Writers' Congress in August, he took the initiative of engaging his writer-friend Alexei Tolstoy in a conversation about the tsar. They agreed, among other things, that Ivan differed from Peter in surrounding himself with Russians, not foreigners.[14] The obliging count was doubtless pleased to encourage the

pro-Ivan direction of Stalin's thinking. Another who did so, perhaps unwittingly, was Gorky. He had long ago confided to paper the thought that
the Russian common people, judging by their songs and stories in which
Ivan appears as a wise and just tsar, regarded Ivan's terror against the
boyars as a heroic struggle. Now, in the context of an argument for the
importance of folklore as an historical source, Gorky told the Writers'
Congress that folk opinion on Ivan and his fight against the feudal lords
was very different from the negative views of later historians.[15] Gorky was
the main speaker at that well-publicized event, and Stalin, who could
follow its proceedings in *Pravda* from his vacation retreat at Sochi on the
Black Sea, must have appreciated the favorable mention of Ivan.

In his talk with Eisenstein and Cherkasov, Stalin found the explanation for post-Ivan Russia's Time of Troubles in the tsar's passion for prayer
that enabled five feudal families to survive the antiboyar purge. No such
number is recorded in history books. How did Stalin come by it? A Soviet
historian has reasonably hypothesized that he derived the idea from the
classic Russian play *Tsar Fedor Iovannovich,* by the nineteenth-century
writer Alexei K. Tolstoy. The Moscow Art Theater, which was Stalin's
favorite, produced this play in Stalin's time and performed it often. A
character in it says that Ivan Grozny, in dying, "turned *Rus'* over to five
boyars."[16]

It is easy to see how and why Stalin thought of himself now as a latter-
day Ivan. It was a powerful rationalization, enabling him to dramatize
himself, in the midst of his murderous conspiring, as one who was acting
rightfully at a critical point in the history of Russia and Communism. The
basis of his rationalization was a perceived parallel between Russia's situation now and the mid-sixteenth century. Both times, as he apparently saw
it, a gifted and resourceful leader devoted to the interests of a unified
Russian state found himself beset by treasonable opposition of an entrenched aristocracy that stood in the way of progress and the pursuit of a
wise foreign policy—of westward expansion. Both times the aristocratic
opposition operated through oligarchical institutions: the Boyar Council
then, the party congress, Central Committee, and Politburo now.

Whether Stalin's dramatizing mind contrived to see Kirov (at his
Leningrad post in the Livonian direction) as his Kurbsky or Staritsky may
never be known, but it is plain from his statements through the years that
he regarded the Old Bolshevik leadership as an aristocracy. Ivan's epistle
to the fugitive Prince Kurbsky referred slightingly to the *vel'mozhi* (grandees). In the 1920s this archaic expression was not generally used by
Bolsheviks, but Stalin repeatedly used it in contemptuous reference to
Bolshevik bigwigs. Speaking at the Thirteenth Congress in 1924 of the
need for periodic party purges, he said that "Soviet *vel'mozhi*" must be

made to understand that "there is a master who can demand account for their sins against the party." Then he used another Grozny symbol—the broom on the *oprichnik*'s saddle—by adding: "I think it's mandatory for the master to move through the party ranks from time to time with a broom in his hands."[17] In a private letter of 1929 he spoke up for young, obscure party writers against unnamed prominent ones whom he called "literary *vel'mozhi*."[18] Then, at the just concluded Seventeenth Congress, he used the archaic word three times in a passage about the need to remove from office persons "with certain past merits" who had become "haughty *vel'mozhi*."[19] It is open to speculation that in having himself publicly identified in the congress' aftermath as simply "secretary" rather than "general secretary," Stalin was mindful of Ivan's styling himself simply "prince of Moscow Ivan Vasilievich" rather than "tsar" during the *oprichnina* terror.

As his chief enemies were *vel'mozhi*, he was Grozny. By chance the initials of Stalin's given name and patronymic, Iosif Vissarionovich, were the same as those of his identity-figure, Ivan Vasilievich. An ex-insider reports that he used "Ivan Vasilievich" as his pseudonym in secret-police correspondence during the Great Purge.[20] As he prepared that purge, which would involve (as Ivan's had) arrests, imprisonment, torture to extract confessions, treason trials, and executions, he could see himself in mortal battle against Bolshevik grandees' sedition. By creating the *oprichnina* as an instrument of autocratic rule and means of purging the Russian land of boyar treason, Ivan was acting in the deepest interests of Russian statehood. Now a new "Ivan Vasilievich" would do the same, but with a difference: just as he, Stalin, had succeeded where Peter failed in making Russia industrially strong, so now he would succeed where Ivan failed in carrying through the fight against sedition to a finish.

There is further indication that Stalin was identifying himself with "Ivan Vasilievich" in 1934: this was the year when he decreed the rewriting of Russian history in such a way as to glorify Grozny as a past great Russian revolutionary from above.

Before such a Soviet Russian historiography could develop, the Pokrovsky school had to be dethroned. Pokrovsky himself was ill with cancer from at least 1930. On his death in 1932 he was given a Red-Square funeral befitting a Bolshevik grandee and praised as an eminent figure in historical science. The manner of his passing and the party eulogies made it inexpedient for Stalin to move against the Pokrovsky school immediately. A sign of coming change was visible, however, in the very editorial that Pokrovsky's journal, *Marxist Historian,* ran along with his obituary. It demanded "a decisive reorganization of the historical front" on the basis not only of Pokrovsky's heritage butt also of "a painstaking study of all the works of Lenin and Stalin."[21]

As of then, Stalin's published writings contained very little to which historians could look for guidance on how to reorganize the historical front. Conscious of this and of the challenge that the reorganization presented, Stalin took it upon himself in 1934 to navigate history on its anti-Pokrovsky new course. He did this by revising party policy on historical education in the schools. His views on historical education emerged little by little in a series of Central Committee directives. A decree dated 12 February 1933 established that each school textbook must be approved by the Commissariat of Education and that "for each individual subject there must exist a single mandatory textbook approved by the Commissariat and published by the Educational Publishing House."[22] There followed, on 16 May 1934, three joint party-government decrees signed by Stalin as Central Committee secretary and by Molotov as chairman of Sovnarkom. One reintroduced a more traditional school structure. The second criticized the teaching of geography for being too schematic. The third found history teaching in unsatisfactory shape and contained directives for new approaches in this field.[23]

Shortly before these decrees were published, some Soviet historians were invited to the Kremlin to meet with members of the Politburo and prominent educators for an advance briefing. Over thirty years later, one of them recalled the scene. Stalin held in his hand a textbook (the historian-memoirist noted at the time, with trepidation, that it was one he himself had coauthored), and began by saying: "My son asked me to explain what's written in this book. I took a look and also couldn't comprehend it." He went on for five or ten minutes, saying that texts should be written differently, that what they needed was not general schemes but precise historical facts—and while he talked he repeatedly hitched up his trousers in the mechanical manner of one-time prison inmates used to wearing trousers without belts. The historian also recalled that everyone present was silently fixated on Stalin, as though drawn to the speaker by an irresistible force. "I remember that moment with a thought about present-day debates: did everyone believe in Stalin or did more sober skeptics 'grasp everything from the start'. I think they believed."[24]

Though the decree on history teaching made no mention of Pokrovsky, its anti-Pokrovsky orientation was clear from its criticism of abstract historical schemes and the demands for chronological factuality and "characterizations of historical figures." The latter point was especially stressed in *Pravda*'s editorial on 16 May, when the decrees were published. How radical a change it meant may be seen from the fact that previous observance of the rule of ignoring individuals had been so strict that one university professor received a severe dressing down for merely including a brief characterization of Martin Luther in a lecture on the German Reformation.[25] Now the way was open for taking account of influential individuals.

The decree on history teaching directed that history faculties be restored in Moscow and Leningrad universities by September 1934 and that new school history texts be prepared by June 1935. When prospectuses for texts on the Soviet Union and modern world history were submitted soon afterward Stalin personally undertook to pass judgment on them. He availed himself of the assistance of Zhdanov, who apparently helped him organize his thoughts on paper. A second helper, recruited over protest, was Kirov.

In the late summer of 1934 Kirov was summoned to Sochi where he found Stalin and Zhdanov at work preparing comments on the prospectuses. Stalin wanted him to go to Kazakhstan to supervise the gathering of the harvest. The local leaders were, it seemed, nervous in face of the prospect of a bumper crop. Then Kirov must move to Moscow. "After all," said Stalin, "you're a secretary of the party Central Committee!" Kirov accepted the Kazakhstan assignment but tactfully declined the move to Moscow, pleading the need to stay in Leningrad until the conclusion of the city's reconstruction at the end of the Second Five-Year Plan.[26] He returned to Leningrad for Air Force Day, 18 August, and then spent nearly the whole of September in Kazakhstan. While he was there an attempt was made to arrange his assassination.[27] The manhunt was on.

During the meeting at Sochi, Stalin had a further demand. He wanted Kirov to stay there for a week or so to take part in discussing (as Kirov's post-Stalin biographer puts it) "the thoughts expressed by Stalin" on the prospectuses for history textbooks. Embarrassed, Kirov said: "Iosif Vissarionovich, what kind of historian am I"—to which Stalin replied. "Never mind, sit down and listen!"[28] When the comments thus prepared in 1934 were published in *Pravda* on 27 January 1936, they bore the signatures of Stalin, Zhdanov, and Kirov. Stalin thus established in advance that he and Kirov were in close collaborative relations during the latter's last months.

And when, in 1937, the Stalin-approved new history text appeared, it presented Tsar Ivan Grozny as a hero of Russian history. "Under the reign of Ivan IV," it said, "Russia's possessions were enlarged manifold. His kingdom became one of the biggest states in the world." It did so, the book indicated, only by virtue of the tsar's war on boyar treason. For after the first defeats in the Livonian war, "Ivan discovered that he was being betrayed by the big patrimonial boyars. These traitors went into the service of the Poles and Lithuanians." The text went on:

Tsar Ivan hated the boyars, who lived in their patrimonies like little tsars and tried to limit his autocratic power. He began to banish and execute the rich and strong boyars. He had to fight the boyars in order to crush these little tsars and to strengthen his position as sole ruler. To fight the boyars he recruited from among the landowners a special force, several thousand strong. This force he called the *oprichniki.* The *oprichniki* wore a special uniform. Attached to his saddle each *oprichnik* had a dog's head and a broom. This was the emblem of their office: to ferret out and track the enemies of the tsar, and to sweep away the boyar-traitors. . . . In this way, Ivan Grozny strengthened autocratic power in the Russian state by destroying the privileges of the boyars. Thereby, as it were, he completed the work started by Ivan Kalita, of gathering together the scattered appanage principalities into one strong state.[29]

What had once been regarded as the monarchist view of Ivan was now a part of the elementary education of every Soviet schoolchild.

Internal Détente

Machiavelli, with whose book *The Prince* Stalin was familiar, advises a ruler how to guard against conspiracies: acquire a great reputation ("for he will not be easily attacked, so long as it is known that he is capable and reverenced by his subjects"), and avoid unpopularity: "And one of the most potent remedies that a prince has against conspiracies, is that of not being hated by the mass of the people; for whoever conspires always believes that he will satisfy the people by the death of their prince; but if he thought to offend them by doing this, he would fear to engage in such an undertaking, for the difficulties that conspirators have to meet are infinite."[30]

Safeguarding himself against conspiracies was a matter of special concern to Stalin now. Apart from his personal proneness to suspect a conspirator in everyone, there were realistic grounds for concern. The move to replace him with Kirov at the time of the congress had failed, but his forthcoming purge would certainly bring far more serious trouble. The terror after Kirov's assassination would cause consternation among many in high places, and that would in turn lead to an additional danger of a concerted highlevel effort to remove him from power. To allay it, he must not only attend closely to arrangements for his personal security and the surveillance of others. He must also create a climate discouraging to would-be conspirators. Hence, he had good reason to be mindful now of Machiavelli's advice.

His great reputation was assured by the personality cult, which was keeping his name, picture, sayings, theoretical precepts, past exploits and present doings constantly before the minds of Soviet people, starting with the youngsters whose classrooms featured the slogan, "Thank you, Comrade Stalin, for our happy childhood." But all this was no guarantee of being well liked. The congress experience, if nothing else, had taught him the difference between the reality of popularity (Kirov's) and its semblance. If he was to become really popular, his actions must be directed, and seen to be directed, to the people's welfare. So Stalin in 1934 became, within limits, a vigorous exponent of the very politics of reconciliation with the people that Kirov, Gorky, and others had been urging upon him for some time with but indifferent success. He sponsored an extensive and palpable domestic *détente,* a Stalinist peace with the Soviet people.[31]

There were further considerations. Stalin could clearly see the strength of the Kirov-Gorky argument that a respite was needed for stabilizing society and restoring morale in preparation for likely war. He could use a period of calm for concentrating on the next phase of the revolution from above and bringing along the new people who would advance to high position. The impact of the assassination would be all the greater in a relaxed national atmosphere. Finally, by espousing popular measures strongly and visibly, he could lull fears in the minds of future purge victims and exploit their abilities while preparing their doom. So, for example, he allowed Bukharin to assume the editorship of *Izvestia* after the party congress, and went on making good use of Radek's journalistic talents and expertise in German affairs.

Starting in February 1934, step followed step in a steady march of official actions to better the lot of Soviet people. Some were gestures toward the peasantry. A decree published over the signatures of Stalin as Central Committee secretary and Molotov as head of the government cancelled unmet grain-delivery quotas for 1933 and spread out over three years the repayment of government loans of grain for feed and food. *Pravda's* 1st March editorial on this modest measure was blazoned: "In What Other Country Does the Peasantry Receive Such Aid!" In May local Soviet officials were authorized to restore to full citizenship deported kulaks who had worked hard and proved loyal, especially the young. In July Stalin and other Central Committee officials met with a group of regional party secretaries to discuss problems of rural policy. At that time about 70 percent of the peasant households were collectivized. Speaking for the Central Committee, Stalin cautioned against administrative coercion in collectivizing the remainder, and advocated the subsequently taken steps to raise collective farmers' incomes, limit their delivery quotas, and fix the size of their private plots.[32] A reported further topic of discussion at the July meeting was the dissolution of the political departments that had been created in the machine-tractor stations during collectivization. Kirov, who was present, is said to have spoken strongly on this issue, proposing the revival of Soviet power in the countryside."[33] This proposal was within the frame of the policy Stalin was now pursuing, and thus Kaganovich proposed to the Central Committee during its subsequent November 1934 plenary session that the political departments be fused with the regular

district party committees. Adoption of the proposal suggested a return to
rural normalcy.

Stalin's internal-*détente* policy took many other forms. In April 1934
the government issued a decree on the need to spur housing construction
in towns and worker settlements. More goods began to appear in the shops,
and people started to talk about the advent of a "little NEP."[34] The November plenum endorsed a Politburo decision—which Molotov said had been
proposed by Stalin—to end bread rationing as of 1 January 1935. Nearly a
half-century later, a former Soviet citizen, then an émigré in America, told
this writer that he still remembered the joy he felt as a young boy in Odessa
when handed his first piece of nonrationed bread, and his inner surge of
gratitude to Stalin at that moment in his life. Again in November 1935,
speaking at the Stakhanovites' congress in the Kremlin, Mikoyan told how
Stalin had demanded of him that he produce samples of the high-quality
new toilet soap now being manufactured for ordinary people at a Politburo
meeting so that the members could look them over—after which "we
received a special Central Committee decision on the assortment and composition of soap."[35] Not all expressions of Stalin's new populism were
similarly publicized. Khrushchev, then first secretary of the Moscow Party
Committee, received a phone call from him one day saying "rumors have
reached me that you've let a very unfavorable situation develop in Moscow
as regards public toilets. Apparently people hunt around desperately and
can't find anywhere to relieve themselves. This won't do. It puts the
citizens in an awkward position. Talk this matter over with Bulganin and
do something to improve these conditions."[36]

Measures to alleviate material hardship went along with moves to
dispel the *piatiletka*'s atmosphere of austerity. A lighthearted musical
comedy, *The Jolly Fellows,* the first of a series of its kind, appeared on
Soviet screens during 1934. Popular dance halls were opened in Moscow,
Leningrad, and other big cities. There and in worker clubs people danced
the formerly frowned-upon foxtrot to tunes of once tabooed American jazz.
Tennis, previously decried as bourgeois, became respectable. The dining
rooms of Moscow hotels, heretofore patronized almost exclusively by
foreigners, filled up with decorously dressed young men and women representing, the *Times* correspondent reported, "all sections of Soviet business and industry."[37]

Another journalist, on a visit to Russia after an interval of six years,
observing the goods in previously empty stores and the chintzy pictures,
lampshades, tidies, and cushions in the room of a happy shock worker,
wondered if the Soviet upper classes were fated to go through all the
motions that lead up to Grand Rapids Chippendale. "The Soviet Experiment is getting somewhere, certainly," she concluded, "but is it Main

Street?"[38] Similar thoughts went through the mind of the writer Ilya Ehrenburg as he walked Moscow's streets in the hot summer of 1934 and heard the newly popular song, "Masha and I by the Samovar," blaring through open windows. "There were many more Mashas than samovars, but 'Masha by the Samovar' suited the members of boards, the chairmen of town soviets, the clerks: the petty bourgeois tastes of prerevolutionary times seemed to them the criterion of beauty."[39]

A stirring exploit of 1934 helped Stalin appear before the nation as the common man's friend. The icebreaker *Cheliuskin,* carrying a scientific expedition on an attempted voyage from Leningrad to Vladivostok via the Northern Sea Route, sank in ice in the Sea of Okhotsk. The expedition's leader, Professor Otto Shmidt, and 103 members and crewmen made camp on an ice floe from which Soviet airmen rescued them in small groups during March and April. The press featured the story day by day. There was a surge of national pride at the spectacle of the marooned men's fortitude and their rescuers' valor against heavy odds. When it was all over, the airmen were awarded the newly instituted title, Hero of the Soviet Union. But the main hero of the incident was Stalin. His name and portrait dominated the publicity. On the eve of their triumphant homecoming the rescued men wired thanks. The message said: "We knew that thou, Comrade Stalin, wert caring for us, that thou wert the initiator of the grandiose measures to save the polar explorers of the Cheliuskin."[40]

The first Soviet Writers' Congress in August 1934 seemed at the time an omen of cultural liberalism. Zhdanov's brief introductory remarks on Stalin's description of Soviet writers as engineers of human souls hinted at the approaching total political power over literary creation, but what was considered significant at the time was Gorky's keynote speech endorsing literary diversity within a framework of Soviet loyalty. The congress also stressed "socialist humanism" in keeping with the emerging new antifascist line in foreign policy. Bukharin and Radek spoke. Still another seemingly favorable sign was the welcome extended to nonparty writers, who made up 40 percent of the 600 delegates. There were speeches by such nonparty literary notables as Babel, Olesha, and Pasternak, and Alexei Tolstoy gave a major address on dramaturgy. In his remarks at the congress' conclusion, Gorky revealed who was responsible for the new tolerance: "Two years ago, Iosif Stalin in his concern to raise the quality of literature told writer-Communists, 'Learn to write from the nonparty ones'."[41]

Just before the Writers' Congress was due to open, Stalin made another intervention—this time to convey an image of himself to the literary community as a ruler with its interests at heart. It had to do with Mandelstam, who had been arrested in mid-May 1934 after his anti-Stalin epigram made the rounds. His wife Nadezhda appealed to Bukharin, now *Izvestia's*

editor, to intercede on her husband's behalf; and Pasternak, who offered
to help, went to see Bukharin too. Bukharin wrote a letter to Stalin with a
postscript saying that Pasternak was upset by Mandelstam's arrest. Late
one night in July on the eve of the Writers' Congress, a phone call came
from Stalin in the Kremlin to Pasternak in his noisy Moscow communal
apartment.

Mandelstam's case had been examined, Stalin said, and all would be
well. And why hadn't Pasternak interceded for him, he asked, adding: "If
I were a poet and a poet friend of mine were in trouble, I would do anything
to help him." While Pasternak was saying something in reply, Stalin broke
in: "But he's a genius, isn't he?" Afterward Pasternak got Stalin's secretary
on the phone, asked whether he should keep quiet about this conversation,
and was told there was no need at all to make a secret of it. Stalin clearly
wanted it to have the widest possible resonance, Nadezhda Mandelstam
quite rightly observed in her memoirs.[42] If the motive and meaning of his
nocturnal phone call were not understood by Russians at the time and,
indeed, have remained a subject for speculation ever since, that is because
Stalin's action has not been seen in the context of the politics of internal
détente that he was pursuing in his conspiracy from above. He wanted the
cultural community to see him as a caring patron of the arts, a man with a
poetic heart. For the time being, while saved from worse fate, Mandelstam
was sent into internal exile.

Another sphere of the *détente* policy was law enforcement. Stalin
wanted to give professional people and the ordinary man reassurance against
arbitrary mistreatment by lower-level authorities. The Procuracy, which
had been elevated to the rank of an all-union independent agency in 1933
and given power of supervision over the legality of acts by administrative
bodies, including the OGPU, was mobilized for the legality campaign.
Many persons convicted for trivial or inflated misdemeanors were released;
and the police reportedly received orders not to arrest any engineers or Red
Army personnel without a special warrant or consultation with the party
Central Committee.[43] The Procuracy was headed then by an Old Bolshevik, Ivan Akulov. He applied himself energetically to exonerating specialists imprisoned on flimsy charges. His deputy, who succeeded him as
Procurator in 1935, was Stalin's man Andrei Vyshinsky. Stalin's personal
backing of the reform policy was clearly shown by Vyshinsky's champion-
ship of it. He took justice officials to task for the "prosecutorial deviation"
of assuming that every court case must end in a conviction; and sternly
lectured them against harming the regime in the eyes of the people through
unwarranted arrest, improper confiscation of property, and violation of
rights.[44]

Coming as it did during the campaign to correct abuses in law and court practice, the police reorganization act of July 1934 easily went down as a reform measure, a move to clip the police's arbitrary powers. *Pravda*'s editorial, while vowing no relaxation in the fight against traitors, spoke of the regime's enhanced present stability. *Izvestia*'s editorial, which would have been written by Bukharin or under his guidance, went further. Terror had earlier been needed to quell actual resistance, it said, but now "enemies inside the country have in the main been defeated and crushed, which means that the fight, by no means ended, will go on but substantially BY OTHER METHODS; that the role of REVOLUTIONARY LEGALITY grows enormously; that the role of COURT institutions, which examine cases according to definite norms of judicial procedure, grows as well.[45] Stalin must have been well content to see *Izvestia* wishfully expand the meaning of the new police legislation. It served the needs of his conspiracy.

Perhaps the most adroit maneuver in the *détente* policy was a temporary show of preparedness for reconciliation within the party. Although the purge resumed in May 1934 with the formation of purging commissions in nine more regions, it proceeded routinely, expulsions were not the prelude to arrest, and very few from the elder party generation were affected. Meanwhile, some well known ex-oppositionists publicly recanted, declared fealty to Stalin and the General Line, and petitioned for reinstatement in the party. One was Christian Rakovsky, who had been living in internal exile since 1928 and whose prestige in Left opposition circles was second only to Trotsky's.[46]

More significant still, Zinoviev and Kamenev, who had been readmitted to the party in 1933, made modest reappearance in public life. Zinoviev contributed occasional articles to *Pravda* on international affairs and for about three months, between April and July 1934, was listed in successive issues of *Bol'shevik* as a member of its editorial board. Kamenev also appeared in *Pravda* and wrote the preface to a volume of Machiavelli's writings published in November. It lauded *The Prince* for offering "a magnificent picture of the zoological features of the struggle for power in a slave society, in which a rich minority ruled over a toiling majority."[47] This was quite probably an Aesopian message about the Soviet state. But what satisfaction Kamenev derived from making it must have been eclipsed by that of the Machiavellian from whom—very possibly—emanated the suggestion that he dig his own grave deeper by writing that essay on the Florentine. It became evidence against him in the 1936 show trial.

Stalin had a special reason for wanting these men to reappear in public life now. They were, it seems, marked down in his mind as candidates for condemnation in treason trials. They were going to be accused of playing parts in a terrorist conspiracy operating down to the present. Zinoviev and

Kamenev would be charged with prime responsibility for Kirov's murder. It was important to establish in the public mind, and particularly in the party mind, that they were at large at this time and hence *could* have been plotting and perpetrating foul deeds. The real conspirator was seeking to confer plausibility on the intended future case against those to whom his crime would be ascribed, and to deflect possible suspicion from himself.

Murder in Leningrad

If Kirov was to be assassinated, someone in Leningrad had to be in charge of the operation. The man chosen for that role was Ivan Zaporozhets, a high Moscow NKVD official with ties to Yagoda. Stalin must have had Yagoda's help in getting Zaporozhets to undertake so odious a mission, and gaining that help could hardly have been easy.

Some evidence from Yagoda himself to this effect came in part of his testimony in the Moscow purge trial of 1938. In general the Stalin show trials mixed fact and fantasy in certain characteristic ways, as wil! be shown further on. Yagoda confessed—no doubt under duress—to having been one of the ringleaders of a "bloc of rightists and Trotskyists" that was said to have perpetrated Kirov's murder, and planned Stalin's, in an anti-Soviet conspiracy. Yagoda testified that the bloc's intention to kill Kirov was communicated to him in the summer of 1934 by one of its leaders, Yenukidze (who in 1934 was secretary of the Central Executive Committee, as the Soviet parliament was then called). "I tried to object," Yagoda said. "I even argued that I, as a person responsible for guarding the members of the government, would be the first to be held responsible in case a terrorist act was committed against a member of the government. Needless to say, my objections were not taken into consideration. Yenukidze insisted that I was not to place any obstacles in the way; the terrorist act, he said, would be carried out by the Trotskyist-Zinovievite group. Owing to this, I was compelled to instruct Zaporozhets . . . not to place any obstacles in the way of the terrorist act against Kirov."[48]

It is plausible that Yagoda initially sought to resist an order to help arrange the killing of Kirov by sending Zaporozhets to Leningrad for this purpose. If for no other reason, he would have been reluctant for the reason given in his testimony: the action he was being told to abet would reflect ill on him as head of state security. The Yenukidze part of the story is, however, absurd.[49] If he had importuned Yagoda's assistance in arranging for Kirov's murder as part of a plot to overthrow the Soviet regime, Yagoda could have saved himself, Kirov, Stalin, and the Soviet regime by promptly informing on Yenukidze to Stalin. But if Stalin importuned him, there was no one higher to whom he could turn. Thus for "Yenukidze" we may read "Stalin," and we may see in Yagoda's forced confession of guilt a classic case of Stalin's inner need to purge himself of repressed guilt feeling by projecting his villainies onto "enemies of the people." He was thus made to appear blameless, according to the dictates of his idealized Stalin self, and their confessions provided a juridical basis for their condemnation for his crimes.

The chief of the Leningrad regional office of the NKVD was Filipp Medved, a friend of Kirov's. Medved's first deputy, in charge of state security in the region, was a man named Karpov. In 1934, probably by the end of summer, Karpov was transferred out of Leningrad and Zaporozhets was appointed to take his post. Medved objected to the appointment of Zaporozhets to be his first deputy and complained to Kirov about it. Kirov got in touch with Stalin to register the objection, but to no avail.[50] Zaporozhets took over the highly sensitive position and was now able to supervise matters on the ground in Leningrad.

The conspiracy found an unwitting instrument in Leonid Nikolaev, a thirty-year-old Leningrader who was something of a social misfit and a moody young man. He lived in a small apartment with his wife Milda Draul, a Latvian by nationality, who worked in the dining hall of the Leningrad party and government headquarters in the Smolny Institute. His mother also lived in Leningrad. A party member since 1920, Nikolaev had worked in various low-level jobs and then been expelled from the party for refusing to go off on assignment to a "labor front." (Later, however, on instructions from Moscow, his party membership was restored to him.)[51] From April to December 1934 he was unemployed and hence without regular income. This raises the question that Rosliakov asks in his memoir: who supported him materially during those months?[52] That question is all the more apposite in view of the further reported fact that, when a search of their premises were made after Nikolaev killed Kirov, the wife and mother were each found in possession of 5,000 rubles.[53] That was a large sum in those days.

There are various versions of the young man's motivation to become a killer. According to Medvedev, he was embittered by his failure in life and decided to kill Kirov as a dramatic political act in the old Russian terrorist tradition.[54] According to Orlov, he confided in a companion, who was a police informer, that he intended to kill the local Party Control Commission member who had expelled him from the party, and Zaporozhets, after learning about this, encouraged and assisted him to act on his impulse but with Kirov as his victim.[55] A third version has Stalin directly involved. After learning from a check of the central NKVD files on Leningrad party officials that Kirov was in close relations with Nikolaev's wife, Stalin had Nikolaev invited to Moscow for a chat during which he showed sympathy for him in his family plight, thereby inciting the young man to take revenge on Kirov. While in Moscow, Nikolaev (according to this version) told the whole story to his old friend Sorokin, who worked in the Moscow regional branch of the NKVD. Arrested in 1938, as were many other police officials, Sorokin turned up in the same Butyrka prison cell as Pavel Gol'dshtein, who gives the account as he heard it there.[56] Although it seems highly dubious that Stalin would have met in person with Nikolaev, he could have arranged for someone in Moscow to meet with him and inflame his jealousy, referring in the process to Comrade Stalin as an exemplar of virtue who would never condone a colleague's philandering. Moreover, the story of Kirov's attention to Milda Draul could have been a fabrication on Moscow's part.

Whatever the original motivation, Nikolaev proved manipulable. But even with the assistance that Zaporozhets and men working with him could provide, the crime was not easily accomplished. Kirov's bodyguards were loyal to him. Nevertheless, Nikolaev tried in various ways to get close enough to him to kill him. A diary found on him after he finally committed the crime had entries indicating that he had repeatedly requested an audience with Kirov, only to be told by the latter's secretary that Kirov could not receive him but would receive and read a written statement by him. Also found on him was a map of Kirov's route on his frequent walks after work from the Smolny to his apartment on Kamennoostrov Prospekt.

When he walked home, guards would follow in a car and two would accompany him on the street, one walking in front of him, the other behind. During one of Kirov's walks the guards' suspicion was aroused by a man who seemed to be stalking him. Detained, turned over to local NKVD headquarters and searched, the man turned out to be Nikolaev. A loaded pistol and map of Kirov's walking route were found in his possession. F. T. Fomin, Medved's second deputy, who had charge of border and internal guard duty, questioned him. On Zaporozhets' instructions, however, Nikolaev was released and given the pistol back.[57] He made more attempts to come close to Kirov. On two occasions he sought to accost Kirov as he was getting into his car on leaving the Smolny. On the second of these two occasions, which took place in the autumn of 1934, Nikolaev was again detained, searched and found in possession of the revolver. Once more Zaporozhets had him released, this time on the ground that there was no basis for placing him under arrest.[58] That was manifestly absurd.

In the final days of November 1934 Zaporozhets was acting head of the Leningrad NKVD administration. Unexpectedly, he went off on a five-day leave for family reasons without clearing this departure from duty with the NKVD authorities in the normal way but by getting permission from

Yagoda over the telephone, and Fomin became acting director on the spot.[59] A plausible interpretation is that Zaporozhets was under extreme pressure from Moscow to get the planned action accomplished by the start of December and felt it important for him not to be in town at the moment of this shocking crime. His presence could not but reflect ill on him as acting director in Medved's temporary absence and hence would make it necessary for him to be punished with all severity.

From 25 to 28 November Kirov and other top Leningrad party officials were in Moscow for the Central Committee plenum that decided to end bread rationing shortly. On the evening of the plenum's final day the whole group boarded the Red Arrow night train for home and arrived in Leningrad in the morning on 29 November. When interrogated by Fomin after the assassination two days later, Nikolaev said that he had stalked Kirov for a long while and that he had been waiting on the platform when the Red Arrow pulled in on 29 November but was unable to shoot Kirov because officials surrounded him as he walked along the platform.[60]

Kirov was to address a meeting of Leningrad party activists at the Tauride Palace on the evening of 1 December, and give a report the next morning to a plenum of the Leningrad regional and city party committees, which would approve measures for carrying out the decisions taken in Moscow. After his arrival on 29 November Kirov phoned a request for needed statistical materials to his friend Mikhail Rosliakov, who headed the financial department of the city and regional state administration. Later that day Rosliakov received a phone call from the regional second party secretary, M. S. Chudov, who asked him to come to the Smolny at 3 P.M. on 1 December for the meeting of a commission that was preparing the draft of a decision to be taken on 2 December.

On 1 December, a Saturday, Kirov worked at home on the report he was to give the next day. Among the materials he used (a visitor to the Kirov apartment-museum in Leningrad in the late 1970s could see them still lying there on the dining room table) was an open copy of Stalin's *Problems of Leninism*. When Rosliakov phoned him early in the day about the requested economic statistics, Kirov asked him to send them directly to his apartment and to be sure to be in Chudov's office for the commission meeting in the afternoon. When Rosliakov reached Chudov's office on the third floor of the Smolny at the appointed hour, he found the commission, composed of twenty to twenty-five leading city and regional officials, gathered for the meeting.

Some time between 4 and 5 P.M., as they waited for Kirov to arrive, two shots rang out. The commission member nearest the door, A. Ivanchenko, darted out but instantly returned. Darting out after him, Rosliakov found Kirov lying face down in the corridor to the left of the door to

Chudov's reception room. He had been shot in the back of the head; the second bullet, which the killer may or may not have intended for himself, was later found lodged in the cornice. Rosliakov bent down over Kirov saying "Kirov, Mironych." No response. In the corridor to the right of Chudov's door he saw a man lying on his back with his arms lying askew and a pistol in his right hand. He seized the pistol and handed it to A. I. Ugarov, secretary of the city party committee, who was standing by him. In the man's pocket they found a notebook and a party card. Ugarov read out the name on the card: "Leonid Nikolaev." Some others ran up and wanted to kick Nikolaev, but Rosliakov and Ugarov stopped them.

Rosliakov goes on as follows: Someone phoned for first aid and someone called the NKVD to ask that Medved come. Kirov's accompanying bodyguard, a man named Borisov, came up gasping for breath; he had somehow lagged far behind Kirov in the corridor. Rosliakov and others picked Kirov up and placed him on the table in the meeting room. Several foremost Leningrad physicians came, along with other medical personnel and equipment. One of the physicians, Dr. Vasily Dobrotvorsky, was the first to say that the situation was hopeless. But doctors went on trying to resuscitate Kirov. Then a surgeon, Dr. Yustin Dzhanelidze, arrived. He went up to Kirov and then turned to his colleagues saying: "A death report must be drawn up." Medved arrived hatless, his overcoat unbuttoned, his face a picture of total dismay.[61]

Here Rosliakov's firsthand memoir account must be interrupted to say the following. When Medved reached the Smolny he was stopped at the entrance by guards not known to him. They were from Moscow and somehow turned up at the Smolny entrance before Medved did. Furthermore, Borisov was a man of proved personal loyalty to Kirov who, alarmed earlier by the episodes in which the detained Nikolaev was freed and given his gun back, had warned Kirov that his life was in danger.[62] Since Borisov was under strict orders not to be separated from his charge, it is altogether probable that he was briefly waylaid by some ruse after he and Kirov entered the Smolny, and also that the same Muscovites who carried out the ruse had prearranged Nikolaev's presence in the Smolny at that time. For he would hardly have been lurking in the corridor in expectation of Kirov's arrival for an unannounced high-level meeting unless that had been done.

After the doctors' verdict was known, Chudov put through a call by the direct Kremlin line to the Central Committee. Kaganovich answered and, when told that Kirov had been killed, said that he would find Stalin. Several minutes later the phone rang, and Stalin was on the line. Chudov repeated to him the news that Kirov had been killed. Stalin then put a question to him in search of fuller information. Chudov replied that the doctors were drawing up the death report, and Stalin asked for their names.

Hearing that one of them was a Dr. Dzhanelidze, he asked that he pick up the phone. When he did so, Dzhanelidze started to speak with Stalin in Russian but then shifted to both men's native Georgian, a language unfamiliar to the others in the room.[63] Plainly, Stalin was intent on learning without delay the exact medical facts so that he could proceed immediately with his further plans.

Fomin and accompanying Leningrad NKVD officials arrived quickly on the Smolny scene. After taking stock of the whole situation, Fomin returned to his office. No sooner had he arrived there than a call came from NKVD headquarters in Moscow. Yagoda was on the phone. After hearing Fomin's report, he inquired how Nikolaev was dressed and whether any items of foreign origin were found on him. About an hour later Fomin received a second call from Moscow and this time it was Stalin at the other end. After listening to Fomin's report, Stalin also put some questions: What clothes was Nikolaev wearing? Was he wearing a cap? And were there no foreign items on him? Hearing a negative answer to the last question, Stalin, after a considerable pause, hung up. Later on, when analyzing what had happened in Leningrad that day, Fomin came to the conclusion that something had gone awry in the preparation of the Leningrad operation.[64] Why Stalin might have shown special interest in such a detail is not hard to understand. He could have had reason to expect that a foreign cap or other item would be found on Nikolaev, which would confer plausibility on a charge that evil forces abroad had a hand in a supposed conspiracy from below which cost the life of Kirov.

It took a doctor about three hours to bring Nikolaev to his senses. He was then questioned more than once before Stalin arrived the next day and took the investigation temporarily into his own hands. Under initial questioning by Fomin, Nikolaev was evasive, became confused, went into hysterics, said that his shot would be heard all over the world, yet declined to give his motive for killing Kirov.[65] This is consistent on the whole with Khrushchev's report, based on the Shvernik commission's investigation in 1960 and after, that Nikolaev initially declined to answer questions, demanded to be turned over to representatives of the central NKVD apparatus, and said that it was known to Moscow why he acted as he did.[66] However, Rosliakov, again referring to these first questionings, says that Nikolaev gave the desire to take revenge as his motive, claiming that his honor had been blemished and his private life thrown out of kilter.[67]

During the morning of 2 December a delegation of high Leningrad officials went to the station to meet a special train carrying Stalin, Zhdanov, Molotov, Voroshilov, Yezhov, Yagoda, Vyshinsky, and some others. When the train arrived Stalin emerged first without saying a word. He went up to Medved and slapped him across the face with a gloved hand.

Then he listened to a brief report by Fomin. He and the others made a first stop at the hospital where an autopsy had been performed on Kirov during the night and then went on to the Smolny where they set themselves up in Kirov's office for an inquiry. Among those brought in for questioning were Medved, Nikolaev's wife, and Nikolaev. Stalin very harshly rebuked Medved for letting things get out of hand and not preventing Kirov's murder. A shocked and dismayed Milda Draul said that she had known and suspected nothing. Nikolaev, in some sort of semiconscious state when brought in, did not at first recognize Stalin. Only after being shown a picture of him did he realize that Stalin was speaking to him. Speaking unclearly and weeping, he repeated: "What have I gone and done?" "What have I gone and done?"[68] According to Khrushchev's account, when Stalin asked Nikolaev why he had killed Kirov, Nikolaev went to his knees and said he had done it on assignment from and on behalf of the party.[69] Another, not necessarily inconsistent version, has him saying to Stalin, "But you yourself / told / me. . . ." (*Vy zhe sami mne. . . .*), whereupon NKVD guards struck him and hustled him out.[70]

Another person called in for questioning was the bodyguard Borisov, who had been arrested. At this point there was a delay, during which Stalin reportedly went into the outer office and said to those present there: "Nikolaev must be physically brought around. Buy chicken and fruit and feed him up, give him needed medical treatment, and he'll tell everything. To me it is already completely clear that a well-organized counterrevolutionary terrorist organization is active in Leningrad and that Kirov's murder was its deed. A painstaking investigation must be made."[71]

The delay ended when word came that on a sharp turn from Voinov Street enroute to the Smolny, Borisov had somehow fallen to his death out of the open cab of a truck in which he was riding. Rosliakov was told (apparently by one of the Leningrad higher-ups who were in Kirov's inner office with Stalin at the time) that Stalin, when informed of this accident and Borisov's resulting death, exclaimed, in an obvious allusion to the Leningrad NKVD's inefficiency, "They couldn't even do that properly."[72] In truth (and as Stalin no doubt knew would be the case) Borison had been killed on the way to the Smolny.

He did not fall out of an open cab of the truck. He was riding in the closed rear of the truck under a two-man NKVD escort (undoubtedly Moscow NKVD men). By some quirk of fate, the driver of the truck survived to be questioned about the incident in Khrushchev's time. As he told the story, an NKVD man riding beside him in the cab of the truck suddenly reached over and grabbed the steering wheel, causing the truck to swerve into the side of a building. The driver seized the wheel and righted the vehicle so that it struck the building a glancing blow and was not badly damaged. Then he was told that the chief bodyguard had died in the accident. Khrushchev comments: "This was evidently no fortuity, it was a premeditated crime." And further: "Why did Borisov die when none of the others were hurt? Why, later, were the two NKVD men accompanying Kirov's chief bodyguard themselves shot? It means that someone had to see to it that they were destroyed so as to cover up all the traces."[73]

On that day, 2 December, Kirov's coffin was placed in the vestibule of the Tauride Palace. Stalin, Molotov, Voroshilov, Zhdanov, and top Leningrad officials took the first shift in an honor guard as people filed by to pay last respects to the dead Kirov. Not until the night of 3 December, however, did Stalin and the others return to Moscow on a train carrying Kirov in his coffin. During the day-long interval Stalin had a long talk with Nikolaev in his prison cell. This has been reported by a former GULAG inmate, Lev Razgon, who in camp in the later 1930s made the acquaintance of an imprisoned ex-NKVD official named Korabelnikov.

He told Razgon that on the night of 1 December he and numbers of other NKVD men in Moscow were sent by special train to Leningrad where they were taken to the local NKVD headquarters. He and one other NKVD man were assigned to guard Nikolaev in his cell in the inner prison there. The two guards changed shifts every six hours and had orders not to let Nikolaev out of their sight for a single instant. Only on one occasion did they leave him alone: when Stalin came to see him. Stalin and Nikolaev were together for a full hour, alone, while the two NKVD men stood guard outside the cell door and in the presence of very high NKVD officials. What Stalin said to the unnerved young victim of his conspiracy is of course not known, but from evidence about to be mentioned it may reasonably be hypothesized that he gave him the gist of the version of the crime that he wanted publicized, promised to spare his life and even set him free again if he cooperated by testifying accordingly in a forthcoming trial, and threatened him with execution if he refused to do so.

After Stalin took his leave of Nikolaev, Korabelnikov had the next shift of guard duty and returned to the cell. When Razgon asked him how Nikolaev had behaved at that time, Korabelnikov said that he acted as though struck over the head by something. He flung himself on the bunk and tried to cover up his head. Following orders, Korabelnikov forbade him to do that. Then he rushed to and fro in the cell muttering something to himself. Finally he began asking questions of Korabelnikov: How was the weather outside? What was playing in the theater? How did they shoot condemned prisoners?[74] The other guard was a man named Katsafa. He survived Stalin's time and in written testimony to the party Central Committee in 1956 reported that Nikolaev told him that Kirov's murder had been arranged by the secret police and that he had been promised that his life would be saved if he agreed to testify against Leningrad followers of Zinoviev at his trial. And further: Did Katsafa believe that he would be deceived?[75]

Khrushchev, who had come to Leningrad separately as head of a Moscow workers delegation, also took his turn standing in the honor guard. Both he and Rosliakov were there when Stalin and top Politburo members took their places in the last round of the honor guard at 9:30 P.M. on 3 December. Rosliakov saw signs of agitated emotion on the faces of Voroshilov and Zhdanov (but not Molotov). As for Stalin: "Astonishingly calm and impenetrable was the face of I. V. Stalin, giving the impression that he was lost in thought, his eyes gazing upward over Kirov's bullet-struck body, his arms held down at his side, fingers close together, as often observed in the past."[76] Khrushchev's impression was very similar: "He had enormous self-control, and his expression was impenetrable."[77]

Beyond reasonable doubt, the man with the impassive face was responsible for the murder. On this crucial point Khrushchev's later judgment can stand: "Of course, Stalin did not personally give Nikolaev the assignment. Nikolaev was too small a man for that, but I have no doubt that someone prepared him on Stalin's orders. This murder was organized from above. I believe that it was organized by Yagoda, who could have taken this action only on secret instructions from Stalin, received face to face."[78]

Fomin was removed from the investigation of the murder and Ya. S. Agranov, who was Yagoda's deputy in the NKVD and a member of the group traveling with Stalin, replaced Medved temporarily as head of the Leningrad NKVD administration. In 1935 Medved, Zaporozhets, Fomin, and other high Leningrad NKVD officials were charged with criminal negligence and exiled to Siberia for three-year terms. This lenient initial treatment was probably aimed at calming the nerves of others high in the NKVD who now had reason to wonder about their own future fates. Medved was shot in 1937, Zaporozhets in 1938, and Fomin remained in captivity.[79]

In Leningrad on 9 March 1935, a traveling session of the Supreme Court Military Collegium under Ulrikh's chairmanship tried and convicted Milda Draul, Olga Draul, and a Roman Kuliner as "accomplices" of Nikolaev in his act of terror. Ulrikh reported to Stalin on 11 March that death sentences had been carried out on all three.[80] The cover-up was thorough.

Tense December

The truism that Kirov's murder triggered the Terror of the later 1930s is slightly inaccurate: the Terror commenced during the day of the fatal shooting with Stalin's preparation of two directives that were, together, his equivalent of the one-paragraph terror law issued by Hitler at the time of the Röhm purge.

One ordered investigative agencies to speed up cases of those accused of preparation of execution of acts of terror, forbade judicial organs to delay execution of sentence in such cases pending possible clemency, and directed the NKVD to execute those sentences immediately. Khrushchev reports that Stalin, without Politburo approval, took it upon himself to arrange for Yenukidze, as secretary of the Presidium of the Central Executive Committee, to sign this document on the evening of 1 December.[81] *Pravda,* which published the three-point directive on 4 December, said that it had been passed by the Central Executive Committee's Presidium "at a meeting on 1 December." The "meeting" would have been the one between Stalin, himself a Presidium member, and Yenukidze.

The second document was published in *Pravda* on 5 December as an edict of the same Presidium. It bore the dual signatures of Kalinin as the Presidium's chairman and Yenukidze as its secretary. It said that in cases involving terrorist organizations and terrorist acts against Soviet officials, investigation was to be completed in ten days, indictments were to be shown the accused one day before the judicial hearing, cases were to be heard without participation of the accused, sentences were not subject to appeal or petitions for clemency, and capital-punishment sentences were to be carried out immediately.[82]

By the time these two documents were published, the state terror machine was in motion on their basis. The Supreme Court's Military Collegium, under the ever-subservient Ulrikh, was busy dispensing summary justice. On 6 December *Pravda* announced that the cases of seventy-one "White Guardists" arrested in the recent past on charges of preparing to organize terrorist acts against Soviet officials were heard by the Military Collegium on the previous day, that all but five had been sentenced to die, and that the sentences had been carried out. Since these people were in prison when Kirov was killed, they could hardly have been involved in the crime. Their execution was a first example of Stalin's terror law in action. A few days later, twenty-eight more alleged "White Guardists" were executed in Kiev on its basis. Rumors were rife in Moscow about persons being arrested in the small hours of the morning for anti-Soviet activity, and many Muscovites were destroying their pocket address books so as not to endanger friends if they themselves should be arrested.[83]

Meanwhile, the country was declared in mourning, and the floodgates of official adulation for Kirov opened wide. He was the "Soviet people's favorite" and "our Kirov." His home town of Viatka was among the many places given his name. His years in the Siberian underground, in the Civil

War, and in Leningrad were lovingly remembered. His articles and speeches were published in book form. His brain was turned over to the Leningrad Institute for brain research. The instant Kirov cult was blended into the Stalin cult, which took on added lustre. Kirov became "Comrade Stalin's best comrade-in-arms and friend." Stalin was shown in the honor guard, with Kirov in old photos, and as first mourner at the Red Square funeral. "In the first days when Lenin's city was orphaned," editorialized *Pravda,* "Stalin rushed there. He went to the place where the crime against our country was committed. The enemy did not fire at Kirov personally. No! He fired at the proletarian revolution. . . ."[84]

For the conspirator from above, the prime purpose of Kirov's murder was to make possible an official finding that Soviet Russia was beset by a conspiracy that had done away with Kirov as part of a larger plan of terrorist action against the regime. From this followed the need for the campaign of political punitive operations for which Stalin's law of 1 December provided a juridical foundation; these operations opened with the executions of imprisoned "White Guardists." For the requisite definition of the danger situation to be promulgated, Stalin considered it urgently imperative to pin the murder on a group of conspirators who engaged Nikolaev as their agent and to connect this group with another group that was to include some high-level political enemies, eventually cast as leaders of the alleged anti-regime plot. All these things Stalin accomplished, crudely but effectively, during that tense December.

An NKVD statement on 3 December said that the murder was committed by Nikolaev, a former employee of the Leningrad Worker-Peasant Inspectorate, and that investigation was continuing. Stalin went to work on the case. From the Leningrad NKVD office's files he had obtained a document with the names of a group of pro-Zinoviev, anti-Stalin former Komsomol activists who during 1934 were meeting to discuss a book project on Komsomol history. The office had asked Kirov's permission to arrest them. Not considering them dangerous, he had turned the request down. Now Stalin transformed this discussion group or some of its members, on paper, into a terrorist "Leningrad center." On the same sheet of paper, under the heading "Moscow center," he inscribed the names of Zinoviev, Kamenev, and other ex-Zinovievists lately living in Moscow. Some names he shifted back and forth between the columns. This paper, in his handwriting, survived among his effects and was photocopied for the Shvernik commission.[85]

He was acting with extreme haste to place the regime and country before a *fait accompli.* He had to get his false version of events on the public record and officially accepted, lest the finger of suspicion point at him. Hence his eagerness for a lightning trial of Nikolaev together with

"Leningrad center" members and for prompt action against ex-oppositionist leaders indicating that *they* were under suspicion. By 15 December Zhdanov, now Leningrad first party secretary in Kirov's place, knew what the investigation would show. Addressing a meeting of Leningrad party activists, he said that Zinoviev and his supporters were responsible for the murder. On the next day a closed plenum of the city and regional party committees, attended by Rosliakov, listened in tense silence to a report by Agranov that Kirov's murder had been organized by a youth section of the former Zinovievist opposition consisting of I. I. Kotolynov, V. V. Rumyantsev, K. N. Shatsky and other young people acting under the inspiration of Zinoviev, Kamenev, Yevdokimov, Bakaev, and other prominent ex-oppositionists in Leningrad.[86]

Zinoviev, Kamenev, and thirteen associates were under arrest in Moscow by 15 or 16 December. A week later it was announced that the cases of Zinoviev, Kamenev, and five others were, for lack of sufficient data, being referred to the NKVD Special Board with a view to administrative exile; the others' cases were still being investigated.[87] By then a secret circular letter had gone out from Stalin's Central Committee headquarters to party committees around the country. Entitled "Lessons of the Events Surrounding the Evil Murder of Comrade Kirov," it ordered the party purged of "alien elements." All former followers of Zinoviev, Kamenev, and Trotsky were to be expelled immediately. The letter was to be read and discussed in meetings of party cells everywhere.[88]

Meanwhile, NKVD men in Leningrad were preparing quick judicial action in order to get a preliminary form of Stalin's version on the record. Because of the need for speed, not even the pretense of an open trial, requiring as it would the coerced cooperation of the defendants, was considered possible. The main effort was to induce Nikolaev, by the promise of sparing his life and giving him only a light sentence, to testify falsely that he had been associated with the terrorist "center" and had acted on its behalf.

On 22 December came a public announcement that the murder was no loner's act but a political crime committed by Nikolaev on behalf of a group of people linked, at least ideologically, with Zinoviev. Nikolaev was said to have received his orders from Kotolynov, representing an underground "Leningrad center" that sought, by means of terrorist acts against the regime's "principal leaders," to change Soviet policy "in the spirit of the so-called Trotskyist-Zinovievist platform."

An indictment was published on 27 December over the signature of Vyshinsky, deputy procurator of the Soviet Union. Fourteen Leningraders, including Nikolaev, were indicted on charges of having formed an underground Zinovievist group led by an eight-member "Leningrad center."

They had taken money from the Leningrad consul of a foreign state (unnamed) and tried, through him, to make contact with Trotsky and with an anti-Soviet White émigré group on whose behalf they proposed to commit terrorist acts. For conspiratorial purposes they got themselves reinstated in party membership. They began to stalk Kirov, on whom they wanted to take revenge for his fight against the Zinovievist opposition. Kotolynov, according to Nikolaev's preliminary testimony, coached him in the technique of shooting, and another member of the group explained the itinerary of Kirov's walks and suggested the best spots for the killing.

The trial was held behind closed doors and lasted two days. All fourteen accused were pronounced guilty and sentenced to die. When the death sentence was pronounced on Nikolaev and he realized that he had been deceived, he screamed and struggled to break loose from his guards.[89] In accordance with Stalin's law of 1 December, execution followed immediately, on 29 December. No proceedings were published. This was no show trial. The accused members of the discussion group confessed only to their actual anti-Stalin sentiments, denying any involvement in Kirov's murder and any dealings with Nikolaev. One of them, Vladimir Levin, said in a moving final word, which was continually interrupted by the judge (Ulrikh), that the peasants were pauperized, the workers poorer than under the tsar, the Revolution's ideals betrayed, and Russia faced with material and spiritual disaster. Then he added that though he had no knowledge of any terrorist assassination plots or attempts, he had weighed up the life of one against those of the millions whose misfortune he had caused—and at this allusion to Stalin he was hustled out of the courtroom.[90]

Having discussed the secret circular letter from Central Committee headquarters, the party cells proceeded to stage indignation meetings in institutions throughout the land. The report of the trial of the "Leningrad center" appeared at this time, and so these meetings "confirmed" Stalin's version of events. The former leaders of the anti-Stalin opposition in the party were being accused of inspiring, although not yet of actual directing, the killers of Kirov. A flood of denunciations followed in the meetings organized by the party cells. As the purging went forward in local party organizations, *Pravda* declared that there must be no more "rotten liberalism" toward Trotskyites. "More vigilance toward open and secret enemies of socialism," demanded its editorial on the trial and ensuing executions.[91] Stalin's pretense of preparedness for reconciliation with his political enemies was over. The great terroristic purge, which would devastate and transform the society in the next few years, was starting.

Politically perceptive people could see that crude and clumsy machinations were taking place, and some could hardly help suspecting that the murder was a provocation which Stalin was going to exploit for punitive purposes. A young woman journalist then living and working in Rostov, Vera Panova, recalls in a posthumously published memoir that her husband, Boris Vakhtin, managing editor on another local paper, telephoned her late on 1 December and said: "Vera! In Leningrad they've killed Kirov!" She records what then occurred to her:

"Who killed him?" I ask, no answer comes, but I know what will happen now: after all, I've written about the burning of the Reichstag. And that night I have a dream but I don't dare tell it even to Boris: they themselves killed Kirov so as to start a new terror. Against whom? Against the "lefts," against the "rights," against anyone they want. But I can't keep this dream from Boris for long. After vacillating, I tell it to him. He gives me a strange look and is silent.[92]

Leningrad party officials were of the same mind. Ludmilla Chudova, wife of M. S. Chudov, was later incarcerated in a special camp at Tomsk for "members of the families of traitors," that is, purged leaders. There she told another incarcerated wife: "Zinoviev had no need for Kirov's death. It came from the very top, orders of the Boss. My comrades, Chudov included, realized this after the shooting."[93] Even among ordinary Leningrad workers, grieving for their lost Mironych, a ditty was making its whispered rounds (and this might help explain the savage repressions soon to be visited upon the Leningrad working class):

> Oh cucumber, oh pomidor
> Stalin killed Kirov
> In the corridor.[94]

Some men in authority in Moscow must have had a similar thought or suspicion in their minds, but they remained passive while events took their deadly course. We are told that Stalin presented the materials of the hastily concocted case against the "Leningrad center" before a meeting of the Politburo that was held in "an atmosphere of extreme tension." He strongly proclaimed his continued adherence to the internal-*détente* policies with only one qualification: in view of the opposition's refusal to "disarm," the party must now launch a "checkup" of Trotskyists, Zinovievists, and Kamenevists.[95] Thereupon the Politburo agreed to his proposed summary trial of the Leningrad group and continuing investigation of the arrested Moscow Zinovievists.

It is also reported that at a Politburo meeting toward the end of December, possibly the meeting just mentioned, Kuibyshev, reflecting the feelings of some Politburo members who were shocked and aroused by what was happening, proposed the appointment of a special Central Committee commission of inquiry to pursue an investigation parallel with the police investigation already under way.[96] The motion did not carry, and Kuibyshev shortly afterward died suddenly, at 47, of what was then publicly described as heart disease and later, in 1938, as medical murder resulting from a heart attack brought on by malpractice committed on Yagoda's orders.[97]

The only reported instance of protest involved Gorky. Because of his great prestige and known friendly feelings for Kamenev, Stalin was anxious to get from him some public expression of support. Through Yagoda he conveyed his personal request that Gorky write an article condemning individual terror. Even without mentioning Zinoviev and Kamenev, such an article would cast a shadow on them and serve Stalin well at a critical moment in his life and Russia's. Gorky refused the request and replied through Yagoda: "I condemn not only individual terror, but *state* terror as well."[98] Not long after, there appeared an "Open Letter to A. M. Gorky" from the writer F. Panfyorov, whose criticisms, albeit on literary issues of no large importance, were highly unusual and very likely intended to convey a warning.[99]

Yenukidze also fell into eclipse. On 16 January 1935 *Pravda* published an editorial note entitled "Correction of Errors" denying that he had been—as an earlier article had described him—an organizer of the underground printing press in Baku in 1904. Then came a self-criticism by Yenukidze downgrading his own celebrated revolutionary past in Transcaucasia and confessing that he had not always shown "adequate Bolshevik steadfastness."[100] Soon after he was shunted off to a minor post in Transcaucasia. In June 1935 he disappeared from view after a Central Committee plenum expelled him both from the Central Committee and party membership. During that closed plenum, Yezhov, whom Stalin had elevated in January 1935 to Kirov's vacant post as a Central Committee secretary, reported on the "Yenukidze case." He accused Yenukidze, who had long been responsible for the administration of the Kremlin, of political blindness and criminal complacency, which had made it possible for "counterrevolutionary Zinoviev-Kamenev and Trotskyist terrorists" to feather a nest for themselves in the Kremlin and prepare an attempt on Stalin's life.[101] Evidently, Stalin and Yenukidze had come to a political parting of the ways, and it had something to do with the murder in Leningrad and the case Stalin was now intent on building against the Zinoviev-Kamenev group as the ones responsible for starting the Terror.

Shortly after Kirov's murder and before Zinoviev was arrested, a young follower of the latter went to his Moscow apartment to learn directly from him what the murder might portend. "They will pin this on us," he heard Zinoviev say. A little later the doomed Bolshevik leader stood by the apartment window looking down on an organized street demonstration below. It was demanding death for Kirov's murderers. "This," said Zinoviev slowly, "is the beginning of a great tragedy."[102]

13

POLITICS AND SOCIETY
IN THE PURGE ERA

The Quiet Terror

FROM THE START of 1935 to the summer of 1936 the broom of Stalin's terroristic purge swept through Soviet society at lower levels. Many expelled party members and others were arrested and sent to camps or exiled. Although reflected in the official press, the repressions went on with a minimum of fanfare. Party expulsions occurred under the auspices of announced procedures for a long overdue "checkup of party documents" followed by an "exchange of party cards." With very few exceptions, leading figures in the regime, both in Moscow and the provinces, were little affected. This was the period of quiet terror. The poet Anna Akhmatova called it comparatively "vegetarian."[1] Yet, many a human tragedy was played out in the quietly terrorized Russia of that time.

The command for a campaign of repressions came in a new circular letter, dated 18 January 1935, from Stalin's Central Committee headquarters to all party organizations. It ordered them to mobilize their forces against enemy elements and root out counterrevolutionary nests.[2] It justified the need for this by referring to a new trial, held in secret on 15–16 January in Leningrad, at which Zinoviev, Kamenev, and seven associates were convicted of having formed an underground "Moscow center," which allegedly inspired the young Leningrad oppositionists whose "center" had been accused in the December 1934 trial of inspiring and abetting Kirov's murder. Fiction was being built upon fiction in the drive to pin responsibility for the crime on ex-oppositionist circles.

No account of the trial proceedings was issued. The only materials published were an indictment signed by Vyshinsky and a report on the verdict. According to the latter,

The judicial inquiry established no facts that would provide a basis for describing the crime of the members of the "Moscow center" in connection with the 1 December 1934 murder of Comrade S. M. Kirov as incitement to this dastardly crime. But the inquiry fully confirmed that the participants in the counterrevolutionary "Moscow center" knew about the terrorist sentiments of the Leningrad group and themselves stirred up these sentiments. All the defendants confessed themselves fully guilty of the charges against them.[3]

From this one may infer that the defendants denied all complicity in the murder but made some minimal admission of political culpability under pressure of a combination of threats and promises that were used to extract it from them. The case was flimsy and the two-day affair could have been no more than the travesty of a trial. But it met Stalin's urgent need to stage a vigilance campaign and demand wholesale repressions. It enabled him to put out the line that ". . . driven by blind hatred and malice against the party and its leadership, against Comrade Stalin, the genius-continuer of Lenin's cause, the Zinovievist counterrevolutionary gang actively assisted enemies of the Soviet Union to prepare war against her. It trained the fascist mongrels who raised arms against Comrade Kirov."[4] Here was the embryo of the legend of anti-Stalin, antistate conspiracy that emerged fully formed when the first great show trial opened in the following year.

It was plain by now that the Kirov murder was no passing misfortune but an event that Stalin planned to use as a pretext to embark on a sustained vendetta against political enemies. In private he made no bones about it. Ordzhonikidze, who summoned Lominadze to Moscow from his Magnitogorsk post in January 1935, told the fellow Georgian that Stalin now "was full of self-reproach—it was *he* who had lacked the necessary 'vigilance'! He had been 'too trusting,' but now he would make up for it. It was not enough that the 'chips should fly,' as he had once promised they would; the whole forest of discontent must be felled and uprooted."[5] The feigned earlier lack of vigilance—something never lacking in Stalin—was a convenient ploy for voicing unfeigned fury.

The Central Committee plenum of 1 February 1935 showed by its decisions (the proceedings were unpublicized) Stalin's dominance of the regime. The clearest evidence was Yezhov's appointment to the post that Kirov's murder had vacated in the Central Committee Secretariat. Mikoyan and V. Y. Chubar were advanced from candidate membership to Kirov's and Kuibyshev's seats as full members of the Politburo, while Zhdanov and R. I. Eikhe became candidate members.[6] Further evidence of Stalin's secure control came at the end of February with Yezhov's appointment to head the Party Control Commission.

During the 1 February Central Committee plenum, Stalin took a step toward fulfilling, or seeming to fulfill, his December promise to the Politburo to continue internal *détente* policies: he championed the idea of democratizing the Soviet Constitution. The Central Committee decided—on his initiative—to propose constitutional changes aimed at "further democratizing" the Soviet electoral system.[7] So, as the quiet terror developed under Stalin's covert direction, the press poured forth a stream of constitutional discussion in praise of him as a democratizer.

Meanwhile, the repressions were in full swing. Leningraders were a prime target. During March 1935 former aristocrats, civil servants, officers, and merchants were deported from Leningrad *en masse*. Together with their families, they were ejected from lodgings, often in cellars of homes they had once owned and of which they had become caretakers, and sent away on twenty-four-hours' notice. A local resident learned that the deportees were chosen through denunciations and by finding out who was still alive and living in Leningrad of those listed in an old social register, *All Petersburg*.[8] But the repression was not really class-conscious. Between thirty and forty thousand Leningrad workers were sent to destinations all across northern Siberia with their wives and children.[9] Other thousands were arrested on one ground or another. Ambassador Bullitt heard a report from the British vice-consul in Leningrad that 100,000 persons had been exiled from the city.[10] In the camps, to which many were sent, the Leningraders were variously known as the "Kirov torrent" and "Kirov's assassins." Deportations on a smaller scale took place in Moscow.

By February 1935 a nationwide vigilance campaign was raging as party committees complied with the demand of the secret circular of 19 January to root out enemy elements and counterrevolutionary nests. It was a repetition, on a far greater scale and with differences, of the witch-hunt unleashed by Stalin's letter of 1931 to *Proletarian Revolution*. Now political as well as ideological offenses were "exposed," intellectuals were not the sole target, and expulsion from the party frequently meant not only loss of work but arrest and concentration camp. Not a few of the victims were

Old Bolsheviks or persons who had become active in party affairs during the 1920s.

Some representative examples may be cited. The Old Bolshevik Belousov was arrested as a counterrevolutionary for failure to denounce a fellow Old Bolshevik, Timofey, who shortly before the Seventeenth Congress privately had suggested to him that as congress delegates they should vote to replace Stalin as general secretary. Belousov had fled in terror and then avoided Timofey when they later chanced to meet at the Society of Old Bolsheviks. Another old worker, Communist Nikolai Yemelyanov, who hid Lenin and Zinoviev in his cottage at Razliv near Petrograd in July 1917, was arrested and sentenced to five years in camp on suspicion of possessing a copy of Lenin's "testament" and because in his cottage, which had become a museum where he served as guide, he would mention names of persons now fallen into disgrace. Joseph Berger, a founder of the Palestine Communist Party, who worked in the early 1930s as head of the Comintern's Near East Department and took Soviet citizenship, received five years in camp for "counterrevolutionary Trotskyist activity" consisting in some disparaging remarks about Stalin that had been reported to the authorities.[11]

Another case involved a younger party historian, Nikolai Elvov, who had contributed a chapter on 1905 to the Yaroslavsky-edited party history that Stalin criticized in his letter to *Proletarian Revolution*. After that letter appeared, Elvov was transferred from Moscow to Kazan, capital of the Tatar Autonomous Republic, where he worked as a teacher, as a journalist on the paper *Red Tartary,* and as an activist on the town party committee. Mentioned now in *Pravda* as a "Trotskyist contrabandist," he was arrested.[12] Very many others suffered similar fates. Word reached the *Bulletin of the Opposition* that hundreds of people in any way connected with the opposition, even if long ago, as well as relatives and friends of theirs or persons who at some point had abstained on a vote, were being arrested and sent into exile; and that oppositionists already in exile were being rearrested for dispatch to still more remote places or confinement.[13] An example typical of many: The arrest of a young ex-oppositionist, Mark Poliakov, in the Ukraine in February 1935 led, one week later, to the expulsion of his cousin, Lev Kopelev, from the Komsomol and from Kharkov University "for connections with a Trotskyist relative."[14]

The mechanism of guilt by association multiplied the effect of the purge and spread fear through the party's lower ranks. Eugenia Ginzburg, the wife of a leading party official in Kazan, had befriended Elvov in the Pedagogical Institute, worked with him on *Red Tartary,* and helped him prepare a source book on Tatar history. Shortly after his arrest, she found herself under attack for not having denounced Elvov as a purveyor of

Trotskyist contraband, and for not having critically reviewed his source book. When she asked, "Has it been proved he's a Trotskyist?" some people replied: "Don't you know he's been arrested? Can you imagine anyone being arrested unless there's something against him?" Many who were less proud and more fearful than she sought safety in breast-beating repentance of their own past "lack of vigilance" and "rotten liberalism." Some whose past records made them especially vulnerable outdid themselves in self-criticism and also in denouncing others.[15] She herself was fortunate enough to be let off, for the time being, with a party reprimand for "slackening of political vigilance."

Another representative victim of the quiet terror was Vera Panova's husband, Boris Vakhtin. In February 1935 he was fired from his job as managing editor of the Rostov paper *Molot* and expelled from the party for "Trotskyism" at a denunciation meeting where it came out that he neglected to mention in his party records that as a Komsomol member earlier in life he had for a time supported the opposition. The good offices of a family friend got him a worker's job. Then, very early one morning, the police came to arrest him and searched the apartment under the eyes of his terrified mother, wife, and children. For many weeks Panova would take parcels for him to a prison window in Rostov where they sometimes were accepted and sometimes not and where she met and befriended similarly bereaved women. Eventually Vakhtin was transferred for further interrogation to Moscow, whence the news came in mid-summer that he and some other expelled Communists from Rostov had been sentenced to ten years in the Solovetsk Islands concentration camp in the Far North. Meanwhile, Panova herself had been dismissed from her job (as had the kindly editor who made the mistake of waiting five days before dismissing her). When some free-lance writing that she did in a desperate attempt to feed her family led to a denunciatory article about her in a local paper, she slipped away with the children to an obscure country place and solely for this reason managed to survive the time when, as her memoir puts it, "The accursed *oprichnina* broom swept men and women away."[16]

To grasp the workings of the Terror at this new stage, we must note a term that came into constant use at the start of 1935: *dvurushnik,* meaning a "two-faced person" or double-dealer, that is, a person accused of being a carrier of antiparty sentiments and perpetrator of counterrevolutionary deeds behind a mask of party and Soviet loyalty. "Enemies in Soviet masks" was a related expression. Zinoviev and Kamenev were said to have been at their loathsome worst as double-dealers when they defended party policy at meetings earlier in the 1930s, when they condemned their own oppositional pasts at the Seventeenth Congress, and especially when they dared submit obituary articles to *Pravda* after Kirov's murder. All this had been done to conceal their deadly conspiring behind a screen of pro-Soviet probity.

The presence in the society of double-dealers masked not only as loyal citizens and party members but as attractive human beings was the theme of a movie called *Party Card,* produced at this time by the Mosfilm studio. The *dvurushnik* Pavel finds work in a factory where, on the instructions of his espionage organization, he steals his wife Anna's party card for future villainous use; and she, a shockworker and party member of irreproachable character, is expelled from the party for loss of the card. Ultimately he is unmasked and arrested. According to a review, "This is a truthful story about life, a call to class vigilance: the enemy is still alive and not dozing."[17]

Many thousands of obscure party people, not to mention active ex-oppositionists, were vulnerable to the double-dealer charge. The majority had become supporters of the General Line by 1929 and worked hard to help fulfill the *piatiletka,* but almost everyone had some lapse or blemish in his or her party past, recorded in the protocols of old party meetings. One had abstained in the vote on the opposition's platform in 1923, or voted in favor. Another had expressed a view made deviant by some later Stalin statement condemning it. No matter how staunch the subsequent political orthodoxy, or how impeccable the performance on the job, such a person could be exposed now as a double-dealer all along. And how to disprove the accusation? By its cruel logic, the more vocal one's latter-day support of the party's line, the more duplicitous and hence dangerous he or she was said to be. No wonder that so many rushed in fear to purge themselves of guilt by public confessions.

While no real counterrevolutionary activities were going on, and no terrorist conspiracies were being hatched against Stalin, there was a slender reality base for his obsession with double-dealers: the private thoughts and attitudes of many party people were at variance with the official views they uttered when they spoke in public. They didn't see Stalin as the Lenin-like hero leader of Russia's revolutionary leap to socialism that he deemed himself to be and that the Soviet media portrayed. Eugenia Ginzburg, for example, confesses that in early 1935 she had not the slightest doubt of the rightness of the party line and would have given her life for the party, but could not bring herself to idolize Stalin, "as it was becoming the fashion to do."[18] She and others were party loyalists without being, in their hearts, Stalin loyalists. Only in this sense were they "two-faced," but it was enough to condemn them in his mind.

The duality was deepest among the surviving ex-revolutionaries who belonged to the Society of Old Bolsheviks and a companion elite organization, the Society of Former Exiles and Political Convicts. Dubious that the new society taking shape in the 1930s was socialist, aware of Stalin's earlier obscurity in party history, knowledgeable about the lapses and blemishes in *his* revolutionary biography, and appalled at the falsifying of party history that his letter to *Proletarian Revolution* was generating, they could not regard him as Lenin's true and rightful successor.[19] From his point of view, therefore, the society and its branches in provincial centers were hotbeds of double-dealers. In May 1935, when numbers of Old Bolsheviks were already under arrest or in the camps, a curt decree came out, over the signature "Central Committee," liquidating the society (at its own request, it said) and setting up a commission of Stalin operatives, including Yaroslavsky, Shkiriatov, and Malenkov, to take over its property and "work out proposals for better use of the literary and other materials of the society."[20] The action may have been taken at this time because, reportedly, the society had collected signatures on a petition to the Politburo against the possible use of the death penalty against accused Old Bolsheviks like Zinoviev and Kamenev, recalling Lenin's injunction, "Let no blood flow between you."[21] But such a petition could only have hastened the society's inevitable demise in the course of the Great Purge.

The cryptic reference to "better use" of its literary and other materials takes on special meaning when we realize that the records and publications, like those of the companion society, were a major repository of the party past that was now being rewritten according to Stalin's canons. From this point of view, the closing was part of a book purge taking place all over Russia. The Smolensk archives show that the Soviet censorship organization, *Glavlit,* was ordering libraries to confiscate the works of Trotsky, Kamenev, and Zinoviev along with other "Trotskyist-Zinovievist counter-revolutionary literature" that included, according to a directive of 21 June 1935 to the Lenin Library of Smolensk, books by A. Shliapnikov, E. Preobrazhensky, former Commissar of Education Lunacharsky, and the well-known party historian V. I. Nevsky, who himself was fired from the directorship of Moscow's Lenin Library and arrested in early 1935 after he refused a written instruction from Stalin to remove a lot of political literature from the library, saying: "I am not running a baggage room. The party directed me to preserve all this."[22] Among librarians there was understandable confusion about the extent of the book purge. They plied *Glavlit's* offices with questions like: What is to be done with anthologies of Marxism that Lenin edited jointly with Zinoviev? The edition of Lenin's works edited by Kamenev? John Reed's *Ten Days That Shook the World* (wherein now exposed traitors to the Revolution were included among its foremost leaders)? And if Trotsky had an article in a certain issue of *Communist International,* should the whole issue be confiscated? There is no record of the answers.[23]

I have suggested that Russia's numerous "two-faced persons" were guilty not of criminal acts but of what George Orwell in *1984* called "thought-crime," one or another degree of inner lack of enthusiasm for Stalin and his leadership. But the *dvurushniki* of the Stalinist purge were being accused of having become members of conspiratorial secret societies to commit counterrevolutionary terrorist deeds like the murder of Kirov. How shall we interpret Stalin's thinking in this regard? First, he seems to have considered anti-Stalin talk as tantamount to actual conspiring. The reality behind the legend of the "Moscow center" responsible for Kirov's murder was that friends of Kamenev and Zinoviev would gather at one or the other of their Moscow apartments of an evening and engage in informal political conversation, sometimes critical of Stalin.[24]

Secondly, Stalin's vision of the double-dealers as active agents of a terrorist antiparty conspiracy derived from his own deep-seated subconscious tendency to project upon his enemies whatever was unacceptable, discordant with the idealized Stalin, in his own life and conduct, and punish them for it. There *was* a terrorist antiparty conspiracy in Russia then: Stalin's. His image of it appeared in an article called "Despicable Double-Dealers." It said: "Having nothing in their hearts but animosity and hatred for the party, for the Soviet regime, Trotsky, Zinoviev, Kamenev, and their hangers-on have made terror the main method of their foul activity and in doing so are acting like Jesuits."[25] This was Stalin projected on his enemies. Filled with animosity against the old Bolshevik party, many of whose leading figures and members rejected him, and against the Soviet regime as then constituted, he was turning to terror from above as his main method and he was acting with supreme duplicity—concealing his own antiparty conspiracy by accusing the very party people he meant to destroy of being counterrevolutionaries.

In May 1935 he placed his conspiracy on an organized basis by secretly forming a "state security commission" to supervise the conduct of the purge. He was the chairman; Yezhov, Zhdanov, Shkiriatov, and Malenkov were members. The commission set up a "political state-security department" consisting of Poskrebyshev and Malenkov from the Central Committee, Agranov and I. A. Serov from the NKVD, Shkiriatov from the Party Control Commission, and Vyshinsky (now Procurator General in place of Akulov) from the Procuracy, to direct and coordinate the day-to-day purge operations. This information comes from an NKVD colonel who helped organize the political state-security department's executive arm and later defected to the West. Headed by Serov and numbering over 150 persons plus service staff, the executive arm was subdivided into operational groups for the various industries and for trade, education, the press, party personnel, and so on. It had special representatives in the

NKVD offices in the republics and provinces and created operational groups in and for those various parts of the country. At first its work consisted largely of gathering information from police and party archives on the personnel files of party members with oppositional pasts or connections with one or another political grouping. It took over the voluminous files of the soon-to-be-dissolved *ad hoc* party purge commission set up in 1933.[26]

As the party-police machinery of full-scale terror was being organized in secret, Stalin proposed at an Orgburo meeting that a checkup of party members' documents be carried out to "set our party house in order." His proposal was adopted.[27] On 13 May 1935, a "closed letter" went out from the Central Committee to all party organizations saying that a Central Committee inquiry had uncovered numerous cases in which "enemies of the party and working class" had fraudulently obtained party membership cards and carried on subversive activities under cover of them. It ordered a verification and updating of documents on the basis of a careful investigation of the credentials and party pasts of every single party member.[28]

The checkup was a calculated move in the conspiracy from above. An obvious major purpose was to serve the informational needs of the above-mentioned operational groups, each of which had NKVD special representatives in the localities who assisted the district and town party secretaries in carrying out the operation and took custody of the updated documentation. The latter covered not only rank-and-file party members but the secretaries themselves.[29] Hence the checkup gave Stalin's political operatives more precise information on many officials of the party apparatus who would themselves fall victim to the purge in the violent new phase that opened in 1936. In the present phase, however, these officials were being used rather than repressed.

The checkup was also a purge under another name. Said *Pravda:*

One must not forget that our country lives in a capitalist encirclement. This is not simply a geographical concept. . . . Inside the country there are still no few accursed enemies of socialism, splinters of smashed classes hostile to the proletariat, concealed counterrevolutionary Trotskyists, White Guard scum, Zinovievists. . . . It must be understood that if we want to destroy all enemies in the shortest possible time, our first task is to overcome the organizational disorders in our own ranks, to put our own party house in order.[30]

The total numbers expelled from the party between May and 1 December 1935 have been estimated at 190,000.[31] A secret progress report sent out from Central Committee headquarters to the provincial party committees in July 1935 gives some sense of what was happening. Dozens of individual cases of expulsions resulting from the checkup were listed under such categories as: "Spies and Suspected Spies," "White Guardists and Kulaks," and "Trotskyists and Zinovievists" (the most numerous category). Among those listed in one or another category were: a Leningrad Zinovievist named Mirkin, expelled for concealing that his father had been a well-off merchant and for having "actively supported" a now deported Zinovievist named Zelikson; a Trotskyist factory director in Ivanovo province named Birbrauer, who had maintained ties with an expelled "active Trotskyist" woman named Charonskaia; a Princess Ilinskaia who had been working in a polyclinic cafeteria under an assumed name and who had relatives with valuables and money in a French bank; a man of Polish extraction who had listed himself as Ukrainian on his party records and maintained ties with two brothers in Poland through a third living in Canada; a man named Keil in Odessa who had visited the Czechoslovak Embassy and applied for an exit visa to Czechoslovakia where he had a businessman brother. Keil was listed under the spies category.[32] Some of these cases reflect the growing danger to Soviet citizens with relatives abroad, and help explain the observation by Ambassador Bullitt, in a letter of 1 May 1935, to Roosevelt, that "almost no one dares have any contact with foreigners and this is not unbased fear but a proper sense of reality."[33]

The power of the NKVD was growing constantly, for arrests were taking place on its decision.[34] Yet, during this first phase of the terror operation, Stalin still relied heavily on the party apparatus. Hardly any of its members were victims themselves, nor were high government officials.[35] The "grandees" were going to fall in the second phase, accused, among other things, of harboring in their organizations the enemies being uncovered now. Perhaps it was a troubled sense of that possibility, along with other motives, that explains a certain foot-dragging and even resistance to wholesale purging that occurred among local party functionaries at this time. In some cases, moreover, pressures for economic performance made them reluctant to throw out individuals who worked all the more diligently in order to live down lapses in their party pasts.

The very insidiousness of Stalin's developing conspiracy kept Bolshevik veterans in local authority from foreseeing the radical expansion of the Terror in the near future, and some acted according to their party consciences in individual cases. Lev Kopelev got reinstated in Kharkov University by going to Kiev and telling his tale to a girlfriend's Old Bolshevik father, who in turn was a friend of the Ukrainian Commissar of Education, Zatonsky, and of the NKVD representative for the Ukraine, Balitsky.[36] Eugenia Ginzburg's party reprimand was rescinded and replaced with a mild reproof when her appeal reached the secretary of the province party committee.[37] Ivan Rumiantsev, party secretary of the Western Province, raised the possibility of a "mistake" in a penned notation on an anguished letter from a woman whose life was being destroyed through guilt by association with an exiled husband with whom she had long since parted.[38] There must have been many such cases, for a resolution of the Central Committee plenum of 21–25 December 1935, based on a report by Yezhov, referred to party officials who "in spite of repeated warnings from the Central Committee" had failed to grasp the checkup's significance "and in some instances showed outright resistance to this most important measure for strengthening the ranks" of the party.[39]

No sooner was the checkup completed in early 1936 than a new operation was launched, again a purge under another name: "exchange of party cards." The party house was to be put in still better order by replacing the existing, 1926-model party membership cards with an improved new version designed to ensure, as *Bol'shevik* explained, "really centralized registration of Communists." But the exchange, it stressed, was no mere technical procedure: "The checkup of party documents purged the party of enemies. The exchange of party documents must continue the purging of the party's ranks." The declared main aim of the continued purging was, however, to rid the party less of enemy elements than of passive members who lacked "organic connection" with the party, took no interest in its history, didn't study its policy, and avoided agitation and propaganda activities.[40]

As there were plenty of passive elements, the exchange saw a mass of further expulsions through denial of new party cards. Most of these were apolitical, and Stalin intervened on the side of leniency and understanding—toward them. In the Central Committee plenum of 1–4 June 1936 he protested against wholesale expulsion of "passives." Industrious women textile workers in Ivanovo province should not have been expelled, for example, because of insufficient political literacy; it was the party organizations' business to improve their political literacy.[41] The same point was made earlier in an unsigned *Pravda* editorial written in the hyper-peremptory tone that usually reflected Stalin's personal inspiration. "It is generally known that the son does not answer for the father," it said, "and still less the grandson for the grandfather." Why, then, had the brothers Mikhail and Alexei Popov been expelled from the party, with resulting loss of work, because their grandfather, now twenty years dead, owned a meat shop in Michurinsk? The purge should be conducted less as a campaign against passive members. Its main target must be "enemy and alien elements." Genuine Bolshevik vigilance lay in the ability to identify—and pitilessly unmask—the real enemy as distinguished from the mere violator of party discipline or party ethics.[42] Real enemies were people like the director of the Smolensk electric station, who was purged at this time because he had once been overheard saying, "the material situation of the workers is growing worse."[43]

The Birth of a Treason Trial

All this was only the prelude to the massive terror that Stalin launched when preparations were complete. These involved far more than the checkup, the exchange of cards, and the organizing of the purge machinery.

In the coming new stage, the purge would engulf the Bolshevik ruling stratum. To justify a terror operation of that nature, Stalin needed a far weightier political warrant than the version of events already on the record from the quick closed trials of the "Leningrad center" and "Moscow center," in which the ex-oppositionist leaders had admitted only moral and political responsibility for the Kirov assassination. He required a version adequate to his sense of having been, himself, the object of a monstrous conspiracy in the recent past. He needed a shockingly sensational revelation of a several-years-old and widely ramified counterrevolutionary plot against his own and Kirov's lives and for the overthrow of the Soviet system, involving persons who had held high posts in the party-state.

To make the case dramatically persuasive, the charges would have to be confirmed by the testimony of the plot's ringleaders in a public or semipublic trial. Hence the twofold task of Stalin and those assisting him in this affair—Yezhov, Yagoda, and the latter's immediate NKVD subordinates—was to work out the conspiracy legend in detail and to induce Zinoviev, Kamenev, and others, including prominent Bolsheviks of Trotskyist past, to confess openly that there really had been a big terrorist conspiracy and that they themselves, under Trotsky's direction from afar, had played leading parts in it. This would provide a plausible publicity backdrop for massive terror, prepare the way for a series of further high-level arrests by implicating other ex-oppositionists in treasonable activities, and fulfill Stalin's need for a vindictive triumph over the hated enemies who would be publicly disgraced and condemned in the trial.[44]

To persuade the intended trial defendants to cooperate in the scheme by confessing to participation in a nonexistent conspiracy was no easy matter; preparations went on for about a year and a half. After their conviction in the January 1935 trial, Zinoviev, Kamenev, and others were sent to the Verkhne-Uralsk political prison. Ciliga, who saw them there, reported later that Zinoviev arrived with a bunch of books on fascism, a subject in which he was showing special interest, and that during the summer of 1935 he and Kamenev were returned to Moscow where they were put on trial a second time in secret, along with thirty-four others, on charges of preparing an attempt on the life of Stalin. Although Kamenev's brother, the painter Rosenfeld, was a prosecution witness against him, he categorically denied all charges. As a consequence, the five-year sentence he received in the January 1935 trial was doubled. Ciliga learned about the second trial after Zinoviev and Kamenev were brought back to Verkhne-Uralsk.[45] The decisive period in the trial preparation still lay ahead.

Meanwhile, in April 1935, about 300 ex-oppositionists had been shipped from their various places of confinement to the Liubianka, the central NKVD headquarters in Moscow. By some time in May about fifteen of them had been coerced into agreeing to make confessions of sufficient plausibility for use in the planned show trial. What methods of coercion were used may be guessed from the boast of the then deputy commissar of internal affairs, L. M. Zakovsky, a vicious one-time common criminal convicted of murders before the Revolution, that he could make Marx himself confess that he had worked for Bismarck. A month before the show trial opened in August 1936, a secret instruction sent on Stalin's initiative authorized use of any methods of interrogation (that is, torture included) on "spies, counterrevolutionaries, White Guards, Trotskyists, and Zinovievists." Apropos the still resistant Kamenev, Stalin said threateningly to interrogator L. G. Mironov at that time: "Don't come to me without Kamenev's confession."[46]

In addition to the genuine Old Bolshevik leaders chosen for defendant roles in the trial, the cast included several who took part, in one instance willingly and in others after pressuring, as fictitious defendants whose function was to aid the interrogators by furnishing false testimony on demand and implicating the principals in nefarious activities. These fictitious defendants included V. Olberg, an NKVD agent; I. Reingold, an official of the Cotton Syndicate who once had an association with Kamenev; and Zinoviev's one-time personal secretary, R. Pickel. The strategy of trial preparation consisted of first constructing the conspiracy legend out of the fictitious defendants' testimony and then confronting the principals with it; and of confronting still resisting principals with those who had already been broken and were then used to influence the holdouts.[47]

Even using this strategy, it took the special squad of interrogators many months of relentless pressure to break down the resistance of the prospective main defendants to the demands that a fiercely insistent Stalin was making upon them. A Stalin-originated saying current among the interrogators was: "Mount your prisoners and don't dismount till they have given you the testimony."[48] The pressure ran the gamut from sleepless periods of up to ninety hours on the conveyor to threats against the lives of loved ones to appeals to serve the party's needs. The ultimate pressure was the threat of death along with the promise that the lives of the defendants' and their loved ones and those of other ex-oppositionists would be spared on condition of unstinting cooperation in the planned show trial.

Stalin devised a frightful form of mental torture in order to induce these people, and others later, to put on a seemingly voluntary performance in court. It took the form of a law, "On Measures Against Crime Among Minors," which made children of twelve and over subject to "all measures of criminal punishment" (including death) for crimes of violence, murder, or attempted murder. *Pravda*'s editorial on this law noted in passing that some individuals had even used children for "personal-criminal, counter-revolutionary, antistate purposes," thereby hinting that threats to children might be employed against prospective purge-trial defendants.[49] The law was so used in particular to threaten Kamenev, who was told (on Stalin's direct instructions) that his young son had been on the lookout for Stalin's car on a road outside of Moscow.[50] The front-paging of this barbarous law in *Pravda* was clearly designed to convince present and future participants in purge trials that the threat to their children's lives was meant with all seriousness. When people whom Stalin perceived as enemies were involved, the son did answer for the father.

In addition to acting by remote control as the trial's chief producer, Stalin took a hand in creating the script. In doing so he applied to serious political business a dramaturgical bent that was rooted in his self-dramatizing nature. This tendency led to occasional interventions by him in the work of playwrights. One, which has come to light since his death, is especially instructive. A successful younger playwright, Alexander Afinogenov, wrote a play in 1933 called *Lies*. It was a tale of intrigue in a provincial factory town where two lowly career-seeking party members denounce Nina, the wife of the plant's deputy director—whose post they covet—by reading out in a party meeting an entry in her diary, which has come into their hands. Nina is a sincerely believing Communist, but a troubled one. "Collectivization we have only in the countryside," reads one of her diary entries. "In our personal lives we are all alone, each putting on a good face before others and all of us wearing masks."[51] Her life is further bedeviled by a friendship with Nakatov, an old revolutionary who has been exiled to the factory directorship for earlier oppositionism and who, unknown to Nina, is still conducting secret oppositional activities. In the end, under the inspirational influence of still another Old Bolshevik, she tells Nakatov, who has revealed the activities to her, that she is resolved to expose his underground antiparty group.

Afinogenov was a believing Communist, like his heroine, and the play expressed, among other things, his apparent disquiet over such developing realities as false denunciation and fear of speaking one's mind. Conscious of its political sensitivity, he sent copies to Gorky and Stalin and asked for their reactions. Gorky replied from Sorrento with a kindly but severe critique suggesting that such a play could at best be given a closed showing before a picked audience of a thousand staunchly Leninist enthusiasts of the General Line. But the real Soviet theatrical audience was made up not primarily of socialists but of "sons-of-bitches of the past, expelled from the destroyed paradise of philistine living." They would take the play in an anti-Communist spirit. [52]

Stalin also read the play and replied. He was rudely critical, yet also interested enough to make marginal comments and alterations in the play's text, which he returned to Afinogenov with his letter. He found the Communist characters ill-drawn save for Nakatov, who at least followed a consistent line ("duplicity," explained Stalin in parentheses). He showed a literalness of mind in marginal comments that, for example, took umbrage ("What nonsense!") at a remark *intended* by Afinogenov to show a character's misguided attitude. By a monologue of Nina's deploring that the press wasn't writing the truth and people weren't speaking at home the way they did at meetings, he wrote: "Why this dreary boring gibberish?" But he also took it upon himself to rewrite the play in places. He struck out whole scenes and monologues. Here and there he crossed out remarks and substituted or added others of his own. The general drift of his comments and alterations was to make villains always appear as villains, especially as being "two-faced" (a word added repeatedly), and to insist that everything be set before the audience in elementary black and white. Afinogenov revised the play in accordance with Stalin's directions. It had a successful premiere in Kharkov in November 1933 and was scheduled to open in the Moscow Art Theater in early December. But it was withdrawn when Afinogenov, after again soliciting Stalin's opinion, received a note from him saying: "I consider the second version unsuccessful."[53] Even after his own editing, *Lies* was too true for Stalin.

This episode is part of a larger body of evidence that artistic creativity held a fascination for him when it dealt with political themes, and that he felt competent to improve upon the work of literary professionals. Far from being the nonintellectual some have pictured, Stalin was articulate, interested in ideas, and had a certain Marxist-Leninist and historical learning. What he lacked was creativity. This tormented him, helped make him moody at times of triumph, and fed his resentment of more creative minds, such as Bukharin or Radek, even as he used them for his own ends. In one area, however, Stalin showed himself truly original. Because his mind worked conspiratorially, he had a fertile imagination in all matters concerning conspiracy.

In 1935–36 he turned this peculiar creative capacity to his uses in the conspiracy from above. He became a playwright in devising the script for the first of the great political dramas staged by the NKVD, Vyshinsky, and Ulrikh as treason trials. The script's fundamental idea had lain in his mind since the crisis time toward the end of 1932 when he found himself beset by criticism in the country and oppositional talk in the party over the staggering human costs of his economic October. Unable to relinquish or scale down his view of himself as a Lenin-like genius of revolutionary politics, his only possible response was to see the critics and oppositionists as being, behind their appearance of loyalty to the party-state, conspiring enemies of it aiming to wreck the revolutionary cause by removing him as its successful leader.

Stalin's seminal creative contribution is reflected in the transformation that the conspiracy legend underwent from the version of Kirov's murder put out in January 1935 to the script enacted in the show trial of August 1936. First, the conspiracy turned into a large-scale, high-level affair involving a "bloc" between foremost Zinovievists and foremost Trotskyists acting under Trotsky's guidance from abroad. Second, this conspiratorial "united center" was said to have been formed toward the end of 1932. Third, it became a terrorist conspiracy primarily against Stalin; his removal from the scene by murder was the supreme object. Kirov's murder thus receded from the center of events and became merely the one success scored by their conspirators in their plan to kill Stalin and various of his close associates. Fourth, ties between the conspirators and the Gestapo became a part of the story. Finally, the anti-Stalin plot was said to have been motivated by the very successes achieved under his leadership in the building of socialism in the Soviet Union; these, it was said, showed the oppositionists' politico-ideological bankruptcy and fanned their desire to avenge themselves on the Soviet government for their political failure by resorting to terrorism.

When the conspiracy legend that Stalin had created came back to him in the form of confessional testimony from the future performers, starting with those serving as accomplices in the trial preparation, he used his editorial pen—just as in the case with Afinogenov—to improve upon the draft text. Some of the corrections he made have been reported. Reingold, for example, testified that Zinoviev, in a conversation in his apartment in August 1934, explained his instructions to murder Kirov by saying that he was Stalin's closest assistant. Stalin strengthened this point, and heightened the literary effect, by inserting in Reingold's testimony: "Zinoviev said: 'It is not enough to fell the oak; all the young oaks growing around it must be felled too.' " Presumably in an effort to gratify Stalin's pride of authorship, this phrase was cited not once but twice in the official indictment. Again, at the point where Reingold was testifying to Kamenev's line of argument on the necessity of terrorist actions, Stalin inserted a statement by Kamenev saying: "The Stalin leadership group has become as strong as granite. Therefore, we must create a schism." This phrase too was duly incorporated into the portions of testimony cited in the official indictment.[54]

So, behind the scenes, the script took shape for the first of the show trials of Old Bolsheviks. In it Stalin's own conspiratorial *Weltanschauung* was elaborated in full fictional details that he himself probably considered true in the way great art is, if not as altogether factual history.

The New Service Nobility

The Terror of the later 1930s is comprehensible as a political action only if seen in the larger setting of the revolution from above as Stalin conceived and was attempting to carry it out. Following the example of Ivan Grozny, he was creating an *oprichnina,* a "special court" consisting of high party and police officials answerable to him alone and charged, like its sixteenth-century predecessor, with the task of stamping out the treason that he felt was rampant in the land.

But the historical *oprichnina,* in the Stalinist view as set forth in the *Great Soviet Encyclopedia* in the later 1930s, was not solely an instrument of terror. It was not rightly seen, in the picture drawn by some older historians, as "just a bloody epic of senseless murders, a mad whim of a vengeful tsar-tyrant seeking to do away with boyars whom he saw as an untrustworthy and a threat to his power." Nor was Kliuchevsky accurate in his description of it as simply a higher police force for affairs of boyar treason. Correctly viewed, as by Platonov and Wipper, the *oprichnina* was a "major reform" of the prevailing agrarian system. It had "great political meaning" as a weapon of struggle not only against certain persons but also against certain political institutions. It was a whole complex of political measures designed by Ivan Grozny to foster the armed strength and centralized power of the Moscow state by crushing the old hereditary landed aristocracy.[55]

Stalin, too, was engaged in a major transformation of the Soviet order, beyond the *piatiletka*'s revolution of collectivization and industrialization. His complex of political measures was designed to foster the military strength and centralized power of the new Muscovite Soviet state. The established party aristocracy, the Old Bolshevik grandees in their majority, were his treasonous boyars. But while purging the Soviet land of them, he had also to apply himself to further construction. A revolution, whether from below or from above, is a radical reconstitution of a sociopolitical order. As such it necessitates rebuilding as well as destruction. The ruling stratum, in particular, must not merely be displaced but replaced by new people who meet the requirements of the transformed order.

Conscious of this need, Stalin devoted much attention to bringing along the new generation of men (women were scarce in it) who would fill the purge-depleted ruling stratum in the near future. This element of his state-building activity had been adumbrated as early as the mid-1920s when he showed a partiality for the young and unsung along with animosity toward great Bolshevik grandees like Pokrovsky and Lunacharsky; when, in 1931, he told a conference of business executives that they should stop being afraid to promote able "nonparty comrades" to managerial posts in industry, for "our policy is not at all to turn the party into a closed caste"; and when, in 1933, he told a conference of *kolkhoz* shock workers that party members must not shut themselves in their party shell and preen themselves on party membership, for all of them, including Old Bolsheviks with a twenty- or thirty-year party past, had at one time or another been nonparty people.[56]

Just as the Great Purge began, Stalin made public his resolve to pursue the policy of opening the party to new members in all earnest. Addressing a reception for metal workers in the Kremlin on 26 December 1934, he recalled the party slogan of the *piatiletka,* "Technology is all-decisive," and said that the main concern now was the *people* in charge of technology. Then this lover of gardening resorted to a metaphor inspired by his hobby: "People must be carefully and attentively cultivated the way a gardener cultivates a favorite fruit tree."[57] Several months later, in his talk at the Red Army graduating ceremony in the Kremlin, he returned to the theme. Leaders should show the utmost solicitude for workers high and low in every sphere, cultivate them painstakingly, assist them in time of need, encourage them when they showed signs of succeeding, and help them along in their careers. Stalin punctuated the thought with a memory from his days of Siberian exile. Thirty fishermen went across the river to fetch some wood and returned at night minus one of their number, saying he must have drowned. Then one remembered that it was time to water the mare, and when reproached by Stalin that they cared more for their animals than for people, answered: "We can always make people, but a mare—just try to make a mare." The story's moral was that "we must above all learn to value people, to value cadres, to value every worker who can be of use to our common cause. We must finally understand that of all the valuable forms of capital in the world the most valuable and decisive capital are people, cadres. We must remember that under our present conditions, cadres are all-decisive."[58]

When many loyal citizens of socialist persuasion were disappearing by Stalin's fiat into the concentration camps, it was Machiavellian duplicity for him to describe "people" as precious capital and plants to be cultivated with loving care. But it was also an expression of his revolutionizing statecraft from above. The all-decisive cadres, the capital to be conserved, the plants to be cultivated, were especially the *little people* destined for places in a radically reconstituted ruling elite. Stalin coined yet another phrase for them. At a Kremlin reception for participants in the May Day 1935 parade, he addressed the assembled Red Army men as "party and nonparty Bolsheviks" and thereupon explained—in words that would have left Lenin speechless with shocked astonishment—that "one can be a Bolshevik without being a party member." Later that month, *Pravda* quoted these further words from his toast:

A Bolshevik is one who is devoted to the end to the cause of the proletarian revolution. There are many such among nonparty people. Either they haven't had time to enter the party's ranks or they see it as so holy that they want to prepare better to enter the party's ranks. Oftentimes such people, such comrades, such fighters stand even taller than many and many a party member. They are faithful to it to the grave.[59]

As examples *Pravda* cited the heroic fliers of the Cheliuskin rescue epic, who only afterward formally joined the party.

Stalin had begun wooing the "nonparty Bolsheviks" still earlier. At the Kremlin reception for metal workers in December 1934, a prominent older-generation nonparty engineer, Academician I. Bardin, was chosen to give a short speech on the metal industry's behalf. He said that its achievement of a pig iron output of 10 million tons in 1934 was a big political victory in the industrial revolution proceeding under the guidance of Stalin and the Communist Party. Stalin said in reply that the party alone was not responsible for this success, any more than it alone, with only 130,000 members at the time, could have carried out the revolution of October 1917. The production victory was due in large measure to "nonparty and old specialists, people like yourself," he told Bardin. The party's main role had been to weigh the possibilities and choose a correct target figure, 10 million tons, rather than an unduly low one or an unduly high one (17 million tons) that had been proposed for the *piatiletka*.[60] Stalin refrained from recalling his own responsibility for imposing the unreal 17-million-ton target, later revised downward on Kuibyshev's insistence.

Another celebrated nonparty Bolshevik was the Donbas coal miner Alexei Stakhanov. On the night of 30–31 August 1935, he mined a record 102 tons (the norm per six-hour shift was 7.3 tons) by strenuous effort and a novel division of labor under which he kept hewing while other workers performed his usual duty of reinforcing the worked-over coal face between bouts of hewing. Only later did he join the party. The government held up his feat for emulation and other labor heroes, often of peasant origin like Stakhanov, appeared in many spheres. So arose the "Stakhanov movement" for higher productivity by intensifying and rationalizing work processes. Addressing a conference of 3,000 Stakhanovites in the Kremlin, Stalin hailed it as a "revolution" in industry that had occurred "almost spontaneously" and to some extent "against the will of management," and said it showed the need for higher work norms. It showed, too, that "we leaders of the party and government must not only teach the workers but also learn from them."[61] The press called the meeting a "congress of party and nonparty Bolsheviks."

Stakhanovism accentuated pay differentials because the voluntary speed-up exploits were based on piece-work pay; and the press widely publicized the newly won prosperity of renowned labor heroes like Stakhanov himself and Pyotr Krivonos, the locomotive engineer who found a way to drive his freight train at passenger-train speed. The movement thus tapped the potent incentive of high monetary reward in the post-rationing situation of 1935–36 when the supply of consumer goods went on growing and the ruble's value was stabilized. Stalin alluded to this when he explained in his speech why the movement began when it did: "Life has become better, comrades. Life has become gayer. And when life goes more gaily, the work goes faster."[62] The internal *détente* remained in force for the deserving. Even some former anti-Bolsheviks found themselves among them. A governmental decree amnestied Ramzin and eight fellow convicts in the Industrial Party trial for their successful work on boiler design while in prison. Along with the decree was printed a letter of thanks for clemency in which Ramzin and three others took note of the "solicitude for man" that the NKVD had shown during their five-year imprisonment by providing all conditions for continued scientific work.[63]

Seeking the middle nobility's assistance in his battle against the grandees, Ivan Grozny recruited many of his *oprichniki* from among low-born nobles and assigned confiscated boyar lands to them in service tenure. Now Stalin was acting in like fashion—quite probably in full consciousness of that fact—by cultivating a new Soviet Russian service nobility of which the Stakahanovite labor aristocracy was one small part. Along with material rewards, he used for this purpose the extensive awarding of orders of merit to party and nonparty Bolsheviks whose assistance and loyalty he was courting. From the time of Peter the Great, who instituted them, orders of merit were a conspicuous element in tsarist Russia's monarchical culture.[64] Under new names they made a strong comeback in the culture of Russian national Bolshevism during Stalin's time.

A military Order of the Red Banner was instituted in Soviet Russia in 1918, and later a Red Banner of Labor. But it was in the 1930s that a whole system of orders and associated privileges emerged. In 1930 the Order of Lenin was created for "special merits in socialist construction," and the Order of the Red Star for "special merits in defense." Later, in 1936, came a fifth order, the Badge of Honor. Associated with the orders were such privileges as lifetime monthly pay bonuses (for instance, 25 rubles monthly for an Order of Lenin), apartmental rental reductions, free tram service, annual free rail trips, and preferential school admission for one's children.[65] In 1935 Stalin began showering orders on deserving party and nonparty members. In this he took care to make his personal initiative clear. At a Kremlin reception for women heroines of *kolkhoz* labor, he announced the decision to confer the Order of Lenin on the group leaders among them and the Red Banner of Labor on the others. Soon after, he ended his speech to the Stakhanovites in similar fashion: "So we've come to the decision that we'll have to recommend some 100–150 of you for the highest award." A month later, at a Kremlin reception for representatives of Armenia on that republic's fifteenth anniversary of joining the Soviet Union, Molotov announced that on Stalin's initiative the government would confer orders on them all.[66] These events were heavily publicized. Around that time the front pages of leading dailies began featuring long lists of the names of the meritorious workers in various trades and professions on whom orders were being conferred. Stalin was thus securing the devotion of many whom he lifted out of obscurity into a privileged position in society.

The new service nobility acquired titles and ranks as well as orders. This first period of the Terror saw an outpouring of rank- and title-creating statutes. In September 1935 officer ranks, topped by "marshal," were restored, together with corresponding insignia, in all the armed forces; and the Red Army staff was renamed "General Staff" in accordance with Russian tradition.[67] The NKVD's armed forces also received military ranks, and a special rank system was created for its Chief Administration of State Security (sergeant, junior lieutenant, lieutenant, senior lieutenant, captain, major, senior major, commissar of state security third rank, commissar second rank, commissar first rank).[68] Distinction in the arts received recognition with the creation of the title of "People's Artist," initially conferred on the noted directors of the Moscow Art Theater, Konstantin Stanislavsky and Vladimir Nemirovich-Danchenko, and the famous actors Vasily Kachalov and Ivan Moskvin.[69]

In late 1935 Stalin and Molotov issued, over their signatures, a new education decree that underlined the need for discipline in the schools, restored the traditional five-mark system (one = very poor, two = poor, three = average, four = good, five = excellent), and prescribed a return to pupils' uniforms (a pre-1917 Russian practice) starting in several main cities in 1936. Not long afterward, arrangements were decreed for the conferring of personal ranks on teachers: "primary school teacher," "secondary school teacher," and "distinguished school teacher"; and school administrators again got the rank of "director" as in the past.[70] Fixed gradations of salary and privilege accompanied these hierarchical rank-

ings. In the mid-1930s, there were seven classes of salaries for state officials, ranging from 500 rubles a month for people's commissars and other
high-ranking persons (class seven) down to 250 rubles a month for class-
one officials such as secretaries and section heads of district Soviets.[71] In
addition to their regular salaries, certain very high officials received monthly
packets of cash in recognition of particularly meritorious services. Although this practice was unpublicized, it became known to many.[72]

Less than twenty years before the Great Purge, Russia had a much-
betitled upper class of rank-holding servitors of the state. Memories of it
were still fresh. A representative of it, Stalin's writer-friend Alexei Tolstoy, was prominent in Soviet society. Speaking at the Congress of Soviets
in 1936, Molotov said: "The well-known writer A. N. Tolstoy has spoken
before me. Who does not know that he is the former *Count* Tolstoy. And
now? One of the best and most popular writers of the Soviet land—*Comrade* Alexei Nikolaevich Tolstoy. The guilt for this is history's, save that
the change was for the good. All of us, along with A. N. Tolstoy himself,
are in agreement with this."[73] From count to comrade was the message;
that a comrade could be a count was the subtle subtext.

Building on the Muscovite tradition of the nobility's obligatory state
service, Peter the Great introduced his Table of Ranks based on the principle of advancement and even ennoblement according to merit; a commoner acquired noble status with the crucial promotion to the eighth class,
where one obtained the rank of major on the military side and collegiate
assessor or collegiate senior commissar on the civilian side. The rank
system was swept away by the revolutionary storm of 1917. Its incipient
revival in Stalin's Russia of the mid-1930s was not taking place by popular
demand although there was doubtless a receptivity to it and, among some
perhaps, a nostalgia for it reflecting the tenacity of the centuries-old Russian political culture. The revival was a product of statecraft, a calculated
series of moves in Stalin's refashioning of the society from above on the
model of the tsar-transformers whom he saw as, along with Lenin, his
predecessors at the head of Russia.

As the Table of Ranks was implemented in the eighteenth century,
the original principle of rank's accessibility to talent irrespective of social
origin gave way in practice to drastic class restrictions.[74] In the mid-1930s,
the resurrected hierarchical system was open to virtually all the upwardly
mobile. The advance of able, ambitious citizens of working-class or peasant origin up the ladder of rank was welcomed. No section of society,
except the underclass of prison laborers, was excluded from the possibility
of entering the new Soviet service nobility.

This privileged order rose at the same time when Soviet Russia was
declared a genuinely socialist society in the new Constitution of 1936.

How could this be reconciled with Marxism and Leninism, which held that socialism meant the advent of a society without classes? Indeed, how could it be reconciled with the claim made at the time of the Seventeenth Party Congress, two years earlier, that a classless society would emerge under the Second Five-Year Plan (1933–37)? Stalin managed it by removing a foundation stone of Marxism and Leninism, the notion that socialism entailed an end to the division of society into classes. According to Article One of the new Constitution, the Soviet Union was "a socialist state of workers and peasants," that is, a two-class state. Stalin also said, in his speech of 25 November 1936 on the draft Constitution, that these were nonantagonistic "friendly classes," in addition to which there was a third social group, the intelligentsia, now 80 to 90 percent worker or peasant in origin. The intelligentsia was not exactly a class but a stratum *(prosloika)*, yet in no way was it inferior in rights to the workers and peasants whose interests it served. Thereby the notion of a class-differentiated socialist society, accommodating the new service nobility especially in its third social group, became embedded in an ideology that was still called Marxist-Leninist although it had lost rightful claim to such a title.[75]

Stalin knew that not only much of the theatrical audience but most of the people were at heart the "sons of bitches of the past" of whom Gorky spoke in his letter to Afinogenov. Attachment to Russian tradition was still strong, especially among the peasantry, a class to which Stalin looked for recruits to the new elite that was moving into posts vacated by arrested persons. So, he pursued during the purge era a policy of selective restoration of Russian tradition. The policy also reflected his personal predilections and his orientation on preparing the nation for war.

Popular traditionalism was strongest of all in simple attachment to Mother Russia. During the Civil War the Bolsheviks had appealed to this sentiment in peasant Russian souls, and many must have felt it in their own. But ideologically Bolshevism had tried to remain true to a Marxism on whose banners were inscribed the *Communist Manifesto's* words: "The working men have no country." Now, with Stalin's backing, the Soviet regime espoused the principle that the people did have a country in which it was their right and duty to take national pride. "Soviet patriotism" became the watchword.

Stalin had set an example with his statement, "we have a fatherland," in his no-more-beatings-of-Russia speech of 1931. The propaganda of Soviet patriotism began in earnest, however, in 1934, the year in which he organized his antiparty conspiracy. The Russian word for motherland, *rodina,* was reintroduced into official usage in the statute of 9 June 1934 incorporating the concept of high treason into the legal system (the Russian phrase for high treason is *izmena rodine,* "betrayal of the motherland").

From then on, *rodina* reacquired full right of citizenship in the Soviet lexicon. Radek led the way with an article, "My *Rodina*," in which he told how a Bolshevik like himself, who was (he explained) a Germanized Polish Jew by origin, worshipped at the altar of Soviet patriotism.[76]

The country in which Soviet citizens were invited to take patriotic pride was defined specifically as *Soviet* Russia led by Stalin. An astute presentation of this theme came from David Zaslavsky, a clever journalist of anti-Bolshevik past who was placing his pen at Stalin's service. He argued that patriotism, which yearned in vain for a worthy object in old Russia, had finally found it now. He quoted from Gogol's *Dead Souls* the mystically nationalist lines that apostrophize Russia as a fleet troika speeding God knows where: *"Rus', whither fliest thou? Answer me! No answer. The little bell emits a wonderful sound, wind splits the air: everything on earth rushes by, and other states and peoples, looking around, turn aside and make way for her."* But they didn't turn aside, Zaslavsky went on. They looked back on laggard Russia with scorn and beat her mercilessly and systematically—until now, when the people finally had a *Rus'* worthy of their patriotic pride.[77]

There was more than linguistic coincidence in the resurrection of *rodina* when high treason reentered official usage: the politics of purge and the politics of populist traditionalism were closely interlinked. In 1935 a writer named Boris Levin made this connection the basis of a play called *Rodina*. He explained in an interview that the play was both about the new meaning that patriotism had acquired and the need for vigilance against enemies. The plot involved a conflict between Soviet citizens who were true patriots and Russian émigré spies who were not.[78] The willingness to be on the alert for enemies and to assist Stalin's regime in destroying them was being made into an essential ingredient of Soviet patriotism.

By 1935 the daily press was regularly publishing commemorative articles about such prerevolutionary Russian figures as the radical writers Chernyshevsky, Belinsky, and Dobroliubov, the eighteenth-century scientist Lomonosov, the nineteenth-century playwright Ostrovsky, and the painter Repin. Also in that year, a 48-member All-Union Pushkin Committee, headed by Gorky, was formed to popularize Pushkin's poetry and prepare measures for marking, in 1937, the centenary of the poet's death. Soon after the October Revolution, Mayakovsky had written: "We are shooting the old generals! Why not Pushkin?" Now *Pravda*'s editorial accompanying the announcement of the coming centenary celebration was called "The Great Russian Poet."[79]

Russian folk songs and dances were brought back into fashion. Stalin attended a dress rehearsal of the concert that the army's Red Banner Ensemble was to perform for the Seventh Congress of Soviets in 1935. He especially praised four sailors' rendering of the Russian folksong "Kali-nushka," and suggested that it be included in the regular repertoire.[80] Later that year the party elite attended a concert in the Bolshoi Theater. When a trade union group performed such old-time favorites as "Kamarinskaya" to the accompaniment of folk instruments, Stalin—in whose national Bol-shevik soul there also lurked a "son-of-a-bitch of the past"—was observed applauding lustily. The next day's *Pravda,* reporting this, editorialized: "The ever rising interest in folk dances and folk songs is a healthy and vital phenomenon. It is also the right path for the whole of Soviet musical art."[81]

He took pains to publicize himself as the champion of national tradi-tion. The Cossack corps, which had served as a punitive force of the old regime against the revolutionary movement, then formed a backbone of the White armies in the Civil War, and been disbanded by the Bolsheviks, was restored in the Red Army, with traditional Cossack uniforms, during 1935. The revival was dramatized in Stalin's presence during the party celebration in the Bolshoi Theater on 6 November 1936. This time the Red Banner Ensemble started the concert with a rendering of "Dubinushka." Then Don and Kuban Cossacks appeared on the stage, sang a song to Stalin followed by several old Cossack melodies, and wound up with a resound-ing Cossack "hurrah" for Stalin as their caps shot up in the air.[82] To many Old Bolsheviks, some of whose faces bore scars from Cossack sabres, such a spectacle was blasphemous.[83]

Reviving some Russian traditions, Stalin slightly curbed party efforts to combat another: religion. Soviet culture was antireligious in opposing the traditional religions on behalf of the new state orthodoxy of Marxism-Leninism. Antireligious propaganda was carried on in the schools, by the Komsomol, and by a special party auxiliary called the League of Militant Atheists, headed by Yaroslavsky. The *piatiletka* saw mass closure of churches and much persecution of the clergy, yet religious attachment survived among very many, especially in the countryside where, according to Ya-roslavsky in a pamphlet of 1937, perhaps as many as two-thirds of the people remained believers.[84] One reason for the tenacity of religious feel-ing in the face of the drive against it is that when hundreds of thousands of younger mothers took jobs during the *piatiletka,* their children—despite being children of the Revolution, born in the 1920s—came under stronger influence of grandparents, many of whom remained traditionally devout, kept the family icons, surreptitiously took the children to churches to be baptized, and by their whole bearing made the little ones feel foolish when they came home from school saying "God doesn't exist."

The antireligious campaign was relaxed in 1934. The League went into decline, its newspaper *Bezbozhnik* (The Atheist) closed down, and its membership dropped precipitously in numbers. At Easter time in 1935 the government authorized renewed sale in the markets, and later in state stores, of the special ingredients needed for the traditional Russian Easter cake.[85] Toward the end of that year, the traditional Russian Christmas tree, proscribed after the Revolution, made—unquestionably with Stalin's approbation—an officially sponsored comeback as "New Year's tree." Since Russian Christians observe Christmas according to the Orthodox Church calendar, on 7th January, the eve of the new year was an appropriate time for the religiously inclined to set up the tree. Stalin wanted the populace to identify him with the policy of easing up a little on religion. That became clear when Komsomol delegates met in Moscow in April 1936 for the organization's Tenth Congress. One principal speaker, E. L. Fainberg, revealed in his report that Stalin, in preliminary discussion of a draft of the new bylaws, rejected a clause that would have obliged the Komsomol to combat religion "decisively, mercilessly." All it should do was to "explain patiently the harm of religious prejudices."[86]

Soon afterward, in his speech before the Eighth Congress of Soviets on the draft new Constitution, Stalin opposed two suggested antireligious amendments. One, which would have prohibited religious worship outright, was "not in accord with the spirit of our Constitution." The other would have deprived not only ex-White Guardists and "former people" not engaged in useful work, but also clergymen, of voting rights, or, alternatively, of the right to be elected. In opposing this proposal (in both forms) Stalin said the time had come to repeal the long-standing Soviet law depriving nonlaboring and exploiter elements of voting rights. "In the first place, not all former kulaks, White Guardists, or priests are hostile to the Soviet regime," he said.[87] This was one of the most highly publicized of his speeches, and came at a time when Bolsheviks were being denounced by the thousands in the new, unbridled phase of the terror that started in the autumn of 1936.

A People's Vozhd'

Neither the tsar-carpenter nor his princely predecessors in early Muscovy were resplendently remote royal figures. The Muscovite prince, observed Platonov, became "a *vozhd'* of the people, relying on the whole mass of the people and leading it not only to national unity but also to international primacy in all the Orthodox countries."[88] Wipper's Ivan Grozny was just such a leader making war on the treasonous boyar aristocracy by compact with the Russian people and for Russia's good. As if in conscious emulation, Stalin took it upon himself now to be a *vozhd'* of the people, a tsar with a populistic aura. And when he convened the Congress of Soviets in late 1936 to adopt the new Constitution that would bear his name, he may have been mindful of Ivan's calling the first Russian Assembly of the Land during *his* time of terror.

In acting the part of a Russian tsar, Stalin was taking advantage of the traditional disposition to view the reigning monarch as a stern yet just and caring *tsar-batiushka* (tsar-father). "The Russian people is really a tsaristic people; *it needs a tsar,*" he is reported to have said to Alexander Svanidze, the brother of his Georgian first wife, during a game of billiards sometime around 1934.[89]

In February 1935, he took part in drafting a new model collective farm charter at the second all-union congress of *kolkhoz* shock workers, and here his populism showed a propeasant flavor. He defended a position on private peasant garden plots directly contrary to the position he took in secret at the end of 1929 when initiating the rural October. Opposing a proposal that the garden plot be limited to one-tenth of a hectare, he insisted that the personal interests of the collective farmers must be reckoned with, and went on: "Some think you can't allow them a cow, others that you can't allow them a sow. In general you want to squeeze the *kolkhoznik*. That won't do. That's wrong. . . . So long as the family, children, personal needs, and personal tastes exist, these things have to be considered."[90] With Stalin as their vocal defender, the peasants received provisions in the new model charter that the garden plots could vary between one-quarter and one-half hectare and be up to a hectare in special districts, and that each household could have at least one cow, two calves, one sow and its progeny, up to ten sheep or goats, unlimited poultry and rabbits, and up to twenty beehives. The revised articles of association were, moreover, publicized as a charter of *kolkhoz* democracy on the ground that they made provision for approval by the collective farm's general assembly of many decisions—such as those affecting the production plan and output norms—heretofore made by the governing board or the chairman acting alone.[91]

Stalin again presented himself as a peasant's advocate when, during a Kremlin conference of combine drivers in December 1935, one of them complained that the local authorities hadn't wanted to send him to Moscow to attend the conference because he was the son of a kulak. That was when Stalin said: "The son doesn't answer for the father." Soon afterward, his Central Committee headquarters sternly—on *Pravda*'s front page—overruled the refusal of a Machine Tractor Station deputy director for political matters to permit a young collective farm woman to take a tractor driver's course on the ground that she was the daughter of a deported kulak. The accompanying editorial pointed out that following Stalin's just-quoted statement, the government, on 29 December 1935, had repealed restrictions on entry into higher education or vocational schools on grounds of social origin or parents' deprivation of rights. All citizens, irrespective of social origin, had an equal right to education.[92]

Although Stalin was a reclusive man, not one to mingle with the masses, he appeared before and among the people extraordinarily often just at this time. Since his appearances were largely an artefact of official publicity, little relaxation of the customary supertight security precautions was required. Still, they enabled him to play the part of a people's *vozhd'*. Together with Molotov, Kaganovich, and Ordzhonikidze he went to inspect Moscow's new metro system, and took a ride in what was described as "a car with passengers—workers of Moscow."[93] In company with Kaganovich, Ordzhonikidze, and Yagoda, he went to a place outside Moscow to view the workings of one of the locks on the recently built Moscow-Volga canal. Two excursion boats, one called "In Memory of Kirov," were going through. The deck band struck up "The Internationale" when the passengers recognized Stalin standing on the shore. They applauded, waved handkerchiefs, cheered, and called out: "Thank you, Comrade Stalin, for the happy life."[94]

He shared the publicity limelight with the Soviet airmen—"Stalin's falcons," as they came to be called—whose exploits of the mid-1930s commenced with the rescue of the Cheliuskin crew and culminated in the extraordinary 5,288-mile first nonstop flight over the Pole from Russia to North America in a single-engine monoplane flown by Valery Chkalov and two others and bearing the name "Stalinist Route." Photos of him appeared daily in the Soviet press, now in genial pipe-smoking profile, now walking with his comrades across the Kremlin grounds, now hugging a returned airman-hero at the Moscow airport, now surrounded by young Pioneers, now in a country setting with an arm around his ten-year-old daughter Svetlana. He was shown holding little girls who were invited to the reviewing stand atop the mausoleum during events in Red Square to present him with a bouquet of flowers, and their stories of the memorable moment would appear under headlines like "How I Got Acquainted With Comrade Stalin." Filial as well as fatherly, he took a short publicized trip to Tiflis for a farewell visit with his aged and ailing mother, to whom he jestingly explained that he had come on Svetlana's orders to fetch a jar of her nut preserves.. When she noted gray streaks in his hair, he told her that he felt very fit. Much later, he privately told his daughter Svetlana that his mother also said to him on that occasion: "What a pity you never became a priest."[95]

The standard form of Stalin's appearances among the people was the reception in the Great Hall of the Kremlin for large groups of meritorious representatives of some branch of the economy or section of the populace. There were receptions for railway workers, nonferrous metallurgists, Central Asian collective farmers, wives of Red Army commanders, wives of heavy-industry executives, and many others. Stalin was always the central figure. Usually he would give a short speech and propose to his invariably agreeable Politburo associates that orders be bestowed on some or all of the guests. On occasion he would show by a gesture his tsar-like magic power to make life-dreams come true. At the reception for heroines of *kolkhoz* labor, for example, he asked the champion sugar-beet grower, Maria Demchenko, if she would like to study, and she replied: "So much that I can't describe it to you." At that he turned to his colleagues and said: "You know, comrades, Demchenko's going to study and be an agronomist."[96]

The cult of the people's *vozhd'* showed exuberant further growth at this time. His name grew talismanic. Fighter planes streaked across the sky over Red Square in a formation that described the six letters, S-T-A-L-I-N; student athletes paraded through the Square in that formation; and fifty-one mountain climbers nearing the peak of Mount Kazbek were photographed from the air in S-T-A-L-I-N formation.[97] The name was sung in verse by poets from as far away as Kazakhstan where the folk bard Djambul improvised lines like: "When I was over seventy, Lenin and Stalin brought light to me." By decision of the Central Committee, the Institute of Marx-Engels-Lenin was instructed to publish Stalin's collected writings. On Stalin's initiative a Central Lenin Museum was opened in Moscow. The main theme of its exhibits was the collaboration of the "two titans" in the Russian Revolution.[98]

Although the personality cult remained dual, Stalin was more and more the center of attention. A writer, A. Avdeenko, described the opening of the Seventh Congress of Soviets on 28 January 1935. When Stalin and his Politburo colleagues appeared in the Great Hall of the Kremlin, 2,000 delegates leaped from their seats, applauding, shouting, smiling at Stalin. "I looked back, and on all those faces, in all those eyes, I saw love, devotion, selflessness." A woman factory worker sitting beside the writer gripped his hand and whispered: "How simple he is, how modest. And see how he smiles—so gaily; makes you want to smile too." "Dearer than the dearest," said a male worker neighbor with tears in his eyes. When Avdeenko, himself a delegate, took the floor two days later, he ended his speech by saying: "And when the woman I love presents me with a child, the first word it shall utter will be—*Stalin!*"[99]

Lest Avdeenko's contemporary report seem a fabrication, we may cite here the post-Stalin memoir by the writer Ilya Ehrenburg, who visited Moscow in 1935 from his Paris post as an *Izvestiia* correspondent and attended a session of the Stakhanovites' congress. Everyone rose when Stalin appeared, the applause went on for ten or fifteen minutes, and Stalin clapped in response. When, at last, they all sat down, a woman's wild cry went up, "Glory to Stalin!" Then the 3,000 jumped to their feet again and resumed clapping. Everyone, Ehrenburg included, kept intently watching Stalin during the proceedings. On the way home afterward, Ehrenburg felt uneasy about it all, but concluded that he did not understand the psychology of the masses and was judging things as a member of the intelligentsia. The acclamations had just been "a curious way of expressing emotion, a kind of declaration of allegiance."[100]

Perhaps so. The cult was promoted in countless ways by official action, yet the feelings it engendered among ordinary people, especially the meritorious ones received in the Kremlin, were often unfeigned. Stalin's Machiavellian strategy of seeking popularity as security against conspiracies to overthrow him—a danger that still existed and could grow as high-placed persons began to perceive the true extent of his purge plans—was succeeding. Testimony to this came many years later when Khrushchev and a few other survivors of the Great Purge tried to explain to the nation why no one in high position acted to bring about Stalin's removal at the time of the Terror. Referring to the cult atmosphere of the 1930s, they wrote that ". . . if anyone in that setting took action against Stalin, he would have had no support among the people."[101] There was a grain of truth in this lame excuse.

But insurance against a possible counterconspiracy was not the sole object of the projection of Stalin as a great leader and popular idol. He wanted to *be* those things. The Soviet Russian state to which the new service nobility owed its allegiance was to have him as its personification and ideal; it would be a Stalin-led state with a Stalin-centered class of servitors and populace. Not only opposition-minded Old Bolsheviks but very many party officials who had been Stalin supporters in the 1920s and held posts of higher or lower responsibility during the *piatiletka* knew about his failings as a leader and were aware of facts of party history that he needed to repress. But consciousness of these matters was hazy or nonexistent among the emergent new constituency of "party and nonparty Bolsheviks," which the political gardener was cultivating in popular soil. By virtue of their youth in many instances, their simple peasant backgrounds in many others, these people *could* see him as a blemish-free "real Bolshevik" in the sense of his 1931 letter to *Proletarian Revolution* and as one of the greats of Bolshevism on a par with Lenin. In their history-conditioned Russian souls they could even revere him as the people's tsar of a Russia resurgent under Soviet auspices. He could tell that from the enthusiastic acclamations of the excursionists on the Moscow-Volga canal, and from the shining eyes of the common folk with whom he was consorting in the Kremlin's Great Hall.

What was still needed was a depiction of him as a Bolshevik titan on a par with Lenin in a history book or biography or both. No such work existed, although his letter of several years ago to *Proletarian Revolution* might have suggested the need for one. In earlier revolutionary history as presented in the standard text by N. Popov Stalin made but a skimpy appearance. Even its latest, 1935 edition, mentioned him only a few times in the two hundred plus pages about the period up to the formation of Bolshevism as a separate party in 1912.

There was not much more about his formative period in the revised edition of the first volume of Yaroslavsky's party history issued in 1934, despite all the effort the editor must have made to show Stalin as an important early figure. He fared a little better in V. Knorin's widely read *Short History* of the party, but even there his revolutionary activities up to 1912 were mentioned only in five places.[102] As late as 1934–35, Stalin's role in the beginnings of Bolshevism was still being truthfully presented in the major party histories as rather modest.

The man who undertook to transform this state of affairs was Stalin's sycophantic Georgian protégé and confidant, Lavrenti Beria. Notwithstanding all his lack of qualifications to be a party historian, even where Transcaucasian party history was concerned, he employed his power as party chief of Transcaucasia to intervene in this field. In January 1934 he informed a Georgian party congress in Tiflis that everything so far written on the early history of the revolutionary movement in Transcaucasia was defective in its failure to bring out "the authentic, real role of Comrade Stalin, who in fact led the struggle of the Bolsheviks in the Caucasus for many years." In order to remedy matters it had been decided to set up in Tiflis a Stalin Institute, which would gather all pertinent materials to show the "true picture of Comrade Stalin's gigantic role in our revolutionary movement."

Even before the institute's creation, Beria knew what the materials would show. For he declared in his lengthy speech to the Tiflis party congress: *"Comrade Stalin is the founder of the Bolshevik movement in Georgia and in the Transcaucasus."*[103] Working on the basis of this speech, some Georgian historians produced a book called *On the History of the Bolshevik Organizations in the Transcaucasus.* Soon afterward they were shot[104] and the work came out as Beria's. He read it aloud before a two-day meeting of Tiflis party activists. The Russian text was published in eight long installments in *Pravda* in July–August 1935 and then in book form.

The standard writings on Transcaucasian party history then were those by Filipp Makharadze, Mamia Orakhelashvili, and Abel Yenukidze. Even the more recent among them accorded Stalin's initial decade as a revolutionary, 1898–1908, hardly more than the limited attention it merited.

Beria struck out at the standard texts as error-ridden and stated the prime point that hadn't been made clear but must be: "The whole history of the Transcaucasian Bolshevik organizations, the whole revolutionary movement of Transcaucasia and Georgia, have, from the first days of their rise, been linked inseparably with the work and name of Comrade Stalin."[105]

Although filled with a mass of quotations and references to real events, the "Beria" book was essentially a fantasy-picture of Transcaucasia's revolutionary past. It constructed a legend in which the youthful Stalin was— just as he would have retrospectively seen himself in his self-adulating imagination—Transcaucasia's Lenin. Citing as source material the undated oral testimony of various Georgian Old Bolsheviks, without archival references, the book made out Stalin and two early-deceased party comrades, Lado Ketskhoveli and Alexander Tsulukidze, to have been the core of a proto-Bolshevik revolutionary minority in the Georgian Marxist milieu at a time when the dominant, Zhordania-led majority was proto-Menshevik. It falsely pictured Stalin as the senior member of the trio, the *vozhd'* to whom the other two turned for instructions and advice. It catered to Stalin's true-Russianism by linking the radical minority with Russian Marxist emissaries then in Tiflis. It placed him in the center and leadership of events in which his actual role was at most peripheral, such as the Batum strikes of 1901–2 and the political turbulence of 1905 in Georgia. It treated his insignificant, derivative philosophical tract of 1906–7, *Anarchism or Socialism?*, as a path-finding work of Marxist thought.

In order to portray Stalin as a revolutionary hero of all-Transcaucasian and not merely Georgian dimensions, the book appropriated for him the leadership of the Baku Social Democratic organization around the time of its emergence in 1901. Decades later, a Politburo member of Stalinist past, M. A. Suslov, wrote that Beria's "no-account little book" *(knizhonka)* pictured Stalin as the founder of the Baku party committee in 1901 "although, as is known, he never came to Baku before 1904."[106] The role Beria falsely ascribed to Stalin was played by Yenukidze, a fact stated in the biographical article about him in the *Great Soviet Encyclopedia*. The retrospective affirmation of Stalin in that historical role necessitated the retrospective negation of Yenukidze. It has been noted that Yenukidze's fall in early 1935 was heralded by a *Pravda* editorial note referring critically to Yenukidze's Baku period. The self-critical historical article with which Yenukidze responded was notable for his disclaimer that he had created the Baku committee in 1900–1901, but also for the fact that he gave the main credit for that to Ketskhoveli and none to Stalin.[107] The Stalin-Beria politics of biography were a powerful reinforcing, if not primary factor in Yenukidze's downfall, which, not coincidentally, was publicized a month or so before the Beria book appeared.

Only in the last chapter, where Stalin's Great Russian nationalism was reflected in an account of his battle in the early 1920s against the "national deviationism" of the Georgian Bolshevik leadership, did the book depart the ground of legend for that of real history and coming purge politics. Otherwise, its appearance was a giant early step in the creation of a radically falsified new history of Bolshevism that presented the past according to Stalin's self-glorifying view of the parts that he and others had played, or should have played, in it. Beria moved along the path that Stalin hacked out with his letter to *Proletarian Revolution*. By holding up the book as an example in a leading article, *Pravda* invited other party historians to follow in his footsteps.[108] Not long after the Beria book came out, the press took up the cult of the young Stalin as Transcaucasia's Lenin by publishing old workers' reminiscences of Stalin's early exploits as organizer and leader of the Bolshevik organizations there.

But for all the significance of these contributions to the further growth of the personality cult, something was still missing: a biography of Stalin. For quite a while there had been hope that Gorky would turn his still potent writing talent to the project. Gorky's vivid little book of reminiscences of Lenin was well known. After sending materials for a Stalin biography to him, the head of the association of state publishing houses, A. B. Khalatov, inquired in a letter of January 1932 whether more were needed. Having returned for good to Moscow, Gorky bowed to the pressure and every morning for several months closeted himself in his study with documents sent to him by special courier from the Central Committee. But in the end he gave up the effort, pleading inability to fulfil the task on the requisite high level.[109]

Discussions also went on with prominent foreign writer-friends of the Soviet Union—Lion Feuchtwanger, André Gide, and Henri Barbusse—and the latter, a member of the French Communist Party, undertook the project with Moscow's full cooperation.[110] He died of illness in Moscow in August 1935 shortly after the Seventh Comintern Congress, in which he took part. By then the completed biography, *Stalin: A New World Seen Through One Man,* was out in France. *Pravda* marked the 7 November holiday by printing a Russian translation of the book's foreword, in which Barbusse called Stalin the most eminent man in the world, yet also the most unknown, and described the simplicity with which he lived, with his three children, in a four-room apartment in a small building once used as servants' quarters in the Kremlin, on a monthly ruble salary of something between twenty and forty English pounds. A Russian translation of the whole book appeared in early 1936 in an initial printing of 300,000 copies at a price almost any citizen could afford, one ruble. Soviet press reviews were lavishly laudatory. It was the glorifying biography that Stalin required.

"He is the Lenin of today," a phrase that occurred toward the end of the book, was its leitmotif throughout. After introducing Koba the heroic young Transcaucasian revolutionary, in the first chapter written in Beria's vein, the book devoted chapter 2 to Lenin ("The Giant"), but really to Lenin-Stalin because its key theme was the formation of *two* giants' fighting partnership in the years before, during, and shortly after 1917. "Lenin put the greatest value on Stalin's writings," it said in one place. "Too little is known of the decisive part played by Stalin at the time of the Treaty of Brest" in another, and "Lenin never let a day pass without seeing Stalin" in still another.[111] Beyond being the Lenin of today, Stalin was the man Lenin could not have done without yesterday. And the heroization of his political biography went along with the humanization of the hero. Stalin— like Lenin—was a man given to Homeric laughter. He was a hard worker who regularly went to bed at four in the morning. He did not employ thirty-two secretaries, like Mr. Lloyd George, but only one, Comrade Poskrebyshev. He did not sign what others put before him, but wrote it himself. What were his traits that most impressed those who knew him? "His kindness, his delicacy," said Barbara Djaparidze, who had fought beside him in the old days in Georgia. "His gaiety," said Orakhelashvili. "He laughs like a child."[112]

"The new Russia worships Stalin," wrote Barbusse in conclusion, and the publication of his book there helped the statement come true. Stalin assisted too with a reference to Lenin as "our father and mentor."[113] By the canons of the dual cult, it meant that Stalin was the father and mentor of today. So the public attitude grew increasingly reverential, as the celebrated French writer André Gide learned in an instructive way on his trip to Russia in 1936.

In announcing Gide's arrival on 19 June, *Pravda* said that he was born in 1869 "in an aristocratic Protestant French family." The quite unusual reference to a foreign guest's religious affiliation was certainly connected with the fact that in Russian transliteration his family name was *Zhid*, the Russian word for "Yid" or "Kike." Evidently, *Pravda* thought it desirable to inform the Soviet public that Gide was not a *zhid*.

A prominent cultural figure known for his pro-Soviet attitude, Gide received a warm official welcome, met Stalin, and was taken on a tour of the country that included Stalin's birthplace, Gori, in Georgia, where Beria had erected a museum building to enclose and preserve the hut in which Soso Djugashvili was born in 1879.

In *Return From the U.S.S.R*, the subsequently published record of disillusion that made its author a Soviet *bête-noire*, Gide told of having his car stop in front of Gori's post office so that he could send his high host a telegram of thanks for the hospitality being accorded him everywhere. He handed in the text, which read, "Passing through Gori, in the course of our wonderful journey, I feel the need to send you my most cordial. . . ." Here the translator paused, and said: "I cannot let you speak like this. 'You' is not enough when that 'you' is Stalin." Gide's escorts consulted among themselves and suggested: "You, leader of the workers," or "You, lord of the peoples." Gide protested in vain; the telegram was only accepted after he agreed to the addition.[114]

What the escorts knew, and the famous Frenchman of Protestant persuasion did not, was that in Russia one did not address a tsar as simply "you." The customary usage was, rather, "Your Majesty" or "You, Sire."

14

STALIN AND FASCISM

Popular Front Politics

IF THE VICTORY of fascism in Germany had a place in Stalin's policy design, further spread of fascist power did not. A tidal wave of fascism could not only preclude the very division of Europe into opposing armed camps on which he was counting, but could also expose Soviet Russia to a deadly danger of attack by a fascist phalanx of states. He had therefore to do everything possible to keep remaining European democracies and above all France—the keystone of any anti-German grouping—from going fascist, and to encourage them to take a stand against German aggression. So, he abandoned the extremist left tactics that eased Hitler's path to power and through Comintern authorized for other Communist parties what he had denied their German comrades: united fronts with other working-class parties to preserve democratic institutions and bar the road to fascism.

In effecting the Comintern's shift of position, Stalin found a useful instrument in the Bulgarian Communist Georgi Dimitrov. When the Reichstag was set afire in 1933, Dimitrov was in Berlin. Arrested by the Nazis and put on trial in Leipzig as one of the alleged culprits, Dimitrov courageously defied the Nazi court's charges and gained international fame. Released from a German prison after the Soviet government conferred its citizenship upon him, he arrived in Moscow in late February 1934 convinced of the need for a new policy for international Communism. In mid-March he requested an interview with Stalin, who received him in the presence of his Comintern representative, Manuilsky, engaged him in lengthy discussion, and allowed him to carry the day. On the way out Manuilsky confided: "Your meeting with Stalin will have historic importance later on."[1] Dimitrov was brought into the Political Commission of the Comintern Executive Committee where he plunged into the work of developing the new tactics and lining up foreign Communists' support in preparation for the Comintern's coming Seventh Congress.[2]

Since France was the core country of nonfascist Europe, and its Communist party the main one now after the crushing of German Communists, it was the logical proving ground for the new policy, all the more so as the demonstration by antidemocratic extremists in Paris on 6 February 1934 awakened many Frenchmen to the fascist danger at home. In May 1934 the united-front line was launched in *Pravda* with an endorsement by the French Communist leader Maurice Thorez, an editorial appeal for a united front, and an antifascist manifesto on "proletarian humanism" by Gorky.[3] At their national conference in Ivry the following month, the French Communists adopted the policy of antifascist unity of the Left. In July they signed a unity pact with the French Socialists (no longer "social-fascist"), the first of numerous such agreements concluded by Communist parties in other European countries within the next few years.

Before the French cantonal elections in October 1934, Thorez took the significant further step of calling for a broader antifascist "Popular Front" coalition of the two left-wing parties and the nonsocialist Radical Socialists, who drew their support from the peasants and middle strata. Whereas Communist united-front tactics toward Socialists had a history going back to 1921–23, coalition politics with "bourgeois" parties was a departure from Leninist theory and practice and made sense only because Stalin's goal in the Popular Front policy was not to make a revolution but to stop fascism from taking power. When Thorez called on him in Moscow in 1935, Stalin congratulated him on a policy that he called uniquely audacious and in conformity with the spirit of Leninism. "You have found a new key to open the windows of the future," he added.[4] Responsibility for the new key was Stalin's.

Formal adoption of the Popular Front policy came at the Seventh

Comintern Congress, which met in Moscow in July–August 1935 with some 500 delegates, representing sixty-five Communist parties, in attendance. Dimitrov, who was elected Comintern general secretary at this congress, set forth the new line. In doing so he emphasized that fascism as a mode of government ("the open terrorist dictatorship of the most reactionary, most chauvinist, most imperialist elements of finance capital") was separated by a gulf from the democratic form of bourgeois government. This implicitly modified Stalin's old dictum that fascism and Social Democracy were "not antipodes but twins" and that Social Democracy was "objectively the moderate wing of fascism."[5] Communist parties were now enjoined to defend democratic rule against fascism by forming united fronts with Social Democratic parties and, where feasible, broader antifascist popular fronts. They were to give their support to united-front or popular-front governments and possibly participate in them. They were also encouraged to don the mantle of patriotism. Yet, as some scholars have observed, this was the most "Russocentrist" congress of all Comintern congresses inasmuch as defense of the Soviet Union, even in alliances it might conclude with imperialist colonial powers, was made the supreme task of foreign Communists.[6] It was also the most orchestrated. A Finnish Communist delegate, noting the absence of actual discussion or debate and the textually approved speeches with their obligatory genuflections to Stalin, could not help recalling his experience of the Third Congress in 1921, where many speeches were extemporaneous and speakers clashed in open debate.[7]

Stalin prescribed the line of this congress, appeared at it, and was elected to its presidium. Yet, he did not address it, and neither during nor afterward did he publicly express his view of the Comintern's new policy. "This was more tacit agreement with the congress's decisions than active support of them," comment two latter-day Soviet historians.[8] Apart from a desire to gloss over the reversal of the left sectarianism of the previous period, Stalin had a reason for his aloofness: reluctance to be too openly identified in person with a political line that would belie the seriousness of secret diplomacy that he was already developing vis-à-vis Berlin.

Given that its theme was cooperation with non-Communist forces to ward off the fascist danger, the Comintern's Seventh Congress played down the organization's official mission of fostering world Communist revolution. Nevertheless, Dimitrov duly stipulated in his address that while Communists were ready to support united-front parliamentary governments, only Soviet power would bring "final salvation." This, and the participation of American delegates in the proceedings, was enough to arouse official American protests that Moscow was in violation of the Litvinov pledge of noninterference on which U.S. recognition of the USSR was predicated.[9] In the opposite political camp, a disgusted Trotsky damned the meeting as "the liquidation congress of the Third International" and called the Popular Front the "politics of prostration."[10] Before long Stalin seemed to lend weight to that opinion by telling Roy Howard that the Soviet Union had never harbored world revolutionary intentions.[11]

When popular-front governments arose in France and Spain in 1936, Soviet policy appeared to bear out Stalin's unrevolutionary words. The Spanish elections of February 1936 produced a Communist-supported popular-front government of liberals and Socialists under Manuel Azaña; the French elections of May 1936, a Communist-supported popular-front government of Socialists and Radicals headed by the Socialist Léon Blum. A spontaneous strike movement of unprecedented proportions erupted in France before the Blum government took office. Worker occupation of plants gave it a radical character. This was ominous from the standpoint of Stalin's policy of supporting a strong and stable status-quo France. In Litvinov's words to a correspondent of *Pétit Parisien:* "What is essential is that France should not allow her military strength to be weakened. We hope no internal troubles will favour Germany's designs."[12] When the strikers numbered two million, Thorez, certainly acting on Stalin's instructions, ordered the Communists of Paris to end the strike, and the French Communist Party put out the slogan: "The *Front Populaire* is not the revolution." With Communist help the mass strike was damped down.

The Dual Diplomacy

Stalin's popular-front politics went along with a realignment of his diplomacy toward collective security against aggression. Soviet entry into the League of Nations in September 1934, whereby Moscow joined forces with the Versailles powers in the previously maligned league, was a turning point in this development, underpinning vigorous efforts to assist the formation of an anti-German grouping of European states.

Fear of further spread of fascism was not the only reason for Stalin's new course in diplomacy; actions on the German side influenced him as well. After consolidating his power in Germany, Hitler's initially cautious and conciliatory moves in foreign policy gave way to greater boldness. By early 1934 his anti-Soviet stance was manifested, among other ways, in German-Polish relations. During 1933 Poland's strongman, Marshal Piłsudski, signaled through informal channels a desire for an understanding with Moscow, and sounded out France and Great Britain about a preventive war against Hitler's Germany while she was still too weak for effective resistance. When it became clear that no positive response was coming, he concluded a nonaggression pact with Hitler on 26 January 1934. Although he thereupon sent his foreign minister to Moscow to convey assurances that Poland had no anti-Soviet intent, Stalin could hardly be in doubt of the new pact's anti-Soviet meaning for Hitler.[13] In March 1934 representatives of the Krupp firm traveled to Moscow to cancel a five-year contract for training Soviet technicians and supplying machinery and steel. To test the changing situation, Moscow at the end of March proposed to the Germans a joint statement on the independence of the Baltic states. The reply from Berlin in mid-April was negative. That was the month when Soviet-French negotiations for a mutual-assistance pact started in earnest.

But Stalin did not forsake his earlier orientation on a new and greater Brest—a divisive diplomacy leading to a new European war in which Moscow would remain neutral until a time of its choosing and then carve out his envisaged "socialist borderland." Evidence of this is contained in a letter of 19 July 1934 to his Politburo colleagues rejecting a plan by the editor of Bol'shevik, Adoratsky, to reprint Friedrich Engels's essay of 1890, "The Foreign Policy of Russian Tsarism," in the journal's forthcoming special issue for the twentieth anniversary of the outbreak of the World War. Engels had forecast the war on the basis of an acute analysis of the emerging division of European powers into opposed camps. He had also shown an anti-Russian bias, portraying Russian foreign policy since Catherine II's time as a never-ending search for world domination by a talented but unscrupulous cabal of foreign-born adventurers, which he called a "new Jesuit order" and a "secret society."

In his 1934 letter (first made public in Bol'shevik in May 1941), Stalin took Engels to task for explaining Russia's policy of aggrandizement more by the presence of the gang of adventurers than by the need for outlet to seas and seaports for enlarged foreign trade and strategic positions. Engels, he wrote, had exaggerated Russia's role by suggesting that war could be averted by the overthrow of tsarism, from which it would follow that a war by bourgeois Germany against tsarist Russia would be a war of liberation. What room did this leave for Lenin's policy? When war broke out in 1914, Lenin refused to support either side, seeking to turn the war between the rival imperialist camps into a series of revolutionary civil wars in the belligerent countries. In making specific reference to that position of Lenin in mid-1934, Stalin was suggesting that Moscow should adopt a position of noninvolvement in the approaching second imperialist war. But he knew that for this war to be advantageous for Moscow, it must be protracted, and for that both sides must be formidably strong.

The Soviet-French talks begun in April 1934 were accompanied by attempts to create an "Eastern Locarno"—an East European security system linking the USSR, Poland, Czechoslovakia, Finland, and the Baltic states, along with France and Germany, in mutual-assistance guarantees. These efforts foundered first on German, and then on Polish opposition. Moscow and Paris proceeded, however, to sign their bilateral pact on 2 May 1935, and a similar mutual-assistance pact was signed two weeks later between the Soviet Union and Czechoslovakia. It bound the USSR to come to the defense of Czechoslovakia in case of invasion after France did. At that time, French Foreign Minister Pierre Laval paid a visit to Moscow. The communiqué on his talks noted that Stalin expressed "full understanding and approval of the policy of state defense that France is pursuing in order to maintain her armed forces at a level appropriate to her security needs."[14] Since it had been Communist policy to withhold parliamentary support for military preparations of bourgeois governments, Stalin's statement caused a sensation. French Communists called off their campaign against the government's plan to extend the period of military service from one to two years. From Litvinov, who had read *Mein Kampf*, Stalin knew about Hitler's long-held notion of conquering France first and then turning on Russia. If Hitler were to open the coming new war, as Stalin hoped he would, by marching against France, Stalin wanted France to be militarily strong enough to keep from being overrun and speedily conquered.

A similar design informed his policy toward Britain at that stage. At the end of March 1935, following a visit to Berlin with British Foreign Secretary Sir John Simon, Sir Anthony Eden, who was then lord privy seal, paid a visit to Moscow and was the first Western statesman of high rank to have a personal interview with Stalin. After reporting to Litvinov on the talks which Simon and he had just conducted with Hitler, Eden was received in the Kremlin by Stalin, Molotov, Litvinov, and the Soviet ambassador in London, Ivan Maisky. He found Stalin well informed, quiet-spoken ("the quietest dictator I have ever known, with the exception of Dr. Salazar"), a good listener prone to doodling, a man of pragmatic temper whose personality made itself felt without effort, whose quality of mind he could not help respecting, and whose courtesy "in no way hid from us an implacable ruthlessness."[15]

Stalin got down to business by asking Eden whether he thought the present European situation "as alarming as, or more alarming than, the situation in 1913." When Eden replied that he would say "anxious" rather than "alarming," Stalin said he considered it basically worse because in 1913 there was one potential aggressor, Germany, and now there were two, Germany and Japan. He spoke of the Germans as a great and capable people with understandable resentment of the Versailles treaty. To Eden he seemed "perhaps more understanding of the German point of view than Litvinov, in the sense that he was less scrupulous and had no prejudice against the Nazis as such, which Litvinov no doubt felt for their treatment of the Jews." Stalin argued for "some scheme of pacts" to deter German aggression. Then he walked to the world map on the wall and "remarked in friendly tones upon the power and influence of so small an island as Britain." He thus made it clear that he could see positive value in the British Empire, and *a fortiori* in its preservation. And as if to warn Eden not to put credence in Hitler's anti-Bolshevism, he remarked on the "duplicity of German policy" as expressed first, in the offer of 200-million-mark credit to the Soviet government and German willingness to include some important contracts for war matériel in the bargain; and, secondly, in the spreading of a story by Germans that Deputy War Commissar Tukhachevsky had made contact with General Goering and pressed some anti-French scheme upon him.[16]

In retrospect Eden expressed puzzlement over Stalin's reference to Tukhachevsky in a pro-Nazi light. For on 31 March, while the British visitor was still in Moscow, *Pravda* published a strikingly anti-Nazi article by Tukhachevsky. It cited *Mein Kampf* on territorial conquest in Russia and its border states as the Nazis' future aim, and called Hitler's anti-Soviet posture a convenient cover for revanchist plans in the West and South. It calculated that by the summer of 1935 Germany would have an army of 849,000 men, 40 percent more than France and nearly as many as the 949,000 under arms in the Soviet Union. The article's factual tone only enhanced its alarming message, which was probably intended—with Stalin's knowledge—to underscore the argument to Eden on the need for collective security. Lest anyone overlook its significance, it was reprinted in *Izvestiia* and *Red Star* the next day. It caused a furor in the German Embassy. Count Schulenburg, who had taken Nadolny's place as ambassador, cabled a translation to Berlin and expressed his indignation that so high-ranking a personage should cite "such bogus figures for the purpose of anti-German propaganda." Behind the scenes Stalin had personally edited this article in draft, somewhat toning it down in the process.[17]

An advocate of mechanized forces in the Red Army and of tactics based on offensive operations by powerful tank formations and motorized troops, Tukhachevsky foresaw that future German military operations would be based on mechanized invasion armies. He believed that Hitler was lulling France to keep her from increasing her military forces and that he had revanchist plans in the West as well as designs on Russia. In 1936, he and Litvinov were sent to represent the USSR at the funeral of King George V in London. British military men and others in high circles were favorably impressed by the Soviet marshal, not alone for his tactful and dignified bearing and knowledge of foreign languages but also for his impressive expertise in military matters, leading *The Manchester Guardian* to comment on 1 February 1936 that "Tukhachevsky's friendly talks with a number of influential persons may be regarded as marking a new period in relations between Britain and the USSR."[18] In Paris on the way home, Tukhachevsky spoke with General Gamelin and visited military installations. Soon after returning he was promoted to first deputy defense commissar and made head of the Red Army's newly formed Administration of Combat Readiness.

In September 1936, M. Gekker, head of the Defense Commissariat Foreign Relations Department, told Wing Commander Collier of the British Embassy in Moscow that France was an unstable country and the only way to secure peace in Europe was to conclude an Anglo-Soviet alliance.[19] Voroshilov, who was host to British Major General A. P. Wavell, head of the British delegation visiting Soviet maneuvers that month, said to Wavell that Germany would start a war before long and the British should quicken their rate of preparation, "especially as regards the army." Germany, even a few years ago, might have attacked the Soviet Union with some chance of success, he went on, but now would find them ready. "When Germany realized this, she might turn instead on the less prepared France and England."[20]

By his collective-security diplomacy, in combination with his popular-front tactics in the Comintern, Stalin was assisting events to take their course toward a European war. An accord with Germany remained a basic aim because it would offer an opportunity to effect a westward advance of Soviet rule while turning Germany against the democracies in what Stalin envisaged as a replay of World War I, a protracted inconclusive struggle that would weaken both sides while neutral Russia increased her power and awaited an advantageous time for decisive intervention. But to make sure that the European war *would* be protracted, he wanted Britain and France to be militarily strong enough to withstand the onslaught that Germany under Hitler was becoming strong enough to launch against them. That explains his moves to encourage ruling elements in both these major states to rearm with dispatch, and his orders to the French Communists to support the French military buildup.[21]

Stalin's collective-security diplomacy was a calculated effort of coalition building in Europe. He earnestly sought to bring about the formation of a strong politico-military anti-German grouping based on France and Britain. But, as we shall see, *it was not a coalition in which he wanted the Soviet Union to participate when war came.*

Stalin's design seems not to have been lost on his tough-minded foreign commissar, Litvinov, who himself was an ideal instrument of the collective-security diplomacy because, as a Moscow *Westler*, he genuinely believed in it and therefore could be a persuasive advocate of it, whether in diplomatic talks or in great public gatherings such as those of the League of Nations in Geneva. In a private conversation after World War II, Jacob Suritz, who was Soviet ambassador in Berlin in the mid-1930s, told his friend Ehrenburg that he had been summoned to Moscow in 1936 for a high-level conference at which Litvinov presented his position and Stalin, after concurring, laid his hand on the other's shoulder and said, "You see, we can reach agreement," to which Litvinov replied: "Not for long."[22] The foreign commissar really meant it when he said, in the phrase that grew world famous at that time, "Peace is indivisible." But for Stalin, who was in charge of Soviet diplomacy, peace was divisible.

Hitler was practicing divisive diplomacy of his own, and doing so at Russia's expense by playing the card of anti-Bolshevism in seeking Western acquiescence in his moves to restore German power. Thus in March 1935, shortly after letting it be known that Germany had rebuilt a military air force and was reintroducing conscription with the goal of a thirty-six-division army, he received the above-mentioned visit by Simon and Eden for two days of talks during which, while obdurately defending his military moves, he denounced Soviet Russia and offered German support for Britain in exchange for the return of former German colonies.[23] Meanwhile, he publicly declared that he had no claims on France and no aggressive designs on his Western neighbors. If Hitler was thus employing anti-Bolshevism for *his* political purposes, Stalin must have reasoned, why should he not make corresponding use of antifascism for his?

His coalition building was made all the more imperative by a tendency visible in French and especially British diplomacy to seek good relations with Germany. Hitler naturally encouraged this tendency. Desiring to head off an anti-German coalition, he responded to the Franco-Soviet pact with a speech of 21 May 1935 in which he gave assurances of nonaggression to his neighbors (except Lithuania, which allegedly oppressed Germans in Memel), attacked Soviet Russia as a state ruled by a doctrine totally antithetical to Germany's National Socialism, and particularly proffered the hand of peace to France. In the following summer and fall, Laval sought a French rapprochement with Germany. In June 1935, acting on its own, the British government concluded a bilateral naval agreement with Germany, allowing the latter 35 percent of British naval strength in violation of the Versailles treaty.[24] In January 1936 the German military attaché in London hinted to General Dill of the War Office that a Russo-German rapprochement might come about if the British did not forestall it by themselves coming to an understanding with Germany.[25] That, indeed, was then becoming an objective of the British government, which decided that a cabinet committee should "investigate the possibility of a general understanding with Germany" and recommended all precautions in this connection, including nonacceptance of an invitation that Ambassador Maisky tendered to the Secretary of State for War, Duff Cooper, to pay an official visit to the Soviet government.[26]

Influential forces in France and especially in Britain were seeking to tilt official diplomacy toward an accord with Germany. Hitler found a British friend in Lord Lothian, who, after a visit to Germany, wrote in the *London Times* that the new Germany did not want war but only "real equality" and that its very devotion to race would keep it from seeking to annex other nations.[27] In June 1935 the Prince of Wales spoke in support of contact between British and German war veterans' organizations. Lothian and others wanted to turn Hitler eastward. As Sumner Welles, who became U.S. undersecretary of state in 1937, put it later: "In those prewar years, great financial and commercial interests of the Western democracies, including many in the United States, were firm in the belief that war between the Soviet Union and Hitlerite Germany could only be favorable to their interests. They maintained that Russia would necessarily be defeated, and with this defeat Communism would be destroyed; also that Germany would be so weakened as a result of the conflict that for many years thereafter she would be incapable of any real threat to the rest of the world."[28]

On 7 March 1936 Hitler took the bold and risky step of marching his forces into the demilitarized Rhineland. At that time his resurgent army was still no match for the army of France. Seeing the potentially decisive change in the power balance that would occur if Hitler's move succeeded, a worried French government considered military action but was dissuaded by London.[29] Britain's orientation on an understanding with Hitler's Germany was showing itself in British promotion of inaction at a critical moment in the drift toward war.

All this went on under watchful Moscow eyes. The Western powers were working both sides of the diplomatic street. So was Hitler. And so was Stalin. In fact, he had resumed his diplomacy of accord with Germany in advance of the developments just mentioned, and he pursued it concurrently with the coalition-building diplomacy of collective security. Aware of Hitler's inclination toward a war against France as a prelude to a *Drang nach Osten,* he could not help knowing that he held a card of great value in the current diplomatic game: the capacity to assure Germany of Soviet neutrality in event of war in the West. Stalin started probing Berlin as soon as Ambassador Schulenburg took up his Moscow post. When the ambassador presented his credentials on 3 October 1934, President Kalinin expressed hope for improved German-Soviet relations. "Too much importance should not be attached to the outcry in the press," he went on. The peoples of the two countries were "in many ways dependent upon each other," and he believed that a way would be found of restoring friendly relations.[30] In the following month the new Soviet ambassador in Berlin, Suritz, told a German foreign-office official that Soviet distrust of Germany "could only be dispelled and the atmosphere calmed on a realistic basis. . . ."[31]

On 8 May 1935, six days after the signing of the Franco-Soviet pact, Litvinov told Schulenburg that he hoped the pact would be followed by a "general pact" involving Germany. That would "lessen the significance of the Franco-Soviet Pact" and "lead to an improvement in relations with Germany, which the Soviet Government desired above all things and which they now considered possible."[32] In the late spring of 1935, Gustav Hilger, Russian-born counselor of the German Embassy in Moscow, took a trip to Kiev where the German consul gave a reception in his honor. Among the several high local functionaries who attended was one Vasilenko, chairman of the Executive Committee of the Kiev Regional Soviet. He said to Hilger that recently some workers had told him they could not understand the current party line toward Germany, which was only trying to free herself from the Versailles shackles. Instead of helping her, the Soviet government was making a pact with Germany's oppressors. "In short," Vasilenko went on, "Litvinov's policy does not convince the masses, and history will soon pass over Litvinov. How absurd of Soviet Russia to ally herself with a 'degenerate' state like France! Peace would be secure only through friendship with Germany. Who cares about the racial concepts of National Socialism?"[33] An experienced Russian hand like Hilger could not but know that such statements by a Soviet official would hardly be coming from the "masses."

The Soviet trade mission in Berlin, offering a channel of communication apart from Litvinov's Narkomindel, played a key role in Stalin's German diplomacy. Between 1935 and 1937 it was headed by a Georgian, David Kandelaki, who let it be known that he was in direct contact with Stalin and enjoyed his confidence. Soon after Kandelaki's arrival at the Berlin post, trade talks that had dragged on since mid-1934 came to favorable fruition in a new agreement signed by him and Reich Minister of Economics Hjalmar Schacht on 9 April 1935. The agreement stipulated that Moscow would pay off half of its outstanding 200-million-mark credit in gold and foreign exchange, the other half in goods, and would place additional orders to the extent of 200 million marks with German industrial firms on the basis of a new five-year credit from a German banking consortium.[34]

Matters took a new turn when Schacht, in June 1935—the month in which Germany concluded the naval agreement with Britain—raised the possibility of increasing the volume of Soviet-German trade with a 500-million-mark credit extended for a ten-year period. Kandelaki took this news to Moscow, where Stalin put a political interpretation upon it. "Well, now, how can Hitler make war on us when he has granted us such loans? It's impossible," he reportedly said at a Politburo meeting.[35] On returning to Berlin, Kandelaki called on Schacht on 15 July to deliver the reply. Just beforehand his authority was enhanced, and the importance attached to his activity underlined, by a decree awarding him the Order of Lenin for "outstanding merits, energetic efforts, and initiative in the foreign-trade field."[36] Kandelaki told Schacht that he had spoken with Stalin, Molotov, and Foreign Trade Commissar Rosengolts. They had approved the substance of the new conversations, but wanted further arrangements postponed pending completion of the trade program already under way. Then, as Schacht reported it, "after some embarrassment, M. Kandelaki expressed the hope that it might also be possible to improve German-Russian political relations." Schacht told him that on such matters the Soviet government must approach the Foreign Ministry through its ambassador.[37]

Undeterred, Stalin persisted in his overtures. It was indicated to the Germans that such known adversaries of theirs as Litvinov and Tukhachevsky would constitute no obstacle to an accord. At the end of October 1935 the departing counselor of the German Embassy, von Twardowski, was surprised when Tukhachevsky (unquestioningly acting on orders emanating from Stalin) appeared among others at a farewell reception for him. He and the German military attaché, General Koestring, had an hour's talk during which the marshal professed great respect for the German army and declared that, although he was a good Communist and a soldier who knew nothing about politics, he hoped that Germany and the Soviet Union would come together again. Twardowski's report on the conversation noted that after Voroshilov, Tukhachevsky was regarded as the most influential man in the Red Army "and is in general reputed to be pro-French."[38] At a dinner on the eve of the 7 November holiday shortly afterward, Litvinov raised his glass to the German ambassador and drank "to the rebirth of our friendship."[39]

Then, as if to follow up on Schacht's suggestion, overtures were made through the Soviet Embassy in Berlin. On 2 December 1935, Embassy Counselor Sergei Bessonov told a German Foreign Ministry official that efforts should be made to achieve a *détente* in Soviet-German relations, and agreed that expanded economic relations could serve as a starter. A week later, he called on von Twardowski and solicited his opinion on how German-Soviet relations could be improved.[40] Ambassador Suritz pursued the same theme when von Twardowski paid a courtesy call on him at that time. He asked: what could be done to improve German-Soviet relations, what effect would a strengthening of economic relations have on the political situation, were more active cultural relations possible, and should he intensify his social activities in Berlin? Suritz also stressed that Litvinov should not be regarded as an opponent of German-Soviet relations.[41] On 20 December Bessonov went to the German Foreign Ministry, expressed optimism about the trade negotiations, and broached to the official with whom he was speaking the idea of a bilateral Soviet-German nonaggression pact, something that he said had already been discussed in a private German-Soviet conversation at the beginning of 1935.[42] Between late November and early December, similar Soviet soundings were made through the German Embassy in Moscow and in Tiflis, where the German consul general was approached by the Narkomindel's man in Georgia, Georgi Astakhov.[43]

Stalin's probes drew no positive response. For Hitler they were premature. Improved German-Soviet relations, not to mention a nonaggression pact, were ruled out by his need to exploit anti-Bolshevism while strengthening Germany's position, as he did with the reoccupation of the Rhineland, which opened the way for his subsequent moves to annex Austria and vanquish Czechoslovakia. Only with those objectives accomplished would he be ready for war in the West, and not until then would he be responsive to overtures from the East. Stalin undoubtedly took this into account. His probes did, however, signal that Moscow would be ready when Berlin was.

Lest there be any doubt of this, Stalin made his position public via Molotov. Interviewed by a French journalist on the Soviet response to the German reoccupation of the Rhineland, the Soviet premier replied as follows to a question whether there were any tendencies in the Soviet Union toward a rapprochement with Germany: "There is a tendency among certain sections of the Soviet public towards an attitude of thoroughgoing irreconcilability to the present rulers of Germany, particularly because of the ever repeated hostile speeches of German leaders against the Soviet Union. But the chief tendency, and the one determining the Soviet Government's policy, thinks an improvement in Soviet-German relations possible."[44]

Counterintervention in Spain

In Spain, where society was sharply polarized between rich and poor, the electoral success of the Popular Front aroused social unrest and, in July 1936, led to the Morocco-based generals' revolt under Francisco Franco. The ensuing three-year Civil War in turn ignited widespread social revolution.

The generals' revolt might have been quelled in fairly short order but for two circumstances. First, Italy, Germany, and Portugal supplied the insurgents with munitions and fighting men. Second, the Republic, sorely lacking in arms, expert military leadership and organization, received no corresponding flow of aid from abroad. In Paris, Premier Blum was unable to respond positively to the Republic's appeal for arms because the British would not support it, and the French cabinet was itself divided on the matter. So, in hopes of restraining the intervention of fascist governments, he proposed a general nonintervention policy aimed at bringing the fighting to a stop for lack of arms.[45] An official Nonintervention Committee was set up in London. Germany and Italy joined, but their continuing aid to the insurgents rendered the nonintervention policy ineffectual.

The situation urgently called for Soviet response. The Spain of the Popular Front was a prime example of the type of "bourgeois democracy" that Stalin's new Comintern tactics were designed to support. The country's takeover by the generals, with German and Italian aid, would gravely weaken France as the anchor-state of what remained of nonfascist Europe, and would strengthen the tendency of small European states, already reinforced by Hitler's unopposed reoccupation of the Rhineland, to seek accommodation with Germany. In addition to all else, Hitler's respect for Stalin's Russia as a serious power would hardly be enhanced if she stood passively by while Germany and Italy were seeing to the destruction of republican Spain.

Stalin had to act. He knew that his response must not antagonize France and Britain, but rather encourage them to give military aid to Loyalist Spain. Initially, therefore, the response did not go beyond a clamor in the Soviet press against the fascist-supported Franco revolt and strong support for the nonintervention policy, plus public donations for food and medical supplies to the Republic. As it became clear that Italy, Germany, and Portugal would not abide by the nonintervention formula and that the insurgent forces were winning, Stalin decided to intervene. He called a special Politburo meeting at the end of August 1936 and proposed a plan for "cautious intervention" in the Spanish Civil War. Two days later Krivitsky, in Holland, received orders by special courier to mobilize all available agents and resources for buying arms and sending them to Spain. Anxious to avoid direct entanglement in the war, Stalin passed the order down to all Soviet personnel involved to "Stay out of range of the artillery fire!"[46]

The covert operation, rapidly organized, got planes, other arms, and fighting men to hard-pressed Loyalist Spain by mid-October 1936, just in time to stave off the fall of Madrid to the insurgents. Spain's gold reserve, in 7,800 boxes, with a total value of $518 million,[47] was shipped to Russia to finance the Soviet aid effort. Some 500 foreign Communists resident in

Russia were sent to Spain to form the nucleus of the volunteer International Brigade, whose ranks eventually numbered between 30,000 and 50,000, with Frenchmen, Germans, Italians, Poles, Americans, Englishmen, Belgians and men from the Balkans represented.[48] The brigade's leader, Emil Kleber, billed as a naturalized Canadian soldier of fortune, was a Bukovina-born Soviet citizen named Stern who had worked in military intelligence and as an instructor in Comintern military schools.[49]

Stalin sent Marcel Rosenberg to Spain as the Soviet ambassador, but placed a Polish-born Soviet ex-military man, Arthur Stashevsky, nominally the trade envoy in Barcelona, in charge of the whole Spanish operation. All Comintern activities were controlled by the NKVD, whose chief representative in Spain was Nikolski, alias Schwed, alias Lyova, alias Orlov.[50] Soviet military personnel sent to Spain, including pilots and tank officers who saw combat, numbered between 500 and 600 and were commanded by General Yan Berzin, formerly chief of Red Army military intelligence. Moscow derived its dominant influence in Spanish republican affairs not from the numbers of men directly involved but from being the chief military supplier and using the Spanish Communist Party as its agent.[51]

In mid-October 1936 Stalin cabled greetings to the head of the Spanish Communist Party, José Díaz, saying that the working people of Soviet Russia were only doing their duty by rendering what aid they could to Spain's "revolutionary masses." Social revolution was, indeed, afoot in the Loyalist zone of the war-divided land, especially in Catalonia where the Anarcho-Syndicalists and a dissident Communist party called the Partido Obrero de Unificación Marxista were quite influential. "The war and the revolution are inseparable," ran their slogan, expressing the idea that revolutionary measures such as worker control of production would best inspire the people to fight and win the war. This clashed with Stalin's political purposes, which were linked with his diplomacy of coalition building in Western Europe.

His desire to keep Popular-Front Spain "bourgeois" was expressed in a letter that he, Molotov, and Voroshilov dispatched on 21 December 1936 to Premier Largo Caballero advising that the peasants' economic interests be favored, that the petty and middle bourgeoisie be protected from confiscation, that representatives of nonleftist republican parties be attracted to the government's side, and that no encroachment on foreigners' property interests be tolerated in Spain.[52] Hence the line prescribed by Moscow for the Spanish Communists was: "We can't talk of revolution until we've won the war."[53] But given the exigencies of his diplomacy, a clear-cut victory in the war was hardly Stalin's aim. His concern, rather, was to prevent or, failing that, to delay the Republic's defeat.[54]

The Mask of Antifascism

It was characteristic of Stalin to find multiple uses in a single line of action. So, now, he made his international antifascist stance serve the needs of his purge politics at home. He did so, in part, by fabricating criminal connections between the alleged conspirators and Nazi Germany. The NKVD interrogators were given the task of compelling Zinoviev, Kamenev, and other defendants to confess that their conspiracy had threads leading to the Gestapo, hence was a Trotskyist-*fascist* one.

What Stalin stood to gain from this is plain. There would necessarily be a din of publicity from the first and later treason trials of famous revolutionaries, and the fall of many a Bolshevik grandee could not be hidden from public knowledge. If the terror could be given an appearance of antifascist political prophylaxis by tarring its most prominent victims and by implication myriad others with the brush of fascism, the shock effect upon opinion, including influential liberal and leftist opinion abroad, would be softened.

In line with these tactics, Stalin set about presenting his regime as the democratic, humanistic, culture-prizing antithesis of a fascist one. At the birth time of the Popular Front, he encouraged his cultural spokesmen at the 1934 Writers' Congress to identify the Soviet Union with humanism and the defense of culture against Nazi barbarism. Soviet representatives and foreign Communists emphasized these same themes at the Communist-backed International Writers' Congress for the Defense of Culture, which was held in Paris in June 1935.

Such celebrities as Gide, Heinrich Mann, André Malraux, and Aldous Huxley were in attendance. The Soviet delegation, shepherded by Stalin's rising party protégé Alexander Shcherbakov, included Ehrenburg, who was one of the organizers, Alexei Tolstoy, Mikhail Kol'tsov, Vladimir Kirshon, and others. So, while books were being purged from libraries in Russia, Soviet writers joined their foreign colleagues in proclaiming the need to preserve the cultural heritage. While people were disappearing into prisons and concentration camps in the quiet terror going on under the guise of the checkup of party documents, emissaries from Moscow were contrasting the "socialist humanism" of the Soviet Union with state terrorism in Nazi Germany. And while Kandelaki and others were secretly sounding out the Nazi chiefs about a political deal, leading lights of Soviet literature were denouncing fascism in Paris. As individuals they may not have been more than dimly aware of the parts they were playing in this obfuscation.

Stalin's main expedient for camouflaging the terror operation was his

constitutional undertaking. Soon after he initiated the idea of democratizing changes in February 1935, a constitutional commission was set up
under his chairmanship. It met in July and formed twelve subcommissions,
two of which were chaired by Stalin: general constitutional questions and
the drafting subcommission.[55] Proposals were submitted, and in mid-April
1936 a draft prepared by Ia. A. Iakovlev, A. I. Stetsky, and B. M. Tal' of
Stalin's drafting subcommission was discussed in four days of conferences
with him and Molotov. Stalin wanted clause one to describe the Soviet
Union as a "socialist state of workers and peasants" rather than simply "a
state of free laborers of town and country" (thereby emphasizing that
socialism really was built). In line with his populist politics, he added two
clauses. One permitted some small-scale individual peasants (then still
numbering about a million) and craftsmen to ply their trade; the other
guaranteed the right of personal property in earnings, savings, housing
space, garden plots, and personal items, and the right to inherit such
property.[56] On the other hand, he excluded proposed clauses on the right
of legislative initiative and freedom of scientific experiment.[57] At the end
of April, Stalin, other Politburo members, Vyshinsky, Litvinov, and Bukharin met as the drafting subcommission to finish the work. The resulting
draft was reviewed by the full constitutional commission and Politburo on
15 May, approved by a plenum of the party Central Committee at the
beginning of June, and published on 12 June 1936 for nationwide discussion.

In his interview with Roy Howard in March 1936, Stalin had stated
that the new constitution would be "the most democratic of all the consti-
tutions in the world." Under it the suffrage would be universal, direct,
secret, and equal. Candidates would be nominated not only by the Communist Party but also by all sorts of nonparty public organizations, and a
lively electoral struggle would be "a whip in the people's hands against
poorly functioning government organs."[58] As soon as the draft was published, the press christened it "Stalin Constitution" and made much of its
being the "most democratic." The nationwide discussion gave a new theme
to the leader cult, enunciated by Radek: "The architect of socialist society
has become the builder of socialist democracy."[59] When the Congress of
Soviets met on 25 November to enact the new charter, *Pravda* featured on
its front page a sketch of the constitution giver towering over the Soviet
land like a colossus.

Under the previous constitution, adopted in 1924, those elected to
each tier of soviets elected those at the next higher tier, from the village
tier at the bottom to the town, region, and republic soviets in the middle,
and to the USSR Congress of Soviets at the apex. The proportionality
arrangements favored worker over peasant votes (on a ratio of one to five),

and there was no provision for the secret ballot (so ill-wishers would have to show their hand). Such "soviet democracy" was officially considered higher than "bourgeois" parliamentary democracy because of its open proletarian class character. From that classical Bolshevik standpoint, universal, direct, equal, and secret suffrage was retrograde and, sure enough, Trotsky flayed the innovation from abroad. In its formal institutional structure the Stalin state could no longer properly be called "soviet"; it was no longer the regime of a proletarian dictatorship. "The new constitution abolishes the soviets by dissolving the workers in the general mass of the population," he wrote, with the aim of replacing the "decayed" regime of soviets with *"Bonapartism on a plebiscitarian foundation."* Plebiscitarianism, he added acidly, had evolved a long way from Napoleon III to Goebbels' recent techniques.[60]

So Trotsky. But in Russia, Stalin's constitutional initiative seems to have evoked hopes if not the "real happiness" that according to Louis Fischer pervaded the land upon its announcement in 1935.[61] Such hopes were harbored also by some in higher circles. With his constitutional initiative, and by enlisting the help of Bukharin, Radek, and others in the drafting process, Stalin apparently managed, at least initially, to convince people that he seriously meant to take some humanizing, democratizing measures now that the danger from Hitler's Germany was becoming more and more manifest. When the distinguished French writer Romain Rolland visited Russia in 1935, Gorky spoke to him about the coming new constitution with great optimism.[62]

Analysis of the final text, however, would have raised doubt about the credibility of Stalin's forecast of a lively electoral struggle with, presumably, competing candidates for the Supreme Soviet (as the Congress of Soviets was renamed) and with the people flogging malfunctioning government organs. Article 126 made the single-party monopoly a constitutional feature of the polity for the first time by stipulating that the Communist Party was "the guiding nucleus of all the working people's organizations, both public and state." This brought into the state's constitution the provision of the party's bylaws giving the party cell of every state or public institution the right of control over that institution's administration. Candidates nominated by, say, a Soviet plant or collective farm or hospital would thus have to have the party cell's approval, and the cell was bound by the party bylaws to obey directives from higher party authorities. The latter would hence be the ones to decide whether there should be one or more candidates for election to the Supreme Soviet in any particular district and who they should be.

The clauses on civil rights, presumably drafted by Bukharin's subcommission, attracted keen attention. Article 125, a constitutional innovation, guaranteed the freedoms of speech, press, assembly, and street marches and demonstrations, but only "in accordance with the interests of the working people and for purposes of strengthening the socialist system," and this qualification was not only heavily stressed by the Central Committee's journal *Bol'shevik* but construed to mean that the aim of Article 125 was to "further strengthen the dictatorship of the working class."[63] Other nominal guarantees were correspondingly hedged. Article 112, which would have been Vyshinsky's contribution, stated that "Judges are independent and subordinate only to the law." But the courts being state institutions, judges were constitutionally obligated to follow directives from appropriate party organs. Similarly, the inviolability of person guaranteed by Article 127, and the rule therein that no one could be arrested save by court order or procurator's sanction, were conditional upon the preceding article on the party's pervasive control.

All of this notwithstanding, Stalin succeeded, by the mobilizing efforts of tens of thousands of party cells throughout the land, in enlisting masses of people in organized discussion of the constitution. Between the draft's publication on 12 June and adoption in slightly altered form on 5 December 1936, nearly 40 million citizens attended a total of 458,441 meetings in plants, collective farms, and other organizations to discuss the document, making 83,571 suggestions for change, and 3,471,864 persons participated in 164,893 plenary meetings of local soviets and their bodies, with a harvest of 40,619 suggested changes.[64] When he addressed the Congress of Soviets on 25 November, Stalin dismissed some proposed changes as inappropriate on the grounds that they were historical in character or had to do with current legislative concerns rather than constitutional ones. He dismissed others either as merely semantic or as mistaken. On the ground, for example, that the intelligentsia was not a "class" but only a "stratum," he rejected a proposal to amend Article One (which defined the Soviet Union as a two-class "socialist state of workers and peasants") by adding the intelligentsia as the third class. He accepted proposals for creating a Commissariat of the Defense Industry, for direct elections not only to the Supreme Soviet's Council of the Union, as the draft provided, but also for its Council of Nationalities, and some others of like or lesser consequence.[65]

In the midst of the nationwide constitutional discussion, on 26 May 1936, the government published a draft of new family legislation for "broad discussion." It provided for the outlawing of abortion save when childbirth would endanger the mother's life or health, state allowances for mothers of many children (to those having seven children, an annual allowance of 2,000 rubles for five years for each subsequent child, and to those having eleven children a bonus of 5,000 rubles on the birth of each subsequent child and an annual allowance of 3,000 rubles for four years); an expanded network of maternity homes, nurseries and kindergartens; and made divorces more costly. This moved far toward the family policies of Nazi Germany and Fascist Italy.[66] Because people's deep concerns were affected and the constitutional discussion atmosphere offered encouragement, a great outpouring of letters to the newspapers followed. Since the housing shortage was still dire for the vast majority in the towns and contraceptives were unavailable or unreliable, very many were critical of the proposed outlawing of abortion. "A categorical prohibiton of abortion will confront young people with a dilemma: either complete sexual abstinence or the risk of jeopardizing their studies and disrupting their life," wrote a married engineer with a five-year old son. "Very often it is the lack of living quarters that is the reason behind an abortion," wrote a student signing herself K. B. "If the bill included a clause assuring a room for married couples expecting a baby, it would be a different matter." Writing in refutation of K. B., a student in the Institute of Red Professors, G. F., objected that "she approaches the problem of childbearing as though it were a private matter." A collective farm woman thought that a nursing mother who became pregnant should be allowed an abortion. Another such woman, the mother of five, suggested that state allowances should begin as early as for the fifth child, "for it is no easy job to rear a family of five."[67]

More than the constitutional discussion, this one had a democratic flavor: the issue was important and opinions were expressed on both sides. The government's handling of the discussion was, however, another matter. The small selection of letters published in *Pravda* and *Izvestiia*, for example, out of the huge flood received by both papers, was weighted on the side of the antiabortionist "ayes," which also received strong editorial support. The published letters approving the draft law were largely from the peasant population, and some were signed by officials, whereas the published "nayes" were mainly from white collar employees, students, and workers. But when Louis Fischer's wife went around to the editorial offices of Moscow newspapers and was allowed to look at the files of incoming letters, she found so few being received in support of the new law that the editors were printing all of those while their desks were piled with hundreds of letters opposed to the law, and not only from college girls, ballerinas, factory workers, and housewives but even from illiterate peasant mothers who dictated their opinions to school children.[68]

The discussion was allowed to continue for just one month, after which, on 27 June 1936, the family legislation was enacted by decree in the form proposed, with only one minor change (the family allowances went into effect after the sixth and tenth child rather than after the seventh and eleventh). The people had lost an important freedom brought by the

Revolution, and any intelligent person could see how little the official talk about growing socialist democracy meant. Many people were heard expressing indignation in private, and many women denied relief from unwanted pregnancies reportedly committed suicide. Maurice Hindus, who was in Tiflis when the law was enacted, found that birthcontrol literature, which remained legal, suddenly disappeared from bookshops and newsstands. When an incensed Louis Fischer vehemently attacked the new law in conversation with Health Commissar G. N. Kaminsky, the latter said simply: "The Boss says we must have more children."[69]

Meanwhile, the draft new constitution was being lauded as a "constitution of socialist humanism." In support of this claim the press pointed to the clauses guaranteeing the rights to work, leisure, education, medical treatment, old-age assistance, and equality of sexes. There was also a clause on equality of all citizens irrespective of race and nationality, which was cited to contrast englightened Soviet practice with that of the fascist states. Yet, nationalism was finding an echo in official writings that extolled the Great Russians as a nation. "Russian culture," said a *Pravda* editorial, played a huge part in the development of the numerous peoples liberated by the October Revolution. "And Russian workers, Russian working people, can only take pride in the fact that the honor fell to them to help the working people of other nationalities become truly free members of the socialist commonwealth of peoples of the USSR."[70]

This editorial appeared just a few days after the publication (on 27 January 1936) of Stalin's critical comments, cosigned by Zhdanov and Kirov, on draft outlines of new history texts, the document that inaugurated the Stalin school of nationalism in Russian history writing. Almost immediately the Stalin school announced its Great Russian chauvinism with a scathing attack on *Izvestiia* editor Bukharin for having taken an unpatriotic view of the Russian people in an article for the anniversary of Lenin's death on 21 January 1936. Bukharin credited Lenin with designing, and Stalin with bringing into existence, a new highly organized society of bold, energetic, and remarkably fast-working Stakhanovites, which was a world apart from the only semi-integrated old Russia notorious for its slovenly disorganization, Asiatism, and laziness, whose most universal characteristic was its Oblomovism, and which was, in fact, "a *nation* of Oblomovs." Some days later an *Izvestiia* editorial said the Russian people were first among equals in the Soviet Union and had fraternal relations with non-Russian Soviet peoples for whom, in the past, the very word "Russian" connoted the gendarme, the priest, and the greedy merchant and was a byword for policies that brought starvation, illness, extinction, and decline of national cultures.[71]

Pravda upbraided Bukharin's "rotten conception" of old Russia as a "nation of Oblomovs." How could such a nation have produced the most revolutionary class of the world proletariat in the Russian workers and its most revolutionary party in the Bolsheviks? How could it have produced such giants as Pushkin and Lermontov, Lomonosov and Mendeleev, Belinsky and Chernyshevsky, Herzen and Dobroliubov, Tolstoy and Gorky, Sechenov and Pavlov? Where was the "Russian revolutionary sweep" that Stalin had designated as the heart of Bolshevik style in work, and the Leninism which Stalin had found to be "the highest achievement of *Russian culture?*" Nor had the word "Russian," as *Izvestiia*'s editorial said, connoted simply the gendarme, the priest, and so on, to Azerbaijanis, Georgians, Armenian, and other workers who fought side by side with Russian workers for revolution.[72]

It may well have been this article, along with the Stalin-Zhdanov-Kirov critical comments on history outlines, that prompted Nazi Foreign Office officials to question Andrei Smirnov, a member of the Soviet Embassy in Berlin, about the meaning of the rising nationalistic trend in Russia.[73] It was a worried interest, for it was not good news to the Nazi officials that a country regarded as a future enemy was adopting an outlook so potent as they knew from Nazi experience that extreme nationalism could be. As 1936 unfolded, the Russian nationalism grew still more pronounced.

What most of all gave the lie to Stalin's pose of antifascism was the developing terror. In the peroration of his address of 25 November, he declared that "the new Soviet Constitution will be an act of indictment against fascism saying that socialism and democracy are invincible. The new Soviet Constitution will be a moral aid and real lift for all those now waging the fight against fascist barbarism." By that time, the purge was entering upon its climacteric phase and Stalin's regime was surreptitiously becoming, like German fascism, a terroristic dictatorship headed by a *Fuehrer*. Still earlier, a whole vast region of the country, from the Urals east across Siberia and from the Far North to the Karaganda coal mines in Kazakhstan, had become a world of repression dotted with concentration camps, political isolators, and exile colonies. The Yugoslav Communist Anton Ciliga, who was deported from the USSR at the end of 1935, gave the *Bulletin of the Opposition* a picture of it based on his experience. He spoke of Leningraders being shipped into Siberia by the trainload after Kirov's murder; of Yugoslav and Hungarian Communists as well as very many Old Bolsheviks seen in various isolators; of sentences of political offenders being automatically extended on completion; of peasant women inmates of the camps being forced to serve men sexually in a system of semiregulated prostitution, and so on.[74]

A subsequent issue of this journal carried an open letter to Gide by the Belgian-born writer and revolutionary Victor Serge, who was let out of Russia in April 1936, after three years of prison and exile, by the personal intercession of Romain Rolland with Stalin and after leading French writers pressed the case—despite Soviet opposition—at the Paris Writers' Congress in 1935.[75] He touched on the mass exiling of Leningraders in early 1935; the arrests of many thousands of long-time Communists taking place; the concentration camps filling up; the minute regimenting of literature from above; the existence of a literary mandarinate, thoroughly organized, living well, and docile, while eminent men of culture like the historian of Russian social thought Ivanov-Razumnik, the symbolist poet Vladimir Piast, the authority on Italian Fascism German Sandomirsky, the initiator of the first Soviet encyclopedia Novomirsky, the historian of the Civil War Anyshev, the literary historians Gorbachev, Lelevich, and Vardin, the Leningrad agronomist Dingelshtedt, and the sociologist Yakovin were in prisons or camps. "We're fighting fascism," Serge concluded. "But how do we fight fascism with so many concentration camps in our rear?"[76]

Bukharin, it seems, had taken an active part in Stalin's constitutional initiative in the hope that the democratic principles enunciated in the new constitution, however hedged in practice, would sketch a possible perspective for Soviet political development at a time when conditions—notably the need for an antifascist foreign policy course in company with Europe's democracies—favored it. He had not completely surrendered this hope when, in February 1936, on a Politburo decision taken at Stalin's initiative,[77] he went to Paris as head of a three-man delegation to negotiate with the German Social Democrats for Soviet purchase of parts of the Marx-Engels archives that were spirited out of Germany when Hitler took over. The Russian Menshevik Boris I. Nicolaevsky, who was instrumental in shipping the documents out of Berlin and was their caretaker in Paris, had repeated talks with Bukharin during his stay abroad, as did Nicolaevsky's Menshevik colleague Fedor Dan.

As Izvestiia's editor, Bukharin had asked his old friend Ehrenburg to be the paper's regular Paris correspondent, and the two met often during Bukharin's stay there. "I don't know," Ehrenburg much later recalled him saying, "perhaps it's a trap."[78] His foreboding was sound: Stalin would use his Paris talks with the Mensheviks against him in his coming trial. In conversation with the Menshevik contacts, Bukharin was very pessimistic at times, saying "He'll finish us all off," "He's Satan," and "We're all doomed."[79] Yet, his fear for the worst seems to have been tempered by some hope against hope that the worst was avoidable. The hope was linked with the new constitution, of which he spoke with Nicolaevsky at length, mentioning that the idea of elections with competing candidates had come up in the constitutional commission. He saw policies inspired by "humanism" as necessary antidotes to fascism, something he was constantly studying in theoretical pamphlets on fascism picked up during his one-day stopover in Berlin en route to Paris.

Soon after his return to Moscow at the end of April 1936, it must have become clear to Bukharin that his hope had been illusory and his worst fears realistic. Figures released in March on the checkup of party documents showed that at least 300,000 expulsions had resulted, and now the exchange of party cards was under way. Even editorials on the new constitution were sounding an ominous note, as when *Bol'shevik* wrote in one: "It must not be thought that the verification and exchange of party documents have wholly purged the party of enemies. Conspiratorial accursed enemies are still lurking in the party, not all two-faced people have been exposed."[80] Given Bukharin's continuing access to higher circles through his work on the constitutional commission, his post as *Izvestiia* editor, his Central Committee status, Kremlin apartment and many friends, he may have got wind of the coming trial and heard that soundings were being made in Berlin with a view to a Soviet-Nazi accord.

He saw now with stark clarity that Stalin was a master of deceit who was making use of the public discussion of the "most democratic" constitution as a smokescreen for moves to transform the Soviet regime into something approximating a fascist one. He opened his own two-part article on the just published draft constitution by indicating that what he meant by fascism was a "terroristic dictatorship."[81] Soon after, he made an audacious attempt to inform his readers of what was happening in Russia. Since it was impossible to do it openly, he drew upon the mastery of Aesopian language that he, like some other revolutionaries, acquired under the old regime. He wrote an editorial article entitled "Routes of History," with a subtitle ("Thoughts Aloud") that alerted the knowing reader, by its very unusualness in the Soviet press, to expect something especially significant. It appeared in *Izvestiia* on 6 July 1936 and was Bukharin's last signed article.

Starting with lavish praise of the Stalin Constitution, it argued that "real history" had not proceeded in our time along the routes previously predicted. Certain "false prophets" (by subtle allusion Stalin was indicated to have been foremost among them) had failed to foresee that fascism would emerge as the greatest international problem. It is a "paradox of history," the article went on, that though the masses are regarded by the fascist ideologues as *Untermenschen,* the rulers in order to retain control must deceive the people by creating an illusion of being with and for the masses. In actuality, whereas socialism raises the mass, enriches the content of personality, and elevates the intellectual functions, fascism "creates a depersonalized mass, with blind discipline, with a cult of Jesuitical obedience, with suppression of the intellectual functions." Thus deception is the essence of fascism: "An intricate network of decorative deceit (in words and deeds) is the extraordinarily essential characteristic of fascist regimes of all kinds and complexions." And while the deceitful fascist elite allows that the people own the means of production only "spiritually," for its own part it means to own "cannon," "airplanes," and "lands in the east of Europe" not in a "spiritual" sense only, but materially. But this deception must sooner or later come to light: "Its perpetrators have it in mind to gain for themselves an historical respite by sending everything into the yawning abyss of war. However, this is a game of winner take all in which they will lose everything."

This essay in anti-Stalinist Aesopian communication may be deciphered as follows: Do not take the Stalin Constitution and its democratic phraseology seriously. It is only a decorative facade of political deceit behind which Stalin is moving to create, by means of a huge blood purge, a new Soviet regime of fascist complexion that will be a denial of the Marxist ideals of the Bolshevik Revolution. It will be a totally despotic regime based on police terror and suppression of the intelligentsia ("intellectual functions"). Stalin is seeking by these means to pave the way for an alliance with the German fascists, which will precipitate a second world war in which he expects to remain at least temporarily uninvolved while we build cannon and airplanes and assimilate East European territories that we will occupy under the deal. But the whole plan will lead only to disaster.

Why Bukharin thought Stalin's plan would lead to disaster was explained shortly after in another *Izvestiia* editorial, which was unsigned but bore indications (for example, the characteristic touch of quoting from Shelley's "Masque of Anarchy") of Bukharin's authorship. "It would be unforgivable blindness," it said, "not to see that it is the land of Soviets that attracts the most savage hatred of the unbridled adventurists." It was folly, in other words, to suppose that Hitler could be deflected for long from attacking the USSR. The article also made an emotional appeal to the British ruling circles to take a firm stand against the Nazis. Picturing Lords Lothian, Londonderry, and others as fawning on Hitler, it recalled the war dead of 1914–18 and asked: "How are the sons of England sleeping in Flanders fields?" Entitled "War and Peace," this editorial appeared on 1 August. Later that month the trial began, and with it denunciations of Bukharin.[82]

The End of Maxim Gorky

Gorky died in June 1936. Since it would have been out of the question to get his endorsement of the condemnation of his friend Kamenev and other Old Bolsheviks soon to appear in the dock, and yet his public silence would be intensely embarrassing at such a moment, his death came at a highly opportune time for Stalin.

Kirov's murder had been a shattering emotional blow to Gorky, who said just that in a letter to the writer Konstantin Fedin, adding: "I very greatly loved and respected that man."[83] Gorky was in the Crimea for his health when the murder occurred. Late in the night of 1 December 1934, a car containing armed guards came rumbling up the road to the house where Gorky and his entourage were staying. They were amazed by this. Since his life was not in need of protecting, the thought could not fail to occur: "The Boss may be protecting not him from someone, but himself from him. God forbid that the old man should take it into his head to do something strange, such as going off somewhere or making a public statement that the Boss would not like him to make."[84]

Back in Moscow later, Gorky's situation grew tense. One one occasion, the distinguished elder writer, M. Prishvin, called on him at his home on Povarskaya Street and was denied entry by his secretary, Kriuchkov, whom many considered an agent of Yagoda's. Prishvin pushed his way past Kriuchkov and entered Gorky's study. Informed of what had just happened, Gorky said: "Why, don't you realize that I'm under house arrest?"[85] Still, he continued to take an active interest in three journals he had founded (*The Collective Farmer, Our Achievements,* and *The USSR in Construction*). But his movements were restricted, on the doctors' pretext of his poor health, to his home in Moscow, his country place nearby, and occasional trips to the Crimea. Because of this, he was avid for news and read *Pravda*. But the copy of *Pravda* that came to him was one especially made up for him, in which reports of arrests were replaced by news about the crab catch and the like.[86]

He needed a warm winter climate because of his lung condition. He reportedly sought and failed to get a visa to go to Sorrento for the winter of 1935–36. Just before leaving for the Crimea instead, he complained to Ilya Shkapa, a Soviet journalist friend who served as his assistant for the journal *Our Achievements,* that he was terribly tired and felt surrounded: "Hemmed in. . . . Neither backward nor forward. . . . I'm not used to this kind of thing."[87] He traveled to the Crimea. One who was with him on that trip, and who was an acquaintance of the writer Galina Serebriakova, later told her something about it. The door of Gorky's room was kept locked at night, on the doctors' orders, to prevent him from going out and catching cold. But once Gorky outwitted the doctors. He crawled out of his window at midnight and went into the garden. Serebriakova's source witnessed the following scene. Gorky looked up at the sky. Then he walked to a tree, clasped its branches in his arms, and stood there weeping.[88]

He returned to Moscow on 27 May 1936, and turned his attention to some uncompleted writing. On 1 June he came down with influenza. On 6 June the Soviet press started to print daily bulletins on his health—something normally done when a fatal outcome was beyond doubt. On 8 June Stalin, Voroshilov, and Molotov paid him a visit. Later he scribbled sentences on one subject and another. When no longer able to write, he spoke his last words: "End of novel, end of hero, end of author."[89] Death came on 18 June, just two months before the Zinoviev-Kamenev trial opened.

The official medical bulletin said that he died of cardiac arrest arising from a chronic lung ailment. Among its seven signatories were two prominent physicians from the Kremlin hospital, Lev Levin and Dimitry Pletnev. In the show trial of March 1938, they testified that on Yagoda's orders, and as part of an anti-state plot of which Bukharin and Rykov were ringleaders, they had caused Gorky's death by deliberate malpractice (administering overly strong doses of properly indicated medicines). Dr. Levin received the death penalty. Dr. Pletnev received a twenty-five-year sentence as an accessory to the crime, but was shot in 1941. Both have been officially exonerated of the charges to which they pleaded guilty.

Exactly how Gorky died remains a subject of speculation. Published eyewitness reports by persons who attended him in his final days indicate that he died a natural death, yet in commenting on these reports the keeper of the Gorky archive in Moscow's Gorky Institute of World Literature wrote that it would be premature to say that the case has been conclusively clarified.[90] And Shkapa, speaking by phone in October 1988 at the age of over ninety, declared: "I am convinced that Gorky was murdered by Stalin, just as Bukharin, Krestinsky, and others were."[91]

Before he died, Gorky sent an urgent message to his French Communist writer friend, Louis Aragon, asking him to come to Moscow; he had something important to convey to him.[92] Aragon arrived in Moscow on 15 June 1936, but was unable to see his friend during the ensuing last three days of Gorky's life. What the intended message, or missive, may have been is indicated by the report that a secret diary was found by the group of writers who were sent to go through Gorky's literary archives after he died. Those present hurriedly glanced through the document in fascinated silence.

It began by noting that someone had calculated that if a miserable flea were magnified so many thousandfold, the resulting creature would be the world's most awful beast, beyond human control. Sometimes monstrous grimaces of history produced those things in reality: Stalin was such a superflea, magnified to unbelievable proportions by party propaganda and hypnotic fear.

The leader of the writers' group, editor of *Our Achievements* Vasily

Bobryshev, phoned the NKVD, whose representatives quickly appeared and took the document away. Those present were made to sign pledges not to reveal what they had read. Although Gorky had made known to the Soviet government his desire that his three journals be maintained after his death, with editorial staffs unchanged, they were closed within two weeks after his death and their staff members, along with others in Gorky's entourage, were arrested.[93] Yagoda, on reading the story about the flea that swelled into an uncontrollable monster, responded with a curse and a Russian proverb: "No matter how well you feed a wolf, he keeps looking back toward the woods."[94]

Gorky was buried with full honors as befitted the country's premier man of letters, and his great friendship with Stalin entered into Soviet legend.

15

THE FORGING OF
AUTOCRACY I

Old Bolsheviks on Trial

B Y MID-SUMMER 1936, the preparations for the treason trial were
nearly complete. When the leading figures had been brought by
relentless inhuman pressures to the point of final capitulation to
Stalin's demands, Zinoviev stipulated that the promise to spare
their and others' lives be made to them by Stalin in person, and Kamenev
insisted that this be done in the Politburo's presence. These terms were
accepted.

When the two men were taken to the Kremlin in the company of
G. A. Molchanov, head of the NKVD Secret Political Department, the
Politburo materialized in the form of what Stalin described as its "commission," consisting of himself, Voroshilov, and Yezhov, who was not yet a
Politburo member. Stalin was deaf to Zinoviev's anguished argument that
the planned trial would besmirch not only the accused men but the party
itself. But when, at the end, Stalin said, "We don't want to shed the blood

of Old Bolsheviks, no matter how grave were their past sins against the party," the two broken ex-triumvirs exchanged glances and Kamenev said that they would proceed on condition that none of the Old Bolsheviks scheduled for trial would be executed, that their families would not be harmed, and that no other former oppositionists would be put to death. "That goes without saying," Stalin responded. The police leaders, Yagoda included, were much relieved when word spread among them afterward that there would be no executions.[1]

Once they had given their consent, the leading defendants found their daily regime transformed into something resembling that of a sanatorium. The final trial preparations included a rehearsal under the direction of Vyshinsky, who would serve as the prosecutor. The spectacle about to be performed would not be a trial with elements of a show, but a show with elements of a trial.

Because the preparations had gone on in secret, special steps were taken to prepare the country for the impending event. The closed circular letter of 29 July gave local party officials advance notice and particulars. Then a suitable public atmosphere was created. On 15 August came the announcement that in 1936 the NKVD had uncovered a Trotskyist-Zinovievist plot to murder Stalin and other leaders and that the plotters had killed Kirov. The case would be heard by the Supreme Court's Military Collegium in open judicial session starting 19 August. "Enemies of the People Caught Red-Handed" was the headline of *Pravda*'s editorial on the day of the announcement. It treated the monstrous conspiracy as a fact and the charges as true and even knew what the punishment must be: there was "only one penalty" for such crimes. The next day's editorial said that the checkup and exchange of party documents had shown that vigilance was lacking in many places: "We have in the party not a few liberals playing at democracy when what's called for is a revolutionary's iron hand." By then the press was reporting mass meetings in institutions across the land, at which people were condemning the "foul agents of bestial fascism."

The proceedings opened at mid-day of 19 August. The venue was not the Hall of Columns on the ground floor of the House of Unions, where the Shakhty trial was staged, but the smaller upstairs October Hall. Its ornamented walls once rang with the music of balls for the nobility and it offered accommodation for not more than about 350 spectators. This afforded excuse for excluding not only families of the accused but also party and government leaders, many of whom were personally known to the defendants. The audience consisted mainly of lower-level NKVD employees in civilian clothes who were rotated session by session, and various higher police officers in uniform.[2] Foreign correspondents and representatives of foreign embassies attended. A recessed gallery up above the scene at the rear, where orchestras once played, offered space for another spectator behind dark windows covered by thin gauze, and the puffs of pipe smoke visible from time to time behind the gauze gave indication that this spectator was Stalin.[3] By special arrangement the proceedings were also transmitted by wire to his Kremlin study. He was in Moscow during the trial and surely would have attended on occasion.[4] It was, after all, his own production.

At the front of the hall, on a raised platform, sat the three judges—Ulrikh and his associates Matulevich and Nikitchenko—and the other performers. On the audience's left were Prosecutor Vyshinsky and his secretary, and opposite Vyshinsky, behind a low balustrade, sat the sixteen defendants flanked by NKVD guards with fixed bayonets. Behind the defendants was a door to a passageway leading to several rooms, in one of which Yagoda and others monitored the performance as transmitted by wire.[5]

The prominent Old Bolsheviks among the defendants were Zinoviev and Kamenev; G. E. Yevdokimov, an ex-Zinovievist who once headed the Leningrad Soviet and had been a Central Committee member; I. F. Bakaev, an ex-Zinovievist who played a notable part in the Civil War and headed the Leningrad Cheka; I. N. Smirnov, an ex-Trotskyist who led the Fifth Army that defeated Kolchak and then was in charge of party work in Siberia; S. V. Mrachkovsky, an ex-Trotskyist Civil War hero; and ex-Trotskyist V. A. Ter-Vaganian, a party intellectual and founder of the monthly *Under the Banner of Marxism*. Two defendants, E. S. Holzman and E. A. Dreitzer, were minor Bolshevik figures with past oppositionist ties. Several were to serve as state's witnesses in defendant guise: Valentin Olberg, an NKVD operative experienced in German affairs; Richard Pickel, who had once headed Zinoviev's secretariat; Isak Reingold, a one-time acquaintance of Kamenev's who had recently headed the Cotton Syndicate. The pseudodefendants also included three Soviet citizens who had worked for the NKVD in the German Communist Party apparatus: I. I. Fritz David (Ilya Krugliansky), Alexander Emel (Moissei Lurye), and K. B. Berman-Yurin. Then there was Dr. Nathan Lurye, an obscure person with involvement in German affairs. Two other principals were Trotsky and his son Lev Sedov, who were being tried *in absentia*—Trotsky as the archconspirator. The *New York Times* correspondent covering the trial noted in his first day's dispatch that while the distinguished-looking white-haired Kamenev seemed his usual self, the once stout Zinoviev looked thin, haggard, crushed, and apathetic.[6]

The proceedings went on for six days. From the indictment, the testimony, Vyshinsky's summing-up, the last statements, and the judges' verdict, the following sequence of events was concocted.[7] In the fall of

1932, pursuant to instructions by Trotsky from abroad, an underground Trotskyist organization in Russia joined forces with an underground Zinovievist organization to form a conspiratorial "united center" consisting of Smirnov, Mrachkovsky, and Ter-Vaganian for the Trotskyists and Zinoviev, Kamenev, Yvdokimov, and Bakaev for the Zinovievists; its goal was the seizure of power. Since the Soviet Union was advancing to socialism with signal success under Stalin's inspired leadership, the conspirators could not count on popular support, hence adopted terrorist methods to displace him and other Soviet leaders by murder. They were also motivated by hate and malice against Stalin because his policies were bringing the country out of its difficulties.

The terrorist design began in March 1932 when Trotsky appealed in an open letter—a copy of which was found between the double walls of Holzman's suitcase—for Stalin's removal, meaning his murder. Trotsky led the conspiracy from Norway, Zinoviev and Kamenev acted as ringleaders (despite being in exile in 1932–33 and under arrest in 1935–36), and Smirnov (who was in prison from 1 January 1933) communicated with his outside Trotskyist contacts by code. The center intended to do away with the direct perpetrators of terrorist acts and other police accessories so as to cover up the traces of the crimes.

With the help of an offshoot, the underground Nikolaev-Kotolynov terrorist group in Leningrad, the center brought off the murder of Kirov. No other terrorist attempts succeeded although many were planned and prepared. In the fall of 1932, acting on instructions from Smirnov, Holzman met Sedov in Berlin and then Sedov and Trotsky in Copenhagen's Hotel Bristol, where Trotsky said it was necessary to murder ("remove") Stalin. Bakaev, Reingold, and Dreitzer failed twice in plans to assassinate Stalin in 1934. In 1935 Berman-Yurin and Fritz David intended to kill Stalin at the Seventh Comintern Congress but failed—the former because he could not gain entry and the latter because, although admitted and with a Browning pistol on him, he was seated too far from Stalin to be able to shoot him. Olberg was prevented by his own arrest from carrying out Trotsky's orders, conveyed by Sedov, to kill Stalin in Moscow on May Day of 1936. Nathan Lurye was unable to fulfill his assignment to kill Kaganovich and Ordzhonikidze when they visited Cheliabinsk. Then he failed to shoot Zhdanov during the May Day parade in Leningrad in 1936 because he was too far way in the line of marchers. Voroshilov, Kosior, and Postyshev were also objects of assassination plans that failed.

The Gestapo, Nazi Germany's secret police, rendered practical assistance to the conspirators, for example by providing Olberg with a false Honduran passport and by giving assurance that all persons involved in preparing and committing terrorist acts would be given refuge in Germany.

A German fascist named Franz Weitz, representing SS chief Himmler, organized the group headed by Trotsky's agent Moissei Lurye, which was sent into the Soviet Union to murder Stalin and others. When Lurye queried Zinoviev about the conspirators' connections with the Gestapo, the latter justified an alliance with the Nazis for anti-Soviet purposes by recalling that Lassalle wanted to use Bismarck in the interests of German revolution.

The principal defendants were presented as monsters of duplicity. Zinoviev wrote to the Central Committee in May 1933, when preparations for terrorist acts were in full swing, pleading for reinstatement in the party and vowing loyalty to it. He and Kamenev published articles in *Pravda* renouncing past sins and pledging future support. During 1934 Kamenev revealed his real political philosophy by calling Machiavelli a "master of political aphorism and a brilliant dialectician" in a preface to a Russian edition of *The Prince,* published by the Academia Publishing House, of which he was then head. After the terrorist center organized the murder of Kirov, Zinoviev's perfidy went to such lengths that he sent to *Pravda* an obituary letter mourning the "extinguished beacon," and after Bakaev and Yevdokimov were arrested he wrote a letter to Yagoda asking to be summoned so as to establish that he, Zinoviev, had nothing to do with the murder. At their trial in January 1935 Zinoviev denied that anything like a Zinovievist center had existed after 1926–27, and Kamenev said: "I lived to the age of fifty and did not see this center in which, it turns out, I myself was active," and "I was not opposed to talking. I talked."

In summing up for the prosecution, Vyshinsky said it was one of the most striking cases in history when the word "mask" acquired its real meaning. Machiavelli was nothing but "a puppy and a yokel" compared to the double-dealers in the dock. "Liars and clowns, insignificant pigmies, little dogs snarling at an elephant, that is what this gang represents!" There were no words for the perfidy, duplicity, sacrilege, and cunning of Zinoviev's act in writing an obituary for Kirov with hands stained with Kirov's blood. The diatribe rose to a concluding crescendo of vehemence in Vyshinsky's shouted words: "I demand that the mad dogs be shot—every one of them!" Outside the October Hall the masses were said to be seething with indignation, and the daily editorials were typified by *Pravda*'s "Crush the Loathsome Creatures!" "The People's Wrath is Mighty and Terrible," "Trotsky-Zinoviev-Kamenev-Gestapo," and "The Mad Dogs Must be Shot!" Zaslavsky's reportage from the courtroom was a venomous invective against the accused, and Demyan Bedny contributed a poem, "No Mercy!," which combined the title theme with glorification of the accuser:

> WE PROTECTED STALIN.
> WE CANNOT BUT PROTECT HIM!
> WE GUARD HIM AS OUR HEAD
> AS OUR OWN HEART!

We caught a snake, and not just one.
Zinoviev! Kamenev! On the first bench!
Yours the honor of being the first to
Touch your lips to the cup of death![8]

In their last pleas the accused (with the exception of Smirnov who, as in earlier testimony, contested the charges concerning his activity after his arrest) outdid one another in confessions of guilt. "I depart as a traitor to my party, as a traitor who should be shot," said Mrachkovsky. "The difference between us and the fascists is very much in our disfavor," said Yevdokimov. Reingold, echoing Vyshinsky's conclusion, said the defendants should be shot "like mad dogs." Pickel said the accused were "nothing more nor less than a detachment of international fascism." Kamenev, after pleading guilty to serving fascism and counterrevolution, concluded his statement movingly (to those present, for the published summary of the proceedings omitted this part) by addressing his three sons, one a Red Army aviator, and saying that they should devote their lives to Stalin's cause. He hailed Stalin as the great leader who had made the dream of socialism a reality, collapsed, and was helped from the room by a guard.[9] Zinoviev's last plea dwelt on the conspirators' affinity with fascism: "My defective Bolshevism became transformed into anti-Bolshevism, and through Trotskyism I arrived at fascism. Trotskyism is a variety of fascism, and Zinovievism is a variety of Trotskyism."

Yet curiously, as Denny noted (and the published proceedings did not), Ulrikh twice during the trial interrupted to stop defendants' attacks on Nazi leaders.[10] Stalin evidently wanted to brand the accused as fascistlike and hence to portray the trial and the mass terror it heralded as an antifascist undertaking, but to do this without unduly ruffling the highplaced men in Berlin with whom he was continuing to deal and hoped to reach an accord. If those men were paying close attention to the Moscow events, they would have noted that eleven of the sixteen men on trial were Jews[11] (or thirteen of eighteen if we include Trotsky and Sedov). More than that, they would have perceived that in the three leading accused—Trotsky, Zinoviev and Kamenev—Stalin was prosecuting those who most epitomized what Nazis, in a book on *Bolshevism and the Jews,* called the "Jewish element in the leadership of Bolshevism."[12]

After the judges retired to deliberate, the prisoners had to wait more than seven hours before the court reconvened late at night to pronounce death sentence on them all. The next morning, 25 August, the press announced that the sixteen were executed after the Presidium of the USSR Central Executive Committee rejected pleas for clemency made by fifteen of them (Holzman was not listed among those filing pleas). *Pravda*'s editorial said that millions of working people were starting their working day with the joyful feeling that a loathsome creature had been crushed.

The reference to pleas for clemency, implying a modification of the 1 December 1934 law excluding them in terrorist cases, is additional evidence that a deal had been struck—the defendants' lives in return for their performances in the show trial.[13] With the exception of the recalcitrant Smirnov, they had fulfilled their part of the bargain; Stalin had broken his.

From a juridical point of view, the six-day spectacle in the October Hall was a mockery of a trial. The only evidence offered, save for the confessions of the accused, was Olberg's forged Honduran passport, and no witnesses were produced save Smirnov's wife Safonova, herself in NKVD custody on charges of involvement in the conspiracy. So clumsy were the NKVD fabricators of events that Copenhagen's only Hotel Bristol, where Holzman testified that he had received terrorist orders from Trotsky and Sedov in 1932, proved to have been razed in 1917; and Trotsky was able to furnish documentary proof to the Dewey Commission, which met in Mexico in early 1937, that his son Sedov was not in Denmark in 1932.[14] The master-plan document for terrorism, Trotsky's 1932 letter calling for Stalin's "removal" by murder, was nothing other than the "Open Letter" of March 1932 (printed in the *Bulletin of the Opposition*), in which Trotsky replied to the Moscow decree of the previous month, depriving him and his family of Soviet citizenship, with a political tract that accused Stalin of leading the party and country into a blind alley and concluded by saying: "It is necessary, finally, to carry out Lenin's last, insistent counsel: *remove Stalin.*" As the *Bulletin* observed in late 1936, this made Lenin "the first terrorist." Yet the equation "removal = murder" was the foundation of the whole affair. The reality behind it all was that in the fall of 1932, when Russia was in deep crisis due to Stalin's misguided project of an economic October, talk of his removal from power was rife among party members, including some of those who had just been condemned.

But however flimsy the trial was juridically, it met Stalin's needs: first, for an event that would smash once and for all the taboo on physical annihilation of Old Bolsheviks of once high standing and thereby open the way for his intended transformation of the elite by terror, and second, for the visitation of terrible punishment upon the many who had incurred his murderous enmity by all manner of word and deed, however inconsequential, which impugned the idealized Stalin. And while the trial *qua* trial was a farce, as it was correctly called by the knowledgeable Norwegian minister in Moscow in conversation with his American colleague at the time,[15] there were those abroad who, for various reasons, were taken in. The former Moscow correspondent Walter Duranty wrote from Paris, "It is inconceivable that a public trial of such men would be held unless the authorities had full proofs of their guilt,"[16] and the English jurist D. N. Pritt, who attended the trial, entitled his article for the *News Chronicle*

"The Moscow Trial Was a Fair Trial." *Pravda* promptly reproduced the headline in bold letters.

For Stalin, the execution of Zinoviev and Kamenev, in violation of his promise to spare their lives, represented the final measure of vindictive triumph over loathsome enemies. He not only humiliated, exploited, and destroyed them, but he caused them to die knowing they had publicly abased and besmirched themselves and very many others, taken on the guilt for *his* murder of Kirov, *his* supreme duplicity, and *his* terrorist conspiracy against the party-state. They had confessed to representing a variety of fascism when he was introducing just that in Russia by, among other things, this very pseudo-trial; and they wound up groveling at their murderer's feet and glorifying him—*all for nothing but to serve his purposes.*

Years after Stalin's death, Anastas Mikoyan reportedly gave oral testimony that Stalin sent Voroshilov to the Lubianka to observe the execution and confirm the deaths. After carrying out this assignment, he reported (though it may be doubted that he reported these particulars to Stalin) that, as they faced their executioners, Zinoviev shouted, "This is a fascist coup!" Kamenev said: "Stop it Grisha. Be quiet. Let's die with dignity." The last words were Zinoviev's: "No! This is exactly what Mussolini did. He killed all his Socialist Party comrades when he seized power in Italy. Before my death I must state plainly that what has happened in our country is a fascist coup."[17]

Next Steps

Although it went down as the "trial of the sixteen," this first show trial implicated many more people than those in the dock plus Trotsky and his son. Not only did the defendants name as accomplices various persons who were convicted along with Zinoviev and Kamenev in the January 1935 trial but did not appear as defendants now. Their testimony also— unquestionably because Stalin so decreed—implicated various other prominent Bolshevik politicians in ties with the "center," including Radek, Piatakov, Rykov, Tomsky, Bukharin, Uglanov, Shliapnikov, Lominadze, Okudzhava, Serebriakov, Sokolnikov, Riutin, Slepkov, Sten, Shatskin, and Putna. Especially ominous in the hint it gave of far-reaching purge plans was the mention of the ex-Rightist leaders and of Putna, a military leader. Reingold testified that Zinoviev and Kamenev "found common ground" with Tomsky and Rykov in 1932 while liaison with Bukharin was maintained by Karev, a Zinovievist linked with Eismont's and Slepkov's "terrorist groups." Kamenev testified: "We counted on the Rightist group of Rykov, Bukharin, and Tomsky," and said that the center, in case of its coming to grief, designated Radek, Sokolnikov, and Serebriakov as a "reserve group" for terrorist activity. Zinoviev testified: "Tomsky expressed complete solidarity with us." Dreitzer testified that Corps Commander Vitovit Putna, Soviet military attaché in London, was "one of the active participants in the terrorist work." In August Putna was recalled from London and arrested. The suggestion of high-level military involvement was further indicated by the arrests of Division Commander Dimitry Schmidt in Kiev in July, of Corps Commander Vitaly Primakov, deputy commander of the Leningrad military district, soon after the August trial, and of two high-ranking officers in the Ukraine.

In its special issue on the August 1936 trial, the *Bulletin of the Opposition* counted a total of 139 incriminated individuals, including those on trial, and pointed out that, with a few exceptions, they were the best-known representatives of Bolshevism. Five (Kamenev, Rykov, Tomsky, Trotsky, and Zinoviev) were, along with Lenin and Stalin, the seven full members of Lenin's Politburo of 1923, and Bukharin was then a candidate member. Eighteen had been or (in the cases of Bukharin and Rykov) were now Central Committee members. Most striking, the list of miscreants included five of the six men mentioned by Lenin in his testament-letter as potential successors to the leadership (Trotsky, Zinoviev, Kamenev, Bukharin, and Piatakov), leaving only Stalin both alive and in good standing.[18] Except for lesser Bolsheviks and pseudodefendants, those accused of treason or of connections with the traitors constituted an Old Bolshevik Who's Who, soon to become a Who Was Who, lending weight to the *Bulletin*'s characterization of the Moscow proceedings as a "trial of October."

At the close of the evening session of 21 August, Vyshinsky stated that he had ordered an investigation of testimony implicating Tomsky, Bukharin, Rykov, Uglanov, Radek, and Piatakov in criminal activities, and that Sokolnikov and Serebriakov, about whose counterrevolutionary crimes the authorities had evidence, were to be prosecuted. The next day Tomsky committed suicide. His son Yuri, who survived the Stalin era, years later reported that his father shot himself after Stalin came to his home with a bottle of wine and the two men closeted themselves in the study for a talk that ended with Tomsky ordering Stalin to leave, showering him with curses, and calling him a murderer as Stalin stalked out in a rage, the bottle still under his arm.[19] Further history of Soviet Russia, and of Europe and the whole world would have changed in many ways, for the better, if Tomsky had shot his visitor instead of or along with himself. But to solve great state problems by killing a leader was as alien to Tomsky's Marxist and Bolshevik political culture as it was to that of Zinoviev, Kamenev, Trotsky, and others.[20] The only notable Old Bolshevik capable of "individual terror" as a political act was Stalin.

He faced a dilemma now. He intended the first trial to be the starting point for a transformation of the regime through terror and not simply what his police chiefs and other higher-ups thought it would be, namely, a final settling of accounts with a group of old oppositionists, after which Soviet life and policy would resume their normal course. The trial served his purposes by implicating many who were not yet under arrest and whom it would be premature to arrest because his power position, although immensely formidable now, was not yet so impregnable that he could strike out indiscriminately at all those marked down in his mind for destruction. So it was possible that various persons whom the trial had placed on notice might, by suicide, foil his further purge-trial plans. It was very likely with this concern in mind that he went to Tomsky to offer reassurance and perhaps, in doing so, to solicit some helpful action, perhaps an article condemning those on trial. Such a desire to reassure would explain why Bukharin's name still appeared on *Izvestiia*'s masthead as editor-in-chief even as it published damning trial testimony about him, and why Radek, Preobrazhensky, Piatakov, Rakovsky, and other noted ex-oppositionists still at large were allowed (or encouraged, with a hint that it would fortify their positions) to publish philippics against the "mad dogs."[21] These articles were, moreover, of use to Stalin as endorsement by famous revolutionaries of charges that were hard for many to believe. Later they were treated as examples of dastardly duplicity.

Rykov was on the point of committing suicide after Tomsky did but was dissuaded by family members, who later bitterly regretted their action.[22] Stalin thereupon took special care to keep Bukharin alive, while he remained at liberty, by periodic injections of hope. Having been on vacation in the Pamir mountains of Central Asia during the Moscow trial, and having read about it in local papers, Bukharin flew back to Moscow half expecting to be arrested on arrival. Instead, he was met by his young wife, Anna Larina, with their chauffeur-driven car and taken to their Kremlin apartment. Bukharin immediately sought a meeting with Stalin, only to learn that after the trial he departed for a holiday at Sochi on the Black Sea.[23] However, some reassurance came when the press, on 10 September, published a statement by Vyshinsky's office that investigation of testimony about Bukharin and Rykov (no mention was made of Tomsky, whom the official suicide report had accused of complicity in criminal activity) had established "no justification in law" for proceedings against them and therefore the case was closed. Very likely Stalin ordered Vyshinsky to put out this statement as a means of persuading the two prospective leading defendants in a future purge trial not to elude their roles by suicide.[24] He made another such gesture when Bukharin, using the pass issued to him as

Izvestiia's editor, appeared in Red Square for the annual parade on 7 November 1936 and took a place with his wife on a side-stand—only to have a guard approach him, salute, and say: "Comrade Bukharin, Comrade Stalin asks me to inform you that you are in the wrong place. Would you please proceed to the stand above the Tomb?"[25] That was where Stalin and the other top leaders stood.

In fright because no exonerating mention was made of him in the statement of 10 September, Radek appealed to Bukharin the following evening to intercede for him with Stalin. He wanted Stalin himself, and not Yagoda, to deal with his case, and for Stalin to be reminded of the loyalty that he, Radek, showed in 1929 when, without opening Trotsky's letter brought to Moscow by Bliumkin, he sent it to Stalin via Yagoda. A few days later Radek was arrested. As he was being led away, he called out to his daughter: "Whatever may be said about me, don't believe it."[26] After his arrest Bukharin conveyed his message to Stalin in a letter that ended, however, with the phrase: "But who knows him anyhow?"[27]

Great as it was by now, Stalin's power was not yet unlimited. The Central Committee elected by the Seventeenth Congress was still in being and formally in supreme authority. Most of the party leaders whom Stalin intended to eliminate were not only at liberty but in influential posts in Moscow and the provinces. Above all, neither of the two great organizations for violence, the political police and the military, was yet under his absolute control. In the wake of the August trial, he concentrated on the police, first of all by replacing Yagoda with Yezhov.

Between these two there was an important distinction. Although by no means a renowned old revolutionary, Yagoda had party credentials going back, it seems, to 1907 and was, with his colleagues in the NKVD leadership, representative of a cohort of old Chekists who, whatever their lack of squeamishness, were mostly Old Bolshevik members of the generation destined in Stalin's mind to go under.[28] He had cooperated, however reluctantly, in the machinations leading to Kirov's murder and presided over the NKVD during the preparation of the August trial.

How zealously he sought to gratify the emerging dictator is shown by an initiative he took in January 1935 to toughen the regime of ex-"kulak" deportees in distant places by keeping them there after their three- or five-year terms of exile expired. Under an edict of 27 May 1934 (adopted in the spirit of internal *détente*), kulaks who had been deported to labor colonies for five years, or three years if for work in gold or platinum mines, were to have their civil rights restored afterward, provided that local OGPU representatives certified that they had worked conscientiously and loyally served the regime. Now, on 17 January 1935, Yagoda sent Stalin a memorandum on NKVD stationery saying that many whose civil rights were being restored on expiration of their terms were being allowed by local authorities to leave these "unpopulated areas," to the detriment of their development. He proposed that the 1934 edict be amended by a clause specifying that restoration of rights not include the right to leave the place of forced resettlement. On 25 May 1935 Stalin made and initialed a hand-written notation in the margin by this proposal: "Right" *(pravil'no)*. On that very day a corresponding edict of the Central Executive Committee was issued over the signatures of Kalinin and Yenukidze.[29]

Yagoda had served Stalin well. On the other hand, he had past ties with the Rightist leaders and was privy to some of Stalin's darkest deeds. He was a Jew (figuring in the above-mentioned Nazi book on *Bolshevism and the Jews*), and his replacement by a non-Jew would be further evidence for the Germans that the Stalin regime was reducing its Jewish component. Finally, the political play producer undoubtedly could already cast Ya-goda, in his mind's eye, in a spectacular future trial role as a confessor of villainies that he, Stalin, would have felt driven to expunge from his own mental record.

The man to lead the police in all-out terror could only be Stalin himself. But as formal head of the NKVD he needed someone who would function unquestioningly, automatically, as transmitter of his orders and executor of his wishes. Ideally this man should be someone of intelligence, experience, and total servility, a political nobody who could take on the appearance of a somebody without ever seeking, much less acquiring, the reality of it. Such a person was Nikolai I. Yezhov. Born in Petersburg in 1895, orphaned early, he had begun factory work at the age of fourteen, joined the party in 1917 or 1918, served in the Civil War and then in local party work in Kazakhstan. He became deputy commissar of agriculture in 1929–30 before joining the Central Committee staff. Diminutive in stature (just five feet tall), he impressed others as an ordinary person and not a cruel one, "But from the moment he first met Stalin, he fell completely under the total unconditional, almost hypnotic influence of the general secretary."[30] Groomed by his recent experience of deputy chief and chief of Party Control Commission for the job of assistant purger-in-chief, he was just the man to be the figurehead chief of the NKVD now. It is a measure of Stalin's guile and the general lack of understanding of the realities at the summit of power that the approaching time of total terror, which was wholly Stalin's doing, would go down in the public mind as the *Yezhovshchina*, "Yezhov's rule."

From Sochi, on 25 September 1936, came a telegram addressed to Kaganovich, Molotov, and other Politburo members. It said: "We consider it absolutely necessary and urgent that Comrade Yezhov be appointed to the post of people's commissar of internal affairs. Yagoda has definitely shown himself clearly incapable of exposing the Trotskyist-Zinovievist bloc. The OGPU is four years behind in this matter."[31] Although the telegram carried Zhdanov's signature along with Stalin's, Zhdanov was probably asked to sign so as to obscure somewhat that Stalin was acting on his own. The criticism of Yagoda and the mention of the police being "four years behind" were the telltale signs of Stalin's authorship, indicating that his time of trouble four years earlier remained an obsessive memory.

The Politburo recipients obeyed with alacrity. Government edicts appointing Yezhov commissar of internal affairs and Yagoda commissar of communications (concerned with posts, telegraph, and telephone) were issued the next day and published 27 September. Shortly afterward, one of Yagoda's NKVD deputies, G. E. Prokofiev, was appointed his first deputy in the new job. Yezhov did not immediately clear out the Yagoda-era police leadership. Thus L. M. Zakovsky, Stalin's brother-in-law S. L. Redens, and A. A. Slutsky were kept on, the latter because he was chief of the NKVD's Foreign Department and his hasty removal would have encouraged defection by NKVD officers stationed abroad.[32] Molchanov, however, was soon replaced as head of the Secret Political Department by M. P. Frinovsky, a Stalin favorite who had previously commanded the frontier troops; and by the beginning of 1937 Molchanov was under arrest. So was Yagoda's chief of construction of the White Sea canal, Firin, who had been shown in a Nazi publication, Streicher's *Stürmer,* as one of a group of "Jewish Bolshevik plutocrats."[33]

The main initial move, however, in the Stalin-Yezhov takeover of the NKVD was to assign three hundred men from the Central Committee's (that is, Stalin's) special purge apparatus as assistants (in effect apprentices) to Moscow and provincial NKVD chiefs, whom they subsequently replaced in early 1937. These men constituted, in Krivitsky's words, "a parallel OGPU, responsible only to Stalin personally."[34] They differed from the old Chekists in that they lacked significant Bolshevik pasts, and were more readily willing to conduct the interrogations under torture— which became, according to Khrushchev, standard practice in 1937.[35] When, following Yagoda's replacement by Yezhov, Molchanov called a special meeting of leading NKVD officials to meet their new chief in his capacity as commissar, Yezhov reportedly finished his speech to them by saying: "Comrade Stalin is the first Chekist."[36] If so, he never made a truer statement.

Conquest of the military presented a far more formidable problem, and Stalin needed Yezhov in place at the head of the NKVD partly to serve him in a systematic effort to solve it.

The Antimilitary Conspiracy

There were many reasons why Stalin was driven to crush the existing military establishment, no matter what the resulting damage to Soviet military strength, morale, and preparedness.

Those in the high command who looked to Tukhachevsky as their leader were men now in their early to mid-forties who, whatever their lack in some cases of Old Bolshevik credentials (Tukhachevsky was a junior officer of the Imperial army in World War I) belonged to the Bolshevik Civil War generation. They had memories of serving under War Commissar Trotsky, strong ties of sympathy with the Kirov-Kuibyshev-Ordzhonikidze group in the later leadership, and a history of protest against the way in which the collectivization drive was conducted.[37] They were loyal Soviet soldiers but, especially in Tukhachevsky's case, men of independent mind and character who defended their viewpoints in high councils. Apart from the fact that three of them—Yakir, Gamarnik, and Feldmann—were Jews, this cohort of Bolshevik military professionals was strongly anti-Nazi in spite of its respect for German military prowess, and Stalin knew that it could not easily stomach the kind of accord with Hitler that he contemplated. Further, he had a burning resentment against Tukhachevsky over the debacle (for which he himself was heavily responsible) in the Soviet-Polish war of 1920,[38] and in his pride of being a military genius he no doubt credited himself with the capacity to provide the strategic guidance that a military purge would cost the Soviet Union. Finally, the Tukhachevsky command along with the military establishment that looked to it for leadership was, by its very existence, an obstacle to the totally autocratic new state that Stalin was forging.[39] As such it could even become a threat to him in the course of the radical new phase of terror getting started in the summer and fall months of 1936.

Although Putna's incrimination in the Zinoviev-Kamenev trial and the arrests of Primakov and Schmidt were bad portents for the high command, Stalin let it alone for the time being. He also took some steps to calm the minds of military men as much as possible. On 17 August, two days before the trial opened, the Soviet press featured prominently a government decree awarding orders of merit to 1,500 military men—an unprecedented number to be honored in this way all at once. And in the wake of the trial, Yakir, unaware of ominous doings in the Liubianka that involved him, headed a Red Army delegation sent to observe military maneuvers in France. Meanwhile, in deep secrecy, Stalin prepared the great military purge. Characteristically, he conspired against the military establishment by fabricating a Tukhachevsky-led conspiracy against the Soviet state. The name he gave to the fabricated conspiracy was: "Anti-Soviet Trotskyist Military Organization in the Red Army."

In the summer of 1936, before formally taking over the NKVD, Yezhov went to work under Stalin's minute supervision to bring a "military-Trotskyist organization" into being in the Red Army. Over at the Liubianka he directed and took part in the interrogation of prisoners with the aim of forcing them to give false testimony that various top military leaders and some lesser ones were participants in the nonexistent organization. Methods of pressure and torture ("impermissible methods") were used. Among those thus victimized were several defendants-to-be in the second major show trial, coming in early 1937, including E. A. Dreitzer, S. V. Mrachkovsky, and I. I. Reingold. Primakov, arrested on 14 August 1936, and Putna, whose arrest followed on 20 August, were of special use for Stalin's conspiratorial purposes since, unlike most of the other military notables, they had supported the Left opposition in the 1920s.[40]

The same barbaric methods were used on them as well. Putna, who at first only admitted that he had taken part in the Left opposition in 1926–27 and renounced it thereafter, was brought to testify on 31 August that there had been various "centers" of the "Trotskyist-Zinovievist bloc" and that he, along with Primakov, had taken part in a Trotskyist military organization. Primakov proved harder to break. For a long time he kept sending statements to Stalin protesting his innocence. But there was a limit to even this very brave man's capacity to withstand the treatment inflicted on him in Moscow's dreaded Lefortovo prison. Finally, on 8 May 1937 he wrote a statement to Yezhov confessing that for nine long months he had held out against admitting his participation in the Trotskyist counterrevolutionary organization and that he had been so "insolent" as to go on denying guilt "at the Politburo before Comrade Stalin." Stalin, the statement went on, said "Primakov is a coward, to claim innocence in an affair of this kind is cowardice." It really was cowardice on my part, the statement said further, and false shame for having been deceitful. "I hereby state that after returning from Japan in 1930 I got in touch with Dreitzer and Schmidt and via Dreitzer and Putna with Mrachkovsky, and started Trotskyist work about which I will provide full testimony." From this document, found in Stalin's personal archive, the Soviet inquest learned that Stalin not only directed Yezhov's work of fabrication but personally participated by putting pressure on Primakov, who then, in his interrogation of 14 May 1937, named Yakir as a co-conspirator and said "The Trotskyist organization thought Yakir the one must suited to take the post of people's commissar in place of Voroshilov."[41]

Further evidence of the important place allotted to Yakir in the fabricated military conspiracy comes from the treatment of Division Commander Schmidt following his arrest on 5 July 1936. This bluff ex-cavalryman, a Civil War hero who fought at Tsaritsyn when Stalin was in charge there, incurred Stalin's enmity during the Fifteenth Party Congress in 1927, before which Schmidt supported the Left opposition. When he chanced to encounter Stalin in the Kremlin grounds, he accosted him with rude military language and, motioning with a hand toward his saber, threat-ened to lop off Stalin's ears.[42] Later he received command of a special tank brigade in the Kiev military district. Ion E. Yakir, the Kiev district com-mander, was a famed military leader, an intimate associate of Tukhachev-sky, a general so highly respected in Berlin that he was known there as the "Soviet Moltke." Schmidt's arrest aroused concern among his fellow offi-cers in the Kiev district, and Yakir, deeply troubled, went to Moscow to intercede with Stalin, but he got no farther than Yezhov. The latter bran-dished documents purportedly containing proof that Schmidt was guilty of having—as Vyshinsky charged during the August trial—plotted to kill Defense Commissar Voroshilov while the commissar was observing ma-neuvers in the Kiev District.[43]

Yakir was, however, given an audience with Schmidt and another of the high officers recently arrested in the Ukraine, B. Kuzmichev. He found Schmidt emaciated, apathetic looking, sluggish of speech, and with the appearance, as he later told his family, of a "man from Mars." Neverthe-less, in Yakir's presence, Schmidt retracted his confession to plotting Voroshilov's murder. He put this retraction in writing although the police forbade him to add any particulars to the denial of guilt. Yakir transmitted this piece of paper to Voroshilov and returned to Kiev somewhat heart-ened, only to receive, later, a phone call from Voroshilov who said that Schmidt, on further interrogation, had confirmed his earlier confession and admitted that, in retracting it, he had sought to deceive both Voroshilov and Yakir.[44] What agonies his courage in retracting the false confession cost him may never be known; he was executed soon after.

What Yakir did not know was that Schmidt had been accused by his interrogators at the Lubianka of plotting to murder Voroshilov in Kiev *so that Yakir could take over his post*. Their only material evidence of guilt was a schedule of Voroshilov's movements that was distributed to all commanders involved in the Ukrainian military exercise that Voroshilov was observing. When Schmidt denied this charge, they confronted him with another: before leaving in 1934 for medical treatment in Vienna, *Yakir ordered him to prepare his tank brigade for an anti-Soviet uprising*.[45]

An intrigue involving the Nazis, which almost certainly instigated by Stalin, also figured in events preceding the military purge. In December 1936 a Russian émigré, General N. Skoblin of the Union of Tsarist Veter-ans in Paris, approached Reinhard Heydrich, head of the Nazi party's

Security Service, with a report that Tukhachevsky and fellow generals were plotting with the German General Staff to overthrow Stalin's regime. He said that his motive in passing on this information was to take revenge on Tukhachevsky, with whom he had served in the Imperial army, for going over to the side of the Revolution despite being of noble origin.[46] Apropos this explanation, it is curious that Skoblin would have chosen precisely December 1936 to settle scores with his one-time fellow officer, and that he would have wanted to serve what he, as an anti-Soviet Russian émigré, should have considered the Revolution's cause by undermining a plot against it, even if the plot were led by a personal enemy.

Some accounts have indicated, or at least left open the possibility, that this intrigue originated with the Germans.[47] On the other hand, the view that Stalin initiated it has been voiced by two Soviet sources whose testimony has appeared abroad: Major V. Dapishev of the Soviet General Staff, and Ernst Genri (S. N. Rostovsky), a Soviet citizen who lived abroad in the pre–World War II years, and whose antifascist books, *Hitler Over Europe?* and *Hitler Over Russia?*, were published in various languages, including Russian in Soviet editions of 1935 and 1937. "The forgery was prepared by the Gestapo but the idea came from Stalin," says Dapishev. "He planted it with the fascist ringleaders through General Skoblin."[48] According to Genri, "the real initiator of the forgery was Stalin himself, who utilized the services of the Gestapo via Skoblin."[49] It is more than likely that Skoblin served as a double agent. He suddenly disappeared from Paris in September 1937 around the time when the leader of the Russian émigré community there, General Miller, was kidnapped by Soviet agents. And Skoblin's wife, the singer Nadezhda Plevitskaya, was tried by a French court and convicted on charges of aiding and abetting the kidnapping. After serving three years of a twenty-year sentence, she died mysteriously in prison.[50]

At the time of Skoblin's visit to Berlin in December 1936, a veteran German intelligence officer named Jahnke warned Heydrich that Skoblin may have acted on orders from Stalin aimed at weakening the German General Staff and destroying the Tukhachevsky group with German help. But Heydrich, scenting a triumph for his relatively new intelligence organization and a chance to humble the German officer corps in revenge for his having earlier been cashiered as a naval officer on moral grounds, bit the bait. He went to his immediate superior, H. Himmler, who headed the S.S. (Gestapo), and to Hitler with his news and pressed them to cooperate in the undoing of the Red Army leaders. Hitler, after some hesitation, agreed.[51]

Once he had the green light, Heydrich used General Hermann Behrens of the Security Service to obtain a specimen of Tukhachevsky's signature from the German High Command's archives, which were burgled. This signature was on the secret Soviet-German agreement of 1926 on military cooperation, signed on the German side by General von Seeckt. A bulky dossier was produced, partly consisting of authentic materials from the time of the secret collaboration of the 1920s between the two governments, but also containing a forged exchange of letters over a year's period in which senior German generals promised Tukhachevsky and his associates their support in a *putsch* against Stalin. Because Heydrich (it is said) used the services of a Soviet agent who had volunteered to help the Gestapo forge the documents, Behrens came to the conclusion that the NKVD had conceived the notion of framing Tukhachevsky and that Heydrich was functioning as a tool of Moscow.[52] Precisely how the dossier reached Moscow, if it did, is not known.

During secret talks in Berlin in January–February 1937, a German negotiator, Graf Trautmannsdorff, told the Czech ambassador, Vojtěch Mastný, that according to information Hitler had received from Russia, a coup was due there to remove Stalin and Litvinov and establish a military dictatorship. Although Czech President Beneš said in memoirs published in Prague in 1947 that he immediately transmitted to Moscow what he had learned concerning the Mastný-Trautmannsdorff talks, the Soviet Union's Foreign Policy Archives contain no confirmation of his statement.[53] In March 1937, however, Vladimir Potemkin, Soviet ambassador in Paris, reported back to Moscow a conversation in which Edouard Daladier, then French defense minister, told him that the ministry had received from "Russian émigré circles" information on a planned coup in the Soviet Union involving high elements of the Red Army hostile to the Soviet system of government. The "circles" were General Skoblin.[54]

V. Falin, the head of the Soviet party Central Committee's International Department in 1989, stated that he had seen (presumably in Moscow) "papers prepared by Schellenberg on Tukhachevsky and others."[55] The official inquest found documents in Stalin's personal archive "confirming that German intelligence circles strove to bring disinformational material to him about M. N. Tukhachevsky,"[56] but the report on the inquest does not say whether the doctored dossier is part of this material.

However the matter of the dossier may stand, and whatever was the original source of the intrigue, the latter was not responsible for the catastrophe that later befell the Red Army and the nation it was ready stoutly to defend. The entire blame for that rests with the conspirator in the Kremlin and those who voluntarily served his villainous purposes. He had conceived and embarked on his conspiracy many months before Skoblin came to Berlin in late 1936 with his message for Heydrich. In that awful time, when denunciations of innocent "enemies of the people" were heard across the length and breadth of the Russian land, there was a real archenemy of the people at the very center of political events, wrecking his country's military establishment: Stalin.

The Terror Deepens

When Stalin sent his secret telegram from Sochi making clear to his Politburo colleagues that he intended greatly to expand the purge in the near future, an intensified terror campaign had already been in progress for two months. Even as the August trial took place, *Pravda* conveyed the message that the Trotskyist-Zinovievist conspiracy was not simply history but the focal point of an insidious anti-Soviet movement that had ramifications all over the country and *was still going on.* Beria, whose influence on Stalin was at a new peak due to his glorifying book on him as Transcaucasia's revolutionary hero, fired the opening salvo. He announced the exposure in Armenia of a "Trotskyist-nationalist group" headed by that republic's former commissar of education, Nersik Stepanian, and wrote that the just deceased first secretary of the Armenian Communist Party, Aghasi Khanchian (whose death by suicide was announced in Erevan in July) had sought to take Stepanian and the group under his protection.[57]

As soon as the trial ended, Stalin's old Chekist friend G. Yevdokimov, now secretary of the North Caucasus Regional Party Committee, weighed in with an exposure of terrorist and wrecking activities by groups of masked enemies in that section of the country, suggesting that local replicas of the central conspiracy were to be uncovered everywhere.[58] The next day's *Pravda* editorial, "Rotten Liberals Are Enemy Accomplices," said that the sixteen ringleaders of conspiracy were destroyed but it would be "the greatest crime" to think that thereby accounts had been settled with all enemies and one could go to sleep now. The trial had shown that not all foul double-dealers had yet been exposed. No, the enemy was putting on a mask and showing himself to be cunningly duplicitous. Unfortunately, the party contained not a few rotten liberals who substituted ringing speeches for real vigilance, as happened in Dniepropetrovsk where liberal dupes, including the head of the Regional Soviet Administration, provided work refuge to a Trotskyist returned from exile, Katsnelson, and helped enemies of the party named Kaplan and Vaisberg to regain party membership. "One must expose in Stalin's way the rotten liberals, all those whose revolutionary intuition has gone bad and who lack Bolshevik vigilance." This was an order to party and government officials not to obstruct the developing purge process, and a warning that they were in danger of falling victim to it themselves if they did.

Already at the time of the trial, fear invaded the publishing world and other parts of the bureaucracy. "Trotskyist nests" were uncovered in agencies under the State Administration of Publishing Houses (headed by Tomsky prior to his suicide). Its unit, the State Social-Economic Publishing House, had done business with "fascist dogs" Fritz David and Berman-Yurin. The head of its foreign section, now dismissed, had failed to report to the party organization that a Trotskyist named Domrachev had asked his advice about where best to conceal Trotsky's works. And among the foreign section's collaborators was one Pankov, who visited Zinoviev in his apartment in 1934, and Radek's secretary Tivel, now arrested as an enemy of the people.[59]

Denunciations also began in the Writers' Union, of which, it transpired, Pickel had been a member. Ivan Marchenko, secretary of the union's party committee, was fired and arrested for having given shelter and support to Galina Serebriakova, Tarasov-Rodionov (author of *Chocolate*), and other writers "linked with class enemies."[60] In Serebriakova's case, on which we have details, the "link" was marriage. She had been married for eleven years to a prominent Old Bolshevik, G. Y. Sokolnikov, who, although he supported the Left opposition in 1925–26, subsequently served as Soviet ambassador to London, deputy commissar of foreign affairs, deputy commissar of the timber industry, and was elected a candidate member of the Central Committee at the Seventeenth Party Congress. Earlier she had been married to L. G. Serebriakov. Vyshinsky, as noted above, named both these men during the August trial as persons to be prosecuted.

Serebriakova's story bears recounting as one of the Stalin terror's countless tragedies stemming from relations with other victims. With her mother and two daughters she spent 26 July 1936 at their dacha near Moscow. Sokolnikov did not appear after work. Toward midnight ten NKVD officers came, searched the place in silence, and went away. This told her that her husband was under arrest. But as the August trial had not yet taken place, she could not know then that the aim was to impress him into service as a cooperative defendant in a second show trial coming later. She knew him only as a supporter of party policy. The next day she called on Marchenko at the Writers' Union headquarters in Moscow and told him what had happened. His response was that of a rotten liberal: he knew her, and believed in her party loyalty. Others were afraid. No friends phoned at the family's Moscow apartment, over which police agents now kept constant watch. On 5 August, at a meeting of the district party committee, she was assailed by those present and told that what linked her with her husband, twenty years her senior, was not love but counterrevolutionary ideas and underground anti-Soviet activity. The committee expelled her

from the party for "loss of vigilance and ties with an enemy of the people."
Later in the year the new party secretary of the Writers' Union, Vladimir
Stavsky, held Marchenko up to scorn for having, among other sins, praised
Serebriakova as a "literary Stakhanovite" before her link to an enemy of
the people was uncovered: "What kind of vigilance is this! This is loss of
vigilance, and rotten liberalism."[61]

Shortly after the August trial, at which Vyshinsky announced that
Sokolnikov was going to be prosecuted, Serebriakova received a phone
call from Yagoda's deputy, Agranov. Later that day she was picked up by
a police car and delivered to the Lubianka where, after a five-hour wait,
she was received in a big brightly lit room by Agranov and Yagoda. Soon
they were joined by Yezhov, whose "tiny size and old dwarf's face"
terrified her. Yagoda, although he didn't yet know it, was performing one
of his last services for Stalin as NKVD chief. For Serebriakova it was the
first in a series of all-night interrogations in the course of which Agranov
demanded that she save herself and her family from a terrible fate by
"earning our confidence." This she could do by telling how, on 10 December
1934, standing outside the door of the study, she heard her husband
and father conversing about preparations for a terrorist act against Stalin.
She indignantly refused, and accused her high interrogators of conspiring
to deceive Stalin and the Central Committee with forged documents. Agranov
gave her one day to think things over. During it, after vainly trying to
bring herself to commit suicide, she had a nervous breakdown and was
sent to a mental hospital, where she received good care and gradually
recovered.

Then she was taken to Moscow's Butyrka prison, stripped naked, and
put in a cold dark cell with rubber walls. Once the cell door opened, a light
shone in, someone touched her back with the tip of his boot, and she heard
a man say, "Those enemies of the people sure knew how to pick their
women." Another time the door opened, a flashlight was trained on her,
she heard a man's outcry, and thought the voice was her husband's. When
released and sent home shortly after this, she learned that her mother had
recently been summoned to the Lubianka and commanded to write a letter
to Sokolnikov telling him that Galina was free and well and that her books
were in print (which was no longer true.)[62] That is part of the story of how
he was induced to play the criminal conspirator role in the second Moscow
show trial: they had shown him in a harrowing way what kind of fate they
were prepared to inflict upon his young wife if he refused to do so. The
other part of the story was the promise of a prison sentence instead of
execution on condition of his full cooperation.

A similar promise appears to have been made to Radek as a means of
inducing him to confess publicly that he had joined with Trotsky, Sokol-

nikov, Piatakov, Serebriakov, and others in a plot to overthrow the Soviet regime. Although Radek was not noted for being strong-willed (Trotsky told the Dewey Commission in 1937 that his character would utterly disqualify him for conspiratorial action[63]), he reportedly held out against the NKVD's pressures and blandishments for some time after his arrest but then became supercooperative after Stalin came to the Lubianka and had a long talk with him.[64] Being a gifted writer with imagination and insight into the strange workings of Stalin's mind, Radek thereupon took it upon himself, doubtless with cues that Stalin had given him in their talk, to write the script for the political play in which he himself would have a starring villain role. And being Russia's premier German expert, his fantasied conspiracy easily became, with Stalin's inspiration, one involving treasonous dealings by Trotsky, himself, and others with the Nazis.

Stalin assigned another feature part to Yuri L. Piatakov, who was incriminated by testimony in the August 1936 trial and taken into custody around that time. A Bolshevik since 1910, a leading figure in the Revolution who headed the Soviet government of the Ukraine, a member of the Trotskyist opposition expelled from the party in 1927 but reinstated the following year, the now forty-six-year-old Piatakov had since served as vice-president of Gosplan, Soviet trade representative in France, head of the Soviet State Bank, and then as Ordzhonikidze's deputy at the Heavy Industry Commissariat, where he became the chief administrator of industrialization under the five-year plans. Along with Bukharin he was one of two younger potential leaders noted by Lenin in his testament-letter ("a man undoubtedly distinguished in will and ability, but too much given over to administration and the administrative side of things to be relied on in a serious political question"). Although he was one of those Old Bolsheviks for whom the idea of building socialism was inseparably linked with better workers' conditions and moving toward a classless society,[65] he nevertheless threw himself with enormous energy into his work and was a major brain of Stalinist industrialization.

His arrest was a shocking blow to Ordzhonikidze. Apart from personal feeling for Piatakov, Ordzhonikidze—who was not himself a technologically sophisticated man—leaned strongly on him for leadership of heavy industry. He remonstrated with Stalin, who appears to have held out hope for Piatakov's release while soliciting Ordzhonikidze's help in persuading Piatakov to cooperate in the coming pseudotrial, very likely by offering him the opportunity to continue, afterward, being of use in the economy.[66] Piatakov's agreement was also, according to Orlov, extorted by a promise that neither his wife nor his greatly valued assistant, Kolya Moskalev, would come to harm or be called in as witnesses. And while Ordzhonikidze's fiftieth birthday was officially marked in late October

1936 with congratulatory messages in the press, Stalin put coercive pressure on him by arranging, without publicity, the arrest of his brother Papuliia, who lived in Georgia.[67] Beria, whose relations with Ordzhonikidze had long been bad, was certainly pleased to take this step, but would not have done so without directions from Stalin.

The focal theme of the first trial was terrorist designs on Stalin and other Soviet leaders, and Gestapo ties in this connection. The second show trial would prominently add the theme of industrial and other sabotage, or "wrecking," raising against Bolshevik managers the same sort of charges as those brought against "bourgeois specialists" in the Shakhty trial and its successors in the early 1930s. This was important for Stalin since the prime function of his show trials was to supply a rationale for mass terror throughout the country: it could hardly be maintained that Russia was swarming with hundreds of thousands of would-be terrorists seeking to kill Stalin and a few other leaders, but it was possible to accuse people in managerial positions everywhere of wrecking, all the more so as accidents and breakdowns, resulting mostly from the pressures of bacchanalian planning and Stakhanovite record-fever, could be represented as deliberately caused by malefactors in Communist disguise. So, if Piatakov, the chief manager of the industrialization drive, and Y. A. Lifshitz, the deputy commissar for railways (another defendant in the 1937 show trial), could be made to confess that they organized sabotage, then thousands of their subordinates, in all parts of the country, could be arrested as accessories to their crimes.[68]

As a buildup for the (still unannounced) forthcoming second Moscow trial, a trial of alleged wreckers was staged in Novosibirsk on 19–23 November 1936 and publicized nationwide. The choice of the Siberian locale is largely explained by the fact that some who would be accused as transmitters of instructions to the wrecking group in the Kemerovo coal mines of Siberia's Kuznetsk basin, and then put on trial in Moscow in January 1937, were prominent ex-Left oppositionists, notably Y. N. Drobnis and M. I. Muralov. They had been given administrative jobs in Siberia after recanting their oppositionism in 1929–30. Although the Soviet press described the Novosibirsk trial as "open," no foreign diplomats or correspondents were present.

Nine administrators and engineers, one of the latter a German citizen named E. I. Strickling, were accused of wrecking activities in the Kemerovo mines in 1935–36: deliberate disorganizing of mine operations by arson (among other means), artificial holding down of output, and violation of safety rules resulting in the gassing of two miners to death in December 1935 and the murder of ten more in a mine explosion on 23 September 1936. I. Noskov, I. Shubin, and M. Kurov, three alleged leaders of the local wrecker group, were said to be Trotskyists, and a fourth, I. A. Peshekhonov, lately chief engineer of the Kemerovo mines, had been convicted in the Shakhty trial in 1928. The entire conspiratorial wrecking effort was laid to Trotsky, who was charged with working in league with the Gestapo and to have transmitted sabotage instructions to the local wrecker group via Piatakov, Drobnis, and Muralov. Depositions by these three, who were under arrest in Moscow, were cited. And sure enough, Piatakov's article denouncing the defendants in the August 1936 trial was now said to have been written "to hide his personal participation in the criminal antipeople Trotskyist conspiracy, so as to preserve in his own person the root from which could subsequently grow the tree of a new conspiracy."[69]

Although the main theme of the Novosibirsk trial was wrecking, allegedly designed to do economic damage and arouse worker discontent, the political terrorism theme of the August Moscow trial was not omitted. The Siberian wreckers were charged with planning an attempt on the life of the head of the West Siberian Regional Party Committee, Politburo member Eikhe. And as if to compensate Molotov for his omission from the list of the intended victims of the united center, he was now said to have been the target of an assassination attempt when he visited the West Siberian mining center of Prokopievsk in the fall of 1934. According to the charges, Piatakov instructed A. A. Shestov, a mining manager in that area, to see that Molotov was murdered. Shestov entrusted the job to the head of the Prokopievsk Trotskyist group, one Cherepukhin, who in turn assigned it to a subordinate, V. V. Arnold. As the driver of Molotov's car in Prokopievsk, Arnold was to sacrifice himself and kill Molotov by driving over a precipice. The attempt failed, however, because Arnold lost his nerve and did not drive fast enough, so that the car only capsized.[70] Forty-five years later, on 24 October 1961, a Politburo member and chairman of the CPSU Central Committee's Party Control Committee, N. M. Shvernik, told the Twenty-Second Soviet Party Congress that when Molotov was in Prokopievsk in 1934 the car in which he was driving got its right wheels lodged in a roadside rut. The passengers were not harmed. Shvernik went on: "This episode later became the basis of a version about an 'attempt' on the life of Molotov, and a group of completely innocent people were convicted for it."[71]

Since Piatakov, Shestov, and other Soviet industrial executives paid visits to Germany earlier in the 1930s to supervise Soviet purchases of German equipment for new industrial centers like the Kuznetsk basin, and numbers of German workers and engineers, such as Strickling, were employed in these centers, it was not hard for the NKVD conspiracy experts to produce an appearance of Nazi involvement by coercing defendants-to-

be to testify to this effect. And the German connection bulked large in the
Soviet publicity about the trial:

In Berlin the Trotskyist murderers—Piatakov, Sedov, Smirnov—conferred under
the Gestapo's wings. From Germany an overseas bird flew to the Kuzbas: the
fascist Strickling, one of the main participants in the Kemerovo crime. From
Germany came directives to organize fascist cells in the Kuzbas. . . . Strickling
systematically reported to foreign intelligence on his fascist wrecking actions
when he went on vacation trips abroad.[72]

Yet Stalin had no wish to unduly antagonize the Nazi leaders with whom,
at this time, he was pursuing quiet diplomacy. When death sentences were
passed on all nine defendants at the trial's end, Joachim von Ribbentrop,
then Hitler's ambassador in London with the rank of undersecretary of
state in the Foreign Office, reportedly asked Prime Minister Stanley Bald-
win to inform Moscow that Germany would sever diplomatic relations
with Russia if the death sentence on Strickling was carried out, whereupon
that sentence, along with those of two Soviet defendants (charged with
being "White Guards" rather than Trotskyists), was commuted to ten years
in prison.[73]

In late 1936 arrests slackened in connection with the countrywide
ceremonies attending formal adoption of the new constitution and the
changeover in leadership of the secret police.[74] But the new rule that every
Bolshevik must prove the genuineness of his Bolshevism by showing the
capacity to recognize enemies, no matter what their guise, was having its
deadly effect in a swelling stream of denunciation letters to the authorities,
some signed, some anonymous.

A Kiev journalist, for example, noted in a diary entry in October 1936
that editorial offices were receiving letters with unconfirmable wrecking
charges against district and regional officials. "Someone is encouraging
suspicions," he observed. "There's a rising tide of denunciations of leaders—party officials, managers, scientists." A type that made its appearance
around this time was the eager and indefatigable denouncer. The journalist's diary had an entry in November 1936 about one such person, a woman
named Nikolenko, who wrote letters accusing officials of the Ukrainian
party Central Committee and the Kiev regional and city party committees
of being enemy accomplices because they were harboring many Trotskyists and Zinovievists to whom, "through connections," new party cards
were issued in the recent exchange. The Kiev City Party Committee investigated the case and expelled her from the party as—the diarist said—a
"lesson to all slanderers."[75] Apparently, local officials, here and elsewhere,
were getting worried now that the flood of denunciations from below,
which had been generated from above by the Central Committee's circular

letter of 29 July and various newspaper editorials, was threatening them.

It was certainly with the approval, and quite possibly on the initiative, of Pavel Postyshev, then first secretary of the Kiev Regional Party Committee and a candidate member of the Politburo, that Nikolenko was expelled from the party for making baseless accusations against local officials. That act was his undoing. Not long afterward *Pravda* editorially assailed certain local party organizations, those of Kiev and Rostov included, for harboring enemies of the people, resisting their exposure, and (in the case of Rostov) for having leaders who were themselves "cunningly masked Trotskyists." Of the Kiev organization it said that two-faced persons from the Trotskyist-Zinovievist pack had got into some top posts in the party apparatus and skillfully deployed their own kind for planned wrecking and terrorist activities. Personnel selection here had been insufficiently painstaking.[76]

In January 1937 Kaganovich was sent down to Kiev with instructions to end resistance there to the growing purge. At a Regional Committee plenum that he arranged, Nikolenko was eulogized as a "heroine" and "exposer of enemies," and the Kiev party organization was charged with losing vigilance and protecting enemies. Postyshev was relieved of his duties as Regional Committee first secretary on the flimsy pretext that he could not (as he had been doing) combine them with those of Republic Central Committee second secretary; and the Regional Committee's second secretary, Ilin, was removed on vague charges of political errors. The journalist's diary entry for 25 January 1937, recording all this, ended: "Can it be that Stalin won't correct this mistake?"[77]

The pathetic concluding question shows how far even politically literate people were from understanding what was happening in the country, who was behind it, and why.

RADEK: You are a profound reader of human hearts, but I must nevertheless comment on my own thoughts in my own words.

VYSHINSKY: I know that you have a fairly good stock of words behind which to conceal your thoughts, and it is very difficult for a man, even a good reader of human hearts, to understand you and induce you to say what you are really thinking. But I would ask you to reason here not so much as a journalist who has specialized in international affairs, but as a man accused of treason.

—FROM THE PIATAKOV-RADEK TRIAL

16

THE FORGING OF
AUTOCRACY II

THE QUIET TERROR of 1934–36 struck directly at very few influential people, and only now were some among them growing anxious about their own fates. To many citizens the replacement of the unpopular policeman Yagoda by the hardly known party man Yezhov had seemed an omen of better times. Very likely a mood of uneasiness prevailed among ranking persons—those belonging to the "nomenclature" in Soviet parlance—as they partied on 31 December 1936. But not many Soviet functionaries realized then that they would remember "thirty-seven"—if they survived it—with a shudder.

Looking back after her ordeals of the ensuing quarter-century, Eugenia Ginzburg recalled the New Year's eve party that she and her son attended at a country place for the privileged elite in Astafyevo, near Moscow, as a Masque of the Red Death. Her husband, still party secretary in Kazan, had sent them there to relieve the awful pressure on her at home. She reflected in retrospect that nine-tenths of those high-level celebrants, whose ladies were dressed in finery and whose children, if their fathers were of imported Lincoln or Buick rank, looked down on those (like Ginzburg's) whose fathers rated only Fords, would exchange their pleasant suites for bunks in Butyrka prison in the next few months.[1]

Pravda, Stalin's anonymous voice, hinted in its New Year's day editorial that stormy political weather lay ahead. "The Soviet ship is well fitted out and well armed," it concluded. "It has no fear of storms. It follows its own course. Its hull has been fashioned by the genius-builder to breast angry seas in the epoch of wars and proletarian revolutions. It is piloted by the genius-helmsman, Stalin." Even the next few days' flurry of publicity for the oncoming Pushkin centenary struck a macabre note in an article on the poet's death. Pushkin died in February 1837 at the age of thirty-seven in a duel with a man named Dantes, a foreign adventurer in Russian service. The article cited as "new documents" some century-old diplomatic dispatches by the Netherlands minister in Petersburg indicating that Pushkin was provoked to challenge Dantes by a court intrigue stemming from Tsar Nicholas I himself and involving the spreading of rumors about Pushkin's wife, the aim being to rid the realm of a freedom-loving figure who was a hero for the "party" of Russian progressives of that time.[2] So, it seemed, Russia's great national poet fell victim to a politically motivated murder plot in which a tsar and a foreigner were villains.

The German Jewish writer in exile, Lion Feuchtwanger, well known (as Gide had been before his visit in 1936) as a friend of the Soviet Union, arrived in Moscow at the start of the year and was received by Stalin.[3] No interview transcript was published. Elizabeth Poretsky, then in Moscow, learned from a close friend—a Comintern and military-intelligence operative of Austrian background who served as an interpreter in the talk—that it did not go well. Feuchtwanger spoke disapprovingly of the ubiquitous Stalin-worship (in the pro-Soviet book he later published, *Moscow 1937,* he recalled pointing out to Stalin that he saw his bust even in an exibition of Rembrandt), which visibly angered Stalin, who then ended the talk after saying it wasn't his fault if the people felt that way toward him.[4] Interviewed by Moscow radio two days later, Feuchtwanger hinted at a blunt exchange by saying of Stalin: "He is not overly polite, but on the other hand doesn't take offense when his interlocutor attacks him."[5] Then Russian political wit went to work, and a ditty made the rounds:

> There at the door stands
> A man with eyes of bead.
> Oh, let us hope this Jew
> Does not turn out a *Zhid.*[6]

But Feuchtwanger had ended his comment by saying, "Stalin, as he comes across in colloquy, is not only a great statesman, a socialist, an organizer—

he is, above all, a real Man," and the outcome was a second meeting that went smoothly.

Stalin's Radek and Radek's Stalin

The terror storm was heralded by the announcement of a new treason trial, to open in Moscow on 23 January. The announcement stated that Piatakov, Radek, Sokolnikov, and Serebriakov, following instructions from Trotsky, formed a "parallel center" in 1933. It organized sabotage and terrorist groups that engaged in wrecking in a number of plants, especially defense plants, prepared terrorist acts against leaders, and spied for foreign states. The aim was to undermine Soviet military strength, to hasten a military attack on the country, to help foreign aggressors take territories from the Soviet Union and dismember it, and to overthrow the Soviet regime and restore capitalism.[7]

The seventeen named as defendants included, in addition to the four well-known Old Bolsheviks and ex-Left oppositionists just mentioned, three other ex-members of the Left opposition: N. I. Muralov, Y. N. Drobnis, and M. S. Boguslavsky. Some were economic executives. Yakov Lifshitz, a one-time Trotsky supporter, had been deputy to Kaganovich at the Railways Commissariat; I. A. Knyazev had been assistant head of that commissariat's Central Traffic Department; and Y. D. Turkov held an executive post with the Perm Railway. S. A. Rataichak had headed the Central Administration of the Chemical Industry under Piatakov in the Heavy Industry Commissariat, and G. E. Pushin was a subordinate of his as chief of the Gorlovka Nitrogen Fertilizer Plant. B. O. Norkin was chief of construction at the Kemerovo Chemical Works in the Kuznetsk basin. A. A. Shestov, also a wrecker according to the Novosibirsk trial, appeared now as a defendant, as did V. V. Arnold, the hapless driver of Molotov's car the day its wheels got stuck in a rut. Two of the accused, Shestov and I. Y. Hrasche, were ex-NKVD secret agents in industry and functioned as state's witnesses in defendant guise.[8]

On the appointed day, 23 January 1937, the macabre play opened in the October Hall for its single performance. After Vyshinsky read the indictment, Piatakov was called. Evgeni Gnedin, who attended as the Narkomindel's press chief responsible for censoring foreign correspondents' dispatches, recalls the once strong-willed organizer of industry as he appeared there, "his manly face transformed into a death mask." The first five rows of spectator seats were filled with "strange, unpleasant characters, some with massive square faces, others sharp-nosed and mean-looking."[9] They were the interrogators, placed there to monitor their charges' performances and to warn them, by their very presence, of the unendurable torment that any undue straying from the script would cost them.

The prearranged conspiracy story, as it emerged in Piatakov's answers to Vyshinsky's questions, went as follows. In 1931, while he was in Berlin on Soviet governmental business, he met twice with Trotsky's son Sedov. In Moscow later that year, he received through Shestov a letter from Trotsky on the need to remove Stalin and his immediate assistants by violence and to conduct wrecking in the economy. Kamenev visited him in the fall of 1932 in Moscow, informed him about the united center, and said it had established close ties with the Rightists on a platform of Stalin's overthrow and abandonment of the construction of socialism. The parallel center grew active in 1933 when Lifshitz and others organized wrecking groups in the Ukraine, Shestov and others in Western Siberia, Serebriakov in the Transcaucasus and in railway transport. Wrecking methods included deliberate misplanning, construction delays, incendiarism and explosions, putting unfinished coke ovens into operation, dissipating resources, buying unneeded materials, and intentionally making life hard for workers to arouse discontent, with the overall aim of discrediting Stalin's leadership.

Piatakov testified that Trotsky directed all this from afar. From mid-1935, by which time the united center had been broken up, to early 1936, the parallel center came into its own as the main one, while seeking, especially via Tomsky, organized ties with the Right. Trotsky's directives reached Piatakov through Radek, who toward the end of 1935 received a long letter from Trotsky. It envisaged the center's coming to power either before a war through terrorist acts against Stalin and his lieutenants, or, as was more probable, during a war with Germany and possibly with Japan. That required reaching prior agreement with those governments. While in Berlin on business in late 1935, Piatakov met a Trotskyist, Dmitri P. Bukhartsev, then *Izvestiia* correspondent in Berlin, who arranged for Piatakov to fly to Norway for one day to see Trotsky. On or about 12 December 1935, bearing a German passport, Piatakov was flown in a special airplane from Tempelhof airdrome in Berlin to Oslo and driven from the Oslo airfield by car to the suburb where Trotsky lived. There the two men had a two-hour conversation.

In it Trotsky said that socialism could not be built in one country alone, that war was inevitable, that it would come in 1937, that the conspirators must engage in wrecking activities to become the gravediggers of the Stalin state, in order to prevent it from consolidating itself by economic achievements and by the support of the new, young cadres who saw it as a truly socialist state. Looking to a *coup d'état* that would bring a Trotskyist government to power, it was necessary to take account of the real forces in the international situation, primarily the fascists, and establish contact with them in preparation for taking power before a war or following the defeat of the Soviet Union in the course of war. Trotsky said he had conducted negotiations with the vice-chairman of Nazi party, Hess. They had reached an agreement under which, in return for Nazi support for the Trotskyist-Zinovievist bloc if it should come to power in a war, the bloc would compensate the Nazis by allowing them to set up a German protectorate in the Ukraine and thus begin the dismemberment of the USSR, and by retreating domestically toward the restoration of capitalism. Piatakov accepted Trotsky's program as a directive. The first day's court session concluded with testimony from Bukhartsev, who gave details of his role in arranging Piatakov's flight to Oslo through Trotsky's emissary, whom he identified as a mysterious stranger named Gustav Stirner. Piatakov confirmed the truth of this testimony.[10] Embarrassingly, however, Norwegian official sources soon revealed that no planes landed at Oslo airfield in December 1935. It was a case of Copenhagen's missing Bristol Hotel all over again.

In a dispatch to London about this trial, Ambassador Chilston of the British Embassy in Moscow commented that the prisoners "confessed to the most heinous crimes without any hesitation or emotion, like a well-coached class being put through an oral examination on a familiar and not very interesting subject."[11] Piatakov, with his death-mask face, acted his trial role in that perfunctory manner. But with Radek, who was called on the second day, it was a rather different story. Whether in expectation of a promised lighter sentence, or simply because of his irrepressible nature as an intellectual performer, he and not Vyshinsky dominated his testimony and he carried it off as a condemned politician's confession, with marks of his own authorship and even, on careful reading, of Aesopian *apologia*. This impression accords with the recollection of George F. Kennan, the then American Embassy secretary who accompanied the new American Ambassador Joseph E. Davies to the trial as interpreter. He remembers Radek as he stood to testify, looking his normal self, speaking with a certain aplomb, occasionally taking a sip from a cup of tea he held in his hand as he spoke.[12]

In "February–March 1932," Radek said (resisting Vyshinsky's efforts to get him to say "February"), he received a letter from Trotsky concluding that "we must raise the question of removing the leadership." He received the letter from *Izvestiia* correspondent Vladimir Romm, whom he met during a trip to Geneva that spring. Radek's addition of the word "March" was a tacit reference to Trotsky's anti-Stalin open letter published by the *Bulletin of the Opposition* in March 1932, which is indicated by the immediately following remark: "The word terrorism was not used, but when I read the words 'removing the leadership,' it became clear to me what Trotsky had in mind."[13] And how did he learn that a conspiratorial struggle was being organized? Radek said:

For instance, once when I was walking home from the offices of *Izvestiia,* I saw Smirnov on the Tverskaya with his former, if one may so express it, "Chief of Staff"—Ginsburg. Observing me, they turned down Gnezdnikovsky Pereulok. And I immediately realized that something was in preparation, that something was brewing. But they did not come to me, and did not speak to me openly.

Thus he in fact said that nothing really happened. But, to a mind like Stalin's, such seeming inaction as the *non*-meeting with Smirnov could appear to conceal sinister plotting.

Continuing his testimony, Radek admitted that he had joined the conspiracy in earnest in the fall of 1932. As his story went, at some point in late October or early November 1932 he had a talk with Mrachkovsky, who asked: "Have you received a letter from the old man?" "Old man" *(starik)* was the customary way of referring to Trotsky, Radek explained (the "letter" in question was presumably again Trotsky's open letter in the March *Bulletin of the Opposition*). Then he went on:

He asked me: what have you decided? I replied that if you had not guessed what I had decided, you would not have put that question to me. I have decided to go with you. Then I asked him how they visualized the struggle. . . .

Mrachkovsky replied, according to Radek, that "the struggle had entered the terrorist phase and that in order to carry out these tactics they had now united with the Zinovievists and would set about the preparatory work." Vyshinsky then asked: "What preparatory work?" Radek replied: "It was clear that since terrorism was the new position, the preparatory work must consist in assembling and forming terrorist cadres." In the following testimony, which Vyshinsky extracted with occasional reference to passages in several volumes of the defendant's pretrial testimony under police interrogation, Radek mentioned specific "terrorist groups" in Moscow headed by Dreitzer and Zaks-Gladniev, in Leningrad headed by Prigozhin, in Rostov headed by Beloborodov, in Tula headed by Diliateva, in the Urals headed by Yulin, in Western Siberia headed by Muralov, in Georgia headed by Mdivani, and a "historical or hysterical" group under the leadership of Friedland (an historian of the Pokrovsky school who had come under attack after Stalin's letter appeared in *Proletarian Revolution*); and he agreed that these terrorist groups were preparing attempts on the lives of party and government leaders.[14]

Observing the trial in Ambassador Davies' company, George Kennan had the "distinct impression" that the defendants and the prosecutor himself "were talking in symbols—that many of the expressions which they used repeatedly . . . had different meanings in their minds than in the minds of the spectators—that these expressions, in other words, were algebraic equivalents behind which real values were concealed." In a memorandum about the trial, he supported his thesis by referring to an exchange in which Piatakov denied that he specifically instructed Rataichak to get in touch with German agents, saying, "I gave the instruction in a more algebraical formulation, in a general form, without being specific . . . ," to which Vyshinsky replied, "I know what you mean by algebra, but I must now deal not with algebra but with facts."[15]

In order to comprehend the "algebra" of this and the other purge trials, we must recall that the early 1930s were a time of deep disenchantment with Stalin and his leadership; that oppositional groups were forming in the party with anti-Stalin platforms such as Riutin's; that both former Leftists and Rightists, even while abstaining from active opposition, were speaking critically of Stalin in their intimate circles; and that severe opposition to Stalin and his policies was being voiced openly in Trotsky's Paris-based *Bulletin of the Opposition,* copies of which or news about which filtered into Russia, in part because a Stalin adviser and *Izvestiia* commentator like Radek was authorized to read all material published abroad concerning Soviet affairs.

The "algebra" was a set of equivalents between real events and the meaning or interpretation placed upon them in what may be called the trial "system," which was an elaborated expression of Stalin's mind, that is, his characteristic ways of coming to terms with certain sorts of actual events. A basic algebraical equation in the trial system was: criticism of Stalin's leadership equals "Trotskyism." Anti-Stalin articles in the *Bulletin* were "Trotsky's letters." Meetings among friends in which anti-Stalin political thoughts were expressed were examples of conspiratorial "struggle." When the talk touched on the desirability of removing Stalin from power, such talk was "terrorism" and the groups engaging in it were "terrorist groups" (the algebraical formula being: "remove" equals "kill"). Thus Radek's trial testimony concerning "terrorist activity" in which he became involved in late 1932 had a real basis in the anti-Stalin intraparty discussions of that time; but only through the algebraic formulas of the system did it take on the aspect of intended "assassination of the leadership."

Further, there were two systems of terrorist (that is, anti-Stalin) struggle, the "guerrilla system" of individual terrorism, which Radek testified he did not support, and "a systematic, regular, organized group struggle" (that is, political opposition over a protracted period), which he preferred. After Kirov was murdered, he wrote a postcard to Dreitzer, who was in Krivoi Rog, "in veiled language," saying that "after the disaster that had befallen father we had to settle what to do next" (that is, was there any way to stop Stalin now from proceeding further down the path he had taken?) Here, as if casually, Radek testified that in seeking to get in touch with Dreitzer he had asked the help of Putna, who "came to see me with some request from Tukhachevsky."[16] This did not incriminate Tukhachevsky, but linked him with an already implicated military associate under arrest, and so was a danger signal.

A fundamental presupposition of the trial system was that all the conspiring terrorists (= party members critical of Stalin and his leadership) were, despite their being scattered in places all across the country, despite their diverse erstwhile political affiliations, *members of a single community* under the unified external direction of Trotsky. Trotsky, in turn, was seen as a diabolic monster of conspiracy who devoted all his energy in every waking moment to the one and only objective of destroying Stalin and his state. Since no such unified and ramified anti-Stalin conspiratorial group really existed, we may call it a "murderous pseudo-community."[17] All those condemned or incriminated in the great purge trials in Moscow and the many local purge trials held on their model, along with the mass of victims who were arrested, interrogated, and executed or sent to camps without a formal trial in the terror period, formed Stalin's murderous pseudocommunity.

Much of the trial testimony referred to actual events in terms of the algebraical equivalents of the trial system, but some parts were pure or partial fabrication. Thus, when Vyshinsky turned to the question of relations between "the bloc" (= the pseudo-community) and the Nazis and Japanese (while cautioning that no mention must be made in open court of the names of official foreign institutions or officials), Radek said that he received letters from Trotsky in April 1934, December 1935, and January 1936. The first said that with the coming of the fascists to power in Germany, war was inevitable and would result in the defeat of the Soviet Union, creating favorable opportunities for the bloc's accession to power. Trotsky had already informed "semi-official circles" in Germany and Japan ("a certain Central European state" and "a certain Far Eastern state," as Radek put it in Vyshinsky's own algebra) that the bloc stood for a bargain with them and was ready to make both economic and territorial concessions. The letter demanded that bloc leaders in Moscow make known to those states' representatives their agreement with his steps. Sokolnikov, using a normal contact afforded by his post as assistant foreign affairs commissar, did so inform the representative of "a certain Far Eastern state."

Then Radek testified that at a Moscow diplomatic reception in the fall of 1934 he spoke with a "Central European" diplomat who, after expressing regret that the two countries were throwing mud at each other in their newspapers, said that "our leader" was aware that "Mr. Trotsky is striving for a rapprochement with Germany" and "wants to know, what does this idea of Mr. Trotsky's signify?" Radek said that he knew this man must be informed about Trotsky's dealings with the Germans because he, Radek, "read everything written by Trotsky" and knew that "he never advocated the idea of a rapprochement with Germany in the press." He told his foreign interlocutor that "sole attention must not be paid to these newspaper alter-cations," and that "realist politicians in the USSR understand the signifi-cance of a German-Soviet rapprochement and are prepared to make the necessary concessions." He explained that he was speaking for "the bloc." As we know, Radek, around that time, was acting as Stalin's unofficial intermediary with German representatives in Moscow. Gnedin notes in his memoir that when Radek gave the above testimony, "well informed people understood that the exchange really took place, but it took place on instruc-tions from Stalin or Molotov and not at all in connection with secret designs of the 'conspirators.' "[18] The "realist politicians" in question and "the bloc" in this context were Stalin and Molotov. And if, as Vyshinsky thereupon compelled Radek to confess, his conversation with the German diplomat was an act of treason, the traitor was Stalin.

Radek proceeded to testify that in the next letter, which he received at the outset of December 1935, Trotsky was more specific on the defeatist program: the Ukraine would go to Germany, the Amur and Maritime regions to Japan, plants would be transferred to private ownership, collec-tive farms disbanded, capitalism restored. Further, the social structure of the Soviet Union would be brought into line with that of the victorious fascist states. Soviet power would be replaced by what Trotsky called "a Bonaparte government," meaning "fascism without its own finance capi-tal."[19] Here it should be noted that Trotsky published in the April 1935 issue of the *Bulletin of the Opposition* a long, important article arguing that Soviet Russia's "Thermidor" (which he had once seen as merely threaten-ing or as an ongoing process) was, in fact, a long-ago passed stage and that

the present-day political regime of Soviets is extraordinarily reminiscent of the first consul's regime and, indeed, of the Consulate's end when it was verging on the Empire. If Ṣtalin lacks the luster of victories, he at least surpasses the first Bonaparte in a regime of organized sycophancy. . . . The present political regime of the USSR is a "Soviet" (or anti-Soviet) regime of Bonapartism, closer in type to the Empire than to the Consulate.

Trotsky found support for this thesis in the generous use the Stalin regime was making of the services of one-time anti-Bolsheviks: Maisky the ex-Menshevik ambassador in London; Troyanovsky the ex-Menshevik am-bassador in Washington; Khinchuk and Suritz the ex-Menshevik past and present ambassadors in Berlin; the ex-bourgeois history professor Potemkin, who was ambassador in Paris; the ex-Right SR Grinko, who was finance commissar; and the ex-Right Bundist specialist in gutter journalism, Zaslavsky. Finally, he raised the possibility that Stalinism would be the prelude to "fascist-capitalist counterrevolution" in Russia.[20] That is what Stalin, through Radek, was now accusing Trotsky of seeking to bring about by the strategy of wartime defeatism. Having read Trotsky's article, Radek knew that the Trotsky of his testimony was the mirror image of Trotsky's Stalin; and this article may well have been the algebraical referent of Trotsky's second "letter." At any rate, Radek was making Trotsky out to be the agent of Soviet Bonapartism that the Trotsky article accused Stalin of being.

Vyshinsky then raised the subject of a directive in Trotsky's letter on wrecking. Radek denied that the letter gave any "specific instructions on this score," but ascribed to Trotsky the argument that in order to be taken seriously by the "countries concerned," the bloc must show its strength by terrorist actions, by wrecking, and by acting to undermine army morale and discipline. Defense industry and rail transport, because of their obvious wartime significance, were to be especially important wrecking objectives. Piatakov, Serebriakov, and Lifshitz, then called as witnesses, confirmed that they had received and acted upon Trotsky's directive.

Toward the end of his testimony, Radek contended in his own defense that Trotsky's defeatist program, which had made sense to him in 1933–34, no longer did by 1935 when the economy was in much stronger shape, and that, albeit in a vacillating way, he had toyed with the thought of organizing a conference of leading bloc members to argue for opposing Trotsky's December 1935 directives.[21] When Vyshinsky questioned his veracity on this score, noting that for about three months after his arrest he had untruthfully denied all the charges that the police investigators brought against him, Radek replied: "Yes, if you ignore the fact that you learned about the program and about Trotsky's instructions only from me, of course it does cast doubt on what I have said."[22] His point was that the prosecution could not consistently take the parts of his story that it liked— and for which he was the sole source—as true while dismissing the part it disliked as untrue on the ground that he was a liar. At this, after a few final words, the florid-faced ex-Menshevik prosecutor of Bolsheviks ended his interrogation of Radek.

During the five ensuing days, prisoners confessed in grisly detail to crimes of wrecking and sabotage in industry and transport aimed at causing embitterment at Stalin and the government and weakening the state's war potential and preparedness. They testified that they committed these crimes on orders from the parallel center and representatives of foreign governments. The crimes included coal mine explosions, fires, breakdowns in chemical works, all involving casualties, and numerous train wrecks, especially of troop trains and freight trains, again with many casualties. Since a number of the key confessed plotters were Trotskyists in Siberian exile, Siberia was naturally the locale of much of the wrecking and Japan was heavily implicated as the Far Eastern "military fascist state" at whose behest the parallel center acted. Thus Ivan Knyazev confessed to having accepted from a Japanese, "Mr. Ha——" a directive to organize, in event of war, the burning of military depots and the infecting of troop trains and canteens with virulent bacteria.[23] His testimony was punctuated by such sanguinary passages as that in which he told of causing (as chief of the railroad involved) a troop-train wreck in which twenty-nine Red Army men were killed and the same number injured, the latter including cases of "heads pierced, arms broken, ribs broken, legs broken."[24]

Wrecking involved the trial's algebra. It was a fundamental algebraical principle of this and other purge trials—as of the earlier trials of "bourgeois specialists"—that *nothing is accidental,* and that events which have the appearance of unfortunate accidents are, in actuality, products of a great conspiracy. As Lord Chilston drily observed, "When one reflects that (as I have previously reported) there was a period when an accident happened every five minutes on the Soviet railway system, it must be conceded that this group, of which only seventeen persons have been brought to trial, was ubiquitous indeed."[25]

This comment was prophetic in a way that the writer may not have seen at the time. For each of the executives on trial—and the majority of the defendants held executive posts, from assistant commissar down—was the superior of many lesser executives and administrators, who in turn were superiors of mine foremen, locomotive drivers, and other workers. Since the head of a railroad, like Knyazev, could not personally wreck a train, someone below him and then someone below that person, and so on, had to be an accomplice, as, for example, Arnold was supposed to act on orders from Cherepukhin, which the latter received from Shestov, and Shestov from a higher source, to kill Molotov in a car accident. In the trial algebra, the hiring of a subordinate by an "exposed" higher executive was the "recruiting" of that person into the conspiratorial pseudocommunity.[26] Consequently, wrecking did indeed become "ubiquitous." A wave of arrests began in the aftermath of this trial, and as more and more of Stalin's targeted magnates fell in the ensuing months, repressions ramified through the society and the limited terror of the past two years turned into the holocaust of 1937–38. No wonder that Stalin, at the trial's climax, expressed his approval to Yezhov by conferring on him the rank—previously held only by Yagoda, but no longer—of commissar general of state security. To help people gain the impression that "Yezhov's rule" was upon them, the announcement was accompanied by a large photo of the little commissar general.[27]

Vyshinsky's summing-up speech for the prosecution on 28 January was an hours-long performance. Almost immediately it rose to a vituperative pitch that might have inspired George Orwell's later depiction, in *1984*, of the daily Two Minute Hates against "Goldsteinism": "This is an abyss of degradation! This is the last boundary of moral and political decay! This is the diabolic infinitude of evil!" *Pravda* kept in step with an editorial that day entitled "Trotskyist-Wrecker-Saboteur-Spy," and on inside pages it reported resolutions of collective hate sessions in plants, schools, *kolkhozy,* and elsewhere, under headlines like: "Crush the Reptile!" "Death to the Traitors to the Motherland!" and "Smash Judas-Trotsky's Band to Pieces!"

Along with the shrill invective, Vyshinsky offered a replay of the history of Bolshevism as he knew Stalin wanted to view it. "While Lenin was alive these people fought against Lenin," his story ran, "and after his death they fought against his great disciple. . . ." While Lenin and Stalin were organizing the party early in the century, Judas-Trotsky was squirting "venomous saliva" at Lenin's ideas in a 1904 pamphlet, *Our Political Tasks.* In 1911–12 he organized the anti-Lenin "August bloc," a precursor of his later anti-Stalin Trotskyist-Zinovievist bloc. For many years after the defeat of the "new opposition" in 1926–27, such active Trotskyists as Piatakov, Radek, Sokolnikov, Serebriakov, Drobnis, Muralov, Lifshitz, Boguslavsky, Shestov, and others claimed that they had abandoned Trotskyism. But this was a way of camouflaging the hatred they continued to harbor for the Soviet system and socialism. They used scoundrels like Rataichak, Knyazev, Arnold, Stroilov, and Hrasche to work as spies and wreckers. They went to the ultimate length of duplicity when, just a few months ago, they published articles condemning their fellow-criminals in the Kirov murder, Zinoviev and Kamenev, for—among other things—having been duplicitous. "And so, covering up the traces of his own foul deed, Radek talks about exposed double-dealers who had been handed over to the law. . . . Radek thought he was writing about Kamenev and Zinoviev. A slight error! This trial will rectify Radek's error. He was writing about himself."

In order to show a reality basis for the fantastic accusations against the trial defendants, Vyshinsky resorted to the algebra of the trial system. First he cited an article printed in the *Bulletin of the Opposition* of April 1930 in which, he alleged, Trotsky declared "retreat" to be inevitable and called for an end to the ongoing mass collectivization, the "hurdle race" of industrialization, and the policy of economic autarchy. This Vyshinsky

made out to be an implicit formulation of the program for capitalist restoration. Then, to support the charge of Trotsky's defeatism in war, he
mentioned a reference Trotsky had made to Clemenceau in a party document of July 1927, during the showdown between the dominant Stalin
faction and the United opposition. Stalin, in his speech to the Fifteenth
Party Congress later that year, accused Trotsky on this basis of defeatism.
Should an enemy come within eighty kilometers of Moscow, Stalin then
said, Trotsky, believing that the Soviet regime was degenerating, would
seize upon that situation to bring in a new Clemenceau, that is, a Trotskyist
regime. Now, Vyshinsky went on, Trotsky and his accomplices had adopted
his Clemenceau thesis as "real preparation, in alliance with foreign intelligence services, for the defeat of the USSR in war." Trotsky and his kind
had degenerated "into a fascist vanguard, into the storm battalion of fascism." They all deserved death by shooting.[28]

Trotsky had no trouble disposing of the "Clemenceau-thesis" argument when he testified before the Dewey Commission later in 1937. He
had, indeed, referred to Clemenceau's action, but Clemenceau had sought
a change of government in 1917 to keep France from being defeated, not
to hasten her defeat, and consequently went down in memory as the "father
of victory." And he had referred to Clemenceau in response to the charges
being made in 1927 that the war danger ruled out the freedom of criticism
of party policy that the opposition was demanding. As for defeatism, he
had been four-square for defense of the Soviet Union then and, despite all,
still was now.[29]

In all but one case, the accused men's last statements were brief and
perfunctory, typified by Piatakov's abject admission that he had landed in
"counterrevolution of the most vile, loathsome, fascist type, Trotskyist
counterrevolution." The exception was Radek, who took advantage of
what he knew would be his final appearance in the public limelight to make
a statement; and mustering all his still formidable power of intellect, he
made it a politically meaningful one. First, he sought to serve Stalin's
need—political and psychological—in a more effective way than Vyshinsky did with his interminable bombast. Secondly, he contrived to include
an element of self-defense that made it more difficult for Stalin to break
his pretrial assurance of a relatively lenient sentence—an assurance that
Radek undoubtedly considered worthless. Thirdly, he conveyed some
messages in Aesopian language.

To such an extent was the statement a political speech that at one
point—very likely in mock forgetfulness of being on trial for high treason—Radek addressed the court as "comrade judges," then duly corrected
himself when Ulrikh intervened to order him to say "citizen judges." It had
something of the quality of Radek's 1934 article on "The Architect of
Socialist Society" in that it wove selected facts into a fictional composition,

in this case with a dramatic plot that Radek thought would gratify Stalin's grandiosity and craving for vindictive triumph over political enemies, himself included. To this end he presented himself not as a criminal type but as a political man gone wrong, who in a party career spanning thirty-five years committed the grievous error of linking up with Trotsky and Trotskyism, which led eventually to his criminal complicity in the evil doings of the parallel center. But he was admitting his guilt "from motives of the general benefit that this truth must bring" (that is, worthy political motives); and to doubt him on this point, he implied, was to doubt the whole basis of the trial, which rested on "the evidence of two people—the testimony of myself, who received the directives and the letters from Trotsky (which, unfortunately, I burned), and the testimony of Piatakov." This was his self-defense on the ground of having been Stalin's main support for staging this trial.

Next he referred to Bukharin, whom he had implicated. Starting with a manifestly ludicrous remark, he said that he was not tortured while under interrogation; rather it was he who had tortured the investigators for two and a half months by compelling them to perform a lot of useless work. Even then, however, he "stubbornly refused to testify with regard to Bukharin," though he knew the latter's position was as hopeless as his own. "But we are close friends, and intellectual friendship is stronger than any other kind." He seems to have been saying to Bukharin: I held out as long as I could, old comrade, but in the end to no avail.

Radek's peroration was ostensibly for Stalin. The "old Trotskyists," he had observed earlier, considered it impossible to build socialism in one country, yet later on "nobody could help but see that socialism in our country had been built." Hence Trotsky put his stake on Hitler and the destruction of socialism in the one country. At present what the penitent Radek wanted to say to "those elements who were connected with us" was this: the government would take care of terrorist organizations like the Trotskyist one. "But there are in our country semi-Trotskyists, quarter-Trotskyists, one-eighth Trotskyists, people who helped us not knowing of terrorist organization but sympathizing with us. . . ." His message to all such elements was that the country was in a period of supreme tension, a prewar period, and that "whoever has the slightest difference with the party" was in danger of turning into a saboteur and traitor "if he does not thoroughly heal that difference by complete and utter frankness to the party."[30] It was a final piece of agitation for Stalin's regime and an act of prostration before the "architect" himself. Some of those in attendance or those who read the verbatim trial report were repelled by the seeming suggestion of a need to root out even "one-eighth" Trotskyists—but they missed Radek's Aesopian last message.

There is a legend that *Pravda*'s version of Radek's concluding pas-

sage (unlike the passage in the verbatim report) read: "All the Old Bolsheviks were essentially Trotskyists, if not completely, then halfway, and if
not halfway at least a quarter or one-eighth."[31] It is not so: *Pravda*'s version
coincided with the verbatim report. Like many legends, however, this one
has sense to it despite its factual inaccuracy. It shows that Radek's message
got through to at least some Old Bolsheviks. What he was conveying in
his reference to "one-fourth" and even "one-eighth" Trotskyists still at
large was a truth that must have dawned on him through his experience in
the Lubianka between his arrest in September and his trial appearance in
January: that Stalin was embarking upon the radical project of exterminating virtually the whole Bolshevik party insofar as it remained, as it especially did among Old Bolsheviks, a Leninist one.

Such was the import of the passage in question when read together
with Radek's definition of "Trotskyism" as disbelief in the possibility of
building a socialist society in a single country. For that disbelief was
something Trotsky had shared with Lenin, who bequeathed it to the party
as part of his theoretical legacy. In those terms, not only Lenin was a
"Trotskyist" to the end of his life, but so was Stalin as late as May 1924
when he repeated in his lectures on the "Foundations of Leninism" the
proposition that it was impossible "to achieve final victory of socialism
without the concomitant efforts of the proletarians of several leading countries." Only later in 1924, under the influence of his version of national
Bolshevism, did Stalin revise his position, remove that passage from the
text of the "Foundations," and disavow the heretofore generally accepted
Bolshevik tenet that the victory of socialism in a single country was not
possible.[32] Thus Radek's Aesopian message was that, in its developing
new stage, Stalin's revolution from above was aimed at eliminating that
seven-eighths or so of the Leninist Bolshevik party, including especially the
Old Bolshevik part, which was not fully imbued with Stalin's kind of
Russian national Bolshevism and the Stalin-worship that went along with
it. Lenin himself, were he still alive, would have logically belonged to the
core of the doomed seven-eighths. The new arrests that some in attendance
at the trial believed Radek to be provoking with his reference to "one-
fourth" and "one-eighth" Trotskyists[33] were arrests that he knew were in
the offing whether he provoked them or not.

At 7:15 p.m. on 29 January the court retired to "confer," and reconvened at three the next morning to deliver its verdict. All the accused were
pronounced guilty, thirteen sentenced to be shot, and four given prison
sentences. Radek and Sokolnikov, as members of the center but "not
directly participating in the organization and execution" of terrorist and
other such acts, received ten-year sentences, Arnold a ten-year sentence,
Stroilov an eight-year one. As Radek filed out behind a soldier who took

charge of him, he looked back at the assembled spectators with a pathetic farewell smile.[34] To his wife's perplexed questions in a post-trial interview that was granted them, he replied: "I had to do it" *(Tak nado bylo).*[35] Radek and Sokolnikov were fated to live out only two of the ten years to which they were sentenced. Post-Stalin official records give 1939 as the year in which both died. Radek was killed in camp by criminals especially sent for that purpose.[36] Sokolnikov's wife, Serebriakova, having served the purposes of the organizers of the trial, was exiled to far-off Kazakhstan.

"The country welcomes the just verdict," *Pravda* wrote the day after the trial ended. And, again as if to inspire *1984*'s picture of public Hates against "Goldstein" and his "ism," it reported that the working people had already held mass meetings in Moscow, Leningrad, and elsewhere to cheer the condemnation of the Trotskyist band of murderers, spies, saboteurs, and traitors and send curses to enemy of the people Trotsky, whose death sentence *in absentia* was editorially pronounced as follows: "Let the foulest of the foul, the furious enemy of the workers of the world, the fierce fomenter of a new war, Judas-Trotsky, know that the people's wrath will not pass him by."[37] In Moscow upward of 200,000 people were herded into Red Square and adjoining streets, at a temperature of 27 below zero centigrade, to demonstrate that—as one of the placards read—"the court's verdict is the people's verdict." There to address them was the forty-two-year-old secretary of the Moscow Party Committee, Nikita Khrushchev, who reviled Judas-Trotsky and his band and said: "By raising their hand against Comrade Stalin, they raised their hand against all the best that humanity has, because Stalin is hope. . . . Stalin is our banner. Stalin is our will. Stalin is our victory."[38] Stalin himself made no personal appearance.

Among the foreign observers at the trial was Feuchtwanger. Interviewed by *Pravda* on the final day, he opined that the defendants' guilt was proved beyond doubt, that Trotskyism had been smashed in the Soviet Union and abroad, and that the trial was a major contribution to the anti-fascist cause.[39] Probably it was at this point that he had his second and more cordial meeting with Stalin. His subsequently published *Moscow 1937,* although it duly referred to the Stalin bust in the Rembrandt exhibit, presented a Stalin who was the "most unpretentious" man of power of the author's acquaintance, and went on:

He shrugs his shoulders at the vulgarity of the immoderate worship of his person. He excuses his peasants and workers on the grounds that they have had too much to do to be able to acquire good taste as well, and laughs a little at the hundreds of thousands of portraits of a man with a moustache which dance before his eyes at demonstrations.[40]

The book was published in Moscow in a Russian translation with a large circulation. Stalin must have been pleased that "this Jew" did not turn out a *Zhid*.

Foreign envoys in Moscow had been allowed to attend the trial in person accompanied by one interpreter. The German and Japanese ambassadors did not attend. It seems that the question uppermost in embassy observers' minds and conversations did not concern Stalin's purposes in staging this judicial frame-up. The foreigners rather wondered whether these charges and confessions deserved credence, and most of them believed that they did not. A notable exception was U.S. Ambassador Davies who, while chatting with foreign press correspondents during a trial intermission was heard by George Kennan to say: "They're guilty. I've been a district attorney, and I can tell."[41] This foreshadowed the opinion Davies expressed in a letter of 4 February 1937 to President Roosevelt that the trial established "a definite political conspiracy to overthrow the present government."[42] Most members of the diplomatic corps showed more political acumen. "To take this case at anything like face value involves an intolerable strain on the faculty of belief," reported Ambassador Chilston in a dispatch to London, adding that none of the foreign representatives with whom he had spoken believed in the genuineness of the trial and most agreed that "the facts cannot be adequately explained without assuming that unavowable methods were employed on the prisoners."[43]

But what of the trial's meaning as a political event? If the alleged conspiracy was real, the trial's meaning lay in its exposure and the punishment of those guilty. But for diplomatic observers in Moscow who could not believe in the conspiracy's genuineness, the trial's meaning as a political event remained mysterious. To experience history unfolding—even from the vantage point of the October Hall—was, in this case, of small help toward its comprehension. Ambassador Chilston found the chief motive in the desire to utterly discredit Trotsky and his adherents as a danger to the peace of the world. That was superficial. He dismissed as fanciful the informal suggestion by Boris Steiger—a Soviet official of aristocratic background who was authorized to have social contact with members of the diplomatic corps—that it might be worth recalling the example of "the boyars under Ivan the Terrible."[44]

However astute, the minds of diplomats stationed in Moscow at that time were not attuned to patterns of earlier Russia that had bearing on current events. They were unable to take the hint that Steiger, himself a former baron and guardsman, seems to have dropped—that in Stalin's Russia a new *oprichnina*-state, with a new Ivan-like tsar at its head, was gradually displacing the original Bolshevik party-state, and that the trial they had just witnessed was a calculated action undertaken with that end in view. They did not understand that the trial's theme of terrorism presaged a great wave of state terrorism against all "enemies of the people" accused of being involved in the just uncovered great conspiracy; that the charges of widespread wrecking and sabotage, however absurd on their face, were indicative of an intent to transform the regime from above by decimation of the still extant party-linked ruling elite; and that what I have called the "trial system" was the melodramatic expression of Stalin's own belief system, which was now being established, through the trial and the confessions and the Terror, as the new Communist faith both in the Soviet Union and abroad. Nor, finally, did they understand the trial's significance as a vehicle of Stalin's foreign-policy purposes although Ambassador Chilston attributed to unnamed colleagues the view that "Stalin may be preparing some radical change of policy, to which the few remaining Old Bolsheviks, unless they were exterminated, would be strongly opposed."[45] He did not know how right he was.

Stalin Woos Hitler

While the trial was in preparation, and even while the prisoners in the dock were confessing under duress to mythical efforts by Trotsky and other conspirators to reach an accord with the Nazis, Stalin was methodically engaged behind the scenes in actual efforts toward that end.

Talks between Schacht and Kandelaki resulted in the signing on 29 April 1936 of an economic agreement for 1936 favorable to both sides. In early May, Herbert L. W. Göring, an official in the Economics Ministry, arranged for his cousin, Minister President Hermann Göring, to receive Kandelaki and his assistant at the Trade Mission, Lev Friedrichson (an NKVD man), for a talk of which Herbert Göring wrote:

Their visit to the Colonel General passed off in a very pleasant and almost friendly way, and Kandelaki and Friedrichson were in every respect delighted by the Colonel General's charming manner. . . . Göring suggested to the Russians that if ever they had any wishes with which they were making no headway they should apply to him direct; he was prepared at all times to assist by word and deed. This naturally constituted a considerable success for the Russian gentlemen. Kandelaki, I hear, left for Moscow yesterday evening in order to report, among other things, on this most agreeable reception by Göring.

A marginal note by another official said Kandelaki did not leave the next day but called on Schacht, "who poured some water into the wine." Still, the "Russian gentlemen" must have been pleased with Göring's comments, especially as he told them, according to a further minute by his cousin, that the newly signed treaty "would also be a pacemaker on the road to further political understanding between these two great nations. All his efforts were directed towards making closer contacts with Russia again, politically too, and he thought that the best way would be through intensifying and expanding mutual trade relations." What the Russians did not know was that Göring, in talking with German industrialists a few days later, and stressing to them the importance of developing business with Russia, said he "had decided to discuss this subject sometime very seriously with the *Fuehrer,* whose attitude to it, admittedly, was not very sympathetic."[46]

It would have been natural, however, for Stalin to construe Göring's words as indicative of thinking shared by Hitler. When, on 22 May 1936, Ambassador Suritz came to bid Foreign Minister Neurath farewell before going on leave in Carlsbad, he expressed satisfaction over the outcome of the economic negotiations and "asked whether any change in political relations might be expected in the near future." Neurath said he did not see preconditions for that at present but hoped political relations would once again develop satisfactorily.[47] Some weeks later the Soviet Embassy in Berlin must have been instructed to probe the possibility of a nonaggression agreement. A German Foreign Ministry official, Hencke, reported in a memorandum of 3 July 1936 that Embassy Counselor Bessonov raised the question of a nonaggression pact and spoke of three possibilities. Germany might feel there was no need for one in the absence of a common border. Second, Germany might reject the idea because of existing Soviet treaties with France and Czechoslovakia. Third, Germany might be prepared to supplement the 1926 Berlin treaty with a nonaggression clause. Hencke replied that he could take no position on these conjectures, that nonaggression pacts were indeed appropriate for neighbor states only, but that Germany definitely had no desire to attack the Soviet Union.[48]

The diplomatic pleasantries of Göring, Neurath, and Hencke were— although Stalin had no way of knowing this—quite out of line with Hitler's attitude, which was unremittingly hostile. At about that time Hitler decided to institute a Four-Year Plan in Germany and place Göring in charge of it, and in August 1936 he wrote a memorandum in this connection. When he showed a copy of it to Albert Speer in 1944, he said it had been prompted by the lack of understanding by the Reich Ministry of Economics and the opposition of the German business world to "all large-scale plans." The memorandum's master theme was the necessity of war. Hitler left no doubt about whom and what the war would be against. The world, the memorandum said, was moving with ever increasing speed toward a conflict with Bolshevism, whose essence and aim "is solely the elimination of those strata of mankind which have hitherto provided the leadership and their replacement by worldwide Jewry." At present only two states in Europe,

Germany and Italy, were firm against Bolshevism. Considering how rapidly the Red Army had been growing in power, one could see how menacing it would be ten, fifteen, or twenty years hence. In face of that danger, the *Wehrmacht* must be transformed in the shortest time into the first army of the world. The final solution lay in extending overpopulated Germany's living space and/or the sources of its raw materials and foodstuffs. The memorandum concluded that the German army must be operational, and the economy ready for war, in four years.[49]

Unaware of Hitler's secret determination to make war on Russia within four years, Stalin persisted in his overtures for closer ties. In September 1936 Kandelaki and Friedrichson requested that Göring receive them for continued economic negotiations. The request was not granted.[50] Not daunted, Stalin then directed his agents to use the normal channel— Schacht. At Kandelaki's request, Schacht received the two men toward the end of December 1936. Judging by Schacht's later account of the conversation in a letter to Neurath, Kandelaki raised the topics of both economic and political relations for discussion. Schacht responded that the Soviet ambassador and German Foreign Ministry were the proper channel for political discussions. As for economic relations, he could see a possibility of a brisk trade development if the Russian government would make the political gesture of abandoning all Communist agitation abroad. "Mr. Kandelaki," said Schacht, "indicated, evidently unwillingly, his sympathy with my view." Kandelaki then returned to Moscow to report to Stalin.[51] In that same month, December 1936, Krivitsky received orders to "throttle down" Soviet intelligence work in Germany.[52]

The trial of the "parallel center" in the following month, with its charges and confessions of dealings between the anti-Stalin opposition and Nazi leadership, could hardly help but roil Soviet-German relations somewhat, especially as reference was made in the Soviet press to a treasonable interview that Radek supposedly had with a German Embassy "press attaché" during a diplomatic reception. On 25 January 1937 *Pravda* said in an editorial that Radek had supported Trotsky's deal with German fascism in personal conversations in Moscow with a fascist "military attaché"—a transparent reference to General Köstring.

Yet, Stalin did what he could to keep Berlin tempers unruffled. Early on in the trial, Georgi Astakhov, now posted to the Narkomindel's press department, invited Dr. Schüle, Moscow representative of the German press agency D.N.B., to breakfast. The German Embassy's note on their conversation said that he did so "spontaneously." Only on instructions from the highest level, however, would Astakhov have taken this step. The trial was not directed against Germany, he said to Schüle, and there was no reason for a further worsening of complicated Soviet-German relations. Schüle said that the trial astonished him and mentioned the agreement that according to Piatakov's testimony was reached between Trotsky and Hess. To this Astakhov replied: "Please take into consideration that Trotsky could have been lying when he told this to Piatakov."[53] This sly intimation that a key accusation of the trial was false points to Stalin's desire to prevent the trial from derailing his effort to come to terms with Hitler.

For reasons of his own, stemming from the hope of preserving normal German-Soviet relations, Ambassador Schulenburg sought to soften the trial's impact upon the Nazi higher-ups. In a telegram of 28 January 1937 to Berlin, he called the trial "pure theater" and said that it should not be taken too seriously. He advanced various reasons why the real effect was nil—among them Astakhov's breakfast comments a few days earlier and also the fact that all the German firms against which accusations were made in the trial had closed down their Russian operations prior to the trial's opening.[54] As for the trial's meaning, the embassy note on the Astakhov-Schüle breakfast exchange found it in Stalin's taking revenge against malcontents in the country and all who had once signed the platform of Trotskyist opposition. The anti-German charges were not to be treated seriously, for "Nobody can believe that Germany would attack the Soviet Union to bring Bronstein and Sobelsohn to power."

Göring stated in a Reichstag speech of 30 January that the trials were regarded as "theater only" and that no suspicions existed concerning Germans who had been incriminated, particularly Reichsminister Hess. Schulenburg cited this statement in a further telegram, dated 4 February 1937, as a support for his advice not to protest the charges against German public figures.[55] The Nazi party organ, *Völkischer Beobachter*, commented editorially on 3 February: "If Stalin is right, the Russian Revolution was the work of a gang of abominable criminals including only two honest men, Lenin and Stalin. Yet for years these two have governed Russia in collaboration with this scum." If former trials, it went on, had the object of producing scapegoats, this one had the further object of incriminating Germany and Japan. "More interesting than this, however, is the number of Jews among recent victims; in fact the original Jewish gang has been largely exterminated and substituted by Caucasians." Radek, "the most poisonous of all Soviet Jews," and "Sokolnikov-Brilliant" were among the victims. Although a further Jewish group remained, headed by Litvinov and Kaganovich, the fact was that Stalin "has made himself an oriental despot on the pattern of Genghis Khan or Tamerlane. . . ."

The timing of Stalin's next overture to Hitler is especially notable. Upon returning from Moscow to Berlin, Kandelaki sought and obtained another interview with Schacht. It took place on 29 January 1937, the next to last day of the Moscow trial. Kandelaki, accompanied by Friedrichson, told Schacht that in Moscow he had conferred with Stalin, an old "school comrade" of his, and with Molotov and Litvinov. Then, speaking from a prepared text and in the name of Stalin and Molotov, he said that the Russian government had never declined to negotiate with the Germans politically (to Schacht's question, when had that been, Kandelaki replied that it was at the time of the negotiations on the Franco-Soviet pact). The Russian government did not intend to direct its policy against German interests. It was prepared for negotiations with the Reich government on improved relations and general peace. The negotiations could proceed through diplomatic channels, and the Russian government was prepared to handle all talks and negotiations confidentially. Schacht reminded Kandelaki of his (Schacht's) December statement that such proposals should go through diplomatic channels. Kandelaki accepted this, but asked Schacht to sound out the situation. Reporting all this to Neurath, Schacht suggested that Kandelaki be told that abandonment of Comintern agitation would be a precondition for the talks in which Moscow was interested.[56]

We may be sure that Stalin deliberately timed the approach to Berlin during the Moscow trial. He knew that the Nazi leaders knew that the charges of a secret deal between Trotsky and the German government were groundless. It would have been characteristic of his subtle and wily political mind to believe that he was demonstrating—by his overture *during* the trial—that they should not take its antifascist rhetoric too seriously; that, in fact, he was not only not opposed to an accord with them but, on the contrary, interested in one, provided only that it serve Russia's state interests rather than injure them as the condemned men were accused of having been willing to do. Thus both his probe via Kandelaki and his treason trial put a Soviet-Nazi accord on the agenda, albeit in strikingly different ways.

Since the probe was secret, Stalin's hint about the spuriousness of the trial was for the Nazis only. For the rest of the world there remained the show of antifascism, and a message that the developing new Stalin terror was prophylaxis against an anti-Stalin opposition, which in desperation had descended to the lower political depths by collusion with the fascist powers. What Stalin stood to gain from this antifascist theme was, in the first place, a softening of the negative impact that the Terror was bound to provoke on foreign and home opinion. Insofar as foreign sympathizers like Feuchtwanger, and Russians as well, could be deluded into thinking that Old Bolshevik ex-oppositionists had made common cause with fascism, and for purposes of dismembering the Soviet state, the dismay that very many people felt at the spectacle of the Moscow trials would be allayed somewhat. Further, the trial conveyed to the Soviet public—always fearful of war, especially with Germany—the message that Stalin's internal ene-

mies were bent on fomenting war with Germany and Japan and, by implication, that the Stalin regime was shoring up peace by acting against them.

Finally, the trial's antifascist dressing was useful for Stalin's coalition-building diplomacy of collective security. True, it could suggest that
a state so riddled with treason might be a weak reed as a military partner
(although Ambassador Davies, for one, did not see it in this way). However, it presented the picture of an official Russia professing antifascism
and thus being a country that could be viewed as a potential ally against
fascist aggression. Probably more important in Stalin's calculations in the
diplomatic game being played out across Europe, the antifascist publicity
surrounding the treason trial, when juxtaposed with Hitler's ranting anti-
Bolshevism, would encourage Western political leaders to see an unbridgeable ideological chasm between Russia and Germany and therefore
make them less active, hence less dangerous competitors for rapprochement with Germany.

Stalin's latest probe through Kandelaki proved fruitless. Having received Schacht's account of it, Neurath some days later reported to Hitler
what Kandelaki had said in the name of Stalin and Molotov. Hitler's
reaction was negative. Negotiations with the Russians at present, he said
to Neurath, would only be used by them to form a closer military alliance
with France and seek better ties with England. A Russian statement on
dissociation from Comintern propaganda would have no practical use. "It
would be something else," Hitler added (according to Neurath's letter to
Schacht), "if the situation in Russia should develop in the direction of an
absolute despotism supported by the military. In that case, to be sure, we
must not miss the right moment for involving ourselves again in Russia."[57]
Neurath further told Schacht that he should answer Kandelaki's inquiry by
saying that no success could be expected from political negotiations at the
present time, "that is, so long as the close tie of the Comintern with the
Russian government exists."

Even that, however, was less than a total rebuff and it did not cause
Stalin to change his basic policy orientation. He had made it crystal clear
to Hitler that he was interested in a political accord, and he expected Hitler
to respond sooner or later. Meanwhile, he sought to mollify the Germans
by withdrawing a request for the recall of General Köstring from his
Moscow post. The lesser German Embassy member who had been mentioned in the trial as a "press attaché," one Herr Braun, was to be sent back
to Germany, but even this was compensated on the Soviet side by an
undertaking quietly to drop pending cases against thirty or forty arrested
German nationals. The favorable disposition of the Köstring case (for lack
of "compromising data," Deputy Foreign Commissar Krestinsky told Ambassador Schulenburg on 6 March 1937) was all the more meaningful a

gesture on Stalin's part in view of the fact that Köstring's relations with the Red Army were very good.[58]

Having fulfilled his mission for Stalin, Kandelaki was transferred to Moscow in April 1937 and there had a private audience with Stalin, who at first rewarded him for his services with an appointment as deputy commissar for foreign trade.[59] Krivitsky, who was also in Moscow at this time, had talks with Yezhov on the situation in Germany. Hitler had made Germany the strongest power in Europe, Yezhov said, and no one in his senses could fail to reckon with this. Then: "For Soviet Russia there is but one course. And here he quoted Stalin: 'We must come to terms with a superior power like Nazi Germany.' "[60]

After the Trial

After the Piatakov-Radek trial, a pall of fear descended on party people throughout the land as repressions multiplied. Many victims at this stage were people arrested earlier and given relatively lenient sentences. They were recalled and condemned to more severe punishment. Many others had been marked down as potential victims but not yet taken into custody; now they were.

The case of Eugenia Ginzburg was fairly typical. On 7 February 1937 she was called to her district party committee in Kazan and expelled from membership. Although her husband, Aksyonov, remained nominally a figure of importance as a secretary of the regional party committee, he was helpless: the police were running things now. She and he lay awake through the nights in fear that one of the police vehicles coursing through the streets would stop at their door. They purged their home library by burning books by Bukharin, Radek, and others. On 15 February she was summoned by phone to local NKVD headquarters and placed under arrest. A team of interrogators kept her sleepless on the "conveyor" for seven-day periods, pressuring her to confess that she had belonged to a secret terrorist organization on the newspaper *Red Tartary,* headed by Elvov. When she protested, "This is a Soviet institution where people can't be treated like dirt," her interrogators answered: "Enemies are not people. We're allowed to do what we like with them. People indeed!"[61]

Pravda made it clear that wrecking charges were now to be made on a mass scale. It said that the command staff of industry must "identify the enemy in the field of technology and science." In Zaporozhie, which was cited as an example, various accidents and breakdowns were treated by local engineer-Communists as mere "malfunctions." An inquiry, however, showed them to have been organized by "the dirty hands of wreckers." This lack of Bolshevik vigilance raised questions concerning the Zaporozhie City Party Committee (Comrade V. Strup, secretary) and the party organizations of the main factories there.[62]

The next day's editorial assailed sycophancy toward local party chiefs. Thus, Comrade Ryndin, secretary of the Chelyabinsk Regional Party Committee, was publicly eulogized by the head of the South Urals railway line, where the spy Knyazev did his wrecking, and there were quite a few others who tolerated sycophantic praise by their subordinates.[63] This article, like the aforementioned one, was a warning to high-placed party officials not to protect their protégés, not to shrink from "identifying the enemy" among them, if they did not want to be identified themselves as the enemy. But once these high party officials surrendered subordinates to the NKVD's tender mercies, might they not find themselves denounced by those unfortunates as partners in crime? Many must have asked themselves that question now. The flood waters of the Great Purge were finally lapping at the feet of party bosses. Ryndin, for example, was a full member of the Central Committee elected by the Seventeenth Congress.

The time had come for Stalin to call a plenary session of this sovereign party body and secure its endorsement of actions he had been taking without consulting it and other actions yet to be taken. The proceedings of the "parallel center" trial now provided him with material needed for obtaining the acquiescence and indeed the complicity of the Central Committee in the developing Terror. To be sure of success, he had to make certain that the Central Committee—many of whose members were already condemned in his mind as enemies—was itself sufficiently intimidated to sanction the nationwide purge campaign. He was shrewd in his choice of a means of intimidation. From around the time when Yezhov became head of the NKVD, Stalin made it a practice to circulate to all Central Committee members, marked "Secret," copies of the depositions being extracted from ranking persons under arrest, such as Piatakov.[64] This meant that all members of the high body could see in advance the accusations being brought against some of their number, notably Rykov and Bukharin, could sense that awful things must be happening to the arrested persons in order to force them to sign such lies, and had to wonder whether and when their own names would appear in someone's denunciations.

Awful things were in fact happening at the Lubianka. Months earlier, many ex-Rightists had been brought from distant places of confinement to Moscow. Their interrogators already had in mind a scheme into which their depositions were to fit. The gist of it was that the Right opposition's leaders had long harbored terrorist designs and conspired with the "Trotskyist-Zinovievist bloc" to destroy the Soviet order. This was the leitmotif of an unpublished tract by Yezhov, "From Factionalism to Open Counter-revolution." He had begun work on it in 1935, shortly after the Kirov murder. When he finished, Stalin carefully edited the document and suggested ways of improving it.[65]

The interrogators' job was to extract false testimony in support of this fictional scheme. Their methods ran the gamut from promises to spare the prisoner's life and appeals to serve "the interests of the party," on one hand, to shouts, threats, blackmail, and outright physical pressure or torture on the other. Stalin followed the results closely. Yezhov regularly sent him protocols of the interrogations and testimony. Thus on 7 October 1936 Stalin received a protocol containing testimony by Tomsky's former personal secretary, M. Stankin, that a terrorist group of which he had been a member planned to commit an act of terror against Stalin during the annual meeting on 6 November 1936 in the Bolshoi Theater to mark the anniversary of the Revolution. Sixty such protocols went to Stalin between September 1936 and February 1937.[66]

Among the victims of these atrocious methods were Riutin and another prominent former follower of Bukharin, A. N. Slepkov. Both responded by going on hunger strikes and attempting suicide. On one such occasion Riutin was pulled out of a noose that he had fashioned for himself. In a protest statement written in November 1936 and found decades later in the archives, Riutin said that the interrogators were treating as incitement to terror various passages in his illegal "documents" (meaning the "platform" and "appeal"). Having held out against the inhuman pressures, he was shot later on. Others were less iron-willed. Broken by merciless interrogation, Bukharin's erstwhile disciple V. N. Astrov became a limp instrument in the hands of his masters, ready to agree to any depositions asked of him (in a most rare act of clemency, Stalin subsequently had him freed and returned home, and he was still living in 1989). Protocols of his and others' similar false depositions went from Yezhov to Stalin, who had copies circulated to all the full and candidate members of the Central Committee, then numbering close to the 139 elected to membership by the Seventeenth Congress. Ninety-eight of them were destined to disappear.

In early December 1936 Stalin had enough depositions in hand to call the Central Committee in session. Its proceedings were unpublicized. He evidently wanted to use the meeting to ensure the high body's acquiescence in the expulsion of Bukharin and Rykov during a publicized plenum to be held in early 1937. Yezhov was the rapporteur, and he accused Bukharin and Rykov, on the basis of false depositions which he cited at length, of being the ringleaders of a major "center" of the great conspiracy that had to be uprooted. Bukharin flatly rejected all the false charges and denied that a Rightist "center" had ever existed. He went so far as to declare at one point: "Whatever you may declare, whatever you may decree, whatever you may believe or not believe, I assure you that always, to the last minute of my life, I will stand by our party, by our leadership, by Stalin." Rykov told the plenum that the charges being made against him in the depositions were "lies from beginning to end." Personal confrontations with arrested men were arranged for Bukharin and Rykov during breaks in the Central Committee meeting. The men under arrest duly repeated orally, in confrontation with Bukharin and Rykov, the accusations that had been extorted from them at the Lubianka. Stalin took an active part in these nightmarish affairs, occasionally intervening with a charge of his own.[67]

By putting on this secret meeting, he managed to cow the members of the high party body. Now he could count on its acquiescence in the expulsion of Bukharin and Rykov at the publicized plenum coming up. At that zero hour in the history of Soviet Russia, the committee members must have been motivated above all by fear for their lives and the lives of their loved ones if they came out openly against the budding tyrant. The only possible salvation lay in a violent act of tyrannicide by someone brave enough to undertake it in a meeting hall that must have been under constant surveillance by Stalin's guards.

Originally scheduled for 19 February, the publicized plenum was postponed for nine days due to Ordzhonikidze's death on the 18th. The timing of his death was not coincidental. Now that Kirov and Kuibyshev were gone, Ordzhonikidze's position in the party was second only to Stalin's, and if there was anyone to whom industry and other sectors looked for protection against the growing terror, it was he. He could be deceived and manipulated by Stalin, but unlike others in the entourage, such as Molotov and Voroshilov, he could not be broken in spirit. By virtue of his very old intimacy with Stalin, their common Georgian origins, his tendency to become infuriated to the point of ignoring dictates of prudence, and his loyalty to the party's cause, Ordzhonikidze was the one prominent leader left who was capable of openly resisting Stalin at the upcoming plenum and possibly becoming the core figure in a last-ditch concerted opposition to the general secretary's rampage of terror. Stalin had, at all cost, to forestall that.

The January trial and its aftermath brought things to a head between the two. If, as hypothesized above, Stalin manipulated Ordzhonikidze into soliciting Piatakov's cooperation in the trial, with a promise that he could thereby save the life of his right-hand man at the commissariat, Piatakov's execution served as final proof of Stalin's perfidy; and the instant burst of the witch-hunt in heavy industry in early February told Ordzhonikidze that all he had tried to build up during the five-year plans was tottering. Stalin's response to his protests against the arrest of high executives in heavy industry was to propose that he, Ordzhonikidze, give a speech at the coming plenum on wrecking in industry.[68] This would have cast him in the (for him) unthinkable role of Stalin's accomplice in destroying valuable personnel *en masse* in his own empire. Meanwhile, he was sent falsified records of his older brother Papulia's interrogation (under torture) in Georgia and similarly extracted depositions by arrested commissariat officials containing accusations *against himself,* with a note from Stalin: "Comrade Sergo, look what they are writing about you."[69] That was not all. Ordzhonikidze's dear friend Alexander Svanidze, Stalin's brother-in-law by his Georgian first wife, received the death penalty at this time.[70] Finally, Stalin ordered a search of the Ordzhonikidzes' Kremlin apartment. Enraged, Ordzhonikidze got Stalin on the phone—after fruitless attempts throughout the night—and was told: "That organ can make a search even of my place. It's nothing special."[71]

On the morning of 17 February, Ordzhonikidze had a long talk with Stalin, described by his post-Stalin biographer, who had access to archives, as follows:

Several hours, eyeball to eyeball. A second conversation, by phone, after Sergo came home. Unchecked rage, mutual insults, Russian and Georgian profanity. No more love, no more faith. All destroyed. Shared responsibility for what he could no longer avert—that Sergo couldn't do. He didn't want to play a villain's part, that would blot out his whole past life. Nothing left but to exit.[72]

Ordzhonikidze had been thinking about suicide. A few days earlier he had taken a walk around the Kremlin grounds with Mikoyan, to whom he said he could no longer tolerate what Stalin was doing to the party, and could not go on living.[73] On 18 February he stayed all day in his bedroom in the apartment, took no food, and wrote something—most likely a farewell letter indicting Stalin for the terrible things happening to the party and country. At 5:30 p.m., a shot rang out. His wife, Zinaida, ran in and found him dead on the bed. Her sister, Vera, who ran in too, saw and picked up some papers he had left on his desk. Stalin, whom Zinaida phoned, came over immediately and said "Shut up, you idiot," when she screamed at him: "You didn't protect Sergo for me or for the party." When he saw the sheets of paper that Vera was clutching in her hand, he tore them away from her. Joined by Molotov and Zhdanov (and Beria, who then disappeared after Zinaida tried to slap his face and called him a scoundrel), Stalin said it must be reported that Ordzhonikidze died of a heart attack. Ordzhonikidze's secretary, Makhover, said when he came: "They killed him, the scoundrels." His long-time personal aide at work, Semushkin, raved and made a terrible scene. Subsequently, Semushkin and his wife were arrested, as were many of Ordzhonikidze's close associates at the commissariat. His deputy, Vannikov, was summoned to Yezhov's office a few days later and ordered to write a report about "wrecking" directives written by Ordzhonikidze.[74]

On 19 February the Central Committee announced with "deep sorrow" the sudden demise of "the ardent, fearless Bolshevik-Leninist and outstanding leader of economic construction in our country." The official medical report, published that same day, gave the cause of death as a heart attack. It was signed by Commissar of Public Health G. N. Kaminsky and three medical men in the Kremlin hospital, including the ill-fated Dr. Levin. On 15 March, for unexplained reasons, Kaminsky was replaced in his post as public health commissar. He might have protested the misuse of his name on the medical report. The funeral was held with full honors, the cremated body interred in the Kremlin wall, the country declared in mourning for several days. The North Caucasus Territory was renamed Ordzhonikidze Territory.

The Fall of the Central Committee

The way was now clear for Stalin to proceed with the plenum. It opened, without public announcement, in a Kremlin building on 25 February. The official information bulletin, published 6 March, said only that the plenum discussed and passed a resolution on the party organizations' task in connection with the forthcoming Supreme Soviet elections under the new constitution, and that it discussed other questions, including the antiparty activity of Bukharin and Rykov, who were expelled from party membership. The accompanying *Pravda* editorial said, however, that the plenum would go down as one of the most important pages in the party's history. That it did.

The first day or so was largely devoted to a seemingly routine subject. On 26 February, Zhdanov reported on what the coming nationwide elections, based on the new constitution, meant for the party organizations. He foresaw a tense election struggle "with hostile agitation and hostile candidacies." And "while our people are dozing and rocking themselves, enemies are active and preparing hard for the elections." To give leadership to the election campaign, the party organizations must enforce the innerparty democracy required by the party rules. But the rules were widely violated, for example by the common practice of bringing various leading figures into local plenums and party committees by cooptation rather than by election. People were serving as secretaries of party committees who had not been elected members of them. It was a wide practice to appoint new party committee secretaries without putting their candidacies up for discussion by the membership. And there must be no more voting for the officers of party organs "by lists" and openly; the voting must be secret and on an individual basis, with retention by party members of full right of criticism and rejection of candidates.[75] After a discussion the following day, the plenum adopted a resolution endorsing the report's theses. All leading party organs were to become elective, with secret ballot, and new elections of party organs were to be held by 20 May. How this party reform measure was linked to the purge will be explained presently.

Next, Stalin proceeded to secure the expulsion of Rykov and Bukharin from Central Committee and party membership—technically the *sine qua non* of arresting them. By periodically injecting some hope into the flow of warning signals of disaster, he had kept Bukharin from committing suicide during the last grim period of waiting in his Kremlin apartment. Bukharin would sit in the study holding his personal revolver with its gold-plated handle that said, "To a leader of the Proletarian Revolution, N. I. Bukharin, from Klim Voroshilov," but could not bring himself to pull the trigger.[76] Meanwhile, more and more protocols of extorted false depositions came to him and to Rykov at their apartments, and defamatory articles appeared in the press, such as one in *Pravda* calling Bukharin "an agent of the Gestapo." In letters to the Politburo and to Stalin, Bukharin denied the truth of the depositions and, in protest against them and the press campaign, declared that he was going on a hunger strike. This he did as the plenum approached.[77]

When the question of expelling Bukharin and Rykov came up at the plenum, what ensued was not so much a discussion as a political lynching party led by a now openly domineering Stalin. The rapporteur was Yezhov, who repeated the charges made by him in the recent unpublicized plenum. Instead of ending opposition, as they promised to do in 1929, Bukharin and Rykov had kept their "underground organization" in being as the center of a conspiratorial effort in league with the Trotskyists and others to overthrow the state and seize power by violent means. Mikoyan gave what amounted to a coreport in the same vein. In it he said that Bukharin's letters to the Central Committee represented an attempt at "intimidation" of the Central Committee.[78]

In vain the two doomed men sought to defend themselves. With Stalin giving the cues, the terrified assembly subjected Bukharin and Rykov to a savage baiting. Their attempts at a self-defense were dismissed as examples of duplicity and as a heinous effort to discredit the NKVD. A published excerpt from the transcript can illustrate what went on:

BUKHARIN: In an extraordinary, exceedingly difficult time, I wrote about it (in the letters to the Central Committee). There was no element of either ultimatum or intimidation.

STALIN: And the hunger strike?

BUKHARIN: About the hunger strike, I haven't even now renounced it, I told you
and wrote to you why I undertook it in desperation. I wrote to a narrow circle
of people because, with the sort of charges now being made against me, my
life has become impossible. I can't shoot myself with a revolver because then
they would say that I killed myself so as to do harm to the party, but if I die
as though from an illness, why what do you lose? (Laughter.)

VOICES: Blackmail!

VOROSHILOV: Foul play. A plague on you. Dastardly. Just think about what you
are saying.

BUKHARIN: But you must understand, it's hard for me to live.

STALIN: And is it easy for us?[79]

A commission was appointed, with Mikoyan as its chairman, to review the case and a two-day recess was called. Perhaps in order to take
personal revenge on them, Stalin arranged for Krupskaya and Lenin's
sister, Maria Ulyanova, to be included as members along with a large
number of men on whom he knew he could depend. No one opposed
expulsion of Bukharin and Rykov from the Central Committee and from
party membership. When polled, however, some added: "To be arrested,
brought to trial, and shot," whereas others said: "To be brought to trial,
without execution." Stalin, when polled, said: "Not to be brought to trial,
but send the case of Bukharin-Rykov to the NKVD." (This of course meant
that he had the two men in mind as star performers in a third great show
trial yet to come.) Krupskaya and Ulyanova, with what must have been
very heavy hearts, joined others in voting "For Comrade Stalin's proposal," and the latter carried.[80]

During the recess Bukharin prepared a short letter entitled "To a
Future Generation of Party Leaders," had his wife learn it by heart, and
then burned it. Before leaving home for the last time, he kissed his nine-
month-old son and begged his wife's forgiveness. He and Rykov arrived
together at the building where the plenum was taking place. They were not
admitted to hear its verdict, which was a foregone conclusion. Eight waiting men intercepted them near the doorway and took them straight to the
Lubianka.[81]

So succumbed the Central Committee, sealing the fate of the party-
state for the coming quarter century as well as that of the majority of the
committee members themselves, who did not long survive the event. The
high body's compliance was a crowning act of acquiescence in Stalin's
terror project. Was any significant opposition shown at this juncture?
The available evidence points to a negative answer. According to Khrushchev's Twentieth-Congress report, "many members" at that plenum "questioned" the policy of mass repression, and their "doubts" were ably expressed

by Pavel Postyshev.[82] The question is whether these doubts, which certainly must have been widely shared at the plenum, were *openly* expressed by anyone other than Postyshev himself.[83]

It doubtless took great courage on Postyshev's part to speak up at all. How ably he did so is another matter. The point of his statement, as quoted by Khrushchev, was to defend a fellow member of the Ukrainian Central Committee, Karpov. He did not question the purge in general or the victimizing of Bukharin and Rykov in particular. After speaking of the hard years of collectivization and industrialization when some "joined the camp of the enemy" and "healthy elements" fought for the party, Postyshev went on:

I never thought it possible that after this severe era had passed, Karpov and people like him would find themselves in the camp of the enemy. And now, according to the testimony, it appears that Karpov was recruited in 1934 by the Trotskyists. I personally do not believe that in 1934 an honest party member who had trod the long road of unrelenting fight against enemies, for the party and for socialism, would now be in the camp of the enemies. I do not believe it. I cannot imagine how it would be possible to travel with the party during the difficult years and then, in 1934, join the Trotskyists. It is an odd thing.[84]

Stalin interrupted at one point to ask, "What are you?" and Postyshev replied, "I am a Bolshevik, Comrade Stalin, a Bolshevik."[85] After the plenum, during which his work in the Ukraine was criticized, Postyshev was transferred to the party secretaryship of the Kuibyshev region—the last stop on his path to perdition.

Molotov gave a major report on wrecking in industry. He said that Piatakov was the chief organizer of wrecking in heavy industry. Because he held so high a post, wreckers and spies had every opportunity to place their people in the chief administrations, trusts, and enterprises. Then Molotov made it clear that the purge in heavy industry was already far along: "Not just a single hundred industrial leaders with party cards, but also 'nonparty' engineers and technicians who had key posts in institutions of the Heavy Industry Commissariat and for years carried on criminal wrecking work there have now been exposed." Drawing heavily on materials of the January trial, he drew a picture of an economy infested with wrecking by "Japanese-German-Trotskyist agents" plus—now that this was settled—Bukharinist and Rykovist wreckers of the Right.

Brushing aside all justification for caution in the hunt for wreckers, Molotov rejected the argument of some industrial managers that plan fulfillment and overfulfillment proved that wrecking was not a serious problem. True, Rataichak's chemical-industry section of the Heavy Industry Commissariat overfulfilled its plan for 1935 and 1936, but it only proves that "Even wreckers can't spend all their time wrecking, else they wouldn't survive." Prime responsibility for exposing wreckers rested with the NKVD. But industrial managers themselves bore responsibility too. Receiving signals from their administrative staffs, they should sense danger from enemies and take action. They must develop the capacity to identify enemies in their midst.[86]

A long speech by Stalin on 3 March climaxed the proceedings. Before analyzing it let us consider the problem that he faced at this point. The development of purge events since Kirov's murder, culminating in the two big purge trials, had seemed to many to be Stalin's vengeful settling of accounts with old enemies, ex-oppositionists, who numbered in the few thousands. But the trials were far more than that: a rationale for the tidal wave of repression now rising. People had not expected mass terror, they had not foreseen that hundreds of thousands of supposedly conspiring, secretly anti-Soviet "two-faced" persons, high and low, were going to be arrested, compelled to confess their duplicity and criminality, shot or sent away. Stalin's task now was to communicate to the Central Committee members the vision of a society swarming with enemies wearing masks of party and Soviet loyalty. But he was addressing not simply the 130 or so highly placed Communists meeting in secret in the Kremlin. His speech would shortly appear in *Pravda*. Its audience was the nation and the outside world. Stalin's speech was thus his *apologia* for the unfolding terror project and he tried very hard to make it convincing.

He began by defining the situation as he wanted people to see it. Agents of foreign states had penetrated all or nearly all economic, administrative, and party organizations; had penetrated high posts as well as low; and certain leading comrades, locally and in the capital, showing themselves careless, complacent and naive, had failed to spot the wreckers, spies, and murderers How so? Not for lack of warning signals. There had been, first, the Kirov murder, showing that enemies would act duplicitously behind Bolshevik masks; then the Central Committee's secret circular letter of 18 January 1935, which decried the notion of the enemy growing weaker with the country's progress as "a belch of the Right deviation"; then the secret circular letter of 19 July 1936, which demanded maximum vigilance of the party organizations. The warning signals did not, however, dispel carelessness, complacency, and blindness among party comrades.

For this there were a number of reasons. First, the comrades "forgot" about the capitalist encirclement, whose agents were bound to activate wreckers, spies, and murderers inside the Soviet borders. Second, the comrades "overlooked" the fact that present-day Trotskyism was no longer the political current in working-class politics that it had been seven or eight years ago, but had degenerated into a band of wreckers, spies, and murderers—highway robbers ready to commit any foul act, not excluding espionage and outright high treason. They hadn't "noticed" this and so had not adopted in time new, more decisive ways of combatting the Trotskyists. Finally, the comrades had "overlooked" the important difference between present-day wreckers and those of the Shakhty-trial period. Unlike the latter, who were openly hostile to the Soviet system, the present-day Trotskyist wreckers were mainly people with party cards who would praise and play up to their superiors so as to gain their trust. They therefore had access to all our institutions, something, again, that our comrades "did not notice." And all this political "blindness" was largely a result of Soviet economic successes, which had their shady side in that they led people to disregard the things just mentioned and pay little attention to the "strange people" in the Central Committee offices who kept calling attention to wrecking.

The solution for the problem was "political education," which would help party comrades see the phenomena to which they had been blind. Party and nonparty Bolsheviks must be *made aware* of the aims and techniques of wrecking and espionage by foreign intelligence services. They must be made to understand that not the old "methods of discussion" but new methods were needed in order to fight present-day Trotskyism. The slogan, "master technology," must give way now to new ones, "master Bolshevism" and "liquidate our political trustfulness." It all meant that some "rotten" theories have to be discarded.

First, the theory that the class struggle would lessen as the socialist society advanced, whereas in fact successes only aroused more malice among enemies and led them to go to further extremes, with ready help from abroad, in harming the Soviet state. Second, the idea that wreckers do nothing but wreck and never show successes in work, whereas a "real wrecker" *must* show occasional successes so as to stay in place and be trusted—in order to continue wrecking. Third, the idea that wrecking could be blocked by systematic plan fulfillment, for existing plans were too low and failed to allow for huge reserves in the economy; besides, wreckers aim to do their work not in peace time but on the eve of war or during war and hence must be dislodged in advance. Fourth, the idea that wrecking could be checked by promoting the Stakhanov movement. Fifth, the idea that the Trotskyists had run out of reserves, for two-thirds of the Trotskyist Fourth International, such as the Sheflo group in Norway, the Souvarine group in France, the Ruth Fischers from Germany, the Max Eastmans in America, were spies and saboteurs. Sixth, the rotten theory that wrecking was not a serious problem because the Bolsheviks had the support of millions whereas the Trotskyist wreckers were a mere handful in number.

For whereas millions were needed to build a Dnieper dam, for example, it needed only a few dozen to blow it up; and several spies in an army or even an army-division staff could betray military plans to an enemy.

So, it was chiefly a problem of teaching party cadres how to orient themselves in the internal and international situation as mature Leninists. The party's leadership stratum, consisting of 3,000–4,000 higher leaders, or party "generals," 30,000–40,000 middle-ranking leaders, or party "officers," and 100,000–150,000 lower command staff, or party "noncoms," must receive better ideological education; and fresh forces, in line for advancement, must be added to them. Each party leader, from republic and regional party secretaries to secretaries of party cells, should select two other persons "capable of being their real deputies." Cell secretaries and afterward their deputies will be sent to four-month "party courses" in the regional centers. First secretaries of district party organizations and their deputies will go to eight-month "Leninist courses" in one of ten major centers. First or second secretaries of city organizations and then the most capable members of these organizations will attend six-month "courses in party history and policy" to be organized in the Central Committee. And regional secretaries as well as secretaries of republic central committees will attend a six-month "conference on internal and international politics." These comrades must provide not one but several shifts of possible replacements for leaders of the party Central Committee itself. Could all this be done? Yes, given only the willingness to part with the absurd and idiotic disease of carelessness, complacency, and political myopia. Then no enemies, internal or external, need be feared, "for we will smash them in the future just as we are smashing them in the present and did smash them in the past."[87]

So Stalin sought to "educate" the party to see what he saw. Had he been addressing a forum of free political men (only four members of that Central Committee were women), he would have received a crushing rebuff. His argumentation was forced, fearfully weak, not backed up by facts. The man recently executed as the foremost wrecker of industry, the ex-Trotskyist Piatakov, was in fact the highly capable, hard-driving, dedicated leader of Soviet industrialization. Trotsky and other ex-oppositionist leaders had not been conspiring with the Nazis. Trotskyist oppositionists were a negligible handful in Soviet society, if that. Industrial accidents, while widespread, were rarely the work of deliberate wreckers. Class struggle, insofar as it had existed at all in the early 1930s, was dampening down. Nobody had been plotting to kill Stalin, and Kirov's murder was not the work of those charged with it. Because the vision of reality that Stalin sought to impose was false, he could not have convincingly maintained it had he been confronted with fellow party leaders who spoke their minds, questioned his contentions, demanded hard evidence, and insisted on investigating (as Bukharin had proposed) the strange things happening behind the party's back at the Lubianka.

But it was not such an assembly that he was addressing. Although it included the party-state's highest dignitaries, among them five top professional commanders of the armed forces (Tukhachevsky, Yakir, Gamarnik, Bliukher, and Yegorov), the Central Committee was cowed into silence. How intimidated its members were is suggested by the freedom with which Stalin could and did reveal the radical extent of his purge plans by telling all party secretaries, high and low, each to choose two people "capable of being their real deputies," that is, their replacements, and again by his reference to the need for "several shifts" of replacements *for the Central Committee leaders themselves*. He could hardly have hinted more openly at the shortness of tenure of very many of those present. He was telling them in advance what lay ahead and what would be summed up by Khrushchev in 1956: "Of the 139 members and candidates of the party's Central Committee who were elected at the Seventeenth Congress, 89 persons, that is, 70 per cent, were arrested and shot (mostly in 1937–38)."[88]

So far were they from opposing Stalin that when he took the floor again two days later to give a concluding speech after the discussion of his report, he started by saying: "The discussion has shown that we now have complete clarity, that we comprehend the tasks, and are ready to liquidate the deficiencies in our work." Some of those present had outdone themselves in calling for punishment of all who had ever had the most tenuous ties with Trotskyists or Trotskyism. This we may infer from the fact that Stalin now cautioned against demands "heard here at the plenum" for casting out not only "real Trotskyists" but also those who had once oscillated toward Trotskyism but then turned away from it, and even those who had occasion "to walk along the same street as a Trotskyist." An individualized approach was needed, he said. Some one-time Trotskyists had really reformed, and some non-Trotskyists had maintained personal ties with individual Trotskyists for a time. But such comrades must not be lumped together with the Trotskyists.[89]

Then Stalin spoke about personnel matters, raising the question of the criteria higher officials should use in choosing their coworkers. There were two proper criteria: the coworkers should be (1) politically trustworthy and (2) qualified in a practical way. But too often those chosen were, instead, "acquaintances, friends, home folks, personally devoted people, masters at eulogizing their patrons." So arose "family groups" of people who sought to live in peace with one another, glorify one another, and not offend one another. Two examples were Comrade Mirzoian, regional party secretary in Kazakhstan, and Comrade Vainov, his counterpart in Yaros-

lavl region. The former brought thirty to forty of "his own people" with
him from Azerbaijan and the Urals, where he previously worked, and the
latter brought his "tail" of over a dozen people with him from the Donbas.

This glimpse into a Soviet political society permeated with patron-
client relations illuminates a serious problem confronting Stalin in the
Great Purge. First, let it be said that he was no less guilty than Mirzoian
and Vainov of having a "tail." Starting in the 1920s, he had built up his
own "family group" consisting of old party comrades like Molotov and
Voroshilov, home folks from the Transcaucasus like Ordzonikidze and
Mikoyan, admiring younger protégés like Zhdanov and Khrushchev,
"masters at eulogizing" their patron like Kaganovich and Beria, and totally
reliable staffmen like Yezhov, Poskrebyshev, and Mekhlis, who were as
personally devoted to him as they were dependent upon him. His own
political career was an archetypal case of the phenomenon that he vividly
depicted—and decried.

But it is clear why he now decried this phenomenon. The ties of
mutual solidarity among party and other Soviet officials were an obstacle
to the Terror in its incipient new phase. Patrons would be reluctant to
"identify the enemy" among their own clients, and clients would be reluctant to denounce their patrons. As Stalin's choice of provincial examples
indicates, the problem might be particularly troublesome for him outside
the capital, where provincial party bosses were all-dominant figures in
their regions and might even have "their own people" in the local NKVD
offices.

He cautioned party officials against carrying their "tails" with them
when transferred from one region to another. This, we may note, pointed
to one possible way of counteracting the practice: Moscow higher-ups
could see to it that an official being transferred to another region *not* take
his clients along. But as very many regional and, indeed, central officials
remained in place for the present, with their "family groups" intact, that
expedient would be of limited value, and Stalin went on to indicate, guard-
edly, how he intended to deal with the problem: he was going to introduce
certain democratic principles into his revolution from above. To what
extent the Central Committee members, and his subsequent nationwide
audience, understood him is another matter.

How, Stalin inquired, should officials' performance on the job he
checked? Some comrades considered it a matter of leaders checking up on
their subordinates "from above," but that was only one part. Another and
vitally important part was "from below" when the masses checked up on
leaders by critically noting their errors and ways of rectifying them. Bolsheviks, as Lenin had said, must have the courage openly to recognize and
correct their errors. And here Stalin cited a remarkable case to illustrate

that proposition: the error committed by "our party comrades" in 1930 when they forgot about the voluntary principle in organizing *kolkhozy,* under which collectivization would take several years, and tried to collectivize the peasantry in three or four months by the use of "administrative pressure," and the Central Committee had to restrain the overzealous comrades from their dizziness with success. Although the criticism aroused hostility, that did not keep the Central Committee from going against the current and setting the comrades onto the right path.

Only in the presence of terrorized people could Stalin have gotten away with this perversion of a history still fresh in many Bolshevik memories, a history of his own bungling of collectivization by the use of terror methods and his own attribution of the "error" to lower-level collectivizers. Now he compounded the offense by repeating the misattribution in a sermon on Bolshevik leaders' need to be brave in acknowledging their mistakes. Many in his plenum audience must have been outraged, but none dared speak up.

Warming to his populist theme, Stalin said ties with the masses must not be severed. The voices of rank-and-file party members, of "little people," must be heeded. Their view from below was a necessary complement to leaders' view from above, as shown some years ago when Central Committee members successfully interviewed some ordinary workers in search of a solution, which had eluded the Heavy Industry Commissariat, for the problem of raising coal output in the Donbas. Then Stalin cited a more topical example of heeding "simple people from down below." It was the case of Nikolenko, whose name he spelled Nikolaenko, the wholesale denouncer in Kiev who was expelled from the party as a lesson to slanderers and had been reinstated with honor, as a "heroine," after a special visit to Kiev by Kaganovich. Who, Stalin asked, is Nikolaenko? An ordinary "little person" who for a whole year gave signals that things were not well in the Kiev party organization, exposed "familyism" and the presence of Trotskyist traitors. Instead of heeding her, they shied away from her as though from a persistent fly, and finally expelled her. Only the Central Committee's intervention brought to light the fact that Nikolaenko was right and the Kiev organization wrong.

Here Stalin drove home the importance of keeping in touch with the people by recalling the Greek myth of Antaeus, the hero son of Poseidon, God of the Sea, and Gaea, Goddess of the Earth. The secret of Antaeus's power lay in the fact that whenever he was hard-pressed, he touched the earth, his mother, and gained new strength. His conqueror in the end was Hercules who, lifting him into the air, separated him from mother earth and vanquished him. The Bolsheviks, like Antaeus, were strong in keeping contact with their mother, the masses. In his reply to birthday greetings in

1929, Stalin had referred to the Bolshevik party as his mother. The maternal theme still occupied his mind save that now the mother was the people and very many Bolsheviks were his enemies. Nikolaenko was, Stalin indicated, no exception, since "One could cite dozens and hundreds more such cases." His revolution from above was reaching out now to the "simple people from down below," the Nikolaenkos, whose help he was soliciting for denouncing leading Bolshevik figures, together with their "family groups," as enemies of the people.[90]

He had still another plan for overcoming patron-client solidarities in the purge process. Zhdanov's report at the start of the plenum spoke of restoring inner party democracy by ensuring that party committees become truly elective, with observance of the secret ballot. Stalin returned to this theme in his concluding speech, saying that "unconditional electiveness of party organs, the right to nominate and withdraw candidates, closed voting, freedom of criticism and self-criticism" were necessary means of facilitating checkup on leaders by the party masses.

The plenum's resolution on Zhdanov's report specified that intraparty elections were to be held by 20 May. Reporting on the outcome, *Pravda* stated editorially that the elections "improved the composition of the party's leading cadres." In Moscow, for example, 40 percent of the members of party-cell committees (4,409 out of 10,799) were elected for the first time.[91] Whether improved or not, the composition had undergone a large change: 40 percent of the previous members had lost their cell-committee memberships. Party elections were likewise held at higher levels. The Moscow city and party committees were reelected, also with use of the secret ballot, by delegates to an all-Moscow party conference. Many years after, Khrushchev, who in 1937 was first secretary of the Moscow regional and city party committees, revealed how those secret intraparty elections took place:

I remember the following state of affairs at the Moscow party conference of 1937. All candidates nominated for membership on the Moscow city and regional committees had to be screened and "sanctioned" by the NKVD. Neither the Central Committee nor the party at large could promote its own members. The NKVD had the last word in assessing the activities of any party member and in deciding whether or not he could be elected to top party posts.[92]

Stalin's "intraparty democracy" was thus a smokescreen. Secrecy of the ballot, along with a show of democratism in the nominating process, were mechanisms employed to take party election results out of the hands of "leading party cadres," many of whom were marked down for extinction, and turn matters over to the NKVD.

Stalin ended the speech by presenting himself as the common man's friend, a compassionate leader, incensed against bureaucrats in the party apparatus who thought nothing of expelling "thousands and tens of thousands" of people from the party, chiefly for "passivity" or failure to master the party's program. He was referring, though he did not say so, to expulsions under the 1935–36 checkup and exchange of party documents. It was an outrage, he said, that a heartless policy resulted in the casting out of remarkable workers and splendid Stakhanovites from the party on such grounds, when they could have been dealt with considerately by being given a warning or a reprimand. Besides, Lenin's formula, enshrined in the party rules, required only *acceptance,* not full intellectual mastery of the program; otherwise it would be a party of intellectuals only.

These wholesale expulsions, Stalin said, were "antiparty" because they were bound to produce bitterness in one section of the party. The Trotskyist two-faced people followed the practice of picking up such embittered comrades and drawing them into the swamp of Trotskyist wrecking. Numerically, the Trotskyists had never been a big force. When the last party discussion occurred, in 1927, only 4,000 party members out of 854,000 voted for the Trotskyists, 2,600 abstained, and 123,000 did not take part in the voting, many because they were on travels. At most, then, only about 12,000 members sympathized with Trotskyism, and many of them later departed from it. "And if, in spite of this, the Trotskyist wreckers still have certain reserves around our party, that's because the wrong policy of certain of our comrades in the question of expulsion and reinstatement of expelled people, the heartless attitude of certain of our comrades toward the fate of individual workers, artificially multiply the numbers of the discontented and embittered and thereby create these reserves for the Trotskyists."[93]

Thus Stalin contrived to train his sights on the party leadership even while presenting himself as a force for moderation in the party purge, to identify himself with the simple people against the bigwigs, and to imply that the enemies were many even as he cited statistics on how few Trotskyists there really were, or had been, in the party. Just as he unloaded his responsibility for the miscarriage of collectivization on the grassroots collectivizers, so he unloaded his responsibility for much of the party purging of recent years on the "certain comrades" who had carried out his directives for the 1935–36 checkup and exchange—and now were being charged with abetting the Trotskyist wreckers by what they had done.

As they left the Kremlin after Stalin gave the concluding speech on 5 March, the plenum's last day, some of the many doomed Central Committee members may have reflected that they had witnessed a performance by one of history's grand masters of political guile, whose capacity for evil knew no bound.

The Storm Breaks

Almost from the day of the plenum's ending, the terror storm began. "Vigilance, vigilance, and still more vigilance—that's what the Central Committee demands of us! The party organizations did not draw all the conclusions, as the Central Committee demanded immediately after the dastardly murder of S. M. Kirov by the Trotskyist-Zinovievist scoundrels."[94] This was *Pravda*'s editorial message accompanying publication of Stalin's main plenum report. By then the Central Committee no longer existed as a collective political force, only as Stalin's personal apparatus of power acting in its name.

Meetings of party activists were called at town and district levels, in commissariats and other institutions, down to plants, *kolkhozy,* and regiments, to discuss the plenum. The commissariat meetings were, typically, three-day affairs, attended by several hundred persons, "nonparty Bolsheviks" included. The commissar would lead off with a report on the plenum and its implication for the commissariat, several dozen individuals would speak, others would hand in written materials on "deficiencies in the work," that is, denunciatory reports, and the meeting would close by adopting a resolution approving the plenum's results and undertaking to act in its spirit. Thus the resolution of the Heavy Industry Commissariat, now headed by V. I. Mezhlauk, called on heavy-industry workers to "expose enemies of the people to the end."[95] Mezhlauk himself fell victim to the Terror later on.

Kaganovich opened a three-day activists' meeting of his Commissariat of Railways on 10 March with a speech in which he said: "I cannot name a single railroad, a single rail network, where there was no Trotskyist-Japanese wrecking. What's more, not a single branch of railway transport is without such wreckers." His deputies at the commissariat, nearly all directors of railways, the heads of railway political departments, and other leading transport officials were thereupon arrested on the basis of lists sent to the NKVD.[96] Kaganovich's example was probably an egregious one, yet shows clearly what was only hinted in the newspaper reports at the time—that these were mostly denunciation meetings, followed by mass arrests.

Among the organizations struck by the terror storm was the NKVD itself. There are two versions of how Yezhov conducted the police purge in the aftermath of the plenum; both may be true. According to Orlov's account, he assembled heads of the NKVD's central departments one evening in March (date not given) and told them that they were being sent out to various regions to check on local party officials' political reliability.

Among the few not so assigned were A. G. Slutsky and Redens. Those receiving the assignments departed by train for the localities and were arrested en route; their assistants, sent two days later to join them, were similarly arrested before news of their chiefs' fate reached Moscow.[97] According to Krivitsky, Yezhov called a meeting of senior NKVD officials on 18 March in the club room of the Lubianka annex and gave a speech accusing Yagoda of having been a spy who served the Okhrana before the Revolution and the Germans ever since. The Yagoda-era officials among those present, having served under this spy and lived in his close proximity for many years, were themselves suspect now, and mutual denunciations began.[98] If both versions are true, this meeting would have taken place after the one reported by Orlov.

Having removed all but a very few leading holdovers from Yagoda's time, Yezhov proceeded to arrest those who had served as interrogators in preparing the first two Moscow trials. Preferring quick death to worse fates, some avoided arrest by suicide, either shooting themselves or jumping out of windows—the Lubianka's or their apartment houses'. One suicide was Chertok, a particularly brutal interrogator of Kamenev, who leaped from the balcony of his twelfth-floor apartment. From Moscow the police purge spread to NKVD offices in the provinces, claiming, it is estimated, the lives of over 3,000 operatives in 1937.[99]

Once the police purge was basically accomplished, Stalin, with the solid support of Yezhov's NKVD, was free to proceed with the most delicate operation of all: the beheading of the Red Army, to be followed by a full-scale military purge. There had been advance warning with the incrimination of Putna in the January trial and the casual mention of Tukhachevsky's name in that connection. A British Embassy message to London on 2 February 1937 passed on a rumor then current in Moscow that 525 Red Army officers were under arrest for Trotskyist activities. Stalin's seemingly hypothetical statement at the February–March plenum about the harm some spies could do in an army staff carried ominous overtones at the time of its publication. Voroshilov called and addressed a post-plenum meeting in the Defense Commissariat, attended by 2,000 people, but there is no indication that Tukhachevsky or other army chiefs came under attack at this point.[100] Rumors of Tukhachevsky's arrest that nevertheless began to circulate in the foreign colony were officially denied. In April he attended a dinner party given by Ambassador Davies for Red Army officers, and in that same month it was announced that he would be among the Soviet representatives at the coronation of King George VI in May.[101] Apparently, Stalin wanted to reassure Tukhachevsky and indirectly his army associates while preparations for the coup against them, involving special NKVD troops under Frinovsky, went forward in secret.

On 4 May 1937, as the time approached for Tukhachevsky's departure for London, the British Embassy was informed that owing to illness he would not go. The unofficial explanation given Tukhachevsky, who was not ill, was that an attempt on his life was being prepared in Warsaw.[102] Meanwhile, the marshal appeared in Red Square for the May Day parade.

Events moved rapidly from then on. On 11 May the Soviet press announced key personnel shifts: Tukhachevsky was moved to command of the Volga Military District; Marshal A. I. Egorov, chief of the General Staff, was appointed to Tukhachevsky's post as first deputy defense commissar; Army Commander B. M. Shaposhnikov became chief of the General Staff; and Yakir was shifted from his Kiev command to command of the Leningrad Military District. Simultaneously came the announcement of a reorganization of control of the armed forces with the creation of military soviets and of the revival of the Civil War institution of political commissars in all troop units and administrations. Under a subsequently published decree, the military soviets, consisting of the district commander, his chief of staff, and an unidentified third member, were placed in charge of all army and naval districts.[103] Under the guise of reestablishing party control of the armed forces as in the Civil War period, police control was being instituted in preparation for the wholesale military purge.

The doomed military chiefs were arrested separately and by stealth. Tukhachevsky conducted himself with characteristic quiet dignity during his last days of freedom. When his devoted driver, Ivan Kudriavtsev, suggested that he write a letter to Stalin, he said he had done so and that the letter was in Stalin's hands. Shortly after mid-May, accompanied by his wife, he departed by train for Kuibyshev to take over the new post. On arrival, he left his wife and daughter in the dining car of the train, then standing in the train station, and went off to local party headquarters to report to the regional party secretary, Postyshev. He was arrested while waiting in the outer office.[104] His wife and daughter returned to Moscow where she was arrested a day or two later along with Tukhachevsky's mother, sisters, and brothers Nikolai and Aleksandr. Later his wife and both brothers were killed on Stalin's orders, three sisters were sent to camps, his young daughter Svetlana was placed in a home for children of "enemies of the people" and arrested and sent to a camp on reaching the age of seventeen, and his mother and one sister died in exile.[105]

Putna and Primakov were already in custody. The other six who were to be accused of participating in the alleged plot were Yan Gamarnik, chief of the Red Army's Political Administration; A. I. Kork, head of the Frunze Military Academy; B. M. Feldman, chief of the Command Staff Administration; Robert P. Eideman, head of the Society for Air and Chemical Defense; I. P. Uborevich, commander of the Belorussian Military District;

and Yakir. They were all taken into custody during the month of May, with the exception of Gamarnik, who shot himself to death when the NKVD came to arrest him on 31 May at his Moscow apartment.

Archival materials made public for the first time in 1989 shed light on what happened next. The arrested army chiefs were pressured and physically tortured into willingness to testify that they had been involved in a conspiracy to overthrow the Soviet state. Their torturers also used the familiar device of promises to spare their lives and those of their loved ones if they performed on trial in accordance with the conspiracy script. Tukhachevsky, who at first denied guilt, gave in after "all measures were taken to break down his resistance." How brutal these measures were becomes clear in the light of the finding that some greyish brown spots on pages of the protocols of his interrogation are bloodstains whose unusual shape indicates that they came from a body in motion, in other words that Tukhachevsky was reeling from blows to his head or body at the moment of "confessing." Similar savage treatment was meted out to others among the arrested military leaders who initially resisted confessing, and with similar results. Stalin personally followed all this day by day. He received protocols of the interrogations, had meetings with Yezhov nearly every day, and twice, on 21 and 28 May, saw Yezhov's deputy, M. P. Frinovsky.

Before the end of May he circulated, as a Politburo document, a message to the Central Committee members and candidates saying that the "Central Committee" had obtained materials exposing Central Committee member Rudzutak and candidate member Tukhachevsky as participants in an anti-Soviet Trotskyist-rightist conspiratorial bloc and espionage work against the USSR on behalf of fascist Germany, and proposing that the Central Committee members and candidates vote to expel the two men and refer their cases to the NKVD. The Central Committee members and candidates were polled and of course the proposal carried. Similar proposals went out in the following several days concerning Yakir, Uborevich, Gamarnik (before his suicide), and some others.[106]

An expanded session of the military council of the Defense Commissariat was held behind closed doors between 1 and 4 June. In addition to the regular members of the council (twenty of whom were under arrest as "conspirators" by 1 June), the participants included 116 military officers from the provinces and the central apparatus of the Defense Commissariat. Reporting to the council as defense Commissar, Voroshilov announced that the NKVD had uncovered at the level of the army leadership a long-active but deeply concealed counterrevolutionary fascist organization, and he used some of the already extorted false depositions of the arrested military leaders to back up this contention. On the following day, 2 June, Stalin took the floor and, again with references to the false confessions, he declared that "a military-political conspiracy against the Soviet regime, stimulated and financed by the German fascists," had existed in the Soviet Union. Its leaders, he alleged, were Trotsky, Rykov, Bukharin, Rudzutak, L. M. Karakhan (Soviet ambassador to Turkey at the time), Yenukidze and Yagoda, and also the military men now under arrest. The leaders of the plot, he went on, systematically carried on relations with the German fascists, especially with the German *Reichswehr,* and "shaped all their work to suit the tastes and orders of the German fascists." Speaking of Tukhachevsky Stalin said that "He gave our operational plan, the operational plan—our holy of holies—to the German *Reichswehr.* He had a meeting with representatives of the German *Reichswehr.* A spy? Yes, a spy." He followed with similar allegations concerning Yakir, Uborevich, Kork, and Karakhan. All of them were spies and participants in the plot to sell out Soviet Russia to fascist Germany.

Then Stalin went on to make the same charge against still other military officers, accusing them of espionage. At this point he continued his tirade as follows:

This was a military-political conspiracy. It was a handwritten product of the German *Reichswehr.* I think that these men are dolls and puppets in the hands of the *Reichswehr.* The *Reichswehr* wants systematic deliveries of military secrets from these gentlemen, and these gentlemen passed military secrets to the *Reichswehr.* The *Reichswehr* wants the government that exists here to be overthrown and they undertook to accomplish this, but didn't succeed. The *Reichswehr* wanted to make sure that in event of war all would be in readiness, wanted the army to take the course of wrecking so that the army would not be ready for defending the country, that's what the *Reichswehr* wanted. . . . That's the basic thing. It follows that this conspiracy is not so much an internal affair as a product of external conditions, not so much a matter of internal policy in our country as it is a policy of the German *Reichswehr.* They wanted to make a second Spain out of the USSR and the recruited spies who were active in this cause. That's the situation.

Stalin went on to say that three to four hundred military men were already under arrest, and then accused the Soviet intelligence organs of criminal laxity, saying that there had been uncovered in the intelligence organs a whole group of people working for Germany, for Japan, for Poland. He voiced dissatisfaction over the absence of warning signals from the localities about such people, and demanded such signals (that is, denunciations), adding: "Even if only five percent of it were the truth, even that would be something." At the end the members of the military council sharply condemned the "conspirators" and gave assurances of their boundless devotion to the party and the government. However, thirty-four of the forty-two who spoke up in the discussion of Voroshilov's report were themselves soon under arrest as conspirators.[107] The fact that this military council meeting had taken place became known to the public on 13 June when an order of the day by Voroshilov was published. In it he called the session an "enlarged one," with "members of the government" taking part, but did not mention that Stalin was a participant.

The trial and condemnation of Tukhachevsky, Yakir, Kork, Uborevich, Eideman, Feldman, Primakov, and Putna took place behind closed doors before a special tribunal which Stalin personally selected. It was called a "special judicial session of the Supreme Court of the USSR." Stalin included in the membership of it, in addition to Ulrikh, some prominent military figures: Ya. I. Alksnis, V. K. Bliukher, S. M. Budenny, V. M. Shaposhnikov, I. P. Belov, P. E. Dybenko, and N. D. Kashirin. He chose these particular military men for the role assigned to them as judges because, during the military council meeting and in Stalin's presence, they had all voiced bitter condemnation of Tukhachevsky and the other arrested military men as "conspirators."[108] Belov, Bliukher, Alksnis, Kashirin, and Dybenko would soon afterward find themselves accused of having been participants in the nonexistent military conspiracy and pay with their lives.

Stalin personally supervised every step in the preparation for the special judicial session. On 5 June, in company with Molotov, Kaganovich, and Voroshilov, he received Yezhov and Vyshinsky to give the text of the act of indictment a final going-over. On 9 June Vyshinsky briefly interrogated the accused men so as to confirm as prosecutor the authenticity of their depositions. Lest any hitch occur, the interrogators of the arrested men were present on this occasion (perhaps as a warning of what could happen to anyone who sought to retract his confession). Stalin received Vyshinsky twice that day and Vyshinsky signed the act of indictment. It said that the accused had formed a military-Trotskyist organization in 1932–33 on instructions from the German General Staff and Trotsky. It had engaged in wrecking, sabotage, terror, and preparations for the overthrow of the government and restoration of capitalism. Late at night on 9 June, Stalin, Molotov and Yezhov received *Pravda* editor Mekhlis to arrange for publication on 11 June of an official announcement of the uncovering of the conspiracy.[109]

Before the special judicial session took place on 11 June, the accused men were invited to submit repentant appeals for clemency to Stalin and Yezhov. This was done so as to give them the illusion that they could preserve their lives by cooperating fully in the pseudo-trial. On the copy of Yakir's statement, in which he affirmed his love for Stalin, the party, and the country, appear notations by Stalin, Molotov, Voroshilov, and Kaganovich. Stalin's says: "A scoundrel and a prostitute." Molotov's and Voroshilov's say: "An absolutely precise formulation." Kaganovich's reads: "For the scoundrel, bastard and s. (slut), only one punishment, execution."[110] By circulating such materials to his close associates, Stalin was giving them the opportunity to purchase their own continued well-being and that of their families by complicity in his action, and they paid the price, becoming still more broken men in the process.

The last act in the tragedy was a one-day pretense of a trial. The interrogators accompanied the victims to the special judicial session and were with them in the waiting room as well as in the room where the special panel met. After the reading of the indictment, the accused men duly confessed themselves guilty and in the ensuing cross-examination they confirmed, in the main, their depositions. When military men on the panel addressed specific questions to them, however, they tended to reply in noncommittal ways or deny knowing anything about the matter in question. Thus when Bliukher asked Tukhachevsky if he could confirm that his espionage activity began before 1932–33, Tukhachevsky replied to this allusion to his contacts with the *Reichswehr* in the 1920s by saying: "I don't know whether that could be considered espionage." Questions of this kind led Tukhachevsky to say at one point: "I feel as if I'm dreaming."[111] No use was made during the trial of disinformational materials from Germany although documents of this sort were found much later in Stalin's personal archive.[112]

On Stalin's personal orders in advance of the trial, all the defendants were sentenced to die, and the sentences were carried out on 12 June. But while the trial was still in session on 11 June, Stalin sent out over his own signature the following message to the authorities in the republics and regions: "In connection with the trial taking place of the spies and wreckers Tukhachevsky, Yakir, Uborevich and others, the Central Committee asks you to organize meetings of workers and, where possible, peasants, and meetings of Red Army units, and pass resolutions on the necessity of applying the supreme measure of repression. The trial should be finished tonight. The announcement of the sentences will be published tomorrow." Within nine days of the trial, 980 military commanders and high-ranking political officers in the army were under arrest as participants in the alleged military conspiracy. They too were tortured into giving false depositions and these in turn led to the arrest of a host of other innocent men.[113] The great military massacre was now under way, and Russia would very nearly pay with her life for Stalin's success in bringing it off.

His coup against the military leaders was the culminating act in the year-long implementation of the conspiracy from above. It highlighted, if only briefly, what was happening at that time: a protracted, masked takeover of all power by a man resolved to make himself an absolute autocrat. It is a measure of Stalin's supreme skill as an engineer of such takeovers that hardly anyone, at home or abroad, seems to have comprehended clearly, as Bukharin did toward the end, that a kind of *coup d'état* was occurring.

The floodgates of terror were wide open now. And while a few Bolsheviks had the courage to express opposition, even face-to-face with Stalin, to the terror raging in the country—and suffered lethal consequences—they did so as individuals. There is no evidence that the party offered any concerted resistance as it was going down. At appalling cost to the country, Stalin managed to overthrow the collective party regime bequeathed by Lenin *without any overt sign that this was happening*. Thus a dispatch written in the U.S. Embassy, signed by Ambassador Davies, said that diplomatic circles in Moscow attributed responsibility for the execution of the army leaders not to Stalin personally but "to the 'action of the party' through its party leaders," among whom Stalin was simply "by far the strongest character."[114]

Periodically published reports that the Central Committee had met in plenary session for such-and-such discussions supported the false appearance of continued rule by the sovereign party body. Thus *Pravda* announced on 30 June 1937 that a regular Central Committee plenum took place a few days earlier, that it discussed agricultural matters (on which its decisions were also published), and approved a draft statute on elections to the Supreme Soviet. What *Pravda* did not say, and what was revealed only after Stalin died, is that this plenum also saw a mass denunciation session in which Central Committee members, in an atmosphere that must have bordered on hysteria, strove to meet Stalin's demand for "Bolshevik criticism and self-criticism."

"Comrades! Everyone is making a speech saying what he knows about everyone else," Khrushchev later quoted the ex-Commissar of Public Health, G. N. Kaminsky, as saying on that occasion. Kaminsky went on:

I also have something I want to say for the information of the party. When I worked in Baku there were rumors rampant that during the occupation of Baku by English troops, Beria worked for the counterintelligence service of the Mussavat government. Since the Mussavat counterintelligence service was under the control of the English, it was said that Beria must be an English intelligence agent operating through the Mussavatists.

Beria, Khrushchev further recalled, made no reply to the accusation, and Kaminsky disappeared immediately after the plenum ended. Lest it be inferred that Kaminsky's exposé of Beria was a thrust against Beria's patron Stalin, we should note that Malenkov also criticized Beria on that occasion, albeit only for "self-glorification," and that he made the same charge against the secretary of a Central Asian party bureau, who was later arrested.[115] Thus, terrorized Central Committee members were now vying with one another for the favor of their sovereign master, the autocrat Stalin. Most did not receive it.

So ended the party regime created in the Bolshevik Revolution of 1917–21. It was subverted from within and overthrown by its general secretary. A fitting epitaph for it would be the reported last words of Marshal Tukhachevsky before the tribunal that condemned him on June 11:

And so, citizen judges, including you Ulrikh, and you Shaposhnikov, and you Bliukher, and you Budenny, I want you to know that both you and we here on the prisoners' bench are involved in the circle of guilt. To look on all this and remain silent is a crime. And for all these years we have looked on and remained silent. And for this both you and all of us deserve to be shot.[116]

Stalin and champion sugar beet grower Maria Demchenko.

Mikhail Tomsky, Voroshilov, and Yan Rudzutak, 1933. *Staatsbibliothek Berlin*

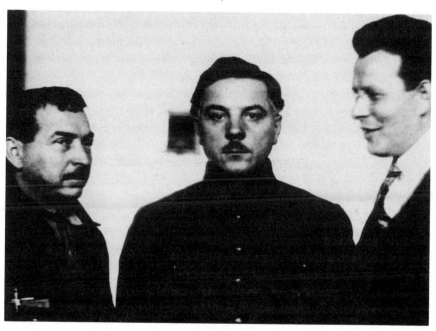

Gerasimov's cult painting of Stalin and Voroshilov in Kremlin.

Lev Kamenev, 1935. *Staatsbibliothek Berlin*

Painting of Stalin at Kirov's bier.

Stalin looks over his new ZIS-101, 1935.

Stalin with children, 1936.

Stalin statue at Paris World Fair, 1937.

Stalin and Zhdanov, 1936.

Above, Nikolai Bukharin shortly before
his arrest in 1937.

Anna Larina, Bukharin's wife.

Prison laborers building the Belomor Canal between the Baltic and the White Sea.

Chief prosecutor Vyshinsky at the Moscow trial. *David King Collection*

Stalin shaking hands with Ribbentrop, Moscow, September 1939.

Molotov in Berlin, 1940. Gustav Hilger translates for von Ribbentrop.

One would have to write about it in a way to make the heart stop
beating and the hair stand on end.

—BORIS PASTERNAK, *I Remember*

17

THE TERROR PROCESS

STALIN now unleashed the full fury of the Great Purge. With the
Central Committee cowed, the NKVD under Yezhov and his men,
the military chiefs shot, the purge machinery in place, documentation on very many victims in hand, and the existence of a vast
antistate conspiracy established as dogma by the purge trials, he proceeded
with the radical project of remaking Soviet political society.

A firestorm of repressions enveloped the society's upper and middle
strata from March and April 1937 and did not finally subside until 1939.
The statistics of victimization, still a subject of study and debate, will be
discussed below. Suffice it to say here that no major nation has ever
suffered state terrorism of such ferocity as Russia did then, that those
arrested and put to death or consigned to slave-labor camps numbered in
the millions, and that the grief and hardship borne by their loved ones defy
computation. The moral, spiritual, economic, military, and cultural dam-

age to the Soviet state was likewise incalculably great.

Memoirs of some who lived through that time say that by the hot summer of 1937 they had the impression that madness was abroad in the land. True, there were worker settlements beyond city limits that remained fairly tranquil.¹ Possibly things were tranquil, too, in various rural places. At the height of the Terror, Stalin made a special point of granting concessions to the peasantry. A decree on 21 March 1937 cancelled arrears on collective-farm and individual peasants' grain deliveries to the state for 1936, and allowed peasants to sell surplus grain immediately instead of waiting until they had delivered requisitioned grain to the state. Such propeasant acts, combined with the fortuitous fact that fine weather made 1937 a bumper crop year, unlike 1936 with its prolonged drought in many areas, were conducive to good feeling among peasants. Many may have taken grim satisfaction that Communists, who had inflicted the ordeal of collectivization and famine upon them not long ago, were now receiving their just deserts. When the Terror claimed Politburo member Kosior, who as secretary of the Ukrainian Communist Party had overseen the famine in the Ukraine, a peasant-born young Ukrainian army officer, Grigorenko, considered it "just retribution for his activities against the people."²

For upper- and middle-level urban Russia this was the time of terrible travail. Arrests took on epidemic proportions. "People are not arrested, they just disappear," said a firsthand report that appeared in the *Bulletin of the Opposition* abroad. "In the midst of a meeting, a man goes to the bathroom and doesn't come back. That way it's less conspicuous. Where he ended up nobody, of course, asks."³ But very many arrests occurred where people lived. Black NKVD cars called ravens rumbled through city streets at night. For many, especially those of any standing, the nights, particularly between 11 p.m. and 2 a.m., were not for sleeping but for agonized waiting. When a young girl who went out partying one night came home late and rang her apartment doorbell after finding that she had forgotten her key, she had to wait a long while and ring again before her father appeared at the door, ashen-faced and fully dressed. He stared at her for a long minute and then, instead of heaving a sigh of relief, vented his tension by slapping her uncomprehending face.⁴ Starting in 1937, Litvinov kept a revolver on his night table. The foreign commissar was determined to kill himself if they came for him rather than let them put him to death.⁵

Some older persons had the good sense to retire and live in lonely isolation; the greater danger was to belong to a work collective where purge meetings went on and the institution's NKVD-manned special section was checking out potential victims. Some went to distant places and disappeared from view. A few whose life chances were low survived by lucky accident: someone in the NKVD forgot to include their names on a list of people to be picked up.[6] Many sought to drown their fear as the cheerful drunkenness of earlier years gave way to a widespread drunkenness of desperation in the later 1930s.[7] The lively political discussions that had previously gone on in Communist intellectuals' apartments died away into whispered conversations among intimate friends on the one remaining subject of supreme interest: the reasons for the purge.[8]

Stalin's Role

Adept at the tactics of dissimulation, Stalin now kept inconspicuous. After his speeches at the February–March 1937 plenum, he gave no major public address for two years. He spoke for publication only twice more in 1937 and only once in all of 1938, and on these occasions no more than alluded to the Terror. He had Molotov give the annual 6 November address in both 1937 and 1938, although the former occasion was special as October's twentieth anniversary, and it fell to Mikoyan to give the NKVD-glorifying main speech at the celebration in late 1937 of the twentieth anniversary of the Cheka's founding. Stalin absented himself from the high party officials in attendance, whose group photo appeared in the press, and only showed up for the concert put on afterward in the Bolshoi Theater, where the event was held. Meanwhile, he moved his personal work quarters and key parts of the Central Committee Secretariat from Staraya Square into the Kremlin.[9] Never one to mingle freely with the people, this Kremlin-dweller now became more remote than ever.

He thereby encouraged people to believe that the Terror was not of his doing and that those responsible for it might not even be keeping him informed about it. Ehrenburg, who spent the early months of 1938 in Moscow on leave from his war-correspondent work in Spain, much later recalled the eminent theater director Meyerhold saying to him: "They conceal it from Stalin." Pasternak, whom Ehrenburg met while walking his dog one night in Lavrushensky Lane, waved his arms amid the snowdrifts and said: "If only someone would tell Stalin about it." Both probably understood more than they let on. The writer Isaak Babel, a friend of Yezhov's wife, went to see her to "find a key to the puzzle," and reported: "It's not a matter of Yezhov. Of course he plays his part, but he's not at the bottom of it." Yet, Ehrenburg claims that he himself was inclined to attribute responsibility to Yezhov and says: "We thought (perhaps we wanted to think) that Stalin knew nothing about the senseless violence committed against the Communists, against the Soviet intelligentsia."[10]

Another theory attributed the blame, both for the Terror and Stalin's ignorance of it, to mysterious anti-Communist enemies in high places. In memoirs published after Stalin's death a man who commanded a military district at the time recalls a conversation with the commissar of a rifle division, who said:

What's going on? . . . I don't believe that there are so many enemies in the party. I don't believe it. Maybe people alien to us are sitting at some high level in the party, in the security organs. It seems as though the party's cadres are deliberately being destroyed. I'll bet my head that Iosif Vissarionovich doesn't know about it. Signals, complaints, and protests are intercepted and don't get to him. Stalin has got to be apprised of it. Otherwise, disaster. Tomorrow they'll take you and then me. We can't be silent.[11]

This theory of stealthy counterrevolution was held also by some prisoners in the camps, who reasoned that fascists had wormed their way into powerful places.[12] Evidence now on the record shows that such views were a product of Stalin's deviousness and that they also resulted from the resistance of many to the idea that he was the driving force of what was increasingly shaping up as the destruction of the Leninist regime.

Behind the scenes, he was the Terror's director general. His Kremlin office was the command post. Those who played prominent parts in public, like Vyshinsky and Ulrikh, were his puppets. Yezhov, who was elevated to candidate membership of the Politburo in 1937 and lent his name to the epoch, remained throughout a subservient underling. He would come to Stalin every day with a thick sheaf of papers and confer with him for three to four hours, receiving orders.[13] He would turn over to Stalin, for his approval, lists of prospective victims with proposed sentences indicated on them. During 1937–38, Stalin approved 383 such lists, with the names of 44,000 party, government, Komsomol, military, economic, and other officials as well as cultural figures.[14] These were mostly persons of sufficient standing for Stalin to identify them or have a sense of who they were; decisions on far larger numbers of lesser victims were made by others. Sentencing, often *in absentia,* followed as a matter of course.

Stalin actively supervised the terror process, directing preparations for the coming third Moscow trial, issuing arrest orders on his own initiative, busying himself with details of ongoing interrogations, specifying on occasion what form of torture should be used on this or that party victim, reprimanding NKVD men if they failed to extract the required confessions of guilt, and even arranging face-to-face confrontations in his office between accused leading figures and those who had been tortured into being their accusers.[15] He personally intervened to ensure the bloodbath in the armed forces ushered in by the destruction of the Tukhachevsky group— by appearing at a secret conference of armed-force political officers in

August 1937 and demanding the extermination of alleged enemies in the military. When one participant asked, "Can we raise our voices to the full concerning enemies of the people?" Stalin answered: "To the whole world. You absolutely must."[16] Thereupon Voroshilov and Yezhov issued an order declaring that an elaborate espionage network existed in the armed forces and demanding denunciation of suspects, after which the NKVD carried out massive repressions in the Red Army in the latter part of 1937.[17]

The dutiful Yezhov and other servitors had difficulty keeping up with Stalin's unlimited demands. On his copy of the depositions of one person under arrest, Stalin penned the notation: "Comrade Yezhov. Those by whose names in the text I've put the letters 'ar.' should be arrested, if they've not already been." On a Yezhov document with lists of persons under arrest and data on others being "checked out" for arrest, his notation read: "They should not be checked out, but arrested."[18] These were not isolated cases. While visiting the office of Mekhlis, now head of the Main Political Administration of the armed forces, the *Pravda* journalist Mikhail Kol'tsov was shown a thick document containing the depositions of the recently arrested *Izvestiia* editor, Tal'. On it was scrawled in red pencil Stalin's laconic message to Mekhlis and Yezhov ordering the arrest of all persons mentioned in them.[19] Not even Stalin's trusted purge collaborator Shkiriatov, working as Yezhov's deputy, could always divine his master's desires. When Stalin commissioned him to look into charges by a Komsomol official, Olga Mishakova, against A. V. Kosarev, then head of the Komsomol, Shkiriatov suggested that Kosarev be let off with reprimand. "If something is not right," he said in his memorandum, "you will correct me."[20] Stalin's correction was Kosarev's arrest and the destruction of the whole Komsomol leadership. On rare occasions, for reasons of his own, Stalin would grant the gift of life. "We won't touch the wife of Mayakovsky," he said to Yezhov concerning Lily Brik,[21] and according to unconfirmed rumor he wrote "Don't touch this cloud-dweller" by the name of Pasternak when it appeared on one of the lists of the provisionally condemned.

But how could Stalin work his terrorist will on a nation of 165 million? The people's history-bred passivity in the face of governmental power was a help, as was the discipline that went with party membership. Careful advance planning and organization in the stage-by-stage conspiracy from above, along with the reshaping of the security police into a new *oprichnina* under Stalin's personal direction, also played a big part. One other factor was the incomprehension in Bolshevik minds of what was happening. Kol'tsov, famous now for his *Pravda* reportage from Spain and his *Spanish Diary,* a man who saw Stalin often, paced his brother's room saying:

I think, I think. And I can't understand anything. What is happening? How did it suddenly turn out that we have so many enemies? These are people we've known for years, side by side with whom we've lived! Army commanders, Civil War heroes, old party men! And for some reason, hardly have they disappeared behind bars than they instantly confess that they're enemies of the people, spies, agents of foreign intelligence. What's it all about? I feel I'm going out of my mind.[22]

Stalin's mind and motives, hence also his actions, were a closed book to such otherwise knowledgeable people. Not understanding him, they could not understand the meaning of his Terror. Their incomprehension played into his hands.

Also noteworthy is the extraordinary cunning and duplicity that Stalin showed in his dealings with various individuals who were condemned in his own mind to destruction. He would convincingly reassure them that they had nothing to worry about. He toasted the Civil War hero, D. F. Serdich, and proposed that they drink to *Brüderschaft*—shortly before Serdich's arrest. He saw and reassured the historian Yuri Steklov, who had asked for an appointment because of worry over arrests; Steklov was arrested that very night. He spoke warmly with Marshal Bliukher a few days before this military leader was taken. A. Serebrovsky, deputy commissar of heavy industry, was picked up at a hospital two days after Stalin phoned his wife to express concern that she was going about on foot and told her that he was putting a Kremlin car at her disposal.[23]

Assistants showed similar duplicity. One day, as Mekhlis sat in Kol'tsov's *Pravda* office, he warned Kol'tsov that a trusted long-time *Pravda* man named Avgust was a masked enemy. Kol'tsov replied that Avgust was an utterly honest Bolshevik who had endured penal servitude under the tsar, to which Mekhlis rejoined that the tsarist secret service had recruited provocateurs from among precisely such "most honest" ones. Just then Avgust came into the office to present newspaper columns for Kol'tsov's signature. Mekhlis was transformed. "Ah, Comrade Avgust," he said, "happy to see you. How are you getting along, dear friend, how's your health?" The unwittingly condemned Avgust was deeply touched by Mekhlis' solicitude.[24] Around that time Kol'tsov had a three-hour session with Stalin, who questioned him on Spain and solicitously named him "Don Miguel." There was only one strange moment. As he was going out the door, Stalin called to him: "Comrade Kol'tsov, do you possess a revolver?" When Kol'tsov, surprised, answered affirmatively, Stalin asked: "But you don't intend to shoot yourself with it?" Assured that he had no such intention, Stalin said: "Splendid! Once again thank you, Comrade Kol'tsov. So long, Don Miguel!"[25] Not long afterward, Kol'tsov was arrested.

Even with all this working for him, Stalin could not have carried off the monstrous mass repressions of 1937–38 without an army of active helpers, from Politburo members and other high officials down to the thousands of NKVD interrogators in prisons all over the country, overseers and guards of the burgeoning camp population, personnel of the NKVD special sections in Soviet institutions, secret informers throughout the society, press writers who inveighed against enemies of the people, and rank-and-file party members and "nonparty Bolsheviks" who contributed denunciations. How did he manage to mobilize this army? Part of the answer is that he compelled all those in his entourage and in high administrative posts to become his accomplices in the terror process. Those whom he could not so compel, or feared that he could not, he destroyed. Rudzutak, for example, who was a candidate member of the Politburo as well as a full member of the Central Committee, was arrested in May 1937 while entertaining friends at his country dacha near Moscow, and later executed.[26] By this time, Stalin was simply disregarding the rule that a Central Committee plenum's sanction was needed for a member's arrest. Other Politburo members or candidates whom he destroyed were Kosior, Chubar, and Postyshev. Petrovsky he reduced to a wreck by destroying his son. With Kirov, Kuibyshev, and Ordzhonikidze out of the way, only Andreev, Kaganovich, Kalinin, Molotov, Voroshilov, and Mikoyan, in addition to Stalin, remained of the fifteen Politburo members and candidates elected after the Seventeenth Congress. Zhdanov, Khrushchev, and Yezhov were added, and Beria and Shvernik after Yezhov's removal at the end of 1938. They all paid the price of survival by becoming Stalin's active accomplices.

An exception of sorts was Kalinin, who was useful as a symbolic benign figure in the powerless post of chairman of the Supreme Soviet's presidium. When Ivan Akulov, who had served under Kalinin in the executive organ of the parliamentary body, was arrested in 1937, the weak but well-meaning Kalinin sought to intercede for this prominent Old Bolshevik who was his very close friend. Stalin dismissed the matter, saying, "Thou always wert a liberal, Mikhail Ivanovich." And to impress upon him the futility of such efforts, Kalinin's wife, Ekaterina, was arrested and kept in confinement for many years.[27] During all that time the nominal president of the Soviet state sat in the Politburo with Stalin, without whose orders no one would have dared to arrest his wife. She was released shortly before he died in 1946, and after his death sent back into exile. Another aide whom Stalin broke in this way was Otto Kuusinen, a leading Comintern operative, whose wife and son were arrested. When Stalin asked Kuusinen why he didn't seek his son's freedom, Kuusinen meekly replied, "Evidently, there were serious reasons for his arrest," whereupon Stalin ordered the son's—but not the wife's—release.[28]

One method of making accomplices out of subordinates was to require them to cosign condemnatory documents. Khrushchev testifies:

When an investigation was concluded and Stalin considered it necessary for others besides himself to put their signatures to the report, he would sign it then and there, at the meeting, and after that it would be passed around to the rest of us, and we would sign without reading it, as if we knew all about it from the information Stalin gave, the views he stated. And thereby, so to speak, it was already, so to speak, a kind of collective sentence.[29]

In other cases, Stalin would pass a death-sentence document to a particular associate for cosigning. One that came from Yezhov contained four lists of persons to be tried by the Military Collegium (whose action would consist in automatically rubber stamping Stalin's decision): a general list, a list of military men, a list of NKVD men, and a list of "wives of enemies of the people." Yezhov wrote: "I request sanction to condemn them all under the first category" (the "first category" meant death). Stalin's signature, along with the word *za* (in favor) appeared under each list, and beneath his was a second signature: V. Molotov.[30]

Stalin also kept confederates in line by having dossiers compiled on them for possible later use. When he sent Khrushchev to Kiev in January 1938 to take charge of the Ukrainian Republic, Khrushchev arranged to bring along a competent official of his acquaintance, one Lukashov, to run the republic's trade commissariat. Lukashov was arrested. Later, after his release, he told Khrushchev that he had been tortured into denouncing him as a member of a conspiracy.[31] In other cases—Kaganovich's was one— the NKVD would arrest a member of the man's personal retinue, a chauffeur or bodyguard for example, as a source of enforced testimony against him, and the danger such an arrest represented would be obvious to the man. He would then be all the more eager to remain in Stalin's good graces.

The Twenty-Second Congress put some illustrations on the record. When Stalin received a letter in June 1937 saying that G. I. Lomov, an Old Bolshevik who was commissar of justice in Lenin's government of 1917, had been on friendly terms with Rykov and Bukharin, he appended a notation: "Comrade Molotov, what about this?" Molotov answered, "In favor of immediate arrest of that bastard Lomov," whose arrest and execution followed.[32] On a document sanctioning the imprisonment, but not execution, of the wives of many arrested officials, Molotov wrote by the name of one of them "VMN" (initials for "supreme measure of punishment," death by shooting).[33] In the case of a professor working in Narkomindel who wrote asking his intercession for his arrested father, Molotov penned a note to Yezhov, "Is this professor still in Narkomindel and not in the NKVD?"[34] In addition to securing the arrest of railway officials by lists, which included his deputies and all heads of railways, Kaganovich wrote thirty-two personal letters demanding the arrest of eighty-three leading transport officials.[35] In May 1937 Zhdanov called a meeting of the Leningrad regional party committee and announced that two of its high officials, Chudov and Kadatsky, had been exposed as enemies. As the meeting ended he was approached by a committee member, D. A. Lazurkina, who said she was sure that Kadatsky, a party member since 1913 and a man who had fought all the intraparty oppositions, was loyal, whereupon Zhdanov said: "Lazurkina, cut that talk, or things will go badly for you."[36] They did. She was arrested and spent seventeen years in camp.

Still another way of making accomplices out of leading figures was to send them on purge expeditions into the provinces, whence they reported on their findings and took action according to Stalin's instructions. Although they let it be known locally that they were acting on his authority, no mention of this was ever made in the press.[37] On arriving in the regional center of Ivanovo in June 1937, Kaganovich wired Stalin that the regional party secretary should be arrested and that wrecking was rife in industry, agriculture, supply, trade, public health, education, and political work. "The apparatuses of regional institutions and the regional party committees have proved to be exceedingly infested," he said.[38] The regional party and government officialdom was repressed *en masse* following receipt of Stalin's approving reply. Meanwhile, Kaganovich and his team proceeded to Smolensk, where the long-time party secretary, Ivan Rumyantsev, and his clientele were arrested on charges of being traitors and spies for German-Japanese fascism. The ravages of this particular operation can be seen from a report published three months later by Rumyantsev's successor, D. Korotchenkov, that about a thousand new persons had been installed in higher party, Komsomol, and government posts in the region.[39] Malenkov went on such purge missions with Yezhov to Belorussia and with Beria to Armenia. Andreev, Mikoyan, and Shkiriatov were sent on like missions as well. In Moscow, Malenkov and Beria alternated in visiting Lefortovo prison, where they personally tortured Communists under interrogation.[40]

In addition to members of Stalin's immediate entourage, heads of various agencies were made to become accomplices in the terror process by placing their signatures on death lists received from the NKVD. An example that has come to light since Stalin died is Alexander Fadeev, who in 1937–38 was a key figure in the leadership of the Writers' Union (he became its secretary in 1939). In 1956, after official Russia was staggered by Khrushchev's revelations about the Stalin Terror in his Twentieth-Congress secret speech, Fadeev told a writer friend that Stalin, who behaved as a loving father toward him and gave him many suggestions (including one that he write a novel entitled *Ferrous Metallurgy* on the basis of materials to be supplied to him about the uncovering of a wreckers' conspiracy in the iron and steel industry), had showered him, as well as others in comparable positions, with money and honors. He said that in 1937 the Politburo passed a decision that arrests of persons associated with one or another organization had to be sanctioned by the heads of these organizations and that, as a leader of the Writers' Union, he repeatedly sanctioned writers' arrests. He asked this friend whether he would be able to go on living if he learned that he had assisted in destroying very many honest people. The friend said that he probably couldn't. On 13 May 1956, a few hours after their last conversation, Fadeev shot himself to death.[41]

"We all took the easy way out by keeping silent in the hope that not we but our neighbors would be killed," writes Nadezhda Mandelstam of 1937–38.[42] This generalization is broadly true, but there were exceptions. Acting alone and usually at the cost of their lives, some had the courage to protest or otherwise resist the terror process. Aron Sol'ts, a prominent Old Bolshevik who was known among fellow ex-revolutionaries as the "party's conscience" and who had shared a bunk with Stalin when the latter came to Petersburg in 1912 after escaping from exile, was working in the Procuracy in 1937 as Vyshinsky's assistant. He began to demand proofs of the guilt of accused enemies. He clashed with Vyshinsky over the arrest of an Old Bolshevik and Civil War veteran, Valentin Trifonov, demanding the case materials and saying he didn't believe Trifonov was an enemy. Vyshinsky said, "If the organs took him, that means he's an enemy," to which Sol'ts rejoined: "You lie. I've known Trifonov for thirty years, and I know you as a Menshevik!" Shunted off to Sverdlovsk in the Urals, he took the rostrum at a party meeting in October 1937 and proposed a commission of inquiry into Vyshinsky's activities, whereupon he was dragged off the platform, fired from the Procuracy, denied the interview with Stalin that he demanded, and finally, after he went on hunger strike, confined in a psychiatric hospital from which he emerged in a demented state to die during World War II.[43]

Another who protested was I. M. Vareikis, a Bolshevik since 1913 and now a Central Committee member as well as first secretary of the Far East Regional Party Committee. He telephoned Stalin from Khabarovsk in September 1937 to ask the reasons for the arrest of a number of Communists. To his wife's question, "What was Stalin's answer?," he said:

It's horrible even to say. At first I thought wasn't Stalin at the other end, but someone else. But it was Stalin. He shouted, "It's none of your business. Don't interfere where you shouldn't. The NKVD knows what it's doing." Then he stated that only an enemy of the Soviet regime could defend Tukhachevsky and others, and slammed down the receiver.

A few days later, Vareikis was urgently summoned to Moscow. On 9 October, at a small station stop outside the capital, he was arrested. Four days later his wife, herself a party member since 1919 and the mother of three, was arrested in Khabarovsk. He was killed in 1939; she shared his fate.[44]

There were also cases of resistance in the military. After Yakir's execution, senior commanders and armed-forced political workers were arrested in his Kiev military district. In August 1937 a division commander in the district, A. V. Gorbatov, was summoned to a meeting in which it was said that his now arrested superior, corps commander Piotr Grigoriev, had "proved" to be an enemy of the people. Called on to speak, Gorbatov said he had known Grigoriev for over fourteen years, that he had never vacillated on party policy, and was one of the best commanders in the whole army. Accused of "liberalism" by the head of the corps political section, Gorbatov was soon expelled from the party for "contacts with enemies of the people," shifted to another district, and finally, in 1938, arrested.[45] Corps commander Georgi Shtern, who was posted to the Far East after Marshal Bliukher's arrest there and who played a distinguished part in commanding Red Army forces in battles with the Japanese along the Khalkin-Gol River in 1938, is credited with having written a bold report to Stalin on the dangerous situation created in the Far East by the destruction of the local officer corps, after which the arrests came to an end. As he headed for his new post in the Moscow area after Hitler's armies attacked Russia in 1941, Shtern, who was Jewish, was arrested and shot as a "German spy."[46]

Even in the police organization there were some who refused to take part in the carnage. T. D. Deribas, who directed the Far Eastern NKVD in 1937, was arrested and shot, reportedly for opposing the repression of party and government officials. I. M. Leplevsky, the Belorussian commissar of internal affairs, was arrested and shot after having refused to apply the "new methods" (torture). M. S. Pogrebinsky, NKVD director in Gorky Region, and some other old Chekists committed suicide rather than follow orders.[47] One of them, Mikhail Letvin, left a suicide note saying "I can no longer take part in the murder of innocent people and the fabrication of spurious cases." A. K. Artuzov, who had worked under Dzerzhinsky and Menzhinsky, was arrested after protesting at a meeting in 1939 against the "sergeant-major's" style of leadership that had come in since Menzhinsky's death. He wrote on his cell wall before being shot: "It is an honest man's duty to kill Stalin."[48]

Krupskaya's unavailing efforts on behalf of individual victims can serve as a symbol of the futility of resistance at this late stage. Her most courageous act was speaking up at the June 1937 Central Committee plenum

for Central Committee member I. A. Piatnitsky, a Bolshevik since 1898,
a close associate of Lenin's, and former secretary of the Comintern's
Executive Committee. On the eve of the plenum he and a few other Old
Bolsheviks had discussed over tea, in someone's apartment, the grim
situation in the party and what should be done about it, and one person
present turned informer. At the plenum Piatnitsky was accused of having
been a tsarist police agent.[49] Krupskaya's intercession did not save him
from immediate arrest, subsequent terrible torture, and execution in 1939.
When she asked Yezhov about some arrested Old Bolsheviks' fate during
the annual Lenin memorial meeting in January 1937, he simply turned
away. She was helpless to stay the arrest and execution of Education
Commissar Andrei Bubnov, another Old Bolshevik comrade of Lenin's,
and major educationists who were taken in the sweeping purge of the
Commissariat of Education.[50] At the peak of the Terror she regularly received over 400 letters a day, many no doubt from persons seeking her
intercession for arrested relatives or friends,[51] but her sole recorded success
was the release of one I. D. Chigurin, who issued Lenin a party card in
April 1917. Meanwhile, as will be seen, she remained an object of Stalin's
smoldering animosity.

Denunciation

Informing, and specifically the denunciation of persons as traitors,
has a long history in Russia. Developing a practice established under
earlier Muscovite rulers, Ivan Grozny required of his *oprichniki* a pledge
to report anything they might know or hear about "anything evil" being
contemplated against him. Under Ivan's successors, informing continued
and by the mid-seventeenth century "Muscovites of whatever rank and
standing were bound in law to serve as political informers against each
other, to report whatever they knew or heard about disloyal acts, or even
thoughts, of their fellow citizens—to spy or die."[52] In the nineteenth century, this function was professionalized in Nicholas I's Gendarmerie, a
corps of officers stationed all over the country whose task was to report
directly to him whatever they felt he should know. As a result, "an incautious word or a foolish joke at the expense of the Government was too
often magnified into an act of high treason."[53]

Denunciations did not disappear during the early years of Bolshevik
rule. Lenin was so bothered by false denunciations that in December 1918
he drafted a proposal that false denunciations be made punishable by
shooting—but his proposal was not adopted.[54] During the NEP the Sovnarkom issued a decree over his signature that made a consciously false

denunciation or false court testimony punishable by a one-year sentence, or by two years if accusation of a serious crime was involved, if the motives were self-seeking, or if artificial fabrication of evidence occurred.[55]

The Stalinist 1930s turned the clock back to forced denunciation and informing. Governmental encouragement of denunciation, founded or unfounded, was revived and magnified during collectivization. Peasants were invited to denounce "kulaks" or "kulak accomplices" for withholding grain from the state. The regime glorified a boy named Pavlik Morozov as a denouncer. Later biographical research has disclosed that the real-life Pavlik was born in 1918 in the Urals village of Gerasimovka; that his father, Trofim Morozov, a poor peasant become chairman of the village soviet, was brought to trial in 1932 on charges of bribe taking; that Pavlik, called as a witness, testified that his father had appropriated property confiscated from kulaks; and that Pavlik's infuriated grandfather Sergei and cousin Danil stabbed him and his small brother to death in the woods.[56] But as told in Stalin's time, the story was that Morozov's father secretly helped local kulaks by selling them false documents, for which Pavlik denounced him in court as a traitor; and that when Pavlik later denounced village kulaks for hiding and spoiling their grain, some of them waylaid and killed him in the woods, for which they received death sentences. Such was the legend as recounted in Stalin's time. Morozov's supposed denunciatory act was set before the minds of children and others as an example worthy of emulation.

Denunciation became a basic mechanism of the Terror and goes far to explain its huge extent. The conclusion of the closed letter of 29 July 1936 from Stalin's Central Committee offices—"The inalienable quality of every Bolshevik under present conditions must be the ability to see through the enemy of the party, no matter how well he may be masked"— was the formula. *To see through and expose the masked enemy*—these code words for the duty to denounce became an insistent refrain. *Pravda* informed its nationwide audience that it was "a crime against the party and people for a Communist not to see through the enemy in good time and expose him, if only in some small matter, for a larger hostile action can be concealed behind a small one."[57]

Communists, however, were not the only ones whose duty it was to see through and expose. The "nonparty Bolsheviks" were duty bound too. *Pravda* characterized them as people committed to defending the motherland and explained: "To defend the motherland is to be vigilant! He who defends the motherland is the one who is able, conclusively and in good time, to expose the enemy, no matter how he may mask himself.[58] Then the journal of party organization said that such exposing was "the *sacred duty* of every Bolshevik, party *and nonparty."*[59] Stalin personally crowned this campaign with his praise of the zealous denouncer Nikolaenko and the many other "little people" like her as heroes and heroines of vigilance.

The mastering of Bolshevism that he called for at the February– March plenum meant, in large part, learning to see through and expose masked enemies. The first two big show trials were lessons in such "party education" because they offered a plethora of examples of ways in which enemies could act as traitors behind masks. To localize the lessons, lesser show trials were held in republics, provinces, and districts in later 1937, and reported in the local press. The accused would be district party and government officials.[60] Meanwhile, in the middle and later months of 1937, a large literature poured forth on the ways of the enemy at home and abroad. Vyshinsky made a major contribution with a long article on "The Wrecking-Sabotage Work Methods of the Trotskyist-Fascist Agents," published as a pamphlet in a mass printing. It was a gloss on Stalin's two plenum speeches. A similar manual by one S. Uranov, "On Some Cunning Techniques of the Recruiting Work of Foreign Intelligence Services," appeared in *Pravda* and as a pamphlet with a circulation of 650,000. The Leningrad NKVD chief, Leonid Zakovsky, a man notorious for his cruelty, published an article in *Leningrad Pravda* in 1937 giving advice on how a "Soviet person" should behave. If for example one noticed that one's neighbor was living beyond his means, one should report this to the organs. In one case a bookkeeper, who was a priest's daughter, "proved" to be an enemy after a worker reported suspicion of her. Lack of factual evidence should not stand in the way of reporting such suspicions: the organs had ways of verifying them.[61]

Other articles coached people in the art of seeing through and exposing. Enemy machinations, it was said, could be concealed behind appearances of routine misconduct. Thus a signal from a nonparty bookkeeper in the Agricultural Bank led to exposure of one K., who was given to overspending state funds, as a member of a terrorist center using these funds to finance counterrevolutionary activity. The moral: "People who squander state funds right and left usually prove to be either enemies or their direct accomplices."[62] On this theory persons convicted under the law of 7 August 1932, which made theft of state property a capital crime, not only received the prescribed ten-year sentence but could be, and in various cases were, classified as "enemies of the people." A young woman then in training in the Moscow Procuracy learned by experience that they included several poor women who, to feed their hungry children, stole cookies from the Bolshevik Candy Factory where they worked.[63]

Bol' shevik explained enemy ways in the press and publishing. Professor Barkhin's textbook of stylistics, published in 1936, asked pupils to write essays starting: "The plant where my father (mother, brother) works," and then to answer such questions as: Location? Size? Type and horse-power of machines made? Fuel used? Size of work force? Where do the products go? From such an exercise, the party journal said, any spy who penetrated the school system could gather useful information needed by bourgeois intelligence. The article also mentioned misprints, through which enemies exploited printers' lack of vigilance to write, for example, "ter-rorist level" in place of "theoretical level," "brotherly peace" in place of "Brest peace," "victorious" (pobednaia) in place of "such a (podobnaia) wrecking program." Conclusion: "Wrecking in this area (and not without the participation of hostile editorial folk) takes very many forms."[64]

These examples show that instruction in methods of exposure com-municated a kind of artificial political paranoia akin to that involved in what has been described above as the trial system. Paranoid persons char-acteristically place sinister interpretations on events that may have no sinister bearing, and attribute hostile motives to acts that may have no hostile intent. In their mental world, nothing is accidental, and they devise highly imaginative explanations to convince themselves and others that what appeared accidental was done with an ulterior harmful purpose by a malevolent person or persons. Just such thought patterns were now being prescribed by Central Committee publications. They were teaching people how to invent sinister, counterrevolutionary motives for common everyday occurrences in their society, where some did misappropriate state funds, steal cookies, fail to correct misprints, and issue textbooks with exercises or passages like those decried as espionage trickery. Since it was Stalin who at the February–March plenum had called for "education" in the enemy's insidious ways, it can hardly be doubted that he was the prime source of these paranoid ways of thinking that the nation was told to adopt. We do not know whether he seriously shared them or simply found it expedient to prescribe them for his political purposes, but they evidently came readily to his mind.

A torrent of denunciations was flowing by the spring of 1937. They started during the party meetings held after the February–March plenum to discuss the plenum documents, Stalin's speeches in particular. These were repetitions on a huge scale and with more deadly effect of the meet-ings held in academic institutions in 1931 to discuss Stalin's letter on party history assailing "Trotskyist contraband" and "rotten liberalism." Those now denounced, however, were no mere rotten liberals or historian-contra-bandists but "enemies of the people" subject to arrest and swift or slow destruction.

Communists were in greater danger than nonparty people of being denounced, and higher-ranking ones in greater danger than lower. Yet, as the examples just cited show, hardly anyone was safe. Notwithstanding the macabre humor of the time (in one anecdote a nocturnal knock on the door is answered by a man who says to the policemen outside, "You've made a mistake—the Communists live upstairs"), lack of party membership was no protection against denunciation and arrest. Great numbers of quite nonpolitical people fell victim. Many were relatives of arrested persons, students of arrested professors, secretaries of arrested officials, subordinates of arrested army officers, and the like. Such persons were subject to denunciation for "ties" or "family connections" with an enemy of the people. One might, for example, be a worker in a plant or other institution whose director and other officials were arrested as heads of a wrecker ring, and be denounced as a member of that ring. Guilt by work association goes very far to explain the lightning swift spread of denunciations and the tenfold rise in arrests between 1936 and 1937, which Khrushchev reported in his closed speech to the Twentieth Congress.

Article 58, section 10, of the Criminal Code made it a counterrevolutionary crime, punishable by five to eight years in a camp, to engage in "propaganda or agitation" with intent to overthrow or weaken the regime, and included under this heading the dissemination or mere possession of literature of such content. Many were denounced under this article, in some cases for possessing a copy of that seditious document, Lenin's testament (which was officially branded as a forgery). Many peasants, workers, and shop girls, known among fellow prisoners as "babblers," were sentenced under Article 58–10 as a result of an imprudent remark.[65] For example, a peasant was denounced in 1937 for having said at some point that he lived better before collectivization.[66] A cleaning woman who worked in a government office was denounced after she was overheard saying as she approached a portrait of Stalin on the wall with her rag, "Now my dear little pockmarked one, I'll clean thy face."[67]

The most innocent accident, past or present, could seal one's doom. A man was denounced for having rented a room in a country dacha owned by an arrested historian.[68] A peasant who tossed a hatchet that accidentally pierced a Stalin portrait lying nearby was arrested as a terrorist (under Article 58, section 8, covering terror) and condemned to eight years.[69] A young actor who worked as an extra in Moscow's Vakhtangov Theater and supplemented his earnings by wall painting in a factory club room was denounced by the club director, and then arrested, for the disrespect shown to Stalin by the act of stacking his portrait along with a reproduction of Repin's "The Volga Boatmen" against another wall while painting the one where they hung.[70] A woman streetcar driver in Kharkov lost her job because her former husband had signed an opposition statement ten years earlier.[71]

Klara Angilovich, a Communist who taught literary theory in a Leningrad institute, was denounced by students as a Trotskyist for having commented, in evaluating a thesis on the Trotsky school of literary scholarship, that it cited little Trotskyist literature.[72] A sixty-five-year-old peasant woman from a collective farm near Moscow was somehow denounced as a *trotskistka* (Trotskyist), a term she was so far from understanding that she confused it with *traktoristka* (tractor driver), and said to cellmates in prison, "They don't put old women like me on tractors." Having received a ten-year sentence for Trotskyist terrorism, she asked one cellmate, who happened to be Eugenia Ginzburg, "Are you one of those *traktoristki* too, dearie?"[73] One Maria Ivanovna, a seventy-year-old teacher, who was giving private lessons, assigned a poem from her own copy of a third-grade text of 1923 vintage that happened to contain a photo of Trotsky, a fact she overlooked. Her pupil noticed the photo and showed the book to the head teacher, who turned it over to the NKVD, and two days later Maria Ivanovna disappeared forever after being arrested for "counterrevolutionary Trotskyist activity."[74]

As this shows, children were enlisted in the army of denouncers. Pavlik Morozov, glorified in song and story, came fully into his posthumous own now. His denunciatory exploit was presented to children as an heroic example of a child's placing of devotion to the state and Stalin above filial loyalty at the cost of his own life. The singer Galina Vishnevskaya, writing abroad from her memories of being a small girl in Russia then, recalls the young being told at Pioneer and Komsomol meetings that it was their duty to report all suspicious events, following Pavlik's example. The implicit message was: "Children, if you're good little boys and girls, if you inform on Mama and Papa, songs may even be sung about you."[75]

The Komsomol, for young people from sixteen to twenty-three, played its part in the terror process as well. A *Pravda* correspondent in the Stalingrad Region complained that too little vigilance was shown in the just completed election meetings of the region's 1,525 primary Komsomol organizations. In very few cases had discussions of candidates "exposed offspring of fascist agents who wormed their way into the Komsomol."[76] What effect such articles had is clear from a document that made its way West many decades later, the handwritten minutes of a Komsomol meeting of 7 September 1937 at Moscow University. The bureau of the university's primary Komsomol organization presented draft resolutions concerning students whose parents had been arrested. One case involved a girl student whose arrested father had served as a deputy commissar of agriculture and whose aunt (the father's sister), uncle, and stepmother had been arrested as well. Asked about her attitude toward her father, she said: "Since the NKVD organs arrested him, it's clear that he committed a crime and is an

enemy of the people." She claimed, however, that her father's party record
was impeccable and that all conversations on political themes that she had
overheard were "correct." Lengthy discussion of her case was punctuated
with such comments as: "Exposure of her father was possible, her uncle's
arrest already provided a signal." The girl was expelled from the Komsomol.[77] Such meetings were being held all across the country. For the rising
generation they offered object lessons in the "Bolshevism" that Stalin
wanted all the people to master.

Denunciation from below was being generated from above. First,
"above" and "below" were relative matters. Republic, regional, town, and
district party leaders, who were "above" for people in their areas, were
"below" for Stalin. The closed letter of 29 July 1936, with its demand to
see through and expose, put heavy pressure on them to show zeal as
denouncers. A response on which the Smolensk archive provides detailed
evidence was that of the party secretary of the Western Region's Kozelsk
district, Piotr Demenok, with whom (as the archive shows) Stalin was in
direct touch, as with all other district party chiefs, through Poskrebyshev
and the Special Sector. Immediately on receiving his copy of the closed
letter, Demenok began writing denunciations right and left, directing them
in some cases to the Regional Party Committee and in others to the head of
the district NKVD. On 4 August 1936, at an enlarged meeting of the bureau
of the Kozelsk district party committee, speakers vied with one another in
denouncing people as enemies.[78]

The February–March plenum intensified pressure on intermediate
authorities to denounce. The tone of the demand grew threatening. As
noted above, a *Pravda* dispatch from Stalingrad berated the regional party
committee there for not purging the regional Komsomol, whose secretary,
it said, was covering up enemies. The reluctance of regional party leaders
to do what was demanded is understandable: by complying, they would
open themselves up to charges of complicity in an earlier cover-up of
enemies.

In other cases some central party organ, acting as Stalin's mouth-
piece, would directly attack regional party leaders in such a way as to
instigate denunciation of them from below. *Pravda,* for example, called
on Omsk Bolsheviks to "raise their voices to the full" against their regional
leaders, headed by Comrade Bulatov, who had protected Trotskyist-Bukharinist spies in various regional posts.[79] Here we see a further important
political use of the plan that Stalin, via Zhdanov, championed at the February–March plenum for revitalizing "inner-party democracy." The latter
comprised not only secrecy of the party ballot but also the ordinary party
members' right to criticize their superiors in party meetings. This they
would normally never dream of doing. A party member would not speak

up against his little Stalin in Omsk, Comrade Bulatov, or his little Stalin in Smolensk, Comrade Rumyantsev. But now, under the slogan of taking "inner-party democracy" seriously, they were being mobilized to do just that, to attack Bulatov and other Omsk leaders for failing to ferret out enemies and Stalingrad leaders for laxity in purging the Komsomol.

The destruction of Ivanovo's bureaucratic elite shows this use of "inner-party democracy." In the wake of Kaganovich's visit to Ivanovo in June 1937 and Stalin's subsequent approval of his finding that the local party and government bureaucracies were thoroughly "infested," *Party Construction*—of which Malenkov was editor in 1937—took the Ivanovo Regional Party Committee heads to task for having earlier expelled many worthy party members for "passivity" (in this the officials were following the Central Committee's instruction on the exchange of party documents in the first half of 1936, which said that "chief attention must be paid to eliminating passive people who do not justify the lofty title of party member and came into the CPSU(b) ranks accidentally").[80] The expelled "passives," said *Party Construction,* proved to be Stakhanovite workers who temporarily lessened their participation in party life or were in arrears on party dues. So, while expelling such honest workers, loyal to the cause of Lenin-Stalin, the regional and many district committees failed to expose masked Trotskyist-Bukharinist saboteurs and spies.[81]

By charging the local leaders with misconduct in expelling "passives" and lack of vigilance toward real enemies, the journal solicited denunciation of the Ivanovo elite from below, which gave the purge an appearance of rank-and-file party members exercising their right of criticism under "inner-party democracy." Meanwhile, a *Pravda* correspondent in Ivanovo, citing figures on hard times for collective farmers in 1936, when 998 of the region's 5,401 collective farms paid the peasants nothing per workday unit and 3,303 paid under ten kopecks, accused local agricultural officials of being wreckers and asked whether it was only "political myopia," or something worse, that explained the regional committee's long toleration of enemies in the agricultural organs.[82] *Pravda* thereby managed both to stigmatize the doomed Ivanovo bureaucracy and ingratiate Stalin's regime with the peasantry by attributing its woes to traitors in that bureaucracy. If and when historians gain access to Ivanovo's secret files for 1937, they will surely find, among the denunciatory letters about party and government officials, some signed by peasants.

By singling out the party leaders of certain regions for such exemplary, well-publicized condemnation, the central press put all others on notice that failure to produce large numbers of denunciations in their jurisdictions would endanger them. Many appear to have responded as Stalin wanted them to. Local party secretaries who, upon arrest, moved from the close-mouthed lives they had led in public to the freedom of speech that, paradoxically, prevailed in some prison cells, told of questioning party members as to the numbers of enemies they had denounced. "If you want to stay a member of the party, see that you denounce its enemies" was their response to someone who said he didn't know of any enemies.[83] On the other hand, their very success in producing the denunciations that Moscow demanded placed them in danger of denunciation for harboring masked enemies in their local midst. For most there was no way out. This undoubtedly entered into Stalin's calculations.

Responses to the demand to "see through and expose" varied widely. At one end of the spectrum were unimportant people and also some more important ones who went through it all without denouncing anybody. At the other end were the zealots, such as the woman who got up at a party meeting in Kiev and pointed to a regional health official named Medved: "I don't know that man over there, but I can tell from the look in his eyes that he's an enemy of the people." Medved shot back: "I can tell from the look in her eyes that she's a whore." Only by thus taking the counteroffensive did he save himself.[84] She may or may not have been the woman of whom Khrushchev told the Yugoslav ambassador in 1956 that Kievites were in such fright of her that they would cross to the other side of the street so that she would not see them. This "very sick person" and "those who used her" were responsible, he said, for the deaths of an estimated 8,000 people.[85] Since Khrushchev did not give names, we also do not know whether this woman, or one of them if there were two, was Stalin's exemplary Nikolaenko. There were other wholesale denouncers. Some proposed a norm of one hundred denunciations to prove one's political vigilance.[86] A delegate to a Moscow party conference in 1937 boasted that he had exposed over 100 enemies in four months.[87]

Such prodigious denouncers must have been a rarity compared to the far larger number who denounced but not in a wholesale way. Among these, motives varied widely. Some denounced for fear of being denounced if they failed to turn in someone who had told a political anecdote in a group conversation. Some denounced persons they disliked. Some wanted to gain possession of the room or apartment of the person they denounced, whose family would likely be evicted once he was arrested. Some wanted to eliminate rivals for athletic glory or other desired goals. And not a few were actuated by career ambition to denounce persons senior to them who stood in their way.

And thus while the political hierarchy was being hollowed out by mass repressions, many not only survived but prospered by rising to middle and higher rungs. They were the "promotees" *(vydvizhentsy)* of yesteryear, younger people of mostly humble worker or peasant origin who had been readied by specialized education or on-the-job training for advancement to responsible posts. Not all cleared the way for their further advancement by denunciation, but many did take that road. Beck and Godin note the zeal with which many students denounced their professors, junior officials those higher up, rank-and-file party members those in responsible posts; and describe this ambition-driven "revolt of subordinates" as a most significant feature of the period.[88] Evgeni Gnedin recalls that certain ambitious young men, including such comers of Soviet diplomacy as Malik, Tsarapkin, and Podtserob, would meet in a nearby pub to choose prospective victims from among their elders, and then, at meetings of the Narkomindel's party organization, denounce those persons for "ties with enemies of the people" (for instance, arrested ex-colleagues).[89]

Lest the reader infer that the revolution from above was becoming one from below, it must be said that no "revolt of subordinates" would or could have taken place without the permission, incitement, and pressure to denounce that came from Stalin and his accomplices. There is evidence, moreover, that some of the denouncing occurred under supervision. When Godin (Shteppa), a professor of ancient history at Kiev University, was being denounced at party meetings at the university for "Trotskyism," with mentions of his social origin (he was a priest's son), the leading denouncer was his assistant and favorite graduate student, one Efromenko, who acted on instructions. "This was the system: to commission students to criticize their teacher with a view to later taking his place."[90] The NKVD was in touch with the lives of millions through its special sections in plants and every kind of institution. The Tsarapkins, Maliks, and self-promoting young counterparts elsewhere could get cues for denunciation from their institution's special section or make sure that it approved their provisional choices of targets.

A rich source of forced denunciations from below was the legion of secret informers—people of all kinds impressed by the NKVD into becoming its part-time helpers. Their continuing employment in regular jobs ensured them access to fellow citizens' conversations at the workplace and elsewhere. And now they were asked to see through and expose the machinations of masked enemies. Since there were no such machinations, only the occasional disgruntled citizen voicing a critical opinion on, say, the new antiabortion law or repeating a political anecdote, the informers had a hard time complying with their new task. NKVD mentors had to teach them how to "interpret" what they overheard, how to read hidden meanings in statements that in fact had no sinister meaning. If, for example, someone said something to a foreigner about insufficient housing, the informer learned to translate that statement into "espionage." Tellers of anti-Stalin jokes became "instigators of terrorism," and informal friendly groupings became anti-Soviet "organizations."[91] Thus were secret informers initiated into the world of artificial paranoia.

A Spearman's Maneuver

While terror victims were disappearing by night in the last months of 1937, daytime public life centered on festive preparations for electing a Supreme Soviet under the new constitution. The election campaign dramatized Stalin's politics of populism by the stress put on nonparty people and the name given to the full slate of candidates—"bloc of party and nonparty people." In Stalin's electoral district in Moscow, it was a nonparty woman worker who took the floor at the first nomination meeting to plead: "Comrade Stalin, don't refuse, be our candidate for the Supreme Soviet."[92]

Official claims that this would be a truly democratic election, complete with secret ballot, lent the proceedings an air of expectancy. All the more so as the press published a sample ballot implying, by its instruction to cross out all names but one, that there would be multiple candidacies—as Stalin had intimated in his 1936 interview with Roy Howard. A temporary appearance of multiple candidacies was created by the fact that in all but a very few of the 1,143 electoral districts Stalin or some one of his Politburo associates was nominated along with another, usually local candidate (preselected by the authorities). Then, on the eve of the election, each Politburo member accepted nomination in one district only. Hence, when 91 million voters went to vote on 12 December, their ballots carried only one candidate's name for each of the Supreme Soviet's two chambers. Although the ballots still carried the instruction to leave in one name and cross out others, there was no reason for anyone to enter the booths set up to ensure secrecy except to cross out a single candidate's name. Not surprisingly, nearly 90 million votes went to "bloc" candidates; there was no one else to vote for. The election was an official celebration of the regime rather than a test of its popularity.

On 11 December Stalin gave a speech accepting nomination in one of Moscow's electoral districts. "The impending elections aren't just elections, comrades," he said. "They are a holiday of our workers, peasants, our intelligentsia. Never in the world have there been such truly free and democratic elections, never!" He advised the people to demand of their deputies that they be as fearless in battle and as merciless to enemies of the people as Lenin was, as free from any hint of panic at times of danger as Lenin was, as wise and unhasty in resolving complex problems as Lenin was, and that they love the people as Lenin did. He could not say whether all the candidates met these criteria. There were individuals, including some Bolsheviks, of whom you couldn't say whether they were good or bad, brave or cowardly, *for* the people to the end or *for* the enemies of the people. There was a black sheep in every family. After this allusion to the Terror, Stalin urged the voters to influence their deputies to keep "the great image of the great Lenin" before their minds and imitate Lenin in all things.[93] The traits he chose to ascribe to Lenin were probably revealing of what he imagined his own to be. As Demyan Bedny had written in 1929, Stalin's image of Lenin was a subconsciously executed self-characterization.[94]

Shortly after the election publicity subsided, *Pravda* printed an article that struck an unusual note by assailing indiscriminate denouncers. Its author was Kol'tsov, whom the Nazi publication on *Bolshevism and the Jews* called "Friedland-Kolzoff" and presented as one of the prominent "Jews behind Stalin" in journalism. He related the case of a student in a Moscow training institute who had been expelled from the party and then from the institute on the basis of a denunciatory letter accusing him of duplicity, careerism, and sycophancy. Instead of investigating the charges, which were groundless, the institute's party secretary had quickly arranged to have him expelled from the party as an enemy of the people. Such individuals, Kol'tsov said, were ready to defame, calumniate, expel, and dismiss quite innocent people just to protect themselves. But the party, the government, the courts, and the public would clip the paws of those who by slander and heartlessness violated the rights and darkened the quiet working life of any citizen.[95]

A month later came a follow-up article, also by Kol'tsov, on false denouncers. He divided them into three groups: spearmen who would hurl denunciatory spears in all directions, so as to appear politically righteous and thereby to divert attention from their own dark deeds or pasts; careerists who denounced for self-advancement; and soulless bureaucrats who, for self-protection, would take instant action on receiving any spearman's piece of paper. The NKVD, Kol'tsov concluded, would unerringly find its way to all these slanderers, whom it rightly saw as haters of the Soviet order.[96]

Since denouncers of all kinds were legion now, acting under pressures from above, Kol'tsov's articles could only have appeared if commissioned by *Pravda*'s editor on instructions from Stalin's offices. No doubt he was happy to fulfill the commission in hope that his articles might portend an early end to the terror process that so mystified and troubled him. Two days after the second article appeared, the press published a lengthy Central Committee decree for which the articles must have been a curtain raiser: "On Errors of Party Organizations in Expelling Communists, and on Formalistic Bureaucratic Treatment of Appeals by Those Expelled, and Steps to Eliminate These Defects." An introductory note said that the decree was adopted by a regular Central Committee plenum that took place in the past few days, and that the plenum relieved Postyshev of his post as a candidate member of the Politburo and appointed Khrushchev a candidate member of that body. It did not say who spoke at the plenum.

Citing such facts as those described in Kol'tsov's articles, the decree excoriated unnamed heads of various local party committees for mechanically approving wholesale expulsions of Communists innocent of wrongdoing. Individual cases were cited. A biology teacher in the Ukraine lost her job after the local paper printed a piece—subsequently found to be slanderous—saying that her brother was a nationalist. Careerist Communists were striving to distinguish and advance themselves, and insure themselves against charges of insufficient vigilance, by indiscriminate repressions. They were ready to expel dozens of Communists just to look vigilant. Some were in fact masked enemies who sought to cover up their hostility by cries for vigilance. One such enemy, now unmasked, was a secretary of the Kiev regional party committee, Kudriavtsev, who would turn to speakers at a party meeting and ask: "And have you submitted at least one denunciation?" As a result nearly half the members of the Kiev city party organization were subjects of denunciatory reports, most of them false. It was high time to unmask such criminal double-dealers as Kudriavtsev, to have done with the soulless bureaucratic attitude toward appeals by expelled party members, and to destroy every last disguised enemy in the party's ranks.[97]

Did this decree reflect, as has been hypothesized, a defensive campaign by party officialdom to deflect Stalin from the purge?[98] By no means. It was a maneuver by Stalin to deflect responsibility for the Terror that he and his helpers had driven to frenzied extremes. All the phenomena that the decree castigated and attributed to careerists, soulless bureaucrats, and masked enemies were responses to pressure for denunciation coming from above. Now local party authorities were being blamed for them.[99]

By having the decree put out, Stalin was not only diverting responsibility from himself. He was using it as a denunciatory spear to bring down various high-ranking party officials in the provinces who had been serving as his instruments in the terror process. After returning home from the February–March plenum in 1937, many of these men must have felt goaded by that plenum's purge message to go all out in unmasking enemies of the people, and they doubtless pressured their regional and district subordinates to act accordingly. In obeying the crafty dictator's charge to prove their worth as purgers, they necessarily disregarded his calculated concluding words of caution at the plenum on the need for a careful approach to each individual case of expulsion, his warning against "heartlessness." This now proved their undoing. It laid them open to the accusations of heartless indiscriminate purging that the decree levelled against them.

The chief target of Stalin's decree was Postyshev. After trying and failing to stop the pathological denouncer Nikolaenko in Kiev and then speaking up at the February–March plenum in defense of a purged associate, his fate was sealed. Two weeks after that plenum, he was relieved of his post as second secretary of the Ukrainian Central Committee and appointed secretary of the party committee of the Volga province of Kuibyshev. He also received an unpublicized reprimand for protecting enemies of the people[100] (presumably including persons denounced by Nikolaenko). After being installed in the new post, he was pressured into pushing the purge there so severely that Kuibyshev earned citation in the January decree as an egregious case of a province where party members were being expelled wholesale as enemies of the people without justification.[101] The NKVD organs, said the decree, had found no basis for arresting many of those expelled from the party in Kuibyshev region. Since the organs' inquisitional methods were finding "bases" for the arrest of countless utterly innocent people all over the country, we may be certain that the inability of the Kuibyshev organs to find grounds for arrests had its source in instructions from Moscow.

The last act in Postyshev's political downfall was played out at the January 1938 plenum. It took place while members of the Central Committee were in Moscow for the first meeting of the Supreme Soviet elected in December. The committee had by then been decimated by the purge. Those present at this "regular plenum" numbered a mere twenty-eight, fifteen of whom were Politburo voting members and candidates, among them Postyshev. The rapporteur on errors in expelling party members was Malenkov. He was not yet a member of the Central Committee although, as head of that body's Department of Leading Party Organs, he was serving as a right-hand man for Stalin in the Terror. His nonmembership in the committee explains the failure of the plenum announcement to mention his name as the speaker on the subject of the decree on expulsions.

After he gave statistics on Communists wrongfully expelled in Kuibyshev region, Postyshev was grilled about the matter. Were there no "honest" people in Kuibyshev leading circles, asked Nikolai Bulganin, then a Central Committee candidate member. Hardly a one, Postyshev replied, adding: "Does this really surprise you?" The obvious implication was that in approving wholesale expulsions he had followed the prevailing general practice. Molotov accused Postyshev of exaggerating. Beria asked him how many members of the Kuibyshev regional party committee remained unpurged. Postyshev answered twenty-five out of sixty-one. Malenkov ended the discussion by condemning Postyshev for failure to recognize his errors "as fixed in the Politburo's decision, where your actions are pronounced plainly provocational in all their consequences."[102] The interrogation and its outcome had been prepared in advance. Postyshev was arrested soon afterward, and subsequently shot.

The January decree was Stalin's doing, a spearman's maneuver. After a short lull in expulsions, a flurry of press articles on the decree's themes, and reinstatement in party membership of numbers of low-level expelled persons, the reign of terror resumed as before. And any lingering hopes for an early end to mass repressions were dashed when announcement came that another public treason trial would open in Moscow on 2 March 1938.

Inquisition

As denunciations multiplied, so did arrests. The prisons of main and provincial cities were filled to overflowing, with a hundred or more prisoners jammed into some cells originally built for no more than twenty. Emergency barracks went up to accommodate still more. All sorts of structures, from monasteries to bathhouses, came into service as prisons. The wax figures in some prisons that had been preserved as museums, including Moscow's ancient Lefortovo, were replaced with real people as prison functions resumed.[103] Each cell contained a large lidded tub, into which the prisoners relieved themselves. This so-called *parasha* was emptied out and cleaned daily, but the stench persisted. A newcomer received a place nearest it and moved farther away as prior arrivals departed after their interrogations ended. When prisoners were called out "with belongings," it meant that they were being transferred to another prison or sent to camp. "Without belongings" was the dread message that they were to be shot.

People remaining at large had only a faint idea of what went on in the prisons into which relatives, friends, work associates, neighbors, and others vanished. What little they learned came partly from the nightmarish appearance of the one out of thousands who was set free. Now, from post-Stalin official testimony and memoirs of purge victims who survived, we know what happened. After arrest as masked enemies, the victims were "unmasked," one by one, in interrogations that forced them, first, to confess that they had been two-faced persons working against the regime and, second, to name accessories in crime. This procedure corresponds to that of the medieval Inquisition, on which a Soviet historian writes: "The extortion of confession was the basic element of the inquisitional judicial procedure," and "In order to save himself, the accused had first to confess himself guilty of the charge made against him and then to give away real or imagined accomplices. . . ."[104]

The task of bringing legal theory into line with inquisitional practice fell to Vyshinsky, who was now, in addition to his other duties, Stalin's chief legal theorist and scourge of prior Soviet legal theorists and theories. Addressing a meeting of party activists at the Procuracy in March 1937, he advanced the view that in cases of crimes against the state the confession was the main and decisive evidence. In support of this position he said that "One must remember Comrade Stalin's proposition that there are times, moments in the life of society and in our life in particular, when laws turn out to be obsolete and have to be set aside."[105]

Until a month or more following the February–March plenum, the methods used to extort confession, although brutal, normally fell short of torture in the strict sense—the infliction of physical pain by beating and other means. They comprised verbal abuse, threats, including threats against loved ones, and interrogation on the "conveyor." It was still possible for an exceptionally strong and stout-hearted victim, such as Eugenia Ginzburg, to resist confessing. Arrested in mid-February 1937 and charged with having organized a Tatar writers branch of a terrorist group to which she belonged, she was subjected to threats, blandishments, and the ordeal of being kept sleepless on the conveyor for seven days while a team of interrogators worked over her in shifts. Having steadfastly refused to confess, she later counted herself lucky that her interrogation was over before outright physical torture began in April.[106]

We have Stalin's word for it that torture was introduced in 1937. On 20 January 1939 he dispatched a coded telegram to party and NKVD authorities around the country saying that "methods of physical pressure" came into use in 1937 by permission of the "Central Committee," that such methods were used by "bourgeois" intelligence services and there was no reason why the "socialist" one should be more humanitarian, and that "physical pressure should still be used obligatorily as an exception applicable to known and obstinate enemies of the people, as a method both justifiable and appropriate."[107] By 1937 the words "Central Committee" on such a document meant Stalin.

In mid-July 1937, after some time in a transit prison in Kazan, Ginzburg was transferred to Moscow's Butyrka where, on the first day, she made friends with two young German women Communists in her cell, Greta and Klara, who told her about torture. Klara lay down, pulled up her skirt to show hideous welts on her thighs and buttocks, and said: "This is Gestapo." Then she held out blue and swollen hands and said: "This is NKVD." At night, all of a sudden, they heard through open cell windows the screams of people being tortured and their torturers' curses and shouts. That went on every night from 11 p.m. to 3 a.m. On 1 August Ginsburg was taken to Lefortovo where a Supreme Court military tribunal, after a seven-minute "trial" that included two minutes for private deliberation, sentenced her to ten years imprisonment in solitary confinement for participation in a terrorist group. In many other cases, people were sentenced *in absentia* by NKVD special boards.[108] At that time, under legal provisions dating from 1922, the maximum punishment short of death by shooting was ten years of confinement. Later in the year, a decree signed by Stalin's broken Soviet president, Kalinin, raised the maximum term to twenty-five years.[109] This was for almost all the death penalty in another guise.

If, as is likely, Stalin's coded telegram of January 1939 repeated key words of the order sent out by the "Central Committee" in 1937, the latter made mandatory the torturing of "known and obstinate enemies of the people." Now all persons arrested as enemies were "known" (by the organs) to be such; the "obstinate" ones were those who refused to confess. Hence, readiness to confess would normally—except in specific cases in which Stalin prescribed torture—enable the victim to avoid torture. This inference accords with testimony from various sources that interrogators initially would try to persuade the prisoners to confess and that many, especially ordinary workers and peasants whom the other prisoners called "babblers," readily confessed, say, to having complained of goods shortages, and received sentences of three to seven years of forced labor for "counterrevolutionary agitation." There were also cases of high-level victims, such as the famed aircraft designer A. N. Tupolev, who, when apprised of the situation by a prisoner who had already suffered torture, confessed straightaway to avoid that fate.[110] Torture, which was usually by beating—with fists, chair legs, or rubber truncheons—came into play when victims resisted persuasion and threats to themselves and family members. Many prisoners decided to confess after the horrifying experience of hearing frenzied screams of others being tortured.

The prisoner's guilt was taken for granted from the start of interrogation. For, as the NKVD men would say, "The NKVD *never* makes mistakes." Any protestation of innocence thereby became a political statement against the regime. What had to be decided was the nature of the prisoner's guilt and willingness to acknowledge it formally by signing a written confession detailing his or her offenses. The prisoner's cooperation in fleshing out the mythical record of crime was demanded. Even when the NKVD had in hand its own version of such a record, it was shown to the prisoner, if at all, later on.[111] At first the interrogator would indicate the nature of the charge and then solicit pertinent specifics. The interrogator of the arrested young high school history teacher, Pavel Gol'dshtein, began by mentioning the names "Nana" and "Lyova" (two young Russians who had reemigrated from Manchuria after Moscow sold the Chinese–Far Eastern Railway in 1935 and had studied in Gol'dshtein's father's violin class and his stepmother's piano class, respectively). Then he ordered Gol'dshtein to tell how his father had introduced him to "the Japanese intelligence agents and how they recruited you," meaning that Nana and Lyova were Japanese spies and that the elder Gol'dshtein and Pavel had joined their espionage ring.[112]

Prisoners were pressured, and if necessary tortured, into collaborating with their interrogators in concocting cases against themselves. Some sought and received assistance from cellmates in this work; and to make it easier for those with insufficient fantasy to invent confessions, the authorities would move experienced "consultants" from cell to cell to help them out.[113] The requisite creative imagination centered in the supplying of sinister conspiratorial motives for prisoners' past actions. The paranoidal thought pattern that we found in the "trial system," and in the ascribing of hidden meanings to actions for which people were denounced, thus confronts us again in the fabricating of confessions. For example, the NKVD built a case against a young man named Vasily Konstanovich, the champion stamp collector in the north Caucasian town of Kholodnogorsk, on the ground that his collection contained a German stamp with Hitler on it as well as an English one with Queen Victoria that was worth more than its Soviet one with Lenin. "So, you rate the queen of our class enemies above Lenin, and Hitler still higher," the interrogator said to Vasily, who was compelled to confess that he "led a counterrevolutionary organization engaged in criminal anti-Soviet agitation and cunningly masked as a stamp collector society."[114] All organized philatelic activities were closed down in Russia in 1937.[115]

Further examples come from the prison experience of Yakir's son in Astrakhan. All the priests of Astrakhan and Stalingrad, about forty in number, became an anti-Soviet organization of "Heliodorites" on the basis of the fact that the Archimandrite of Tsaritsyn (later Stalingrad), Heliodor, wrote letters to some of them from abroad after fleeing Russia during the Civil War. A man who once lived with his parents in Poland became a spy on the ground that his purpose in going fishing in the Volga, which he used to do, was to count the steamers plying the river and pass this information to Polish intelligence.[116]

Prisoners, many of whom were highly cultivated and ingenious, concluded from their observations that cases were fabricated on the basis of victims' "objective characteristics," such as being a senior party official, a senior military officer, or a former Red Partisan in the Revolution and Civil War.[117] Another such characteristic, foreign origin or ties, was regularly

taken as a basis for forcing people to confess that they were spies. Thus
Stalin's brother-in-law Redens, who was of Latvian origin and a high
official of the Moscow NKVD, was compelled, upon his arrest in 1937, to
confess that he had been a spy on Latvia's behalf.[118] So expert did some
prisoners become that they could quickly forecast the section of Article 58
under which a new arrival in their cell would be charged as soon as they
learned key facts about that person.

When, for example, Professor Kalmanson, who held a chair in zool-
ogy and was assistant director of the Moscow Zoo, entered the Butyrka
cell occupied by Ivanov-Razumnik and others, they classified him as a
"spy" when he told them that he was born of émigré parents in Bulgaria,
attended German universities, came to Moscow in 1930 with a German
wife, and corresponded with relatives abroad. They were dumbfounded
when Kalmanson returned from his first interrogation and announced that
he was a "wrecker" on the charge that 16 percent of the zoo's monkeys,
for whose feeding rations he was responsible, had died in the past year—a
charge apparently arising from the fact that the professor had criticized the
zoo's director, who was on good terms with the NKVD, in a recent article.
When he answered that the deaths were caused by the weather and that the
London Zoo's statistics showed that 22 percent of *its* monkeys died of
tuberculosis in the same period, his interrogator impulsively replied: "Well,
that means that England has its wreckers too," then checked himself and
said: "We can't take England as an example." In the next session he
touched only lightly on the wrecking charge and went on: "We'll now turn
to the main question—your spying activities on behalf of Germany."[119]

For actors in purge productions of high political importance, special
playwriting services were available. The Leningrad NKVD in 1937 was
preparing a local purge trial in which the principal accused were Nikolai
Komarov, a candidate member of the Central Committee, one-time chairman of the Leningrad Regional Executive Committee, and a close collaborator of Kirov's along with other high Leningrad officials under arrest
(including Old Bolsheviks Mikhail Chudov, Fyodor Ugarov, Boris Poz-
ern, and Chudov's wife Shaposhnikova). They were to be members of a
conspiratorial "Leningrad center." One Rozemblum, a Bolshevik since
1906, was tortured into confessing and then brought to Zakovsky, who
informed him that he would be a witness in the trial and said:

You yourself will not need to invent anything. The NKVD will prepare for you a
ready outline for every branch of the center; you will have to study it carefully and
to remember well all questions and answers which the court might ask. This case
will be ready in four–five months, or perhaps a half year. During all this time you
will be preparing yourself so that you will not compromise the investigation and
yourself. Your future will depend on how the trial goes and its results.[120]

When confessions were needed, there were brutish specialists in torture who would go to any length to break victims' will to resist the demand to confess. One such individual, Rodos by name, subjected Kosior and Chubar to prolonged torture. "He is a vile person, with the brain of a bird, and morally completely degenerate," Khrushchev said to the Twentieth Congress.[121] Such was undoubtedly the character of many among the "promotees" in the security organs. A similar drive for self-advancement that motivated careerists to denounce their colleagues and superiors was at work among younger interrogators. To excel as a fabricator of plots and show oneself an expert in persuading or torturing victims into confessing was a route to promotion in the NKVD.

Hardly anyone, even among proverbially tough Russians, held out under the tortures to which recalcitrant prisoners were subjected. One of the few who did was Division Commander Gorbatov. Called out on his fourth day in the Lubianka, he was given pen and paper by the interrogator, who said simply: "Describe all the crimes you have committed," to which the young officer replied: "There's nothing to write." He repeated this later with another interrogator. Meanwhile his cellmates, including an army brigade commander and a high official of the Commissariat of Trade, informed him that they had written nonsensical self-incriminating statements and told him shocking stories of torture. When the police saw that Gorbatov would not be easily broken, they remanded him to Moscow's dreaded Lefortovo. There he was interrogated five times under torture. Each time he had to be carried out covered with blood. Soon began another series of five such sessions, in which three brawny torturers worked over him mercilessly. When a third round began, he longed to die. Finally they gave up, handed him a fifteen-year sentence, and sent him to the Butyrka. He was the only one in his cell there who had not signed a fictitious confession. In wartime 1941 he was recalled to Moscow from the Kolyma camps, released after signing a promise to be silent, reinstated in rank, and received by the army leader, Marshal S. K. Timoshenko, to whom he reported his return from "a long and dangerous mission."[122]

Of the thousand odd cases with which he became personally acquainted in prisons during the Terror, Ivanov-Razumnik found no more than a dozen who successfully resisted inquisition under torture. The methods of torture ran the gamut from the "standing torture" and torture by thirst to such indignities as being forced to drink the contents of a spitoon and on to such horrors of cruelty as the crushing of fingers in doors, being burned with cigarettes on face and body, and being beaten across the genitals with a rubber truncheon.[123] Hardly less cruel were threats to torture loved ones or, in some cases, the actual torturing of them. Pavel Gol'd-shtein, having resisted confession at the Butyrka and having been beaten bloody in Lefortovo, suffered his worst moments when he heard through the wall of the interrogator's room the agonized voice of a woman saying: "On my knees I am begging you, do not beat me," whereupon his interrogator said to him: "That can be repeated with your mother. I'll tell the section head and tomorrow she'll be here."[124] The young man did not immediately give in. This was early 1939 when the tidal wave of terror was starting to subside, and he got off with a five-year sentence.

Sexual abuse of prisoners was uncommon but not unheard of. In the north Caucasian town of Piatigorsk a boy of twelve named Zhenie, who had unusual artistic talent, was denounced by the house superintendent who had pressed him into service as a designer of counterfeit ten-ruble notes, in return for which he would give the boy a little money to buy milk for his sick mother (the father had died). Under interrogation no torture was needed to get a confession. But Zhenie one day returned to the cell in tears and revealed that his interrogator, a Lieutenant Krylov, handcuffed him and forced him to commit a homosexual act. The prisoners in the cell made a protest to the duty officer, after which Zhenie no longer had to go to Krylov. Then the boy was called out late one night "without belongings"—to be shot.[125] Around that time, in 1937, *Pravda* published a photo of the one who was known as the childrens' best friend: Stalin holding his twelve-year-old daughter Svetlana in fond embrace.

Inquisition was not over when victims confessed under duress to fantasied misdeeds; it entered a further and for some a still more agonizing stage. After the admission of guilt, the demand came to expose confederates in crime. And while the crime was fictitious, the confederates had to be real. "Who recruited you" and "Whom did you recruit" were the stock questions. The victim had to name at least one person who brought him into the conspiracy and as many as possible whom he brought in.[126] Some NKVD prisons had norms for such denunciation, for instance, a minimum of twenty denunciations if one were an arrested second secretary of a regional party committee and at least forty if one were a first secretary, whereas an ordinary victim could get off by denouncing only a half-dozen innocents.[127]

Responses of other prisoners varied widely. Some, like the Armenian priest who incriminated all those he had buried in the past three years, sought to comply in a way they knew could not harm anyone. One might denounce persons known to be already under arrest, although in that case one's depositions, possibly leading to a face-toface confrontation with the denounced person in the interrogator's office, could be used to break a person who had hitherto refused to confess. One woman was cynically willing to denounce as many people as her captors desired in order to secure an easy prison existence, and another was tricked by the NKVD into denouncing all those in a group that it "knew for certain" was committing awful crimes.[128] Not all of those whom prisoners incriminated were then arrested. The NKVD was interested in building dossiers against some people at liberty, including Politburo members and prominent intellectuals, so as to have them in reserve for use whenever Stalin might turn against them; and that could be at any moment. Through depositions of arrested purge victims, for example, the NKVD had a dossier on ex-Promparty defendant Tarlé, now Academician Tarlé and high in Stalin's favor as an historian, in which he figured as a conspiratorial counterrevolutionary.[129]

The number of denunciations extorted from prisoners during interrogation must have exceeded, perhaps by many times, those generated outside of prison by the means described earlier. Prisoners in different parts of the country independently devised large-scale denouncing, reasoning that the only way to end the witches' sabbath was to drive it to such grotesque extremes that society would collapse unless it was halted. So they denounced wholesale when the demand came to name fellow conspirators whom they had recruited. An imprisoned doctor, who was president of Kharkov's medical council, pleaded guilty at once and later listed on paper the several hundred doctors of Kharkov, all of whom he knew by name, as enemies whom he had recruited. When his interrogator balked at depriving Kharkov of all its doctors, the prisoner wrote to the local NKVD chief that this interrogator was trying to shield other members of the counterrevolutionary organization, probably for his own counterrevolutionary motives, and demanded the chief's intervention. He employed these tactics after recalling that during the Inquisition in medieval Germany an arrested young theologian pleaded guilty and then named all the members of the Inquisition, including the Grand Inquisitor, as his confederates, after which the local inquisition was called off.[130] No such historical knowledge was needed for others to adopt the same tactic.

Those who chose this desperate expedient were only intensifying the pace of a terror process that by virtue of the pressure for denunciations, both in prison and outside, was spreading like a prairie fire. During the fall of 1937 and in 1938, with a short respite at the start of the latter year, the great punitive operation cut a wider and wider swath in the society. By the close of 1938, it has been suggested, there were dossiers on practically the whole adult population of the country.[131] As in collectivization, when Stalin deliberately started a process that got out of hand and took a catastrophic turn as sullen peasants slaughtered their livestock, so now his carefully prepared and precipitated reign of terror took on a spontaneous momentum of its own with results that he probably had failed to foresee.

The total number of arrests, followed in almost all cases by forced confession and sentencing, is not known. According to the historian Volkogonov, who has had access to pertinent archival sources, from four and a half to five and a half million persons were arrested in 1937 and 1938, and from 800,000 to 900,000 of them received the death penalty. The others in nearly all cases went to prisons or labor camps from which few ever returned. Volkogonov believes that the camps and prisons held three to four million inmates in those years.[132]

For the majority whose sufferings were not ended by a bullet in prison, the terror process continued somewhere in the far-flung system of concentration camps to which they were dispatched in frightful month-long trips in prison railway cars marked "special equipment." In later 1937 the rumor circulated in prison that Stalin had said at the June Central Committee plenum that conditions of confinement should be made more severe,[133] and indeed they were. With large new batches of prisoners constantly arriving in the camps, the camp regimes had to be adapted to ensure a rapid turnover. On a ration of 500 grams of bread or gruel daily for ten to twelve hours of heavy physical labor in mines or forests, an inmate's average life on what was called "general work" was about six months, and NKVD men quickened the rate of turnover by mass shootings euphemistically called "cleansing actions."[134]

The places of confinement became death camps in all but name. A piece of evidence of Stalin's personal responsibility for this is noteworthy. In late 1937 one K. A. Pavlov replaced E. P. Berzin, who had presided over a relatively humane regime in the Kolyma camps in northeast Siberia from 1932 on, when the main purpose was to mine gold. Soon afterward, some local officials sent Stalin a telegram critical of Pavlov's murderous new regime, to which Stalin replied with a message printed in the newspaper *Sovetskaia Kolyma* on 17 January 1938 rejecting their protest as "demagogical and unfounded."[135]

The Why of Forced Confession

The reason for the Terror's inquisitorial character remains obscure. There is no mystery why those chosen for roles in the purge trials were coerced into confessing: that was a necessity of the trials as staged political events. But why were millions of others similarly forced to confess, at the cost not only of intense suffering on their part but also of countless man-hours of pressuring and torturing by their interrogators? The records of their signed confessions were never made public; they stayed in NKVD secret archives in folders marked "To be preserved forever." To what end? It does not suffice to say that prisoners could not be forced to denounce others unless they confessed their own criminality, for great numbers of denunciations were secured from people who were not arrested.

The answer must lie inside Stalin. By mid-1937 he effectively *was* the regime. No high group or institution any longer set bounds to his power or opposed his dictates. The few who raised voices against the Terror or protested individual arrests were destroyed or, as with Krupskaya, silenced. The most probable cause of forced confessions could only be Stalin's insistence that his police produce them. The question then becomes, why did he need them? The fact that he needed them is patent. Not only did he follow closely the interrogations of important persons under arrest. If one refused to sign, he reportedly grew restless and couldn't sleep. In one such case, that of his brother-in-law Redens, by then under arrest and refusing to confess, Stalin arranged for Reden's wife, Anna Alliluyeva, to be brought to him in Lefortovo with a promise of freedom for him and safety for her and their three children *if he would admit that he was a counterrevolutionary.* After trying to explain to her that Stalin could not be trusted in anything, Redens asked the duty officer to take her away.[136]

Stalin believed that the party and the society were full of people hostile to the Revolution and to him as its leader, who hid their hostility behind appearances of Soviet and Communist loyalty and of devotion to him. "Everywhere and in everything he saw 'enemies,' 'two-facers,' and 'spies'," Khrushchev testifies concerning Stalin at this time in his life.[137] His urge to unmask, his overpowering need for confessions, was at bottom a need for reassurance, *for proof,* that he was right. He craved certainty that the multitude of people whom he suspected of being enemies were in fact the two-faced ones, the *dvurushniki,* that he believed them to be. To suspect, after all, is to be somewhat less than certain. The proofs of their perfidy were their written and signed confessions. Naturally, they would strive at all cost to keep their masks on; they would resist confessing with all their might. But the refusal to confess threatened Stalin's sense of being right about the suspect, and therefore, in his mind, all means of extorting confessions must have seemed justified. Being shrewd, he very likely reckoned that some among the great numbers taken into custody, particularly if not personally known to him, were innocent of the masked hostility of which they were accused. But this must have seemed a small price to pay for the total purgation of society that he deemed supremely necessary.

As we push our way further in the explanatory quest, a next question arises: why did he suspect so many fellow Bolsheviks and others of being masked enemies? That he did so is beyond serious doubt, not only in view of the positive testimony that has been citied. For on the alternative hypothesis—that he was cynically aware of the groundlessness of the mass treason charges and had no other motive in the Terror than to absolutize his power by the prophylactic destroying of all those who might conceivably be inwardly resistant to it, and to intimidate the rest—he would have felt no urgent need to extract secret confessions of counterrevolutionary guilt from the victims.

There is no avoiding the question: Why was Stalin driven to believe things that he had no grounds for believing about the huge numbers of people who were victimized? The answer takes us back to his idealized self. Only by believing in the victims' treasonous designs or deeds could he come to terms with their failure to share his grandiose beliefs about himself, their actual or suspected disbelief in his supreme greatness as the party-state's leader of genius. *And this was something for which he did have evidence.*

Still fresh in his memory was the Seventeenth Congress, on the eve of which a few high-level Bolsheviks conspired to replace him with Kirov as general secretary and at the end of which a minority of congress delegates secretly voted against his candidature for the new Central Committee. Since he did not know just who they were, he had to suspect the great bulk of them of being among their number. So, the exuberant display of Stalin-adulation that marked the congress' formal proceedings must have struck him in retrospect as villainously duplicitous. People really against him pretended to be for him. And given the pervasive clientelism of the whole party-state, his suspicion had to fall on the multitude of their associates in central and regional party and government agencies. Farther back in time—but Stalin's memory was long—were the Riutin, the Syrtsov-Lominadze, and other anti-Stalin manifestations in the early 1930s along with the criticism of him over the calamitous (as it seemed to others, but not to him) outcome of his collectivizing from above.

Stalin had considerable evidence of his unpopularity in Bolshevik, and especially Old Bolshevik circles and beyond. What's more, the people who disparaged him and his works seemed to think of themselves as good Bolsheviks and right-minded Soviet citizens. This had to be unbearable to him because of his unshakable belief in himself as a brilliant revolutionary leader and thinker. The only way in which he could live with his knowledge of their anti-Stalin feelings was to suspect that, behind their pretense of Bolshevik and Soviet loyalty, they were scheming enemies of the *party's* cause. For then they would have to be opposed to him *because* he was a leader of genius. They would be against him *because* of the epochal contributions that he had made and would still make to Soviet Russia's progress at home and the revolutionary cause abroad. But to be absolutely certain about the antiparty, anti-Soviet, and counterrevolutionary motives of those anti-Stalin people who pretended to be devoted to the party and to him (and many of whom *were* devoted to him), he had to have their confessions of duplicity, of counterrevolutionary hostility behind a mask of pro-revolutionary faith.[138] Only if they had been *dvurushniki* all along could he be Stalin the great. Their confessions were an imperatively needed support for Stalin's inner personality cult.

Their confessions enabled him to live at ease with awareness of his low popularity among elements of the political class. For they gave him confirmation—and confirmation that would be preserved forever for the benefit of any future doubters—that all who had belittled his merits and regarded him with hostility did so because of their hatred for the revolutionary regime and nation that had in him a sterling leader. This reasoning helps to explain why the Terror struck with particular ferocity at party members and those of higher rank and longer party standing; at very many in the generation of Bolsheviks who had been strong Stalin supporters against the oppositions in the 1920s; and at many among the capable and energetic industrializers who went through thick and thin to make a success of the *piatiletka* in spite of the disruptive effects of the unrealistic planning. The Communist party was by his own definition, now become official, a party of Lenin-*Stalin* followers. Stalin felt that he had a claim to unconditional fidelity and reverential tribute on the part of these members, but for that reason they were also in greatest danger of falling under suspicion as two-facers. Stalin would hardly expect to be idolized by dekulakized peasants laboring in the frozen North, or by old-regime holdovers who might, nevertheless, render valuable service to the Soviet state as Russian patriots. No more than by foreign statesmen with whom he dealt and who perceived him as above all a matter-of-fact man, a "realist." He could be just that—with them. Not expecting their adulation, he had no need to suspect them of duplicity, except for the conscious pragmatic duplicity that went with the business of statesmanship.

One final step may be taken in the analysis. There *was* a two-faced individual at the center of political life in Russia: Stalin. He would consciously deploy duplicity with great skill, as when he convincingly reassured people marked down in his mind as purge victims that they had nothing to fear. But he was also unconsciously duplicitous because of his need to blot out of his mind the disparities between the idealized Stalin with whom he identified himself and the scheming, bungling, blemished, evil-doing Stalin that he very often had been and still was, never before so vilely as now. In his private letters he was always telling people to be modest, and in his public deportment he was simple and unassuming, like Lenin. Behind a mask of modesty, he concealed an arrogant inner picture of himself as a paragon of revolutionary statesmanship.

Since this was the Stalin in whose reality he had to believe, he could not help unconsciously hating and condemning the much different Stalin that he actually was. His way out of the predicament was to find in others the faults, the blemishes, the machinations, and the double lives that he could not face in himself. That Stalin might be blameless, countless innocents had to be blamed. In them he perceived a conscious duplicity of sworn enemies of the revolutionary state. He was driven to "see through and expose" in others the duplicity that he had to remain blind to in himself. Then, with a sense of only meting out justice, he could and did visit on those unfortunates the rage and fury that he could not bear to direct at himself. No torture, he seems to have thought, was too cruel as punishment for *their* villainy. As a result, he virtually wrecked Soviet Russia in the great manhunt against "wreckers," and by means of the Terror that purported to cleanse the land of enemies, he made very many loyal citizens into real covert enemies of his state.

At this point in our trek through Russia's Stalinist 1930s we may recall Joseph Conrad's story, *The Heart of Darkness,* and the protagonist Marlow's discovery on his trip up the great river into the African interior that the true heart of darkness lies inside a man.

The way we have scurried to and fro in the twentieth century, trapped between Hitler and Stalin.

—NADEZHDA MANDELSTAM, *Hope Against Hope*

18

TERROR, RUSSIAN NATIONALISM, AND FOREIGN POLICY

AS 7 NOVEMBER 1937 approached, Russia went through the motions of celebrating the Revolution's twentieth anniversary. The Marx-Engels-Lenin Institute issued a set of theses telling the Revolution's story as a twenty-year epic struggle culminating in the victory of socialism under Stalin's leadership. Press editorials elaborated upon this theme. On 29 October, at a Kremlin reception for executives of the iron, steel, and coal industries, Stalin spoke briefly on the need for leaders to value the people's trust. "Leaders come and go but the people remains," he told them. "Only the people is immortal. All else is transitory."[1] Since not a few prominent leaders were "going" by then, this allusion to the Terror did not escape some *Pravda* readers.

An anniversary ceremony took place in the Bolshoi Theater on the evening of 6 November. Stalin and fellow Politburo members were present along with a select Soviet audience, foreign Communist leaders, and the diplomatic corps. Stalin, his hair turned gray and his face deeply lined, had noticeably aged in the past three years; he would turn fifty-eight in a few weeks. Molotov gave a long address on the history of the Revolution, hailing Stalin at the end as a symbol of the victories of socialism. After an intermission, a new sound film was shown, *Lenin in October,* produced especially for the anniversary.

A more accurate title would have been *Lenin-Stalin in October.* As Lenin's train from Finland nears Petrograd in April 1917, he orders his worker-guard, Vasily, to arrange a meeting with Stalin, and then, as an afterthought, asks that Krupskaya be informed of his impending arrival. The next day he has a four-hour meeting with Stalin in his hideaway house to learn what's happening in Russia. They part at nightfall with a manly embrace. Stalin has the revolutionary situation well in hand. At the 10–11 October Central Committee meeting, Lenin, surrounded by Stalin, Dzerzhinsky, Sverdlov, and Uritsky (all except Stalin now deceased) passionately denounces Trotsky, Zinoviev, and Kamenev as strikebreakers of revolution and brands their behavior as "total treason." When the Provisional Government plots to behead the revolution by murdering its leadership, the chosen victims are Lenin, Stalin, Dzerzhinsky, Sverdlov, and Uritsky. A repulsive hired assassin, when given a description of Lenin's physical characteristics, asks: "A Jew?" The answer: "No." Viewers may have been reminded that the strikebreakers were.

Lenin appears in this film as a fussy little man, a sort of professor of revolution who needs a practical genius to accomplish something, and Stalin as his right-hand man, the real mastermind of October. Toward the end Lenin arrives at the Smolny and sits on a bench with gauze covering half his face until Stalin stops by to pick him up and take him to the backroom. There the two pace back and forth discussing the plans. Trotsky is nowhere to be seen. As the uprising proceeds, Stalin, shown as about three inches taller than Lenin, stands by a map explaining what is going on. At the close, when Lenin appears before the crowd at the Smolny to announce the victorious outcome, Stalin steps to a respectful place just behind him to the left, unmistakably the successor moving into position, the strong silent man who has carried it off for Lenin, the Bolsheviks, and history. The film was a fantasy of October as Stalin would have been pleased to remember it and have all good Soviet citizens think back on it, with him and Lenin as the Revolution's heroes and Trotsky, Zinoviev, and Kamenev, then as later, as its villainous enemies. From the glowing press accounts of the film we can infer that he enjoyed it. The only sign of less than total satisfaction was a directive to the government's film agency to make it still better by adding scenes showing the seizure of the Winter Palace and the arrest of the Provisional Government.

A second thematic accompaniment of the anniversary was Russia's history. This was the subject of the new school text, *Short Course of History of the USSR,* edited by A. V. Shestakov, which appeared in early October in a first printing of five million copies. Illustrated mainly with portraits of leaders from Prince Oleg, who founded the Kievan state in the tenth century, to Stalin, who led the building of socialism in the twentieth, the book presented 1917–37 as the finale of embattled Russia's long march through history from humble beginnings to world leadership and greatness under Lenin-Stalin. The implicit message was that Soviet Russia, notwithstanding the revolutionary break of 1917, was an organic extension of historic Russia.

A third of the book's 216 pages dealt with earlier Russian history. It told of the rise of Muscovy in the fourteenth century under Ivan Kalita (Ivan the Money-Bag) and subsequent "gatherers" of Russian lands. One chapter described how Muscovy under Ivan III liberated itself from Tatar subjugation, united neighboring principalities under its rule despite their leaders' efforts to ally themselves with the Tatars and Lithuania, and finally conquered Novgorod. How the "autocrat tsar" Ivan Grozny continued the unification and expansion was the subject of another chapter. Shestakov's Ivan Grozny, following Wipper's, was a hero of Russian history. After his first defeats in the war against the Poles and Lithuanians for the Baltic coast, he discovered that the big patrimonial boyars were engaged in treason, having entered the service of the enemies, and he formed his *oprichnina* in order to smash these "little tsars and to strengthen his position as the sole ruler." He thus "completed the work, started by Ivan Kalita, of gathering together the scattered appanage principalities into one strong state."[2]

The Lenin-Stalin theme of *Lenin in October* was prominent in the last part of the Shestakov text. When Lenin went abroad after the 1905 Revolution, Stalin stayed behind in Russia where "his seething energy inspired the Bolsheviks in their hard and persistent labors." Lenin abroad, and Stalin working underground in Russia, "continued the great struggle for socialism, ready to give all their blood, drop by drop, for the cause of the working class." After Lenin-Stalin led the Bolsheviks to victory in 1917 and organized the Soviet Russian state, Lenin died, Stalin took over, collectivization was accomplished against furious resistance from the kulaks, who had the support of a clique of traitors headed by Bukharin and Rykov, and the fulfillment of the Five-Year Plan then ensured the victory of socialism. Fascist spies penetrated and found active assistants in Trotsky, Rykov, and their followers, whose aim was to restore capitalism, "to surrender the Ukraine to the Germans and the Far East to the Japanese, and to prepare for the defeat of the Soviet Union in the event of war."[3]

Iosif Grozny

Having fathered this history text with his contest earlier in the decade, Stalin surely must have read the finished product when it came off the press as the anniversary approached. The parallel it implied between Grozny's fight against traitors who wanted to sell Russia out to foreign states and Stalin's supposed similar struggle was striking. It seems that the Grozny tsar was on his mind now as a role model in the Terror, and there is indirect evidence of that in an informal talk that he gave when he met with Politburo members and a few others, including Comintern chief Dimitrov, in the Kremlin on 8 November 1937. His impromptu speech on that occasion and the accompanying dialogue with Dimitrov were not published. They were, however, recorded verbatim by a person who was present and had permission to do so. Eventually, a copy of the verbatim record made its way abroad.[4]

This is a holiday and everyone is in a holiday mood, Stalin began. But he would speak about the twenty-year existence of the Soviet state rather than about the holiday. *Rus'* was built up over the centuries as a state for tsar and landowners, and there were many bad things about it. But what is a state? An integral, territorially unified organism, closely interconnected economically. The tsarist state lacked such integration. Vladivostok was linked with the center by no more than seven pairs of trains. Now all is unified, there are no neglected borderlands. It is a colossal state, closely integrated economically and politically—which can frighten an enemy and keep him in fear. And a state for the people. Among its equal nations, the most Soviet and the most revolutionary is the Russian nation. Anyone who dares to weaken the might of the USSR will be considered an enemy of the people and destroyed as a clan *(Unichtozhim ikh, kak rod)*.

Warming to the subject of treason, Stalin then said that there were people in Soviet Russia who wanted to weaken the country. Foreign enemies, knowing how hard it would be to conquer it from outside, encouraged them. Trotsky, Radek, Bukharin, Rykov, Zinoviev, Kamenev, Piatakov, and others, seeking power at any price, agreed to cede the Ukraine to the Germans, Leningrad, Baku, the Transcaucasus and Caucasus, Turkmenistan, and Uzbekistan to the British, the Far East and Maritime Region to the Japanese, and the Crimea, Black Sea, and Donbas to the French, with a view to preserving a small, economically weakened state in the center and placing the rest under protectorates of these foreign states. The strength of the Soviet peoples lay in their economic and political unity. Hence, anyone, even if a former leader, a party member, even an Old Bolshevik, who should undertake in deeds or even in thoughts to detach a small piece of the USSR and place it under a protectorate, would be physically destroyed together with his clan *(my budem ego unichtozhat' vmeste s ego rodom fizicheski).*

Then Stalin referred to Lenin and himself as leaders who had never barred an able and honest party member from the road to power. The state apparatus and the governing of the peoples, he went on, is no affair of philosophical study circles about the teachings of Plato and Aristotle. Then he proposed a toast to the health of the builders of the new Soviet state, ending with the words: For the destruction of traitors and their foul line! *(Za unichtozhenie izmennikov i ikh podlogo roda!)*

Replying, Dimitrov recalled that he had seen Lenin's greatness when he sat in a German prison. But after Lenin died, Comrade Stalin's name was inseparable from Lenin's and it was for the good of humanity's struggle that Stalin took Lenin's place. With these words he proposed a toast to Stalin's health. Comrade Dimitrov, Stalin answered, is mistaken, even in Marxist methodology. Personalities always appear if the cause that puts them forward is not a lost one. They come and go, but the people stays forever and a personality will appear if the cause is not a lost one.

Moved to resume, Stalin asked: What was the main error of the oppositionists? It was that they sought to solve all issues by getting a Central Committee majority and not by trying to proceed as desired by the middle element, the party's backbone *(kostiak)*. After Lenin's death, Kamenev, Zinoviev, and Bukharin joined forces. It was well known that Trotsky hadn't been a Bolshevik, he came to the Bolsheviks with his program of permanent revolution. Many said the Republic was Lenin and Trotsky. He was an orator. Then all the famous figures—Trotsky, Bukharin, Rykov, Tomsky, Zinoviev, Piatakov, and God knows who else— joined forces, plus Nadezhda Konstantinovna (Krupskaya—R.T.), who always supported those "left" Communists. As for me, Stalin, they knew me but not as they did Trotsky—be brave and don't ascribe something that wasn't so. There are people who are cowardly in politics, which mustn't be confused with physical cowardice. There are fainthearted people who fear bullets and crawl on the ground, but they're very brave in politics. And don't be afraid of looking truth in the eyes. The famous ones were Trotsky, Kamenev, Zinoviev, Tomsky, Bukharin, Rykov. Whom did we have on our side? Well, I was in charge of organizational work in the Central Committee. Well, what was I compared with Ilyich? An unimpressive fellow *(zamukhryshka)*. There were comrades Molotov, Kalinin, Kaganovich, Voroshilov—all unknown people. Lenin was an eagle and those famous figures were chickens. Let the eagle blow on them and the chickens scatter. We were practicians and they were renowned figures, with the constant support of Nadezhda Konstantinovna.

How did we win out over that group? It happened because that is what the party wanted. Why did it so decide? Comrade Dimitrov, you and I are friends and I don't want to offend you, but you're wrong in what you said about me. The fact is that the oppositionists didn't reckon with the party, especially with its middle element, that's the backbone of the party and it knows how to evaluate people at their practical worth, while those famous figures were good just at making speeches. Compared with their oratorical talents, I'm a poor orator. Apparently, we have people in the party who vote in a practical way, not like rams. They intuitively recognize and advance their young leaders who develop talents and abilities in the course of the work. And at that moment these newly promoted leaders bend all their efforts to justify the trust that the party and people place in them. That trust can't be violated. Fear of letting them down forced many of us to work differently, to learn to work from the masses, from the middle people *(seredniaki)*. And we vindicated the trust of the masses.

When people have experience, when an army has well-trained officer cadres, they show good results in their work. If the generals who lead them are poor and the army suffers losses, the officers throw out the generals. The people itself advances those who lead it to victory. Personalities appear and disappear in history, the people remains and it never errs. If we didn't have the backbone in the party, that foundation of foundations, those "famous" figures might have won out. Personality isn't the crux. It's very hard to say who educated me. You me or I you? You'll say that I'm an outstanding man, it isn't so. Holy fear *(strakh blagorodnyi)* of not justifying the trust that the masses and the people placed in you in the fight with those figures—that's what proved decisive, fear of failure, and we emerged as leaders. Comrades Molotov, Voroshilov, Kalinin, Kaganovich, Mikoyan, and others worked hard. To the middle element, to the officer stratum in the economy, party, and military, to the masses of people who acquire experience and promote even unimpressive ones! Be able to see and value the middle-level people of the officer stratum! Trotsky thought it wasn't the middle level that decides the issue of war and victory but select general staff men. But they went over to Kaledin, Denikin, Wrangel, and Kolchak. It was the noncommissioned cadres and corporals who remained behind with their huge experience of military and economic construction. To the party, which is the vessel of wisdom, to the health of the middle-level people in all spheres of the national economy and military affairs!

Here Dimitrov intervened to say that now he understood that nothing could succeed without the backbone. But that backbone wouldn't have taken shape in such numbers and quality in so short a time had not Comrade Stalin worked to achieve it. Stalin responded that 720,000 party members voted for the Central Committee's line in 1927. They were the basic backbone that voted for the unimpressive ones. Four to six thousand voted for Trotsky, and 20,000 abstained. The party's officer element takes form only with real leadership and training and the generalizing of experience.

Plekhanov was a remarkable man, Stalin said in conclusion. Lenin knew his works by heart. Plekhanov was a talent, a scholar. Lenin was a student of his works and was considered his disciple. If there are no party cadres, party officer element, you will accomplish nothing, no matter what ideal proposals the generals make. Even in war, if there are no well-trained cadres on whom one can rely, nothing will come of it. The party's backbone, the popular masses, will make the right choice themselves. But bear in mind that our middle-level element hasn't yet received recognition, we still don't know it well. Every leader must be in holy fear of failing in the work, so that the people's trust in him will be upheld.

So ended this monologue by the one person in Russia who enjoyed real freedom of speech. In its blunt, ungraceful, wandering way, it was revealing of Stalin's inner world. He was troubled by a party past that he could not live down in memory save by a feat of rationalization that made out his relation to Lenin to be that of a lesser light who was yet a potent practical doer capable of realizing Lenin's designs, just as Lenin was earlier a lesser light himself, a disciple who made history by realizing the designs of the learned theoretician, "general" Plekhanov (here was the theme of *Lenin in October*). By the same mode of reasoning, Stalin and not the famous orators was the chosen leader of the party's middle masses and, as such, the rightful victor in the post-Lenin succession fight. What he had to blot out of memory was that in 1927 the 720,000-strong party "backbone" voted for a leadership group that included, along with himself, his enemies Rykov, Bukharin, and Tomsky, and that most or very many of those 720,000 were already, or soon would be, among the victims of his Terror.

In the picture of himself as leader of the middle stratum lay the link between his role as Lenin's successor in party history and a latter-day Ivan Grozny in Russian history. The high Bolsheviks of speech-making fame were grandees like the great boyars of yore. They too turned traitorous by making common cause with Russia's foreign foes. Like Grozny, Stalin lined up with the middle stratum and lower orders against the grandees' treason. Significant here is Stalin's refrain about exterminating the traitors "as a clan." The term "clan" had no place in the political vocabulary of Bolshevism. But he knew from his reading that it was Grozny's practice, when he turned against a boyar whom he perceived as an enemy, to destroy along with him his whole extended family and retinue, his *rod* or clan. And so when a high Bolshevik fell in the Terror, both his personal family and his official family of political clients went with him. Wives, if not shot, were sent to special concentration camps for "members of traitors' families," and children, if small, went to special orphanages and thence to camps when old enough.

It was Iosif Grozny who spoke in the Kremlin that night. It transpired from his words that he, an unimpressive fellow, rightfully became leader by winning the trust of the party's backbone; and the speech-making famous figures, bested in the party struggle, tried to sell out Soviet Russia to foreign powers by offering them protectorates over peripheral territories. Like the Grozny of Shestakov's history text, Stalin was preserving Russia as a unified state organism against the intrigues of high-placed traitors with hostile governments abroad. In the midst of his Terror and the unspeakable crimes being committed by his servitors on his orders, he had to see himself as a hero of the Revolution's history and Russia's, which were merged in his mind.

Terror in the Non-Russian Republics

At one point in his impromptu speech on 8 November, Stalin called the Russians "the most Soviet and the most revolutionary" of the country's nations. In this statement and throughout the speech he seemed intent on making the Soviet Union a new Russia One and Indivisible, impregnable to the hostile outside world, crushing all traitors and their political clans in the process.

The new Stalin Constitution laid the legal groundwork for extreme centralism. It took away from the union republics the right to have civil and criminal law codes and judicial legislation of their own. It gave all-union commissariats jurisdiction over foreign affairs, defense, foreign trade, rail and water transport, communications, and heavy and defense industries throughout the country. Hybrid "union-republic" commissariats, in which the republic body of that name functioned as an agency of the union one in Moscow, ran the food industry, light industry, lumber industry, agriculture (that is, collective farms), state farms, finance, internal trade, internal affairs, justice, and public health—leaving only education, local industry, communal economy, and social security under autonomous republic commissariats. Although the Russian Federation was in these respects no better off than the Ukraine, Belorussia, the three Transcaucasian and the five Central Asian union republics, its capital was Moscow. The union government was the imperial Russian one in all but name.

When Stalin spoke informally in the Kremlin on 8 November 1937, the purge was mowing down the national leaderships of the outlying republics to the accompaniment of baseless charges of plotting to sever their republics from the union, of "bourgeois nationalism" and "nationalist-terrorist activity." Ethnic Russians in many cases took the places of non-Russian purge victims.

The two westernmost union republics, the Ukraine and Belorussia, lost not only their central and local political elites but the bulk of their scholars, writers, and artists as well, not to mention ordinary people who were taken. The Terror struck the Ukraine with full force in mid-1937 after Postyshev's transfer to Kuibyshev. Arrests of Ukrainian party members alone totalled more than 150,000 that year.[5] First Secretary Kosior, who was Polish by nationality, was shifted to a high government post in Moscow before being arrested. With the sole exception of the Ukraine's president, Petrovsky, who wound up as custodian of the Museum of the Revolution in Moscow, the entire Ukrainian Politburo of mid-1937 perished in the Terror, including Kosior, N. Gikalo, P. Liubchenko, V. Zatonsky, S. Kudriavtsev, M. Khataevich, and N. Popov. Between Molotov's purge mission to Kiev in August 1937 and Khrushchev's arrival there in January 1938 to take over as party boss of the republic, the Ukraine's governing elite was virtually wiped out. The Ukrainian Communist leader Vlas Chubar, who became a full member of the Politburo in the mid-1930s, was shunted to a minor provincial post in 1938 before being arrested and killed. He had been deeply upset by the purges because he couldn't believe that his already arrested best friends had been spies and traitors.[6]

The terror in Belorussia was no less savage. During the 1935–36 verification and exchange of party documents, half its party members had been expelled on the basis of charges brought by Malenkov and Yezhov that a ramified anti-Soviet underground existed in the republic. When the Belorussian premier, Nikolai Goloded, questioned this at a plenum of the republic's party Central Committee in 1937, he was arrested. Following Malenkov's arrival in Minsk at that time, Central Committee secretaries, people's commissars, heads of local party and government bodies and many members of the creative intelligentsia disappeared.[7] The republic's party first secretary, Vasily Sharangovich, presided over the terror process until he too was arrested in mid-1937 and then impressed into service as a defendant in the third Moscow purge trial. Belorussia's president, A. G. Cherviakov, earlier the founder of the republic, committed suicide in 1937, and all those active in building the republic in the 1920s were arrested. Their replacements were mostly Russians, among them V. V. Kisilev, who became premier, and A. A. Nasedkin, who took over the Belorussian NKVD.[8] Before being shot or sent away to camps—fates of nearly all of them—the arrested Belorussians were forced to sign false confessions of treason, when necessary under torture. Thus, the Old Bolshevik Liubovich, deputy premier and chairman of Belorussia's Gosplan, who had been deputy commissar of communications in Lenin's government of 1917, was seen in the Minsk central prison in 1938 lying on the floor and screaming "mama!" as NKVD men lashed him with rubber truncheons.[9]

The Great Purge in Transcaucasia proceeded under the direction of Beria, who acted with guidance from Stalin. In Georgia about 13,000 persons, one fourth of the republic's party membership, were expelled during the quiet terror of 1935–36. Then, in 1937–38, came the turn of the Georgian elite. The toll is evident in the fact that 425 of the 644 delegates to the republic's May 1937 party congress were subsequently arrested and then shot or sent to camps. They included nineteen of the twenty-seven delegates from Georgia to the ill-fated Seventeenth Congress in Moscow.[10] Among the many victimized Georgian Bolsheviks were Yenukidze, whose execution was announced in late 1937; the former first secretary of the Georgian party and a founder of the republic, Orakhelashvili; Stalin's old Georgian opponent, Budu Mdivani; the brother of Stalin's Georgian first wife, Alesha Svanidze, charged with being an agent of German intelligence; and Ordzhonikidze's brother Papuliia. One who survived, in spite of Beria's efforts to get him purged for inattention to Stalin in his book written long ago on the early history of Transcaucasian Bolshevism, was Filipp Makharadze, who held the powerless post of president of the republic.[11] For some reason of his own Stalin spared him.

Nowhere were victims subjected to more atrocious treatment than in Georgia. Orakhelashvili, as his wife was forced to look on, had his eyes gouged out and his eardrums perforated. Nestor Lakoba, the popular party chief of Georgia's Abkhazia region bordering on the Black Sea, was poisoned on Beria's orders in 1936, buried with honors, only to be exhumed in 1937 and posthumously execrated as an enemy of the people. Then his wife was tortured to death, part of the time in the presence of her fourteen-year-old son, in a vain effort to force her to defame her dead husband by signing a document entitled "How Lakoba Sold Abkhazia to Turkey." She had been told that her son would be killed if she refused. He and three friends were sent to a camp. When, later, they wrote to Beria requesting release to resume their studies, he ordered them returned to Tiflis and shot.[12]

In Armenia the Terror peaked in September 1937 with the arrival in Erevan of Malenkov, Beria, and Mikoyan, accompanied by a detachment of secret police, to take part in an Armenian Central Committee plenum. In Erevan alone, over 1,000 people were arrested in the following month.[13] Some prominent Armenian Communists, including the late Khanchian and Premier Ter Gabrelian (who was hurled from a window to his death after interrogation under torture) were accused of having formed an underground organization in a plot to establish a bourgeois nationalist Armenian regime under protection of a capitalist government. Old and second-generation leading Armenian Bolsheviks were among the many thousands who fell victim. Armenia's prisons were so jammed that the basements of government buildings had to be used as prisons. The Armenian Communist Party's Bureau lost seven of its nine members. Not one of the Erevan City Party Committee's fifty-six members elected in early 1937 was reelected in April 1938, and nine of the new members were Russians. Later a Russian replaced an Armenian as head of the republic's NKVD.[14]

In Baku, capital of Soviet Azerbaijan, the first party secretary was Mir Dzhafar Bagirov, one-time head of the Transcaucasian Cheka and an old confederate of Beria's. He played his part as Stalin's purger of this mainly Moslem republic with extreme brutality, mandating terrible tortures to extract confessions and taking advantage, as Beria did, of the opportunity to destroy his own enemies in the terror process. He and his helpers provoked a flow of denunciatory letters numbering in many thousands. The party committee of one Baku district received 600, leaving hardly a single party member in the district undenounced. Newspaper editors would gather their staffs and ask: "Who has denunciatory material, the paper can't come out without it." Early leaders of Soviet Azerbaijan were arrested on fabricated charges of bourgeois nationalism, espionage for Turkey, and desire to sever Azerbaijan from Soviet Russia. The already deceased and much honored Nariman Narimanov, first head of Soviet Azerbaijan's government, and Agamli-ogly, its first president, became enemies of the people posthumously. Most members of the Old-Bolshevik and second-generation national leaderships perished along with thousands of others.[15]

Across the Caspian Sea, Moslem-populated Soviet Central Asia also felt the full fury of the Terror. In the main republic, Uzbekistan, two well-known figures led the long list of victims: the Uzbek party's first secretary, Akmal Ikramov, and its premier, Faizulla Khodzhaev. Still young then (in 1937 Ikramov was just under forty, Khodzhaev just over), both were minority-nation Communists of Leninist formation who rose to high posts under Stalin at the start of the 1930s. They were, like so many of their contemporaries, Soviet nation builders and opponents of the local nationalism they now stood accused of fomenting. Arrested on Stalin's personal orders after he made some sort of nonpublic protest against the mounting purge,[16] Ikramov was replaced in 1938 by a Russian named Yusupov. In the Tadzhik, Turkmen, Kirghiz, and Kazakh republics, events followed the same pattern. Native-born leaders were arrested on charges of being bourgeois-nationalist spies plotting to sever their republics from the Soviet Union and make them colonies of foreign states. For every leader who disappeared, large numbers of lesser ones did as well.

In the 1920s numerous areas within union republics inhabited by smaller national minorities had received the status of autonomous regions or republics, in which local languages were taught and used along with Russian. Now their elites too fell victim on charges of spying and wrecking motivated by bourgeois nationalism. Thus the leaders of the Karelian Autonomous Republic, situated along the frontier with Finland in the Russian Republic, allegedly wanted to turn Karelia over to the "Finnish fascists." Another example was the Jewish Autonomous Region of Birob-idzhan, founded in the early 1930s in an inclement area of the Soviet Far East bordering on Manchuria. In 1936 its population of 64,000 included 19,000 Jews. Along with Russian, Yiddish was an official language. In 1937 the Terror claimed, among many others, the region's president, Joseph Liberberg, and its party secretary, M. Khavkin. Jewish purge victims were accused of being "masked Trotskyist nationalists" or "Japanese spies." The rank-and-file victims included very many of the 1,400 Jews who had come from abroad to help colonize a non-Zionist Soviet Jewish homeland.[17]

By Stalin's earlier definition the cultures of the Soviet nations were proletarian or socialist in content and national in form.[18] A major element of "national in form" was the right of national minorities to the use of their native tongues in schools, courts, and other public institutions. Now Stalin's Russian centralism made cultural and linguistic Russification the order of the day. Ukrainian "nationalists" were assailed for publishing in 1937 a new Russian-Ukrainian academic dictionary that sought to "purge" the Ukrainian language of various Russian terms in common currency throughout the country, and bourgeois-nationalist enemies of the Tadzhik people for cutting Tadzhik children off from Russian culture and the great Russian language in school.[19] The Karelian leaders who allegedly wanted to turn over Karelia to the Finnish fascists were said to have introduced the Finnish language in schools and ignored Russian—"the language of socialist revolution."[20] Russification also overtook primitive peoples and tribes that in the 1920s had been given written languages using Roman letters. In 1937 their Roman alphabets were replaced by Russian's Cyrillic one. Shestakov's history text, now coming out in the national-minority languages for school adoption, made the history of Russia the national past of all Soviet children. Soviet identity was thus becoming Soviet *Russian* identity.

One of the faces of Great Russian nationalism in pre-1917 imperial Russia was anti-Semitism. As the former made a comeback now, the latter did as well. The two went together in Stalin, whose assumed Russian self-identity was coupled with anti-Semitism, shown, for example, in his strong disapproval of his son Yakov's marriage in 1936 to a Jewish woman.[21] Earlier, responding to opportunities for assimilation and advancement opened by the revolutions of 1917, very many Jews flocked into careers in the party, the government, and the professions. The numbers of Jewish purge victims were, accordingly, quite high. It has been argued that Jews were not a special target but suffered greatly because they were represented in disproportionately large numbers in the hardest-hit categories: the intelligentsia and party-government personnel; within those categories the party members; and within that category the members of long standing.[22]

This reasoning is not incompatible, however, with the view that anti-Semitism took on new life during and owing to the Great Purge. In the Soviet Union of 1937 Maurice Hindus sensed a growing hostility to Jews, which he attributed to the prominence of Jewish Communists among the purge victims.[23] Jewish culture came under attack in 1937–38 with the closing of Yiddish schools and Yiddish sections of the academies of science in the Belorussian and Ukrainian republics, the areas of heaviest Jewish concentration where the Pale of Settlement was located in tsarist Russia. In Belorussia, where Jews made up 41 percent of the urban population and were strongly represented in the party and government leadership, the Terror made a clean sweep of them: no Jews remained in Belorussia's leadership as reconstituted after 1938, and only two Jews, out of a total of 304 deputies, remained in the Ukraine's Supreme Soviet as reelected in 1938.[24] At the all-union level there were a few Jewish survivors, notably Kaganovich, his brother M. M. Kaganovich as commissar of defense industry, Mekhlis as chief editor of *Pravda,* and Litvinov as foreign commissar. But the latter's days in office were numbered now, as were those of others whose pictures appeared in a Nazi publication of 1938 on the heavy Jewish representation in the Soviet establishment.[25] By its publication time the book had been largely outdated by the purge, and soon still more of its Jewish Bolshevik subjects joined the earlier victims.

The Terror by no means spared ethnic Russians. But none, so far as is known, came to grief on charges of Russian nationalism. Back in 1923, under heavy pressure from an ill Lenin, Stalin told the Twelfth Party Congress that although local nationalisms were a serious danger, a still greater one was the renascent great-power chauvinism "that seeks to obliterate everything non-Russian, gather all threads of government into Russian hands and stifle everything non-Russian."[26] Far from being a deviation now, such great-power chauvinism was in full command in the person of the new tsar-autocrat, Iosif Grozny.

The Great Purge Trial

The case of the "Anti-Soviet Bloc of Rightist and Trotskyists," it was called. Bukharin and Rykov led the list of twenty-one accused. The others were the one-time leading Left oppositionist, Rakovsky; the Soviet ambassador to Germany from 1921 to 1930 and deputy foreign commissar from 1930 to 1937, Krestinsky, who was a member of Lenin's Politburo, a Central Committee secretary in 1919–20, and a Trotsky supporter in the early 1920s; the counselor of the Soviet Embassy in Berlin from 1931 to 1937, Bessonov; the recent commissars of internal affairs, Yagoda; foreign trade, Rosengolts; finance, Grinko; agriculture, Chernov; and timber industry, Ivanov; the recent head of the consumer cooperatives, Zelensky; the Uzbek leaders Khodzhaev and Ikramov; the Belorussian first secretary, Sharangovich; doctors Levin, Pletnev, and Kazakov from the Kremlin hospital; Yagoda's private secretary, Bulanov; Gorky's secretary, Kriuchkov; Kuibyshev's secretary, Maksimov-Dikovsky; and a middle-level agricultural official, Zubarev. Nine of the twenty-one—Bukharin, Rykov, Chernov, Ivanov, Zelensky, Grinko, Rosengolts, Ikramov, and Yagoda—were elected to the Central Committee at the Seventeenth Congress.

Only formally was this a trial of twenty-one. The indictment and trial testimony were strewn with names of those convicted in the previous two Moscow purge trials; others, such as Mdivani and Okudzhava, who had been put on trial in other parts of the country, in their case Georgia; the deceased Tomsky; the Tukhachevsky group, which now went on public trial posthumously as a "military conspiratorial organization" linked with the larger "Bloc" conspiracy, and many others. And Yenukidze, whose execution on espionage charges without public trial, along with the prominent soviet diplomat Karakhan and others, had been announced in late December 1937, appeared now as a key conspirator. The inclusion of the Right opposition's leaders in a "Bloc" with the Left signified a great enlargement of the circle of the accused, which was now opened to anyone, even members of the old Stalin faction, who had worked in the Soviet government under Rykov before 1930.

All this led Trotsky to comment from Mexico that the whole Soviet state, including early Politburo members Trotsky, Zinoviev, Kamenev, Tomsky, Rykov, Bukharin, and Rudzutak, Premier Rykov, a majority of people's commissars, top diplomats, economic leaders like Piatakov, military leaders, heads of the Russian and all other Soviet republics, and police chiefs of the past decade headed by Yagoda, appeared in this trial as a "centralized apparatus of high treason."[27] Indeed, had the Soviet regime been put on trial by a counterrevolutionary Russian monarchist regime, the cast of the accused could hardly have been much different save for the inclusion of Stalin and those he allowed to survive as his helpers or as seeming Old Bolshevik representatives of political continuity.

The spectacle played out in the October Hall between 2 and 13 March was the supreme production in the Stalin genre of political show trial. As the cast of accused was greatly enlarged, so the imaginary conspiracy was pushed far back in time. The trial portrayed a Revolution led by Lenin and Stalin that was beset from the start by machinations of scheming enemies who played roles of prominent party and government leaders until they were exposed as people who, in the words of Vyshinsky's summing-up speech, "spent the whole of their lives behind masks. . . ."[28] At the time of their opposition to the Brest-Litovsk treaty in 1918, Bukharin and his Left Communists organized with the Left Socialist-Revolutionaries, and with Trotsky, a plot against Lenin. Bukharin proposed not to stop short of arresting the Soviet government and killing its leaders, above all Lenin and Stalin. Fanya Kaplan made her attempt on Lenin's life in August 1918 on instructions not only from the Left SR's but also from Bukharin. From 1921 "Judas-Trotsky" was an agent of German intelligence, and from 1926 an agent of British intelligence as well. Bukharin and Rykov were also linked with foreign intelligence services, and Krestinsky, Rosengolts, and Rakovsky were agents of foreign powers from the early 1920s. The Left and Right had never been genuine political oppositions but subversive movements in oppositionist guise.

In 1932–33, when the futility of open oppositional activity was obvious, the two subversive groups formed, on instructions of foreign intelligence services, a conspiratorial center of the "Bloc." Deputy Foreign Commissar Krestinsky ordered Bessonov, who was about to return to Berlin in 1933 as Embassy counselor, to be Trotsky's liaison in dealings with the Nazis, and also to use his Berlin post to hamper and if possible prevent a normalizing of diplomatic relations between the Soviet Union and Germany. Trotsky negotiated an agreement with the Nazis looking to the defeat of the USSR in a coming war in which the Tukhachevsky group's mission would be to open the front to the Germans. Karakhan was also involved in negotiating with the Nazis to help the "Bloc" overthrow the Soviet regime, in return for which Germany would receive the Ukraine. In January 1934, pursuant to an idea broached earlier by Tomsky, preparations were made by a military conspiratorial organization set up in the Kremlin under Yenukidze to carry out a coup by arresting the assembled Seventeenth Party Congress. The project was not carried through only because the government's broad popularity in the country made it hopeless. In his meetings with Nicolaevsky in Paris in 1936, Bukharin made contact on behalf of the "Bloc" with the Mensheviks and the Second

International. In March 1937 Tukhachevsky confided in Rosengolts and Krestinsky that he intended to carry out a military coup in early May, seize the Kremlin, and murder the regime's leaders—from which it followed that the Tukhachevsky group's arrest came just in the nick of time.

Our information is still incomplete on how the accused men were coerced into playing their parts in the trial. Sharangovich, it appears, was a police agent in defendant's guise. Bessonov, one of the three who received long prison terms instead of the death penalty (the other two were Rakovsky and Dr. Pletnev), told a friend whom he met in a Butyrka cell in 1938 that he was kept on the conveyor for seventeen days without food or sleep and then beaten methodically to break his will to resist.[29] Bukharin said in his final statement at the trial that he held out for three months after arrest before agreeing to testify. We have reason to believe that one means of coercion used during that time was the threat to harm his wife and baby son. Although shunned, she was left in their Kremlin apartment at first, where she received a note from him a month or so after his arrest requesting some books and saying that he had started to write one of his own, *The Degradation of Culture Under Fascism*. Then the police compelled her to write him a note saying that she was living in the Kremlin as before and receiving rations.[30] After Bukharin began cooperating, she was exiled to Astrakhan and later sent to a Siberian camp for "members of traitors' families." How Rykov was broken is not known. To British trial observers he gave the impression of a man gone to pieces: decayed appearance, incoherent statements, inane giggle.[31]

Krestinsky chose a course that he must have known would cost him death by torture. He produced the demanded pretrial depositions unresistingly. Then, when called to testify in the very first trial session, he caused a serious *contretemps* by retracting his pretrial confession. Confronted by Vyshinsky with Bessonov's testimony that Krestinsky had directed him in 1933 to be liaison with Trotsky and hamper the normalizing of Soviet-German relations in his Berlin post, Krestinsky declared in a ringing voice that Bessonov was mistaken, that he had broken with Trotsky and Trotskyism in November 1927, that in speaking with Bessonov in May 1933, before the latter left Moscow to return to Berlin, he instructed him to work for normal Soviet relations with Germany, and that he signed false and involuntary pretrial depositions as the only way to secure the chance to assert his innocence in open session. This exchange was left out of the purported verbatim account of the first session carried in the press on 3 March, hence was a sensation only for those present in the October Hall, newspaper readers abroad, and the few Soviet citizens who perused the 800-page verbatim trial report when it appeared as a book later in 1938. Meanwhile, on 3 March a woman doctor in Lefortovo prison saw Krestinsky savagely beaten and covered with blood; and to courtroom spectators personally acquainted with him, the Krestinsky who reappeared and obediently confessed in a mechanical voice on later days seemed a different man, possibly a double.[32]

The police producers of this show evidently acted under orders to dramatize in all possible ways the contention in Stalin's unpublicized talk of 8 November 1937 that the conspirators sought the dismemberment of the Soviet Union. They aimed, it was said, to undermine the revolutionary power of central Russia by severing its border regions. Grinko pleaded guilty to having plotted on behalf of Ukrainian nationalists to turn the Ukraine over to the Germans; Ivanov, who had headed the Northern Region in the early 1930s as party secretary, to conspiring to cut off Archangel in event of war so that the British could seize it and its surrounding forest areas for the benefit of Britain's timber industry; Sharangovich to conspiring to cede Belorussia to Poland; and Khodzhaev and Ikramov to plans to give the British a protectorate over Uzbekistan and the rest of Soviet Central Asia. Japan was to be recompensed with the Maritime Region for helping the "Bloc" to overthrow the Soviet regime. Bukharin and Rykov were pictured as ringleaders of the entire dismemberment project.

This trial presented the murderous pseudo-community, which now took larger shape as the "Bloc," as having plotted murder on a monstrous scale and perpetrated it in several instances. It was responsible for failed terrorist attempts on the lives of Stalin, Molotov, Kaganovich, Voroshilov, and Yezhov, in the latter's case by poisoning the air in his office with mercury dissolved in an acid. The chief murderer on behalf of the "Bloc" was Yagoda, who confessed to having set up in 1931–32 a Rightist group of high OGPU men. In the summer of 1934 Yenukidze told him that the Trotskyist-Zinovievist group was plotting to murder Kirov, that the "Bloc" had decided on this action, and that he should order Zaporozhets not to place any obstacles in the operation's way.

Yagoda further confessed to forcing doctors Levin, Pletnev, and Kazakov to shorten the lives of high-placed targets of the conspiracy: Menzhinsky, Kuibyshev, Gorky, and Gorky's son, Maxim Peshkov. For some reason, Yagoda balked at confirming in court his pretrial confession that he procured the medical murder of his predecessor Menzhinsky. What then took place behind the scenes in unknown, but Yagoda reappeared a few hours later looking ten years older and readily confirmed everything in his pretrial depositions. He confessed to having enlisted Gorky's secretary Kriuchkov in the effort to do away with Gorky. Kriuchkov tried to induce illness by lighting bonfires along the path of Gorky's long walks in the Crimea in the winter of 1935–36. Then, on Yagoda's orders, in May 1936 he persuaded Gorky to return from the warm Crimea to a cold Moscow, where, after he visited his granddaughters who were ill with the flu, he came down with pneumonia, entered the hospital, and succumbed to medical murder when doctors Levin and Pletnev administered digitalin. And why did the "Bloc" find Gorky's death necessary? Because, Yenukidze had explained to Yagoda, Gorky was dangerous as a staunch supporter of Stalin's leadership.

In order to turn the people against the regime and prepare the way for its defeat in war, the "Bloc" leaders, it was charged, inspired or themselves committed innumerable acts of sabotage and espionage. Wrecking was rife throughout the economy. In this field the present trial far outdid its two predecessors. To cite only a few examples of alleged wrecking acts, Grinko mismanaged the Soviet ruble and deliberately incensed the public by causing depositors to waste a huge amounts of time in savings banks and encounter endless insolence on the part of bank employees. In agriculture Chernov, while serving as Ukrainian trade commissar during collectivization, tried on Rykov's instructions to incense the middle peasants by extending to them the government's repressive measures intended for kulaks. After becoming agriculture commissar, he muddled seed preparation, misplanned crop rotation, arranged to have cattle infected with various bacteria and pigs with the plague, and brought about the destruction of 25,000 horses to hurt the Red Army. Zelensky took advantage of his post as head of consumer cooperatives to have glass and nails mixed into butter, and in testimony that elicited a gasp of horror from the (Muscovite) courtroom audience he confessed to causing destruction to fifty carloads of eggs destined for Moscow. Sharangovich undermined Belorussia's peat industry and arranged the destruction of 30,000 horses. As timber industry commissar, Ivanov managed to disorganize timber-floating operations as well as destroy paper and cellulose factories. "It is now clear," Vyshinsky concluded from such testimony, "why, with our riches and abundance of products, there is a shortage first of one thing, then of another. It is these traitors who are responsible for it."[33]

One other charge especially stressed in this trial was that of having served the tsarist police before 1917. Three of the accused—Ivanov, Zelensky, and Zubarev—pleaded guilty to it. All admitted to having been recruited as secret agents of the Okhrana to inform on revolutionaries. Zubarev confessed to having been recruited as an informer in 1908 by a local police inspector named Vasiliev, who twice paid him thirty rubles for his services (those "thirty pieces of silver," Vyshinsky interrupted, were "twice as much as Judas received"). Vasiliev himself, now a man of sixty-eight, was brought in at this point to confirm Zubarev's testimony. He said that he arrested young Zubarev and got from him a pledge to work as an informer for the tsarist police under the cover-name of "Vasily."

In his summing-up speech Vyshinsky showered the accused, both those in the dock and their fellow conspirators and accomplices in the larger "Bloc," with a torrent of vituperative abuse. They were the "scum of humanity" and "a foul-smelling heap of human garbage." Their masks having finally been ripped off, their "bestial countenance" was now revealed. Bukharin, in particular, was a false and wily creature whose hypocrisy and perfidy exceeded the most monstrous and perfidious crimes known to the history of mankind. How many times had he kissed the great teacher, Lenin, with the kiss of Judas the traitor! Looking meek and mild, he organized wrecking, espionage, and murder. "Here is the acme of monstrous hypocrisy, perfidy, jesuitry, and inhuman villainy." Insidious, brutal, and vengeful, the traitors had not let a year, month, or day go by for twenty years without seeking to harm the Soviet state. Time would pass and their graves would grow over with weeds and thistle while the happy nation would march as before, over a road cleared of the last scum and filth of the past, led by its beloved leader and teacher, the great Stalin, onward and onward, toward Communism![34]

Before sentence was pronounced, the defendants made their final statements, which in all but one case were abject. The exception was Bukharin. Vyshinsky forecast in his summing-up speech that Bukharin would take advantage of the opportunity afforded by his last plea to engage in "preposterous circus acrobatics," and he was right. But the "acrobatics" were anything but preposterous.

During the trial itself, even though he had to speak in conformity with a script prepared in advance to suit his accusers, Bukharin fought constantly. He pleaded guilty to "the sum total of crimes committed by this counterrevolutionary organization," but thereupon suggested that not only did he not take part in but he even lacked knowledge of "any particular act" involved. He declared that "the accused in this dock are not a group." He disclaimed all knowledge of his supposed connections with Nazis, denied ever having spoken of opening the front in time of war, rejected the charge of plotting the assassination of Lenin, Stalin, and Sverdlov in 1918, categorically denied all dealings with foreign intelligence services as well as any complicity in the murders of Kirov, Kuibyshev, Menzhinsky, and Gorky and his son. During Vyshinsky's summing-up speech, he was observed furiously taking notes. His final statement was so little pleasing to Stalin that it was printed in much abridged form in the next day's press. And foreign observers at the trial were impressed by his fighting demeanor. Fitzroy MacLean, who attended for the British Embassy, pictures Bukharin, in giving his final statement, as standing there "fail and defiant," admitting in principle the justice of the case against him and then proceeding "to tear it to bits, while Vyshinsky, powerless to intervene, sat uneasily in his place, looking embarrassed and yawning ostentatiously."[35]

Bukharin's purpose was not to defend himself but to convict his accuser. He had long since come to see Stalin as a bungler who was leading Soviet Russia to ruin out of a monstrous appetite for personal power. Already before his arrest he had pictured Stalin as engaged in transforming Soviet Communism into something akin to fascism, and tried to warn that he was scheming to make common cause with Hitler in a great and ill-starred political gamble that would bring on World War II and destroy the Soviet Union. That the thought of making his final statement a final accusation of Stalin would occur to him was all the more likely in view of a tradition in the Russian revolutionary movement—the tradition of turning political trials into antitrials. The crux of this maneuver was that a revolutionist on trial would turn the tables upon the accusers and put them on trial before the court of public opinion and history. He or she would do this by foregoing a speech of defense and delivering a revolutionary oration, a denunciation of the accusers, their motives, their policies, and their social order.

There was no possibility for Bukharin to deliver such an oration. Still, he found a way of achieving his purpose. It required, first, simply the willingness to go on trial—something he was in any event being coerced to do. Second, it required the pursuit of certain tactics. Stalin was insisting that he appear as chief defendant in this trial. Well and good. He would do so, and try to save his family by complying with that irreducible demand. But he would do it in his own way, speaking his lines according to the Stalin-Vyshinsky script but saying between them what he could to make his own point. Knowing Bukharin, Stalin must have realized that he would do this. But he evidently thought it a tolerable price to pay for the great success of making Bukharin confess himself guilty of counterrevolutionary conspiracy.

Bukharin thus had a twofold objective in the trial: to comply with Stalin by confessing and to turn the tables on him. He tried to make it two trials in one. He himself said this in Aesopian language in his final statement. Speaking of the puzzlement that foreign intellectuals were showing over the Moscow trials and especially the confessions, he stressed that he had retained his clarity of mind and dismissed fanciful hypotheses that would explain the confessions by hypnotism or a "Slavic soul." Going on, he said "the first thing to be understood" is that he and any others like him ("the enemy") had "a divided, a dual mind." What he meant by this was indicated by further statements a little later on. Here we may note that he could not, without being too obvious, present a whole sequence of his own points in any one passage but had to confine himself to saying one thing at a time. So, we must look for the sequence of his Aesopian argument in a series of passages each of which contains one component of it. A telltale sign of the presence of an Aesopian point in a passage is a certain suggestion of incoherence at that place. A presupposition of this mode of communicating is that symbols have multiple meanings. In one of its meanings, a symbol belongs to the show trial; in another, to the antitrial. Thus "Trotsky" means "counterrevolutionary" in terms of the show trial and "person living abroad" in terms of the antitrial. Bukharin in one place referred to "my terminology" to convey that he was using some terms in special ways of his own.

The trial, Bukharin said, has an aspect of confession, but that is not the crux: "The confession of the accused is not essential. The confession of the accused is a medieval principle of jurisprudence." Here he was saying between the lines that in one of its aspects this trial is a witchcraft trial, and that we should not take the confession itself seriously since in such a trial the witch, as a matter of course, has to confess. And the other aspect? Bukharin communicated this by observing that Feuchtwanger's *Moscow 1937,* which had been shown him in prison, did not get to the core of the matter, "when, as a matter of fact, everything is clear. World history is a world court of judgment." The crucial message is contained in Hegel's dictum that world history is the world's court of justice. In its second aspect, Bukharin was saying, this trial is taking place before the court of history.

If in the one aspect it was a trial of Bukharin, in the other it was a trial of Stalin for desecrating the memory of Lenin, betraying what the Revolution stood for, and crushing the old Bolshevik party. What enabled Bukharin to put Stalin on trial for those transgressions was his own stature. He himself was a symbol. If any surviving Old Bolshevik had special claim to representing the Bolshevik heritage and the link with Lenin, it was Bukharin. He was therefore in a position to dramatize by his own self-immolation in the show trial what Stalin was doing to the party as earlier constituted. By undergoing the ordeal of defamation to which Vyshinsky subjected him, he was able not only to convict Stalin of putting the Leninist regime on trial but to catch him, as it were, red-handed in the act and show him up before the world in the process (how well the world understood this is another matter, unfortunately). And this is what I believe he was trying to communicate when he said in his final statement that in the face of "the absolutely black vacuity" confronting him, he wanted to die for something.

But the antitrial was no mere passive act of self-sacrifice to dramatize what Stalin was doing to the Revolution. Bukharin made an active attempt to transform the trial into an antitrial, and his tactics were precisely calculated to fit the needs of this strategy. First, he made a special effort to underline his own great guilt. Thus he accepted full responsibility for the mass of counterrevolutionary acts by the "Bloc," although in doing so he insisted that this was *political* responsibility. And he repeated several times during the trial that he wished not to defend but to accuse himself. "I did not want to minimize my guilt, I wanted to aggravate it,' he said in one place. "This is not my defense, it is my self-accusation," he said elsewhere. "I have not said a singe word in my defense." All this was to say: My tactics in the antitrial are tactics of self-accusation. By stressing how terribly guilty I, an Old Bolshevik leader, am in Stalin's eyes, I am showing implicitly how guilty *he* is of murderous attitudes and acts against those who embody Lenin's Bolshevism. Hence my tactics of self-accusation are my way of placing him on trial for his crimes against Lenin's Bolshevism.

The view that Bukharin was not trying to defend himself may seem contradicted by his denial of guilt under various specific criminal charges. But only superficially was that a defensive move. He rejected the criminal charges not with a view to pleading innocent but rather with a view to making clear where his real guilt lay—in the political field. For this purpose, he had to point out that he was *not* guilty of certain things. So, the denial of the criminal charges was an organic part of the antitrial strategy. Only if the public or history should see the accused Bukharin as a political man would it see that the accuser Stalin was destroying a political tendency. So it was vital to Bukharin's case in the antitrial to show that he had been a Bolshevik oppositionist in relation to Stalin and not, as Vyshinsky was trying to argue, a criminal masquerading for long years as a revolutionary. The duel that raged between the two throughout the trial was thus one in which Vyshinsky argued that all Bukharin's purported political acts were really crimes, and Bukharin maintained that all his alleged crimes were really political acts. If he came off well in the encounter, despite all the disadvantages of his situation compared with Vyshinsky's, the reason is that his contention was true.

So intensely life-loving was this man, then forty-nine years old, that though he made no public plea for clemency, he wrote a note to Stalin after death sentence was pronounced on him and seventeen others on 13 March. It began: "Koba, why do you need me to die?" The note, along with Lenin's note of 1923 threatening to cut off relations with Stalin because of his rudeness to Krupskaya, was among documents found in Stalin's desk drawer after he died in 1953.[36] Bukharin and the others were put to death on 15 March.

Stalin attended the trial in two different ways: by having the proceedings transmitted to his Kremlin quarters via microphones placed in the October Hall, and by viewing the scene in person at times from the darkened room at the rear where, on one occasion, a clumsily directed beam of light suddenly made his yellowish face and drooping moustache visible to attentive spectators. Despite the embarrassment caused at the start by Krestinsky's public exposure of the affair as a frame-up and the impression made by a defiant Bukharin at the end, the trial must have met his needs, both personal and political, as the principal playwright and producer.

What unfolded in the trial was again a gigantic texture of fantasy into which bits and pieces of falsified real history were woven along with outright fiction, such as espionage for foreign powers and plans of the purported conspirators to overthrow the Soviet regime and dismember the USSR. Many things alluded to in the trial really happened. Bukharin did oppose the Brest-Litovsk treaty, and no doubt Krestinsky as ambassador to Berlin did have talks with German military men. There were peasant outbreaks and great livestock losses in the early 1930s. An abortive cabal to remove Stalin from the post of general secretary did take place on the eve of the Seventeenth Congress. In the aftermath, Kirov was murdered, with Yagoda and Zaporozhets playing parts in the crime. Kuibyshev's fatal heart attack may have been hastened by foul play. Gorky's life probably was shortened to prevent him from trying to protest a big political event in the offing, the Zinoviev-Kamenev trial. Savings banks were mismanaged, timber-floating operations disorganized, vegetable sowings misplanned. There were manifold goods shortages, which indeed aroused much discontent. Quite possibly nails and glass turned up in Soviet butter. But these events did not occur as elements of a conspiracy by a "Rightist-Trotskist Bloc." There was no such bloc and no such conspiracy.

What Stalin beheld in the courtroom drama was nothing less than Soviet history as he would have wished it to occur, with all credit redounding to him and all evil and unhappy events for which he was responsible attributed to camouflaged enemies of the Revolution. In accordance with what I have called the "trial system," with its algebraic equivalents, it attributed to an enemy conspiracy all the deeds and misdeeds of that other, despised Stalin that had no place in his idealized image of himself, and thereby it performed a cathartic function for him. On them, whom he hated, was projected the Stalin who became embroiled in conflict with Lenin, who bungled collectivization, who caused a terrible famine, who insisted on industrializing in a way that caused all manner of breakdowns and shortages, the Stalin who became the object of widespread party criticism in the early 1930s, the Stalin whom some wanted to unseat from power at the time of the Seventeenth Congress, the would-be negotiator of an accord with the Nazis, the villainous conspirator from above who used his police to procure Kirov's murder and possibly others, and even, it may be, the ex-part-time Okhrana informer with the cover-name of "Vasily."[37]

All that Stalin would have felt compelled to expunge from his view

of himself, from his record as a revolutionary and political leader, was
now, by their own public admission, the work of his enemies. This was
something more exciting than a mere rewriting of history. It was a story of
atrocious villainy being reenacted before his eyes and ears by the putative
villains themselves. They were telling it as he would have wanted to retain
it in memory. By taking his guilt upon themselves, they were exculpating
him and hence indirectly testifying to his heroic excellence, his unblemished genius as a leader in Lenin's footsteps. They were validating the
idealized Stalin by impersonating the despised one, and if they failed to do
this Vyshinsky did it for them, especially when he imputed to Bukharin,
who had loved Lenin devotedly, the Stalin who had kissed Lenin with the
kiss of Judas the traitor, and who indeed represented "the acme of monstrous hypocrisy, perfidy, jesuitry, and inhuman villainy." It must have
been a supreme experience of vindictive triumph for Stalin to see hated
men taking on themselves, before the Soviet and world public, the blame
for all that he had to repress in himself and his past, and explaining why
they had committed *his* misdeeds. And, at the end, to see them abasing
themselves before him, as totally broken Yagoda did when he ended his
final plea by saying: "Comrade Chekists, Comrade Stalin, if you can,
forgive me."[38]

But this climacteric trial was not only a theatrical enactment of the
dictates of Stalin's psyche. There was political calculation in it as well.
The incorporation of the Right opposition in the alleged conspiracy and the
defendants' confessions of forming terrorist groups in various commissariats provided a rationale for the ensuing new wave of arrests that made
1938 equal or exceed 1937 in numbers of terror victims. And like its
predecessors, this trial had foreign-policy meaning. Although the antifascist theme remained salient, there was a definite anti-British note in the
espionage charges and the claim that the "Bloc" aimed to turn over parts
of a future dismembered Soviet Union to Great Britain. Nor was this trial
consistently anti-Nazi in thematic content. It opened with Bessonov being
made to plead guilty on behalf of the conspirators to receiving and acting
on Krestinsky's orders to obstruct normalization of Soviet-German relations after the Nazis came to power in 1933. The anti-Stalin Communist
opposition was thus cast in the role of frustrator of fruitful Soviet-Nazi
relations. Some of those accused in the trial, above all Bukharin and
Tukhachevsky, were well known as strongly antifascist Communists and,
as in the previous trials, some of the defendants were Jews.

Stalin, moreover, made this trial, as he had the previous one, a vehicle
of exculpation in advance for his contemplated coming accord with Hitler.
Such prominent Communist antifascists as Trotsky and Bukharin were
presented not only as having dealings with the Nazis but as being profas-

cist. Thus Vyshinsky, in the summing-up speech, said of Bukharin: "Like a true watchdog of fascism, he barked joyfully expressing his admiration for German fascism." This smearing of the accused as both fascist in mentality and bent on collaborating with the Nazis was preparation for Stalin's collaboration with them—in the sense that it undermined the idea that Communism stood for antifascism and tainted in advance the thought that the other Old Bolsheviks, unlike Stalin, would have avoided a Soviet-Nazi pact on antifascist principle. In sum, it tended, if not to establish in advance the political respectability of Stalin's hope to work out a deal with Hitler, at least to diminish its disreputability. In these terms the trial, like the previous ones, was saying: If the anti-Stalin Communists were ready and willing to bargain with the Nazis for anti-Soviet purposes, what is so bad about striking a bargain with them that will serve Soviet interests by expanding our territorial possessions and keeping us out of war while Germany and the West fight it out?

Whether these subtle messages came through to German official minds is another matter. Although Ambassador Schulenburg and his diplomatic staff at the German Embassy were oriented all along on a rapprochement between Russia and Germany, the purge trials so aroused Schulenburg's indignation that he forbade staff members to attend them and was bewildered that his American colleague, Ambassador Davies, did attend them and found the prosecution's case credible.[39] Ambassador Chilston's post-trial dispatch to London spoke of "this repellent travesty of justice which the Soviet authorities have graced with the name of a trial," and a question in the House of Commons drew the reply from the prime minister that the trial, with its baseless charges against Britain, was "extremely prejudicial to Anglo-Soviet relations." The non-Communist French press universally condemned the affair, which *Le Temps* saw as dealing a serious setback to the Soviet government's international authority. The Norwegian Labor Party paper *Arbeiderblad,* known for a pro-Soviet attitude in the past, accused Stalin of being a despot suffering from persecution mania who was getting rid of all the best men. The Nazi press gloated over the situation. "Even the great democracies," commented *Völkischer Beobachter,* "will now have their eyes opened."

An appreciative reaction, however, came from Italy. Reacting to the trial as it was taking place, the fascist paper *Popolo d'Italia* asked on 5 March 1938 whether "in view of the catastrophe of Lenin's system, Stalin could secretly have become a fascist." In any event, it went on, "Stalin is doing a notable service to fascism by mowing down in large armfuls his enemies who have been reduced to impotence." The article's author was a one-time socialist who founded fascism through an inflamed Italian nationalism. His opinion carried no small weight. His name was Mussolini.

Antiforeign Terror

Stalin periodically lectured the Soviet people on the deadly perils of the capitalist encirclement. At the February–March plenum in 1937 he reiterated that "The capitalist encirclement is no empty phrase but a real and unpleasant phenomenon." The show trials dramatized his contention. They pictured foreign enemies bristling with hostility to Russia, plotting the Soviet regime's overthrow and the dismemberment of the USSR, recruiting spies and wreckers among persons living inside the country or traveling abroad.

Accordingly, foreigners resident in Russia, Russians who returned from abroad to live in their homeland, and Soviet citizens with foreign connections became suspect, and very many fell victim to the Terror. And so, in the later 1930s, still another pattern in the culture of old Muscovy came to life again: xenophobia. Returning to Moscow in January 1938 to rejoin the U.S. Embassy after a three-year interval elsewhere, Charles Bohlen noticed that the Russian man on the street, who had been open and friendly in 1934, now avoided all contact with foreigners. When his wife joined a queue before a Moscow shop, Soviet women near her vanished as soon as they guessed, by her coat, that she was a foreigner.[40]

Countless innocent people came to grief because of foreign origin, past foreign residence, or foreign ties. Some from Eastern Poland or a Baltic country who had entered Russia as tourists or crossed the border illegally in search of better lives under what they thought was socialism were arrested, made to confess that they had been recruited by foreign intelligence services as spies, and sent to camps.[41] A Russian Jewish woman, who emigrated to England before 1917 and returned as a widow with four children in 1933 to rejoin her relatives, soon afterward disappeared. Her eldest daughter, Flora Leipman, was arrested in 1937 at the age of eighteen, interrogated for months on charges of being a British spy, sent to a Siberian camp in 1939, and released in 1941 to live in exile.[42] In 1938 the ailing small daughter of the only British correspondent in Moscow was placed in a peasant family in the countryside near Moscow for recuperation, and within days half the peasant family and several of its village relatives were arrested. Russian émigrés who had worked on the Chinese–Far Eastern Railway in Manchuria before its sale in 1935 and then returned to Russia full of patriotic feeling were arrested *en masse* as spies for the Japanese and Manchurian intelligence services. Even Ustrialov, the father of émigré national Bolshevism, was swallowed up by the Terror after publishing an article glorifying the Stalin Constitution upon his return.[43]

One day all citizens of Persian origin in Astrahan were rounded up and those who had lived there before the Revolution were dispatched to camps, while those who had fled to Russia in 1929 after the uprising against Reza Shah were forcibly returned to Persia where many of them faced execution.[44] In 1937 over three hundred members of Kharkov's Armenian colony were arrested. Letts, Germans, Poles, Finns, Estonians, Chinese, and members of other ethnic groups living in Kharkov were arrested as spies for the respective foreign governments.[45] Similar fates befell people of foreign extraction in other places.

The antiforeign terror was lethal for large numbers of Soviet citizens, high and low, whose official duties involved dealing with foreigners. Although Stalin spared Litvinov and some of his subordinates because he still needed him to pursue his antifascist coalition-building diplomacy in Europe, the foreign commissar was helpless to prevent the victimizing of virtually a whole generation of well-educated, talented, and experienced officials of the commissariat and its foreign service. The broken Krestinsky, or his double, confessed in the trial that he had recruited numerous adherents in the foreign commissariat. As deputy commissar from 1930, his association with everyone of importance in the commissariat was a basis for establishing their guilt as agents of the "Bloc" under cover of their official contracts with foreign representatives.

The execution of Boris Steiger, the authorized social contact of the Moscow diplomatic corps, who had understood Stalin as Iosif Grozny, was announced along with that of Lev Karakhan in December 1937; espionage for foreign powers was the charge. A careful study of the Terror's ravages in the diplomatic establishment shows that at least 62 percent of the top level Narkomindel officials left over from the 1920s fell victim in 1937–38, another 14 percent having died or defected before that time; that the Terror victims included, along with deputy foreign commissars Krestinsky and Sokolnikov, Soviet ambassadors to Finland, Hungary, Latvia, Poland, Norway, Germany, Turkey, Rumania, Spain, Afghanistan, Mongolia, and Denmark along with many department heads and lesser officials of foreign diplomatic missions; that the NKVD assumed greater and greater control of the Narkomindel, especially with the appointment of the policeman V. G. Dekanozov as deputy foreign commissar in 1939; and that whereas ethnic Russians had comprised only 43 percent of the veteran Soviet foreign service officers earlier on, they comprised fully 80 percent of the new generation of diplomats promoted during the Terror.[46] Two high diplomats—Alexander Barmine, who was chargé d'affaires in Athens, and F. F. Raskolnikov, a revolutionary and Civil War hero who was ambassador to Bulgaria—fled when summoned to Moscow to what they knew would be their deaths. After settling in Paris, Raskolnikov wrote a blistering open letter to Stalin pointing out that he had destroyed Old Bolsheviks, slaughtered party and state cadres who rose in the Civil War and five-year plans, massacred the Komsomol, staged trials that surpassed in absurdity of their accusations the medieval witch trials, defamed and shot Lenin's old associates, and was destroying the Red Army on the eve of war. Raskolnikov died under mysterious circumstances in September 1939 shortly before his open letter appeared in print. Under Khrushchev he was restored to posthumous honor in Soviet annals and his open letter was praised.[47] Under Gorbachev, the letter was published.

During the Great Purge, no group was more totally terrorized than foreign Communists who had sought asylum in Russia or simply gone there to work or study. Their plight and the response of some of them to it were symbolized by a scene in the Lubianka in 1936. A young Italian woman lying on the floor in a jammed women's cell said in French, "You've had a fascist coup." When Russian women prisoners remonstrated, she said, "What else if they're arresting Communists?" They replied: "What are you saying? The Communist Party is still in power," to which she answered: "Why are you trying to trick me? This is a fascist coup for certain. I know what one looks like."[48] Later she was shot.

Foreign Communist militants of many nationalities fell victim. An illustrative case is the Markhlevsky Communist University for National Minorities in Moscow. Its 700 or so students were enrolled in up to twenty different sections, including Polish, German, Hungarian, Bulgarian, Yugoslav, and Jewish ones. Leopold Trepper, a Communist from Palestine, studied there in 1932 in the Jewish section under Professor Dimenshtein, who had been a vice-commissar for nationalities under Stalin in the 1920s, had known Lenin well, and liked to cite his remark, "Anti-Semitism is counterrevolution."[49] One night in the late 1930s the NKVD arrested every single Markhlevsky University teacher save one who happened to be out of town. Their wives were shipped to camps, their children placed in NKVD orphanages, and the institution was closed.[50] No doubt many of the students were taken too. Foreign Communists disappeared *en masse* from Moscow's Hotel Lux, where many lived, and from various buildings for foreigners such as the Weltoktober cooperative apartment house where in 1937 and 1938 they would be arrested at night in groups according to profession or nationality, such as "all" Hungarians or "all" Estonians or "all" Poles. Their wives lost apartments and jobs. Wives who were themselves party members were expelled and banished from Moscow. Not a few were arrested and sent to camps for the crime of belonging to "the family of an enemy of the people." Their children went into NKVD orphanages. While awaiting their fates, many stayed in a rundown building behind the Lux for the families of arrested Communists.[51]

A large colony of foreign Communists in Russia were the Germans, the most staunchly antifascist foreigners of all. The majority of them succumbed to the Terror. One of the first to be taken, in August 1936, was the actress Carola Neher, who played Polly in Brecht and Weill's *Three Penny Opera*. After receiving a ten-year sentence, she refused an attempt by the NKVD to recruit her to work for them, and later was shot.[52] By April 1938 the German representative on the Comintern's Executive Committee had counted 842 German antifascists who had been arrested.[53] German terror victims included Hugo Eberlein, who took part in the original Comintern congress; Werner Hirsch, a close associate of Ernst Thälmann; Leo Flieg, secretary of the German Central Committee; German Politburo member Hermann Remmele; German Central Committee members Heinz Neumann and Hermann Schubert; chief editor of *Rote Fahne,* Heinrich Susskind; the well-known German antifascist writer George Born; the German Jewish composer Hans W. David; the actor Alexander Granach; and nearly the whole editorial staff of the German Communist paper *Deutsche Zentral-Zeitung*. The famous Swiss revolutionary Fritz Platten, who saved Lenin from assassination in 1938, likewise disappeared.[54]

Tragedy also struck a German school that Moscow had given in 1934 for the children of Vienna workers who had resisted the Austrian government's shelling of their tenements. It was closed in 1938. Many of the resident families were arrested and deported to dread fates in Austria. After a young German geography teacher at the school named Kurt was arrested one night, his wife Isolde, a literature teacher in the school, was forced to return to Germany to what she knew would be a concentration camp.[55]

No less cruel a fate overtook foreign refugees from other lands in Russia's vicinity. According to the then general secretary of the Finnish Communist Party, who resided in Moscow during the 1930s until he moved to Stockholm in 1938, as many as 20,000 Finns were sent to Soviet concentration camps and a like percentage of Communists from other Soviet border countries came to grief. The toll of Latvians and Lithuanians was, by his reckoning, still greater, and the numbers of Polish victims of Stalin's Terror ran into very many thousands.[56]

Foreign Communists working in the Comintern offices in Moscow and foreign party leaderships resident there—an interlocking group—were, with exceptions, no less hard hit than rank-and-file foreign Communists, sympathizers, and family members. In fact, so savage was the terror against foreign Communists in Stalin's Russia of 1937–38 that arrested Communists in all anti-Communist countries other than Germany had a much greater chance of survival. Thus Matyas Rakosi survived prison in Horthy's Hungary to become Stalin's puppet leader of that country after World War II, and "Red Anna" Pauker was likewise spared in royalist Rumania to reemerge later. Similarly, lower-level Finnish Communists imprisoned under Finland's "White terror" (as Soviet publications called it) were far more likely to survive than their superiors in Moscow.[57]

Bela Kun, who led the short-lived Hungarian Communist revolution in 1919, the most famed international Communist still living, was another victim for whom the Kremlin's bell tolled. In 1935 he had helped write the theses for the Seventh Comintern Congress. In the summer of 1936 he asked for and had an interview with Stalin about his further work. Stalin asked him to remain in the Comintern, to which he replied that he could not work with Manuilsky (who, as a member of the Comintern's Secretariat and its Executive Committee's presidium, was Stalin's liaison with the organization). Manuilsky, Kun said, was a hypocrite who said one thing today, another tomorrow. When Stalin asked what work he would like, Kun asked to be appointed head of the Red Army's Political Department so as to help prepare the army for war against the fascists, since "Hitler will attack us sooner or later." Molotov, who was present, objected to someone with such an "explosive name" heading the Red Army's Political Department. After the first Moscow show trial, Kun received a phone call from Yezhov, who by then headed the NKVD. Yezhov summoned him for a talk in which he invited Kun to write a pamphlet against the "enemies of the people." Kun refused and asked to be assigned to work as a provincial or district party secretary.[58] His downfall came at the end of June 1937.

The scene was a meeting of the Comintern Executive Committee's presidium, with Dimitrov presiding and Manuilsky acting as prosecutor. The charge was that in a pamphlet Kun wrote for Communists working in Hungary, he said that the Soviet party was ineffectually represented in the Comintern. To Manuilsky's statement that this criticism was directed against Stalin (who was a member of the Comintern presidium but rarely attended its meetings), Kun hotly replied that his target had been Manuilsky himself, who was "no Bolshevik at all." Then Manuilsky accused Kun of having had contacts with the Rumanian secret police and betraying the Hungarian revolution in 1919 while ostensibly leading it. NKVD men waiting in the outer office arrested Kun as he left the meeting; death came to him in 1939. Nearly all the other members of the Hungarian party's Central Committee living in Moscow were arrested during the next few days, and only a few survived the camps or exile to which those not shot were condemned. Hundreds of other Hungarians were likewise arrested and sent to camps.[59]

Soon after, at a similar Comintern presidium session, the bell tolled for the Polish party. Although this party was small in total size—its membership numbered between 9,000 and 10,000 in 1934, an estimated one-fifth to one-fourth of whom were Jewish[60]—the Polish contingent was important in Communism. Some of its leaders were renowned old revolutionaries from Lenin's time, and many Poles had settled in Russia and risen high in the Soviet apparatus. Poles were prominent in the Comintern and its affiliates.

Two Polish Communist leaders, Lenski and Bronkowski, were members of the Comintern Executive Committee's presidium. They did not attend the presidium session that condemned the Polish leadership; they were already under arrest. Again Manuilsky served as accuser. He told a fantastic tale: A Polish regiment of 700 that surrendered during the Soviet-Polish war of 1920 and then settled in Russia, where many of its members found high posts in military and political life, had proved to be an army of trained Polish spies who for seventeen years worked to subvert the Soviet state. Hence, the Polish party's entire high command had been arrested.[61] A pogrom of Russia-based Polish Communists ensued. Those destined for prominent postwar careers, including Bierut and Gomulka, had the good fortune to be languishing in Polish prisons. An NKVD man arrested in the 1940s told a fellow camp inmate, who later came West, that 10,000 Poles were shot in Moscow at that earlier time. Far larger numbers of émigré and Russified Poles, possibly numbering up to 50,000, were arrested and sent to camps.[62]

In the summer of 1938 the Polish Communist Party was dissolved, unquestionably on orders from Stalin. So were the Communist parties of Western Ukraine and Western Belorussia. These were autonomous parts of the Polish Communist Party representing the easternmost provinces of pre-1939 Poland, whose inhabitants included large numbers of ethnic Ukrainians and Belorussians. No formal dissolution decree was published. But Comintern publications stopped mentioning the Polish Communist Party in the second half of 1938, and official confirmation of its dissolution and that of the other two parties came later.[63]

Although no other parties were formally dissolved,[64] several were crushed insofar as their leaders and other militants were available in Russia for victimizing or could be lured there on one or another pretext. The Terror was especially lethal for Communists of neighboring countries. The Latvian party's Central Committee was disbanded, many of its leaders arrested, and a mass purge of Latvian Communists occurred, amounting, as a post-Stalin Soviet historian puts it, to the party's "factual dissolution."[65] The leaderships of the Estonian and Lithuanian parties were likewise liquidated. So thorough was the slaughter that when Communist governments were set up in the Soviet-occupied Baltic states in 1940, their leaderships were made up of former Social Democrats, bourgeois professors, and the like: the prewar Baltic Communists had gone to their deaths in Russia.[66] Another victim of severe repression was the Communist Party of Bessarabia, a border territory that belonged to Rumania before World War II.

Especially hard hit by the anti-Comintern terror were the Communist parties of Finland, Rumania, Bulgaria, Greece, and Yugoslavia along with those of Poland and Germany. Tito, whose family name was Broz and who went by the name of Walter in the movement, came to Moscow in 1935 but, fortunately for him, failed to get Soviet approval to be the Yugoslav party's representative on the Comintern Executive Committee; he departed Russia in 1936. When he returned in 1938, the Yugoslav leadership had been so decimated that he was appointed "caretaker" general secretary of a wholly new Central Committee yet to be created, and in talks with Dimitrov he became aware of a tendency to dissolve the Yugoslav party.[67] All that saved the Bulgarian party leaders from a like fate was Dimitrov's presence in Moscow as official Comintern chief. Nevertheless, the numerous Bulgarian victims included even Dimitrov's codefendants in the Leipzig trial, Blagoi Popov and Vasil Tanev; and only by hiding in Dimitrov's apartment and getting him to intercede with the NKVD did Chervenkov, the husband of Dimitrov's sister, save himself from imminent arrest. The Italian party, not a few of whose leaders (Togliatti excepted) disappeared, was saved from far worse victimizing by the circumstance that most of its leaders and other militants had settled not in Russia but in France. It was only members of legal Communist parties of democratic countries who could live through Russia's Terror, and not all did. Their citizenship and freedom to go home gave them some protection.[68]

The antiforeign terror was conducted not only on Soviet soil but beyond—in Spain. Not only did a multitude of NKVD operatives keep close watch on the 2,000 Soviet pilots, tank officers, staff men, engineers, and technicians who carried out Russia's military intervention in Spain. Under direction of NKVD officer Alexander Orlov, who subsequently defected to avoid victimization, they purged people on the Loyalist side who were critical of Stalin or simply independent-minded. The purge operations included forced confessions and summary executions. Some who fell afoul of them were members of the International Brigade, which was composed of non-Soviet foreign Communist and other volunteers and led by a Soviet military man named Stern who was known in Spain as "General Emil Kleber." In pursuit of Stalin's political objectives, the Spanish Communists were induced to act against the anarchists, syndicalists, and Socialists who were strong in Catalonia. So harmful were these actions to the war effort that General Yan Berzin, the ex-Soviet chief of military intelligence who had come to Spain to organize and direct the Loyalist war for survival, complained about them to Voroshilov. Berzin, who had ties with the Soviet military chiefs, was recalled to Moscow shortly after their destruction in June 1937 and vanished, as did Arthur Stashevsky, the Polish-born Soviet Communist who played a leading part in the intervention under the modest official title of trade envoy in Barcelona and who, like Berzin, was critical of the NKVD's conduct in Loyalist Spain.[69]

Why did the antiforeign terror strike hardest at the party leaderships and parties of neighboring countries and Germany? For light on this question we may turn to Stalin's only public pronouncement on foreign policy in 1938. It came in the form of a reply to a letter from one Ivan Filippovich Ivanov, an obscure Komsomol staff propagandist in a central Russian village, who was accused by two regional Komsomol officials of Trotskyist heresy for having said at a seminar of propagandists, on the basis of Stalin's earlier writings, that the victory of socialism in the Soviet Union was not yet final. Ivanov's superiors, first secretary of the Kursk Regional Komsomol Committee, ordered Ivanov to close the Stalin volume from which he was quoting, and declared: "Comrade Stalin said that in 1926 but this is 1938; then we did not have final victory but now we have it and now we don't have to think of intervention and restoration at all. We now have the final victory of socialism and we have a complete guarantee against intervention and the restoration of capitalism." Ivanov appealed to Stalin to adjudicate the dispute.

In his letter of reply Stalin came down strongly on Ivanov's side. He cited as still fully valid the argument in his own *Problems of Leninism* (1926) that a workers' revolution, "if only in several countries," was a necessary condition of the final victory of socialism in the USSR and of a full guarantee against attempts at intervention and restoration. This problem, he said, "has not yet been resolved and still remains to be resolved." It could only be resolved by "combining serious efforts of the international proletariat with still more serious efforts of our whole Soviet people." Concerning the latter Stalin spoke of strengthening the Soviet armed forces, keeping the people in a state of mobilized readiness, strengthening international proletarian ties with the working class of the bourgeois countries, organizing the latter's political assistance to the USSR in event of a military attack on it, and assistance by the Soviet working class to the working classes in bourgeois countries.[70]

Stalin's studiously nebulous phraseology could be understood only by minds attuned to his distinctive blend of Bolshevism and Russian nationalism—and these did not include the minds of Moscow's foreign diplomatic corps of 1938. He was reasserting the validity of his old view that the security of Russia's revolution required its extension, "if only" to several countries. As I have noted,[71] the countries he had in mind were neighboring ones. His Russian national Bolshevism equated the further spread of Communist revolution with the outward thrust of Soviet Russia's power.

There were two ways in which he could envisage this happening. One was the scenario of his still secret speech of January 1925, in which the

Soviet Union would remain neutral while two coalitions of European states bled each other white in a repetition of World War I. The USSR would then intervene at a time of its choosing to achieve its aims. The other, which overlapped with the first, was an accord with Hitler's regime that would give him a free hand to expand in Eastern Europe while Hitler made war in the West. Such expansion would plausibly mean the recovery of lands that had been parts of imperial Russia and lost during the revolutionary period—eastern Poland, the Baltic states, Finland, and Bessarabia. Stalin must have preferred the latter variant. If it occurred in the near future, it would offer the prospect of an easy, possibly bloodless westward advance at a time when his armed forces, even if the Great Purge had ended by then, would still be far from recovered from its ravages and in no shape to wage large-scale warfare effectively. Later, however, in the aftermath of a slogging war in the West, they would be under command of a well-trained new officer corps and his regime would be fully positioned to move into the rest of Poland, the Balkans, and perhaps deeper into Europe.

Such is the mental context in which his decisions affecting the Comintern and especially the Communist parties in nearby lands and their leaderships make political sense. A new partition of Poland, this time between Stalin's Russia and Hitler's Germany, could not conceivably be palatable to a Polish party with a leadership of Lenin-era lineage and younger leaders and militants formed under its influence. Hence the drastic action of dissolving that party along with those of the Western Ukraine and Western Belorussia. As for the Baltic-state parties, old-line Communists of independent mind and judgment would have been deemed undesirable agents by a Stalin intent on reincorporating those states in an expanded Soviet Russia. Dependably servile functionaries with no notable Communist credentials would be much more preferable as leaders of parties of foreign territories within possible Soviet reach. Meanwhile, the extensive purge of Russia-based Finns combined with preservation of the party as such and permission for its general secretary, Tuominen, to base himself in Stockholm from 1938 on while the Soviet Communist of Finnish nationality, Kuusinen, remained in Moscow to oversee Finnish affairs, made political sense too, since that was a party whose members inside Finland might have to be mobilized revolutionarily in a Soviet confrontation with Finland in the near future. And only in the context of a contemplated agreement with Hitler's Germany is Stalin's slaughter of the Russia-based leadership and militants of German Communism politically intelligible.[72]

Despite the lack of encouraging response from Hitler to the recent overture through Kandelaki, Stalin was poised for possible collaboration with Berlin. He knew that he held a trump card in Hitler's need for peace in the East in order to proceed with the long-standing strategy of striking first against France. Still, the road to accord was a rocky one. It ran through Munich.

Stalin and Munich

Hitler's annexation of Austria in March 1938 placed Czechoslovakia at the top of his war-making agenda. The Third Reich now surrounded over a third of Czechoslovakia's territory, including the well-fortified hilly border area inhabited by the Sudeten German minority whose grievances Hitler exploited through the Sudeten leader Konrad Henlein, his tool, as a pretext for threatening Prague. Yet, as *Pravda* editorially assessed the situation, the Czechoslovak battle-ready army, 1,500,000-strong when fully mobilized, was excellently equipped by a first-class war industry. The republic was not isolated, as Austria had been, but part of a collective-security system, and its people were prepared to fight for the country's independence.[73]

That contemporary Soviet estimate tallies with Churchill's retrospective one, according to which a deputation of German generals that sought (in vain) an audience with Hitler on 26 September 1938 left a memorandum expressing extreme pessimism about a war at that time and forecasting, in an appendix, that even fighting all alone the Czechoslovak army could hold out against available German forces for three months, during which hostilities were unlikely to remain isolated (the Czechs' own estimate, conveyed to the Russians, was four months[74]). So worried were most of the German generals about embarking on a potentially big war for which their country was still inadequately prepared that, according to a much later account by Franz Halder, who was chief of the German general staff in 1938 and survived World War II, they plotted the forcible overthrow of Hitler and other Nazi leaders. They abandoned the plot only after British Prime Minister Neville Chamberlain's flight to Berchtesgaden on 14 September 1938 and his meeting with Hitler the next day, when it began to seem that Hitler would win his way in Czechoslovakia without the war that he wanted and they feared.[75]

As the crisis over Czechoslovakia developed, Litvinov was in the limelight as Soviet spokesman for collective security. As early as 17 March 1938, a few days after Hitler's annexation of Austria, he warned in a press interview against international passivity in the face of aggression and announced that the Soviet Union remained ready to take part in collective actions decided upon with its participation, inside or outside the League of Nations.[76] No doubt Litvinov personally was strongly in favor of this policy. But in all that he did then he acted as Stalin's man. A sign of his total subordination was the existence in a room adjoining his Narkomindel Office of a special phone line to Stalin in the Kremlin. If a visiting foreign envoy raised a question the answer to which required any kind of policy decision, Litvinov would communicate with Stalin before replying.[77] He took no serious decisions on his own.

Stalin, it seems clear, would have been satisfied to see the Western powers become involved in a protracted war with Germany, but he did not expect them to go to war over Czechoslovakia. Should they do so, the first of his above-mentioned two war scenarios would be realized. For at least two reasons, a European war over Czechoslovakia would have seemed opportune. First, Germany's forces and western fortifications were not yet up to planned strength. Second, the loss of Czechoslovakia to Hitler by default would adversely affect the power balance in Europe and open up the Balkans to further German depredations. As *Pravda* put it, if Czechoslovakia ceded the Sudetenland to Germany under French and British pressure, that would end her independence, clear Germany's way to hegemony in Central and Southeastern Europe, enable Germany to step up her Spanish intervention by securing her rear and raw material sources, and deprive France of her last strong points in Europe.[78]

The question is, what was Stalin prepared to do beyond encouraging Prague to hold fast, France to fulfill her treaty obligation to come to Czechoslovakia's defense if she were attacked, and Britain to take a strong stand against German aggression? Whatever he might have preferred to do, it is, first of all, doubtful that he *could* have done much. Soviet society, its armed forces in particular, were as racked by terror as in 1937 if not more so. Over 3,000 naval commanders and 38,679 armymen were ordered shot from 27 February 1937 to 12 November 1938.[79] Out of 101 members of the high command, 91 were arrested and over 80 of these were shot. Seven of the 10 not arrested belonged to Stalin's military clients of the Tsaritsyn group, including Voroshilov, Budenny, G. I. Kulik, and S. K. Timoshenko. The 91 repressed members included three of five marshals, three of four army commanders, the one first-rank army commissar, all 15 second-rank army commanders, both first-rank fleet commanders, and 51 of 57 corps commanders. Lower-level victims included at least 140 of 186 division commanders, over 200 commanders of rifle corps, divisions and brigades, and others of comparable rank. A. I. Todorsky, an arrested corps commander who survived seventeen years in camp, reports hearing Stalin say to Voroshilov at a military conference in the fall of 1938: "Klim, do you still have some lieutenants capable of taking command of divisions?"[80] Such was the shambles to which Stalin had reduced his armed forces around the time of Munich.

If he had been prepared to risk serious Soviet involvement in a conflict over Czechoslovakia, he would have stopped the Terror in March, when Austria fell, rather than intensify it following the great purge trial just at that time. Further, Soviet Russia faced a serious danger then in the Far East. Having taken Peking, Shanghai, and Nanking in the second half of 1937 in their war against China, the Japanese continued to probe the Soviet borders in a series of skirmishes climaxed by a big clash near Lake Khasan in early August 1938. These attacks had to be repulsed by substantial Red Army forces. Even *if* Stalin had been inclined toward it, serious participation in a coalition war against Germany was not an option open to him at that time given his insistence on completing the Great Purge. And the available facts do not show a Soviet Union disposed to fulfill her treaty obligation to join a war in defense of an embattled Czechoslovakia if France did.

As foreign diplomats in Moscow saw numbers of their own nationals victimized, their consulates in Soviet cities being closed down, and the Narkomindel being denuded of intelligent officials with whom they had long dealt, the Russia of the Great Purge seemed to be retiring into international semi-isolation. The U.S. chargé, Loy Henderson, saw signs of Soviet departure from the stance of the 1933–36 "Geneva period." He noted that in stressing the capitalist encirclement before the February–March 1937 plenum, Stalin did not make the previously common Soviet distinction between "friendly or democratic countries" and "fascist aggressors," that the ongoing antiforeign campaign warned Soviet people to beware of foreigners of all nations, not distinguishing between "friendly" and "hostile" ones, that in demanding the closing of a large number of foreign consulates the Soviet government was making no distinction between those of friendly states (like Czechoslovakia, whose newly opened Kiev consulate was closed) and unfriendly ones, and that Zhdanov's speech of 14 January 1938 before the Supreme Soviet contained a diatribe against France.[81]

Henderson also noted an unsigned article that appeared on *Pravda*'s front page. In an authoritative tone the article discussed foreign press reports on the possibility that the Soviet Union might go to war against Japan, and scathingly denounced the authors of these reports as war provocateurs. Neither British nor other war instigators, it said, would live to see the USSR making policy on cues from outside or under pressure from outside. The Soviet government would make war "only against aggressors, only against violators of peace, violators of Soviet frontiers."[82] The concluding equation of peace violation with Soviet border violation was not restricted geographically and suggested that Russia would stay out of developing war situations so long as no one violated Soviet borders.

The embassies of "friendly countries" weren't the only ones that led a hard life during the Terror; Germany's did too. Some German nationals in Russia on business were molested (as in the Novosibirsk affair), and the German Embassy's contacts with the Narkomindel and Soviet citizenry were largely cut off. And yet, the German Embassy's hardships were not as great as might have been expected. The Soviet authorities *did* make a small distinction in their policy of closing foreign consulates—in Germany's favor. Although its consulates in the Soviet Union were under harassment and pressure to close, they were not all closed down until the very eve of war in 1941.[83] German diplomats were allowed to travel to distant parts of Russia. Normal trade relations between the USSR and Germany, broken off for a short period at the outset of 1938, were resumed when, on 1 March, the trade and payments agreement of 24 December 1936 was renewed through the end of 1938.[84]

That Stalin did not desire unduly to ruffle tempers in Berlin at that time is clear from an episode that has since come to light. In the spring of 1938 Demyan Bedny wrote and sent off to *Pravda* a strongly anti-Nazi article called "Inferno." Written as if by a German worker, by whose name it was signed, it compared Nazi Germany to Dante's Inferno. At 2:00 a.m. the next night Bedny was summoned to the office of *Pravda* editor Mekhlis, who showed him the manuscript with a notation in Stalin's handwriting saying: "Tell this newly appeared 'Dante' that he can stop writing." After that, recalls Bedny's son, to whom the poet recounted these events when they happened, Bedny's access to the press was completely cut off.[85]

Despite the emerging crisis over Czechoslovakia, Stalin did not curtail business with Germany. According to information received by the U.S. Embassy in Moscow from the German Embassy in June 1938, discussions were held in April with the head of the Soviet Trade Delegation in Berlin. The Germans were interested in obtaining such commodities as manganese and the Russians wanted to get modern military equipment. A. F. Merekalov, the new Soviet ambassador to Germany, told Schulenburg before his departure for Berlin in June 1938 that he was interested in developing commercial relations with Germany. V. P. Potemkin, who had replaced Krestinsky as deputy foreign commissar, went further, telling Schulenburg "that *unfortunately* the development of commercial relations was the only positive element in Soviet-German relations at the present time."[86] In the early summer of 1938 rumors cropped up in European capitals that a Soviet-German rapprochement might be in the offing.

A surprise meeting between departing U.S. Ambassador Davies and Stalin—the latter's first with a foreign ambassador—took place on 5 June 1938 when the ambassador called on Premier Molotov in his Kremlin office to pay respects. No sooner was Davies ushered into Molotov's office than Stalin entered by the same door, giving the ambassador his first contact with the Soviet leader at close range. He was shorter than Davies had imagined. "There was a suggestion of the sagginess of an old man in his physical carriage," the ambassador added. "His demeanor is kindly, his manner almost deprecatingly simple; his personality and expression of reserve strength and poise very marked." To Davies' admiring opener that Stalin would go down in history as "a greater builder than Peter the Great or Catherine" in view of the extraordinary achievements of the Soviet Union in industrializing under his leadership, Stalin replied that the credit belonged to Lenin, who conceived the plan, 3,000 able planners, and the "Russian people." Most of the ensuing discussion dealt with two topics that Stalin must have raised with awareness of Davies' potential as a channel to President Roosevelt: a proposed contract for construction of a Soviet battleship by an American firm, and a U.S. credit out of which the Kerensky government's still outstanding debt to the United States would be settled.

Davies did not let pass the opportunity to sound out Stalin, if only briefly, on the European situation, which had taken quite a menacing turn in late May. Stalin called the outlook for European peace very poor. But it is notable that his critical shafts were directed more against British policy than against Hitler. Making no reference to collective security, the need to stop Hitler from taking over Czechoslovakia, France's and Russia's obligations to defend that country, he said that the aim of the Chamberlain government was to make Germany strong so as to increase French dependence on Britain and strengthen Germany against Russia, but the Soviet Union had every confidence that it could defend itself.[87] It has been noted that Stalin's special interest in acquiring a battleship that would take three or four years to build did not suggest that he considered Soviet engagement in a major war a contingency of the immediate future.[88]

Late in June, Schulenburg reported to Berlin on the Soviet government's attitude during the German-Czechoslovak crisis of late May, noting that articles appearing in Soviet newspapers at this time made *no* mention of Soviet treaty obligations, that in Paris, London, and Prague Soviet diplomacy undoubtedly recommended firmness toward Germany, and that Litvinov regularly pointed out that Soviet fulfillment of its treaty obligations was contingent on others' fulfilling theirs. Because of its internal situation and fear of a two-front war, the Soviet government, he concluded, would hold aloof from military enterprises for the present and was not likely to allow the Red Army to march to the defense of a bourgeois state although it would try to mobilize other powers to do so.[89]

In late July 1938 Schulenburg's private secretary Herwarth received the permission for an automobile trip that he had requested back in May. With an accompanying driver he proceeded by car across the Ukraine to

Odessa on the Black Sea. Along the way he found no indication of Soviet troop movements. The lack of evidence takes on heightened meaning from the fact that as they were starting out, he informed the men in the NKVD car behind them that he would be taking tourist pictures as a record of the journey, had no wish to get them into trouble, and hence would be appreciative if they would sound their horn twice whenever he entered a military district so that he would refrain from taking pictures until they signalled again that it would be all right.[90] They complied with his request. Since there is no reason to attribute gross stupidity to the NKVD counterintelligence agents who proved so cooperative, we may infer that higher authority in Moscow *wanted* the German Embassy to observe for itself and report to Berlin on the absence of Soviet troop movements in the Czechoslovak direction as the decisive moment approached. No one then in the German Embassy, Herwarth recalls, thought that the Russians would go to war over Czechoslovakia or were in a position to do so.

Berlin bombarded its Moscow Embassy with inquiries concerning a feared Soviet build-up of air power in Czechoslovakia. General Köstring did not believe that the Soviet government would do more than place a few training planes in Czechoslovakia.[91] At the end of August Herwarth passed on an Italian Embassy report that some time earlier forty Soviet aircraft were flown to Czechoslovakia over Polish territory at a great height.[92] According to present information, the Russians sent a small number of medium bombers to Czechoslovakia in the summer of 1938 in partial recompense for Czechoslovak specialized infantry weapons and heavy artillery pieces ordered by Moscow between January and July 1938 and the training of dozens of Soviet technicians at the Skoda Armament Works in Pilsen.[93]

As the final crisis came in late August and September, there was feverish activity in concerned governments. The British, French, and Germans all sought to clarify the Soviet government's position. It hedged.

On 22 August Schulenburg talked with Litvinov. Germany's aim was to annihilate Czechoslovakia, Litvinov told him. Should it go to war for this purpose, France would mobilize, Britain would no longer retreat, and the Soviet Union would keep its promise to support Czechoslovakia. But what form this support would take Litvinov declined to say despite Schulenburg's repeated attempts to find out. After discussing matters with his military and naval attachés, the German ambassador informed Berlin of his opinion that Moscow was trying to press France and Britain to take the initiative against Germany. For its part, however, the Soviet Union would hold back while using every opportunity to supply Czechoslovakia with war material, especially aircraft. It would be hard for it to send troops although military technicians might be dispatched. It was the overwhelming view of the Moscow diplomatic corps, Schulenburg concluded, that if it came to armed conflict with Czechoslovakia, France would attack Germany and Britain would be at France's side, while the Soviet Union would do "as little as possible, so that at the end of the war she will have an intact army at her disposal."[94]

Britain's foreign secretary, Lord Halifax, invited Ivan Maisky, Soviet ambassador in London, for a talk on 17 August. He asked what Maisky thought about the situation in Central Europe. Maisky said the fate of Czechoslovakia depended primarily on whether or not Britain and France took a firm position against the aggressor at this critical hour. On 29 August Robert Vansittart, chief diplomatic adviser to the British government, invited Maisky for a private luncheon talk during which he stressed that Czechoslovakia was "a key position for all future Europe," that the situation would be equally dangerous to both Britain and Russia if it fell, and therefore now was the time to act. Only the Soviet Union was silent, and London and Paris did not know what it intended to do in Central Europe. Maisky's reply was evasive. He said that it would be hard to determine in advance just what steps the Soviet government would take in the hypothetical event to which Vansittart was referring, but that the USSR would fulfill obligations it had undertaken. Besides, were London and Paris informing Moscow of their plans and actions in Central Europe? Why should Moscow act differently?[95]

Two days later Maisky went to dinner with Churchill, who played an important political role at that time without being in the government. Churchill was in great agitation, Maisky reported. He did not exclude the possibility of war in the coming weeks. If the Germans attacked, he was sure the Czechs would fight and this would bring about a situation in the West in which France would come to their aid and even Britain would come into motion although perhaps not from the start. British attitudes, both public and governmental, had shifted in the past ten days in Czechoslovakia's favor and against Germany. If guns went off in Central Europe, matters could take a turn that would lead Britain to war. Churchill's plan was as follows: at the moment when the attempt to reach a compromise with Germany collapsed and Hitler started to brandish the sword, Britain, France, and the USSR would send him a collective note protesting German threats against Czechoslovakia. Less important than its exact content was the very fact of the three powers' collective action, which would frighten Hitler and might stop the threatened aggression. Churchill had presented his plan on paper to Halifax, who was to take it up with Chamberlain. He hoped for support from Vansittart, who was again acquiring notable influence. Churchill inquired about Soviet reaction to his plan. Maisky answered that he couldn't say anything on behalf of the Soviet government and referred to Litvinov's public statement of 17 March. His urgent telegram to Moscow ended by saying that Churchill spoke of Germany with fierce hatred and even had thought up a new slogan: "Proletarians and free-thinking people of all countries, unite against the fascist tyrants."[96]

Had the three governments accepted and acted on Churchill's plan, Hitler would probably not have been deterred, the German military opposition might well have taken its contemplated action against him and his Nazi cohorts, and World War II could have been averted.

On 2 September the French chargé in Moscow, Payart, called on Litvinov. He came on instructions from the French foreign minister, Georges Bonnet, to ask what help Czechoslovakia could count on from the Soviet Union. Litvinov began by reminding Payart that France was obliged to help Czechoslovakia regardless of Soviet help, whereas the latter was conditional on French help. Then he said that if France rendered aid, the USSR was fully resolved to fulfill all its obligations under the Soviet-Czechoslovak pact, using "all paths accessible to us for this purpose" (implying conditionality). Should Poland and Rumania raise obstacles, their conduct, and especially Rumania's, could be changed if the League of Nations were to pass a decision on aggression. Since the League's machinery might work very slowly, necessary measures must be taken now, as provided by the League Charter's Article 11 in event of a threat of war. To Payart's expression of doubt whether a unanimous League decision was possible, Litvinov said that even a majority decision would have huge moral significance, especially if Rumania itself were in agreement with the majority. As for concrete aid, a conference of the Soviet, French, and Czechoslovak armies should be called for preliminary discussion of practical steps by military experts. Finally, a conference should be held of states interested in peace. If it took place at present, with Britain, France, and the USSR participating, and adopted a general declaration, the chances of deterring Hitler from a military adventure would improve.[97]

Payart's talk with Litvinov did not give Paris the assurance it sought about Moscow's intent to uphold Soviet treaty obligations if Czechoslovakia were attacked. Litvinov's proposals meant a time-consuming and, as Payart observed to him, uncertain expedient of lining up support in the League. Indeed, events were moving too rapidly by then for such procedures to have practical meaning. Moreover, the declared Soviet readiness to help Czechoslovakia on condition that France did was contingent on a solution of the transit problem. Since Moscow's relations with Poland were quite strained and the Polish government had designs on Czechoslovakia's Těšín district, this problem primarily involved Rumania. As a member of the Little Entente and endangered by German designs on its oil and grain, Rumania was more amenable to cooperation against Hitler despite Moscow's unrenounced claim to her Bessarabian province. But George Kennan, stationed in Prague at the time of Munich, was told by the German military attaché there that even with Rumanian permission for Soviet troop passage, the rail network in the area of Rumania that the Soviet forces would have to cross was so primitive that it would take about three months to move a Russian division into Slovakia.[98] However that may have been, France was concerned to clarify the situation, both as to Soviet willingness to use the land route through Rumania to Czechoslovakia and Rumania's willingness to allow Soviet forces to move across its territory.

In the early days of September, shortly after Payart's interview with Litvinov, the French ambassador, Coulondre, returned to his Moscow post. He spoke with his diplomatic colleagues. The Bulgarian minister, Antonov, though convinced that the Soviets would "march," wondered how far Stalin could become involved in Czechoslovakia without compromising his regime. Referring to the disorganization evident all around in consequence of the Terror, Antonov said, "It's more than disarray, it's the beginning of paralysis." Lord Chilston shared that feeling. So far as he knew, the Russians had not yet taken a single special measure of military security. The Lithuanian minister, Baltrousaitis, was struck by the anti-British feeling in higher circles in Moscow, caused by the suspicion that Britain was pushing Germany against Russia. The Rumanian minister, Dianou, gave the impression that Rumanian policy was undergoing a switch favorable to the Allies. Dianou, however, was not encouraged by his first contacts with Litvinov, with whom he had spoken before the latter's departure for Geneva some days earlier. Litvinov hardly mentioned the war danger and hadn't a word to say about what the Soviet Union expected of Rumania. On 11 September Coulondre was received, in Litvinov's absence, by Potemkin. He told Potemkin that Litvinov's response to Payart did not suffice to inspire in the French government the confidence on which concerted action by the powers called upon to oppose Hitler's armed action must rest. Formal conferences were tardy when the house was burning. It was a question of knowing whether each of the three powers interested in peace was ready to oppose aggression against Czechoslovakia by placing all its forces in the service of the common cause. This plea for a clear statement of the Soviet stand was met by "total muteness of my interlocutor."[99]

On Stalin's interpretation of the British and French probes of Soviet intentions, evidence is lacking. Considering the view of British policy that he voiced to Davies, and his tendency to project his own thought-ways onto others, he probably saw in the Western powers' approaches to Moscow a desire to entangle Soviet Russia in hostilities with Germany over Czechoslovakia while remaining, themselves, in the background or minimally involved.[100] If so, his assessment would only have stiffened his resolve not to be outdone, but to outdo them, in this diplomatic contest.

In Geneva, between 9 and 13 September, Litvinov was in contact with Rumania's foreign minister, Comnène, on the latter's initiative. Comnène indicated that the Rumanians might agree to the passage of Soviet forces without a League decision and even without explicit recognition by the Soviet Union of the territorial integrity of Rumania. Comnène's later memoirs suggest that Litvinov showed little interest. And Litvinov did not inform Bonnet of the talks he was conducting with Rumania's foreign minister.[101] Held on Stalin's tight leash, Litvinov at that zero hour was unable to pursue the collective security diplomacy that might have influenced the outcome and that he surely would have pursued with full vigor had he been permitted to do so.

Events followed in rapid order. After Chamberlain's meeting with Hitler in Berchtesgaden on 15 September, the British and French governments worked out a plan providing for cession of border areas with over half German population and a new international guarantee of the rest of Czechoslovakia against unprovoked aggression. On 19 September they pressed Prague to accept the plan as the price of peace. In this agonizing predicament, President Beneš of Czechoslovakia called in the Soviet ambassador, S. S. Aleksandrovsky, and asked urgently for answers from Moscow to two questions: How would the USSR act if France fulfilled her treaty obligations, and what would be its position if France did not do so but Czechoslovakia held out? Aleksandrovsky withheld the answers overnight. He brought them to Beneš on 21 September, after the Prague government had decided at a night-time meeting to yield to the Anglo-French pressure. Moscow's answer to the first question was affirmative. On the second, it demanded recourse to the League, prompting Beneš to answer that "this would not be enough for us. . . ."[102]

Stalin had written Czechoslovakia off. *Pravda*'s leading article on 21 September said as much in its last paragraph: "The Soviet Union takes a calm view of the question of which imperialist predator rules in this or that colony, this or that dependent state, for it sees no difference between German or British predators." The next day its leading article said that "the clouds of a second imperialist war have gathered over the world." By definition, an "imperialist war" was one in which Russia would not be participating.

That day, 22 September, Chamberlain had his second meeting with Hitler, now at Bad Godesberg, where Hitler escalated his territorial demands. Public opinion in Britain and France hardened and both countries started mobilizing. Czechoslovakia mobilized on 23 September. According to Beneš' later account, its army was one of the best in Europe, fighting fit in morale and equipment, and the republic was prepared for war.[103] General Gamelin informed Voroshilov of French military preparations, and Voroshilov conveyed word via the Soviet military attaché in Paris that Moscow was arraying thirty infantry divisions, motorized divisions, and air forces along the USSR's western frontiers. Voroshilov's message was, however, belied by reports from German and Polish sources that no Soviet military preparations were detectable, not even such preliminary steps toward mobilization as Belgium, the Netherlands, and Switzerland were taking. Moscow did not reply to, nor inform Prague and Paris of, a Rumanian note received 24 September with Bucharest's formal agreement to Soviet troop passage through Rumania and large-scale overflights across it. Nor did it reply to a Czechoslovak appeal for immediate Soviet air support, sent to Moscow just before Germany's expected invasion on 27 September.[104] "They, too, play a game of their own," Beneš said of the Russians at the time to his private secretary, Prokop Drtina, adding: ". . . if they should get us into it, they will leave us in it."[105]

The rest is unhappy history. The brief military activization in the West subsided with the French and British leaders' decision to go to Munich, where agreement on Hitler's terms was signed on 30 September. Although it was Chamberlain and Daladier who sat around the table with Hitler and Mussolini in Munich and staved off war for a time by appeasement, Stalin also helped pave the way for Hitler's undoing of Czechoslovakia. Even when Beneš called Ambassador Aleksandrovsky early the next morning to ask if the USSR was willing to give full military help in event of a Czechoslovak refusal of the Munich *Diktat,* and said he had to have the answer by noon, Alexandrovsky waited until 11:20 a.m. to telegraph his query to Moscow, which duly replied in the affirmative *after* the Germans marched unopposed into the Sudetenland on 2 October.[106]

Stalin's diplomacy during the months before Munich, both covert and public, was the last act in his coalition-building strategy in the West. There is no reason to believe, and ample reason to doubt, that he was ever prepared to commit Russia's military power, such as it was then, to a war in tandem with France and Czechoslovakia to prevent the latter's obliteration by Hitler. What he sought to encourage was a protracted war pitting Czechoslovakia and the Western democracies against Germany, a war in which the USSR would be uninvolved, or only insignificantly involved, while recovering from the havoc caused by his Terror and positioning itself to intervene at a time of his choosing in order to carry its revolution into Eastern Europe and the Balkans.

On the evidence presented above it is extremely doubtful that Stalin ever took very seriously the possibility that France, with Britain's support, would fulfill her treaty obligation to defend Czechoslovakia. In any event, now that Czechoslovakia had fallen, there remained the alternative, to which Stalin all along had inclined, of a war in the West preceded and unleashed by a Moscow-Berlin accord. In Munich's immediate aftermath his diplomacy steered straight in that direction. Even as the Germans were taking over Czechoslovakia's ceded borderlands in October, Litvinov and Schulenburg reached an oral understanding (first bruited by Schulenburg in the summer of 1938) to play down press and radio attacks between their two states as well as personal attacks on Hitler and Stalin; and in December 1938 the trade agreement between the two governments was renewed without the delay experienced a year earlier, paving the way for further Soviet-German economic talks that had been proposed by the Soviet trade mission in Berlin.[107]

Further, while Hitler ensured Franco's final victory in Spain by refurbishing the German-led and German-equipped Condor Legion, Stalin did not correspondingly bolster the Republican forces, which as late as July 1938 mounted a successful offensive across the Ebro River. Rather, he reduced the Soviet contribution to support of Republican Spain. Although aid to the Republic continued in diminished quantities and the Spanish Communists received instructions in February 1939 to continue last-ditch resistance (the Civil War ended on 1 April 1939 in the Republic's total defeat), a cooling of Soviet interest in Spain was observable in the autumn of 1938. With Moscow's approval, the International Brigade was withdrawn.[108] In November the head of the Republican government, Juan Negrin, appealed to Stalin despairingly for increased military aid. There is no record of a response.[109] No longer would Stalin allow the Spanish cause to stand in the way of better relations with Berlin.

As the intervention in Spain was wound up, Russians who had gone there to risk their lives in the antifascist fight, and who survived, came home, in most cases, to death in Russia. Army officers, fliers, diplomats, policemen, journalists (with the notable exception of Ehrenburg) were swallowed up by the Terror. Among the prominent victims were General Kleber; Vladimir Antonov-Ovseyenko, who in 1936 was sent to serve as Soviet consul general in Barcelona; and Stalin's "Don Miguel" of *Spanish Diary* fame, Kol'tsov, who was arrested in December 1938. When his younger brother, the well-known cartoonist Boris Efimov, sought to intercede for Kol'tsov at a high level, Ulrikh said to him: "Don't you understand that if he was arrested, there was proper authority for it?"[110]

In a Lefortovo cell in early 1939 Pavel Gol'dshtein briefly met and spoke with General Kleber, who rightly predicted that he was about to be executed and explained: "I knew too much as commander of the International Brigade in Spain and earlier in my work in the United States under the name of 'Fred' and before that in the Comintern as 'Stern.' "[111] In 1938 the arrested son of Mikhail Tomsky, who survived the Stalin period to write about this event, met Antonov-Ovseyenko in a Butyrka cell. He had been recalled in the second half of 1937, briefly appointed RSFSR commissar of justice after being received by Stalin for a talk on Spanish affairs, then arrested. He told his fellow prisoners in the cell that he had refused to sign a confession of guilt. When his interrogator called him an enemy of the people because of that, he had said: "You yourself are an enemy of the people, a real fascist," to which the interrogator had replied that the people "trusts us, and you will be destroyed. Why, I'll receive an order of merit for you."[112] Later that day the Old Bolshevik was taken out to be shot.

What virtually all the Russian and foreign Communists who fought in Spain and survived to come to Moscow must have shared was deep anti-fascist conviction. This was enough to make them a political liability to a Stalin bent on doing business with Hitler. Numbers of them ended up in the labor camps along with old and younger Bolsheviks, many of Jewish origin, German, Polish, and other foreign Communists, and still others who could not easily have stomached a collaboration of the Soviet and Nazi regimes to carve up Eastern Europe between them.

No wonder that before the end of 1938 politically astute camp inmates were predicting the Stalin-Hitler pact on the basis of the categories of prisoners coming into the camps.[113]

19

THE REVOLUTION
OF BELIEF

An Elite Transformed

WE HAVE GIVEN no little attention to Stalin's motives for the Terror, and yet this greatest murder mystery of the twentieth century demands further explanation. To provide it, we must first consider the full dimensions of the terror process and view it in relation to another that went on simultaneously: the advancement of new people.

When the Eighteenth Party Congress assembled in Moscow in March 1939, the Communist elite of the Lenin and post-Lenin periods had been virtually wiped out and a new Soviet elite was taking its place. The repressed political generation comprised a very heavy proportion of those who were active in the party before or during the Revolution along with those who joined subsequently and went through the Civil War.[1]

The Terror did not eliminate the whole Old Bolshevik contingent. Apart from Stalin and his Politburo associates of pre-1917 standing (Molotov, Voroshilov, Kalinin, Kaganovich, Andreev, Shvernik, and Zhdanov), some others survived and a few remained in office. R. S. Zemliachka, who was not only an Old Bolshevik but that extreme rarity among leading political figures under Stalin, a woman, became one of six deputy chairpersons of Sovnarkom in 1939. K. I. Nikolaeva remained a Central Committee member, and Alexandra Kollontai was Soviet ambassador in Stockholm. Among other Old Bolshevik survivors there were some with close ties to Lenin, including Krupskaya, Krzhizhanovsky, M. A. Bonch-Bruevich, N. A. Semashko, M. K. Muranov, and Lenin's secretary, Yelena Stasova. Signatures of 538 surviving Old Bolsheviks appeared under a message in *Pravda* on 7 November 1947, October's thirtieth anniversary, to him "whose name personifies the Russian Revolution, with words of love and gratitude for all the great things you have given our party, the working class, and the peoples of our country." Why these few hundreds, and others who survived the Terror but died between 1939 and 1947 went unarrested in the later 1930s has no single answer. In some cases such as that of Sergei Kavtaradze, who was arrested, released in 1940, received affably by Stalin, and appointed head of the Narkomindel's Middle East Department, Stalin must have had personal reasons for saving someone who he knew could be useful to him. The likely main reason, however, is implicit in the fulsome tribute to Stalin just cited. He probably wanted to obscure the radical discontinuity of regime that his Terror caused, embracing as it did the political extinction of the Old Bolsheviks, by allowing some to live on as docile witnesses to testify that he was the personification of the Revolution and that his revolution from above was the fulfillment of Lenin's revolution—although few of them could possibly have believed it.[2]

Below the Politburo and Central Committee levels, the other institutions of party-state rule suffered wholesale depredations. Among the arrested people's commissars were those of justice, internal affairs, education, defense industry, light industry, timber industry, internal trade, public health, state farms, water transport, machine building, and produce collection. The defense and foreign-affairs commissariats were no less hard hit for the fact that Voroshilov and Litvinov survived. With the arrested commissars would go their vice-commissars and other administrative staff, section chiefs and others, down to and including leading personnel of units under the commissariat's jurisdiction. Among the commissariats, few if any were harder hit than the one on which the economic growth of the Soviet Union depended most, the Commissariat of Heavy Industry, which after 1937 was subdivided into about a dozen separate industry commissariats. The Terror swept away a very large proportion of the generation of Soviet industrializers under the five-year plans. Officials from assistant

commissars on down disappeared after Piatakov's condemnation and Ordzhonikidze's suicide in 1937, and major plants across the country were
purged of their own leaders in the wake of those arrests, disrupting operations and causing a serious decline of output in 1937–38.[3] The members
of regional party committees and Soviet executive committees disappeared
en masse, as, in many instances, did their replacements, and then *their*
replacements. In Gorky region, as if in a counterrevolution, the whole
party committee and Soviet executive committee were imprisoned.[4]

As the Terror victimized the Revolution-born political generation,
promotion moved a new one into its place. Appeals for promoting new
party members and nonparty people to responsible posts alternated during
those years with pressure for denunciation of masked enemies. The basic
criterion for promotion was not a lengthy work or party record, but "unlimited devotion to the party, closest ties with the masses, boundless hatred
for enemies of the people, and ability to master the Bolshevik style of
work."[5]

Orders came from the top to accelerate party recruitment, which had
resumed on 1 November 1936 for the first time since it ended in January
1933. The pressure got results. By the outset of 1939 more than 1,850,000
members, nearly 60 percent of those who belonged to the party at the start
of 1933, no longer did—but during the year over one million new members
joined.[6] Stalin reported to the Eighteenth Congress that since the previous
congress, in 1934, 500,000 young Bolsheviks, "party members and persons in close association with the party," had been promoted to leadership
posts in the party and government.[7] He had made good by then on his
earlier resolve that a generation must go, and a new political generation
was now in place.

It was a time of dizzying upward mobility. A future Soviet premier,
Alexei Kosygin, became commissar of the USSR's textile industry in 1939
at thirty-five. A future party general secretary, Leonid Brezhnev, joined
the party in 1931 and by 1939 was head of the Dniepropetrovsk City Party
Committee at thirty-three. Another future general secretary, Yuri Andro-
pov, joined the party in 1939 and by 1940, at twenty-six, was secretary of
the Karelo-Finnish Republic's Komsomol organization. A third future
general secretary, Konstantin Chernenko, joined the party in 1931 and was
secretary of the Krasnoyarsk Regional Party Committee in 1941 at thirty.
A future defense minister, Dmitry Ustinov, was director of a Leningrad
arms plant by 1937 and by 1941, at thirty-three, Soviet commissar for
armaments. The future commander of the Soviet navy, Sergei Gorshakov,
became a rear admiral in 1941 at thirty-one. The future Soviet foreign
minister, Andrei Gromyko, joined the party in 1930, took a postgraduate
degree in economics in Moscow, and in 1939, at thirty, was shifted to the
purge-devastated Narkomindel to head the American Department.

Those moved into the places of the purged political elite were, as a rule, products of specialized education and practical work experience in the early to mid-1930s. In his Eighteenth-Congress report, Stalin christened this administrative and specialist elite the "new Soviet people's intelligentsia," and said that they "poured new blood into the intelligentsia and revitalized it in a new, Soviet way."[8] His metaphor was revealing. In the persons of the promotees new blood had been transfused into the corpse of a Communist Party from which terror had drained most of the old blood.

Could the needs of modernization have made this forced turnover of elite generations necessary?[9] Were the younger, less experienced cadres with on-the-job training or technical education professionally better qualified for managerial jobs in the new, industrially more developed Russia than those they displaced? No doubt, some among the purged managers were technologically undereducated or aging, and not a few among the newcomers proved able. An example was A. S. Yakovlev, the talented young aircraft designer whose "Yak" fighter planes became a mainstay of the Soviet air force in World War II.

Still, the above hypothesis finds no warrant in the known facts. The slain or imprisoned industrial, military, scientific, and other experienced personnel were a large part of the country's precious human capital and included many of her best minds. Stalin understood this, as suggested by what happened when Yakovlev was promoted. Stalin had the veteran aircraft designer A. N. Tupolev arrested, along with an estimated 450–500 engineers of the Commissariat of the Aviation Industry. Fifty to seventy were executed, about a hundred dispatched to camps, and the rest set to work in prison design bureaus created in 1938–39 to produce new planes.[10] In some ways, the new managerial cadres were less functional for a modern industrial society than the more free-spoken men who were arrested: they came into posts that called for initiative, but they were products of the Stalinist school, which spawned initiative- and responsibility-shunning bureaucratic types. Instead of being creative, it was "good to be a telegraph pole," as the saying went at Magnitogorsk.[11]

The notion that the Terror fostered modernization is most dramatically refuted by its impact on the state's defense potential. Military modernizers who foresaw the urgent need to prepare for a new kind of motorized war, as the Germans were doing, went to their deaths with Tukhachevsky, while such uncomprehending believers in the horse cavalry's continuing key role as Voroshilov and Budenny remained in top posts. "The Contours of Coming War," a book manuscript finished in early 1937 by the then forty-nine-year-old Valentin Trifonov, an Old Bolshevik who fought in the Civil War, foresaw the inevitability of a war with fascism that would start with a potentially devastating surprise attack on Russia for which it was necessary to prepare in advance, partly by moving industries eastward.

Stalin, Molotov, and Voroshilov, to whom he sent copies for comment, did not reply. Trifonov's arrest and condemnation came later in 1937.[12] Another would-be military modernizer, air force chief Yan Alksnis, went to death not long after having presciently prescribed a concentration on producing speedy, maneuverable fighter planes rather than more of the Tupolev-type huge long-distance models that the Stalinist "falcons" flew in quest of world records.[13]

The motto of Stalin and his circle was, "We must beat the enemy in his lair." They were under the influence (as others were elsewhere) of the theory of the Italian general, Douhet, that the heavy bomber would be decisive in future war; and Voroshilov duly reported to the Eighteenth Congress that the heavy-bomber proportion of the air force had doubled since 1934, while the proportion of light bombers and assault and reconnaissance planes had been halved.[14] A year earlier, in February 1938, the defense commissar had stated that while the horse cavalry had been virtually eliminated in many armies, "The Red Cavalry remains a victorious and crushing armed force that can and will accomplish great missions on all battlefronts."[15]

May it have been that the greatest virtue of the new cadres, in Stalin's eyes, was their loyalty to him and sure submissiveness to his imperious will? It is very plausible that this figured in his reasoning. The new elite was a reliable support stratum for Stalin's now absolute autocracy. It was purged of independent-minded Bolsheviks who considered themselves Stalin's equal, would freely voice their ideas in party councils, and might vote against him—as some did at the Seventeenth Congress. Now, at last, he could give free rein to the superior policy-making capacities that he believed he possessed, do Soviet Russia's thinking for it, make all the major decisions and very many minor ones without fear of his views being contested.

Yet this explanation does not solve our problem. For massive repressions were not required to ensure a compliant elite. A far smaller, selective terror, with replacement of the victims by obedient state servitors, could have achieved that goal. In the end, the question still remains: why the huge dual process of repression and promotion? For light on it, we may turn to a book on which Stalin lavished a lot of time and energy during this period.

Stalin as Party Historian

The big Soviet news event in September 1938, the month of Munich, was not the gathering of war clouds over Europe. Heavily publicized as that was, it took second place to a book called *History of the All-Union Communist Party: Short Course.* Starting 9 September, *Pravda* serialized it chapter by chapter. Editorials and long signed articles supplied glowing commentary and exegesis.

No author was named on the title page. It left authorship vague, saying: "Under the editorship of a Commission of the Party Central Committee," to which was added a further phrase: "Approved by the Central Committee." This showed that the *Short Course* had high-level sponsorship. Soon after, Stalin was identified as author of a section in chapter 4, entitled "Dialectical and Historical Materialism," and then the whole 350-page book was said to have been produced "on the initiative and with the direct personal participation of Comrade Stalin."[16] After World War II Stalin appropriated authorship of the book.[17]

It was not his first foray into party history. A sketch by him of "The Party Before and After Taking Power" appeared in *Pravda* on 28 August 1921, a whole decade before he intervened on the party-history front with his letter to *Proletarian Revolution.* He had more than a little to do with the appearance and content of Beria's book of 1935 on early Transcaucasian Bolshevism. In 1934 he also involved himself in a project, initiated by Gorky, for a history of the Civil War. Volume 1 of *The History of the Civil War in the USSR,* dealing with 1914 through October 1917, came out in mid-1935. Stalin took a larger part in the shaping of it than has been known abroad. Publicly he was one member of an editorial group. The draft was prepared by a larger group of seventeen, including Gorky, Tovstukha, and I. I. Mints, but while the book was being written, Stalin discussed sections of it with Gorky on visits to the latter's dacha near Moscow. Mints took notes on those discussions.[18]

When the full draft of Volume 1 was ready, Stalin read it carefully and made many suggestions, which were duly incorporated into the published text. While the book was in press, Mints wrote an article, "Stalin as an Editor," and sent it to Stalin's office for advance approval before submitting it for publication at the time of the book's appearance. Receiving no response, he sought and secured an interview with Stalin, who proved reluctant to have his extensive editorial role publicized. Mints suggested replacing Stalin's name, wherever it appeared, with "Chief Editorial Board" *(Glavnaia redaktsiia).* To this Stalin agreed and the article appeared in print under a new title.[19] Decoded, it is revealing about Stalin as an editor.

He was pedantically insistent on formal exactitude. He replaced "Piter" in one place with "Petrograd," "February in the Countryside" as a chapter title (he thought that suggested a landscape) with "The February Bourgeois-Democratic Revolution," "Land" as a chapter title (a "modernism," he called it) with "The Mounting Agrarian Movement." Grandiloquence was mandatory too. "October Revolution" had to be replaced by "The Great Proletarian Revolution." There were dozens of such corrections. And from the book's published text one can see that "Chief Editorial Board" wanted to see the Revolution portrayed in dramatic, even melodramatic form, with Stalin as well as Lenin playing a heroic part and with Trotsky and others as villains.

All this culminated in Stalin's great project: a new party history that would replace existing ones and be the sole authoritative text. Ever since 1932 he had foreseen the need for such a work. In 1935 he set up a committee under Zhdanov to prepare it, but the resulting drafts did not satisfy him. So, in early 1937, he personally wrote a letter to the drafters laying out the guidelines for the book he wanted. He said in it that existing party history texts were unsatisfactory and gave pointers on how to remedy their defects. He made it clear that the book should be thoroughly didactic, not "a light and unintelligible tale of things past," and that the drafters should look for guidance to the corpus of his own writings and speeches. He proposed a new periodization of party history by giving the titles of twelve chapters and the time periods to be covered by each (when published, the book had exactly these twelve chapters). On 16 April 1937 the Politburo instructed the drafting group to base its work on Stalin's letter and freed its three members (Yaroslavsky, V. Knorin and P. Pospelov) from other work to carry out this assignment. The drafting devolved mainly on Yaroslavsky and Pospelov because, in the course of the work in 1937–38, Knorin was arrested and became a Terror victim.[20]

A high-level commission, consisting of Stalin, Molotov, and Zhdanov, was appointed as the book's collective editor. The draft went to these three and to other members of the Politburo, but Stalin himself was the only one to take an active part in editing and reworking it. His changes and additions, preserved on photocopied pages in the Central Party Archive, show to what an extent he placed his personal imprint on the work. Here and there he struck out passages or altered the wording of a chapter title. He specified the exact wording of the title page (which said that the book was edited by a "Commission of the Central Committee" and was approved by the Central Committee). More important, he made a number of substantive additions. One was a philosophical section in chapter four, "On Dialectical and Historical Materialism." Another added passage made more emphatic the theme that the Bolshevik party's real founding took place at the Prague Conference of 1912. Still another was an attack on West European Social Democracy. And not least, he added a passage that highlighted the historic significance of collectivization as a "revolution from above."[21]

And so, at the height of the Terror, Stalin was thinking about the party's history and directing preparation of a book about it.

The *Short Course* as Autobiography

For Old Bolsheviks whose lives were interwoven with the Bolshevik party before and after 1917, especially if they were among its leaders, their own biographies and the party's history were inseparable. Of no one was this more true than Lenin. As Zinoviev observed in honoring him on his fiftieth birthday, ". . . to speak of Lenin is to speak of our party, to write a biography of Lenin is to write the history of our party."[22] Whether Stalin remembered those words or not, the idea they expressed was in his mind too, and the *Short Course* was a book-length application of it to himself, a history of the party enmeshed with his own biography as its coleader with Lenin and single supreme leader after Lenin's death.

The style is dry, dogmatic, impersonal. The chapters give a recital of facts and events with a textbookish "Brief Summary" at the end of each. Chapter 1 follows the conventions set by earlier texts of reviewing Russia's conditions in the later nineteenth century, the rise of the revolutionary movement, and the beginnings of Russian Marxism. Even here a rush to get to the history in which Stalin figured is visible in the omission of so much as a paragraph on the *narodnik* movement as the precursor of the Marxist one. The *narodniki* are only introduced as opponents of the Marxist current, which originated in the 1880s. Then follows a summary of Lenin's early revolutionary career. Toward the close of the first chapter, Stalin makes his first appearance, though not yet as an historical actor, by being quoted on how, in 1900, when only disconnected Marxist groups existed in Russia, "ideological confusion was the characteristic feature of the party's internal life."[23]

Stalin arrives on the scene in Russia's revolutionary turmoil of 1905, covered in chapter three. "Comrade Stalin was carrying on tremendous revolutionary work in Transcaucasia," we read. Thus he said at a workers' meeting in Tiflis: "We need three things: first—arms, second—arms, third—arms and arms again." He and Lenin met for the first time at the Bolsheviks' conference in Tammerfors, Finland, in December 1905, having until then "maintained contact by correspondence and through comrades."[24] No evidence of this correspondence and contact through comrades has ever been made public.

How was it possible for Stalin to portray the Bolsheviks as a party of Lenin-Stalin when he himself was so obscure a local underground figure in it during its early years? In the *Short Course* he had himself portrayed as the party's coleader with Lenin from the time of the party's creation by the simple expedient of making out the 1912 Prague Conference to have been that moment, and by altering history to make it appear that he was elected to the Central Committee at Prague, not coopted.

With Stalin in the thick of events in Petrograd, the book recounts the saga of 1917 as a Lenin-Stalin one. Stalin's several divergences from Lenin are blotted out. He, rather than Trotsky, is pictured as having directed the seizure of power as head of a "party center" in the (Trotsky-led) Revolutionary Military Committee. Although such a center was elected, it did not function as the "leading core" of the committee and Stalin's doings on the day of the takeover remain a mystery. Moreover, Trotsky, who did direct the takeover, appears in the *Short Course* account as having sought to wreck it by proposing that it be delayed (as it was) to coincide with the convening of the Second Congress of Soviets—in order to forewarn the Provisional Government and give it time to take premptive counterrevolutionary action.

The *Short Course* has Stalin working hand in glove with Lenin against disruptive efforts not only by Trotsky but also by other prominent Bolsheviks who would be accused in the purge trials of the later 1930s of having all along been two-faced enemies of the Revolution: Zinoviev, Kamenev, Bukharin, Rykov, Piatakov, and Radek. It has Trotsky in league with the then Left Communists Bukharin, Radek, and Piatakov in a plan to wreck the Bolshevik peace talks with the Germans at Brest-Litovsk in early 1918 and thereby provoke a German offensive that would threaten the infant Soviet regime—and this "sinister scheme" thwarted by Lenin and Stalin, who insisted that peace should be signed (in fact, Stalin waffled on the issue of signing the German ultimatum and was sharply criticized for that by Lenin).[25]

Chapter 8, on the Civil War, has Stalin covering himself with martial glory while Trotsky, abetted now by Tukhachevsky, pursues his treacherous course in his capacity as chairman of the Revolutionary Military Council. Stalin is hailed as author of the winning strategy used against General Denikin's White forces on the southern front in 1919, and Trotsky, who devised that strategy, is depicted as the source of the mistaken one that in act he successfully opposed.[26]

Then the book fictionalizes Stalin's disastrous role in the Soviet-Polish war of 1920, in which he had to be recalled from the southern front for insubordination (as its political commissar, he kept the Red forces fighting to take Lvov after they had been ordered by the Politburo to move northwest to protect the flank of Tukhachevsky's army facing Warsaw on the western front, resulting in the Red Army's rout there). In the *Short Course* version of those events, the Reds' advance on Warsaw "proceeded in an absolutely unorganized manner" through fault of Trotsky and Tukhachevsky. That made it easy for the Poles to breach the western front. To make matters worse, Trotsky ordered the mounted army's transfer from the southern to the western front "although it was not difficult to see that the best and in fact only possible way of helping the western front was to capture Lvov." So, the Red Army's defeat was due to the "wrecker's order issued by Trotsky . . . to the joy of the Polish gentry."[27]

The treatment of the rest of the Soviet period, from 1921 through mid-1938, is no less skewed. We read that the Kronstadt rising of 1921 was a product of counterrevolutionary scheming by class enemies and put down by forces headed by Voroshilov (that dubious honor was Tukhachevsky's). But the misrepresentation of reality is most egregious in the disappearance of divergences between Lenin and Stalin. The reader, for example, would never know that the federal structure of the Soviet Union created by the 1922 Constitution, far from having stemmed from a "proposal of Lenin and Stalin" as the *Short Course* has it, came about after a sharp conflict between them in which Stalin took a position of great Russian chauvinism. No sooner does Lenin die, in the *Short Course* account, than Stalin steps into place as the party's and country's infallible new *vozhd'*.

Industrialization and collectivization appear in the *Short Course* as policies pursued by the Stalin-led party with strong popular backing, and no inkling is given of the horrific human cost. The capitalist countries are said to have done everything possible to impede the industrialization out of fear that its success would threaten the existence of capitalism, and internal oppositionists to have collaborated with them by espionage and wrecking efforts, as in the Shakhty affair, in which the wreckers were linked with "a foreign military espionage service" (no mention made of Germany here).[28]

Collectivization appears in Stalin's book as the climacteric success of Soviet history after Lenin, a huge revolutionary advance to socialism through voluntary decision of the peasants, who "would come in great numbers to the state farms and machine and tractor stations to watch the operation of the tractors and other agricultural machines, admire their performance and there and then resolve: 'Let's join the collective farm.'"[29] Insofar as mistakes were made, these were "'Left' distortions by local authorities," condemned by Stalin in his article "Dizzy with Success."

The book comes to a close with the Soviet state scoring one achievement after another under Stalin's leadership. After he formulates the new slogan, "Cadres are all-decisive," in 1935, Stakhanov hews 102 tons of coal in a single shift, and the Stakhanov movement springs up with examples of new cadres being decisive for economic progress. The government passes an antiabortion law "in view of the rising standard of welfare of the people." In 1936 comes the adoption of the new constitution, drafted by a commission under Stalin's chairmanship and embodying worker-peasant democracy. In 1937, after new facts come to light regarding the "fiendish crimes of the Bukharin-Trotsky gang," the trials take place, showing that the accused conspired against the party-state ever since the October Revolution. The Soviet people approve the extermination of the "White Guard insects" and turn to the next order of business, electing a Supreme Soviet under the new constitution.[30] On 11 December 1937 Stalin addresses the voters of his electoral district. Next day, 91,000,000 citizens go to the polls and 89,844,000 of them enthusiastically vote for the candidates of the Communist and nonparty people's bloc, thereby confirming the victory of socialism in the USSR.

Such earlier texts as Pópov's *Outline History of the CPSU*—now withdrawn from circulation—were far more factual and informative. But they lacked the *Short Course*'s melodramatic quality. It is a story of deadly combat between forces of good and evil. It has two shining heroes. Lenin is the embodiment of revolution in the earlier chapters, with Stalin as his *alter ego* and destined successor. Stalin comes fully into his own in the later ones. At the end he receives the grateful plaudits of the people.

Such was the make-believe world that the subservient drafters produced under Stalin's guidance. The ideal Stalin became real, and those who had incurred his hatred became the villains of history. Without the show trials on the record, and the mass repressions that accompanied them, Stalin's book could not have been written.

Returning now to the question posed earlier—why Stalin needed the massive dual process of repression and promotion—we may first give the floor to him. He told the February–March plenum of 1937, and through it the country, that it was urgently necessary for the cadres to "master Bolshevism." And while he spoke in this connection of learning to see through the techniques and designs of masked enemies, he also made it clear that more was involved. The time had come to replace the old Shakhty-era slogan of mastering technology with the new one of "political education of cadres."[31] The cadres being advanced to responsible posts in place of those disappearing in the Terror were mostly people with on-the-job training or formal technical education, but now they also had to be "politically educated." That it was the *Short Course* mission to provide political education in Stalin's Bolshevism is stated in its introduction.

What this "Bolshevism" basically comprised has been described. In essence it was a fictitious version of his life, his arrogated autobiography as a revolutionary hero, writ large in the party's history. Whether Stalin managed to believe this, and to repress his memory of much that contradicted it, will probably never be known. But certainly he deeply needed to believe it and to know that people in Soviet society did. Evidence of this is the great effort he invested in the story's production and publication and the elaborate measures he decreed for inculcating it in the new elite and younger citizens coming up through the educational network.

After the book was published, he made sure that it would fulfill the purposes he had in mind for it. These were set forth in a Central Committee decree published in *Pravda* on 15 November 1938. It said that the *Short Course* must become the basis of the Soviet system of political education. By providing a "unitary guidance," it would end confusion in the telling of party history and the "abundance of diverse viewpoints" on theory and history found in earlier texts. The decree ordered a radical restructuring of the network of political indoctrination by making central to it the mastering of the *Short Course* by "leading cadres" of party, Komsomol, economic and other officials, as well as the whole party and nonparty intelligentsia, which was lagging—it said—in theoretical and political knowledge.

The book was printed in huge numbers. Again and again, fresh hundreds of thousands of copies rolled off the presses. By the time Stalin died, the book had appeared in 300 reprints, with a total print run of 42,816,000 copies in 67 languages. Years before, in his letter to *Proletarian Revolution,* Stalin implied that the "real" Bolsheviks were Lenin-Stalin loyalists. Now he had seen to the creation of a manual of the fundamentals of "real" Bolshevism and he wanted Soviet people and Communists the world over to accept them as true. The unavoidable shakiness of his pride structure, caused by subconscious knowledge that much had been falsified, made it all the more essential to him that Soviet citizens, and especially the new leading stratum, form a society of the faithful, a community of true believers in *Short Course* Bolshevism.

The mass repressions were the other side of the coin. They were no less motivated by Stalin's need for a society of the faithful than was his mass promotion of new younger cadres for whom the *Short Course* would be dogma. Without being purged of most or very many of those who, by virtue of their memory, if nothing else, could not be expected to be believers in Stalin's "real" Bolshevism, the society could not be what he wanted it to become: a society that saw reality as he did.[32] Since people who had in their minds a different view of the party's and Stalin's past could pass it on to the newcomers, their very presence in the party and among the citizenry would be subversive. They could spread disbelief.

Not being under Stalin's inner pressure to repress the memory of facts and events inconsistent with his compulsion to be the ideal Stalin, their discordant memories could only be extinguished in an external way by "repressing" those people in the Soviet meaning of the term, that is, by making them disappear. His psychological repression necessitated their being arrested, coerced, or tortured into confessing themselves guilty of counterrevolutionary crimes, and then being shot or sent away to endure

lives of suffering in forced-labor camps. We may speculate that his awareness of their presence in the camps, as a countercommunity of the damned,
satisfied his need always to be inflicting punishment on enemies.

Of course, far from all of who disappeared were victimized because
of their discordant memories. We have seen how mass denunciations caused
the terror process to mushroom in 1936–38 and bring the arrest of very
many nonpolitical people whose tragedies had nothing to do with guilty
knowledge of a party history divergent from Stalin's. Yet, party members
and ex-members were very heavily victimized as a group because their life
experience in very many instances had informed them, directly or by
hearsay, of things about which the *Short Course* was silent or mendacious.
Many had been initiated into a truer party history as previously expounded.

This analysis sheds light on the question of why so many Stalinists
fell victim in 1936–38. Whereas those arrested between Kirov's murder
and mid-1936 usually had some large or small oppositional blot on their
records, very many among the huge numbers repressed in the rampant
phase of the Terror were not only free of past oppositional leanings but had
been stout supporters of Stalin's General Line and enthusiasts of the *piatiletka;* some were prominent in the party's Stalin faction. Why did they
come to grief? The answer has to do with the difference between his
Bolshevism and theirs.

Most of these people had been "Stalinists" in the sense that they
accepted the need for the policies he advocated. They were sincere and
fervent Communist believers in higher proportion than those who displaced them and survived. But their belief system differed from the system
now being implanted in the newcomers. Theirs was a faith in a party that
had a prophet and supreme authority figure in Lenin and a practical doer in
Stalin. This was not the Bolshevism propagated by the *Short Course*.

Moreover, many of these ex-Stalin supporters had heard about Lenin's testament and its postscript, and some were knowledgeable about
Stalin's responsibility for the disaster brought about by the *blitzkrieg* collectivization. Their form of Bolshevik faith being subtly deviant from his
and their memories not reliably in conformity with those the *Short Course*
prescribed, they along with others in their party generation had to be
suspect in his eyes. On the other hand, the mass denunciations of persons
in low to middle ranks of administrative authority inevitably victimized
quite a few of the promotees of the early 1930s, who *were* true believers in
Stalin as a genius-leader and who, on turning up in the camps as prisoners,
went on professing their loyalty and believing that, while other prisoners
were being properly punished as traitors, mistakes had been made in their
own cases.[33]

Stalin gave a personally inscribed proof copy of the *Short Course* to his daughter Svetlana, then in her teens. In a book of her own written three decades later in America, where she settled after departing her homeland, she revealed that she found it boring and that he was angry when he learned that she hadn't read it. "He wanted me to study the history of the party," she added.[34] What she seems not to have realized is that the boring book was more than a party history; it was also her father's self-aggrandizing autobiography, in which he needed to believe and to have her, along with all other good Soviet citizens, believe as well.

The Only Authoritative Marxism

Marxism has spawned many interpretations in its history. Proceeding from Lenin's, Soviet theorists developed views in the 1920s and 1930s on such topics as dialectical and historical materialism, the state and law, and education and the family. With the appearance of the *Short Course,* many of these views were proscribed. A Marxism according to Stalin became mandatory.

An experience of this writer's one evening in Moscow in 1945 brought home the situation. A Soviet student met at a public lecture said in conversation afterward that he was studying Marxism at Moscow University. Asked how this subject was taught, he replied, "Marxism is the history of the party." That seemed questionable but turned out a moment later to be the literal truth: the required course on the fundamentals of Marxism-Leninism had as its text Stalin's *Short Course.*

The society of the faithful was to be composed not only of people who believed in Stalin's greatness as a revolutionary doer; they were to believe, too, in his genius as a Marxist thinker and treat all his writings as canonical texts. His every theoretical word became sacred dogma for commentary, exegesis, and cautious elaboration with examples. His corpus of past writings and speeches was combed for pearls of Marxism wisdom. Thus his *Anarchism or Socialism?,* an unfinished fifty-page youthful essay originally published in Georgian party periodicals in 1906–7 as a Marxist's polemic against the Georgian anarchists, and containing elementary didactic statements about Marxism (such as "Why is this system called dialectical materialism? Because its *method* is dialectical, and its *theory* is materialistic"[35]) now became a Marxist-Leninist classic.

The transformation of Leninist Marxism into Stalinist scholasticism was fostered by terror. As the chorus of denunciations swelled in 1936, Stalin's philosophical swordbearers, particularly M. Mitin and P. Yudin, assailed numerous fellow philosophers as enemies of the people. Those denounced were arrested. Others fell silent. Philosophy came wholly into the hands of Mitin-type careerists willing to devote their pens to Stalin's service, primarily by testifying in their writings to his greatness as a Marxist.

Emblematic of Stalin's elevation to lonely philosophical eminence is the fact that the *Short Course* essay on dialectical and historical materialism was not devoted, as would have been appropriate in an "encyclopedia of Marxism-Leninism," to a summary of Lenin's version of Marxism; it appeared as an exposition by Stalin. The book did call Lenin a "master theoretician," adding that after him "Stalin and other disciples of Lenin have been the only Marxists who have advanced Marxist theory"[36] (those other than Stalin went unnamed), but the essay was devoted only to Stalin's interpretation.

Stalin's Marxism attached unprecedented importance to great men. It thereby squared his role as a man whose acts and thoughts were decisively influencing history with an original Marxist theory that saw social classes and their struggles as history's moving forces. Stalin had foreshadowed his position in his interview of 1931 with Emil Ludwig by rebuffing Ludwig's statement, "Marxism denies that personalities play an important role in history." Not at all, said Stalin. He then explained that great men can play commensurably great parts in history if they correctly understand existing conditions and "know how to alter them."[37]

He had some support from Plekhanov here although he made no reference to him in the interview. Plekhanov fathered Russian Marxism partly in polemics against the *narodnik* notion that "heroes" make history by influencing the "crowd." This left him with the problem of accounting as a Marxist for the influence that outstanding individuals can have on the historical process. In a pamphlet of 1898, *The Role of the Individual in History,* he argued that while the underlying determining forces of history are socioeconomic, a gifted individual, *if* his particular talents make him more suited than others to the social needs of his time and *if* the existing social order permits him to rise high, can significantly influence history by helping to accelerate its advance in the direction it was bound to take anyhow.

Plekhanov had come under something of a cloud after Stalin belittled his philosophical merits in his conversation with philosophers in 1930. But he made a comeback in chapter one of the *Short Course*. His argument was expounded to the effect that ". . . outstanding people can become really outstanding personalities if their ideas and wishes correctly express the requirements of society's economic development, the requirements of the advanced class." Then Stalin's book went Plekhanov one better by asserting that "it is not heroes that make history, but history that makes heroes." And further: "Heroes, outstanding personalities, may play a serious role in the life of society only to the extent that they manage to understand rightly the conditions of society's development, to understand how to change them for the better."[38] There was no need to mention Stalin as a case in point of history making a hero; the whole book was testimony to it.

Concerning the dialectical and historical materialism of *Short Course*, little need be said. Marx and Engels could not have viewed so simplistic a statement as a useful summary of their philosophical position. For it omitted reference to the key dialectical principle of "negation of the negation," by which Hegel, followed in their own way by Marx, Engels, and later Lenin and his disciples (Sten for example) conveyed that reality develops through a stage that is revolutionarily "negated" by a next stage (feudalism by capitalism, for instance), the second stage then being revolutionarily negated and yet preserved in a third, higher stage (in this instance, socialism) in which the material accomplishments of capitalism abide in a more advanced, classless society.

After dialectical materialism came historical materialism, introduced as a teaching about modes of production as foundations of history's successive socioeconomic orders: slave society, feudalism, capitalism, and socialism. In its stress on fierce class struggles as a prime feature of the first three of these, Stalin's essay was in accord with both classical and Leninist Marxism. So, too, in its emphasis on revolution as the mode of transition from one social order to the next in the sequence.

When it reached the Bolshevik revolution, the essay stressed the revolutionaries' use of the newly won state power in razing the old social order. Marx and Lenin would have agreed with the idea—since it was theirs—that an anticapitalist revolution would use political power to socialize the means of production and quell resistance by the old ruling class. But the *Short Course* went on to state in its final chapter that the collectivizing revolution from above had established rural socialism in the USSR[39] That coercive state power would be used not only to displace the capitalist ruling class but later on to *build socialism* from above was an idea alien to both classical and Leninist Marxism. No matter that it found expression in a part of the book other than the essay on dialectical and historical materialism; the whole book is what Marxism came to mean under Stalin.

The Statist Realm of Socialism

The word "state" is missing from the *Short Course* account of past forms of society. This omission calls for explanation. The likely one is that use of the term would have called for a Marxist definition of it, and Stalin wouldn't have wanted that.

Let us repair the omission. For Marx and Engels the state is "a special repressive force" (Engels' words) that arises historically in class-divided societies in which a dominant minority class (slave-owners in classical antiquity, feudal nobility in the Middle Ages, and capitalists in the modern period) wield coercive power via armies, police, the law, courts, and the like to hold an exploited majority class of slaves, then serfs, then proletarians in subjection. As a repressive force the state will live a short afterlife in a dictatorship of the proletariat to enforce the workers' seizure of the means of production and suppress their erstwhile exploiters. This final revolution will yield a nonexploitative classless society of free associated producers in which, since repression will not be needed, the state will "die out" or "wither away."[40] In *The State and Revolution* (1917) Lenin cited Engels' definition of the state as a special repressive force. In the coming transition from capitalism to communism, he wrote, repression would still be necessary under the proletarian dictatorship, but this would be repression of ex-exploiters by the worker-peasant state, which would be a "transitional state" already *beginning* to wither away in the first phase of communist society (socialism).[41]

This was the context in which Soviet political and legal thought evolved in the 1920s. The law codes promulgated under the NEP, drawn largely from West European models, were not considered socialist law but law of the transition period from capitalism to socialism. The regnant theory, put forward by E. B. Pashukanis, held that NEP Soviet law was based on the principle of equivalence expressed in commodity exchange. As the NEP ended in 1928–30, legal theorists proclaimed the withering away of law to be close at hand. Although Stalin told the Sixteenth Party Congress in 1930 that the proletarian dictatorship was growing stronger, Pashukanis, in the heady atmosphere of "cultural revolution" that gave legal radicals an illusory sense that their time had arrived, took a different tack. "Now we are achieving the revolutionary transition from capitalism to socialism," he wrote in 1930. Law, he averred, would disappear and be supplanted by policy once all production of petty goods was absorbed into the dominant sector. He even made bold to forecast the withering of the Soviet state by the end of the Second Five-Year Plan in 1937 on the ground that socialism would be achieved by then, classes would have disappeared, and a state would no longer be needed.[42]

To Stalin, whose Russian national Bolshevism envisaged a great and mighty Soviet Russian state and whose revolution from above was building a centralized, bureaucratic, coercive state power using law as one of its instruments, such thinking was repugnant. He tolerated it only so long as he found use for the enthusiasm of Communist intellectuals like Pashukanis for "storming the heights of socialism" during the Great Turn. By

1935, having understood the direction of Stalin's policy, Pashukanis espoused the view that intensified class struggle internally and needs of defense against foreign foes rendered a stronger dictatorship imperative and made talk of the withering of Soviet statehood dangerous.[43]

But despite his turnabout, Pashukanis' cause and that of the school of Soviet Marxist jurisprudence that he led was hopeless. With the enactment of 1936 of the Stalin Constitution, whose first article declared the existing Soviet state and by implication its law to be "socialist," the theory of Marx, Engels, and their disciple Lenin on the disappearance of classes, law, and the state in a fully socialist and later communist society had to be condemned as a "wrecker" theory. How could Stalin be the successful builder of socialism if the state over which he presided and its laws were not socialist?

The revolution in state and law theory, like the revolution of belief as a whole, was bloody. On 20 January 1937 *Pravda* announced that Pashukanis was an "enemy of the people." Arrested, he died that year in prison. The jurisprudential cohort that he led was condemned as a group of wreckers in the legal disciplines. Many of his colleagues suffered fates similar to his, as did ex-Commissar of Justice Krylenko. Stalin's philosopher Yudin excoriated the condemned legal radicals for having taught that state and law, as bourgeois categories, cannot be filled with socialist content. Later, he set forth the Stalinist tenets that Soviet law was now "entirely and completely the law of socialist society in form and content alike."[44]

Stalin had prepared the way for a new legalism when he called for "stability of the laws" in his speech of November 1936 on the new constitution. The man who emerged as spokesman of this legalism was Vyshinsky. He began with a mass purge of the procuracy that carried off many prosecutors who had until then tried to mitigate the extremes of the Terror. In the provinces, 90 percent of the prosecutors were victimized.[45] Meanwhile, new law textbooks were hastily prepared to train up a new generation of jurists in the spirit of Vyshinsky's definition of law in 1938 as "the aggregate of rules of conduct or norms, yet not only of norms but also of customs and rules of community living, sanctioned by state authority and coercively protected by it."[46]

The new doyen of jurisprudence fashioned for Stalin a law and order administration in which professionalized legal education and a measure of procedural formality served as cover for terror-law. He gave theoretical justification for terror-law when, in his *Theory of Judicial Evidence* (1941), he ranked the accused person's depositions as the decisively important evidence in cases of conspiratorial anti-Soviet groups—thereby making it obligatory for interrogators to extract confessional depositions in cases of counterrevolutionary crimes covered in the fourteen paragraphs of the

Article 58 of the criminal code; and when he wrote in his book *The Soviet Judicial System* (1940) that "Not only the courts and their verdicts but also administrative measures through such organs of the proletarian dictatorship as the NKVD's Special Board (instituted under the law of 10 July 1934) are a mighty weapon of the Soviet regime in the struggle against enemies."[47] As mentioned earlier here, the three-men NKVD special boards condemned people *in absentia* secretly, without right of defense or appeal. Of this Stalinist legality the acid-tongued British correspondent, A. T. Cholerton, quipped that whatever might be the case with *habeas corpus*, the authorities strictly observed *habeas cadaver*.[48]

Behind the scenes, in internal documents and oral statements, Vyshinsky prescribed terror-law in brutal forms. He issued orders and circulars to prosecutors and interrogators that blurred the distinction between nonpolitical and political crimes. As the Terror mounted in late 1936, he ordered all criminal cases of major fires, accidents, and production of poor-quality goods reexamined with a view to finding counterrevolutionary intent in them. Deliberate burning of state or public property was to be prosecuted, regardless of motive, under Article 58, paragraph 9 (sabotage). Counterrevolutionary intent was to be imputed in all cases linked with harvesting deficiencies. When it transpired that ticks infected some crops harvested in 1937, Vyshinsky demanded that this be attributed to counterrevolutionaries and many people were condemned accordingly. He repeatedly justified the referring of cases to special boards on the grounds that when it was a matter of destroying the enemy, that could be done without a trial. By saying "Personally, I prefer half a confession signed by the accused in his own handwriting to a full confession recorded by the interrogator," he recommended to prosecutors and interrogators that they make it a practice to prepare handwritten records of depositions, thereby creating a false appearance of voluntary confessions in cases where the accused held out against writing such documents themselves. When Beria demanded of him that prosecutors not insist (as some had been doing) on recording in the protocols of interrogations the protests of accused persons against unlawful methods used by their interrogators, Vyshinsky wrote a letter informing Beria that he had issued instructions not to record such statements in the protocols. At a meeting in 1938 he said that it was pointless to review all the numerous citizens' complaints against sentences pronounced on themselves or family members, and ordered that such complaints be treated "responsibly," that is, left in most instances uninvestigated.[49]

Even after the mass terror subsided in 1939, terror-law held sway. In Stalin's state people could be sent to a concentration camp if overheard and reported to have told a political anecdote. Ten-year sentences were common if a citizen was reported for telling an anecdote that placed the sacrosanct person of Stalin in an unfavorable light.

Despite a let-up in wartime 1941–45, when voluntary public support was a *sine qua non* of the Stalin regime's survival, low-level terror remained a fixture of Russia's life until the day the dictator died; a subtle change began some days after.

The Outcome

Stalin thus used his tyrannical power not only to decide policy and prescribe doctrine but also to impose on society a radically flawed private version of history. By mass repression of old believers (to borrow a term from Russia's pre-1917 religious past) and the training of the transformed elite and the young as new believers in *Short-Course* Bolshevism, this political playwright managed to stage the fantasied drama of his life as though it were reality itself unfolding.

The question arises, with what results? How far did Stalin succeed in creating a community of the faithful, a society that revered him as a leader of genius and caring father of his people, had no memory of facts about him discordant with the official image, loathed those condemned in the purge trials as monsters of deceit and conspirators, believed that it was truly living now under socialism, and accepted his Marxism as its own? Briefly, in some ways the undertaking succeeded, and in others it failed.

The censoring of social memory contributed significantly to the revolution of belief. By eliminating old believers, who carried to perdition knowledge and beliefs that Stalin sought to extirpate, and by cowing those not arrested into silence, the Terror helped to eliminate from society memories and thought-ways at variance with his. The now heretical literature of earlier vintage on party history, Marxist theory, the state and law, and other subjects disappeared from libraries. Those who had copies of such books or of other incriminating materials, such as Lenin's testament or photos, generally took care to destroy them as a safety precaution. Knowing that confidences could bring disaster on the family, many were censorious in what they told their children. Some children were not told that an absent father or grandfather was in prison camp; he was "away on state business." But in other cases young people learned from their elders things that they also learned never to repeat in the presence of strangers. So it was, as a Soviet intellectual testified long after in emigration, that "All people had to become actors and live a double life: duality and wearing a mask provided a certain protection.[50]

The new system of mass indoctrination often had an effect different from that desired by its initiator. In order to complete party study circles, or graduate from higher educational institutions in which party history and dialectical materialism *(diamat,* the students called it) were required courses, people had to study well the *Short Course.* This did not necessarily make them sincere, much less ardent new believers. Many mastered *Short Course* Bolshevism by rote memory and duly parroted it on appropriate occasions. Some made public statements in their actor roles, as Academician Bakh very likely did when he said in a newspaper article: "The *Short Course* is a turning point in my life."[51] A young woman geneticist who in 1939 wanted work in Moscow's Institute of Evolutionary Morphology had to pass an examination in Marxism in order to be accepted. She did so in part by showing detailed knowledge of the *Short Course* theoretical section. In memoirs written in emigration decades later, she wrote: "The *Short Course* appeared in 1938. Impossible to read without revulsion; you had to know it by heart."[52]

Among young people who had to study the *Short Course* to pass the required ideological courses in a higher educational institution, Svetlana Stalin was not the only one who found it boring. In one such Moscow institution, the women students in *diamat*—this was wartime when very few students were men—informally called their woman teacher "dia-mama" and cribbed their way through the examination by concealing notes under their skirts above the knee. The two required courses were taught by departments of Marxism-Leninism. Some Soviet students, knowing that courses in theology were required for university students in tsarist Russia, took to calling their Department of Marxism-Leninism the "theological faculty." Stalin's reduction of Marxist and Leninist theory to a set of crude dogma probably had the effect of killing interest in the subject among a majority of the educated youth at the end of the 1930s and after. A few who did retain an interest moved in a dissident direction. In the 1940s a few small groups of educated young people began to study Lenin's writings with a view to disentangling what Lenin really thought from Stalinist statism.[53] One could now read parts of Lenin's *The State and Revolution* as a dissident tract, and they did so.

What about the belief that Soviet society, with its huge centralized state, stratification, semiclandestine system of privilege for the upper strata, and poor to modest living conditions for the masses, was now living under socialism? There were doubters. One, who in 1936 was twenty-six years old and in training as an engineer, recalled much later in emigration that he, "like the majority," was surprised and shocked to hear Stalin proclaim in his speech on the new constitution that now socialism had been achieved. For he associated socialism with abundance and freedoms.[54] Whether his was actually a majority view is uncertain. Many were simply indifferent to ideology, but there was an activist element of the youth whose idealistic devotion to the regime and enthusiasm for socialism somehow persisted.

One member of it was Raisa Orlova, born in 1918. When the *piatiletka* ended in 1933 she knew by heart the children's incantation "518 and 1,040" (518 plants built and 1,040 machine and tractor stations set up). Stalinist Communism was a "second religion" for her, so much so that, as a student and Komsomol organizer in Moscow's Institute of Philosophy, Literature, and History in 1938, she "marveled at the clarity of the *Short Course*," which, she says, served as a standard reference bible and was "meant for the masses."[55] Another true believer was Lev Kopelev, whom Orlova would later marry. As a twenty-one-year-old collectivizer in the Ukraine, he believed Stalin's claim that the fight against the kulak was a struggle for socialism. When Kirov was murdered, he accepted the official explanation that Zinovievite ex-oppositionists were to blame and decided that "terror was indispensable."[56] Such young people did not live behind masks—or not yet. How numerous they were we do not know.

Idealism aside, career advancement was a potent incentive for joining Stalin's community of the faithful. Whether it was the colossal sweep of the purge broom or the continuing growth of the industrial economy and party-state organs that opened up desirable places for them in the middle and upper strata, the beneficiaries were likely to become Stalin loyalists, if not Stalin adulators. A document found in the archives by the Soviet historian Yuri Borisov reveals that the purges had created 100,000 vacancies in the party apparatus alone by the beginning of 1938.[57] An authority on the military purge says that it won for Stalin outright religious adoration on the part of the new higher command staff of the army.[58] The same undoubtedly could be said of many promoted plant directors, deputy directors, chief engineers, and their counterparts in other state institutions. They could see Stalin as their benefactor and take pride in the system in which they did so well. Very likely the simple schematic Marxism taught in the *Short Course* was all that most of them felt any need to know. And as higher or up-and-coming party-state functionaries, why should they doubt that this system was indeed the socialist one that Stalin had proclaimed it to be, that socialism was a form of society in which a bureaucratic centralized state took charge of everything, and that those in authority, themselves included, had every right to the special shops, special dining rooms, special clinics, and special rest homes that served them and their families? Since most were of peasant or worker origin, it was natural for them to think of the late-1930s Russia as the worker-peasant state that it officially claimed to be, although they themselves were no longer members of either of these classes.

We come now to the question of how contemporaries reacted to the Terror. Did they believe in the guilt of those who fell victim? In many instances people knew that loved ones who disappeared were Stalin followers of impeccable party-line rectitude. Yet, that did not necessarily imply to them that the purge trials were a sham and the great anti-Soviet conspiracy a political myth. They could believe that ex-oppositionists had conspired against the regime and organized a network of helpers, but that the arrest of their innocent relatives and friends as members of the ring was a mistake. They could also believe that Stalin was uninformed of such miscarriages of justice and try to appeal to him over the NKVD's head by writing anguished letters to him. In old Russia a folk saying, "God is high above and the Tsar is far away," reflected the monarchist faith that not the tsar but his ministers were responsible for sufferings endured by the people. Since much of the tsarist political culture was reborn under Stalin, it is hardly surprising that such thinking appeared as well.

Not all believed the story of a vast counterrevolutionary conspiracy. "Not for a single minute," said Viktor Levin, a Moscow University student at the end of the 1930s, when asked much later whether he believed it at the time. Nor did his father and brother. When asked what they thought underlay the trials and arrests, Professor Levin said that they attributed these events to political conflict in the regime and the settling of political scores as a result.[59] They were not alone in taking such a view. However, a former Soviet philosopher who was, like Levin, a student at the time, believes that while some people thought the purge trials reflected a political settling of scores, the majority, intellectuals included, accepted the claim that a conspiracy had been exposed.[60] The charges brought against lower-level victims in public meetings were not generally believed, say Beck and Godin, "But most Soviet citizens believed that something lay behind the arrests, if only an incautious though by no means wicked remark, or a previous connection or acquaintance with someone who had really been guilty."[61] The picture that emerges is one of widespread willingness to believe in the guilt of at least the prominent figures among the accused, and possibly of others as well.[62]

How is this to be explained? The show trials with their elaborate confessions of high-level guilt, the public meetings and the press campaign about enemies of the people are only a part of the answer. A further and in this writer's view indispensable part is incomprehension of the Terror's causation. Unaware as they were of Stalin's role, of his personal need for history to be rewritten according to his life-script and for the rewritten history to be believed by the people, and hence of the link between the repressions and the formation of the new elite, politically conscious minds were baffled by what was going on; and the only apparent explanation was that at least some of the alleged enemies were indeed guilty of treasonable or other serious offenses. For it was incredible that people would be arrested all over the country without any justification at all.

This line of reasoning also helps to explain why many felt no fear for themselves during that time of terror: they knew themselves to be innocent of any wrongdoing.[63] Only on the supposition of a definite connection between guilt and arrest would awareness of one's own innocence of wrongdoing bring with it a sense of immunity from arrest. Had it been otherwise, had citizens in the mass known (or failed to resist and blot out the thought in case it occurred to them) that the alleged conspiracy was a fabrication and that there were no enemies of the people—other than Stalin and those assisting him in the Terror—they would all have had to live in incessant deadly fear for themselves and their families. But in countless cases people discovered after being arrested that their sense of security associated with innocence had been a false one. Once imprisoned they learned, under the brutal ministrations of their interrogators, that no "mistakes" had been made in regard to them, as at first they thought, and that they had to sign fabricated confessions of guilt as the only alternative to unbearable torture.

When all is said, it seems that Stalin engineered the revolution of belief with substantial success albeit at catastrophic cost to the society, economy, culture, military potential, and general well-being. He made himself into the unblemished cult figure, and all the condemned ones went down as enemies of the people. Stalin's singular Marxism became official dogma, as did his vision of the system formed in the revived state-building process as a truly socialist one and his views on any subject whatever as soon as they were made public. So long as he lived, and for a few years thereafter, the immense disparity between the glorious Stalin of his institutionalized make-believe world and the Stalin of historical actuality remained a secret to all but a few.

It has been suggested that psychologically disturbed political leaders eventually stumble in power and go down to defeat.[64] Stalin was one of history's notable exceptions. He repeatedly stumbled but did not go down to defeat; he dragged his party, state, and society down. In this devastating and unspeakably tragic instance, the leader managed, at ghastly cost, to impose his skewed view of himself and the world, his belief system, upon his society. Not he but the country came to grief.

The twin processes of repression and promotion had done their work, but with what must have been an unanticipated result. In the seemingly successful effort to fashion a society of the faithful, Stalin had brought into being a society of conformists. People wore masks of conformity in public, but he knew that some viewed him critically or hated him in their hearts.

Not all of those who professed devotion to him and approval of his policies were speaking their true minds. Some, in short, were two-faced, but there was no easy way of knowing just which ones they were. Hence in the eyes of this scourge of double-dealers, virtually every Soviet citizen, and every bigwig in particular, was a potential double-dealer. And whereas conspiring double-dealers were pretty much a figment of Stalin's imagination in the 1920s, nonconspiring ones were not at all a rarity in the later 1930s— and so, paradoxically, he had fostered the very phenomenon that oppressed him. A sense of this made him both morbid and deeply dangerous. To the end of his life he would go on yielding now and then to the urge to rip masks off the faces of suspected conspiring double-dealers.

20

THE SCRIPTED CULTURE

Culture's Dictator

WE HAVE SEEN Stalin asserting philosophical authority in 1930, intervening in the field of party history in 1931, having the school history texts revised, editing Afinogenov's *Lies,* giving guidance to historians of the Civil War, having the party's history rewritten with him as the chief hero, issuing as his own what became the canonical version of Soviet Marxism, and exercising his dramatic flair in producing political trials as theatrical events. This list of his forays into cultural life is far from complete. Not only did he take a keen interest in Soviet culture; he radically reshaped it. Literature, the theater, the cinema, music, painting, architecture, education, learning, and science—all showed the deep influence of his tastes and ways of thought. During the 1930s, he effected a cultural revolution from above.

It negated in various ways what went by the name "cultural revolution" in 1928–31, when party zealots in self-styled proletarian art organizations imposed their canons on literature, music, art, education, and scholarship. That movement Stalin utilized as a source of revolutionary esprit for the *piatiletka*. Its militant spirit and doctrinaire intolerance were congenial to him, but it ran counter to his preferences on several counts. First, the would-be cultural revolutionaries, typified by Pokrovsky in history and Pashukanis in legal theory, were not his minions. Although they flung themselves into the cultural side of what they thought was to be the construction of socialism, they were not the submissive agents of the state and Stalin that *his* cultural revolution required. They were men with ideas of their own deriving from a Leninist Marxism that linked the advent of socialism with the withering away of the state. They were Bolsheviks of the left whereas Stalin encouraged, and infused into Soviet culture, statist and Russian nationalist Bolshevism of the radical right.

A standard-bearer of the leftist cultural movement was the RAPP, the 3,000-member Russian Association of Proletarian Writers that dominated literary life in 1928–31. RAPP's leadership included the organization's secretary Leopold Averbakh, whose sister was married to Yagoda, the writer Vladimir Kirshon, and the critic V. Yermilov. It preached a literary theory called "dialectical materialism," according to which writers should disclose in their characters the inwardly discordant "living person" as a mixture of positive and negative qualities. This had no appeal to Stalin, under whose soon-to-be-imposed "socialist realism" writers would be constrained to depict heroes as thoroughly heroic and villains as totally depraved. RAPP's rallying cry, "ally or enemy," excluded fellow-travelers from the ranks of allies. Lack of party membership would be no bar to entry of nonparty writers, such as Pasternak and Stalin's favorite, Alexei Tolstoy, into the new, all-embracing Soviet Writers' Union and similar organizations for the other creative arts, which were formed following the Stalin-inspired Central Committee decree of 23 April 1932 dissolving RAPP and other proletarian art organizations.[1]

That action was foreshadowed in 1929 in an exchange of letters between Stalin and the playwright Vladimir Bill-Belotserkovsky concerning Mikhail Bulgakov and his play *Days of the Turbins*. The son of a Kiev professor of theology and a doctor by training, Bulgakov published in 1925 a novel called *The White Guard,* which he then made into the play just mentioned. It is set in Kiev in the waning days of the Civil War and shows a White Russian family like his own, divided finally between some who decide to emigrate and others who for patriotic reasons stay and link their fates with a Bolshevik-ruled state which for them represents the real and eternal Russia. The Moscow Art Theater, founded in 1898 by Konstantin Stanislavsky and V. I. Nemirovich-Danchenko and famous for Chekhov productions, staged Bulgakov's play as its first Soviet play. Stalin loved it and according to several Soviet reports went to see it as many as fifteen times. Probably he thrilled to the play's message that Lenin's movement was quintessentially Russian.

In its heyday in 1928 RAPP was hotly critical of Bulgakov's play. Averbakh and Kirshon attacked it for sympathetic portrayal of White officers, and another leftist writer stigmatized it for Great Russian chauvinism. Bill-Belotserkovsky, though not himself a RAPP member, went so far as to suggest in a letter to Stalin in 1928 that Bulgakov's play be banned. In his belated reply, dated 2 February 1929, Stalin demurred, saying *Days of the Turbins* is "a demonstration of the all-conquering power of Bolshevism."[2] RAPP's pressure was, however, effective enough to persuade the Art Theater to cancel the play. Then Bulgakov wrote a letter to Stalin raising the possibility of his going abroad for lack of useful work at home. On 18 April 1930, just four days after Mayakovsky's suicide, Stalin telephoned Bulgakov at night (possibly out of fear of a rash of suicides by notable creative figures) and, having received the writer's assurance that he would rather be of use at home than go abroad, saw to it that Bulgakov was appointed an assistant director at the Art Theater, after which *Days of the Turbins* was revived.[3]

Having been badgered by RAPP, Mayakovsky had reluctantly joined it two months before his suicide. Afterward, the official custodians of literature did not treat him kindly. In 1935 his long-time woman friend and keeper of his memorabilia, Lily Brik, wrote to Stalin complaining of their unresponsiveness to her efforts to set up a museum in Mayakovsky's Moscow apartment and promote publication of his works. Stalin penned on her letter a note to Yezhov directing him to help Brik because: "Mayakovsky was and remains the best and most talented poet of our Soviet epoch. Indifference to his memory and works is a crime."[4] Some days later *Pravda* carried an unsigned article in praise of Mayakovsky. It favorably contrasted his interest in public affairs with aesthetes' interest in pure poetry, said that Mayakovsky succeeded in overcoming his earlier futurism, berated bureaucrats who hadn't yet established the apartment-museum and were not doing enough to publish his works, and ended by quoting Stalin's description of Mayakovsky as "the best and most talented." Next to the article appeared an extract from Mayakovsky's 1925 poem "Homeward!" containing the lines:

> I want the pen to be on a par
> >   with the bayonet;
> And Stalin
> >   to deliver his Politburo
> reports
> >   about verse in the making
> as he would about pig iron
> >   and the smelting of steel.[5]

Had not Mayakovsky taken his own life, Stalin's Terror very likely would have victimized him as it did other leftist cultural luminaries of the early Soviet years. But he was safely deceased, and Stalin's praise canonized him. The apartment-museum was set up. Monuments were erected to him. Streets, squares, steamships, and a Moscow metro station were named after him. Mass editions of his works came out, research on his work became a scholarly industry, and "For what do I love Mayakovsky?" became a standard question on graduating examinations in Soviet schools. Yet, *The Bedbug* and *The Bathhouse,* plays that an increasingly depressed Mayakovsky wrote not long before his suicide—the former a satire on a Communist future in which flamboyant characters like himself would be freaks, the latter a savage lampoon of pompous bureaucrats of the early Stalin era who were hemming him in—stopped being performed not long after Mayakovsky died.

In private letters Stalin made occasional disclaimers of literary expertise. But they were disingenuous, as shown by the fact that he would thereupon voice his authoritative word on the question at hand.[6] More to the point, he indulged literary impulses of his own. Having written a few youthful poems in his native Georgian, he felt at home in poetry. At the height of his Terror he found time to work over a translation into Russian of Shota Rustaveli's twelfth-century Georgian epic poem, *The Knight in a Tiger's Skin,* a tale of love and glory on which he doted. The translator, Shalva Nutsubidze, had been arrested by 1937 along with most of the Georgian intelligentsia. Friends managed to salvaged a copy of his already prepared translation and somehow it found its way to Stalin. Liking its literal exactitude, he ordered Nutsubidze released, invited him to dinner, discussed the translation, and proposed refinements of his own, after which *The Knight* came out in a handsome new edition, also partly designed by Stalin, and without mention of his involvement in the project.[7]

In music, as in the other arts, Stalin's tastes became law. He had a liking for patriotic Russian operas of the nineteenth century, such as Glinka's *Ruslan and Liudmilla,* which was revived in 1937. But mostly his musical tastes were those of a simple man: they ran to the tuneful and traditional. In addition to Russian folk songs, he had a Georgian favorite, "Suliko." For Soviet opera the right path, he thought, was that taken by the composer Ivan Dzerzhinsky in his opera *The Quiet Don.* It had melodic folk music from the Kuban Cossack setting of the Sholokhov novel on which it was based. After attending a performance in 1936, Stalin and Molotov congratulated the company and made suggestions on how to improve the staging.[8]

A few days later, Stalin went to see another opera, *Lady Macbeth of Mtsensk District.* The score was by Dmitri Shostakovich, already a world-famous composer at age twenty-nine. Based on a novelette of 1865 by Nikolai Leskov, a tale of erotic passion and crime in the world of the provincial Russian merchant class, *Lady Macbeth* had played with signal success in Moscow and Leningrad as well as abroad since its first performance in 1934. Stalin, however, was incensed, and a vituperative unsigned article, "Muddle Instead of Music," followed in *Pravda*. Shostakovich's cacophonous opera, the article said, was "leftist muddle instead of natural human music." It seemed coded for aesthete-formalists who had lost all healthy taste. It embodied not socialist realism but the crudest naturalism, typified by the big double bed on which most of the action occurred. A hymn to merchant lust, it borrowed nervous, convulsive, jerky rhythms from jazz to represent passion in its heroes. Its success abroad was due to its appeal to the perverted bourgeois taste for the neurotic in music. Such clearly dangerous "leftist deformity" in opera stemmed from the same source as leftist deformity in painting, poetry, pedagogy, and science.[9]

Lady Macbeth was taken off the stage, meetings were held to discuss the muddle, and people turned away from the composer. Although he regained official favor with his somberly melodic Fifth Symphony in 1937, Shostakovich never composed operatic music again and never got over his bitterness. Meanwhile, the abusive attack on him in 1936 inaugurated a campaign against "formalism" in all the arts. What formalism meant was left unclear although it seemed a synonym for whatever was avantgarde, modern, experimental, or leftist. The true test of an art work's value was its popular character *(narodnost')*, its accessibility to ordinary people and capacity to please them.

A wave of party-organized meetings provided forums for denouncing others' formalist errors, contritely confessing one's own, and promising to become more *narodny*. The press struck out at "cacophony" and "pseudo-revolutionary innovationism" in architecture, whose prime representative was the architect Konstantin Melnikov; at "daubers" who smeared leftist deformity into their illustrations for children's books; at painters who thought that painting should represent not real objects but the artist's inner vision; at antipopular literary formalism that ignored what supposedly the people wanted, namely, to see itself, its happy life, shown with the simplicity found in the writings of Lenin and Stalin.[10] Efforts to put music on the right path produced a festival of folk songs and dances in Moscow later in 1936, after which one of its organizers, Igor Moiseev, established a State Folk Dance Ensemble featuring a blend of ballet with traditional Russian folk dances and those of other Soviet nationalities. This was acceptable musical art.

"Muddle Instead of Music" sounded an ominous note for the "jerky rhythms" of jazz. From then on life grew difficult for genuine jazz as played by Alexander Tsfasman and his band, and others, which had become popular earlier in the 1930s. The decline of jazz was masked by the inauthentic continuance of it played by a large State Jazz Orchestra of the USSR formed in 1938. But even this orchestra got into trouble when its beautiful new singer Nina Donskaya, who could sing real jazz, displeased Stalin by her way of doing it when the orchestra played at one of his gala evenings in the Kremlin for the Soviet elite, after which the band lost the "USSR" from its title, and Nina her job with it.[11] He had no objection, however, to Soviet pop music so long as the jazz element did not get out of bounds.

Stalin had a passion for movies and a keen appreciation of their strong influence on the public, which was as movie-crazy as any Western audience of the time. He, not the head of the Chief Administration of Cinematography, was the cinema's commissar. He had his own projection room where he previewed new films before they could be released for the public screens. Thus his personal blessing, at a special advance showing for Politburo members, was needed to clear the way for Grigori Aleksandrov's musical comedy *The Jolly Fellows,* in which the much beloved jazz conductor Leonid Utesov played the part of a shepherd who becomes a jazz conductor. At the end of the viewing, those present awaited Stalin's reaction and sighed with relief when he said: "Good! I feel as if I'd been off on a month's holiday."[12] The film appeared on Soviet screens in December 1934, the month of Kirov's murder, and was a huge hit nationwide. Its lighthearted melodies, some borrowed from American sources, helped keep people's minds off events unfolding during the quiet terror. This kitsch suited Stalin's political calculations as well as his musical taste.

In 1936 came *Circus* (also directed by Aleksandrov), in which an American circus performer who has to emigrate because she is the mother of a black child finds refuge in Moscow where she falls in love with the circus director. The joyous and tuneful words of the director's "Song of the Motherland" were endlessly sung by many in those years. It began:

> Broad is my native land,
> Full of fields, rivers and trees.
> I know of no other country
> Where a man so freely breathes.

Some jazz played by Tsfasman and his band survived in this film as music of the sinful racist America that the heroine left behind.

But Stalin's special favorite among the new musicals, repeated for him so often that he knew its punch lines by heart was Aleksandrov's *Volga Volga,* which came on the screens in 1938. In part a spoof on bureaucracy, it told the story of competing amateur groups in a provincial town. They race one another in boats along the Volga enroute to Moscow, where their "Song of the Volga" is sung jointly. The girl folk singer, who composed it, falls in love with the orchestra conductor and they win first prize in an all-union folk music contest for amateurs. So it was that a stream of joyful songs flooded Russia as repressions reached their peak in 1938.[13]

Gratifying the dictator's wishes and tastes, Aleksandrov got along with him. So did Mikhail Romm, who directed *Lenin in October* under Stalin's personal supervision, and, most of all, Mikhail Chiaureli. Discovered by Beria in Georgia, Chiaureli ingratiated himself with Stalin by glorifying him in films like *Great Dawn* and *The Fall of Berlin.* Meanwhile, such master film makers as Vsevelod Pudovkin, Dziga Vertov, Alexander Dovzhenko, and Sergei Eisenstein fell on hard times.

They showed remarkable artistic individuality so long as they could experiment and improvise as autonomous producer-directors, with such results as Vertov's pioneering documentary *Kino-Eye* in 1924, Eisenstein's immortal *Battleship Potemkin* in 1926, Pudovkin's *The End of St. Petersburg* in 1927, and Dovzhenko's *Earth* in 1930. By then Stalin's cultural dictatorship was closing in on them. Stalin proposed to Eisenstein in 1926 a film on the need for collectivization. After an interruption to make a film for the tenth anniversary of the Revolution and having Stalin censor parts of his resulting creation, *October,* Eisenstein finished the film about the need for collectivizing, which he called *The General Line.* Then he and his collaborator Aleksandrov were called in by Stalin, who had previewed it. He gave them a lecture on Marxism and film making, proposed changes, and suggested a new title, *Old and New,* which was used.[14]

The system of the "cast-iron" scenario that developed in the 1930s hobbled the film masters' creativity. Under it, elaborately detailed scripts for new films—the subjects of which were often prescribed by Stalin—had to be precensored in the State Committee for Cinematography, and the film director had to work with colleagues whose task it was to see to strict execution of the approved plan.[15] This regime kept Eisenstein, who was brimming with fresh ideas and projects, from completing a successful new film between *Old and New* of 1929 and *Alexander Nevsky* of 1938. The latter was itself another assignment from Stalin and produced according to the cast-iron scenario method. Later, Eisenstein was mobilized for Stalin's project of showing Ivan Grozny on film as a Russian national hero.

Dovzhenko's tribulations under culture's dictator were similar. In early 1935 Stalin suggested to him that he produce a film about the legendary Ukrainian Civil War commander Nikolai Shchors on the model of the recently released and much acclaimed *Chapayev,* a film about Chapayev's Civil War exploits as a Red Army commander and his death in battle.

Dovzhenko dutifully went home to the Ukraine to fulfill the task, and the film finally appeared in 1939. Shchors himself having died an early death, there was no problem showing him as a fearless division commander fighting internal and, in 1919, Polish foes of the Revolution in the Ukraine. But many who fought alongside him had, by the time of the film's shooting, fallen victim to the Terror, hence Dovzhenko had to surround his hero with fictional fighting comrades. Every single episode and all decisions on the film had to be cleared with higher authority in Moscow and there were midnight interviews with Stalin, including—as Dovzhenko afterward confided to Moscow friends—one nightmarish meeting in which a baleful Stalin refused to speak with him and Beria, who was present, accused him of being involved in a Ukrainian nationalist conspiracy.[16]

As Eisenstein was a creator of Soviet Russia's innovative cinema, so his teacher, Vsevelod Meyerhold, was founder of her avantgarde theater. Forty-four years old and well known when Lenin's party took power, he welcomed the Revolution, joined the party, and proclaimed the advent of a "theatrical October." In the 1920s, Moscow's Meyerhold Theater became a Mecca for leftist theater lovers from abroad, and its director was known in the Soviet theatrical world as the "master." He staged *The Bathhouse* and *The Bedbug* while his friend Mayakovsky yet lived, and tried vainly to produce Nikolai Erdman's hilarious satire on contemporary Soviet life, *The Suicide*.[17] None of these initiatives could have gone down well with Stalin.

Some Meyerhold productions were updated versions of old Russian classics. Thus Griboyedov's *Woe from Wit,* on nineteenth-century Russian philistinism, became Meyerhold's *Woe to Wit,* in which the final scene was a mimed one with dressed-up wax dummies as the pompous gossips: the play was not about Griboyedov's Russia only. In 1933 Meyerhold made a bow to theatrical realism by producing, but in his own special way, the younger Dumas' *Camille.* His beautiful wife, the actress Zinaida Raikh, played the title role. The sentimental French period-piece, staged with exquisite elegance, charmed Muscovite theatergoers. So did Meyerhold's subsequent production of Tchaikovsky's opera *The Queen of Spades,* based on a tale by Pushkin.

An omen of approaching disaster for him and his experimental theater was a line in "Muddle Instead of Music" saying that Shostakovich's leftist operatic music derived from "Meyerholdism," which rejected simplicity and realism in the theater. But the master was untamable so long as he remained free to speak out. He did not chime in with the chorus of recanting "formalists" in the public discussion that ensued in the spring of 1936. When, in the terror-stricken atmosphere of 1937, all theaters prepared to stage an appropriate Soviet play for the twentieth anniversary of October, he chose to produce a play based on the ideologically impeccable novel *How the Steel Was Tempered,* by Nikolai Ostrovsky. But he could not help being his own creatively innovative self in the way he produced it.

Although written before socialist realism was officially imposed on the arts, Ostrovsky's autobiographical novel was emblematic of what was now demanded of literature: its positive hero, Pavel Korchagin, is an enthusiast of the Revolution, a dedicated Komsomol member who fights in the Civil War, then stars as a worker and, when stricken by blindness and a terminal paralyzing disease, becomes a writer in his refusal to give up the fight for the party's cause. Meyerhold's stage adaptation was called *One Life.* As the anniversary date approached, there was a high-level preview by officials of the government's All-Union Committee for Art Affairs, with some prominent Moscow actors present. One of them told Jelagin at the time that it was a brilliantly produced play with tragic over-tones. Never had the Civil War's horrors been shown on the stage so graphically, with one stunning scene in which a girl trudged silently across the front of the stage—having been raped by a squad of Red Armymen.[18]

That brought a thunderbolt from on high. The play was rejected for showing, and a vicious attack on Meyerhold's theater appeared in *Pravda* some weeks later. Alone among 700 professional Soviet theaters, wrote the head of the Committee for Art Affairs Platon Kerzhentsev, Meyer-hold's had failed to produce a play for October's twentieth anniversary. From 1920, when Meyerhold produced a play in praise of traitor Trotsky, through his attempt to libel the Soviet family by staging Erdman's *The Suicide* and his formalist twisting of Russian classics to his disgraceful failure to make a play based on Ostrovsky's optimistic novel, he showed that art had no need for such an "alien theater." Then came a Committee edict closing down Meyerhold's theater.[19]

Like various other leading exponents of experimentalism in the arts, Meyerhold was a Communist. Now that his theater was shut down and leftist art banished from the Soviet stage, were conditions perhaps more favorable for purely professional, realistic art, represented most notably in the theater Stalin personally frequented and patronized, Stanislavsky's Moscow Art Theater? It has been suggested that such was the case,[20] but facts do not bear out that view. After the fall of its leftist RAPP critics, when the Art Theater's situation should have improved, it worsened. True, it became an official government theater subordinate no longer to the Education Commissariat but directly to the Central Executive Committee of the Congress of Soviets. Personal lifetime pensions, orders, titles, trips abroad for health purposes—all this came its way, and a street was named after Stanislavsky.

But the benefits came at a steep price, writes the Art Theater's literary director of a later era: Stalin in person became the theater's supreme censor, as Tsar Nicholas I had become Pushkin's personal censor a century before. Although he authorized the revival of Bulgakov's *Days of the Turbins* in the early 1930s, he did not allow the Art Theater to stage two good plays—Bulgakov's other Civil War drama, *Flight,* and Erdman's *The Suicide.* After the seventh performance (in 1936) of Bulgakov's *Cabal of the Hypocrites,* a play about Molière's relation to tyrant Louis XIV, the patron-censor banned its further showing. But the heaviest price was not the banned plays; it was "the incurable moral corrosion of a unique creative organism. . . ."[21]

Stalin also ventured to resolve various issues in science and technology. Thus in 1937 he took part in a meeting to discuss the proposal of an engineer named Nikolaev to defend Soviet tanks against enemy bullets by shielding them with an outer layer of hard steel separated from a cast-iron inner layer—on the theory that bullets would ricochet harmlessly off the inner layer after spending their main force penetrating the outer one. Given the floor, Nikolaev said that under his plan armor would be "active" rather than "passive" in that it would "protect while being destroyed." Stalin liked that. "Protects while being destroyed," he repeated after Nikolaev. "Interesting. Here's the dialectic in action." Then he asked for the assembled experts' views. None dared register the objections, and the useless idea was approved.[22]

Stalin made his most notorious intervention into scientific life by supporting an upstart plant breeder, Trofim Lysenko, in a series of sensational projects to make agriculture flourish, which came to nothing, and a crusade to destroy the science of genetics, which succeeded. Lacking in scientific biological education, the peasant-born Lysenko knew old peasant recipes and was gifted at self-promotion. In 1929 he announced that he could dramatically raise crop yields by "vernalization," a process of soaking and chilling seed, especially winter wheat.[23] As mass collectivization went forward, followed by crisis and famine, the Soviet press was hungry for hopeful news about food prospects, and Lysenko came into prominence in the early 1930s. He also received support from the world-renowned leader of Soviet biology and agronomy, Academician Nikolai Vavilov, who headed the Lenin Academy of Agricultural Sciences and the Institute of Genetics. Science was under heavy pressure then for practical achievements, and in 1931 Vavilov had many packets of diverse plant seeds sent to Odessa, where Lysenko was working, to be tested by vernalization. Around that time Lysenko found an invaluable confederate in an opportunist philosopher named Isai Prezent, who provided him with a theoretical platform in so-called "progressive biology," meaning Lamarck's theory of inheritance of acquired characteristics. "Creative Darwinism," he also called it, and later "Michurinist Darwinism" in tribute to the native Russian plant breeder Ivan Michurin, who died in 1935.[24]

Testing of vernalization produced no positive results, and some leading scientists began to criticize Lysenko because his position violated
elementary genetic principles. When Vavilov gently tried to bring his
young protégé around, that only aroused his ire. Then came the watershed
event in Lysenko's life. In February 1935, a few weeks after Kirov's
slaying and the start of the quiet terror, he got the chance to speak at a
Kremlin meeting of *kolkhoz* shock workers with Soviet leaders, Stalin
among them. After touting his achievements, he spoke of a class war "on
the vernalization front" where his scientific opponents were acting as
wreckers. As he went on in this way, Stalin was unable to contain himself.
He rose from his seat at the dais, applauded, and shouted, "Bravo, Comrade Lysenko, bravo!"[25] From then on the young charlatan was a favorite
of Stalin's. Apart from being susceptible to Lysenko's flattery and pleased
by his evident eagerness to assist the developing Terror, Stalin must have
been drawn to him by the practical bent of his work. A "people's academician," as the press had dubbed Lysenko, and one who promised to
produce big practical results in agriculture, was very welcome.

Lack of positive results from testing of vernalization did not stop
Lysenko. When one of his sensational schemes to revolutionize agriculture
failed to pay off, he would divert attention from the failure by coming up
with a flashy new one. Naturally, he encountered opposition from respectable professional scientists in the field. At the end of 1935, when he had
another chance to speak out in Stalin's presence, he intensified his accusation that some people were nefariously interfering with his efforts to
bring benefits to Soviet agriculture. Sitting at the dais with Stalin, Ya.
Yakovlev, until recently Commissar of Agriculture (he would be shot in
1938), interrupted him by asking: "Whom exactly are you referring to,
why no names?" Lysenko answered with several names, first among them
Vavilov's.[26] Next day he was awarded the first of his eight orders of Lenin.

Portentous as it was, that event did not end the struggle. Some agron-
omists of integrity, led by Vavilov, fought a losing battle for the continued
existence of genetics. The Lysenkoites were borne aloft on the great wave
of terror that followed the February–March plenum of 1937. Lysenko and
Prezent used themes in Stalin's major plenum speech to stigmatize their
scientific foes as enemies of the people. Geneticists began disappearing
into prison. By early 1938 Lysenko was in administrative command as
president of the Lenin Academy of Agricultural Sciences, from whose
presidency Vavilov had been removed in 1935, and his followers were
taking over key posts in all related scientific institutions. He was on his
way to the total pogrom of genetics that he would carry through in 1948
with Stalin's blessing.

Conformism was a hallmark of the scripted culture of administrative *diktat.* Creative originality was fettered and a reign of mediocrity prevailed. Whether at public meetings or in books and plays, or even in small gatherings (in which, people knew, an NKVD informant might be present), one spoke as one knew one should. People became what it was dangerous not to become—textualists repeating ideas that they knew were orthodox and safe because they had a seal of Stalinist approval.

To what an extent the Stalinist culture was scripted may be shown by an example. As a professor recalled at a much later time, the following scene occurred in an oral examination on party history at Moscow University. "How does our party stand?" came the question. "The party stands unshakably, firmly, confidently," answered the student. "Wrong," the examiner said. "You don't know the *Short Course*—our party stands 'like a promontory'."[27]

Stalinist cultural scripts took on retrospective force. As Orwell's totalitarian world came alive in the *Short Course* transformation of eminent revolutionaries into unpersons or worse, so comparable processes went on in other fields of culture. Thus, after Stalin declared in 1935 that Mayakovsky was "the best and most talented poet of our Soviet epoch," it turned out that he *always had been* the best and most talented, and that those who had said critical things about him before Big Brother delivered his dictum, be they RAPPists like Averbakh or critics like A. Voronsky, *had therefore always been* enemies of the people.

There were a few brave souls who defied Stalin's cultural *diktat* in the face of death. One was the non-Communist Vavilov. In 1940, when his portrait disappeared from the Moscow Agricultural Exhibition's section on the work of his All-Union Institute of Plant Breeding, he said: "What can you do? Evidently, I'll have to go to the cross."[28] Arrested on 6 August of that year, he refused under torture to confess to charges of involvement in an anti-Soviet conspiracy and received the death penalty. It was commuted in 1942 to twenty years of confinement, and in 1943 he died of exhaustion in Saratov's prison.

Another unbreakable one was Meyerhold. After his theater was closed and its troupe scattered to other theaters, he was unemployed. Then the aged Stanislavsky, his one-time teacher, courageously offered him work. Explaining that he was no longer in control of his Art Theater, he offered to employ Meyerhold as a producer in his small opera studio. But the Committee on Art Affairs, now purged of Kerzhentsev and his team for having tolerated Meyerhold for too long, would not approve this appointment. Then Stanislavsky took the disgraced man on as a teacher in the studio. There he worked for several months. Stanislavsky died in August 1938. In June 1939 Meyerhold was given a chance to recant his formalist sins at an all-union conference of theater directors organized by the Committee on Art Affairs. When his turn came to speak on the second day of the conference, the audience, which included Juri Jelagin, warmly applauded him.

A small, gray-haired man, he spoke haltingly at first, then took fire. He admitted guilt for not having done more to discourage the "Meyerhold mania" of would-be imitators who distorted his artistic method in their efforts to apply it, and allowed that there was some truth in the charge that he had experimented unduly with some Russian classic plays. But he would not confess to formalism. A master, he said, must have the right to express his creative individualism experimentally. And why should this be called "formalism"? Putting the question in reverse, Meyerhold went on:

What is socialist realism? Apparently socialist realism is orthodox antiformalism. I would like to consider this question in practical rather than theoretical terms. How would you describe the present trend in the Soviet theater? Here I have to be frank: if what has happened recently in the Soviet theater is antiformalism. . . , I prefer to be considered a formalist. I, for one, find the work of our theaters at present pitiful and terrifying. This pitiful and sterile something that aspires to the title of socialist realism has nothing in common with art. . . . Go to the Moscow theaters and look at the colorless, boring productions which are all alike and differ only in their degree of worthlessness. . . . In your effort to eradicate formalism, you have destroyed art![29]

Meyerhold was arrested a few days later. Shortly thereafter Zinaida Raikh was found murdered in her apartment, with seventeen knife wounds. Very likely someone high up in authority preferred the appearance of a criminal attack to arrest in her case. What happened to Meyerhold came out a half-century later. His chief interrogator was the bestial, bird-brained Boris Rodos. On 13 January 1940, having given in at last, Meyerhold wrote a long letter to Vyshinsky, with a copy to Molotov, detailing the ghastly tortures to which the degenerate had subjected him in order to extract the needed confession of treasonable guilt. Three weeks later, he was shot.[30]

Heroes and Their Deeds

Stalinist culture had thematic content. Its master theme was heroism in struggle for the right cause against all obstacles, ranging from natural forces to villainous opposition from hostile political forces. The culture's centerpiece, the supreme hero, was Stalin.

Heroism was not, to be sure, a new Soviet theme in Stalin's time.

Eisenstein's *Potemkin* had a collective hero in the battleship's mutinous sailors, and other early Soviet films focused on the mass as hero. Lenin as hero of Russian and world revolution was salient in the cult of him that arose when he died. Such classic novels as D. Furmanov's *Chapayev* (1923) and Fadeev's *The Rout* (1927) featured hero-types in the dashing Civil War guerrilla leader Chapayev and the more complex Civil War commander Levinson.

The mass as hero made a comeback in literature of the *piatiletka*. It featured "little men," in Gorky's phrase, as the nuts and bolts of a great machine—society—that had the party as, in the title of a novel of 1931, its "driving axel."[31] Then high Stalinist culture brought individual heroes into their own. Zhdanov pronounced the watchword—"heroization"—in his directive speech on socialist realism at the First Congress of Soviet Writers in 1934. He called for a literature of revolutionary romanticism that would depict "reality in its revolutionary development" toward the great goal of communism, and said: *"Soviet literature should be able to portray our heroes; it should be able to glimpse our tomorrow."*[32]

By chance a useful exemplar of the individual hero was at hand in 1934 in the Pavel Korchagin of Ostrovsky's earlier written novel. Its subject was Pavel's tempering as steel in the Civil War, then in economic construction, and finally in the resolute effort to be of use as a propagandist and writer as he lies blind and dying. No "living person" in RAPP's sense of a mixture of positive and negative traits, Pavel is one-dimensionally heroic. He is an ideal enthusiast of the Revolution with no other life than one of faith in the party for whose cause he fights to the very end, when news comes that his manuscript has been accepted for publication. Some critical reviews published when the novel's first part came out in 1932 gave way to uncritical acclaim of the story after 1934 as emblematic of socialist realism.

But in one respect *How the Steel Was Tempered* fell short of fulfilling the socialist realist canon: it was not Stalin-centered in the way that came to characterize products of high Stalinist culture. Another novel of 1934, Yakov Ilin's *The Big Conveyor Belt,* shows this difference. It has as one of its heroes a tractor plant executive, Ignatov, who is depressed by failure to get production going after the plant is built and, in despair, submits his resignation. But then he attends a Kremlin conference of economic executives at which Stalin explains the causes of current difficulties and how to overcome them. Transfixed, Ignatov rushes over to Ordzhonikidze and says: "Send me where you will!" The *vozhd'* has illumined the road ahead, and his listeners go off inspired to follow it in their further work.

In high Stalinist culture, heroes had a leader and teacher, a higher hero: Stalin. There was a hierarchy of hero cults with Stalin's, or Lenin-

Stalin's, at the apex. Below the apex were cults of deceased leaders like Sverdlov, Dzerzhinsky, and Kirov, and then small cults of living comrades of Stalin, notably Voroshilov. Below these were the much publicized heroes from the common folk: labor heroes and heroines like Stakhanov and Maria Demchenko, heroic Polar explorers like Otto Schmidt and his fellow survivors of the Cheliuskin expedition, Stalinist falcons like Chkalov who set new world records for long-distance flights, heroic scalers of heretofore unclimbed mountain peaks, and others.

For the stereotypical hero and heroine of this literature, Stalin was a talismanic figure: a far-seeing leader, an omniscient teacher, and a paternal love-object. As Stakhanov recalled in a (doubtlessly ghost-written) memoir of the Kremlin meeting of Stakhanovites addressed by Stalin, "I could not take my eyes off him" and I "felt a great need to get closer to him."[33] Stalin was in the hearts and minds of airmen heroes as they flew their dangerous missions. He inspired workers and collective farmers to new feats on the labor front. His publicized salutations were treasured by them. He was the hero of heroes. And the young generation was socialized into the hero-minded culture by being offered as a subject for school compositions: "In life there is always a place for heroism."[34]

As befitted the figure at the apex of the hero pyramid, Stalin—along with the mummified Lenin down below—came now into the zenith of scripted glory. The heroism of this fearful man, who lived in elaborately guarded isolation from the populace lest he expose himself to the slightest risk of mishap, became a dominant cultural motif. Newspaper articles, public lectures, pamphlets, plays, films, novels, poems, songs, paintings, and works of sculpture fashioned a fictional Stalin whose revolutionary precocity, daring, courage, fearlessness in struggle, comradeship with Lenin, Marxist foresight, genius as a political leader, and lofty moral stature were transmitted to the Soviet peoples and reflected back to the man.

In Stalinist culture, Stalin covered himself with glory in 1917. Lenin remained at the most the other hero, and dependent on Stalin in being even that. Such, as already noted, was the case in the film *Lenin in October*. So, too, in N. Pogodin's play *Man With a Gun*, produced in 1937. But nothing is more striking in the fabrication of a legendary Stalin in October than writings and paintings telling how a Stalin led Bolshevik center organized the October coup. What Stalin did at that decisive historical moment, other than write articles for *Pravda*, is unknown. The center came alive, however, not only in the *Short Course* but also in paintings that showed its members (minus the terror victim Bubnov, the others having survived politically by virtue of dying before the 1930s) listening intently to their inspired leader, Stalin, giving instructions on what was to be done. Of such pictorial socialist realism Trotsky commented from abroad that the "realism" lay in imitating provincial daguerreotypes of the third quarter of the nineteenth century and the "socialist" in showing events that never happened.[35]

The cult of heroism found a further favorite subject in Stalin as the Revolution's savior in the Civil War. The "workers' count" Alexei Tolstoy—older now, balding, corpulent, alcoholic, living aristocratically with a charming, svelte, smartly dressed (in foreign clothes) twenty-eight-year-old third wife named Liudmilla, and cynical as ever—produced prodigious falsifications of Civil War history in two works: the story *Bread* (1937) and a play, *Road to Victory*.[36] *Bread* portrayed Stalin as a calm, cool, superbly efficient political commissar who took over a disorganized Red-held Tsaritsyn and masterminded its defense, with Voroshilov's Tenth Army, as a result of which grain—hence bread—flowed to the heartland of Russia and saved Lenin's revolution. *Road to Victory* was about the intervention by fourteen states in Russia's Civil War and the heroic part Stalin played in its repulse. In these and other Civil War plays and novels, including Vsevolod Ivanov's *Parkhomenko* (1938), Stalin plays his role as co-organizer of victory with Lenin, thwarting Trotsky's traitorous designs to sabotage the war effort that he was officially supposed to be directing.

Of all Stalin's hero-roles, none was more prominent than that of Builder of Socialism after Lenin died. His private hero-script of out-Lenining Lenin as the architect of a new October found manifold expression in the arts.

In a long lyrical poem about collectivization, *The Land of Muravia* (1936), the then young writer Alexander Tvardovsky, himself the son of a "dekulakized" peasant in the Smolensk region and a future influential literary truth-teller about Stalin's time, portrayed Stalin as a legendary figure who, according to rumor in a hundred thousand villages in that time of turmoil and strife, rode through the countryside on a jet-black horse:

> Past lakes, through hills and woods and fields
> Along the road he rides
> In his grey trenchcoat with his pipe.
> Straight on his horse he guides
>
> He stops and speaks
> To peasantfolk
> Throughout the countryside
> And making necessary notes,
> Goes on about his ride.[37]

Socialist realism directed the arts to depict reality in its revolutionary development, portraying "our heroes" and giving glimpses of "our tomorrow." The exiled writer Andrei Sinyavsky has interpreted this as a teleological cultural canon prescribing that Soviet reality be portrayed in its movement toward a Purpose, future communism.[38] But his otherwise insightful essay fails to highlight the focus of the scripted culture on the historical present, on yesterday and today in its very depiction of movement toward the future Purpose.

Since culture could not show Stalin in his heroic dimension as Builder of Socialism unless socialism had basically been created, the central theme was not the Soviet Union on the way to the future communist utopia but the USSR as the land of socialism realized—and still enroute to communism under Stalin's leadership. The task of culture was to idealize the existing system, to depict the Soviet situation in an idyllic light, to fabricate a present utopia. Thus a poem produced in 1938 by the Belorussian poet Petrusia Brovka told the story of a former poor woman farm laborer, Katerina, who becomes a celebrity due to the *kolkhoz* system. Having shown herself a model worker on the collective-farm fields, Katerina is delegated to attend a Kremlin conference where she sees the great *vozhd'* surrounded by loving people, tells in her speech how "the *kolkhoz* land is flourishing," and addresses words of ardent gratitude to Comrade Stalin.[39]

In place of what actually existed—a still industrializing country with very many workers living in privation, a peasantry in a new enserfment, a huge caste of slave laborers in concentration camps, a privileged service nobility living in relative luxury minus security of tenure, a similarly insecure court circle at the top functioning at the pleasure of a new tsar-autocrat, a heavily terrorized society honeycombed with police informers, in which an overheard careless word or anecdote was a potential ticket to hell—Stalinist culture depicted a democratic Soviet Russia whose nonantagonistic classes of workers and peasants and intelligentsia "stratum" lived in amity, a socialist Russia moving toward the further stage of full communism under an adored Stalin's leadership.

The autocrat himself, living a highly secluded life in the care of his police guards and in the company of reliably compliant subordinates, needed to believe in the reality of this other world. This we have from one of those subordinates, Khrushchev, who spoke from personal memory when he informed the Twentieth Party Congress that Stalin, never traveling anywhere in the provinces and speaking with workers or collective farmers, "knew the country and agriculture only from films. And these films had dressed up and beautified the existing situation in agriculture. Many films so pictured *kolkhoz* life that the tables were bending from the weight of turkeys and geese. Evidently, Stalin thought that it was actually so."[40] How else could he be the hero-builder of socialism if a socialist Russia had not emerged under his leadership?

The Hero-Nation: Russia

In January 1937 the Russian Soviet Federated Socialist Republic adopted its republican version of the all-union Stalin Constitution enacted the previous year. Editorializing on the occasion, *Pravda* wrote that the RSFSR was "the first among equal republics in the Soviet family." With a population of 105 million, its territory stretched from the Baltic to the Pacific. *Pravda* went on:

Russian culture enriches the culture of the other peoples. The Russian language has become the language of world revolution. Lenin wrote in Russian. Stalin writes in Russian. Russian culture has become international, for it is the most advanced, most humane. Leninism is its offspring, the Stalin Constitution its expression![41]

Such was a typical manifestation of an official cult of Russia as a hero-nation that was by then in full flower. The multinational Soviet people was a hero-people in Stalinist culture, but Great Russia, the hero-nation, was first among equals in the family.

Stalin had given an impetus to the glorifying of Russia by calling in 1934 for a new history text for Soviet schools. In 1937 a jury chaired by Zhdanov ruled in favor of Shestakov's entry. The jury's ruling was prefaced with a sketch of the Stalin school of Russian historical thought in the form of lengthy comments on defects of the entries. In dealing with pre-1917 history, various authors had overlooked the progressive impact of the coming of Christianity via the then higher Byzantine culture; had treated the annexation of Georgia and the Ukraine to Russia as an absolute evil, whereas in fact it was the "lesser evil" since for Georgia a Russian protectorate was the only alternative to being swallowed up by Persia and Turkey and for the Ukraine it was the only alternative to being swallowed up by Poland and Turkey; and hadn't correctly assessed the historical significance of the battle on the ice of Lake Chud in 1242 when the Novgorod forces under Alexander Nevsky defeated the Teutonic Knights, who threatened to destroy the peoples they conquered. Finally, some authors had idealized such reactionary movements as the *Streltsy* rebellion against Peter's efforts to civilize the Russia of his time.[42]

This decree expressed Stalin's chauvinistic version of Russian national Bolshevism and desire to exalt the forgers of Russian statehood whom he saw as his and Lenin's precursors. In Shestakov's *Short History,* issued in 1937 as the mandatory textbook for classes three and four in Soviet schools, the children were introduced to a glorification of the Russian state and a long line of its heroic figures from Prince Vladimir of Kiev, who adopted Christianity in 988, to "the great Stalin, leader of the peoples."[43]

The new reverence for Russia's past brought a revolution from above in folklore studies. In the 1920s Soviet folklorists had generally subscribed to a theory of the aristocratic origin of the medieval Russian epic songs *(byliny)*. It held that the tsar-glorifying national folklore reflected a ruling-class ideology, aroused sick fantasies in children, and must be eradicated. Now came a radical change.[44] Gorky's discussion of folklore as folk wisdom, in his address to the Writers' Congress in 1934, was an advance sign of it. Meanwhile, not understanding what was afoot, Demyan Bedny prepared for Moscow's Kamerny Theater the libretto of a comic opera *Bogatyrs (The Epic Heroes)*. He portrayed these characters of Russian legend as drunkards and cowards. The robber outlaws mentioned in the epic songs he depicted as Robin-Hood-like revolutionary elements on the people's side. Prince Vladimir's adoption of Christianity in the tenth century, by leading the people of Kiev into the Dnieper River for a mass baptism in the dead of winter, was ridiculed as an episode in a drunken debauch.

When *Bogatyrs* was approved for showing in November 1936 by Kerzhentsev's Committee on Art Affairs, Molotov came to the opening night's performance—and left fuming after the first act: "An outrage! The *bogatyrs* were great people!"[45] Kerzhentsev himself had to castigate the Kamerny Theater and Bedny, who was thereupon evicted from his Kremlin apartment and expelled from the Writers' Union. The epic heros, Kerzhentsev wrote, were of popular, not aristocratic origin. As leaders of Russia's resistance to Asian invaders like the Tatars, they were dear to Bolsheviks as embodiments of the Russian people's heroic qualities in the distant past. As for the Christianization of *Rus'*, Vladimir was baptized two years before the mass winter event. The adoption of Christianity was progressive because it served Russia's rapproachement with Byzantium and other countries of higher culture, and the priesthood fostered the spread of literacy and learning in the Kievan state. Having once called Russia's history "rotten" and pictured the Russian people asleep on the oven-shelf, Bedny was now guilty of a light-minded, anti-Marxist falsification of the people's past.[46]

Folklore was more than restored; it was created anew. Stalin and Lenin became subjects of old-style new songs *(noviny)* represented as popular in origin. Marfa Kriukova, a talented folk-singer from the far north, was sent with an editor-assistant on a trip to Stalin's Georgian homeland. The resulting "folksong" pictured him walking around in the Kremlin like Vladimir of old:

> Stalin began walking in the middle of the hall,
> Waving his white hands about,

> Shaking his black curls,
> And he thought a mighty thought.
> He summoned his friends and companions. . . .

Kriukova and her helper also composed a "Lay of Lenin" in which Trotsky's treason hastens the ill Lenin's death, Lenin relies on Stalin to destroy the Revolution's enemies, and Stalin in conclusion gives his vow of loyalty to the dead leader.[47] So the fighting friendship of the two Bolshevik *bogatyrs* was celebrated in pseudofolklore.

While the new history text was being written in 1936, press articles anticipated its strident Russian nationalism by glorifying Russia as a hero-nation. One savaged Bukharin for publishing in *Izvestiia* on 21 January 1936, the twelfth anniversary of Lenin's death, an article in praise of Lenin and the Revolution for having transformed "a nation of Oblomovs" into the advanced society of the present. With citations from Stalin to back up its counterargument, the editorial said that Bukharin's image of old Russia as a land of lazy Oblomovs was "stupid, harmful, reactionary claptrap."[48]

The heroism of the Russian nation as embodied in its fighting men led by Prince Alexander Nevsky was the theme of Eisenstein's film, for which Prokofiev wrote the musical score. In one of his statements about it, Eisenstein hinted at a parallel between the noble Nevsky, who rallied the Novgorodians to defeat the invading Teutonic Knights in 1242 on the ice of Lake Chud, and Stalin.[49] The film ended with Nevsky saying to some freed German commanders: "Go and tell everyone in foreign parts that *Rus'* lives. Let them come to us as guests without fear. But anyone who comes to us with a sword will perish by the sword. On this the Russian land stands and will stand!"

A classical Russian opera about heroism, Glinka's *Life for the Tsar,* was revived by the Bolshoi Theater in 1939 as *Ivan Susanin* (Glinka's original title), the name of the Russian peasant who, in the opera as shown before 1917, sacrifices his life in order to save the young Tsar Mikhail from capture by the Poles during the Time of Troubles. He does so by leading the Polish army in winter into a deep forest near Smolensk from which there is no escape. In the new, Stalinist version, Susanin saved not the tsar but Moscow. The hero-leaders of the popular uprising against the Polish invaders were Kozma Minin and Prince Pozharsky. In the final scene the victorious peasant insurgents of the anti-Polish resistance receive a heroes' welcome from the milling, colorful crowd as they march into Red Square to a swelling chorus of "Glory, Glory!" and then, as bells ring and orchestras play, Minin and Pozharsky ride onto the scene on horseback. As *Pravda*'s review described the finale, "This is the moment when the spectators and players merge and it seems that one huge heart beats in the hall. The people salutes its heroic past, its knights, its fearless *bogatyrs*.

A marvelous, unforgettable moment." By his daughter's testimony, Stalin was fond of *Susanin* but only for the sake of the scene in the forest, after which he would go home.[50]

These art works doubtless served, in Stalin's mind, to prepare the populace to fight hostile foreign forces in the war that he hoped would come at a time of his choosing. Their subtext was the readiness of the people to fight foreign foes again. If, with the help of the Russian people, Nevsky had defeated the Germans, Minin and Pozharsky the Poles, and Kutuzov the French, a no longer backward Soviet Russia would surely crush any foreign forces that might try to administer her a beating. The patriotic theme in the presentation of Russia's past mingled with an anti-foreign one.

Xenophobia was making itself felt in the scripted culture of Russian national self-glorification. In mid-1936, as the campaign of denunciations developed, some Soviet scientists, starting with a prominent mathematician, N. Luzin, were denounced for sending their writings abroad before publishing them at home. *Pravda* took up the theme editorially. It condemned "traditions of servility" toward the West handed down from tsarist times when an aristocratic nobility spurned the Russian language, despised the Russian people, and thought "the light of science comes only from the West, only from foreigners." And now, when Soviet Russia had an advanced science, some members of its scientific community (names given) still considered it natural and normal to publish their writings initially or only abroad. Such a situation was intolerable. *"The Soviet Union is not Mexico, not some Uruguay, but a great socialist power."*[51] Hastily convened meetings in Academy of Science institutes condemned Academician Luzin and others as "enemies in Soviet mask" for "a sort of wrecking in science" shown in sending writings for initial publication abroad.[52]

Perhaps for fear of disrupting important scientific work, someone high up soon curbed this campaign and scientists like Luzin did not disappear into prison. Neither, however, did the xenophobic theme disappear. Lysenko and his followers began stigmatizing the genetics that they wanted to purge from Soviet science for being derivative from the work of foreign founders of the field: Gregor Mendel, August Weissman, and T. H. Morgan. Not until the successful culmination of their efforts in 1948 did such epithets as "Weissmanism-Mendelsim" become common currency. But already in 1939 Lysenko was saying that "it is time to eliminate Mendelism in all its varieties from all courses and textbooks."[53] This was a foretaste of the extremes of official xenophobia that the scripted culture featured in the postwar 1940s.

As glorification of the hero-nation's past took over in the later 1930s, the non-Marxist prerevolutionary five-volume *Course of Russian History* by Kliuchevsky was republished. A favorable review praised his vivid portraits of Russian rulers from early times to the eighteenth century and chided him only for seeing in Ivan's *oprichnina* "a higher police for affairs of treason" rather than appreciating its progressive role in history.[54] Meanwhile, Pokrovsky and his non-Russian-nationalist historiography were fiercely denounced. Pokrovsky's death of cancer in 1932 may have saved him from a worse fate. Had he lived into the later 1930s he would have found that he had served the purposes of "Trotskyist wreckers" by, for example, deleting from history the "just wars" that the Russian and other now Soviet peoples had waged in the past. And historians of his school who now fell victim to the Terror were vilified as enemies of the people. Thus the writer of a book on modern European diplomatic history that saw the Franco-Russian alliance of 1896 as having been a provocative act toward Bismarck's empire (hence, by suggestion, the Franco-Soviet treaty as provocative toward the Third Reich) became "the Trotskyist terrorist, Ts. Fridliand."[55]

Against M. N. Pokrovsky's Conception of History, a two-volume collection of essays issued in 1938, flayed Pokrovsky for heinous "errors," among them: he did not see that Muscovy's gathering of Russian lands and the emergence of the autocratic system were progressive; failed to note that the Russians were justified in starting the Livonian war in 1558; forgot to explain that the victory of the German forces over the Russians in the battle at Nevel in 1563 was due to Kurbsky's treason; didn't see that the Russian people waged a heroic just war of liberation against the Poles and deprecated the parts that Minin and Pozharsky played in it. Further, he denied the progressive significance of Peter I's activities; laid responsibility for the Fatherland War of 1812 not on Napoleon but on Russian commercial capital; cast slurs on the great Russian strategist Kutuzov; slandered the Russian peasantry by saying it rose up against the French "for its chickens and geese"; tried to justify Japanese imperialism in the Russo-Japanese war of 1904–5 and denied the Russian soldiers' heroism in defending Port Arthur and in other battles of that war.[56] This catalogue of Pokrovsky's errors was, in reverse, a catalogue of many of the Stalin school's Russian nationalist positions.

Enemies and Their Deeds

"A harmful play. Pacifist. I. V. Stalin." So read Stalin's comment inscribed on a copy of a play, *When I'm Alone,* whose hero, a Soviet intellectual, despaired over backbiting and fighting among people around him. Mikhail Kozakov, the play's author, thereupon fell into disfavor.[57]

Stalin's use of "pacifist" as an epithet tells the story. His element was fighting, struggle against enemies, and vindictive triumph over them. In his real political life the cast of enemies was ever changing. As some went down to defeat and in many cases death, there always were new ones to take their places. And as in real political life, so in the make-believe world of Stalinist culture. It was peopled with enemies against whom heroes fought in the never-ending drama of *Kto—kogo?* The fictional enemy remained always the main character along with the fictional hero. Sometimes the fictional or fictionalized enemy would defeat a fictional or fictionalized hero, for example a little hero Pavlik Morozov or a great hero Kirov. But always another fictional or fictionalized hero, at appropriate times the fictionalized Stalin, would bring the enemies down to defeat and mete out merited punishment to them. No less than the hero image, the enemy image was a focal theme of the culture scripted.

The villains who murdered Pavlik Morozov appeared in the story as told and retold at the Terror's height. And there were variations on its theme. One was *The Wonderful Pioneer Gena Shchukin,* issued in 1938 in 50,000 copies for young people. Gena lives in a remote Siberian village near gold mines that are targets of Trotskyist wreckers. They sabotage mining machinery and also motor transport in order to stop shipment of food and equipment to the mines. Unknown to anyone, Gena's foster-father Akimov is a Trotskyist wrecker in whose apartment the other Trotskyists often gather to plan their operations. Gena overhears them. Finally he informs on them, writing to his Uncle Petya that Akimov and his friends are enemies who ruin machines. Akimov murders the boy, but ultimately has to confess his crime when Uncle Petya forwards Gena's letter to the local authorities. He killed Gena, says Akimov, "because he was a Pioneer" and "knew a lot he shouldn't have." Akimov and his fellow enemies are put on trial. "So," concludes the story, "the little Bolshevik Gena, at the cost of his own heroic life, helped expose enemies.[58]

Assassination of another hero, in this case a fictionalized Kirov named Pyotr Shakhov, secretary of a regional party committee, was the subject of *The Great Citizen,* a Stalin-prize-winning movie of 1939. In the second part of this two-part film, Shakhov in 1934 falls victim to a Trotskyist murder plot whose ringleaders, a fictionalized Zinoviev and Kamenev, are former heads of the party organization later led by Shakhov. Another movie, *Honor,* released in 1938, showed enemy efforts to sabotage the railroaders' movement in 1935 to improve their work indices.

The theme of one's own relatives as enemies of the people was elaborated in *The Stranger,* a play produced in 1938 by the Leningrad Soviet Theater in Moscow. The setting is a family of Stakhanovite workers in a plant in the provinces. Their son Nikolai and his wife unexpectedly arrive from Moscow after a twelve-year absence, because Nikolai has been dismissed from a high post and expelled from the party for links with enemies. Now he penetrates the local plant to commit an act of sabotage. But his relatives expose him. Seeking to save his own skin, Nikolai shoots his sister Galia and wounds his brother Misha before being arrested.

Another such play, *One's Own House,* by B. Romashov, should have pleased Stalin's distaste for "pacifism." In the play the secretary of the regional party committee says that it is the Communists' very love for people which compels them to be vigilant and fight for people's happiness against the villainy that will long still get in the way of this happiness. And the engineer hero, Bulygin, complains that not everyone realizes that there is a war on. A leader in this war is a secret wrecker, factory director Shatov, a former Trotskyist who has concealed this fact. He and fellow enemies light fires in lumber yards, cause accidents at power stations, wound two workers, and set off a factory explosion. The moral of the play is: "The enemy is cruel, foul, and crafty," and further: "We live in our new large Soviet house, work, enjoy life, make merry. And various characters wander around our house trying to blow it up."[59]

In Magnitogorsk in the later 1930s John Scott went to see a play about enemies, *The Face-to-Face Confrontation.* Its action began in a spy school in a country that was obviously Germany, where a master spy named Walter was ready to be sent into the Soviet Union as Ivan Ivanovich Ivanov. Scott noted that most of the people in the audience were sitting on the edge of their seats, and the tension in the theater was contagious. Then the scene shifted to Moscow where Walter is committing foul deeds, such as murdering a girl who, he fears, might betray him. He pushes her under the wheels of a train. Meanwhile, various Soviet citizens, their suspicions aroused, inform the authorities. Caught at last, Walter and his still functioning predecessor-spy, Keller, are brought together in a face-to-face confrontation in the office of the interrogator, who, using each's testimony against the other, brings them both to confess. Walter-Ivanov pleads for mercy, but Keller is defiant to the end, saying: "The decisive battle is ahead of us. I will be shot, but you will go down to defeat." To which the interrogator replies, "We will be the victors." The curtain fell amid wild applause,[60] which suggests that the new nationalism was evoking a strong popular response. So successful was *Face-to-Face Confrontation* that a movie version was made, entitled *Engineer Kochin's Error.* It came on Soviet screens in late 1939, after Stalin concluded his pact with Hitler, and omitted the German setting of the opening scenes in the play version.

Another instance of the need to revise the enemy image in order to keep up with political events may be seen in Fyodor Panfyorov's long novel *And Then the Harvest (Bruski).* The subject was collectivization in a Volga region village. The novel came out in four volumes over a decade, 1928–37. In volume 3, Panfyorov depicted as masked enemies some characters who had figured as positive in volume 2. Moreover, he then revised volume 2, altering characterizations of some of these characters to prepare the reader for their exposure as enemies in volume 3.[61]

In the hero and enemy images we may discern elements of culture's dictator himself. The hero image contains features of the ideal Stalin that he needed to believe was real, to have affirmed by fellow citizens and reflected in culture. And in the enemy image we see features of his hated Stalin—of the duplicity, the conspiratorial behavior, the dissimulation, the craftiness, and the callous cruelty that he displayed in real life but could only admit into consciousness as attributes of others on whom they were projected—enemies.

In addition to appearing in stories, novels, plays, and films offered to the public as works of culture, the image of the enemy appeared in the press as ostensible truth about real people. The pressure from above to denounce produced, as we have seen, a countrywide wave of denunciations. Once under arrest, people were pressured or tortured by their interrogators into producing, with their help, fictional confessions of guilt for antistate crimes they had not committed. The records of their mythical misdeeds and motives comprised a huge mass of material that history must consider a vital component of Stalinist culture as a culture of enemy-invention. Strangely, Beria and other police bosses saw it so themselves. On trial after Stalin died, they called the protocols of interrogations by the likes of Rodos "true works of art."[62]

Examples of such torture-produced art have come to light. Rodos made Meyerhold confess that he was a British and Japanese spy and a Trotskyist from 1923, engaged in subverting theatrical art on orders from Rykov, Bukharin, and Tomsky, and in 1936 was recruited into a Trotskyist organization by Ilya Ehrenburg (who was never arrested). Kol'tsov, according to the confession that he repudiated in his twenty-minute hearing before Ulrikh on the ground that he signed it only after terrible tortures, was an agent of the German, French, and American intelligence services. Babel, who was taken on 16 May 1939, after Yezhov's arrest, confessed that he had been "organizationally linked" with Yezhov's wife in conspiratorial acts against Soviet leaders, that Ehrenburg had recruited him into a Trotskyist espionage group that transmitted secrets about military aircraft to the West via André Malraux and included, among others, the writers Leonid Leonov, Valentin Kataev, Vsevelod Ivanov, Lidiia Seifullina, and Vladimir Lidin, film directors Eisenstein and Aleksandrov, actors S. Mikhoels and A. Utesov, and Academician Otto Schmidt. On the records of each of these persons, all then still at large, there was some black mark from Stalin's standpoint that made it desirable for the police to have incriminating testimony against them ready for use at any moment when Stalin might want their arrest. Babel and Kol'tsov were executed in January 1940. Their relatives received word in the deadly euphemism: "Ten years in remote camps without right of correspondence."[63]

Even without the fictional confessions as documents, we can reconstruct from public denunciations the content of this secret Stalinist literature of cultural enemyhood. The first show trial, in which the drama critic Pickel was one of the cast of sixteen defendants, opened the floodgates of denunciation in the literary world. V. Stavsky, a peasant-born writer who by then was secretary of the Writers' Union board, lashed out at such wreckers in literature as A. Tarasov-Rodionov, author of the novel *Chocolate* (1922), and the critic A. Voronsky, editor of the literary journal *Red Virgin Soil* in 1921–27, who had sided with the Left opposition and then recanted. Voronsky's hostile actions included advocacy of "class peace" in literature. Instead of exposing kulaks as enemies, the writer should seek "the human being" in them, he had argued, whereas—said Stavsky—"no compassion and sniveling humanism can be shown toward enemies of socialism. To 'pity' a kulak, a speculator, a traitor, an enemy of the people, is to feel sorry for the wolf that will respond to the pity with fresh crimes and acts of treachery." Hence "the supreme act of humanism is the destruction of these vicious snakes dispatched by fascism into the land of socialism."[64] It was, in short, a hostile act for a writer to deny culture's need to propagate the image of the enemy.

Soon after Yagoda's arrest, a torrent of abuse, some with an anti-Semitic accent, rained down on his "now exposed" (that is, already arrested) brother-in-law Averbakh. As RAPP's ex-leader, he was an arch-traitor in the literary world, and so was publicly stripped of "the lying mask that hid the wicked face of an enemy." His earlier attacks on Trotsky were camouflage to cover up his continuing fidelity to Trotskyism. His later attacks on Mayakovsky were enemy actions. His wrecker literary theory, "Averbakhism," held that Soviet culture was still only proletarian, denying that it was already socialist. Its call to "remove any and all masks" was itself a masked appeal to artists to portray a nonsocialist Soviet reality. After RAPP's dissolution he had created a "parallel literary center" engaged in counterrevolutionary work in literature.[65]

The list of Averbakh's fellow wreckers in the "parallel center" was topped by the names of Kirshon, Afinogenov, and the Polish refugee (now "supposedly expelled from Poland") Bruno Iasenskii. Afinogenov saved himself from perdition in the only way open to him: by including a fierce denunciation of Averbakh and Averbakhism in an abject public confession of deep guilt for "sliding into the Trotskyist literary swamp."[66] Kirshon and Iasenskii disappeared in 1937. It bears mention that both were fervently antifascist in their writing. Kirshon wrote his last play, *The Big Day,* in 1936. The big day was that on which an enemy state—transparently Nazi Germany—invades the Soviet Union without declaring war, whereupon twenty-six million people immediately volunteer for army service and Soviet airmen fly a daring mission into hostile territory where some are caught but conduct themselves heroically. This play received warm response when shown in Moscow, Leningrad, and Smolensk. But once Kirshon was under arrest, a critic found it to be a "false play" bearing a stamp of deadening RAPPist schematism and pseudopsychologism.[67] Iasenskii was arrested while in the midst of writing an antifascist novel set partly abroad, *Conspiracy of the Indifferent.*[68]

Another, comparable case involved the German Communist refugee writer Georg Born, who (like other prominent German antifascist writers then living in Moscow) "turned out to be a German spy." He had recently published in Russian an anti-Nazi novelette, *The Lone One and the Gestapo,* which told a tale of Gestapo terrorism abroad against the German antifascist emigration. Once Born had disappeared into prison, his ostensible antifascism was pictured as cunning cover for his fascism, his anti-Nazi novel as "the mask of a German spy." How else explain that it had nothing to say about how the Gestapo recruited spies like Born, and the Trotskyist aid that enabled German counterintelligence to penetrate the USSR?[69] Thus, masked internal enemy forces were represented as being in league with enemies abroad. Prone to seeing conspiracy everywhere, culture's dictator implanted this way of thinking in Stalinist culture.

The Shadow Culture

Mother Russia is resourceful. Even during Stalin's time some of her talented sons and daughters had the fortitude to go on in their creative ways. Working in secret from all but perhaps a family member or friend, they produced literature that only became known to the world long after most had died.

To realize what courage it took to confide thoughts about the Stalinist phenomenon to paper, we must note that the Terror struck the cultural world with hardly less fury than it did other sectors of society. Writers, including critics and literary scholars, were hit hardest of all in the creative arts. Such prominent figures as Pil'niak, Babel, Kirshon, Kol'tsov, Mandelstam, Pavel and Ivan Vasiliev, Ivan Kataev, Nikolai Erdman, Nikolai Zabolotsky, Alexander Voronsky, Alexei Gastev, Alexander Tarasov-Rodionov, Nikolai Kluyev, D. S. Mirsky, Alexander Zavalishin, Vasily Kni-

yazev, Sergei Tretyakov, Peter Dreshin, and Sergei Amaglobeli were only
the better known victims. Research by Eduard Beltov shows that in the
Stalin period as a whole, from the start of the 1930s to the 1950s, 1,000
writers were put to death and other 1,000 or so survived in captivity.[70] The
great majority of the 2,000 writer-victims would have been arrested between 1934 and 1940. Not even so loyal a Stalinist as Sholokhov was safe
in those days. In October 1938 he learned that the local NKVD authorities
in Veshenskaia District were torturing arrested acquaintances of his into
denouncing him as a counterrevolutionary, whereupon he went with friends
to Moscow, got an interview with Stalin, and received absolution.[71] His
case was an exception.

But the statistics of victimization cannot convey a full sense of what
it meant to be a writer of integrity in the later 1930s. Since so many writers
disappeared, those not arrested had to live in fear of that fate, a fear often
intensified by the disappearance of a loved one or a close friend and by
helpless concern for family members.

One contribution to the shadow culture is the diary of a classical
philologist, Olga Freidenberg, who studied and taught at the Leningrad
Institute of Philosophy, Language, Literature, and History and privately
corresponded over many years with her cousin, Pasternak, who lived in
Moscow. In 1932 the institute's new young director, Gorlovsky, persuaded her to organize its department of classical philology. At the outset
of 1935, as the quiet terror developed, he was dismissed, went to Moscow
to find out why, and didn't return. On 14 January 1935, the institute
newspaper responded to his disappearance with an editorial printed under
a large headline: DISCOVER PEOPLE'S THOUGHTS. Then began what
Freidenberg called in her diary "demagogic devastation" as students, chiefly
of working-class origin, intrigued against and informed on others, chiefly
of middle class origin. Soon after, disaster struck her.

Her doctoral thesis, which she defended in June 1935, came out as a
book, *Poetics of Plot and Genre,* in May 1936 and sold well for three
weeks, after which it was withdrawn from bookshops. The campaign
against "formalism" was then raging in the press. In September an *Izvestiia*
article, "Harmful Gibberish," attacked her book. She wrote in her diary:
"Oh, the news we were forever expecting in fear and trembling: News that
reached one by phone, that overtook one on the street, that came crashing
into one's home, that ripped off the door of every refuge: It is highly
improbable that anyone in the future will understand how terrible it was,
how sinister and ominous." Faculty friends urged her to admit minor errors
publicly so as to save the book, and warned that her failure to do so might
endanger them too. She wrote a letter to Stalin and kept silent about it.
Meanwhile, people avoided her on the street and friends stopped phoning.

Whispers and rumors about her abounded and she attended institute meetings where colleagues and students isolated her in a ring of empty chairs. Then came a summons to Moscow, a talk there with a deputy commissar of education (to whom her letter to Stalin had been given), and assurance from him that she need not worry. Back in Leningrad, people smiled and congratulated her. The atmosphere was transformed. Then it grew grim again when another hostile article appeared in *Izvestiia,* after which Pasternak wrote a letter in her defense to Bukharin who, however, was by then under house arrest. "No one who has not lived in the Stalin era can appreciate the horror of our uncertain position," she wrote in her diary. "A person's life was poisoned secretly, invisibly, as witches and sorcerers were hounded in the Dark Ages."

She was not arrested, but her brother Sasha was, in August 1937, a time when so many were under arrest that one had to wait in line in the street for days to reach the prison information window in quest of news. In January 1938 Sasha was sentenced to Siberia for five years "on suspicion of espionage," and the thought of him being there with only the summer clothes he was wearing when arrested nearly drove Olga mad. "All hope was gone," ran her diary entry. "Everyone knew the horrors of Stalin's camps and his so-called 'construction projects'—working in swamps up to the waist, beaten almost to death, broken bones, fractured skulls, freezing to death." Sasha never returned.

By encouraging denunciation of others as a patriotic act, Stalin and Stalinism not only bred mediocrity; they brought out the worst in people, their envy, animosity, and conspiratorial behavior. Freidenberg was especially struck by this when Stalin's 1950 pronouncements on linguistics upset what had long been orthodoxy in this field and caused havoc in all the humanities. She described in her diary the *skloka* (feuding) implanted in the culture of daily life. "Wherever you looked, in all our institutions, in all our homes, *skloka* was brewing," she wrote. "It stands for base, trivial hostility, unconscionable spite breeding petty intrigues, the vicious pitting of one clique against another. It thrives on calumny, informing, spying, scheming, slander, the igniting of base passions. . . . *Skloka* is the alpha and omega of our politics."[72]

Another contribution to the shadow culture is the novel *Sofia Petrovna,* written by Lidiia Chukovskaya in Leningrad in 1939–40. Sofia Petrovna Lipatova, an ordinary nonparty person, is widowed early in the 1930s and then takes a typist's job in a Leningrad publishing house to help her son Kolya get a higher education. One day he comes home from his high school with a story of how his best friend, Alik Finkelstein, was called a "Yid" by a loutish student named Pashka Gusev, after which the class decided to try Pashka before a "comrades' court" with Kolya as its "public prosecutor." Later Alik and Kolya are admitted to an engineering institute after passing entry exams with high marks. After a time they are sent as technicians to the Uralmash works in Sverdlovsk.

The Moscow trial of January 1937 brings home to Sofia Petrovna the huge dimensions of the conspiracy that has menaced the Soviet state. A sincere believer in Stalin, she is indignant at the traitors on trial who not only killed Kirov but wanted to murder Comrade Stalin and had agents who committed awful deeds like blowing up mines and causing train wrecks. Then her own institution finds in its midst enemies who have masqueraded as loyal citizens. They disappear, as does a respected Leningrad physician whom she has known. She finds it hard to believe that he or her director were enemies. One night in 1937, Alik comes from Sverdlovsk with the shocking news that Kolya is under arrest. In agony now, Sofia Petrovna joins a line of hundreds of other women awaiting their turn to get news of loved ones. A prosecutor informs her that her son has been sentenced to ten years in "far camps" for a terrorist act to which he has confessed. The horror deepens when Sofia Petrovna reads an article in the wall newspaper of her publishing house assailing her for having spoken up in defense of her close friend and coworker Natasha Frolenko, whose suspicious identity as an old-regime officer's daughter has come under public scrutiny. After work she goes to her apartment, where Natasha is waiting with the news that Alik has been arrested.

The last blow falls when she gets a letter sent by Kolya via an unknown acquaintance. He writes that he is innocent, that Pashka Gusev testified to having recruited him into a terrorist group, that his interrogator, Rudnev, beat him into signing a confession. He pleads with her to intercede quickly because "you can't survive here for long." She wants to write an appeal to higher authority based on the letter's facts, and rushes to the arrested physician's apartment for help. The physician's wife, who is about to be evicted and exiled, takes Sofia Petrovna into the kitchen, away from the room with the telephone that she knows is tapped, and says: "For your son's sake, don't write. . . . They forgot to evict you, but if you write the statement they'll remember to, and will send your son still farther away." Sofia Petrovna goes home, and keeps thinking of the line in the letter: "Mamochka, interrogator Rudnev beat me. . . ." Then, a still uncomprehending destroyed person, she puts a match to the letter and lets it singe her fingers as it burns.

This heartrending tale of how Stalin's Terror made life into hell for a legion of simple Sofia Petrovnas survived the war years in safe hands, and appeared in print abroad after Stalin died.[73] The author lived to see it published in the Soviet journal *Neva* in 1988.

Among the bereaved mothers in Leningrad was one of Russia's greatest poets, Anna Akhmatova, a close friend of Chukovskaya's. Her husband and fellow poet Nikolai Gumilev, who served as an officer in World War I, was shot in 1921 on false charges of participation in a monarchist plot against the Bolshevik regime. In the quiet terror of 1935 her son, Lev Gumilev, was arrested and sent to a camp, released a year or so later, then rearrested in 1938, not to be released until 1956. Between 1935 and 1940 Akhmatova produced one of the great works of the shadow culture, a set of poems called *Requiem* (also first published in Russia in 1988). Worth quoting in full is her "Instead of a Preface" to it:

In the terrible years of the *Yezhovshchina* I spent seventeen months waiting in line outside the prison in Leningrad. One day somebody in the crowd identified me. Standing behind me was a woman, with lips blue from the cold, who had, of course, never heard me called by name before. Now she started out of the torpor common to us all and asked in a whisper (everyone whispered there): "Can you describe this?" And I said: "I can." Then something like a smile passed fleetingly over what had once been her face.[74]

Not only could she describe it; in *The Requiem,* on which she was secretly at work when that exchange occurred, she did. The poems are about the time when

> The stars of death shone high above
> As innocent *Rus'* writhed
> Under bloody boots
> And the wheels of black ravens.

But *The Requiem*'s subject is not what we think of as the Terror: the denunciation meetings, the disappearances, the interrogations under torture, and the camp experience. They are about the mass of unarrested victims who had to live in their "empty house" (a phrase from one of the poems) after a loved one was taken, about the toll the Terror took on the spirit of those millions of mothers, wives, and children of loyal dutiful citizens who were arrested. So we read:

> I have learned how faces fall to bone,
> how under the eyelids terror lurks
> how suffering inscribes on cheeks
> the hard lines of its cuneiform texts,
> how glossy black or ash-fair locks
> turn overnight to tarnished silver,
> how smiles fade on submissive lips,
> and fear quavers in a dry titter.
> And I pray not for myself alone
> but for all who stood outside the jail,
> in bitter cold or summer's blaze,
> with me under that blind red wall.

And at the end the poet writes in one of the poems that if her country should ever set up a monument to her, she would want it to be placed not by the sea or in the tsar's gardens, but

> here, where I spent three hundred hours
> in line before the implacable iron bars.
> Because even in blessed death I fear
> to miss the rumbling of the black ravens
> and the old woman's howling like a wounded beast.

Akhmatova was a friend and confidante of Mandelstam, whose place of exile in 1935–37 was Voronezh. She visited the Mandelstams there in 1936 and in a poem, "Voronezh," gave testimony to the sense of doom with which Mandelstam lived then:

> And the town stands locked in ice:
> a paperweight of trees, walls, snow. . . .
> But in the room of the banished poet
> Fear and the Muse stand watch by turn,
> and the night is coming on,
> which has no hope of dawn.

Living there with his wife Nadezhda in a rented room, Mandelstam kept forming in his mind verses which Nadezhda copied out in notebooks, whence their later title *The Voronezh Notebooks*. A Voronezh school-teacher friend, Natalya Shtempel, kept copies through the war years and later turned them over to the widow, who had committed many to memory.

As the Terror bore down in early 1937, Mandelstam made a desperate effort to save, if not himself, then his wife by writing an Ode to Stalin. But being Mandelstam, his incapacity to produce hack work made even this bow to the tyrant, it has been argued, more poetically meaningful than the scripted panegyric literature of the time.[75] It may indeed have helped ensure his wife's survival, hence his poetry's, after his own arrest in 1938, followed at the end of that year by his death in a transit camp near Vladivostok. And the self-compelled writing of the Ode touched off in Mandelstam, in January–February 1937, a last burst of lyric poetry of un- and anti-Stalinist complexion that made *The Voronezh Notebooks* a vital part of the shadow culture. Defiant lyrics evoke the landscape, Europe's culture, and the approach of death at the hands of the "idol" whom he had execrated in his epigram of 1933. And the poet's haunting sense of his niche in history:

> I was born on the night of two-three
> January of the unreliable year
> eighteen ninety-one, and the
> centuries surround me with fire.[76]

Bulgakov was not arrested in the Terror and died of uremia in 1940 at the age of forty-nine. Censorship largely silenced him in the later 1930s.

He forced himself to write a play, *Batum,* as an obeisance to Stalinist culture. It portrayed the young Djugashvili as a revolutionary hero at the turn of the century and was to be shown in 1939. But at the last minute it was banned from on high, reportedly because Alexei Tolstoy, to whom Stalin had sent a copy for his opinion, found offensive a scene in which the future *vozhd'* suffered physical blows.[77] Meanwhile, Bulgakov worked in secret during the 1930s on a book that he had begun in 1929, *The Master and Margarita.* He started on it anew in 1932 after burning the portion he had written earlier. When published long after his and Stalin's death, it proved to be Russia's greatest twentieth-century work of fiction. It too belongs to the shadow culture.

Most of the action takes place in a fantasied Moscow of black magic performed by the Devil, who pays a visit there as Professor Woland, accompanied by a strange crew: an interpreter named Koroviev, a fanged demon named Azazello, a black cat named Begemot, and a lovely witch named Gella. "Never Speak to Strangers," the title of the first chapter, evokes a time of terror when careless words in a stranger's presence could lead to perdition, as they do in the case of the writer Berlioz, who converses with Woland on the latter's arrival and then, as Woland has just foreseen, falls to his death under a streetcar, after which Woland and company take over his Moscow apartment.

The novel's action also takes place in Jerusalem, as narrated by Woland, on the day of Christ's interrogation by Pontius Pilate and Crucifixion. These same events are the subject of a Moscow writer, the Master, who, crushed by criticism of his manuscript, burns it and takes refuge in an insane asylum. The Master's consort, Margarita, wins Woland's favor by her performance as the Queen Witch at the Witches' Sabbath that he stages in Moscow. In gratitude he returns to the Master his book, saying "Manuscripts don't burn," and at the end gives him everlasting peace.

More than one contemporary experienced the later 1930s in Russia as a Witches' Sabbath. The Jerusalem story finds a fitting place in the Muscovite events of the time. Like so very many in Stalin's Terror, Yeshua (the name given to Christ in the narrative) is victimized by a false denunciation. He is accused of having spoken about Caesar in a treasonable way in Judas' presence, and Pilate, who fears that his own failure to confirm the death sentence might result, as it would have in the Moscow of the Terror, in his own downfall, therefore reluctantly confirms it. In doing so he also confirms Yeshua's statement that cowardice is one of the worst of human sins. This Christ-figure was a doomed man in Jerusalem/Moscow because he would not surrender his faith that all men are potentially good.

The satanic nature of the world Stalin brought to life is this work's master-theme. Bulgakov portrays a society where truth (Yeshua), creativity (Master), and love (Margarita) can barely survive, or may be crushed.[78]

Bulgakov knew that it could not be published or made known during his lifetime. His wife, Elena Sergeevna, told a family friend later about his last hours. As he lay speechless and unseeing, he made little motions indicating that he had a request to make of her. She went onto her knees, stroked his head, and asked what he wanted. No answer. Divining his message, she asked: "You want me to keep *The Master and Margarita,* you want me to have it published. I promise to do it!" At this Bulgakov drew himself together, raised his head slightly, and said: "I want them to know."[79]

Decades later, they knew.

21

CULMINATIONS, 1939-1940

A JOINT party-government decree of 1 January 1939 imposed disciplinary measures on workers and office employees who were late for work without valid reason. If under 20 minutes late, one would be penalized; if over, fired as a shirker and evicted from job-related housing. Workers and employees were, further, not to take too long off for meals, leave work early, or loaf during working hours. "Liberal-conciliatory" bosses were to be brought to trial for failure to enforce labor discipline. Local prosecutors received orders from Vyshinsky to prosecute any who stood aside from the fight against "flyers" (who flitted from job to job) and loafers.

This was one of a series of edicts that tightened the fetters of administrative control during the culminating two years of the revolution from above. Labor books, containing one's employment history and records of awards and penalties, were introduced in January 1939 as a method of enforcing labor discipline. To add a carrot to the new sticks, awards were instituted for exemplary work, each carrying material benefits: the title Hero of Socialist Labor, a medal for Labor Valor and one for Labor Distinction. Stalin's law of 27 May 1939 formalized *barshchina* by making it compulsory for collective farmers to work a specified number of days per year on the *kolkhoz*. All these steps foreshadowed the decree of 26 June 1940, which prohibited voluntary departure from jobs and replaced dismissal with court trial as the penalty for shirking; and the decree of 12 October 1940, which empowered industrial commissariat chiefs to transfer workers and their families from place to place in the country. Two to three million people were sent to camps for violating these draconian laws of 1940.[1]

Tsar Peter had attached serf workers to munitions factories. Appropriately, part 2 of *Peter I* came on Soviet screens in 1939 and received favorable reviews praising the crowned revolutionary as a heroic Russian statesman whose zeal to serve state interests led him to turn over his own son for execution.

The Party Congress and After

Toward evening on 10 March 1939, some 1,900 delegates gathered in the Kremlin for the first session of the Eighteenth Party Congress. Most were men in their thirties—"healthy young representatives of a healthy young people," wrote Vsevolod Vishnevsky in next day's *Pravda*. Molotov gave a brief opening speech. As Stalin then made his way to the rostrum to present the main political report, all rose and gave him an ovation. When he signaled for silence, the roar of applause grew still louder. When he finished, all rose again to applaud.

The previous such meeting five years earlier had been dubbed the "Congress of Victors." Now most of the victors had become victims, the elite and party had been transformed, and the new gathering could have been called the Congress of Submissive Servitors. A small incident illustrates this point. In his report to the Congress, Stalin grossly mispronounced the term for the Agricultural Commissariat (saying *Narkomzyom* instead of *Narkomzem*), whereupon subsequent speakers who had occasion to refer to that Commissariat, Molotov included, mispronounced the term as he did. When informally queried about this forty years later, Molotov explained that "If I had said it right, Stalin would have felt that I was correcting him" and, being "touchy and proud," he would have taken offense.[2] As this implies, Stalin needed to be treated as the perfect figure he believed himself to be, and those terrorized dignitaries acted accordingly, albeit at the expense of their dignity.

The dual process of repression and promotion had done its work. As if to symbolize what had happened, Krupskaya, who was to be a delegate, died a few days before. Her seventieth birthday, on 26 February, was marked with press articles in her praise. The next morning, according to an official announcement, she died of a serious illness. Stalin helped carry the urn with her ashes to its Red Square burial place. Then his loathing of her found expression in an order to the publishing house she had headed in the Commissariat of Education that not a word about her was to be published. Her books disappeared from library shelves, and she became, posthumously, a virtual unperson in Stalin's Russia.[3]

Starting his congress speech with foreign affairs, Stalin said that a new imperialist war, redividing the world by military means, was already in its second year. It had not yet turned into a world war. A bloc of aggressor states—Germany, Italy and Japan—was arrayed against the interests of Britain,-France, and the United States. In combination the democracies were "unquestionably stronger" than the fascist states, both economically and militarily. Yet, they were making concessions and conniving at aggression under the flag of nonintervention. A hullabaloo in their press about German intentions to seize the Soviet Ukraine was an attempt "to provoke a conflict with Germany without visible grounds." The democracies wanted the aggressors to embroil themselves in war with the Soviet Union. After the two sides had weakened and exhausted each other, the nonwarring states could step in, fresh and strong, and dictate conditions to the enfeebled belligerents. Soviet policy in this situation was to preserve peace and carry on business relations with all countries so long as they maintained like relations with it and made no effort to violate its interests. Secondly, "to be cautious and not allow our country to be drawn into conflicts by warmongers who are used to having others pull chestnuts out of the fire for them." And thirdly, to strengthen the might of its armed forces.[4]

Turning to internal affairs, Stalin pictured the Soviet Russia of 1939 as a land of socialism realized and en route to full communism. The economy was thriving, cultural standards were progressing, political life was "completely democratized." The purge of spics, assassins, and wreckers had not shaken and demoralized the system, as some foreign journalists were saying. Rather, it rid the system of those "who kowtowed to the world abroad, were imbued with slavish servility toward every foreign bigwig and ready to render him service as spies," and who did not realize that "the last Soviet citizen, being free of capital's fetters, stands head and shoulders above any high-placed foreign bigwig whose neck wears the yoke of slavery."

Such was the state of Soviet Union according to Stalin. In reality, the Communist Party no longer existed save as an organ of his autocracy subordinate to his police. Far from being in healthier shape than before, the now fully state-regimented society was a limp, fear-stricken mass. The Terror had wrought such havoc in the economy that in the critically important iron and steel industry, for example, there was zero growth in 1937–39, and so vital a part of it as the Magnitogorsk works, with only 8 engineers and 66 trained technicians left on its staff, had to rely on 364 mere "practicals" (workers without special training) to take the places of the qualified people it lacked.[5] Only 12.3 percent of the population, and only 1.8 percent of the collective farmers, had as much as seven years of schooling in 1939.[6] And that the Terror gravely weakened the Soviet system, among other things by denuding the armed forces of up to 50,000 loyal, patriotic, highly trained top- and middle-ranking commanders, is best indicated by the later testimony of Marshal Georgi Zhukov: "Stalin didn't want to fight. We weren't ready. In effect we had no real regular army up to 1939. Just territorial conscripts' formations." Further: "He destroyed. Destroyed the army's whole top echelon (golovka). We entered the war without the army's top echelon. There wasn't anybody." And apropos of Tukhachevsky: "A giant of military thought, a star of first magnitude in our Motherland's military constellation."[7]

Stalin's political report gave the total Soviet population at the time of the congress as 170 million. How did he arrive at this figure? There was a national census in January 1939, but the results were not known to Stalin until April, the month after the congress. Another national census had been taken in January 1937, the first since December 1926. The 1926 census showed a population of 147 million. In the later 1920s the population was growing by 3 million yearly. In early 1936 Stalin had a talk with I. A. Kraval, who headed the Central Economic Accounts Administration, which included the census bureau. He told Kraval that he supposed the forthcoming new census would show a figure of about 170 million. He must have derived it by projecting the 3 million annual growth figure over the seven intervening years. That was to disregard the monstrous losses due to mass deportations during collectivization, the great famine, and terror operations to date. But Kraval, O. A. Kvitkin, and others responsible for the 1937 census were honest. The census showed a Soviet population of 162 million.[8] When Stalin learned the results, which remained unpublished, the census was publicly condemned as a "wreckers' census," and those involved, Kvitkin included, were shot as enemies of the people. The 1939 census showed a figure of 161.5 million, to which 5.8 million military service people and prisoners were added for an indicated total of 167.3 million.[9] But the census officials, fearfully mindful of their predecessors' fate in 1937, gave Stalin the figure he announced at the congress. By autocratic fiat, he blotted out the demographic disaster caused by his revolution from above.

Stalin's contribution to ideology in his congress report was a further enthronement of Soviet statehood. He made bold to correct Engels' proposition in his book *Anti-Dühring* that the future proletarian state—a repressive force, like any other state—was fated to "wither away" for lack of a repressive function as class antagonisms die down. Since he still claimed to be a Marxist, Stalin could no more disown the idea of the state's ultimate disappearance than a formally Christian sovereign could disown the idea of an afterlife, but he went as far as he could in this direction. It transpired that Engels was right only "in the abstract." He had failed to foresee the situation of a socialist state that remains in a capitalist encirclement and hence in need of a strong army, punitive organs, and intelligence service to guard it against foreign attack. In a continuing encirclement a powerful state would be necessary *even under full communism*. Consequently, there must be no more underestimating the role and importance of "our socialist state" and no more idle chatter about how its intelligence service and the Soviet state itself would soon be "relegated to the museum of antiquities" (Stalin refrained from attributing this phrase to its original author, Engels). Citizens must never forget that foreign espionage services will smuggle spies, murderers, and wreckers into the Soviet Union, and therefore must strengthen the intelligence service and help it defeat and extirpate enemies of the people.

This was ominous language. Elsewhere in the report, however, a passage seemed to portend an easing of internal fear and tension. There was no further need for "mass purges," Stalin said. Elaborating in his report to the congress on party affairs, Zhdanov cited egregious cases in which party functionaries had shown themselves to be "masked enemies" by making wholesale denunciations in order to disorganize the party and destroy its apparatus through the victimizing of honest Communists. One Siberian party official, for example, had such a big denunciation business that he divided those to be denounced into different categories on paper: "big enemies," "little enemies," "tiny enemies," and "wee enemies."

Beria addressed the congress as the NKVD's new chief in place of Yezhov, whom he had replaced in December 1938. He pledged that the organization would extirpate all enemies of the people. At present, he said, it was purging itself of enemy elements who had wormed their way into it (that is, Yezhov-era officials) and taking on tested new cadres. Yezhov, now commissar of water transport (a job he was given in April 1938 when Beria became his deputy at the NKVD), attended the congress as a delegate but was not reelected to the Central Committee. Stalin saw to that by appearing at a closed session of higher-ups to select the candidates for election and there accusing Yezhov of involvement in a high-level NKVD plot to kill him and of being responsible for arresting innocent people. Yezhov then left the congress. Arrested some days later, he was shot on 1

April 1940 after performing his necessary last service for Russia's true terrorizer—composing a confession of anti-Soviet crimes.[10] His enduring legacy was the memory of horror and the misnomer *Yezhovshchina*.

The wave of arrests receded at the outset of 1939. Beria, having become a candidate member of the postcongress Politburo in March, suggested at one of its sessions that the time had come to arrest fewer people or else there would soon be no one left to arrest.[11] Several thousand terror victims were then released from custody, very likely because Stalin wanted people to believe that the fallen Yezhov was the prime terrorizer. The maneuver had a certain success. Baffled as they were by their grim fates, not a few arrested people reasoned in prison that fascists had taken over the NKVD in an anti-Soviet plot; and now, it seemed, Yezhov had been one of them. After her release from prison in early 1939, a woman scientist, Ts. L. Yankovskaya, hurriedly wrote a letter to the government saying: "Believe me, all the hundred people in my cell are innocent, fascists have penetrated the NKVD." The Leningrad NKVD got around to arresting her after the war on account of that letter.[12]

Although the prison population diminished by the end of 1939, terror operations continued on a smaller scale. Thousands of cases started under Yezhov went on being handled in the usual ways and with the usual punitive outcomes. Other, new ones kept the organs busy. For example, as late as April 1941 a dozen students were arrested in the town of Saratov, most of them not even known to one another, and condemned as comprising an underground anti-Soviet youth organization, the "Literary Circle." According to N. Porzhin, one who survived, they were all forced by methods of interrogation "not inferior to the Gestapo's" to confess their guilt and implicate others. Then came prison or camp.[13]

In Beria, Stalin had an NKVD chief who would see to the fulfillment of his cruel directive of 20 January 1939 on obligatory continued use of torture not only out of obedience to orders but also because of the sadistic pleasure he apparently took in torturing people or having them tortured in his presence. This went along with his habit of having attractive young women whom he saw on the street, as his car drove by, picked up by his subordinates and brought to a place of his where he would force them into sexual acts. He had a private office in each Moscow prison containing political prisoners. Nearly every night he would show up in one of them and conduct interrogations under torture. After he departed toward morning, the Military Collegium would convene in the office and pass sentence on condemned persons.[14]

The released prisoner Yankovskaya was not alone in theorizing that fascists had penetrated the NKVD. Some other Communists in the camps subscribed to this view; according to one version of it, spoken in whispers, there was just one fascist in the USSR: Stalin.[15] Why some prisoners' minds inclined to a theory of fascist takeover is not hard to see. They knew that loyal Communists like themselves were being victimized *en masse*. Since they also knew that they were not guilty of the crimes to which they were compelled to confess, there had to be some other explanation. They knew that fascist regimes persecuted Communists, sent them to concentration camps, and so the "fascist theory" of the Great Purge was a natural inference.

The whispered version was not mistaken: in the person of Stalin a fascist-like leader had taken over dictatorial power. With the help of many minions, ranging from Molotov, Kaganovich, Zhdanov, Yezhov, and Beria to brutal interrogators, camp guards, and executioners who shot batches of condemned persons and dumped their bodies into pits, he was doing what fascist dictators were known to do: conducting terror against Communists. Yet—and this helps to explain why the "fascist theory" was only one of many theories voiced in the camps—Soviet Communists were being destroyed in the name of Communism itself. To obscure matters still more, the ringleaders of the supposed great conspiracy were accused of having been in league with German fascism in seeking to overthrow the Communist party-state and Stalin as its true Leninist leader.

However confusing these things were for contemporaries, they need not confuse later historians. Stalin's was a Bolshevism of the radical right. As such it was wayward, deeply deviationist, and questionably Bolshevist save insofar as it could and did lay claim to all that was harsh, repressive, and terrorist in Lenin's legacy. And this shows what was sound in the "fascist theory" that focused on Stalin. In all its varieties, Nazism included, fascism was (and is) an extremist movement or regime of the radical right. As a Bolshevism of the radical right, Stalin's Russian national Bolshevism was akin to Hitler's German National Socialism.

Kinship is not identity. There were differences, among them the fact that Stalin's Bolshevism, despite its covert and after the war increasingly overt anti-Semitism, did not preach a biological racism like Hitler's. But the likenesses were many and deep. Both regimes, with the proviso just mentioned in Stalinism's case, were anti-Communist. Both were chauvinist, and idealized elements of the national past. Both were statist and imperialist. Both were enemy-obsessed. Both were terroristic and practiced torture in their prisons. Under both regimes state terrorism was linked with a theory of international conspiracy: a Jewish anti-Aryan conspiracy in Hitler's case and an anti-Soviet one in Stalin's. Both were regimes of personal dictatorship with a leader cult. Both featured cults of heroes and heroism. Both exalted youth, physical strength, and motherhood. The one emphasized what was *narodny;* the other, what was *volkisch*. Both favored grandiosity in architecture. Both were antiliberal, anticosmopolitan, and antimodernist. They were both radicalisms of the right.

In the nature of its ruler and his autocratic regime, Stalin's Russia of mid-1939 was, therefore, readier for the step it was about to take in foreign policy than its own people, Communists elsewhere, and foreign publics and governments realized.

The Path to the Pact

When Stalin in his party congress speech attributed to the democracies a plan of embroiling the fascist states in war with the Soviet Union, he was projecting onto them a scenario that had lain in his own mind since at least 1925 and animated his diplomacy subsequently. It envisaged a war between two European coalitions with the USSR remaining neutral until an advantageous moment and then intervening to advance the Communist cause. The task of diplomacy was to help this division of Europe come about.

Having pursued the divisive diplomacy and observed the emergence in Europe of two potentially warring coalitions, Stalin in his party congress speech set in motion talks leading to an alignment with Berlin. He did so by professing a desire for peace and business relations with "all" interested states and disclaiming any intention of "pulling chestnuts out of the fire" for others. That raised the possibility of a negotiated neutrality which would insure Hitler against what he had to fear most: a two-front war. This, Stalin could calculate, would enable Hitler to unleash aggression and him, while remaining neutral, to take over territories in Eastern Europe on an agreed-upon basis. And given his expressed belief that the democracies were stronger than the fascist states, he could and evidently did calculate also that the oncoming war between them would be a protracted one that would result in their mutual weakening or exhaustion while Soviet Russia was at peace and rebuilding its own strength. In conversation after World War II, Voroshilov said: "We in spite of it all thought that if Germany attacked Britain and France, it would bog down there for a long time. Who could have known that France would collapse in two weeks?"[16]

Five days after Stalin addressed the party congress on 10 March, Hitler seized the remainder of Czechoslovakia, setting up a protectorate over the Czech lands and a "free state" of Slovakia. This dramatic demonstration that appeasement would not satiate Hitler catalyzed change in the Anglo-French stance. A diplomatic flurry ensued, involving Poland and Rumania as well as Britain and France. The Poles were nonresponsive to German demands on the Free City of Danzig and to the idea, conveyed on 21 March by Hitler's foreign minister, Ribbentrop, to Jozef Lipski, Poland's ambassador to Germany, that a German-Polish understanding would have to include anti-Soviet provisions.[17] On 31 March Chamberlain made public in the House of Commons a guarantee to Poland in event of her independence being threatened. France quickly concurred in this, and during March the two governments started political talks with Moscow for an alliance against further aggression. On 6 April a Polish-British communiqué announced a reciprocal defensive agreement between the two countries. When Admiral Canaris, head of German counterintelligence, brought confirmation of this news to Hitler, the enraged dictator dashed across the room pounding his fists on a marble table, shrieked a stream of curses, and said: "I shall prepare a diabolic beverage for them." An associate of Canaris interpreted this as the first hint of a pact with Stalin.[18] A directive from Hitler to the *Wehrmacht,* dated 11 April, ordered preparations to go forward for war against Poland.

Moscow's diplomatic response to the German takeover of Czechoslovakia was mild, and its response to the change in Anglo-French policy was disinclination to take it seriously.[19] A TASS statement of 4 April denied press reports that the USSR was undertaking to supply Poland with military equipment and withhold raw materials from Germany in case of war. Ehrenburg's antifascist reports from Paris under the pseudonym of Paul Jocelyn stopped appearing in *Izvestiia* from mid-April.[20] On 17 April the new Soviet ambassador to Berlin, Alexei Merekalov, called on Ernst von Weizsäcker, state secretary in the German Foreign Office. He said that ideological differences need not be a stumbling block in Russian-German relations, that Soviet Russia had not exploited the present friction between Germany and the Western democracies and had no desire to do so, and went on: "There exists for Russia no reason why she should not live with [you] on a normal footing. And from normal, the relations might become better and better."[21]

Stalin followed up this démarche with a major new move. On 3 May Molotov, while retaining the premiership, was appointed foreign commissar and Litvinov was dismissed from that post. Reporting this in a telegram to Berlin the next day, the German chargé in Moscow, Werner von Tippelskirch, recalled Stalin's caution in his party congress speech against allowing the Soviet Union to be drawn into conflicts, and added: "Molotov (no Jew) is held to be 'most intimate friend and closest collaborator' of Stalin."[22] The dismissal of Litvinov, who was not only Jewish but known for his pro-Western orientation, did not fail to arouse Hitler's interest. Two days later Gustav Hilger was called home from his Moscow Embassy post and taken by Ribbentrop to see the *Fuehrer* in Berchtesgaden. When Hitler, who kept chewing his fingernails during the interview, asked what might have caused Stalin to dismiss Litvinov, Hilger stated his belief that he had done so because Litvinov favored an understanding with England and France whereas Stalin thought they wanted him to pull chestnuts out of the fire for them. This seemed to make sense to Hitler, who then asked Hilger whether he thought Stalin might be ready for an understanding with Germany. Again Hilger made reference to the 10 March speech. When asked, finally, for his view of developments in Russia, Hilger mentioned its growing economic strength, the serious weakening of its military power caused by repression of 80 percent of the Red Army's high-ranking officers, and the ideological shifts away from Communist doctrines toward Russian nationalism, parental authority, school discipline, and anti-experimentalism in the arts. As Hilger later learned, Hitler afterward told Ribbentrop that if his, Hilger's, estimate of Soviet trends was correct, then measures must be taken as soon as possible to prevent further consolidation of Soviet power.[23] Far from softening Hitler's attitude toward Russia, Hilger had only hardened it by describing developments under Stalin. An agreement with Stalin could only be, for Hitler, a short-term expedient on the way to the conquest of Russia.

Unaware of Hitler's reaction to Hilger and not comprehending the man's obsessive personality, Stalin plodded further down the road that would bring his country to near destruction in 1941–42. On 20 May Molotov received Ambassador Schulenburg for an interview in which the new foreign commissar suggested, although without amplifying what he meant, that for the then stalled Soviet-German economic negotiations to be resumed, "political bases" must be built. Reporting this to Berlin, Schulenburg counseled caution lest proposals from the German side be used by the Kremlin to put pressure on England and France,[24] with which Soviet discussions were then taking place. In an address on 31 May to the Supreme Soviet, Molotov referred to these and to the inadequacy of the guarantees that the two Western democracies were offering the USSR. He also noted that those talks in no way inhibited the Soviet government from developing business ties with countries like Germany and Italy, adding that negotiations for a new trade agreement and new credits with Germany had begun.

Then Stalin, through Molotov, took another step: The Soviet chargé in Berlin, Georgi Astakhov, visited the Bulgarian minister on 14 June and had a talk that he knew would be reported to the German authorities. Moscow, he said, was vacillating between three possibilities: a pact with England and France, a hands-off position ("further dilatory treatment of pact negotiations"), and a rapprochement with Germany. The third option was closest to its desires, but there were problems, for instance, the Soviet Union did not recognize Rumania's possession of Bessarabia and had to fear a German attack via the Baltic states or Rumania. Were Germany to declare that she would not attack the USSR or that she would conclude a nonaggression pact with her, the USSR would probably refrain from concluding a treaty with England. Since, however, she did not know what Germany really wanted, she might opt for continuing the negotiations with England in a dilatory manner and having a free hand in any conflict that might break out.[25] In the ensuing weeks Berlin began to show interest in a political rapprochement.

As the mutual probing to this end went forward, secret events in Beria's domain bespoke Stalin's resolve for an accord with Hitler. Litvinov's dismissal was accompanied by a purge of remaining Litvinov-era figures from the Narkomindel and their replacement by men like young Gromyko with little or no experience in foreign affairs. Most of the purged officials, among them Evgeni Gnedin, were arrested. Following his arrest on 11 May and incarceration in Lubianka's inner prison, Beria and his henchman Kobulov, who now headed the NKVD's special investigations division, took personal charge of his case. Kobulov apprised Gnedin that he had been arrested as a "major spy" and demanded that he come clean about his "ties with enemies of the people." Gnedin denied these charges. Then he was taken to Beria's office where, in the presence of Beria, Kobulov, and an NKVD lieutenant, he learned that he was "no longer in the office of the superspy, your former chief," that is, Litvinov. To compel his help in concocting a case against a Litvinov-led group of enemies in the Narkomindel, Gnedin was forced to lie face down on a carpet in front of Beria's desk and then brutally beaten with rubber truncheons all over his bared body. Repeated such sessions were even more painful, but he did not give in. Other arrested Litvinov men, among them the diplomat E. V. Girshfeld, were unable to hold out. Gnedin was shown a protocol of his interrogation of 15–16 May containing the statement that Litvinov "with anti-Soviet intentions was inciting war."[26] Such, apparently, would have been a public charge against Litvinov and his ex-subordinates had Stalin decided on so dramatic a demonstration of his desire for a deal with Hitler.

As secret exchanges between Moscow and Berlin continued during the summer months, Stalin heightened pressure on Hitler by having Molotov engage simultaneously in discussions with the British and French for a mutual assistance pact between the three powers. The fact of these talks, and that William Strang, head of the Foreign Office's Central European Department, was in Moscow for that purpose, was public knowledge. He departed Moscow in early August without an agreement having been reached, but British and French military missions arrived on 11 August for staff talks on a three-power pact. Voroshilov headed the Soviet negotiating team. Much of the time he stalled. The stumbling block in the end was Anglo-French inability to secure Warsaw's acceptance of the demand that the Red Army be allowed to march through Poland to "make contact" with the enemy. While interested in Russia's aid in munitions and war mate-rials, the Polish government feared a Soviet occupation of eastern Poland too much to accede to such terms.[27]

It was not alone the specter of a new Triple Entente that put Hitler under pressure to come to quick agreement with Moscow. His plan was to crush Poland speedily before the French and British could intervene on her behalf. For this to succeed, his army had to move by the start of September, before autumn rains interfered by slowing operations.[28] "The Reich gov-ernment is of the opinion that there is no question between the Baltic and the Black seas which cannot be settled to the complete satisfaction of both countries," Ribbentrop cabled to Schulenburg in Moscow on 14 August. After an ensuing flurry of communications on the terms of the agreement to be signed, Hitler wired Stalin to say that he wanted a pact "as a long-range German policy," accepted Molotov's draft of one, and was sure the supplementary protocol wanted by Moscow could be quickly clarified if a responsible German statesman could come to negotiate.[29] This elicited from Stalin the invitation for Ribbentrop to come to Moscow on 23 August. From a German who was with Hitler when he received Stalin's commu-nication, Hilger learned that the *Fuehrer*'s response was ecstatic joy. Drumming his fists against the wall, he cried out: "Now I have the world in my pocket!"[30] Then he stole a march on events by announcing on 20 August to a stupefied Western world that Germany and Russia had agreed to conclude a nonaggression pact.

On the afternoon of 23 August Ribbentrop, accompanied by assis-tants, arrived in Moscow in Hitler's personal Focke-Wulf Condor plane. Received with honors as five swastika banners waved from Moscow's airdrome building, he was put up in the former Austrian Embassy and later driven to the Kremlin in a swastika-bedecked American car. There, to his pleasurable surprise, Stalin as well as Molotov awaited him. The negotia-tions proceeded with dispatch, and the agreements were signed after mid-night. The ten-year nonaggression treaty bound the two parties to desist from attacking one another, to withhold support from any third power that might attack either one, to consult on problems involving common inter-ests, not to participate in any grouping of powers aimed at the other, and to settle all disputes by peaceful means. The secret supplementary proto-col, a photocopy of which fell into British hands in Germany after World War II, put Finland, Estonia, and Latvia (but not Lithuania) in Russia's sphere of influence, noted its interest in Bessarabia, and specified a Ger-man-Russian demarcation line along the Vistula, the San, and the Bug rivers "in event" of a rearrangement of Polish territories.

A late supper was served after the signing of the pact. Among the toasts was Stalin's to Hitler: "I know how much the German nation loves its *Fuehrer;* I should therefore like to drink to his health." Molotov raised his glass to Stalin and said it was Stalin who, through his speech in March, which was well understood in Berlin, brought about the reversal in political relations. During the informal table talk, Ribbentrop joked that Berliners, known for their wit, had lately been saying, "Stalin will yet join the anti-Comintern pact." Stalin opined that Britain's army was weak but France's was "worthy of consideration," to which Ribbentrop replied that her forces were numerically weaker than Germany's and that Germany's Westwall was five times stronger than France's Maginot line.[31] Supper ended around 2:00 a.m. and Ribbentrop flew home on 24 August.

Decades later, two Germans who were with Ribbentrop on that Moscow trip, Gebhardt von Walther and Karl Schnürre, shared with me their memories of it. When asked what had most impressed him about Stalin in his dealings with the Germans, von Walther replied, "his charm," and added: "He could charm anyone." Evidently Stalin deployed his charm to persuade Ribbentrop and those accompanying him that he could be trusted as an alliance partner. To Schnürre, Stalin seemed a believer in the alliance with Germany that the pact symbolized. At the time of the signing of the accord, he appeared solemn and rather emotional, as if he had made his choice, was conscious of its implications, and convinced of the rightness of his step. At one point during the evening, he said: "And if in the coming period Germany should be forced to her knees, I would come to her aid with a hundred Red divisions on the Rhine!"[32]

On the night of 24 August, after Ribbentrop's departure for Berlin, Stalin had some Politburo members, Khrushchev among them, as dinner guests at his dacha outside Moscow. He had set the policy all by himself and carried it out with the help of Molotov. How closely he had kept the secret of what they were up to is indicated by the fact that Khrushchev first heard from Stalin that Ribbentrop was coming to Moscow on the day before his arrival, and responded to this news by wondering aloud if Ribbentrop was defecting. With Stalin's encouragement he went duck hunting the next day with Bulganin and Malenkov in nearby Zavidova, where Voroshilov joined them. In the evening they brought along the ducks they had bagged to Stalin's dacha. They found him in a rare good mood, cracking jokes, and clearly pleased with himself. He said that Ribbentrop had brought with him a draft of a friendship and nonaggression treaty, which had been signed. The British and French would hear about it on the morrow and go home. The talks with them had been fruitless. They weren't serious about an alliance, their real goal was to incite Hitler against Russia, and it was good that they should leave. As for Hitler, Stalin had this to say: "Of course it's all a game to see who can fool whom. I know what Hitler's up to. He thinks he's outsmarted me, but actually it's I who have tricked him." Stalin also told the assembled Politburo members that "because of this treaty the war would pass us by for a while longer. We would be able to stay neutral and save our strength. Then we would see what happened."[33]

Stalin summoned Voroshilov's adjutant, General R. P. Khmelnitsky, and ordered him to tell Voroshilov to end the talks with the Western military missions. Khmelnitsky passed a note to Voroshilov saying: "Klim! Koba said you should shut down the barrel organ."[34] On 25 August Voroshilov called the heads of the two missions, Admiral R. A. Drax and General Joseph Doumenc, to the Kremlin and informed them that there was no use continuing the talks in view of the changed circumstances. He angrily blamed the Poles on the ground that they had kept saying they did not want Soviet help.[35] He shut down the barrel organ with a bang, and the Westerners left for home. On 1 September, secure in the knowledge that Russia would remain uninvolved, Hitler hurled the full force of the *Wehrmacht* against Poland. True to their obligations, Britain and France declared war on Germany. World War II had begun.

Collaborating with Germany

People abroad were dumbfounded by the Hitler-Stalin accord. British humor rose to the occasion with David Low's famous cartoon showing the two uniformed pistol-packing dictators, hats in hand and bowing deep, with Hitler saying "The scum of the earth, I believe?" and Stalin replying "The bloody assassin of the workers, I presume?" Russians were no less astonished to learn from their newspapers that Russia and Germany were now to be linked in friendship.

Addressing the Supreme Soviet on 31 August to ask its ratification of the pact, Molotov criticized the Western democracies' conduct of talks with Moscow, implying that they had instigated Poland's refusal to accept Soviet military aid. He also implicitly condemned Litvinov (who was in the audience as one of the deputies) for his pro-Western orientation, saying that some had been "obsessed with simple antifascist formulas" and hence inclined to overlook "the danger attending machinations by provocateurs in the so-called democratic countries." This anti-Litvinov jibe casts further light on the tortures to which Gnedin and others were being subjected. As for friendship with Russia's new pact partner, Molotov declared:

Yesterday the fascists of Germany were pursuing a hostile foreign policy toward the USSR. Yes, yesterday we were still enemies in the foreign-policy sphere. Today, however, the situation has changed and we have ceased being enemies.[36]

Those words must have inspired the episode in Orwell's *1984* in which Oceana, which has been in alliance with Eastasia against Eurasia, suddenly switches and becomes Eurasia's ally against Eastasia.

But unlike Oceana's subjects in *1984,* the masses of Russians did not make the required mental switch in response to the policy reversal. Many had memories of Germans as enemies in World War I; some had fought them then and were ready to again. Leaving aside the automatically responsive Stalin loyalists well represented among the promotees, many people were dismayed, shocked, and full of shame.

Although we have no evidence of people reasoning that Stalin's Bolshevism of the radical right had an affinity with fascism, there was malaise about the news. Even so devout a young believer as Raisa Orlova felt troubled: "So, if we were for Hitler, then what were we supposed to do about the antifascists, the novels of Willi Bredel and Feuchtwanger, the stories about the tortures and the staunchness of the Communists, the Jewish pogroms, and bonfires of books?"[37] When Tupolev in his prison aircraft design bureau on Moscow's outskirts was shown a copy of a Soviet newspaper of 29 September (which published the text of a second agreement, the "German-Soviet Boundary and Friendship Treaty," signed by Molotov and Ribbentrop), he crumpled it in his hands and shouted: "What kind of friendship? What's going on with them over there, have they gone out of their minds!"[38]

Nor was the pact popular among ordinary workers. In Moscow's First State Ball-Bearing Plant, recalls an American-born black who went to Russia during the Depression, became a Soviet citizen, and was working in that plant in 1939, some workers in his shop wept openly; others just looked grim. He did not know a single Russian who did not hate the Nazis.[39] Some made hostile remarks in the hearing of secret informants about German fascism—and were arrested for doing so.[40] In Moscow parks where groups gathered to hear from agitators about the pact's meaning, views were voiced that the pact was bound to be short-lived, that Germany was not to be trusted, and that a German attack on Russia was imminent.[41]

For his part Stalin was punctilious in seeing to observance of the new line that Russia and Germany were good neighbors. *Pravda's* dispatch from Berlin on 3 September reporting that the war had started was headlined simply "Military Actions Between Germany and Poland." Its review of the "actions" on 11 September was headed "The German-Polish War." Schulenburg cabled to Berlin on 6 September that Soviet press coverage of Germany was utterly transformed and that anti-German literature had disappeared from bookshops.[42] A Moscow dispatch of the same date in *The New York Times* reported that the anti-Nazi films *Professor Mamlock* and *The Oppenheimer Family* had disappeared from Soviet screens, that the Vakhtanov Theater's production of Alexei Tolstoy's *The Road to Victory,* about Germany's part in the Civil War intervention, had been withdrawn, as had Eisenstein's *Alexander Nevsky*. As readers of *1984* will remember, it was a function of Oceana's Ministry of Truth to alter all historical records so as to show that Oceana *never had* been Eurasia's enemy.[43]

As the German armies advanced eastward across Poland, many Russians, being in the dark about the secret arrangements for Poland's partition, grew apprehensive that the Germans would not stop at the Soviet-Polish frontier. Official announcements of the call-up of reserves for army service heightened these fears, and a run on food shops ensued. Meanwhile, in secret exchanges, Hitler pressured Stalin to send his forces into Poland according to their agreement. Stalin, not wanting his own people and the world to realize that he had colluded with Hitler, wanted to delay his forces' entry as long as he could. But the swiftness of the German advance made lengthy delay impossible and on 17 September Soviet troops marched into Poland. Another indication of Russian popular feeling came in reports reaching the U.S. Embassy in Moscow that workers in factories jumped on machines and cheered when they heard this news because they assumed that the Red Army was going to fight the Germans.[44]

Instead, it was embarking on a collaborative venture. This was mainly evident behind the scenes, however, as in Molotov's telephone message to Schulenburg on 9 September asking him to convey his congratulations and greetings to the Reich Government on the entry of German troops into Warsaw.[45] After learning via Schulenburg that the Soviet forces would begin operations without delay, Ribbentrop was only unhappy about the Soviet proposal to explain the action publicly as a move to protect the Ukrainian and Belorussian ethnic majorities in eastern Poland, as this would "expose the two states before the whole world as enemies."[46]

Stalin and Molotov tried to mollify Berlin without, however, abandoning the pretext that the Red Army was moving into Poland to protect West Ukrainian and West Belorussian "blood-relatives," as Molotov put it in his radio speech of 17 September announcing the operation. The Polish army having been all but routed then by the Germans, the Soviet occupation of eastern Poland met only light resistance and proceeded swiftly. The territory taken over comprised about 200,000 square kilometers and had a population of nearly thirteen million, of whom ethnic Ukrainians numbered over seven million, ethnic Belorussians over three million, Poles over one million, and Jews over one million. The Red Army's casualties in the operation, according to Molotov, were 737 killed and 2,599 wounded.[47]

The Soviet press reported that the Red Army was being greeted with jubilation by the fraternal Ukrainians and Belorussians across the old border. *Pravda* on 22 September featured a large front-page drawing of a Ukrainian or Belorussian peasant embracing a young Red Army man as though it were his long-lost son. And indeed, the invading Red Army units were welcomed by many Ukrainian, Belorussian, and Jewish inhabitants of this territory where the dominant Poles were an ethnic minority living mainly in the towns and the non-Polish population suffered discrimination.[48] Attitudes soon changed as Stalin's system was imposed on these new millions of his subjects.

Further high-level exchanges led to Ribbentrop's second visit to Moscow and the German-Soviet Boundary and Friendship Treaty of 28 September. Stalin proposed in advance a deal whereby Lublin province and a part of Warsaw province situated east of the demarcation line as determined in August should go to Germany and Lithuania to Russia. This was agreed in a new secret supplementary protocol amending the one of 23 August. The treaty itself referred to the agreement on the new state boundaries in the middle of what had been Poland and contained a clause calling the settlement "a firm foundation for a progressive development of the friendly relations" between the two countries. Published along with it was a joint declaration saying that it would serve the interest of all countries to end the war between Germany and France and Britain and that Germany and the Soviet Union would consult on further measures if their efforts to this end should prove fruitless.[49] In the new spirit of friendship Ribbentrop was royally feted in Moscow. A special performance of *Swan Lake* was put on in his honor. And so congenial was the atmosphere during a Kremlin banquet with Politburo members and high Germans accompanying Ribbentrop that one of them, the *Gauleiter* of Danzig, told him on the return flight that he had almost imagined himself "among old party comrades.[50]

Stalin lost no time putting into effect his understanding with Hitler that all three small Baltic countries belonged to his sphere of influence. To avoid the onus that outright invasion would incur, he adopted a two-stage procedure. Stage one was the conclusion of mutual-assistance pacts whose provisions for the stationing of "limited contingents" of Soviet troops and the establishment of Soviet naval and air bases on the territories of the Baltic states would render nugatory their pledges of respect for these states' sovereign rights. How highhandedly Stalin acted may be seen from the experience of the first of the Baltic foreign ministers to be summoned to Moscow, from Estonia. Having been invited for what was to be a discussion of trade relations and the like, he was called from the Bolshoi Theater at night to meet Molotov in the Kremlin and confronted with the demand that Soviet forces be stationed in his country. At a further meeting Molotov set the number of troops at 35,000, to which the Estonian replied that this was more than the whole Estonian army. At that point Stalin walked in and innocently asked what the problem was. Then (in a ploy that would be repeated to good effect in relations with the Anglo-American allies during the Soviet-German war) he graciously lowered the number of Soviet troops to 25,000.[51] The pact with Estonia was signed on 28 September; those with Latvia and Lituania followed in early October.

With what had been eastern Poland under secure occupation, Stalin moved in October to annex all of it except the city of Wilno (and surrounding area), which was ceded to Lithuania and became its capital as Vilnius. The occupiers quickly organized sham elections for national assemblies of the Western Ukraine and Western Belorussia. These bodies formally petitioned the USSR's Supreme Soviet to admit Western Ukraine and Western Belorussia to the Soviet Union as part of the Ukrainian and Belorussian republics. The Supreme Soviet granted the petitions during its meeting of 31 October–2 November.[52]

Poland and the defenseless Baltics were easy pickings for Stalin; Finland was a different matter. With its fortified Mannerheim Line, its greater space in which to fight, its sturdy small army, and rugged will to resist encroachment, Finland stood up for its rights. When its high-level representatives were summoned to Moscow in early October, they rejected a mutual-assistance treaty of the sort being imposed on the Baltic states, on the ground that it would violate their country's neutrality. Then concrete military-strategic demands were made on them: to move back the Finnish border north of Leningrad on the Karelian isthmus by several dozen kilometers to eliminate its proximity (about twenty miles) to Leningrad, in return for some Soviet Karelian territory east of Finland's border; to dismantle the Mannerheim Line; and to lease some territory to the USSR to set up a Soviet naval base near the port of Hanko at the northern entrance to the Gulf of Finland.

On 31 October Molotov reported to the Supreme Soviet on foreign relations. It was the most ignominious speech of his diplomatic career. It had taken, he said, only a short blow against Poland, first by the German army and then by the Red Army, for nothing to remain of "this ugly offspring of the Versailles Treaty." Then he flayed the British and French ruling circles for portraying their war against Germany as an ideological war for democracy and destruction of Hitlerism:

One can accept or reject the ideology of Hitlerism, just as one can any other ideological system, that's a matter of political views. But anybody can understand that an ideology can't be destroyed by force, that one can't put an end to it by war. So, it is not only senseless but criminal to wage such a war as a war to "destroy Hitlerism" under the false flag of a struggle for "democracy."

As for Soviet-German relations, they were now based on a firm foundation of mutual interests. The Soviet view had always been that a strong Germany was a necessary condition of a stable peace in Europe. Now relations with the German state were based on friendly ties, readiness to support Germany's peaceful aspirations, and desire to foster economic ties.[53]

To Soviet people high and low in authority, these friendly words about Hitler's Germany, and others like them in other Molotov speeches of that time, carried a political message. It was heard even in Arctic slow-death camps of Kolyma. A kindly fellow prisoner, Doctor Petukhov, assigned the recently arrived Eugenia Ginzburg as a medical assistant in a ward for women prisoners with babies. There the head doctor, Evdokia Ivanovna, herself a prisoner, conducted periodic political classes consisting of her reading aloud Soviet newspaper articles to other imprisoned doctors and nurses. One day she read a report by Molotov containing warm words about Germany. Then, lowering her voice, she advised her fellow prisoners not to say "fascists" any more but rather "German National Socialists."[54] The Nazis were to be spoken of with respect, even in Kolyma.

Stalin's pact and ensuing line on friendship with Nazi Germany stunned the international Communist movement and larger circle of Soviet sympathizers abroad. Although the Terror had decimated the Moscow-based leaderships of the German, Polish, Rumanian, Austrian, Hungarian, and Baltic Communist parties, rank-and-file party members and sympathizers in foreign countries were unaware of its scope and anti-Communist character. Whatever the rigors of recent years in Russia, Communism still connoted to them a set of humanistic ideals, and the affinity of Stalin's form of Russian National Bolshevism with Hitler's German National Socialism was not understood. So, the world movement was shocked by the events of August–September 1939.

The new line handed down to the Comintern by Stalin and imposed on the foreign Communist parties was that the war now taking place was a conflict between rival imperialisms in which the parties' duty was to deny their governments support and work for a negotiated peace. As Dimitrov spelled it out on 11 November, Popular Front tactics were no longer suitable save in colonial countries, because Communists must not make common cause with the imperialists in their "criminal antipopular war.[55] The term "fascism" disappeared from Comintern publications, and divisions arose in various Communist parties as many members quit in disgust. By opposing the antifascist war in this way, Stalin engaged in *de facto* political collaboration with Hitler. He also collaborated diplomatically with him by establishing relations at the ambassadorial level with the German puppet Slovak state, and, later, with the pro-German Vichy government in France, while breaking diplomatic ties with a number of governments of German-occupied countries that found refuge in London.

Having divided and demoralized the international Communist movement, Stalin proceeded to bring down worldwide opprobrium on his country by moving to take over Finland by force. Instead of leaving this small neutral neighbor with its four million people to its devices, he acted under his collusive secret agreement with Hitler to claim it as his own. On the false pretext, so like Hitler's methods, that Finns had begun shelling Soviet positions, Moscow on 28 November 1939 denounced its nonaggression treaty with Finland and then, on the night of 30 November–1 December, without a declaration of war, attacked Finland by land, sea, and air. Soviet planes bombed Helsinki and other Finnish open cities, killing hundreds of noncombatants.

Stalin was not content to demand from the Finns that they accept in full the claims Moscow had made on them in the foregoing negotiations and that they had been seeking to meet by concessions within reason. In his vaulting ambition he sought to make Finland into a Soviet satellite merged with neighboring Soviet Karelia in a "Karelo-Finnish" union republic of the USSR. On 1 December Soviet citizen and Comintern operative Otto Kuusinen became "representative of the People's Government and Minister for Foreign Affairs of Finland," in which capacity he proclaimed establishment of a "Finnish Democratic Republic," which was thereupon recognized by the Soviet government. Moscow then announced that Finns in the region of Terioki, a town by now taken by Soviet forces inside Finnish borders, had set up a revolutionary government that would conquer Helsinki with its own troops and create a democratic government. Kuusinen would head it. All this prompted *The New York Times* to comment that "The difference between the new Russian method and the Hitler method is not so large."

On 1 December that paper expressed the wrath widely aroused by Stalin's moves in a thundering editorial. "In the smoking ruins of the damage wrought in Finland lies what remained of the world's respect for the government of Russia," it said. "The bombs that rained on Finnish workers and peasants finally shattered a mighty illusion. The defeat in this battle will not be Finland's. It will be the defeat of the Russian revolution and of the power of the idea which gave what dominion it had to the Communist International." Some days later, as the Finns put up a sturdy resistance that must have come as a nasty surprise for Stalin, the League of Nations in Geneva, responding to a Finnish government appeal for a negotiated settlement with Moscow, invited the Soviet government to cease hostilities and agree to negotiate with the Finnish government. Molotov declined on the ground that the USSR was not at war with Finland. On 14 December the League informed Moscow that the USSR was no longer its member.

To the international furor caused by Stalin's Hitlerite methods was added now the humiliation of his armed forces' inability to conquer Finland by *blitzkrieg*. Her forested terrain and multitude of lakes made the Russian commanders' reliance on tank forces disadvantageous. Although vastly outnumbered, the Finnish forces gave a good account of themselves. White-robed sharpshooters on skis took their toll of enemy soldiers, and fought off tanks by hurling gasoline-filled bottles, which became known as "Molotov cocktails." Perhaps it should be added to the credit of the Russians that they had little stomach for a war of aggression; they are doughty warriors only in defense of Mother Russia. Nor was the war popular at home, especially as casualties mounted, food supplies grew scarce, and the government doubled the price of vodka to soak up purchasing power. The Finns held out all through December and after, but were compelled to sue for peace in early March 1940.

Their prime minister flew to Moscow and was received by Molotov as Finland's representative, nullifying Kuusinen's claim to be Finland's political leader. Talks begun on 8 March ended in the signing of a peace agreement under which hostilities were to cease at 12 noon on 13 March. Assuming that the war was over, Finnish soldiers began leaving their positions that morning. Several Soviet divisions then attacked the town of Vipuri, and fierce battles ensued as the Finns there took up arms in rage and fought from house to house. By noon they had to surrender and the town (renamed Vyborg) was in Soviet hands. Stalin thus salved his vanity at the cost of several thousand Soviet lives; and then, just ten minutes before the 12 noon truce came into force, he took his revenge on Finland for having dared to stand up against him by needlessly having his forces fire a final intensive barrage all along the front.[56]

Although the peace terms were quite harsh on Finland, which lost the Karelian Isthmus, the shore of Lake Ladoga and more, it remained a free country within the land it retained. The Winter War cost the Soviet Union 200,000 lives, according to Finnish estimates. Molotov's account to the Supreme Soviet on 29 March 1940 gave the Soviet casualties as 48,745 dead and 158,863 wounded. The 30,000 captured Soviet prisoners returned by the Finns at the war's end were immediately arrested and sent to concentration camps for terms of five to eight years; the returned officers were shot.[57]

The real culprit of this shameful, ill-conceived war of conquest was of course Stalin. His massacre of the officer corps had left the Red Army all but leaderless. Voroshilov, under whose command the Soviet forces at first fought in the Finnish war, was by then a morally broken man whose will had weakened to the point that he feared taking any responsible decisions. So he appeared to young Admiral Kuznetsov, then commissar of the Soviet navy, during the Finnish campaign.[58] Stalin, whose idealized self-image precluded any recognition of faults in his own conduct, was furious with the military and Voroshilov. At his dacha near Moscow he rose in a rage and began to berate Voroshilov. According to Khrushchev, who observed the scene, Voroshilov for once defended himself. He too leaped up and shouted to Stalin: "You have yourself to blame for all of this. . . . You're the one who annihilated the army's Old Guard; you had our best generals killed!" Rebuffed then by Stalin, Voroshilov lost his self-control, picked up a platter of suckling pig, and smashed it down on the table.[59] After that outburst he was replaced by Timoshenko as commander in the Finnish war.

On the day of Ribbentrop's first arrival in Moscow, 23 August 1939, contact began between the NKVD and the Gestapo. As two young German Embassy secretaries, Hans von Herwarth and Gebhardt von Walther observed the scene at the airport, von Walther grabbed von Herwarth by the arm and called his attention to the way in which the Gestapo officers who had disembarked from Ribbentrop's plane were shaking hands with their NKVD counterparts among those meeting the plane, and smiling at one another. "They're obviously delighted finally to be able to collaborate," he said to his companion. "But watch out! This will be disastrous, especially when they start exchanging files."[60]

An experience of Gnedin's in the Lubianka in November 1939 suggests that von Walther's remark may have been prescient. During an interrogation in which a senior lieutenant of the NKVD accused Gnedin of having been a German spy, Gnedin was told that incriminating evidence on this point had been secured by the NKVD from the Gestapo. The two countries were now in friendly relations, said the officer, and then added with a touch of mystery, as if revealing a professional secret: "So, we are exchanging materials with the Gestapo." Gnedin afterward wondered whether they might be planning to organize a public trial of him and other active Soviet antifascists as promoters of a policy of encirclement of Germany.[61]

The lieutenant who told Gnedin about the exchange of files may have been lying, but the fact of at least one-sided collaboration between the two dread agencies is not in doubt. One-sided because what the Gestapo did for the NKVD is not known, whereas we do have information on some services performed for the Gestapo by the NKVD. Soon after the Stalin-Hitler pact was signed, the NKVD issued orders that all Germans and former Austrians be sent from prisons or concentration camps where they were then being kept to Moscow's Butyrka, where for a time they were well treated in preparation for their coming transfer to the Gestapo at the demarcation line in Poland. Specialists and ordinary workers of German nationality were included along with Communists, other German anti-Nazis, and Jewish refugees, among them Alexander Weissberg. Some had once held high positions in the German Communist Party. The imprisoned

Margarete Buber, wife of Heinz Neumann, who had perished in the Terror, was a victim of this brutal operation. When told in the Butyrka that he was to be expelled to Germany, Weissberg reminded the young NKVD officer who showed him the expulsion order that he was Jewish and asked that he be sent to Sweden. Others similarly protested, but to no avail. They were all turned over to the Gestapo between the fall of 1939 and the spring of 1940.[62] Many would later die at Auschwitz.

Another field of collaboration under the pact was trade. Talks begun in October 1939 led to the conclusion on 11 February 1940 of a barter agreement under which very large amounts of Soviet strategic raw materials, including feed grains, oil, iron ore, scrap and pig iron, manganese, and platinum, were exchanged for German industrial products, machinery, and armaments. The latter, however, included not the three battle cruisers sought by Moscow but just one. Stalin's effort to solidify his new political relationship with Berlin economically was a big boost for the German war effort, in part because it helped circumvent British efforts to impose an economic blockade on Germany.[63] Until the very last moment—3 a.m. on 22 June 1941, the day of Hitler's attack on Russia—long trainloads of Soviet grain, ore, and other materials regularly crossed the demarcation line although, from the outset of 1941, Germany stopped reciprocal deliveries, especially of machine tools, to Russia. The Germans would show the tools to Soviet inspectors in Germany, the inspectors would accept them, but the tools were never delivered.[64]

Saluting Stalin at Sixty

As Stalin turned sixty in December 1939, the regime celebrated him in speech, song, and story as the beloved *vozhd'* of a land of socialism triumphant.

Already on 19 December about half of *Pravda*'s six pages were devoted to the birthday, with dispatches from all over the country about the people's reverent observance of it. Next day, five of *Pravda*'s six pages were filled with an adulatory short biography of him. All this blotted out news of the Finnish war, in which heavy Soviet losses were arousing much concern. Muscovites on streetcars were overheard saying "We thought it would be over in four or five days. The Finns seem tough guys. It seems they are not all against the White regime as we thought."[65] On 21 December, the birthday itself, Soviet papers did not report, as Western ones did, that Soviet forces were in retreat on the Far Northern front in face of a strong Finnish counterdrive. For Stalin, who very likely received that news, it was not a good birthday present.

That day the press was filled with lavish tributes to him by Politburo members and others, and these were later collected into a book issued in 300,000 copies. A tally in it said that Stalin had received 10,150 birthday messages from various organizations and 5,155 from individuals, plus 1,508 from children.[66] An edict of the Supreme Soviet's Presidium made him a Hero of Socialist Labor. A Sovnarkom decree created Stalin Prizes.

Ten years earlier Stalin was hailed on his fiftieth birthday as the party's best Leninist, under whose leadership Soviet Russia would build socialism. Now the master theme was that he had brilliantly fulfilled that mission in history. The birthday tributes, drawn up according to the scripted culture of *Short Course* Bolshevism, sketched a make-believe reality in which Stalin had proved himself in life as a revolutionary leader.

Molotov led off the individual tributes with one that made out Stalin to have demonstrated by his thoughts and deeds the truth of what he had said in his published reply to the birthday tributes to him in 1929: "You need have no doubt, comrades, that I am prepared in the future, too, to devote to the cause of the working class, the proletarian revolution and world Communism, all my strength, all my ability, and, if need be, all my blood, drop by drop." Voroshilov published a glowing account of Stalin the military and political genius. Now, he went on in a phrase soon to be belied by events, the five-year plans had built a defense potential "fully ensuring the inviolability of the frontiers of our socialist state." And here was his picture of the Stalinist war of aggression against Finland: "With the name of Stalin on their lips, units of the Leningrad front are waging battles to defend the approaches to Leningrad and are liberating the Finnish people from its enslavers."

Citing Marx's phrase about revolutions as the locomotives of history and Lenin's gloss on it about the need to "speed up the locomotive and keep it on the tracks," Kaganovich called Stalin "the great engine-driver of history's locomotive." As such he had driven it down sharp descents and up hard rises, through twists and turns. Along the way, he had crushed the Trotskyist and Bukharinist traitors who, in attacking the locomotive, had aimed all their poisoned arrows at the engine-driver. For Khrushchev, "Comrade Stalin's biography [was] the glorious history of the Bolshevik party." For Beria, Stalin was "the greatest man of the present age, the deepest theorist of our epoch and the genius of the strategy and tactics of the proletarian revolution." So went the encomia from men of the auto-crat's entourage, who lived at his pleasure, governed their spheres accord-ing to his dictates, and knew how their self-aggrandizing lord and master would like to see himself and be seen by contemporaries and posterity.

How Stalin reacted to the unprecedented outpouring of adulation we do not know. He may have been moody in late December because of a submerged realization that he had badly bungled the dealings and war with

Finland and thereby lowered Hitler's respect for Russia's military might and prowess. And as the stereotyped eulogies were by now a fixture of Stalinist culture, they may have grown boring to him despite his never-ending need for them.

On 23 December *Pravda* printed some congratulatory birthday messages to Stalin from foreign leaders, among them Generalissimo Chiang Kai-shek of China, Dr. Joseph Tiso, who headed Hitler's fascist state of Slovakia in dismembered Czechoslovakia, and the foreign minister of Turkey. Heading the list were messages from Hitler, who wished Stalin good health and "a happy future for the peoples of the friendly Soviet Union," and Ribbentrop, who recalled his "historic hours in the Kremlin" and extended "warmest" birthday congratulations. Stalin's replies were also printed. He asked "Head of the German State, Mr. Adolf Hitler," to accept gratitude for his greeting and thanks for the good wishes to the Soviet peoples. And to Ribbentrop Stalin wrote: "I thank you, Mr. Minister, for your congratulations. The friendship of the peoples of Germany and the Soviet Union, sealed in blood, has every reason to be lasting and firm."

Stalin was no doubt feigning friendship in these shameful words about a friendship sealed in the blood of German and Soviet soldiers who fell in collaborative conquest of Poland. Still, he might not have written them had he been informed about something Hitler had said to his armed force chiefs of staff just one month earlier, on 23 November 1939: "At the present time Russia presents no danger. . . . But treaties are kept only as long as they are expedient. . . . Now Russia still has far-reaching aims, particularly the strengthening of her position on the shores of the Baltic Sea. We can oppose her only if we are free in the West."[67]

War Clouds Gather

The poor showing of his terror-ravaged forces in the Finnish war made clear to Stalin that improvements were urgently needed in the military sphere. Shortly after that war ended in March 1940, a series of steps followed to rectify the situation. Troop training was greatly intensified. New models of tanks and other weapons were introduced. The need was recognized to train military cadets and officers in methods of modern warfare. New measures for strategic deployment were proposed. More infantry divisions were created, airborne forces were increased in numbers, and separate armed and mechanized divisions were formed.[68]

On 10 May 1940 the low-intensity "phony war" that had gone on in the West since September 1939 ended abruptly as Hitler made his offensive move. Massed German mechanized forces swept around the Maginot Line through Holland, Belgium, and northern France, encircling France's main army and forcing the remnants of Britain's forces on the continent to take to boats back to their home island. On 15 May Holland surrendered. Brussels fell to the advancing Germans two days later, and in mid-June they took Paris. Hitler danced his famous jig when the surrender terms were signed.

Stalin reacted to this turn of events exactly as might be expected—by going into a depression. This we have directly from Khrushchev:

I remember we were all together in the Kremlin when we heard the news over the radio that the French army had capitulated and that the Germans were in Paris. Stalin's nerves cracked when he learned about the fall of France. He cursed the governments of England and France. "Couldn't they put up any resistance at all?" he asked despairingly.

Nor did Stalin take heart as time went on. Khrushchev, who was with him in Moscow shortly before the Soviet-German war started, later recalled:

He'd obviously lost all confidence in the ability of our army to put up a fight. It was as though he'd thrown up his hands in despair and given up after Hitler crushed the French army and occupied Paris. As I've said, I was with Stalin when we heard about the capitulation of France. He let fly with some choice Russian curses and said that now Hitler was sure to beat our brains in.[69]

The readers of this book will understand why Stalin despaired. France's swift collapse under Hitler's onslaught exploded the assumption of a protracted war in the West on which he had based his foreign policy in the 1930s, and now Russia was exposed to deadly danger of destruction. Cunningly careful in the one sphere in which he excelled—accumulating personal power—Stalin was a gambler and a bungler in high politics involving the power and interests of the nation. The calamity brought on by his gamble with terroristic collectivizing of the peasantry showed this at the outset of the 1930s, and the fiasco of his foreign policy showed it now. What made him a gambler and a bungler was the sublime faith in his own superior judgment that this man of limited and flawed leadership capacity attributed to himself because he believed that he was great and wise as a political leader.

Shaken as he was by the Anglo-French debacle in the West, Stalin moved to take advantage of Germany's involvement there in order to secure the remaining territories whose inclusion in his sphere of influence he had negotiated with Hitler. As the German campaign against France was ending, stage two of the takeover of the Baltic states began. A Soviet ultimatum of 14 June demanded that Soviet troop units be admitted on the ground that the air and naval forces already stationed there were not sufficient to meet security requirements. The three governments accepted the ultimatum, and the occupation proceeded without incident. In Moscow that month, Molotov gave Lithuania's vice-premier, Vincas Kreve-Mickevicius, a Stalin-like explanation, saying that ever since Ivan Grozny, Russian tsars had sought to reach the Baltic Sea for reasons of state.[70]

As Soviet tanks and truckloads of troops passed through Baltic towns and villages, whose clean, attractive small houses and well-kept fields amazed the soldiers, local people stood on the streets watching with glum faces. Soon the shelves in local shops emptied as Soviet soldiers, disobeying instructions, found their way to them and snapped up all their wares at what to them were ridiculously low prices in rubles or bond obligations, which the storekeepers innocently accepted in payment. The weak local Communist organizations arranged meetings at which citizens would welcome their occupiers as liberators. But so sullen were the faces of those pressured into attending these meetings that photos taken by Soviet reporters sent in for the occasion were not deemed fit for publication by newspaper editors back home.[71] After single-list "elections" held in July 1940, the securely controlled newly elected national assembles petitioned the Supreme Soviet for admission to the USSR, and in early August the Baltic states became union republics.

Meanwhile, Rumania's turn had come. Its Bessarabian province, which had belonged to the tsarist empire, had figured in the Stalin-Hitler accords of August–September 1939. But as no full clarity existed on this issue, Germany's diplomatic help was needed now. On 23 June 1940 Molotov informed Schulenburg that the Bessarabian problem had to be resolved immediately, and also that Moscow expected to claim Bukovina, also a part of Rumania, on account of its largely Ukrainian population. Two days later Berlin agreed to the demand for Bessarabia but said nothing about Bukovina, whereupon Molotov reduced the Soviet demand to northern Bukovina but coupled this lesser demand with a request for German intercession with the Rumanian government to ensure compliance with the Soviet demands. After Ribbentrop sent an affirmative reply, Moscow issued an ultimatum, with which Rumania complied. Hitler gave way on these questions, but the outcome was to harden his resolve to settle accounts with Stalin's Russia.[72] Northern Bukovina and a part of Bessarabia went to the Soviet Ukrainian Republic, and the greater part of Bessarabia, along with what had been the Moldavian Autonomous Republic in the Soviet Ukraine, became a new Moldavian Soviet Republic with its capital in Kishinev.

The newly acquired territories were all scenes of coercive revolutions from above, complete with nationalization of banks and plants, confiscation of landowner estates, collectivization, and repression of "socially alien" elements. The stark savagery of Stalinism found reflection in the scale and character of these repressions, which took diverse forms: mass arrests in what had been eastern Poland, the interning of captured remnants of the Polish army, arrests and deportations in the Baltic states, Bessarabia, and northern Bukovina. The victims numbered, all told, about two million.[73] To grasp the meaning of this figure, it must be realized that for a horrifyingly high number of these victims, "repression" meant execution or early death. Executions began in the eastern Polish lands in the first weeks of the occupation and went on all through 1939–40. Approximately 1,200,000 people were deported from these areas into the Soviet interior, many to Siberia, and it is estimated that about one-quarter of these died in exile or in concentration camps by the end of the summer of 1941. It is also estimated that as many as 100,000 people were executed by the NKVD during the evacuation of prisons in the Western Ukraine and Western Belorussia in June–July 1941.[74]

Special note must be taken of one Stalinist crime that received worldwide attention when, in 1944, the then retreating German occupants announced their discovery in the Katyn forest near Smolensk mass graves containing he remains of 4,443 executed Polish officers (the fates of another 10,000 Polish officers interned after Soviet conquest of eastern Poland in 1939 are still unknown). In the ensuing furor the Stalin government accused the Nazis of the crime. It has, however, been acknowledged by Moscow that the officers were executed by the NKVD between the end of March and start of May 1940.[75] The Katyn forest was the mass grave not only for those murdered Polish officers, but also for thousands upon thousands of Soviet terror victims whom the NKVD transported there, from 1935 to 1941, for execution, and for 135,000 Soviet prisoners of war executed by the Nazis during the occupation.[76]

The occupied Baltic states, Bessarabia, and northern Bukovina fared no better than the territories taken from Poland. In Estonia, for example, repressions started right after the Soviet forces occupied the republic in June 1940 and prior to its formal annexation in July. Political leaders, government officials, and army officers were convicted for actions taken while in the service of independent Estonia. Many people were executed and many others deported in cattle cars to unknown destinations from which no letters or news of their fates ever came. Over 7,200 Estonians were arrested in 1940 and 1941, and then, on the night of 14 June 1941, the NKVD deported over 10,000 Estonians—80 percent of them old people, women, and children—to Siberia. So terrifying were these events that after the Germans took Estonia in 1941, some 75,000 to 90,000 Estonians fled westward in 1942–43 to escape a possible repetition of these events in the future.[77] The repressions in Latvia and Lithuania followed the pattern of those in Estonia. Local Communists were, moreover, among the first to be arrested.

An individual terrorist act perpetrated at this time, on Stalin's orders, was the murder of Trotsky. The assassin was a Spanish agent of the NKVD, Ramon Mercader. Under the name of "Jacson" he insinuated himself into Trotsky's good graces on the pretext of being himself a Trotskyist. Trotsky and his wife, Natalya Sedova, were living in a villa in a suburb of Mexico City, Coyoacan. Guarded around the clock by Mexican police, reinforced by Trotskyist volunteers, the dwelling had the character of a small fortress under siege. In the spring of 1940 dissension raged in Trotsky's following, some of whose prominent American leaders, including Max Shachtman, were incensed at Trotsky for his refusal to condemn the Soviet takeover of eastern Poland and the war in Finland and for his call for "defense of the Soviet Union."[78] A large-scale terrorist attempt occurred at 4 a.m. on 24 May, when the sentries were taken by surprise by unknown assailants who fired at many as 200 shots into the bedrooms of the villa; Trotsky and his wife and their grandson escaped by lying on the floor. Then, on 20 August, 1940, Mercader, standing with Trotsky in his study, felled him from behind by plunging a pickax deep into his skull. Mortally wounded, Trotsky grappled with his assailant before succumbing, and died the next day. A letter found in the pocket of the arrested murderer made him out to have been a disillusioned Trotsky follower, which version *Pravda* repeated in its brief notice of Trotsky's death.[79]

The period following Hitler's stunning success in Western Europe was one of great international tension. Germany and Britain were still at war, and Britain had America's growing support. The British Isles were open to possible German invasion by sea. Very likely in the hope of cementing Soviet-German ties and thereby encouraging Hitler to continue the war in the West rather than give top priority to aggression against Russia, the fearful Stalin sought to mollify him by taking an anti-Anglo-French line in official discourse. On 5 July 1940 *Pravda* published lengthy summaries of German "White Books" containing captured French official documents, including secret Anglo-French staff correspondence of early 1940 on contingent plans for military action against Russia in support of embattled Finland. *Pravda*'s blistering editorial that day, "Documents Exposing the Anglo-French Organizers of War," said that the British and French ruling circles had long been preparing the ongoing second imperialist war. The documents showed that the war organizers had done their best to embroil Belgium and the Netherlands into their plans, and that the entry of German forces into the Low Countries had simply preempted the allies' use of them as a base for attacking Germany. "And only the wise Stalinist policy of the Soviet government diagnosed the warmongers' nefarious designs in good time and averted the attack on our country that was being prepared by the British and French."

The Soviet press announced on 1 August that a recently held plenary session of the party Central Committee heard and approved a report on the government's foreign policy. Nothing further was said about this report. However, what may have been a sanitized version of it for publication appeared in *Pravda* on 2 August as a Molotov report of the previous day to the Supreme Soviet. He reviewed developments in international relations over the past year, taking note at the outset of France's speedy defeat and capitulation. Soviet-German relations, he said, remained fully in accord with the new course specified in the agreement concluded between the two governments a year earlier. "This agreement," Molotov went on, "which our government is adhering to strictly, eliminated the possibility of frictions in Soviet-German relations as measures were being taken along our western frontier and, at the same time, gave Germany calm confidence in the East." Molotov could have illustrated this crucial last point by adding that Hitler, with the guarantee of Soviet nonintervention that the August–September 1939 accords gave him, had been able to send 136 divisions—the great bulk of his armed forces—against the Western democracies in May 1940, leaving a mere four infantry divisions on the new Soviet-German border and another six to police their rear.[80]

The rapporteur on foreign policy at the just-mentioned Central Committee session of late July must have been Molotov. The meeting, at which Litvinov lost his seat on the Central Committee, witnessed a dramatic scene. After Molotov raged against the ex–foreign commissar, accusing him, among other things, of "Anglophilism," Litvinov broke the dead silence of the assembly by declaring that a German attack was inevitable. Then he said that he failed to see why he had been displaced from his Foreign Commissariat post and why so many people of Vyshinsky's type were in the party now. Finally, he addressed himself directly to Stalin, saying: "So, how do things stand, do you regard me as an enemy of the people?" Stalin, pacing beside the table of the presidium, pointed at Litvinov and slowly enunciated the words: "We do not consider Papasha an enemy of the people. Papasha is an honest revolutionary." (Papasha was a name by which Litvinov had long been known in the Bolshevik movement.) Nevertheless, preparations for a trial of "enemy of the people Litvinov" proceeded after this plenary session. Beria and Kobulov tried to make Gnedin and other former Litvinov underlings testify against him. The Soviet source of this account surmises that the trial was not staged because Stalin decided to hold Litvinov in reserve, "just in case."[81]

An event of the fall of 1940 reflected Stalin's strong desire to preserve good relations with Hitler and fear of provoking him. The Soviet historian

Arkady Yerusalimsky had prepared a Russian-language edition of Otto von Bismarck's memoirs. *Thoughts and Recollections,* and equipped it with a 14-page introductory essay portraying that nineteenth-century chancellor as a proponent of peace with Russia. He had built up the German Empire by a "revolution from above" effected through foreign wars, but in all his empire-building activity was guided by the principle of never allowing Germany to go to war against Russia. So much so that young Kaiser Wilhelm, under whom Bismarck was retired, considered him a "Russophile." It was no doubt the theme of Bismarckian amity between the two countries that underlay Molotov's personal sponsorship of this very unusual publication by a Soviet professor. Whether the book, when published in 1940, was brought by the German Embassy in Moscow to Ribbentrop's personal attention is not known, but the latter claimed in his own memoirs that all through the winter and spring months of 1941 he kept reminding Hitler of Bismarck's Russian policy.[82]

Page proofs of the introduction to Yerusalimsky's book went to Stalin before the book could be published. After World War II Yerusalimsky gave the proofs, with Stalin's penciled notes and comments scrawled on them, to a younger colleague, Mikhail Gefter. Following old habits of a one-time *Pravda* editor, Stalin made stylistic corrections. But there were substantive comments as well. He disliked the implicitly warning tone of Yerusalimsky's concluding passages. He struck out entirely a vivid sentence saying that Bismarck "always had a high evaluation of the moral qualities of the Russian army, and forever imprinted on his mind was the image of the simple Russian soldier ready in the name of duty to freeze in a snowstorm on the Shipka Pass but never leave his post." He also commented that a passage on Bismarck's repeated warnings against involvement in a war with Russia was inappropriate *(ne to)* as a final paragraph of the introduction. Around 1 November 1940 Yerusalimsky had a personal interview with him in the presence of Molotov and Zhdanov. When Yerusalimsky timidly sought to defend the placement of his final paragraph on the ground of its political topicality, Stalin replied: "But why do you frighten them? Let them try."[83]

While those thoughts were on Stalin's mind, quite different ones were on Hitler's. In the wake of the defeat of France, the German generals had been working on a plan under the code name of "Sea Lion" for an early invasion of the British Isles. At the end of July of 1940, however, Hitler announced in secret to heads of the *Wehrmacht* that he had decided to postpone the invasion of Britain in order to settle accounts first with Russia. That, he thought, would render Britain's situation untenable. As General Halder confided to his diary: "It was decided that in order to resolve the problem, Russia must be destroyed in the spring of 1941. The sooner we crush Russia, the better. [84] All preparations for Operation Sea Lion ended in the first half of October. This was the very thing that Stalin desperately hoped would not happen. Intelligence reports about it went to Moscow,[85] but he did not heed them.

As German preparations for invading Russia went forward in the summer and fall, Hitler wanted to delude Stalin concerning his aggressive intentions. With this in view, he took steps to encourage the belief that Soviet-German relations might take a further turn for the better. In correspondence between Berlin and Moscow during the summer, the Germans pressed the Soviet government to send a high-level delegation to Berlin for a new round of negotiations that would take account of changes in the world situation since Ribbentrop's visits to Moscow in 1939. On 22 October 1940, Molotov handed Schulenburg in Moscow a letter to Ribbentrop from Stalin saying "I agree with you that a further improvement in the relations between our countries is entirely possible on the permanent basis of a long-range delimitation of mutual interests." Herr Molotov, Stalin went on, agrees that he is under obligation to pay you a return visit to Berlin and accepts your invitation.[86] In taking this decision, Stalin did precisely what Hitler wanted him to do.

On 11 November Molotov departed Moscow by train for Berlin accompanied by sixteen security guards, a physician, and three personal servants. He arrived the next morning for what turned out to be a forty-eight hour stay during which he had two three-hour sessions with Hitler, meetings with Rudolph Hess, Herman Göring, and Ribbentrop, including a final two-hour session with Ribbentrop in his personal air-raid shelter while British planes bombed Berlin. To what extent the whole affair was a charade, a diversionary maneuver on Hitler's part, is best indicated by a secret order that he issued on 12 November saying that whatever the outcome of the diplomatic talks staring that day, "all the previously envisaged earlier preparations for the East should be continued."[87] And Hitler's conduct in the talks supports the view that his aim was to lull fears that would presumably be aroused in Moscow by signs of the now ongoing German preparations for war in the East and thereby to keep Stalin from putting the Soviet armed forces on mobilized alert and the whole nation in a state of conscious readiness to defend the homeland.

So, it was an expansive, friendly *Fuehrer* whom Molotov met in person for the first time on 12 November, a German chancellor in the Bismarckian mould with whom one could discuss in the manner of imperial statesmen the delineation of two world powers' spheres. Russia and Germany, Hitler declared, were two great nations that need not by nature have any conflict of interests, and it should be possible for them to reach a settlement that would lead to peaceful collaboration beyond the life-span of the present leaders. Molotov voiced his full agreement with these points, and with Hitler's further point that the political collaboration between them during the past year had been of considerable value to both countries. Molotov also observed that one of the benefits was that Germany had received a "secure hinterland" which had been of great importance for events during the year of war.

If Germany and Russia stood together, Hitler continued, it would be advantageous to both countries, to which Molotov replied that this was entirely correct and would be confirmed by history. Then Hitler described military operations being carried out against England and said that as soon as weather conditions improved, Germany would be poised for the great and final blow against England. Apropos future Russian-German collaboration, he said some colonial expansion in Central Africa was necessary and Germany needed certain raw materials, but "the Russian empire could develop without in the least prejudicing German interest." Molotov said that this was "quite correct." Hitler observed that he fully understood Russia's attempts to get ice-free ports with secure access to the open sea and would be prepared to help effect an improvement for Russia in the regime of the Black Sea Straits.

Responding, Molotov first stressed that Stalin had given him exact instructions and everything he was about to say was identical with Stalin's views. As regards the Tripartite Pact of 27 September 1940 between Germany, Italy, and Japan, to which Russia's adherence had been raised as a possibility, what was the meaning of the New Order in Europe and Asia and what role would the USSR have in it? Further, the Finnish question was still unsolved (he was referring to the presence of German troops there), and he would like to know whether the previous year's German-Russian agreement on Finland was still in force. There were issues to be clarified regarding Russia's Balkan and Black Sea interests. After hearing Hitler respond, Molotov said that Russia's participation in the Tripartite Pact appeared to him fully acceptable in principle, provided that Russia was to cooperate as a partner and not be merely an object.[88]

So taken in was Molotov by Hitler's play acting that in their next long conversation he boldly went ahead to stake out some claims in coming collaborative rearrangements in the world. On Finland, he said that his remark related to the secret protocol (in which Finland had been placed in Russia's sphere of influence), to which Hitler replied that Germany was very interested in deliveries of nickel and lumber from Finland and was not interested in acquiring Finnish territory. After the coming dissolution of the British Empire, Germany, France, Italy, Russia, and Japan would have to concern themselves with its partition. Molotov expressed interest in the regime of the Black Sea Straits, and sounded out Hitler on the idea of Russia giving Bulgaria a guarantee like the one Germany and Italy had given Rumania. Hitler said that he did not know of any Bulgarian request for such a guarantee, to which Molotov replied that Moscow would like to settle with Turkey the question of security from an attack by way of the Straits and that a guarantee to Bulgaria would alleviate that situation. Hitler said he would have to talk this over with Mussolini and then turned to plans regarding a division among the interested powers of "the British Empire's bankrupt estate." After supper on 14 November, Ribbentrop and Molotov talked at length in the air-raid shelter about future collaboration between the countries of the Tripartite Pact and Russia, and proposed the draft of an agreement on this matter that would be made public. In the end Molotov referred to Stalin's letter of 22 October and agreed that a delimitation of spheres of influence must be sought.[89]

Not only did Stalin/Molotov play into Hitler's hands by the trip to Berlin and discussions there; they also reinforced still further his resolve to march on Russia. Ribbentrop recalled of Hitler that as a result of Molotov's visit "his reticence regarding Russia became striking, and there was many a sign that strong forces were at work, urging him to take a decision against Russia.[90] Not knowing this and assuming that they were in a game of give-and-take with Hitler, Stalin made a next move in response to Hitler's and Ribbentrop's expressions of interest in Russia joining the Tripartite Pact. In a memorandum that Molotov turned over to Schulenburg on 26 November, agreement to join the pact was made contingent on fulfillment of the following conditions: withdrawal of German troops from Finland; conclusion of a mutual assistance pact between the USSR and Bulgaria; the establishment of a base for Soviet land and naval forces within range of the Bosporus and Dardanelles under a long-term lease; recognition of the area south of Batum and Baku in the Persian Gulf direction as the center of Soviet aspirations; and Japanese renunciation of her rights to concessions for coal and oil in Northern Sakhalin.[91]

Although a move of this kind on the diplomatic chessboard was only what Hitler and Ribbentrop had solicited in Berlin, Stalin unwittingly confirmed Hitler in his bellicose intentions. No reply to the memorandum came from Berlin. The effect on Hitler was to hasten his preparations for war. General Halder recorded in his diary that on receipt of Schulenburg's telegram containing the Molotov document, Hitler declared: "Russia must be brought to her knees." He then ordered his General Staff to accelerate the preparation of a concrete plan for war in the East. He approved it on December 5 under the code name "Otto Plan."[92] On 18 December he approved it in a fuller final form under the code name "Barbarossa Plan." It stated: "The German Armed Forces must be prepared *to crush Soviet Russia in a quick campaign* even before the conclusion of the war against

England." The directive said that preparations for the attack were to be completed by 15 May 1941, and that it was of utmost importance that the intention to attack not be discovered.[93] Thus was the die cast. Russia was now in the gravest danger she ever confronted, and it was compounded a thousandfold by the fact that her citizens, in their great majority, remained unaware of it and that urgently needed defensive measures to meet the danger were not being taken.

After the signing of the pact with Hitler in August 1939 Stalin boasted that he had "tricked" Hitler, but in truth, it was the other way around. Not only did Hitler, by his quick victory over France, invalidate Stalin's firm assumption that the war in the West would be protracted and thereby work to his advantage. Now he had outsmarted Stalin by encouraging him to believe that he was disposed to enter into arrangements under which the two of them would more or less dominate the world in tandem. Stalin never seems to have comprehended the full force of Hitler's fanaticism and the impossibility of doing that sort of business with him. According to his daughter's recollection, he never stopped regretting that the condominium scenario did not come to pass. "Ekh, together with the Germans we would have been invincible," he went on repeating already after the war was over."[94]

22

THE RECKONING

GIVEN the efficiency of Soviet intelligence and the scale of the German preparations for war in the east, it was impossible to keep those preparations a secret in accordance with the Barbarossa directive. Richard Sorge, Moscow's spy in Tokyo, reported without delay on the German decision for war, and the Red Army chiefs received weekly updates on German preparations. By the beginning of 1941 they had precise information on the planned operation.[1] By the month of March rumors of the coming invasion were rife in Berlin, where Berezhkov was stationed. Different dates for it were being bruited: 6 April, 20 April, 18 May, and 22 June.[2]

All this information went, of course, to Stalin. But knowledge of a set of circumstances is not a diagnosis of what they mean and what, accordingly, should be done in response to them. In diagnosing situations, Stalin was not one to trust his military intelligence chiefs, six of whom he had arrested between 1936 and 1940.[3] According to Mikoyan, he convinced himself that Hitler would not risk a two-front war by attacking Russia before he had prevailed over Britain, and this, he reasoned, could not happen before the middle or end of 1942.[4]

Given that assessment of the situation, what did Stalin do? At the beginning of 1941 he wrote a personal letter to Hitler saying that German troop concentrations in the east were creating the impression that Hitler intended to make war on the Soviet Union. Hitler answered with a personal and, as he put it, "confiding" letter admitting the presence of those troop concentrations. But he gave Stalin his assurance (on his word of honor as *Reichschancellor*) that these forces were not aimed against the Soviet Union because he intended strictly to observe the German-Soviet pact. The explanation was that western and central Poland were within range of British air observation and under bombardment by British planes. That was why he had been forced to keep large German troop contingents in eastern Poland. General Zhukov, who became chief of the General Staff in February 1941, and who read Hitler's letter, reported later that it conveyed the impression that Hitler was keeping his forces in eastern Poland in preparation for operation Sea Lion.[5]

Although these soothing lies from Hitler had an effect on Stalin, we should not assume that he was unaware that the country was in great danger. That he was quite apprehensive is perhaps best indicated by his action of quickly recognizing on 5 April 1941 a new Yugoslav government that took power by a coup; Germany invaded Yugoslavia the next day. Stalin very likely hoped that because of Yugoslavia's rugged terrain and will to resist, the Germans' campaign there might slow down preparations to the point of their being unable to move against Russia in the spring of 1941.[6] However, the German army overcame Yugoslavia quickly.

Still, Stalin went on hoping against hope for a delay. In April 1941 the Soviet General Staff received a report through intelligence channels that the German decision for war was final and that invasion would come soon with a *blitzkrieg* against the Ukraine followed by an advance to the east. Nevertheless, in May, just one month before the attack came, Stalin opined in a small group that "A conflict will become inevitable in May of next year."[7] This wishful thinking ruled his mind. Zhukov much later recalled of the days just before the war: "All his thoughts and acts were inspired by one desire—to avoid war—and confidence that he could do it." Zhukov added that "It never even occurred to anyone to raise doubt about his judgments and assessments of the situation."[8]

What decisions Stalin did take at Russia's zero hour were utterly disastrous. His mind was fixated on the latter part of what he had said to the Sixteenth Party Congress in 1930: "Not a foot of foreign territory do

we want, but not a single inch of our own land will we give up to anyone."
Now he had expanded "our own land" by many thousands of square miles
beyond the old 1939 borders, and not a single inch *of it* could be given up
to anyone. That expanded domain was the one tangible fruit of all his
diplomacy from the outset of the 1930s. And he insisted that the war plans
worked out by his General Staff provide for keeping it. As they were being
formulated in the fall of 1940, no account was taken of a possible breakthrough by hostile forces. When a defensive strategy in depth was bruited
during one strategic war game, Stalin venomously remarked: "Why cultivate defensive attitudes? What is this, are you planning a retreat?"[9]

Because of his refusal to consider a strategy of defense in depth, an
action inimical to Russia's most vital security interests was taken in the
spring of 1941. On Stalin's orders, a 1,200-kilometer-long line of strong
fortifications extending the entire distance between the Baltic and Black
seas, built during the 1930s at huge cost and effort, was partially disman-
tled and partially abandoned with a view to constructing a new line of
fortifications along the new borders to the west. However, the plans made
in 1940 to build the new line were calculated for several years and by June
1941 had no more than begun to be carried out.[10] Had the recently acquired
western territories been held as a lightly defended buffer region and the old
fortified line preserved, the Red Army would out of necessity have received ample warning of the German invasion and could have fought
effectively along that line as only Russians can and will fight when they
are in a position to defend Russia against a mortal enemy. What's more,
the old fortifications were no Maginot line around which the Germans
could have swept as they did in May 1940 through the low countries.

Meanwhile, Stalin moved a large proportion of his 170 divisions to
positions not far from the new borders. Also stationed there, vulnerable to
capture or destruction by the Germans (which in fact occurred) were 25,000
railway carloads of munitions—30 percent of all Russia's reserves—and
half of the army's fuel reserves. Furthermore, in the period just preceding
the invasion, hundreds of German reconnaissance units were allowed to
cross the border for their purposes on the pretext of "searching for graves,"
and German planes were not only allowed to enter Soviet air space (324
such intrusions took place in the first half of 1941) for reconnaissance but,
when forced to land because of engine trouble, were graciously repaired
by the Russians and sent home with their fuel tanks refilled.[11]

Molotov closed his foreign policy report to the Supreme Soviet on 1
August 1940 by quoting Stalin as having said that it was "necessary to
keep our whole people in a state of mobilized readiness in the face of the
danger of military attack, so that no 'accident' and no tricks of our foreign
foes could take us by surprise." Far from doing that as the danger grew to

alarming proportions, Stalin did just the reverse. He spiritually *demobilized* the nation by having a Soviet official statement put out on 14 June 1941 dismissing rumors of imminent German invasion as "clumsy fabrications." It said that "according to Soviet information, Germany, like the USSR, is also strictly observing the provisions of the Soviet-German non-aggression pact and, therefore, in the opinion of Soviet circles, rumors of Germany's intentions to violate the pact and open an attack on the USSR are devoid of all foundation." Military historian Volkogonov says that this statement was issued in order to solicit new talks with Hitler, the aim being to stave off war through June and July, after which August would be too close to autumn for invasion and war would have to be postponed until the spring of 1942. Stalin, he adds, said in private as late as 15 June that war was unlikely, at least until the following spring.[12] One result of the 14 June statement was that on Sunday, 22 June, a fine day in European Russia, people went out for their weekend leisure pursuits unmindful of the fact that their country was already under attack by 152 German divisions.

Before the invasion, warnings of its imminence came from a multitude of sources other than Soviet intelligence. One came in a telegram from Winston Churchill, the now embattled Britain's prime minister. This was one of the warnings that Stalin failed to pass on to his General Staff; he saw it as an effort to hasten a collision between him and Hitler.[13] The bravest warning act was undertaken by Ambassador Schulenburg. He invited Dekanozov, who was then in Moscow on a trip back from his new post as Soviet ambassador in Berlin, to have lunch at the German Embassy. The lunch, at which Hilger and von Walther were also present, took place on 19 May 1941.

During it, as Mikoyan much later told the historian Kumanev, Schulenburg turned to Dekanozov and said:

Mr. Ambassador, this may be unprecedented in the history of diplomacy, since I am about to reveal to you state secret number one: tell Mr. Molotov, and he, I hope, will inform Mr. Stalin, that Hitler has taken the decision to begin war against the USSR on 22 June. Why, you may ask, do I tell you this? I was brought up in the spirit of Bismarck, and he always opposed war with Russia.

The lunch ended at this point. Schulenburg had upheld the honor of the German nation by betraying Hitler. Dekanozov rushed off to inform Molotov of what he had learned. Later that day, Stalin told the assembled members of the Politburo about Schulenburg's message, and commented: "We shall consider that disinformation has now reached the level of ambassadors."[14]

Two further incidents of that time call for notice. Shortly before the invasion General Kirponos, chief of the Kiev Special Military District, reported to Stalin that the German armies were preparing an attack in the very near future and proposed that a strong defense be prepared with evacuation of 300,000 people from the border areas, organizing of several strong points there as well as antitank ditches and trenches. The answer from Moscow was that this would be a "provocation" and that the Germans were not to be given any pretext for military action.[15] The other incident, reported by Stalin's secretary, Poskrebyshev, was a visit to Stalin on 13 June by Admiral Kuznetsov, then the Soviet naval commissar. He informed Stalin that the Germans had withdrawn all their ships from Soviet ports and requested permission to withdraw all Soviet ships from German ones. Stalin sent him on his way, saying "Can the admiral not have read today's TASS report refuting the provocational rumors about a German attack on the Soviet Union? Everywhere provocations. All our enemies and false friends are trying to sick us on Hitler in their own interests."[16]

This situation was unprecedented in history. Soviet Russia's fate was in the hands of an absolute autocrat who fancied himself a political and military leader of genius but was unable at the critical moment to perform the prime functions of a leader: to diagnose the country's problem situation realistically, prescribe measures designed to meet it, and implement those measures. How are we to explain his inability to rise to the challenge? It does no good to suggest "insanity" as an answer. He did have a diagnosis of the multitudinous warnings from his agents and others: "provocations." And he drew from this diagnosis a logical prescription for action, or rather for inaction. To respond by taking defensive measures in preparation for an expected attack was to tell Hitler that he, Stalin, was mistrustful of him and thereby make absolutely certain that Hitler *would* attack. By acting as he did to leave the country peacefully unprepared for invasion, he sought to persuade Hitler that he need not have any fear of Russia and hence no need to invade.

This was one of the most monumental acts of leadership folly in human annals, yet historians must try to explain it. I suggest that the explanation goes back to what Stalin had least of all expected—the swift fall of France under Hitler's onslaught—and the reaction of despair that, as we know from Khrushchev, this caused in him. The semi-paralyzed Stalin of June 1941 was still the utterly stunned, despairing Stalin of June 1940 who foresaw a thrashing by Hitler now that he had beaten the allies in the West. Stalin did not believe in his country's ability to stand up—as it proceeded to do under the worst imaginable circumstances—against attack by Hitler's massed forces. That being so, his only apparent recourse was to dismiss the many warnings of coming invasion as "provocations" and take no defensive action in response to them in the anguished hope that Hitler as a result would hold off and thereby give him another year in which to get ready for war.

This hypothesis accords with what happened when the dread news of the invasion reached him. Stalin went to bed late at night on 21 June, sleeping as usual on the couch at his Kuntsevo dacha. At 4 a.m. a bodyguard, contrary to all rules, knocked on his door to tell him that General Zhukov was on the phone. Stalin donned a robe, picked up the receiver, and answered. Zhukov told him that enemy planes were bombing Kiev, Minsk, Sevastopol, Vilnius, and other cities. No answer. Then came Zhukov's voice: "Did you understand me, Comrade Stalin?" The man at the other end breathed heavily into the phone and said nothing. "Comrade Stalin," Zhukov repeated, "did you understand me?"[17] As Zhukov later related, Stalin stayed silent for two whole hours while troops and civilians were dying, bombs were falling, and planes were being destroyed by the Germans on airfields where they stood. Only after those endless two hours did permission come from him to give the order to resist. Afterward, Stalin was in so deep a state of shock that he received no one for a week.[18] It was left to Molotov, who was no longer head of the Soviet government (Stalin had assumed that post on 6 May 1941), to announce over the radio that Russia was at war and appeal to the people to fight the invaders. Not until 3 July was Stalin able to address his people by radio. Even then, according to the testimony of a young Moscow girl who listened to the broadcast, he spoke in an unsteady voice and one could hear clinking sounds as he reached with trembling hands to pour water from a pitcher into his glass.[19]

How shall we explain Stalin's state of deep shock at that time? A part of the answer is deadly fear that the cause was lost. But another part, which follows from the interpretation of Stalin and his actions presented in this book, is that he, who had all along been a hero of history in his own eyes, was for once, and inescapably, confronted with the reality of himself as a colossal bungler of high policy and, as such, an enemy of the people.

NOTES

Introduction: Toward a New October

1. I. V. Stalin, *Sochineniia*, 13 vols. (Moscow, 1946–52), VI, 46. Three additional volumes appeared in the United States: XIV (I)–XVI (III), ed. Robert H. McNeal (Stanford, 1967). Hereafter cited as *Stalin*.
2. Aleksandr Bolotin, "Chto my znaem o Liapidevskom?" *Ogonyok,* no. 14, 2–9 April 1988, p. 20. When Anatoly Liapidevsky, a famous Soviet flyer, was feted in the Kremlin in 1934, Stalin approached him, bottle in hand, and said: "Comrade Liapidevsky, your father was a priest, mine was priest too. In case of need, get directly in touch with Comrade Stalin." Bolotin's sources for his article included the now deceased Liapidevsky's wife and daughter.
3. For this analysis of the neurotic personality, see Karen Horney, *Neurosis and Human Growth* (New York, 1950). For more on its applicability to Stalin, see Robert C. Tucker, *Stalin as Revolutionary, 1879–1929: A Study in History and Personality* (New York, 1953), chaps. 3 and 12.
4. *Stalin*, III, 25.
5. *Stalin*, XI, 224. The occasion was a 1928 speech.
6. *X s"ezd RKP/b/, mart 1921 goda* (Moscow, 1960), pp. 202–3. "Russia One and Indivisible" was a slogan of the Whites during the Civil War of 1918–20.
7. *Stalin*, V, 71. This piece of writing by Stalin was first published after World War II. The emphasis is Stalin's. (In all subsequent quotations the emphases are in originals, unless noted otherwise.)
8. *Stalin*, VIII, 215, 220. The statements appear in Stalin's theses for the Fifteenth All-Union Party Conference, originally published in *Pravda* on 26 October 1926.
9. Robert C. Tucker, *Politics As Leadership* (Columbia, Mo., and London, 1981), chap. 2.
10. *Stalin*, XIII, 38–39. The poem cited was "Who Lives Well in *Rus'?*" by the nineteenth-cen-

tury poet Nikolai Nekrasov. *Rus'* is the name
by which the territories that formed the core
of the modern Russian state, centered in the

grand principality of Kiev, were known in
early times.

1. The Tsardom's Rise

1. V. O. Kliuchevsky, *Kurs russkoi istorii*
(Moscow, 1937), II, 130. Kliuchevsky (1841–
1911) held the chair of history at the University of Moscow in the 1880s and 1890s. His
5-volume *Kurs,* based on his university lectures, was first published in 1904–8.
2. George Vernadsky, *Russia at the Dawn of
the Modern Age* (New Haven, 1959), p. 68
and *passim.*
3. Pavel Nikolaevich Miliukov, *Ocherki po istorii russkoi kul'tury,* 5th ed. (St. Petersburg,
1904), I, 144, 145.
4. Miliukov, *Ocherki,* I, 143; and *Russia and
Its Crisis* (New York, 1962), pp. 121–23.
The latter book is largely based on Miliukov's lectures of 1903 at the University of
Chicago.
5. Richard Hellie, *Enserfment and Military
Change in Muscovy* (Chicago and London,
1971), p. 103. Hellie's examination of the
evidence leads him to affirm (p. 264) "the
primacy of the role of the state power in the
enserfment."
6. Miliukov, *Ocherki,* I, 133–34, 143–44. But
Miliukov repeatedly stresses the underlying
causal primacy of the external factor—"the
primacy of external growth over internal" (p.
144).
7. Miliukov, *Russia,* p. 122.
8. Kliuchevsky, *Kurs,* II, 208–9. In *Ivan Grozny*
(Moscow, 1975), p. 20, R. G. Skrynnikov
also writes that Ivan showed a vicious streak
at twelve and at fourteen took friends on wild
violent rampages on horseback in Moscow.
9. Skrynnikov, *Ivan Grozny,* p. 36.
10. Kliuchevsky, *Kurs,* II, 179. The authenticity
of the Grozny-Kurbsky correspondence has
been challenged by Edward L. Keenan in *The
Kurbskii-Groznyi Apocrypha: The Seventeenth-Century Genesis of the "Correspondence" Attributed to Prince A. M. Kurbskii
and Tsar Ivan IV* (Cambridge, Mass., 1971),
but upheld by Skrynnikov and other histori-

ans, whose position I accept.
11. Kliuchevsky, *Kurs,* II, 196; Skrynnikov, *Ivan
Grozny,* pp. 130–32. Skrynnikov cites the
authors of unofficial chronicles as taking the
view that "there was no actual conspiracy"
although there were "careless conversations"
by malcontents who favored Prince Vladimir
Andreevich, and these were reported to the
tsar.
12. Skrynnikov, *Ivan Grozny,* p. 101.
13. *Ibid.,* p. 104. Anastasia, the first of Ivan's
seven wives, died a lingering death of illness
in 1560.
14. Kliuchevsky, *Kurs,* II, 189–90; Skrynnikov,
Ivan Grozny, pp. 105–7.
15. Kliuchevsky, *Kurs,* II, 191. The following
account draws heavily on this source.
16. Skrynnikov, *Ivan Grozny,* p. 179.
17. Kliuchevsky, *Kurs,* II, 197.
18. T. V. Lokot', *Smutnoe vremia i revoliutsiia*
(Berlin, 1923), p. 24. Viewing 1917 as a new
Time of Troubles, Lokot' foresaw the possibility of a "national movement for rebirth of
Russia" headed by a new Ivan, "a dictator
who leads the people out of the chaos of revolution to firm foundations of national statehood" (pp. 91–92).
19. My sketch of Peter's revolution from above
draws upon Michael T. Florinsky, *Russia: A
History and an Interpretation* (New York,
1955), I, chaps. 12–15, as well as vol. IV of
Kliuchevsky's *Kurs.*
20. Kliuchevsky, *Kurs,* IV, 225; Florinsky, *Russia,* II, 390.
21. Kliuchevsky, *Kurs,* IV, 223.
22. Leonard Hubbard, *The Economics of Soviet
Agriculture* (London, 1939), p. 19.
23. Kliuchevsky, *Kurs,* III, 11.
24. A. I. Gertsen (Herzen), *Dvizhenie obshchestvennoi mysli v Rossii* (Moscow, 1907),
pp. 46–47, 154–55. This book was first published in 1851 in Germany.

2. Lenin's Legacy

1. *The State and Revolution* (1917), in *The Lenin
Anthology,* ed. Robert C. Tucker (New York,
1975), p. 328.
2. T. H. Rigby, *Lenin's Government: Sovnarkom, 1917–1922* (Cambridge, England,
1979), p. 235.
3. *Lenin Anthology,* p. 490. The word here
translated "cudgel" is *dubinka,* literally a
"club."
4. Both citations from E. H. Carr, *Socialism in
One Country, 1924–1926,* II (New York,
1959), 424–25. Carr notes that the original
function of the concentration camps was "not
punitive, but preventive."
5. V. I. Lenin, *Polnoe sobranie sochinenii,* 5th

ed., 55 vols. (Moscow, 1958–65), XLV, 190.
Hereafter cited as *Lenin.*
6. *Lenin,* XXXVI, 316.
7. *"Left-Wing" Communism—An Infantile Disorder,* in *Lenin Anthology,* p. 569.
8. Lenin said *(ibid.):* "We in Russia (in the third
year since the overthrow of the bourgeoisie)
are making the first steps in the transition
from capitalism to socialism or the lower stage
of communism."
9. *Lenin Anthology,* p. 674. In *The Communist
Party of the Soviet Union* (New York, 1959),
p. 264 n., Leonard Schapiro notes that at
about this same time Lenin told a visiting
Spanish socialist, Fernando de los Rios, that

the transition period might last "perhaps forty or fifty years."

10. "The Importance of Gold Now and After the Complete Victory of Socialism" (1921), in *Lenin Anthology*, pp. 512–13.

11. For fuller discussion of this thesis, see Robert C. Tucker, *Political Culture and Leadership in Soviet Russia: From Lenin to Gorbachev* (New York, 1987), chap. 3.

12. *Lenin*, XXXVI, 30. Lenin's words about Peter were a paraphrase of Marx's. In 1865 Marx wrote to J. B. Schweitzer: "If Peter the Great defeated Russian barbarism by barbarity, Proudhon did his best to defeat French phrase-mongering with phrases." Karl Marx and Friedrich Engels, *Selected Correspondence, 1846–1895*, trans. and ed. Dona Torr (New York, 1942), p. 175.

13. "On Cooperation," in *Lenin Anthology*, pp. 707–13.

14. *Ibid.*, p. 713.

15. *Lenin*, XXXVIII, 204. He made this statement in 1919.

16. "Better Fewer, But Better," in *Lenin Anthology*, pp. 745–46.

17. Leon Trotsky, *Literature and Revolution* (Ann Arbor, 1960), p. 94.

18. Vera T. Reck, *Boris Pil'niak: A Soviet Writer in Conflict with the State* (Montreal, 1975), p. 96. The author notes (pp. 5–6) that Stalin, who refers to *The Naked Year* in his lectures of 1924 on *The Foundations of Leninism*, was one of Pil'niak's readers.

19. William Henry Chamberlin, *The Russian Revolution, 1917–1921* (New York, 1935), II, 42.

20. Speech of 6 December 1920, *Lenin*, XL, 56.

21. *Smena vekh*, 2nd ed. (Prague, 1922), pp. 50, 56–59, 62–63, 68, 89, 146, 182–83. For Ustrialov's "national Bolshevism" as the proper tactics for Russian patriots, see his article "Natsional-bolshevizm," in his *Pod znakom revoliutsii*, 2nd ed. (Harbin, China, 1927), pp. 47–53. On Ustrialov and his influence in Russia, see M. Agursky, *Ideologiia natsional-bolshevizma* (Paris, 1980).

22. *Lenin Anthology*, pp. 526–27.

23. "Our Revolution (Apropos of N. Sukhanov's Notes)" (1923), *ibid.*, pp. 705–6.

24. For the details of Lenin's indictment of Stalin for Great Russian chauvinism and his failed effort to purge Stalin from party power, see Tucker, *Stalin As Revolutionary* (New York, 1973), chap. 7. "Derzhimorda" is a Russian colloquialism for a police bully, derived from a character in Gogol's play *The Inspector General*.

25. *Lenin*, XLV, p. 309.

26. *Pravda*, 23 April 1920.

27. "Lenin," *Novosti zhizni*, 24 January 1924. Dmitry Donskoy was a prince of Muscovy in the second half of the fourteenth century. It is virtually certain that Stalin read this article. He repeatedly referred to Ustrialov in speeches of 1925–26, and in one (*Stalin*, IX, 71) he said, "Ustrialov's articles in praise of Lenin are known to our whole party."

28. On the rise of the Lenin cult, see Tucker, *Stalin As Revolutionary*, pp. 279–88, and for the full story of it see Nina Tumarkin, *Lenin Lives! The Lenin Cult in Soviet Russia* (Cambridge, Mass., 1983).

29. Nikolai Valentinov, *Doktrina pravogo kommunizma: 1924–26 gody v istorii sovetskogo gosudarstva* (Munich, 1960), p. 16.

30. Cited by Stephen F. Cohen in *Bukharin and the Bolshevik Revolution: A Political Biography, 1888–1938* (New York, 1973), p. 188. For the Left's charge of "national narrow-mindedness," see *loc. cit.*

31. William Reswick, *I Dreamt Revolution* (Chicago, 1952), pp. 255, 164.

32. For particulars, based on an unpublished essay on "Thermidor and Anti-Semitism," written by Trotsky in 1937, see Joseph Nedava, *Trotsky and the Jews* (Philadelphia, 1971), pp. 174–78.

33. *Stalin*, XII, 343. The occasion was his report to the Sixteenth Party Congress in 1930.

34. *Stalin*, VIII, 142–43.

35. *Ibid.*, XIII, 25. Italics added. On the exchange of letters, see I. Eventov, *Zhizn' i tvorchestvo Demyana Bednogo* (Leningrad, 1967), pp. 205–8.

3. Stalin's Program

1. Speech of 1 November 1926, *Stalin*, VIII, 263. Italics added.

2. *Ibid.*, V, 109. Italics added.

3. *Ibid.*, VI, 396–97, 398–99.

4. *Ibid.*, VII, 281–82.

5. Discussion with first American worker delegation, *Stalin*, X, 135. The discussion took place in September 1927.

6. Speech of 27 January 1925 to a Moscow province party conference. *Stalin*, VII, 27.

7. *Ibid.*, VII, 261–63, 281–82, 288, 296–97.

8. *Ibid.*, VII, 11–14. First published after World War II.

9. *Ibid.*, 38. Earlier in the speech Stalin had listed the Western proletariat and the colonial peoples as the first and second allies. But the third ally was the "greatest."

10. *XIV s"ezd VKP(b), 18–31 dekabria 1925 g.* (Moscow and Leningrad, 1926), part 1, p. 959.

11. *Stalin*, II, 303–4.

12. *Ibid.*, V, 34, 15–16.

13. On Stalin's "daily norm," see Yuri Sharapov in *Moskovskie novosti*, 18 September 1988; on his underlining in Lozinsky's book, see O. Volobuev and S. Kuleshov in *Sotsialisticheskaia industriia*, 25 June 1988. On the organization of the personal library and Russian history books in it, see Dmitrii Volkogonov, "Triumf i tragediia: Politicheskii portret I. V. Stalin," *Oktiabr'*, no. 12 (1988), pp. 64–65, 101.

14. M. S. Aleksandrov (M. Ol'minsky), *Gosudarstvo, biurokratiia, i absolutizm v istorii*

Rossii, 2nd ed. (Moscow and Petrograd, 1919), pp. 85–86, 233–34, 240.

15. M. N. Pokrovsky, *Russkaia istoriia v samom szhatom ocherke* (Moscow, 1934), p. 86 and *passim.*

16. *Lenin,* LII, 24.

17. M. N. Pokrovsky, *History of Russia from the Earliest Times to the Rise of Commercial Capitalism,* trans. and ed. J. D. Clarkson and R. M. Griffiths (New York, 1931), pp. 283, 285, 304, 322, 326, 341.

18. Leon Trotsky, *1905,* trans. Anya Bostock (New York, 1971), pp. 4–8.

19. Pokrovsky's review was first published in the journal *Krasnaia nov'* (no. 3, 1922), then republished in his collection, *Marksizm i osobennosti istoricheskogo razvitiia Rossii* (Moscow, 1925).

20. *Pravda,* 1 and 2 July 1922, English translation in *1905,* pp. 327–45.

21. *Pravda,* 15 July 1922. For the statements quoted from Marx, see *The Marx-Engels Reader,* ed. Robert C. Tucker, 2nd ed. (New York, 1978), pp. 436–37.

22. This article first appeared in the journal *Kommunisticheskii internatsional,* no. 3 (40) (1925). For the material quoted from *Capital,* see *Marx-Engels Reader,* pp. 433–34.

23. *Stalin,* IX, 176. What appears here is Stalin's answer to Tsvetkov and Alypov (minus one portion that has been put on the record since Stalin's death, for which see below). Since the phrase I have cited appears in quotation marks in Stalin's reply of 7 March 1927, we may infer that they used it in their letter to him, which has never been published. His reply first appeared in his collected works after World War II.

24. O. Sokolov, "Ob istoricheskikh vzgliadakh M. N. Pokrovskogo," *Kommunist,* no. 4 (March 1962), p. 77, citing a documentary source in the Central Party Archive of the Institute of Marxism-Leninism. Stalin deleted this part of the letter when editing it for publication in vol. IX of his collected works. The deletion is understandable, since both Trotsky and Pokrovsky were proscribed figures at that time. Point 4 evidently came at the end of the letter, which consists of three points as printed in vol. IX.

25. *Stalin,* VII, 43, first published in Stalin's collected works in 1947.

26. *Ibid.,* IX, 21.

27. Iu. Larin, *Sovetskaia derevnia* (Moscow, 1925), pp. 15, 17, 142, 144, 175, 179–80, 193–94.

28. *XIV konferentsiia RKP(b)* (Moscow and Leningrad, 1925), p. 189.

29. *Ibid.,* p. 142.

30. *Stalin,* VII, 373. In his *Stalin: A Political Biography,* 2nd ed. (New York, 1967), p. 319, Isaac Deutscher mistakenly attributes the "second revolution" idea to Larin and mistakenly comments that Stalin, in the speech just referred to here, "ironically treated his view as a cranky idea." It was Bukharin's polemical twist that fastened the "second revolution" idea on Larin.

31. G. V. Plekhanov, *Osnovnye voprosy marksizma* (Moscow, 1922), pp. 102–3.

32. M. Voloshin, *Stikhotvoreniia,* I, ed. B. A. Filippov *et al.* (Paris, 1982), pp. 344–48. I am indebted to Professor Alec Nove for calling my attention to Voloshin's poem.

33. Aleksandrov, *Gosudarstvo,* pp. 102–3. For the information about Stalin's reading of *The Forefather of Russia* I am indebted to Dmitrii Volkogonov in a conversation in Moscow in June 1989. The name of the book's author is Maksimov (initials unknown).

34. S. F. Platonov, *Petr Velikii* (Leningrad, 1926), pp. 102–13. In high Soviet circles at that time, Stalin was informally called *khozyain.*

35. N. A. Gredeskul, *Rossiia prezhde i teper'* (Moscow and Leningrad, 1926), *passim.* The author of the foreword was S. Desnitsky. I am indebted to Professor M. Ia. Gefter of Moscow for calling my attention to this book.

36. *Stalin,* XI, 248–49. Stalin's mention of Peter's "leap" suggests his familiarity with Plekhanov's reference to his "revolutionary leap."

37. Trotsky writes in *My Life* (New York, 1930), p. 467, that Lenin would say of Stalin (in private conversation, of course): "This cook will make only peppery dishes."

4. Starting the Second Revolution

1. *Stalin,* X, 298–99.

2. Boris I. Nicolaevsky, *Power and the Soviet Elite,* ed. Janet D. Zagoria (New York, 1965), pp. 135 and 135 n.

3. *Stalin,* XI, 248.

4. Alexander Baykov, *Soviet Foreign Trade* (Princeton, 1946), Appendix, Table IV. The figure for grain exports in 1913 comes from Iu. A. Moshkov, *Zernovaia problema v gody sploshnoi kollektivizatsii sel'skogo khoziaistva v SSSR (1929–1933 gg.)* (Moscow, 1966), p. 16. It is 9.6 million tons; Baykov shows 9.2 million.

5. *Stalin,* XI, 176–78. This speech was first published after World War II. Six hundred million poods are roughly equivalent to ten million tons. Stalin may have deliberately overstated the contrast between prewar and late-1920s levels of marketed grain. On this, see Jerzy F. Karz, "Thoughts on the Grain Problem," *Soviet Studies,* no. 4 (April 1967), esp. p. 405.

6. Report to the Eleventh Party Congress, *The Lenin Anthology,* ed. Robert C. Tucker (New York, 1975), p. 529.

7. Moshe Lewin, "Who Was the Kulak?" *Soviet Studies,* no. 2 (October 1966), pp. 189–90. In *The Economics of Soviet Agriculture* (London, 1939), p. 100, Leonard E. Hubbard writes that "the more energetic and prosperous" farmers called kulaks in the later 1920s "bore no resemblance whatever to the typical

pre-War kulak, who was a man of substance and much the social superior of the average peasant small-holder. The pre-War kulak had been destroyed during War Communism, if not physically eliminated; he had, so to say, been reduced to the ranks."

8. Levin, "Who Was the Kulak?" pp. 191–98. A commonly used criterion for defining the kulak was possession of twenty-five to forty acres of sown area.

9. V. P. Danilov, "Sotsial'no-ekonomicheskie otnosheniia v sovetskoi derevne nakanune kollektivizatsii," *Istoricheskie zapiski*, no. 55 (Moscow, 1956), pp. 109–10. He also reports here that in 1926–27 the combined proportion of poor peasants and farmhands comprised no more than about 35 percent of the rural population as against 65 percent on the eve of the Revolution.

10. *Ibid.*, p. 110. On the discriminatory tax policy, see this source, p. 130.

11. L. S. Rogachevskaia, *Likvidatsiia bezrabotitsy v SSSR, 1917–1930 gg.* (Moscow, 1973), p. 144. According to this source, nearly four million persons went from the villages to the towns for work in 1927–28.

12. Anton Ciliga, *The Russian Enigma* (London, 1940), p. 10. A Yugoslav Communist, Ciliga spent the years 1925–35 in Russia, the last five of them in prison and exile.

13. Maurice Hindus, *Broken Earth* (London, 1926), pp. 277–79, 284–85. See also Hubbard, *Economics*, p. 103.

14. V. P. Danilov, ed., *Ocherki istorii kollektivizatsii sel'skogo khoziaistva v soiuznykh respublikakh* (Moscow, 1963), pp. 21, 26. By the end of 1928, according to Pavel Penezhko ("Kak udarili po 'Chayanovshchine'," *Ogonyok*, no. 10, 5–12 March 1988, p. 7), about 28 million persons, comprising one out of three farmsteads, were involved in one or another form of cooperative.

15. P. I. Liashchenko, *Istoriia narodnogo khoziaistva SSSR*, III (Moscow, 1956), 245.

16. Rogachevskaia, *Likvidatsiia* p. 213.

17. *Stalin*, XI, 246, 247, 248.

18. Louis Fischer, *Russia's Road from Peace to War: Soviet Foreign Relations, 1917–1941* (New York, 1969), p. 172. On the war scare see this source, pp. 165–79, and John P. Sontag, "The Soviet War Scare of 1926–27," *The Russian Review* (January 1975). Sontag writes here that the war scare was genuine, yet "grossly and crudely manipulated by Soviet politicians in 1927."

19. *Stalin*, IX, 322.

20. *Ibid.*, X, 281, 288.

21. On the fabricating of circumstances by leaders, see Tucker, *Politics As Leadership* (Columbia, Mo., 1981), pp. 64–67.

22. Roy A. Medvedev, *Let History Judge: The Origins and Consequences of Stalinism*, trans. Colleen Taylor, eds. David Joravsky and Georges Haupt (New York, 1971), p. 112.

23. Abdurakhman Avtorkhanov, *Stalin and the Soviet Communist Party: A Study in the Technology of Power* (New York, 1959), pp. 28–30. On the personal relationship between

Yevdokimov and Stalin, see Alexander Orlov, *The Secret History of Stalin's Crimes* (New York, 1953), p. 14.

24. Medvedev, *Let History Judge*, p. 113.

25. William Reswick, *I Dreamt Revolution* (Chicago, 1952), p. 247. See this source and Eugene Lyons, *Assignment in Utopia* (New York, 1937), chap. 5, for eyewitness accounts of the trial. I have drawn on both for the trial description here presented.

26. Medvedev, *Let History Judge*, p. 312.

27. Interview in November 1979, with Pyotr Rabinowitch, an émigré who served many years as a Soviet jurist.

28. Lyons, *loc. cit.*

29. *Stalin*, XI, 53–54.

30. *Ibid.*, XII, 302, 303. The occasion was his report to the Sixteenth Party Congress in 1930.

31. *Stalin*, XII, 20–21, and Franz Borkenau, *World Communism: A History of the Communist International* (Ann Arbor, 1962), pp. 336–37.

32. Bertram D. Wolfe, *A Life in Two Centuries* (New York, 1981), pp. 430–32.

33. A copy of Kamenev's notes on the conversation is in the Trotsky Archives at Harvard University (Document T1897), and will be cited here as "Bukharin-Kamenev Conversation."

34. Vladimir Tikhonov, "Chtoby narod prokormil sebia," *Literaturnaia gazeta*, 3 August 1988, and "Pora zemel'noi reformy," *Moskovskie novosti*, 7 August 1988. Academician Tikhonov, a senior scholar at the All-Union Lenin Academy of Agricultural Sciences in Moscow, states in the first of the sources cited here that Stalin's personal intervention to depress grain prices and raise peasants' taxes was "concealed by politicians and in later years by historians."

35. *Stalin*, XI, 11.

36. *Ibid.*, 3–7. Described here as a short record of Stalin's speeches on the Siberian trip, this document was first published in his collected works after World War II.

37. Moshe Lewin, *Russian Peasants and Soviet Power: A Study of Collectivization* (Evanston, Ill., 1968), p. 229.

38. On Stalin being out of step with Mikoyan, who on 12 February 1928 called for restraint in a *Pravda* article, see Lewin, *Russian Peasants*, p. 232.

39. *Ibid.*, pp. 238–42.

40. *Ibid.*, pp. 393–94.

41. This account is based on a transcript of Bukharin's unpublished speech in the Trotsky Archives at Harvard University (Document T1901).

42. Speech of 9 July 1928, *Stalin*, XI, 159, 169.

43. *Ibid.*, 170–72.

44. "Bukharin-Kamenev Conversation." For further details on the clandestine conversations and their repercussions, see Tucker, *Stalin as Revolutionary* (New York, 1973), pp. 416–18.

45. *XVI konferentsiia VKP(b), aprel' 1929 goda* (Moscow, 1962), p. 744. For the moderates' use of this phrase in February, see this source,

pp. 806–7. For Stalin's dismissal of the charge, see *Stalin*, XII, 3.

46. *Stalin*, XI, 256. Rykov's remarks are cited from documentary sources in F. M. Vaganov, *Pravyi uklon v VKP(b) i ego razgrom (1928–1930 gg.)* (Moscow, 1970), p. 180.
47. *Stalin*, XII, 90.
48. Vaganov, *Pravyi uklon*, pp. 149, 179–86.
49. *XVI konferentsiia VKP(b)*, p. 623.
50. Speech to the July 1928 Central Committee plenum, *Stalin* XI, 163.
51. *Stalin*, XII, 37.
52. *Lenin*, XLIII, 331–32.
53. *Stalin*, XII, 305.
54. *Lenin*, XXXVIII, 194–96, 200.

55. *Stalin*, XI, 174–75 and XII, 166.
56. *Ibid.*, XII, 49–55.
57. *Ibid.*, 33. Lenin made the quoted statement during the short-lived Hungarian Communist revolution of 1919. See *Lenin*, XXXVIII, 386–87.
58. "Fright at the Fall of the Old and the Fight for the New," *Lenin Anthology*, pp. 424–26.
59. *Ibid.*, pp. 125, 151.
60. Nadezhda Krupskaya, *Vospominaniia o Vladimire Ilyiche Lenine v piati tomakh* (Moscow, 1960), I, 490.
61. *Bol'shevik*, no. 19–20, 31 October 1930, p. 95. The letter first appeared in a book published in 1924 but not widely circulated.

5. The Five-Year Plan in Four!

1. *Lenin*, XXXIV, 55.
2. W. H. Chamberlin, *Russia's Iron Age* (London, 1935).
3. *Stalin*, XII, 229, 234.
4. G. V. Kuibysheva, O. A. Lezhava, V. V. Nelidov, and A. F. Khavin, *Valerian Vladimirovich Kuibyshev: Biografiia* (Moscow, 1966), p. 280.
5. *Planovoye khoziaistvo*, no. 1 (1929), p. 109. Cited by Moshe Lewin, "The Disappearance of Planning in the Plan," *The Slavic Review*, no. 2 (June 1973), p. 272. See also, in this issue, Holland Hunter's article, "The Over-Ambitious Soviet First Five-Year Plan," and the commentaries on it by R. Campbell and S. F. Cohen.
6. Kuibysheva *et al.*, *Kuibyshev*, p. 287.
7. Cited by Lewin, "Disappearance of Planning," from G. F. Grin'ko, "Plan velikikh rabot," *Planovoye khoziaistvo*, no. 2 (1929), pp. 9–10.
8. Medvedev, *Let History Judge* (New York, 1971), p. 103.
9. *Stalin*, XII, 278, 345–47.
10. A. F. Khavin, *U rulia industrii* (Moscow, 1968), pp. 77–78. The author, a personal acquaintance of Kuibyshev's, was then a journalist working on various economic newspapers.
11. *Stalin*, XIII, 41.
12. This term is Naum Jasny's. See his *Soviet Industrialization, 1928–1952* (Chicago, 1961), pp. 73ff., for specifics.
13. Speech of January 1933, *Stalin*, XIII, 182.
14. Antony C. Sutton, *Western Technology and Soviet Economic Development, 1930 to 1945* (Stanford, 1971), pp. 321, 346, 363–72.
15. On Grinevetsky's influence on the plan, see Leon Smolinsky, "Grinevetskii and Soviet Industrialization," *Survey* (April 1968).
16. *Stalin*, XII, 325; *Politicheskii slovar'*, ed. G. Aleksandrov *et al.* (Moscow, 1940), p. 592.
17. *A Blow at Intervention* (Moscow and Leningrad, 1931), p. 128. The Soviet transliteration of Russian names into English differs somewhat from the current usage.
18. From the memoirs of a friend of Lurie's, the Old Bolshevik V. E. Gromov, *Politicheskii dnevnik, 1964–1970* (Amsterdam, 1972), pp.

381–82. On the Industrial Party case, see Medvedev, *Let History Judge*, pp. 117–24, and Kendall E. Bailes, *Technology and Society Under Lenin and Stalin: Origins of the Soviet Technical Intelligentsia, 1917–1941* (Princeton, 1978), chap. 4. Bailes' hypothesis that one of the motives of the affair was to discredit pretensions of the technical intelligentsia to a greater political role in society (p. 97) seems weak for lack of substantiating evidence.
19. *Stalin*, XII, 302, 303, and Bailes, *Technology and Society*, p. 98.
20. Raphael R. Abramovitch, *The Soviet Revolution, 1917–1939* (New York, 1962), p. 423 n. For the 1931 report on arrests of engineers, see this source, p. 382.
21. E. Kol'tsman, "Vreditel'stvo v nauke," *Bol'shevik*, no. 2, 31 January 1931, pp. 73–75. Since *vreditel'* means both wrecker and agricultural pest, Kol'tsman accused *Okhrana prirody* of covering up its wrecking purposes with a pretense of struggle against wreckers (that is, pests).
22. Cited by Sheila Fitzpatrick, "Cultural Revolution as Class War," from a pamphlet by Krinitsky published in 1928, in *Cultural Revolution in Russia, 1928–1931*, ed. Sheila Fitzpatrick (Bloomington and London, 1978), p. 10.
23. *Stalin*, XIII, 66, 67.
24. Sheila Fitzpatrick, *Education and Social Mobility in the Soviet Union, 1921–1934* (Cambridge, England, 1979), pp. 186–88, 198.
25. G. Zaidel' and M. Tsvibak, *Klassovyi vrag na istoricheskom fronte* (Moscow and Leningrad, 1931), p. 103.
26. S. F. Platonov, *Ivan Grozny* (Petrograd, 1923), p. 156.
27. *Stalin*, XIII, 5–6.
28. *The Lenin Anthology*, ed. Robert C. Tucker (New York, 1975), pp. 374–78.
29. Robert Sharlet, "Pashukanis and the Withering Away of Law in the USSR," in Fitzpatrick, *Cultural Revolution*, pp. 178, 179, 185.
30. Gail Warshofsky Lapidus, "Educational Strategies and Cultural Revolution," *ibid.*, pp. 94–99.
31. S. Frederic Starr, "Visionary Town Planning

During the Cultural Revolution," *ibid.*, pp. 210–11, 226.
32. *Stalin*, XII, 369–70.
33. *Ibid.*, XIII, 72, 73.
34. Edward J. Brown, *The Proletarian Episode in Russian Literature, 1928–1932* (New York, 1971), chaps. 10–11 and Conclusion, and *idem, Russian Literature Since the Revolution* (London, 1963), pp. 209–12.
35. *Stalin*, XI, 326–29.
36. Brown, *Proletarian Episode*, p. 189.
37. *Pravda*, 23 April 1932.
38. Brown, *Proletarian Episode*, pp. 200–201, 214–15. Stalin's personal responsibility for the decree was reported by Kaganovich at the Seventeenth Party Congress in 1934.
39. Alec Nove, *An Economic History of the USSR* (London, 1969), p. 213. I am indebted to this source, pp. 212–14 and 264–66, and two other sources for details in this discussion: Andrei Y. Vyshinsky, ed., *The Law of the Soviet State*, trans. Hugh W. Babb (New York, 1948), pp. 399–413, and S. S. Studenikin *et al., Sovetskoe administrativnoe pravo* (Moscow, 1950), *passim.*
40. But even these, producing goods from local materials for local consumption, had to meet standards and specifications set in Moscow and were subject to local party authorities subordinate to higher ones in Moscow. On this see Leonard E. Hubbard, *Soviet Labour and Industry* (London, 1942), p. 115.
41. Cited in Robert C. Tucker, *The Soviet Political Mind: Stalinism and Post-Stalin Change* (2nd ed., New York, 1971), p. 177. Pervukhin made the remark informally during a Moscow diplomatic reception in 1955 in my hearing.
42. Mark Popovsky, "Iubileiinoe," *Novoye russkoye slovo*, 29 July 1979. The author, a specialist in agricultural research, emigrated from Russia in the 1970s.
43. Data on military developments from B. S. Tel'pukhovsky, "Deiatel'nosti KPSS po ukrepleniiu oborony SSSR v gody sotsialisticheskoi rekonstruktsii narodnogo khozaistva (1929–1937 gg.)," *Voprosy istorii KPSS*, no. 8 (1976) pp. 88–94.
44. Cited by Robert S. Sullivant, *Soviet Politics and the Ukraine, 1917–1957* (New York, 1962), pp. 150–53, 360. I am indebted to this source for the data on the Ukraine in this paragraph. Compare the situation in the Armenian Soviet Republic, where the capital, Erevan, "lost most of its already limited independence of Moscow" and ". . . most of the commissariats of the Armenian government lost their formal autonomy." Mary Kilbourne Matossian, *The Impact of Soviet Politics in Armenia* (Leiden, 1962), pp. 117–18.
45. *Stalin*, XII, 368.
46. In *Russian Realist Art: The State and Society, The Peredvizhniki and Their Tradition* (Ann Arbor, 1977), p. 173, Elizabeth Valkonier writes that the creation of this committee "was a decisive step in establishing central control over Soviet art, music, theater and cinema."
47. For an account of the transformation, see Loren R. Graham, *The Soviet Academy of Sciences and the Communist Party, 1927–1932* (Princeton, 1967).
48. Hryhory Kostiuk, *Stalinist Rule in the Ukraine: A Study of the Decade of Mass Terror (1929–1939)* (New York, 1960), pp. 49–50, 56–57, 63. The attack on Ukrainian nationalism in orthography came in a *Pravda* article of 27 April 1933 by B. Levin, noted by Kostiuk (p. 57 n.)
49. *VKP(b) v rezoliutsiakh i resheniakh s"ezdov, konferentsii i plenumov TsK*, II, *1925–1939*, 6th ed. (Moscow, 1941), p. 511.
50. *Narodnoe khoziaistvo SSSR v 1958 godu: Statisticheskii ezhegodnik* (Moscow, 1959), p. 698. Citing these statistics in *The Prophet Outcast: Trotsky, 1929–1940* (London, 1963), p. 100 n., Isaac Deutscher comments: "It was therefore in a literal sense that, by means of inflation, Stalin took half the worker's wage to finance industrialization."
51. *Stalin*, XIII, 56–57.
52. A. Zimin (pseudonym), *Sotsializm i neostalinizm* (New York, 1981), pp. 18–23. This *samizdat* study by E. Leikin was written in Moscow. For Marx's position, see "The Critique of the Gotha Program," in *The Marx-Engels Reader*, ed. Robert C. Tucker (New York, 1978), pp. 529–30.
53. Nove, *Economic History*, p. 208, and, for the old scale, Manya Gordon, *Workers Before and After Lenin* (New York, 1941), p. 179.
54. Zimin, *Sotsializm i neostalinizm*, p. 182, n. 29.
55. Lidiia Shatunovskaia, *Zhizn' v Kremle* (New York, 1982), pp. 66–70. The author lived in Government House from 1931 until her arrest in 1947. In later years she emigrated.
56. Fitzpatrick, *Education and Social Mobility*, pp. 216–17, 316–17.
57. John Scott, *Behind the Urals: An American Worker in Russia's City of Steel* (Cambridge, Mass., 1942), pp. 30, 38–40, 80–81, 85, 86–88, 209–10, 231–33.
58. G. M. Malenkov, *O zadachakh partiinykh organizatsii v oblasti promyshlennosti i transporta* (Moscow, 1941), p. 39.
59. *Stalin*, XIII, 104–5.
60. Alexei N. Tolstoy, *Polnoe sobranie sochinenii* (Moscow, 1946–51), IV, 393.
61. *Ibid.*, X, 652–53, 602.
62. R. Ivanov-Razumnik, *Pisatel'skie sud'by* (New York, 1951), pp. 39–43. On the three versions of Tolstoy's play about Peter, see Spencer E. Roberts, *Soviet Historical Drama: Its Role in the Development of a National Mythology* (The Hague, 1965), chap. 5.
63. Tolstoy, *Polnoe sobranie*, I, 87.
64. *Ibid.*, III, 535.
65. *Ibid.*, XIII, 535. The *strel'tsy* were linked with high-level supporters of Peter's sister.
66. Tolstoy, *Polnoe sobranie*, IX, 662. The second part was completed in 1934.
67. Yuri Annenkov, *Dnevnik moikh vstrech*, II

(New York, 1966), p. 149. "Ehrenbriuki" (literally "Ehrenpants") was a derisive reference to the writer Ilya Ehrenburg. The "second" and "third" variants referred to by Tolstoy were evidently the revisions of his play *On the Rack.*

68. Tolstoy, *Polnoe sobranie,* IX, 784, 785. This statement was made at a meeting in Lenin-grad in March 1933 to mark the fiftieth anniversary of the death of Marx.

69. Tolstoy, *Izbrannye sochineniia,* VI (Moscow, 1953), pp. 535–36. The statement was made in 1933. The Mordovians are a non-Russian nationality of Finnish origin dwelling mainly in the Volga area southeast of Moscow.

6. The Making of a Rural Upheaval

1. Speech of Yan Rudzutak at the Sixteenth Party Congress. *XVI s"ezd VKP(b), 26 iunia–13 iuliia 1930 g.* (Moscow, 1930), II, part 2, 1239–40.

2. Eugene Lyons, *Assignment in Utopia* (New York, 1937), pp. 387–88.

3. *Stalin,* XIII, 107–8. Areopagus was the hill in ancient Athens where the highest court sat. As reelected by the Sixteenth Party Congress in 1930, the Central Committee actually had 49 voting and 53 candidate members. In party practice, a candidate member of the Politburo or Central Committee is a participant in its discussion but without right of vote.

4. T. H. Rigby, *Lenin's Government* (Cambridge, England, 1979), pp. 55–56, 102–3, 110; E. B. Genkina, *Lenin—predsedatel' Sovnarkoma i STO* (Moscow, 1960), pp. 6, 10–11, 31.

5. Rigby, *Lenin's Government,* pp. 178, 188–89. Lydia Bach, a contemporary observer, is cited here as writing that in 1922 the Sovnarkom had "ceased to be a body with a will of its own" and had "lost its importance and its authority."

6. Aleksandrov (A. S. Michelson), *Kto upravliaet Rossiei? Bol'shevitskii partiino-pravitel'stvennyi apparat i 'Stalinizm'* (Berlin, 1933), pp. 262–65, 316–20. On the 1930 reorganization, see *Partiinoe stroitel'stvo,* no. 2 (4) (February 1930), pp. 70–72, and no. 3–4 (5–6) (February 1930), pp. 86–87. On the Orgburo work plans, *Pravda,* 15 May 1928 and 5 March 1931.

7. S. Dmitrievsky, *Sovetskie portrety* (Stockholm, 1932), p. 103. A first secretary of the Soviet Embassy in Stockholm when he defected in 1930, Dmitrievsky had headed the Foreign Commissariat chancellery in 1924 and was well informed.

8. *Bol'shaia sovetskaia entsiklopedia,* XLVI (Moscow, 1940), 514. My account of Stalin's power structure draws heavily upon Niels Erik Rosenfeldt, *Knowledge and Power: The Role of Stalin's Secret Chancellery in the Soviet System of Government* (Copenhagen, 1978), and his extension of the book in "The Consistorium of the Communist Church," *Russian History,* parts 2–3 (1982), pp. 308–24.

9. Rosenfeldt, *Knowledge and Power,* pp. 31–32 and 129–60; Dmitrievsky, *Sovetskie portrety,* pp. 108–9; Abdurakhman Avtorkhanov, *Stalin and the Soviet Communist Party* (New York, 1959), chap. 14; and Alexander Barmine, *One Who Survived: The Life Story of a Russian Under the Soviets* (New York, 1945), pp. 260–62.

10. "Diktator Sovetskogo Soiuza," *Sotsialisticheskii vestnik,* no. 19 (1933), pp. 3–6. This article appeared under the pseudonym "Iv." Its author was Boris I. Nicolaevsky, editor of this émigré Menshevik journal, who based his account on testimony from Soviet sources. Some confirmatory information on the layout comes from Lyons, *Assignment,* pp. 383–84. Lyons interviewed Stalin in his Central Committee office.

11. Leon Trotsky, *Stalin: An Appraisal of the Man and His Influence,* ed. and trans. Charles Malamuth. New ed. (New York, 1967), p. 388.

12. Rosenfeldt, *Knowledge and Power,* pp. 92–94.

13. *Biulleten' oppozitsii,* no. 1–2 (July 1929), p. 14; no. 9 (February–March 1930), p. 16; no. 14 (August 1930), pp. 17–19; no. 12–13 (June–July 1930), pp. 25, 29.

14. *Stalin,* XI, 316–17. The initials "ACP(b)" stand for "All-Union Communist Party (Bolsheviks)." The document was reprinted in this volume of Stalin's works with the notation "published for the first time" and without reference to the 1929 *Pravda* editorial version. The fact that it did appear as a *Pravda* editorial indicates that the memorandum, or draft article, received the approval of a Politburo majority.

15. *Biulleten' oppozitsii,* no. 1–2 (July 1929), p. 3.

16. For further details on the Bliumkin affair, see Simon Wolin and Robert M. Slusser, eds., *The Soviet Secret Police* (New York, 1957), pp. 45–46, and Isaac Deutscher, *The Prophet Outcast: Trotsky, 1929–1940* (London, 1963), pp. 84–89. Bliumkin, a former Left SR, had participated in the assassination of the German ambassador, Count Mirbach, in 1918 and had a somewhat unsavory career in the Cheka thereafter. For details see Clarence Brown, *Mandelstam* (Cambridge, England, 1973), pp. 71–74.

17. Speech to First All-Russian Congress of Peasant Deputies (1917), *Lenin,* XXXII, 186, 188.

18. *Pravda,* 22 December 1929. For particulars on the birthday celebration, and on the one for Lenin in 1920, see Tucker, *Stalin As Revolutionary* (New York, 1973), pp. 58–59 and chap. 13.

19. *Kommunisticheskaia revoliutsiia,* no. 22–23 (December 1929), p. 66.

20. Konstantin Popov, "Partiia i rol' vozhdia," *Partiinoe stroitel'stvo*, no. 3 (1930), pp. 5–9. *Iskra* was the party paper abroad at the turn of the century. Lenin's statement about the will of thousands occurs in his *Immediate Tasks of the Soviet Government* (1918), but with reference to directors of production, "leaders of labor."

21. M. L. Bogdenko, "K istorii nachal'nogo etapa sploshnoi kollektivizatsii sel'skogo khoziaistva SSSR," *Voprosy istorii*, no. 5 (May 1963), pp. 20–21.

22. *Ibid.*

23. *Ibid.*

24. N. A. Ivnitsky, "O nachal'nom etape sploshnoi kollektivizatsii (Osen' 1929–vesna 1930 gg.)," *Voprosy istorii KPSS*, no. 4 (1962), pp. 64–65.

25. Fedor Belov, *The History of a Soviet Collective Farm* (New York, 1955), pp. 5–6.

26. Bogdenko, "K istorii," p. 30.

27. N. A. Ivnitsky, *Klassovaia bor'ba v derevne i likvidatsiia kulachestva kak klass (1929–1932 gg.)* (Moscow, 1972), p. 159.

28. Iu. A. Moshkov, *Zernovaia problema v gody sploshnoi kollektivizatsii* (Moscow, 1966), pp. 61–62.

29. *Ibid.*

30. *Ibid.*, p. 65.

31. Maurice Hindus, *Humanity Uprooted* (New York, 1929), pp. 165–67. See also Leonard Hubbard, *The Economics of Soviet Agriculture* (London, 1939), p. 103.

32. B. A. Abramov, "Kollektivizatsiia sel'skogo khoziaistva v RSSFSR," in *Ocherki istorii kollektivizatsii*, ed. V. P. Danilov (Moscow, 1963), p. 96. Abramov adds: "By proclaiming in the article that the middle peasants were entering the collectives by whole districts, I. V. Stalin was thereby orienting the party organizations on wholesale conduct of collectivization."

33. Ivnitsky, *Klassovaia bor'ba*, pp. 76–77.

34. In Danilov, *Ocherki istorii*, p. 96, Abramov writes: "Stalin's article exerted pressure on the party cadres and even on the course of the discussion of the collective farm movement at the November plenum."

35. *Ibid.*, p. 97.

36. V. Molotov, "O kolkhoznom dvizhenii," *Bol'shevik*, no. 22, 30 November 1929, pp. 11, 12, 13. Molotov's comments on the success of the grain collections campaign and creation of a large inviolable grain reserve, if true, refute the explanation for mass collectivization offered by E. H. Carr in *The October Revolution: Before and After* (New York, 1969), p. 104: "A third successive annual crisis of the grain collections loomed ahead. The problem of supplying town and factories had become completely intractable. Gradualism was not enough."

37. Molotov, "O kolkhoznom dvizhenii," pp. 16–17.

38. *VKP(b) v rezoluitsiakh*, II, 1925–1939, (Moscow, 1941), 363, 374.

39. B. A. Abramov, "O rabote komissii Politbiuro Tsk VKP(b) po voprosam sploshnoi kol-lektivizatsii," *Voprosy istorii KPSS*, no. 1 (1964), p. 33. Baranov's letter was read out by S. I. Syrtsov, who was chairman of the Russian Federation's Council of People's Commissars.

40. Abramov, in Danilov, *Ocherki istorii*, p. 96.

41. Abramov, "O rabote komissii Politbiuro," p. 33.

42. Ivnitsky, "O nachal'nom etape," p. 64; Danilov, *Ocherki istorii*, p. 43. G. N. Kaminsky was a cochairman of the *Kolkhoz* Center.

43. *Stalin*, XII, 152–53.

44. Trotsky Archives at Harvard University (Document T1693). The source is an unpublished letter of June 1928 by Moshe Frumkin, then the deputy finance commissar and an adherent of the moderates. In the Russian, the Molotov statement cited by Frumkin reads: "Nado udarit' po kulaku tak, shtoby seredniak pered nami vytianulsia."

45. *Stalin*, XII, 149, 166–68, 170. Italics added.

46. Abramov, "O rabote komissii," pp. 33–35.

47. Ivnitsky, "O nachal'nom etape," p. 63.

48. Abramov, "O rabote komissii," p. 36; M. A. Vyltsan, N. A. Ivnitsky, and Iu. A. Poliakov, "Nekotorye problemy istorii kollektivizatsii v SSSR," *Voprosy istorii*, no. 3 (1965), p. 12.

49. Abramov, "O rabote komissii," p. 36; Vyltsan, Ivnitsky, and Poliakov, "Nekotorye problemy," p. 12.

50. Abramov, "O rabote komissii," p. 40; Ivnitsky, "O nachal'nom etape," p. 68.

51. Abramov, "O rabote komissii," p. 40; Bogdenko, "K istorii," p. 26 n.; Vyltsan, Ivnitsky, and Poliakov, "Nekotorye problemy," pp. 6, 12.

52. Bogdenko, "K istorii," pp. 26, 31. For the reduction in timetable in the North Caucasus and the Lower and Middle Volga, see Abramov, "O rabote komissii," p. 40. Abramov observes further: "Stalin's changes gave an orientation on accelerating the collective farm movement and introduced lack of clarity into one of the basic questions of collective farm construction—the procedure for socializing possessions when organizing the collectives."

53. Abramov, "O rabote komissii," pp. 40–42. Abramov comments: "Ryskulov's changes relegated the principle of voluntary membership into the background and made pressure on the peasant masses the basis of organizing the collectives." Since Ryskulov was not a man of high political stature and would thus have been loath to take the initiative that he did on his own, it is likely that he acted at Stalin's instigation.

54. Vyltsan, Ivnitsky, and Poliakov, "Nekotorye problemy," pp. 6, 12.

55. Abramov, "O rabote komissii," pp. 41, 42.

56. According to L. S. Rogachevskaia, *Likvidatsiia bezrabotitsy v SSSR* (Moscow, 1973), pp. 142, 173, there were 1.5 million unemployed in April 1928, but by the latter part of 1929 shortages were being felt, especially on the big construction projects. For the November plenum's stress on timber exports,

see *VKP(b) v rezoliutsiakh,* p. 363.
57. *Stalin,* XII, 170.
58. Bogdenko, "K istorii," p. 28.
59. Ivnitsky, "O nachal'nom etape," p. 66.
60. See, for example, Isaac Deutscher, *Stalin: A Political Biography* 2nd ed. (New York,

1966), pp. 273, 295, and E. H. Carr, *Socialism in One Country, 1924–1926,* I, (New York, 1958), 177, 185.
61. Report to the Fifteenth Party Congress, *Stalin,* X, 333.

7. The Cult and Its Creator

1. *Stalin,* XIII, 6.
2. Eugene Lyons, *Assignment in Utopia* (New York, 1937), pp. 263–64.
3. Interview with Svetlana Alliluyeva, Princeton, 1969.
4. *VKP(b) v rezoliutsiakh,* II, 1925–1939 (Moscow, 1941), 428.
5. Mr. Fischer gave me this information in a personal conversation. For the quoted passage, see *The Nation,* 13 August 1930, p. 176.
6. David Joravsky, *Soviet Marxism and Natural Science, 1917–1932* (New York, 1961), p. 170.
7. *Vestnik Kommunisticheskoi akademii,* Kn. 35–36 (1929), p. 390. For note of this list, see Joravsky, *Soviet Marxism,* p. 227.
8. Medvedev, *Let History Judge* (New York, 1971), p. 224.
9. *Pravda,* 7 June 1930.
10. M. Mitin, *Boevye voprosy materialisticheskoi dialektiki* (Moscow, 1936), pp. 43–44 and "Nekotorye itogi i zadachi raboty na filosofskom fronte," *Pod znamenem marksizma,* no. 1 (1936), pp. 25–26. For the date of the interview, see the chronology in *Stalin,* XIII, 401.
11. Genrikh Volkov, "Voznesenie: O tom, kak Stalin sdelalsia velikim filosofom," *Sovetskaia kul'tura,* 7 June 1988.
12. P. Cheremnykh, "Men'shevistvuiushchii idealizm v rabotakh BSE," *Bol'shevik,* no. 17, 15 September 1931, p. 85.
13. A. Slutsky, "Bol'sheviki o germanskoi s.-d. v period ee predvoennogo krizisa," *Proletarskaia revoliutsiia,* no. 6 (1930), pp. 37–72.
14. See chapter 6, p. 126, above.
15. *Stalin,* XIII, 84–102. The letter appeared originally in *Proletarskaia revoliutsiia,* no. 6 (1931).
16. *Stalin,* XI, 281–82, 284.
17. V. A. Dunaevsky, "Pis'mo I. V. Stalina 'O nekotorykh voprosakh istorii bol'shevizma' (Okt. 1931 g.) i ego posledstviia dlia sovetskoi istoricheskoi nauki i sudeb istorikov." Unpublished paper (Moscow, 1989), p. 32.
18. *Vsesoiuznoe soveshchanie o merakh uluchsheniia podgotovki nauchno-pedagogicheskikh kadrov po istoricheskim naukam, 18–21 dekabria 1962 g.* (Moscow, 1964), p. 363.
19. Paul H. Aron, "M. N. Pokrovskii and the Impact of the First Five-Year Plan," in *Essays in Russian and Soviet History in Honor of Geroid Tanquary Robinson,* ed. John Shelton Curtiss (New York, 1962), p. 301.
20. *Istoriia VKP(b),* gen. ed. E. M. Yaroslavsky, IV (Moscow and Leningrad, 1929),

part 1, p. 230, part 2, p. 291. Yaroslavsky said in his editorial foreword that the volume had been in preparation for the tenth anniversary of the Revolution (1927), "but for a whole series of reasons was delayed for a year." He did not explain what the reasons were.
21. *Vsesoiuznoe soveshchanie,* pp. 19, 75, 362, 457. See also V. A. Dunaevsky, "Bol'sheviki i germanskie levye na mezhdunarodnoi arene," in *Evropa v novoe i noveishee vremia: Sbornik statei pamiati Akademika N. M. Lukina* (Moscow, 1966), pp. 508–9.
22. Dunaevsky, "Bol'sheviki," pp. 509–12. The Russian word here translated as "glorifiers" is *alliluishchiki.*
23. *Pravda,* 12 December 1931. Dunaevsky, "Bol'sheviki," p. 511, observes that "Kaganovich's speech, filled with shouted threats, was designed to pin the label of Trotskyist on all who from now on would dare to deviate from Stalin's propositions."
24. Yaroslavsky's letter appeared in *Pravda* on 10 December 1932; Radek's on 12 December; Popov's on 8 December.
25. *Pravda,* 29 December 1931.
26. *Stalin,* XIII, 126–30. The quotations from Olekhnovich, whose letter, like Aristov's, remained unpublished, are found in Stalin's reply.
27. *Pravda,* 22 January 1932.
28. Dunaevsky, "Bol'sheviki," pp. 511–12.
29. Eugene Lyons, *Moscow Carrousel* (New York, 1935), pp. 140–41.
30. *Stalin and Khashim (1901–1902 gody): Nekotorye epizody iz batumskogo podpolia* (Sukhumi, Georgia, 1934).
31. *Pravda,* 22 February 1933.
32. Noting that a "need for vindictive triumph" is a regular ingredient of the search for glory in some neurotic personalities, Karen Horney writes: "The aim of the neurotic vindictive revenge is not 'getting even' but triumphing by hitting back harder. Nothing short of triumph *can* restore the imaginary grandeur in which pride is invested. It is this very capacity to restore pride that gives neurotic vindictiveness its incredible tenacity and accounts for its compulsive character." *Neurosis and Human Growth* (New York, 1950), pp. 101, 103.
33. "Bukharin-Kamenev Conversation," Trotsky Archives (Document T1897).
34. Isaac Deutscher, *The Prophet Unarmed: Trotsky, 1921–1929* (London, 1959), pp. 296–97, citing Victor Serge, *Vie et mort de Trotsky* (Paris, 1951), whose account is based on eyewitness testimony by Trotsky's wife, Na-

talia Sedova.

35. Deutscher, *Stalin* (New York, 1966), p. 290.
36. Svetlana Alliluyeva, *Twenty Letters to a Friend*, trans. Priscilla Johnson McMillan (New York, 1967), pp. 59, 78.
37. See Marc Jansen, *A Show Trial Under Lenin: The Trial of the Socialist Revolutionaries, Moscow 1922* (The Hague, 1982).
38. John Scott, *Behind the Urals* (Cambridge, Mass., 1942), pp. 186–87.
39. Pavel Penezhko, "Kak udarili po 'Chayanovshchine'," *Ogonyok*, no. 10, 5–12 March 1988, pp. 6–8.
40. *Protsess kontrrevoliutsionnoi organizatsii men'shevikov (1 marta—9 marta 1931 g.)* (Moscow, 1931), pp. 11, 37.
41. N. Valentinov, "Iz proshlogo," *Sotsialisticheskii vestnik*, no. 4 (752), (April 1961), pp. 68–72; R. Abramovitch, "Menshevitskii protsess 1931 g.," *ibid.*, no. 2–3 (750–51) (February–March 1961), esp. pp. 50–51. Abramovitch attributes Stalin's ire against the Mensheviks also to the outcry raised by the Menshevik Delegation Abroad against collectivization by terror and the misfortunes caused by Stalin's breakneck industrialization.
42. "Pis'mo men'shevika Mikhaila Yakubovicha General'nomy Prokuroru SSSR o protsesse men'shevikov v 1931 g." For an incomplete translation of this *samizdat* document, see Medvedev, *Let History Judge*, p. 125–31.
43. Anton Ciliga, *The Russian Enigma* (London, 1940), p. 227. Yakubovich's deposition confirms this account. In *Let History Judge*, Medvedev reports that Sukhanov, released after several protests by hunger strike, was shot in 1937.
44. Rubin's experiences have been related by his sister. See Medvedev, *Let History Judge*, pp. 132–36.
45. Victor Serge, *Memoirs of a Revolutionary, 1901–1941*, trans. and ed. Peter Sedgwick (London and New York, 1963), 251.

8. Terror and Calamity: Stalin's October

1. Quoted by E. H. Carr, *Socialism in One Country, 1924–1926*, II (New York, 1959), p. 446, from *V vserossiiskii s"ezd deiatelei sovetskoi iustitsii* (Moscow, 1924), p. 233.
2. David Dallin and Boris I. Nicolaevsky, *Forced Labor in Soviet Russia* (New Haven, 1947), pp. 52–54. According to S. Swianiewicz, *Forced Labour and Economic Development: An Enquiry into the Experience of Soviet Industrialization* (London, 1965), p. 14, the total number of inmates by the end of the 1920s may have come to 200,000. But this number would include inmates of regular prisons, as well as forced-labor camps.
3. Dallin and Nicolaevsky, *Forced Labor*, pp. 88–90, 208, 212. The canal's strategic purpose was to enable Soviet naval vessels to be shifted from the Baltic, if necessary, to the White Sea.
4. A. P. Serebrovsky, *Na zolotom fronte* (Moscow, 1939), pp. 15–17. See also John D. Littlepage and Demaree Bess, *In Search of Soviet Gold* (New York, 1937), for the experiences of an Alaskan gold-mining engineer whom Serebrovsky recruited to work for the Soviet Gold Trust in the 1930s.
5. Dallin and Nicolaevsky, in *Forced Labor*, pp. 50–51, write: "Any forced labor camp with a population exceeding 3,000 or 5,000 constitutes a town. The deportation of millions of kulaks to labor camps was thus reflected in the census figures as a rapid growth of towns; and, in general, the expansion of labor camps is an element of the proud growth of 'cities' evidenced in Soviet statistics."
6. *Istoriia KPSS*, 2nd enl. ed. (Moscow, 1962), p. 442 (hereafter cited as *Istoriia*); D. M. Ezerskaia and N. A. Ivnitsky, "Dvadtsatipiatitysiachniki i ikh rol' v kollektivizatsii sel'skogo khoziaistva v 1930 g.," *Materialy po istorii SSSR*, chief ed. A. A. Novosel'sky, I, *Dokumenty po istorii sovetskogo obshchestva* (Moscow, 1955), p. 394.
7. Anton Ciliga, *The Russian Enigma* (London, 1940), pp. 108, 111. For a full account of the twenty-five-thousanders see Lynne Viola, *The Best Sons of the Fatherland: Workers in the Vanguard of Soviet Collectivization* (New York, 1987).
8. "Na vysote sovesti," *Literaturnaia gazeta*, 14 May 1986.
9. Case related to the author by Vladimir Gurfinkel, a Soviet émigré now living in the United States. His grandfather was the collectivizer. For a similar account see M. Frolov, "Kak ya zagonial krest'ian v kolkhoz," *Rodina*, no. 4 (1989), pp. 26–27.
10. John Scott, *Behind the Urals* (Cambridge, Mass., 1942), pp. 17–18.
11. Swianiewicz, *Forced Labour*, p. 119. Before World War II, the author was professor of political economy at the University of Wilno.
12. Merle Fainsod, *Smolensk Under Soviet Rule* (New York, 1958), p. 246. This book is based on the archives of the Smolensk province (then Western province) party committee. The province is situated just east of the Belorussian Soviet Republic, which borders on Poland. The advancing German army overran it so quickly in 1941 that the Smolensk city party authorities had no time to destroy their records. Captured by the Germans, these archives were shipped to Berlin where they were found by the American army in 1945. They are now in the National Archives in Washington, D.C.
13. Fainsod, *Smolensk*, pp. 242–46.
14. Victor Kravchenko, *I Chose Freedom: The Personal and Political Life of a Soviet Official* (New York, 1946), pp. 88–89. Katya and her sister Shura had accidentally escaped when, near Kharkov, they were allowed out to get some water, though the guard said it was against his rules; when they returned to

the station with some milk given them by strangers, the train had left.

15. Fainsod, *Smolensk,* pp. 244–45.

16. *Stalin,* XII, 310.

17. V. P. Danilov, ed., *Ocherki istorii kollektivizatsii* (Moscow, 1963), pp. 41, 44, 110; N. A. Ivnitsky, "O nachal'nom etape sploshnoi kollektivizatsii, *Voprosy istorii KPSS,* no. 4 (1962), p. 65.

18. Danilov, *Ocherki istorii,* pp. 110–11. Ivnitsky, "O nachal'nom etape," p. 65, cites further examples of negative phenomena reported in the informational bulletins that went to Stalin.

19. In "Nekotorye problemy istorii kollektivizatsii SSSR," *Voprosy istorii,* no. 3 (1965), p. 7, M. A. Vyltsan, N. A. Ivnitsky, and Iu. A. Poliakov attribute "the serious difficulties of that time" to Stalin's "underestimation of the complexity of shifting peasants onto the path of collectivization, the calculation that private farming could be ended swiftly with a single blow."

20. M. L. Bogdenko, "K istorii nachal'nogo etapa sploshnoi kollektivizatsii," *Voprosy istorii,* no. 5 (May 1963), p. 35.

21. Vylstan, Ivnitsky, and Poliakov, "Nekotorye problemy," p. 12.

22. M. L. Bogdenko, "Kolkhoznoe stroitel'stvo vesnoi i letom 1930 g.," *Istoricheskie zapiski,* no. 76 (1965), p. 21.

23. Bogdenko, "K istorii," p. 7, citing a source in the Central State Archives of the National Economy of the USSR.

24. See *Istoriia,* p. 443, as well as Bogdenko, "K istorii," p. 27, for Stalin's personal responsibility for this *Pravda* leading article and particularly for its statement that the 75 percent target was "not maximal."

25. Vyltsan, Ivnitsky, and Poliakov, "Nekotorye problemy," p. 18. For the 15 percent figure, see *Istoriia,* p. 443.

26. V. P. Danilov, "Ne smet' komandovat':" *Znanie-sila,* no. 3 (1989), p. 2, and Roy A. Medvedev, *Let History Judge: The Origins and Consequences of Stalinism,* rev. and exp. ed. (New York, 1989), p. 234.

27. V. Tikhonov, "Chtoby narod prokormil sebia," *Literaturnaia gazeta,* 8 August 1988. In "Sotsializm i kooperatsiia," *Don,* no. 2 (1989), p. 122, Tikhonov offers a somewhat higher estimate of the numbers of people repressed.

28. Quoted by Swianiewicz, *Forced Labour,* p. 21.

29. *Istoriia,* p. 442.

30. Markoosha Fischer, *My Lives in Russia* (New York, 1944), p. 50. The author was the wife of Louis Fischer, then working as the Moscow correspondent of *The Nation* magazine.

31. *Istoriia,* p. 444.

32. Danilov, *Ocherki istorii,* p. 45.

33. N. A. Ivnitsky, *Klassovaia bor'ba v derevne i likvidatsiia kulachestva kak klass* (Moscow, 1972), pp. 250–54.

34. M. L. Bogdenko, "Kolkhoznoe stroitel'stvo," pp. 28–29.

35. *Khrushchev Remembers,* trans. and ed. Strobe

Talbott (Boston, 1970), p. 73.

36. *Istoriia,* p. 445. On the threat of a breakdown of the spring sowing and a resulting famine, see Bogdenko, "Kolkhoznoe stroitel'stvo," p. 29.

37. *Istoriia,* pp. 444–45.

38. Danilov, *Ocherki istorii,* pp. 110–11.

39. *Istoriia,* p. 445. The Politburo members and regional party leaders involved are not identified by name. For the Ukrainian Central Committee's decision of 21 February, see Bogdenko, "Kolkhoznoe stroitel'stvo," p. 26 n.

40. *Istoriia,* p. 445.

41. The title character of Chekhov's short story "Unter Prishibeev" is a nosey, officious, prying, and insufferably bossy ex-noncom in retirement, who is finally sentenced to a month in jail for making the lives of his fellow villagers miserable by his perpetual petty interference.

42. Bogdenko, "Kolkhoznoe stroitel'stvo," p. 28.

43. N. A. Ivnitsky, "O nachal'nom etape," p. 66.

44. See R. W. Davies, *The Socialist Offensive: The Collectivisation of Soviet Agriculture, 1929–1930,* 2 vols. (Cambridge, Mass., 1980), for full details on the process of collectivization in 1929–30.

45. Vyltsan, Ivnitsky, and Poliakov, "Nekotorye problemy," p. 9.

46. *Stalin,* XIII, 190–91.

47. *Ibid.,* 225–27, 229–30.

48. *Khrushchev Remembers,* p. 73.

49. Danilov, *Ocherki istorii,* p. 55. For Molotov's role, see I. E. Zelenin, "Politotdely MTS (1933–1934 gg.)," *Istoricheskie zapiski,* no. 76 (1965), p. 43.

50. Zelenin, "Politotdely," pp. 53–54.

51. The full text of the document has been published in *Sotsialisticheskii vestnik,* no. 2–3, (February–March 1955), pp. 50–52, with an explanatory foreword by S. Volin.

52. Alexander Baykov, *Soviet Foreign Trade* (Princeton, 1946), Appendix, Table IV. According to *Istoriia,* p. 448, the USSR imported 2.3 million tons of iron and steel in 1930–31.

53. V. P. Danilov and N. V. Teptsov, "Kollektivizatsiia: Kak eto bylo," *Pravda,* 16 September 1988. On weather conditions in 1931–32, see William Henry Chamberlin, *Russia's Iron Age* (London, 1935), pp. 83, 86; and *Stalin,* XII, 216–17.

54. Iu. A. Moshkov, *Zernovaia problema v gody sploshnoi kollektivizatsii* (Moscow, 1966), p. 226; and M. Maksudov (pseud.), *Poteri naseleniia SSSR* (Benson, Vt., 1989), p. 57.

55. Danilov and Teptsov, "Kollektivizatsiia." When the law was published in *Pravda* on 8 August 1932, no mention was made of Stalin's personal authorship of it. His authorship of it was first revealed in *Stalin,* XIII, p. 392, a volume of Stalin's works first published in 1952.

56. Danilov and Teptsov, "Kollektivizatsiia."

57. James William Crowl, *Angels in Stalin's Paradise: Western Reporters in Soviet Russia, 1917 to 1937: A Case Study of Louis*

Fischer and Walter Duranty (Lanham, Md., 1982).

58. Chamberlin reported his observations of the famine in *Russia's Iron Age*, pp. 82–88, 367–69. Eugene Lyons spoke later of "the whole shabby episode of our failure to report honestly the gruesome Russian famine of 1932–33" (*Assignment in Utopia* [New York, 1937], pp. 572ff.). For a full account of Western coverage and the lack of it, see Robert Conquest, *The Harvest of Sorrow: Soviet Collectivization and the Terror-Famine* (New York and Oxford, 1986), chap. 17.

59. Fedor Belov, *The History of a Soviet Collective Farm* (New York, 1955), pp. 12–13.

60. Fred E. Beal, *Proletarian Journey: New England, Gastonia, Moscow* (New York, 1937), pp. 305–7.

61. Lyons, *Assignment*, p. 577. The statement by Kalinin is quoted by Chamberlin, *Russia's Iron Age*, p. 369. For a detailed account of the "Potemkin Village" aspect of Eduard Herriot's travel in the Ukraine, see Ewald Ammende, *Human Life in Russia* (London, 1936), chap. 6.

62. Beal, *Proletarian Journey*, pp. 287, 291, 297.

63. *Khrushchev Remembers*, p. 74.

64. *Pravda*, 26 May 1964.

65. *Pravda*, 10 March 1964. This exchange was revealed by Khrushchev, who said in a speech of 8 March 1964 that the letters had recently been found in the archives.

66. In *Communism and the Russian Peasant* (Glencoe, Ill., 1955), p. 35 n., a book based on interviews with former Soviet citizens who became displaced persons after World War II (a group that included not a few former Ukrainian peasants), Herbert Dinerstein reports that "Soviet citizens of varying degrees of sophistication hold, with impressive unanimity, that Stalin made and willed the terrible famine of 1932 and 1933." He quotes them as saying, "He did it to make the power feared. There was no discipline at first, but after the famine there was terrible fear."

67. Kravchenko, *I Chose Freedom*, p. 130.

68. An estimate of 3 or 4 million famine deaths is given by Stephen G. Wheatcroft in "New Demographic Evidence on Excess Collectivization Deaths," *The Slavic Review*, no. 3 (Fall 1985), p. 508. Murray Feshbach gives an estimate of 5 million in "The Soviet Union: Population Trends and Dilemmas," *Population Bulletin*, no. 3 (August 1982), p. 7, but he has informed me (17 November 1989, personal conversation) that in the light of recently revealed new statistics on the Soviet censuses of 1937 and 1939, his estimate of famine deaths is 7 to 10 million. Robert Conquest offers an estimate of 7 million famine deaths (divided into 5 million in the Ukraine, 1 million in the North Caucasus, and 1 million elsewhere) in *The Harvest of Sorrow*, p. 303. The estimate of 3 million children deaths in the famine comes from M. Maksudov (pseud.), "Losses Suffered by the Population of the USSR, 1918–1958," *The Samizdat Register* II, ed. Roy A. Medvedev (New York,

1981), p. 235.

69. Chamberlin, *Russia's Iron Age*, p. 79, citing both sayings. For other references to the peasant perception of the collective farm as a revival of serfdom, see Victor Serge, *From Lenin to Stalin*, trans. Ralph Manheim, 2nd ed. (New York, 1973), p. 62, and Leonard Hubbard, *The Economics of Soviet Agriculture* (London, 1939), p. 116.

70. Fainsod, *Smolensk*, p. 251.

71. A prerevolutionary Russian encyclopedic dictionary defines "barshchina" as "compulsory agricultural work of peasants for a landowner before the emancipation of the peasants in 1861." See F. Pavlenkov, *Entsiklopedicheskii slovar'* (St. Petersburg, 1913), p. 206.

72. *S"ezdy sovetov Soiuza sovetskikh sotsialisticheskikh respublik: Sbornik dokumentov, 1922–1936 gg.*, III (Moscow, 1960), p. 188.

73. Belov, *History*, pp. 11, 16–17.

74. Vyltsan, Ivnitsky, and Poliakov, "Nekotorye problemy," p. 10. The authors, who cite an archival source here, do not say how Molotov replied.

75. *Spravochnik po zakonodatel'stvu dlia ispolnitel'nykh komitetov sovetov deputatov trudiashchikhsia*, I (Moscow, 1946), pp. 239–41. A further decree of 13 April 1942 sharply raised the norms specified in 1939.

76. In Russian, the phrase he used was "*sploshnaia barshchina.*" The person to whom I put the question was my father-in-law, Konstantin G. Pestretsov (1897–1961), whose father was of peasant origin.

77. *Pravda*, 29 April 1933. A full description of the revived internal passport system appears in *Sovetskoe administrativnoe pravo* (Moscow, 1940), pp. 198–200. For Khrushchev's testimony that it was introduced on the personal decision of Stalin, see *Pravda*, 7 March 1964.

78. *Biulleten' oppozitsii*, no. 17–18 (November–December 1930), p. 37.

79. *Stalin*, XIII, 172–73, 178–82, 214.

80. Aleksandr I. Solzhenitsyn, *The Gulag Archipelago*, II (New York, 1975), 100–102. On Stalin's cruise, see M. Gorky, L. Auerbach, and S. G. Firin, eds., *Belomor* (New York, 1935), pp. 304–5.

81. *Proletarian Journey*, p. 289.

82. Alec Nove, *An Economic History of the USSR* (London, 1969), p. 191. These statistics are derived from Soviet sources. For the point about the aggregate percentages, see this source, p. 192. It should be noted that one plan target, that for oil, was fulfilled (21.4 million tons produced in 1932 as compared with the projected 22).

83. A. A. Barsov, "Sel'skoe khoziaistvo i istochniki sotsialisticheskogo nakopleniia v gody pervoi piatiletki (1928–1932)," *Istoriia SSSR*, no. 3 (1968), pp. 81–82.

84. Holland Hunter, "The Overambitious First Soviet Five-Year Plan," *The Slavic Review*, no. 2 (June 1973), p. 256. See p. 243 for the estimate that industrial output expanded by at least 50 percent over five years.

85. James R. Miller, "Mass Collectivization and

the Contribution of Soviet Agriculture to the First Five-Year Plan: A Review Article," *The*

Slavic Review, no. 4 (December 1974), pp. 764–66.

9. Stalin's Time of Trouble

1. Introduction by Yevgeny Yevtushenko to Andrei Platonov, *The Fierce and Beautiful World,* trans. Joseph Barnes (New York, 1970), p. 14.
2. Nadezhda Mandelstam, *Hope Against Hope: A Memoir,* trans. Max Hayward (New York, 1970), pp. 13, 22–23, 146–49. There have been rumors, never confirmed, that Stalin was part Ossetian. The Ossetes are a numerically small mountain people of Iranian origin, given to the vendetta, in the north of Georgia.
3. Merle Fainsod, *Smolensk Under Soviet Rule* (New York, 1958), p. 248.
4. Medvedev, *Let History Judge* (New York, 1971), pp. 88–89. Medvedev cites as his sources two party members who were delegates to that conference and personally remembered Krupskaya's remarks, which were not published in the Soviet press.
5. *Khrushchev Remembers* (Boston, 1970), pp. 44–46. See also Robert H. McNeal, *Bride of the Revolution: Krupskaya and Lenin* (Ann Arbor, 1972), pp. 280–81.
6. *Ocherki istorii kollektivizatsii,* ed. V. P. Danilov (Moscow, 1963), pp. 46–47.
7. Markoosha Fischer, *My Lives in Russia* (New York, 1944), p. 51.
8. *Pravda,* 17 November 1964. According to this memorial article, Nazaretian lost the Urals job owing to intrigues, was then given administrative work in the Central Committee through the good offices of Maria Ulyanova (Lenin's sister), and perished in the later purges.
9. O. Bogdanova, A. Stanislavsky, and E. Starostin, "Soprotivlenie," *Ogonyok,* no. 23, 3–10 June 1989, pp. 10–11.
10. *Pravda* 2 December 1930; *Bol' shevik,* no. 21 (1930), pp. 25, 29.
11. Joseph Berger, *Shipwreck of a Generation* (London, 1971), p. 166. One of the founders of the Communist Party of Palestine, Berger was posted to Moscow on Comintern business in 1931 and reports Lominadze's statement to the above effect in a conversation he had with him in that year. This was after the exposure of the "bloc." Lominadze, after being relieved of his high posts, was appointed party secretary at the new power station in Magnitogorsk.
12. *Biulleten' oppozitsii,* no. 31 (November 1932), pp. 20–21; no. 28 (July 1932), pp. 2–3.
13. "Krasivee, luchshe li budet zhizn'? Iz dnevnikov Mate Zalki," *Moskovskie novosti,* 24 July 1988.
14. *Vsesoiuznoe soveshchanie o merakh uluchsheniia podgotovki nauchno-pedagogicheskikh kadrov po istoricheskim naukam* (Moscow, 1964), p. 291.
15. Arkadii Vaksberg, "Kak zhivoi s zhivymi," *Literaturnaia gazeta,* 29 June 1988, and Lev Razgon, "Nakonets!" *Moskovskie novosti,* 26

June 1988. The full text of the Appeal, along with notes and commentary by Vaksberg, appears in *Yunost',* no. 11 (1988). These materials confirm, but also render far more precise, a much earlier account of the Riutin affair in "Letter of an Old Bolshevik," in Boris I. Nicolaevsky, *Power and the Soviet Elite* (New York, 1965), originally published by Nicolaevsky in 1937 in the émigré Menshevik journal *Sotsialisticheskii vestnik.* Nicolaevsky's account was based on information given him by Bukharin (the article's "Old Bolshevik") when the latter visited Paris in 1936.
16. Dmitrii Volkogonov, "Triumf i tragediia: Politicheskii portret I. V. Stalina," *Oktiabr',* no. 12 (1988), p. 49. In "Kak zhivoi s zhivymi" Vaksberg writes that Ordzhonikidze, Kuibyshev, and "certain other Politburo members" joined Kirov in opposing Stalin's demand.
17. Vaksberg, "Kak zhivoi," and Razgon, "Nakonets!"
18. *Stalin,* XIII, 206–7, 214.
19. A. F. Khavin, *Kratkii ocherk istorii industrializatsii SSSR* (Moscow, 1962), p. 200. It was on 1 January 1933 that the Second Five-Year Plan was officially opened.
20. *XVII konferentsiia VKP(b)* (Moscow, 1932), p. 148.
21. Self-quotation in L. Trotsky, *The Revolution Betrayed,* trans. Max Eastman (New York, 1937), p. 61.
22. This man, Piotr Kamyshov, was an uncle of my wife, who told me about the incident.
23. Berger, *Shipwreck,* p. 90.
24. *Ibid.,* pp. 64, 67, 73, 74.
25. Svetlana Alliluyeva, *Twenty Letters* (New York, 1967), pp. 34, 35, 105.
26. *Khrushchev Remembers,* pp. 43, 44.
27. Alliluyeva, *Twenty Letters,* p. 105. For further testimony on Nadya's critical attitude toward Stalin, from a person who met her at a party at the academy during the final period, see G. A. Tokaev, *Betrayal of an Ideal* (Bloomington, In., 1955), pp. 160–61.
28. Alliluyeva, *Twenty Letters,* p. 106.
29. Alexander Barmine, *One Who Survived* (New York, 1945), p. 263. In 1937, while serving as Soviet chargé d'affaires in Athens, Barmine defected under threat of purge and stayed in the West.
30. Conversation in Moscow in June 1984 with Bukharin's widow, Anna M. Larina.
31. This account follows Alliluyeva's in *Twenty Letters,* pp. 108–9, 112–13.
32. Aino Kuusinen, *Before and After Stalin: A Personal Account of Soviet Russia from the 1920s to the 1960s,* trans. Paul Stevenson (London, 1974), pp. 91–92, and Lidiia Shatunovskaia, *Zhizn' v Kremle* (New York, 1982), pp. 198–99.
33. Alliluyeva, *Twenty Letters,* pp. 122–23. The

author explains this inner change by her mother's death and the circumstances surrounding it. For all that event's great importance, it must be seen as one of a larger set of precipitants.

34. Whether this marked the onset of a condition falling somewhere on the spectrum of mental states psychiatrically designated as "paranoid" is not for an historian to say. The question of Stalin's psyche has lately come under discussion in the Soviet press. See O. Moroz, "Poslednii diagnoz," *Literaturnaia gazeta,* 28 September 1988; V. O. Topliansky, "Noch' pered rozhdestvom v 1927 godu," *Ogonyok,* no. 14, 1–8 April 1989; and especially "Konsilium," *Literaturnaia gazeta,* 2 August 1989, the report of a round-table discussion by prominent Soviet psychiatrists of the question: "Was Stalin mentally ill?" Although nearly all pronounced him in varying degree psychopathological, none found him psychotic or insane. According to Dr. A. Lichko, deputy director of the Bekhterev Institute in Leningrad, however, "In the final months of his life Stalin was psychotic and apparently in that period he was insane. The whole time prior to that he had paranoidal psychopathology and hence was sane. Therefore, responsible for his actions." Dr. Lichko

expressed himself to the same effect in a personal interview with this author in Leningrad in April 1989.

35. Smolensk archive in the National Archives, WKP499 (T87 / 43), p. 1. An English translation of the secret letter appears in *Resolutions and Decisions of the Communist Party of the Soviet Union,* III, *The Stalin Years: 1929–1953,* ed. Robert H. McNeal (Toronto, 1974), pp. 167–81.

36. *Pravda,* 6 May 1935. The reference to bullets carried an allusion to the assassination of Kirov in late 1934 as well as to a threat of Stalin's assassination.

37. *Stalin,* XIII, 207–12, 214.

38. *Ibid.,* 210–11.

39. *VKP(b) v rezoliutsiakh* II, *1925–1939* (Moscow, 1941), 523.

40. McNeal, *Stalin Years,* pp. 125–26. The fourth, fifth, and sixth categories were: "degenerates who have merged with bourgeois elements"; "careerists, self-seekers, and bureaucratized elements"; and "moral degenerates."

41. On the history of the Central Control Commission and the indications of Stalin's disfavor, see Paul M. Cocks, "Politics of Party Control," unpublished Ph.D. dissertation presented to Harvard University (1968), chaps. 2 and 7.

10. The Diplomacy of Rapprochement with Germany

1. Thomas D. Campbell, *Russia: Market or Menace?* (London and New York, 1932), pp. 16–17.

2. *Stalin,* I (XIV), 121. (A volume prepared by Robert H. McNeal; see Bibliography.)

3. *Writings of Leon Trotsky, IV (1932–33),* eds. George Breitman and Evelyn Reed (New York, 1972), p. 21. Trotsky's article provoked from Stalin, who had not publicized his interview with Campbell, a denial of the latter's recollection of their conversation (*Stalin,* XIII, 146–48).

4. Leon Trotsky, *The Revolution Betrayed* (New York, 1937), p. 186.

5. Orville H. Bullitt, ed., *For the President, Personal and Secret: Correspondence Between Franklin D. Roosevelt and William C. Bullitt* (Boston, 1972), pp. 68–69; United States, State Department, *Foreign Relations of the United States, Diplomatic Papers: The Soviet Union, 1933–1939* (Washington, D.C., 1952), pp. 60–61.

6. "From a Publicist's Diary (Theme for Elaboration)," *Lenin,* XXXV, 189. The document appeared in 1929 in *Leninskii sbornik* (Moscow), XI.

7. *Stalin,* XIII, 115–16.

8. *Ibid.,* 115–17.

9. *Lenin,* XLII, 68.

10. Harvey Dyck, *Weimar Germany and Soviet Russia* (New York, 1966), pp. 103, 141. On the diplomacy of Rapallo, see Renata Bournazel, *Rapallo: Naissance d'un mythe* (Paris, 1974).

11. *Stalin,* VI, 36.

12. Ruth Fischer, *Stalin and German Communism: A Study in the Origins of the State Party* (Cambridge, Mass., 1948), pp. 287, 313, Brandler, notes the author, wrote in the German party organ *Rote Fahne:* "Beat the fascists whenever you meet them."

13. "Letter to Comrade Me——rt" (actually, to the German left Communist Arkadi Maslow), in *Stalin,* V, 43, 45.

14. *Stalin,* VII, 98–99.

15. Dyck, *Weimar Germany,* pp. 229, 235. In this and the following two paragraphs I rely heavily on the detailed documented record presented by Dyck.

16. Bukharin told Kamenev in July 1928 ("Bukharin-Kamenev Conversation," Trotsky Archives (Document T1897)) that Stalin was taking the line in the Politburo that there should be no death sentences in the Shakhty case. In the event, the three Germans placed on trial were acquitted.

17. Dyck, *Weimar Germany,* pp. 236, 242–44.

18. Karl Dietrich Bracher, *The German Dictatorship: The Origins, Structure, and Effects of National Socialism,* trans. Jean Steinberg (New York, 1970), chap. 14; Joachim C. Fest, *Hitler,* trans. Richard and Clara Winston (New York, 1975), part 4, chaps. 3–4, part 5, chap. 1.

19. Leon Trotsky, *The Struggle Against Fascism in Germany* (New York, 1971), pp. 125–29, 139. In "The German Communists' United-Front and Popular-Front Ventures," in *The Comintern: Historical Highlights,* ed. Milorad M. Drachkovitch and Branko Lazitch (New

York, 1966), p. 115, Babette L. Gross writes from experience that for members of the German Communist party at that time, "the Nazi bully squads were the main adversary; they had to be counterattacked, their blows warded off."

20. A. Ascher and G. Lewy, "National Bolshevism in Weimar Germany," *Social Research* (Winter 1956), pp. 464–66, 472, 478–79. For the Comintern directive see *Kommunisticheskii Internatsional' v dokumentakh, 1919–1932*, part 2 (Moscow, 1933), p. 946.

21. Gross, in Drachkovitch and Lazitch, *Comintern*, p. 117. The author, sister of Margarete Buber-Neumann (Heinz Neumann's wife), also reports here (p. 116) that on a visit to Moscow in April 1931 Neumann heard Stalin criticize the KPD for having cooperated with the SPD in Thuringia in bringing about a no-confidence vote for the Nazi minister of the interior, Wilhelm Frick.

22. Ex-Insider, "Moscow—Berlin 1933," *Survey*, no. 44–45 (October 1962), p. 162. Theodore Draper and Leopold Labedz have informed me that the pseudonymous interviewee was Joseph Berger.

23. Stampfer subsequently settled in the United States where he revealed this information in an interview. See David J. Dallin, *Russia and Postwar Europe*, trans. F. K. Lawrence (New Haven, 1943), pp. 61–62 n.

24. Quoted by E. H. Carr, *The Interregnum, 1923–1924* (New York, 1954), p. 187. See also Trotsky, *Struggle Against Fascism*, pp. 111–12. Although Stalin did not include the letter in his collected works, he acknowledged its authenticity in a Central Committee plenum of 1927. See *Stalin*, X, 61–62.

25. Margarete Buber-Neumann, *Von Potsdam nach Moskau: Stationen eines Irrweges* (Stuttgart, 1957), p. 284. The author adds here: "I haven't forgotten Stalin's question to Neumann because it was the first thing Heinz shared with me when he arrived at the Friedrichstrasse Station in Berlin."

26. Gustav Hilger and Alfred G. Meyer, *The Incompatible Allies: A Memoir-History of German-Soviet Relations, 1918–1941* (New York, 1953), p. 253.

27. Erich Wollenberg, *The Red Army: A Study of the Growth of Soviet Imperialism* (London, 1940), p. 278. Wollenberg was one of the editors of *Rote Fahne* in 1932.

28. *Ibid.*, p. 237.

29. In his memoir, *Moscow-Tokyo-London: Twenty Years of German Foreign Policy* (Norman, Okla., 1952), p. 81, Herbert von Dirksen observes that Litvinov was "no dyed-in-the-wool Rapallo man but only rendered lip-service to that policy" and that "the coming of National Socialism provided him with the welcome pretext to be one of the first to leave the foundering Rapallo-policy."

30. *The Speeches of Adolf Hitler*, ed. N. H. Baynes (London, 1942), II, 1019, quoted by Max Beloff, *The Foreign Policy of Soviet Russia, 1929–1941* (London and New York, 1947), I, 25.

31. Report of 28 April 1933 from Khinchuk, in *Dokumenty vneshnei politiki SSSR*, chief ed. A. A. Gromyko (Moscow, 1970), XVI, 271.

32. Karl Radek, *Podgotovka bor'by za novyi peredel mira* (Moscow, 1934), pp. 92–94.

33. Walter Laqueur, *Russia and Germany: A Century of Conflict* (London, 1965), pp. 154–58; and Ascher and Lewy, "National Bolshevism," pp. 469, 474–78.

34. Karl Heinz Niclaus, *Die Sowjetunion und Hitlers Machtergreifung* (Bonn, 1966), pp. 120, 121, 127, 138, citing from German archival sources a secret report of 17 August 1933 from Dirksen to State Secretary Bulow in Berlin.

35. Dirksen, *Moscow-Tokyo-London*, pp. 116; and Hilger and Meyer, *Incompatible Allies*, pp. 260–61, apropos the persuading of Hitler.

36. Evgeni Gnedin, *Iz istorii otnoshenii mezhdu SSSR i fashistskoi Germaniei* (New York, 1977), pp. 22–23. Gnedin was deputy chief of the Foreign Department of *Izvestiia* in the early 1930s, first secretary of the Soviet Embassy in Berlin in 1935–37, and chief of the Narkomindel Press Department in 1937–39.

37. United States, State Department, *Documents on German Foreign Policy, 1918–1945*, Ser. C, II (Washington, 1959), p. 41.

38. Gnedin, *Iz istorii*, p. 13.

39. Dirksen, *Moscow-Tokyo-London*, p. 118.

11. The Congress of Victims

1. I. E. Zelenin, "Kolkhozy i sel'skoe khoziaistvo SSSR v 1933–1935 gg.," *Istoriia SSSR* (September–October 1964), p. 14 n.

2. Boris I. Nicolaevsky, "Letter of an Old Bolsheviks," in *Power and the Soviet Elite* (New York, 1965), pp. 30, 44.

3. *Ibid.*, pp. 31–33.

4. *Stalin*, XIII, 410.

5. Interview with I. I. Mints at the Institute of USSR History in Moscow, June 1977.

6. Nicolaevsky, *Power*, pp. 15–16. According to the "Letter," Gorky, in bruiting his idea of a loyal second party, had the support of another world-famous Russian, Ivan Pavlov.

7. *Stalin*, VI, 422.

8. Among Kirov's sympathizers was a nineteen-year-old Leningrader with religious leanings, who said in a memoir written abroad more than forty years later: "Kirov was the only (in the Soviet regime's time) popular leader. He alone was relatively accessible, regularly walked his dog. It was comparatively easy to get an audience with him and in most cases he would be responsive and grant the request." A. Krasnov-Levitin, *Likhie gody, 1925–1941: Vospominaniia* (Paris, 1977), p. 265.

9. S. Sinel'nikov, *Kirov* (Moscow, 1964), p.

321. For more examples, see pp. 321–22.
10. *Ibid.*, p. 311. To illustrate the comparative deliberateness of the pace of the collectivization drive in Leningrad region, Sinel'nikov notes that only 6.6 percent of the peasant households were collectivized by 1 January 1931, 45.1 percent by 1 January 1932, 45.4 percent by 1 January 1933, and 54.2 percent by 1 January 1934.
11. Personal communication from Professor Mikhail Gefter in Moscow.
12. *Khrushchev Remembers* (Boston, 1970), p. 61.
13. Sinel'nikov, *Kirov*, p. 360.
14. Kendall E. Bailes, *Technology and Society Under Lenin and Stalin* (Princeton, 1978), chaps. 6 and 7. For an earlier example of Ordzhonikidze's protection of a victimized Soviet engineer, see Marietta Shaginyan's article in *Izvestiia*, 6 November 1964.
15. Semen Gershberg, *Rabota u nas takaia: Zapiski zhurnalista-pravdista tridtsatykh godov* (Moscow, 1971), pp. 164–65.
16. Nicolaevsky, *Power*, p. 34. The "Letter" adds that Kalinin reportedly was reprimanded (by whom it is not said) for his outburst. On Voroshilov as a possible sympathizer, see Isaac Deutscher, *Stalin* (New York, 1966), p. 354.
17. Lev Nikulin, *Tukhachevsky: Biograficheskii ocherk* (Moscow, 1964), pp. 167–69. On the 1920 origins of Stalin's animosity toward Tukhachevsky, see Tucker, *Stalin As Revolutionary* (New York, 1973), pp. 203–5. Nikulin reveals (pp. 176–77) that during a discussion of Civil War history in the Frunze military academy in Moscow in 1930, Tukhachevsky was blamed for the Red debacle at Warsaw ten years earlier, and then wrote a letter to Stalin in protest against the unjust charge.
18. *VKS(b) v rezoliutsiakh*, II, *1925–1939* (Moscow, 1941). For the Ordzhonikidze-ch-Zaveniagin interview with Stalin, see Gershberg, *Rabota*, pp. 199–200. Gershberg, a *Pravda* correspondent for economic affairs in the 1930s, was told of the interview by Zaveniagin shortly after it took place.
19. R. W. Davies, "The Soviet Economic Crisis of 1931–1933" (University of Birmingham, Soviet Industrialisation Project Series, no. 4), pp. 14–17. Cited by permission of the author.
20. Nicolaevsky, *Power*, pp. 47–48.
21. See chapter 9, pp. 221–22, above for the directive.
22. *Bol'shevik*, no. 9, 15 May 1933, pp. 7, 8. Yaroslavsky's description of the new purge as a "general" one appeared in *Bol'shevik*, no. 7–8, 30 April 1933, p. 18.
23. Nicolaevsky, *Power*, pp. 34–35, 45–46.
24. *XVII s" ezd VKS(b), 26 ianvaria–10 fevralia 1934 g.* (Moscow, 1934), p. 303. All citations from congress speeches below are from this volume.
25. L. S. Shaumian, in *Pravda*, 7 February 1964.
26. Unpublished document, dated 5 September 1988, by Olga Shatunovskaia. A party member since 1916, Shatunovskaia was arrested in Stalin's Terror and spent sixteen years in confinement. She became a member of a Politburo commission, chaired by N. M. Shvernik, which was formed in 1960, pursuant to a decision of the Twentieth Party Congress, to investigate the purge trials of the 1930s. For some of the names mentioned, see Roy Medvedev, *Let History Judge*, rev. and exp. ed. (New York, 1989), p. 331. That the Ukraine-based Petrovsky was one of the Old Bolsheviks who wanted Stalin replaced is confirmed in a Soviet biography of him: F. Bega and V. Aleksandrov, *Petrovsky* (Moscow, 1963), p. 303.
27. N. S. Khrushchev, "Vospominaniia," *Ogonyok*, no. 28, 9–15 July 1989, p. 29. Some of this portion of Khrushchev's memoirs, released for publication in Moscow by his family, did not appear in *Khrushchev Remembers*.
28. Shatunovskaia document.
29. A. I. Mikoyan, "V pervyi raz bez Lenina," *Ogonyok*, no. 50, 12–19 December 1987, p. 6. This is a previously unpublished part of Mikoyan's memoirs.
30. Nicolaevsky, *Power*, p. 35.
31. G. A. Trukan, *Yan Rudzutak* (Moscow, 1963), pp. 91, 92. The author adds: "An authoritative and full-powered control organ evidently interfered with I. V. Stalin's concentrating of all power in his own hands." For further testimony to this effect, see *Kommunist*, no. 18 (December 1962), p. 37.
32. Trukan, *Rudzutak*, p. 92.
33. *Ibid*.
34. Interview with Walter Duranty, *Stalin*, XIII, p. 280.
35. United States, State Department, *Documents on German Foreign Policy, 1918–1945*, Ser. C, II (Washington, D.C., 1959), 274. Hereafter cited as *DGFP*.
36. M. Litvinov, *Vneshniaia politika SSSR* (Moscow, 1937), pp. 74–96.
37. *DGFP*, Ser. C, II, 319, 321, 322, 324.
38. *Ibid.*, 333–34.
39. *Ibid.*, 435–36.
40. Quoted by Max Beloff, *The Foreign Policy of Soviet Russia* (London, 1947), I, 99.
41. S. M. Kirov, *Stat' i i rechi, 1934* (Moscow, 1934), pp. 39, 40, 41, 45–46.
42. Made less apparent by the fact that the final quoted passage and Kirov's definition of fascism as a terroristic dictatorship were deleted from the somewhat condensed version of his precongress speech printed in *Pravda* on 24 January 1934.
43. The name of the *oprichniki*, Ivan Grozny's terroristic henchmen, lingered on in Russian memory as a byword for brutality, and was often applied by revolutionaries to the tsarist secret police. Rudzutak's reference to beheading was an allusion to the beheading of four German Communists by the Nazis in August 1933.
44. *Pravda*, 31 January 1934. The "prolonged" was deleted in the subsequently published congress transcript. The discrepancy has been noted by Stephen F. Cohen in *Bukharin and the Bolshevik Revolution* (New York, 1973), p. 464.

45. Franz Borkenau, *World Communism: A History of the Communist International* (Ann Arbor, 1962), pp. 382–83.
46. Gustav Hilger and Alfred G. Meyer, *The Incompatible Allies* (New York, 1953), p. 271.
47. "Skol'ko delegatov XVII s"ezda partii golosovalo protiv Stalina?" *Izvestiia Ts.K. KPSS*, no. 7 (1989), p. 114.
48. Khrushchev gives the number of votes cast against Stalin as "either 260 or 160" in a previously unpublished portion of his memoirs (N. S. Khrushchev, "Vospominaniia," *Ogonyok*, no. 28, 9–15 July 1989, p. 29). Mikoyan gives the number as nearly 300 in a previously unpublished part of his own memoirs ("V pervyi raz bez Lenina") p. 6.
49. Mikoyan, "V pervyi raz bez Lenina," p. 6.
50. Verkovykh, "Skol'ko delegatov," p. 120.
51. *Khrushchev Remembers*, p. 49.
52. Svetlana Alliluyeva, *Twenty Letters* (New York, 1967), pp. 137–38. Alliluyeva gives Olga Shatunovskaia as her source here.
53. M. Ilin, "Vystrel v Smol'nom," *Sovetskaia kul'tura*, 15 August 1989. This article consists of excerpts from a still unpublished memoir by M. V. Rosliakov, "Kak eto bylo (k ubiistvu S. M. Kirova)," located in the Kirov Museum in Leningrad. Rosliakov, a close associate and friend of Kirov's, was present at the Seventeenth Congress as a delegate.
54. B. Nicolaevsky, "Stalin i ubiistvo Kirova," *Sotsialisticheskii vestnik* (December 1956), p. 241. This article is reprinted in Nicolaevsky, *Power*, pp. 69–97.
55. *Stalin*, IX, 66.

56. In revealing that 1,108 of the 1,966 delegates were later arrested, Khrushchev gave no breakdown of arrests in the two categories. The proportion of arrests was presumably higher among the voting delegates.
57. Medvedev, *Let History Judge* (1971), p. 156.
58. A. Mel'chin, *Stanislav Kosior* (Moscow, 1964), p. 71.
59. Walter G. Krivitsky, *In Stalin's Secret Service* (New York and London, 1939), p. 151. The author, who escaped from Russia in 1937, was found dead in a Washington, D.C., hotel room in 1941 under circumstances pointing to murder.
60. Nicolaevsky, *Power*, pp. 60, 61. "Old Bolshevik" pictures Stalin as having come to this view after Kirov's assassination. For reasons adduced here, I consider it certain that he reached it by February 1934.
61. *The Lenin Anthology*, ed. Robert C. Tucker (New York, 1975), p. 90. For the epigraph, see p. 12.
62. "The Tax in Kind," *Lenin*, XLIII, 234. Stalin's spokesman Cherviak quoted this passage in his article on Lenin and terror (*Bol'shevik*, no. 19–20, 31 October 1930, p. 96).
63. *Stalin*, VI, 57–59. An illustration cited here by Stalin was Lenin's position in the small minority of radically antiwar Social Democrats during the World War.
64. *Ibid.*, XII, 358. Stalin also had a special liking for Lenin's essays entitled *Against the Current*. See *ibid.*, VII, 18.
65. *Ibid.*, X, 369–70.
66. *Ibid.*, 371.

12. The Coming of the Great Purge

1. See chap. 9, p. 219 above.
2. Boris I. Nicolaevsky, "Letter of an Old Bolshevik," in his *Power and the Soviet Elite* (New York, 1965), p. 45.
3. *XVII s"ezd VKS(b), 26 ianvaria–10 fevralia 1943 g.* (Moscow, 1934), pp. 561–62.
4. For the information on this meeting I am indebted to Professor Aron Katsenelinboigen, who emigrated from Russia in 1975. His source had firsthand knowledge of the episode.
5. *Pravda*, 9 June 1934. Although the statute referred to armed service personnel, it was interpretable as applying to anyone of official status.
6. It appeared in *Sobranie zakonov i rasporiazhenii raboche-krest'ianskogo pravitel'stva Soiuza sovetskikh sotsialisticheskikh respublik*, no. 11, 7 March 1935, pp. 139–40. The Special Board was abolished after Stalin died.
7. P. A. Zaionchkovsky, *Krizis samoderzhaviia na rubezhe 1870–1880 godov* (Moscow, 1964), p. 406, and by the same author, *Rossiiskoe samoderzhavie v kontse XIX stoletiia* (Moscow, 1970), p. 155. Stalin's own several exiles had been by decision of the Special Board.
8. Karl Dietrich Bracher, *The German Dictatorship: The Origins, Structure, and Effects of National Socialism*, trans. Jean Steinberg (New York, 1970), pp. 239–40. The author estimates the number of victims of the Röhm purge at 150–200. Other estimates have run as high as 1,000 to 2,000.
9. Walter G. Krivitsky, *In Stalin's Secret Service* (New York, 1939), p. 183.
10. Valentin Berezhkov, "Prigovor vynosit vremia," *Nedelia*, no. 31 (August 1989). Berezhkov gives his source as Mikoyan. Since Mikoyan was a candidate member of the Politburo in 1934, he would have been in a position to speak from personal memory of Stalin making the quoted statement. Berezhkov served in the Soviet Embassy in Germany at the close of the 1930s and later became an interpreter for Stalin.
11. R. Wipper, *Ivan Grozny*, trans. J. Fineberg, 3rd ed., (Moscow, 1947), pp. 73, 93, 98, 106–8, 127–29, 146, 171.
12. In chap. 3, p. 52.
13. N. K. Cherkasov, *Zapiski sovetskogo aktera* (Moscow, 1953), pp. 380–82. The interview took place on 24 February 1947, with Molotov and Zhdanov present.
14. Interview of 28 June 1977 with I. I. Mints at the Institute of History of the USSR, Mos-

cow. Mints spoke to me on the basis of his personal notes concerning the conversation.

15. *I vsesoiuznyi s"ezd sovetskikh pisatelei, 1934* (Moscow, 1934), p. 10.
16. Vladimir Kobrin, "Vozhd' i tsar'," *Moskovskie novosti,* 7 August 1988.
17. *Stalin,* VI, 229
18. *Ibid.,* XII, 114.
19. *Ibid,* XIII, 370.
20. Alexander Orlov, *The Secret History of Stalin's Crimes* (New York, 1953), p. 206.
21. *Istorik-Marksist,* no. 1–2, 1932, p. 10.
22. *Direktivy VKP(b) i postanovleniia sovetskogo pravitel'stva o narodnom obrazovanii,* comp. N. I. Boldyrev (Moscow and Leningrad, 1947), I, 159, 168.
23. *Ibid.,* 169–71.
24. A. I. Gukovsky, "Kak ia stal istorikom," *Istoriia SSSR,* no. 6 (1965), p. 97. Stalin's son Vasily would have been about fourteen years old at that time.
25. Konstantin F. Shteppa, *Russian Historians and the Soviet State* (New Brunswick, N.J., 1962), p. 126. The author, a history professor in Kiev in the 1930s, speaks of this incident from personal knowledge.
26. S. Krasnikov, *S. M. Kirov v Leningrade* (Leningrad, 1966), pp. 187–88. The final year of the Second Plan was 1937.
27. Medvedev, *Let History Judge* (New York, 1971), p. 158.
28. S. Krasnikov, *Sergei Mironovich Kirov: Zhizn' i deiatel'nost'* (Moscow, 1964), p. 196.
29. *A Short History of the USSR,* ed. A. V. Shestakov (Moscow, 1938) pp. 49–50. The Russian edition appeared in 1937: *Kratkii kurs istorii SSSR.*
30. Niccolo Machiavelli, *The Prince* (New York, 1952), pp. 104–5. For the report in high Soviet circles around 1930 that *The Prince* was a bedside book of Stalin's, see Anton Ciliga, *The Russian Enigma* (London, 1940), p. 134. I was told by the late Boris Nicolaevsky that Kamenev, with whom Stalin shared Siberian exile for a time during World War I (and with whom Nicolaevsky was well acquainted) observed Stalin poring over *The Prince* by the hour.
31. In *Power and Soviet Elite,* pp. 92–93, 95–96, Nicolaevsky interprets the internal-chdétente policy as a sign of Stalin's postcongress defeat in a "duel between Stalin and Kirov" for political supremacy. The only evidence cited, however, is the policy itself, plus the fact that Stalin was not called "general" secretary in the announcement of the postcongress Central Committee session. If, as I contend, Stalin willed the policy, Nicolaevsky's interpretation of it collapses.
32. *Leninskii kooperativnyi plan i bor'ba partii za ego osushchestvlenie* (Moscow, 1969), pp. 129–30. This meeting was not publicized at the time, and the text of Stalin's remarks has not been published.
33. Medvedev, *Let History Judge,* p. 157.
34. Louis Fischer, in *The Nation,* 8 May 1935, p. 530, for the growing prosperity in 1934, and A. Sergeev, *Novoye russkoye slovo,* 21

March 1975, for a personal recollection of talk about a "little NEP."
35. *Pravda,* 20 November 1935.
36. *Khrushchev Remembers* (Boston, 1970), pp. 62–63. Nikolai Bulganin was then chairman of the Moscow City Soviet. Khrushchev thought this conversation occurred before the Seventeenth Congress, but did not remember the exact time of it. He became first secretary of the Moscow party committee after the congress.
37. Walter Duranty, "Soviet Revives Gayety and Games," *The New York Times,* 19 March 1934.
38. Anne O'Hare McCormick, "Russia's Trend—To Main Street?" *The New York Times Magazine,* 13 February 1934, p. 20.
39. Ilya Ehrenburg, *Memoirs: 1921–1941,* trans. Tatiana Shebunina with Yvonne Kapp (Cleveland and New York, 1964), p. 283.
40. *Pravda,* 19 June 1934.
41. *I s"ezd,* p. 675. Stalin must have said this on a social occasion.
42. Nadezhda Mandelstam, *Hope Against Hope* (New York, 1970), pp. 6, 25, 146–47.
43. Louis Fischer, *Men and Politics: An Autobiography* (New York, 1941), p. 226–27. Also, Fischer, in *The Nation,* 8 May 1935, p. 529. As a pro-Soviet resident journalist in Moscow during much of the 1930s, Fischer had sources of information in high Soviet circles. A report in the Soviet paper *Za industrializatsiiu,* 16 May 1934, illustrates the opportunities that existed for correcting abuses: half the engineers and technicians in many coal mines around the Siberian mining center of Prokopievsk were working as convicts under sentence for minor or imaginary neglect of duty.
44. *Bol'shevik,* no. 18, 30 September 1934, p. 45. Akulov became a purge victim in 1937.
45. *Pravda* and *Izvestiia,* 11 July 1934.
46. His statement appeared in *Pravda* on 18 April 1934. See also the recantation by the ex-Trotskyist L. Sosnovsky, *Pravda,* 27 February 1934.
47. Chimen Abransky, "Kamenev's Last Essay," *The New Left Review,* no. 15 (May–June 1962), p. 40. A full translation of the essay appears here. Articles by Zinoviev appeared in *Pravda* on 1 May, 31 May, and 14 July 1934; an article by Kamenev, on 6 November. I am indebted to Dr. John Sontag for pointing out to me the fact of Zinoviev's appearance and disappearance from *Bol'shevik's* editorial board during 1934.
48. *The Great Purge Trial,* ed. Robert C. Tucker and Stephen F. Cohen (New York, 1965), p. 493.
49. This point is made by Robert Conquest, *The Great Terror: Stalin's Purge of the Thirties,* rev. ed. (New York, 1973), p. 76. He also cites the Yagoda testimony as otherwise probably accurate.
50. V. Lordkipanidze, "Ubiistvo Kirova: Nekotorye podrobnosti," *Argumenty i fakty,* no. 6 (1989), pp. 5–6. The author describes his own father, T. I. Lordkipanidze, as having

been an NKVD official and devoted to Kirov, with whom he was acquainted.

51. *Ibid.*
52. "Vystrel v Smol'nom," *Sovetskaia kul'tura,* 15 August 1989.
53. Lordkipanidze, "Ubiistvo Kirova," p. 6.
54. Medvedev, *Let History Judge,* p. 158.
55. Orlov, *Secret History,* p. 15.
56. Pavel Gol'dshtein, *Tochka opory: V Butyrskoi i Lefortovskoi tiur'makh 1939 goda* (Jerusalem, 1978), pp. 10–13. Gol'dshtein was a young high-school history teacher when arrested in 1938. He survived Stalin's time and later emigrated to Israel where he wrote and published this memoir.
57. Lordkipanidze, "Ubiistvo Kirova," pp. 5–6.
58. "Vystrel v Smol'nom,"
59. Lordkipanidze, "Ubiistvo Kirova," p. 5.
60. *Ibid.,* p. 6.
61. "Vystrel v Smol'nom."
62. Medvedev, *Let History Judge,* p. 159.
63. "Vystrel v Smol'nom."
64. Lordkipanidze, "Ubisstvo Kirova," p. 6.
65. *Ibid.*
66. N. S. Khrushchev, "Vospominaniia," *Ogonyok,* no. 28, 9–15 July 1989, p. 30.
67. "Vystrel v Smol'nom."
68. *Ibid.*
69. Khrushchev, "Vospominaniia," p. 30.
70. Personal conversation with N. Kirshon, whose father, Voroshilov's adjutant R. Khmel'nitsky, heard this from Voroshilov shortly after he returned with Stalin from Leningrad.
71. Lordkipanidze, "Ubiistvo Kirova," p. 5. Fomin is given as the source here.
72. "Vystrel v Smol'nom."
73. Speech of 27 October 1961 to the Twenty-Second Party Congress, *Pravda,* 28 October 1961.
74. Lev Razgon, *Nepridumannoe* (Moscow, 1989), pp. 164–67.
75. Medvedev, *Let History Judge,* p. 163.
76. "Vystrel v Smol'nom."
77. Khrushchev, "Vospominaniia," p. 30.
78. *Ibid.*
79. Lordkipanidze, "Ubiistvo Kirova," p. 6.
80. D. Volkogonov, "Triumf i tragediia: Politicheskii portret I. V. Stalina," *Oktiabr',* no. 12 (1988), p. 53. Olga was probably Milda's mother and Roman Kuliner the mother's husband.
81. *Khrushchev Remembers,* Twentieth Congress speech, p. 575. Khrushchev's closed speech to the XXth party congress was first published in the Soviet Union in *Izvestiia Ts.K. KPSS,* no. 3 (1989).
82. In Moscow in June 1989 Professor Volkogonov made available to me a facsimile copy of the original typewritten text of this edict. It has a handwritten signature by Yenukidze, but none by Kalinin under *his* typed signature. A notation, "For publication," initialed by Stalin, appears to have been added by Sta-

lin on 4 December 1934 immediately on his return from Leningrad to Moscow.
83. Harold Denny, "Russian Arrests Spreading Terror," *The New York Times,* 16 December 1934.
84. *Pravda,* 5 December 1934.
85. Olga Shatunovskaia document of 5 September 1988, p. 2.
86. "Vystrel v Smol'nom." Rosliakov, himself a victim of the ensuing Stalin terror, as were many other Leningrad officials, returned home in 1956 after many years in Stalin's camps, completed his memoir in 1970, and died in 1985.
87. *Pravda,* 23 December 1934.
88. Merle Fainsod, *Smolensk Under Soviet Rule* (New York, 1958), p. 222.
89. Medvedev, *Let History Judge,* p. 163.
90. Joseph Berger, *Shipwreck of a Generation* (London, 1971), pp. 161–62. In a Moscow prison in 1937, Berger learned the story of the trial from an eyewitness, Dmitry Ivanov, who was associated with the accused but not included among the defendants in that trial.
91. *Pravda,* 30 December 1934.
92. "Glavy iz vospominanii Very Panovy," *SSSR: Vnutrennie protivorechiia,* no. 3 (1982), pp. 279–80. Panova, who subsequently became a well-known writer, died in the 1970s. Her memoirs, *O moei zhizni, knigakh i chitateliakh,* were published in 1975 minus chap. 28, from which the citation comes.
93. Conversation with Anna Mikhailovna Larina, widow of Bukharin, in Moscow, June 1977.
94. Conversation in 1982 with the exiled writer Lev Kopelev, who related the story from personal memories of that time. In Russian *pomidor* means tomato.
95. Nicolaevsky, *Power and Soviet Elite,* p. 51. For this information Bukharin would have been Nicolaevsky's source.
96. Lidia Nord, *Marshal M. N. Tukhachevsky* (Paris, 1978), p. 120.
97. Kuibyshev died on 25 January 1935. Post-Stalin Soviet biographies have described his death as a natural one caused by a heart attack.
98. Orlov, *Secret History,* p. 276.
99. *Pravda,* 28 January 1935. This literary attack on Gorky has been noted by Leonard Schapiro, *The Communist Party of the Soviet Union* (New York, 1959), pp. 402–3.
100. *Pravda,* 8 June 1935.
101. G. Trukan, "Avel' Yenukidze," *Agitator,* no. 12 (1989), p. 42. The full proceedings of that plenum remain unpublished as of 1989.
102. Conversation with the late Elkon G. Leikin, Moscow, June 1977. Mr. Leikin was the young follower. Arrested in 1935, he spent many years in camps and returned to Moscow in Khrushchev's time.

13. Politics and Society in the Purge Era

1. Nadezhda Mandelstam, *Hope Against Hope* (New York, 1970), p. 99.

2. The letter is mentioned and partially quoted in the subsequent secret circular of 29 July

1936, in Smolensk Archive, at the National Archives, WKP 499 (TB7/53).

3. *Pravda*, 18 January 1935. The nine members of the alleged "Moscow center," together with eight others said to be associated with them, received prison sentences ranging from five to ten years, and seventy-six others said to be connected with the group were administratively sentenced by the NKVD Special Board to concentration camps or exile.

4. *Pravda* leading article, 17 January 1935.

5. Joseph Berger, *Shipwreck of a Generation* (London, 1971), p. 167. Berger was told this at the Mariinsk camp in 1935 by Lominadze's close friend and second in command at Magnitogorsk, who had been arrested soon after Lominadze returned from the Moscow mission and related his conversation with Ordzhonikidze. Lominadze himself committed suicide around that time after receiving orders to report to Chelyabinsk, which he knew meant his own arrest (*ibid.*, p. 168)

6. *Pravda*, 2 February 1935.

7. See Molotov's speech, *Pravda*, 7 February 1935, on Stalin's initiative.

8. A. Krasnov-Levitin, *Likhie gody* (Paris, 1977), p. 269. On 20 March 1935 *Pravda* announced that 1,074 "former people" had been deported from Leningrad, but this appears a gross understatement. It is reported on good authority that in February 1935, 4,000 Leningrad "former" families were deported to Astrakhan alone, and this was only one of the deportees' destinations. See Piotr Yakir, *A Childhood in Prison* (New York, 1973), p. 29.

9. Anton Ciliga, *The Russian Enigma* (London, 1940), p. 71.

10. Orville H. Bullitt, ed., *For the President* (Boston, 1972), p. 151.

11. Berger was arrested at the end of January 1935, and the other two during February. See Berger, *Shipwreck*, pp. 8, 56–57, and 74–75. He reports that Yemelyanov received parcels and letters from Lenin's sister, Mariya Ulyanova, and from Krupskaya, who wrote: "I wish we could do more for you, but we can't." That was in mid-1935.

12. *Pravda*, 5 February 1935. For his activities in Kazan, see Eugenia Semyonovna Ginzburg, *Journey into the Whirlwind*, trans. Paul Stevenson and Max Hayward (New York and London, 1967), pp. 2–8.

13. *Biulleten' oppozitsii*, no. 43 (April 1935), p. 15.

14. Lev Kopelev, *Khranit' vechno* (Ann Arbor, 1975), pp. 264, 277–78.

15. Ginzburg, *Journey*, pp. 9–12.

16. "Glavy iz vospominanii Very Panovoi," *SSSR: Vnutrennie protivorechiia*, no. 3 (1982).

17. *Pravda*, 14 March 1936. Produced in 1935, the film was first shown in early 1936.

18. Ginzburg, *Journey*, p. 3.

19. On the feelings of the society members about the falsifying of party history and the majority view of Stalin as "a traitor to the revolution," see Alexander Orlov, *The Secret History of Stalin's Crimes* (New York, 1953), pp. 32–33.

20. *Pravda*, 25 May 1935. A similar decree, published soon after, liquidated the Society of Former Exiles and Political Convicts. Yezhov was made a member of its liquidation commission.

21. Boris I. Nicolaevsky, "Letter of an Old Bolshevik," in his *Power and the Soviet Elite* (New York, 1965), p. 56.

22. Medvedev, *Let History Judge* (New York, 1971), p. 167.

23. Merle Fainsod, *Smolensk Under Soviet Rule* (New York, 1958), pp. 374–75.

24. Nicolaevsky, *Power*, p. 54.

25. *Pravda* leading article, 13 August 1936. In Bolshevik vernacular, "acting like Jesuits" meant acting duplicitously.

26. "Na sluzhbe u Stalina (ispoved' chekista)," ed. A. Tikhomirov, unpublished ms., Columbia University Library, pp. 57–60. The composition of the above-mentioned takeover commission for the Society of Old Bolsheviks suggests that its files too were wanted as a source of information on likely purge victims. This point has been made by Leonard Schapiro in *The Communist Party of the Soviet Union* (New York, 1959), p. 404.

27. Stalin's initiative in this matter, and the quoted words from his statement at the unpublicized Orgburo session, were revealed by Khrushchev in a later speech (*Pravda*, 20 January 1936). The checkup was in the planning stage as early as September 1934 when Kaganovich, speaking of the tasks of the new departments of leading party organs in the Central Committee, republic and province party committees, complained about the disorderly state of the party's documentation on its members. See *Partiinoe stroitel'stvo*, no. 23 (November 1934), pp. 2, 7.

28. See the Smolensk Archive (WKP 499) for a copy of this secret circular letter, which was never published.

29. Tikhomirov, "Na sluzhbe," p. 61.

30. Leading article, 26 May 1935.

31. John A. Armstrong, *The Politics of Totalitarianism* (New York, 1961), p. 30.

32. The progress report, a copy of which is in the Smolensk archive, was signed by Yezhov and Malenkov, then head and deputy head, respectively, of the Central Committee's Department of Leading Party Organs.

33. Bullitt, *For the President*, p. 116. He also said that ". . . the least of the Muscovites, as well as the greatest, is in fear."

34. Berger, *Shipwreck*, p. 168, reports, for example, that at Magnitogorsk in early 1935 arrests were taking place at the discretion of the NKVD without consultation with the local party secretary.

35. Fainsod, *Smolensk*, p. 230; Medvedev, *Let History Judge*, p. 167. Fainsod notes, however, that some local government officials, such as the director of the Smolensk post office, and others in executive posts in economic and Soviet work, fell victim; and Medvedev notes that a few middle-level local party officials were arrested. The cases of Yenukidze and Lominadze were exceptional.

36. Lev Kopelev, *I sotvoril sebe kumira* (Ann Arbor, 1978), p. 330.
37. Ginzburg, *Journey*, p. 11. She quotes him as saying "What on earth are they reprimanding her for? Everybody knew Elvov. He was trusted by both the regional and the town committees. Is it for walking down the street with him?"
38. Fainsod, *Smolensk*, pp. 225–29.
39. *Pravda*, 26 December 1935. One likely reason behind the resistance would have been the understandable fear among local party chiefs of the implications for themselves of too numerous cases of masked "enemies" having gone for long undetected in their districts, towns, or provinces.
40. *Bol'shevik*, no. 4, 15 February 1936, pp. 5–6. For the 14 January 1936 Central Committee instruction setting forth the purposes and procedures of the exchange, see Smolensk archives (WKP 54) and Fainsod, *Smolensk*, p. 232.
41. *Bol'shevik*, no. 13, 1 July 1936, pp. 9–10.
42. *Pravda*, 15 March 1936.
43. Fainsod, *Smolensk*, p. 233.
44. For his repeated voicing of venomous hatred for them during the prolonged preparation of the trial, see Orlov, *Secret History*, p. 117.
45. Ciliga, *Russian Enigma*, pp. 282–83, and *Biulleten' oppozitsii*, no. 47 (January 1936), p. 3. In the Moscow purge trial of August 1936, reference was made to the July 1935 date of the second Zinoviev-Kamenev trial and to the doubling of Kamenev's sentence at that time. See *The Case of the Trotskyite-Zinovievite Terrorist Centre*, reprint of the Moscow edition (New York, 1967), p. 174.
46. E. Ambartsumov, "Yadovityi tuman rasseivaetsia," *Moskovskie novosti*, 19 June 1988.
47. Orlov, *Secret History*, p. 157, reports that five of the defendants, the three here mentioned and two others (Fritz David and K. Berman-Yurin) were NKVD accomplices; and in chap. 4 explains the strategy of using their testimony against the principals. Orlov was in Moscow during the preparation of the August 1936 purge trial and attended it as a spectator. The account given here of its preparation has been checked against that given by him earlier to Boris I. Nicolaevsky in an unpublished 68-page manuscript, "Tainy Stalinskoi vlasti," now in the Hoover Institution archives, Stanford, Fund N. 227, Box 3.
48. *Ibid.*, p. 74. Stalin, according to Orlov, first used this phrase in 1931 when talking with a police official who was pressuring Sukhanov to agree to some point of false testimony in the Menshevik trial then in preparation.
49. *Pravda*, 9 April 1935. The text of the law appeared in the previous day's issue.
50. Orlov, *Secret History*, pp. 38–41, 118, 121–22. He adds (p. 41), ". . . every inquisitor of the NKVD was obliged to have on his desk during the interrogation of the arrested Bolsheviks the law which decreed the application of the death penalty to children." Kamenev, then fifty-two, had three sons, one

of them a young boy (*ibid.*, p. 166).
51. A. Karaganov, *Zhizn' dramaturga: Tvorcheskii put' Aleksandra Afinogenova* (Moscow, 1964), p. 282.
52. *Ibid.*, p. 287. The author refers to the text of Gorky's letter, printed in *Gorkii i sovetski pisateli: Neizdannaia perepiska* (Moscow, 1963), pp. 31–34. The phrase about "sons-of-bitches of the past" does not appear there, although the thought does, and editorial marks indicate an omission at that point; Karaganov evidently cited the omitted words.
53. Karaganov, *Zhizn' dramaturga*, pp. 295–305, 334–35. The author had access to, and cites, a photocopy of the play's text, containing Stalin's comments and alterations, now preserved in the Central State Literary Archives.
54. Orlov, *Secret History* pp. 69–70; *The Case of the Trotskyite-Zinovievite Terrorist Centre*, pp. 16, 32, 35.
55. Article on the *Oprichnina*, in *Bol'shaia sovetskai entsiklopediia*, XL (Moscow, 1939), pp. 226–28.
56. *Stalin*, XIII, 68, 250–51.
57. *Ibid.*, XIV (I), 49.
58. *Ibid.*, 62–64. The speech was given on 4 May 1935.
59. *Ibid.*, 65–66; *Pravda* leading article, 30 May 1935.
60. *Pravda*, 7 November 1935.
61. *Stalin*, XIV (I), 80, 86–87, 95, 100. The conference took place in November 1935.
62. *Ibid.*, 89.
63. *Pravda*, 6 February 1936.
64. Eight different orders were extant in the early 20th century: the orders of St. Stanislav, St. Anna, Prince Vladimir, St. Georgi, the White Eagle, Prince Alexander Nevsky, St. Catherine, and St. Andrei. F. Pavlenkov, *Entsiklopedicheskii slovar'* (St. Petersburg, 1913), p. 1665.
65. *Sobranie zakonov i rasporiazhenii*, no. 26, 19 May 1930, pp. 286–89; *Pravda*, March 16, 1936.
66. *Stalin*, XIV (I), 76–77, 101; *Pravda*, 31 December 1935.
67. *Ibid.*, 23 September 1935.
68. *Ibid.*, 8 October 1935. Yagoda, who had the unique rank of "Commissar General of State Security," later issued an order specifying the exact form of the police officers' uniforms and insignia (*Pravda*, 5 January 1936). The blue trousers prescribed for them had the same color as those worn by the uniformed political police of tsarist Russia.
69. *Pravda*, 7 September 1936. The title "Distinguished Master of Sport" had been created in 1934.
70. *Pravda*, 4 September 1935 and 11 April 1936.
71. *Sobranie zakonov i rasporiazhenii*, no. 10, 28, February 1934, pp. 135–37.
72. See, for example, Mandelstam, *Hope Against Hope*, p. 231, where it is indicated that the system of packets was established by the mid-1930s, if not earlier.
73. V. M. Molotov, *Stat'i i rechi, 1935–1936* (Moscow, 1937), p. 255.
74. James Hassell, "The Implementation of the

Russian Table of Ranks During the Eighteenth Century," *The Slavic Review*, no. 2 (June 1970), pp. 286–87.

75. *Pravda*, 26 November 1936, for Stalin's speech, and A. Zimin, *Sotsializm i neostalinizm* (New York, 1981), pp. 44–59, on the tacit departure from Marxism-Leninism. For the Marxist view that "friendly classes" would be a contradiction in terms, see Robert C. Tucker, *The Marxian Revolutionary Idea* (New York, 1969), chap. 1, esp. pp. 13–14.

76. *Izvestiia*, 6 July 1934.

77. *Pravda*, 7 November 1935. In *Biulleten' oppozitsii*, no. 43 (April 1935), pp. 10–11, Trotsky described Zaslavsky as "a perfect type of hired bourgeois slanderer," who went over to the Soviet regime in 1923 after writing for White publications in Kiev during the Civil War. Lenin's articles of 1917, Trotsky recalled, contained frequent mentions of "Zaslavsky and scoundrels of his kind."

78. *Pravda*, 7 May 1935.

79. *Ibid.*, 17 December 1935. For Mayakovsky's remark, see Maurice Friedberg, *Russian Classics in Soviet Jackets* (New York and London, 1962), p. 12.

80. Recollection by the ensemble's director, A. Aleksandrov, in *Pravda*, 16 January 1939.

81. *Ibid.*, 10 November 1935.

82. *Ibid.*, 10 November 1936.

83. Orlov, *Secret History*, pp. 35–36.

84. John Shelton Curtiss, *The Russian Church and the Soviet State* (Gloucester, Mass., 1965), pp. 250–67; N. S. Timasheff, *Religion in Soviet Russia, 1917–1942* (New York, 1942), pp. 38–45. Yaroslavsky's 1937 estimate is cited by Timasheff (p. 65) from E. Yaroslavsky, *Ob antireligioznoi propagande* (Moscow, 1937).

85. Timasheff, *Religion in Soviet Russia*, p. 46.

86. *Pravda*, 22 April 1936. Noted by Ralph Talcott Fischer, Jr., *Pattern for Soviet Youth: A Study of the Congresses of the Komsomol, 1918–1954* (New York, 1959), p. 353 n.

87. *Pravda*, 26 November 1936. It must, however, be mentioned that Article 124 of the new "Stalin Constitution" granted citizens "freedom of worship and freedom of antireligious propaganda." The implicit denial of the right of proreligious propaganda was illiberal in comparison with the 1918 Soviet Constitution's granting of "freedom of religious and antireligious propaganda." See *Istoriia sovetskoi konstitutsii (v dokumentakh), 1917–1956* (Moscow, 1957), pp. 145, 174.

88. S. F. Platonov, *Smutnoe vremia* (Petrograd, 1923), p. 15. Available in English as *The Time of Troubles*, trans. John T. Alexander (Lawrence, Kansas, 1970).

89. Anton Antonov-Ovseyenko, *The Time of Stalin: Portrait of a Tyranny* (New York, 1981), p. 223. The author had access to various high-level survivors of the Stalin era in preparing this *samizdat* study, but it must be used with critical caution. See also Stalin's remark of 1926 in a small circle (Medvedev, *Let History Judge*, p. 325), "Don't forget we are living in Russia, the land of the tsars. The

Russian people like to have one man standing at the head of the state."

90. Speech of 15 February 1935, reported in *Pravda* on 13 March 1935. See also *Stalin*, XIV (I), 53–54.

91. "On *Kolkhoz* Democracy," *Pravda*, 2 April 1935. A translated text of the 1935 model charter appears in Leonard E. Hubbard, *The Economics of Soviet Agriculture* (London, 1939), pp. 131–46.

92. *Pravda*, 30 March 1936. The peremptory tone of both the decision, signed simply "Central Committee," and the editorial suggests a personal intervention by Stalin.

93. *Pravda*, 23 April 1935.

94. *Ibid.*, 25 June 1935. Yagoda's participation in this event can be explained by the fact that the canal was built by prisoners under NKVD supervision.

95. *Pravda*, 27 October 1935; Svetlana Alliluyeva, *Twenty Letters* (New York, 1967), p. 154.

96. Maria Demchenko, "I Was With Stalin," *Pravda*, 11 November 1935.

97. *Ibid.*, 1 July, 7 July, and 5 October 1935.

98. *Ibid.*, 29 April 1936. On the decision to publish Stalin's collected writings, see *ibid.*

99. *Pravda*, 29 January and 1 February 1935.

100. Ilya Ehrenburg, *Memoirs: 1921–1941* (Cleveland, 1964), pp. 323–24. Apropos Stalin's widely quoted remark that people must be cultivated lovingly the way a gardener cultivates a fruit tree, Ehrenburg suggests here that people "rejoiced at the thought that they would be treated carefully and lovingly."

101. CPSU Central Committee resolution of 30 June 1956, "On Overcoming the Cult of Personality and Its Consequences," *Spravochnik partiinogo rabotnika* (Moscow, 1957), p. 330.

102. *Istorik-Marksist*, no. 10(50), 1935, p. 140.

103. *Pravda*, 14 and 20 January 1934.

104. S. Mikoyan, "Sluga," *Komsomol'skaia pravda*, 21 February 1988. Another source (B. Popov and V. Oppokov, "Berievschina," *Trud*, 26 August 1989) says that the main ghostwriter, a man named Bediia, was executed.

105. *Pravda*, 29 July 1935. All following citations from Beria are from the text as originally printed in *Pravda*, 29 July–5 August 1935. Entitled *K istorii bol'shevitskikh organizatsii na Zakavkazii*, the book by 1939 was in its fourth, revised edition.

106. *Kommunist*, no. 3 (February 1962), p. 20.

107. *Pravda*, 16 January 1935. The biographical article on Yenukidze appeared in *Bol'shaia sovetskaia entsiklopediia*, 1st ed., XXIV (Moscow, 1932), pp. 522–24. It is indicative of Beria's methods that he presented the subject of the article as being also its author, thereby converting Yenukidze, who was noted for his modesty, into a seeming braggart.

108. *Pravda*, 10 August 1935.

109. *Politicheskii dnevnik*, II, *1965–1970* (Amsterdam, 1975), p. 217, citing *M. Gorky i sovetskaia pechat': Arkhiv Gor'kogo*, X, book 1, p. 260. See also V. Kostikov, "Illiuzion

schast'ia, *Ogonyok,* no. 1, 30 December–6 January 1990, p. 14.

110. Roy A. Medvedev, "New Pages from the Political Biography of Stalin," in *Stalinism: Essays in Historical Interpretation,* ed. Robert C. Tucker (New York, 1977), p. 207 n.

111. Henri Barbusse, *Stalin: A New World Seen Through One Man,* trans. Vyvyan Holland (New York, 1935), pp. 45, 60.

112. *Ibid.,* pp. 277, 278.

113. *Pravda,* 5 December 1935. The phrase appeared in a talk he gave on 4 December to a conference of collective farmers.

114. André Gide, *Return from the U.S.S.R,* trans. Dorothy Bussy (New York, 1937), pp. 45–46.

14. Stalin and Fascism

1. Jean Merot, *Dimitrov, un revolutionnaire de notre temps* (Paris, 1972), pp. 184–187.

2. For documents on his activity, see "Novy dokument G. Dimitrova," *Izvestiia Ts.K. KPSS,* no. 3 (1989), and K. K. Shirinia, "Iz istorii podgotovki VII kongressa Kommunisticheskogo internatsionala," *Voprosy istorii KPSS,* no. 8 (1975), pp. 50–61.

3. *Pravda,* 23 May 1934. On the backstage preparation of the new line, see Celie and Albert Vassart, "The Moscow Origins of the French 'Popular Front,' " in *The Comintern: Historical Highlights,* ed. M. M. Drachkovitch and B. Lazitch (Stanford, 1966), and Daniel R. Brower, *The New Jacobins: The French Communist Party and the Popular Front* (Ithaca, 1968), chap. 2.

4. Maurice Thorez, *Fils du peuple* (Paris, 1960), p. 102.

5. Article of September 1924, *Stalin,* VI, 282. Dimitrov's definition of fascism has been ascribed to Stalin. See B. M. Leibzon and K. K. Shirinia, *Povorot v politike Kominterna* (Moscow, 1965), p. 123.

6. Fernando Claudin, *The Communist Movement from Comintern to Cominform* (New York and London, 1975), I, 189–91.

7. Arvo Tuominen, *The Bells of the Kremlin: An Experience in Communism,* trans. Lily Leino, ed. Piltti Heiskanen (Hanover and London, 1982), pp. 141, 142.

8. Leibzon and Shrinia, *Povorot,* p. 308. They also note here that no transcript of the congress proceedings was published.

9. United States, State Department, *Foreign Relations of the United States, Diplomatic Papers: The Soviet Union, 1933–1939* (Washington, 1952), pp. 218 ff. Further referred to as *US Foreign Relations.*

10. *Biulleten' oppozitsii,* no. 46 (December 1935), pp. 5, 7.

11. *Pravda,* 6 March 1936.

12. Claudin, *Communist Movement,* I, 201–3.

13. Boguslaw Miedzinski, "The Road to Moscow," in *Kultura Essays,* ed. Leopold Tyrmand (New York, 1970); Louis Fischer, *Russia's Road from Peace to War* (New York, 1969), p. 234.

14. *Pravda,* 16 May 1935.

15. Anthony Eden, *Facing the Dictators: The Memoirs of Anthony Eden* (Boston, 1962), pp. 170–71.

16. *Ibid.,* pp. 171–74. The now published German documents show that in fact the Nazi government introduced new restrictions on trade with Russia in February 1935. United States, State Department, *Documents on German Foreign Policy, 1918–1945,* Ser. C, II, (Washington, D.C., 1959) 935–40, 960–61. Hereafter cited as *DGFP.*

17. "Nakanune voiny (Dokumenty 1935–1940 gg.)," *Izvestiia Ts.K. KPSS,* no. 1 (1990), pp. 161–69.

18. Lev Nikulin, *Tukhachevsky: Biografitcheskii ocherk* (Moscow, 1964), pp. 179, 186. The author comments: "Naturally, these talks alarmed the Nazi Embassy in London and the Hitlerite intelligence, which saw in Tukhachevsky a gifted military theoretician and future commander of an especially important front." On Tukhachevsky's activities in London, see also I. M. Maisky's contribution to *Marshal Tukhachevsky: Vospominaniia druzei i soratnikov* (Moscow, 1965), pp. 227–30.

19. Great Britain, Foreign Office, *Documents of British Foreign Policy / Russia Correspondence* (for full reference see the Bibliography), report of 19 September 1936 from D. MacKillop in Moscow to the Foreign Office. Further referred to as *DBFP.*

20. *Ibid.,* report of 21 September 1936 from MacKillop to Eden.

21. In his book *In Stalin's Secret Service* (New York, 1939), pp. 20–21, Walter G. Krivitsky, who was chief of Soviet military intelligence in Western Europe in the mid-1930s and subsequently defected to the West, argues (as do I) that Stalin was pursuing "two simultaneous courses of action," the collective-security diplomacy and the search for an accord with Hitler, and he interprets Stalin's moves in the campaign for collective security as "designed only to impress Hitler, and bring success to his undercover maneuvers which had but one aim: a close accord with Germany." Although the desire to "impress Hitler" may well have figured as an additional motive, the main one, in my view, was to forge an anti-German grouping in the West.

22. Ilya Ehrenburg, *Post-War Years, 1945–1954,* trans. Tatiana Shebunina (Cleveland and New York, 1967), p. 278. On Litvinov's foreign-policy outlook, see Iu. Denike, "Litvinov i Stalinskaia vneshniaia politika," *Sotsialisticheskii vestnik,* no. 5 (653) (May 1952), pp. 84–87.

23. Eden, *Facing the Dictators,* pp. 148–53.

24. *The Speeches of Adolf Hitler,* ed. Norman H. Baynes (London, 1942), II, 1218–47; Gerhard L. Weinberg, *The Foreign Policy of Hitler's Germany: Diplomatic Revolution in Europe, 1933–36* (Chicago and London,

1970), pp. 214–15, 219.

25. *DBFP/Russia Correspondence,* letter of 24 January 1936 from the Foreign Office to Ambassador Chilston.

26. *Ibid.,* letter of 19 February 1936 from D. E. Sargent to the secretary of state. Sargent added that Ambassador Bullitt, who had passed through London a few days earlier, said to Lord Lothian that the chief desire of "the boys in the Kremlin" was "to see the European states go on quarrelling with each other," so that "in the end, with luck, there would be a European war with chaos and communism as a result." This is consistent with the view expressed by Bullitt in a dispatch of 19 July 1935: "To keep Europe divided and to postpone the war which will certainly come if Europe remains divided is the substance of Russian policy in Europe." *US Foreign Relations,* p. 226.

27. *London Times,* 31 January and 1 February 1935. Cited by Louis Fischer, *Men and Politics* (New York, 1941), p. 266.

28. Sumner Welles, *The Time for Decision* (New York, 1944), p. 321.

29. George F. Kennan, *Russia and the West Under Lenin and Stalin* (New York, 1960), p. 286. Lack of French will was a factor too. On this see Weinberg, *Foreign Policy,* p. 254.

30. *DGFP,* Ser. C, III, 455.

31. *Ibid.,* 683.

32. *DGFP,* Ser. C., IV, 138. Schulenburg reported: "I listened without comment."

33. Gustav Hilger and Alfred G. Meyer, *The Incompatible Allies* (New York, 1953), p. 269.

34. *Ibid.,* pp. 28–29. For German information on Kandelaki's direct contact with Stalin, see Schulenburg's communication of 20 February 1937 to Berlin, in National Archives, roll 282, serial 393, frame 212218.

35. Krivitsky, *In Stalin's Secret Service,* p. 15. Krivitsky heard this report on one of his trips to Moscow. It came from a high NKVD official.

36. *Pravda,* 12 July 1935. The decree listed five other trade officials, below Kandelaki's name, as recipients of the lesser Order of the Red Banner of Labor.

37. *DGFP,* Ser. C, IV, 453–54.

38. *Ibid.,* 782–83.

39. *Ibid.,* 813.

40. *Ibid.,* 870–71, 897–98.

41. *Ibid.,* 898–99.

42. *Ibid.,* 931–33. No further information exists on this private conversation.

43. Weinberg, *Foreign Policy,* p. 222 and 222 n. citing preserved German documents on these contacts.

44. Statement of 19 March 1936. Jane Degras, ed., *Soviet Documents on Foreign Policy,* III, *1933–1941* (London, 1953), p. 184.

45. Gabriel Jackson, *The Spanish Republic and the Civil War, 1931–1939* (Princeton, 1965), pp. 251–52.

46. Krivitsky, *In Stalin's Secret Service,* pp. 80–81.

47. Burnett Bolloten, *The Spanish Revolution: The Left and the Struggle for Power During*

the Civil War (Chapel Hill, 1979), p. 144.

48. Pierre Broué and Emile Témime, *The Revolution and the Civil War in Spain,* trans. Tony White (Cambridge, Mass., 1979), pp. 376–77.

49. Krivitsky, *In Stalin's Secret Service,* pp. 97–98.

50. *Ibid.,* pp. 82–83, 93. This Alexander Orlov would defect in 1938 in fear of the purge, live out his life incognito in North America, and bear witness to much that he had learned as a high-ranking officer of the Soviet political police.

51. Bolloten, *Spanish Revolution,* p. 154.

52. *The New York Times,* 4 June 1939. The letter was released by the former Loyalist ambassador in France, Luis Araquistain. On the unrevolutionary character of Stalin's Spanish policy, see David T. Cattell, *Communism and the Spanish Civil War* (Berkeley and Los Angeles, 1955), pp. 211–12; Claudin, *Communist Movement,* I, 239–42; Bolloten, *Spanish Revolution,* parts 2 and 3; Isaac Deutscher, *Stalin* (New York, 1966), pp. 424–25; and Leon Trotsky, *The Spanish Revolution (1931–1939)* (New York, 1973), p. 250 and *passim.*

53. George Orwell, *Homage to Catalonia* (New York, 1972), p. 67.

54. In *The Spanish Civil War* (New York, 1961), p. 613, Hugh Thomas writes that "Stalin followed a policy similar to that of Hitler: prevention of his protégés' defeat, without ensuring their victory."

55. *Pravda,* 8 July 1935. The other subcommissions and their heads were: economic (Molotov); finance (Chubar); juridical (Bukharin); electoral system (Radek); judicial organs (Vyshinsky); central and local government organs (Akulov); education (Zhdanov); labor (Kaganovich); defense (Voroshilov); foreign affairs (Litvinov). According to S. I. Iakubovskaia, "Sovetskaia istoriografiia obrazovaniia SSSR," *Voprosy istorii,* no. 12 (1962), p. 16, the hundred or so persons involved in the drafting work also included Education Commissar Bubnov, Justice Commissar Krylenko, Marshal Tukhachevsky, and his military colleague Yan Garmarnik.

56. I. B. Berkhin, "K istorii razrabotki konstitutsii SSSR 1936 g.," in *Stroitel'stvo Sovetskogo gosudarstva: Sbornik statei k 70-letiiu E. B. Genkinoi* (Moscow, 1972), p. 7.

57. Iakubovskaia, "Sovetskaia istoriografiia," p. 16.

58. *Pravda,* 5 March 1936.

59. *Ibid.,* 7 July 1936.

60. *Biulleten' oppozitsii,* no. 50 (May 1936), p. 6, and also Lev Trotsky, *The Revolution Betrayed* (New York, 1945), chap. 10. In referring to Goebbels' techniques, he had in mind the Nazi's handling of the 1935 Saar plebiscite.

61. L. Fischer, *Men and Politics,* p. 333.

62. *Pravda,* 13 July 1936, reporting Rolland's comments on the newly published constitutional draft.

63. *Bol'shevik,* no. 14, 15 July 1936, p. 4.

64. Berkhin, "K istorii," p. 76.
65. *Pravda*, 26 November 1936.
66. On the German family policy, see Richard Grunberger, *The 12-Year Reich: A Social History of Nazi Germany, 1933–1945* (New York, 1971), chap. 16. Nazi policy provided, among other things, for family allowances, and it made abortion "one of the most heinous crimes in the Nazi statute book" (p. 238).
67. These four letters appeared in *Izvestiia* on 29 and 30 May and 2 June 1936. Translations in Rudolf Schlesinger, ed., *The Family in the USSR: Documents and Readings* (London, 1949), pp. 255–57. The new legislation, as enacted, is translated on pp. 269–79 of this source book.
68. Markoosha Fischer, *My Lives in Soviet Russia* (New York, 1944), pp. 136–37.
69. L. Fischer, *Men and Politics*, p. 347. For the indignation and suicides, see M. Fischer, *My Lives*, p. 138. The wave of suicides is also reported by Maurice Hindus, *House Without a Roof: Russia After Forty-Three Years of Revolution* (Garden City, N.Y., 1961), pp. 143–44.
70. *Pravda*, 1 February 1936.
71. *Izvestiia*, 2 February 1936. Although unsigned, this article was treated by *Pravda*, soon afterward, as Bukharin's.
72. *Pravda*, 10 February 1936.
73. Hindus, *House Without a Roof*, p. 164. Smirnov, stationed in Teheran in 1942, told this to Hindus when the latter stopped over in Teheran en route to Russia to report on the Soviet-German war.
74. *Biulleten' oppozitsii*, no. 47 (January 1936), pp. 1–4.
75. Victor Serge, *Memoirs of a Revolutionary* (London, 1963), pp. 316–19.
76. *Biulleten' oppozitsii*, no. 51 (July–August 1936), pp. 9–11. Piast, he said, committed suicide in exile.
77. Roy A. Medvedev, *Nikolai Bukharin: The Last Years*, trans. A. D. P. Briggs (New York, 1980), p. 112.
78. *Ibid.*, p. 115. Ehrenburg told this to Medvedev in the 1960s.
79. "An Interview with Boris Nicolaevsky," in Boris I. Nicolaevsky, *Power and the Soviet Elite* (New York, 1965), pp. 15–17.
80. *Bol'shevik*, no. 12 (15 June 1936), p. 24.

81. *Izvestiia*, 14 June 1936.
82. The last three paragraphs are taken verbatim from my essay "Stalin, Bukharin and History as Conspiracy," originally printed as the introduction to *The Great Purge Trial*, ed. Robert C. Tucker and Stephen F. Cohen (New York, 1965). For the suggestion that "War and Peace" was from Bukharin's pen, in part because of the reference to Shelley, see Robert M. Slusser, "The Role of the Foreign Ministry," in *Russian Foreign Policy: Essays in Historical Perspective*, ed. Ivo J. Lederer (New Haven, 1962), p. 221, n. 32.
83. Vadim Baranov, " 'Da' i 'net' Maksima Gor'kogo," *Sovetskaia kul'tura*, 1 April 1989.
84. *Ibid.*
85. "Gor'kii i Stalin," *Politicheskii dnevnik*, III, no. 37 (October 1967), p. 58, reproduced in Stephen F. Cohen, ed., *An End to Silence: Uncensored Opinion in the Soviet Union* (New York, 1982), p. 76. For Victor Serge's similar experience of trying to see Gorky and having his way barred by Kriuchkov, see Serge, *Memoirs*, p. 69.
86. Baranov, " 'Da' i 'net.' "
87. Ilya S. Shkapa, *Sem' let s Gor'kim: Vospominaniia* (Moscow, 1966), pp. 383–84. A few days later, Shkapa was arrested, and spent the next twenty years in confinement.
88. Galina Serebriakova, *O drugikh i o sebe* (Moscow, 1968), p. 198.
89. Baranov, " 'Da' i 'net.' "
90. V. S. Barakhov, "A. M. Gor'kii: Poslednie dni zhizni: svidetel'stva ochevidtsev i nedokazannye versii," *Literaturnaia gazeta*, 12 July 1989. The eyewitness reports just mentioned are published here.
91. Baranov, " 'Da' i 'net.' "
92. Louis Aragon, *La mise à mort* (Paris, 1965), p. 41. For Aragon's arrival in Moscow on the morning of 15 June 1936, see *Pravda*, 16 June 1936. I am indebted to the late Evgeni A. Gnedin of Moscow for drawing my attention to this episode.
93. Gleb Glinka, "Dnevnik Gor'kogo," *Sotsialisticheskii vestnik*, no. 1 (667) (January 1954), pp. 19–20. The information reported in this article is attributed by the author to an eyewitness of the diary's discovery.
94. Alexander Orlov, *The Secret History of Stalin's Crimes* (New York, 1953), p. 276.

15. The Forging of Autocracy I

1. Alexander Orlov, *The Secret History of Stalin's Crimes* (New York, 1953), pp. 125–29. Molchanov was Orlov's source for this meeting in the Kremlin.
2. Orlov, *Secret History*, p. 148. One of the higher officers in attendance was Orlov himself.
3. Evgeni A. Gnedin, *Katastrofa i vtoroe rozhdenie: Memuarnye zapiski* (Amsterdam, 1977), p. 282. Gnedin was chief of the Narkomindel's press section in 1937–38 and in that capacity attended the 1937 and 1938 trials.

4. Roy A. Medvedev, *Nikolai Bukharin* (New York, 1980), p. 124 for Stalin's presence in Moscow during the trial and p. 153 for his ability to listen in on trial proceedings from his Kremlin study.
5. Orlov, *Secret History*, pp. 159–60.
6. Harold Denny, in *The New York Times*, 20 August 1936. See also Orlov, *Secret History*, p. 160, where the haggard appearance of the majority of the defendants is contrasted with the "robust health and carefree bearing" of the pseudodefendants.

7. *The Case of the Trotskyite-Zinovievite Terrorist Centre* (New York, 1967), a translation of *Sudebnyi otchet po delu Trotskistsko-Zinovievskogo terroristicheskogo tsentra* (Moscow, 1936).
8. *Pravda*, 21 August 1936.
9. Denny, in *The New York Times*, 24 August 1936.
10. *Ibid.*
11. United States, State Department, *Foreign Relations* (Washington, 1952), p. 302. Further referred to as *US Foreign Relations*.
12. See Herman Fehst, *Bolschewismus und Judentum: Das jüdische Element in der Führerschaft des Bolshewismus* (Berlin and Leipzig, 1934), where photos of Trotsky, Zinoviev, and Kamenev are featured prominently.
13. Walter G. Krivitsky, *In Stalin's Secret Service* (New York, 1939), pp. 207–8 and Alexander Barmine, *One Who Survived* (New York, 1945), pp. 285, 294–95, report that a decree restoring the power of pardon was issued prior to the trial. I have not been able to find the text of such a decree in the press or statute book of that time, but it is possible that such a decree was prepared to show the defendants as proof that the promise to spare their lives was serious.
14. *The Case of Leon Trotsky: Report of Hearings on the Charges Made Against Him in the Moscow Trials* (New York, 1937), pp. 146, 148, 149, 167–68.
15. *US Foreign Relations*, p. 302.
16. *The New York Times*, 17 August 1936.
17. Anton Antonov-Ovseyenko, *The Time of Stalin:* (New York, 1981) pp. 145–46.
18. *Biulleten' oppozitsii*, no. 52–53 (October 1936), pp. 19–20.
19. Roy A. Medvedev, "New Pages from the Political Biography of Stalin," in *Stalinism*, ed. Robert C. Tucker (New York, 1977), p. 213.
20. How far such politics of the pistol were from Old Bolshevik minds was reflected in a thought expressed by Lominadze to a friend before he committed suicide in 1935: "A hundred thousand suicides among prominent party members might possibly make Stalin reflect." Joseph Berger, *Shipwreck of a Generation* (London, 1971), p. 168, reports that he heard this in the Mariinsk camp in 1935 from the person, then a fellow inmate, to whom Lominadze said it.
21. Radek, "The Trotskyist-Zinovievist Fascist Band and Its Hetman Trotsky," *Izvestiia*, 21 August 1936; Piatakov, "Mercilessly Destroy the Despicable Murderers and Traitors," *Pravda*, 21 August 1936; Rakovsky, "There Must Be No Mercy!" *Pravda*, 21 August 1936; Preobrazhensky, "For the Supreme Measure of Treason and Villainy the Supreme Measure of Punishment," *Pravda*, 24 August 1936.
22. Medvedev, "New Pages," p. 213.
23. Medvedev, *Bukharin*, pp. 123–25.
24. Some Western scholars, for instance Leonard Schapiro, *The Communist Party of the Soviet Union* (New York, 1959), p. 409; Robert

Conquest, *The Great Terror* (New York, 1973), p. 215; and Robert C. Tucker, *The Soviet Political Mind*, rev. ed. (New York, 1971), p. 60, have taken the 10 September statement as a strong indication that Stalin was encountering high-level party opposition from behind the scenes to his planned purge of the ex-Rightists. My own view on that has since changed.
25. Medvedev, *Bukharin*, p. 129.
26. E. Guseinov and V. Sirotkin, "Litso i maski Karla Radeka," *Moskovskaia pravda*, 14 May 1989.
27. Medvedev, *Bukharin*, pp. 126–27.
28. Orlov, *Secret History*, pp. 255–56, writes that Yagoda falsified his political biography by giving himself a pre-1917 party past that he lacked and that Stalin, on learning this, kept the information as a means of control over him. Robert M. Slusser argues persuasively (private letter of 20 March 1980) that, as post-Stalin official materials indicate, Yagoda did become a Bolshevik in 1907 (he would have been about seventeen years old then). On Yagoda, see also S. Wolin and R. M. Slusser, *The Soviet Secret Police* (New York, 1957), pp. 43–46, and Conquest, *Great Terror*, p. 217.
29. I am indebted to Professor Dmitry Volkogonov for giving me a photocopy of the typed original of Yagoda's memorandum to Stalin. For the 1934 and 1935 edicts here referred to, see *Sobranie zakonov i rasporiazhenii raboche-krest'ianskogo pravitel'stva SSSR*, no. 33, 4 July 1934, pp. 465–66, and no. 7, 11 February 1935, p. 60.
30. Medvedev, in Tucker, *Stalinism*, p. 213.
31. Khrushchev, Twentieth Party Congress speech on Stalin, in *Khrushchev Remembers*, p. 575. For a different view of the meaning of "four years behind," a view I do not accept because of the weakness of the evidence advanced for it, see Robert H. McNeal, *Stalin: Man and Ruler* (New York, 1988), pp. 189, 184.
32. Orlov, *Secret History*, p. 223. Two who did defect, in 1937, were Ignace Reiss (Poretsky), who not long afterward was found murdered in Switzerland, and Walter Krivitsky; Orlov himself defected subsequently. Others were recalled during the purge and became victims of the Terror.
33. Elisabeth K. Poretsky, *Our Own People: A Memoir of 'Ignace Reiss' and His Friends* (London, 1969), pp. 178, 200–201. For Molchanov's replacement, see John A. Armstrong, *The Politics of Totalitarianism* (New York, 1961), p. 53.
34. Krivitsky, *In Stalin's Secret Service*, p. 146; also Orlov, *Secret History*, pp. 208, 213.
35. Twentieth Party Congress Speech on Stalin, *Khrushchev Remembers*, p. 586.
36. V. Posdniakov, "Kak Yezhov prinimal NKVD," *Narodnaia pravda*, vol. 5 (1949), p. 21. The account is purportedly an eyewitness one.
37. On this last point, see Armstrong, *Politics of Totalitarianism*, p. 62, and Krivitsky, *In Stalin's Secret Service*, p. 224.

38. Robert C. Tucker, *Stalin As Revolutionary* (New York, 1973), pp. 203–5.

39. ". . . the Red Army command—independent of Stalin, self-created, an equal at least in its own estimation to its political master—was hopelessly and irretrievably guilty of being the ultimate barrier to absolute power." John Erickson, *The Soviet High Command: A Military-Political History, 1918–1941* (London, 1962), pp. 427–28.

40. "Delo o tak nazyvaemoi 'Antisovetskoi Trotskistskoi voennoi organizatsii' v Krasnoi Armii," *Izvestiia Ts.K. KPSS*, no. 4 (1989), pp. 43–45. This is a report on an inquest carried out in the Politburo Commission on Further Study of Repressions of the 1930s–1940s and early 1950s. It is based on documentary materials from the archives of the party Central Committee, the KGB, the Procuracy, and the Central Committee's Institute of Marxism-Leninism.

41. *Ibid.*, pp. 47–48.

42. Barmine, *One Who Survived*, p. 90. "Stalin listened without saying a word," Barmine adds, "but his face was dead white and his lips were drawn in a tight line."

43. I. Dubinsky, *Naperekor vetram* (Moscow, 1964), pp. 243, 248, 249. The report of Yakir's Berlin repute is here (p. 260) attributed to General Gamelin of the French General Staff.

44. P. I. Yakir, "Bud' nastoiashchim, syn!" in *Komandarm Yakir: Vospominaniia druzei i soratnikov* (Moscow, 1963), pp. 224–25.

45. Dubinsky, *Naperekor*, p. 261. Italics added.

46. F. Sergeev, " 'Delo' Tukhachevskogo," *Nedelia*, no. 7 (1989), p. 10. Although Tukhachevsky's father was of the nobility, his mother was of peasant and, indeed, serf origin. For this see A. Kotlova-Bychkova, "Riadom s marshalom," *Vechernaia Moskva*, 5 April 1989.

47. See, for example, Gunter Preis, *The Man Who Started the War* (London, 1960), pp. 77–78, and Sergeev, " 'Delo' Tukhachevskogo."

48. Session of the Section on the History of the Great Patriotic War, Institute of Marxism-Leninism, 18 February 1966, on A. M. Nekrich's *June 22, 1941*, a book written in the Soviet Union but later published in English translation in the United States (ed. and trans. V. Petrov, Columbia, S.C., 1968). A Russian transcript of the discussion appears in *Posev*, 13 January 1967. The statement here cited appears on p. 4.

49. Ernst Genri, "Otkrytoe pis'mo pisateliu I. Erenburgu," *Grani*, 63 (1967), p. 195. A Soviet biography of Genri appears in *Literaturnaia entsiklopediia*, IX (Moscow, 1978), 224–25.

50. Nikolai Abramov, "The New Version of the 'Tukhachevsky Affair': Declassified Documents from the U.S.S.R. Foreign Policy Archives," *New Times*, no. 13 (1989), p. 38.

51. Wilhelm Hoettle, *The Secret Front: The Story of Nazi Political Espionage* (London, 1953), pp. 78–81, 20–21; Walter Schellenberg, *Hitler's Secret Service* (New York, 1956),

52. Hoettle, *Secret Front*, pp. 81–83; Schellenberg, *Hitler's Secret Service*, p. 43.

53. Abramov, "The New Version," pp. 38–39; F. N. Kovalev, "Stranitsy istorii: Dokumenty polpredstva SSSR v Prage, otnosiashchiesiia k 'delu Tukhachevskogo,' " *Vestnik Ministerstva innostrannykh del SSSR*, no. 8 (42), 1 May 1989, p. 43; *Memoirs of Dr. Eduard Benes: From Munich to New War and New Victory*, trans. Godfrey Lias (London, 1954), pp. 12–20.

54. Abramov, "The New Version," p. 38.

55. V. Falin, "Dva raznykh dogovora," *Argumenty i fakty*, no. 33, 19–25 August 1989.

56. "Delo o 'Antisovetskoi Trotskistskoi organizatsii," p. 61.

57. *Pravda*, 19 August 1936. The facts are that Stepanian, a leader of the Armenian Bolshevik opposition to Beria, secretly wrote a book entitled "The Actual History of the Transcaucasian Bolsheviks," which was a refutation of Beria's Stalin-glorifying one, and tried unsuccessfully to run it off on the Armenian state press; and that Khanchian, a supporter of Stepanian, was condemned for "nationalist errors and entanglements" at a high-level party session on 9 July 1936, and then was killed not by his own hand but by Beria's. Ts. P. Agaian, *Nersik Stepanian* (Erevan, 1967), pp. 50–53; Mary K. Matossian, *The Impact of Soviet Policies in Armenia* (Leiden, 1962), pp. 129–31. That Beria personally murdered Khanchian in his office was confirmed by A. N. Shelepin at the Twenty-Second Soviet Party Congress. See *XXII s"ezd KPSS, 17–31 oktiabria 1961 goda* (Moscow, 1962), II, 404. Henceforth cited as *Twenty-Second Congress*.

58. *Pravda*, 26 August 1936.

59. *Ibid.*

60. I. Lezhnev, in *Pravda*, 27 August 1936.

61. *Literaturnaia gazeta*, 15 October 1936.

62. Galina Serebriakova, *Smerch, passim*. This memoir was reportedly in press in Moscow in 1964 when Khrushchev was ousted from power, then taken out of press, and partly lost. The preserved part was serialized in *Novoye russkoye slovo*, 8–30 December 1967.

63. "Radek's outstanding characteristics, as a matter of fact, are impulsiveness, instability, undependability, a predisposition toward falling into panic at the first sign of danger, and exhibiting extreme loquacity when all is well. These qualities make him a journalistic Figaro of first-rate skill, an invaluable guide for foreign correspondents and tourists, but utterly unsuited for the role of conspirator." (*Case of Leon Trotsky*, p. 523).

64. Orlov, *Secret History*, pp. 198–99. Radek's shift from resistance to supercooperation is also reported by Medvedev, *Bukharin*, p. 133. "It was probably due to Radek's forced assistance," he adds, "that the 1937 trial was prepared so quickly and went so smoothly."

65. Berger, *Shipwreck*, p. 88.

66. For indirect evidence on the remonstrating and the hope, see Alexander Weissberg, *The*

Accused, trans. Edward Fitzgerald (London, 1951), p. 56; and for Ordzhonikidze's reported visit to Piatakov in prison, during which he said, "I gave battle for you and I won't stop fighting for you. I talked to *him* about you," see Orlov, *Secret History,* pp. 180–81.

67. Medvedev, *Bukharin,* p. 128. Medvedev also says that several of Ordzhonikidze's friends were arrested at this time, but does not name them.

68. Weissberg, *The Accused,* p. 9.

69. *Pravda,* 23 November 1936.

70. *Ibid.,* 22 November 1936. Both Shestov and Arnold appeared as defendants in the January 1937 Moscow trial. For Shestov's testimony

on the failed attempt on Molotov, see *Report of Court Proceedings in the Case of the Anti-Trotskyite Centre,* Moscow, 23–30 January 1937 (Moscow, 1937), pp. 262–63.

71. *Twenty-Second Congress,* p. 216.

72. *Pravda,* 23 November 1936.

73. Raphael R. Abramovitch, *The Soviet Revolution, 1917–1939* (New York, 1962), p. 400. I have not succeeded in finding confirmation of the reported action by von Ribbentrop.

74. Medvedev, *Let History Judge* (New York, 1971), p. 171.

75. T. Mariagin, *Postyshev* (Moscow, 1965), p. 291.

76. *Pravda,* 4 January 1937.

77. Mariagin, *Postyshev,* p. 294.

16. The Forging of Autocracy II

1. Eugenia Semyonovna Ginzburg, *Journey Into the Whirlwind* (New York, 1967), pp. 37–38.

2. *Pravda,* 1 January 1937.

3. *Ibid.,* 9 January 1937. This announcement of the previous day's talk, which it said had lasted three hours, was accompanied by a large photo of the two in Stalin's Kremlin office.

4. Elisabeth K. Poretsky, *Our Own People,* (London, 1969), p. 177, and Lion Feuchtwanger, *Moscow 1937: My Visit Described For My Friends,* trans. Irene Josephy (New York, 1937), p. 77. Feuchtwanger also wrote here: "I spoke frankly to him about the vulgar and excessive cult made of him, and he replied with equal candour."

5. *Pravda,* 13 January 1936.

6. Poretsky, *Our Own People,* p. 177, where the ditty is given in Russian and an unrhymed English translation.

7. *Pravda,* 20 January 1937. The existence of a "parallel center" was hinted in the August 1936 trial's testimony that the "united center" had a "reserve group" consisting of Radek, Sokolnikov, and Serebriakov. Now Piatakov was added and the "group" became a "center."

8. Alexander Orlov, *The Secret History of Stalin's Crimes* (New York, 1953), p. 173.

9. Evgeni A. Gnedin, *Katastrofa i vtoroe rozhdenie* (Amsterdam, 1977), p. 281.

10. *Report of Court Proceedings in the Case of the Anti-Trotskyite Centre,* Moscow, January 23–30, 1937 (Moscow, 1937), pp.. 46–80. Henceforth cited as *Piatakov-Radek Trial Report.*

11. Dispatch no. 53, 6 February 1937, Great Britain, Foreign Office, *Documents of British Foreign Policy* (for full reference, see Bibliography). Further referred to as *DBFP.*

12. Personal interview in 1974.

13. *Piatakov-Radek Trial Report,* p. 87.

14. *Piatakov-Radek Trial Report,* pp. 86–95.

15. United States, State Department, *Foreign Relations* (Washington, 1952), p. 364, for Kennan's comments in his memorandum of 13 February 1937; and *Piatakov-Radek Trial*

Report, pp. 188–89, for the Piatakov-Vyshinsky exchange.

16. *Ibid.,* pp. 99–105.

17. This term is used by Dr. Norman A. Cameron in his chapter on "Paranoid Reactions" in *Comprehensive Textbook of Psychiatry,* eds. A. M. Freedman, H. I. Kaplan, and H. S. Kaplan (Baltimore, 1967), p. 670. Elsewhere this authority on paranoia has spoken of a "paranoid pseudo-community" and has characterized it as "an imaginary organization of real and imagined persons, whom the patient represents as united for the purpose of carrying out some action upon him" and as "a unified group, with some definite plot of which he is the intended victim." Norman Cameron, "Paranoid Conditions and Paranoia," in *American Handbook of Psychiatry,* ed. Silvano Arieti (New York, 1959), p. 519. By using the phrase "murderous pseudo-community," I am leaving open the question whether Stalin's pseudo-community was a paranoid one.

18. Gnedin, *Katastrofa,* p. 279. The trial testimony in question appears in *Piatakov-Radek Trial Report,* p. 109.

19. *Ibid.,* pp. 113–15.

20. "The Worker State, Thermidor, and Bonapartism," *Biulleten' oppozitsii,* no. 43 (April 1935), pp. 9–13.

21. Curiously, no further reference was made by either Radek or Vyshinsky to the letter that, according to his earlier testimony (*Piatakov-Radek Trial Report,* p. 106), he received from Trotsky in January 1936. He only mentioned seeing Piatakov in January 1936 after the latter's supposed visit with Trotsky in Norway.

22. *Piatakov-Radek Trial Report,* p. 135.

23. *Ibid.,* pp. 381, 384.

24. *Ibid.,* p. 367.

25. Dispatch no. 53, 6 February 1937, *DBFP,* p. 148.

26. On "recruiting" as the trial's meaning of hiring, see the informative article by David J. Dallin on "The Piatakov-Radek Trial" in his *From Purge to Coexistence: Essays on Stalin's and Khrushchev's Russia* (Chicago, 1964), p. 85, where he writes: "If a people's

commissar, revealed to be a Trotskyite, had appointed ten or fifty persons to various jobs, these appointees are his protégés, his friends, his supporters; and since he is a 'terrorist,' he chose these people with special intent. They are co-plotters, co-members of the 'terrorist organization.' "

27. *Pravda*, 28 January 1937.
28. *Piatakov-Radek Trial Report*, pp. 416–516, *passim; Stalin*. X, 342.
29. *The Case of Leon Trotsky: Report of Hearings on the Charges Made Against Him in the Moscow Trials* (New York, 1937), pp. 283–88, 575–77.
30. *Piatakov-Radek Trial Report*, pp. 541–51. At a number of points I have altered the wording of the translation in the interest of literal accuracy.
31. Anton Antonov-Ovseyenko, *The Time of Stalin:* (New York, 1981), p. 141, reports this as fact.
32. *Stalin*, VIII, 61; Tucker, *Stalin As Revolutionary* (New York, 1973), p. 379.
33. Gnedin, *Katastrofa*, p. 282.
34. *Ibid.*, p. 281, and Feuchtwanger, *Moscow 1937*, p. 127.
35. E. Guseinon and V. Sirotkin, "Litso i maski Karla Radeka," *Moskovskaia pravda*, 14 May 1989.
36. *Ibid.*, and Warren Lerner, *Karl Radek: The Last Internationalist* (Stanford, 1970), pp. 170–71.
37. *Pravda*, 31 January 1937.
38. *Ibid.*
39. *Pravda*, 30 January 1937.
40. *Moscow 1937*, pp. 76–77.
41. Personal interview with George F. Kennan.
42. Joseph E. Davies, *Mission to Moscow* (Garden City, 1943), p. 30.
43. Dispatch no. 53 of 6 February 1937, *DBFP*.
44. *Ibid.* Steiger was executed in December 1937, a purge victim.
45. *Ibid.*
46. United States, State Department, *Documents on German Foreign Policy, 1918–1945*, Ser. C, V, 571–72. Hereafter cited as *DGFP*. On Göring's interest in better economic relations with Russia because of Germany's foreign exchange shortage, see Gerhard L. Weinberg, *The Foreign Policy of Hitler's Germany: Diplomatic Revolution in Europe, 1933–36* (Chicago and London, 1970), pp. 310–11.
47. *DGFP*, p. 574.
48. J. W. Brugel, comp., *Stalin und Hitler: Pakt gegen Europa* (Vienna, 1973), p. 38.
49. "Memorandum by Adolf Hitler on the Tasks of a Four Year Plan," *DGFP*, Ser. C, V, 853–62. Göring was appointed Commissioner for the Four-Year Plan on 18 October 18 1936.
50. *DGFP*, Ser. C, V, 989.
51. Letter of 6 February 1937 from Schacht to Neurath. U.S. National Archives, Documents on German Foreign Policy, 1918–1945, roll 282, serial 393.
52. *In Stalin's Secret Service* (New York, 1939), p. 21.

53. Note of 31 January 1937 from the German Embassy in Moscow to the Foreign Ministry. Piatakov-Radek (Trotsky Prozess) (January 1937), I. Political Archive of the Foreign Ministry, Bonn, Germany.
54. *Ibid.*
55. *Ibid.*
56. Letter of 6 February 1937 from Schacht to Neurath. The German Foreign Ministry queried Ambassador Schulenburg in Moscow regarding Kandelaki's claim of a school relationship with Stalin. Schulenburg replied that as Stalin was older, he and Kandelaki could not have been schoolmates, but that Kandelaki had often told the German Embassy of his close contact with Stalin and there was no reason to doubt that he enjoyed Stalin's confidence.
57. Letter of 11 February 1937 from Neurath to Schacht. U.S. National Archives, Documents on German Foreign Policy.
58. Innere Politik, Parlaments- und Parteiwesen, II. Political Archive of the Foreign Ministry, Bonn, Germany.
59. *Pravda*, 3 April 1937. Later in 1937 he disappeared, one of the many who paid with their lives for knowing Stalin's secrets.
60. *In Stalin's Secret Service*, pp. 21–22.
61. *Journey*, pp. 39–63.
62. *Pravda*, 8 February 1937.
63. *Ibid.*, 9 February 1937.
64. Medvedev, *Bukharin*, p. 128.
65. "O partiinosti lits, prokhodivshikh po delu tak nazyvaemogo 'antisovetskogo pravotrotskistskogo bloka,' " *Izvestiia Ts.K. KPSS*, no. 5 (May 1989), pp. 72–73. This article, based on archival materials of the Central Committee, the KGB, and the Institute of Marxism-Leninism, presents the documented results of an inquest carried out under Politburo auspices.
66. *Ibid.*, pp. 73–74, 77.
67. "O partiinosti lits," pp. 75–76.
68. Roy A. Medvedev, *Let History Judge* (New York, 1971), p. 193.
69. *Ibid.*
70. Before being shot, according to Khrushchev (*XXII s" ezd KPSS, 17–31 oktiabria 1961 goda* [Moscow, 1962], II, 587; further referred to as *Twenty-Second Congress*), Svanidze was told that Stalin would forgive him if he would ask for clemency. Svanidze replied: "What is there to ask clemency for? I've committed no crime."
71. I. Dubinsky-Mukhadze, *Ordzhonikidze* (Moscow, 1963), p. 6.
72. *Ibid.*, pp. 6–7.
73. *Khrushchev Remembers* (Boston, 1970), p. 85. Only after Stalin died was Khrushchev told this by Mikoyan.
74. Medvedev, *Let History Judge*, pp. 194–96. Medvedev's detailed account of Ordzhonikidze's death is based on the eyewitness account given by his brother, Konstantin K. Ordzhonikidze, in 1966 and printed in the *samizdat* source, *Politicheskii dnevnik*, I, *1964–1970* (Amsterdam, 1972), no. 3 pp. 540–43.

75. Zhdanov Plenum Report, 26 February 1937, *Bol'shevik*, no. 5–6, March 15, 1937, pp. 8, 10, 11, 15, 19.
76. Medvedev, *Bukharin*, pp. 129–35.
77. "O partiinosti lits," p. 77.
78. *Ibid.*, p. 77–78. The text of Yezhov's plenum speech was not published.
79. *Ibid.*, p. 78.
80. *Ibid.*, pp. 79–81.
81. Medvedev, *Bukharin*, pp. 136–37.
82. *Khrushchev Remembers*, p. 577.
83. Antonov-Ovseyenko, *Time of Stalin*, p. 121, writes that Rudzutak, Eikhe, and Chubar tried to intervene on behalf of Bukharin and Rykov. Medvedev says (*Bukharin*, p. 135) that Postyshev's speech was the only one to express any doubts about the propriety of arresting a close colleague who had never indulged in oppositional activity.
84. *Khrushchev Remembers*, p. 577.
85. *Ibid.*, p. 613–14.
86. V. M. Molotov, "Uroki vreditel'stva, diversii i shpionazha Iapono-Nemetsko-Trotskistskikh agentov," *Bol'shevik*, no. 8, 15 April 1937, pp. 12–45.
87. *Pravda*, 29 March 1937.
88. *Khrushchev Remembers*, p. 572.
89. At the very time Stalin made this statement, reports Medvedev, "thousands of such people were being arrested." *Let History Judge*, p. 291.
90. That the Nikolenko mentioned in chap. 15 and the Nikolaenko referred to by Stalin was one and the same person is confirmed in *Ocherki istorii Kommunisticheskoi partii Ukrainy*, 2nd enl. ed. (Kiev, 1964), p. 466.
91. *Pravda*, 17 May 1937.
92. *Khrushchev Remembers*, p. 81.
93. *Pravda*, 1 April 1937. The speech was given on 5 March.
94. *Pravda*, 29 March 1937.
95. *Ibid.*, 18 March 1937.
96. Speech of N. M. Shvernik to the Twenty-Second Congress, October 24, 1961. *Twenty-Second Congress*, II, 215. The portion of the speech reported by Shvernik in 1961 was not cited in *Izvestiia*'s 18 March 1937 account of the three-day meeting, nor was reference made there to the ensuing arrests.
97. Orlov, *Secret History*, p. 214. Although in

Spain at this time, Orlov was in regular contact with NKVD visitors from Moscow and receiving information from them.
98. Krivitsky, *In Stalin's Secret Service*, pp. 146–151. Krivitsky was in Moscow at this time.
99. Orlov, *Secret History*, pp. 215, 216, 219.
100. *Izvestiia*, 18 March 1937.
101. Nikolaus Basseches, *Stalin*, trans. E. W. Dickes (London and New York, 1952), p. 302 for the rumors; Davies, *Mission to Moscow*, p. 121, for the dinner and April announcement.
102. Lev Nikulin, *Tukhachevsky* (Moscow, 1964), p. 190. The author comments: "This excuse naturally aroused doubt: Tukhachevsky could have gone to London by warship."
103. *Pravda*, 17 May 1937, for the decree's text.
104. A. Kotlova-Bychkova, "Riadom s marshalom," *Vechernaia Moskva*, 5 April 1989.
105. Lev Nikulin, "Poslednye dni marshala," *Ogonyok*, no. 13 (1963), p. 26; Nikulin, *Tukhachevsky*, p. 191; Lidiia Shatunovskaia, *Zhizn' v Kremle* (New York, 1982), p. 97.
106. "Delo o tak nazyvaemoi 'Antisovetskoi Trotskistskoi voennoi organizatsii' v Krasnoi Armii," *Izvestiia Ts.K. KPSS*, no. 4 (1989), pp. 50–52.
107. *Ibid.*, pp. 52–54.
108. *Ibid.*
109. *Ibid.*, pp. 54–56.
110. *Ibid.*, p. 56.
111. *Ibid.*, pp. 56–57, 61.
112. Nikulin, *Tukhachevsky*, p. 191.
113. "Delo," pp. 57–58.
114. Davies, *Mission to Moscow*, p. 119. The dispatch was dated 29 July 1937.
115. *Khrushchev Remembers*, pp. 100–101. The reference to Kaminsky's attack on Beria also appears in Khrushchev's Twentieth-Congress report on Stalin, but in briefer form. The Mussavats were anti-Bolshevik Moslems in the Transcaucusus.
116. Pavel Gol'dshtein, *Tochka opory: V Butyrskoi i Lefortovskoi tiur'makh 1939 goda* (Jerusalem, 1978), p. 64. Gol'dshtein heard of Tukhachevsky's last words directly from one of the high officers present on 11 June, Ilya Pavlovich Kit-Voitenko, with whom he shared a prison cell.

17. The Terror Process

1. See, for an example, N. Otradin, "Poputnye zametki," *Novoye russkoye slovo*, 11 October 1975. In the late 1930s, Otradin worked in a plant near a small district center in the Upper Volga region. He recalls: "The terror was going on above—but we down below heard only rumors; in our plant and in the settlement beside it, nobody suffered."
2. Petro G. Grigorenko, *Memoirs* (New York, 1982), p. 37.
3. "V GPU (Iz rasskazov tov. Raissa)," *Biulleten' oppozitsii*, no. 60–61 (December 1937), p. 20.
4. Dina Kaminskaya, *Zapiski advokata* (New York, 1984), p. 14.

5. Ilya Ehrenburg, *Post-War Years, 1945–1954*, trans. Tatiana Shebunina (Cleveland and New York, 1967), p. 277.
6. Lidiia Shatunovskaia, *Zhizn' v Kremle* (New York, 1982), pp. 109–11, reports such a case based on personal experience.
7. N. P. Poletika, *Vidennoe i perezhitoe* (Jerusalem, 1982), p. 416.
8. Markoosha Fischer, *My Lives in Russia* (New York, 1944), p. 205.
9. Anton Antonov-Ovseyenko *The Time of Stalin* (New York, 1981), p. 115.
10. Ilya Ehrenburg, *Memoirs: 1921–1941* (Cleveland, 1964), pp. 426–27. See also Medvedev, *Let History Judge* (New York,

1971), pp. 290–91. When the train on which Ehrenburg and his wife were traveling later in 1938, en route to Western Europe, crossed the Soviet border into Finland, he hugged her and said, "We're saved." A. Gladilin, *Novoye russkoye slovo*, 26 November 1980. Now in emigration. Gladilin was one of a group of young writers to whom Ehrenburg told this in 1961.

11. A. Ya. Vedenin, *Gody i liudi* (Moscow, 1964), p. 55.

12. F. Beck and W. Godin, *Russian Purge and the Extraction of Confession*, trans. Eric Mosbacher and David Porter (New York, 1951), p. 223. Godin is the pseudonym of Konstantin F. Shteppa, a Kiev University professor arrested in 1938; Beck is the pseudonym of a German scientist with whom he shared a cell. Both were sent to camps.

13. Medvedev, *Let History Judge*, p. 296. The source of this information was a camp survivor, P. Shabalkin, who was told the story in camp by a fellow prisoner who, as a police official, had been a member of Stalin's personal bodyguard and observed Yezhov's comings and goings.

14. Twentieth Congress Report, *Khrushchev Remembers*, p. 584; Medvedev, *Let History Judge*, 294.

15. Twentieth Congress Report, *Khrushchev Remembers*, pp. 584–85; Medvedev, *Let History Judge*, pp. 295–96.

16. Iu. P. Petrov, *Partiinoe stroitel' stvo v Sovetskoi armii i flote: Deiatel' nost' KPSS po sozdaniiu i ukrepleniiu politorganov, partiinykh i komsomol' skikh organizatsii v vooruzhennykh silakh (1918–1961 gg.)* (Moscow, 1964), p. 300.

17. Medvedev, *Let History Judge*, p. 210.

18. N. R. Mironov, "Vostanovlenie i razvitie leninskikh printsipov sotsialisticheskoi zakonnosti (1953–1963 gg.)," *Voprosy istorii KPSS*, no. 2 (1964), p. 19.

19. *Mikhail Kol' tsov, kakim on byl* (Moscow, 1965), p. 71. The source is Kol'tsov's brother, the cartoonist Boris Yefimov, to whom Kol'tsov related the story at the time.

20. Medvedev, *Let History Judge*, p. 292.

21. *Dvadtsaty vek*, no. 2 (1977), p. 75.

22. *Mikhail Kol' tsov*, p. 71.

23. Medvedev, *Let History Judge*, p. 291.

24. *Mikhail Kol' tsov*, p. 70.

25. *Ibid.*, p. 66.

26. G. A. Trukan, *Yan Rudzutak* (Moscow, 1963), pp. 94–95.

27. A. Tolmachev, *Kalinin* (Moscow, 1963), pp. 226–27; A. Blinov, *Ivan Akulov* (Moscow, 1967), pp. 76–77.

28. Medvedev, *Let History Judge*, p. 309.

29. Nikita Khrushchev, *Vospominaniia: Izbrannye otryvki* (New York, 1979), I, 193.

30. Speech of Z. Serdiuk, Twenty-Second Party Congress. *XXII s" ezd Kommunisticheskoi partii Sovetskogo soiuza, 17–31 oktiabria 1961 goda* (Moscow, 1962), III, 152. Hereafter cited as *Twenty-Second Congress*.

31. *Khrushchev Remembers* (Boston, 1970), p. 108. When Khrushchev told this story to Sta-

lin, the latter replied: "They've been gathering evidence against me too."

32. Shelepin's speech, *Twenty-Second Congress*, II, 404.

33. M. A. Suslov, cited by Medvedev, *Let History Judge*, p. 246.

34. Shvernik's speech, *Twenty-Second Congress*, II, 216.

35. *Ibid.*, p. 215.

36. Lazurkina's speech, *Twenty-Second Congress*, III, 120.

37. Medvedev, *Let History Judge*, p. 292.

38. Serdiuk's speech, *Twenty-Second Congress*, III, 153.

39. Merle Fainsod, *Smolensk Under Soviet Rule* (New York, 1958), p. 60. Korotchenkov's report is cited by Fainsod from *Partiinoe stroitel' stvo*, no. 19, 1 October 1937.

40. Medvedev, *Let History Judge*, p. 348.

41. *Politicheskii dnevnik* II, *1965–1970* (Amsterdam 1975), p. 124–25.

42. Nadezhda Mandelstam, *Hope Against Hope* (New York, 1970), p. 108.

43. Yuri Trifonov, *Otblesk kostra* (Moscow, 1966), pp. 25–27, 52. The late author was Valentin Trifonov's son.

44. D. Lappo, "Vernyi syn partii," *Pravda*, 18 September 1964.

45. *Years Off My Life: The Memoirs of General of the Soviet Army A. V. Gorbatov*, trans. Gordon Clough and Anthony Cash (New York, 1964), pp. 104–9. This is an abridged version of Gorbatov's autobiography, published in the Soviet journal *Novy mir*, March–May 1964.

46. Grigorenko, *Memoirs*, pp. 115–16.

47. Medvedev, *Let History Judge*, pp. 215–16.

48. Lev Nikulin, *Mertvaia zyb'* (Moscow, 1966), p. 368.

49. *Let History Judge*, p. 199. For a report that Krupskaya begged Stalin to spare the lives of Zinoviev, Kamenev, and others tried in August 1936, see Elisabeth K. Poretsky, *Our Own People* (London, 1969), p. 172.

50. *Let History Judge*, p. 199.

51. Robert H. McNeal, *Bride of the Revolution: Krupskaya and Lenin* (Ann Arbor, 1972), p. 287.

52. A. M. Kleimola, "The Duty to Denounce in Muscovite Russia," *The Slavic Review*, no. 4 (December 1972), pp. 771, 799.

53. Sir Donald MacKenzie Wallace, *Russia* (London, 1912), pp. 384–85.

54. V. M. Shapko, in *Voprosy istorii KPSS*, no. 1 (January 1963), p. 74.

55. "O nakazaniiakh za lozhnye donosy." *Sobranie uzakonenii i rasporiazhenii rabochego i krest' ianskogo pravitel' stva*, no. 77, 24 December 1921, p. 787.

56. V. Kononenko, "Pavlik Morozov: pravda i vymysel," *Komsomol' skaia pravda*, 5 April 1989.

57. "Prezrennye dvurushniki," *Pravda*, 15 August 1936.

58. "Partiinye i nepartiinye bol'sheviki," *Pravda*, 9 September 1936.

59. Leading article, *Partiinoe stroitel' stvo*, no. 2, 15 January 1937, p. 15. Emphasis added.

60. Medvedev, *Let History Judge,* p. 236.
61. A. Krasnov-Levitin, *Likhie gody* (Paris, 1977), p. 315; *The Memoirs of Ivanov-Razumnik,* trans. P. M. Squire (London, 1965), p. 209. Vyshinsky's article appeared in *Bol'shevik,* no. 10, 15 May 1937.
62. R. Rubenov, "Formy maskirovki trotskistskikh i inykh dvurushnikov," *Partiinoe stroitel'stvo,* no. 15, 1 August 1937, p. 27.
63. Kaminskaya, *Zapiski advokata,* p. 17.
64. P. Vinokurov, "Nekotorye metody vrazheskoi raboty v pechati i nashi zadachi," *Bol'shevik,* no. 16, 15 August 1937, *passim.*
65. Ginzburg, *Journey,* pp. 180–81.
66. Simon Wolin and Robert S. Slusser, eds., *The Soviet Secret Police* (New York, 1957), p. 185.
67. N. Belinkova, "Kholodnyi smekh," *Novoye russkoye slovo,* 29 May 1979.
68. Walter G. Krivitsky, *In Stalin's Secret Service* (New York, 1939), p. 153.
69. Beck and Godin, *Russian Purge,* p. 42.
70. Juri Jelagin, *Ukroshchenie iskusstv* (New York, 1952), p. 164.
71. *Biulleten' oppozitsii,* no. 60–61 (December 1937), p. 20.
72. Krasnov-Levitin, *Likhie gody,* pp. 319–20.
73. Eugenia Semyonovna Ginzburg, *Journey into the Whirlwind* (New York, 1967), pp. 181–82.
74. Krasnov-Levitin, *Likhie gody,* p. 317.
75. *Galina: A Russian Story,* trans. Guy Daniels (San Diego, New York, London, 1984), p. 23.
76. *Pravda,* 10 July 1937.
77. Document in the author's possession.
78. Fainsod, *Smolensk,* pp. 234–36.
79. M. Gorinsky, "Pora Omskim bol'shevikam zagovorit' polnym golosom," *Pravda,* 29 September 1937.
80. Fainsod, *Smolensk,* p. 232.
81. *Partiinoe stroitel'stvo,* no. 14, 15 July 1937, pp. 55–56.
82. B. Levin, "Politicheskaia blizorukost'?" *Pravda,* 30 June 1937.
83. Alexander Weissberg, *The Accused* (London, 1951), p. 312.
84. *Khrushchev Remembers,* pp. 114–15.
85. Veljko Micunovic, *Moscow Diary,* trans. David Floyd (Garden City, N.Y., 1980), pp. 28–29. "If you could only have seen how Stalin looked as I told him that," Khrushchev added, apropos Kievites' fright.
86. Beck and Godin, *Russian Purge,* p. 23.
87. Abdurakhman Avtorkhanov, *Stalin and the Soviet Communist Party* (New York, 1959), p. 221.
88. Beck and Godin, *Russian Purge,* p. 24.
89. "V narkomindele, 1922–1939: Interv'iu s E. A. Gnedinym," *Pamiat': Istoricheskii sbornik,* no. 5 (Moscow, 1981; Paris, 1982), p. 380. Elsewhere (*Katastrofa i vtoroe rozhdenie* [Amsterdam, 1977] pp. 248–59), Gnedin writes: "Young careerists pushed their way straight to positions, especially to posts abroad."
90. K. F. Shteppa, "Volna massovykh arestov v Sovetskom Soiuze (po lichnym vospomina-

niam)," ms. no. 203, Boris I. Nicolaevsky Collection, The Hoover Institution, Stanford, California, pp. 4–5.
91. Beck and Godin, *Russian Purge,* p. 206.
92. Vs. Vishnevsky, "U vsekh na ustakh—Stalin," *Pravda,* 23 October 1937.
93. *Ibid.,* 12 December 1937.
94. Cited in Tucker, *Stalin As Revolutionary* (New York, 1973), pp. 470–71.
95. *Pravda,* 19 December 1937.
96. *Ibid.,* 17 January 1938.
97. *Ibid.,* 19 January 1938. Full translation in Robert H. McNeal, ed., *Resolutions and Decisions of the Communist Party of the Soviet Union,* III, *The Stalin Years, 1929–1953* (Toronto, 1974), pp. 188–95.
98. Robert H. McNeal, "The Decisions of the CPSU and the Great Purge," *Soviet Studies,* no. 2 (October 1971), pp. 184, 185; and *idem, Stalin: Man and Ruler* (N.Y., 1988), pp. 210–11.
99. "By adopting this decree Stalin and his retainers tried to shift the guilt for the mass repressions away from themselves and pin it on local organizations." *Ocherki istorii Kommunisticheskoi partii Azerbaidzhana,* ed. M. Iskanderov (Baku, 1963), p. 542.
100. T. Mariagin, *Postyshev* (Moscow, 1965), p. 298.
101. Georgii Kumanev, "No istina dorozhe," *Ogonyok,* no. 33, 15–21 August 1989, p. 21. The pressure consisted of sending Politburo member Andreev to Kuibyshev in August 1937 to command Postyshev to take measures against "enemies."
102. "K padeniiu Postysheva: Iz stenogrammy plenuma TsK VKP(b)," *Pamiat',* no. 3 (Moscow, 1978; Paris, 1980), pp. 403–5; also Kumanev, *loc. cit.*
103. *Let History Judge,* pp. 238–39.
104. I. R. Grigulevich, *Istoriia inkvizitsii (XIII–XIX vv.)* (Moscow, 1970), pp. 117, 128. A two-volume Russian translation of J. A. Llorente, *A Critical History of the Inquisition of Spain* (English ed., 1823), was published in Moscow in 1936 (*Kriticheskaia istoriia ispanskoi inkvizitsii*) and may have been consulted in the NKVD.
105. Mironov, "Vostanovlenie," p. 19. Stalin's statement must have been made orally. It does not appear in speeches published in his lifetime.
106. Ginzburg, *Journey,* pp. 60–89. One other method used before April and belonging to the category of torture was the "standing cell," confinement in a box so narrow that the prisoner could only stand with arms at his side. See *ibid.,* p. 79, for its use on a prisoner confined in the cell next to Ginzburg's in Kazan.
107. Twentieth Congress speech, *Khrushchev Remembers,* p. 586.
108. Ginzburg, *Journey,* pp. 152–54, 159–60, 170–73. For other cases of prisoners overhearing screams from interrogation cells, see Beck and Godin, *Russian Purge,* p. 40.
109. *Pravda,* 3 October 1937. Confinement was normally in camp rather than prison.

110. *Ivanov-Razumnik*, pp. 246, 153; Beck and Godin, *Russian Purge*, p. 44.
111. Arrested on 29 September 1937, Ivanov-Razumnik was shown the NKVD's charge sheet on him on 2 November, after lengthy interrogation (Ivanov-Razumnik, p. 273).
112. Pavel Gol'dshtein, *Tochka opory: V Butyrskoi i Lefortovskoi tiur'makh 1939 goda*, I (Jerusalem, 1974), 58–59.
113. Beck and Godin, *Russian Purge*, p. 45; and more fully in Shteppa (Godin), "Volna massovykh arestov," chap. 6, p. 11. Shteppa personally met such "consultants" in Kiev prisons at the time. The Soviet historian of the Church Inquisition observes that "specially trained provocateurs" were placed in victims' cells to help persuade them to confess (Grigulevich, *Istoriia inkvizitsii*, p. 122).
114. Mikhail Boikov, *Liudi sovetskoi tiur'my* (Buenos Aires, 1957), II, 178, 221–25.
115. I am indebted for this information to Mr. William Shinn of the U.S. Foreign Service.
116. Piotr Yakir, *A Childhood in Prison* (New York, 1973), pp. 36, 38, 40.
117. Beck and Godin, *Russian Purge*, p. 56.
118. *Ivanov-Razumnik*, pp. 266–67.
119. *Ibid.*, pp. 305–6.
120. Twentieth Congress speech, *Khrushchev Remembers*, pp. 582–83.
121. *Ibid.*, p. 586.
122. Gorbatov, *Years Off My Life*, pp. 110–19, 151–52.
123. *Ivanov-Razumnik*, pp. 248–51; Grigorenko, *Memoirs*, p. 99. On the "penalty kick" by Lefortovo Colonel Sidorov at male prisoners' genitals, see Aleksandr I. Solzhenitsyn, *The Gulag Archipelago*, I (New York, 1974), 116.
124. Gol'dshtein, *Tochka opory*, II, 48–49.
125. Boikov, *Liudi*, I, 173–88.
126. Beck and Godin, *Russian Purge*, p. 122.

127. Medvedev, *Let History Judge*, p. 340; Weissberg, *The Accused*, p. 313.
128. Ginzburg, *Journey*, pp. 134–35, 185–86. For the Armenian priest, see Beck and Godin, *Russian Purge*, p. 46. For a case of denouncing others known to be under arrest, Evgeni A. Gnedin, *Katastrofa*, pp. 132–33.
129. *Ivanov-Razumnik*, pp. 284–86. "The NKVD had a dossier for every important official, stamping him as a counter-revolutionary, spy, and traitor" (Beck and Godin, *Russian Purge*, p. 47).
130. Weissberg, *The Accused*, pp. 314–17. See also Gorbatov, *Years Off My Life*, p. 110; Ginzburg, *Journey*, p. 75; Medvedev, *Let History Judge*, p. 340.
131. Beck and Godin, *Russian Purge*, p. 47.
132. D. V. Volkogonov, *Triumf i tragediia: Politicheskii portret I. V. Stalina*, 2 vols. (Moscow, 1989), I, 239–40.
133. Ginzburg, *Journey*, p. 253.
134. Krasnov-Levitin, *Likhie gody*, p. 326. On mass shootings of Trotskyists in camps in the winter of 1937–38, see Solzhenitsyn, *Gulag*, II, 387–89. The literature on the camps is huge. For a summary account, see Conquest, *Great Terror*, chap. 10, and for a valuable case study, see his *Kolyma: The Arctic Death Camps* (New York, 1978).
135. *Let History Judge*, p. 297. "This letter," Medvedev adds, "provoked an even greater orgy of terror in the Kolyma region, against Chekists as well as prisoners."
136. Antonov-Ovseyenko, *Time of Stalin*, p. 118. As mentioned earlier, Redens was shot.
137. Twentieth Congress speech, *Khrushchev Remembers*, p. 585.
138. This pattern of Stalin's rationalization has been analyzed in Tucker, *Stalin As Revolutionary*, pp. 450–52.

18. Terror, Russian Nationalism, and Foreign Policy

1. *Pravda*, 31 October 1937.
2. *A Short History of the USSR*, ed. A. V. Shestakov (Moscow, 1938), pp. 49–50.
3. *Ibid.*, pp. 167, 235, 245–47.
4. The talk was recorded by Voroshilov's adjutant, General R. P. Khmelnitsky, whose daughter, Natalya Kirshon, has authorized me to cite and paraphrase the material. A two-sentence excerpt from the speech is quoted in "Komintern: Vremia ispytanii," *Pravda*, 7 April 1989.
5. Roy A. Medvedev, *Khrushchev: A Political Biography*, trans. Brian Pearce (New York, 1983), p. 25. On the Ukrainian terror, see also Hryhory Kostiuk, *Stalinist Rule in the Ukraine* (New York, 1960), pp. 127–31, and Robert S. Sullivant, *Soviet Politics and the Ukraine* (New York, 1962), pp. 219–23.
6. V. Drobizhev and N. Dumova, *V. Ya. Chubar: Biograficheskii ocherk* (Moscow, 1963), pp. 67, 71.
7. Speech of K. T. Mazurov, *XXII s" ezd KPSS* (Moscow, 1962), I, 291.
8. Ivan S. Lubachko, *Belorussia Under Soviet*

Rule, 1917–1957 (Lexington, Ky., 1972), pp. 123, 125.
9. Unpublished memoirs of Ya. Drobinskii, cited by Roy A. Medvedev, *Let History Judge* (New York, 1971), pp. 266–67.
10. *Ocherki istorii Kommunisticheskoi partii Gruzii (1921–1963 gody)* (Tbilisi, 1963), II, 160. This source says that 70 percent of the Georgian delegation to the Seventeenth Congress fell victim. The congress transcript shows twenty-seven who listed Georgia as their party organization.
11. Suren Gazarian, "O Berii i sude nad Beriavtsami v Gruzii," *SSSR: Vnutrennie protivorechiia*, no. 6 (1982), pp. 118–19. This article comes from Gazarian's *samizdat* work, *Eto ne dolzhno povtorit' sia*.
12. *Ibid.*, pp. 141–42; Medvedev, *Let History Judge*, pp. 264, 269; Anton Antonov-Ovseyenko, *The Time of Stalin: Portrait of a Tyranny* (New York, 1981), p. 148.
13. *Kommunist* (Erevan), 15 November 1961, cited by Borys Levytsky, ed., *The Stalinist Terror in the Thirties: Documentation from*

the Soviet Press (Stanford, 1974), p. 327.

14. For these and further particulars on the Armenian purge, see Mary K. Matossian, *The Impact of Soviet Policies in Armenia* (Leiden, 1962), chap. 8.

15. *Ocherki istorii Kommunisticheskoi partii Azerbaidzhana*, ed. M. Iskanderov (Baku, 1963), pp. 540–42; David Tarsky, "Bagirovshchina," *Novoye russkoye slovo*, 12 and 13 March 1982. Bagirov lived to be tried and sentenced to death in a trial in Baku in 1956, which Tarsky attended.

16. "Vernyi boets partii," *Pravda*, 9 April 1964.

17. C. Abramsky, "The Biro-Bidzhan Project, 1927–1959," in *The Jews in Soviet Russia Since 1917*, ed. Lionel Kochan (London, 1970); article "Birobidzhan," *Encyclopedia Judaica*, IV (1971), 1044–50; W. Kolarz, *Russia and Her Colonies*, 3rd ed. (London, 1956), p. 177. By a decree of the RSFSR Supreme Soviet presidium, dated 2 December 1981, the Jewish Autonomous Region—long since become a fiction—was formally dissolved.

18. Speech of 18 May 1925, "On Political Tasks of the University of Eastern Peoples," *Stalin*, VII, 138.

19. *Pravda*, 4 October and 28 December 1937.

20. Speech of M. V. Gorbachev, *Pravda*, 16 August 1938. Karelians speak a Finnic language.

21. Svetlana Alliluyeva, *Twenty Letters* (New York, 1967), p. 159.

22. B. D., "Russkii yevrei vechera i segodnia," unpublished ms., cited by Roy A. Medvedev, *On Stalin and Stalinism* (Oxford, 1979), p. 114.

23. *House Without a Roof* (Garden City, N.Y., 1961), p. 310. See also S. M. Schwarz, *Antisemitizm v Sovetskom Soiuze* (New York, 1952), p. 8.

24. M. Agursky, "The Birth of Byelorussia," *The Times Literary Supplement*, 30 June 1972, p. 744; William Korey, "The Origins and Development of Soviet Anti-Semitism: An Analysis," *The Slavic Review*, no. 1 (March 1972), p. 118.

25. *Juden hinter Stalin*, comp. R. Kommoss (Berlin and Leipzig, 1938).

26. *Stalin*, V, 239, 245. On the background of his speech, see Tucker, *Stalin as Revolutionary* (New York, 1973), pp. 249, 264–65.

27. "Itogi protsessa," *Biulleten' oppozitsii*, no. 65 (April 1938), p. 3.

28. The summing-up speech and a condensed text of the verbatim report of the trial, along with notes, annotations, and an interpretive introduction, appears in *The Great Purge Trial*, ed. Robert C. Tucker and Stephen F. Cohen (New York, 1965). For the full text of the verbatim report, see *Report of Court Proceedings in the Case of the Anti-Soviet "Bloc of Rights nad Trotskyites"* (Moscow, 1938).

29. Medvedev, *Let History Judge*, p. 187.

30. Medvedev, *Nikolai Bukharin* (New York, 1980), pp. 144–46.

31. "Trial of 'Right Trotskyist Bloc,'" dispatch of 28 March 1938 from Ambassador Chilston in Moscow to the Foreign Office. Great Britain, Foreign Office, *Documents of British Foreign Policy* (for full reference, see the Bibliography).

32. Medvedev, *Let History Judge*, pp. 186–87; Evgeni A. Gnedin, *Katastrofa i vtoroe rozhdenie* (Amsterdam, 1977), p. 281.

33. Tucker and Cohen, *Great Purge Trial*, p. 565.

34. For Vyshinsky's speech, see Tucker and Cohen, *Great Purge Trial*, pp. 514–86.

35. Fitzroy Maclean, *Eastern Approaches* (New York, 1949), pp. 107–8. For Bukharin's final statement, see Tucker and Cohen, *Great Purge Trial*, pp. 656–68. My account here of Bukharin's conduct at the trial and his last statement is taken from my introductory essay in *Great Purge Trial*, pp. XLII–LVIII. For other accounts, see Stephen F. Cohen, *Bukharin and the Bolshevik Revolution* (New York, 1973), pp. 374–80, and Medvedev, *Buhkarin*, chap. 12.

36. *Ibid.*, p. 161.

37. On "Vasily" as a cover-name that might possibly have been used by Stalin in pre-1917 dealings with the tsarist police (although this remains unproved speculation), see Tucker, *Stalin as Revolutionary*, p. 11.

38. Gnedin, *Katastrofa*, p. 281.

39. Hans von Herwarth with S. Frederick Starr, *Against Two Evils*, (New York, 1981), pp. 110, 112.

40. Charles E. Bohlen, *Witness to History, 1929–1969* (New York, 1973), p. 46. See this source, p. 46, for Stalin's having visibly aged in the past three years.

41. For cases in point, see Iu. B. Margolin, *Puteshestvie v stranu Ze-ka* (New York, 1952), pp. 6–9.

42. *Novoye russkoye slovo*, 9 February 1985. She was allowed to return to England in 1985.

43. *Izvestiia*, 13 December 1936.

44. Piotr Yakir, *A Childhood in Prison* (New York, 1973), pp. 61–62.

45. Alexander Weissberg, *The Accused* (London, 1951), p. 10. "It almost seemed," comments the author, "as though the G.P.U. were determined to ensure the racial purity of Russia's towns by administrative action."

46. Teddy J. Uldricks, "The Impact of the Great Purges on the People's Commissariat of Foreign Affairs," *The Slavic Review*, no. 2 (June 1977), pp. 188, 190, 191, 195.

47. The letter was printed in the Russian émigré paper *Novaia Rossiia* on 1 October 1939.

48. Antonov-Ovseyenko, *Time of Stalin*, p. 145.

49. Leopold Trepper, *The Great Game: The Story of the Red Orchestra* (London, 1977), pp. 38–39.

50. Personal conversation in Moscow in June 1984 with Vladimir Maletsky, the son of one of the executed teachers.

51. David Pike, *German Writers in Soviet Exile, 1933–1945* (Chapel Hill, 1982), pp. 320, 324, 330–31.

52. *Ibid.*, pp. 313, 345.

53. Medvedev, *Let History Judge*, p. 222.

54. Pike, *German Writers,* pp. 325, 326, 328, 333.
55. Markoosha Fischer, *My Lives in Russia* (New York, 1944), pp. 189–90.
56. Arvo Tuominen, *The Bells of the Kremlin* (Hanover, N.H., 1983), p. 234.
57. *Ibid.*, p. 229.
58. Mrs. Bela Kun, *Bela Kun (Memoirs)* (Budapest, 1966), pp. 416–18.
59. Tuominen, *Bells of Kremlin,* pp. 222–23. Tuominen was present at the presidium meeting here described. For 1939 as the year of Kun's death, see his widow's memoir. For the hundreds of other Hungarians victimized, see Zoltan Vas, *Szepirodalmi Konyokiado* [Homecoming, 1944] (Budapest, 1970), p. 18.
60. Abraham Brumberg, "The Ghost in Poland," *The New York Review of Books,* 2 June 1983, p. 37, n.4.
61. Tuominen, *Bells of Kremlin,* pp. 225–26. Tuominen attended this session as well.
62. Ex-Insider, "The Party That Vanished," *Soviet Survey,* no. 33 (July–September 1960), pp. 104, 105.
63. M. K. Dziewanowski, *The Communist Party of Poland* (Cambridge, Mass., 1959), p. 151; *idem,* "Stalin and the Polish Communists," *Soviet Survey* (January–March 1961), p. 62. For the dissolution of the Western Ukrainian and Western Belorrusian parties, see *Kommunist,* no. 8 (1964), pp. 76–78, cited in Levytsky, *Stalinist Terror,* pp. 331–32.
64. The Korean party may have been. See Vladimir Dedijer, *Tito* (New York, 1953), p. 115, where Tito brackets the Korean party with the Polish, and Medvedev, *Let History Judge,* p. 221, where he writes: "The entire Korean section of the Comintern was arrested."
65. A. K. Rashkevits, in *Vsesoiuznoe soveshchanie o merakh uluchsheniia podgotovki nauchno pedagogicheskikh kadrov* (Moscow, 1964), p. 286.
66. Tuominen, *Bells of Kremlin,* pp. 227–29; Levytsky, *Stalinist Terror,* pp. 332, 335–36.
67. Dedijer, *Tito,* pp. 107–8, 115.
68. Branko Lazitch, "Stalin's Massacre of the Foreign Communist Leaders," *The Comintern: Historical Highlights,* ed. Milorad M. Drachkovitch and Branko Lazitch (Stanford, 1966), pp. 141, 167–68, 169.
69. Particulars in this paragraph are drawn from Walter G. Krivitsky, *In Stalin's Secret Service* (New York 1939), chap. 3.
70. *Pravda,* 14 February 1938. Ivanov's letter was dated 18 January 1938, Stalin's reply 12 February.
71. Chap. 3 above, p. 46.
72. According to Tuominen, *Bells of Kremlin,* p. 239, "the German Communists would have found it even more difficult than the others to accept fraternization with Hitler." The only members of the German Central Committee to survive, he points out, were Wilhelm Pieck and his assistant, Walter Ulbricht.
73. K. Velikanov, "Germanskaia ugroza Chekhoslovakii," *Pravda,* 2 April 1938.

74. Telegram of G. A. Astakhov, Soviet chargé in Berlin, to Moscow, 15 September 1938, reporting a talk with the Czechoslovak chargé there. *Dokumenty vneshnei politiki SSSR,* ed. A. A. Gromyko *et al.,* XXI (Moscow, 1977), 497. Hereafter cited as *Dokumenty.*
75. Winston S. Churchill, *The Second World War: The Gathering Storm* (New York, 1961), pp. 227, 279–81. That Hitler desired the military conquest of Czechoslovakia in 1938 rather than the bloodless quasi-solution that the Munich settlement gave him is persuasively argued by Gerhard L. Weinberg in *The Foreign Policy of Hitler's Germany: Starting World War II, 1937–1939* (Chicago and London, 1980), esp. pp. 389–90. On the existence of a generals' plot against Hitler at that time, see *ibid.,* p. 458, and Karl Dietrich Bracher, *The German Dictatorship* (New York, 1970), p. 398.
76. *Izvestiia,* 18 March 1938.
77. Personal interview with Evgeni Gnedin in Moscow, June 1977. As Litvinov's press officer, Mr. Gnedin was in close daily contact with him. When, on one occasion, he himself inadvertently lifted the receiver on the backroom phone, he heard Stalin's voice at the other end—and gently put the receiver down.
78. International review by "Observer," *Pravda,* 17 September 1938.
79. G. Kumanev, "22-go na rassvete," *Pravda,* 22 June 1989.
80. I. Makhovkov, "Unichtozhenie komandnykh kadrov Krasnoi Armii," *SSSR: Vnutrennie protivorechiia,* no. 3 (1982), pp. 204–10. On Stalin's sparing of the Tsaritsyn group, see John Erickson, *The Soviet High Command* (London, 1962), p. 462.
81. Dispatch of 18 February 1938, United States, State Department, *Foreign Relations of the United States, Diplomatic Papers: The Soviet Union, 1933–1939* (Washington, 1952), pp. 515–17. Further referred to as *U.S. Foreign Relations.*
82. *Pravda,* 11 February 1938.
83. Von Herwarth, *Against Two Evils,* p. 78. Von Herwarth was Ambassador Schulenburg's private secretary, with the embassy rank of third secretary.
84. Gustav Hilger and Alfred G. Meyer, *The Incompatible Allies* (New York, 1953), pp. 275, 282–85.
85. D. Pridvorov, "Ob otse," in *O Demiiane Bednom* (Moscow, 1966), p. 222.
86. Telegram from the chargé in Moscow, Kirk, to the secretary of state, June 22, 1938, *U.S. Foreign Relations,* pp. 584–85. Emphasis added.
87. *Ibid.,* pp. 571–77.
88. Weinberg, *Starting World War II,* p. 417.
89. *Documents on German Foreign Policy, 1918–1945,* Series D *(1937–1945),* II, *Germany and Czechoslovakia, 1937–1938,* pp. 423–26. Hereafter cited as *DGFP,* Ser. D, II.
90. Von Herwarth, *Against Two Evils,* pp. 122–23.
91. *Ibid.,* p. 122.
92. *DGFP,* ser. D, II, p. 667.

93. Jiří Hochman, *The Soviet Union and the Failure of Collective Security, 1934–1938* (Ithaca and London, 1984), p. 148. The author gives no precise number of bombers sent. In *Russia's Road from Peace to War* (New York, 1969), p. 312, Fischer writes that he was told by the French minister of aviation Pierre Cot (he does not say when) that the USSR delivered 300 aircraft to Czechoslovakia between the late May 1938 crisis and the Munich conference at the end of September.

)4. *DGFP*, Ser. D, II, 629–31.

)5. *Dokumenty*, pp. 436, 458–59.

96. *Ibid.*, pp. 464–65.

97. *Ibid.*, pp. 470–71.

98. George F. Kennan, *Russia and the West Under Lenin and Stalin* (New York, 1962), pp. 304–5.

99. Robert Coulondre, *De Staline à Hitler: Souvenirs de deux ambassades, 1936–1939* (Paris, 1950), pp. 157–59.

100. On British and French policies prior to Munich, see Jonathan Haslam, *The Soviet Union and the Search for Collective Security, 1933–1939* (New York, 1984), and Telford Taylor, *Munich: The Price of Peace* (Garden City, N.Y., 1979).

101. Hochman, *Soviet Union*, p. 160, and p. 236 n., where Hochman cites the memoirs of Comnène, *Preludi del grande drama* (Rome, 1947), pp. 83, 86, 10.

102. Hochman, *Soviet Union*, p. 161.

103. *Memoirs of Dr. Eduard Beneš* (London, 1954), p. 29.

104. Hochman, *Soviet Union*, pp. 164, 166–67, with full documentation in notes.

105. Prokop Drtina, *Československo můj osud* (Toronto, 1982), I, 202, cited in Michael Kraus, "The Soviet Union, Czechoslovakia, and the Second World War: The Foundations of a Communist Rule," Ph.D. dissertation, Princeton University, 1985, chap. 1, p. 57. On Benes' doubts see also J. W. Bruegel, "Dr. Benes on the Soviet 'Offer of Help' in 1938," *East Central Europe*, no. 1 (1977), pp. 57–58, and Edward Taborsky, "President Edvard Beneš and the Crises of 1938 and 1948," no. 5, part 2 (1978), pp. 205–6.

106. Hochman, *Soviet Union*, p. 166.

107. Hilger and Meyer, *Incompatible Allies*, pp. 288–89; von Herwarth, *Against Two Evils*, p. 142.

108. Hugh Thomas, *The Spanish Civil War* (New York, 1961), pp. 556–58, 566, 613. For the instructions to the Spanish Communists, see Burnett Bolloten, *The Spanish Revolution* (Chapel Hill, 1979), p. 473.

109. E. H. Carr, *The Comintern and the Spanish Civil War*, ed. Tamara Deutscher (New York, 1984), p. 71.

110. *Mikhail Kol'tsov, kakim on byl* (Moscow, 1965), p. 76.

111. Pavel Gol'dshtein, *Tochka opory: V Butyrskoi i Lefortovskoi tiur'makh 1939 goda*, II (Jerusalem, 1978), 42–43.

112. *Novy mir*, no. 11 (November 1964), p. 212. For Antonov-Ovseyenko's talk with Stalin and brief governmental appointment prior to arrest, see Anton Rakitin, *Imenem revoliutsii (Ocherki o V. A. Antonov-Ovseyenko)* (Moscow, 1965), p. 178. Anton Rakitin is the pseudonym of Anton Antonov-Ovseyenko, the executed man's son.

113. F. Beck and W. Godin, *Russian Purge* (New York, 1951), p. 234.

19. The Revolution of Belief

1. T. H. Rigby, "The CPSU Elite: Turnover and Rejuvenation from Lenin to Khrushchev," *The Australian Journal of Politics and History*, no. 1 (1970), pp. 16, 17.

2. A similar interpretation is suggested by Medvedev, *Let History Judge* (New York, 1971), p. 308.

3. Kendall E. Bailes, *Technology and Society Under Lenin and Stalin* (Princeton, 1978), p. 287. On the purge of industrialists see also Jeremy R. Azrael, *Managerial Power and Soviet Politics* (Cambridge, Mass., 1966), p. 100, and Barbara G. Katz, "Purges and Production: Soviet Economic Growth, 1928–1949," *The Journal of Economic History*, no. 3 (September 1975).

4. Medvedev, *Let History Judge*, p. 203.

5. *Pravda*, 14 August 1937.

6. A. L. Unger, "Stalin's Renewal of the Leading Stratum: A Note on the Great Purge," *Soviet Studies*, no. 3 (January 1969), pp. 325, 329.

7. *XVIII s"ezd VKP (b), 10–21 marta 1939 g.* (Moscow, 1939), p. 30.

8. *Ibid.*, p. 37.

9. For indications of such reasoning, see Bar-rington Moore, Jr., *Terror and Progress USSR: Some Sources of Change and Stability in the Soviet Dictatorship* (Cambridge, Mass., 1954), p. 177; and Sheila Fitzpatrick, *The Russian Revolution* (Oxford, 1982), p. 59.

10. Bailes, *Technology*, pp. 394–98, citing the *samizdat* memoir by an arrested survivor, G. A. Ozerov, *Tupolevskaia sharaga* (Frankfurt, 1971). For Yakovlev and his career, see Bailes, *Technology*, pp. 403–5, and A. S. Yakovlev, *Tsel' zhizni*, 2nd enl. ed. (Moscow, 1968).

11. John Scott, *Behind the Urals* (Cambridge, Mass., 1942), p. 196. On the inhibiting effect of the purge on technological innovation, as shown in the disruption of the Soviet radar program, see Bailes, *Technology*, pp. 420–21.

12. Yuri Trifonov, *Otblesk kostra* (Moscow, 1966), pp. 188–90.

13. Bailes, *Technology*, pp. 394–95, citing Alksnis' article in *Industriia*, 18 August 1937. As Bailes shows, even in the prison design bureau Tupolev himself sought to switch his own efforts from the huge models he had earlier designed.

14. *XVIII s" ezd*, p. 195, and Bailes, *Technology,* pp. 399–401. Trifonov's unpublished book was critical of Douhet's doctrine.
15. *Voenno-istoricheskii zhurnal,* no. 12 (1964), p. 11.
16. *Politicheskii slovar'*, eds. G. Aleksandrov, V. Fal'ianov, and N. Rubinstein (Moscow, 1940), pp. 285–86.
17. *Bol'shevik,* no. 1 (January 1946), p. 52. According to Khrushchev *(Khrushchev Remembers,* p. 607), Stalin, when editing the proofs of the *Short Biography* of him that was to be published in 1947, inserted a passage saying that in 1938 appeared the *Short Course,* "written by Comrade Stalin and approved by a commission of the Central Committee."
18. For this information and that which follows here, I am indebted to Mints, whom I interviewed at the Institute of History of the USSR in June 1977.
19. I. Mints, "Podgotovka velikoi proletarskoi revoliutsii: K vykhodu v svet pervogo toma "Istorii grazhdanskoi voiny v SSSR," *Bol'shevik,* no. 12, 15 November 1935, pp. 15–30.
20. Nikolai Maslov, " 'Kratkii kurs istorii VKP(b) —entsiklopediia kul'ta lichnosti Stalina," in *Surovaia drama naroda: Uchenye i publitsisty o prirode stalinizma* (Moscow, 1989), pp. 337–40, 345. Stalin's letter appeared in *Pravda* on 6 May 1937 and was entitled "On a Textbook of Party History: Letter to the Drafters of the Textbook of History of the All-Union Communist Party (Bolsheviks)."
21. Maslov, " 'Kratkii kurs,' " pp. 340–45.
22. *Pravda,* 23 April 1920.
23. *History of the Communist Party of the Soviet Union (Bolsheviks): Short Course* (Moscow, 1945), p. 24. Hereafter cited as *Short Course.* No published source is given for the quoted statement. It may have been made orally by Stalin to members of the drafting group.
24. *Ibid.*, pp. 81–82.
25. *Ibid.*, p. 216, Tucker, *Stalin As Revolutionary,* pp. 177–78.
26. *Short Course,* pp. 238–39; Tucker, *Stalin As Revolutionary,* pp. 201–3.
27. *Short Course,* pp. 241–42; Tucker, *Stalin As Revolutionary,* pp. 203–5.
28. *Short Course,* pp. 282, 292. For the significant omission of reference to German engineers accused of sabotage in the Shakhty case, see Robert M. Slusser, "The Role of the Foreign Ministry," in *Russian Foreign Policy: Essays in Historical Perspective,* ed. Ivo J. Lederer (New Haven and London, 1962), p. 225.
29. *Short Course,* pp. 297–98.
30. In order to culminate in the December 1937 election, the *Short Course* had to suggest that the Bukharin-Rykov trial of March 1938 took place in 1937.
31. *Pravda,* 29 March 1937.
32. See Alexander Weissberg, *The Accused,* (London, 1951), for a similar interpretation. He does not, however, see the promotions process as the other side of the same coin.
33. In *The Gulag Archipelago,* II, chap. 11, Solzhenitsyn, with only a minor qualification, lumps these true believers in Stalin with other "orthodox Communists" under the overall rubric of "loyalists." His failure to distinguish between the differing forms of Bolshevik faith results in a misleading picture.
34. Svetlana Alliluyeva, *Only One Year* (New York, 1969), p. 368.
35. Joseph Stalin, *Anarchism or Socialism?* (New York, 1953), p. 10.
36. *Short Course,* p. 358.
37. *Stalin,* XIII, 106.
38. *Short Course,* p. 14.
39. *Ibid.*, p. 305.
40. Friedrich Engels, "Socialism: Utopian and Scientific, in *The Marx-Engels Reader,* ed. Robert C. Tucker, 2nd ed. (New York, 1978), pp. 713.
41. *The Lenin Anthology,* ed. Robert C. Tucker (New York, 1975), pp. 323, 373–75.
42. John N. Hazard, "Housecleaning in Soviet Law," *American Quarterly on the Soviet Union,* no. 1 (April 1938), p. 12. Pashukanis' 1930 statement appears in his "The Soviet State and the Revolution in Law," in *Soviet Legal Philosophy,* trans. Hugh W. Babb (Cambridge, Mass., 1951), p. 278. For the body of Pashukanis' writings, see *Pashukanis: Selected Writings on Marxism and Law,* eds. Piers Beirne and Robert Sharlet (London, 1980).
43. E. Pashukanis, "Uchenie Lenina i Stalina o gosudarstve i novyi etap razvitiia sovetskogo demokratizma," *Pravda,* 22 February 1935.
44. P. Yudin, "Protiv putanitsy, poshlosti i revizionizma," *Pravda,* 20 January 1937; and "Sotsializm i pravo," *Bol'shevik,* no. 17, 1 September 1937, pp. 31–48. English translation in Babb, *Soviet Legal Philosophy,* pp. 281–301.
45. N. V. Zhogin, "Ob izvrashcheniakh Vyshinskogo v teorii sovetskogo prava i praktike," *Sovetskoe gosudarstvo i pravo,* no. 3 (March 1965), p. 26. On Vyshinsky's career, see Robert Sharlet and Piers Beirne, "In Search of Vyshinsky: The Paradox of Law and Terror," *International Journal of the Sociology of Law,* no. 12 (1984), pp. 453–77.
46. A. Ya. Vyshinsky, *Voprosy teorii gosudarstva i prava* (Moscow, 1949), p. 84. English translation in Babb, *Soviet Legal Philosophy,* p. 337.
47. *Ibid.* pp. 7–8. On Vyshinsky's "jurisprudence of terror," see Robert Sharlet, "Stalinism and Soviet Legal Culture," in *Stalinism,* ed. Robert C. Tucker (New York, 1977), pp. 155–80.
48. Malcolm Muggeridge, *Chronicles of Wasted Time* (London, 1972), p. 244. In "Soviet Criminology: Its Demise and Rebirth, 1928–1963," *Soviet Union,* no. 2 (1974), Peter H. Solomon writes: "The 'stability of law' became the new slogan, but the terror went on; and legalism came to serve as a facade for it." See also Peter H. Juviler, *Revolutionary Law and Order* (London, 1976), chap. 3.
49. Zhogin, "Ob izvrashcheniiakh Vyshinskogo," pp. 23–25, 27, 29.

50. N. P. Poletika, *Vidennoe i perezhitoe (iz vospominanii)* (Israel, 1982), p. 408. Professor Poletika emigrated in 1973; in the late 1930s he was in his early thirties and living in Leningrad. Compare the quoted statement with Nadezhda Mandelstam's that ". . . leading a double life was an absolute fact of our age, and nobody was exempt." *Hope Against Hope: A Memoir*, trans. Max Hayward (New York, 1970), p. 203.

51. *Ibid.*, p. 231.

52. Raisa Berg, *Sukhovei: Vospominaniia genetika* (New York, 1983), p. 43.

53. For the story of one such group and its cruel fate, see Anatoly Zhigulin, "Chernye kamni," *Znamia*, July 1988, pp. 10–75, and August 1988, pp. 48–119.

54. A. Fedoseev, *Zapadnia: Chelovek i sotsializm* (Frankfurt am Main, 1979), p. 52.

55. Raisa Orlova, *Memoirs*, trans. Samuel Cioran (New York, 1983), pp. 40, 57, 65.

56. Lev Kopelev, *The Education of a True Believer*, trans. Gary Kern (New York, 1980), pp. 226, 300.

57. "Stalin—chelovek i simvol," *Novoye russkoye slovo*, 12 June 1987. This article reproduces a discussion of 13 April 1987 in Moscow's Central Writers' Club following a lecture by Borisov on Stalin.

58. I. Makhovikov, "Unichtozhenie komandnykh kadrov krasnoi armii," *SSSR: Vnutrennie protivorechiia*, no. 3 (1982), p. 220.

59. Interview at the Kennan Institute in Washington, D.C., in December 1983. Professor Levin became a noted Soviet linguist. He emigrated in the 1970s.

60. Personal communication of 1 January 1987 from Professor I. Yakhot, now living in Israel.

61. F. Beck and W. Godin, *Russian Purge* (New York, 1951), p. 34.

62. For further corroborative evidence on this point, see Robert W. Thurston, "Fear and Belief in the U.S.S.R.'s 'Great Terror'. Response to Arrest, 1935–1939," *The Slavic Review*, no. 2 (Summer 1986), pp. 213–34.

63. On this point, see Aleksandr I. Solzhenitsyn, *The Gulag Archipelago*, I, 12, where he writes: "The majority sit quietly and dare to hope. Since you aren't guilty, how can they arrest you?" See Thurston, "Fear and Belief," for evidence of lack of fear associated with the sense of innocence.

64. Edmund Wilson, cited by Alexander and Juliette George, *Woodrow Wilson and Colonel House: A Personality Study* (New York, 1964), p. 317.

20. The Scripted Culture

1. On RAPP see Edward J. Brown, *The Proletarian Episode in Russian Literature* (New York, 1971), For Stalin's initiative in dissolving it, *Pravda*, 23 April 1937, and Boris Souvarine, "Poslednye razgovory s Babelem," *Kontinent*, no. 23 (1980), p. 348.

2. *Stalin*, XI, 328. Bill-Belotserkovsky's letter to Stalin was never published, but is mentioned in A. Smeliansky, *Mikhail Bulgakov v Khudozhestvennom teatre* (Moscow, 1986), p. 129. For the charge of Great Russian chauvinism brought against the play, see N. A. Gorchakov, *Istoriia sovetskogo teatra* (New York, 1956), p. 234 n.

3. For a full account of Bulgakov's letter and Stalin's nocturnal phone calls, see Ellendea Proffer, *Bulgakov: Life and Work* (Ann Arbor, 1984), pp. 315–23.

4. S. M. Chertok, *Poslednaia liubov' Mayakovskogo* (Ann Arbor, 1983), pp. 34–39.

5. *Pravda*, 5 December 1935. "Homeward!" appears in Vladimir Mayakovsky, *The Bedbug and Selected Poetry*, trans. Max Hayward and George Reavey (Bloomington and London, 1975), pp. 187–89. For an account of Mayakovsky's life and work, see Patricia Blake's Introduction to this volume.

6. See, for example, his letter to the writer A. Bezymensky, *Stalin*, XII, 200–201, beginning: "I'm no judge of literature and of course no critic. However, since you insist, I can give you my personal opinion."

7. Boris Gass, *Zadui vo mne svechu* (London, 1984), pp. 146–48, 152–59. Nutsubidze reworked the translation under Stalin's guid-

8. *Pravda*, 20 January 1936.

9. *Ibid.*, 28 January 1936. On 7 February *Pravda* again assailed Shostakovich for the "aestheticizing formalism" of his music for a ballet then showing, *Clear Stream*.

10. *Pravda*, 20 February, 1 and 6 March, and 3 April 1936. On Melnikov see S. Frederick Starr, *Melnikov: Solo Architect in a Mass Society* (Princeton, 1978).

11. Juri Jelagin, *Taming of the Arts*, trans. Nicholas Wreden (New York, 1951), p. 266. Jelagin was then a member of the State Jazz Orchestra, having earlier played in the orchestra of Moscow's Vakhtangov Theater. On jazz in the 1930s see this source, pp. 255–67, and S. Frederick Starr, *Red and Hot: The Fate of Jazz in the Soviet Union* (New York, 1985), chaps. 7 and 8.

12. G. V. Aleksandrov, *Epokha i kino*, 2nd ed. (Moscow, 1983).

13. Vladimir Frumkin, "The Cultivation of Mythological Reality: 'Double Think' in the Soviet Mass Song of the Thirties," unpublished MS, Oberlin College, 1980.

14. Jay Leyda, *Kino: A History of the Russian and Soviet Film* (New York, 1973), pp. 268–69, citing Aleksandrov's account of the meeting with Stalin in *Iskusstvo Kino*, December 1939.

15. Herbert Marshall, *Masters of the Soviet Cinema: Crippled Creative Biographies* (London, 1983), pp. 24, 40, 172, 216–17.

16. Leyda, *Kino*, p. 354, referring to Dovzhen-

which occurred the following comment: "ance between 1937 and 1939; it was published in 1941.

ko's friends as his source. A foreigner, Leyda worked in the Moscow film world in the 1930s.

17. Gorchakov, *Istoriia,* pp. 175–79; Jelagin, *Taming of the Arts,* p. 155. *The Suicide* only got as far as the dress rehearsal.

18. Juri Jelagin, *Temnyi genii (Vsevolod Meyerhold).* 2nd enl. ed. (London, 1982), p. 380.

19. P. Kerzhentsev, "Chuzhoi teatr," *Pravda,* 7 December 1937; "O likvidatsii teatra im. Vs. Meierkhol'da," *ibid.,* 8 January 1938. -

20. By Sheila Fitzpatrick, in "Culture and Politics Under Stalin: A Reappraisal," *The Slavic Review,* no. 2 (June 1976), pp. 225, 231.

21. A. Smeliansky, ". . . Naveki, odnazhdy i navsegda," *Sovetskaia kul'tura,* 16 January 1988.

22. V. Yemelyanov, "O vremeni, o tovarishchakh, o sebe," *Novy mir* (February 1967), pp. 87–89. The author was one of those present at the meeting.

23. David Joravsky, *The Lysenko Affair* (Cambridge, Mass., 1970), pp. 58–60.

24. Mark Popovsky, *The Vavilov Affair* (Hamden, Conn., 1984), pp. 56, 62–63.

25. *Pravda,* 15 February 1935. Valerii Soifer, "Gor'kii plod," *Ogonyok,* no. 1, 2–9 January 1988, p. 27.

26. Soifer, "Gor'kii plod," p. 27. For Lysenko's way of coming up with new schemes to cover the failure of others, see Popovsky, *Vavilov Affair,* pp. 77–78.

27. Genrikh Volkov, "Byt' li nam mankurtami?" *Sovetskaia kul'tura,* 4 July 1987.

28. Evgenia Al'bats, "Genii i zlodeistvo," *Moskovskie novosti,* 15 November 1987, p. 10.

29. Jelagin, *Taming of the Arts,* pp. 162, 169–73; *idem, Temnyi genii,* pp. 383, 406–10.

30. Arkadii Vaksberg, "Protsessy", *"Literaturnaia gazeta,* 4 May 1988.

31. Katerina Clark, "Little Men and Big Deeds: Literature Responds to the First Five-Year Plan," in *Cultural Revolution in Russia, 1928–1931,* ed. Sheila Fitzpatrick (Bloomington and London, 1978). See also Clark's *The Soviet Novel: History As Ritual* (Chicago and London, 1985), chap. 4.

32. *I vsesoiuznyi s"ezd sovetskikh pisatelei, 1934* (Moscow, 1934), pp. 4, 5.

33. A. Stakhanov, *Rasskaz o moei zhizni* (Moscow, 1937), cited by Katerina Clark, "Utopian Anthropology As a Context for Stalinist Literature," in *Stalinism,* ed. Robert C. Tucker (New York, 1977), p. 187.

34. V. Kardin, "Uncharted Destinies Are Waiting for Us," *Moscow News,* no. 13, 5–12 April 1987.

35. "Iskusstvo i revoliutsiia," *Biulleten' oppozitsii,* no. 77–78, (May–July 1939), p. 8.

36. This picture of him at the time comes from Jelagin, *Taming of the Arts,* pp. 123–24, describing a country outing for the couple arranged by Vakhtangov Theater persons, Jelagin included, with the aim of getting Tolstoy's agreement for their theater to produce *Road to Victory* in 1938.

37. Alexander Tvardovsky, *Selected Poetry,* trans. [of this poem] D. Rottenburg (Moscow, 1981), pp. 236–37. The word *muravia* could be translated "plenty" or "greenery."

38. Abram Tertz, *The Trial Begins* and *On Socialist Realism,* trans. Max Hayward *(Trial)* and George Dennis (New York, 1965), pp. 149–50. Abram Tertz was the pseudonym Sinyavsky used when these writings appeared abroad and he remained in Moscow.

39. G. S. Cheremin, *Obraz I. V. Stalina v sovetskoi khudozhestvennoi literature* (Moscow, 1950), p. 19.

40. *Khrushchev Remembers,* p. 610.

41. "Konstitutsiia geroicheskogo naroda," *Pravda,* 16 January 1937.

42. *Ibid.,* 22 August 1937.

43. Shestakov, *A Short History of the USSR* (Moscow, 1938), *passim.*

44. Felix J. Oinas, "The Political Uses and Themes of Folklore in the Soviet Union," *Journal of the Folklore Institute,* no. 2–3 (1975), pp. 157–58.

45. Jelagin, *Taming of the Arts,* pp. 150–51.

46. *Pravda,* 15 November 1936.

47. Oinas, "Political Uses," pp. 163, 166–68, and *idem,* "Folklore and Politics in the Soviet Union," *The Slavic Review,* no. 1 (March 1973), p. 50. For other such materials, see N. P. Andreev, *Russkii fol'klor* (Moscow, 1938), pp. 617–50.

48. "Ob odnoi gniloi kontseptsii," *Pravda,* 10 February 1936. Writing in *Pravda* on 8 March 1922, Lenin said: "There was a character type in Russian life—Oblomov. He lay in bed all the time and drew up plans. Much time has gone by, but the Oblomovs have remained. . . . One has only to take a look at us, how we hold meetings, how we work in committees, to see that the old Oblomov has survived, and he'll have to be washed, cleaned, shaken up, and thrashed for a long time if anything is to be made of him."

49. Harlow Robinson, *Sergei Prokofiev: A Biography* (New York, 1987), p. 350.

50. Svetlana Alliluyeva, *Only One Year* (New York, 1969), p. 390. For the cited review, see *Pravda,* 4 April 1939.

51. *Ibid.,* 9 July 1936.

52. *Ibid.,* 13 July 1936.

53. Joravsky, *Lysenko Affair,* p. 211, citing Lysenko's article "Po povodu stat'i akademika N. I. Vavilova," *Sotsialisticheskoe zemledelie,* 1 February 1939.

54. N. Rubinshtein, "Kliuchevsky i ego *Kurs russkoi istorii,*" *Pravda,* 15 August 1937.

55. *Istorik-Marksist,* no. 2 (1937), p. 143.

56. *Protiv istoricheskoi kontseptsii M. N. Pokrovskogo,* B. Grekov *et al.* eds., 2 vols. (Moscow, 1939); *Istorik-Marksist,* no. 4 (1939), pp. 157–62; and article on Pokrovsky in *Bol'shaia sovetskaia entsiklopediia,* XL (Moscow, 1940), 856–69.

57. M. Kozakov, "Risunki na peske: Fragmenty iz knigi," *Ogonyok,* no. 8, 20–27 February 1988, p. 29. This article's author, Mikhail Kozakov's son, does not date *When I'm Alone.* It probably was written after World War II.

58. E. Smirnov, *Slavnyi pioner Gena Shchukin* (Moscow, 1938).

59. B. Romashov, "Rodnoi dom," *Znamia,* no.

3 (March 1938), pp. 42, 66.

60. John Scott, *Behind the Urals* (Cambridge, Mass., 1942), pp. 197–203.

61. These changes have been noted by F. Beck and W. Godin, *Russian Purge* (New York, 1951), p. 28.

62. Vaksberg, "Protsessy."

63. *Ibid.*

64. "Za bol'shevitskuiu bditel'nost' v literature," *Novy mir*, no. 6 (1937), pp. 196–97.

65. *Ibid.*, p. 194; L. Plotkin, "Trotskistskaia agentura v literature," *Zvezda*, no. 7 (1937), pp. 210–13. For the accent of anti-Semitism in a denunciation of Averbakh by Pavel Yudin, see Edward J. Brown, *Russian Literature Since the Revolution* (London, 1963), p. 217.

66. *Literaturnaia gazeta*, 1 May 1937.

67. G. Lebedev, "Melkaia spekuliatsiia na bol' shoi teme," *Literaturnyi kritik* (May 1937), pp. 109–10. The play's text appeared in *Novy mir*, no. 2 (February 1937). For a personal memoir of Kirshon by his widow, see Rita Korn, *Vospominaniia* (Moscow, 1982).

68. The completed part, along with a foreword by Iasenskii's widow, Anna Berzin, appeared in *Novy mir*, no. 5 (May 1956).

69. R. Voinov, "Masirovka shpiona," *Molodaya gvardiia*, no. 8 (1937), pp. 182–83. See also Pike, *German Writers in Soviet Exile* (Chapel Hill, 1982), p. 326.

70. "Eto nuzhno ne mertvym—zhivym," interview with Beltov in *Knizhnoe obozrenie*, no. 25, 17 June 1988.

71. Petr Lugovoi, "S krov'iu i potom: Iz zapisok sekretaria raikoma," *Literaturnaia Rossiia*, 27 May 1988.

72. *The Correspondence of Boris Pasternak and Olga Freidenberg, 1910–1954*, ed. Elliott Mossman, trans. Elliott Mossman and Margaret Wettlin (New York and London, 1982), pp. 157–58, 162–68, 179–81, 303–4.

73. As *Opustelyi dom* (Paris, 1965). Translated as *Sofia Petrovna* (Evanston, Ill., 1988).

74. *Poems of Akhmatova*, selected, trans. and introduced by Stanley Kunitz with Max Hayward (Boston, 1967), p. 99. All further citations from Akhmatova here are from this source, although I have made small changes in some translations.

75. Gregory Freidin, "Mandel'shtam's Ode to Stalin: History and Myth," *The Russian Review* (October 1982), where the Ode's text appears in English translation on pp. 424–26. For the self-compulsion involved in the poem's creation, see Mandelstam, *Hope Against Hope* (New York, 1970), chap. 43.

76. Osip Mandel'shtam, *Voronezhskie tetradi* (Ann Arbor, 1980), p. 95. I have drawn here on the interpretation of the Voronezh lyrics by Ronald Hingley, *Nightingale Fever: Russian Poets in Revolution* (New York, 1981), pp. 212–18.

77. Lev Ostrovsky, "Zakat khudozhestvennogo teatra," *Novoye russkoye slovo*, 2 January 1979. The text of *Batum* appears in *Neizdannyi Bulgakov*, ed. Ellendea Proffer (Ann Arbor, 1977), pp. 137–210.

78. I owe this formulation to Lars T. Lih.

79. Aleksei Adzhubei, "Te desiat' let," *Znamia*, no. 7 (1988), p. 82.

21. Culminations, 1939–1940

1. Roy A. Medvedev, in *Argumenty i fakty*, 3 February 1989.

2. Dmitry Pavlov, "Dve poslendnie vstrechi s V. M. Molotovym," *Literaturnaia gazeta*, 18 April 1990.

3. *Let History Judge* (New York, 1971), p. 199. Antonov-Ovseyenko's contention *(The Time of Stalin* [New York, 1981], p. 140) that Krupskaya died of food poisoning is contradicted by V. Dridzo, her personal secretary, who was with her in her last hours and claims that she died a natural death of an intestinal blood clot. See "O Krupskoi," *Kommunist*, no. 5 (March 1989), pp. 105–6. However, historians I. Kulikov and V. Kumanev consider that the circumstances of Krupskaya's death "demand further and objective study." *Pravda*, 5 January 1990.

4. *XVIII s"ezd VKP(b) 10–21 marta 1939 g.* (Moscow, 1939), pp. 12–15. In his congress speech on Comintern affairs, Manuilsky placed heavy stress (p. 57) on Stalin's theme that the democracies were stronger than the fascist states. All further references to Stalin's and other congress speeches are to this source.

5. Viktor Danilov, "Fenomen pervykh piatiletok," *Gorizont*, no. 5 (1988), p. 36.

6. Vadim Churbanov, "Chto proiskhodit s nashei kul'turoi," *Ogonyok*, no. 37, 10–17 September 1988, p. 19.

7. Elena Rzhevskaya, "V tot den', pozdnei osen'iu," *Znamia*, no. 12 (1986), pp. 169–70. The article was first published twenty-one years after the author's interview with Zhukov in November 1965.

8. Mark Tol'ts, "Repressirovannaia perepis'," *Rodina*, no. 11 (1989), p. 59. On Kraval, his 1936 conversation with Stalin, and later fate, see A. Berezin, "Ivan Kraval," *Vestnik statistiki*, no. 7 (1988), pp. 56–57.

9. Tol'ts, "Perepis'," p. 60.

10. Anatolii Golovkov, "Ne otrekaias' ot sebia: Is istorii sovremennosti," *Ogonyok*, no. 7, 14–21 February 1988, p. 27. For the closed session at which Stalin assailed Yezhov, see Medvedev's account, based on notes of an eyewitness, in *Stalinism*, ed. Robert C. Tucker (New York, 1977), pp. 218–19.

11. S. Mikoyan, "Sluga," *Komsomol'skaia pravda*, 21 February 1988.

12. Irina Shcherbakova, "Odin iz sta, iz piatisot, iz tysiachi," *Moskovskie novosti*, 30 October 1988. Beck and Godin, *Russian Purge* (New York, 1951), pp. 223–25, report that the "fascist theory" was one of the most common

among the seventeen different theories of the Great Purge advanced by prisoners in prisons and camps at the time.

13. N. Porzhin, "O voine my uznali ot Vavilova," *Sovetskaia kul'tura,* 24 December 1988.

14. Arkadii Vaksberg, "Protsessy," *Literaturnaia gazeta,* 4 May 1988. On Beria's criminal form of womanizing, see B. Popov and V. Oplokov, "Berievshchina," *Trud,* 26 August 1989.

15. Beck and Godin, *Russian Purge,* pp. 223–25.

16. V. M. Kulish, "U poroga voiny," *Komsomol'skaia pravda,* 24 August 1988. For a prediction that Germany would be defeated in a war against the Western democracies, see the unsigned book review, "Razoblachennyi mif," *Pravda,* 14 August 1939.

17. Max Beloff, *The Foreign Policy of Soviet Russia, 1929–1941* (London, 1949), II, 232.

18. *Diplomat in Berlin, 1933–1939: Papers and Memoirs of Josef Lipski,* ed. Waclaw Jedrzejewicz (New York, 1969), pp. 522–24.

19. Gerhard L. Weinberg, *The Foreign Policy of Hitler's Germany* (Chicago, 1980), pp. 552–53.

20. Ilya Ehrenburg, *Memoirs: 1921–1941* (Cleveland, 1964) p. 477.

21. Memorandum by Weizsäcker, in *Nazi-Soviet Relations, 1929–1941. Documents from the Archives of the German Foreign Office,* eds. R. J. Sontag and J. S. Beddie (New York, 1948), pp. 1–2.

22. *Ibid.,* pp. 2–3.

23. Gustav Hilger and Alfred G. Meyer, *The Incompatible Allies; A Memoir History of German-Soviet Relations, 1918–1941* (New York, 1953), pp. 293–97.

24. Sontag and Beddie, *Nazi-Soviet Relations,* pp. 5–8.

25. German Foreign Office memorandum, 15 June 1939, *ibid.,* pp. 20–21.

26. Evgeni Gnedin, "Sebia ne poteriat'," *Novy mir,* no. 7 (July 1988), pp. 179–85. This article is extracted from Gnedin's memoir, *Katastrofa i vtoroe rozhdenie: Memuarnye zapiski* (Amsterdam, 1977).

27. Bohdan B. Budurowycz, *Polish-Soviet Relations, 1932–1939* (New York, 1963), pp. 157–60.

28. Weinberg, *Foreign Policy,* p. 582.

29. Sontag and Beddie, *Nazi-Soviet Relations,* pp. 50–68.

30. Hilger and Meyer, *Incompatible Allies,* p. 300.

31. Sontag and Beddie, *Nazi-Soviet Relations,* pp. 71–78.

32. Interview with von Walther in Bonn on 23 March 1970 in the offices of the German Society for Foreign Policy, which he then headed, and with Schnürre in his office in Bad Godesberg on 25 March 1970. In the late 1930s Schnürre worked under H. Schacht on economic ties with Russia.

33. *Khrushchev Remembers* (Boston, 1970), pp. 127–28.

34. Kulish, "U poroga voiny." According to Professor G. Kumanev (personal conversation in

Moscow, May 1989), the note transmitted by Khmelnitsky was written by Stalin's assistant, Poskrebyshev.

35. Budurowycz, *Polish-Soviet Relations,* p. 168.

36. *Pravda,* 1 September 1939.

37. Raisa Orlova, *Memoirs,* trans. Samuel Cioran (New York, 1983), p. 218.

38. Y. Golovanov, "1,367 dnei iz zhizni Andreia Tupoleva," *Literaturnaia gazeta,* 9 November 1988.

39. Robert Robinson, with Jonathan Slavin, *Black on Red: My 44 Years Inside the Soviet Union* (Washington, D.C., 1988), p. 137.

40. Beck and Godin, *Russian Purge,* p. 75.

41. Moscow dispatch by G. Gedye, *The New York Times,* 9 September 1939.

42. Sontag and Beddie, *Nazi-Soviet Relations,* p. 88.

43. For an analysis of Orwell's novel in relation to Stalin's Russia, see Robert C. Tucker, "Does Big Brother Really Exist?" in *1984 Revisited,* ed. Irving Howe (New York, 1983), pp. 89–102.

44. Charles E. Bohlen, *Witness to History* (New York, 1973), p. 90.

45. Sontag and Beddie, *Nazi-Soviet Relations,* p. 89.

46. *Ibid.,* pp. 93–94.

47. Speech of 31 October 1939, published in *Pravda* on 1 November 1939.

48. Jan T. Gross, *Revolution from Abroad: The Soviet Conquest of Poland's Western Ukraine and Western Belorussia* (Princeton, 1988), pp. 29, 31.

49. Sontag and Beddie, *Nazi-Soviet Relations,* pp. 102–8. The treaty and declaration were published in the Soviet press on 29 September 1939.

50. *The Ribbentrop Memoirs* (London, 1954), pp. 131–32. Ribbentrop wrote these unfinished memoirs in 1946 while on trial in Nuremberg as a Nazi war criminal.

51. Bohlen, *Witness to History,* p. 91. Bohlen's source was a member of the Estonian Legation in Moscow.

52. For details concerning the elections, see Gross, *Revolution from Abroad,* chap. 2.

53. *Pravda,* 1 November 1939.

54. Evgenia Ginzburg, *Krutoi marshrut,* II (Milan, 1979), 52.

55. *The Communist International, 1919–1943.* Documents selected and edited by Jane Degras, III (London, 1971), 455–56.

56. N. Volkov, "Prolog mirovoi voiny," *Novoye russkoye slovo,* 7 May 1985.

57. Joseph Berger, *Shipwreck of a Generation* (London, 1971), p. 171. Berger, then confined in the Norilsk camp, observed a convoy of these prisoners sent to Norilsk.

58. N. Kuznetsov, "Krutye povoroty: Stranitsy istorii," *Pravda,* 29 July 1988.

59. *Khrushchev Remembers,* p. 154. Khrushchev does not give a date for this incident.

60. Hans von Herwarth with S. Frederick Starr, *Against Two Evils* (New York, 1981), p. 165.

61. Gnedin, "Sebia ne poteriat'," pp. 146–47.

62. Alexander Weissberg, *The Accused* (London, 1951), pp. 502–6; Beck and Godin, *Russian Purge,* pp. 126–27. For Margarete

Buber-Neumann's experience of expulsion and transference, see Margarete Buber, *Under Two Dictators,* trans. Edward Fitzgerald (London, 1949), pp. 150–75.

63. Hilger and Meyer, *Incompatible Allies,* pp. 316–17.
64. Kulish, "U poroga voiny."
65. G. F. R. Gedye, "Stalin's Birthday Eclipses the War," *The New York Times,* 21 December 1939.
66. *Stalin: K shestidesiatiletiiu so dnia rozhdeniia* (Moscow, 1940), p. 382. The tributes to him cited below are printed in this book.
67. Hilger and Meyer, *Incompatible Allies,* p. 314.
68. N. Volkov, "Prolog," 8 May 1985; A. M. Nekrich, *June 22, 1941,* ed. V. Petrov (Columbia, S.C., 1968), 128.
69. *Khrushchev Remembers,* pp. 134, 166.
70. Alexander Dallin, "The Baltic States Between Nazi Germany and Soviet Russia," *The Baltic States in Peace and War, 1917–1945,* eds. V. S. Vardys and R. J. Misiunas (University Park, Md., 1978), p. 108.
71. N. Volkov, "Prolog," 8 May 1985.
72. Gerhard L. Weinberg, *Germany and the Soviet Union, 1939–1941* (Leiden, 1954), pp. 101–4; and for Hitler's reaction, M. M. Hitchens, *Germany, Russia, and the Balkans* (New York, 1983), p. 257.
73. Roy Medvedev, "Nash isk Stalinu," *Moskovskie novosti,* 27 November 1988.
74. Gross, *Revolution from Abroad,* pp. 228–29.
75. "Gorbachev Hands Over Katyn Papers," *The New York Times,* 14 April 1990.
76. "Tainy katynskogo lesa," *Moskovskie novosti,* 6 August 1989.
77. Evald Laasi, "Crime Against Humanity," a broadcast in English from Tallinn, *Lodumaa,* 23 November 1988; and article in *Sirp ja Vasar,* an Estonian cultural weekly, 27 November 1987.
78. Isaac Deutscher, *The Prophet Outcast: Trotsky, 1929–1940* (New York, 1963), pp. 472–75.
79. *Ibid.,* pp. 483–508 *passim.* For a Soviet historian's reconstruction of the murder along these lines, and affirmation of Stalin's responsibility for the crime, see N. Vasetsky, "Likvidatsiia," *Literaturnaia gazeta,* 4 January 1989.

"Likvidatsiia," *Literaturnaia gazeta,* 4 January 1989.
80. For these figures, see Kulish, "U poroga voiny."
81. Zinovii Sheinis, " 'Venkov ne nado. . . .': Zhizn' i sud'ba Maksima Litvinova," *Sovetskaia kul'tura,* 7 January 1989.
82. *Ribbentrop Memoirs,* p. 151.
83. M. Gefter, "Stalin umer vchera," *Inogo ne dano,* ed. Yu. N. Afanasiev (Moscow, 1988), p. 322. I am grateful to Professor Gefter for showing me his copy of the proofs with Stalin's penciled corrections and comments.
84. Cited by Valentin Berezhkov, *S diplomaticheskoi missiei v Berlin, 1940–1941* (Moscow, 1966), p. 43. A German-speaking specialist on German affairs, Berezhkov worked in the Soviet trade mission in Berlin in 1940.
85. Leopold Trepper, *The Great Game: The Story of the Red Orchestra* (London, 1977), p. 125.
86. Sontag and Beddie, *Nazi-Soviet Relations,* p. 216.
87. Cited by Berezhkov, *S diplomaticheskoi missiei,* p. 49, Berezhkov here uses the phrase "diversionary maneuver" to describe the affair. For the details of Molotov's train trip to Berlin, see Hilger and Meyer, *Incompatible Allies,* pp. 321–22.
88. Sontag and Beddie, *Nazi-Soviet Relations,* pp. 226–33. The document cited is a record of the conversation, which was attended by Ribbentrop and Deputy Soviet Foreign Commissar V. G. Dekanozov. Hilger and V. N. Pavlov were the interpreters. See Hilger and Meyer, *Incompatible Allies,* p. 323, for Hilger's summary of what Hitler said and his memory that when he afterward accompanied Molotov to his quarters, "he seemed relieved at Hitler's amiability."
89. Sontag and Beddie, *Nazi-Soviet Relations,* pp. 234–54.
90. *Ribbentrop Memoirs,* p. 150.
91. Sontag and Beddie, *Nazi-Soviet Relations,* pp. 258–59.
92. Berezhkov, *S diplomaticheskoi missiei,* p. 51.
93. Sontag and Beddie, See *Nazi-Soviet Relations,* pp. 260–64, for the full text of Barbarossa.
94. Svetlana Alliluyeva, *Only One Year* (New York, 1969), p. 392.

22. The Reckoning

1. Leopold Trepper, *The Great Game: The Story of the Red Orchestra* (London, 1977), pp. 125–26.
2. Valentin Berezhkov, *S diplomaticheskoi missiei v Berlin* (Moscow, 1966), p. 91.
3. V. M. Kulish, "U poroga voiny," *Komsomol'skaia pravda,* 24 August 1988.
4. G. Kumanev, "22-go, na rassvete," *Pravda,* 22 June 1989.
5. Dmitry Volkogonov, "Nakanune vony," *Pravda,* 20 June 1988. For Zhukov's reading of Hitler's letter, see Elena Rzhevskaya, "V

tot den', pozdnei osen'iu," *Znamia,* no. 12 (1986), p. 169.
6. In Gustav Hilger and Alfred G. Meyer, *The Incompatible Allies* (New York, 1953), p. 326, Hilger offers such an interpretation.
7. Volkogonov, "Nakanune."
8. Rzhevskaya, "V tot den'," p. 169.
9. Volkogonov, "Nakanune."
10. I. T. Starinov, *Miny zhdut svoego chasa* (Moscow, 1964), p. 176; A. M. Nekrich, *June 22, 1941,* ed. V. Petrov (Columbia, S.C., 1968) p. 129; Petro G. Grigorenko, *Memoirs*

(New York, 1983), p. 47. According to Grigorenko, the old line was destroyed on Stalin's personal orders.

11. Kulish, "U poroga voiny," and G. Kumanev, "22-go."

12. Interview with Volkogonov, *Trud,* 19 June 1988.

13. Volkogonov, "Nakanune."

14. Kumanev, "22-go." See also Hilger and Meyer, *Incompatible Allies,* p. 331. Hilger was the one who suggested the step to Schulenburg.

15. *Khrushchev Remembers,* p. 590.

16. O. Gorchakov, "Nakanune, ili tragediia kassandry," *Nedelia,* no. 40, 31 October–6 November 1988. Although published on 14 June, the TASS statement was dated 13 June and would have been seen by high officials that day.

17. Volkogonov, "Nakanune."

18. Rzhevskaya, "V tot den'," p. 170.

19. The Moscow girl was Eugenia Pestretsova, who later became my wife.

BIBLIOGRAPHY

I. Archival Sources and Governmental Documents

Degras, Jane, ed. *Soviet Documents on Foreign Policy*. Vol. III, *1933–1941*. London, 1953.
Dokumenty vneshnei politiki SSSR, chief ed. A. A. Gromyko. Vol XVI. Moscow, 1970. Vol. XXI. Moscow, 1977.
Great Britain. Foreign Office. *Documents of British Foreign Policy / Russia Correspondence*. F. O. 371, film rolls 17250–22287, 1934–38. Wilmington, Del., 1976.
Hoover Institution Archives, Stanford, California. Fund N. 227, Box 3.
Political Archive, Foreign Ministry, Bonn. Innere Politik, Parlaments- und Parteiweisen, Bd. 2., and Piatakov-Radek (Trotsky Prozess) (January 1927).
Smolensk Archive in the U.S. National Archives. Washington, D.C. WKP 499 (T87 / 53).
Sobranie zakonov i rasporiazhenii raboche-krest'ianskogo pravitel'stva Soiuza sovetskikh sotsialisticheskikh respublik. Moscow, 1924–37.
Trotsky Archives. Harvard University. Cambridge, Mass. Documents T1693, T1897, T1901.
United States. State Department. *Documents on German Foreign Policy, 1918–1945*. Series C and D *(1937–1945)*. Washington, D.C., 1959
United States National Archives. Washington, D.C. Documents on German Foreign Policy, 1918–1945. Role 282, serial 393.
United States. State Department. *Foreign Relations of the United States, Diplomatic Papers: The Soviet Union, 1933–1939*. Washington, D.C., 1952.

II. Congresses, Conferences, Other Proceedings

X s"ezd RKP(b), mart 1921 goda. Sten. otchet. Moscow, 1960.
XIV s"ezd VKP(b), 18–31 dekabria 1925 g. Sten. otchet. Moscow and Leningrad, 1926.

XVI s"ezd VKP(b), 26 iunia–13 iuliia 1930 g. Sten. otchet. Moscow, 1930.
XVII s"ezd VKP(b), 26 ianvaria–10 fevralia 1934 g. Sten. otchet. Moscow, 1934.
XVIII s"ezd VKP(b), 10–12 marta 1939 g. Sten. otchet. Moscow, 1939.
XXII s"ezd KPSS, 17–31 oktiabria 1961 g. Sten. otchet. 3 vols. Moscow, 1962.
IX konferentsiia VKP(b). Sten. otchet. Moscow and Leningrad, 1925.
XVI konferentsiia VKP(b), april 1929 goda. Moscow, 1962.
XVII konferentsiia VKP(b). Sten. Otchet. Moscow, 1932.
VKP(b) v rezoliutsiakh i resheniakh s"ezdov, konferentsii i plenumov TsK. 6th ed. Vol. II, *1925–1939.*
      Moscow, 1941.
S"ezdy sovetov Soiuza sovetskikh sotsialisticheckikh respublik: Sbornik dokumentov, 1922–1936 g. Vol.
      III. Moscow, 1960.
I vsesoiuznyi s"ezd sovetskikh pisatelei, 1934. Sten. otchet. Moscow, 1934.
Protsess kontrrevoliutsionnoi organizatsii men'shevikov (1 marta–9 marta 1931 g). Stenograma sudeb-
      nogo protsessa. Moscow, 1931.
A Blow at Intervention. Moscow and Leningrad, 1931.
Sudebnyi otchet po delu Trotskistko-Zinovievskogo terroristicheskogo tsentra. Moscow, 1936.
The Case of the Trotskyite-Zinovievite Centre, reprint of the Moscow ed. New York, 1967.
Report of Court Proceedings in the Case of the Anti-Trotskyite Centre. Moscow, 23–30 January 1937.
      Moscow, 1937.
The Case of Leon Trotsky: Report of Hearings on the Charges Made Against Him in the Moscow Trials.
      New York, 1937.
Report of Court Proceedings in the Case of the Anti-Soviet "Bloc of Rights and Trotskyites." Moscow,
      1938.

III. Books in Russian

Afanasiev, Yu. N., ed. *Inogo ne dano.* Moscow, 1988.
Agaian, Ts. P. *Nersik Stepanian.* Erevan, 1967.
Agursky, M. *Ideologiia natsional-bolshevizma.* Paris, 1980.
Aleksandrov (A. S. Michelson). *Kto upravliaet Rossiei? Bol'shevitskii partiino-pravitel'stvennyi apparat i*
      'Stalinizm'. Berlin, 1933.
Aleksandrov, G., V. Fal'ianov, and N. Rubinstein, eds. *Politicheskii slovar'.* Moscow, 1940.
Aleksandrov, G. V. *Epokha i kino.* 2nd ed. Moscow, 1983.
Aleksandrov, M. S. (M. Ol'minsky). *Gosudarstvo, biurokratiia, i absolutizm v istorii Rossii.* 2nd ed.
      Moscow and Petrograd, 1919.
Andreev, N. P. *Russkii fol'klor.* Moscow, 1938.
Annenkov, Yuri. *Dnevnik moikh vstrech.* Vol. II. New York, 1966.
Bega, F., and V. Aleksandrov. *Petrovsky.* Moscow, 1963.
Berezhkov, Valentin. *S diplomaticheskoi missiei v Berlin, 1940–1941.* Moscow, 1966.
Berg, Raisa, *Sukhovei: Vospominaniia genetika.* New York, 1983.
Beria, Lavrenti P. *K istorii bol'shevitskikh organizatsii na Zakavkazii.* 4th ed. Moscow, 1939.
Blinov, A. *Ivan Akulov.* Moscow, 1967.
Boikov, Mikhail. *Liudi sovetskoi tiur'my.* 2 vols. Buenos Aires, 1957.
Bol'shaia sovetskaia entsiklopediia. 65 vols. Moscow, 1926–47.
Cheremin, G. S. *Obraz I. V. Stalina v sovetskoi khudozhestvennoi literature.* Moscow, 1950.
Cherkasov, N. K. *Zapiski sovetskogo aktera.* Moscow, 1953.
Chertok, S. M. *Poslednaia liubov' Mayakovskogo.* Ann Arbor, 1983.
Chukovskaya, Lidiia. *Opustelyi dom.* Paris, 1965.
Danilov, V. P., ed. *Ocherki istorii kollektivizatsii sel'skogo khoziaistva v soiuznykh respublikakh.* Moscow,
      1963.
Direktivy VKP(b) i postanovleniia sovetskogo pravitel'stva o narodnom obrazovanii, comp. N. I. Bol-
      dyrev. Vol. I. Moscow and Leningrad, 1947.
Dmitrievsky, S. *Sovetskie portrety.* Stockholm, 1932.
Drobizhev, V., and N. Dumova. *V. Ya. Chubar: Biograficheskii ocherk.* Moscow, 1963.
Dubinsky, I. *Naperekor vetram.* Moscow, 1964.
Dubinsky-Mukhadze, I. *Ordzhonikidze.* Moscow, 1963.
Eventov, I. *Zhizn' i tvorchestvo Demyana Bednogo.* Leningrad, 1967.
Fedoseev, A. *Zapadnia: Chelovek i sotsializm.* Frankfurt am Main, 1979.
Gass, Boris. *Zadui vo mne svechu.* London, 1984.
Genkina, E. B. *Lenin—predsedatel' Sovnarkoma i STO.* Moscow, 1960.
Gershberg, Semen. *Rabota u nas takaia: Zapiski zhurnalista-pravdista tridsatykh godov.* Moscow, 1971.
Gertsen (Herzen), A. I. *Dvizhenie obshchestvennoi mysli v Rossii.* Moscow, 1907.
Ginzburg, Evgenia. *Krutoi marshrut.* Vol. II. Milan, 1979.
Gnedin, Evgeni A. *Katastrofa i vtoroe rozhdenie: Memuarnye zapiski.* Amsterdam, 1977.
———. *Iz istorii otnoshenii mezhdu SSSR i fashistskoi Germaniei.* New York, 1977.
Gol'dshtein, Pavel. *Tochka opory: V Butyrskoi i Lefortovskoi tiur'makh 1939 goda.* 2 vols. Jerusalem,
      1974–78.

Gorchakov, N. A. *Istoriia sovetskogo teatra*. New York, 1956.
Gor'ki i sovetskie pisateli: Neizdannaia perepiska. Moscow, 1963.
Gredeskul, N. A. *Rossiia prezhde i teper'*. Moscow and Leningrad, 1926.
Grekov, B., *et al.*, eds. *Protiv istoricheskoi kontseptsii M. N. Pokrovskogo*. 2 vols. Moscow, 1939.
Grigulevich, I. R. *Istoriia inkvizitsii (XIII–XIX vv.)*. Moscow, 1970.
Istoriia KPSS. 2nd enl. ed. Moscow, 1962.
Istoriia VKP(b), gen. ed. E. M. Yaroslavsky. Vol. IV. Moscow and Leningrad, 1929.
Istoriia sovetskoi konstitutsii (v dokumentakh), 1917–1956. Moscow, 1957.
Ivanov-Razumnik, R. *Pisatel'skie sud'by*. New York, 1951.
Ivnitsky, N. A. *Klassovaia bor'ba v derevne i likvidatsiia kulachestva kak klass (1929–1932 gg.)*. Moscow, 1972.
Jelagin, Juri. *Temnyi genii (Vsevolod Meyerhold)*. 2nd enl. ed. London, 1982.
———. *Ukroshchenie iskusstv*. New York, 1952.
Kaminskaya, Dina. *Zapiski advokata*. New York, 1984.
Karaganov, A. *Zhizn' dramaturga: Tvorcheskii put' Aleksandra Afinogenova*. Moscow, 1964.
Khavin, A. F. *U rulia industrii*. Moscow, 1968.
———. *Kratkii ocherk istorii industrializatsii SSSR*. Moscow, 1962.
Khrushchev, Nikita. *Vospominaniia: Izbrannye otryvki*. Vol. I. New York, 1979.
Kirov, S. M. *Stat'i i rechi, 1934*. Moscow, 1934.
Kliuchevskii, V. O. *Kurs russkoi istorii*. 5 vols. Moscow, 1937.
Komandarm Yakir: Vospominaniia druzei i soratnikov. Moscow, 1963.
Kommunisticheskii Internatsional' v dokumentakh, 1919–1932. Part 2. Moscow, 1933.
Kopelev, Lev. *Khranit' vechno*. Ann Arbor, 1975.
———. *I sotvoril sebe kumira*. Ann Arbor, 1978.
Korn, Rita. *Vospominaniia*. Moscow, 1982.
Krasnikov, S. *S. M. Kirov v Leningrade*. Leningrad, 1966.
———. *Sergei Mironovich Kirov: Zhizn' i deiatel' nost'*. Moscow, 1964.
Krasnov-Levitin, A. *Likhie gody, 1925–1941: Vospominaniia*. Paris, 1977.
Krupskaya, Nadezhda. *Vospominaniia o Vladimire Il'iche v piati tomakh*. Vol. I. Moscow, 1960.
Kuibysheva, G. V., O. A. Lezhava, V. V. Nelidov, and A. F. Khavin. *Valerian Vladimirovich Kuibyshev: Biografiia*. Moscow, 1966.
Larin, Iu. *Sovetskaia derevnia*. Moscow, 1925.
Leibzon, B. M., and K. K. Shirinia. *Povorot v politike Kominterna*. Moscow, 1965.
Lenin, V. I. *Polnoe sobranie sochinenii*. 5th ed. 55 vols. Moscow, 1958–1965.
Leninskii kooperativnyi plan i bor'ba partii za ego osushchestvlenie. Moscow, 1969.
Leninskii sbornik, Vol. XI. Moscow, 1929.
Liashchenko, P. I. *Istoriia narodnogo khoziaistva SSSR*. Vol. III. Moscow, 1956.
Litvinov, M. M. *Vneshniaia politika SSSR*. Moscow, 1937.
Llorente, J. A. *Kriticheskaia istoriia ispanskoi inkvizitsii*. Moscow, 1936.
Lokot', T. V. *Smutnoe vremia i revoliutsiia*. Berlin, 1923.
Maksudov, M. (pseud.) *Poteri naseleniia SSSR*. Benson, Vt., 1989.
Malenkov, G. M. *O zadachakh partiinykh organizatsii v oblasti promyshlennosti i transporta*. Moscow, 1941.
Mandel'shtam, Osip. *Voronezhskie tetradi*. Ann Arbor, 1980.
Margolin, Iu. B. *Puteshestvie v stranu Ze-ka*. New York, 1952.
Mariagin, T. *Postyshev*. Moscow, 1965.
Marshal Tukhachevsky: Vospominaniia druzei i soratnikov. Moscow, 1965.
Mel'chin, A. *Stanislav Kosior*. Moscow, 1964.
Mikhail Kol'tsov, kakim on byl. Moscow, 1965.
Miliukov, Pavel Nikolaevich. *Ocherki po istorii russkoi kul'tury*. 5th ed. Vol. I. St. Petersburg, 1904.
Mitin, M. *Boevye voprosy materialisticheskoi dialektiki*. Moscow, 1936.
Molotov, V. M. *Stat'i i rechi, 1935–1936*. Moscow, 1937.
Moshkov, Iu. A. *Zernovaia problema v gody sploshnoi kollektivizatsii sel'skogo khoziaistva SSSR (1929–1932 gg.)*. Moscow, 1966.
Nikulin, Lev. *Tukhachevsky: Biograficheskii ocherk*. Moscow, 1964.
———. *Mertvaia zyb'*. Moscow, 1966.
Ocherki istorii Kommunisticheskoi partii Gruzii (1921–1963 gody). 2 vols. Tbilisi, 1963.
Ocherki istorii Kommunisticheskoi partii Azerbaidzhana, ed. M. Iskanderov. Baku, 1963.
Ocherki istorii Kommunisticheskoi partii Ukrainy. 2nd enl. ed. Kiev, 1964.
Ozerov, G. A. *Tupolevskaia sharaga*. Frankfurt, 1971.
Pamiat': Istoricheskii sbornik. No. 3. Moscow, 1978; Paris, 1980. No. 5. Moscow, 1981; Paris, 1982.
Panova, Vera. *O moei zhizni, knigakh i chitateliakh*. Leningrad, 1975.
Pavlenkov, F. *Entsiklopedicheskii slovar'*. St. Petersburg, 1913.
Petrov, Iu. P. *Partiinoe stroitels'stvo v Sovetskoi armii i flote; Deiatel'nost' KPSS po sozdaniiu i ukrepleniiu politorganov, partiinykh i komsomol'skikh organizatsii v vooruzhennykh silakh (1918–1961 gg)*. Moscow, 1964.
Platonov, S. F. *Smutnoe vremia*. Petrograd, 1923.
———. *Petr Velikii*. Leningrad, 1926.

Platonov, S. F. *Ivan Grozny*. Petrograd, 1923.
Plekhanov, G. V. *Osnovnye voprosy marksizma*. New York, 1922.
Pokrovsky, M. N. *Marksizm i osobennosti istoricheskogo razvitiia Rossii*. Moscow, 1925.
———. *Russkaia istoriia v samom szhatom ocherke*. Moscow, 1934.
Poletika, N. P. *Vidennoe i perezhitoe (iz vospominanii)*. Jerusalem, 1982.
Politicheskii dnevnik. Vol. I, *1964–1970*. Amsterdam, 1972. Vol. II, *1965–1970*. Amsterdam, 1975.
Proffer, Ellendea, ed. *Neizdannyi Bulgakov*. Ann Arbor. 1977.
Radek, Karl. *Podgotovka bor'by za novyi peredel mira*. Moscow, 1934.
Rakitin, Anton. *Imenem revoliutsii (Ocherki o V. A. Antonov-Ovseyenko)*. Moscow, 1965.
Razgon, Lev. *Nepridumannoe*. Moscow, 1989.
Rogachevskaia, L. S. *Likvidatsiia bezrabotitsy v SSSR, 1917–1930 gg*. Moscow, 1973.
Schwarz, S. M. *Antisemitizm v Sovetskom soiuze*. New York, 1952.
Serebriakova, Galina. *O drugikh i o sebe*. Moscow, 1968.
Serebrovsky, A. P. *Na zolotom fronte*. Moscow, 1939.
Shatunovskaia, Lidiia. *Zhizn' v Kremle*. New York, 1982.
Shkapa, Ilya M. *Sem' let s Gor'kim: Vospominania*. Moscow, 1966.
Sinel'kov, S. *Kirov*. Moscow, 1964.
Skrynnikov, R. G. *Ivan Grozny*. Moscow, 1975.
Smeliansky, A. *Mikhail Bulgakov v Khudozhestvennom teatre*. Moscow, 1986.
Smena vekh. 2nd ed. Prague, 1922.
Smirnov, E. *Slavnyi pioner Gena Shchukin*. Moscow, 1938.
Sovetskoe administrativnoe pravo. Moscow, 1940.
Spravochnik partiinogo rabotnika. Moscow, 1957.
Spravochnik po zakonodatel'stvu dlia ispol'nitelnykh komitetov sovetov deputatov trudiashchikhsia. Vol. I. Moscow, 1946.
Stakhanov, A. *Rasskaz o moei zhizni*. Moscow, 1937.
Stalin i Khashim (1901–1902 gody): Nekotorye epizody iz batumskogo polpolia. Sukhumi, Georgia, 1934.
Stalin, I. V. *Sochineniia*. 13 vols. Moscow, 1946–52. Vols. XIV(I)–XVI(III), ed. Robert H. McNeal. Stanford, 1967.
Stalin: K shestidesiatiletiiu so dnia rozhdeniia. Moscow, 1940.
Starinov, I. T. *Miny zhdut svoego chasa*. Moscow, 1964.
Stroitel'stvo Sovetskogo gosudarstva: Sbornik statei k 70-letiiu E. B. Genkinoi. Moscow, 1972.
Studenikin, S. S., *et al. Sovetskoe administrativnoe pravo*. Moscow, 1950.
Surovaia drama naroda: Uchenye i publitsisty o prirode stalinizma. Moscow, 1989.
Tolmachev, A. *Kalinin*. Moscow, 1963.
Tolstoy, Aleksei N. *Polnoe sobranie sochinenii*. 15 vols. Moscow, 1946–51.
———. *Izbrannye sochineniia*. Vol. VI. Moscow, 1953.
Trifonov, Yuri. *Otblesk kostra*. Moscow, 1966.
Trukan, G. A. *Yan Rudzutak*. Moscow, 1963.
Ustrialov, Nikolai. *Pod znakom revoliutsii*. 2nd ed. Harbin, China, 1927.
Vaganov, F. M. *Pravyi uklon v VKP(b) i ego razgrom (1928–1930) gg*. Moscow, 1970.
Valentinov, Nikolai. *Doktrina pravogo kommunizma: 1924–26 gody v istorii sovetsksogo gosudarstva*. Munich, 1960.
Vedenin. A. Ya. *Gody i liudi*. Moscow, 1964.
Volkogonov, D. A., *Triumf i tragediia: Politicheskii portret Stalina*. Moscow, 1989.
Voloshin, N. *Stikhotvoreniia*. Vol. I, ed. B. A. Filippov *et al*. Paris, 1982.
Vsesoiuznoe soveshchanie o merakh uluchsheniia podgotovki nauchno-pedagogicheskikh kadrov po istoricheskim naukam, 18–21 dekabria 1962 g. Moscow, 1964.
Vyshinsky, A. Ya. *Voprosy teorii gosudarstva i prava*. Moscow, 1949.
Yakovlev, A. S. *Tsel' zhizni*. 2nd enl. ed. Moscow, 1968.
Yaroslavsky, E. *Ob antireligioznoi propagande*. Moscow, 1937.
Zaidel', G., and M. Tsvibak. *Klassovyi vrag na istoricheskom fronte*. Moscow and Leningrad, 1931.
Zaionchkovski, P. A. *Krizis samoderzhaviia na rubezhe 1870–1880 godov*. Moscow, 1964.
———. *Rossiiskoe samoderzhavie v kontse XIX stoletiia*. Moscow, 1970.
Zimin, A. *Sotsializm i neostalinizm*. New York, 1981.

IV. Books in Other Languages

Abramovitch, Raphael R. *The Soviet Revolution, 1917–1939*. New York, 1962.
Akhmatova, A. A. *Poems of Akhmatova*, selected, trans., and introduced by Stanley Kunitz with Max Hayward. Boston, 1967.
Alliluyeva, Svetlana. *Twenty Letters to a Friend*, trans. Priscilla Johnson McMillan. New York, 1967.
Ammende, Ewald. *Human Life in Russia*. London, 1936.
Antonov-Ovseyenko, Anton. *The Time of Stalin: Portrait of a Tyranny*. New York, 1981.
Aragon, Louis. *La mise à mort*. Paris, 1965.
Armstrong, John A. *The Politics of Totalitarianism*. New York, 1961.
Avtorkhanov, Abdurakhman. *Stalin and the Soviet Communist Party: A Study in the Technology of Power*. New York, 1959.

Azrael, Jeremy R. *Managerial Power and Soviet Politics*. Cambridge, Mass., 1966.

Bailes, Kendall E. *Technology and Society Under Lenin and Stalin: Origins of the Soviet Technical Intelligentsia, 1917–1941*. Princeton, 1978.

Barbusse, Henri. *Stalin: A New World Seen Through One Man*, trans. Vyvyan Holland. New York, 1935.

Barmine, Alexander. *One Who Survived: The Life Story of a Russian Under the Soviets*. New York, 1945.

Basseches, Nikolaus. *Stalin*, trans. E. W. Dickes. London and New York, 1952.

Baykov, Alexander. *Soviet Foreign Trade*. Princeton, 1946.

Beal, Fred E. *Proletarian Journey: New England, Gastonia, Moscow*. New York, 1937.

Beck, F., and W. Godin. *Russian Purge and the Extraction of Confession*, trans. Eric Mosbacher and David Porter. New York, 1951.

Beloff, Max. *The Foreign Policy of Soviet Russia, 1929–1941*. 2 vols. London and New York, 1946–49.

Belov, Fedor. *The History of a Soviet Collective Farm*. New York, 1955.

Beneš, Eduard. *Memoirs of Dr. Eduard Beneš: From Munich to New War and New Victory*, trans. Godfrey Lias. London, 1954.

Berger, Joseph. *Shipwreck of a Generation*. London, 1971.

Bohlen, Charles E. *Witness to History, 1929–1969*. New York, 1973.

Bolloten, Burnett. *The Spanish Revolution: The Left and the Struggle for Power During the Civil War*. Chapel Hill, 1979.

Borkenau, Franz. *World Communism: A History of the Communist International*. Ann Arbor, 1962.

Bournazel, Renata. *Rapallo: Naissance d'un mythe*. Paris, 1974.

Bracher, Karl Dietrich. *The German Dictatorship: The Origins, Structure, and Effects of National Socialism*, trans. Jean Steinberg. New York, 1970.

Broué, Pierre, and Emile Temime. *The Revolution and the Civil War in Spain*, trans. Tony White. Cambridge, Mass., 1979.

Brower, Daniel R. *The New Jacobins: The French Communist Party and the Popular Front*. Ithaca, N.Y., 1968.

Brown, Clarence. *Mandelstam*. Cambridge, England, 1973.

Brown, Edward J. *Russian Literature Since the Revolution*. London, 1963.

———. *The Proletarian Episode in Russian Literature, 1928–1932*. New York, 1971.

Brugel, J. W., comp. *Stalin und Hitler: Pakt gegen Europa*. Vienna, 1973.

Buber, Margarete. *Under Two Dictators*, trans. Edward Fitzgerald. London, 1949.

Buber-Neumann, Margarete. *Von Potsdam nach Moskau: Stationen eines Irrweges*. Stuttgart, 1957.

Budurowycz, Bohdan B. *Polish-Soviet Relations, 1932–1939*. New York, 1963.

Bullitt, Orville H., ed. *For the President, Personal and Secret: Correspondence Between Franklin D. Roosevelt and William C. Bullitt*. Boston, 1972.

Campbell, Thomas D. *Russia: Market or Menace?* London and New York, 1932.

Carr, E. H. *The Interregnum, 1923–1924*. New York, 1954.

———. *Socialism in One Country, 1924–1926*. 3 vols. New York, 1958–1964.

———. *The October Revolution: Before and After*. New York, 1969.

———. *The Comintern and the Spanish Civil War*, ed. Tamara Deutscher. New York, 1984.

Cattell, David T. *Communism and the Spanish Civil War*. Berkeley and Los Angeles, 1955.

Chamberlin, William Henry. *Russia's Iron Age*. London, 1935.

———. *The Russian Revolution, 1917–1921*. Vol. II. New York, 1935.

Chukovskaya, Lidiia. *Sofia Petrovna*. Evanston, Ill., 1988.

Churchill, Winston S. *The Second World War: The Gathering Storm*. New York, 1961.

Ciliga, Anton. *The Russian Enigma*. London, 1940.

Clark, Katerina. *The Soviet Novel: History As Ritual*. Chicago and London, 1985.

Claudin, Fernando. *The Communist Movement from Comintern to Cominform*. 2 vols. New York and London, 1975.

Cohen, Stephen F. *Bukharin and the Bolshevik Revolution: A Political Biography, 1888–1938*. New York, 1973.

———, ed. *An End to Silence: Uncensored Opinion in the Soviet Union*. New York, 1982.

The Communist International, 1919–1943. Documents selected and edited by Jane Degras. Vol. III. London, 1971.

Conquest, Robert. *The Great Terror: Stalin's Purge of the Thirties*. Rev. ed. New York, 1973.

———. *Kolyma: The Arctic Death Camps*. New York, 1978.

———. *The Harvest of Sorrow: Soviet Collectivization and the Terror-Famine*. New York and Oxford, 1986.

Coulondre, Robert. *De Staline à Hitler: Souvenirs de deux ambassades, 1936–1939*. Paris, 1950.

Crowl, James William. *Angels in Stalin's Paradise: Western Reporters in Soviet Russia, 1917 to 1937. A Case Study of Louis Fischer and Walter Duranty*. Lanham, Md., 1982.

Curtiss, John Shelton, ed. *Essays in Russian and Soviet History in Honor of Geroid Tanquary Robinson*. New York, 1962.

———. *The Russian Church and the Soviet State*. Gloucester, Mass., 1965.

Dallin, David J. *Russia and Postwar Europe*, trans. F. K. Lawrence. New Haven, 1943.

———, and Boris I. Nicolaevsky. *Forced Labor in Soviet Russia*. New Haven, 1947.

Davies, Joseph E. *Mission to Moscow*. Garden City, 1943.

Davies, R. W. *The Socialist Offensive: The Collectivisation of Soviet Agriculture, 1929–1930*. 2 vols. Cambridge, Mass., 1980.

Dedijer, Vladimir. *Tito*. New York, 1953.

Deutscher, Isaac. *The Prophet Unarmed: Trotsky, 1921–1929*. London, 1959.

———. *The Prophet Outcast: Trotsky, 1929–1940*. London, 1963.

———. *Stalin: A Political Biography*. 2nd ed. New York, 1967.

Dinerstein, Herbert. *Communism and the Russian Peasant*. Glencoe, Ill., 1955.

Dirksen, Herbert von. *Moscow-Tokyo-London: Twenty Years of German Foreign Policy*. Norman, Okla., 1952.

Drachkovitch, Milorad M., and Branko Lazitch, eds. *The Comintern: Historical Highlights*. Stanford, 1966.

Dyck, Harvey. *Weimar Germany and Soviet Russia*. New York, 1966.

Dziewanowski, M. K. *The Communist Party of Poland*. Cambridge, Mass., 1959.

Eden, Anthony. *Facing the Dictators: The Memoirs of Anthony Eden*. Boston, 1962.

Ehrenburg, Ilya. *Memoirs: 1921–1941*, trans. Tatiana Shebunina with Yvonne Kapp. Cleveland and New York, 1964.

———. *Post-War Years, 1945–1954*, trans. Tatiana Shebunina. Cleveland and New York, 1967.

Erickson, John A. *The Soviet High Command: A Military-Political History, 1918–1941*. London, 1962.

Fainsod, Merle. *Smolensk Under Soviet Rule*. New York, 1958.

Fehst, Herman. *Bolshewismus und Judentum: Das judische Element in der Führerschaft des Bolshewismus*. Berlin and Leipzig, 1934.

Fest, Joachim C. *Hitler*, trans. Richard and Clara Winston. New York, 1975.

Feuchtwanger, Lion. *Moscow 1937: My Visit Described for My Friends*, trans. Irene Josephy. New York, 1937.

Fischer, Louis. *Men and Politics: An Autobiography*. New York, 1941.

———. *Russia's Road from Peace to War: Soviet Foreign Relations, 1917–1941*. New York, 1969.

Fischer, Markoosha. *My Lives In Russia*. New York, 1944.

Fischer, Ralph Talcott, Jr. *Pattern for Soviet Youth: A Study of the Congresses of the Komsomol, 1918–1954*. New York, 1959.

Fischer, Ruth. *Stalin and German Communism: A Study in the Origins of the State Party*. Cambridge, Mass., 1948.

Fitzpatrick, Sheila. *The Russian Revolution*. Oxford, 1982.

———, ed. *Cultural Revolution in Russia, 1928–1931*. Bloomington and London, 1978.

———. *Education and Social Mobility in the Soviet Union, 1921–1934*. Cambridge, England, 1979.

Florinsky, Michael T. *Russia: A History and an Interpretation*. Vol. I. New York, 1955.

Freedman. A. M., H. I. Kaplan, and H. S. Kaplan, eds. *Comprehensive Textbook of Psychiatry*. Baltimore, 1967.

Friedberg, Maurice. *Russian Classics in Soviet Jackets*. New York and London, 1962.

George, Alexander, and Juliette George. *Woodrow Wilson and Colonel House: A Personality Study*. New York, 1964.

Gide, André. *Return from the U.S.S.R.*, trans. Dorothy Bussy. New York, 1937.

Ginzburg, Eugenia Semyonovna. *Journey into the Whirlwind*, trans. Paul Stevenson and May Hayward. New York and London, 1967.

Gorbatov, V. A. *Years Off My Life: The Memoirs of General of the Soviet Army V. A. Gorbatov*, trans. Gordon Clough and Anthony Cash. New York, 1964.

Gordon, Manya. *Workers Before and After Lenin*. New York, 1941.

Gorky, M., L. Auerbach, and S. G. Firin, eds. *Belomor*. New York, 1935.

Graham, Loren G. *The Soviet Academy of Sciences and the Communist Party, 1927–1932*. Princeton, 1967.

Grigorenko, Petro D. *Memoirs*. New York, 1982.

Gross, Jan T. *Revolution from Abroad: The Soviet Conquest of Poland's Western Ukraine and Western Belorussia*. Princeton, 1988.

Grunberger, Richard. *The 12-Year Reich: A Social History of Nazi Germany, 1933–1945*. New York, 1971.

Haslam, Jonathan. *The Soviet Union and the Search for Collective Security, 1933–1939*. New York, 1984.

Hellie, Richard. *Enserfment and Military Change in Muscovy*. Chicago and London, 1971.

Herwarth, Hans von, with S. Frederick Starr. *Against Two Evils*. New York, 1981.

Hilger, Gustav, and Alfred G. Meyer. *The Incompatible Allies: A Memoir-History of German-Soviet Relations, 1918–1941*.

Hindus, Maurice. *House Without a Roof: Russia after Forty-Three Years of Revolution*. Garden City, N.Y. 1961.

———. *Broken Earth*. London, 1926.

———. *Humanity Uprooted*. New York, 1929.

Hingley, Ronald. *Nightingale Fever: Russian Poets in Revolution*. New York, 1981.

History of the Communist Party of the Soviet Union (Bolsheviks): Short Course. Moscow, 1945.

Hitchens, M. M. *Germany, Russia, and the Balkans*. New York, 1983.

Hitler, Adolf. *The Speeches of Adolf Hitler*, ed. N. H. Baynes. Vol. II. London, 1942.

Hochman, Jiří. *The Soviet Union and the Failure of Collective Security, 1934–1938*. Ithaca and London, 1984.

Hoettle, Wilhelm. *The Secret Front: The Story of Nazi Political Espionage*. London, 1953.

Horney, Karen. *Neurosis and Human Growth*. New York, 1950.

Howe, Irving, ed. *1984 Revisited*. New York, 1983.
Hubbard, Leonard E. *The Economics of Soviet Agriculture*. London, 1939.
———. *Soviet Labor and Industry*. London, 1942.
Ivanov-Razumnik, R. *The Memoirs of Ivanov-Razumnik*, trans. P. M. Squire. London, 1965.
Jackson, Gabriel. *The Spanish Republic and the Civil War, 1931–1939*. Princeton, 1965.
Jansen, Marc. *A Show Trial Under Lenin: The Trial of the Socialist Revolutionaries, Moscow 1922*. The Hague, 1982.
Jasny, Naum. *Soviet Industrialization, 1928–1950*. Chicago, 1960.
Jelagin, Juri. *Taming of the Arts*, trans. Nicholas Wreden. New York, 1951.
Joravsky, David. *Soviet Marxism and Natural Science, 1917–1932*. New York, 1961.
———. *The Lysenko Affair*. Cambridge, Mass., 1970.
Juvilier, Peter H. *Revolutionary Law and Order*. London, 1976.
Keenan, Edward L. *The Kurbskii-Groznyi Apocrypha: The Seventeenth-Century Genesis of the "Correspondence" Attributed to Prince A. M. Kurbskii and Tsar Ivan IV*. Cambridge, Mass., 1971.
Kennan, George F. *Russia and the West Under Lenin and Stalin*. New York, 1960.
Khrushchev, Nikita. *Khrushchev Remembers*, trans. and ed. by Strobe Talbott. Boston, 1970. Vol. II, *Khrushchev Remembers: The Last Testament*, trans. and ed. by Strobe Talbott. Boston, 1974.
Kochan, Lionel, ed. *The Jews in Soviet Russia Since 1917*. London, 1970.
Kolarz, W. *Russia and Her Colonies*. 3rd ed. London, 1956.
Kommoss, R., comp. *Juden hinter Stalin*. Berlin and Leipzig, 1938.
Kopelev, Lev. *The Education of a True Believer*, trans. Gary Kern. New York, 1980.
Kostiuk, Hryhory. *Stalinist Rule in the Ukraine: A Study of the Decade of Mass Terror (1929–1939)*. New York, 1960.
Kravchenko, Victor. *I Chose Freedom: The Personal and Political Life of A Soviet Official*. New York, 1946.
Krivitsky, Walter G. *In Stalin's Secret Service*. New York and London, 1939.
Kun, Mrs. Bela. *Bela Kun (Memoirs)*. Budapest, 1966.
Kuusinen, Aino. *Before and After Stalin: A Personal Account of Soviet Russia from the 1920s to the 1960s*, trans. Paul Stevenson. London, 1974.
Laqueur, Walter. *Russia and Germany: A Century of Conflict*. London, 1965.
Lederer, Ivo J., ed. *Russian Foreign Policy: Essays in Historical Perspective*. New Haven, 1962.
Lerner, Warren. *Karl Radek: The Last Internationalist*. Stanford, 1970.
Levytsky, Borys, ed. *The Stalinist Terror in the Thirties: Documentation from the Soviet Press*. Stanford, 1974.
Lewin, Moshe. *Russian Peasants and Soviet Power: A Study of Collectivization*. Evanston, Ill., 1968.
Leyda, Jay. *Kino: A History of the Russian and Soviet Film*. New York, 1973.
Lipski, Josef. *Diplomat in Berlin, 1933–1939: Papers and Memoirs of Josef Lipski*, ed. Waclaw Jedrzejewicz. New York, 1968.
Littlepage, John D., and Demaree Bess. *In Search of Soviet Gold*. New York, 1937.
Lubachko, Ivan S. *Belorussia Under Soviet Rule, 1917–1957*. Lexington, Ky. 1972.
Lyons, Eugene. *Moscow Caroussel*. New York, 1935.
———. *Assignment in Utopia*. New York, 1937.
MacLean, Fitzroy. *Eastern Approaches*. New York, 1949.
Mandelstam, Nadezhda. *Hope Against Hope: A Memoir*, trans. May Hayward. New York, 1970.
Marshall, Herbert. *Masters of the Soviet Cinema: Crippled Creative Biographies*. London, 1983.
Marx, Karl, and Friedrich Engels. *Selected Correspondence, 1846–1895*, trans. and ed. Dona Torr. New York, 1942.
Matossian, Mary Kilbourne. *The Impact of Soviet Politics in Armenia*. Leiden, 1962.
Mayakovsky, Vladimir. *The Bedbug and Selected Poetry*, trans. Max Hayward and George Reavey. Bloomington and London, 1975.
McNeal, Robert H. *Bride of the Revolution: Krupskaya and Lenin*. Ann Arbor, 1972.
———, ed. *Resolutions and Decisions of the Communist Party of the Soviet Union*. Vol. III, *The Stalin Years: 1929–1953*. Toronto, 1974.
———. *Stalin: Man and Ruler*. New York, 1988.
Medvedev, Roy A. *Let History Judge: The Origins and Consequences of Stalinism*, trans. Colleen Taylor, eds. David Joravsky and Georges Haupt. New York, 1971. Rev. and exp. ed. New York, 1989.
———. *On Stalin and Stalinism*. Oxford, 1979.
———. *Nikolai Bukharin: The Last Years*, trans. A. D. P. Briggs. New York, 1980.
———, ed. *The Samizdat Register II*. New York, 1981.
———. *Khrushchev: A Political Biography*, trans. Brian Pearce. New York, 1983.
Merot, Jean. *Dimitrov, un revolutionnaire de notre temps*. Paris, 1972.
Micunovic, Veljko. *Moscow Diary*, trans. David Floyd. Garden City, N.Y., 1980.
Miliukov, Pavel Nikolaevich. *Russia and Its Crisis*. New York, 1962.
Moore, Barrington, Jr. *Terror and Progress USSR: Some Sources of Change and Stability in the Soviet Dictatorship*. Cambridge, Mass., 1954.
Mossman, Elliott, ed. *The Correspondence of Boris Pasternak and Olga Freidenberg, 1910–1954*, trans. Elliott Mossman and Margaret Wettlin. New York and London, 1982.
Muggeridge, Malcolm. *Chronicles of Wasted Time*. London, 1972.

Nedava, Joseph. *Trotsky and the Jews*. Philadelphia, 1972.
Nekrich, A. M. *June 22, 1941*, ed. and trans. V. Petrov. Columbia, S.C., 1968.
Niclaus, Karl Heinz. *Die Sowjetunion und Hitlers Machtergreifung*. Bonn, 1966.
Nicolaevsky, Boris I. *Power and the Soviet Elite*, ed. Janet D. Zagoria. New York, 1965.
Nove, Alec. *An Economic History of the USSR*, London, 1969.
Orlov, Alexander. *The Secret History of Stalin's Crimes*. New York, 1953.
Orlova, Raisa. *Memoirs*, trans. Samuel Cioran. New York, 1983.
Orwell, George. *Homage to Catalonia*. New York, 1972.
Pike, David. *German Writers in Soviet Exile, 1933–1945*. Chapel Hill, 1982.
Platonov, Andrei. *The Fierce and Beautiful World*, trans. Joseph Barnes. New York, 1970.
Platonov, S. F. *The Time of Troubles*, trans. John T. Alexander. Lawrence, Kansas, 1970.
Pokrovsky, M. N. *History of Russia from the Earliest Times to the Rise of Commercial Capitalism*, trans.
    and ed. J. D. Clarkson and R. M. Griffiths. New York, 1931.
Popovsky, Mark. *The Vavilov Affair*. Hamden, Conn., 1984.
Poretsky, Elisabeth K. *Our Own People: A Memoir of 'Ignace Reiss' and His Friends*. London, 1969.
Preis, Gunter. *The Man Who Started the War*. London, 1960.
Proffer, Ellendea. *Bulgakov: Life and Work*. Ann Arbor, 1984.
Reck, Vera T. *Boris Pil'niak: A Soviet Writer in Conflict with the State*. Montreal, 1975.
Reswick, William. *I Dreamt Revolution*. Chicago, 1952.
Ribbentrop, Joachim von. *The Ribbentrop Memoirs*. London, 1954.
Rigby, T. H. *Lenin's Government: Sovnarkom, 1917–1922*. Cambridge, England, 1979.
Roberts, Spencer E. *Soviet Historical Drama: Its Role in the Development of a National Mythology*. The
    Hague, 1965.
Robinson, Harlow. *Sergei Prokofiev: A Biography*. New York, 1987.
Robinson, Robert, with Jonathan Slavin. *Black on Red: My 44 Years Inside the Soviet Union*. Washington,
    D.C., 1988.
Rosenfeldt, Niels Erik. *Knowledge and Power: The Role of Stalin's Secret Chancellery in the Soviet
    System of Government*. Copenhagen, 1978.
Schapiro, Leonard. *The Communist Party of the Soviet Union*. New York, 1959.
Schellenberg, Walter. *Hitler's Secret Service*. New York: 1956.
Schlesinger, Rudolf, ed. *The Family in the USSR: Documents and Readings*. London, 1949.
Scott, John. *Behind the Urals: An American Worker in Russia's City of Steel*. Cambridge, Mass., 1942.
Serge, Victor. *Vie et mort de Trotsky*. Paris, 1951.
———. *Memoirs of a Revolutionary, 1901–1941*, trans. and ed. Peter Sedgwick. London and New York,
    1963.
———. *From Lenin to Stalin*, trans. Ralph Manheim. 2nd ed. New York, 1973.
Shestakov, A. V., ed. *A Short History of the USSR*. Moscow, 1938.
Shteppa, Konstantin F. *Russian Historians and the Soviet State*. New Brunswick, N. J., 1962.
Solzhenitsyn, Aleksandr I. *The Gulag Archipelago: An Experiment in Literary Investigation*, trans. Thomas
    P. Whitney. 3 vols. New York, 1974–78.
Sontag, R. J., and J. S. Beddie, eds. *Nazi-Soviet Relations, 1929–1941: Documents from the Archives of
    the German Foreign Office*. New York, 1948.
Soviet Legal Philosophy, trans. Hugh W. Babb. Cambridge, Mass., 1951.
Stalin, Joseph. *Anarchism or Socialism*. New York, 1953.
Starr, S. Frederick. *Melnikov: Solo Architect in a Mass Society*. Princeton, 1978.
———. *Red and Hot: The Fate of Jazz in the Soviet Union*. New York, 1985.
Sullivant, Robert S. *Soviet Politics and the Ukraine, 1917–1957*. New York, 1962.
Sutton, Antony C. *Western Technology and Soviet Economic Development, 1930 to 1945*. Stanford, 1971.
    Page 197.
Swianiewicz, S. *Forced Labour and Economic Development: An Enquiry into the Experience of Soviet
    Industrialization*. London, 1965.
Taylor, Telford. *Munich: The Price of Peace*. Garden City, N.Y., 1979.
Tertz, Abram. *The Trial Begins* and *On Socialist Realism*, trans. Max Hayward *(The Trial)* and George
    Dennis. New York, 1965.
Thomas, Hugh. *The Spanish Civil War*. New York, 1961.
Thorez, Maurice. *Fils du peuple*. Paris, 1960.
Timasheff, N. S. *Religion in Soviet Russia, 1917–1942*. New York, 1942.
Tokaev, G. A. *Betrayal of an Ideal*. Bloomington, In., 1955.
Trepper, Leopold. *The Great Game: The Story of the Red Orchestra*. London, 1977.
Trotsky, Leon. *My Life*. New York, 1930.
———. *The Revolution Betrayed*, trans. Max Eastman. New York, 1937, 1945.
———. *Literature and Revolution*. Ann Arbor, 1960.
———. *Stalin: An Appraisal of the Man and His Influence*, ed. and trans. Charles Malamuth. New ed.
    New York, 1967.
———. *The Struggle Against Fascism in Germany*. New York, 1971.
———. *1905*, trans. Anya Bostock. New York, 1971.
———. *Writings of Leon Trotsky*, IV, *(1932–33)*, eds. George Breitman and Evelyn Reed. New York,
    1972.

———. *The Spanish Revolution (1931–1939)*. New York, 1972.
Tucker, Robert C. *The Marxian Revolutionary Idea*. New York, 1969.
———. *The Soviet Political Mind: Stalinism and Post-Stalin Change*. 2nd ed. New York, 1971.
———. *Stalin As Revolutionary, 1879–1929: A Study in History and Personality*. New York, 1973.
———, ed. *The Lenin Anthology*. New York, 1975.
———, ed. *Stalinism: Essays in Historical Interpretation*. New York, 1977.
———, ed. *The Marx-Engels Reader*. 2nd ed. New York, 1978.
———. *Politics as Leadership*. Columbia, Mo., and London, 1981.
———. *Political Culture and Leadership in Soviet Russia: From Lenin to Gorbachev*. New York, 1987.
———, and Stephen F. Cohen, eds. *The Great Purge Trial*. New York, 1965.
Tumarkin, Nina. *Lenin Lives! The Lenin Cult in Soviet Russia*. Cambridge, Mass., 1983.
Tuominen, Arvo. *The Bells of the Kremlin: An Experience in Communism*, trans. Lily Leino, ed. Piltti Heiskanen. Hanover, N.H., and London, 1982.
Tvardovsky, Alexander. *Selected Poetry*. Moscow, 1981.
Tyrmand, Leopold, ed. *Kultura Essays*. New York, 1970.
Valkonier, Elizabeth. *Russian Realist Art: The State and Society, The Peredvizhniki and Their Tradition*. Ann Arbor, 1977.
Vardys, V. S., and R. J. Misiunas, eds. *The Baltic States in Peace and War, 1917–1945*. University Park, Md., 1978.
Vas, Zoltan. *Szepirodalmi Konyokiado* [Homecoming, 1944]. Budapest, 1970.
Vernadsky, George. *Russia at the Dawn of the Modern Age*. New Haven, 1959.
Viola, Lynne. *The Best Sons of the Fatherland: Workers in the Vanguard of Soviet Collectivization*. New York, 1987.
Vishnevskaya, Galina. *Galina: A Russian Story*, trans. Guy Daniels. San Diego, New York, and London, 1984.
Vyshinsky, Andrei Y., ed. *The Law of the Soviet State*, trans. Hugh W. Babb. New York, 1948.
Wallace, Sir Donald MacKenzie. *Russia*. London, 1912.
Weinberg, Gerhard L. *Germany and the Soviet Union, 1939–1941*. Leiden, 1954.
———. *The Foreign Policy of Hitler's Germany: Diplomatic Revolution in Europe, 1933–36*. Chicago and London, 1970.
———. *The Foreign Policy of Hitler's Germany: Starting World War II, 1937–1939*. Chicago and London, 1980.
Weissberg, Alexander. *The Accused*, trans. Edward Fitzgerald. London, 1951.
Welles, Sumner. *The Time for Decision*. New York, 1944.
Wipper, R. *Ivan Grozny*, trans. J. Fineberg. 3rd ed. Moscow, 1947.
Wolfe, Bertram D. *A Life in Two Centuries*. New York, 1981.
Wolin, Simon, and Robert M. Slusser, eds. *The Soviet Secret Police*. New York, 1957.
Wollenberg, Erich. *The Red Army: A Study of the Growth of Soviet Imperialism*. London, 1940.
Yakir, Piotr. *A Childhood in Prison*. New York, 1973.

V. Newspapers and Periodicals in Russian

(All of them published in the Soviet Union unless noted otherwise.)

Agitator
Biulleten' oppozitsii (Paris, New York)
Bol'shevik
Don
Gorizont
Grani (Frankfurt)
Istoricheskie zapiski (ed. A. L. Sidorov)
Istoriia SSSR
Istorik-Marksist
Izvestiia
Izvestiia Ts.K. KPSS
Knizhnoe obozrenie
Kommunist
Kommunisticheskaia revoliutsiia
Kommunisticheskii internatsional'
Komsomol'skaia pravda
Kontinent (Paris)
Literaturnaia Rossiia
Literaturnaia gazeta
Literaturnyi kritik
Molodaia gvardiia
Moskovskaia pravda
Moskovskie novosti

Narodnaia pravda (Paris)
Nedelia
Novoye russkoe slovo (New York)
Novosti zhizni
Novy mir
Ogonyok
Oktiabr'
Partiinoe stroitel'stvo
Planovoe khoziaistvo
Pod znamenem marxizma
Pravda
Proletarskaia revoliutsiia
Rodina
Sotsialisticheskii vestnik (Berlin)
Sotsialisticheskaia industriia
Sovetskaia kul'tura
Sovetskaia Rossiia
Sovetskoe gosudarstvo i pravo
SSSR: Vnutrennie protivorechiia (New York, ed. Valerii Chalidze)
Trud
Vechernaia Moskva
Vestnik Kommunisticheskoi akademii

Vestnik Ministerstva innostrannykh del SSSR
Vestnik statistiki
Voenno-istoricheskii zhurnal
Voprosy istorii
Voprosy istorii KPSS

Yunost'
Za industrializatsiiu
Znamia
Znanie-sila
Zvezda

VI. Articles in Russian

Abramov, B. A. "Kollektivizatsiia sel'skogo khoziaistva v RSFSR." In *Ocherki istorii kollektivizatsii,* ed. V. P. Danilov.

――――. "O rabote komissii Politbiuro Tsk VKP(b) po voprosam sploshnoi kollektivizatsii," *Voprosy istorii KPSS,* no. 1 (1964).

Abramovich, R. "Menshevitskii protsess 1931 g.," *Sotsialisticheskii vestnik,* no. 2–3 (February–March 1961).

Adzhubei, Aleksei. "Te desiat' let," *Znamia,* no. 7 (1988).

Barsov, A. A. "Sel'skoe khoziaistvo i istochniki sotsialisticheskogo nakopleniia v gody pervoi piatiletky (1928–1932)," *Istoriia SSSR,* no. 3 (1968).

Berezhkov, Valentin. "Prigovor vynosit vremia," *Nedelia,* no. 31 (August 1989).

Berezin, A. "Ivan Kraval," *Vestnik statistiki,* no. 7 (1988).

Berkhin, I. B. "K istorii konstitutsii SSSR 1936 g." In *Stroitel'stvo Sovetskogo gosudarstva: Sbornik statei k 70-letiiu E. B. Genkinoi.*

Bogdanova, O., A. Stanislavsky, and E. Starostin. "Soprotivlenie," *Ogonyok,* no. 23, 3–10 June 1989.

Bogdenko, M. L. "K istorii nachal'nogo etapa sploshnoi kollektivizatsii sel'skogo khoziaistva SSR," *Voprosy historii,* no. 5 (May 1963).

――――. "Kolkhoznoe stroitel'stvo vesnoi i letom 1930 g.," *Istoricheskie zapiski,* no. 76 (1965).

Bolotin, Aleksandr. "Chto my znaem o Liapidevskom?" *Ogonyok,* no. 14, 2–9 April 1988.

Cheremnykh, P. "Men'shevistvuiushchii idealizm v rabotakh BSE," *Bolshevik,* no. 17, 15 September 1931.

Churbanov, Vadim. "Chto proiskhodit s nashei kul'turoi," *Ogonyok,* no. 37, 10–17 September 1988.

Danilov, Victor P. "Sotsial'no-ekonomicheskie otnosheniia v sovetskoi derevne nakanune kollektivizatsii," *Istoricheskie zapiski,* no. 55 (1956).

――――. "Fenomen pervykh piatiletok," *Gorizont,* no. 5 (1988).

――――. "Ne smet' komandovat'!" *Znanie-sila,* no. 3 (1989).

"Delo o tak nazyvaemoi 'Antisovetskoi Trotskistkoi voennoi organizatsii' v Krasnoi Armii," *Izvestiia Ts.K. KPSS,* no. 4 (1989).

Denike, Iu. "Litvinov i Stalinskaia vneshniaia politika," *Sotsialisticheskii vestnik,* no. 5 (653) (May 1952).

Dunaevsky, V. A. "Bol'sheviki i germanskie levye na mezhdunarodnoi arene." In *Evropa v novoe i noveishee vremia: Sbornik statei pamiati Akademika N. M. Lukina.* Moscow, 1966.

"Eto nuzhno ne mertvym—zhivym" (interview with E. Beltov). *Knizhnoe obozrenie,* no. 25, 17 June 1988.

Ezerskaia, D. M., and N. A. Ivnitsky. "Dvadtsatipiatitysiachniki i ikh rol' v kollektivizatsii sel'skogo khoziaistva v 1930 g." In *Materialy po istorii SSSR,* chief ed. A. A. Novosel'sky. Vol. I. *Dokumenty po istorii sovetskogo obshchestva.* Moscow, 1955.

Falin, V. "Dva raznykh dogovora," *Argumenty i fakty,* no. 33, 19–25 August 1989.

Frolov, M. "Kak ya zagonial krest'ian v kolkhoz," *Rodina,* no. 4 (1989).

Gazarian, Suren. "O Berii i sude nad Beriavtsemi v Gruzii," *SSSR: Vnutrennie protivorechiia,* no. 6 (1982).

Gefter, M. "Stalin umer vchera." In *Inogo ne dano,* ed. Yu. N. Afanasiev.

Genri, Ernst. "Otkrytoe pis'mo pisateliu I. Erenburgu," *Grani,* 63 (1967).

Glinka, Gleb. "Dnevnik Gor'kogo," *Sotsialisticheskii vestnik,* no. 1 (667) (January 1954).

Gnedin, Evgeni. "Sebia ne poteriat'," *Novy mir,* no. 7 (July 1988).

Golovkov, Anatolii. "Ne otrekaias' ot sebia: Iz istorii sovremennosti," *Ogonyok,* no. 7, 13–20 February 1988.

Grin'ko, G. F. "Plan velikikh rabot," *Planovoe khoziaistvo,* no. 2 (1929).

Gukovsky, A. I. "Kak ia stal istorikom," *Istoriia SSSR,* no. 6 (1965).

Iakubovskaia, S. I. "Sovetskaia istoriografiia obrazovaniia SSSR," *Voprosy istorii,* no. 12 (1962).

"Iv." (Boris I. Nicolaevsky). "Diktator Sovetskogo soiuza," *Sotsialisticheskii vestnik,* no. 19 (1933).

Ivnitsky, N. A. "O nachal'nom etape sploshnoi kollektivizatsii (Osen' 1929–vesna 1930 gg.)," *Voprosy istorii KPSS,* no. 4 (1962).

"K padeniiu Postysheva: Iz stenogramy plenuma Ts.K. VKP(b)," *Pamiat': Istoricheskii sbornik,* no. 3 (Moscow, 1978; Paris, 1980).

Khrushchev, Nikita S. "O kul'te lichnosti i ego posledstviiakh," *Izvestiia Ts.K. KPSS,* no. 3 (1989).

――――. "Vospominania," *Ogonyok,* no. 28, 9–15 July 1989.

Kol'tsman, E. "Vreditel'stvo v nauke," *Bol'shevik,* no. 2, 31 January 1931.

Kostikov, V. "Illiuzion schast'ia," *Ogonyok,* no. 1, 30 December–6 January 1990.

Kovalev, F. N. "Stranitsy istorii: Dokumenty polpredstva SSR v Prage, otnosnashchiesiia k 'delu Tukhachevskogo,' " *Vestnik Ministerstva innostrannykh del SSSR,* no. 8 (42), 1 May 1989.

Kozakov, M. "Risunki na peske: Fragmenty iz knigi," *Ogonyok,* no. 8, 20–27 February 1988.

Kumanev, Georgii. "No istina dorozhe," *Ogonyok,* no. 33, 15–21 August 1989.

Lebedev, G. "Melkaia spekuliatsiia na bol'shoi teme," *Literaturnyi kritik* (May 1937).

Lordkipanidze, V. "Ubiistvo Kirova: Nekotorye podrobnosti," *Argumenty i fakty,* no. 6 (1989).

Mahkovikov, I. "Unichtozhenie komandnykh kadrov Krasnoi Armii," *SSSR: Vnutrennie protivorechiia*, no. 3 (1982).
Maslov, Nikolai. " 'Kratkii kurs istorii VKP(b)'—entsiklopediia kul'ta lichnosti Stalina." In *Surovaia drama naroda: Uchenye i publitsisty o prirode stalinizma.*
Medvedev, Roy A. "O Staline i stalinizme," *Istoriia SSSR*, no. 4 (July–August 1989).
Mikoyan, A. I. "V pervyi raz bez Lenina," *Ogonyok*, no. 50, 12–19 December 1987.
Mints, I. "Podgotovka velikoi proletarskoi revoliutsii: K vykhodu v svet pervogo toma 'Istorii grazhdanskoi voiny v SSSR,' " *Bol'shevik*, no. 12, 15 November 1935.
Mironov, N. R. "Vostanovlenie i razvitie leninskikh printsipov sotsialisticheskoi zakonnosti (1953–1963 gg.)," *Voprosy istorii KPSS*, no. 2 (1964).
Mitin, M. "Nekotorye itogi i zadachi raboty na filozofskom fronte," *Pod znamenem marxizma*, no. 1 (1936).
Molotov, V. M. "O kolkhoznom dvizhenii," *Bol'shevik*, no. 22, 30 November 1929.
———. "Uroki vreditel'stva, diversii i shpionazha Iapono-Nemetsko-Trotskistskikh agentov," *Bol'shevik*, no. 8, 15 April 1937.
"Nakanune voiny (Dokumenty 1935–40 gg.)," *Izvestiia Ts.K. KPSS*, no. 1 (1990).
Nicolaevsky, B. "Stalin i ubiistvo Kirova," *Sotsialisticheskii vestnik* (December 1956).
Nikulin, Lev. "Poslednye dni Marshala," *Ogonyok*, no. 13 (1963).
"O Krupskoi," *Kommunist*, no. 5 (March 1989).
"O partiinosti lits, prokhodivshikh po delu tak nazyvaemogo 'antisovetskogo pravotrotsistkogo bloka,' " *Izvestiia Ts.K. KPSS*, no. 5 (May 1989).
Panova, Vera. "Glavy iz vospominanii Very Panovoi," *SSSR: Vnutrennie protivorechiia*, no. 3 (1982).
Penezhko, Pavel. "Kak udarili po 'Chayanovshchine,' " *Ogonyok*, no. 10, 5–12 March 1988.
Plotkin, L. "Trotskistskaia agentura v literature," *Zvezda*, no. 7 (1937).
Popov, B. and V. Oplokov. "Berievschina," *Trud*, 26 (August 1989).
Popov, K. "Partiia i rol' vozhdia," *Partiinoe stroitel'stvo*, no. 3 (1930).
Posdniakov, V. "Kak Yezhov prinimal NKVD," *Narodnaia pravda*, vol. 5 (1949).
Pridvorov, D. "Ob otse." In *O Demiiane Bednom*. Moscow, 1966.
Romashov, B. "Rodnoi dom," *Znamia*, no. 3 (March 1938).
Rubenov, R. "Formy maskirovki trotskistskikh i inykh dvurushnikov," *Partiinoe stroitel'stvo*, no. 15, 1 August 1937.
Rzhevskaya, Elena. "V tot den', pozdnei osen'iu," *Znamia*, no. 12 (1986).
Serebriakova, Galina. "Smerch," *Novoye russkoe slovo*, 8–30 December 1967.
Sergeev, F. " 'Delo' Tukhachevskogo," *Nedelia*, no. 7 (1989).
Shirinia, K. K. "Iz istorii podgotovki VII kongressa Kommunisticheskogo internatsionala," *Voprosy istorii KPSS*, no. 8 (1975).
Slutsky, A. "Bol'sheviki o germanskoi s.-d. v period ee predvoennogo krizisa," *Proletarskaia revoliutsiia*, no. 6 (1930).
Soifer, Valerii. "Gor'kii plod." *Ogonyok*, no. 1, 2–9 January 1988.
Sokolov, O. "Ob istoricheskikh vzgliadakh M. N. Pokrovskogo," *Kommunist*, no. 4 (March 1962).
Souvarine, Boris. "Poslednye razgovory s Babelem," *Kontinent*, no. 23 (1980).
Stavsky, V. "Za bol'shevitskuiu bditel'nost' v literature," *Novy mir*, no. 6 (1937).
Tel'pukhovsky, B. S. "Deiatel'nosti KPSS po ukrepleniiu oborony SSSR v gody sotsialisticheskoi rekonstruktsii narodnogo khoziaistva (1929–1937 gg.)," *Voprosy istorii KPSS*, no. 8 (1976).
Tikhonov, V. "Sotsializm i kooperatsiia," *Don*, no. 2 (1989).
Tol'ts, Mark. "Repressironannaia perepis'," *Rodina*, no. 11 (1989).
Topliansky, V. O. "Noch' pered rozhdestvom v 1927 godu," *Ogonyok*, no. 14, 1–8 April 1989.
Trotsky, Leon. "Iskusstvo i revoliutsiia," *Biulleten' oppozitsii*, no. 77–78 (May–June 1939).
Trukan, G. "Avel' Yenukidze," *Agitator*, no. 12 (1989).
"V GPU (Iz rasskazov tov. Raissa)," *Biulleten' oppozitsii*, no. 60–61 (December 1937).
"V narkomindele, 1922–1939: Interv'iu s E. A. Gnedinym," *Pamiat': Istoricheskii sbornik*, no. 5 (Moscow, 1981; Paris, 1982).
Valentinov, N. "Iz proshlogo," *Sotsialisticheskii vestnik*, no. 4 (April 1961).
Verkhovykh, M. V. "Skol'ko delegatov golosovalo protiv Stalina?" *Izvestiia Ts.K. KPSS*, no. 7 (1989).
Vinokurov, P. "Nekotorye metody vrazheskoi raboty v pechati i nashi zadachi," *Bol'shevik*, no. 16, 15 August 1937.
Voinov, R. "Maskirovka shpiona," *Molodaia gvardiia*, no. 8 (1937).
Volkogonov, Dmitrii. "Triumf i tragediia: Politicheskii portret I. V. Stalina," *Oktiabr'*, no. 12 (1988).
Vyltsan, M. A., N. A. Ivnitsky, and Iu. A. Poliakov. "Nekotorye problemy istorii kollektivizatsii v SSSR," *Voprosy istorii*, no. 3 (1965).
Yakir, P. I. "Bud' nastoiashchim, syn!" In *Komandarm Yakir: Vospominaniia druzei.*
Yemelyanov, V. "O vremeni, o tovarishchakh, o sebe," *Novy mir*, no. 2 (February 1967).
Yudin, P. "Sotsializm i pravo," *Bol'shevik*, no. 17 (1 September 1937).
Zelenin, I. E. "Politotdely MTS (1933–1934 gg.)," *Istoricheskie zapiski*, no. 76 (1965).
———. "Kolkhozy i sel'skoe khoziaistvo SSSR v 1933–1935 gg.," *Istoriia SSSR* (September–October 1964).
Zhigulin, Anatoly. "Chernye kamni," *Znamia*, July 1988, August 1988.
Zhogin, N. V. "Ob izvrashcheniiakh Vyshinskogo v teorii sovetskogo prava i praktike," *Sovetskoe gosudarstvo i pravo*, no. 3 (March 1965).

VII. Articles in Other Languages

Abramov, Nikolai. "The New Version of the 'Tukhachevsky Affair': Declassified Documents from the U.S.S.R. Foreign Policy Archives," *New Times*, no. 13 (1989).

Abransky, Chimen. "Kamenev's Last Essay," *The New Left Review*, no. 15 (May–June 1962).

———. "The Biro-Bidzhan Project, 1927–1959." In *The Jews in Soviet Russia Since 1917*, ed. Lionel Kochan. London, 1970.

Agursky, M. "The Birth of Byelorussia," *The Times Literary Supplement*, 30 June 1972.

Aron, Paul H. "M. N. Pokrovskii and the Impact of the First Five-Year Plan." In *Essays in Russian and Soviet History in Honor of Geroid Tanquary Robinson*, ed. John Shelton Curtiss.

Ascher, A., and G. Lewy. "National Bolshevism in Weimar Germany," *Social Research* (Winter 1956).

Bruegel, J. W. "Dr. Beneš on the Soviet 'Offer of Help' in 1938." *East Central Europe*, no. 1 (1977).

Brumberg, Abraham. "The Ghost in Poland," *The New York Review of Books*, 2 June 1983.

Cameron, Norman. "Paranoid Conditions and Paranoia." In *American Handbook of Psychiatry*, ed. Silvano Arieti. New York, 1959.

Clark, Katerina. "Little Men and Big Deeds: Literature Responds to the First Five-Year Plan." In *Cultural Revolution in Russia, 1928–1931*, ed. Sheila Fitzpatrick.

———. "Utopian Anthropology as a Context for Stalinist Literature." In *Stalinism: Essays in Historical Interpretation*, ed. Robert C. Tucker.

Dallin, Alexander. "The Baltic States Between Nazi Germany and Soviet Russia." In *The Baltic States in Peace and War, 1917–1945*, eds. V. S. Vardys and R. J. Misiunas.

Dallin, David J. "The Piatakov-Radek Trial." In his *From Purge to Coexistence: Essays on Stalin's and Khrushchev's Russia*. Chicago, 1964.

Dziewanowski, M. K. "Stalin and the Polish Communists," *Soviet Survey* (January–March 1961).

Ex-Insider. "The Party That Vanished," *Soviet Survey*, no. 33 (July–September 1960).

———. "Moscow-Berlin 1933," *Survey*, no. 44–45 (October 1962).

Feshbach, Murray. "The Soviet Union: Population Trends and Dilemmas," *Population Bulletin*, no. 3 (August 1982).

Fitzpatrick, Sheila. "Culture and Politics Under Stalin: A Reappraisal," *The Slavic Review*, no. 2 (June 1976).

Freidin, Gregory. "Mandel'shtam's Ode to Stalin: History and Myth," *The Russian Review* (October 1982).

Gross, Babette L. "The German Communists' United-Front and Popular-Front Ventures." In *The Comintern: Historical Highlights*, ed. Milorad M. Drachkovitch and Branko Lazitch.

Hassell, James. "The Implementation of the Russian Table of Ranks During the Eighteenth Century," *The Slavic Review*, no. 2 (June 1970).

Hazard, John N. "Housecleaning in Soviet Law," *American Quarterly on the Soviet Union*, no. 1 (April 1938).

———. "The Soviet State and the Revolution in Law." In *Soviet Legal Philosophy*.

Hunter, Holland. "The Overambitious First Soviet Five-Year Plan," *The Slavic Review*, no. 2 (June 1973).

Joravsky, David. "Stalinist Mentality and Higher Learning," *The Slavic Review*, no. 4 (Winter 1983).

Katz, Barbara G. "Purges and Production: Soviet Economic Growth, 1928–1949," *The Journal of Economic History*, no. 3 (September 1975).

Karz, Jerzy F. "Thoughts on the Grain Problem," *Soviet Studies*, no. 4 (April 1967).

Kleimola, A. M. "The Duty to Denounce in Muscovite Russia," *The Slavic Review*, no. 4 (December 1972).

Korey, William. "The Origins and Development of Soviet Anti-Semitism: An Analysis." *The Slavic Review*, no. 1 (March 1972).

Lapidus, Gail Warshofsky. "Educational Strategies and Cultural Revolution." In *Cultural Revolution in Russia, 1928–1931*, ed. Sheila Fitzpatrick.

Lazitch, Branko. "Stalin's Massacre of the Foreign Communist Leaders." In *The Comintern: Historical Highlights*, ed. Milorad M. Drachkovitch and Branko Lazitch.

Lewin, Moshe. "The Disappearance of Planning in the Plan," *The Slavic Review*, no. 2 (June 1973).

———. "Who Was the Kulak?" *Soviet Studies*, no. 2 (October 1966).

Maksudov, M. (pseud.). "Losses Suffered by the Population of the USSR, 1918–1958." In *The Samizdat Register II*, ed. Roy A. Medvedev.

McCormick, Anne O'Hare. "Russia's Trend—To Main Street?" *The New York Times Magazine*, 13 February 1934.

McNeal, Robert H. "The Decisions of the CPSU and the Great Purge," *Soviet Studies*, no. 2 (October 1971).

Medvedev, Roy A. "New Pages from the Political Biography of Stalin." In *Stalinism: Essays in Historical Interpretation*, ed. Robert C. Tucker.

Miedzynski, Boguslaw. "The Road to Moscow." In *Kultura Essays*, ed. Leopold Tyrmand.

Miller, James A. "Mass Collectivization and the Contribution of Soviet Agriculture to the First Five-Year Plan: A Review Article," *The Slavic Review*, no. 4 (December 1974).

Oinas, Felix J. "The Political Uses and Themes of Folklore in the Soviet Union." *Journal of the Folklore Institute*, no. 2–3 (1975).

———. "Folklore and Politics in the Soviet Union," *The Slavic Review*, no. 1 (March 1973).

Rigby, T. H. "The CPSU Elite: Turnover and Rejuvenation from Lenin to Khrushchev," *The Australian Journal of Politics and History*, no. 1 (1970).

Rosenfeldt, Niels Erik. "The Consistorium of the Communist Church," *Russian History*, parts 2–3 (1982).

Sharlet, Robert. "Stalinism and Soviet Legal Culture." In *Stalinism*, ed. Robert C. Tucker.

———. "Pashukanis and the Withering Away of Law in the USSR." In *Cultural Revolution in Russia, 1928–1931*, ed. Sheila Fitzpatrick.

———, and Piers Beirne, "In Search of Vyshinsky: The Paradox of Law and Terror." *International Journal of the Sociology of Law*, no. 12 (1984).

Slusser, Robert M. "The Role of the Foreign Ministry." In *Russian Foreign Policy: Essays in Historical Perspective*, ed. Ivo J. Lederer.

Smolinsky, Leon. "Grinevetskii and Soviet Industrialization," *Survey* (April 1968).

Solomon, Peter H. "Soviet Criminology: Its Demise and Rebirth, 1928–1963," *Soviet Union*, no. 2 (1974).

Sontag, John P. "The Soviet War Scare of 1926–27," *The Russian Review* (January 1975).

Starr, S. Frederick. "Visionary Town Planning During the Cultural Revolution." In *Cultural Revolution in Russia, 1928–1931*, ed. Sheila Fitzpatrick.

Taborsky, Edward. "President Edvard Benes and the Crises of 1938 and 1948," *East Central Europe*, no. 5, part 2 (1978).

Thurston, Robert W. "Fear and Belief in the U.S.S.R.'s 'Great Terror': Response to Arrest, 1935–1939," *The Slavic Review*, no. 2 (Summer 1986).

Tucker, Robert C. "Does Big Brother Really Exist?" In *1984 Revisited*, ed. Irving Howe, New York, 1983.

Uldricks, Teddy J. "The Impact of the Great Purges on the People's Commissariat of Foreign Affairs." *The Slavic Review*, no. 2 (June 1977).

Unger, A. L. "Stalin's Renewal of the Leading Stratum: A Note on the Great Purge." *Soviet Studies*, no. 3 (January 1969).

Vassart, Celie and Albert. "The Moscow Origin of the French 'Popular Front.' " In *The Comintern: Historical Highlights*, ed. Milorad M. Drachkovitch.

Wheatcroft, Stephen G. "New Demographic Evidence on Excess Collectivization Deaths," *The Slavic Review*, no. 3 (Fall 1985).

VIII. Unpublished Material

Cocks, Paul M. "Politics of Party Control," Ph.D. dissertation. Harvard University, 1968.

Davies, R. W. "The Soviet Economic Crisis of 1931–1933." University of Birmingham, Soviet Industrialisation Project Series, no. 4.

Dunaevsky, V. A. "Pis'mo I. V. Stalina 'O nekotorykh voprosakh istorii bol'shevizma' (Okt. 1931 g.) i. ego posledstviia dlia sovetskoi istoricheskoi nauki i sudeb istorikov." Unpublished paper. Moscow, 1989.

Frumkin, Vladimir. "The Cultivation of Mythological Reality: 'Double Think' in the Soviet Mass Song of the Thirties." Unpublished MS. Oberlin College, 1980.

Kraus, Michael. "The Soviet Union, Czechoslovakia, and the Second World War: The Foundations of a Communist Rule." Ph.D. dissertation. Princeton University, 1985.

Orlov, A. "Tainy Stalinskoi vlasti." Unpublished MS. Hoover Institution Archives, Fund N. 227, Box 3.

Rosliakov, M. V. "Kak eto bylo (K ubiistvu S. M. Kirova)." Unpublished memoir. Kirov Museum. Leningrad.

Shteppa, K. F. "Volna massovykh arestov v Sovetskom soiuze (po lichnym vospominaniiam)." MS. no. 203, Boris I. Nicolaevsky Collection. The Hoover Institution, Stanford, California.

Tikhomirov, A., ed. "Na sluzhbe u Stalina (ispoved' chekista)." Unpublished MS. Columbia University Library.

INDEX